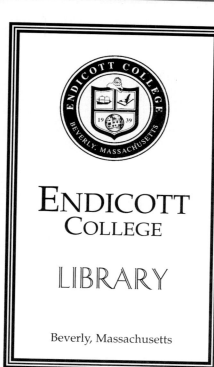

Encyclopedia of the
AMERICAN
RELIGIOUS
EXPERIENCE

Encyclopedia of the AMERICAN RELIGIOUS EXPERIENCE

Studies of Traditions and Movements

Charles H. Lippy and Peter W. Williams, *EDITORS*

Volume II

CHARLES SCRIBNER'S SONS · NEW YORK

Copyright © 1988 Charles Scribner's Sons

Library of Congress Cataloging-in-Publication Data

Encyclopedia of the American religious experience.

Bibliography: p.
Includes index.
1. United States—Religion.   2. North America—
Religion. I. Lippy, Charles H. II. Williams, Peter W.
BL2525.E53   1987   291'.0973   87-4781
ISBN 0–684–18062–6 Set
ISBN 0–684–18861–9 Volume I
ISBN 0–684–18862–7 Volume II
ISBN 0–684–18863–5 Volume III

Published simultaneously in Canada
by Collier Macmillan Canada, Inc.

3 5 7 9 11 13 15 17 19   Q/C   20 18 16 14 12 10 8 6 4 2

Printed in the United States of America.

The paper in this book meets the guidelines for permanence and
durability of the Committee on Production Guidelines for Book Longevity
of the Council on Library Resources

CONTENTS

CONTENTS

CONTENTS

CONTENTS

CONTENTS

CONTENTS

Encyclopedia of the
AMERICAN
RELIGIOUS
EXPERIENCE

Part IV
RELIGIONS OUTSIDE THE JEWISH AND CHRISTIAN TRADITIONS

BUDDHISM

Charles S. Prebish

THE religious tradition that has come to be known as Buddhism can be traced to the preachings of a man known as Siddhārtha Gautama who lived in India from 563 to 483 B.C. Born into a royal family, he was raised in princely opulence until, at the age of twenty-nine, he became concerned with the old age, sickness, and death around him and renounced the world in order to seek an antidote to this suffering through religious means.

Siddhārtha studied with the foremost religious teachers of the time, but found their systems lacking. He wandered India with other religious ascetics, but found no peace through bodily austerity either. Having experienced extremes of poverty and riches, he concluded that salvation could only be found through a carefully mapped-out middle path, and devoted himself to strenuous meditative practice aimed at actualizing the potential that he believed all human beings to have. Within a short period, he attained his goal, formally called *nirvāṇa* (the blowing-out of passion), and set out to preach his method to others. Now known as the *Buddha* (one who has awakened), he addressed all the ills of people's lives. Traditionally, in India, the termination of life was thought to be followed by rebirth in a new form, prolonged into eternity. Each individual was afforded no release from this continuing cycle (known as *saṃsāra*). Buddha argued that this continual rebirth established all life as suffering. In addition, he posited the cause of suffering as human craving. It was possible, according to Buddha, to terminate this endless craving and to do so required following a basic (eight-membered) path. These four points (suffering, its cause, its cessation, and the path) constitute the cornerstone of Buddhism, and are called the "Four Noble Truths." Buddha also preached other doctrines, collectively called his Dharma, and he offered a disciplinary tract known as his Vinaya.

The basic religious practice in Buddhism centered around an initial period of striving for moral perfection, subsequent direct involvement in meditation, and, finally, the acquisition of wisdom. For the individual who followed the path to its full conclusion, nirvāṇa (and freedom from rebirth) was the goal. Religious life focused on both a lay and monastic community. Further, it was emphasized that both men and women had equal opportunity to attain the goal. Buddha died at the age of eighty, after preaching for a period of forty-five years. By the time of his death, his following was judged to be immense.

Within a hundred years following Buddha's death, the original community began to splinter into subgroups. By around 200 B.C., the religion split into two major groups, *Hīnayāna* (lesser vehicle) Buddhism and *Mahāyāna* (greater vehicle) Buddhism. Each group persists today: Hīnayāna Buddhism is largely found in South Asia, while Mahāyāna predominates in Southeast and East Asia. Also, within a thousand years of the Hīnayāna-Mahāyāna split, a third major school of Buddhism, known as *Vajrayāna* (diamond vehicle), developed, stressing the esoteric side of the Buddhist tradition.

It is only logical to expect that, as Buddhism moved into modern times, it would appear in the West. With increased communication and readily available forms of transportation, contact between Buddhist cultures and the West has been on the rise for several centuries. The following essay attempts to document this contact, and also explores the implications of the Buddhist movement for those Americans who have become involved in it.

BUDDHISM

Although it is now quite common to refer to the Oriental influences in the writings of such prominent American literary figures as Henry David Thoreau, Ralph Waldo Emerson, and Walt Whitman, and to point to the impact of the Theosophists on the Oriental movement in America, the more genuine beginnings of Buddhism in America can be traced to the Chinese immigrants who began to appear on the West Coast in the 1840s. Prior to the discovery of gold at Sutter's Mill, the number of Chinese immigrants was small, but with the news of the golden wealth in the land, the figure increased exponentially. One source (Fields) points out that by 1852, 20,000 Chinese were present in California; less than ten years later, perhaps 10 percent of Californians were Chinese.

By the mid-1850s, temples began to appear in the Chinatown section of San Francisco; within a quarter century, several hundred temples dotted the California coastline. The sort of religious practice operative in these Chinese temples was clearly eclectic in nature, combining elements of Buddhism, Taoism, and Confucianism. A number of Buddhist priests were in residence at these temples, but the presence of a distinctly Chinese Buddhism in America did not appear until much later.

The Japanese presence in America was much slower to develop than the Chinese, but it had a much greater impact. In the 1870s, when the Chinese influence was already apparent, there were few Japanese listed in the census, and that number had barely reached 2,000 by 1890, despite the diligent efforts of many of these Japanese immigrants to adjust to American customs and ideals. Nonetheless, the World Parliament of Religions, held in conjunction with the Chicago World's Fair in 1893, changed the entire landscape for Buddhism in America.

Among the various representatives of Oriental religions at the parliament were two Buddhists: Sōyen Shaku, who was to return to America a decade later and promote the school of Rinzai Zen (Japanese branch of Zen Buddhism, founded by Eisai 1141–1215), and Anagarika Dharmapala, the main proponent of the Mahabodhi Society in America. Sōyen Shaku visited America for a second time in 1905 at the invitation of Mrs. Alexander Russell. Through her courtesy, he was able to visit and lecture in several American cities, thus establishing a basic ground for the entry of Zen (a meditative school of Buddhism, started in India but developing fully in China and Japan). When Shaku returned to Japan in 1906, three of his most immediate disciples were selected to promote the Rinzai lineage in America.

The first of these, Nyōgen Senzaki, came to California in 1905 but delayed his mission to teach Zen until 1922. Shaku's second disciple, Sōkatsu Shaku, lived in America from 1906 to 1908, and again from 1909 to 1910, but he eventually returned to Japan. Shaku's most noted disciple, and the man who made the most impact on the growth of Buddhism in America, was Daisetsu Teitaro Suzuki. Suzuki followed his teacher to America, working as an editor for the Open Court Publishing Company in LaSalle, Illinois, from 1897 to 1909. Although he returned to Japan in order to pursue his literary career in Buddhist studies, he reappeared in America in 1936 and stayed until World War II. After the war Suzuki returned to America for a third visit, between 1950 and 1958, during which he lectured frequently in major American universities and cities. Suzuki served as president of the Cambridge Buddhist Association, founded in 1957, and worked closely with the Zen Studies Society of New York, founded in 1956. In addition to his numerous lectures designed to enhance public awareness of Rinzai Zen in America, Suzuki was a prolific writer. He is best known for his *Essays in Zen Buddhism* (in three series), *Manual of Zen Buddhism,* and *The Training of the Zen Buddhist Monk.*

The Rinzai Zen lineage was not the only one to develop on the American scene. Sōtō Zen (a Japanese form of Zen, introduced by Dōgen, 1200–1253) began to appear in America in the 1950s. In mid-decade, the Chicago Buddhist Temple was founded by Soyu Matsuoka Rōshi (*Rōshi,* master). Eventually leaving the Chicago organization in the hands of his American disciple Richard Langlois, Matsuoka Rōshi went on to serve many other Zen groups in America. The most influential Buddhist in the Sōtō lineage to date has been Shunryu Suzuki Rōshi. Within two years of his arrival in America in 1959, he had founded the San Francisco Zen Center and had attracted a more-than-substantial following of new American Buddhists. Suzuki Rōshi died in 1971, appointing as his successor Richard Baker Rōshi, one of the few Westerners to be considered a "master" in the tradition. The Sōtō Zen lineage in America also includes one of the few women Rōshis: Jiyu Kennett. British by birth, she was the first woman admitted to train at Sōjiji Temple in Japan since the fourteenth century. In 1968 she was licensed as a full teacher, and in 1969 she came to America to establish a Zen monastery on Mount Shasta in northern California.

In addition to the traditional forms of Rinzai and Sōtō Zen, still another form of Zen has appeared in America. This group, owing its American origins to Sogaku Harada, attempts to harmonize the major doctrines and practices of each Zen school into a workable, unified whole. Curiously, Harada, instrumental in bringing the approach to this country, never traveled to America himself. Instead, he sent three of his primary disciples in his place. The first of these was Taizan Maezumi Rōshi; arriving in America in 1956, he established the Zen Center of Los Angeles. This center trains both priests and lay disciples, and maintains an active program of temple pursuits that includes a rigorous schedule of Zen publications. Harada's second disciple, Hakuun Yasutani Rōshi, visited the United States in 1962, holding Zen meditation sessions in many major American cities. He returned to the United States regularly until his death in 1973, after having served a variety of American Zen societies.

Harada's third disciple is also the most interesting. American by birth, Philip Kapleau first came into contact with Japanese culture while serving as a court reporter in 1946 during the War Crimes Trials held in Tokyo. Back in America, he attended the lectures of D. T. Suzuki in 1951, then returned to Japan to escape what he called "intellectual" Buddhism. Kapleau studied Zen in Japan from 1953 to 1966. Upon his return to America, he founded the Zen Meditation Center in Rochester, New York, and published an American version of his now classic book, *The Three Pillars of Zen.* Of Harada's three disciples, Kapleau has worked hardest at adjusting Zen to its American environment. Indeed, his attempts to Americanize Zen led to his break with Hakuun Yasutani Rōshi in 1967.

Zen was not the only tradition to benefit from the World Parliament of Religions. Indeed, the tradition represented by Anagarika Dharmapala has also had an interesting history in America,

influencing the development of yet another school of Buddhism, Theravāda (an early school of Buddhism; literal translation, "those who hold the doctrine of the elders"). Prior to his appearance at the Chicago meeting, Dharmapala had founded the Mahabodhi Society in Colombo, Ceylon (1891). Under the direction of Henry Steel Olcott, the organization sought to return Bodh-Gaya (in India) to the Buddhists of the world. Paul Carus, the general editor of Open Court Publishing Company, and close friend of D. T. Suzuki's, supported Dharmapala's efforts, becoming founder of the American branch of the Mahabodhi Society. Dharmapala returned to America several more times during his lifetime, promoting his cause in primarily intellectual circles. Although there have been numerous Theravāda advocates in the aftermath of Anagarika Dharmapala, the first noteworthy Theravāda organization was not begun until 1966, when the Buddhist Vihara Society was founded in Washington, D.C., primarily to serve the international community in the nation's capital. There are currently Sinhalese and Thai temples in North Hollywood, California, as well as the Stillpoint Institutes, founded by an American Buddhist monk known as Anagarika Sujata. Since the early 1970s, the Theravāda meditation technique known as *vipassanā* (insight) has been quite popular on the American scene, particularly as practiced at the Insight Meditation Center in Barre, Massachusetts.

It has been noted that "to a large degree, the history of Buddhism in America up to 1960 is, with the exception of Buddhist Churches of America, really a history of Zen in America" (Prebish). It is important to realize, though, that Buddhist Churches of America is a profoundly important exception to a simple identification of American Buddhism with Zen Buddhism in America. Its history in America began with a fact-finding tour in 1898 in which two missionaries were sent from the home temple in Japan to San Francisco. As a result of the ensuing report, two priests, Shuei Sonoda and Kakuryo Nishijima, arrived in San Francisco in 1899 to establish an organization that they called the Buddhist Mission of North America. Although the two priests were especially successful in ministering to the Japanese immigrant families, their efforts were hampered by acute racism.

Just as the Chinese Immigration Exclusion

Act of the late 1880s limited access to America by the Chinese, the Japanese Immigration Exclusion Act of 1924 hampered Japanese efforts to gain entry to America. Further, Japanese immigrants were not allowed to become naturalized American citizens. Nonetheless, the Japanese immigrants utilized the constitutional guarantee of religious freedom to establish temples and religious communities. By 1931, thirty-three main temples were active. The outbreak of World War II witnessed the relocation of over 100,000 Japanese immigrants to internment camps. More than half of these individuals were Buddhist and roughly two-thirds were American born.

In 1942, the name of the Buddhist Mission of North America was officially changed to Buddhist Churches of America. Unlike the Zen organizations currently operative in America, Buddhist Churches of America represents a part of the Buddhist tradition that is nonmeditative. Thus it provides a stark contrast to the prevailing image of a Buddhist monk sitting in a quiet room calmly staring into a blank wall. Rather, this organization presents a rich liturgy and a lively sequence of religious festivals.

The Chinese are once again making their presence visible in American Buddhism. Although not nearly so active as the Japanese Buddhist groups, several Chinese Buddhist organizations have appeared in the last twenty years. Most notable of these is a largely monastic group in San Francisco known as the Sino-American Buddhist Association, under the direction of a venerable monk named Hsüan-Hua. Chinese Buddhist groups can also be found in the Catskill Mountains of New York and in the Bronx, New York. Closely related to Chinese Buddhism, Korean and Vietnamese Buddhist groups have lately begun to appear in America, generally emphasizing the meditative pattern stressed earlier.

The Buddhist culture to enter America most recently is the Tibetan. Although a few Tibetan Buddhist groups appeared in the West prior to 1960, the majority came after the Tibetan holocaust, during which the Communist Chinese made every effort to extinguish religion in Tibet. Following an immediate exile in India, Bhutan, Nepal, and Sikkim, the diaspora has widened, with many Tibetans seeking to reestablish their sacred lineages on American soil. Communities from each of the four major Tibetan Buddhist sects can now be found in America, but perhaps the most well known are the Tibetan Nyingma Meditation Center, founded by Tarthang Tulku, and the various communities of Vajradhatu and Nalanda Foundation, established by a young exile known as Chögyam Trungpa (representing the tradition of bKa-rgyud-pa, the Buddhist sect founded by Mar-pa, 1012–1096).

The Tibetan groups are the most colorful Buddhist groups now prospering in America, possessing a rich tradition of Buddhist art and a powerful psychological approach to mental health. They also seem to be growing faster than any other Buddhist organizations in America. It is no wonder, then, that they quote the thousand-year-old saying of the sage Padmasambhava to explain their rapid growth: "When the iron bird flies, and horses run on wheels, the Tibetan people will be scattered like ants across the World, and the *Dharma* [doctrine or teaching] will come to the land of the Red Man."

Outlining the historical details of the Buddhist movement in America tells but a small part of the story, for the growth of American Buddhism is far more than its history. Rather, it represents a struggle to acculturate and accommodate on the part of a religious tradition that appears to be wholly foreign to the American mindset. It is important to realize from the outset that two radically differing groups were primarily responsible for Buddhism's earliest growth in America. On the one hand, Buddhism was the native religion of a significant group of Asian immigrants. On the other hand, it became the religion, or at least subject of serious personal interest, for a group of Caucasian Americans who embraced Buddhism primarily out of intellectual attraction.

It has become the norm in dealing with the acculturation process in American Buddhism to define time periods on which interest can be focused. In *American Buddhism* I suggest that the most convenient periods include (1) Buddhism's earliest history in America, 1893–1960; (2) its adjustment to an interval of political, social, and religious turmoil in America, 1961–1970; and (3) a period of growth and development, 1971–1980. Each of these time spans presents a unique set of circumstances and problems for the Buddhist movement; consequently, each needs to be considered in order.

Prior to 1893 (selected because it is the date

of the World Parliament of Religions in Chicago), Buddhism in America was largely recognized as a scholarly endeavor undertaken primarily as an attempt to understand the Asian tradition through a careful study of its literary works in their original languages. Leaders in this enterprise included Charles Rockwell Lanman and Henry Clarke Warren, two Sanskritists who collaborated to produce the *Harvard Oriental Series,* the first volume of which offered Hendrik Kern's translation of the Buddhist *Jātakamālā* (birth stories). The scholarly tradition of Lanman and Warren continued, but it ran parallel to the developing pursuit of Buddhism as a living religion practiced on American soil.

For Americans venturing into its practice as an expression of intellectual concern, Buddhism was a profoundly unusual religion. It presented a radically different notion of time, portrayed as a continuous cycle that has no beginning or end, and from which there is no escape without diligent religious effort. It argued that rebirth follows death, and that each rebirth is dictated by the quality of one's moral actions (called *karma*). Unlike traditional Western religion, it is nontheistic, regarding its founder simply as an extraordinary man and not a deity. It suggests that suffering is the basic common denominator of all human existence and defines salvation (in some accounts) as a termination of suffering. Religious practice, in most Buddhist groups, involved neither prayer nor liturgy, and focused on a silent meditative process that many Westerners misunderstood as self-hypnosis.

In contrast to the Buddhism of the essentially Caucasian intellectuals, Buddhism served the Japanese immigrant communities that emerged on the West Coast and gradually appeared on the Eastern Seaboard as well. As noted earlier, these Buddhists represented two basic groups: Zen (both Rinzai and Sōtō) and Pure Land (Buddhist Churches of America). Although each of these groups purportedly attempted to adjust to their new American environment, their religious life reflected a ritual enactment that remained largely Japanese. In other words, although the temple was located in America, the sacred center of the tradition remained essentially Japanese in character. It was not until after World War II that the situation changed for both the Asian and non-Asian Buddhists in America.

Following the war, Asia remained more than ever in the American consciousness and sphere of influence. Asian studies began to appear in the curricula of many American universities, and many more Americans became exposed to the Buddhist tradition through academic courses and the growing number of English language translations of important Buddhist texts and scriptures. Equally important, Asian-American communities began to crop up throughout the land, expanding more fully to both coasts as well as Middle America. Community life has always been a central, unifying aspect of the Buddhist tradition in its Asian homeland, and as Asian-American Buddhist communities expanded in postwar America, the community was to play an equally significant role.

The postwar era in America, especially during the 1950s, provided new and serious problems for America. Crime, mental-health disorders, drug addiction, and racism began to grow rapidly, especially in urban America. All of these issues are dealt with straightforwardly and aggressively in Buddhist ethics (which, for example, uses meditation as a therapeutic purgative for drug addiction and tolerance to combat racism), providing the Buddhists in America with perhaps their first genuine opportunity to address American problems from the Buddhist perspective. The 1950s provided the proverbial foot-in-the-door by which Buddhism was able to begin its Americanization process. Also during the 1950s, a quasi-bohemian movement began in largely literary circles, calling itself the Beat generation. Drawing from more traditional sources, its proponents offered a new literature, language, philosophy, and life-style, some of which was borrowed, in perverted form, from Zen Buddhism. The champions of "Beat Zen"—Jack Kerouac, Allen Ginsberg, and others—became celebrities in the subterranean culture of the 1950s. They misunderstood Zen, certainly, prostituting the supposed ecstasy of the Zen meditative experience, perverting its ethics, and offering in their place an antinomianism supported nowhere in the Buddhist tradition. Nonetheless, the Beats were highly visible, prolific in their writing, and attractive to the heirs of the "lost generation." Through their efforts, Buddhism, however unauthentically presented, became known to thousands of Americans.

In addition to the Buddhism of the Beats, two other kinds of Buddhism were emerging in the

1950s. Proponents of the first, typified by writers like Gary Snyder, actually went to Asia (usually Japan) and studied with masters of the various traditions. The second approach to Buddhism (which included the popular Buddhism stressed by pseudoauthorities such as Alan Watts) dramatized its benefits, offered simplified explanations of its tenets, and made it appear eminently beneficial as an American religious practice. Unfortunately, it was also profoundly inaccurate as well. As a result, by 1960 Buddhism had consolidated some growth, was much more visible in America, and yet had still not solved what was becoming an obvious identity crisis.

During the period from 1961 to 1970, Buddhism experienced a rapid, dynamic growth in America, but its swift growth brought with it a myriad of problems that have not yet been resolved. America was gaining a much more sophisticated knowledge of Asia. In less than twenty years, the United States had concluded two wars on Asian soil and had begun an undeclared, unpopular military effort in Vietnam. Further, each of the cultures encountered in these wars was a Buddhist culture. From the umbrellalike classification of Asian studies, the independent discipline known as Buddhist studies emerged. First, in a doctoral program at the University of Wisconsin under Richard Hugh Robinson, and later, at Columbia University (and others), it became possible to forge a career out of the study of the Buddhist tradition.

Theodore Roszak's influential book *The Making of a Counter Culture,* published at the end of the 1960s, argued that the counterculture witnessed in the social environment was "essentially, an exploration of the politics of consciousness. . . ." The "consciousness explosion," as it is sometimes called, provided an enormous boost to the Buddhist endeavor in America. The counterculture was the drug culture, and whatever its liabilities, drug experience initially promised huge insights in its psychedelic frenzy. As the real dangers of drug experimentation became known, many of the leading "hippie" spokesmen praised the pursuit of Buddhist meditative techniques as a safer alternative to the drug experience.

The Buddhist movement in America also benefited from the turmoil that beset traditional religion in America during the 1960s. The "death of God" theologians had created a furor in the academy, and Harvey Cox's *The Secular City,* published in 1965, asked a whole new set of questions about how to be religious in precarious times. The sociologist Peter Berger summarized the situation well when he noted that secularization encourages a pluralistic occasion and that, religiously, a de-monopolization of clientele results. One of the results is a new interest in ecumenicity. This is important for Buddhist growth in America, for with the religious clientele up for grabs, Buddhism could compete for its fair share of the market. In addition, with an increased push for ecumenicity, Buddhism was able to hop on the ecumenical bandwagon, and in so doing, gain a deeper foothold in American soil. And of course it was a non-Asian constituency that 1960s Buddhism pursued.

Buddhism has always been praised for its immense emphasis on psychological wholeness as a clear manifestation of progress in the religious life. As a result, the religion was to benefit from the interest in new psychological techniques that appeared in the decade. The general movement was dubbed the "Human Potential Movement" as an expression of its concern to maximize the fruits of being fully human. Such therapies as Gestalt and Primal Scream became part of idiomatic speech on the "consciousness circuit." Many individuals, trying to realize their full psychological potential, embraced Buddhism as just another product in the "spiritual supermarket"; some stayed, some strayed. Nevertheless, Buddhism gained a new measure of interest in the 1960s marketplace.

During the same decade, Asian immigrants in America were still searching for a life-style that was consistent with their traditional religious enterprise while not compromising their role in modern American society. They remained the most populous group of American Buddhists, and they largely remained Buddhists-in-America rather than genuinely American Buddhists in their ideas and activities. For these Asian-American Buddhists, religious tradition was characteristically both a city and lay movement. And while they were committed to their religion and community, they did not cope successfully with establishing a means of reinforcing community identity through recreational activities. Consequently, they did not develop what Rosabeth Kanter has called a transcendence-facilitating tradition. Communal ambiguity developed as a result of self-definition in terms of what was rejected rather than what was affirmed. A great proliferation of Buddhist sects had become established in America, and in the absence of a developing group identity this situation only exacerbated the dilemma of Buddhist community life in America.

By 1970 virtually the full extent of Asian Buddhist sects was represented in America. From the Japanese tradition came both the Pure Land (Japanese Buddhist school founded by Hōnen, 1133–1212) and True Pure Land (Japanese Buddhist school founded by Shinran, 1173–1262) groups, Rinzai Zen, Sōtō Zen, Syncretistic Zen, Nichiren Shōshū (Japanese Buddhist school founded by Nichiren, 1222–1282), and Shingon (Japanese Buddhist school founded by Kūkai, 774–835). From China, both Ch'an (Chinese Buddhist school founded by Bodhidharma in 520) and Pure Land groups were present. The Korean Chogye Chen (meditative school) and South Asian Theravāda traditions were active as well. Finally, the Tibetan Buddhist schools dGe-lugs-pa (founded by Tsong-kha-pa, 1357–1419), rNying-ma-pa, bKa-rgyud-pa, and Sa-skya-pa (founded by 'Brog-mi) had taken up residence in America. All are struggling against falling into the trap that Agehananda Bharati calls the "aloha-amigo" syndrome.

Emma Layman, author of one of the first comprehensive books on Buddhism in America, suggested that in the 1970s Buddhism was beginning to look for an internal ecumenicity:

> This is taking several forms: (1) establishment of nonsectarian or intersectarian churches and monasteries; (2) intersectarian sharing of resources, for example, Sunday School materials and visual aids; (3) exchange of priests or ministers on occasion; (4) integration of meditational-type approaches into ceremonial-type churches; and (5) joint services involving different sects and/or non-Buddhist groups. In each of these ways Buddhists of different sects do get together in comfortable interaction, co-existence, or union.

The sort of cooperation that Professor Layman describes might well have promoted harmony rather than fragmentation. It was only minimally visible early in the decade, but by the end of the period in question was becoming more effective. Buddhism was also faced with an internal re-

luctance to confront modernity (no place more visible than in its ethical system, which has remained unchanged for almost 1,500 years) and an unwillingness to come to grips with advancing technology. Nonetheless, in the calm that persisted after the war in Vietnam, it was able to begin some attempts at consolidation. In so doing, some of the distinctions that weakened the movement early in its American history were dissolved.

Up to now we have been considering the historical and cultural context in which Buddhism emerged as an American religious phenomenon. We must now focus on a series of specific issues that effect the Buddhist tradition in America. The first of these is basic: namely, how do we decide just what constitutes a Buddhist?

On the surface, the issue of determining Buddhist standing seems especially uncomplicated. One just asks the question, "Are you a Buddhist?" Unfortunately, such an approach does not always yield a fruitful or accurate result. Holmes Welch discovered, in preparing his book *The Practice of Chinese Buddhism, 1900–1950,* that Chinese refugees in Hong Kong might answer in the affirmative to the above question. However, if one followed the initial question with another, "Are you a Taoist?" the same individual might well answer in the affirmative again. In other words, some individuals had no difficulty whatsoever in professing multilateral religious affiliations. Welch found a clearer and more accurate way of determining Buddhist standing. He asked whether an individual had taken the *three refuges* ("I go to the Buddha for Refuge, I go to the Dharma for Refuge, I go to the Saṃgha for Refuge") and the *five vows of the laity* (not to lie, kill, steal, take intoxicants, or engage in illicit sex). These two items reflect the traditional Buddhist requirement for standing in the community or *saṃgha.* If this traditional approach to Buddhist membership were applied to the American Buddhist community, formal membership rolls would be found to include very many persons who did not fit the normative requirement for *saṃgha* membership.

The issue of Buddhist identity and membership becomes even murkier when we consider that many Buddhist groups in America determine membership by incredibly looser criteria than the traditional Buddhist standards. Items such as frequent attendance at church and meditation sessions, financial gifts to the organization, and simply placing one's name on a mailing list have been used by one or another American Buddhist group for determining membership status. None of these criteria considers the quality of membership or commitment to the tradition. At a time when very many non-Asian Americans are finding their way into Buddhist organizations, it is becoming essential to find some criteria that reflect commitment to the Buddhist tradition and awareness of a prior American heritage on the part of the adherent. The appearance of books like Dom Aelred Graham's *Zen Catholicism* (1963) and William Johnston's *The Still Point* (1970) suggests that such a possibility exists. Scholars like Harvey Cox (and to a lesser extent, Martin Marty) have even suggested that multiple allegiances may be beneficial. Nevertheless, any standardized procedure remains a desideratum for American Buddhists today.

A second concern in considering the Buddhist movement in America is to determine just who these American Buddhists are. Who is attracted to Buddhism? What is their heritage? What is the general style of the Buddhism that has been imported? These questions will help us get a handle on the nature of the Buddhist movement as it exists today.

Prior to World War II, nearly all Buddhists in America were of Asian ancestry, despite the fact that many were born in this country. With the increasing emphasis on Buddhism as an intellectual focus of study, more and more Caucasians began to consider themselves religiously Buddhist. Today, there are clearly more non-Asian Americans in the Buddhist movement than Asian-Americans. Nearly all non-Asian Buddhists are white, middle class, and between twenty and forty-five years old; as a group they have an unusually high level of education. Individuals rather than families seem to be attracted to Buddhism.

Why do these individuals choose to turn to the Buddhist tradition? Emma Layman, in her ground-breaking work on Buddhism in America, outlines eleven motivational factors that she deems useful in understanding just why many Americans are professing Buddhism:

1) familial-cultural affinity
2) intellectual, scientific appeal
3) appeal of a rational cure for a sick society
4) appeal of pageantry, symbolism, and the esoteric
5) do-it-yourself appeal
6) a wish to transcend the ordinary
7) need for a wise and benevolent authority figure
8) need to rebel against the establishment
9) need for relief from suffering
10) need for a fuller, richer, more effective life
11) need to seek the truth

There is no question at all that Layman's eleven factors present a reasonable approach to understanding Buddhist growth in modern America. These factors, however, are also met by the more traditional forms of Western religion. Consequently, our concern for understanding why so many individuals have turned to Buddhism remains, to a large extent, unresolved. To be sure, the art and esotericism of the Buddhist tradition is interesting and exciting, but it tells only a very small part of the story, especially when Buddhists are making every effort to "demystify" the traditional religion for its American audience.

In its homeland, the Buddhist religion placed an exceedingly high priority on a monastic style of life. For the monk or nun, nomadism provided a solitude and freedom from societal burdens in which it became possible to actualize the Buddha's message on a personal level, resulting in true religious growth and attainment. Within perhaps a hundred years of the leader's death in 483 B.C., the wandering way of life of the monks and nuns began to disappear in favor of a stable, settled monastic life. Such a life still provided ample opportunity for the attainment of enlightenment, but it also fostered a harmonious relationship between the monastic order and the laity. Virtually all the Buddhist cultures of South, Southeast, and East Asia developed thriving monastic traditions. In the United States, however, this has not been the case. The imported Buddhism that is now taking root in American soil remains for the most part limited to the laity. There are monasteries and religious professionals, but they are clearly neither the majority nor the normative model.

During the earliest period of Buddhism's entry into America, the explanation for its lay character is clear. The Pure Land tradition that served the Japanese immigrant community represents a nonmeditative strand of the Buddhist tradition in which emphasis is placed on positing one's faith in the saving grace of Amida Buddha. In this tradition, the ardent follower has little need to withdraw from the world. Rather, he or she maintains an active involvement in secular life while cultivating a proper interior environment. Zen, also, was an intellectual curiosity for Americans, and although they took meditation instruction from Zen priests, these teachers had home monasteries in Japan, not America.

The situation has changed only somewhat today. Some meditative groups have established monasteries and even suggest formal retreats for their disciples, but few groups have suggested that its members actually withdraw from secular life in favor of a monastic vocation. Of course there are a few groups that ordain monks and nuns, but these groups represent only a minimal part of the Buddhist tradition in America. One group, though, has established a proper ordination lineage for monks and nuns in this country in accord with the precepts outlined in the Buddhist disciplinary rules (Vinaya). It appears that, for the immediate future, Buddhism will remain an almost exclusively lay community in America. It also appears that, with the exception of the Pure Land and Nichiren Shōshū groups (about which we shall say more later), the American Buddhist tradition is placing increasing emphasis on a meditative life-style as the primary religious practice.

How many Buddhists are there in America and just where do we find them? Neither of these questions is easy to answer with any real accuracy. The raw numbers may be very deceptive. Buddhist Churches of America generally claims to have in excess of 100,000 members. If we add to this figure *Life* magazine's 1970 estimate of 200,000 members in Nichiren Shōshū, the preliminary total rises to 300,000. By adding in another factor for the combined meditative groups, along with some estimate for the miscellaneous Buddhist groups and individuals in the United States, it becomes possible to postulate approximately 500,000 Buddhists in America. This figure is probably not accurate, nor can it be verified. Most Buddhist groups in America do not keep the kinds of records necessary to provide accurate figures.

The issue of where American Buddhists reside is a somewhat simpler matter. Not surprisingly, Buddhism in America has been, and continues to be, a city movement. The city provides the widest of all possible audiences for Buddhist preachers and teachers. Consequently, they have sought disciples in large urban centers. At least one Buddhist group is listed in the telephone directory of any major American city. There have been rather superficial movements on the part of some Buddhists to leave the urban areas for the serenity of the countryside. The assumption seems to have been that once removed from the hustle and bustle of city life, enlightenment would be immediately forthcoming. Needless to say, that did not prove to be the case. More responsible Buddhist groups have emphasized working on the root of religious delusion wherever one resides, in New York City or the wilds of Montana. But because Buddhists can benefit from retreats and extended sessions of withdrawal from the workaday world, many groups have erected country centers to supplement their city centers. In this way, modern American Buddhists are able to strike a balance between urban dwelling and rural retreat—and of course, Buddhism has been referred to as the "middle path" for over 2,000 years.

Can we estimate the growth rate of the Buddhist tradition on American soil? It is unlikely that we can assign some growth factor to the tradition and plot its rise on a graph. It does seem, however, that the meteoric growth of the 1960s has subsided considerably. In its place is a much more gradual but stable rise, influenced by a variety of factors. For example, Buddhist growth can be (to some degree) linked to the publication of popular books by famous Buddhist teachers. In this way, well-known preachers can reach an audience that might never be accessible on a personal level. Adhering to Buddhist principles in earning a living has become a viable mode of bringing the Buddhist message to a wide audience. Few television viewers are aware that the famous New York Deli featured on the comedy series "Mork and Mindy" is owned by Buddhists, as are scores of other American businesses, and utilized as a low-key but creative and effective means of making the Dharma available to Americans. The variables are impossible to total; yet the rise in numbers of American Buddhists is continuous.

Having taken a brief look at the questions of who, why, where, and how many, it is time to examine some of the specific Buddhist groups in America. Since the Japanese tradition appears to be the one with the largest number of adherents, we shall consider it first. In addition, it presents a wide diversity in terms of Buddhist practice and direction.

As we noted earlier, Buddhist Churches of America, a Buddhist group in the Jōdo Shin-shū, or "True Pure Land," tradition of Japanese Buddhism, was one of the earliest Buddhist organizations to appear on American soil. Present before the turn of the twentieth century, it has maintained national headquarters in San Francisco during this entire period. Since the end of World War II, it has established eight primary districts throughout the United States, encompassing more than sixty independent churches and forty branches. A sophisticated administrative structure governs the organization, under the direction of a bishop. In addition to its purely religious branches, it maintains two major educational centers (the American Buddhist Academy in New York and the Institute of Buddhist Studies in California). Being a Pure Land establishment, its religious practice focuses on a liturgy that emphasizes faith in and praise for the saving grace of Amida Buddha.

Attendance at church services is stressed, and the church follows a rich and full festival season. Buddhist Churches of America maintains several periodical publications and pursues a rigorous training program for its clergy. The problem of identity is acute for the organization, since it primarily serves the Japanese-American community and has never had a very large non-Asian following. Second-generation Japanese-Americans have sought to accommodate American ideals through the various practices and activities of the church. In so doing, they have alienated their children, who are eager to reassert and emphasize their Japanese heritage. This situation represents a convoluted generation gap in reverse. As a result, Buddhist Churches of America, although the oldest Buddhist group in America, is the one having accomplished the least acculturation. It is a predicament that is not likely to improve.

Equally nonmeditative in its orientation is Nichiren Shōshū of America. The name of the organization is something of a misnomer, for this religious unit is actually part of the Japanese Sōkagakkai movement. The parent group in Japan is self-consciously political in motivation, utilizing religious ideals and practices in a quest for wealth and power as well as spiritual ends. The Sōkagakkai movement has roots in the formal Japanese school of Buddhism known as Nichiren, founded in the thirteenth century by a prophet bearing the same name, and arguing that the famous Indian Buddhist text known as the Lotus-sūtra was the only efficacious religious document for troubled times. Exported to America in the early 1960s, the sect appealed to many downtrodden Americans by promising wealth and satisfaction merely in return for chanting a liturgy that centers around the phrase "homage to the Lotus-sūtra."

From its American infancy in 1960, Nichiren Shōshū of America had established 258 chapters with over 200,000 members by 1974. In order to effect such dramatic results, the organization depended on an ingenious and well-managed administrative staff, headed by George M. Williams (born Masayasa Sadanaga in Seoul, Korea, of Japanese parentage). Wherever he lectured, Williams emphasized the American character of his religion, and argued that it was the true Buddhism and the true humanism. In addition, he continually spotlighted Nichiren Shōshū's concern for world peace, a goal he and his group hope to bring to fruition no later than 2200. By adding several slick publications and through reliance on testimony from its members for attracting and reinforcing new and prospective members, the organization grew rapidly through the 1970s. The problem that faces it is the aggressive tactic utilized by the parent group. The word for its recruitment effort, *shakubuku* (smash and flatten), rather accurately depicts the way in which new members are brought into the social unit. Further, it is the only Buddhist school that tends to emphasize its uniqueness at the expense of other Buddhist schools. Nonetheless, with a keen awareness of American marketing techniques, and with an ample audience from which to attract members, it seems that Nichiren Shōshū of America will be a force to be dealt with in the future.

The meditative strand of Japanese Buddhism is primarily represented in America by the Zen tradition. It is impossible to offer a generalized outline of Zen practices, primarily because there are so very many groups and the practices particular to each are so varied. If one were to pick a prototypical Zen center to focus on in elucidating both the Zen style and its mode of practice in America, it might well be the San Francisco Zen Center. Begun in 1961 by Shunryu Suzuki Rōshi, who arrived from Japan two years earlier, it has been stable in growth and direction and a leader in its community.

The Zen Center is not just a city center. In addition to its main headquarters in a somewhat seedy section of town, it has developed Zen Mountain Center (affectionately known as Tassajara) in Monterey County and a farm (called Green Gulch) that produces food for the parent community. San Francisco Zen Center has been a leader in community renovation, trying diligently to breathe new life into a once lovely section of San Francisco. It has several affiliated groups, constituting an effective outreach program. Despite the death of its founder in 1971, the center has fared well under the direction of its American Rōshi, Richard Baker. The group offers several types of membership (general member, practicing student, affiliate member, annual member), but each adherent is encouraged to practice the staple of the Zen tradition, meditation, and to visit the center as often as is practical. The organization has published a fine journal called *Wind Bell* and sponsors several periods of intense practice each year (known formally as *sesshins*). In addition, it has realized substantial profits from Suzuki Rōshi's book *Zen Mind, Beginner's Mind,* and from Edward Espe Brown's two volumes, *The Tassajara Bread Book* and *Tassajara Cooking.* Most of San Francisco Zen Center's members are non-Asian, and this is no real surprise. As early as 1971, Claude Dalenberg, one of the center's leading members, wrote:

> Zen Center should be in harmony with American society, capable of existing on its own two feet in the middle of that society. Now that we're thrown into this neighborhood and subject to the pressures of living here, I hope we will be forced to grow up, to mature, and not continue to be dependent on Japanese surroundings.
>
> (*Wind Bell*, 9 [1970–1971], p. 15)

Countless other Zen groups might equally well reflect the style and vitality of Zen in America, such as the Zen Center in Rochester, New York, and Maezumi Rōshi's Zen Center in Los An-

geles. Many of these groups are cataloged in Rick Fields's *How the Swans Came to the Lake* and Emma Layman's *Buddhism in America.* Here, it is sufficient to say that the Zen movement in America is the first Japanese-based organization to cultivate a non-Asian membership and to emphasize a meditative, reflective life-style as the staple of a new approach to being complete and whole in modern America.

The most prominent of the remaining Japanese Buddhist schools in America is that of Shingon, which represents the esoteric dimension of the Buddhist tradition, generally referred to as Tantra. Shingon came to America in 1912 with the founding of the Koyasan Buddhist Temple in the "Little Tokyo" section of Los Angeles. Although it has never gained many followers, or been considered fashionable among intellectuals, it remains present and active on the American scene.

The Tantric tradition in Buddhism has been more fully reflected in the Tibetan Buddhist groups that have taken up residence in the United States. Perhaps the earliest of these to become established was a dGe-lugs-pa group that took up residence in Freehold Acres, New Jersey. The leader of this group was a Kalmuck (Mongolian) known as Geshe Wangyal who, within three years of his arrival in 1955, had founded the Lamaist Buddhist Monastery, where he was able to share his vast knowledge with a group of eager and talented American students. The most notable of these is Robert Thurman, ordained by the Dalai Lama as the first American dGe-lugs-pa monk. Present in America almost as long as the dGe-lugs-pa tradition is that of the Sa-skya-pa. Until recently, the most significant figure in this lineage was Deshung Rinpoche, a brilliant lama who worked with Buddhological scholars at the University of Washington. Within the last decade, the appearance of Sa-skya-pa groups, with resident lamas, has been on the rise.

Far more visible are a rNying-ma-pa group known as the Tibetan Nyingma Meditation Center and a bKa-rgyud-pa group known as the Vajradhatu and Nalanda Foundation. The former organization is the brainchild of a learned lama named Tarthang Tulku. Identified early in his life as an incarnate lama, Tarthang began an intensive thirteen-year training period (in meditation and scholarship) at age fourteen. After the Communist Chinese invasion of Tibet, Tarthang fled to Sikkim, where he continued his studies. Prior to the death of his chief teacher, the young scholar-monk was instructed to bring his lineage to the West. Following six and one-half years at the Sanskrit University in Benares, Tarthang came to the West, settling in Berkeley, California.

Within a year of his arrival in America, Tarthang Tulku's students began the Tibetan Nyingma Meditation Center, and by 1971 they had expanded to a new home in the Berkeley hills. In 1973 the Nyingma Institute was founded, and the organization has been expanding continuously since then. They have established affiliate centers in several cities, a thriving publishing enterprise called Dharma Press, a human development training program, and several other major undertakings. By far their most ambitious activity is the construction of a self-sufficient community known as Odiyan, conceived according to a grandiose plan. Although Tarthang Tulku is keenly aware of his American setting, he is working diligently to provide his students with a Buddhist religious training that preserves its Asian heritage while speaking to their American background and circumstance. As such, his training can be categorized under five basic headings: (1) foundation practice (or *bum-nga*) in which five basic activities are repeated 100,000 times each; (2) *pūja*, or ceremonies of devotion and offering; (3) sūtra chanting in which traditional Tibetan texts are chanted along with the prayer to Guru Rinpoche, the Refuge vow, and the *Bodhisattva* (Buddha to be) vow; (4) rituals on sacred days in the religious calendar; and (5) seminars and workshops devoted to particular topical issues. To be sure, some students cannot maintain their commitment throughout this vigorous training. Nonetheless, those disciples who do remain in the tradition form a solid foundation on which a lasting lineage in America can be built.

Also of interest is Chögyam Trungpa, an incarnate lama from the bKa-rgyud-pa lineage. Trungpa's holiness was also identified at a very early age, as he was installed as the head of the Surmang monasteries at the age of thirteen months. During the years of educational training that ensued, a regent was appointed to rule in his stead. Trungpa took his novice's ordination at eight and his Bodhisattva vow at eleven. A few years later he was forced to flee over the mountains into India by the invading Communist Chi-

nese. He was fortunate in being aided in his Western education by a remarkable woman named Freda Bedi, and eventually studied at Oxford.

Chögyam Trungpa founded his first Western community in Scotland in 1967 and came to the United States several years later to reside at Tail of the Tiger, a meditation center in Barnet, Vermont, founded by several of his students. Energetic and aggressive, within a few short years Trungpa had built the most developed Buddhist organization in the United States, possessing both a religious and secular division. He sought to preserve his important lineage while speaking to what he perceived as an acute American religious dilemma. Time and again demonstrating both a remarkable wit and a profound insight, Trungpa took his message to the people in a continuous series of seminars in major American cities. In this way, he developed a sizable following. In addition, the tapes of his seminars were edited into book manuscripts by his most advanced students and published. Precisely because they were so timely and interesting, Trungpa was able to expand his following exponentially.

By the mid-1970s, Trungpa had moved his central headquarters to Boulder, Colorado, and begun a Buddhist university known as Naropa Institute. This organization is unusual in that it combines traditional scholarly studies with non-verbal enterprises such as dance in an exciting and personally fulfilling way. And in its short history, Naropa Institute has attracted some of the most talented and best-known scholars and artists on the American scene.

Trungpa has been important to the Tibetan tradition in America in that he insists on basic meditational practice for all of his students. He does not emphasize the colorful and esoteric parts of the Tibetan Buddhist tradition until such time as they can be contextually understood by his disciples. His organization seems to have adjusted to a period of perhaps too speedy growth in the 1970s, and is now advancing at a manageable pace.

Loosely allied with the meditative strands of the Japanese and Tibetan tradition is that of the Sino-American Buddhist Association. The Chinese Buddhist tradition has never developed a significant following in America, but this group suggests the flavor and mood of Chinese Buddhist practice. In the first place, it is eclectic in nature, combining elements of Ch'an, Vinaya, T'ien-t'ai (an early school of Chinese Buddhism), Tantra, and Ching-t'u (Pure Land) in its practices. Second, it emphasizes a great reliance on the traditional master, in this case embodied in the Venerable Hsüan-Hua. Third, the organization reflects the energy and diligence of the Chinese Buddhist approach in order to accomplish highly ambitious goals.

The leader of the group, Hsüan-Hua, is considered to be the first Ch'an patriarch in America. His lineage supposedly traces back to the historical Buddha, and Hsüan-Hua is noted to be forty-fifth in that line. He was born in 1908, became a monk after his mother's death, and pursued an incredibly vigorous course of training during his middle years. He traveled throughout the world on behalf of his lineage, finally coming to San Francisco in 1962 at the request of the San Francisco Buddhist Lecture Hall. Unlike most of the other Buddhist teachers in America, Hsüan-Hua has emphasized a monastic way of life for his disciples. Though he is also interested in maintaining an active laity, he has gone to great lengths to establish a valid ordination lineage for monks and nuns on American soil. To accommodate this monastic emphasis, Gold Mountain Dhyāna Monastery was established in 1971, and in 1976 his charges began work on the "City of Ten Thousand Buddhas," to be erected on a 237-acre tract near Ukiah, California.

Although a substantial part of the organization's practices include involvement with the Pure Land tradition, cultivation of the Vinaya and a heavy dose of meditation are incumbent on all followers. Periods of intensive meditation are a regular part of the calendar, with some sessions spanning the traditional 108 days. Further, during these periods, the daily routine generally begins at 4:00 A.M. and runs to 10:00 P.M. without interruption. During other periods, the group pursues a highly active translation and publication effort. Through the Buddhist Text Translation Society the organization is training highly competent individuals who are capable of translating important Buddhist texts into English; the master's commentary is appended.

Emma Layman considers several other Chinese Buddhist groups that have appeared on the North American continent. Included are Temple Mahayana, which serves as a retreat center for the Eastern States Buddhist Association of New York City, and the Temple of Enlightenment in the Bronx, New York. These groups are certainly interesting, but space limitation restricts their coverage here. In addition, the various Korean and Vietnamese Buddhist groups can only be mentioned but not discussed.

The remaining tradition to be considered here is that of the Theravāda, which permeated South Asia following the missionary enterprise of the Indian King Aśoka in the third century B.C. and which continues today. The primary representative of the Theravāda tradition on American soil is the Buddhist Vihāra Society, founded in 1965, in Washington, D.C., under the direction of the Venerable Thera Bope Vinita, a monk from Vajirarama Temple in Sri Lanka. The founding of the organization was the culmination of several years' work following the American visit of Madihe Pannaseeha Thera, who noticed much interest in Buddhism but little opportunity for Americans to pursue active involvement. In 1967, Thera Bope Vinita was succeeded by Mahathera Dickwela Piyananda, and later Mahathera Henepola Gunaratana also took up residence in the *vihara* (dwelling), which by then had established permanent residence on 16th Street N.W.

The group has maintained close ties with its parent organization in Sri Lanka, the Sasana Sevaka Society. In addition, although it has a rather widespread mailing list, it has no affiliated groups in the United States. Consequently, its membership remains small, and it fulfills primarily a service role for the international community in the U.S. capital. Regular services are held for its membership, augmented by observation of several festival days and Uposatha retreats. A modest library and bookstore are maintained, and a newsletter, known as the *Washington Buddhist,* is published regularly. Beyond this, the Buddhist Vihara Society has little more to offer Americans interested in the Theravāda tradition, possibly because the center is unwilling to exploit the "vipassana explosion," in which a faster, flashier brand of Theravāda meditation has become more popular than the traditional form of satipaṭṭhāna meditation stressed by the vihara.

There is no doubt that we could go on describing various Buddhist groups in America ad infinitum. However, now that we have offered something of a historical overview, attempted to place the groups in cultural context, outlined their membership in terms of numbers, commitment, concern, and affiliation, and described some of the most prominent and influential American Buddhist groups, we will conclude by examining the impact that these groups have made on America: where they fit into the modern American religious picture, where they might be going in the immediate and distant future, and whether they will ever become major, driving forces in American religiosity.

However sympathetic one might be, it must be admitted that Buddhism itself has made very little direct impact on America. Indeed, it is possible that Oriental culture as a whole has influenced America more profoundly; Buddhism in and of itself remains in its infancy here. If we draw on its history in its Asian homeland (whether in India, Tibet, Burma, or another country), it is clear that Buddhism took many centuries to form a cultural amalgam consistent with its own teaching and reflective of the host culture. We should expect the same gradual development in America.

If we consider American Buddhism one of what Jacob Needleman calls the "new religions," then several related concerns come into focus. Perhaps the foremost of these is the American public's fear of new religious movements. Harvey Cox makes this point clear in *Turning East: The Promise and Peril of the New Orientalism* (1977). His reference to a friend's calling Cambridge, Massachusetts "Benares-on-the-Charles" reflects the suspicion that Buddhism in America is somehow a cult, and by association with other, dangerous cult groups, to be both feared and avoided. Robert Ellwood, in *Religious and Spiritual Groups in Modern America* (1973), has outlined fifteen characteristics of cults. Curiously, not only are many of these attributes not negative in nature, most of them can be found in the major religious traditions of the world. The fact, for example, that Buddhism is godless theologically does not indicate that Buddhism has no conception of ultimate reality. It simply does not employ the specific symbol of God to represent that conception.

Buddhism in America can only be transformed into a truly American Buddhism when it can offer distinctly Buddhist answers to specifically American problems. Although we might not now argue for its inclusion in that complex of cultural events called civil religion, we can still attest to the efficacy of an American Buddhist art, ritual life, music, and seasonal festival cycle as a means of escalating the acculturation process. Much that was once considered part of the so-called counterculture has elevated itself from the domain of the "underground" to the realm of the ordinary. Now, as we increasingly demystify the so-called inscrutable East, it is becoming possible for Buddhism to emerge in modern America as an important aspect of the current religious situation.

BIBLIOGRAPHY

Van Meter Ames, *Zen and American Thought* (1962); Leonard Hal Bridges, *American Mysticism from William James to Zen* (1970); Harvey Gallagher Cox, *Turning East: The Promise and Peril of the New Orientalism* (1977); Heinrich Dumoulin and John Maraldo, eds, *Buddhism in the Modern World* (1976); Robert S. Ellwood, *Religious and Spiritual Groups in Modern America* (1973) and *The Eagle and the Rising Sun* (1974); Rick Fields, *How the Swans Came to the Lake: A Narrative History of Buddhism in America* (1981); Charles Y. Glock and Robert N. Bellah, eds., *The New Religious Consciousness* (1976); Dom Aelred Graham, *Conversations: Christian and Buddhist* (1968); Robert Greenfield, *The Spiritual Supermarket* (1975).

Christmas Humphreys, *Sixty Years of Buddhism in England, 1907–1967* (1968); Louise Hunter, *Buddhism in Hawaii* (1971); Tetsuden Kashima, *Buddhism in America: The Social Organization of an Ethnic Religious Institution* (1977); Gyomay Kubose, *American Buddhism: A New Direction* (1976); Emma McCloy Layman, *Buddhism in America* (1976); Martin Marty, *A Nation of Behavers* (1976); H. Neill McFarland, *Rush Hour of the Gods* (1967); Robert S. Michaelsen, *The American Search for Soul* (1975).

Jacob Needleman and George Baker, eds., *Understanding the New Religions* (1978); Louis Nordstrom, ed., *Namu Dai Bosa: A Transmission of Zen Buddhism to America* (1976); Charles S. Prebish, *American Buddhism* (1979); Charles Reich, *The Greening of America* (1971); Theodore Roszak, *The Making of a Counter Culture* (1969) and *Unfinished Animal: The Aquarian Frontier and the Evolution of Consciousness* (1975); Peter Rowley, *New Gods in America* (1971); Irving Zaretsky and Mark Leone, eds., *Religious Movements in Contemporary America* (1974).

[See also "Cults" in the Late Twentieth Century; Hinduism, Islam in North America; Occult Movements in America; and Shinto and Indigenous Chinese Religion.]

HINDUISM

John Y. Fenton

WESTERNERS have been aware of India since the time of the ancient Greeks. Indeed, the discovery of America was an unintended side effect of the search for a shorter trade route to India. Early American colonists shared a general European fantasy about India as a place of great wealth, fabulous kingdoms, and exotic mysteries. And, through eighteenth-century British colonists in India as well as through other Europeans, Americans came to perceive the Hindu tradition as a philosophy with possibly the oldest extant religious scriptures. From the eighteenth century to the present, the "ancient wisdom" of India appears in American traditions as the "perennial philosophy," the original core and central message of all of the great spiritual leaders of the past.

Hinduism offered those dissatisfied with institutional, traditional Christianity a religious and philosophical alternative. Others, caught up in the continuous American tradition of religiosity, an alternative to Christianity and Judaism, found in Hindu mysticism another avenue to ecstatic or occult religious experience, to conversion, to personal transformation. Prior to the twentieth century, however, most Americans knew little about the actual Hindu religious tradition, and many Christians were inclined to regard it as inferior, pagan, and probably idolatrous.

Current Hindu influence upon American culture and religion can be traced through the development of American spiritualism (concerned with the occult, contacting spirits, and the like), through literary and philosophical influences, through the missionary activities of Hindu emissaries and religious movements among Americans, and through the transplanting of Hindu traditions to America by Asian Indian immigrants.

HINDU TRADITION IN AMERICA

In the eighteenth and early nineteenth centuries most Americans' understanding of India came through commercial and missionary activity. Although initial contact was secondhand, through descriptive and interpretive European literature and missionaries' reports, direct accounts of India and its religions became available through increasing American trade, travel, and missionary activity. The growing interest in Hinduism was, however, primarily confined to New England and included Cotton Mather and John Adams. Joseph Priestly, the discoverer of oxygen and a foundational figure in English Unitarianism, published *A Comparison of the Institutions of Moses with Those of the Hindoos and Other Ancient Nations* in 1799, after his immigration to the United States.

More serious interest began in the 1820s and 1830s with the appropriation, in altered Americanized forms, of ideas from the Hindu Upanishads by transcendentalists such as Ralph Waldo Emerson, Henry David Thoreau, and Walt Whitman. "Philosophical" Hinduism was discussed and debated among Unitarians in the *Edinburgh Review* (popular in New England) and the *North American Review* and was of continued interest among Americans discontented with mainline Christian traditions. Yet, European and American Christian missionaries reported about popular rather than philosophical aspects of Hindu tradition, and often with derogatory overtones.

By the middle of the nineteenth century reasonably adequate translations of selected Hindu scriptures, such as the Bhagavad-Gītā and the Laws of Manu, were available. Sanskrit language studies were inaugurated at Yale University in 1841—but by scholars trained in Europe (especially in Germany) rather than in India. Once established in America, these Sanskrit professors trained other scholars primarily in philology and literature rather than in Hindu religious tradition or philosophy. The American Oriental Society was founded in Boston in 1842 by ministers, theologians, and missionaries with Asian field experience. By the second generation the society was run by professional orientalists who produced important philological research but still had no experience in India.

From the 1870s the series *Sacred Books of the East,* edited by F. Max Müller, provided the first good translations from Chinese, Hindu, and Buddhist religious traditions. Around this time, Americans also gained firsthand knowledge of Buddhism and Chinese religious traditions as travel became even easier and missionary activities in East Asia increased.

The beginnings of Theosophy in the mid-1870s exhibit the persistent connection between the American preoccupation with occult experience and "ancient wisdom," heavily influenced by both the eighteenth-century Swedish author Emanuel Swedenborg and the mysticism of Asian religions. The Theosophical Society, whose blend of various Asian religions, including Buddhism and Hinduism, with rationalism later helped to make Asian religions popular, began as a spiritualist group. Madame Blavatsky and Colonel Olcott first identified their teachings as Hindu and Buddhist during their trip to India and Ceylon (Sri Lanka) in 1878. The enthusiasm of Westerners for Hindu and Buddhist traditions catalyzed renewed interest among Indians in their own native traditions and cultures. Mohandas K. Gāndhī, the major figure in the Indian independence movement, for example, first came to appreciate the Bhagavad-Gītā during his student years in England at the urging of British Theosophical Society acquaintances.

In 1893 the World's Parliament of Religions was held in conjunction with the World's Fair in Chicago. For the first time, delegates from Asia gathered in America to expound their traditions and exchange their religious views with large American audiences. That there was such a gathering at all evidenced a new world vision and a new Protestant and Roman Catholic attitude toward other world religions.

One of the charismatic stars of the parliament was a delegate from India, Swami Vivekānanda. Encouraged by his success, Vivekānanda stayed in the United States for several years, lecturing and organizing local chapters of his Vedanta Society. The first was founded in New York City in 1894; other centers were soon established in a dozen cities across the United States. The Vedanta Press in Hollywood, California, was the primary American source of published Hindu scriptures and philosophy in America until the 1960s.

In 1920, Swami Yogānanda came to Boston to attend the International Congress of Religious Liberals, and became the first Hindu missionary to settle permanently in America. His Self-Realization Fellowship and branches of his Church of All Religions blended Hindu and Western ideas and religious practices. Yogānanda's and the Vedanta Society's missions set the dominant patterns for the Hindu movements that became so numerous in the United States after World War II.

Hindu influence upon American culture increased in a variety of ways in the first half of the twentieth century. Hindu themes were prominent in the writings of some literary figures such as W. B. Yeats and T. S. Eliot. Gerald Heard, Aldous Huxley, and Christopher Isherwood had personal connections with the Vedanta Society and wrote about the philosophy of non-dualism, intuitive absorption in ultimate reality, and unusual states of consciousness. World religions courses began to penetrate college curricula during the 1930s, although they did not become widespread until after World War II.

The Indian independence movement, and especially the activities of Gāndhī, were widely covered in American books and the press. Gāndhī's campaign subsequently provided the model for Martin Luther King, Jr.'s nonviolent resistance movement against racial repression in the 1950s and 1960s. Solid American scholarship on the Indian subcontinent and the Hindu tradition first began to have an impact in the mid-1960s, anticipating the social upheavals of the student and anti-war movements of the following decade.

RELIGIOUS TRADITIONS AMONG INDIAN IMMIGRANTS BEFORE 1965

Before 1965, when immigration from India and other Asian countries increased greatly, Indians in the United States and Canada constituted only a small fraction of Indian immigrants; the vast majority had settled in such areas as east, south, and central Africa, Sri Lanka, British Guyana, the Fiji Islands, Trinidad, and the United Kingdom. Although a small number of Indians were admitted to the United States in 1820, significant immigration began only in the late 1890s, when Indian immigrants were lured primarily from the Punjab (in northwest India) by commercial transporters with the promise of work on the Canadian railroad. Approximately 900 of these drifted south into Washington State. About 3,000 Indians arrived in America from India in 1907 and 1908. Before 1960 fewer than 12,000 Indians (including about 3,000 who entered illegally through Mexico) entered the country. During this period Indian immigration was much smaller than that of the Chinese and Japanese.

Perceived by white Americans as labor rivals, Indians were harassed and persecuted. In 1907 riots in Bellingham and Everett, Washington, caused the expulsion of about 1,000 Indians. While some went to Canada, others moved on to California to work temporarily on the railroads. Driven out of that industry by worker hostility, the Indians subsequently turned to agricultural labor.

Immigration to California from India over the years was complicated by changing immigration and naturalization policies. Immigration was closed in 1917; naturalization was an uncertain possibility; and land ownership was threatened until 1946, when an act of Congress gave Asian Indians the right of citizenship and an annual immigration quota of 100 individuals.

Most of the first-generation immigrants were illiterate and remained so, learning little English. Immigration restrictions allowed very few women to enter the country. Some of the men married Mexican-American women and became generally accepted in the Mexican-American community. Most Indians, being the object of prejudice, withdrew into their own society, linking their difficulties in an alien social environment with the anticolonial struggle for independence at home in India. In 1911 Indian farmers in the United States formed a political movement, called the Ghadr party, that fused Indian nationalism with immigrant identity and their own racial pride.

Almost all of the Indians in California came from the Punjab, Gujarat, Bengal, and the United Provinces. The majority were Sikh while the remainder were Hindu and Muslim. Sikhs, whose monotheistic devotional tradition was founded in the Punjab in the sixteenth century, formed a relatively closed rural social system in California. The first Sikh *gurdwārā* (temple; literally, gateway to the guru) was established in Stockton in 1909 by the Pacific Coast Khalsa Diwan Society. A second *gurdwārā* was not organized until 1948 in El Centro. The non-sectarian Indian Society of Yuba and Sutter Counties was founded in 1945, followed by the India American Cultural Society. These societies celebrated annual religious festivals and events of both political and religious importance.

Before 1945 Indian Hindus had small temples in San Francisco and Los Angeles, and a few worshiped with the Vedanta Society. Indian Muslims had a small meeting place in Stockton. And before 1965 Indian immigrants contributed little to the general spread of their religious ideas among Americans; outside of California they were scattered in small groups.

RELIGION AMONG INDIAN IMMIGRANTS SINCE 1965

The total number of persons originating in India who live in other parts of the world is estimated to be between 5 and 6.5 million. The largest population movement began in the first half of the nineteenth century following the abolition of slavery within the British Empire in 1835. The indenture system, developed to recruit cheap labor, accounts for a great proportion of the early immigrants, although a significant minority migrated as self-paid passengers.

Indians constitute the majority of the population in Mauritius, Fiji, and Guyana, are close to a majority in Trinidad, and are large minorities in Sri Lanka, Malaya, and Singapore. Asian Indians are small minorities (generally less than 3 percent of the total population) in east, central, and southern Africa, the United Kingdom, and Canada.

With the liberalization of U.S. immigration laws in 1965, the rate of Asian Indian immigration dramatically increased. Census figures for 1980 show a total of 387,223 Asian Indians in the United States (.17 percent of the total population); the largest number, 84,000, are in the New York City metropolitan area (24,000 of them concentrated in Queens). Sixty thousand reside in California (primarily in Los Angeles and San Francisco), 34,000 in Chicago, and more than 10,000 each in Washington, D.C., Detroit, Philadelphia, and Houston. Twelve other cities have Asian Indian populations of between 2,500 and 6,000. The Population Reference Bureau estimated the Asian Indian population in the country to be 525,600 in September 1985 and projects a total of 1,006,305 for the year 2000.

In contrast to most other immigrant groups in America, the majority of Indians arriving in America since 1965 are highly educated, fluent in English, technically and professionally trained, of the middle and upper class, and metropolitan in origin. While these Indians acculturate fairly easily in public situations, at home and among other Indians they remain ambivalent toward American culture and are strongly attached to Indian life-styles, Indian cultural tradition, and idealized valuations of India. They are bicultural, moving back and forth between private and public, indigenous and alien cultures. They adopt American material culture traits, but not typical middle-class values. And their Indian identity is reinforced by frequent return trips to India, by the tendency of the men to secure their brides from home, by participation in secular and religious voluntary associations, and by the heavy use of movies, music, news, and other cultural materials from India. Only 25 percent of them are U.S. citizens, often for purely practical reasons.

Among themselves, Indians organize primarily along regional and religious lines because of their strong sense of social boundaries. Moreover, regional cultures and religious traditions are much more concrete than "Indian culture" or "Hinduism" for them. Both locally and nationally, Indians have great difficulty forming organizations that represent *all* Indian immigrants. However, caste restrictions among Indians in America are largely nonfunctional except for choice of marriage partners.

Asian Indian Hindus in America are culturally and religiously quite heterogeneous. Within the borders of the Republic of India sixteen major languages and a host of minor dialects are spoken. The only language spoken and understood throughout the country is a foreign one: English. Cultural and regional differences correspond to linguistic differences; and cults, rituals, and primary deities vary within these cultural regions. Local variations (often called "little traditions" by social scientists) are at least as important for understanding the Hindu religious tradition as are general characteristics shared by the tradition as a whole (often called the "great tradition" or "Sanskrit tradition"). At the time of their immigration to America, most Asian Indian Hindus knew their religious tradition primarily as practiced in its local variations—in which Hinduism is conveyed and supervised by a variety of religious specialists, very few of whom have come to America. Local religious structures in India are bound together with cultural structures and have been transplanted only fragmentarily to America.

The term *Hindu* is as much a cultural as a religious designation. While the Hindu tradition of Asian Indians often shares much that is characteristic of export Hinduism (discussed later in this essay), it also tends to celebrate regional culture as well as religion, frequently including rituals conducted in Sanskrit in traditional fashion against a background of Hindu mythology. In addition, Hindu tradition includes a strong sense of familial duties and obligations, a culturally transmitted sense of social duty, and a variety of customary practices.

The Sikh tradition was founded in the sixteenth century by Gurū Nānak and brought to completion under the tenth guru, Gobind Singh, in the seventeenth century. Sikhs stress the devotional and mystical love of the one true transcendent and invisible God, the Sat Nām (True Name). Sikhs are initiated into the *khalsā* (the pure, the community; originally a military fraternity) with the new common family name Singh (lion). Women have the common name Kaur. Men are obligated to wear their hair uncut, to carry a small saber, and to wear a comb, khaki shorts, and a steel bracelet. After the death of Gobind Singh, the Sikh scriptures, the Ādi-Granth or Guru Granth Sāheb, replaced the living guru.

Communal worship takes place in the *gurdwārā* (temple) where the Ādi-Granth is kept and honored. Sikh communal worship generally includes readings from the Ādi-Granth, hymn singing, a lecture, supplications to God, distribution of food that has been offered to God, and sharing food from the community kitchen. The major annual festivals fall primarily in the period from October to January, celebrating the birthdays, martyrdoms, and release from prison of several of the first ten gurus, and the installation of the Ādi-Granth as the eleventh and last guru.

Jainism began to become a vigorous movement with Nataputta Vardhamāna, called Mahāvīra (great hero), in the sixth century B.C.E. It was an ascetic tradition intended to lead to liberation. According to Jain tradition Mahāvīra was the twenty-fourth in a line of Tīrthaṅkaras (ford makers—across the stream of suffering and rebirth) that stretches back many additional centuries. This rigorously ethical and ascetic tradition required of monks and nuns absolute *ahimsā* (nonviolence) to any living being, truthfulness, celibacy, taking only what is given, and complete detachment. For laity a system of lesser vows, ideally leading to monasticism, was eventually developed requiring nonviolence, truthfulness, chastity, simplicity, limiting greed, nonstealing, giving alms, and spending temporary periods fasting, in meditation, and as monastics. For the laity there is also a religious cult with temple rituals resembling Hindu *pūjā* (worship), in which flowers and fruits are offered before the images of the Tīrthaṅkaras as an aid to detachment. Jains in America are almost exclusively lay persons from northwest India.

Individual and Family Religion. The primary social context for the practice of Hindu, Jain, and Sikh religions in America is the individual in the context of an extended family, even if most members of the family live in another state, or in India. Personal religious practice seems to have changed little since immigration, although parents of older children sometimes become more observant. The vast majority of first-generation Asian Indians are married, in their thirties, and live in nuclear families with not more than two children. Personal religious practice is in part carried out, especially by the wife, for the benefit of the family. Perhaps three-quarters of the women do some form of personal devotion each day; this is true of less than half of the men. The form of devotion is usually simple and brief, some mantras or a brief meditation. A few Indians practice Transcendental Meditation or yoga. Perhaps three quarters of the homes contain small religious shrines, but in some cases no one worships there. Many women fast several days a year to promote their husbands' health.

Pūjās are performed by many Hindu families for annual religious festivals connected with particular deities. The majority of festivals fall between October and December. Rites of passage are less observed and less elaborate than in India, although *pūjās* for birth are observed with some frequency. The typical young male returns to India for a bride as well as for the marriage ceremony. Birthdays of children receive more attention in America, and Christmas has been adopted as a festive occasion. Rituals are sometimes performed upon moving into a new house, to give thanks for something good that has happened, or to ensure success in new ventures. Some Indians consult astrologers about auspicious times for planned events. In general, timetables for rituals are fitted into American weekends.

Most Indian immigrants return to India at least once every five years and, while there, visit shrines and temples and partake in family religiosity. In addition to overtly religious practices, adult Hindu males frequently understand themselves as *karma-yogis*—persons who are fulfilling their moral and religious duties while performing their vocations within society, thus adhering to a "Hindu way of life."

Sikhs and Jains display similar patterns. Most Sikhs do not have a copy of the Guru Granth Sāheb in their homes because the Granth requires a separate room and worship both morning and evening. Some Sikhs who do have the Granth curtail worship to once a day.

Temples. In the strict sense a Hindu temple is the abode of one primary deity permanently present in an image before which a Sanskrit-language *pūjā* is performed daily by a Brahman priest. Construction and maintenance of temples is financially feasible only when the local population is relatively large. In such cases, as in the New York City area, religious institutions tend to revert to the more restricted cultural and religious boundaries that are common in India. The Hindu Temple of New York devoted to the deity Gaṇeśa was established with the cooperation of a temple foundation in south India. Sanskrit *pūjās* are conducted daily. *Pūjās* are also performed at the request of individuals and for the major annual festivals. Sunday worship attracts less than one hundred persons, primarily from south India.

The New York Geeta Temple is devoted to several deities, attracts several hundred north

Indians, conducts brief rituals in Hindi rather than Sanskrit, and devotes the bulk of worship to vernacular discourses and *bhajans* (individual and group devotional hymn singing). The Swami Nārāyana cult, which has become very popular in England, has also established temples in New York and Chicago. Appealing primarily to Gujaratis, Swami Nārāyana venerates its founder, born in the late eighteenth century, as a form of the god Vishnu. Sunday services, and especially major Hindu festivals, at the ISKCON temple in New York and Washington, D.C., attract large numbers of Indians.

Jains, who constitute a small minority of Indian immigrants, have temples in New York City, Boston, Chicago, Cleveland, and several locations in California. The majority of Sikh *gurdwārās* are in California, with others in New York, Washington, D.C., Chicago, and Houston. A traditional Hindu temple to Meenākshī has been built in Houston. Hindu temples have been completed or are in various stages of construction in many urban centers. There are two temples in Hawaii, one in San Francisco, California, three in Berkeley, and one temple each in San Leandro, Morago, Los Angeles, Livermore, Fremont, Glendale, Norwalk, and Oakland in California. Denver, Colorado, and Yuma, Arizona, have a temple each. In New Jersey there are temples in Morris Plains, Garfield, and Berlin. Maryland has one temple in Bethesda and two in Silver Springs. Pittsburgh has three temples and there are temples in Stroudsburg and Harrisburg, Pennsylvania. There are two temples in Flushing, New York, and one in Wellesley Hills, Massachusetts. Flint, Michigan, has two temples. There are temples in Lemont and Urbana and two in Chicago, Illinois, and one each in Cincinnati, Beavercreek, and Toledo, Ohio. Houston and San Antonio, Texas, have temples. There are also temples in New Orleans, Louisiana, Nashville and Memphis, Tennessee, and Augusta, Georgia. Atlanta, Georgia, has two temples.

The attempt of Hindus in Pittsburgh to construct a temple split the community into two groups, one of north Indians favoring a "modern" temple with many deities, the other of south Indians choosing a one-deity temple in south Indian architectural style. This Śrī Venkateswara Temple in Pittsburgh was built with the cooperation of an Indian temple foundation connected to the famous Śrī Venkateswara temple in south India that also supported the Hindu Temple of New York, and also attracted substantial donations not from just the immediate area but from all parts of the United States. A variety of traditional rituals are conducted all day long in Sanskrit by resident priests, and individual *pūjās* can be sponsored for a fee. The temple also has a cultural hall for a large number of cultural events. The north Indian group has recently dedicated a second Pittsburgh temple, and a third temple is planned.

Because the Indian population is highly mobile, in terms of both occupation and personal travel, Indians who do not live near temples nevertheless visit them. The Śrī Venkateswara Temple in Pittsburgh and others perform *pūjās* for people in other locations and mail the *prasāda* in dry form to the sponsors. The Satyanārāyana Pūjā for success is particularly popular. Temples also print rubrics and explanatory literature to help in the performance of some rituals at home. Temple-produced tape cassettes are used by some, both for the Sanskrit-spoken portions of the ritual and for instructions for performance. A few temples have priests who make tours to other communities, and a few freelance priests travel about the country for special events such as weddings. Some Hindus sponsor *pūjās* to be performed in India. Sikh associations distant from *gurdwārās* also arrange for *granthīs* (scripture readers) and *rāgīs* (hymn singers) to visit their worship for occasions such as Gurū Nānak's birthday.

The ritual needs of Hindus in communities without temples or professional priests can be met by temporary, part-time priests. Some of these learned to perform *pūjās* in India; others learned the rites from manuals sent from India. While in some cases scrupulous care is taken to maintain the rite in traditional form, in most the rite is shortened and explanations of the rite and new stories are introduced. In these cases, as when a professional priest conducts a *pūjā* outside a temple, the deities are invoked into the space used only for the duration of the ritual.

Voluntary Associations. Voluntary associations organize gatherings for worship, fellowship, entertainment, and to celebrate regional and linguistic identity in all Indian communities. When there are sufficient numbers in a particular community, people from the same Indian region who speak the same native language form associations to sponsor celebrations of annual religious festivals, cultural events, and entertainment. New York City, for example, has organizations representing every Indian region from which there are immigrants. An autumn celebration of Durgā Pūjā (the mother goddess), for example, may attract Bengalis from several states. Since Indians typically do not live in primarily Indian neighborhoods, the observance of the elephant-headed god's festival, Gaṇeśa Caturti (Gaṇeśa's fourth), in late summer might be the primary occasion for Maharashtrians to assemble. Some associations meet periodically specifically for the purpose of worship. *Pūjās* are followed by a communal, vegetarian meal.

There are also umbrella associations in almost any sizable Indian community that attempt to bring together and to represent Indians of each religion or language. These organizations, generally more successful in the smaller Indian communities, put most of their emphasis on the celebration of Indian culture and the fostering of good relations with non-Indian Americans. For example, the India-America Cultural Association in Atlanta has been reasonably successful in uniting an Indian community of about 3,000; funds have been raised to purchase a church building that serves as a cultural and religious center. Two rooms have been set aside and renovated as a temple shrine. Other space in the building is available for worship by Jains and Sikhs as well as Hindus; however, many in the local Sikh community have opted to attempt to build a *gurdwārā* instead.

Where the Vedanta Society is active, it attracts Hindus from all areas of India. Vishwa Hindu Parishad is another international organization that attempts to promote and to preserve Hindu culture and religion. Local voluntary associations also exist in many cities. Arya Samaj is active in some areas, particularly in California and New York. ISKCON attracts large numbers of Indian Hindus in the major American cities, especially for the celebration of Krishna's birthday. Some Hindus also participate in smaller communities, particularly in those where there is no Hindu temple. A fairly large number of Hindu gurus and swamis lecture in various Indian communities with considerable regularity. One of the most popular, Swami Chinmāyānanda of the Chinmāya Mission, also has some followers outside the Indian community.

Future Prospects. The Hindu religious tradition in America will no doubt be bolstered by continued immigration from India. But the future of Hindu, Sikh, and Jain traditions in America is to a large degree dependent on the second and future generations of the immigrants. There is very little long-term organized religious education for children. There are some Sunday programs, short courses, summer camps, language courses, and classes in Indian dance. Children also accompany their parents on trips to India. They are frequently brought with the family to worship occasions, but most grow up with little knowledge and little real feeling for the traditions.

The Indian behavioral-cultural-sanctional context for child rearing is missing. Parents have to compete with the American educational system and the peer interests of American children. Parents themselves are often ambivalent, undecided whether they are migrants who will one day retire in India or permanent immigrants. Negative aspects of American culture such as crime, dishonesty, broken families, pornography, and drugs are viewed by first-generation Asian Indians with perhaps as much apprehension for their children as the prospect of weakened religious traditions.

While first-generation parents will probably not be able to arrange their children's marriages, the experience of other immigrants suggests that most second-generation Indians will marry other Indians. Second-generation married couples are likely to continue Indian traditions and are more likely to become largely secular than to convert to some other religious tradition. There has been only negligible Christian missionary work among Indians in the U.S., and while Hindus occasionally attend Christian worship, conversions to Christianity are rare.

EXPORT HINDUISM

Many of the Hindu movements exported to America in the twentieth century share some characteristics in common with concurrent developments in India. Most center around gurus, living or deceased, who are believed to embody the highest spiritual realization. The primary attraction of the movements is a belief that the gurus can teach or transmit this experience to those who follow them; all the movements focus on spiritual diagnoses of personal problems and therapeutic transformation of the self. Their basic world view is non-dual: truth is one; personal and impersonal gods are the same; beneath the frustration and disorder of personal and social existence is an underlying unity that is also manifest in the individual self.

Export Hinduism is generally very optimistic about human possibilities, holding that the true self deep within each person can be awakened and put one in touch with the power of the universe at large. The true reality of each person is the same as or part of universal reality. This reality is the true basis of all religions, but transcends them all. There is no possible conflict between science and religion because each points in its own way to the same ultimate reality. For adherents of these movements, the process of attaining this ultimate reality is thus a proven scientific technique or path to be followed. The path itself is believed to be simply true and is no more religious in a sectarian sense than mathematics or physics. Export Hinduism represents the general Hindu tradition rather than particular sectarian Hindu traditions, and it claims as well to represent the fundamental spiritual tradition of all humankind.

Missionary movements from India enjoyed their greatest popularity in the 1960s and 1970s, appealing primarily—but not exclusively—to young, middle-class, white Americans not yet married and settled in their own families. Export Hinduism, packaged for American consumption, was an attractive alternative faith for much the same reasons as were other Asian religions and secular psychological transformation movements. In a time of great cultural, spiritual, and moral change and upheaval in the face of the Great Society—a time of the apparent decline of the symbolic integration of American society—Asian religious movements filled a moral and spiritual vacuum for the marginal, helping them to make moral sense of their lives. Asian mysticism offered a sense of family and community to those with weakened familial ties and moral structures, and for young people it promised a sense of control, especially through meditation, to help overcome feelings of impotence generated by the impersonal bureaucracies of technological capitalism.

Continuing the American tradition of spiritualism and counterspirituality, mysticism offered the possibility of one's being transformed into a fully realized and powerful person. This tradition, also present in increasingly popular Western transformational psychologies, was absent from mainline American religious institutions. In fact, the emphasis on experience in these mystical traditions catalyzed the Charismatic movement, religious healing, meditation, and Holiness movements in Christianity.

The content of Asian mysticism was new, but its focus on the personal problems of life was not. Social and structural distress was diagnosed in psychological and spiritual terms, and a spiritual remedy was prescribed. Especially in the Hindu movements, people were offered roots in an inner but universal self already harmoniously related to all things and all persons. Because universal order was hidden, belief in this order could be maintained even when society did not agree. Typically, the way to fulfillment was marked by clear techniques or paths to be followed and by the presence of a manifestation of spiritual power in the figure of the guru, a founder or teacher with the secret of transcendent ecstatic experience and wisdom.

Americans joined not only Hindu movements but also other movements and cults that might offer the best chance of individual or communal fulfillment. There was in fact a great deal of "spiritual shopping": drop-out rates in certain Asian religious groups were typically as high as 50 percent.

The Vedanta Society. As mentioned earlier, the Vedanta Society, oldest of the Hindu missionary movements to America, was founded in New York City in 1894 by Swami Vivekānanda, spiritual heir to Śrī Rāmakrishna. Vivekānanda came to America offering the spiritual riches of India in exchange for the technology and material progress of the West.

Vedānta refers to the "end or purpose of the Upanishads, as interpreted by the tradition stemming from Śankara, the great ninth-century Hindu theologian and as modified by Vivekānanda. God or Ultimate Reality (the Brahman) is non-dual but nevertheless manifest in the ordinary world of multiplicity. The Brahman is *sat-*

chitānanda (being, consciousness, bliss) and is immanent in the world though in a veiled manner. In its higher, transcendent reality the Brahman is absolutely indescribable. The Brahman is present in human beings as their *ātman* (true self), so that the human body is the temple of the divine spirit. Caught up in ignorance of their true nature, human beings suffer from the fragmentary nature of their apparent level of existence and are subject to rebirth after death until they come to the realization of their true nature, the fundamental unity of all reality.

Realization that the self *(ātman)* is the self of the world (Brahman) occurs primarily as a matter of insight or intuition that results from the inherent capacity of the self to become one with ultimate reality. But realization is catalyzed by correct teaching, by meditation, by the presence and impact of a teacher who has already realized the highest truth, and by service in the concrete, ordinary world in ways that manifest the divine unity of all things. The ideal of *vedānta* is a spiritually balanced and harmonious life of devotion, wisdom, service, and meditation.

Vivekānanda, emphasizing the universality of this message, taught that *vedānta* is the heart of all religious traditions and is at odds with none that are truly spiritual. For him, ultimate reality manifested itself at various times in perfectly realized beings who are descended forms *(avataras)* of the Brahman. Avatars of the past include such figures as Krishna, Jesus, and the Buddha. Many members of the Vedanta Society regard Śrī Rāmakrishna as the *avatara* of the present age.

There are twelve Vedanta Society centers in the United States, all under the supervision of the Rāmakrishna Mission in Calcutta, India. The American organizational center of the Vedanta Society is now located in Los Angeles. A spiritual retreat for the Chicago center is currently being built in Ganges Town, Michigan.

The organizational core of the Vedanta Society consists of monastics, some of whom become swamis (self-mastered persons) after at least nine years of training. Although the majority of the swamis in the United States are Indians, about twenty American men have been ordained since 1956 and twelve women have taken monastic vows. Lay members are active in the affairs and programs of local societies. The society currently has about 220 monks and 3,000 lay members.

The programs of the Vedanta Society have a strong philosophical or intellectual emphasis, appealing in America primarily to the educated middle classes; meditation and spiritual instruction for individuals are also offered. *Pūjā* (ritual worship), followed by *bhajans* (devotional songs), is conducted according to an annual lunar calendar for the birthdays of Rāmakrishna; his wife, Śrī Sārada-devī; and Swami Brahmānanda, an immediate disciple of Rāmakrishna; and also for prominent Hindu festivals such as Śivarātri, Krishna's birthday, Kālī Pūjā, and Christmas. *Āratī* (the offering of fire) is performed daily in the society centers.

The Vedanta Society has a uniquely wide appeal to Americans, to Asian Indian immigrants, and to persons from other cultures as well. Its press publishes scripture translations, philosophy, and guides for the spiritual life. Many of the society's basic religious ideas are shared by other Hindu missionary movements, and its modes of operation have become models for the propagation of other types of export Hinduism in America.

The Self-Realization Fellowship. As noted earlier, Paramahaṇsa Yogānanda was the first Hindu yogi to remain permanently in America. The Self-Realization Fellowship, which he founded in 1925, taught classical forms of yogic meditation and *kriya-yoga.* Meditation is paying attention selectively. Classical yoga is a meditation technique for stopping all of the modifications of ordinary awareness so that a person may become conscious only of his or her spiritual nature. The technique includes behavior modifications that cut dependence upon sensory stimulation, body posture that is steady and erect, lowering the metabolic rate by slowing the rate of breathing, and finally, concentrating upon an appropriate object to such an extent that everything but the object disappears from awareness. One must then learn to concentrate without an object of concentration until the spirit within becomes conscious of itself.

Kriya yoga is intended to be a form of God-realization. It employs breath control and the repetition of sacred sounds, or mantras, to energize and reintegrate the seven *chakras* (psychic centers) ranged from the bottom of the spinal column to the top of the brain. Yogānanda explained Hindu yoga in Western psychological terms, modified for American conditions, and combined with Christian concepts. His books *Autobiography of a Yogi* (1946) and *Whispers from Eternity* (1929) have sold widely. His successful publications set a model for the heavy use of print and other media to spread Hindu teachings in America.

The Self-Realization Fellowship today includes both lay persons and monastics. Yogānanda's Church of All Religions combines Hindu and Christian forms of worship, and, like Christian fellowships, meets on Sunday mornings. Sister Daya Mata (Faye Wright) is the current head of the forty-four groups in the United States, headquartered in Los Angeles. Other yogic organizations derived from the Self-Realization Fellowship include the Self-Revelation Church of Absolute Monism, in Washington, D.C. (led by Swami Premānanda), which also emphasizes the life and teachings of M. K. Gāndhī; Prema Dharmasāla (founded by Vasudevas and Devaki), in Virginia Beach, Virginia; the Temple of Kriya Yoga, led by Swami Kriyānanda (Melvin Higgins), in Chicago; and the Ananda Meditation Retreat, founded by another Swami Kriyānanda (J. Donald Walters), near Nevada City, California.

The International Society for Krishna Consciousness. The International Society for Krishna Consciousness (ISKCON), whose members are popularly known as "Hare Krishnas," derives from a Vaisnava (Vishnu) devotional tradition initiated by Caitanya in Bengal, India, in the sixteenth century. A. C. Bhaktivedanta Swami Prabhupāda came from India to New York City in 1965 to spread a modern version of Krishna devotion. At first gradually, then more rapidly, he attracted disciples. In the late 1960s he transferred the center of the movement to Los Angeles.

Easily the best known form of export Hinduism, the Hare Krishnas are a familiar sight on American city streets. Wearing saffron robes or saris, they solicit funds, sell the movement's magazine and books, and chant the Krishna mantra: "Hare Krishna Hare Krishna Krishna Krishna Hare Hare Hare Rama Hare Rama Rama Rama Hare Hare." (Rama is the name of another avatar of Vishnu in Hindu tradition. In ISKCON Rama is regarded as another name of Krishna. Hare is an invocation of Krishna's consort, Rādhā.)

The movement is based on *bhakti* (ecstatic devotion) to Krishna, a figure who in much of Hindu tradition is regarded as one of the avatars of Vishnu, but who is the Supreme Personality of the Godhead in ISKCON. For the devotees Krishna is *the* God who is also known in other religious traditions under other names. Krishna is the hero–divine guru of the Bhagavad-Gītā and the divine being in descent form (avatar) in the scripture called the Bhāgavata Purāṇa, which tells of Krishna's birth, playful childhood, and adolescent love for the *gopīs* (cow maidens) in Vrindavan in north India. The account in the Bhāgavata Purāṇa (called the Śrīmad Bhāgavatam in this movement) provides the paradigm for the devotional life, which calls for ecstatic devotion as *gopīs* longing for the presence and grace of Krishna.

Devotional life is based upon the repetitive chanting of the Krishna mantra. The mantra is repeated subvocally when it is not being proclaimed aloud so that the devotee may be constantly reminded of Krishna. In a Krishna temple, God is believed to condescend to come down to be present in his image. The temple becomes a symbolic Vrindavan in which Krishna is the permanent divine guest of his devotees.

One or more persons in the temple take responsibility for the proper care of and service to the images. The altar includes images of the guru (Bhaktivedanta Swami), Caitanya (the founder of the tradition in Bengal), Rādhā (the eternal consort of Krishna), and Krishna. The daily ritual resembles that of a traditional Hindu temple. The *pūjārī* (ritualist) rises at 3:30 A.M., chants with prayer beads, wakes up the deities with a bell, takes them out of their beds, dresses them, and offers them food on trays in front of the altar. The food (called *prasāda*) is the deities' grace, or gift, to the devotees. At 5 A.M. everyone in the temple compound attends the *ārātrika* (fire offering) *pūjā* (worship, doing honor) for half an hour, and all eat the food that is left over from what had been offered earlier to the deities. The *pūjārī* then bathes the deities and dresses them again. Breakfast *prasāda* is served at 8:45 A.M. Lunch and dinner also consist of *prasāda;* in fact, no food should be taken that has not first been offered to the deities. After lunch the deities are undressed for afternoon rest, and later awakened and dressed again. After dinner and before the devotees retire, the deities are undressed and put to bed for the night. In the evening there are two more *ārātrikas* and the worship of the *Tulasī* plant, which is sacred to Krishna. For special occasions deity images are put in ornate swings and entertained in the evening. Since the temple is the abode of Krishna and the other deities, it is Vrindavan on earth (a heaven on earth).

The daily schedule of other ISKCON devotees may include the studying of scripture and doctrine, performing chores around the temple, handling temple business, and, for most, excursions in groups to public places for chanting, selling the magazine *Back to Godhead* or books written by Bhaktivedanta Swami, soliciting funds, explaining ISKCON to interested persons and inviting them for evening *prasāda*. The daily round is heavily scheduled and highly regimented. The life of the devotee in a Krishna temple is relatively isolated in a highly structured environment totally symbolically transformed. The temple society serves as a new, enlarged family.

Men and women are segregated in most situations in the temple; women are treated as subordinates, as is often the case in Indian tradition; unmarried devotees are required to be celibate. Married devotees have sexual relations only for the purpose of procreation. Some devotees take a lifelong vow of celibacy and are initiated as monastics. Governance is hierarchical, from the guru (or his representatives; Bhaktivedanta Swami died in 1977) to the guru-appointed temple president on down. Social control of membership from the top is strong. Devotees and lay followers of ISKCON are, except for Asian Indians, almost entirely middle-class whites. The guru-disciple relationship is fundamental, the disciple laying all of his or her spiritual destiny in the hands of the guru with total trust and without criticism. The sincere devotee regards the guru's interpretations and translations of the scriptures with a literalistic attitude and reads only what is recommended or permitted by the guru.

Bhaktivedanta Swami wrote a large number of scholarly theological books, including translations and commentaries on the scriptures central to the Krishna tradition; perhaps most important are *The Bhagavad-gītā As It Is* (1972) and *The Śrīmad Bhāgavatam* (1962). The books are published and distributed by the organization's Bhaktivedanta Book Trust. In addition to donations received from supporters, ISKCON derives considerable income from the sale of the guru's books, the magazine *Back to Godhead,* and small businesses.

There are over sixty Krishna temples in major cities across the United States with probably about 2,500 residents, and several thousand additional persons who regularly or occasionally attend temple worship. Asian Indians attend in the hundreds in some cities, especially for annual festivals such as Krishna's birthday. In 1969 a large temple and monastic compound called New Vrindavan was founded in West Virginia near Wheeling. There are also several hundred full-time ISKCON members and fifteen to twenty temples in India as part of the effort to spread this type of Krishna devotion in India.

Bhaktivedanta Swami appointed a governing body commission in 1970 to help manage the international organization. After his death in 1977, leadership passed to this body of twelve persons. Now with twenty-three members, the governing body commission presides over six zones in the United States and Canada and approximately fourteen zones in the rest of the world. What the future of ISKCON will be without its founding guru remains to be seen.

Transcendental Meditation. Transcendental Meditation (TM) is undoubtedly the most popular form of export Hinduism in America. More than 600,000 Americans are said to have paid the meditation training fee. Maharishi Mahesh Yogi, a disciple of Guru Dev in India, launched TM in America through the Spiritual Regeneration Foundation in 1959. Subsequently the Students' International Meditation Society (SIMS) promulgated "the science of creative intelligence" among college students. The movement grew slowly until the mid-1960s, when the Beatles and several movie stars became temporary followers and TM received heavy media coverage. In the late 1960s and early 1970s TM organizations sponsored scientific studies to prove that the practice of TM lessens stress and has other apparent physical and psychological benefits. And in the late 1970s and early 1980s TM was given periodic television exposure in popular programs such as "The Mike Douglas Show." A very sophisticated packaging and merchandising campaign has also boosted TM's popularity.

In 1974 the general TM governing body, the World Plan Executive, bought a college campus in Fairfield, Iowa, and founded the Maharishi International University, which offers both bachelor's and master's degrees. A second TM university has been established in Switzerland. Other branches of TM in America include the American Foundation for the Science of Creative Intelligence, which teaches TM to business people; the Spiritual Regeneration Movement, which works with middle-aged and older persons; and the American Association of Physicians Practicing the Transcendental Meditation and TM-Siddhi Programs, which claims five thousand doctors as members.

TM centers of one or another sort exist in virtually every major American city. Advanced courses in TM are offered at a resort in Livingston Manor, New York, and on Majorca. Some large corporations offer TM programs for their employees; the U.S. Army has experimented with TM to combat drug abuse; and, for a while, TM was offered as a course in five public schools in New Jersey. (In 1979 the U.S. Court of Appeals in Philadelphia ruled that Transcendental Meditation was a religion and that it therefore could not be taught in the public schools.)

Transcendental Meditation is popular for a variety of reasons. It claims that it is not a religion but is instead the science of creative intelligence; it is relatively easy to learn and to practice; positive results start early in the practice; the cost of initiation and training is moderate; and it makes no demands for changes in life-style or behavior. TM consists primarily of a form of meditation called *japa*—the repetition of the names of deities or of brief verses (mantras), usually from the Hindu scriptures.

In Hindu tradition *written* scriptures are secondary and nonessential. The Vedas are not revealed by a god or gods, but were intuited by great seers of the ancient past. The truth they embody is only partially contained in the meaning of the words and phrases. The sounds themselves, regardless of their intellectual meaning, embody the truth and conform to the basic structure and principles of ultimate reality. The oral repetition of such mantras attunes or aligns the meditator to ultimate reality and allows him or her to tap the energy of the universe itself.

Although the traditional theory of the use and meaning of the mantra in Hindu tradition is not explicit in Transcendental Meditation, it nevertheless appears to be its implicit background and context. In his book *The Science of Being and Art of Living* (1963), the Maharishi says that his science of being and form of meditation teach people how to contact ultimate reality, the absolute field of pure being. The ultimate goal of TM is "to achieve the spiritual goals of mankind in this generation." TM can be regarded as nonreligious to the extent that spiritual techniques can be regarded as nonreligious.

Transcendental Meditation is also promoted as a means of relieving stress and tension. A recent newspaper advertisement proclaims: "Get Rid of Stress. The Transcendental Meditation Program provides: deep rest, increased energy and mental alertness, improved interpersonal relationships" (*Atlanta Constitution,* 21 May 1984). After an introductory lecture and payment of a fee, a person who wishes to try TM undergoes a brief initiation, and is given a mantra that a teacher decides is personally appropriate. After learning the mantra the initiate is instructed to repeat it silently while sitting in a relaxed posture. The meditator is not to concentrate upon the mantra but rather to return to its silent repetition whenever he or she notices that attention has wandered. Gradually, repeating the mantra becomes an easy and natural process. The meditator agrees to practice TM for two twenty-minute periods each day, with the teacher or "checker" consulting with the initiate several times subsequently to handle any problems that may arise.

Testimonials from TM practitioners are frequently very positive about its benefits. A large number of Americans have carried out the technique for many years. Published scientific studies reporting positive health benefits reinforce the meditator's belief in TM. However, critics have questioned the reliability and use of scientific controls in the published studies. It has also been pointed out that two twenty-minute relaxation periods a day would in themselves be beneficial without meditation; some researchers have achieved similar results with subjects repeating nonsense phrases instead of mantras.

After some six months of training, those who have a greater interest in TM may become teachers; there are more than six thousand in America. Higher forms of meditation are also taught at retreats. In recent years, meditation courses purporting to make levitation possible have been offered (for much higher fees). Recently the Maharishi has made claims that the practice of TM by 1 percent of the population of a city would reduce crime rates, and that if 1 percent of the world population would meditate, there would be no more wars.

The Divine Light Mission. The DLM was launched with the tours of Guru Maharaj Ji in America in 1970. Within three years the mission had some twenty-four centers and 50,000 followers (called *premies,* lovers of God) in the United States and Canada. In 1971 and 1972, Maharaj Ji's American tours were accompanied by massive advertisements and media coverage. The boy savior mixed apparently adolescent play, pranks, and self-amusement with his public appearances before potential followers. Followers explained his playfulness as *līlā,* the *māyā* or magic spell and sport of the divine incarnation who is different from any other teacher or prophet and whose actions as the *avatar-satguru* (perfect master) could not be predicted or fitted into any stereotype.

Maharaj Ji's father, Shri Hans Ji Maharaj Ji, headed the Prem Nagar Ashram and the Divine Light Mission in India for some forty years and was considered by his followers to be a *satguru.* At his death in 1966 the succession was claimed by one of his younger sons, Maharaj Ji, at the age of eight years. According to Maharaj Ji, each age has its perfect master. Salvation requires complete devotion to him as an embodiment of God, the *satguru* of this age.

Followers are initiated into the movement by the guru's Divine Light representatives, called *mahātmas,* who transmit a direct experience of God as divine light, celestial music, and divine nectar. The technique of initiation, called "the giving of knowledge," consists of four parts: pressing the knuckles forcefully into the eyeballs until flashes of light are seen; plugging the ears with the fingers and concentrating on internal sounds; meditating upon the sound of one's breathing; and curling the tongue backward against the rear of the soft palate until the nectar is tasted. These techniques are practiced daily by *premies.*

In 1977 the DLM reported that some 50,000 people were involved in the mission and that more than 10,000 were actively involved in fur-

thering its work. Maharaj Ji's marriage to his American secretary in 1974, his financial extravagance, his abandonment of a vegetarian diet, and his general self-indulgence prompted his mother to declare that he was not the true successor to his father and to transfer the succession to his eldest brother. Disagreement within the guru's family prompted some *premies* to leave the movement; but, although the number of *premies* has declined to perhaps a few thousand, DLM continues among dedicated followers. While about a tenth of the *premies* live together in communes and surrender their possessions to the Divine Light Mission, most of the remaining members have employment and homes of their own. A brand of spiced tea produced by *premies* still sells well, and some *premies* run vegetarian groceries and restaurants.

Meher Bābā. Meher Bābā declared himself to be the avatar of the Age, God, and infinite consciousness in human form. Calling himself the "ancient one" who appeared in previous avataric forms in such religious figures as Zoroaster, Krishna, Rama, Buddha, Jesus, and Muḥammad, he claimed to manifest the essence of the teachings of all the great religious traditions, affirming them as revelations of God.

Born Merwan Sheheriarji Irani, of Persian parents in Poona, India, he was reared in an atmosphere of Zoroastrian and Sufi (Islamic mysticism) traditions. According to the faithful, his awakening to his true nature began in 1908 at age nineteen under the stimulus of one of the five perfect masters (who exist in every age to oversee the spiritual welfare of the world). Working with first one and then another of these masters, Irani's gradual awakening continued until 1921. Irani reported that the last of the masters saluted him as the Avatar of the Age. He then began his mission as avatar in India by working with the poor, the sick, the mentally ill, and the untouchables. His early disciples called him Meher Bābā (compassionate father).

Although different avatars have brought different messages, Bābā declared that the message of divine love is always the same. Each avatar in his own individual style compassionately takes on the suffering of the world. From 1925 until his death in 1969, Bābā voluntarily did not speak. He proclaimed that he would at some time break his silence, but he died without having done so.

His silence was explained as the means by which the Word of God must be spoken in our time, not aloud, but in the depths of the human soul. It was his intent to awaken divine love in each person rather than to bring new religious teachings. Bābā communicated non-orally, first with an alphabet board and later by means of hand gestures. Through this process he dictated books, such as *God Speaks* (1955), which are in close accord with both the non-dual *vedānta* Hindu tradition and Sufi doctrines. The teachings in books were given secondary importance; his message was centered in his person, which his silence accentuated. The absence of spoken words was intended to force people to confront the Avatar of the Age rather than doctrines, and to awaken the Word and love within them.

Bābā first came to the West and to America in 1931. During the 1950s and early 1960s he made three more trips to America, attracting several dozen followers. The Meher Spiritual Center was opened in Myrtle Beach, South Carolina, in 1956 as his center in the West; some of his American followers were allowed to come to his ashram in Meherabad, India. After living in seclusion for several years, he summoned his followers to come to Meherabad for *darśana* (viewing, presentation, or blessing) in the spring of 1969. The *darśana* was held, although Bābā had died a few months before. Bābā lovers say that Meher Bābā continues to live in the hearts of everyone who experiences his divine love.

Bābā lovers congregate in informal, scattered groups, often meeting in private homes, relying on love and intuition. Other than the Myrtle Beach center and Meher Bābā bookstores in various cities, there are no formal Bābā institutions. There are several thousand Bābā lovers in the United States. A Sufi organization centered in San Francisco called Sufism Reoriented is also related to Meher Bābā.

The Disciples of Nityānanda. Several disciples of the Indian guru Bhagwan Śrī Nityānanda established yoga centers in America. Nityānanda's Kashmīr Śaivite tradition of *siddha-yoga* (the yoga of the guru's grace), which he began to teach in the 1930s, is based upon the ability of a *siddha* (a fully realized person) to awaken the female *śakti* or *kundalinī* within by means of *śaktipat* (initiation). *Śakti* is the creative power of nature, the Mother, and the active power of the male transcendent god Śiva. The *kundalinī* is the female power latent within each person that can be reawakened.

Swami Muktānanda Paramahansa received *śaktipat* from Nityānanda in 1947 and is said to have become a fully enlightened being after nine years of inner development. At Nityānanda's death in 1961 Muktānanda became his successor and founded the Gurudev Siddha Yoga Peeth (or ashram). Muktānanda made three Western tours that included the United States in 1970, 1974–1976, and 1979–1981.

The Siddha Yoga Dham of America (SYD) was founded in 1974, first in Oakland, and later in South Fallsburg, New York. There are about fifteen ashrams in the United States and about two hundred centers that offer introductory programs of lectures, chanting, *hatha-yoga*, and celebration of festivals.

The guru is a channel of *śakti*, spiritual power, which he transmits to a disciple in the process of initiation, called *śaktipat*. The absolute and the phenomenal world are identical. The disciple's awareness of this begins with the giving of spiritual power, which works gradually from the lower *chakras* (psychic centers) to the higher until full awareness is eventually achieved. SYD centers are places for learning about and practicing *siddha-yoga*, for the attraction of new disciples, and for mutual support in the spiritual discipline.

Muktānanda passed the succession before his death in 1982 to two young Indian disciples, Swami Nityānanda and his sister Gurumayi Chidvilasananda. Nityānanda retired in 1985, apparently voluntarily. In 1986 Nityānanda charged that he had been forced out of the succession illegitimately. His sister claims that he was asked to resign because of sexual improprieties. About fifty-five Americans have been initiated into the Saraswati monastic order and Siddha Yoga Dham claims nearly 300,000 followers worldwide.

Albert Rudolph, who studied with both Nityānanda and Muktānanda, founded eight independent ashrams in America as Swami Rudrānanda. Franklin Jones worked with both Rudrānanda and Muktānanda but broke away (as Bubba Free John) to establish the Dawn Horse Fellowship (now the Primitive Church of Divine Communion) centered in the Talking God Seminary in California.

HINDUISM

The Disciples of Swami Śivānanda. Swami Śivānanda's influence in America has been through several of his disciples who formed American branches of the Divine Life Society. Swami Śivānanda founded the Śivānanda Ashram in India in 1932, followed by the Divine Life Society in 1936, and the All World Religious Federation in 1945. He taught the practice of love and service together with a combination of the traditional yoga disciplines. His yoga includes bodily postures, meditation, work, devotion, and the repetition of mantras.

The Integral Yoga Institute, with about twelve centers, was started in 1966 in America by Swami Satchidānanda. The True World Order founded by Swami Vishnudevānanda in 1969 succeeded his Śivānanda Yoga Vedanta Center started in 1959. Retreat centers are located in Quebec, California, and the Bahamas. Swami Laksmy Devyāshram founded the Holy Shankaracharya Order in the Poconos and in Virginia and the Rajarajesvari Peetham in Stroudsburg, Pennsylvania, and in Virginia. The International School of Yoga and Vedanta was set up in Miami by Swami Jyotir Maya Nanda in 1969. Swami Radha (Sylvia Hellman) founded the Yasodhara Ashram Society in Canada in 1956.

Ananda Marga. The Ananda Marga Yoga Society was founded in India by Shrii Shrii Ānandamūrti, who was regarded as a miracle worker and as *mahāguru* (similar to avatar). He taught a form of yoga to be practiced after initiation by the guru. After its introduction to America by Āchārya Vimalānanda Avadhuta in 1969, Ananda Marga rapidly grew to over one hundred centers with about 3,000 members. Because of his political activism in India, the Indian government arrested Ānandamūrti for political terrorism and murder in 1972; he was, however, acquitted in 1978. But after 1972 Ananda Marga membership began to decline rapidly.

Sikh Dharma. The Healthy, Happy, Holy Organization (3HO) was established in America in 1968 by Yogi Bhajan as a combination of Sikh religious tradition and *kundalinī-yoga.* Subsequently renamed the Sikh Dharma Brotherhood, the movement is a branch of the Sikh Dharma of Amritsar, the site of the Golden Temple in the Punjab. Although looked on favorably by Indian Sikhs, Sikh Dharma primarily attracts Americans. There are about 150 ashrams with more than 4,000 residents. Male members adopt the uncut hair, turban, beard, steel bracelet, dagger, comb, and khaki shorts of Sikh tradition. Both males and females wear white adaptations of Punjabi dress styles. Meditation consists of a form of *kundalinī-yoga* using hyperventilation and a mantra containing the Sat Nām (True Name). Sikh Dharma members are often more consistently observant of traditional Sikh dress and grooming requirements, vegetarianism, and prohibition of alcohol than Indian Sikhs in America.

The Rajneesh Meditation Center. The Rajneesh Meditation Center was brought to America by disciples of Bhagwan Rajneesh from its headquarters in Poona, India. Rajneesh employs encounter group types of therapy mixed with yoga meditation and various Western psychological techniques, all coupled with a sexually permissive attitude. Rajneesh has written a great many books that have been widely distributed. The organization claims approximately 3,500 followers, called *sannyasi* (a term usually reserved for celibates). The headquarters were moved to a large ranch bought by the movement near Antelope, Oregon (population 40), in 1981. *Sannyasis* bought up much of the town and won the municipal elections in January 1983. Considerable disunity developed within the headquarters in 1985. Rajneesh lost his visa and was deported in 1986.

Rādhāsoāmī Satsang. Founded in India in 1861, the Rādhāsoāmī Satsang movement combines Hindu and Sikh elements to teach a yoga of the universal sound and devotion to the Rādhā Soāmī masters. God is the union of the Rādhā (soul) and the soāmī (master/creator). The movement was begun by Singh Sahab, and the succession was passed for two generations, but dissension about the succession rose after the third leader, and several subdivisions developed. The Rādhā Soāmī Satsang, Beas, which was brought to America in 1910, lists forty-one centers and about 10,000 members in the United States. Kirpal Singh founded the Ruhani Satsang in America somewhat later. Currently there are three divisions of Ruhani Satsang in America with centers in California, Virginia, and New Hampshire.

The Śrī Aurobindo Society. There are several largely autonomous centers connected with the Śrī Aurobindo Society of India in California and

697

on the East Coast. Śrī Aurobindo taught an integral form of yoga in the context of a doctrine that spirit ascends in an evolutionary pattern through matter to higher and higher levels of spirit while, at the appropriate time, supermind descends to transform mind into spirit. A center in New York State called Matagiri follows the discipline of integral yoga and also publishes Aurobindo's many books. Several hundred people are involved in American Aurobindo centers.

Other Indian Missionary Organizations. Satya Sai Bābā, who announced that he is the reincarnation of Sai Bābā of Shirdi, a holy man who died in 1918, attracts a small American following as deity and guru. His teachings are a modernized form of traditional Hinduism, and he is noted for his miracles. Gurudev Chitrabhanu, who established the Jain Meditation International Center in New York City in 1975, teaches a form of *kundalinī-yoga* in the context of the Jain religious tradition. Chritrabhanu has several hundred followers among Indian Jain immigrants and the general population. Śrī Chinmoy Kumar Ghose, who came to America in 1964, has taught yoga and the path of devotion to God to several hundred Americans. He is the director of the United Nations Meditation Group and has published prolifically. There are perhaps several dozen other yogic and meditational Hindu organizations in America.

Secularized and heavily Americanized organizations of Hindu inspiration include the Krishnamurti Foundation of America of Jiddu Krishnamurti, which teaches a philosophical and psychological approach to human development; the Hanuman Foundation of Bābā Rām Dās (Richard Alpert), which teaches service to those in need as a form of *karma-yoga* (the yoga of action); and Gopi Krishna's Kundalini Research Foundation, which teaches *kundalinī-yoga* on a biological basis.

Hindu forms of meditation and therapeutics have also influenced new eclectic religious movements. And new forms of Hindu and Buddhist spirituality in America have stimulated the development of spirituality among mainline Protestant, Catholic, and Jewish institutions.

BIBLIOGRAPHY

Yogi Bhajan, *The Teaching of Yogi Bhajan: The Power of the Spoken Word* (1977) and *Yoga for the Eighties: Kundalini Yoga* (1985); Harold H. Bloomfield, Michael P. Cain, and Dennis T. Jaffe, *TM: Discovering Inner Energy and Overcoming Stress* (1975); Francine Jeanne Daner, *The American Children of Krsna: A Study of the Hare Krsna Movement* (1976); James V. Downton, Jr., *Sacred Journeys: The Conversion of Young Americans to Divine Light Mission* (1979); Robert S. Ellwood, Jr., *Alternative Altars: Unconventional and Eastern Spirituality in America* (1979).

Maxine P. Fisher, *The Indians of New York City: A Study of Immigrants From India* (1980); Jack Foram, *Transcendental Meditation* (1976); Steven J. Gelberg, ed., *Hare Krishna, Hare Krishna* (1983); Norris Hundley, Jr., *The Asian American: The Historical Experience* (1976); Carl T. Jackson, *The Oriental Religions and American Thought: Nineteenth-Century Explorations* (1981); J. Stillson Judah, *Hare Krishna and the Counterculture* (1974); Mark Juergensmeyer and N. Gerald Barrier, eds., *Sikh Studies: Comparative Perspectives on a Changing Tradition* (1979).

H. Brett Melendy, *Asians in America: Filipinos, Koreans, and East Indians* (1977); J. Gordon Melton, ed., *Encyclopedia of American Religions,* 2 vols. (1978); Muktānanda Paramahaṇsa, *Meditate* (1980); Jacob Needleman and George Baker, eds., *Understanding the New Religions,* (1978); A. C. Bhaktivedanta Swami Prabhupada, *KRISHNA: The Supreme Personality of Godhead,* I (1970); Charles B. Purdom, ed., *God to Man and Man to God: The Discourses of Meher Baba* (1975); Archarya Rajneesh, *Flight of the Alone to the Alone* (1970); Thomas Robbins and Dick Anthony, eds., *In Gods We Trust: New Patterns of Religious Pluralism in America* (1981).

Parmatma Saran, *The Asian Indian Experience in the United States* (1985) and, with Edwin Eames, eds., *The New Ethnics: Asian Indians in the United States* (1980); Ganda Singh, *The Sikhs and Their Religion* (1974); Maharaj Charan Singh, *Divine Light* (4th ed., 1976); Wendell Thomas, *Hinduism Invades America* (1930); John White, *Everything You Want to Know About TM* (1976); Raymond B. Williams, "The Lord's Song in a Foreign Land," in his *A New Face of Hinduism: The Swaminarayan Religion* (1984).

[See also BUDDHISM; "CULTS" IN THE LATE TWENTIETH CENTURY; ISLAM IN NORTH AMERICA; OCCULT MOVEMENTS IN AMERICA; SHINTO AND INDIGENOUS CHINESE RELIGION; *and* TRANSCENDALISM.]

SHINTO AND INDIGENOUS CHINESE RELIGION

C. Carlyle Haaland

INTRODUCTION

THE popular view of the United States is that in its beginnings it was inhabited chiefly by Protestant immigrants, if one ignored the Native Americans. Gradually, however, this image has given way to a more pluralistic one. The presence, since colonial times, of Roman Catholic and Jewish traditions was widely recognized by the 1950s, in large part due to the work of Will Herberg.

Still, even this religious trilogy did not define the total national fabric. Also present were religious alternatives to the Jewish and Christian traditions. In the nineteenth and early twentieth centuries there were episodes in which other religions were embraced either by questing Americans of European heritage or by members of Eastern ethnic groups seeking to discover or to maintain their cultural roots—for example, the Transcendentalist effort to embrace Hindu or Buddhist sentiments and the Islamic venture in the black American experience.

In the 1950s and 1960s, however, through the likes of Allen Ginsberg, Philip Kapleau, Jack Kerouac, and Alan Watts, the nation gave fuller attention to the existence of religious forms considered nontraditional by conventional standards. These forms, being non-Jewish, non-Christian, and non-Islamic, rarely were monotheistic. Often they were polytheistic, and sometimes atheistic. They included Hindu, Buddhist, Taoist, Shinto, and Confucianist forms—and reflected the notion that Asia, not Europe, is the source of religious truth.

This article is devoted to some of these Asian religious forms. Bypassing those derived from the Hindu and Buddhist traditions, it will treat of those forms rooted in the Japanese Shinto and indigenous Chinese traditions. Of these, Shinto is the more diverse and will receive more attention. Obviously, this will not exhaust the subject. Research needs to be done on religious forms that have entered the United States from such East Asian countries as South Korea, Taiwan, and Tibet, and such South Asian countries as the Philippines, Indonesia, Sumatra, Malaya, Thailand, Burma, Cambodia, and South Vietnam.

JAPANESE RELIGION

Japan has been called a two-faith nation, meaning that while Shintoism, Buddhism, Confucianism, Taoism, Christianity, and folk religion all exist, most Japanese, perhaps as many as 80 percent, embrace both of the first two in one form or another.

Shintoism and Buddhism have fulfilled different purposes for the Japanese. Shintoism is considered the religion for marriage and other ceremonies celebrating life. It gives meaning and order to the ongoing activities and events of historical, social, and political life. Buddhism is viewed as the religion of burial, emphasizing a different order of reality and preparing one for departure from this life. This practice of embracing more than one religious tradition is obviously not characteristic of the Catholic, Protestant, or Jewish faiths.

A second feature of Japanese religion is that monotheism is not a dominant idea. Indeed, theism in the sense of adherence to a single supreme being is not widespread. For some Japanese there is no god at the center of human existence. There is only emptiness. Thus, transcendence refers not to a transcendent, supreme being but to transcending this futile, empirical world. In contrast, for other Japanese there is a more polytheistic and immanental component in religion. Varieties of physical structures, natural objects, and people are viewed by many as embodying sacredness.

Third, Japanese religion emphasizes the celebration of important times in individual and national life. Birth, coming of age, and burial are important events in the Jewish and Christian traditions. However, these events, as well as annual festivals like the New Year, are the primary occasions for attending to religious obligations in Japanese religion. At such times visits to shrines and temples as well as home celebrations and observances occur. The idea that one tends to most of the important religious activities and obligations on a fixed day of the week, as in the Jewish and Christian traditions, is not dominant in Japan.

Finally, since Japanese view so much as legitimately giving meaning and order to life, religious belief and practice tend to be syncretistic. The sacred and the secular blur, and religious forms blend. Conversely, in the Jewish and Christian traditions it is commonplace to emphasize the distinctive nature of religious groups and the separation of religion from the world.

Origins and Forms of Shinto. Shinto derives from the Chinese *shen-tao,* or way of *kami. Kami* is a term both singular and plural in meaning. It refers to any aspect of existence that inspires a sense of awe because it is perceived as extraordinary in terms of place or position occupied. Thus, waterfalls, rivers, trees, rocks, crops, the emperor, heroes, and, paradoxically, ordinary people can be viewed as representations of *kami.*

Shinto, as a term, came into usage after Buddhism entered Japan from China in the sixth century A.D. Originally used to deprecate indigenous Japanese religion with its emphasis upon *kami* as sacred manifestations in the physical world, Shinto became an honorable title to those who rejected Buddhism and reasserted the value of the indigenous religion.

In the course of time four forms of Shinto developed—Imperial, Folk, Shrine, and Sectarian. The first, Imperial Shinto, emphasized the sacredness of the ruling emperor, guaranteed by direct succession from Amaterasu-O-Mikami, the feminine sun deity and cosmic source. Given such origins, imperial functions and pronouncements took on high significance, commanded

commitment and loyalty, and resulted in a strong sense of a sacred national community composed of a people descending from *kami* and created by *kami.* This tenet of the sacredness of the emperor was written into the Japanese constitution of 1889 and remained in effect until omitted from the new constitution drawn up after World War II. However, belief in the special importance of the emperor, devoid of political implications and emphasizing the symbolic significance of the model human, continues to be held by many today.

Folk Shinto, which derives from the pervasive indigenous religious tradition of Japan, has been the most dominant religious form in the daily life of the Japanese people. Further, it undergirds Imperial Shinto, is compatible with Shrine Shinto, and is an influence upon Sectarian Shinto.

Folk Shinto looks upon natural phenomena, animals, people, households, kinship groups, and villages as manifestations of *kami.* The human spirit, considered an expression of *kami,* is given a special name, *tama.* The spirits of the dead are simply *kami* in a different expression.

Kami tend to be benevolent. If people attend to proper worship and religious observances, and do not transgress certain taboos—such as selecting the proper day for marriage or determining where to erect a house—they can expect a felicitous life. However, if one errs, the *kami* can become vindictive. Moreover, in such cases evil *kami,* otherwise constrained, would be unleashed, resulting in disease, disaster, and calamity. Thus, the ritual activities of individuals, family, and social groups are central to maintaining a harmonious order.

Folk Shinto also tends to guarantee the cycle of the calendar year by sustaining important annual festivals, some influenced by other religious traditions. Among these are Shogatsu (New Year), one week beginning 1 January; Hina Matsuri (Doll Festival), 3 March, for all girls; Haru no Higan (spring equinox), one week including 23 March; Hana Matsuri (Flower Festival), 8 April, associated with planting time; Tango no Sekku (Boy Day), 5 May, for all boys; Oharai (Grand Purification), 30 June, to purge the self of errors and defilement; Tsukumi (Moon Viewing), 15 August, an early harvest celebration reflecting gratitude; and Aki no Higan (autumn equinox), one week including 23 September.

In addition, Folk Shinto emphasizes certain rites of passage—Tanjo (Birth); Shichi go San (three, five, and seven years of age), 15 November; Seijin Shiki (Coming of Age), now celebrated on 15 January for those attaining their twentieth birthday in the calendar year; Konrei (Marriage); Yakudoshi (Year of Peril), for men aged forty-two and women aged thirty-three; Toshi Iwai (Year of Jubilation), at age sixty-one and seventy; and Tomurai (Death).

To assist in the observances, Folk Shinto encourages the establishment of small shrines for households, kinship groups, or villages. Before these shrines, offerings of food and drink are placed for the *kami* associated with these social groups. Other shrines are also established to attend to particular *kami,* such as *inari* (god of harvest and rice) and *kitsune* (fox). Frequently, fox and rice or harvest shrines are integrated, with the characteristic of prosperity attributed to the fox, who is viewed as guaranteeing an abundant rice crop.

Shrines established on regional or national scales to venerate an important leader or the emperor belong to the category of Shrine Shinto, which was historically linked with Imperial Shinto through the idea that Shinto and the Japanese nation are indissolubly yoked.

Shrine Shinto crystallized at important religious centers where physical structures, some of great size, were erected. Here, priests and priestesses resided.

Central to Shrine Shinto is the belief in the sacredness of a particular place associated with specific *kami.* Reverence is expressed through the maintenance of the structure erected on the site. At these shrines important annual festivals and life-cycle rituals were observed, such as New Year, purification, and marriage, and the traditions of religious music and dance developed. The priests would also leave the premises to consecrate the fields for planting, to carry in portions of the harvest, and to consecrate new homes and businesses.

In time, particularly after World War II, shrines also became centers for the development of the Shinto belief system, the seminal elements of which are sincerity in all relationships, the unity of all people under the emperor, and service to humanity without thought of personal reward.

Sectarian Shinto is somewhat like American Protestantism in its denominational structure. It includes numerous small organized variants within the Shinto tradition that are considered compatible with the Imperial and Shrine forms. Sectarian Shinto emerged and expanded in the early nineteenth century. Many of the sectarian groups, as well as others inspired by Buddhism and Christianity, caught the Japanese imagination after World War II, expanded further, and were often referred to as the New Religions of Japan.

SHINTO IN THE UNITED STATES

The Japanese and Japanese-American population group that began to emerge in the late nineteenth century in the United States and in Hawaii has always been relatively modest in size. By 1920 there were 75,000 on the mainland; by 1940, 125,000; by 1960, 260,000. In the mid-1980s there were some 790,000 persons of Japanese birth or ancestry, about 55 percent on the mainland.

Early members of this ethnic group were inclined to adhere to some form of Shinto, even though a substantial portion also embraced Buddhism. In the first half of the twentieth century under the influence of American culture three trends developed. First, almost 40 percent of this ethnic group opted for formal membership in the Buddhist tradition, with the Buddhist Churches of America founded in 1899 and headquartered in San Francisco receiving the greatest number. Second, others from this group gravitated to Roman Catholic and Protestant traditions, with Baptist, Episcopal, Methodist, Presbyterian, and Congregational popular prior to World War II. Third, Sectarian Shinto groups gradually rose to a position of dominance within Shinto in the United States, particularly after World War II. However, while dynamic in character these Sectarian Shinto groups remained relatively small in size, approximating the membership of such other religious groups as the Ethical Culture Movement, Vedanta Society of New York, Beachy Amish and other Mennonite groups, and Amana Church Society.

In the early twentieth century, all four forms of Shinto existed in the United States and continued to function until World War II. In the 1950s and 1960s Shinto groups expanded moderately and were modified as a result of international contacts resulting from the postwar occupation of Japan, increased trade and travel, and additional immigration.

The extent to which Imperial Shinto operated in the late nineteenth century is not clear. However, one should not expect that the Japanese immigrants purged their minds of learned customs, habits, and beliefs, including veneration of the emperor, when they boarded ships to the United States. Indeed, these elements would remain as part of their ethnic identity, continue with them, and find expression in such acts as displaying the Japanese flag. This posture, of course, led to a period of travail and disruption in the twentieth century.

During the early 1940s, when Imperial Shinto fueled the Japanese war effort, there was sufficient concern over its presence in the United States to bolster the enforced relocation of over 100,000 persons of Japanese descent to camps at various distances from the Pacific coastal regions on the grounds that these people constituted a national security risk. Ministers and priests in Japanese religious (especially Shinto) groups were harshly treated. Many clergy were sent to the Crystal City, Texas, detention center, and marked for deportation to Japan after the war. Still, the extent to which Imperial Shinto was expressed in overtly political loyalty remains an unresolved issue.

Folk Shinto also entered the United States with Japanese immigration, solidifying as the family and community structure was established. In continuity with Folk Shinto in Japan and its indigenous flavor, it was popular in form and animistic in nature, and emphasized maintenance of local sacred places, veneration of sacred objects, and observance of periodic rituals of local, regional, or national significance.

Folk Shinto shrines in the continental United States often were small in size and associated with private households. However, in Los Angeles in the 1930s the large Gongen Shrine, dedicated to *inari*, was established, apparently the only significant nature shrine in the United States. Within the relocation centers during World War II small shrines, usually to *inari*, were occasionally erected among the barracks; the symbolism was evident.

Folk Shinto today is publicly manifested chiefly in the Japanese gardens prominent on the West Coast, in the seasonal festivals held in such locales as Nihonmachi (Japan Town) in San Francisco, in the arts of ikebana and bonsai, and in maintaining *kamidana* (*kami* alcoves) in the home. More than attempts to sustain Japanese culture, these forms are meant to inspire the awe properly associated with natural events and phenomena.

Shrine Shinto was established for a short period of time in the United States and Hawaii. *Daijingu* (great shrines), modeled after those in Japan dedicated to the sun goddess, were erected in Seattle, San Francisco, and Los Angeles in the 1930s. Three shrines also were built in Hawaii. At these centers marriages were performed and annual festivals celebrated, reasserting the connection with Japan and its traditions. After World War II these shrines did not regain their prominence.

There were four expressions of Sectarian Shinto during the pre–World War II era—Taishakyo (or Taikyo), Hito no Michi, Konkokyo, and Tenrikyo. The first, Taishakyo, officially recognized as a religious movement by the Japanese government in 1886, was unique in that it had no founder. Its emphasis was upon reverence for and mystical communion with *kami*, rituals of purification, services for the dead, and the integration of Shinto with all things Japanese.

Taishakyo gave rise to three local expressions in the United States—the North American Shinto Church in San Francisco in 1904, later relocated to Los Angeles; the Shinto Church of America in Los Angeles in 1919; and a small group in San Pedro, California, in the 1920s, which had disbanded by 1932. The movement appears to have foundered as a result of World War II relocations.

The second Sectarian Shinto movement was Hito no Michi (Way of Man), which derived from an earlier movement known as Shinto-Tokumitsu-kyo (Divine Way as Taught by Tokumitsu) founded in 1912 by Tokumitsu Kanada. In 1919 a disciple, Tokoharu Miki, assumed leadership, reorganized the movement in 1925 as Jindo-Tokumitsu-kyo (Human Way as Taught by Tokumitsu), and renamed it Hito no Michi in 1931.

Emphasizing the relationship of the mystical quality of nature to the practicalities of family life and social relations rather than to things imperial, Hito no Michi entered the United States in the 1930s. Official disapproval in Japan during World War II resulted in the demise of the group, and in the United States the relocation produced a similar result. The number of its early adherents is not known. After the war it was reorganized again, this time as PL Kyodan, and returned to the United States in that form.

The third expression, Konkokyo (Doctrine of the Golden Light), was founded by Bunjiro Kawate in the late nineteenth century and recognized by the Japanese government as a Shinto sect in 1900. During a serious illness Kawate claimed to have encountered and subsequently embodied Konjin, the dreaded golden *kami*. Restored to health, Kawate began to speak of Konjin as a benevolent *kami,* referring to him as Konko Daijin, the Great Kami of the Golden Light, or Tenchi Kane no Kami, the Golden Kami of the Universe.

In 1885, two years after Kawate's death, Konkokyo was formally organized, with principal emphasis upon mediating between *kami* and humanity. Gradually members moved away from observance of taboos and toward concern for personal faith in a single *kami* in order to achieve insight into the meaning of the universe.

Konkokyo entered the United States in the 1920s; missions were established in Los Angeles, San Jose, Oakland, Sawtelle, and San Francisco, in California, and in Portland, Oregon. During World War II the Konkokyo missions were seized, and many of the priests, defenders of Japan, were arrested and marked for deportation. Subsequently they were permitted to return to California cities, chiefly Los Angeles and San Francisco, where the missions continued, though not to the prewar extent.

Today Konkokyo is headquartered in San Francisco. There are less than 1,000 members, mostly older Japanese-Americans, which suggests that for some people Konkokyo still serves as a link to the homeland. Its priests still provide services customarily performed by Shrine Shinto priests in Japan, such as marriages and dedications. For example, when Japan Air Lines opened a new flight crew training facility in Napa County, California, in 1972, a Konkokyo priest attended and performed the traditional Shinto consecration of the center.

The fourth Sectarian Shinto sect, Tenrikyo (the Religion of Heavenly Wisdom), is undoubtedly the best known, though recently it has sought to shed its Shinto identity. The foundation of Tenrikyo dates to 1838, when Miki Nakayama, a rural woman, had a vision during an illness in which she experienced the presence of a sacred entity, later known as Tenri-O-no-Mikoto (the Ruler of Heavenly Wisdom), also referred to as Oyasama (the Parent Deity).

Tenrikyo has been called the Christian Science of Japan because of its emphasis upon healing through teaching and ritual. However, its primary focus is upon one's personal relationship to the sacred entity through regular prayer, religious ritual, devout labor, and pilgrimage to Jiba, the center in Tenri City near Kyoto.

Tenrikyo appeared in the United States in 1896, but not until 1903 did it become permanent. In that year Tsunetaro Kanzawa immigrated and began part-time preaching in San Francisco; Haruo Higashida did likewise in Los Angeles, establishing a fellowship under California law. The Tenri City headquarters recognized these fellowships in 1927 and 1933, respectively.

The period of greatest Tenrikyo growth was from 1927 to 1934, when more than forty individuals arrived to do religious work among Japanese immigrants, many of whom were from rural areas where groups like Tenrikyo were popular. In 1934 the Daikyokai (Tenrikyo Mission Headquarters and Main Church) was established in Los Angeles to oversee the emergent *bunkyokai* (lesser churches) and *fukyosho* (branch fellowships) in Hawaii, California, Colorado, Utah, Oregon, Washington, and western Canada.

Today there are approximately sixty churches and smaller fellowships in the United States, with a total membership of 3,500, 90 percent of which are of Japanese birth or ancestry. The minimum number of members necessary to maintain a fellowship is sixteen. Churches, which foster and supervise fellowships, generally have one hundred or fewer members. The main church in Los Angeles has more than two hundred members.

In Tenrikyo, leadership, which includes 40 percent women, is based upon heredity. Children or grandchildren succeed elders as heads of churches and fellowships. Adherents maintain a religiously oriented home with prayers or recitations from the foundress's writings undertaken daily at sunrise and sunset. Public worship occurs once a month on Sunday afternoons. On the third Sunday of each month the Los Angeles Main Church also gathers; numerous members from other locales attend. The Main Church also celebrates special festivals each year, including the days marking the birth and death of the foundress.

Public worship, which is conducted in traditional mode with Japanese robes, instruments, and songs, is followed by a period of social play. Japanese food and drink, conversation, and entertainment all provide a link to the Japanese past.

In the period since World War II four new groups derived from Shinto have entered the United States. These are PL Kyodan, Tensho Kotai Jingukyo, Tenkokyo, and Sekai Kyuseikyo.

PL Kyodan (Perfect Liberty Religious Association) traces its origins to Hito no Michi. It blends the Shinto view of the sacredness of mountains with the esoteric Shingon Buddhist idea that all things are expressions of Dainichi (the Great Sun Buddha). In 1946 the present organizational name was taken, making this the only Japanese religious group with Western terms in its official title.

The current leader of PL Kyodan, who is known as the *oshieoya* (teaching parent), is Tokuchika Miki, the son of the founder of Hito no Michi. He is considered to be not only the source of all truth and correct teaching but also the one who mediates divine healing and reconciling power from the sacred entity.

The sacred entity in PL Kyodan is Mioya-O-kami (Sacred Parental Entity). The key teaching is that if people remain in harmony with this source, then family, social, and professional life will be more prosperous, fulfilling, and creative. This teaching is summed up in the Twenty-one Precepts, of which the first is also the group motto, Life Is Art. Receiving *mioshie* (religious instruction) from masters and offering prayers accompanied by *oyashikiri* (hand gestures) assure union of the individual with the sacred entity. Religious services are held each Sunday and include testimonials from members. And on the twenty-first of each month a service is held at which offerings are gathered.

PL Kyodan appeared in the United States in the 1960s. Currently it has approximately six churches and maintains fifteen smaller missions. One of the largest Japanese groups in the United States, its membership is about 5,000, of which half are of Caucasian, black, or Hispanic descent, suggesting the group's broadening appeal. Headquartered in Glendale, California, like most religions of Japanese source it is most successful in the Los Angeles and San Francisco areas.

Tensho Kotai Jingukyo was founded by a woman, Sayo Katamura, who visited the United States three times in the 1950s and 1960s to promote the movement particularly among non-Japanese. Today it has about 1,500 members in twenty centers in the United States, most of them in Hawaii.

This group has two chief characteristics. Since it has no professional leadership, its work is carried on by members gathering and cooperating together. And its emphasis is less on doctrine and more on practice, particularly physical expression in prayer. Thus, it is known as the Dancing Religion.

Like many Japanese groups, this religion has been influenced by several traditions. However, its Shinto roots are found in the emphasis upon the natural world, of which humanity is a part, as inherently orderly and good. Humans, therefore, should seek to live in harmonious relationship with nature.

Tenkokyo (the Religion of Miracles) was founded in 1927 by Tomokiyo Yoshisane. It emphasizes reverence for the sun goddess and a practical asceticism.

In 1958 Terumi Fujita, who had reorganized the movement in 1948, came to the United States. For three months he traveled and preached in twenty-two states to promote the cause. The next year the Los Angeles branch was made the American headquarters, a venture viewed as the first step to worldwide expansion.

Fujita emphasized the need for religion to evolve with changing times, especially in dealing with personal crisis. To accomplish this he stressed simplicity, practicality, and harmonious relationships.

Tenkokyo refers to the sacred entity as Oyagami-sama, the creator of the universe and all things. Human lives and minds are the seeds of this entity, and true devotion will lead to the elimination of all misery, including physical infirmity, the solution of all daily problems, and the general happiness of all through the union of all races. This group has remained relatively small, with about 1,500 members, mainly Japanese-Americans on the West Coast.

Sekai Kyuseikyo (the Church of World Messianity) was founded in 1935 by Mokichi Okada. Nine years earlier Okada underwent a religious experience that led him from a business career to full-time religious activity until his death in 1955. The present organizational name came into use in 1950.

Okada proclaimed himself to be the conduit by which divine power was channeled to humanity. Thus, he took on the proportions of a messianic cult figure and was known by his followers as Meishu-sama.

In many respects this movement bears the least similarity to Shinto of all groups in the United States. It continues the Shinto emphasis upon nature, strongly supporting natural farming techniques. Yet it has a Buddhist influence and appears to have evolved into a form of monotheism, emphasizing the idea of a supreme god who is the creator of the universe, giver of life and power, and source of all light, truth, and revelation. Okada taught that this god revealed a divine plan in which there would be brought into being a new paradisaic age involving a world free from misery, disease, poverty, and conflict.

The central practice of this group is Johrei, in which two individuals sit facing each other. One extends a cupped hand, palm outward, in order to channel divine light to the other person. This process of individual purification is viewed as a precondition for the building of the earthly paradise.

World Messianity, which is headquartered in Atami, Japan, was established in Hawaii in 1953 by a woman minister, Kiyoko Higuchi. The next year she began work in Los Angeles. Currently, there are over 2,000 members each in Hawaii and on the mainland, mostly in a dozen centers in California. The Hawaiian members are chiefly of Japanese descent. The mainland members are approximately half Caucasian, attesting to the fact that the movement has been able to shed its traditional Japanese character. This is aided by the lessened emphasis upon the authority and control of the headquarters in favor of support of local meetings in homes at times convenient to members.

A large number of Japanese-Americans do not claim formal membership in any religious organization, preferring to maintain contact with the current expressions of Folk Shinto or informal association with Buddhist practices. Of those who do claim formal membership in a religious organization, about 40 percent opt for the Buddhist Churches of America, as mentioned earlier, although it should be noted that the church headquarters reports that its members number 700,000, or 90 percent of the total ethnic group. Others, joined by Caucasians, identify with such smaller Buddhist forms as Zen and Nichiren Shoshu. Still others associate with various Christian communions, although the integration of the once separate Japanese-American parishes into the larger denominational structures renders an exact count of these Christian adherents difficult to accomplish. Finally, the number of persons claiming formal membership in groups derived from Shinto does not exceed 15,000, though at least half as many more maintain an informal relationship. In sum, it would be fair to claim that persons of Japanese birth and ancestry are both more religious and less churched than persons tracing their origins to Europe.

CHINESE RELIGION

Origins and Characteristics. At its inception Chinese religion possessed characteristics subsequently evident in Japanese religion. In part this reflected the influence of the former on the latter. In part it reflected the traits common to much early Asian religion. First, religious traditions in Chinese culture were not viewed as mutually exclusive. The use of various traditions to meet different individual and group needs and obligations was considered appropriate and was widely practiced. Second, public religious activity tended to occur in relation to important calendar times or periodic human events, such as the New Year or birth or death. Gatherings were not regularly held on a specific day of the week or month. Third, the sacred and the secular were not considered separate and distinct. Human and natural life were viewed as fraught with dimensions of mystery and change that evoked a sense of profound awe. Fourth, monotheism did not exist except within the Christian and Moslem traditions imported to China. Ethics devoid of any transcendent reality could be paramount in some situations. In others, polytheism dominated. However, commitment to one or another sacred entity in any given moment was considered to be a personal matter, and as a whole, polytheism gave both heaven and earth their meaning, purpose, order, and direction.

In early Chinese religion polytheism was expressed in relation to *shen* and *kwei*. All *shen* (gods or spirits) were viewed as true—that is, as great and good—though some were of a higher order than others. While all *shen* were good, all needed to be influenced by offerings of food, wine, incense, and prayers. Lower gods were especially susceptible to these suasions.

When and how much attention was given to *shen*, however, depended upon individual circumstances. Evil existed in terms of the disruption of cosmic and natural order rather than as something intrinsic to humans or associated with human action. Evil resulted when the *shen* retreated and *kwei* (evil spirits) held sway. At these junctures it was essential that attention be given to the *shen* so as to reestablish order through their return and felicitous actions. Since *shen* met needs at particular moments, one did not need to attend to them routinely. So, for the most part they were acknowledged and kept at a respectful distance.

In the course of time, quite naturally, Chinese religion evolved. Ultimately some sacred entities came to prominence. These included the war god, the god and goddess of the kitchen, the earth god, the fertility goddess, the agriculture god, and the rain god, also known as the dragon god.

In spite of this evidently important apparatus, religion in China played a subordinate and supportive role in society. The superordinate dimension became the family, both nuclear and extended. As people matured, their interpersonal and intergenerational relations became stronger. Chinese society developed a high regard for family progenitors. This came to focus in a cult of ancestors in which adopting correct posture toward elders was followed by performing rituals in respect to the deceased.

Chinese religion, then, came to possess three other characteristics. First, organized religion along Christian or even Shinto lines did not develop to any significant degree. Hence, specific theologies, liturgies, and distinct groups commanding membership and commitment tended not to emerge. Indeed, proselytizing by any tradition was viewed as inappropriate. Second, priests and other religious functionaries were viewed as peripheral to the social fabric and were summoned only when necessary to serve the family needs, particularly at funerals. Third, the male members of the family came to play key roles in sustaining religious belief and practice.

Forms of Chinese Religion. In addition to Buddhism, which came to China as early as A.D. 65 but is not part of our subject here, and indigenous religion, two traditions helped to shape the Chinese attitude toward religion, Confucianism and Taoism.

Confucianism emerged about 500 B.C. and went through a series of changes over time. Confucius himself, however, both emphasized and exemplified *li* (the principles of social order and harmony), which were refined as the Five Great Relationships, the core of Confucianism. These were: kindness in the father, filial piety in the son; gentility in the eldest brother, humility and respect in the younger; righteous behavior in the husband, obedience in the wife; humane consideration in elders, deference in juniors; and benevolence in rulers, loyalty in ministers and subjects. These maxims, essentially ethical, established the basis of Chinese life, gave greater authority to the ancestral cult, and informed many of the attitudes with which one approached the practice of Taoism.

Taoism traces its source to Lao-tzu in the sixth century B.C. Viewing life as good and to be enjoyed, he emphasized a viewpoint that sought to explain the harmony of nature as a whole, heaven as well as earth, and the place of humanity within it. Not gods but *tao,* the Way, was what kept all nature in essential balance and order. To recognize *tao* and live in relationship with it resulted in peace, prosperity, and ultimately longevity and health, even immortality. If all humans did this, these results would be universalized. The great ages in Chinese history were seen by Lao-tzu as times when rulers were in unity with *tao,* and all people prospered individually and collectively. Thus, governmental organization was less important than the worthy actions of the leaders in assuring a good life. And professions were considered dangerous because they tended to complicate the simplicity of natural processes.

The form of Taoism that captured the attention of the ordinary Chinese is called religious Taoism. It gave less attention to monastic practices and study of the canon, and more to the array of traditional popular *shen* informing Chinese life. It also fostered a set of practices and techniques designed to assure the life of felicity.

One of the most important of these practices was alchemy, which developed into two types. *Wai-tan* (exoteric) emphasized the concocting of substances and elements into the elixir of immortality, and *nei-tan* (esoteric) emphasized mental and physical reorientation and reeducation. More important than either of these, however, was the expectation that certain attitudes should be present if alchemy was to be successful. These included a desire to manifest quietness, to extend love toward all things, and to manifest loyalty and virtue in life, the latter being influenced by the Confucianist tradition. Other important practices included yogic and dietary techniques; *t'ai-chi ch'üan*, the slow ballet form of boxing and gymnastics; and *jou-tao*, the "yielding way" of combat.

Just as Confucianism undergirded the sense of social order, Taoism did likewise in terms of natural order. Both provided underpinnings to the idea of historical order. Influencing each other and intertwining with the earliest forms of Chinese religion, they created a milieu of great significance for the Chinese immigrants in the United States.

CHINESE RELIGION IN THE UNITED STATES

Chinese began to arrive in the late eighteenth century and the immigration continued through much of the nineteenth century. The reasons for this eastward movement were the persistence of famine and social and political turmoil in China. Later, the notion that there were mountains of gold across the Pacific, particularly in California, provided further inducement.

Large numbers of these early immigrants came from Kwantung Province in southern China, near the ports from which passage to the United States could be secured. In religion the Kwantung region was strongly committed to the indigenous Chinese system of *shen;* to Confucianist teachings with emphasis upon correct relationships, particularly among family members; to ancestral obligations; and to religious Taoism. The Confucianist and ancestral dimensions in particular made it exceedingly difficult for many Chinese to leave the family. For those who did,

these same dimensions assured the continuance of a links with the family.

Thus, as with all ethnic groups, Chinese immigrants carried with them beliefs and practices rooted in and tying them to their heritage. In the course of time these took hold in a new land with annual celebrations and periodic observances and ceremonies serving as the markers for broadly diffused religious activity.

The nature of this religious tradition tended to assure that the Chinese immigrant was not drawn into membership in Christian communions that required loyalty to the exclusion of all other faiths. Even as late as the mid-twentieth century only 10,000 persons from this ethnic group (which numbered about 500,000) belonged to Chinese Protestant churches, mostly Baptist, Presbyterian, and nondenominational. An equally small number sought membership in the Roman Catholic tradition. This resistance to joining the Christian churches did not deter immigrants from utilizing Christian resources if these were useful. Thus, it was not uncommon for Chinese Christian pastors to be called upon to assist in emergencies, to provide assistance in business ventures, and to arrange courses on the English language and American customs. There is, however, little evidence that Christian beliefs and practices were taken over and incorporated into the traditional Chinese religious mode.

Because Chinese religion tends to be manifested in popular forms—that is, in the life of the people rather than in formal organization—it cannot be approached in the same manner as Sectarian Shinto or, indeed, the spectrum of American denominations. Such elements as leaders, mission work, headquarters established, parishes organized, gatherings held, literature published, and the like simply do not exist. Accordingly, much of the Chinese religion in the United States is in form similar to Japanese Folk Shinto or to popular religion derived from the American experience.

In assessing Chinese religion in the United States, festivals come in for special note. Routinely, most attention is given to the celebration of the lunar New Year in many cities. Lesser-known but equally traditional festivals are also observed, including such calendar events as the Mid-Autumn Festival and the Spring Festival, corresponding to the fall and spring equinoxes. But a fuller awareness of the presence of Chinese religious practice comes through observance of joss houses, district or family associations, and burial and grave-tending rituals.

The term *joss* comes from the Spanish word for God, *Dios*. Thus, the joss houses derived their name from the Spanish Catholic churches that the Chinese immigrants found in California. These churches, colorfully ornamented and full of images, were associated by the immigrants with the temples and shrines of China, and inspired them to erect on American soil edifices as abodes for their sacred entities.

These joss houses were sometimes Buddhist and sometimes Confucianist in character. The former often had images reminiscent of sacred entities in Chinese Buddhism, for example, Kuan-Yin (goddess of mercy), Kuan-Kung (protector god, god of war), and Cai Shen (god of wealth). The latter edifices, while often including such images, placed the image of Confucius centrally, thus asserting the importance of family lineage. In either case it was customary that persons would visit these centers to present food and wine, burn incense, and offer prayers when the need arose to avert misfortune. Many joss houses remain in use in Chinese enclaves in the United States.

Associations were a second phenomenon that served to sustain Chinese religious practice. Some were based on districts of origin in China; others upon family relationships. Some were civic in nature; others, benevolent. Some harkened back to the days when religious, economic, and political elements were mingled in the groups, thus linking more sacred and more secular agendas. In the United States all of the associations in a given area were brought together under the umbrella of a Chinese Benevolent Society in order to assure commonality and cooperation.

One of the main purposes of these associations was to provide support for the burial and remembrance of the deceased. Associations would maintain books of genealogy in which to record one's place in the continuous family lineage, provide assistance at burials, and even arrange to have the remains of the deceased transported back to the place of origin. Though not a uniformly followed practice, the return of one's remains was considered by many as an especially important activity for assuring loyalty to and unity with one's ancestors. In recent years this

practice has died out and the associations now tend to provide a focus for community, identity, social activity, and Chinese values while continuing general support in cases of death.

Since family lineage is so important to Chinese religion, burial and grave-tending practices assumed major importance in all families of immigrants. This continues to the present day.

Memorializing the dead is focused in the important practice of *sao mu* (grave tending; literally, "to sweep the grave"). *Sao mu* is particularly observed during the Ch'ing Ming period, an important annual festival time that coincides with the month of March. Families and friends visit graves and place offerings of food and drink. At other times in the year graves are also visited and offerings placed. Usually these visits occur on Sunday, but some Chinese-Americans consult an almanac for the most propitious date and time.

At funerals as well as grave tendings the quantity of food and drink offered varies according to the means and wishes of the family. Buddhist priests are employed for the interment. Observing these obligatory activities sustains a relationship with the family and social fabric that spans history and helps one avoid the displeasure of the spirits and ensuing calamity. So strong has been the concern for proper attention to the dead that even in families where members have joined Christian groups, all come together and participate in traditional Chinese observances.

Apart from these activities and those that pertain to marriage and birth, one is hard pressed to find signs by which to identify Chinese religious practice in the United States. If one walks the streets of the Chinatowns one will, of course, pass shops catering to those who still seek to placate the *shen* or to purchase the elements with which to create the elixir of immortality. And in addition to an occasional Chinese Buddhist temple, one can find a rare Taoist society or association or a Confucianist shrine dedicated to sustaining insights from those traditions. But that is all.

Even though persons of Chinese birth or descent numbered 894,000 in 1980, the evidences of religious activity are not readily apparent. It is as though in the Chinese community religion has very nearly become the "invisible institution," because it is viewed as a private matter not to be pursued in a public setting. One should not commit the error, therefore, of maintaining that the

Chinese ethnic group as a whole is indifferent to religion. The vast majority have adhered to religion as it fits their needs, and the religion appealed to is an amalgamation of a number of traditions from China.

CONCLUSION

Both Shinto and indigenous Chinese religion have tended to persist in the United States because of the needs of Japanese-Americans and Chinese-Americans. These forms continue to provide a vehicle for maintaining continuity with the lands of origin and, thus, for perpetuating a certain distance from the dominant customs and values of the United States.

In the case of some Sectarian Shinto groups another need is addressed. A few individuals not of Japanese descent have joined some of these groups because they see in them an opportunity to develop a religious affiliation that is distinct from the more dominant Jewish and Christian forms. But the fact that the groups remain in great part culture-bound makes it unlikely that they will attract many non-Asian members.

The Shinto groups and the more diffused Chinese religion tend to be peripheral to much of American life, and it is unlikely that they will ever play major, influential roles within the United States. Perhaps the most revealing point in this regard is that, with the exception of the Buddhist Churches of America, no other religious group of Japanese or Chinese origin is included in the informative *Yearbook of American and Canadian Churches.*

BIBLIOGRAPHY

Jack Chen, *The Chinese of America* (1980); H. Byron Earhart, *Japanese Religion: Unity and Diversity* (1969); Robert S. Ellwood, Jr., *Religious and Spiritual Groups in Modern America* (1973) and *The Eagle and the Rising Sun: Americans and the New Religions of Japan* (1974); Donald Keith Fellows, *A Mosaic of America's Ethnic Minorities* (1972); Will Herberg, *Protestant, Catholic, Jew: An Essay in American Religious Sociology* (1960); Ichiro Hori, Fujio Ikado, Tsuneya Wakimoto, and Keiichi Yanagawa, eds, *Japanese Religion* (1972); Bill Hosokawa, *Nisei: The Quiet Americans* (1969); Francis L. K. Hsu, *The Challenge of the American Dream: The Chinese in the United States* (1971); John A. Hutchison, *Paths of Faith* (1969).

Yamato Ichihashi, *Japanese in the United States* (1969); Constant H. Jacquet, Jr., ed., *Yearbook of American and Canadian Churches* (1985); John B. Noss, *Man's Religions*, 5th ed. (1974); Clark B. Offner and Henry Van Straelen, S.V.D., *Modern Japanese Religions,* with Special Emphasis on Their Doctrines of Healing (1963); Charles S. Prebish, *American Buddhism* (1979); Betty Lee Sung, *Mountain of Gold: The Story of the Chinese in America* (1967); Tenrikyo Overseas Mission Department, ed., *Tenrikyo: Its History and Teachings* (1966); Laurence G. Thompson, *Chinese Religion: An Introduction* (1969); Ryūsaku Tsunoda, William Theodore deBary, and Donald Keene, *Sources of the Japanese Tradition,* 2 vols. (1958); Melford S. Weiss, *Valley City: A Chinese Community in America* (1974). [*See also* BUDDHISM; "CULTS" IN THE LATE TWENTIETH CENTURY; HINDUISM; ISLAM IN NORTH AMERICA; *and* OCCULT MOVEMENTS IN AMERICA.]

OCCULT MOVEMENTS IN AMERICA

Robert S. Ellwood

THE occult bands in the spectrum of American spirituality exhibit superficial diversity, but possess a fairly consistent sociological nature, a set of common themes, and a degree of historical interconnectedness. The term *occult movement* may be broadly defined to include Spiritualism, Theosophy, Rosicrucianism, UFO groups, Neo-Paganism, modern witchcraft, Satanism, and other initiatory and magical orders. The formal doctrine, practice, and tone of these groups vary immensely. Much misunderstanding can result from lumping them together too precipitously, as though adherence to one necessarily implied fraternity with all the others. Followers of modern witchcraft have, very unfairly, been labeled Satanists, and Theosophists as unjustly called Pagans. Nonetheless, fundamental attitudes, and their historical and sociological expression, link the movements together. Those attitudes may be summed up in the term *occultism.*

Occultism refers to "secret truth." Occult movements are those whose adherents believe they are custodians of significant truth about reality—truth unknown to most people either because it has been deliberately concealed or because it is by its very nature unknowable without special training or initiation. This esoteric knowledge characteristically concerns little-known laws of nature, unexplored psychic and spiritual capacities of the human being, or superhuman hierarchies—gods, spirits, masters—ranged between the human being and "ultimate reality." In occult lore, these hidden laws and superior beings invisibly guide the world and assist the sincere aspirant toward higher wisdom. Initiations, rites, and meditation techniques are frequently part of an occult movement's equipment—aids to the attainment of occult truth, and to tapping its power.

Conceptual themes common to most American occultism include affirmation of belief in astrology, psychic phenomena, reincarnation, and spiritual healing. The occult world view typically postulates an impersonal, monistic Absolute, which operates the universe through law rather than by caprice. Hence occultism claims an affinity with the scientific approach. But between the Absolute and the human being, as already suggested, many quite personal intermediaries may operate—masters, Neo-Pagan gods and goddesses, UFO "space brothers," and the spirits of the departed, who are evoked by mediumship. Both the universe and the human being are apt to be viewed in essentially mentalistic terms. Occultists generally hold that mind creates the outward manifestations of reality, and that the human mind/spirit is independent of the physical body, with a separate origin, a separate career reincarnating through many forms, and a separate destiny. Finally, occult wisdom is usually said to be very ancient, though long hidden from most eyes.

Occult movements differ from such other against-the-mainstream religious movements as revivalism, Pentecostalism, or New Thought. The occult orientation is less toward appropriate feelings or mental attitudes than toward appropriate understanding; this leads to an emphasis on study and learning, on the lecture rather than on the hortatory sermon, on the class rather than on the congregation. This does not mean that experience is underrated; it certainly is not, for instance, in witchcraft, Spiritualism, or ceremonial magic. But the emphasis on understanding does mean that experience derived from familiarity with occult truth is thought to be possible only in a tightly controlled setting. The controlling participants must have had adequate preparation and must be highly committed and

711

bonded to the group. For all practical purposes, the core occult group is small, close knit, and, if not secretive, at least wary in its dealings with the outside world. Some meetings or ceremonies may be restricted to initiates, and entry into the group may be structured to allow selectivity and the programming of initiatory experiences.

A related sociological characteristic of occult groups is in the nature of their leadership. The leader, or the founder, of an occult movement is likely to be a person who communicates depth, psychic energy, and a sense that he or she has an easy relationship with forces and entities beyond the ordinary. He or she will not be so much a flamboyant preacher as a demanding teacher, who will nevertheless exercise a magnetic fascination for potential disciples and will display to them extraordinary, magical abilities that confirm commerce with other planes of reality. The leader is, in a word, a magus—a shaman or wizard in the civilized world—displaying "phenomena" as calling cards and imparting secret lore neglected by the modern world. Thus Helena Petrovna Blavatsky and Georges Gurdjieff, for example, are described as persons with unforgettable eyes whose presence and discourse brought the group around them into something like new worlds.

But if a small intensive group were all an occult movement had, it would have little general impact. In fact, most of the groups discussed here have had a noticeable effect on American spiritual history as a whole. Occult movements usually have significant diffuse as well as intensive modes of expression. An inner core of believers follows the esoteric teachings consummately, perhaps in community, serving as disciples of the magus during his or her life-time, and afterward as apostles. But a far larger population may have read one or two of the movement's books, attended one or two lectures, or practiced privately its techniques of meditation or magic. Some contemporary occult groups, in fact, depend heavily on outreach, through the mail and bookstores, and have donated their works to public libraries.

The extent and significance of such diffuse influence are difficult to assess with exactitude. But unquestionably millions of Americans past and present, even in the most remote rural areas, have been affected by the perusal of Spiritualist, Theosophical, or Rosicrucian literature. Its diffuse influence is borne witness by the widespread awareness of such concepts as karma, reincarnation, and astrology, which directly or indirectly have been popularized more by the occult tradition than by academic scholarship. To cite a more recent phenomenon, few women actually engage in the worship of the goddess promulgated by feminist Wicca (witchcraft) groups, but an awareness of such worship has had an undoubted impact on the religious consciousness of thousands more.

The bipolar intensive/diffuse modes of expression typical of groups in the occult tradition are much more clearly marked than in mainstream denominations. Few of the latter have a central core of commitment and practice with quite the flavor of a Theosophical school or a magical order, and few have a comparable informal "outside" following. Non-Lutherans with no real intention of becoming members do not say Lutheran prayers or take Lutheran correspondence courses, but a sizable informal following is typical of Rosicrucians and Spiritualists; many in our pluralistic society combine private occult reading and practice with Sunday-morning worship in a mainstream church.

Perhaps the bipolar styles of adherence are partly explained by the nature of those who are drawn to occult movements. Occultists come from most of the main classes in society: young and old, male and female, rich and poor; in America they are more likely to be of white middle-class background than poor or from racial minorities, except in groups engaged in ethnic-based practices like voodoo. But running through the life of the typical occultist is what sociologists speak of as *status inconsistency*—a sense of dichotomy between what one is within, or has made oneself, and one's outer role in life. A status-inconsistent person might be one with real intellectual gifts who has been unable to get a good academic education and to gain access to the opportunities that go with education. Another might be an intelligent and inwardly individualistic woman who is trapped in traditional feminine roles, or an immigrant landed in a strange land who does not know how to apply his talents toward success.

Such types are clearly discernible among, for example, the followers of early Theosophy in New York in the 1870s. Co-founder Henry Steel Olcott, writing of those years in *Old Diary Leaves*

(1895), depicts self-educated scholars, a house painter learned in Greek philosophy, rising immigrants, and above all Helena Blavatsky herself —that incomparable original, self-exiled from her heritage, the fabulous yet stifling life of a Russian aristocrat, who never accepted that female biology defined her destiny.

Undoubtedly, as education and opportunity have become more widely available, acute forms of status inconsistency have been alleviated. This may be one reason why occultism in the twentieth century has not taken the dramatic and culture-shaking forms it did in the eighteenth and nineteenth centuries, when it often had clear overtones of social protest. (An exception might be the occult elements of the 1960s "counter culture," dominated by young people who manifestly felt status inconsistency in considering the roles they felt the "Establishment" wished to impose on them.)

Yet discrepancies remain that undoubtedly will continue to produce occult and other non-normative spirituality. With increased opportunity, modernity has also begotten radical pluralism, in the form of almost limitless spiritual and life-style options. At the same time, traditional family, community, ethnic, and religious roots are severely tested by the mobility and apparent personal independence of modern life. Indeed, a fundamental reality of modernity is that it compels one, in the face of many options, both traditional and non-normative, to take responsibility for one's own subjectivity, nowhere more than in the spiritual realm. Even if one elects the conventional mainstream religion in which one was raised, that is a choice in a way it would not have been generations ago.

For several reasons, this radical modern pluralism leads some people to occultism today, as it did in the eighteenth and nineteenth centuries when the same forces were gathering. First, occultism's intellectual emphasis affirms the intelligence and learning of those who might otherwise feel overwhelmed by multitudinous choices. Second, occultism's self-proclaimed compatibility with science appears positive in a new and confusing world. Third, particularly in its diffuse mode of expression, occultism fits well with the spirit of modern individualism and pluralism; at the same time, personal occult study and practice need not be inconsistent with participation in conventional religion. Finally, the yearning for

roots often felt in a world in which so many traditionalisms seem shattered is met by occultism's claim to represent antique lore, going back to ancient Egypt or India, or even to the world of the Paleolithic shaman.

The occult experience has planted itself in America in the form of a definite and fairly compact tradition. While occultism has, as we have seen, taken many conceptual and practical forms, it also possesses a definite philosophical core that can be traced back to Greek Pythagoreanism and Neoplatonism, to Hellenistic Hermetism and Gnosticism, and to medieval cabala and alchemy. In the Middle Ages, this heritage, reinforced by European folk religion of pre-Christian origin, offered a covert alternative or supplement to orthodoxy.

In the Renaissance, abetted by the new discovery of its classical sources and by the new science, which seemed initially to consort well with it, this European esotericism exploded in popularity, at least among princes and scholars. It formed a full-fledged world view, finely articulated for readers of English in much Elizabethan literature. The Renaissance and Elizabethan world view's three basic pillars were Ptolemaic astronomy, the great chain of being— the concept of a hierarchy of increasingly superior intelligences linking earth to heaven—and the notion of "correspondences." The last refers to the idea, expressed in the popular occult saying "As above, so below," that relationships and lines of mystical force conjoin the various elements of the universe, with man a microcosm at the center. Planets and zodiacal signs, gemstones, herbs, and organs of the human body thus have connections capable of both philosophical and magical application.

This overall world view easily sustained astrology: alchemy; wizardry, with its evocation of spirits; and classical medicine, based on humors and bodily "airs." Although the term *Rosicrucian* comes from an alleged secret order of occult savants, the Order of the Rosy Cross that was proclaimed by a popular pamphlet of 1614, the term has then and since been used to allude to that Renaissance world view, and to name various groups devoted to its study.

On the same stage, though not of the same classical derivation, was belief in witchcraft. That fascinating dread, derived no doubt from dark corners of the human psyche, was primarily rationalized from orthodox Christian belief in Satan and his power. As the only occult beings thought to have biblical sanction, witches were vigorously accepted even by those who, like the Puritans, attacked astrology as unbiblical. Notwithstanding, the sixteenth- and seventeenth-century idea of witchcraft was influenced by the intellectual occult tradition as well as by folk belief, and its fortunes rose and fell with the Renaissance world view. Modern revivals of witchcraft as a benign faith have borrowed from the occult tradition to flesh out its magical meaning.

The Elizabethan world view came to the New World with the more educated of the early settlers. Its presence was symbolized by the establishment of a Rosicrucian society in Germantown, Pennsylvania, in 1694, to pursue cabalistic and other mystical teachings. But by the eighteenth century, the advance of science and the spirit of the Enlightenment had put that outlook in considerable disarray. The Copernican-Newtonian universe and the new picture of the human body, sparked by Harvey's discovery of the circulation of the blood, were replacing the old Renaissance macrocosm and microcosm. The tension between the two is reflected in the works of such colonial intellectuals as Jonathan Edwards, Cotton Mather, and Benjamin Franklin. The old view declined as inexorably as a receding tide, and with it waned belief among the educated in such matters as astrology and witchcraft. Change was gradual, however. While Franklin ridiculed astrology, almanacs with horoscopic prognostications were widely circulated in the colonies until the last quarter of the eighteenth century. Furthermore, the old world view fragmented as it decayed, so that one might hold to one of its tenets while rejecting others. Some believed in witchcraft while disdaining the Ptolemaic cosmos, or embraced at once spiritual alchemy and the new medicine—as do many modern occultists. Franklin, even as he denied astrology, affirmed eloquently the great chain of being, with its implication that evil is a matter of perspective. But colonial manifestations of the Elizabethan image of the universe, such as Pennsylvania Rosicrucianism and the Salem witch trials of the 1690s, must be seen as essentially rearguard actions of a dying tradition —at least in the context of the times.

Enlightenment rationalism reached its apex in the America of the Revolutionary and immediate post-Revolutionary eras, the America of Franklin, Jefferson, and Paine. But the occult tradition does not so much die out in any age as change and adapt, next appearing in a new age in the vanguard, expressing the new era's finest ideals. An adaptation in the Revolutionary epoch itself is symbolized by the well-known painting of Washington in the garb of a Freemason.

The Masonic lodges, which burgeoned in Europe in the eighteenth century, reached America by 1730, little more than a decade after the founding in 1717 of the London Grand Lodge from which all modern Masonry stems. Freemasonry derived many of its symbols and the idea of a secret initiatory lodge from the occult tradition, adaptively combining them with ideals from chivalry and from the free-thinking spirit of the Enlightenment. Though ornamented by some aristocrats and clerics, eighteenth-century lodges were a spiritual home for numerous progressive-minded middle-class business and professional men—spirits chafing under antiquated despotisms and, in that sense, status inconsistent. Not surprisingly, lodges often became hotbeds of anticlericalism and of advanced thinking about democracy and the rights of man, not insignificant factors in the background of the French and American revolutions.

Some lodges also became deeply involved in an occultism that was the reverse side of the Enlightenment, like that associated with Saint-Germain, Cagliostro, and Saint-Martin in France. But the eighteenth century understood, in a way perhaps more difficult subsequently, that three seemingly disparate causes—Enlightenment rationalism, occultism, and democratic revolution —could go together. From the eighteenth-century vantage point, the three shared the ultimate common values of human dignity and of a universe governed by laws accessible to the human mind; all, moreover, served to undermine autocrats and their religious props. Thus Freemasonry and even rationalism helped make the occult appear again, as in the Renaissance, to be allied with the wave of progress.

Masonry provided models that were to prove of value to more intensely occult movements in America. Its claim to ancient and Eastern wisdom, its symbolism (for example, the eyed sun atop a pyramid, seen on the back of the dollar bill) betokening spiritual reality behind the cosmos, and its work as an initiatory, ritualistic secret society were full of potential for emulation.

Furthermore, by the late eighteenth and early nineteenth centuries, two fresh movements were to offer new guises for occultism. As they developed in America, these movements enabled occultism to accommodate itself to the new spirit of romanticism that superseded Enlightenment reasonableness and to match the expansive mood of the American frontier. These movements were Swedenborgianism and Mesmerism.

Emanuel Swedenborg began his career in Sweden as a scientist. Of brilliant intellect, he did work ahead of his time in several fields. In mid-life, however, his interests moved decisively toward a desire to understand the metaphysical underpinnings of the universe and of humanity. That shift was much aided by a long series of visionary experiences commencing in 1745. Swedenborg believed that he had seen Christ, met God personally, been a witness to the Last Judgment, which he believed began spiritually in 1757, visited the many mansions of heaven and hell, and conversed with the spirits of numerous past worthies. He wrote voluminously on the knowledge gleaned from these encounters and on the interpretation of Scripture.

Central to Swedenborg's thought was the basically Neoplatonic doctrine that phenomena in the material world reflect spiritual counterparts —an aspect of the idea of correspondences. Furthermore, his observations confirmed the educative nature of the Other World. Souls were not sent to irremediable perdition or to bliss, but to places corresponding to their personality and state, where they could learn and mature to higher planes. Moreover, true "conjugial love" begun here continued to flourish in the next world. Swedenborgianism had considerable appeal in its contrast with the forensic character of much conventional religion of the day, and with the materialism implicit in the new science; it perpetuated in Christian wrappings much of what the old occult world view had to offer. Societies were formed that grew into the small but influential Swedenborgian church (properly, the Church of the New Jerusalem, often called the New Church). A society appeared in Baltimore as early as 1792.

Swedenborgian ideas were disseminated more informally in the yeasty atmosphere of the frontier. John Chapman ("Johnny Appleseed") was an avid apostle of the new doctrines, distributing what he called "Good News Fresh from Heaven," as well as seeds, throughout the Middle West. In no small part because of American enthusiasm for Swedenborgianism—which climaxed around the 1840s—the notions that spiritual and mental causes can effect material results, that the departed enjoy a realm of learning and growth and can communicate with this world, and that a new progressive spiritual era is under way slipped into popular consciousness. It needed but a spark for such tinder to become Spiritualism, and then Theosophy and New Thought.

The flint and steel for that spark were provided by Mesmerism. Franz Mesmer, the Austrian father of hypnosis, had a complementary vogue in America around the time of the Swedenborgian wave. Mesmerism was concerned with healing mind and body through suggestion, best applied in trance, and its use correlated with the psychosomatic nature of much illness. But the Viennese doctor also proposed a more speculative philosophy to interpret his strange discoveries about health and the human mind. He maintained that a subtle universal substance gives life and energy; illness is due to its imbalance, which can be corrected through "animal magnetism." Mesmer employed several methods of reinvigorating those whose life energy was dissipated, but all the methods seemed basically to induce a hypnotic state in which the patient was undoubtedly open to positive suggestion. Mesmer's successors devoted much attention to the state itself. Some developed hypnotism in its modern forms, doing much to pave the way for scientific psychology and psychoanalysis.

Others of more occult bent explored the possibility that the mesmeric state was a doorway to transcendent knowledge and power. Mesmer himself firmly contended that animal magnetism could awaken latent human powers, enabling one to penetrate cosmic mysteries and to develop extrasensory perception because it tapped an inner spiritual source in which all time and space are one, with all wisdom buried as a treasure to be uncovered. Mesmer believed that many wonderful phenomena attributed in the past to oracles and wizards were true, though not for the reasons then thought. But the shamanistic practices had in actuality opened the door a bit to extraordinary mental powers he was now prepared to describe, and to induce, more scientifically. The significance of this view for the occult tradition is well witnessed by Madame Blavatsky's later remark that Mesmerism is the most important branch of magic, and, indeed, the true base of what is called magical or miraculous.

The Swedenborgian rediscovery of Neoplatonic spiritual transcendence and the Mesmerist discovery of potent subjectivity helped to stimulate New England Transcendentalism. The sages of Concord and its surroundings established an American style of mystical thought and introduced the spiritual Orient, providing intellectual foundations for later American occult and New Thought movements.

But it was in Spiritualism that the most dramatic potential of Swedenborgianism and Mesmerism was actualized. The Swedenborgian world of spirits was manifested through Mesmerist states of consciousness in mediumship. Spiritualism began as a movement with the celebrated "Rochester Rappings" reported by the Fox sisters in 1848. It was, however, anticipated by earlier enthusiasms, by romanticism with its exaltation of feeling and experience over reason, and by the popularization of the romantic mood that produced what have been called "the sentimental years," the 1840s and 1850s, with their cult of spiritual progress and their yearning to pierce the veil separating those in life from loved ones beyond. A decisive event was the publication in 1847 of *The Principles of Nature, Her Divine Revelation and a Voice to Mankind* by Andrew Jackson Davis. Davis, the leading philosopher of Spiritualism, studied Swedenborgianism and practiced Mesmerism; the book, delivered out of a trance to scribes, offers a Swedenborgian view of spiritual planes beyond earth, a Fourierist utopianism with its hope in a coming socialist paradise, a Deistic naturalism affirming that though God created the world it subsequently followed natural law, and a confident belief in ongoing human progress. His *Principles,* which in many ways sums up the spirit of the expansive 1840s, was widely read and discussed.

The next year, 1848, Margaretta and Catherine Fox, aged fifteen and twelve respectively, of a poor rural family in Hydesville, near Rochester, New York, first heard the mysterious tappings that they and many others took to be messages from departed spirits. Their accounts evoked sensational newspaper stories, much controversy, and widespread imitation of this commerce with the Other World. Within a year or two, spirit circles flourished in most major cities and in innumerable rural areas. Although the Spiritualist craze died down by the end of the 1850s, Spiritualist churches survive to the present, and Spiritualism has enjoyed modest revivals, especially in the 1870s, the 1920s, and the 1960s.

The central feature of Spiritualism is trance mediumship. Spiritualist churches today generally hold services of a basically Protestant structure, although they may contain such unorthodox features as use of the modern *Aquarian Gospel of Jesus Christ* for the Scripture lesson. But the service often ends with "readings" by a minister-medium, in which brief spirit messages are given to attendees. On other occasions, one may be able to visit a séance in which the medium, now probably in deeper trance, delivers sermonlike instruction from great spirit-teachers.

Early American Spiritualism by and large shared Davis' liberal mind. Prominent Spiritualists were associated with progressive or radical ideas, such as abolition, women's rights, and economic reform. Spiritualism manifested itself in utopian communities such as those associated with Robert Owen, Thomas Lake Harris, and the Shakers. The rhetoric of the movement indicated that Spiritualism represented the latest, most "scientific" phase in religion, as progressive causes did in social reform; that it was the most democratic of faiths; and that the spirits were now breaking through in a new way to humankind to inaugurate a new and better age. Spiritualism also shared the open, experimental mood of the frontier, and it owed something to the practice of Native American shamanism. The "Indian Guide" is a common visitant to the séance room, and not a few early mediums claimed to have learned their craft from native shamans, or even to be of partly Indian descent. The Spiritualist faith was, therefore, an indigenous religion, inimitably shaped by nineteenth-century America. Like that other American spiritual export, Pentecostalism, it quickly spread around the world.

Spiritualist churches and denominations alike have tended over the movement's history to be fluid, changing names and affiliations with bewildering rapidity. This is not surprising, since a high percentage of attendees at Spiritualist services are characteristically nonmembers with little interest in institutional structure. They are drawn primarily by an individual minister, an independent medium, or a particular church. The oldest and perhaps largest denomination is the National Spiritualist Association of Churches, founded in 1893 by a medium and two former Unitarian ministers, but there are many others. Doctrinal issues on which Spiritualists have divided include reincarnation and the question of how specifically Christian the movement should be. Other splits have occurred because of personality conflicts and charges of fraudulent mediumship.

Spiritualism has engendered interesting progeny. One set of groups is centered on what J. Gordon Melton has called Teaching Spiritualism. These movements are based on new Scriptures communicated by spiritual beings, typically emphasizing such themes as reincarnation, spiritual evolution, higher planes of reality than the physical, and other worlds. A leading example is the Universal Brotherhood of Faithists, based on the *Oahspe,* a new Bible received through automatic writing (or rather typing) by John B. Newbrough in 1882. It tells of humanity's origin on a now-lost continent in the Pacific and predicts a coming paradisiacal age. Another modern Scripture, the *Urantia Book,* was received anonymously and first published in 1955; it is distributed by the Urantia Foundation of Chicago and is studied by a number of informal groups. *Urantia* offers extensive new information on the spiritual organization of the universe, the religious history of earth, and the life of Jesus.

Also related to Spiritualism are various UFO groups. Almost immediately after the first sightings of "flying saucers" or "unidentified flying objects" were reported in 1947, individuals came forward with claims to being "contactees," persons contacted by the visitors from other worlds who rode the mysterious vessels. Usually the "contacts" were said to be beings so superior to earthlings as to be virtually godlike. They had important messages for us, warning us on our destructive ways, and promising that if earthmen —or believers—reformed, they could be initiated into a higher galactic civilization. So similar in structure were many of these encounters to the religious revelations of the past that the analytic psychologist C. G. Jung spoke of the spacemen as "technological angels," the gods and sav-

iors of another day reclothed in space-age dress. We may, in particular, note a connection with Spiritualism. Not a few of the major contactees had a background in that faith, and communication with the "space brothers" is frequently psychic or in trance. In "circles," comparable to Spiritualist séances, messages are usually delivered in a mediumistic manner. Themes are typically those garnered from Teaching Spiritualism and from the occult tradition.

Like Spiritualist churches, religious UFO groups have tended to be fluid and ephemeral; they were in decline by the 1980s. Some, like the Aetherius Society, founded in England by George King in 1954, and soon planted in America, found that the UFO experience opened up a sense of cosmic spiritual forces, but before long the society gave major attention simply to messages from masters in other worlds. A group that has sustained a UFO focus is Understanding, Inc., established by Daniel Fry in 1955; Fry claimed to have had a UFO ride and conversation with a space being in 1950. Understanding, Inc., has provided a forum for many contactees and UFO-related ideas.

The most important movement to grow out of the Spiritualist awakening, and one that has spawned a further set of occult groups, is Theosophy. The Theosophical Society was founded in New York in 1875 by the Russian aristocrat Helena Petrovna Blavatsky and the New York lawyer and journalist Henry Steel Olcott. Blavatsky had come to America in 1873 to pursue a deepening interest in Spiritualism in its homeland. The next year she met Olcott in Vermont, where both had gone to investigate Spiritualist phenomena. The odd match of Russian noblewoman and middle-class American took; they got along famously and, after returning to New York, were soon sharing an apartment. Olcott, in his delightful *Old Diary Leaves,* tells of being delivered more and more into the wondrous world of his companion's psychic phenomena and her commerce with masters. (These beings were not necessarily on spiritual planes as were the guides of Spiritualism, but might be in this world, though perhaps dwelling in a remote place like Tibet, communicating mentally with their students.) Increasingly, Olcott's tutors became Eastern, and Blavatsky insisted that Eastern Spiritualism was greatly in advance of the Western.

Nonetheless, the first major work Blavatsky produced, *Isis Unveiled* (1877), showed mostly the influence of the Western occult tradition. Said to have been inspired by the masters and to be a preliminary expression of the "Ancient Wisdom" behind the world's religions, it told of a subtle universal energizing substance—like the animal magnetism of Mesmer—which explained apparent magic. It pointed also to a tripartite constitution of man and the universe: matter, the subtle energy usually thought of as spirit, and Consciousness, or the Universal Mind, from which both derive. This view, with its occult roots, was presented as a challenge to both conventional science and religion; Blavatsky made telling jabs at its pretensions. At the same time, India, still largely innocent of the ill fortune that had overtaken the old wisdom in the churchly, scientific, materialistic West, remained a reservoir of lore and power. It is understandable, then, as Indic interests grew, and as the movement dwindled in America despite the success of *Isis,* that the Theosophical Twins (as Olcott liked to call them) journeyed in 1878–1879 to India. There the movement suffered many changes of fortune, ranging from charges of psychic chicanery to enthusiastic support from native Indians and Ceylonese, who saw in its premises far more validation of their culture and religion than they had been accustomed to receive from Europeans in the heyday of the British raj.

In 1888, having moved on to Europe, Blavatsky published her second major work, *The Secret Doctrine.* It added more Eastern material to the world view of *Isis,* placed greater emphasis on reincarnation, and gave a remarkable picture of the spiritual evolution of the solar system and humanity. Contrary to the general impression, however, Theosophy is not simply a compendium of Eastern beliefs; its standard world view remains as much shaped by the Western occult tradition as by Eastern correlates. Theosophical teaching is many-faceted, but a salient feature is the idea of a monistic cosmos grounded in Consciousness, in which universes rise and fall in great cycles, even as do worlds and races on smaller scales. It inculcates the idea that outer forms express prior inner spiritual realities; that through these immense cosmic cycles the individual "monad" or "pilgrim" is reincarnating and evolving in accordance with karma; that

some entities, far ahead of the norm, are masters who invisibly guide the destiny of worlds. Recapitulating the occult tradition with its correspondences and great chain of being, Theosophy teaches lore such as astrology, and about auras and the subtle nature of human beings. But a major source of its appeal has been its reconciliation of the occult tradition with a more modern belief in progress and evolution.

Theosophy has engendered a number of subsequent occult movements. They fall into two broad categories that might be called "Liberal Theosophy" and "New Revelation Theosophy." In the first class is the largely informal movement of followers of the teaching of Jiddu Krishnamurti. Born in India, Krishnamurti was raised under the auspices of Theosophists who expected that he would become a world teacher. In 1929 he left Theosophy, rejecting all organized spirituality, but continued to attract audiences to his path of "choiceless awareness," a total seeing and being beyond mental processes. His work centered in Ojai, California.

Also in the liberal category is Anthroposophy, founded by Rudolf Steiner, a Goethe scholar who lived in Austria, Germany, and Switzerland. He helped organize Theosophy in Germany, but in 1912–1913 broke with it to inaugurate Anthroposophy, giving the Western occult tradition and Christianity more emphasis than he thought they were receiving in the parent movement. Anthroposophy teaches that spiritual development is evolution back to a lost divine condition; it stresses education, art, and agriculture based on spiritual principles. Anthroposophy had come to the United States by 1925; its schools have a distinguished reputation.

Still another group in the first class is the Liberal Catholic Church, founded in England largely by British Old Catholics and Theosophists. A dominant figure was the prolific and sometimes controversial Theosophical writer Charles W. Leadbeater, who became a Liberal Catholic bishop and whose *Science of the Sacraments* (1920) is a basic text. Church ritual centers on the Mass, which is interpreted in terms of esoteric symbolism and of the creation of "thought forms" to channel divine energy. In the United States since 1917, the Liberal Catholic Church is small, and is divided by jurisdictional conflicts, but it presents a significant witness.

Other movements have developed from Theosophical belief in the possibility of new revelations from masters. One such movement is the Arcane School, which promotes teachings delivered through Alice Bailey, a former Theosophist who died in 1949. She believed she had been given a special commission by one of the masters to prepare humankind for "the return of the Christ"; a major activity of the movement is group meditation at the full moon to channel energy to this end.

Another New Revelation movement is I AM, founded by Guy Ballard. Long interested in occultism and Theosophy, Ballard was a mining engineer who claimed that he had met a Theosophical master, Saint-Germain, in 1930 on the slopes of California's Mt. Shasta. I AM teaches much standard Theosophical doctrine, but with special emphasis on reincarnation, on the ongoing teaching role of "ascended masters," and on the spiritual destiny of America. I AM has produced several splinters, the most visible in the 1980s being the Church Universal and Triumphant, originally the Summit Lighthouse, formed by Mark and Elizabeth Clare Prophet in 1958 and carried on by Elizabeth since her husband's death in 1973. She is believed to be a major channel for the ascended masters. Headquarters is at "Camelot" in Malibu, California.

The Theosophical tradition has also had a more general influence on American occultism. Much of modern astrology has been affected by the seriousness with which Theosophy treated that ancient art, saying it had to be understood in a profounder sense than that indicated by popular prognosticators. Astrology has itself been a mainstay of several occult groups, most conspicuously the Church of Light, incorporated in Los Angeles in 1932, which is said to present teachings of an ancient Brotherhood of Light going back to 2400 B.C. in Egypt.

Gnosticism, also viewed favorably by Theosophy, has enjoyed a revival as well. Since the late nineteenth century, several tiny churches endeavoring to revive the ancient Gnostic version of Christianity have appeared in Europe and America. They have usually been much influenced by Theosophy's view that Gnosticism represents the authentic esoteric significance of Christianity. The best-known of these groups in America is probably the Church of the Gnosis, headquartered in Los Angeles, and led by Bishop Stephan Hoeller, a Hungarian-born Theosophist.

Another wing of American occultism that may be theosophically tinctured is the organization that perpetuates the teachings of Edgar Cayce—the Association for Research and Enlightenment (ARE). Cayce, a Kentuckian of limited education, gave clairvoyant readings while in a sleeplike trance. The readings were at first related mostly to healing. After 1922, when Cayce met Arthur Lammers, a Theosophist and astrologer, they came to concern reincarnation and global prophecies as well. ARE, headquartered in Virginia Beach, Virginia, has study groups in many cities.

As we have seen, Rosicrucianism has a separate background from Theosophy, although in the last century they have exhibited much convergence and interaction. Three principal Rosicrucian movements are found in modern America. The oldest continuing U.S. Rosicrucian group is apparently the Fraternitas Rosae Crucis, founded in 1868 by Paschal B. Randolph, later associated with R. Swinburne Clymer; its headquarters are in Pennsylvania. Partly secret, it teaches an occultism based on karma, reincarnation, heavenly hierarchies, and human brotherhood.

The Rosicrucian Fellowship centered in California was established in 1907 by Carl Louis Von Grasshof, a German better known under his pen name, Max Heindel. Its teaching is heavily Theosophical, with substantial influence from Rudolf Steiner, especially in its Christian emphasis. Vegetarianism and astrology are stressed in its churches and fellowships.

The Ancient and Mystical Order of the Rosae Crucis (AMORC) was founded in 1915 by H. Spencer Lewis. Because of its extensive advertising, it is by far the best-known Rosicrucian group. AMORC claims to be a public manifestation of an initiatory tradition going back to ancient Egypt. Its spacious headquarters in San Jose, California, cover a block, and include administration buildings, an auditorium, and a distinguished museum of Egyptology. Much larger in number of adherents than most groups noted in this article, AMORC emphasizes that it is not a religion, but a vehicle for teaching secret knowledge, about human nature and cosmic mind, which can enable those ready for it to live happier and more successful lives.

Other occult groups very broadly of the Theosophical and Rosicrucian type can only be named —Astara, revealed by Theosophical masters to former Spiritualists Robert and Evelyn Chaney; the Mayan Order, claiming to recall ancient Mayan mysteries; Soulcraft, an occult enterprise of William Dudley Pelley, notorious in the 1930s for his pro-Nazi Silver Shirts (a political leaning definitely not shared by all occultism); the eclectic Sabian Assembly, started by the noted astrologer Marc Edmund Jones; and the Builders of the Adytum (BOTA), a Los Angeles group emphasizing cabala and tarot cards.

One of the best-known occult teachers of the twentieth century was Georges Gurdjieff. He left no single organization, but his name is potent with several groups. Gurdjieff was born in Caucasian Russia and traveled widely as a youth. He appeared in Moscow to begin his work on the eve of the Russian Revolution. His maguslike quality attracted devoted followers, whom he taught new states of consciousness to be attained through labor, group exercises, and surprise. We are asleep, Gurdjieff said, and need the shock of wakening to attain our potential. His work continues through centers like the Gurdjieff Foundation in New York and the Prosperos in California.

A set of occult groups of great interest are those centered on ritual or ceremonial magic. The practice of ritual magic is seen by its adherents to be of essentially religious meaning. Not simply private magic for personal ends, this entails rites of cosmic symbolism and transformational significance. Magic, to these groups, is a means of evoking power—in the form of gods and goddesses—through rituals combining emotional intensity with precision. Their sense of tradition goes back to the medieval grimoires (magical texts), and before them to theurgic Neoplatonism.

Ritual magic certainly has antecedents in that Renaissance occultism evidenced in such stories as *Faust*. But the immediate background of contemporary ceremonial magic is the nineteenth-century occult revival associated with Eliphas Levi in France, with the Hermetic Order of the Golden Dawn in England, and, above all, with Aleister Crowley. A member of the Golden Dawn

in its 1890s heyday, Crowley—poet, mountaineer, libertine, drug addict, and magus—was no man to be only a part of someone else's show. In the early twentieth century, he developed his own order, the *Argenteum Astrum* (AA), and later became effective head in the English-speaking world of the more famous *Ordo Templi Orientalis* (OTO). Crowley's magic included evocation of gods and spirits and sexual rites of the tantric sort. Its purpose was to give the practitioner initiation into states of enhanced psychic power, to impart wisdom concerning the secrets of the universe, and finally to unite the mind with universal consciousness. The practitioner acquired infinite energy, his will unimpeded. "Do what thou wilt shall be the whole of the Law" (meaning, Let magic make your will supreme) was the heart of a great revelation Crowley believed he had received in 1904.

American disciples of Crowley began to organize before his death in 1947, and today the major magical groups here are in the Crowley tradition, though also influenced by the Golden Dawn and by medieval and Renaissance texts. Today OTO exists in at least three American groups of that name, in the aftermath of a complex history, and there are several other magical orders more or less influenced by Crowley and by the Golden Dawn. One is OTA (*Ordo Templi Astartes*), headquartered in Pasadena, California; its rather Jungian interpretation of magical operations holds that the evoked entities may be projected archetypes of the unconscious, and the rite a therapeutic process in which they are acknowledged.

Other occult organizations of great fascination are modern witchcraft, or Wicca, groups, and their close allies who are involved in revivalist neopaganism. Both endeavor to reconstruct the best of the pre-Christian religions of Europe or the ancient Near East; in so doing, they present a religious option they feel is better attuned to nature, ecology, and the masculine and feminine dimensions of the sacred than is mainstream Christianity.

Along with ritual magic, Wicca emphasizes initiation and evocation. But its sources are more reconstructed pre-Christian religion (in the English-speaking world, mostly Celtic and Saxon) than they are Neo-Platonist and cabalistic. In Wicca, life is aligned with nature and the turn of the seasons. Its festivals are the seasonal rites carried over from the archaic milieu, like Midsummer Eve and Halloween; its atmosphere is more simple and homey. But ecstatic and sexual elements are not unknown. Some followers of Wicca claim a direct family or "underground" link with archaic religion of the Middle Ages and with the era of the great witchcraft persecutions. But witchcraft groups in their modern form owe much to Gerald B. Gardner, the British author of *Witchcraft Today* (1954), and to the "Craft" groups he inspired.

In the 1950s covens began operating in both England and the United States. Like so much else occult, they burgeoned in the 1960s under the impact of the counterculture spirit, leveling off but not disappearing in the 1970s and 1980s. Indeed, Wicca was given a new impetus by the quest of those decades for a feminist spirituality; it offered a model of a religion in which the Goddess is at least as important as God, and priestesses as essential as priests. Most typically, Wicca worship centers on the evocation of the Goddess, personifying earth or the universe, and of her consort, the Horned God. Some feminist Wicca groups are composed entirely of women and worship only the Goddess. They perceive this as a perhaps transitional but presently necessary stage in the process of finding female spiritual identity.

Revivalist neopaganism shares many of the same concerns but focuses instead on reconstructing the religion of a specific ancient culture. Although much influenced by the writings of Jung and Robert Graves, and anticipated by one or two tiny older groups, neopaganism in America is for the most part a product of the 1960s. Its manifestations have included groups of ancient Egyptian, Greek, Celtic, and Nordic inspiration. More recently, however, the trend in both Wicca and pagan circles has been less toward slavish revival, and more in the direction of finding new ways to express religion in modern American terms. These groups are attuned to the aliveness of nature, polytheism, the seasons, and the masculine and feminine faces of divinity. A good example is Pagan Way, which has affiliates in a number of American cities. It has no secrets or magic in the ritual sense, and it reconstructs no particular pagan past, but it meets according to a regular calendar for celebrations of

nature and the seasons centering on the Goddess. Such celebrations characteristically include dance, liturgical poetry of a romantic cast, and the offering and ceremonial sharing of food and wine.

Satanism is not to be confused with Wicca or neopaganism, for adherents of the latter view themselves simply as non-Christian worshipers. Satanism, on the other hand, is intimately and inseparably related to the Judeo-Christian tradition. It makes a point of worshiping precisely what that tradition sees as the epitome of evil— the antagonist to God. It is an expression of rebellion against that heritage and its Lord, but conditioned by the classic Judeo-Christian world view with its warfare between God and the Devil.

Accounts of alleged Satanism can be found from the Middle Ages to the present, but modern Satanism is a product of the "decadent" romanticism typical of the late nineteenth century. It has manifested itself in Europe and America in a diversity of individuals and groups, the latter generally ephemeral and far more minuscule than their own claims or those of sensationalist exposés would suggest.

Traditional Satanist worship has at its center the evocation of Satan and the Black Mass, which parodies the Roman Catholic rite. It has great emotional intensity and includes strong overtones of ventilation of anger against God and society. Needless to say, Satanism attracts its share of sociopathic persons, though overgeneralizations should no more be made here than in other religions. Indeed, modern Satanists seem to be divided into three groups. Some regard the Devil as a true deity, representing the life force, the Judeo-Christian God as a repressive entity who merely claims to be good. Others worship Satan as evil, hoping to be rewarded by him for their service. A third group, which might be called the liberal wing of Satanism, is represented by the Church of Satan in San Francisco. For it, the most public Satanic group, the tradition's myths and rituals are little more than ways to help people accept their carnal side without guilt—they have perhaps the therapeutic value of psychodrama.

Although socially Satanism may be in the occult subculture, from a technical point of view it is only marginally part of the occult stream because of its essential ties to Judaism and Christianity. Broadly speaking, that stream represents the perpetuation into contemporary times of a world view fundamentally shaped by the notions of correspondences, of a great chain or hierarchy of beings conjoining Earth and the Ultimate. Man as microcosm is integrally related to the universe, and subtle substances or energies can be wielded by Consciousness to enhance power. The occult belief that this wisdom is exceedingly ancient is by no means wholly wrong; it unquestionably has archaic roots. Classically articulated by Pythagoreans and Neoplatonists, it is like a river, sometimes visible and sometimes underground, that has flowed through the centuries of subsequent Western civilization, producing such branches as alchemy, astrology, and ritual magic. Although in early modern times many held occultism to be compatible with Christianity, its profession implies some rejection of orthodox Christianity as a total spiritual system. In the same way, occultism implies that current science is not a seamless whole either, that there may be value in what science has left behind, as well as in what it has not yet discovered.

The lasting appeal of occultism, however, lies not so much in its relation to other systems of thought, whether religious or scientific, as in its own nature. Its beliefs, acted out in practices, give a sense of significance, power, and harmony with the universe on all levels. The underlying message of the occult movements is "You belong." You are, they say, a legitimate part of the universe; in this system, this harmony, you have a proper place. If you know and enact the secrets that give you that place, the meaning and power of the entire universe also are yours.

BIBLIOGRAPHY

Margot Adler, *Drawing Down the Moon: Witches, Druids, Goddess-Worshippers, and Other Pagans in America Today* (1979); Catherine L. Albanese, *Corresponding Motion: Transcendental Religion and the New America* (1977); Slater Brown, *The Heyday of Spiritualism* (1970); Bruce F. Campbell, *Ancient Wisdom Revived: A History of the Theosophical Movement* (1980); Richard Cavendish, *The Black Arts* (1967); Mircea Eliade, *Occultism, Witchcraft, and Cultural Fashions: Essays in Comparative Religions* (1976); Robert S. Ellwood, *Religious and Spiritual Groups in Modern America* (1973) and *Alternative Altars: Unconventional and Eastern Spirituality in America* (1979); Robert C. Fuller, *Mesmerism and the American Cure of Souls* (1982).

J. Stillson Judah, *The History and Philosophy of the Metaphysical Movements in America* (1967); Howard Kerr, *Mediums, and Spirit-Rappers, and Roaring Radicals: Spiritualism in American Literature, 1850–1900* (1972); Howard Kerr and Charles L. Crow, eds., *The Occult in America: New Historical Perspectives* (1983); Herbert Leventhal, *In the Shadow of the Enlightenment: Occultism and Renaissance Science in Eighteenth-Century America* (1976); Arthur Lyons, *The Second Coming: Satanism in America* (1970); George Trobridge, *Swedenborg: Life and Teaching* (1907; rev. 1935); Kenneth Walker, *A Study of Gurdjieff's Teaching* (1957); Frances A. Yates, *The Rosicrucian Enlightenment* (1972).

ISLAM IN NORTH AMERICA

Newell S. Booth, Jr.

ISLAM is the second largest and probably the fastest growing religion in the world. According to Muslims it is also the original, natural religion, built into creation by God. *Islam* means acceptance, or submission; to be a Muslim is to accept one's proper place within God's creation. Every person is naturally "Muslim," but because this has been obscured by ignorance and carelessness, God, in his mercy, has sent a series of messengers, including Abraham, Moses, and Jesus. All of them communicated the same true message, but much of it was misunderstood or forgotten; thus, there was a need for another messenger, through whom it would be correctly understood. The final message is found in the Qur'an, of which Muḥammad is not the "author," only the transmitter. (*Moslem, Mohammed,* and *Koran* are earlier, less accurate, English spellings of *Muslim, Muḥammad,* and *Qur'an.*)

Certain beliefs are stated by the Qur'an to be central to its message. The first is belief in God, who is absolutely and unambiguously One, as indicated in the following passage from the Qur'an:

> Say: "He is God, One,
> God, the Everlasting Refuge,
> who has not begotten, and has not been
>   begotten,
> and equal to Him is not any one."
> (Arberry, *The Koran Interpreted,*
>   Surah 112)

Second is belief in angels, created beings living in the spiritual realm, who act as agents of God. The third belief is in books, which include the Jewish and Christian Scriptures as originally revealed by God. This original no longer exists; the present Bible is believed to be the result of a process of corruption by Jews and Christians and is not generally read by Muslims, for all that is true in it is found in the Qur'an. Fourth is belief in prophets or messengers, of whom twenty-eight are mentioned in the Qur'an, most of them also biblical figures. Jesus is one of the most important prophets, but Muslim beliefs about him differ greatly from those of Christians. Fifth is belief in the Day of Judgment. The final belief is in predestination—everything that happens is determined by the will of God. (Muslims also believe in human responsibility; the relationship between this and God's determination of all things has been one of the major problems of Muslim theology.)

It is wrong to speak of the religion as Muhammadanism; Muḥammad is not divine or even the founder of Islam. He is very important, however, as its final messenger and as the one who provides a perfect example of how life should be lived in accordance with the message. Islam is not only a "religion" in the narrow sense but a whole way of life, following the Shari'a (often inadequately translated as Law), which is based on the Qur'an and on the example of the Prophet, as recalled and interpreted by the *umma,* the Muslim community.

The *umma* came into existence in 622 C.E., when Muḥammad left Mecca and went to Medina; this was the *hijra,* the "emigration," the beginning of Islam as a historical community, the event from which the Muslim era is dated. In Medina, Muḥammad was a leader responsible for the political and economic welfare of his community. Non-Muslims, especially Christians, have criticized his activities in Medina as inconsistent with his prophetic claims, even going so far as to speak of the "fall of Muhammad." From the Muslim point of view this is totally incorrect; Muhammad's undoubted success as a political and military leader is what distinguishes him most clearly from previous prophets, such as Jesus, who communicated the correct message but did not establish a community with the power to implement this message in the world.

The Shari'a includes the so-called five pillars, the basic duties of the Muslim. The first is the *shahada* (witness): "I bear witness that there is no god but God [Allah] and that Muhammad is the Messenger of God." This is sometimes called the "creed" but, more than a theological statement, it is a "pledge of allegiance," a basic affirmation that, said with faith, makes one a Muslim. (The word *Allah* is Arabic for "the God" and is understood to refer to the same God as is worshiped by Jews and Christians; it is not a special name for "the God of the Muslims.") The second pillar is *salat* (ritual prayer), said five times a day, facing Mecca. The third is *zakat* (giving alms), usually a certain percentage of one's income and/or capital. The fourth is *siyam* (fasting) from daylight to dark every day during the month of Ramadan. The fifth is the *hajj* (pilgrimage) to Mecca, at least once in a lifetime, if possible. It should be noted that all of these duties are incumbent upon Muslims as individuals, but they also relate the individual to the community.

The Shari'a includes rules for marriage, divorce, and inheritance. Men and women are equal before God but have different responsibilities. Women are responsible for the home, and men for economic and political activities outside the home. Women must obey their husbands, and when they leave their homes they must dress modestly; the wearing of a veil, however, is not required by the Shari'a.

Islam is basically egalitarian, but this means that everyone is to have the same opportunities, not necessarily the same wealth. It is acceptable to be rich, but the rich have a special responsibility to be charitable. The rule against interest on loans originally protected the poor from exploitation by moneylenders.

The *umma* is not only a worshiping community, but also a political and economic order under the rule of God. It would be wrong to say that Islam believes in the union of religion and the state, because they are not distinct, to be either "united" or "separated," but two sides of the one rule of God over all life. Islam does not necessarily affirm any one political system, only that the ruler must be a Muslim and enforce the Shari'a.

The major division within Islam came over the question of leadership. According to the Sunni (or majority) view, Muhammad made no specific arrangements for a successor. Immediately after his death in 632 C.E., his closest associates chose one of themselves, Abū Bakr, as *khalifah* (caliph), or successor, with responsibility to defend the *umma* and to enforce the Shari'a. There was no need for a successor as Prophet since the message had been fully communicated; ideally, the caliph was successor both as leader of worship and in the defense and expansion of the community.

The minority party, the Shi'i, believes that Muhammad did plan for 'Alī, his cousin and son-in-law, to succeed him, and for the succession to continue through 'Alī's descendants; the word *imam* is used for these leaders. Later, there was disagreement about which person was the true imam; the majority of Shi'is believe in a succession of twelve, the last of whom went into hiding in 873 C.E., is still living, and will return as the Mahdi to establish God's rule on earth. These are the Ithna Asharis, Imamis, or "twelvers," who are dominant in Iran and also strong in Iraq, southern Lebanon, and parts of India. The Zaidis, or "fivers," recognize as imam any descendant of 'Alī who succeeds in establishing himself as ruler; they are found largely in Yemen. The Ismailis, or "seveners," follow the descendants of the seventh imam; the best-known branch recognizes the present Aga Khan as the forty-ninth in succession. Although the divergence between Sunni and Shi'i beliefs was originally political, in time differences developed in belief and practice.

Muslims agree that the community is, in principle, universal, that they have the duty to "strive" (*jahada*) to establish God's rule in the whole world. Wherever possible this is to be done peacefully, but if people refuse to allow the truth to be proclaimed, the *jihad* (struggle) may require the use of violence, within carefully stated limits. Violence may be legitimate in establishing God's rule, but it is not to be employed for the conversion of individuals: "There is no compulsion in religion" (Pickthall, vol. 2, p. 256). Those who worship one God and believe in a messenger and in a book, primarily Jews and Christians, are "protected peoples" (*dhimmī*) within the "realm of Islam."

During the first century of the Muslim era the "realm of Islam" expanded rapidly by conquest, to Spain in the West and to what is now Pakistan in the East. Except in Spain, most people in this area gradually accepted Islam as a religion. There was another period of expansion by conquest in the fourteenth to the sixteenth centuries under the Ottomans, who extended Muslim rule to the Balkans. Here the majority became Muslim in modern Albania and in parts of southern Yugoslavia.

After the first early sweep, the expansion of Islam farther into Africa and Asia was largely associated with trade and with the Sufi brotherhoods. Sufism is the "mystical" side of Islam, with an emphasis on a direct personal relationship with God and, in some cases, on the unity of all things in God. The early Sufis were individual seekers, but beginning about the eleventh century C.E., Sufi brotherhoods developed and attracted new converts in such places as sub-Saharan Africa.

By the eleventh century C.E., Muslims had crossed the Sahara and won the allegiance of people in the area of the Senegal and Gambia rivers. There are stories of Muslims from this part of West Africa sailing across the Atlantic to the Americas. Although the evidence is not conclusive, this is certainly possible; Muslims have been great travelers. There were also Muslims among the slaves brought to the New World. Although most captured Africans came from areas where there were few if any Muslims at the time, some were taken from the Senegal–Gambia area.

A few Muslims from the Middle East, the Balkans, or India are known to have come to North America between the sixteenth and late nineteenth centuries. They came as individuals, and there was no real Islamic presence. There is a reference to "Moors" living in South Carolina in the 1790s. In the 1850s several Muslims came to the United States to assist in introducing camels in the Southwest; after the failure of the project a man called Hajj Ali stayed and became a prospector in California. The first known American convert to Islam was (Mohammed) Alexander Russel Webb, who, in 1887, encountered Islam in the Philippines, where he was consul.

In the late nineteenth century conditions in the Ottoman Empire were deteriorating, especially in Syria (including what is now Lebanon). Around 1875, Christians from the area began to come to North America. Muslims were much more hesitant, knowing that there were few if any Muslims here, but stories of economic opportunities began to interest them—especially Shi'is from southern Lebanon, for whom conditions were particularly bad. Many first came as single men; with no intention of staying permanently, they hoped to earn as much as possible and then return home. Some worked as unskilled laborers, others as peddlers. Many stayed, later bringing wives to join them.

Islam is a highly "portable" religion; the five pillars can be practiced anywhere—except for the pilgrimage, which can begin from anywhere. For proper observance no particular kind of building is necessary, and Islam has no priests who do for people something they cannot do for themselves. In theory, at least, Islam can be practiced by an individual in any place. In practice, however, few are able to remain seriously Muslim for long without community support.

The basic community is the family, but even a lone family will find it difficult to remain more than nominally Muslim. Islam can be seriously practiced only where a number of Muslims live near enough to each other to join in Friday prayers, in festivals, in the education of children, and in providing mates for their young people. The earliest known example of North American Muslims using one of their homes as a mosque, a place for communal prayer, was in Ross, North Dakota, in 1900.

Early in the twentieth century Muslims from Syria, including what is now Lebanon, began to settle in industrial areas in the Midwest. The first significant community may have been in Michigan City, Indiana, but when Henry Ford announced that he would employ anyone in his factory for five dollars a day, greater Detroit became the major area of settlement. Once a few Muslims were there, others were attracted, often from the same home villages. A building was acquired to serve as a mosque in Highland Park, Michigan, in 1919. When Ford established the River Rouge plant in Dearborn, many Muslims moved to the nearby South End. A mosque was begun by the Sunnis in 1936; about the same time, the local Shi'i community acquired a building to be used as a "Hashimite center." The South End of Dearborn developed into the only area in North America with the outward appearance of a Muslim town, complete with coffee houses, grocery stores, and restaurants catering to the Arab-Muslim population. Other early mosques, indicating the presence of significant Muslim communities, were built in Cedar Rapids, Iowa, in 1934 and Edmonton, Alberta, in 1938.

In general, the growth of Islam was slow in North America until after World War II. Up to that time most immigrants were Arabs, mainly from Lebanon; there were also a few Turks, Albanians, Yugoslavs, and Indians. Canadian censuses indicate thirteen Muslim residents in 1871, 300 to 400 in 1901, and 1,500 in 1911. By 1951 there were between 2,000 and 3,000 (Waugh, et al., p. 76). There are no census data from the United States; Abdo Elkholy estimated a little over 100,000 in the early 1960s.

Since then growth has been much more rapid. Along with continued immigration from Lebanon, there have been many Palestinians, some Egyptians, and a greatly increased number of Pakistani and Indian Muslims, especially in Canada. Yemenis came to California as migrant workers, and to eastern cities as industrial and restaurant workers. In recent years a substantial number of Iranians have settled in North America—especially in southern California. Unlike the earlier Syrian-Lebanese immigrants, many of those settling in North America since 1960 have been in the professions or businesses. Some are former students who have stayed or returned, while others were relatively affluent in their homelands and had the resources to leave when the conditions favoring this affluence changed; a number have been quite successful in North America. Still others, with less education or experience relevant to North American life, are industrial workers, waiters, and, in the case of the Yemenis, migrant laborers. The reason for both the recent and the earlier immigration is largely economic opportunity, although many Palestinians and Iranians have come for political reasons. In general, it can be said that Muslims have come to North America in spite of their religion, not because of it.

Beginning in the 1960s the number of conversions increased greatly, especially among black Americans. Although the Nation of Islam, believing that Allah appeared in the person of Wallace Fard Mohammed and that Elijah Muhammad was the messenger of Allah, was far from orthodox, it attracted the attention of black Americans and indirectly encouraged conversions. Warith Deen Muhammad, Elijah Muhammad's son, has led his followers in the American Muslim Mission toward orthodox Islam. Estimates of white American converts vary from 5,000 to 40,000; these have been largely, but not entirely, related to marriage.

Recent estimates give figures of 100,000 to 200,000 Muslims in Canada, while those for the United States range from 1 to 5 million. By adding estimates of Muslims of various national origins, M. Arif Ghayur arrives at a total of 1.2 million, but he includes very few blacks.

There is, of course, some question about who is properly counted as a Muslim. Are all Muslim immigrants and their descendants to be counted, whether or not they are practicing Muslims? Are Sufi and "neo-Sufi" groups on the fringes of Islam to be included? What about the Ahmadiyyas, who have been designated as "non-Muslim" in Pakistan? Although the Nation of Islam, established by Elijah Muhammad and now led by Louis Farrakhan, can hardly be counted, the American Muslim Mission should now be included.

Educated guesses by a number of qualified observers converge on a figure in the vicinity of 3 million Muslims for the whole of North America—a little over 1 percent of the population. About half of those in the United States live in six metropolitan areas: New York, Los Angeles, Chicago, Detroit, Houston, and Washington; and about 40 percent of those in Canada are in the Toronto area. There are also significant communities in smaller cities, including Toledo, Ohio, and Cedar Rapids, Iowa, and even in the little town of Lac La Biche, Alberta.

The percentage of North American Muslims who are Shi'i is probably higher than the world figure of 15 percent because of the large number of immigrants from Iran, southern Lebanon, and North Yemen, most of whom are Shi'i. There are also approximately 25,000 Ismailis, mainly in Canada. North American Muslims tend to minimize the differences between the Sunni and Shi'i traditions, although they have separate institutions in some places. A few traditional Sufi orders have centers in North America, but many who call themselves "Sufi" are actually promoting a syncretistic mysticism that has little to do with any kind of Islam.

Muslims have become much more visible on the national level; in 1952 an Islamic center was built on a prominent site in Washington, D.C., with contributions from Muslim governments. The Federation of Islamic Associations in the United States and Canada (FIA), started in 1954, states its purpose to be "to promote and teach the spirit, ethics, philosophy, and culture of Islam. . . ." This organization has appealed especially to the earlier Syrian-Lebanese immigrants and their descendants. The FIA publishes the *Muslim Star* and holds national conventions, with programs that have tended to be more social than political. The Council of Muslim Communities in Canada was founded in 1972; it publishes *Islam Canada.*

The Muslim Students' Association of the U.S. and Canada, founded in 1963, has taken a more activist stance. From "alumni" of this group who have remained or returned have developed the Association of Muslim Social Scientists, the Association of Muslim Scientists and Engineers, and the Islamic Medical Association. These, together with the Muslim Communities Association and the Muslim Students' Association itself, are now the "constituent organizations" of the Islamic Society of North America (ISNA), founded in 1982. This group appeals especially to students and former students who have settled in North America since the mid-1960s and to converts. The annual conventions attract a significant number of Muslims of various national and racial backgrounds. In *Islamic Horizons,* a monthly journal providing "news and perspectives," the aims of the organization are stated as being "the advancement of unity among Muslims . . . conveying the message of Islam to non-Muslims and removing misconceptions about it and . . . working with Muslims and non-Muslims to address common concerns to improve the quality of life for all." The ISNA also publishes *Al-Itti-had,* "a quarterly journal of Islamic studies."

The Council of Masajid (plural of *masjid,* which has become "mosque" in English) has close ties with Saudi Arabia and is especially concerned with the building of appropriate mosques. The ISNA also sponsors an architectural service that gives assistance to communities wishing to build mosques, and has itself built a large mosque at its new headquarters in Plainfield, Indiana. Another impressive mosque has been built just south of Toledo, Ohio, by that city's Muslim community. There are now about thirty mosques or Islamic centers, built for that purpose in North America, with many more planned. Ritual prayers are probably said regularly in as many as 500 places.

The word *mosque* is sometimes used only for buildings actually constructed for that purpose, but the term can correctly designate any place used regularly for communal prayer. It should be noted that *mosque* does not refer primarily to a group of people, as do *synagogue* and *church;* it refers to a place, usually but not necessarily a building, used regularly for communal ritual prayers. It is not an institution with members and an organization but the place where the local members of the *umma,* the universal community of Muslims, meet together for prayer. In North America, the mosque or Islamic center takes on other functions and becomes an institution that elects officers and raises money. The distinction between a mosque and an Islamic center is sometimes said to be architectural; the former is built to "look like a mosque." Properly speaking, however, a mosque is only a place of prayer, while an Islamic center may also include a social hall, a kitchen, classrooms, a library, and other facilities. An Islamic center is unnecessary in a long-established Muslim community in which life as a whole is lived in a Muslim context. In North America "it becomes the place where Muslim men, women and children can maintain an Islamic identity" (*Islamic Horizons,* vol. XIII, no. 9, p. 11).

A council of imams is made up of the trained leaders of the larger North American mosques and Islamic centers. Strictly speaking an imam is a leader of prayer; any pious Muslim who knows the prayers can function as an imam. (The word *imam* has a technical sense in Shi'i Islam, where it refers to the descendants of 'Alī, who are recognized as leaders of the whole *umma;* the essential meaning of the word in all its uses is "leader"— in a religious context.) In larger mosques the imam becomes a full-time leader, and in North America he takes on many of the pastoral functions of a Jewish rabbi or a Christian clergyman. At present it would appear that all of the full-time, "professional" imams of "main-line" mosques were born outside of North America; several received their training at al-Azhar in Cairo. The American Muslim Mission, of course, has native-born imams.

There has been growing concern for the education of Muslims born and raised in North America. Most mosques and Islamic centers have "Sunday schools," and some have started day schools at various levels. There is also an Islamic Scouting program. An American Islamic College was established in 1983 in Chicago; it has received support from abroad as well as from North American Muslims. Its purpose is to provide opportunity for the study of Islamic history and thought, as well as the Arabic language. Another concern is for the preparation of imams within North America.

A number of Muslim scholars of Arab, Turkish, Iranian, Pakistani, and Indian origin teach in North American universities. As yet there are no prominent native-born Muslim scholars.

In spite of impressive recent growth, Muslims in North America still suffer from the appearance of "foreignness." It is not uncommon for a distinction to be made between Americans and Muslims, even when the latter are themselves second- or third-generation Americans. Although, in places like Detroit, Muslims have some local influence, they are essentially invisible on the national scene in the United States and Canada. When they are noticed, it tends to be for negative reasons. Muslims in North America suffer from the long-standing negative image of Islam in Western society. This sense of alienation has been increased by the Arab–Israeli conflict, the rise in oil prices, and the Iranian hostage crisis. (Many North Americans confuse "Arab" and "Muslim," unaware either that the majority of Arab-Americans are Christian or that most Muslims—including Iranians, Turks, and Pakistanis—are not Arabs.)

The Muslim community in North America is divided into many subgroups of various national origins that do not necessarily share a strong sense of identity with each other. Pakistanis and Arabs may keep to themselves, while Arabs from Lebanon have little in common with those from Yemen. The recent surge of activism in the North American Muslim community has been related to the politico-religious concerns of Muslim countries, such as the Arab–Israeli conflict and the Iranian revolution. Groups such as the

ISNA seek to provide the basis of a North American Islamic community transcending the communities based on national origin.

While "foreignness" may be a hindrance to Muslims who are immigrants or descendants of immigrants, it does provide them with an identity that converts—especially white converts—lack. Black Americans already have the sense of being a group distinct from the majority and can carry this sense with them into Islam. White North Americans, however, generally have no cultural identity except that of American or Canadian; when they become Muslim they take on a new religious identity but not a new cultural identity consistent with it. Their plight illustrates the point that there is as yet no distinctively American or Canadian Muslim identity.

The five pillars certainly can be observed in North America—but with some difficulties. One may "bear witness" that there is one God and Muhammad is the messenger of God—but the fact that this also has the quality of a "pledge of allegiance" suggests the possibility of tension for American and Canadian Muslims. Prayers can be said, facing toward Mecca, but many Muslims have difficulty taking time from work for this purpose. A few gather for the Friday noon prayer at the mosque, but most working people are unable to do so and must gather instead on Sunday. In most places a public "call to prayer" would annoy some of the neighbors; the South End of Dearborn may be the only place in North America where it is given frequently. The ISNA provides for the collection and distribution of *zakat* by means of the North American Zakah Fund, but only a small number participate as yet. As in many Muslim countries, the fast of Ramadan may be the most widely observed pillar. Although North America is distant from Mecca, the relative affluence of North American Muslims makes it possible for more people to go from here on pilgrimage than from many Muslim countries.

Another difficulty for Muslims is the non-recognition of such holidays as *'id al-fitr*, the celebration at the end of the fast of Ramadan; *'id al-adha*, the day of sacrifice during the pilgrimage; the birthday of the Prophet; and Ashura, observed especially by Shi'is in remembrance of the martyrdom of 'Ali's son, Husain. The two *'id* festivals are occasions for large gatherings in some North American cities, often in rented halls. A practical problem of adjustment is that the Muslim calendar is lunar and eleven days shorter than the solar calendar; thus Muslim festivals move gradually through the seasons, completing a cycle every thirty-three years.

Muslim views of appropriate female modesty and the requirement that a wife obey her husband are radically different from prevailing North American standards. (It should be noted, however, that Muslim views on personal morality have much in common with those of conservative Christian groups.) Intermarriage is a serious problem. A Muslim woman is not allowed to marry a non-Muslim; one who does so is usually disowned by her family and lost to Islam. Such marriages are probably the major source of conversion from Islam to another religion, usually Christianity. Although Muslim men are allowed to marry Jewish or Christian women, those who do so frequently drift away from Islam, even if they do not actually convert to another religion.

Muslims who strictly observe the prohibition of alcohol may have problems in certain social situations. Muslims are also forbidden to eat pork or meat not properly slaughtered. In centers with relatively large Muslim populations there are butchers who provide *halal* (lawful) meat; elsewhere, kosher meats may be substituted. The Muslim prohibition of usury makes it difficult for a devout Muslim to use the banking system; the ISNA has established the Muslim Cooperative Project to provide an alternative method of financing without interest.

In spite of the difficulties of Muslim life in North America, there is some evidence that Muslims here are on the average more devout than in Muslim countries. In a Muslim country one is naturally a Muslim, whether or not one takes seriously the practice of Islam. In North America, Islam becomes a conscious element in the sense of identity. A choice must be made: either one practices Islam or one ceases to be, in any true sense, a Muslim.

Even an active local Muslim community with a mosque or Islamic center does not make possible a fully Muslim way of life, because Islam is a political as well as a religious community; such a life can be a reality only where there is a Muslim government. It has been suggested that the only justifiable reason for a Muslim to live in a non-Muslim country is in order to bring such a country to the truth of Islam.

"Serious" Muslims, therefore, are actively engaged in *da'wa,* or the call to Islam. Often they do not speak of conversion but of reversion to Islam as the truth from which humanity has departed. They are confident that when Islam is presented correctly it will be recognized as having the answers to the social, economic, political, and religious problems now faced by North Americans. It will then become the dominant religion of the continent, making possible here a completely Muslim life. Although such expectations are matters of faith rather than of objective statistical evidence, it is true that if recent growth rates through immigration, conversion, and natural increase should continue, Islam could be the second religion of North America in another generation or two.

BIBLIOGRAPHY

Arthur J. Arberry, *The Koran Interpreted* (1955; 1964); Barbara C. Aswad, ed., *Arabic Speaking Communities in American Cities* (1974); Abdo A. Elkholy, *The Arab Moslems in the United States* (1966); M. Arif Ghayur, "Muslims in the United States: Settlers and Visitors," in *Annals of the American Academy of Political and Social Science,* no. 454 (1981); H. A. R. Gibb, *Mohammedanism* (1949; 2nd. ed. 1953); Yvonne Y. Haddad, "The Muslim Experience in the United States," in *The Link,* vol. 2, no. 4 (1979); *Islamic Horizons,* vols. 8–13 (1979–1984).

Emily Kalled Lovell, "A Survey of the Arab-Muslims in the United States and Canada," in *The Muslim World,* vol. 63, no. 2 (1973); Marmaduke W. Pickthall, *The Meaning of the Glorious Koran,* 2 vols. (1977); Fazlur Rahman, *Islam* (1966; 2nd. ed. 1979); Ātif A. Wasfī, *An Islamic-Lebanese Community in the U.S.A.* (1971); Earle H. Waugh, Baha Abu-Laban, and Regula B. Qureshi, eds., *The Muslim Community in North America* (1983).

Sources of up-to-date publications: American Trust Publications, 10900 W. Washington St., Indianapolis, Ind. 46231; The Islamic Center, 2551 Massachusetts Ave., N.W., Washington, D.C. 20008.
[See also BUDDHISM; BLACK MILITANT AND SEPARATIST MOVEMENTS; "CULTS" IN THE LATE TWENTIETH CENTURY; HINDUISM; and SHINTO AND INDIGENOUS CHINESE RELIGIONS.]

FREE THOUGHT AND
ETHICAL MOVEMENTS

Martin E. Marty

LEADERS of free thought movements in America have been united in opposing the claims and power of organized religions. Religion, in their view, has been "unfree," since it binds people to obsolete forms of supernaturalism. It has also been "unfreeing," since it distracts millions from efforts to liberate people from error. Thus, in the militant terms inherited from the Enlightenment, free thought would war against "priestcraft and superstition."

Likewise leaders of formal ethical movements have shared the critical program of freethinkers but have ordinarily worked hard to state their own claims in terms less critical of conventional religion. They put their energies into the proposal that humans can live more fulfilling lives and can better contribute to personal and civic virtue if they dismiss thoughts of a life to come and concentrate on the here and now; and that rather than doing good out of fear of divine punishment or out of hope for divine favor, people can find principles and motives for good living through rational reflection.

Both nonreligious movements have persisted in American life since the late eighteenth century. In a nation that for the most part has seen its citizens agreeing with the Supreme Court dictum of 1952 (*Zorach v. Clauson*) that "we are a religious people whose institutions presuppose a Supreme Being," these movements have always represented distinct minorities.

In Europe, critical and skeptical movements ordinarily have had an established church to oppose. This meant that they could build on the resentments of people against doing honor to faiths they did not believe in. Thus most of the radical and revolutionary fervor in Europe has included anticlerical and antichurch elements. In the United States, where the churches were

disestablished, it has been more difficult to mount resentment against organized religions. Those who do not believe what the religious do tend simply to live their lives apart from relations to the sacred. They simply ignore unobtrusive religion, which tends to leave the free thought and ethical movements in rather lonely isolation.

What has been called *public atheism,* a vision of social life that makes no reference to *Theos* (God), has been very rare until modern times. While the Greco-Roman world produced notable pioneers to whom later freethinkers could look back—Seneca, Lucretius, and Marcus Aurelius are typical in the Western world—the people of Greece and Rome lived by reference to whole arrays of deities and sacral impulses. Furthermore, after the fourth century, Christianity was the official religion of the West, so that formal dissent against the faith was necessarily rare. New forms of paganism and rationalism did make their way into Europe during the Renaissance, though without disrupting the fabric of the officially approved religion in civic and cultural life.

Between 1492 and 1789 the discoverers, explorers, settlers, and founders of the American colonies arrived with a mixture of motives, but most of them paid lip service at least to the Catholic, Protestant, or, in a few cases, Jewish faith. A figure like Thomas Heriot, an associate of Sir Walter Raleigh in the era before English settlement, used the new sciences to probe the skies and earth of the New World, but his type was extremely rare. Most colonies established churches and gave them privilege and support, whether or not these churches were well attended and whether or not people led exemplary ethical lives as a result of their presence.

In the middle of the eighteenth century the

FREE THOUGHT AND ETHICAL MOVEMENTS

European rationalist movements and the Enlightenment had established themselves, chiefly among the educated classes. A philosopher like Voltaire, who may have believed that religion was still necessary to keep the lower classes ethically in line, could shout "Crush the infamy!" at the prevalent and, in his eyes, repressive Catholic church and Christian claim. Mild forms of the Enlightenment found an audience among the educated in the thirteen colonies. Moderate forms made their way into England chiefly through Arminian theology in the churches and marginally through deism. Arminian theology was still Christian, but its view of a benevolent deity and human beings who made contact with each other in genial terms began to make supernaturalism unnecessary. Deism, meanwhile, replaced the personal and living *Theos* of the predominant biblical faith with *Deus,* an impersonal Being, force, power, or principle. In both cases, it was believed that people did not have to be "bound" to superstition, miracle, supernatural revelation, or the hocus-pocus of self-seeking priests in order to live full and rich moral lives.

The first traces of such thought in its critical forms began to appear in the colonies during the French and Indian Wars, when the British military gave voice to them in the late 1750s. Two decades later, when the French sided with the colonists against England, there was also some vogue for French anticlerical rationalist writers. This enthusiasm quickly passed, however, when during the French Revolution in the 1790s militants in France pushed their case too far and, in the eyes of Americans, committed sacrilege by offending the sensibilities of even those not overly pious. In both cases, free thought and ethical movements took some of their inspiration from the European Enlightenment.

Free thought and ethical movement leaders contend that during the first generation, which means the last third of the eighteenth century, most of the nation's Founding Fathers shared their general ethos. They number in their gallery of pioneers and heroes such decisive figures as Benjamin Franklin, John Adams, George Washington, and Thomas Jefferson. Though most of these men remained members of Congregational churches in the North or Anglican churches in the South, this was at a time when the elite of the congregations were themselves tinged by Arminian and deist sentiments. Serving as a delegate of a Congregational church or on the vestry of an Episcopal church was simply a responsibility of lawyers and planters. They would on occasion attend church and, in the case of Washington, speak well of the role of religion and the churches, but clearly there was no support for dogma or mystery. They might, with Franklin, give pennies and publicity to revivalists like George Whitefield, believing that such efforts contributed to moral seriousness, but with no belief in revivalist faith. Or they might, with Jefferson, side with dissenters to help disestablish religion in states like Virginia but break with them over anything supernatural in biblical revelation.

These honored and generally moderate heroes of free thought and ethical movements believed in a religion of natural rights, natural law, and reason. They succeeded in helping disestablish the churches and assure religious freedom. Their approach was consolidated into the federal and state constitutions, and they helped assure the presence of institutions that made no claim for coerced faith or what in their eyes were sectarian and particularized views of a deity. By all accounts, their outlook was reasonably widespread in the late eighteenth century, though articulation was chiefly a part of the salon and library life of well-off, literate, and discreet persons.

There were two notable exceptions among the revolutionary-era leaders. Ethan Allen, a not very highly lettered incendiary from Vermont's Green Mountains, known for military exploits during the war, dabbled in French and English Enlightenment thought and came up with an anything-but-profound compendium of his own, whose shortened title was *Reason the Only Oracle of Man.* Library of Congress cataloging denominated this work the first published American book against the claims of organized religion. Almost no one bought the Allen book, and the press that printed it burned down—a sign, said the pious, of divine disfavor. Allen exerted no influence on more polished statesmen.

Nearer their councils, however, was Thomas Paine, who moved back and forth between England and America and was not only a patriot known as "citizen Tom Paine" but also a freethinking pamphleteer and philosophically minded writer. *The Age of Reason,* published in England in 1794 and 1796, has stayed in print and become a classic of free thought. Paine was a patriot of only marginal respectability, in no small measure because such writings offended churchgoing America. A century and a half later President Theodore Roosevelt would speak of Paine as a "filthy little atheist," though he was in fact none of the three. Paine was actually a deist, a militant moral philosopher who opposed organized religion but spoke for a private sort of faith: "my own mind is my temple," he would claim. Still, Paine was too outspoken to match the climate of a new nation and he lost favor and public influence.

The notion that one's own mind was one's temple, or the individualizing of the religiously moral path, as in the case of Jefferson—who averred that if he had to go to heaven with a group he would not go at all—did little to perpetuate the free thought outlook. If superstitious ideas were fortified and supported by "temples" and "groups" in organized religion, some reasoned that these could be opposed in sustained ways only if there were organized social movements. If in France there had to be "Festivals of the Supreme Being" to counter the Catholic Mass, so in America there had to be ritual and celebration in support of reason. People had to form congregations or communities where they might encourage each other, probe the extensions of liberty, celebrate their freedom, nurture ethics, and oppose churches.

For a brief period during the American Enlightenment there were heady and hopeful expressions that significant free thought and ethical movements could be launched. Yet leaders misread the public climate. Even the slightly resentful were more interested in disestablishing churches and letting them go their voluntary way than in putting them out of business. Too many agreed with Washington about the necessity of religion in the civil realm, and reflexively thought of religion as a modified version of historic biblical faith. Others may have been freethinkers in their parlors but did not want to risk public disfavor, or they may simply have been too apathetic to keep company with others in agencies and institutions that, they thought, aped the churches.

While Freemasonry was popular with Washington and others and was deistic and critical of certain churches and dogmas, it was anything but a free thought or ethical movement as such. In the period after the Revolution, deistic organization was left to individuals like Elihu Palmer, an anticlerical ex-Baptist. His writings were of no consequence, and he was seen as a threat chiefly because he promoted newspapers, lecture programs, and societies to battle churches. In this period there was founded a Theophilanthropic and a Universal Society in Philadelphia, and Palmer himself in 1794 formed a deistic group in New York. He encouraged some ex-Freemasons to form a "Druid" group, to spread the infidel word from place to place. Yet most of the organizations attracted only a few supporters and soon dwindled, leaving unread newspapers like *The Temple of Reason* to founder.

Near the end of the eighteenth and early in the nineteenth century free thought began to lose favor. Reaction to French revolutionary excesses played a part. Backwoods and small-town people and, for that matter, most residents of cities like Boston, New York, Philadelphia, and Charleston found deism to be a cold and facile set of propositions. It did not satisfy the deeper longings of their hearts. The task of keeping a new nation together led citizens increasingly to look to fervent religion as a binding element, and the churches were recovering from a period of some recession. What most historians call the Second Great Awakening spread fervor on the frontier as well as back in coastal cities. To the shocked and then defensive men of the Enlightenment, the Awakening was an outburst of irrationalism and dangerous enthusiasm, but they had no means to counter it. Free thought looked ever less alluring or even safe, and its advocates moved out of formal movements into quiet private pursuits. By 1826 observers could find only one advocate of the Enlightenment in all the South, Thomas Jefferson's friend the scientist Thomas Cooper—who that year lost his position at the University of South Carolina. A little western outpost of free thought, Lexington, Kentucky, saw its Enlightened Transylvania University fall to revival forces. An era had ended, though it left a rich legacy.

At the same time, partly in reaction now to revivalist excesses and partly to meet new social needs, a second generation of small but organized and visible free thought and ethical movements arose to oppose supernaturalism and conventional religion. Leaders of these movements partook of the climate of experiment that came with the Age of Jackson or what historian Alice Felt Tyler called "freedom's ferment." In eastern literary circles some movements, like Brook Farm near Boston, were endeavors of the elite who, in the words of Ralph Waldo Emerson, thought it necessary to "forget historical Christianity." Their motivating outlook, transcendentalism, was, however, religious or quasi-religious and is usually seen as an alternative to the faith of the churches, not an enemy of religion.

More militant antichurch advocates, in the name of social experiment, gravitated to pockets of urban unrest or to the frontier. The late 1820s saw the first stirrings of workers toward patterns of labor organization. Some of them responded to the promptings of people like Frances Wright, the first woman to gain fame in free thought. Like so many new leaders, she was from England and could be dismissed as un-American, though she stated her case in terms of fulfilling the logic of the Declaration of Independence.

While much of the new ferment took the form of religious communities or utopian experiments —this was the time of the Shakers' prime and the rise of Mormonism and Adventism—some communitarianism was explicitly of a free thought sort. Best known among what historian Arthur Bestor called "backwoods utopias" was New Harmony in Indiana. There a small and soon defunct community of European pietist radicals, the Rappites, sold their colony to Robert Owen, who had gained some success and much fame at New Lanark, Scotland, for his advocacy of communal living and cooperative endeavor. He would replace the conventional family and competitive economy with new social forms, and not only did these not need Christian support, they had to be free of it and oppose it.

Owen traveled widely, debating representatives of organized religion. In Cincinnati he took on Catholic bishop James B. Purcell, and Alexander Campbell, the leader of a new frontier religious movement known as the Disciples of Christ. By this time a new relation was becoming visible in American religious life. Owen's colony was not very successful, indeed was patently unsuccessful, and he might well have been an almost invisible figure. Instead, he gained national fame precisely because the churches opposed him. He could exploit their nervousness in order to gain attention. They could exploit his presence in order to advance their own causes.

What this pattern meant was a subtle and then bold symbiosis between church and antichurch, clergy and anticlericals, defenders of orthodoxies and radical heretics. They needed each other. Not a single leader—no Allen or Paine, no Wright or Owen, or lesser figure like frontier agitator Abner Kneeland—would have been remembered for his or her intellectual contributions or organizational ability. None made permanent contributions to the mainstream American political or social heritage. Few of them were people of intellectual power, though some had rhetorical gifts.

Their very scarcity might suggest that the churches suppressed the free thought tradition. The truth was anything but that: most of what is remembered about them results from the fame the churches gave them. This pattern was visible already at the turn of the century, when a Standing Order cleric like Timothy Dwight portrayed the immoralities that would result should Connecticut deviate from Congregationalism's orthodoxy or settled habits. By the 1820s clerics could suggest—indeed shout—that women would be unrespectable if they followed Wright's way, or that free love and economic chaos would replace the family and a free economy. Their claims and free thought's counterclaims came to focus in debates that the press covered well. Thus, if anything, the churches have historically helped free thought and ethical movements gain whatever attention they did get. They served as bogeys to rally the faithful, as negative references to the good ways of Christian America.

As such, and because they depended so much on highly risky and ephemeral social experiments, the leaders of this second generation were quickly silenced, defeated, or disgraced. The charisma of orthodox leaders like Campbell or innovators like Joseph Smith or William Miller, and the apparent plausibility of their often controversial movements, led them to outpace antisupernaturalist elements. While an Emerson or a Henry David Thoreau might utter violently antitraditional expressions, these men were still seen as somehow religious and eventually respectable. When novelists like Nathaniel Hawthorne or Herman Melville revisited the New England Calvinist mythos, they constantly pointed to its dark side. Yet their literary genius and the positive elements in their vision kept them from being finally dismissed as unrespectable and sent off in defeat, as were Wright and Owen when they were more or less forced to retreat.

After the Civil War there was no question that new secular influences were coming to bear in American life. Most notable was the rise of the modern university, which competed with the small colleges that had held the hegemony until then. These earlier colleges, often church sponsored and in any case coherent embodiments of a single moral vision, were superseded in numbers of students by the often state-supported universities. New specialization divided one form of knowledge from another, and religion was segregated in seminaries, shunted aside to campus divinity schools, or dismissed entirely.

A new generation of scholars in the humanities, social sciences, and natural sciences found it necessary to be self-liberated from the hold of childhood religion. Historians of the "new history" school, among them James Harvey Robinson, Frederick Jackson Turner, and Charles Beard, joined philosophers like John Dewey or social service agents like Jane Addams in keeping churches at a distance. Yet none of them found it important or necessary to organize or join free thought movements. They found the university or the social service settlement to be sufficiently free. Sometimes they brought over aspects of their childhood religion and institutionalized these in public schools or settlement houses. At times it was important for them to make alliances with ministers of the Social Gospel. Thus, while they may have made the orthodox uneasy, and while some of them in the years of struggle over Darwinism may have engaged in a "warfare of science versus theology," their energies were not to be captured by the ethical movements. These movements still remained at the edges of the now more secularized culture, just as they had earlier in a more religious American culture.

During the last quarter of the nineteenth century, however, there were a number of developments in free thought and ethical movements. As before, no individual American of charismatic power and intellectual depth appeared. Across the Atlantic there were or were to be titanic "god killers"—Charles Darwin and Karl Marx, Friedrich Nietzsche and Sigmund Freud. They had only minor counterparts in America. Thus the Englishman Thomas Huxley, who was said to have invented the term *agnosticism* during a visit

to America in 1876, spread the Darwinian vision and wanted to exact from its holders more opposition to religion than the master Darwin himself was ever to ask or demonstrate.

Instead of such giants, America saw only one notable "infidel," the major figure for his half-century, Col. Robert Green Ingersoll. Ingersoll was socially and politically a very respectable figure, a Republican politician. He made his living, however, shocking the respectable and attracting a clientele of sympathizers, by attacking biblical teaching and setting out to replace it with an inconsistent pattern of human morality apart from revelation. Typically, Ingersoll would come to a city on the trail of a major advertising campaign, fill a hall, and spellbind the shocked churchgoers and a few of their critics. Then all would go home a dollar poorer, well entertained, and the clergy were motivated to preach Christian truth and the laity to organize its life just as it had before.

In the literary community there were now a number of articulators of antichurch questions. The best known of these was Samuel Clemens (Mark Twain), whose humorous and even acid satires often included profanations of what most Americans regarded as sacred. Yet Twain's humor was disarming, his criticisms were more entertaining than devastating, and works like *Tom Sawyer* (1876) entered the canon of church people who could overlook mild irreverence for the sake of the portraits of Americana that they otherwise took to their hearts. The generation of literary naturalists led by figures like Theodore Dreiser had no positive words for religion but made no campaign or movement to oppose it. Ambrose Bierce came up with *The Devil's Dictionary* (1906) and other sardonic undercuttings of piety. Yet he was seen as too misanthropic and too eclectic to acquire a following, and he had no alternative moral scheme to offer.

Instead, two major movements came closer than any before them to serving as durable if still small consolidations of organized anticlerical thinking in America. Both served as competitors to or, as some thought, surrogates for church religion before the turn of the century. One, the Free Religious Association, spun off and rose in protest against the residual conventionality of liberal Christian movements like Unitarianism. The other movement also attracted people of post-Christian sensibilities but was founded by a

Jew beyond the borders of Reform or liberal Judaism; this was Felix Adler's Ethical Culture movement.

The Free Religious Association developed in reaction to an action by Unitarians who stated in 1866 that they were liberal Christians. This was an act that closed the door on or rendered uncomfortable a movement of independents who thought the world needed no more liberal Christians. Instead, it needed people who would work for human freedom and dignity without reference to Christianity, God, or the supernatural. Octavius Brooks Frothingham was the guiding light of the movement and its first president; his successor as president was Ethical Culture's Felix Adler. This federation was formed in 1867 and looked ahead to prosperous times in the decades in which liberalism and progressivism, or theological modernism, faced their best prospects. Instead, modernism worked against the Free Religious Association, since Unitarianism now came to encompass humanists who found under its more conventional roof a more congenial home. Ethical Culture helped cut the small humanist movement in two and led to divided loyalties.

Felix Adler was the talent behind Ethical Culture, which he formally organized in New York in 1876. He successfully demonstrated that one could ritualize a religious impulse that had no supernatural reference, did not advocate belief in God, and was not denominational. Instead the movement's ceremonies and lectures were designed to show the "supreme importance of the ethical factor" in all of life. The movement spread overseas (the International Ethical Movement) but had stronger outlets in America in St. Louis, Boston, and Chicago. Adler himself rebelled against his role as a Reform rabbi in New York and eventually taught at Cornell and Columbia. Between 1873 and his death in 1933, he grew ever warier of sects and dogmas, and tried to perpetuate the Hebraic prophetic impulse without reference to the God of the Hebrews. His reform energies went into supporting the right of labor to organize, seeking justice in the distribution of medical care, and advocating civic reform and the rights of children. Like the religious whom he countered, he considered it important to reach and minister to children—hence the establishment of Ethical Culture's camps and well-known schools. Ethical Culture, however, never became a mass movement and in 1983 listed only 4,000 members in 22 centers, with only 354 individuals still enrolled in Sabbath and Sunday schools.

This tracing of free thought leaders and ethical movements almost instinctively and necessarily has concentrated on eruptions in the mainstream culture of English-speaking Americans. Yet some of the more expressive efforts to found moral systems on a social basis rather than on revealed religion or supernaturalism occurred among non-English-speaking immigrant groups. Two examples will illustrate the point: the German "forty-eighters," who came after continental revolutionary failures in 1848; and Czech freethinkers who led anticlerical immigrant groups in cities like Chicago or farm areas in sparsely populated counties of states like Nebraska. These were less well known because developments in ethnic ghettos were rarely visible in the larger "Anglo" culture except when radicalism and anarchy were feared. In the course of time the "forty-eighters" turned respectable and found outlets in moderate socialist parties like the one that produced mayors for Milwaukee for some decades. And the Czech free thought movements lost their causes and their potency and largely faded away. Yet in both cases, their presence reveals how American subcultures were held together and what they fought about.

Czech free thought may seem to be a bypath from the mainroads of America, yet it was not without significance. In the era before the Protestant Reformation, critics of Catholicism followed leaders like Jan Hus, who taught Bohemians, Moravians, and Czechs to question authority when it mingled religion and political power. Hussitism remained inside the church, but it also bred a spirit that found the more radical Enlightenment attractive and made moves outside the church easier in the eighteenth century. By the time of the migrations to America, many of these central European peoples had found that Catholicism was often an instrument of their oppression, and they migrated to escape it.

The majority of Czech immigrants were ordinarily at least nominal Catholics, and capable priests worked to organize them in cities like Chicago, to use their loyalties against the infidels in their midst. A minority were Protestants, less involved in this aspect of unsettlement in the communities. Here once again, however, the symbiosis between infidel and faithful worked its effects. The more the priests spoke up, the more the freethinkers could state their case, and each profited from the agitations of the other.

The Czech freethinkers, like the German anticlericals, organized a whole network of parachurch, yet antichurch, agencies. There were Sokols, athletic societies, to match the Germans' Turnvereins. Both had their musical and singing clubs. Lodges on the Masonic model permitted them to enact rituals that would reinforce brotherhood or sisterhood. Mutual benefit societies allowed for fiscal support and there were many life insurance or death benefit groups, which also adopted quasi-religious but intentionally antireligious bearings.

The problem for these groups, which prevailed in some rural areas in Nebraska, was the passage of generations. The children of the immigrants found that the old Hussite or radically anticlerical movements had no rationale in America, where there was no established church. If anything, turn-of-the-century America found Catholicism to be a force of dissent. With the passion of negation gone, loyalties wavered, boundaries between believer and unbeliever seemed smaller. Some of the children intermarried with Czech and non-Czech Christians and either muffled their criticism or eventually brought up their children as Catholics and became Catholic themselves. In any case, by the 1920s leaders of ethical movements were mourning the loss of the unfaithful, the scattering of the old supporters, the passing of passion.

One could visit any number of immigrant groups and find some counterparts. To take but one more example, the Finnish immigrants of Michigan and other Great Lakes states included adherents of free thought and radical movements. As late arrivals, they were forced to take unattractive mining jobs in the Upper Peninsula and elsewhere. Some of them had already been reached and organized by Marxists in Finland. They resented the anti-Marxism of the officially established Lutheran state church in Finland. In many little Michigan towns a labor temple vied with a Lutheran church, a labor newspaper competed with a church paper. Sometimes tensions within the communities would erupt into violence against a preacher or a labor leader. In a tragic incident on Christmas Eve, 1913, in Calu-

met, Michigan, an antichurch surrogate Christmas Eve party for children was subverted by someone who shouted "Fire!" Seventy-three people were killed in the ensuing panic and stampede from the second-floor hall. For years tension and conflict were the legacy of such events. Yet in the course of time, as religious diversity came to the largely Finnish settlements and as the labor movements became part of secular but not anticlerical unions, this form of free thought agency also waned and left few traces.

The twentieth century has seen an America so diverse, so rich in its pluralism, that almost "anything goes" in the churches, leaving free thought with only moving and unstable targets. Antireligious movements prosper best when there is an established church that allows the opposition to state its case with negative reference. When there are only two or three dominant orthodox faiths, it is still possible for there to be an alternative. By the twentieth century, however, the left wing of Unitarianism and Universalism and some forms of Quakerism had moved so far from orthodoxy but not from respectability that they left little room for the Free Religious Association to prosper, and Ethical Culture found it difficult to position itself beyond the humanism of some forms of Reform Judaism. Almost every religious supernaturalism was countered by another supernaturalism or a religious naturalism, leaving the atheist, agnostic, or skeptic confused about how and where to attack. Public and civil life permitted so much ritualization that the organized free thought movements lost their lure as competitors to churches when it came to attracting people who had a love of ceremony. Forms of secular liberalism that did not make supernatural revelation or clericalism their target attracted people who simply did not wish to acquire the social stigma that went with nonconformism or take on the intellectual energies or passions to refute religious claims they found less enthralling than irrelevant.

Despite this landscape, better described as too tangled than as too barren, some "infidels," as they were seen in the public eye, did rise to prominence. In the early decades of this century these included an eccentric firebrand from Waco, Texas, named William Cowper Brann, editor of the *Iconoclast*. He did go about shattering icons, as he felt called to do. In the heartland of Baptist piety, Brann gained a following that drew national notice, for the consistency of his attacks on churches and his argument that morality could take root in reason alone.

Matching Brann in notoriety some decades later was Joseph Lewis, an Alabama-born Jew who made New York his headquarters for a thriving free thought publishing industry. Lewis, who relished combat with the religious, was elected president of the Freethinkers of America in 1915. He held this position until his death in 1968, often without consulting others or having their support. Lewis was early influenced by Ingersoll, but through the years became devoted to, indeed, obsessed with, Thomas Paine, and sought to enhance and protect the Paine heritage in mid-twentieth-century America. His own writings, from *The Bible Unmasked* (1926) through *An Atheist Manifesto* (1951) and many periodical articles, helped sustain his small but visible movement.

While America had no one to announce the death of God, in Baltimore journalist Henry Louis Mencken it had a publicist of moderate Nietzschean proportions. Mencken, a satirical writer of note and a dedicated lexicographer of sorts who wrote *The American Language* (1918), over the decades turned out scores of essays critical of the "booboisie's" and sometimes even the intellectual's assent to revelation. His *Treatise on the Gods* (1930) was a full-fledged attempt at deflation, on a scale unmatched since Ingersoll was in his prime. Yet Mencken was too much the individualist to organize anything, and his was a solitary voice: he was read as much in the churches as beyond them. When he chose to go respectable, his free thought lost its power to shock. When he overasserted free thought, the respectable enjoyed it or dismissed it.

Lawyer Clarence Darrow gained some notoriety as an infidel chiefly because he was the antagonist to William Jennings Bryan in the celebrated Scopes trial in Tennessee in 1925. This was the most public occasion in which the party that was coming to be called Fundamentalist found a cause, antievolution, and a charismatic advocate, Bryan. Darrow was a self-professed agnostic who took his position not to shock the churches but to advocate civil liberties and the free human spirit. Darrow also had admirers but would have felt out of place in an Ethical Culture movement.

At the borderline between agnostic expression and religion were major figures like Jane Addams, whose childhood Quakerism turned into a more or less agnostic devotion to philanthropy and social change. Until her pacifism in World War I rendered her controversial, however, she was coming to be seen as a kind of secular saint, anything but a destroyer of religion. John Dewey opposed sectarianism, though he saw a role for organized churches in some dimensions of life. For public virtue, however, he would trust social processes and support *A Common Faith* (1934) to promote democratic values in the schools. Horace Kallen, at the Jewish libertarian left, wrote *Secularism Is the Will of God,* a provocative defense of secularism that did not make him unrespectable. Walter Lippmann, the era's best-known political columnist, saw no hope for organized religion and sometimes attacked liberalism more than Fundamentalism, yet he hoped for some new nonsupernatural "religion of the spirit" and led no ethical movement.

Such a complex religious landscape, which saw secular intellectuals more often ignoring and dismissing religion than encountering it intellectually, did on several occasions see little organized eruptions. In 1933 John Dewey's was the most visible name on the Humanist Manifesto, which stated many classic humanistic themes: that people could be moral and society could give expression to the virtuous without reference to supernaturalism—indeed, could do so better without such a reference. Most of the signers of the manifesto would have disagreed with each other on many basic elements and made of it anything but a creed for a new organization. The majority of signers moved on as if forgetting their involvement, but several leaders took responsibility for regathering the group decades later. Paul Kurtz, head of the American Humanist Association and publisher of the journal *Free Inquiry,* helped produce a Humanist Manifesto II in 1973 and, later, a Secular Humanist Declaration. Some of the veterans of 1933 were still alive to sign in their emeritus roles. Again, the signers were a disparate group, anything but creedally united. The common ventures in the newer documents were supports for free inquiry, the power of reason, and the suggestion that human cultures were most promising when free of the trammels of religion and the distractions of supernaturalism or a life to come.

During the period between the two manifestos, neither of which drew much attention beyond a small circle of intellectuals, there were efforts at organizing or sustaining free thought and ethical movements. The Free Religious Association and Ethical Culture lived on, and while the American Humanist Association was taking form a minuscule American Association for the Advancement of Atheism was founded. The AAAA never had many members and, its leaders were sorry to say, never much of a budget.

The AAAA was organized in 1925 as the most explicitly antireligious movement of them all. The only creedal requirement was the formal profession of atheism. In its earlier years in particular the already often unrespectable movement was further blighted, in the public eye, by the racism expressed in publications issuing from or supported by headquarters. *The Truth Seeker,* a publication of very limited circulation, was often associated with the movement, though it was independent.

Another group is called American Atheists, Inc., which Madalyn Murray O'Hair first incorporated in 1970 as Poor Richard's Universal Life Church. Mrs. O'Hair was a tireless organizer and promoted a number of other agencies, called variously the Free Thought Society of America and Other Americans, Inc., most of them extensions of her personality. She published the *American Atheist* in Austin, Texas. Other militant organizations like the United Secularists of America, the Rationalist Association, and Free Thinkers of America claimed only 1,000 or 2,000 members each.

Under Madalyn Murray O'Hair, American Atheists, Inc., learned how to gain an audience by presenting challenges to religion in American courts. The most notable successes came in respect to limiting the role of religion in American public schools. Mrs. O'Hair, like Ingersoll and others before her, learned that the best way to gain an audience was by debating church people. Fundamentalist evangelists in particular rose to the bait, and she became a familiar figure on television talk shows and in lecture halls. Civil libertarians may have welcomed the energies she put into removing traces of religious establishment, yet her ideas attracted no intellectuals and her movement as such did not prosper.

The American Humanist Association had as its leader John H. Dietrich of Minneapolis, who remained a Unitarian minister. Yet his movement spun off some independent groups, and in 1929 small humanistic societies were founded in Hollywood and New York. Theirs was the "religious humanism" that helped issue the Humanist Manifesto of 1933. This movement was thoroughly evolutionary, dedicated to faith in democratic social processes. In 1941 these scattered forces organized the American Humanist Association.

As had happened on several previous occasions, free thought and ethical movements, now usually gathered around code words like *secular* and *humanist,* received, thanks to churches, notice beyond what their numbers, prosperity, or potential might have merited. Far from minimizing these movements, conservative Protestants, usually Fundamentalists, exaggerated them, suggesting that it was a conspiracy of organized secular humanism that was subverting American life, spreading debasing sexual practices, perverting the images in public media, and excluding God from the schools. These Fundamentalists gave fame to the hitherto neglected humanist manifestos and convinced their own followers that these documents served as unifying and motivating creeds. The "secular humanist conspiracy" served to frighten the faithful and inspire donations to evangelistic militants' causes.

Such attention did not lead to new prosperity for these organizations. In 1983 Paul Kurtz supplied statistics on the surviving organizations. The AHA had 3,500 members after forty years, and the American Ethical Union claimed 3,500 after a hundred years; a newer Society for Humanistic Judaism had 4,000 adherents and the Fellowship of Religious Humanists 300, while the humanist movement was beleaguered and defensive inside Unitarianism. Kurtz and other advocates of humanism as an organized force once again had to join predecessors of previous generations in saying that humanism was moribund, hardly organized, barely surviving. There were a few tens of thousands of subscribers to *Free Inquiry* or purchasers of Prometheus Books. There were perhaps that many dues payers in humanist organizations. Free Religious associations and Ethical Culture societies lived on, sometimes gathering in major cities, or, as with Ethical Culture, running schools and camps. As before, religion has remained the outlet for respectable, if casual, America, and antireligion attracts the notice chiefly of religious militants who use it as a foil.

None of this means that free thought and ethical movements have played no larger role than to quicken evangelists into opposition. They have often presented provocative ideas and made them respectable in the hands of people who held established places in society. They have served vigilant organizations whose leaders succeeded in getting the courts to prevent establishment or privilege for religion. Often these leaders have been allies of others, from Thomas Jefferson down to the American Civil Liberties Union. At their best they have kept reminding citizens that those who could not or did not wish to believe in God or the supernatural could "naturally" generate systems of ethics that often put to shame those who, in the name of God, were less preoccupied with human dignity, freedom, or justice. As such, they have made their contribution to both religious and secular America.

BIBLIOGRAPHY

Ethan Allen, *Reason the Only Oracle of Man: Or, a Compenduous System of Natural Religion* (1784; facsimile ed. 1940); Arthur Eugene Bestor, Jr., *Backwoods Utopias: The Sectarian Origins and the Owenite Phase of Communitarian Socialism in America, 1663–1829* (1950; rev. 1970); Paul F. Boller, *George Washington and Religion* (1963); Daniel Boorstin, *The Lost World of Thomas Jefferson* (1948; rev. 1960); Melvin H. Buxbaum, *Benjamin Franklin and the Zealous Presbyterians* (1975); Tomáš Čapek, *The Čechs (Bohemians) in America: A Study of Their National, Cultural, Political, Social, Economic and Religious Life,* (1920; rev.

1969); J. Wade Caruthers, *Octavius Brooks Frothingham: Gentle Radical* (1977); Charles Carver, *Brann and the "Iconoclast"* (1957).

Clarence Darrow, *The Story of My Life* (1932); John Hassler Dietrich, *The Humanist Pulpit* (1931); Donald Drew Egbert and Stow Persons, eds., *Socialism and American Life,* 2 vols. (1952); Charles A. Fecher, *Mencken: A Study of His Thought* (1978); Eric Foner, *Tom Paine and Revolutionary America* (1976); Octavius Brooks Frothingham, *Recollections and Impressions* (1891); John F. C. Harrison, *Quest for the New Moral World: Robert Owen and the Owenites in Britain and America* (1969); William A. Hinds, *American Communities and Co-operative Colonies* (1908); Gustav Adolf Koch, *Republican Religion: The American Revolution and the Cult of Reason* (1933); Paul Kurtz, *In Defense of Secular Humanism* (1983).

Tim LaHaye, *The Battle for the Mind* (1980); Orvin Larson, *American Infidel: Robert G. Ingersoll* (1962); Martin E. Marty, *The Infidel: Freethought and American Religion* (1961); Henry Louis Mencken, *Treatise on the Gods* (1930; rev. 1946); Herbert Morais, *Deism in Eighteenth Century America* (1934; rev. 1960); Jerome Nathanson, "What Do They Believe?" in Leo Rosten, ed., *A Guide to the Religions of America* (1955); Thomas Paine, *The Complete Writings of Thomas Paine,* Philip S. Foner, ed., 2 vols. (1945); Stow Persons, *Free Religion: An American Faith* (1947); Albert Post, *Popular Freethought in America, 1825–1850* (1943); William J. Potter, *The Free Religious Association: Its Twenty-five Years and Their Meaning* (1892); Arthur Edwin Puotinen, *Finnish Radicals and Religion in Midwestern Mining Towns 1865–1914* (1979).

Howard B. Radest, *Toward Common Ground: The Story of the Ethical Societies in the United States* (1969); John M. Robertson, *A History of Freethought in the Nineteenth Century,* 2 vols. (1929); Niels Sonne, *Liberal Kentucky 1780–1828* (1939); Gordon Stein, ed., *The Encyclopedia of Unbelief,* 2 vols. (1985); Alice Felt Tyler, *Freedom's Ferment: Phases of American Social History to 1860* (1944); Sidney Warren, *American Freethought, 1860–1914* (1943); Andrew Dickson White, *A History of the Warfare of Science with Theology in Christendom,* 2 vols. (1896; rev. 1960). [*See also* ENLIGHTENMENT; TRANSCENDENTALISM; *and* UNITARIANISM AND UNIVERSALISM.]

"CULTS" IN THE LATE TWENTIETH CENTURY

Thomas Robbins and Dick Anthony

IN his monograph *Experimentation in American Religion* (1978) sociologist Robert Wuthnow maintains that the United States is presently experiencing a period of "religious populism," which entails experimentation with new forms and practices and an erosion of traditional American religious pluralism characterized by distinctive and stable traditions with clearly defined boundaries. Contemporary religious populism includes both the dissemination of Oriental mystical perspectives and charismatic guru movements and the emergence of syncretistic religio-therapeutic movements that combine elements of Oriental mysticism and popular psychology. A third aspect, which appears to be increasingly significant, is the growth of "televangelism" and the related spread of patterns such as Pentecostalism, faith healing, and Fundamentalism, which were once popularly associated with southern, rural, and lower-class milieus. Some of the new churches and fellowships associated with the latter trend have emerged from the broad "Jesus movement" of the early 1970s, which combined a Bible-based evangelical Christianity with countercultural or "hippie" life styles ("street Christians"). Some of the more eccentric neo-Christian groups as well as the less familiar "Eastern" groups and religio-therapeutic movements have tended to be labeled "cults." During the late 1960s and throughout the 1970s these movements appeared to have a particular appeal for young persons, and "cults," along with drug use, have sometimes been viewed as mounting a major threat to American youth.

"CULTS"

For almost two decades there have been commentary and controversy over the proliferation of "cults" in American society. The popular term *cult* embodies an ill-defined category, frequently stereotyped as authoritarian and "totalistic" (that is, absorbing the devotee in its system such that he lives, works, socializes, etc., in the movement), but including a diverse array of groups that are neither clearly churches nor sects. A religious or therapeutic group is likely to be labeled a *cult* if it is 1) unconventional and esoteric; 2) controversial and the target of allegations of harmful acts; 3) authoritarian; 4) close-knit and communal; 5) aggressively proselytizing; 6) intensive and emotional in its indoctrination practices or group ritual; and 7) charismatic in its leadership. However, a group need not possess all or even most of these traits to elicit the popular label.

Several different conceptions of "cult" are used by sociologists of religion; all exclude some groups that are popularly designated as cults. Some sociologists define "cults" according to a looseness and diffuseness of organization and a related ambiguity of group boundaries and internal doctrinal consensus (Wallis, 1975). Another conception employs deviance or a related criterion specifying a radical break with the dominant tradition of the society (Stark and Bainbridge, 1979). Sociological definitions of "cults" generally entail contrasts with "sects," which have been defined as subgroups of a dominant religious tradition and/or as authoritarian, close-knit, dogmatic groups. Thus some groups that are popularly labeled "cults" might be sociologically defined as "sects."

The term *cult* has recently acquired a pejorative connotation that is associated with allegations of "brainwashing," psychopathology, and extreme authoritarianism and "totalism." But this use of the term is incompatible with its use as a general residual category. Some critics of cults, recognizing the diversity of groups lumped under the popular label, have identified "extreme cults" or "destructive cults" as the real objects of their concern. The criteria for the latter generally involve communal totalism, authoritarianism, charismatic (and putatively arbitrary) leadership, manipulative and heavy-handed indoctrination, deceptive proselytization, violence and child abuse, sexual exploitation, emotional intensity in group life, and alleged use of techniques of "mind control." There presently appears to be some confusion as to what are the defining traits of "destructive cults" themselves as opposed to their supposedly harmful consequences. One approach entails the identification of "cultic" coercive and deceptive processes that may emerge in human groups and social systems (Anderson, 1985). The Unification Church, Hare Krishna, The Way, the Children of God, and Scientology are frequently labeled "destructive cults."

Some sociologists prefer to use terms such as *marginal religious groups,* and scholars in religious studies speak of "new religious movements" or NRMs. Whatever the term used, there are always difficulties in specifying its boundaries or applying it to particular groups; how esoteric, deviant, destructive, or even "new" a given born-again Christian group or faith-healing doctrine is, for example, can often be debated.

"CULTS", CULTURE, AND SOCIETY

What is the significance of the proliferation of esoteric religions in a society? How is such spiritual animation related to broad patterns of social and cultural transformation? There are a number of provocative analyses that attempt to address the question of the sources and the significance of the growth of unconventional religious movements in the past two decades.

Cults and Secularity. Observing the surge of religious innovation over the past two decades, some scholars have seen in it a prima facie refutation of what Andrew Greeley (1972) has termed "the secularization myth," which claims a diminishing significance for religion in modern Western society. On the other hand, a few writers have argued that the contemporary proliferation of cults actually represents a reaction to pervasive secularization. Daniel Bell (1977) points out

that when the institutional framework of religions is shaken, many persons become involved in the search for direct religious experience; the rise of cults is hence facilitated.

A related line of thought asserts the ultimate triviality of new movements and forms and, by implication, the continued dominance of secularization. Bryan Wilson (1976) argues that the contemporary dominance of impersonal social control precludes an authentic "great awakening" that could significantly transform American culture and society. Contemporary "new religions" in Europe and North America represent the reduction of religion to an exotic consumer item that has no consequences in dominant social institutions, political power structures, or bureaucratic and technological controls. By contrast, in Africa and Latin America new Christian Pentecostal and Islamic sects can, in Wilson's view, exert a powerful influence on social institutions, culture, and nation building. However, in modern Western society a variety of religious forms and symbolic worlds can coexist in a "spiritual supermarket" precisely because the wider society is securely secular and the variegated and exotic forms are reduced to insignificant consumer items. Wilson thus rebuts the claim that the "new religions" amount to a significant reaction to the trend of secularization. For him, "the cults are likely to be no more than transient and volatile gestures of defiance."

Cults and the Material World. Writing from an economic determinist perspective, anthropologist Marvin Harris (1981) believes that the proliferation of esoteric religio-therapeutic movements in the context of the rising cost of living associated with the "stagflation" of the 1970s represents a pervasive revival of magic in the face of diminishing economic expectations. According to Harris, the rise of cults signifies "a misunderstood attempt to save America's dream of worldly progress by magical and supernatural means." He notes that the pursuit of wealth and power is emphasized in numerous movements, including many evangelical groups as well as quasi-religious therapy movements such as Scientology or Erhard Seminars Training (EST). In the former groups Jesus is sometimes said to assist the follower's upward socioeconomic mobility and also to heal sickness if the believer has faith. In movements such as EST, Scientology, and Silva Mind Control the devotee is taught to "take responsibility" for his thoughts and to impose his thoughts on reality, thereby enhancing his capacity to gain material and social rewards. For Harris these themes are indicative of a "manipulative and power-hungry side of the new consciousness."

Harris also notes that the daily life of many new communal movements seems to be dominated by the need to create the material base for expansion of the movement and its social influence. A number of groups, including the Unification Church and, formerly, the followers of Bhagwan Shree Rajneesh, represent "capitalist success stories" because they have diversified investments and commercial operations that generate substantial funds, according to Laurence Grafstein (1984). The movements claim exemption from governmental regulation of their financial dealings and commercial subsidiaries; however, they are increasingly challenged on this score by the expanding regulatory mandate of the state to ensure the public accountability of profit-making organizations. Grafstein and Richard Delgado (1979–1980) allege that businesses operated by some religious groups derive their viability in part from under-regulation (including tax privileges) and from an emphasis on spiritual rather than material rewards provided in exchange for the labor of devotees, or what some critics have labeled "slave labor."

Cults and the Breakdown of Community. It has often been noted that religious movements proliferating in the 1970s frequently tended to operate as family surrogates and alternative systems of spiritual kinship in which participants were offered unconditional social support and affect (e.g., "Jesus loves you," "We are brothers and sisters") and became devoted to a guru or leader referred to as "father." The pervasive emphasis on familial warmth and closeness has suggested to many observers that the growth of new movements was a response to alienating social changes involving family breakdown, the predominance of impersonal bureaucratic social patterns, and the decline of "mediating structures" such as extended families, churches, and homogeneous neighborhoods, which provided supports for the nuclear family and linkage to the broader society.

In an important essay, "The New Religions: Demodernization and the Protest Against Modernity" (1981), sociologist James D. Hunter interprets the new movements as responding to heightened problems of existence in modern societies, which are increasingly characterized by "a split between public and private spheres of life." A gap is widening between a highly institutionalized public realm dominated by large-scale, formally organized bureaucratic structures, in which thought, behavior, and relationships are expected to be impersonal and controlled by a principle of functional rationality, and an increasingly fragmented and de-institutionalized private realm, in which the norms governing courtship, marriage, child-rearing, sexuality, and leisure are in flux. According to Hunter, the private realm is no longer governed by clear norms guiding the nuances of intimate behavior and conferring meaning on everyday life.

The duality of the "oppressively formidable public sphere" and the precariously de-institutionalized private realm constitutes the "dilemma of modernity" that provides the context for the growth of new social movements. Although secular social movements may also respond to this dilemma, religious groups possess an advantage in their traditional symbolization of sacred kinship and communities of brotherhood, fatherhood, motherhood, and fellowship. Participants in contemporary religious movements sometimes believe that they partake of a special fellowship in which "loving" relations among spiritual brethren are seen to be derivative from each follower's inner liaison with Jesus, the Holy Spirit, an inspired guru, or an immanent godhead.

The capacity of mystiques in religion to create legitimations that confer a universal significance on new patterns of extended communal relations transcending biological kinship ties is an important trend in the new religion. For example, while the Unification Church operates as a surrogate family for the "Moonies," the Unification community is more than merely a family because it is legitimated in terms of universal values whereby the family forms the core and the reflection of the new kingdom of perfection in which harmony will prevail. Thus, despite the childlike quality of some aspects of social interaction within the community, the role of Unification family member has an "adult" quality that derives from its orientation toward broader civic and spiritual values. The Unification community thus combines the rewards of familial warmth and solidarity with an adult concern with universal values and broad social issues. This may partly explain why, in the words of Irving Horowitz (1981), a severe critic of the movement, the Unification Church "does provide an effective therapeutic setting that offers linkage to the larger society without its turmoils."

The deinstitutionalization of the private realm is reflected in the proselytizing themes of the Unification Church, which "constantly emphasizes the breakdown of the American family, corruption and immorality in American life (divorce, pornography, suicide, drugs, and scandal) and, by contrast the work of the church toward the 'perfect family' in a 'perfect world' " (Doress and Porter, 1981). The authoritarian and totalistic communal world of the Unification Church represents, according to Hunter, the option of "total institutionalization—a microcosmic totalitarianism as a means of tangibly reestablishing a home world for its members. Synanon, the Unification Church, and the Children of God are especially notable in this regard."

The vast majority of today's new religious movements are not as tightly communal and authoritarian as the groups referred to above. However, in Hunter's view, many of those that are not totalistic on the level of social organization are nonetheless characterized by an absolutism or totalism that "manifests itself at the cognitive level":

> Within the new religions absolutism is present, almost by definition—the "pure consciousness" advocated by Transcendental Meditation; "eternal bliss" offered by the Hare Krishna movement; "receiving knowledge" from the Divine Light Mission; achieving "God Consciousness" through the Healthy Happy Holy Organization; and undergoing "Transpersonal Experience" (e.g., being, essence, self-actualization, "oneness," "Cosmic awareness," "Transcendence") in the Human Potential Movement, to name a few. All, in one form or another, profess to offer a superlative, providing its possessor with an ultimate system of relevance which transcends the bland ordinariness and meaninglessness of everyday life in the modern world. (pp. 9–10)

Thus, through ideological and sometimes organizational absolutism the new spiritual groups

that developed in the late 1960s and 1970s responded, in Hunter's view, "to the strains imposed by the double-bind of modernity, an overly rational, abstract public sphere and a radically de-institutionalized private sphere." If, however, new movements have arisen in the context of a deinstitutionalized private sphere, then the surge of new religions might be expected to subside somewhat in the face of (tenuous) indicators of an incipient reinstitutionalization of normative patterns in the private sphere, such as a slight dip in the divorce rate or declines in promiscuity or a reaction against the cultural legitimization of homosexuality.

Cults and Cultural Confusion. Much of the scholarly commentary on the recent growth of esoteric and deviant spiritual groups has emphasized the confusion and transformation of American values in the context of the Vietnam War, the Watergate crisis, and the countercultural ferment of the 1960s and 1970s. Worship of the "American way of life," messianic "Americanism," and "civil religion" are said to have been undermined as unifying religio-political ideologies. One result has been the substitution of "a myriad of fragmented visions for the central messianism we once called Americanism" (Appel, 1980). Thus, the politicized evangelical resurgence as well as the extreme anticommunism of the Unification Church of the Reverend Sun Myung Moon can be seen as contributing to an attempted revitalization of the American tradition of extreme ethical dualism—the absolute dichotomy of right and wrong—and the theme of America as a "chosen people." In contrast, the proliferation of "privatized" and "narcissistic" religio-therapeutic groups, which stress individual self-actualization and implicitly reject the infusion of civic values into spiritual meanings, represents an alternative response to the posited normative breakdown of the 1960s and 1970s.

Robert Bellah has been foremost in analyzing the proliferation of new movements in terms of dislocations in "American Civil Religion," which he defines as a constellation of shared religio-political meanings that express a sense of national purpose and identity. In 1975 Bellah commented that "today the American Civil Religion is an empty and broken shell." In a 1976 essay he argued that the new religions flourishing in the 1970s were "successor movements" to the "crisis of meaning" of the late 1960s. According to him, the counterculture and the ferment of the 1960s entailed a revolt against the hegemony of the cultural values of utilitarian individualism, materialism, and "technical reason," whereby the ends of social action are relativized and the emphasis is placed on the rationalization of means. However, as Bellah had anticipated, the values challenged in the late 1960s and early 1970s may be recovering their primacy. Steven Tipton, a student of Bellah's, has analyzed how various movements, including EST, American Zen, and a "Jesus People" group, mediate between resurgent utilitarian individualism and other value orientations that influenced young persons in the 1970s: countercultural excessiveness and fundamentalist biblical literalism. Thus, the EST orientation of "rule egoism" performs the function of accommodating the countercultural ethos of expressive spontaneity ("situational expressivity"; the term focuses on "doing your own thing" and stresses love and exploration and actualization of self) to careerist utilitarian individualism (the term emphasizes the imperative of manipulating things and people as means to attaining one's goals) thereby allowing ambitious young Americans to be "saved from the sixties" (1982).

Bellah's perspective on contemporary spiritual ferment has not gone unchallenged. Harris, who stresses the economic and acquisitive dimension of today's religious movements, has scoffed at the notion that cultists are revolting against materialism and technology. However, Charles Glock, who coedited with Bellah a major 1976 study of the emergence of new religions in the San Francisco Bay area, also stresses the importance of cultural change and shifting values in generating a search for new meanings and forms. Glock stresses the decline of traditional assumptions of personal autonomy and mastery as constituting a basic cultural shift that is undermining traditional normative patterns and enhancing spiritual ferment.

The emergence of new movements can be interpreted as a response to a prevalent climate of moral ambiguity, which reflects shifting moral attitudes toward various behaviors such as sex-role deviations. Pervasive moral ambiguity results from the decline of a cultural tradition of dualistic moral absolutism, a key element of which is the presumption of personal responsibility and mastery. In the face of pervasive moral confusion two comprehensive spiritual world views have emerged. Monistic perspectives characterize "Eastern" cults and religio-therapeutic movements. These patterns of meaning tend to stress the "oneness" or metaphysical unity of experience, the ultimate illusory quality of the phenomenal world, and the consequent primacy of consciousness and its development. The monistic world view entails an implicit moral relativism. In contrast, dualistic perspectives characterizing resurgent evangelical Fundamentalist and Pentecostal religiosity tend to stress more traditional themes of ethical dualism, punitive moral absolutism, and millenarianism, which derive from the evangelical and Puritan traditions in America.

Dualistic faiths tend to highlight the radical transcendence of God and the irrevocable distinctness of creator and creation. In contrast, monistic movements tend to stress immanence and karma/reincarnation. In emphasizing the primacy of consciousness, American monistic systems, such as Meher Baba, Zen, or Rajneesh, can be seen as extrapolating certain "psychologizing" tendencies in liberal Protestant theology as well as relativist and subjective elements in cultural modernism. The present surge of dualistic movements can thus be regarded as a reaction against these modernist tendencies.

The spread of monistic world views in the 1960s and 1970s was related to the "normalization" of psychotherapy as a common experience for affluent Americans. Since the new legions of therapy clients could not plausibly all be "sick," therapy for non-psychotic conditions tended to become detached from the medical model, and the emphasis shifted to personal growth. These tendencies were embodied in the "human potential movement" and the proliferation of new therapeutic groups and mystiques, many of which were influenced by Oriental mysticism. The "triumph of the therapeutic" was congenial to the spread of quasi-monistic premises such as the primacy of inner consciousness and its exploration.

Monistic systems tend to locate ultimate reality in a depth of consciousness or self. Although groups with quasi-monistic systems have been denigrated as "narcissistic" (Cox, 1977), they may nevertheless embody the "cult of the individual," which the sociologist Émile Durkheim identifies as the integrative ideology of a highly modernized society with an extensive division of labor. The fragmentation of human life-space into a multitude of functionally specific roles and limited organizational involvements places a premium on holistic conceptions of personal identity, which may be obtained by extra-vocational spiritual commitments.

In the early 1980s the dynamic momentum appears to have been with dualistic perspectives —varieties of Fundamentalism and evangelicism. The climate of patriotic renewal and conservative moralism is favorable to the surge of variations on traditional dualistic perspectives and is arguably hostile to the expansion of monistic mystiques and perhaps to spiritual deviance and innovation in general. If normative breakdown and the fragmentation of civil religion have given impetus to spiritual innovation and the rise of "cults," then the possibility of normative and cultural reintegration may have negative implications for the growth and survival of esoteric movements.

VARIETIES OF NEW MOVEMENTS

Typologizing and classifying today's new religious movements has been a recent concern of sociologists of religion. Several typologies are reviewed in Roy Wallis' *The Elementary Forms of the New Religious Life* (1984). Wallis further elaborates the distinction between monistic and dualistic movements in terms of a distinction between "charismatic" monistic groups, which stress the importance of identification with an exemplary spiritual master such as Meher Baba or Bhagwan Shree Rajneesh, and "technical" monism, which pursues enlightenment through standardized procedures such as the Hare Krishna chant. It is also possible to distinguish between "one-level" and "two-level" monistic groups. The former accept the premise that spiritual realization or enlightenment is equivalent to learning the tenets and values of the movement and can therefore be accomplished in one lifetime through intensive training. The latter entails a view of spiritual realization as a rare state of karmic evolution that only a few individuals can attain in a given lifetime or incarnation.

The distinction between one-level and two-level monism entails a distinction between a univocal (one-dimensional) monism purveying spiritual meanings assumed to be immediately applicable to the phenomenal world and a multivocal (multi-dimensional) or symbolic monism in which monistic spiritual truths are seen as pertaining to a different level of reality. Large and well-known "consciousness" groups such as EST and Scientology exemplify univocal systems that have been influenced by "Eastern" thought but view spiritual insights as immediately applicable on the material level. Such movements purport to train persons in techniques for attaining a higher consciousness, which is seen as having an immediate payoff in the enhanced efficacy in the devotee's dealings with the material and social world.

Frederick Bird (1979) notes that the term *monism* may obscure significant differences among Buddhist, Hindu, and Taoist traditions, which are also characterized by ethical and ontological dualisms. Bird argues for a typology that identifies three different relationships of followers or seekers to spiritual masters in the new movements. Participants in new movements tend to become 1) "devotees" of a sacred lord or truth; 2) "disciples" of a sacred discipline; or 3) "apprentices" in the mastery of a sacred system of inner power. Apprenticeship groups roughly correspond to one-level monist groups. Bird sees the different types of master–follower relationships as involving different modes of handling moral accountability, which is integral to the appeal of new movements.

Wallis (1984) has developed a more traditional sociological typology of movements based on their essential "orientations to the world." Wallis regards groups such as the Children of God, the People's Temple, the Unification Church, Hare Krishna, and the murderous Manson family as "world-rejecting" movements hostile to the prevailing social order, which is seen as demonic or irrevocably corrupt. Such groups are generally authoritarian and communally totalistic and can sometimes become political activists. In contrast, groups such as Transcendental Meditation, Silva Mind Control, Nichiren Shoshu, and EST exemplify the "world-affirming" type of movement, which claims to provide the means whereby participants may actualize their physical, spiritual, and moral potential without separating from or opposing the world.

World-affirming and world-rejecting types represent poles of a continuum. However, Wallis' "trichotomy" also includes a third type, the "world-accommodating" movement. This label is applicable to many neo-Pentecostal or charismatic groups, such as the Catholic charismatic renewal movement. Such groups stress the enrichment of the spiritual life of the followers as individuals; but compared to the world-accepting groups, there is less emphasis on worldly or instrumental benefits arising from spiritual gnosis. There is also an absence of world-rejecting emphasis on the movement as a new and purified society. World-accommodating movements are similar to movements more traditionally designated as "quietist."

Wallis sees his "types" as ideal models that actual groups will only approximate. A Pentecostal group whose participants report improved health and business success as a consequence of spiritual apotheosis might be seen to be precariously situated on the border separating world-accommodating and world-affirming groups. Some groups may combine elements of all three types in varying degrees. Nevertheless, change and evolution in a movement may often be seen as a shift of position in terms of Wallis' three-pole model. Thus the ill-fated People's Temple became more world-rejecting over time (the movement ended in a mass suicide at Jonestown), although the more usual pattern is for world-rejecting movements to shift toward greater accommodation.

The Unification Church. The Church of the Reverend Sun Myung Moon is the most controversial and best known of the new groups, although its American membership is actually rather small and has probably never exceeded five thousand. It has been extensively studied and has elicited numerous scholarly and journalistic articles, several sociological monographs (Barker, 1984; Bromley and Shupe, 1979; Lofland, 1977), some apologetics, and numerous recriminatory apostate accounts.

Sun Myung Moon was born in Korea, attended a university in Japan, and was imprisoned by the Communist government of North Korea. Although he has had followers in the United States since the late 1950s, his reorganization and reorientation of the American movement in the early 1970s appears to have coincided with a "turn to religion" on the part of many young Americans in the context of the decline of radical political protest (Bromley and Shupe, 1979).

Unificationists view Moon as the Lord of the Second Advent who comes to complete the unfinished work of Jesus Christ and to heal the split between man and God. In *Divine Principle* (1977) Moon claims that God intended Adam and Eve to have perfect children and to form a "God-centered family" (in which relationships among family members are integrated with the members' relationships to God, as well as modeled after relationships to God). However, since Eve allowed herself to be seduced by Lucifer, the subsequent union of Adam and Eve was unconsecrated, and all future generations were centered on Satan rather than God. Man's resulting "fallen nature" keeps him separate from God and subject to depravity and turmoil.

Throughout history, according to Moon, various "central figures" such as Abel, Noah, Abraham, and Jesus have been sent by God to be the instruments of the restoration of God's heavenly kingdom. The willfulness of man has continually undermined such attempts; Jesus succeeded "in restoring the world spiritually but his untimely death prevented physical restoration, i.e., the formation of a family and the initiation of a God-centered lineage" (Bromley, Shupe, and Oliver, 1981).

The family is thus a central concept in Unificationist theology. Most church members spend at least the first years in communally organized groups in which they participate in a symbolic kinship system. "Father" Moon and his wife are designated as "Our True Parents" and members are "brothers and sisters." Marriage is referred to as "blessing" and is an essential sacrament. Moon qua True Spiritual Parent must bless every marriage, and, moreover, uses his spiritual insight to match couples, who are often not acquainted with each other and may be from different ethnic and cultural backgrounds. He has officiated at controversial mass-marriage ceremonies at which hundreds of couples have been "blessed." The progeny of such marriages are expected to be "perfect children" who will constitute the nucleus of a perfected and restored society.

A prerequisite for restoration is "indemnity" or the rendering of some unconditional "payment." On the individual level devotees must recognize Moon's spiritual status, accept direction from the Messiah, and pay a personal indemnity by helping to raise funds and making new converts (or producing spiritual children). They are expected to receive Moon's blessing in marriage and to produce children, thereby helping to build a restored world order of sinless families. Restoration also occurs on the institutional level, which entails devotees' transferring material goods from the dominion of Satan to the messianic dominion of the new world order. The "external" world is seen as dominated by Satan and must be redirected in accordance with the heavenly "internal world." The "external" structures of businesses and states should come to receive direction from "internal" representatives of the Messiah, and business and political leaders should seek to implement his will. Ultimately all major social institutions are to be "restored" (Bromley, 1985).

These ideas legitimate a highly diversified commercial empire involving banks, restaurants, various industries such as ginseng, fisheries, karate schools, and munitions, hotels, and media, as well as far-flung political operations and linkages with authoritarian anticommunist political forces. The wide-ranging political and economic activities taking direction from associates of Moon have elicited sharp opposition and concern. In 1982 Moon was convicted of tax fraud. After fruitless appeals in which issues involving the criteria whereby expenditures designated as "religious" as opposed to "business" and "personal" were highlighted, he entered federal custody and served over a year of an eighteen-month prison sentence.

Opposition to the Unification Church has also been motivated by its highly manipulative tactics of proselytization and indoctrination or "mind control." "Moonies" have probably figured disproportionately in "deprogrammings" (which involve strenuous attempts to deconvert someone from a devalued faith or to induce someone to leave a controversial movement—efforts that sometimes transpire in a context of forcible physical restraint subsequent to abduction) and the stereotype of the deceptive cult that lures unwary persons to an isolated rural retreat where intense peer pressure and "love-bombing" (the showering of prospective converts with strong affection as part of the process of drawing them into the group) impedes exodus is largely based on the Unificationist "Creative Community" project in Booneville, California (now defunct), and has been indiscriminately generalized as the standard modus operandi of "cults." The Unifi-

cation Church has thus become a representative cult.

Despite the impact of "mind control," the movement has a substantial voluntary defection rate, and its numbers may now be dwindling. Yet many of its associated political, economic, and cultural enterprises are flourishing. Notable among these are the anticommunist political organization CAUSA, which is particularly active in Latin America, and the conservative *Washington Times.*

The Unification Church can thus be classified as a stridently "dualistic" movement whose emphasis on "absolute values" enhances the movement's appeal to persons who are disturbed by the flux and confusion of contemporary values. But this dualism also underlies its controversial right-wing political extremism. In Wallis' terms the Unification Church is an austere "world-rejecting" movement that is very tightly knit and regiments its followers but exists in a state of high tension with the broader society.

The Way International. Originally called Vesper Chimes, The Way was founded in 1942 by Victor Paul Wierwille, a minister of the Evangelical Reformed Church. It flourished during the broad "Jesus movement" revival of the early 1970s and continued to expand in the middle and late part of that decade.

The Way operates as a biblical research, teaching, and household fellowship ministry. New members often become involved in The Way by taking the basic twelve-session course "Power for Abundant Living," developed by Wierwille. Later they may attend The Way College of Emporia in Emporia, Kansas, join The Way Corps, or become a one-year missionary or "Word Over the World Ambassador."

Part of the controversiality of The Way is related to its antitrinitarian beliefs, which evoke the classic Arian heresy. Jesus is defined as the Son of God but not God the Son. The Way also believes in receiving the fullness of the Holy Spirit, which is manifested in nine ways including healing, speaking in tongues, prophecy, and miracles. The group's controversiality is also related to allegations of anti-Semitism and to allegations that members receive paramilitary training and are learning to use deadly weapons in preparation for violent attacks on critics of the movement. Defenders of The Way maintain that the latter allegations represent a misinterpretation of the cooperation of The Way College with the state of Kansas' program to promote hunting safety (Melton and Moore, 1982).

The movement currently appears to be undergoing significant changes; Wierwille retired as its active director prior to his death in 1985. Although The Way is widely stigmatized as a "destructive cult," it appears that the life-styles of numerous members do not correspond to the stereotype of the regimented and totalistic communal cult. Followers frequently live in their own private residences and pursue vocations and careers outside of the institutions of the movement. This may be indicative of a tendency of many deviant religious movements to evolve over time in a more adaptive direction entailing the emergence of numerous "householders" or "lay" members who are not encapsulated in communal religious institutions (Wallis, 1984). In some cases, such as the Unification Church, this development may pose a problem because non-encapsulated members are less "deployable" for energetic mobile fund-raising.

Scientology. The late L. Ron Hubbard, a science fiction writer, developed Dianetics, a "science" of mental health providing a practical system for human improvement that became a fad in the early 1950s. Subsequent to its decline, Hubbard organized Scientology, which elaborated Dianetics into a comprehensive philosophical and theological system as well as an elaborately hierarchical spiritual movement that has sought recognition as a church.

The belief system of Scientology is somewhat similar to ancient gnosticism but is otherwise eclectic and includes elements that draw upon Eastern and ancient Greek thought, psychoanalysis, and modern occultism. In *Dianetics: The Modern Science of Modern Health* (1950) Hubbard claims that the mind is a calculator that works best when it is "cleared," a state achieved through Dianetics. Subsequently, Hubbard elaborated ideas about each individual being a latent "Thetan" or vital force possessed of great powers. Most humans have lost consciousness of their Thetan potential but can be trained to become "Operating Thetans" (O.T.'s) through the techniques and knowledge of Scientology.

According to Hubbard, there is a hierarchy of levels of awareness through which a devotee ascends until he becomes "clear," and then he may go beyond "clear" and be finally apotheosized as an O.T. The instrumentalities of this "clearing" process include expensive courses and a counseling process called auditing. The goal of "auditing" is to remove "engrams" or mental images of past negative experiences that are stored in the "reactive mind" and that inhibit mastery of consciousness. In the past auditing has entailed the use of the controversial "E-meter," a machine used to measure psychic reactions in the process of auditing, which brought the movement into conflict with the Food and Drug Administration in the late 1960s.

Scientology has elicited extreme hostility from the medical profession and from the governments of such nations as Great Britain, Australia, New Zealand, and the United States. As J. Gordon Melton and Robert L. Moore point out, no church has been involved in as much controversy and litigation as the Church of Scientology. It has been involved in legal battles with the FDA, the IRS, federal criminal prosecutors, ex-members, and the son of its founder (1982). Scientologists claim that the movement has been persecuted by government agencies using tactics of infiltration and theft. On the other hand, Scientology has itself been accused of using methods of character assassination, theft, and forgery to strike back at detractors. Several high Scientology officials have been convicted of the theft of government documents and sent to prison. Numerous defectors complain of the movement's authoritarianism, financial costs, manipulativeness, stringent social control, and internal power struggles and coups. Nevertheless, Scientology has enormously influenced what might be called the "occult milieu" in Europe and America. Numerous other movements such as EST either have developed as offshoots of Scientology or have been significantly influenced by its doctrines and counseling practices.

EST. Werner Erhard (born Jack Rosenberg) worked at selling automobiles and encyclopedias while receiving training in various consciousness programs and reading psychology-of-success books. He eventually developed Erhard Seminars Training, which was incorporated as a profit-making educational corporation. Erhard's techniques reflect the influence of Zen, Scientology, Dale Carnegie, and the writings of various psychologists such as Abraham Maslow and Carl Rogers.

Erhard's genius appears to have been his ability to accommodate the relativistic and mystical elements of Eastern monism to a more traditional American success ethic and associated "win friends and influence people" techniques (Tipton, 1982).

In addition to charges of financial manipulation, EST is criticized for preaching or sanctifying selfishness. But Erhard has argued that the contemporary language of civic virtue or moral obligation is inauthentic and actually rationalizes unenlightened self-interest. A new language of enlightened self-interest, he claims, will lead to true altruism. When people are free to acknowledge their real needs at a deeper level of awareness, their apparent egoism will be transformed into true concern for others, according to Erhard. He established the Hunger Project to eliminate world hunger, but critics say that it is just a public relations response to charges of "narcissistic" selfishness.

EST has also been attacked for the ruggedness of its therapy sessions, in which participants sit for hours on hard chairs, are not allowed to relieve themselves, and are called "assholes" (a kind of "attack therapy"?).

Technically EST has been discontinued and Erhard's new group is called The Forum. But critics say that this is merely a superficial change.

Tipton (1982) has concluded that EST appealed in the 1970s to young careerists who needed to reconcile the requirements of careerist conformity with the persisting countercultural values of the late 1960s. EST provided an ethic of utilitarian individualism for upwardly mobile young adults but with rationalizing links to the 1960s emphasis on "consciousness raising."

Controversial Aspects of New Movements. Some observers have noted a disturbing tendency for therapeutic communities to evolve into totalistic and manipulative "cults" controlled by charismatic but unbalanced leaders. The classic case is Synanon, once a highly regarded addict rehabilitation movement that by the late 1970s had developed into an authoritarian and allegedly violent quasi-religious group, unsuccessfully seeking recognition as a church. The organization encountered extreme difficulties after two members were convicted of putting a rattlesnake into the mailbox of a prominent critic of Synanon.

Violence also characterized the end of the People's Temple community in Guyana in which nine hundred persons perished in an orgy of mass suicide-murder in November 1978, apparently inspired by its leader, Jim Jones. Originally a Christian group notable for its opposition to racism and segregation, it had evolved in a quasi-Marxist and "paranoid" direction.

Violence and extreme authoritarianism have also been attributed to several "Eastern" groups, such as the International Society of Krishna Consciousness (Hare Krishna) and the movement led by Bhagwan Shree Rajneesh. The former has been accused of stockpiling weapons and at the present writing is appealing a nine-million-dollar civil judgment against it for allegedly imprisoning a minor through "mind control." Rajneesh's followers have lost an extended legal battle to incorporate their settlement in Oregon as a city. Bhagwan Rajneesh has pleaded guilty to immigration fraud and agreed to leave the United States. The Oregon settlement is being disbanded.

TENSIONS OVER "CULTS"

Many controversies are raging around religious movements in America. Conflicts involving "cults" have arisen in numerous areas including tax privileges, commercial diversification, public solicitation, faith healing and rejection of modern medicine, proselytization and indoctrination practices, mental health jeopardy to participants, corporal punishment and child abuse, child custody, and immigration. The shock of the mass suicide at the People's Temple has contributed to the stigmatization of close-knit and esoteric movements and has augmented a growing "anti-cult movement" (Shupe and Bromley, 1980, 1982). Antagonists of "cults" include relatives of devotees, social workers and mental health professionals, clergy, ex-devotees, politicians, and various government agencies, particularly the IRS. Fascinating legal issues have arisen over the alleged use of "brainwashing" by "cults" and the coercive methods that parents have used to "rescue" their children from controversial groups, and scholars of religion have become divided over the issue of scholarly responsibility with respect to controversial and reputedly harmful groups.

Sources of Conflict. Various factors are involved in the underlying sources of tension between contemporary religious movements and the diverse groups and institutions that appear to be ranged against them. Some groups, such as the Unification Church and Hare Krishna, claim a monopoly of spiritual truth and legitimacy. They see themselves as the exclusive beacon of spirituality in a fallen world replete with demonic influences. They might therefore be viewed as "uncivil religions" that arguably contravene the American "religion of civility," which is "intolerant of intolerance" (Hammond, 1981). Many such groups, Hare Krishna and the Unification Church among them, are communal and totalistic and arguably regiment participants in a manner that violates the values of personal autonomy and individualism central to modern Anglo-American culture (Beckford, 1985).

Groups such as Scientology and the Unification Church are highly diversified and multifunctional and therefore compete with and threaten various groups and institutions in modern society. Close-knit "cults" aspire to the role of family surrogate and thereby evoke concern among relatives of converts who may understandably feel that they have "lost" someone who has become encapsulated in a bizarre and highly regimented movement and who may have become detached from conventional career goals.

Furthermore, the new religious movements may diminish the pool of persons available for participation in conventional churches and synagogues; officials of the latter groups may resent the more intense and diffuse commitments that some new movements have been able to elicit from converts. Gurus and faith-healing groups such as the Faith Assembly compete with certified secular healers; moreover, the latter are less accountable and less socially regulated than their secular competitors. The tension between deviant movements and the medical establishment also has an ideological dimension that entails conflict between the secularist and socially adjustive ethos of mental health and alternative values stressing transcendence, ecstasy, mystery, and millenarian reconstruction.

The totalism of some movements encourages a significant dependency on the part of devotees, who may thereby be vulnerable to exploitation, which may be so severe as to violate the Thirteenth Amendment's prohibition of slavery (Delgado, 1979–1980). The close-knit and authoritarian pattern of some movements makes it appear plausible that the movement or its leaders share some responsibility for alleged abuses

in child-rearing among devotees, particularly in the areas of corporal punishment, which is sanctioned by various Fundamentalist groups, and the rejection of modern medicine associated with faith-healing groups. Finally, totalistic and highly diversified or multifunctional movements that control the daily lives of converts and/or have significant political and economic involvements appear to many persons not to "know their place." They contravene the modern cultural expectation that religious and secular spheres of life will be clearly segregated.

Many of the new movements clearly violate certain social norms and outrage cultural values. A few are dangerous and volatile by any standards. These real problems interact with the interests and institutions that are threatened by diversified and dynamic movements operating partly as family surrogates to mobilize a strong and organized resistance to "cults."

"Medicalizing" Deviant Groups. Some movements, such as the Unification Church, Hare Krishna, and Scientology, are now highly controversial and have elicited strong opposition. But in the context of the First Amendment guarantee of freedom of religion, constraining or sometimes even investigating the alleged abuses of religious groups is often difficult. Some concerned citizens believe that the constitutional objection to governmental interference with the "free exercise of religion" is not applicable to "cults" because the commitment of participants is involuntary by virtue of the "coercive" quality of indoctrination and the resulting trauma and psychopathological deterioration of converts, whose capacity to rationally evaluate their continued involvement is reduced (Delgado, 1977). By this argument, authoritarian "cults" that employ "mind control" are not constitutionally protected from state intervention on behalf of "brainwashed" and traumatized devotees. The abuses of "destructive cults" are thus alleged to raise medical and mental health issues that justify intervention under the norm of *parens patriae* or the proper paternalistic concern of the state for the well-being of its citizens.

This approach can be seen to "medicalize" the issues relating to deviant religious groups. A disproportionate amount of scholarly and popular discourse on today's esoteric religious movements has been preoccupied with the dynamics of conversion and persuasion (and "brainwash-

751

ing'') in such groups. The conceptual framework of medicalization meets the needs of several of the groups that are antagonistic toward "cults": mental health professionals, whose role in the proper healing of the pathological effects of cultist indoctrination is highlighted; ex-converts, who find meaning and convenience in interpreting their involvement with unpopular groups as essentially passive and unmotivated; parents, whose opposition to their children's involvement and impulse to consider active countermeasures is legitimated; and clerics, who do not want to appear to be persecuting newer competitors.

Deprogramming. The strategy of applying a medical model has given rise to "deprogramming," which refers to systematic attempts to deconvert adherents of disfavored groups. These attempts are often made in a context of forcible confinement, which supporters of such coercive measures justify by citing the psychological coercion allegedly employed by cults as well as the primacy of mental health considerations. Thus, one deprogrammer has stated, "We deal with the Unification Church as a mental health problem, not a religion." A qualified defense of deprogramming has been made by Delgado (1977), who argues that an adult indoctrinee's refusal to be counseled or treated may be legitimately overridden "if it appears that the indoctrinee is incapable of fully understanding the conditions to which he has been subjected that account for his recent change of outlook." But some critics of this line of thought perceive a "rationalistic fallacy" whereby a faith is not viewed as authentic or meriting legal protection unless the believer can articulate the rational grounds of his faith.

Most legal and philosophical discussion of deprogramming has focused on the role of the state in religious deprogramming and, in particular, on the status of "legal" deprogramming by means of temporary conservatorship and guardianship orders awarded to parents of adult converts by courts. Delgado maintains that the manipulative and "coercive" processes through which persons are inducted into "cults" render cultist involvements "non-consensual" in terms of the standard criteria of "informed consent." Compulsory therapy may be justified if non-consensuality is accompanied by some degree of psychological damage to the convert.

In a counter-formulation Robert Shapiro (1983) maintains that most allegations that someone has been "brainwashed" in a religious cult usually involve claims that the convert has become a different person under the impact of coercive and manipulative processes of persuasion. In such a situation the application of therapy over the protest of the devotee is not justified, as the "new person" is still a person whose beliefs are absolutely protected from state interference under the First Amendment.

"Legal deprogramming" declined after a well-publicized 1977 California case in which a state appellate court invalidated custody orders granted by a lower court to the parents of several followers of Sun Myung Moon. Presently most coercive deprogramming of adults involves an extra-legal abduction of a convert without the explicit sanction of a court custody order. Although attempts to prosecute or sue deprogrammers have brought mixed results, it appears that the number of abductions of adult devotees is declining. There are also indications that the focus of legal controversy over religious movements is shifting from a fixation on the process through which persons enter and leave exotic groups to conflicts over the regulatory prerogatives of the state with regard to the diversified commercial and financial operations of some groups and to issues involving corporal punishment and rejection of modern medicine in born-again groups such as the Faith Assembly and the Northeast Kingdom community. Allegations of pathological mental coercion in "cults" may figure in some of the latter controversies as well as in civil suits filed against religious movements by ex-devotees.

It is worth noting, however, that a number of recent studies have negative implications for the sensational allegations of cultist "brainwashing." Many of the most authoritarian and intensely stigmatized groups, such as the Unification Church, are characterized by a substantial voluntary defection rate such that "coerced" persons nonetheless manage to exit freely. The reputedly powerful methods of cultist indoctrination are usually ineffective and produce only a few converts out of a larger group attending a preliminary indoctrination workshop or seminar. Whether an ex-devotee has been deprogrammed and how much contact he or she has had with the "anti-cult" social network are significant predictors of whether an ex-convert claims to have been brainwashed. Several studies have indicated that involvement in deviant movements is associated with psychological benefits, such as the diminution of neurotic distress symptoms or the absence of mental disturbance (Kilbourne and Richardson, 1984).

The 1960s and 1970s have witnessed substantial scholarly inquiry into contemporary spiritual ferment and the development of new religious movements. There are indications in the mid-1980s that interest in the general phenomenon is to some degree waning as the growth of new religious movements levels off. "Eastern" religions, which were prominent on college campuses in the early 1970s, now elicit a markedly diminished interest among young persons, although "Eastern" religion as well as exotic religio-therapy still have a substantial appeal among affluent persons in their twenties, thirties, and forties. Evangelical, Fundamentalist, and Pentecostal religion may still be gaining new adherents; they show some strength on college campuses, as well as new political muscle.

Nevertheless, the past two decades of "religious populism," like the Great Awakenings of the American past, are likely to make a permanent imprint on the nation's religious pluralism. Some of the "cults" of the 1970s may survive and become stable institutionalized collectivities, even "denominations." This may be particularly applicable to the so-called "Jesus movement," groups that combine evangelical Christianity and countercultural styles. However, some groups will not survive. This is the prognostication of sociologist Bryan Wilson (1976), who argues that the appeal of many of the new religions is based primarily on spontaneity, novelty, and ecstasy and that these are all elements likely to be undermined as the Unification Church or Hare Krishna offer what Max Weber called a "virtuoso" religiosity, which may limit their appeal to the mass of conventional citizens. The appeal of "cults" to youth is in itself a constraint because, as Wilson says, "tomorrow's youth may make its generational protest in different terms." And they may cope with the loss of community and moral certainty in different ways.

Yet, with regard to the survival of today's "cults," Wilson may be unduly pessimistic. His analysis does point to an essential fact: the new

movements will have to undergo changes in order to survive. A non-encapsulated "laity" must emerge, charismatic leadership must be "routinized," and arrangements must crystallize for socializing the children of first-generation members.

Beyond the question of the survival of the new movements is the more intriguing question of their ultimate cultural impact. Wilson, according to one of his students, "incisively demolishes the claim that the new religions herald a significant reaction against the broad trend of secularization" (Wallis, 1984). Has the religious populism of the past decades failed so dismally to "reenchant the world?" In the sociology of religion there is fierce controversy over whether the proliferation of "cults," along with other contemporary phenomena such as the evangelical revival and the politicization of religion via the right-wing Moral Majority or left-wing liberation theology, testifies to the persisting vitality and cultural significance of religion as the primary instrument of humanity's quest to comprehend, appropriate, and transform the world.

BIBLIOGRAPHY

Susan M. Anderson, "Identifying Coercion and Deception in Social Systems," in Brock K. Kilbourne, ed., *Divergent Perspectives on the New Religion* (1985); Dick Anthony and Thomas Robbins, "Spiritual Innovation and the Crisis of American Civil Religion," in *Daedalus* III (1981–1982); Willa Appel, "Satanism in Politics," *The New York Times* (15 January 1980); Eileen Barker, *The Making of a Moonie: Brainwashing or Choice?* (1984); James Beckford, *Cult Controversies* (1985); Daniel Bell, "The Return of the Sacred? The Argument on the Future of Religion," in *British Journal of Sociology* 28 (1977); Robert N. Bellah, *The Broken Covenant* (1975), "The New Religious Consciousness and the Crisis in Modernity," in Charles Y. Glock and Robert N. Bellah, eds., *The New Religious Consciousness* (1976); Frederick Bird, "The Pursuit of Innocence: New Religious Movements and Moral Accountability," in *Sociological Analysis* 40 (1979); David G. Bromley, "Financing the Millennium: The Economic Structure of the Unification Church," in *Journal for the Scientific Study of Religion* 25 (1985); David G. Bromley and Phillip Hammond, eds., *The Future of New Religious Movements* (in press); David G. Bromley and James Richardson, *The Brainwashing–Deprogramming Controversy* (1983); David G. Bromley and Anson D. Shupe, *Moonies in America: Cult, Church and Crusade* (1979), *The New Vigilantes* (1980); David G. Bromley, Anson D. Shupe, and Donna L. Oliver, "Perfect Families: Visions of the Future in a New Religious Movement," in Florence Kaslow and Marvin Sussman, eds., *Cults and the Family* (1982).

Harvey Cox, *Turning East* (1977); Richard Delgado, "Religious Totalism: Gentle and Ungentle Persuasion Under the First Amendment," in *So. California Law Review* 51 (1977), "Religious Totalism as Slavery," in *New York University Review of Law and Social Change* 9 (1979–1980); Irwin Doress and Jack N. Porter, "Kids in Cults," in Thomas Robbins and Dick Anthony, eds., *In Gods We Trust* (1981); Charles Y. Glock, "Consciousness Among Contemporary Youth: An Interpretation," in Charles Y. Glock and Robert N. Bellah, eds., *The New Religious Consciousness* (1976); Laurence Grafstein, "Messianic Capitalism: The Invisible Hand that Feeds Cults," in *New Republic* 190 (1984); Andrew M. Greeley, *Unsecular Man* (1972); Phillip Hammond, "Civil Religion and New Movements," in Robert N. Bellah and Phillip Hammond, eds., *Varieties of Civil Religion* (1981); Marvin Harris, *America Now: An Interpretation of Social Change Since World War II* (1981); Irving L. Horowitz, "The Politics of New Cults," in Thomas Robbins and Dick Anthony, eds., *In Gods We Trust* (1981); James D. Hunter, "The New Religions: Demodernization and the Protest Against Modernity," in Bryan Wilson, ed., *The Social Impact of New Religions* (1981).

Brock K. Kilbourne and James T. Richardson, "Psychotherapy and New Religions in a Pluralistic Society," in *American Psychologist* 39 (1984); John Lofland, *Doomsday Cult* (1966; rev. 1977); J. Gordon Melton and Robert L. Moore, *The Cult Experience: Responding to the New Religious Pluralism* (1982); Thomas Robbins, "Sociological Studies of New Religious Movements: A Selective Review," in *Religious Studies Review* 9 (1983), "Government Regulatory Powers and Church Autonomy: Deviant Groups as Test Cases," in *Journal for the Scientific Study of Religion* 25 (1985); Thomas Robbins and Dick Anthony, eds., *In Gods We Trust* (1981), "Deprogramming, Brainwashing and the Medicalization of Deviant Religious Groups," in *Social Problems* 29 (1982); Thomas Robbins, Dick Anthony, and James T. Richardson, "Theory and Research on Today's 'New Religions,' " in *Sociological Analysis* 39 (1978).

Robert Shapiro, "Of Robots, Persons, and the Protection of Religious Beliefs," in *So. California Law Review* 56 (1983); William Shepherd, *To Secure the Blessings of Liberty: American Constitutional Law and the New Religious Movements* (1985); Rodney Stark and William Bainbridge, "Of Churches, Sects and Cults: Preliminary Concepts for a Theory of Religious Movements," in *Journal for the Scientific Study of Religion* 18 (1979); Steve Tipton, *Getting Saved from the Sixties: Moral Meaning in Conversion and Cultural Change* (1982); Roy Wallis, "The Cult and Its Transformation," in Roy Wallis, ed., *Sectarianism* (1975), *The Road to Total Freedom: A Sociological Analysis of Scientology* (1976), *The Elementary Forms of the New Religious Life* (1984); Frances Westley, *The Complex Forms of the Religious Life* (1983); Bryan R. Wilson, *Contemporary Transformations of Religion* (1976), ed., *The Social Impact of New Religions* (1981); Robert Wuthnow, *Experimentation in American Religion* (1978). [*See also* BLACK MILITANT AND SEPARATIST MOVEMENTS; BUDDHISM; HINDUISM; OCCULT MOVEMENTS IN AMERICA; *and* SHINTO AND INDIGENOUS CHINESE RELIGION.]

BLACK MILITANT AND SEPARATIST MOVEMENTS

Lawrence H. Mamiya and C. Eric Lincoln

THE unique nature of the black experience in America provided an inevitable impetus for the early development of militant/separatist organizations or movements among black Americans. Brought to America as slaves who were rigidly defined by their captors solely in terms of their African ancestry, and universally restricted in their participation in the ordinary ventures of the society, blacks were primed from the beginning for resistance and evasion. Early "black militance" against oppression was both individual and collective. It took such forms as the defiance of pass laws (which controlled the slaves' movements by requiring them to carry passes or permits signed by their owners) and the practice of voodoo, arson, sabotage, outright defiance (as in the legendary "bad nigger" or "crazy nigger"), assault, and insurrection. Perhaps the most common form of individual militance and evasion was running away, an act that not only removed the slave from the circumstances of his distress, but defied his oppressor and robbed him of property as well.

Insurrection, or revolt, was of course the ultimate corporate expression of black militance. American history is sprinkled with instances of localized "uprisings" and some that were of grander proportions, like the slave revolts led by Gabriel Prosser in 1800, Denmark Vesey in 1822, and Nat Turner in 1831. But this form of militance was both universally feared and summarily suppressed. On the other hand, the black church, while constantly monitored to prevent political or insurrectional infiltration, was tolerated on a minimum-risk basis in the hope that it would provide a counterweight for militancy and disruption. Such was not to be. The black church became instead the cradle of black independence, and black religion became the chief instrument of black liberation. The black church developed political awareness, provided the first political training ground (and political offices) for black people, encouraged and facilitated escape, and set the tone for subsequent black militancy. That it did so while remaining outwardly innocuous is a testament to the survival strategies developed by the black experience.

At stake in all black militant and separatist movements are two fundamental concepts or values: freedom and identity. These were the two cardinal virtues lost to slavery and its aftermath, and they were indispensable to peer acceptance and a sense of personal adequacy and responsibility. They are sine qua non to parity participation in the human enterprise, and this has been the traditional object of black militance, however projected or perceived. When Richard Allen founded the first black church denomination in 1816 and called it the African Methodist Episcopal Church, his assertion was both identity and separation. He and his followers would have preferred a *common* identity with other Americans in St. George's, the white Methodist church they had been attending in Philadelphia. But there their identity was externally determined, thrust upon them, as it were. And with such an imposed identity, other impositions were sure to follow, and they did.

Twentieth-century black leaders like Noble Drew Ali, Marcus Garvey, Father Divine, Daddy Grace, Elijah Muhammad, Malcolm X, and all the other militants and separatists to be discussed felt the need to be "separate" in order to be fully acceptable to themselves, to their perceived identities, and to the people who found it previously impossible to accept them or take seriously their humanity. Militance and/or separatism form the peculiar styles that express their refusal to cooperate with their denigration and rejection.

NOBLE DREW ALI AND THE MOORISH HOLY TEMPLE OF SCIENCE

During the first two decades of the twentieth century more than 4 million black people began leaving their way of life as sharecroppers in the rural South; they headed for industrial cities in the Northeast and Midwest. Attracted by ads in Negro newspapers like the *Chicago Defender* and displaced by the devastation of southern agriculture by boll weevil attacks on the cotton crop, a growing mass of black people voted with their feet to leave the Jim Crow segregation and violence of the South. Crowded into the poorer sections of northern cities, these rural migrants found their hopes and dreams for a better future crushed by the harsh realities of de facto racial discrimination; many of them had exchanged southern rural poverty for northern urban poverty.

Among the black migrants was Timothy Drew, who was born in North Carolina in 1866. Not much is known about his early life before he appeared in Newark, New Jersey, as a street-corner preacher. A magnetic and charming personality, Drew had little formal education. In 1913, when he was 47 years old, he founded the first Moorish Holy Temple of Science in Newark. Shrewdly taking advantage of the widespread discontent among the newly arrived black migrants, Drew rapidly established temples in Detroit, Harlem, Chicago, and Pittsburgh, and in numerous cities across the South. It is estimated that active membership in the Moorish Holy Temple of Science movement reached between 20,000 and 30,000 during his lifetime.

"The name means everything"—and confusion about names, national origins, and self-identity struck deeply into the psyche of many black people, who were the primary victims of America's color caste system. Drew himself changed his name to Noble Drew Ali and added the title Prophet. Although he had little formal education, he was exposed to Middle Eastern religious thought and was impressed by its lack of racial consciousness. Could it be that philosophy from the Middle East was a possible solution

to the plight of black people in America, who were principally judged by their skin color? Noble Drew Ali declared that American blacks "must henceforth call themselves Asiatics, to use the generic term, or more specifically, Moors or Moorish Americans" (Fauset, 1944, p. 41).

To confirm this ethnic transformation and inward change of identity, Prophet Ali issued "Nationality and Identification Cards" to his followers. Each card was stamped with the Islamic symbol of the star and crescent, accompanied by an image of clasped hands and a circumscribed 7. It announced that the bearer honored "all the Divine Prophets, Jesus, Mohammed, Buddha, and Confucius" and pronounced upon him the "blessings of the God of our Father Allah." The card identified its presenter as a "Moslem under the Divine Laws of the Holy Koran of Mecca, Love, Truth, Peace, Freedom, and Justice," and concluded with the assertion "I AM A CITIZEN OF THE UNITED STATES." Each card was validated by the subscription "NOBLE DREW ALI, THE PROPHET" (Lincoln, 1961, p. 53).

As the Moorish Science movement grew and spread from the East Coast to the Midwest, trouble arose. In Chicago the movement became a problem for law enforcement officials. Ali's followers, particularly the males, who wore red fezzes, felt an exaggerated sense of security and importance in their newly found "Asiatic" status. Thursdays, the traditional day off for domestics, were designated "bumping days," and aggressive members would accost whites on the sidewalks and in stores by surreptitiously bumping them out of the way, a practice that reversed the Jim Crow custom of southern whites forcing blacks off the sidewalks. The members would then flash their cards or proudly show their lapel buttons and sing praises to their new prophet who had freed them, psychologically at least, from white domination. There was also a belief that possession of the identity card would prevent harm from the white man or European, who was in any case soon to be destroyed, and "Asiatics" would then be in control.

This new change in behavior, however, was not accepted by whites, and racial confrontations increased daily. Noble Drew Ali finally issued a halt to the disorders and urged his followers to exercise restraint. "Stop flashing your cards before Europeans," he ordered, "as this only causes confusion. We did not come to cause confusion; our work is to uplift the nation" (Lincoln, 1961, p. 54).

The growth of the Moorish Science movement during the post–World War I years was accelerated by the recruitment of better educated but less dedicated members, who quickly assumed positions of leadership. These new leaders attempted to trick and exploit the general membership by selling them herbs, relics, magical charms, potions, and literature. Some of these leaders grew rich by peddling these goods to the credulous Moors. When Ali attempted to prevent further exploitation, he was shunted aside, and eventually he was killed.

The circumstances surrounding Noble Drew Ali's death and the responsibility for it remain unclear and unresolved. During an internal struggle among the leaders of the movement in 1927, one leader was killed. Although Ali was not in Chicago at the time, he was arrested upon his return and charged with murder by police officials. No trial ever took place, however, and he was released on bond. A few weeks later he died mysteriously. The cause of his death is attributed to either a beating he received from the police while he was in their custody or a subsequent beating from dissident members during the internal strife that haunted the movement.

Upon Ali's death the cult split into numerous smaller factions, diluting its former strength and influence. Some temples still remain active, especially in Chicago. Some Moors believe in the spirit of Noble Drew Ali, while others feel that he is reincarnated in their present leaders and speaks through the Holy Koran of the Moorish Holy Temple of Science, which is not to be confused with the Qur'an of orthodox Islam. The Holy Koran of the Moorish Holy Temple is limited to the teachings of Prophet Noble Drew Ali and some other esoteric materials related to his movement. In present-day Moorish temples, membership is restricted to "Asiatics," or non-Caucasians who have renounced their former identities as "colored" or "Negro." The terms *el* or *bey* are attached to the name of each member as a sign of his Asiatic status and inward transformation.

Friday is the Sabbath for the Moors, but meetings are held on Wednesday and Sunday. Facing Mecca, they pray three times a day (sunrise, noon, and sunset) and enforce a strict code of personal morality. Although they view themselves as an Islamic sect, Jesus figures prominently in the worship, as do other aspects of Christian ritual, including hymns that have been adapted to their services.

The Moors have continued their aggressive racial stance, exhibiting hostility toward whites, but they do stress obedience and loyalty to the flag of the United States as long as they live in America. Many Moors were among the earliest converts to the Black Muslim movement.

MARCUS GARVEY AND THE UNIVERSAL NEGRO IMPROVEMENT ASSOCIATION

Black militant and separatist movements have always exerted an influence far greater than their membership might indicate. This view holds true for the followers of Marcus Garvey, leader of the largest black social movement in American history. The exact numbers are debatable, ranging from several hundred thousand paid members to upwards of 6 million. The larger estimates represent an international following in the Caribbean, Central America, Europe, and Africa. Undoubtedly, Garvey's movement was the most influential in the first half of the twentieth century. All subsequent black militant movements—the Black Muslims, the Black Panthers, and other black power groups—have been deeply influenced by Garvey's ideology, slogans, and practices.

"Malcus" Mosiah Garvey, Jr., as his birth certificate reads, was born on 17 August 1887 in St. Anne's Bay on the northern coast of Jamaica. As the youngest of eleven children he grew up close to his mother, Sarah, who was deeply religious. His father was a skilled stonemason whose penchant for reading greatly influenced his son. Although Marcus attended a Church of England school, he did not go on to college, due to some business reversals his father suffered. Throughout his life he yearned to be an educated man; it is ironic that the leading black intellectual of his day, Dr. W. E. B. Du Bois of the United States, became a bitter enemy and severe critic later in Marcus' life. At the age of fourteen Marcus became a printer's apprentice and learned aspects of journalism. As a sensitive and precocious lad he also visited churches to observe the preaching and oratorical techniques of Kingston's leading preachers. Marcus was continually fascinated by the power of the written and spoken word.

In 1907 Garvey became one of the leaders of a printers' union strike. Although the strike was successful, he was the only person to be black-listed, and this bitter experience made him suspicious of the value of the labor movement. Through the influence of Dr. Joseph Love, a Jamaican social activist and editor of the Jamaica *Advocate,* Garvey decided that political and cultural activities were to be the focus of his life. Following Love's example, he launched his first publication, the *Watchman.* From 1909 to 1911 he traveled to Central and South American countries, where he witnessed the constant exploitation of black people. In 1912 Garvey was working in London with Dusé Mohamad Ali, a Sudanese-Egyptian scholar and nationalist who influenced his ideas about African redemption, when he came across a copy of Booker T. Washington's *Up From Slavery* (1901), which ignited his imagination:

> I read "Up From Slavery," by Booker T. Washington, and then my doom—if I may so call it—of being a race leader dawned on me. . . . I asked, "Where is the black man's Government?" "Where is his King and his kingdom?" "Where is his President, his country, and his ambassador, his army, his navy, his men of big affairs?" I could not find them, and then I declared, "I will help to make them."
>
> (Hill, ed., 1983, vol. 1, p. 5)

Excited by his new-found purpose and direction, Garvey returned to Jamaica to begin a program for the redemption of the black race. On 1 August 1914 he established a new organization, the Universal Negro Improvement and Conservation Association and African Communities League, later shortened to the UNIA. The purpose was to unite all people of African heritage in a social crusade to rehabilitate the race. The UNIA motto was "One God! One Aim! One Destiny!"

For two years Garvey struggled in Jamaica, organizing UNIA chapters and trying to break through the barriers of a highly stratified color caste system that made light skin and mulatto status a premium among Negroes. Although he made some headway, it was not until he arrived in America that his movement blossomed. He arrived in Harlem on 24 March 1916 with plans of founding a school, like Booker T. Washington's Tuskegee Institute, in Jamaica and of testing the reactions of American Negroes to his ideas. Garvey arrived in the United States at an opportune time. During the World War I era there was a profound disillusionment and sense of unease among the thousands of black migrants in northern urban centers. From 1917 to 1919 American cities saw the first major outbreaks of race riots; during the bloody summer months of 1919, called the "Red Summer," twenty-six race riots occurred in American cities. Returning black veterans, who had offered their lives for their country in war abroad, became disillusioned by the bitter discrimination they encountered at home. The Knights of the Ku Klux Klan also experienced a major resurgence in the South and began spreading rapidly in the North. Booker T. Washington, the national Negro leader, had died in 1915, and an increasing mood of militancy was felt among black intellectuals.

After a year of travel to assess the mood of this new country, Garvey established the New York division of the UNIA, which quickly became and remained the largest chapter. His message of racial pride, uplift, and redemption found a receptive audience. This short, stocky, dark-skinned Jamaican was a gifted, charismatic orator who thundered, "Up, you mighty race, you can accomplish what you will." A black skin for Garvey was not a badge of shame but a symbol of greatness.

By 1919 Garvey claimed more than 2 million members in thirty chapters. The *Negro World,* the UNIA's New York newspaper, rapidly became the largest black newspaper in the country, with a circulation of 200,000. With a column by Garvey and features on black heroes and heroines, the *Negro World* contributed to the process of building racial pride among the disinherited masses.

A master politician and an astute organizer, Marcus Garvey paid careful attention to the influence of religion among black people. His own experiences in Jamaica and his observations in the United States had taught him that material and spiritual needs are often blended together; the successful organization must be able to satisfy both dimensions. So he started with the "fraternal aspect," the deep desire and universal search for security among the masses. As his second wife, Amy Jacques Garvey, has commented:

> He had to start as a fraternal organization, giving sick and death benefits. This was the easiest means of reaching the common man, who wanted security in his distress; hand him this first, then tell him of the spiritual, racial benefits that would come in time.
>
> (Cronon, 1974, p. 61)

The UNIA also fulfilled the need for group sharing through common rites and rituals in weekly meetings, which resembled church meetings, and in massive, colorful parades. In 1920 the UNIA held its first international convention in Harlem with invited delegates from twenty-five countries. The convention began with a massive parade by thousands of men dressed in the dark blue uniforms of the UNIA's African Legion (composed of unarmed men in smart uniforms; the league's existence hinted at the fact that the redemption of the Negro race may have to come through the use of force, although Garvey never preached violence) and women who wore the distinctive insignia of Garvey's Black Cross Nurses. Colorfully robed choirs and children dressed in their Sunday clothes followed. Madison Square Garden overflowed with more than 25,000 people. The crowd sang the new UNIA anthem, "Ethiopia, Thou Land of Our Fathers," and the official colors of the movement became emblematic of black nationalism worldwide: "Red for the blood of the race, nobly shed in the past and dedicated to the future; Black to symbolize pride in the color of its skin; Green for the promise of a new and better life in Africa" (Cronon, 1974, p. 67). At the convention Garvey was named provisional president of the African Republic, whose members pledged to organize the 400 million people of African descent around the world.

Garveyism provided a "common faith" based on the doctrines of African redemption and "race first," which some scholars have interpreted as a surrogate religion, a "civil religion," or a "religion of success" (Burkett, 1978, pp. 1–9; Hill, 1983, pp. xli–1). It certainly possessed all of the characteristics of a religion, and the UNIA often competed with and in some instances was supported by the traditional black Christian churches. While some black clergymen like the Rev. Adam Clayton Powell, Sr., of the Abyssinnian Baptist Church in Harlem were hostile to Garvey's movement, there is evidence that many others, such as Malcolm X's father, worked actively in the UNIA. The Rev. George Alexander McGuire, a West Indian Anglican priest, became chaplain general of the UNIA and founded the African Orthodox Church. But while the African Orthodox Church was closely associated with the UNIA, it never became the movement's official church. Marcus Garvey remained the UNIA's official statesman and its most perceptive theologian. The idea that "God is Black" is partly rooted in Garvey's theology:

> If the white man has the idea of a white God, let him worship his God as he desires. . . . We as Negroes have found a new ideal. Whilst our God has no color, yet it is human to see everything through one's own spectacles, and since white people have seen their God through white spectacles, we have only started out (late though it may be) to see God through our own spectacles. . . . We Negroes believe in the God of Ethiopia, the everlasting God—God the Father, God the Son and God the Holy Ghost, the one God of all ages. That is the God in whom we believe, but we shall worship Him through the spectacles of Ethiopia.
>
> ("Africa and the Negro," *Negro World,* 15, 2 February 1924)

The plans to redeem "Africa for Africans" and to lay the foundations for a black independent economic system of international trade began with the creation of the Black Star Line. From 1919 to 1921 Garvey and his advisers bought several old steamships at exorbitant prices, refitted and renamed them, and sent them into service. The SS *Yarmouth* was renamed the *Frederick Douglass* and the SS *Kanawha* became the SS *Antonio Maceo.* The SS *Shadyside* sank after a short term of service. Although the Black Star Line was a brilliant idea, a tangible means of fulfilling dreams of liberation and reaching Africa, it also marked the beginning of Garvey's problems and his eventual demise. He used the steamships as symbols of prestige, to encourage people to join the UNIA and to sell stock in the company to them. However, the old steamships also became an enormous financial drain on the UNIA's resources, and eventually they involved him in legal difficulties.

BLACK MILITANT AND SEPARATIST MOVEMENTS

In early January 1922 Garvey was arrested on a charge of using the mail to defraud. His difficulties stemmed from his attempt to purchase a fourth ship, the SS *Orion,* renamed the *Phyllis Wheatley.* The sale was held up because a cash flow problem developed within the Black Star Line, and Garvey attempted to raise funds by advertising the sale of stock. Postal authorities charged Garvey and his associates with using "fradulent representation" and "deceptive artifices" in the sale of stock through the mail. In February 1922 Garvey, Elia Garcia, George Tobins, and Orlando H. Thompson were indicted on twelve counts of mail fraud. Garvey dismissed his lawyer and defended himself. Although the evidence against him was meager and weak, his lack of legal experience and his courtroom demeanor resulted in his losing the case. He was fined $1,000 and sentenced to five years in the federal prison at Atlanta.

In 1927 President Calvin Coolidge commuted Garvey's sentence and ordered him released. His felony conviction and the fact that he was not an American citizen led to immediate deportation proceedings against him. In December 1927 Garvey was deported to Jamaica, where he was joyfully received. He continued to organize on behalf of the UNIA and made trips to Europe in this effort.

At the Sixth International Convention of the Negro Peoples of the World held in August 1929 at Kingston, Jamaica, Garvey's attempt to put on a magnificent show of strength unfortunately resulted in a split between himself and the American delegation of the UNIA over the issue of the location of the headquarters. Garvey wanted to move the UNIA headquarters from Harlem to Kingston. Yet New York was his strongest and largest base. The schism foreshadowed the breakup of his organization.

In 1933 Garvey began publishing the *Black Man,* a magazine in which he strongly denounced such black intellectuals as W. E. B. Du Bois, Chandler Owen, A. Philip Randolph, and George Schuyler. He felt they had contributed to his failures in the United States, particularly in the "Garvey Must Go" campaign led by Owen and Randolph in the *Messenger* magazine. As the editor of the *Spokesman,* Du Bois sharply criticized Garvey's movement and lambasted his meeting with a leader of the Ku Klux Klan in 1922 in Atlanta. During the Great Depression, as

black Americans began turning to other leaders and movements, Garvey became highly critical of Father Divine's Peace Mission in Harlem. He and his second wife, Amy Jacques Garvey, moved to London for a brief time. In January 1940 Garvey suffered a severe stroke, and he died in London on 10 June 1940 at the age of 53 and was buried in Kingston, Jamaica.

Although Du Bois had been very critical of Garvey, he also recognized his significance. "Garvey made thousands think," wrote Du Bois in the *Spokesman,* "who had never thought before. Thousands who merely dreamed dreams now see visions."

Marcus Garvey has left an enormous legacy. His ideas of racial pride, individual uplift, and African nationalism influenced all subsequent black mass movements. He was a visionary who kept his feet on the ground. Besides the Black Star Line, he also organized black factories, some of which mass-produced the first black dolls in America. Malcolm X once said, "The entire Black Muslim philosophy here in America is feeding upon the seeds that were planted by Marcus Garvey" (Garvey, 1974, p. 308).

FATHER DIVINE AND THE PEACE MISSION MOVEMENT

Marcus Garvey once prophesied that "a black God is coming. Be ready when he cometh." Father Divine, a charismatic five-foot, two-inch black man, claimed to be God, not only of blacks but of everyone. The exact origins and history of Father Divine prior to 1914 remain obscure. Although there are varying accounts of his date of birth, his followers accept 1882. Most scholars agree that a man named George Baker from somewhere in the Deep South was the "Messenger" from Baltimore who claimed to be God in Harlem.

In 1899 George Baker, a hardworking yard man in Baltimore, Maryland, was attending a "colored" Baptist church and teaching Sunday school. In 1906 he met two men who changed the course of his life, an itinerant Fundamentalist preacher named Samuel Morris and his friend John Hickerson. Morris' literal interpretation of I Corinthians 3:16 became a major religious revelation. He reasoned: "If I am God's temple and God's spirit dwelleth in me; then, I am part of

God and God is part of me; thus, I am God." Morris claimed to be "Father Jehovia," while Baker became "the Messenger" and Hickerson took the title "Reverend St. John Divine Bishop." They preached the message of "God in every man." In 1912 the evangelical trinity split apart, with Baker going to Valdosta, Georgia, where he developed a small but loyal following.

In 1915 Baker arrived in Harlem, the center of black life and culture, and changed his name to Major J. Devine. Under the influence of his old friend Rev. St. John Divine Bishop, pastor of the Church of the Living God in Harlem, he changed the *e* to an *i*—Divine. He also learned about the limitations of the "God in every man" doctrine when he saw Bishop Hickerson's church collapse because of a series of schisms in which several followers formed separate "Temples of God" and in which each dissident claimed to be God. Major Divine would tolerate no competitors to divinity in his celestial heaven.

At Divine's suburban home at 72 Macon Street in Sayville, Long Island, purchased in 1919 under the name of his first wife, Pinninnah, his reputation as a cult leader began. His home also became a major source of controversy. Throughout the 1920s the immaculate Sayville home was the site of numerous worship services during the evenings and Sundays; hearty banquet meals were served free of charge. Divine's following among the black working class of domestic servants and chauffeurs in the affluent Long Island communities grew steadily. In 1926 the first white member joined. The 1929 stock market crash and the Great Depression proved to be a boon for Divine's small Peace Mission movement. As hunger, poverty, and unemployment spread, busloads of people, mainly blacks from Harlem but some whites as well, began arriving to partake of the free meals, fellowship, and worship services. Racial hostility and the fear of declining property values led white neighbors to bring charges against Sayville's "Harlem Colony" for disturbing the peace. Father Divine and eighty followers were arrested on 15 November 1931.

The case of *Sayville* v. *Divine* became a cause célèbre because of the racial overtones and hostilities at the trial. James C. Thomas, assistant district attorney to Gov. Thomas Dewey, offered his services to Divine. Justice Lewis J. Smith, who was known for his outspoken color prejudice and

prejudice against racial mixing, presided over the case. On 25 May 1932 Divine was found guilty of a misdemeanor; he was sentenced by Justice Smith on 5 June 1932 to the maximum punishment of one year in jail and a $500 fine. Three days after Divine's sentencing, the judge, who had been in good health, suddenly died at the age of 56. Smith's death changed the course of Father Divine's career. To his followers, this event was a further proof of Divine's power and divinity. Father Divine is alleged to have remarked, "I hated to do it" (Hoshor, p. 85; Weisbrot, p. 53; Parker, p. 28). The New York State Supreme Court overturned the verdict in January 1933 and Divine was completely vindicated.

After the trial, Father Divine left Sayville and moved his headquarters to 20 West 115th Street in Harlem. Besides his charismatic preaching ability, Divine possessed showmanship and flamboyance, so that his Peace Mission expanded rapidly in urban centers. But he also had a shrewd mind for organizational and financial matters. His disciples lived communally in "heavens," separated by sex; they pooled their economic resources, turning over all income and possessions to him. In return each follower received room, board, clothes, a job, and a small stipend. At the peak of his powers in the 1930s Father Divine's Peace Mission was the largest real estate holder in Harlem. The cooperative economic enterprise system encompassed twenty-five restaurants, six grocery stores, ten barber shops, two dozen vegetable and seafood wagons, a coal business with three trucks, supplied by coal mines in Pennsylvania, a large emporium for meat, fish, fowl, etc., and tailor shops. The mission also owned three apartment houses, nine private houses, and fifteen to twenty flats. The system also extended to the rural areas, especially Ulster County, New York, which was dubbed the "Promised Land," where his followers attempted to practice Divine's "this-worldly religion." Father Divine also acquired twenty-five acres of land near President Franklin Delano Roosevelt's Hyde Park estate, where he put up a large sign with the initials F.D.R., standing for Father Divine's Residence.

The main vehicle for spreading Father Divine's message of inner bliss and interracial harmony was the large banquet meal held twice daily in Peace Mission centers from New York to California. Elaborate, well-prepared meals of over fifty courses became the showpiece and symbol of the movement. Highly ritualized through the passing of plates and integrated seating arrangements, the banquet was part worship service and communion table as well as a bountiful response to physical and social hunger. But above all, it was a symbol and a daily demonstration of Father Divine's power. In the midst of the Depression, he did what neither the federal government nor any other leader could manage to do, namely, feed thousands of people; and there was always food for more. In his sermon of 27 October 1937 he said:

> Because your God would not feed the people, I came and I am feeding them. Because your God kept such as you segregated and discriminated, I came and I am unifying all nations together. That is why I came, because I did not believe in your God.
>
> (*New Day*, 4 November 1937)

The Peace Mission attracted people from all walks of life, black and white, poor and middle class, young and old—a virtual melting pot of the discontented. Women comprised between three-fourths and nine-tenths of the membership, partly due to their inferior status in society and the equal treatment and leadership roles Father Divine gave them. The inner circle closest to him was composed of as many as twenty-five female secretaries, highly skilled and well educated, called "angels." Estimates of membership run from several thousand to over 2 million. However, for the 160 Peace Mission centers, a total of 50,000 is plausible, although Father Divine's influence certainly extended to hundreds of thousands. Politicians like Fiorello La Guardia acknowledged his influence and sought his support. "This city must be cleaned up," said La Guardia to Divine, "and I am willing to clean it up, and I ask for Father Divine's help and counsel, because he knows the spots that have to be cleaned . . ." (Weisbrot, p. 161).

Father Divine remained neutral in political campaigns throughout the Depression; nevertheless, he did become a social reformer par excellence in civil rights matters by filling a vacuum of leadership in the black community. With a firm belief in American political ideals he insisted that "the struggle for justice was the highest religious calling" (Weisbrot, p. 145). The Peace Mission was active in civil rights causes against racial discrimination. It joined the campaign for justice for the famous "Scottsboro Boys" case and provided major support for the NAACP's antilynching campaign. In 1936 the Peace Mission held a Righteous Government Convention, which drew up sweeping economic and social plans.

Besides the belief in Father Divine as God and the requirements of celibacy and communal living, Peace Mission members joined one of four groups: Lily-Buds, composed of older women; Rosebuds, women and girls from early childhood to middle age; Crusaders, men and boys of all ages; and secretaries, an exclusive honor limited to fifteen to twenty-five women and one man, the executive secretary of the Circle Mission Church. (The internal organization of the Peace Mission was originally divided into four mission churches that covered a certain amount of territory; the Circle Mission Church is the only one to survive.) The Peace Mission attempted to foster economic independence through ambition and hard work. It stressed fair play and advised against credit purchases. It emphasized education as a means of social mobility: in 1935 20 percent of the night school enrollees in New York City were Divine's followers. The Peace Mission also attempted to eliminate racial self-hate by emphasizing racial equality, harmony, and integration.

The 1940s saw a decline in the Peace Mission movement. An aging Father Divine could not sustain the energy to maintain a nationwide movement. World War II also brought an economic recovery in America that removed some of the conditions which gave rise to the Peace Mission. After the first Mother Divine, Pinninnah, died in 1937, Father Divine married the second Mother Divine, in 1946, a white blond disciple called "Sweet Angel," the former Edna Rose Ritchings of Canada. In May 1960 he fell into a diabetic coma; he made his last public appearance in 1963. On Friday, 10 September 1965, Father Divine, the "God-in-a-body," died.

The greatly diminished Peace Mission movement continues under the leadership of the second Mother Divine at the Woodmount estate outside Philadelphia. Mother Divine has achieved spiritual elevation and her name is included in daily prayers alongside that of her late husband. The movement has several thousand aging members scattered across the world. It still has some vast real estate holdings, including the shrine at the Sayville home, the Divine Lorraine Hotel in central Philadelphia, and other pieces of property. Because of its belief in celibacy, the Peace Mission is unable to produce a younger generation and will probably suffer the same fate as an earlier celibate American group, the Shakers.

DADDY GRACE AND THE UNITED HOUSE OF PRAYER FOR ALL PEOPLE

> Never mind about God. Salvation is by Grace only. . . . Grace has given God a vacation, and since God is on His vacation, don't worry Him. . . . If you sin against God, Grace can save you, but if you sin against Grace, God cannot save you.
>
> (Fauset, 1944, p. 26)

Of the numerous "black gods of the metropolis" who arose in the Depression, only Sweet Daddy Grace had the potential to rival the influence of Father Divine's Peace Mission movement. Born Marcelino Manoel de Graca to Portuguese and Negro parents on 25 January 1881 in Brava, Cape Verde Islands, Bishop Charles Emmanuel Grace migrated to New Bedford, Massachusetts, around 1900. He worked as a short-order cook on trains and as a salesman and grocer before he developed a religious following in the early 1920s. Like many others in a strict color-caste society, Bishop Grace tried to "pass" as white and denied his Negro heritage. Throughout his life he had a "patronizing" attitude toward the Negroes who made up the vast majority of his following.

After returning from a trip to the Holy Land in 1921, Grace established the first missions of the United House of Prayer for All People in Wareham and New Bedford, Massachusetts. Within two years, his cult following had spread all along the Atlantic seaboard from New Bedford to Charlotte, North Carolina, and Norfolk, Virginia. He did not assume the title Sweet Daddy Grace until after the rapid growth of his movement had catapulted him to national prominence. Bishop Grace was a master of the most dramatic and flamboyant techniques used to capture the attention of the media and to build a solid following. With his shoulder-length hair, three-inch-long fingernails painted red, white, and blue, and flashy jewelry and clothes, he lived in an ostentatious and opulent manner that was applauded by his followers. He had an eighty-four-room mansion in Los Angeles, a twenty-two-acre estate in Havana, and numerous other houses. He understood well the mass psychology of the poor, knowing that by living in such manner he provided a vicarious satisfaction for their needs. His followers could not enjoy the fruits of wealth in their daily lives, but at least their leader would.

Sweet Daddy Grace was the undisputed head of the United House of Prayer for All People. In major meetings he sat on a thronelike chair on an elevated platform that was gaudily decorated with flashing colored lights. His throne symbolized his power, and there were few challengers to his position, for he did not accept any preachers or understudies into the United House of Prayer who were likely to challenge his style or question his authority. The priorities of his preachers were to collect money, conduct services, and preach. There was a strong emphasis on collecting money, and the chief function of the various clubs in the organization was to raise money for Bishop Grace. There was, for example, a ritual of "money musical chairs," where the faithful were kept circling a room while a band played, dropping money into collection plates in the front of the sanctuary. When their money supply was exhausted, the "spent" worshipers sat down in turn until a winner finally emerged. Bishop Grace's ministers were allowed to keep one night's offering each week.

The religious background of most of Grace's followers was the Holiness-Pentecostal movement, which emerged in the rural South during the late nineteenth century. These followers were often referred to in the black community as the "sanctified." Many of the converts to the United House of Prayer were able to keep their Holiness beliefs and practices—such as belief in conversion, sanctification, and intervention of the Holy Spirit. Being born again was not enough; a holy, methodical, and righteous life as well as the second baptism of the Spirit were requisites. Speaking in tongues and being possessed by the Spirit in acts of "falling out" were evidences of the second baptism, which were common occurrences in the United House of

Prayer's ecstatic and enthusiastic worship services. Followers could not smoke, drink, dance, or attend movies, ball games, or other public entertainments.

The major difference between the Holiness movement and the United House of Prayer was the belief that, in Daddy Grace, God's Spirit was made manifest. And, unlike Father Divine, Daddy Grace never claimed to be God. However, the supernatural powers of healing attributed to him and the constant invocation of his name in worship services and prayers made the boundary line between the human and the divine quite thin. As one follower said, "There isn't any leader except Grace. There isn't any religion except through Grace. Grace can heal you. When he puts the *Grace Magazine* on your chest, it is the healing power of the Spirit" (Fauset, 1944, pp. 22–23).

Daddy Grace rivaled Father Divine's ability to capture the attention of the news media through flamboyant practices like "fire hose baptisms" in public, where hundreds of neophytes in the faith —dressed in bathing suits—were baptized with a hose borrowed from the local firehouse. Like Divine, Daddy Grace was an entrepreneur, but on a smaller scale. Products such as soap, writing paper, toothpaste, hair pomade and other toiletries, a magazine, and even cookies all bore the name Daddy Grace and were sold in the canteen at each house of prayer. He also headed a home buying association, an insurance company, and a burial society.

At one point in their rivalry for the allegiance of the black masses in Harlem, Daddy Grace could even brag of putting Father Divine out of his "Heaven" in the early 1930s. After moving from Sayville, Long Island, Divine opened his Harlem headquarters in a building that had been a rented home of one of his followers. Daddy Grace made inquiries about his new rival's place and found out that he could purchase the building, which he did immediately. As the new landlord, Daddy Grace was willing to let Father Divine stay; however, the embarrassment and humiliation of paying rent to a competitor forced Divine to seek a new headquarters. It also taught Divine the value of always purchasing a property before occupying it.

Daddy Grace's tax problems with the Internal Revenue Service and a variety of other legal entanglements concerning his marital life forced him to leave the country for a period of time in the mid-1930s, thus cutting short his rivalry with Father Divine. Partly because of the absence of his charismatic presence, his following never achieved the scope and range of Father Divine's Peace Mission movement. As a result of a heart condition, "Sweet, Sweet Daddy Grace," as he was often called, died in Los Angeles, California, on 12 January 1960. Grace's major contribution was that of a charismatic religious leader who attempted to provide a measure of spiritual relief and solace for the downtrodden masses in enthusiastic worship services. He was not a social reformer or activist in the mold of Marcus Garvey, or Father Divine, or the Honorable Elijah Muhammad. Rather he was content to live above the din in the comfortable style of a cult leader whose opulent life-style symbolized the fantasies and the aspirations of the dispossessed.

Upon Daddy Grace's death, Bishop Walter McCullough, a quiet, uncharismatic, but shrewd associate of Grace's who once owned a tailor and dry cleaning shop in Washington, D.C., survived several legal and political challenges to take over the group in 1962. As a result of his manuevering and longevity, Bishop McCullough is now included in the religious world view of the United House of Prayer. Though Daddy Grace and Bishop McCullough, now called Sweet Daddy Grace McCullough, are considered to be religiously equal, McCullough is Grace's "Son." Both Grace and McCullough are considered to be God's messengers, the "only prophets on earth since Jesus" (Robinson, p. 230).

A man of astute organizational and business acumen, Bishop McCullough has provided stability to the movement by building new houses of prayer and rebuilding its economic base through real estate investments. He also built "God's White House" in Washington, D.C., as the main headquarters, and established a ministerial training school in Richmond, Virginia, in 1967. More significantly, Bishop McCullough has been able to change the United House of Prayer for All People from a "man-worshiping cult" to a Holiness sect with a powerful administrator (Robinson, p. 234). Bishop McCullough's followers continue to be uneducated, lower-class blacks, mostly women, who are attracted to the holiness-sanctified worship services, and who find their chief identity in being a part of the family of Sweet Daddy Grace McCullough.

THE HONORABLE ELIJAH MUHAMMAD, MALCOLM X, AND THE NATION OF ISLAM

The cities of Detroit and Chicago were beacons to the waves of black migrants from the rural South. These cities also provided the background for the development of one of the most militant and separatist black religious movements in America, the Nation of Islam. Sometime in the midsummer of 1930, an amiable but faintly mysterious peddler suddenly appeared in a black ghetto of Detroit called Paradise Valley. At first he came to sell raincoats and silks and other sundries attractive to the residents of the area, but later he began giving advice about the people's health and spiritual development. He also began teaching them about their "true religion"—not Christianity, but the "religion of the Black Men" of Asia and Africa; he used both the Bible and the Qur'an for reference. His gatherings, first held in the homes of his followers, soon overflowed these private facilities and a hall was rented and christened the Temple of Islam. This mysterious stranger who referred to himself as Mr. Farrad Mohammed, or sometimes as Mr. Walli Farrad or W. D. Fard, came to be recognized in 1931 as "the Great Mahdi," or "Saviour," who had come to bring a special message to the suffering blacks in the teeming ghettoes of America.

Master Fard taught his followers about the deceptive character and temporary domination of "blue-eyed devils," or white overlords. He also stressed the importance of attaining "knowledge of self" as a prerequisite for achieving black liberation. He instructed his followers that they were not Americans and therefore owed no allegiance to the American flag. Several hundred years of slavery followed by continued racial discrimination and economic deprivation in America gave a powerful emotional resonance to Fard's message. He wrote two manuals for the movement, *The Secret Ritual of the Nation of Islam,* which is transmitted orally to members, and *Teaching for the Lost-Found Nation of Islam in a Mathematical Way,* which is written in symbolic language and requires special interpretation. Within three years Fard had founded an effective organization with a temple that had its own worship style and rituals and a "University of Islam" with a special curriculum made up largely of Fard's teaching. The "university" was essentially a combined elementary and secondary school, but for his followers, it was the first step toward cultural and psychological freedom. He also established the Muslim Girls' Training Class to teach young women the principles of home economics and their proper role in the Nation of Islam, or Black Muslims. Finally, he created the Fruit of Islam, a quasi-military organization of male Muslims who served as honor guards, ushers, and enforcers of internal discipline within the temples, as well as security agents for the minister of Islam and other leaders.

One of the earliest officers of the movement and Fard's most trusted lieutenant was Elijah Poole, who was given the Muslim name Elijah Muhammad. Born on 10 October 1897, Poole was the son of a rural Baptist minister and sharecropper from Sandersville, Georgia. He and his family migrated to Detroit in 1923 and he and several of his brothers joined the Nation of Islam in 1931. Despite his third-grade education, Elijah Muhammad's shrewd native intelligence enabled him to rise rapidly through the ranks, and he was chosen by Fard to be the chief minister of Islam, to preside over the organization. Elijah Muhammad was almost single-handedly responsible for Master Fard's deification as "God in person," and for the perpetuation of his teachings after Fard disappeared mysteriously in 1934.

Although there were varied stories and conjectures about Fard's disappearance, some claiming that he "returned to the Holy City of Mecca" or that he was murdered by dissidents in the movement, there is no extant evidence to support any of them. However, after Fard's disappearance there was a severe eruption involving several contending factions of the Nation, one of which was led by Elijah Muhammad. Muhammad and his closest followers had to flee Detroit amid threats of death; they settled on the south side of Chicago, where they established Temple No. 2 in 1936. In the late 1930s and 1940s, Muhammad reshaped the Nation of Islam and gave it his own imprimatur. He also provided an answer to Marcus Garvey's prophecy about the coming of a black God. According to Muhammad's teachings, Master Fard became identified with Allah, and he was worshiped with sacrifices and prayer. Muhammad himself assumed the mantle of the departed leader under the title Messenger of Allah.

Under Muhammad's guidance, the Nation began to grow, slowly at first but steadily. He saw the need to develop a two-pronged attack on the problems of the black masses: a stress on the development of economic independence and an emphasis upon the recovery of an acceptable black identity. "Do for Self" was the rallying cry to develop economic self-reliance for black individuals and for the black community. The economic ethic of the Black Muslims has been described as a kind of "Black Puritanism"—hard work, frugality, the avoidance of debt, self-improvement, and a conservative life-style. This formula soon made the Black Muslims conspicuously different from most of their fellows in the same socioeconomic class in the black ghetto. During the forty-one-year period of his leadership, Muhammad and his followers established more than one hundred temples, innumerable grocery stores, restaurants, bakeries, and other small businesses. The Nation itself owned farms in several states, a bank, trailer trucks for its fish and grocery businesses, an ultramodern printing press, and other assets. Muhammad's ministers of Islam found the prisons and streets of the ghetto a fertile recruiting ground. His message of self-reclamation and black manifest destiny struck a responsive chord in the thousands of black men and women whose hope and self-respect had been all but defeated by racial abuse and denigration. As a consequence of where they recruited and the militancy of their beliefs, the Black Muslim movement has attracted many more young black males than any of the other black movements.

Muhammad's uncanny sense of the vulnerabilities of the black psyche during the social transitions brought on by two world wars, and the attendant stresses and their aftermath, enabled him to fashion his *Message to the Black Man*, which diagnosed the problem as a confusion of identity and self-hatred caused by white racism; the cure he prescribed was radical surgery, through the formation of a separate black nation. Muhammad's 120 "degrees," or lessons, and the major doctrines and beliefs of the Nation of Islam all elaborated on aspects of this central message. The white man is a "devil by nature," absolutely unredeemable and incapable of caring about or respecting anyone who is not white. He is the historic, persistent source of harm and injury to black people. The Nation of Islam's central theological myth tells of Yakub, a black mad scientist who rebelled against Allah by creating the white race, a weak hybrid people who were permitted temporary dominance of the world. Whites achieved their power and position through devious means and "tricknology." But, according to the Black Muslim apocalyptic view, there will come a time in the not too distant future when the forces of good and the forces of evil—that is to say, blacks versus whites—will clash in a "Battle of Armageddon," and the blacks will emerge victorious to re-create their original hegemony under Allah throughout the world.

All of these myths and doctrines have functioned as a theodicy for the Black Muslims, as an explanation and rationalization for the pain and suffering inflicted upon black people in America. For example, Malcolm Little (later Malcolm X) described the powerful, jarring impact that the revelation of religious truth had upon him in a Massachusetts state prison when his cellmate whispered to him, "The white man is the Devil." It all began to make sense: the chaos of the world behind prison bars became a cosmos, an ordered reality. The doctrine explained his father's early death in Omaha, Nebraska, at the hands of whites and the extreme poverty endured by his widow and nine children. It gave him a reason for his mother's being taken away to an insane asylum, it rationalized his dropping out of school in the eighth grade, and it made sense of all the years of hustling and pimping on the streets of Roxbury and Harlem as Detroit Red. The conversion and total transformation of Malcolm Little into Malcolm X in prison is a story of the effectiveness of Elijah Muhammad's message, which has been repeated many thousands of times over during the forty-one-year history of the Nation of Islam under Muhammad's leadership. Dropping one's surname and taking on an X, standard practice in the movement, was an outward symbol of inward changes: it meant ex-Christian; ex-Negro; ex-slave. It also signified that the new convert to Islam was "undetermined," no longer the predictable "Negro" created by the white man.

Malcolm Little was born in Omaha on 19 May 1925. After dropping out of school and moving from Lansing, Michigan, to Boston in 1940 to live with his oldest sister, Ella, Malcolm gradually became involved in criminal activities and ran afoul of the law. In 1946 he was arrested and sentenced to a ten-year term for burglary, but he was paroled for good behavior after six years. In 1947, through the influence of his brother Wilfred in Detroit, Malcolm joined the Nation of Islam and began the process of rehabilitating and educating himself in prison by writing and memorizing words from a dictionary. By the end of his prison term, he had read every book in the prison library.

The years between Malcolm X's release from prison and his assassination, 1952–1965, mark the period of the greatest growth and influence of the Nation of Islam. Minister Malcolm X was a man of enormous physical and intellectual energy. After meeting Elijah Muhammad in 1952, he began organizing Muslim temples in Philadelphia, New York, and Boston in the Northeast, in the South, and on the West Coast as well. Malcolm also founded the Nation's newspaper, *Muhammad Speaks,* in the basement of his home; he initiated the practice of requiring every male Muslim to sell an assigned quota of newspapers on the street as a recruiting and fund-raising device. He preached on street corners in Harlem and often participated in "fishing" for lost souls in the bars and cafes and even in front of Christian churches as their Sunday services let out. He rose rapidly through the ranks to become minister of Boston Temple No. 11 and was later rewarded with the post of minister of Temple No. 7 in Harlem, the largest and most prestigious temple in the Nation of Islam after the Chicago headquarters. The Honorable Elijah Muhammad recognized his organizational talents and his enormous charismatic appeal and forensic abilities by naming Malcolm his national representative of the Nation of Islam, second in rank to the Messenger himself. In 1960 Malcolm was also commissioned to represent the Nation abroad in Islamic countries and in the Holy City of Mecca. Under his lieutenancy the Nation of Islam achieved a membership estimated to have ranged from 50,000 to 500,000. But like the other movements of this kind, the numbers involved were quite fluid and the influence of the Nation of Islam refracted through the charisma of Malcolm X greatly exceeded its actual membership.

Malcolm's keen intellect, incisive wit, and ardent radicalism made him a formidable critic of American society, including the civil rights movement. A popular speaker on college campuses and a favorite media personality, his twelve years as a minister in the Nation of Islam overlapped the decisive years of the civil rights leadership of Dr. Martin Luther King, Jr. Malcolm challenged King's central notions of "integration" and the effectiveness and dignity of the nonviolent Christian ethic upon which it depended. More than anyone else, Malcolm predicted that even if King's movement succeeded, the black subculture and its vital contributions to the American experience would be submerged in a sea of whiteness, leaving blacks with no history and no identity. What was at stake at a deeper level than the civil right to sit in a restaurant or even to vote was the integrity of black selfhood and its independence. Malcolm's biting critique of the "so-called Negro" and his emphasis upon the recovery of black self-identity and independence provided the intellectual foundations for the "Black Power" movement initiated by Stokely Carmichael in 1966 and for the black consciousness movement that emerged in the late 1960s and 1970s in American society.

Malcolm's alternative to King's nonviolent stance was clearly enunciated in the time-honored right to self-defense he found in the prevailing Hebraic, Islamic, and American social and political credos. While Malcolm and the Black Muslims never advocated a violent revolution or overthrow of the American government, members were instructed to defend themselves, their families, and their homes "by any means possible." Malcolm constantly reminded his audiences that the American Constitution guarantees all citizens the "right to bear arms." Elijah Muhammad forbade any of his followers to carry arms of any type in an effort to forestall harassment by the police, but in spite of this public renouncement of weapons, in the context of the nonviolent civil rights struggle the Black Muslims were perceived as violent and potentially disruptive. In consequence, the nonviolent civil rights movement derived some public and political leverage that might not have been available to it otherwise. The federal establishment and the American public clearly preferred the tactics of Martin Luther King to those Malcolm X was suspected of deploying. "Never be the aggressor! Never look for trouble," he admonished his followers. "But if any man comes to take advantage of you, lay down your life, and the whole planet Earth will respect you!" (Lincoln, p. 5). Malcolm's very presence and his uncompromising militancy were frightening to the American public. It is possible that he made an enormous contribution to Americans in helping them to come face to face with the consequences of racial paranoia. He articulated the pent-up anger, the frustration, the bitterness, and the rage felt by the dispossessed black masses, the "grass roots." And perhaps more clearly than other leaders of his time, he foresaw the violent consequences of the repressed anger and bitterness that exploded in large-scale urban rebellions in Harlem, Watts, Newark, and Detroit after his death.

From the beginning the Nation of Islam was opposed to America's participation in foreign wars—first because Islam was held to be a religion of peace, but more pointedly because blacks were being required to fight and die for values they could not enjoy in America. The Black Muslims were instructed not to join the military and to refuse the draft to underscore their separatism from American society. Elijah Muhammad and some of his sons spent time in prison for refusing the draft during World War II and the Korean War. Four years before Dr. King's public stand against the Vietnam War in 1967, Malcolm X had voiced his criticisms. Perhaps the most persuasive argument against blacks participating in the American military involvement overseas was made by Muhammad Ali, the heavyweight boxing champion, who had been converted to Islam by Malcolm X in 1964. In refusing to be drafted for the war in Vietnam in 1967, and facing the penalty of being stripped of his crown at the peak of his career and a possible prison sentence, Ali reminded America that "no Vietnamese ever called me a Nigger."

In December 1963 Elijah Muhammad imposed a penalty of silence on Malcolm X for three months, ostensibly as punishment for some thoughtless remarks Malcolm made regarding the assassination of President John F. Kennedy. The order for silence, however, was escalated into a deeper internal dispute among the Muslims, and in March 1964 Malcolm broke with the Nation of Islam and left the movement. Minister Louis X of Boston, also called Louis Farrakhan, took Malcolm's place as national representative and as minister of Temple No. 7 in Harlem.

During the last year of his life, while estranged from the Nation of Islam and under considerable personal strain, Malcolm traveled to Africa and Asia to internationalize the struggle against racism and to decide on an independent course of action at home. After studying orthodox Islam, he made the traditional pilgrimage, or *hajj*, to Mecca, embracing Sunni Islam in the process. Impressed by the unity of all the different races he saw in orthodox Islam, Malcolm became convinced that true Islam could be the solution to the problem of racism in America and in the world. He said:

> We were all the same (brothers)—because their belief in one God had removed the "white" from their minds, the "white" from their behavior, and the "white" from their attitude.
> (Malcolm X and Haley, p. 349)

As el-Hajj Malik el-Shabazz, the Malcolm from the tribe of Shabazz who made the pilgrimage, his new turn was prophetic for the future direction of the Nation of Islam. He was assassinated on 21 February 1965, while delivering a lecture at the Audubon Ballroom in Harlem. Three men were arrested and convicted: Talmadge Hayer, Norman Butler, and Thomas Johnson. Only Hayer has confessed his involvement; he claims that the other two are innocent.

Malcolm's assassination created a controversy that has remained unresolved. There are three basic positions: the Muslims did it upon orders from someone in the hierarchy of the Nation of Islam; it was a conspiracy by the FBI and the New York City Police Department to get rid of Malcolm by taking advantage of an internal Muslim feud; or a combination of the two. It is now known that Muslims have been killed by other Muslims in internal disputes (e.g., the murder of seven members of Hamaas Abdul Khaalis' family in January 1973 in Washington, D.C.); that Gene Roberts, one of Malcolm X's bodyguards onstage at the Audubon Ballroom, was an undercover agent with the Bureau of Special Services (BOSS) of the police department; that someone suddenly called off the police security detail stationed in front of the ballroom before Malcolm's speech; and that no one in the audience was searched for weapons, which was the usual Muslim procedure before an event.

Elijah Muhammad and the Muslim hierarchy denied any involvement in the assassination; yet the Nation of Islam lost some of its members and others stayed away because of a general confusion about who was responsible for killing the popular leader. In the ensuing years, Malcolm has achieved the stature of a martyr in the black community, "our own black shining prince," as the actor Ossie Davis remarked in his funeral oration. Armed with the teachings of the Honorable Elijah Muhammad and his own biting wit, Malcolm was viewed by many as single-handedly responsible for the replacement of "slave terms" like *Negro* and *colored* with *black*. The change in vocabulary in American society was symbolic of deep, internal changes occurring among black people.

The black power and black consciousness movements of the late 1960s and early 1970s sought to reaffirm pride in black history, culture, institutions, and skin. The previous tendencies to assimilate and to blend quietly into the background of American institutions were eschewed as black people on college campuses and in churches, businesses, labor unions, and other social organizations began to form separate caucuses and consciousness-raising groups so they could assert their own agenda. Other more radical political groups like the Black Panthers made their own inferior status into a badge of revolutionary pride as they pressed their demands with rifles in their hands. The bravado of the Panthers was made more frightening and realistic as large-scale urban riots made American cities resemble the bomb-scarred cities of Vietnam. The Vietnam War itself tore at the fabric of American society by alienating large segments of American youth. President Lyndon Johnson's policy of promising "guns and butter" led to a final scuttling of his War on Poverty programs as the cost of the real war increased. American women, mostly white women at first, were radicalized by these events and began to copy the black consciousness movement by forming separate groups to press their own agenda. Just as the abolitionist movement of the nineteenth century gave rise to the women's suffrage movement,

the civil rights and black consciousness movements were midwives for the present feminist movement.

Although the atmosphere of black pride was helpful to the Nation of Islam, the movement tended to become more conservative. Prior to Malcolm's death, Elijah Muhammad began to enjoy the respectable status he was achieving. He felt that Muslims should tone down their militancy and stop calling whites "blue-eyed devils" in public. This conservative tendency contributed to the split between Elijah and Malcolm because Malcolm desired more political participation on the part of Muslims and more radical politics. Malcolm's independent spirit could not be reconciled with Elijah's demand for submission and obedience on the part of all Muslims.

After Malcolm's death, the Nation of Islam enjoyed a period of prosperity, although its membership never surged again. It began to establish farms in Georgia and Alabama in order to produce its own food and create an internal economy. It purchased its own bank and had plans to establish its own university. Minister Louis Farrakhan continued as national representative, and heavyweight champion Muhammad Ali was brought prominently into Muslim events in an effort to replace Malcolm as a showcase figure. But Ali never exerted any strong leadership role, although he had value for the movement as an international celebrity.

In February 1975 the Honorable Elijah Muhammad died, having established an empire worth close to $80 million. One of his six sons, Wallace Deen Muhammad (later Imam Warith Deen Muhammad), was named to succeed him as supreme minister of the Nation of Islam. Two months after his father's death, Wallace shocked his Black Muslim followers and the world by declaring that whites were no longer viewed as devils and that they could join the movement. With that public announcement he began to make radical changes within the organization, disbanding the Fruit of Islam, eliminating racist and separatist teachings, and reinterpreting other doctrines for consistency with orthodox Islam. The rigid disciplinary rules and dress codes instituted by Elijah Muhammad were discontinued, and the Nation was steadily nudged in the direction of orthodox Sunni Islam. These internal changes were reflected externally by changes in the name of the organization from the

Nation of Islam to the World Community of Al-Islam in the West in 1976 and then to the American Muslim Mission in 1980. With a following estimated at 100,000, Imam Warith Deen Muhammad has been accepted by the World Muslim Council and given the responsibility of certifying Americans who make the pilgrimage to Mecca. From its headquarters in Chicago, the American Muslim Mission publishes the *American Muslim Mission Journal,* its official newspaper.

The enormous psychological transformation and changes in religious world view demanded by Imam Warith Deen Muhammad's turn caused an important schism in the Muslim movement. Louis Farrakhan, the former Louis Walcott of Boston and the last national representative appointed by Elijah Muhammad, led a schismatic group in 1978 that succeeded in resurrecting the old Nation of Islam. Farrakhan's Nation, whose base is also in Chicago, retains the black nationalist and separatist beliefs and doctrines that were central to the teachings of Elijah Muhammad. Minister Farrakhan displays much of the charisma and forensic candor of Malcolm X, who was his mentor, and his message of black nationalism is again directed to those blacks mired in the underclass as well as to disillusioned intellectuals. His following is estimated at about 20,000 members, but as with Elijah Muhammad, his influence far exceeds official membership.

The Nation of Islam in its various forms is the longest-lasting and most enduring of the black militant and separatist movements in America. Besides its crucial role in the development of the black consciousness movement, the Nation is important for having reintroduced Islam as a fourth major alternative religious tradition in American society, alongside Protestantism, Catholicism, and Judaism. During the period of slavery, African Muslims constituted up to 20 percent of the slaves on some American plantations. Through the work of the American Muslim Mission, Islam has reemerged as the dominant religious alternative to Christianity in black communities.

Black militant/separatist movements in the United States reflect the persistent difficulties our society has had in adjusting to the realities of our racial and economic insensitivities. Thirty-four million black Americans are still trying to find a more comfortable place in their native land, a place they feel to be consistent with the expectations other Americans take for granted.

The enduring search for respect and respectability, for acceptance and acceptability takes many forms, and the fallout of the effort is not always predictable. But in the long run America is chastened or at least made aware of its dereliction. Black militance in some form will continue to characterize and inform American life as long as the causes from which it derives continue to be prominent in our conventional way of doing things. In the meantime, a prodigious amount of energy and genius will be expended on causes, programs, and ideologies America has sponsored by default.

BIBLIOGRAPHY

Pre–Twentieth Century Militant and Separatist Movements

Gayraud S. Wilmore, *Black Religion and Black Radicalism* (1972; rev. 1983).

Noble Drew Ali and the Moorish Temple of Science

Arthur Fauset, *Black Gods of the Metropolis* (1944; repr. 1971) and "Moorish Science Temple of America," in *Religion, Society, and the Individual,* J. Milton Yinger, ed. (1957); C. Eric Lincoln, *The Black Muslims in America* (1961; rev. 1973).

Marcus Garvey and the UNIA

Randall K. Burkett, *Garveyism as a Religious Movement* (1978) and *Black Redemption: Churchmen Speak for the Garvey Movement* (1978); E. David Cronon, *Black Moses* (1955; rev. 1974); Amy Jacques Garvey, *Garvey and Garveyism* (1963; rev. 1974); Robert A. Hill, ed., *The Marcus Garvey and the Universal Negro Improvement Association Papers,* 3 vols. (1983–1984); Tony Martin, *Race First* (1976).

Father Divine and the Peace Mission Movement

Kenneth E. Burnham, "The Father Divine Peace Mission," in *Black Apostles,* Randall K. Burkett and Richard Newman, eds. (1978), and *God Comes to America* (1979); Sara Harris, *Father Divine* (1953; rev. 1971); John Hoshor, *God in a Rolls-Royce* (1936); C. Eric Lincoln and Lawrence H. Mamiya, "Daddy Jones and Father Divine: The Cult as Political Religion," in *Religion in Life,* XLIX, 1 (Spring 1980); *New Day* (1936–); Robert Allerton Parker, *The Incredible Messiah* (1937); *Spoken Word* (1934–1937); Robert Weisbrot, *Father Divine and the Struggle for Racial Equality* (1983).

Daddy Grace and the United House of Prayer

Afro-American, 6 (27 August 1916); Phillip Casey, series of seven articles in the Washington *Post* (6–11, 13 March 1960): "The Enigma of Daddy Grace: Did He Play God?" "Whatever He Did Was Automatically Right," "Many Setbacks Failed to Deter Daddy Grace," "Parables Served Daddy to Evade Direct Replies," "Friends Say Daddy Didn't Need

Money, He Had Everything," "Daddy's Money Grew on Trees (Manmade)," "Daddy's Outstanding Miracle: Hold on, Flock"; John W. Robinson, "A Song, a Shout, and a Prayer," in *The Black Experience in Religion*, C. Eric Lincoln, ed. (1974); Rufus Walls, "The Secret of Daddy Grace," in *Afro-American*, 5 (5 March 1960); Louise Wilkerson, "Testimonial," *Grace Magazine* (5 August 1967).

Elijah Muhammad, Malcolm X, and the Nation of Islam

George Breitman, ed., *Malcolm X Speaks* (1965) and, with Herman Porter and Baxter Smith, *The Assassination of Malcolm X* (1976); E. U. Essien-Udom, *Black Nationalism: A Search for an Identity in America* (1962); Louis Farrakhan, *Seven Speeches* (1974); Peter Goldman, *The Death and Life of Malcolm X* (1973; rev. 1979); C. Eric Lincoln, "The Black Muslims and Black Acceptance," in *The Black Experience in Religion*, C. Eric Lincoln, ed. (1974), and "The American Muslim Mission in the Context of American Social History," in *The Muslim Community in North America*, Earle H. Waugh et al., eds. (1983); Louis E. Lomax, *When the Word Is Given* (1963); Malcolm X and Alex Haley, *The Autobiography of Malcolm X* (1965); Lawrence H. Mamiya, "From Black Muslim to Bilalian: The Evolution of a Movement," in *Journal for the Scientific Study of Religion*, 21, 2 (June 1982), and "Minister Louis Farrakhan and the Final Call: Schism in the Muslim Movement," in *The Muslim Community in North America*, Waugh et al., eds. (1983); Elijah Muhammad, *Message to the Black Man in America* (1965); Wallace Deen Muhammad, *As the Light Shineth From the East* (1980).

[See also AFRICAN HERITAGE IN CARIBBEAN AND NORTH AMERICAN RELIGIONS; BLACK CHRISTIANITY IN NORTH AMERICA; BLACK RELIGIOUS THOUGHT; and ISLAM IN NORTH AMERICA.]

Part V
MOVEMENTS IN AMERICAN RELIGION

THE GREAT AWAKENING

Stephen A. Marini

T HE Great Awakening was America's first mass religious revival, an intercolonial, interdenominational, multiethnic movement of popular piety, especially among the Calvinist churches, during the second quarter of the eighteenth century. The Awakening was sparked by ministers and itinerant preachers who proclaimed "the necessity of the New Birth"—the doctrine that saving grace came to sinful human beings through a conscious and emotional experience of spiritual transformation. The itinerants' charismatic preaching drew crowds of unprecedented size in colonial America. Their labors bore fruit in abundant and dramatic conversions, especially among women and youth, and rekindled zeal among the faithful. Advocates of the revival claimed it was a special "dispensation" of divine grace for the renewal of true religion, and an eschatological sign of the Second Coming of Christ. They variously interpreted it as the restoration of the apostolic church or the beginning of the millennium, the one-thousand-year reign of the saints, both described in the New Testament Book of Revelation. Opposers of the revival criticized it for reckless innovation, betrayal of tradition, and "enthusiasm," a religious kind of madness.

In most colonial American churches, supporters of the revival pressed for reform. They demanded born-again ministers. They insisted upon stringent membership requirements, admitting only the reborn and requiring them to "separate" or "come out" from worldly society and to "gather" together into intense religious communities modeled on the New Testament. These demands soon divided clergy, congregations, and whole ecclesiastical bodies into rival parties. Prorevival Evangelicals arrayed themselves against a mixed group of Enlightenment liberals and traditional conservatives. Conflict escalated to schism, realigning America's Calvinist denominations and polarizing their theological discourse. The Great Awakening may be defined as this wave of charismatic preaching, widespread conversions, popular religious excitement, schismatic conflict, and theological disputation that gained momentum through the 1720s and 1730s, crested around 1740, and continued through the subsequent decade.

The Awakening also produced consequences of greatest significance in the shaping of American religion. It created a new religious style, revivalism, that became a permanent, powerful, and distinctive feature of American religion. It launched the interdenominational Evangelical movement, whose churches have continued to dominate American Protestantism numerically and geographically ever since. It determined the agenda for a century of American Protestant theology. The Awakening also altered basic institutions of colonial society, families and governments as well as churches. It gave rise to new understandings of self and society and produced conflicts that contributed substantially to the American Revolution; and it inspired a vast indigenous literature of sermons, journals, theological treatises, polemics, pamphlets, tracts, hymns, sacred poetry, spiritual autobiographies, and devotional writing.

All this can justify the larger claim that the Great Awakening was the formative religious episode of the eighteenth century and a lasting influence on subsequent American Protestant history. Most scholars would grant this level of significance to the Awakening, yet the revival has been a source of constant debate since it occurred and it has generated a rich and important interpretive bibliography. There is at present no scholarly agreement, however, on the nature, causes, and consequences of the Awakening, and some interpreters have raised statistical and literary questions about its very existence. In such a hermeneutic situation comprehensiveness is the best approach and it is the one undertaken here.

COLONIAL RELIGIONS IN 1720

The Great Awakening was a complex cultural event, the most extensive popular movement of any kind in America before the Revolution. Many conditions contributed to its outbreak and course of development. The first of these was the conservative sociocultural function of colonial American religions in the early eighteenth century. British North America was a collection of provincial societies, most of which formally observed one religion, and even where no religion was legally established, the church of the original settlers was culturally dominant. The vast majority of Americans lived under the hegemony of a single religion. These churches were aligned, not surprisingly, with the most wealthy and powerful elements of the colony, who patronized them economically and politically. In return the clergy supported or "legitimated" the elite's status and prestige by teaching the divine design and moral virtue of the colonial social order. By 1720 religion's role in the American colonies had become primarily social, providing a hierarchic sacred world that symbolically legitimated provincial elites and morally prescribed the people's deference to them according to St. Paul's maxim, "The powers that be are ordained by God."

In the South, the legally mandated Church of England was intimately allied with the planter elite. But the southern colonies remained an Anglican mission throughout the colonial period, governed by a commissary appointed by the bishop of London rather than an indigenous bishop. Exploiting this ecclesiastical weakness, the Virginia House of Burgesses enacted a Vestry Law in 1643—later imitated throughout the colonies—that established a council of lay overseers for each parish empowered to manage its property and select its clergy. Planter families dominated these self-perpetuating vestries and through them effectively controlled the church's public teaching and moral discipline.

In New England, Congregationalism—the Puritan religion of Massachusetts, Connecticut, and New Hampshire—played a similar role in sustaining traditional authority and mores. In these Puritan commonwealths each town supported a settled minister at public expense and the state was charged with public enforcement of the moral law. The parish minister occupied an honored place in local society, governing and teaching in the church while arbitrating and embodying public morality. University-trained, salaried, and subsidized, ministers comprised a powerful professional class, connected by birth to New England's first families and by office to its political order.

Congregational churches originally were composed of "visible saints," persons elected to membership upon public profession of faith and evidence of sanctified life. These members signed a written covenant pledging obedience to ecclesiastical teaching and discipline. By the mid-seventeenth century, however, few parishioners were willing to submit themselves to the rigors of public testimony and visible sainthood. Yet they wanted to affirm their adherence to Puritan tradition and to have their infant children baptized. In 1662 a synod at Boston approved the "Halfway Covenant," under which baptized adults could obtain membership, though not a vote in parish decisions, without giving testimony and evidence of their regeneration, so long as they agreed to obey the moral teaching and discipline of the church and its ministers. In return their infant children became eligible for baptism. By 1720 the majority of Congregationalists were Halfway members, bound to the church by familial and behavioral ties rather than spiritual experience, while the clergy still maintained their powerful place in New England's deferential society.

Analogous trends appeared among the early religions of the Middle Colonies. The settlers of New Netherland were primarily members of the Dutch Reformed church, a Calvinist communion even more doctrinally strict than Puritanism. The Dutch colony speedily developed into a society dominated by patroons, wealthy landowners whose large estates formed its economic backbone. Religious life was governed directly by the Classis of Amsterdam—the most important synod of ministers in the Netherlands—and Dutch Reformed ministers imparted Old World orthodoxy while supporting the patroon interests. The onset of British sovereignty in 1664 did not break Dutch influence in New York and East Jersey. The patroon society and its church flourished in the Hudson, Hackensack, Passaic, and Raritan river valleys long after 1700, while great English landlords, like William Livingston, took their place alongside the patroons and integrated their planter Anglicanism with conservative Dutch religious culture.

In Pennsylvania and West Jersey, William Penn's Quaker coreligionists quickly established their dominance. Penn's generous distribution of land and mercantile licenses to members of the Religious Society of Friends granted them a privileged position in the phenomenal economic success of Philadelphia and the Delaware Valley. Although the Friends' intense spirituality and radical social teachings imbued Penn's Frame of Government (1682), powerful mercantile families soon invested Quaker meetings with a conservative cultural agenda. After 1700 a policy of "birthright membership," analogous to the Halfway Covenant, conferred membership in meeting upon Quaker children without requiring their personal testimony to the Inner Light. Only a few decades after its organization in 1681, the Philadelphia Yearly Meeting had become the primary religious vehicle for maintaining both the stability of a prosperous province and the social status of its leading families.

There were significant exceptions to this picture of religious homogeneity, hierarchy, and hegemony in almost every American colony by 1720. Yet these elements of religious diversity did not seriously affect the dominance of the major colonial religions. After 1720, however, important new social changes rendered their task of sacred legitimation increasingly difficult. The sustained growth of colonial societies through the early eighteenth century gradually undermined the ability of initially dominant religions to maintain their cultural control. In coastal towns, commercial farm communities, and planter regions, fewer families gained control of more wealth and property. In new settlements and on the frontier the challenge of subsistence fostered a contrasting pattern of relative economic equality. During the early eighteenth century these socioeconomic contrasts helped spawn broader cultural tensions between "cosmopolitan" coastal towns and the "localist" rural back country.

Rising mercantile towns like Salem, Boston, Newport, New York, Philadelphia, Annapolis, and Charleston strove for the sophistication of British imperial cities and maintained strong influence in their commercial hinterlands. But in the interior river valleys and hill country of the colonies, fierce rural loyalties proved resistant to cosmopolitan influence. In the new settlements traditional religious institutions were often slow to develop and costly to maintain; in the cities population increase and social mobility produced an ever-rising number of people who lived outside church institutions altogether.

In both town and country, moreover, traditional norms of social deference were disrupted. Whether it was squire, merchant, and artisan engaging in aggressive and individualistic economic behavior or rural farmer and pioneer seeking security and equality in the new settlements, Americans everywhere after 1720 began to break out of old social patterns and cultural constraints, norms most prominently defined and enforced by traditional religions. In this situation the integrity of those traditional religions began to disintegrate. Charisma and legitimation pulled in opposite directions. Most religious individuals and families lived out their lives in formalistic religious cultures without experiencing the spirituality and sense of community those cultures existed to preserve. Although still secure politically and economically, by 1720 the established colonial churches had begun to fall behind the pace of societal development and to lose the hearts and minds of those still within their institutions.

NEW INFLUENCES FROM THE OLD WORLD

Meanwhile diverse forces in Europe slowly gathered during the early eighteenth century to counter the declining zeal and intellectual defensiveness that afflicted Protestant communions on both sides of the Atlantic. The North American colonies, at the far edge of the Atlantic world, received these influences from ethnic migration as well as literary transmission. Between 1685 and 1735 large numbers of settlers arrived in British North America from France, Germany, Scotland, and Ireland. The religious significance of the new immigration lay in its transmission of renewed piety and innovative theologies from the turmoil of Protestantism in Enlightenment Europe to a colonial American religious world still structured by patterns of the seventeenth century.

From France came Huguenots, Protestants exiled after King Louis XIV's 1685 revocation of the Edict of Nantes, the grant of toleration to Protestants that had marked the cessation of the French Wars of Religion in 1598. Huguenots were rigorous Calvinists, having embraced the teachings of their great countryman John Calvin in the Reformation of the sixteenth century. Thousands of Huguenots unwilling to submit to Catholicism fled into Protestant Europe and its colonies. Many settled in America, with heaviest concentrations in Charleston, Philadelphia, New York, and Boston.

The Scots and Scotch-Irish constituted a second major group of ethnic newcomers to America in the decades before the Awakening. Religio-political conflict roiled Scottish society throughout the early eighteenth century. Abortive rebellions led by James Francis Edward Stuart, "the Old Pretender," in 1708 and 1715 deeply alienated the Catholic Highlander minority from the militantly Calvinist Presbyterian majority and also divided the Presbyterians within. The Crown, meanwhile, undertook forced resettlement of Presbyterian Scots in Ireland as a means to control that restive Catholic dominion. Emigration to North America became a popular escape for the hard-pressed Presbyterians. The religious toleration of Pennsylvania best suited them, and they organized their first American Presbytery at Philadelphia in 1707. From there they aggressively sought out frontier locations in New Jersey and the Delaware and Susquehanna river valleys. Calvinist traditions in the Hudson Valley and New England made those areas also attractive to Presbyterians, though less so than the Middle Colonies.

Germans, most of them from the Palatinate, made up the third major immigrant group, fleeing the enlightened despotism of the Holy Roman Empire after the Peace of Westphalia in 1648. Again, Pennsylvania's full Protestant toleration proved attractive. Germans of all religious types, the "Pennsylvania Dutch," flocked to Pennsylvania, beginning in 1683 with Lutheran settlement at Germantown near Philadelphia and fanning out into a large ethnic subregion that spread north, south, and west from there.

The German immigrants brought to America a continental Protestant movement that had far-reaching importance in sparking revivals on both sides of the Atlantic. That movement, Pietism, was a powerful wave of personal spirituality, moral discipline, and charitable service that swept through central European Protestantism after 1675. The center of Pietism was Halle in Brandenburg, and its leaders were Philipp Jacob Spener and August Hermann Francke. While serving as pastor at Frankfurt during the late 1660s, Spener instituted Pietism by convening in his home *collegia pietatis,* or "associations for piety," biweekly meetings for prayer, testimony, hymn-singing, and discipline.

Spener's 1675 treatise *Pia Desideria (Pious Desires)* gave the movement its manifesto and its name. He called for increased study of the Bible and exercise of spiritual gifts by the laity, revival of preaching among the clergy, stress on practical works of love, and reform of theological education. Spener's controversial program spread quickly through German Protestantism to Lutheran, Reformed, and sectarian alike. In 1694 the elector of Brandenburg established the University of Halle, and under Spener's leadership it became the intellectual and spiritual center of Pietism. After Spener's death in 1705 his successor, Francke, designed the famed Pietist charitable institutions of Halle, including a poor-school, an orphanage, a publishing house, and a dispensary.

The preponderant majority of German immigrants to colonial America were Pietists. Lutheran Pietists were the largest group, but also the one most disrupted by transatlantic migration. Cut off from their ties to the German state church, Pennsylvania Lutherans languished as a poorly served mission during the early eighteenth century. Calvinist German Reformed immigrants suffered similar destitution: the supply of qualified pastors and missionaries lagged far behind the demand of New World congregations. This colonial situation ironically worked to the advantage of Pietist sectarians who brought their ecclesiastical structures with them to America. These groups—Mennonites, Amish,

Dunkers, Seventh-Day Baptists, Ephratans, and Moravians, to name the largest—flourished in the open society of Pennsylvania.

Each of these ethnic groups from the Old World brought militant religious norms that offered new alternatives to the established colonial churches. Both Huguenots and Presbyterians were rigorously Calvinist communions whose strict orthodoxy and moral discipline soon became crucial to maintaining their ethnic identities in America. Their arrival in the Middle Colonies and the South combined with the presence of Dutch Reformed and Congregationalists in the North to bring Calvinism to a new height of influence in American religion. The German Pietists possessed quite a different but no less important kind of spirituality, one characterized by intense emotional identification with the suffering Christ, sustained prayer and sacred song, and a closely knit religious community. This Pietist strain mixed with the new Calvinist migration to fill the interstices and margins of colonial American settlement with new religious populations.

A second source of religious change from the Old World was the intellectual impact of the Enlightenment. During the seventeenth and early eighteenth centuries the scientific revolution of Galileo, Descartes, Leibniz, and Newton had created new methods of empirical observation and inductive logic that philosophers and theologians applied to questions of human and divine nature. In Britain the Enlightenment generated three alternative theories of human understanding during the fifty years between 1690 and 1740—empiricism, rationalism, and skepticism—all of which held theological implications damaging to Reformed Protestantism.

The chief architect of English empiricism was John Locke. His *Essay Concerning Human Understanding* (1690) argued against the Platonic doctrine of innate ideas and depicted the mind as a *tabula rasa,* or blank slate, upon which the reason creates ideas and volitions out of sense perceptions received from the external world. In *The Reasonableness of Christianity* (1695) Locke rejected both subjective religious experience and historical tradition as sources of religious truth, arguing instead for the reason's ability rightly to perceive and comprehend the empirical evidence of Christianity contained in Scripture. While most Anglican theologians granted Locke's religious epistemology, some argued that God transmitted religious truth to the mind directly through self-evident ideas and categories of rational logic. The defense of this position led John Toland in *Christianity Not Mysterious* (1696) to reject the notion of revealed religion altogether and to advocate a "natural religion" restricted to those doctrines strictly consonant with reason. Toland's stress on the existence and sovereignty of a benign and rational Creator God earned his view the label Deism.

For almost a half-century before the American Awakening, British theologians debated the relative claims of Lockean empiricism and Deistic rationalism, only to undermine the credibility of sense and reason themselves in religious epistemology. This development invited skepticism, the position that the mind cannot verify the existence of objective truth at all. The classic expositor of skepticism was Scottish philosopher David Hume, whose *Treatise of Human Nature* (1739–1740) and *Enquiry Concerning Human Understanding* (1748) convincingly demonstrated that no necessary connection exists between perception and reason. Since Hume also accepted Locke's earlier critique of innate ideas, he concluded that what we call truth, rational or religious, is simply the result of arbitrary associations of the will acting under the influence of the passions to seek pleasure and avoid pain.

These new humanistic Enlightenment philosophies of empiricism, rationalism, and skepticism presented a fundamental intellectual challenge to traditional Protestant theology, especially Calvinism. Within the Church of England the dominant theological response combined Latitudinarianism, a tolerant individualism concerning doctrine and practice, with Arminianism, an endorsement of human free will and moral responsibility associated with the seventeenth-century Dutch Reformed theologian Jacob Arminius. Among Dissenters, English Presbyterianism virtually dissolved in the eighteenth century under the Enlightenment's philosophical onslaught on Calvinist orthodoxy.

In America the colonial churches reacted more slowly to the Enlightenment, but by 1720 its disputations had begun to penetrate provincial theological discourse and place traditional theologies on the defensive. The most dramatic early illustration of the Enlightenment's American impact was the shocking defection of Yale

President Timothy Cutler and several members of his Congregationalist faculty to the more liberal doctrines of Anglicanism in 1722. At the same time the new immigrant populations injected a powerful infusion of continental piety and Calvinist belief into colonial society. These intellectual and demographic forces from the Old World made increasing impact in America after 1720, even as the established colonial religions continued to cope with their own institutional weaknesses and spiritual coolness.

EVANGELICAL PIONEERS

About the time the new Pietist and Calvinist populations began to migrate to America, English-speaking theologians on both sides of the Atlantic began issuing imperatives for renewed piety and morality. Among many such figures six stand out as having had the most bearing on the Great Awakening: Isaac Watts and William Law in England; Cotton Mather, Solomon Stoddard, Jonathan Dickinson, and William Tennent, Sr., in America.

Isaac Watts, an Independent (Congregationalist) minister from Southampton, was the first major English Calvinist literary figure after John Bunyan. Watts made a lasting contribution to the emergence of spiritual subjectivism among Dissenters with his instructional and devotional works and, above all, his religious poetry. *Hymns and Spiritual Songs in Three Books* (1707, 1709) was an unprecedented volume of nearly 350 metrical hymns that introduced British Dissent to a new hymnic language of personal devotion. Even more important was Watts's paraphrased psalter, *The Psalms of David Imitated in the Language of the New Testament* (1719), which, as its title indicates, rendered each psalm into explicitly Christian praise expressed from the perspective of the believer's spiritual experience. The impact of these collections cannot be overestimated. In classics of English religious verse, such as "Jesus Shall Reign Where'er the Sun," "O God, Our Help in Ages Past," and "When I Survey the Wondrous Cross," Watts fused biblical narrative with personal religious experience in a powerful new devotional language for individual and congregational worship that stimulated spiritual renewal throughout British Dissent and among its American admirers.

The Anglican William Law contributed enormously important devotional writings influenced by continental Pietism and designed, like Spener's, to promote meditation, moral reflection, and an ascetic Protestant way of life. Law's most important work was *A Serious Call to a Devout and Holy Life* (1728), a treatise that challenged Latitudinarian laxity and insisted on the necessity of the virtuous life—characterized by temperance, humility, self-denial—as a sign of Christian faith. This work and Law's earlier *Practical Treatise upon Christian Perfection* (1726) deeply influenced John and Charles Wesley and their Methodist movement in England and also proved highly popular in America among Anglicans and Calvinists alike.

Both Watts and Law reflected the continental Pietist emphasis on the importance of the "affections," or emotions, as the center of spirituality. Their works gave early popular expression to this crucial counter-Enlightenment response in European Protestantism. In America no poet or spiritual writer of comparable eminence emerged, but the poems of Edward Taylor of Westfield, Massachusetts, unpublished until this century, breathed an eloquent and fervent piety, while Mather, Stoddard, Dickinson, and Tennent made vital contributions that readied colonial Calvinism for revival.

Cotton Mather and Solomon Stoddard represented two different New England Congregationalist approaches to the imperative for spiritual renewal. Mather and Stoddard are usually depicted as bitter opponents, as indeed they were around 1700. At that time they disagreed over Stoddard's practice of inviting all worshipers at his Northampton, Massachusetts, church to the Lord's Supper regardless of their membership status. To Stoddard, the Supper was "a converting ordinance," in itself a means of grace to the regeneration of souls and hence he thought it should be open to all. From Boston Mather, the champion of Harvard orthodoxy, fiercely attacked Stoddard for unconscionably mixing the elect and the reprobate in the solemn celebration of the church's union with Christ.

Stoddard withstood Mather's challenge and became even more aggressive in quest of conversions, preaching the reality of damnation for unrepentant sinners at the Last Judgment. Under Stoddard's urging the Northampton parish experienced five small renewals of religious concern and commitment during the first quarter of the eighteenth century, which some interpreters have claimed as the beginning of the Great Awakening itself. Late in his career Stoddard published a widely read devotional manual, *A Guide to Christ* (1721), that described a proto-Evangelical morphology of conversion based on the achievement of intense states of contrition and humility.

More surprising was Mather's pilgrimage to Pietism. Though trained in scholastic Puritanism and in midcareer attracted philosophically to Enlightenment rationalism, the mature Mather gradually integrated the intensity of his personal devotion with the new continental affectional theology. He began correspondence with Francke in 1710; his version of the Psalms, *Psalterium Americanum* (1718), was published one year before Watts's *The Psalms of David Imitated,* and he followed the lead of his English counterpart in designing his verse to heighten the devotional and meditative experience of the faithful. Mather's most significant theological work, *The Christian Philosopher* (1720), argued the compatibility of "the experimental philosophy" of the new science with "the experimental religion" of the new piety. In 1721 he enlisted with advocates of spiritually and musically heightened congregational singing in the Regular Singing Controversy, and for the rest of his life he urged affectional faith and renewed moral commitment upon his congregation and all New England.

Jonathan Dickinson and William Tennent, Sr., carried the new piety to American Presbyterians. Each man represented a major constituency in the emerging American Presbyterian church. Dickinson embodied the experience and interests of the New England party, English Presbyterians who had found a comfortable niche in America's Puritan commonwealths. Born in Hatfield, Massachusetts, and one of Yale College's earliest graduates (class of 1705), Dickinson quickly received a call from the English Presbyterian congregation at Elizabethtown (now Elizabeth), New Jersey. From this Middle Colony outpost he led the New England party's successful campaign in the Subscription Controversy (1721–1729), an important preliminary to the Great Awakening. By 1716 Scotch-Irish immigration had grown large enough and dispersion of all Presbyterians wide enough to require organization of the Synod of Philadelphia.

Conservative Scotch-Irish insisted that all ordination candidates subscribe in full to the Westminster Confession of Faith (1647), demanding fidelity to this historic definition of British Calvinism as the primary test for the Presbyterian ministry. The New Englanders resisted subscription on the proto-Evangelical ground, articulated in Dickinson's 1722 *Sermon Preached at the Opening of the Synod,* that authentic Christian faith was an irreducibly and uniquely personal experience of grace, one inherently beyond the authority of human creedal formulas. The concern of the church, Dickinson concluded, should be focused more on obtaining a zealous and virtuous ministry than a legalistically orthodox one. After seven more years of bitter dispute the New England party finally achieved a compromise victory in the Adopting Act of 1729, a measure that mandated subscription to "all the essential and necessary articles" of the Confession but permitted individual exceptions subject to the approval of the local presbytery.

William Tennent, Sr., brought the rising intensity of British Dissent from his native Ireland to the Middle Colonies. Educated at the University of Edinburgh, he was ordained in the Church of Ireland (Anglican) in 1706. Over the succeeding decade, however, he rejected both episcopal polity and Latitudinarian theology, embraced Presbyterianism, was ordained, and emigrated to America. Tennent was admitted to the Synod of Philadelphia in September 1718 and was settled permanently at Neshaminy, Pennsylvania, in 1726. He was a tireless itinerant, bringing his demand for experiential regeneration and visible piety to Scotch-Irish settlements of the Delaware Valley in a unique and fiery style of extempore preaching. Of even greater importance was his role as a teacher of ministers. Over the course of nearly twenty years Tennent trained a generation of evangelists, including his three sons, at the "Log College," his household academy so named for its rustic setting on the Pennsylvania frontier.

THE AWAKENING TO 1735

In the late 1720s and early 1730s emergent elements of spiritual renewal began to produce local episodes of popular religious concern that gradually came to reinforce one another. One of the earliest revivals occurred in 1722 among a newly arrived company of Dunkers, or German Baptists. It was led by Conrad Beissel, a mystic who had immigrated to Germantown in 1712 and then moved restlessly about the Middle Colonies for a decade. Back in Germantown he inspired Pietist settlers of all varieties with his powerful preaching in the Dunker revival. His esoteric teaching and severe asceticism, however, soon divided the Dunker congregation.

In 1724 Beissel withdrew to Ephrata on the Cocalico Creek, near present-day Reading, where he formed a monastic community of celibate men and women. The Ephratans were famed for their fervid piety, rigorous discipline, and especially the music of their unique community singing, which Beissel both composed and conducted. The main body of Dunkers regrouped under their founder, Alexander Mack, whose powerful preaching helped sustain Pietist zeal throughout the German community in the 1720s and 1730s.

Across the Delaware River in New Jersey a more complex and significant episode occurred among the Dutch Reformed and Presbyterians. The initiator of this religious renewal was Theodore Jacob Frelinghuysen, who settled as Dutch Reformed pastor at Raritan in 1720. Frelinghuysen was educated at Pietist schools in the Netherlands, and from the outset his Middle Colonies ministry brought controversy. By 1724 his denunciation of mere outward religious conformity, his rigorous definition of authentic regeneration, and his emphasis on the internal witness of the Holy Spirit had divided his four Raritan Valley churches. Conservative opponents published a 250-page *Complaint* against Frelinghuysen, the first of many such attacks, but his evangelistic practices—including *collegia pietatis,* lay exhortation, itinerant preaching, and published sermons—kindled revival in the Raritan churches during and after 1726.

Frelinghuysen's fame and influence spread throughout New Jersey and beyond to William Tennent's Log College at Neshaminy, Pennsylvania. A new and highly significant American pattern of Calvinist interaction began when the Dutch Reformed domine met and gave encouragement to Tennent's son Gilbert, who had accepted a pastoral call to the Presbyterian church at New Brunswick in 1726. When Gilbert fell ill in 1727, Frelinghuysen's letter of support helped rally the young minister to proclaim a more combative, emotional, and explicit Gospel message, one that directly challenged sinners to seek salvation lest they perish in eternal damnation. Gilbert's brothers John and William joined him in the New Jersey ministry, and soon the Tennents' fervent preaching created revivals in most Jersey Presbyterian congregations. So intense were Gilbert's sermons that his hearers sometimes "were compelled to cry out in the public assembly, both under the impression of terror and love." Frelinghuysen and the Tennents supported each other's forceful evangelism in central New Jersey during the late 1720s and 1730s. At this time a stream of young Presbyterian ministers from Neshaminy fanned out to churches in all the Middle Colonies, creating a revivalistic Scotch-Irish party that joined forces with Jonathan Dickinson and the New England Presbyterians.

All these episodes of popular religious renewal predated the famous Northampton, Massachusetts, revival of 1734, the event traditionally cited as the beginning of the Great Awakening. The significance of religious activities at that Connecticut River Valley town, however, should not be underestimated. Under the ministry of young Jonathan Edwards the first large-scale Congregationalist revival commenced, a quickening that Edwards soon advocated as the model for New England's awakening. Edwards was the grandson of Solomon Stoddard, founding minister at Northampton, and the son of Timothy Edwards, minister at East Windsor, Connecticut. He joined his illustrious grandfather in the Northampton pulpit in 1727 after graduating from Yale (class of 1720), undergoing a powerful conversion while serving briefly as a minister in New York City, and tutoring at Yale from 1724 to 1726.

From Stoddard, Edwards gained a thirst for the spiritual renewal of his people and many techniques to encourage it. After Stoddard's death in 1729, however, nearly five years passed without any increase of community religious concern. Then a young people's dance on the Sabbath touched off the most intense local revival to date in America and the first among the original English colonial churches. Edwards' account of the Northampton revival, published in 1738 by Isaac Watts in London under the title *A Faithful Narrative of the Surprizing Work of God,* quickly became the literary archetype for the

Great Awakening and earned Edwards an international reputation as America's leading Evangelical advocate.

News of "promiscuous" dancing by teenagers on the day of sacred rest provoked Edwards to reprimand them and exhort their parents to more vigilant family discipline. During family visitations and youth meetings he appealed directly to his young parishioners to consider the wider implications of their sinful ways: careless of their destiny, they risked divine anger in this life and eternal damnation to come. Edwards' admonition took hold. Several of the young people fell under "conviction" that they were indeed guilty and needful of divine mercy. They obtained an experience of saving grace, immediately abandoned their worldly activities, and testified to their friends. Their example inspired their peers; soon religion was the principal concern of all the town's adolescents.

From the pulpit Edwards delivered a judicious blend of sermons, some vividly depicting the wages of sin and the horrors of the damned, others portraying the regenerate experience and dazzling destiny of the elect. His preaching reached the town's adults as well as its young people. Halfway members of his congregation came under conviction of sin while fully covenanted saints discovered new heights of devotion and spiritual renewal. Edwards visited from house to house urging families to come to Christ and convened small meetings of the repentant and new services and weekly lectures. The town, meanwhile, burst into revival: church attendance swelled and congregational singing reached a new height of emotional expression and vocal skill. Young people as a body rejected worldly ways and embraced piety and Christian virtues, taverns were less frequented, dances and balls were abandoned altogether, and street and parlor conversation centered on religious rather than secular topics. Above all, in Edwards' estimate, "more than 300 souls were savingly brought home to Christ, in this town, in the space of half a year, and about the same number of males as females."

Along with the details of the Northampton events, *A Faithful Narrative* contains accounts of small children, young people, and adults—most of them female—describing dramatic experiences of spiritual transformation. Invalid Abigail Hutchinson, for example, was awakened

. . . by something she heard her brother say of the necessity of being in good earnest in seeking regenerating grace. . . . Her great terror, she said, was that she had sinned against God . . . especially in three things, viz. her original sin, and her sin in murmuring at God's providence, in the weakness and afflictions she had been under, and in want of duty to parents, though others had looked upon her to excel in dutifulness.

(*Works*, vol. IV, p. 192)

After four troubled days she experienced an "easiness and calmness of mind" of a kind she had never known before. Then "these words came to her mind, 'The blood of Christ cleanses [us] from all sin.' . . . By these things her mind was led into such contemplations and views of Christ, as filled her exceeding full of joy" (pp. 192–193).

In a later publication Edwards recorded the charismatic exercises of his wife, Sarah Pierpont Edwards, during the Northampton revival as an example of how the Spirit renewed the souls of covenanted saints: "Often her soul was perfectly overwhelmed, and swallowed up with light and love and a sweet solace, rest, and joy of soul, that was altogether unspeakable; and more than once continuing for five or six hours together, without any interruption." During these transports,

. . . the strength of the body [was] taken away, so as to deprive of all ability to stand or speak; sometimes the hands clinched, and the flesh cold, but senses still remaining; animal nature often in a great emotion and agitation . . . as to cause the person (wholly unavoidably) to leap with all the might, with joy and mighty exultation.

(vol. IV, p. 332)

The revival continued for some months until the suicide of one of Edwards' own uncles, who apparently despaired of salvation, quelled the upsurge of religious concern. Despite its somber ending, the revival left Northampton reunited in a religio-political consensus that at least in Edwards' eyes approached the ancient Puritan ideal of a Christian commonwealth and prefigured the millennial kingdom. And through *A Faithful Narrative*, Edwards transmitted to the English-speaking world his vision that revival not only saved souls; it rescued the youth and renewed the Christian family, it united the town and gathered virtually the entire population into the church, it created higher standards of public and private morality, and it indicated God's particular blessing on New England and the rapid approach of Christ's millennial kingdom.

THE AWAKENING TO 1740

By 1735 American Protestantism had absorbed more than a decade of growing Pietist and Evangelical influence and had produced several significant episodes of revival. In the next five years revivalism exploded across colonial America from Maine to Georgia, fired by yet another infusion of religious zeal and evangelism brought by Methodists from England and Moravians from Germany. The Awakening reached a sudden and powerful peak between 1739 and 1741, driven above all by the dramatic preaching tours of Methodist George Whitefield.

The Moravians and Methodists arrived in America at nearly the same time and grew closely entwined during the ensuing revival, but they came from very different sources within Protestantism. Tracing their origins to the Hussite "Unitas Fratrum," or "Union of Brothers," of fifteenth-century Bohemia, the Moravians had endured more than two centuries of persecution in central Europe for their pacifist, communitarian, nonconformist faith when in 1722 they sought and received sanctuary on the estate of Count Nikolaus von Zinzendorf in Saxony. Zinzendorf, born into a family of aristocratic Lutheran Pietists from Dresden, had been educated at Francke's academy in Halle and at Wittenberg University. Both institutions imbued the young man with an extreme Pietism that found complete expression in the intense devotion, humility, and community of the Moravian refugees.

The count permitted construction on his land of a communal village for the Moravians named Herrnhut ("House of the Lord"). Soon Zinzendorf committed himself wholly to the community, withdrawing from political and secular life to assume office as bishop of a reorganized Moravian Church. During the 1720s he developed Herrnhut into an international model for Pietism and redefined the Moravians as a mission society. From 1730 he sent large groups of Moravians to England and to America, first to Georgia, then to Bethlehem, Nazareth, and Lititz in Pennsylvania, and later to the Wachovia Tract in the North Carolina piedmont. Aboard ship to Georgia one of the earliest companies met two young brothers—the elder an Anglican priest en route to his first mission, the younger on appointment as secretary to James Oglethorpe, founder and governor of the colony. They were John and Charles Wesley, the founders of Methodism.

John and Charles were the fifteenth and eighteenth children, respectively, of the Rev. Mr. Samuel Wesley and his wife, Susannah, and were born and raised in the parsonage of Epworth, Lancashire, and educated at Christ Church, Oxford. In 1726 John was elected to a fellowship in Lincoln College, Oxford, and quickly gathered around him a group of devout scholars known as the "Holy Club," or "Methodists," for their intense piety and moral discipline. During the early 1730s the group included Charles Wesley as well as George Whitefield, the son of tavernkeepers from Gloucester and a precocious servitor scholar at Pembroke College.

To his associates John transmitted the piety of William Law, whom he visited, and the Pietists, whom he read avidly. Whitefield and the other members of the Holy Club yielded to the powerful imperatives of these texts and vowed to follow Wesley into Holy Orders as missionary priests in the Church of England. In 1735 John and Charles traveled to newly settled Savannah, encountering the Moravians, who deeply impressed the young Englishmen with their spiritual zeal and intense feeling of community. The Wesleys' mission in Georgia, however, did not meet with success. Within a year Charles returned to England, and within two John had been driven from Georgia after a series of petulant actions that included publicly denouncing slavery, condemning alcohol consumption, and denying communion to the daughter of a powerful local planter. A disappointed John Wesley landed at Deal, England, on 1 February 1738, only hours before Whitefield sailed from the same port for the Georgia mission. Wesley's hurried note advising Whitefield against the venture did not reach him in time. Wesley never returned to America. In England he met the Moravian Peter Boehler, whose Pietism helped to stimulate John's famed Aldersgate conversion experience in May 1738, when his heart was "strangely warmed" by the infusion of saving grace, which shaped the subsequent course of English Methodism.

Whitefield visited the colonies six times and

became the "Grand Itinerant," the greatest preacher of the Great Awakening and the primal force in the shaping of American Evangelicalism. After a brief but cordial reception at Savannah and Charleston, Whitefield returned to England to receive priestly ordination and collect funds for an orphan-house he planned to build in Georgia modeled after Francke's at Halle. Great crowds attended wherever Whitefield preached in England, but many Anglican bishops and clergy opposed to his homiletic style and theology closed their pulpits to him. Undeterred, he took matters into his own hands and on 17 February 1739 began "field-preaching" in the open air of Hannam Mount, Bristol, where he preached not to the Anglican elite of the city but to a crowd of coal miners. At one stroke this move declared Whitefield's defiance of the ecclesiastical establishment and his intention to carry his message directly to the people. His field-preaching caused a sensation and launched the Evangelical Revival in Great Britain under the leadership of himself and the Wesleys, who soon joined him in field-preaching.

As Whitefield prepared to leave England for America, however, he fell into fundamental disagreement with John Wesley over the nature of "free grace" in the economy of salvation. The issue opened a theological chasm between the two great Methodists, with Whitefield vigorously asserting the Calvinist view that the application of Christ's atoning and regenerating grace is limited to those sinful human souls chosen by God's free and irresistible election, while Wesley argued with equal heat the Arminian position that Christ's atonement is universally available to all souls who freely and sincerely seek it. By the time Whitefield returned to America in October 1739, he brought with him international celebrity and an unprecedented combination of religious identities—Anglican, Pietist, and Calvinist—that could appeal to virtually every Protestant communion in the colonies. And appeal they did, as the twenty-five-year-old evangelist carried the Great Awakening to its zenith in the course of a spectacular fifteen-month preaching tour.

George Whitefield's Preaching Tour, 1739–1741. Whitefield landed on 30 October 1739 at Cape Henlopen, Delaware, where he commenced the *Journals* of his American experience, which he published every few months. They constitute the primary record of his achievement in the Awakening. In Philadelphia, Anglican pulpits were opened to him and large crowds attended his preaching. William Tennent, Sr., and other Presbyterian and Baptist ministers visited him; he was well received by Quakers, including Thomas Penn, proprietor of the colony, and by German Pietists at Germantown and Skippack. At Brunswick, New Jersey, he met Gilbert Tennent. The two evangelists immediately struck up a friendship and Tennent accompanied Whitefield on his progress toward New York, both men preaching wherever opportunity afforded. Commissary Vessey refused permission for Whitefield to preach in the Anglican churches of New York, but Presbyterian ministers there—most notably Ebenezer Pemberton—welcomed him, as did Jonathan Dickinson at Elizabeth and William Tennent later at Neshaminy. Back in the Quaker City, Whitefield spoke to ever-larger crowds that swelled to 10,000 for his last sermon there on 28 November 1740.

The core of Whitefield's message was what he called "the necessity of the New Birth," the claim based on John 3:3 that salvation occurs through a conscious experience of radical personal transformation bestowed by God through the action of the Holy Spirit. Whitefield's preaching dramatized the biblical narrative to convey his Calvinistic understanding of the unconverted soul's desperate situation, sinful in nature and act, violating God's holy law, and justly liable to the divine penalty of eternal damnation. By this rhetorical strategy he provoked his hearers to give up their confidence in traditional religion or rational speculation and to place their faith in Christ as their only hope for salvation. Should God bestow saving grace, he taught, the soul would know it by the spiritual phenomena of the New Birth—first, "conviction," or a candid realization of personal sinfulness; followed by "evangelical humiliation," an often protracted period of prayerful acknowledgment of absolute dependence on God for salvation; and finally regeneration itself, an internal witness of acceptance and cleansing by the Holy Spirit, accompanied by intense relief and joy and often by charismatic gifts such as speaking in tongues, prophecy, vision, trance, and ecstatic "exercise" of the body.

Whitefield pressed his message upon his hearers with an extraordinary combination of homiletic gifts. His voice possessed rare tone, range, and power. According to Benjamin Franklin's calculation, Whitefield could be distinctly heard by an audience of 30,000 people without amplification. To that voice the preacher added a remarkable sense of timing, histrionic pose and gesture, and an easy and familiar manner with all levels of society—gifts attributable at least in part to his early life at the Bell Tavern, Gloucester. David Garrick, the greatest actor of the age, wished he could move audiences as much as Whitefield did simply by uttering the word "Mesopotamia!"

From Philadelphia, Whitefield set out for Savannah to resume his work for his mission parish and the orphan-house project. The journey consumed six weeks, taking him down the coast through Annapolis, Williamsburg, New Bern, Charleston, and Beaufort. Whitefield's message of conversion and new life now included a moral condemnation of slavery, a plea that all true Christians free their slaves, and a plan to open a free school for black children. He received a cool reception from Anglican clergy and vestries, but people flocked to his preaching. One revealing account of Whitefield's impact in the rural South appears in the spiritual autobiography of Hermon Husband, *Some Remarks on Religion,* written about 1750 and published in 1761. When Husband was fifteen he and his parents traveled from the hinterland to hear Whitefield at New Bern, North Carolina:

> There came News of a Man, a Preacher, newly come from England, that both Men and Women were ready to leave all their Livings to follow him. . . . My Father and Mother went . . . and took me along. . . . In comes the Man, George Whitefield by Name, and he took a Text about the wise and foolish virgins. . . . The Spirit of God witnessed to me, and speaking in me says . . . here is One who bears a Testimony to the Truth. . . . Now you have heard something of the Movings or Inspirations of the Spirit indeed.
> (Heimert and Miller, 1967, pp. 637–638)

At Savannah, Whitefield began to construct the orphan-house, which he named Bethesda, and spent several months pastoring to his far-flung parish, including a company of Pietists from Salzburg, Austria, newly settled at Ebenezer, Georgia. But in Charleston, Anglican Commissary Alexander Garden charged Whitefield with "enthusiasm and pride" in his preaching and with "speaking against the generality of the clergy." The two had an argument over Garden's giving permission for balls and parties, which Whitefield had repeatedly condemned as carnal and un-Christian. Garden publicly denounced Whitefield, who in turn defied Garden by preaching at the Congregational, Presbyterian, and Baptist meetinghouses in the city.

Whitefield sailed for Philadelphia on 2 April 1740, only to find that the Anglicans there had also denied him their pulpits. Yet thousands continued to attend his preaching in the fields and in Presbyterian and Baptist meetinghouses from Philadelphia to New York, where many of them were "melted" by Whitefield's emotional appeal to "flee the wrath to come" and cry unto Christ for salvation. By then Whitefield was traveling with an entourage of up to forty men, most of them young Presbyterian ministers from William Tennent's Log College. In the spring of 1740, as the Grand Itinerant proceeded from triumph to triumph and his company of young "sons of thunder" spread his message and preaching style through the center of British North America, the revival seemed to sweep all before it.

Whitefield spent the summer in Savannah and the South, preached his farewell to Charleston before 4,000 people, then sailed to Newport, Rhode Island, where he arrived on 14 September to commence the New England tour that marked the climax of the Great Awakening. His reputation had preceded him to New England: Anglicans suspected him but Congregationalists welcomed him from Newport to Boston. He spoke to overflowing congregations in every Boston church and to crowds of 15,000–20,000 on Boston Common, the largest gatherings ever assembled in New England. He traveled north along the coast as far as York, Maine, then returned to Boston, where he was besieged round the clock by people in the throes of conversion. He preached daily, urging the necessity of the New Birth and denouncing "the pomps and vanities of this world." In mid-October Whitefield crossed Massachusetts to the Connecticut River and Northampton, where he spent several days with Jonathan Edwards, of whom he remarked, "I think I have not seen his fellow in all New England." The last leg of his tour took him down the Connecticut Valley through Springfield, Hartford, and New Haven.

Some of the popular excitement Whitefield aroused in New England itinerancy was captured in the diary of Nathan Cole, a farmer from Middletown, Connecticut, who heard him preach there on 23 October 1740:

> When I saw Mr. Whitefield come upon the scaffold, he looked almost angelical; a young, slim, slender youth, before some thousands of people with a bold undaunted countenance. And my hearing how God was with him everywhere as he came along, it solemnized my mind and put me into a trembling fear before he began to preach; for he looked as if he was clothed with authority from the Great God, and a sweet solemnity sat upon his brow, and my hearing him preach gave me a heart wound. By God's blessing, my old foundation was broken up, and I saw that my righteousness would not save me.
>
> (Heimert and Miller, p. 186)

Cole fell under intense and protracted spiritual crisis after hearing Whitefield's message and experienced the New Birth almost a year later.

Whitefield arrived in New York on 31 October and continued south through his now-familiar stations in New Jersey, where the charismatic manifestations reached new heights under his preaching. He spent the balance of November in Philadelphia and environs, then sailed again to Charleston and Savannah. After celebrating Christmas at the Bethesda orphanage, he preached his farewell sermon to Savannah and, having completed his mission term, he sailed for Britain on 16 January 1741, where he remained until he returned to America in 1744. Whitefield's centrality to the Great Awakening cannot be overestimated. His transatlantic celebrity, charismatic preaching, controversial theology, ecclesiastical defiance, intercolonial itinerancy, and polemical writing provided an ample charge to detonate the potent forces of spiritual renewal that had been gathering in the American colonies for more than two decades.

CONFLICT AND SCHISM: THE MIDDLE COLONIES

Whitefield's 1739–1741 tour marked the zenith of the Great Awakening, when revival burst upon a surprised and delighted religious public. But his evangelism also fomented bitter controversy. In most congregations revival caused new tensions between ministers and their people.

While some pastors embraced Whitefield's imperatives, others rejected them outright or professed an uncomfortable neutrality. These disruptive energies grew along with the Awakening and quickly produced complex and traumatic divisions within American Protestantism.

Yet the Awakening also promoted the first significant American efforts toward ecumenism. The best opportunity for church union existed among the German Pietists, and the role of ecumenist fell to the Moravian leader Nikolaus von Zinzendorf. The unification of the true church was a principal tenet of Moravian teaching, and in its spirit Zinzendorf resigned his office as bishop at Herrnhut to undertake an ecumenical evangelistic campaign in America on the heels of Whitefield's triumph. Zinzendorf arrived in New York late in 1741 and proceeded directly to Pennsylvania, where his charismatic preaching and international fame brought the Awakening to its zenith among the Pietist communions. He urgently proclaimed his mission to form "one congregation of God in the Spirit" and invited the churches to a synod convened for that purpose.

The first synod commenced at Germantown on 12 January 1742 with all the principal German communions represented—Lutherans, Reformed, Mennonites, Schwenkfelders, Dunkers, Seventh-Day Baptists, Ephratans, and Moravians. Seven synods in all were held during 1742, but Zinzendorf's initiative failed primarily due to the inability of the churches to agree on how to distinguish the essentials of their common Pietism from the particulars of their individual doctrines and institutional structures. After a brief term as pastor to the Lutherans in Philadelphia, Zinzendorf left America and never returned. Ironically, his preaching and unity campaign alarmed the churches in Germany enough to supply their American congregations with qualified ministers and missionaries, notably the Lutheran Henry Muhlenburg and the German Reformed Michael Schlatter, capable Pietist leaders who brought stability and coherence to their communions in America. Even Zinzendorf's deep commitment to Pietist ecumenism fell before the Great Awakening's fundamental paradox: even as the revival increased the intensity and importance of personal religion, it weakened and divided colonial religious institutions.

More complex and lasting conflicts took place

among the Calvinist denominations—Presbyterian, Dutch Reformed, Congregational, and Baptist. Whitefield's demands for a purified and fully regenerate church were repeated everywhere by zealous American itinerants following his example. Six months after Whitefield's 1740 New England tour, Gilbert Tennent followed the same itinerary, often achieving even more intense impact than Whitefield himself, while Tennent's brothers and other Log College ministers promoted revival across the Middle Colonies. In New England, Jonathan Edwards and many other prorevival ministers preached by invitation of their Congregationalist colleagues. One such invitation from the Enfield, Connecticut, parish on 8 July 1741 evoked the most famous sermon of the Great Awakening, Edwards' *Sinners in the Hands of an Angry God.* In it Edwards fashioned the ultimate metaphor for awakening sinners, comparing the standing of the innately sinful human soul before a righteous and predestinating God to that of a spider dangled over fire by a slender thread.

Throughout New England and the Middle Colonies, Congregationalist and Presbyterian ministers struggled to guide their people through the confusion of revival, aided—or hindered—by the itinerants. Not surprisingly, it was upon the opponents of the Awakening that the impatient urgency of the revivalists fell. One of Whitefield's most controversial practices was his public criticism of ministers, sometimes by name, for their spiritual deadness. Of South Carolina churches, for example, he wrote in his *Journals,* "they have many ministers . . . but I hear of no stirring among the dry bones," and of the New England clergy, "many, nay most that preach, I fear, do not experimentally know Christ." Such remarks drew the ire of the colonial religious establishments and also encouraged Whitefield's followers to make similar judgments. The most important expression of the revival's clerical critique was Gilbert Tennent's sermon "The Dangers of an Unconverted Ministry," delivered on 8 March 1740 at Nottingham, Pennsylvania. Tennent accused ministers who had not experienced the New Birth of hypocrisy and blasphemy, likening them to "blind Pharisees" who taught the form of religion without its spiritual power. Tennent concluded that unconverted ministers were leading their people as well as themselves to an eternity in hell. His rem-

edy: either remove the unqualified minister or separate the regenerate from his ministration and supply them with truly converted itinerants.

Tennent's manifesto and the controversial itinerancy of his Log College brethren helped polarize the Presbyterian Synod of Philadelphia. Their communion was finally broken, however, by a dispute in the frontier Presbytery of Donegal in Pennsylvania's Susquehanna River Valley. There the clergy was almost entirely antirevival, reflecting the conservative Scotch-Irish traditions of literal subscription to the Westminster Confession of Faith and strict adherence to church polity. Two Donegal ministers, however —Alexander Creaghead of Middle Octorora and David Alexander of Pequea—led revivals in their own parishes and itinerated without permission, for which they were suspended by the Presbytery. The two ministers appealed to the Synod convened at Philadelphia on 27 May 1741. Gilbert Tennent sought to mediate the dispute, but antirevival forces led by Philadelphia's Robert Cross suddenly disrupted the proceedings with a petition declaring that Tennent's own Presbytery of New Brunswick had violated the sense of the Subscription Act by ordaining heterodox Log College ministers and therefore as schismatics had forfeited the right to sit in Synod.

Pandemonium ensued, the antirevival "Old Side" party secured a narrow majority for its protestation, and the prorevival "New Side" ministers withdrew from Philadelphia. The New Side convened on 2 June 1741 at New Brunswick to proclaim the legitimacy of its proceedings and to send itinerants into Old Side territory in the Middle Colonies and Virginia. Although Gilbert Tennent and Jonathan Dickinson labored for reunion, the breach widened as the Awakening continued to grow in intensity and acrimony. Finally on 19 September 1745 the New Side organized its own Synod of New York, and for the next thirteen years the two synods waged constant and bitter warfare for the soul of American Presbyterianism.

Schism also afflicted the Dutch Reformed church in the Middle Colonies. In 1747 the Pietist party of Theodore Frelinghuysen organized the Coetus of New York (a clerical council much like a presbytery), established under the authority of the Classis, or Synod, of Amsterdam in 1747. Some conservative ministers, most of them in New York City, refused to join the Coetus from the beginning; then in 1755 a group of antirevival ministers withdrew from the Coetus in opposition to its plan to gain autonomy from Amsterdam and to build a seminary in America. They joined with the conservative faction to form a "Conferentie," or conference, that appealed to Amsterdam for recognition as the true Dutch Reformed church in America. From 1755 to 1772 the Coetus and the Conferentie did combat over much the same issues that divided New Side and Old Side Presbyterians.

CONFLICT AND SCHISM: NEW ENGLAND

In New England schismatic controversy first emerged in response to the itinerancy of James Davenport, Congregationalist minister at Southold, Long Island, who had toured New England with Whitefield and returned to Connecticut in 1741. Like Whitefield and Tennent, Davenport challenged the Congregationalist establishment of Connecticut by publicly demanding of settled ministers an account of their New Birth. If they refused, he used their refusal as justification to urge their parishioners to separate from their ministration. Davenport gained fame, if not respect, for his uninvited itinerancy and excessive preaching—one exhortation lasted twenty-two hours—and for the frenzied charismatic gifts of his followers and their dramatic practice of exhorting, marching, and singing in the streets.

Davenport and his followers created such a disturbance that in May 1742 the Connecticut General Assembly passed "An Act for Regulating Abuses and Correcting Disorders in Ecclesiastical Affairs," which suspended the salary of any settled Connecticut minister who entered another parish to preach, authorized arrest and exile for any "foreigner or stranger" who preached in a town without a license from the settled minister and a majority of the parish, and prescribed fines and imprisonment for any lay exhorter. Under this law Davenport was finally exiled from Connecticut on 3 June 1742. His brief appearance in Boston brought forth a similar sentence from Massachusetts Bay. In March 1743 Davenport's career as a radical reached its culmination with a public burning of books, finery, and jewelry at New London, Connecticut. Thereafter two other Congregationalist itiner-

ants, Eleazar Wheelock and Solomon Williams, took Davenport in hand, and by the summer of 1744 they had persuaded him to publish his *Confessions and Retractations,* in which he abjured his former excesses.

But Davenport had unleashed disruptive energies that could not be contained by the Congregationalist establishment in church or state. Especially in eastern Connecticut and Plymouth County, Massachusetts, radical and charismatic spirituality continued to spread, urged on by Davenport's former colleagues and especially by lay exhorters who claimed authority to preach based solely on their experience of an internal divine calling. In most cases the radicals separated from the parish and its settled minister, refusing to pay taxes for clerical support. This action challenged the financial and institutional structure of Congregationalism and the government moved quickly to defend it.

Some of the radicals were arrested and tried for nonpayment of ministerial taxes. Many of them had property confiscated in lieu of their outstanding obligations. But legal harassment worked no better than ecclesiastical discipline. The schismatics claimed a natural right to freedom of conscience, denied the authority of the state to govern in matters of religion, and steadfastly persevered in maintaining their own churches. They called themselves Strict or Separate Congregationalists, claiming to have restored the original faith of their Puritan forebears by seceding out from a corrupt state church, ironically the very one their ancestors had erected in New England. The extent of the Separate movement gives some indication of the strength of the Awakening: separations eventually occurred in more than 125 congregations, nearly one-third of all New England churches.

The Separates, moreover, represented only the most traumatic aspect of religious conflict wrought by the Great Awakening in New England. Even as the radicals broke away from the Congregationalist establishment, the Standing Order was riven within by controversy between prorevival New Lights and antirevival Old Lights. The great champion of the New Lights was Jonathan Edwards, who continued to write in support of the revival, though his task became more difficult with the emergence of Davenport's extremism on the one hand and reaction to it on the other. In *The Distinguishing Marks of a Work of the Spirit of God* (1741) Edwards defended the charismatic gifts experienced by converts in the Awakening, including visions, mental "impressions" of Scripture texts, and glossolalia—speaking in tongues—on the argument that while they were not necessarily valid indicators of the Spirit's presence, they were not necessarily invalid ones either.

Edwards' claims, along with the simultaneous zenith of Davenport's evangelism, provoked a negative response, particularly from antirevival Old Light ministers in eastern Massachusetts. Their leader was Charles Chauncy, a native son ordained at Boston's First Church in 1727 and already emerging by 1740 as the city's most liberal and urbane religious leader. Chauncy's first important pronouncement against the revival was his 1742 sermon *Enthusiasm Described and Caution'd Against,* in which he articulated what would become the classic Old Light criticism: that the appeal of the revival rested upon fallible human passions and in extreme form constituted not divine inspiration but delusion, or "enthusiasm," in eighteenth-century psychological language.

Enthusiasm touched off an epic theological controversy that continued for a century and in many ways still remains unresolved. New Lights could not let Chauncy's critique stand unanswered, nor did they want to countenance Davenport and the Separate schismatics. Edwards defended the New Light position at length in *Some Thoughts Concerning the Present Revival of Religion in New England* (1742). Chauncy responded with a systematic Old Light condemnation of the Awakening in *Seasonable Thoughts on the State of Religion in New England,* published in the same year. The Edwards-Chauncy debate pitted the two finest theological minds in New England against each other and drew their allies into a dispute across the entire range of issues raised by the Awakening, from itinerancy and polity to human nature and the economy of grace.

The conflict between Old Lights and New Lights escalated through the mid-1740s and threatened to compound the schisms already introduced by the Separates. Just as the New Lights managed to subdue Davenport, Whitefield landed in New England on 26 October 1744 to rekindle the revival and to rally the radical Evangelical cause. The Grand Itinerant, however, found New England much changed in four

years. Although his preaching still drew great crowds and drove the Separates to a final charismatic paroxysm, he now encountered stiff resistance from much of the Congregationalist establishment. Not only did the Harvard faculty and Boston ministers issue testimonies against him, but, more surprising, so did the Yale faculty and the ministry of New London County, Connecticut.

This pattern signaled the waning of the Awakening in New England and the preservation of union between New and Old Lights. At stake was the remaining integrity of New England Congregationalism: Could New Lights and Old Lights remain in communion despite their fundamental differences? The answer proved to be positive, for although the two factions harbored deep and lasting hostility, as joint heirs to the Puritan vision they agreed on the necessity of a religious establishment, especially at a time of confusion and disorder.

Yet they pursued their common vision in sharply contrasting ways and in clearly differentiated regions: the Old Lights dominated the older cosmopolitan towns of the coastal plain, while the New Lights prevailed in the hill country and upper river valleys of the interior. The crucial institutional issue between the two factions was qualification for church membership. New Lights, pursuing the ideal of a fully regenerate church "gathered" out of a sinful world, rejected the Halfway Covenant and admitted only those who could profess and document their experience of the New Birth. Old Lights preserved the Halfway Covenant and argued the critical importance of its criteria of moral and intellectual assent to church discipline as a principal bulwark against enthusiasm and schism.

Some of the complex tensions wrought by the Awakening in Congregationalist parishes can be illustrated by Edwards' career at Northampton. In the 1740s his congregation engaged in a protracted salary dispute with Edwards, a common enough phenomenon in mid-eighteenth-century parishes. But in 1744 Edwards exacerbated tensions by publicly rebuking and demanding confessions from children—including some from the town's most prominent families—who had been discovered covertly reading an instruction manual on midwifery. His discipline of young people, the action that had sparked the great revival of 1734, worked the opposite effect thirteen years later. Many regarded his actions as exceeding the prerogatives of legitimate pastoral authority, and when he condemned the Halfway Covenant and refused to administer the Lord's Supper to Halfway members, among whom were the families of the offending children, his opponents sprang to the attack. A hostile parish majority convened a church council that demanded and eventually obtained his dismissal on 22 June 1750, without giving him an opportunity to resign. Shortly thereafter he was installed at Stockbridge, Massachusetts, where he ministered eight years as missionary to the Indians and a tiny white settlement.

Edwards' case illustrates the problems that afflicted the Congregationalist establishment in the aftermath of revival. In some measure the Awakening polarized virtually every parish, creating conflict and instability that produced dismissals of many ministers, both Old and New Light, as well as a steady stream of separations by New Lights who rejected the ministry of their Old Light pastors. The end result was a much-weakened ecclesiastical establishment that proved unable to prevent the rise of an alternative Evangelical communion in New England.

In the years after James Davenport's 1744 recantation, Separate Congregationalists in New England struggled to maintain their churches against political and ecclesiastical hostility. Some Separates soon returned to New Light Congregationalist parishes; but most of them would not compromise their separation from the Standing Order. Many of them also embraced the practice of making baptism contingent on a believer's profession of faith. Baptism, they argued, should not be administered to infants but rather only to those who had experienced the New Birth. The practice, they argued, had biblical warrant, and moreover it dramatized their rejection of the Halfway Covenant.

This doctrine of believers' baptism brought these Separates into association with Particular (Calvinist) Baptists in Rhode Island, who possessed a century-long tradition in that colony dating from Roger Williams' original congregation at Providence. By 1752 a number of Separate leaders, including elders Shubael Stearns and Isaac Backus, were calling for "open" communion with the Baptists, while others, notably elders Solomon and Elisha Paine, resisted believers' baptism and demanded "closed" communion only with other Separates. At a 1754 conference at Stonington, Connecticut, the rift became irreconcilable and Backus led his faction into the Baptist communion, overwhelming it with numbers and intense Whitefieldian piety. This new "Separate-Baptist" communion organized formally in 1767 as the Warren, Rhode Island, Baptist Association. The Separate Congregationalists, on the other hand, gradually disintegrated as an ecclesiastical force, their members eventually drifting back to the New Light Congregationalists or into Separate-Baptist churches. By the outbreak of the French and Indian War in 1754, the Awakening had passed in New England, leaving in its wake a shattered Congregationalist establishment divided into Old Light and New Light factions and powerfully challenged by the Whitefieldian revivalism of the Separate-Baptists.

THE AWAKENING IN THE SOUTH

Although sporadic revivals continued to flare up in the back country of New England and the Middle Colonies, after 1745 the center of the Awakening shifted to the South, where first New Side Presbyterians and then Separate-Baptists led the revival through the ensuing decade. During the early 1740s Scots and Scotch-Irish settlers along with a handful of Old Side ministers pushed south and west into the piedmont of Virginia and the Carolinas. In 1742 the New Side Presbytery of New Brunswick commissioned William Robinson to evangelize in Anglican Virginia. At Hanover he encountered a congregation of Dissenters who had embraced the doctrine of the New Birth and whom he organized into the first New Side church in the South. From this beginning the Hanover revival grew steadily under Log College itinerants, assisted by Whitefield's visit in 1745, until Samuel Davies arrived at Hanover in 1747 and initiated the decisive phase of New Side activity in the South.

Davies, born in New Castle, Delaware, and educated by New Side Samuel Blair at Fagg's Manor, Pennsylvania, was ordained by the New Side Presbytery of New Castle in 1746. Dispatched to Virginia, Davies rekindled the revival at Hanover, obtained licenses for seven meetinghouses in five counties, and traveled a vast circuit in the center of the colony. His preaching proved so disruptive that in 1751 the Anglican clergy sought to suspend his license to preach on grounds that itinerancy was subversive to true religion. The Anglicans also argued that the New Side was a schismatic body unprotected by the English Toleration Act of 1689, which required Dissenters to subscribe to the Church of England's Oaths of Allegiance and Supremacy and Thirty-nine Articles of Religion. In short, Virginia Anglicans mounted the same sort of establishmentarian political attack against New Side Presbyterians that Connecticut Congregationalists had against the Separates a decade earlier.

Rather than simply defy the authorities as the Separates had, however, Davies obtained a writ in England sustaining the right of free conscience for Dissenters in the colonies and used that opinion skillfully to win legal recognition of Hanover Presbytery in 1755. That same year Whitefield's third American tour sparked fresh New Side revivals in western counties and the Northern Neck, but before year's end Virginia Presbyterians had suffered devastating attacks on their frontier settlements after Gen. Edward Braddock's defeat by the French and Indians at Fort Duquesne. Until he left the colony in 1758, Davies rallied his coreligionists with sermons that lent the full force of his revival zeal to the military defense of British sovereignty, thereby further integrating the New Side into the cultural establishment of Virginia.

The Baptist role in the Awakening of the South was divided between Regular Baptists, who represented the conservative Calvinist tradition of the Philadelphia Baptist Association (1707), and the more Whitefieldian Separate-Baptists from New England. Regular Baptists first settled along the upper Potomac in Berkeley County in 1743 and spread rapidly across the Appalachians of northern Virginia. Driven eastward by Indian raids, they established a center on Ketocton Creek in Loudoun County in 1755 and grew to sufficient size to be set off as the Ketocton Association in 1765. Through the evangelism of Oliver Hart, Regular Baptists established another southern outpost in South Carolina, organizing the Charleston Baptist Association in 1751.

The Regulars had absorbed only a limited amount of the Awakening's teaching into their orthodox Calvinist style. The Separate-Baptists, on the other hand, represented the very embodiment of Whitefield's radical Evangelicalism and it was they who brought the southern Awakening to its highest pitch. In 1754 Elder Shubael Stearns left Connecticut with his son-in-law Elder Daniel Marshall and their families on an epic evangelistic journey southward. By the year's end they were in Berkeley County, Virginia, and in 1755 they settled and organized a church at Sandy Creek in the North Carolina piedmont. In a short time the Sandy Creek church grew to 600 members as Stearns and Marshall found in the Carolina hinterland a strong popular response to their Whitefieldian itinerancy. Marshall continued on through the piedmont to South Carolina and Georgia, while Stearns spread the Sandy Creek revival north into Virginia. By 1758 they had gathered enough congregations to organize the Sandy Creek Separate-Baptist Association, the first regional body of its kind and the harbinger of future Baptist evangelism in the rural South.

REUNION AND SYNTHESIS

The year 1758 marked the end of the Great Awakening in the South as well as the North. Two events indicated the revival's passing: the reunion of the Presbyterian church and the death of Jonathan Edwards. After seventeen years of schismatic rivalry, the New Side Synod of New York and the Old Side Synod of Philadelphia united under a plan that affirmed the New Side positions on ordination and itinerancy while granting the legitimacy of the Old Side ministers' original protest in 1741. The tenor of this agreement was dictated by the enormous success of New Side evangelism during the hiatus. In 1741 Old Side ministers outnumbered New Side 25 to 22; by 1758 the New Side outnumbered the Old 72 to 22 and had established clear dominance everywhere outside the ethnic Scotch-Irish enclave in Pennsylvania. In addition, the New Side had gained the upper hand in education, establishing the College of New Jersey, now Princeton, in 1746—the year of William Tennent's death and of the closing of his Log College.

Quick turnover in the presidency of the college during its first decade led the trustees in 1758 to call Edwards from Stockbridge to Princeton to lead the struggling school. Since

1745 Edwards had cemented his intellectual reputation with a series of works, including *A Treatise Concerning Religious Affections* (1746) and *A Careful and Strict Enquiry into . . . the Freedom of the Will* (1754), that constructed the outlines of a masterful apologetic for Evangelical Calvinism. He had undertaken the most difficult yet most necessary theological task of his generation: to reconcile the experience of the New Birth with a Calvinist tradition that had rigorously questioned the validity of such spiritual exercises, while at the same time defending the whole against the critiques of Enlightenment philosophy. To this task Edwards brought a wide range of reading, including Calvin and the New England Puritan divines, Locke and a broad range of British Enlightenment theologians and philosophers, the Pietist writings of Spener and Francke, and the French Jansenist theology of Antoine Arnauld, Nicolas Malebranche, and François Fénelon. In pursuing and to a large extent attaining such a goal, he set the course for a century of theological discourse among America's Evangelical Calvinists, Presbyterian, Congregational, Baptist, and Reformed, and earned the status he still enjoys as America's greatest theologian.

Edwards' first great contribution, *A Treatise Concerning Religious Affections*, directly addressed the nature of true religion and delivered an answer as clear as it was uncompromising: "true religion," he wrote, "in great part, consists in holy affections." By affections he meant roughly what we now call emotions, and the holy affections he identified as "fear, hope, love, hatred, desire, sorrow, gratitude, compassion, and zeal." From personal experience and keen observation of the Awakening Edwards was convinced that authentic conversion and spiritual renewal were not in the first instance a matter of rational judgment. To be sure, rational comprehension of Scripture was necessary for the sinner to understand his or her dreadful situation before a righteous God. But the medium through which one received knowledge of salvation and power for regenerate living was the will, exercised through the affections. Regeneration began in the heart, not in the head. Sinners merely know *about* God through their reason; the regenerate come to know God immediately and indubitably through the transformation of their affections by the Holy Spirit.

Edwards severed Evangelical theology from Enlightenment rationalism and committed it to an epistemology of perception and will, sense and emotion, pleasure and pain. In the New Birth the religious affections of the elect are operated upon by the Spirit so that they rightly respond to the infusion of divine grace that inflames and attracts them by its infinite and inherent beauty and excellence. Edwards' affectional definition largely secured the defense of the New Birth against both Deistic rationalism and Humean skepticism. And, just as important, it was consonant with the Calvinist economy of grace. Through the New Birth a predestinating God can and does choose to bestow dramatic evidence of saving grace upon the elect.

The New Birth, then, could make both Enlightened and Calvinist sense, but its sudden and conscious nature contradicted a century of Puritan emphasis on gradual "preparation" for grace as part of a lifelong and often incompletely realized morphology of conversion. In fact, a necessary, conscious, and affectional New Birth was the doctrine that most distinguished Evangelical theology from Puritanism. Puritan spirituality restlessly searched for internal and behavioral evidence of grace while always acknowledging in principle that we cannot finally know whether we are saved while still on earth. The New Birth proclaimed a new dispensation of God's saving grace that could be known with certainty here and now through the irreducibly personal media of emotion and will.

By grounding spirituality in the will, however, Edwards did have to confront a fundamental problem for Calvinism; namely, the freedom of that will, or lack of it, in the economy of grace. Calvinism taught that the action of human will was determined, along with everything else in the process of regeneration, by God. Against this view a diverse group of advocates, including Old Lights, Deists, and John Wesley, argued that since the soul is able freely to will sin, it must also be able freely to will repentance and to petition God for its own salvation. Edwards labeled these positions Arminianism, the term used by orthodox Calvinists to refer to free-will arguments generally (Jacob Arminius was one of the first within the Calvinist churches to suggest an autonomous role for the human soul in the economy of grace).

Edwards tackled the issue in his most philosophically accomplished work, *Enquiry into . . .*

Freedom of the Will. Characteristically, Edwards mounted his strongest argument in the negative mode, demonstrating the impossibility of a fully autonomous and self-determining human will by appealing to the scientific law of cause and effect. All events are caused, including all supposed acts of free will. To be truly free, such acts must be freely determined by some prior cause, which cause must itself be the freely determined effect of yet another cause, and so on. This results in an infinite regress of free and independent causes that must be invoked to explain any single act of free will. For Edwards this is an impossible condition that can only be resolved by the existence of a first cause which is not itself caused, i.e., God. On the positive argument Edwards reversed this logic, claiming that since there is a first cause, we are not free to resist its determinations, but we are free to obey them. In regeneration the elect are not free to resist the New Birth, but their affections freely and naturally respond to the beauty and excellence of divine grace. In this way "necessity is not inconsistent with liberty," and the regenerate will is therefore free in the only meaningful sense of the term; namely, free to choose that which is good, right, pleasurable, and of God.

The inherent beauty and perfection of God and the created order, so central to Edwards' thinking about holy affections and regenerate will, also provided the cornerstone of his moral theology, to which he gave most complete expression in *The Nature of True Virtue* (1765), a treatise written at Stockbridge but published posthumously. In this work Edwards examined the moral qualities of the regenerate will and argued that holy affections produce holy inclination, or benevolence, which is directed first toward God, the source of all being, and then toward all creation. Thus, his fundamental moral axiom: "True virtue most essentially consists in BENEVOLENCE TO BEING IN GENERAL. Or perhaps, to speak more accurately, it is that consent, propensity, and union of heart to being in general, which is immediately exercised in a general good will." This means that the true Christian loves God not for the benefit he or she can obtain from God but rather for what God is and the way God has arranged the universe, regardless of personal consequence. Christian benevolence is therefore "disinterested"; it is governed by what

is most faithful to the divine order, not the human. True saints, then, will exercise good will toward all reality that they encounter, with moral priority accorded to God, church, and nation, and they will categorically oppose evil in all its forms.

In addition to these major works, Edwards wrote on a wide range of other questions. His doctrinal defense of Calvinism included *The Christian Doctrine of Original Sin Defended* (1758) and *A Dissertation Concerning the End for Which God Created the World* (1765; published posthumously). During the Northampton parish controversy he composed his rigorous statement on the terms of communion, *A Humble Inquiry into the Rules of the Word of God* (1749). This concern with visible sainthood also informed his publication of *The Diary of David Brainerd* (1753), the spiritual autobiography of a brilliant young New Light missionary whom Edwards memorialized as the ideal Christian.

Another central interest of Edwards was the working out of God's plan of salvation in human history. He was a consistent postmillennialist, meaning that he reckoned the Last Judgment to occur after the thousand-year reign of the saints described in the Book of Revelation 20:1–6. He therefore looked for signs of that reign's onset in history and identified the Awakening as a harbinger that the millennium was to begin in America. Edwards was at work in Stockbridge revising an extensive sermon series into a systematic theology of history, published in 1779 as *The History of the Work of Redemption,* when he accepted the New Side Presbyterian call to the College of New Jersey. At the opening of his first academic year at Princeton, in 1758, President Edwards demonstrated his confidence in science, another lifelong interest, by obtaining a smallpox vaccination. Six weeks later he died of postinoculation infection.

THE AWAKENING'S AFTERMATH

Edwards' death robbed American Evangelicals of their intellectual leader; Gilbert Tennent's passing two years later deprived them of their greatest revivalist, while throughout the late 1750s the French and Indian War disrupted itinerancy in the back country. The revival impulse returned, however, with the redoubtable Whitefield, who conducted successful American tours in 1764, between the Peace of Paris and the Stamp Act Crisis, and in 1770, during which he died and was buried at Newburyport, Massachusetts. In 1776 Methodist circuit riders dispatched from England by John Wesley sparked their first major revival among Anglicans in Virginia. Separate-Baptists and new sects, including Freewill Baptists, Shakers, and Universalists, fomented the New Light Stir of 1776–1784 in rural New England, and Nova Scotia experienced its own Great Awakening during the same period under the ministration of New Light itinerant Henry Alline. By 1785 the Great Revival had commenced in the South, to be followed after 1800 by the Second Great Awakening throughout the new nation. Under the relentless efforts of Evangelical itinerants, revivalism by the late eighteenth century had been forged into a powerful and permanent shaper of American religion.

The unprecedented success of this continuing revivalism swept Evangelicals into command of America's Protestant churches. Already by 1758 Evangelicals constituted a strong majority of the Reformed communions in America—Congregationalist, Presbyterian, Dutch Reformed, German Reformed, and Baptist—a dominance they retained for more than a century. Among English-speaking Calvinists, the Baptists benefited most from the revivals, creating a rural constituency that outstripped the Congregationalists and Presbyterians during the early nineteenth century. And as revivals continued to flourish in city and country before and after the Civil War, a stream of new sects joined the older Evangelical communions to institutionalize the perennial flow of American converts to the New Birth. In the German churches, too, Pietists maintained control through 1800 and beyond.

Anglicans, by contrast, largely resisted the Calvinist theology of the American Awakening until 1763, when Devereux Jarratt, converted by New Side Presbyterians but loyal to the Church of England, began a highly successful itinerancy from his parish of Bath in central Virginia. Most Anglicans, however, found John Wesley's Arminian Evangelical theology of free will, free grace, and sanctification far more congenial. Massive conversions, gathered by Methodist itinerants like Bishop Francis Asbury and Peter Cartwright after the Revolution, especially among southern Anglicans, propelled the Methodist Episcopal church to the numerical leadership of American Protestantism by 1830.

With the continuing efflorescence of Evangelicalism came the development of an American Evangelical religious culture. The Evangelicals continued their educational efforts after the founding of the College of New Jersey. George Whitefield joined Benjamin Franklin and Anglican rector William Smith in establishing the University of Pennsylvania (1751) at Philadelphia; the Warren Baptist Association organized the College of Rhode Island (1764), now Brown University; and renegade New Light Congregationalist Eleazar Wheelock founded Dartmouth College at Hanover, New Hampshire (1769). The New Lights also published America's first magazine, Joseph Prince, Jr.'s, Boston weekly *Christian History* (1743–1744), a series of ministerial accounts of the Great Awakening in New England towns. By midcentury Evangelicals dominated American religious publishing with their sermons, hymnals, mission magazines, moral and educational writings, tracts, and spiritual autobiographies.

This flood of religious works deeply influenced the emergence of American literature and, through hymnody, music as well. During the Awakening Whitefield introduced the congregational singing of Isaac Watts's hymns into worship and revival meetings. Watts's popularity soared spectacularly; he became the most published author in eighteenth-century America and he inspired a long line of American poetic imitators beginning with Presbyterian Samuel Davies, Congregationalist Timothy Dwight, and Baptist John Leland. In New England the demand for spiritually affecting church song fostered British America's first indigenous musical style, pioneered in the 1770s by Boston's William Billings and spread by itinerant singing masters throughout the new nation.

Intellectually, Edwards' theological synthesis gained acceptance from three generations of New Light Congregationalists and New Side Presbyterians, transmitted to them by College of New Jersey President Aaron Burr, Sr., his son-in-law and successor; by Yale President Timothy Dwight and theologian Jonathan Edwards, his grandson and nephew respectively; and by his own students Samuel Hopkins and Joseph Bellamy. Through these familial, educational, and professional networks, Edwards' theology became the defining framework of Evangelical Calvinist thought for a century, generating successive schools from the New Divinity of Hopkins through the Princeton Theology of Archibald Alexander and Charles Hodge to the New Haven Theology of Nathaniel William Taylor.

From a still wider perspective the Awakening patterned the very structure of nineteenth-century American Protestant thought, as the issues that originally divided Jonathan Edwards and Charles Chauncy—emotion versus reason in religious experience, the freedom of the will, limited versus universal atonement, the constitution of the church—continued to inform debate into the nineteenth century between Evangelical Calvinists and a variety of Arminians including Chauncy, Jonathan Mayhew, and William Ellery Channing, the architects of New England Unitarianism, as well as Francis Asbury and a host of Methodist apologists.

Other dimensions of the Great Awakening also powerfully affected the development of American culture. The experience of the New Birth fostered a psychological style of subjective individualism that helped shape the American self. Spiritual rebirth entailed deep introspection, acknowledgment of dependence on God, emotional transformation, and alteration of behavior, all of which produced a new kind of personal identity grounded in the experience of certainty and change. Socially, the Evangelicals separated themselves from their worldly surroundings. Both physically and culturally, the saints dwelled together as much as possible within the confines of their gathered communities. Typically they wore simple clothing and shunned affluent display; they neither swore nor drank nor smoked; they observed scrupulous standards of fair business practice and sober public behavior. Much of their cultural life centered on the family, a school of piety where children were broken in will early and parents educated by precept and example.

The collective experience of Evangelicals within their gathered churches constituted another vital social dimension of their movement. In Evangelical congregations vast numbers of Americans came together into voluntary associations bound together by intense spiritual, emotional, and moral commitment. Their community was grounded in the revolutionary principle of spiritual equality: each believer was equal in the sight of God and therefore in the church. As their oft-cited slogan went, "God is no respecter of persons." Following this Evangelical principle and relying on the discernment of the Holy Spirit in themselves and their charismatic leaders, they elected their own members and ministers and they judged and disciplined each other based on the terms of written church covenants. They organized their larger communions into representative assemblies, presbyteries and associations, synods and conventions.

For Evangelicals the church represented the highest form of society. Their spiritual governments were constitutional, vesting rights, responsibilities, and authority in members and officers alike. They readily extended these political principles to secular government as well, but Evangelical political theology polarized into libertarian and establishmentarian parties, closely correlated with regional differences and ecclesiastical traditions. The Evangelical movement took root most deeply in the colonial interior. There more extreme communions like Separate-Baptists and New Side Presbyterians flourished and Evangelicals as a group soon predominated. Rural Evangelicalism contributed mightily to the emergent localist culture of the hinterland, reinforcing its values of individualism and local community.

The political theology of these folk was libertarian. They regarded human government with suspicion; insisted on fundamental rights and liberties, above all the right to free exercise of religious conscience; and impatiently awaited the Second Coming of Christ and the millennial kingdom of the saints. They were first politicized during the French and Indian War and zealously defended their rights not only in the Revolution, but also in the 1764–1765 Regulators' Rebellion of the North Carolina piedmont, Shays's Rebellion of 1786–1787 in western Massachusetts, and the Whiskey Rebellion of 1794 in western Pennsylvania.

The other branch of Evangelical political theology, establishmentarianism, reflected orthodox Calvinist teaching on church and state as understood by New Lights and New Sides in the cosmopolitan capitals of Boston and Philadelphia. New Lights had never left the Congregationalist establishment in New England, and Presbyterians gained substantial political power in Pennsylvania after 1756, when Quakers, refusing to sanction military defense in the French and Indian War, withdrew from the colonial government. After the Revolution, these New Lights and New Sides both still adhered to Calvin's vision of government as the partner of the gathered church in a millennial regime on earth. They had besought God for victory and now envisioned an America guided by divine providence, inspired by Christian morality, and clothed in republican virtue.

These libertarian and establishmentarian wings opposed each other in the constitutional debates of the 1780s. Establishmentarians led by Yale President Ezra Stiles and College of New Jersey President John Witherspoon allied with the Federalists to support the plan of the Philadelphia Convention for a strong central government that left the states free to determine their own arrangements between church and state. Libertarians aligned with Antifederalists and demanded a Bill of Rights that included religious liberty precisely in order to prevent political interference with their freedom to dissent. Massachusetts Separate-Baptist Isaac Backus led the Evangelical campaign for religious liberty in New England and later helped swing the libertarian wing into the political camp of Thomas Jefferson, author of the Virginia Statute Establishing Religious Freedom (1786).

In all these ways the Great Awakening proved to be more than simply a religious phenomenon. In its complex pattern of consequences it can be seen more fully as America's first democratic popular movement. During the second quarter of the eighteenth century an unprecedentedly large number of Americans collectively rose up to challenge the constraints of religious, political, and cultural tradition. They were drawn into that challenge by a new kind of religious leader epitomized by Whitefield, charismatic, popular, mobile, who challenged them to address fundamental questions about their eternal destiny and earthly mission. In response they experienced first powerful personal transformations and then intense religious community. They took the message of spiritual equality into their churches,

making of them laboratories for self-government. Gathered together originally to preserve their purity against a corrupt world, Evangelicals gradually reengaged with public society, demanding and defending fundamental political and religious rights. Their revivals continued, their numbers grew, and their religious culture developed. By 1776 Evangelicals had constructed a powerful popular movement based on personal experience, religious community, and egalitarian church institutions. Through their strong support of the Revolution they entered the cultural mainstream of emergent America and stood ready to carry the legacy of the Great Awakening deep into the heart, soul, and mind of the new nation.

BIBLIOGRAPHY

Maurice W. Armstrong, *The Great Awakening in Nova Scotia, 1776–1809* (1948); Isaac Backus, *Isaac Backus on Church, State, and Calvinism: Pamphlets, 1754–1789*, William G. McLoughlin, ed. (1968), and *The Diary of Isaac Backus*, 3 vols., William G. McLoughlin, ed. (1979); Patricia U. Bonomi and Peter R. Eisenstadt, "Church Adherence in the Eighteenth-Century British American Colonies," in *William and Mary Quarterly*, 39 (1982); Richard L. Bushman, *From Puritan to Yankee: Character and the Social Order in Connecticut, 1690–1765* (1967) and, as ed., *The Great Awakening, Documents on the Revival of Religion, 1740–1745* (1970); Jon Butler, "Enthusiasm Described and Decried: The Great Awakening as Interpretive Fiction," in *Journal of American History*, 69 (1982).

C. Conrad Cherry, *The Theology of Jonathan Edwards: A Reappraisal* (1966); Nathan Cole and Michael J. Crawford, eds., "The Spiritual Travels of Nathan Cole," in *William and Mary Quarterly*, 33 (1976); Jonathan Edwards, *The Works of Jonathan Edwards* Perry Miller et al., eds. (1957–).

Norman Fiering, *Jonathan Edwards's Moral Thought and Its British Context* (1981); Edwin S. Gaustad, *The Great Awakening in New England* (1965); Wesley M. Gewehr, *The Great Awakening in Virginia, 1740–1790* (1930); Clarence C. Goen, *Revivalism and Separatism in New England: Strict Congregationalists and Separate Baptists in the Great Awakening, 1740–1800* (1962); Alan Heimert, *Religion and the American Mind: From the Great Awakening to the Revolution* (1966) and, with Perry Miller, as eds., *The Great Awakening: Documents Illustrating the Crisis and Its Consequences* (1967); Stuart Clark Henry, *George Whitefield, Wayfaring Witness* (1957); Richard Hofstadter, *America at 1750: A Social Portrait* (1971); Rhys Isaac, *The Transformation of Virginia, 1740–1790* (1982); Stephen A. Marini, *Radical Sects of Revolutionary New England* (1982) and "Rehearsal for Revival: Sacred Singing and the Great Awakening in America," in Joyce Irwin, ed., *Sacred Sound: Music in Religious Thought and Practice* (1983); Martin E. Marty, *Religion, Awaken-*

ing, and Revolution (1977); Charles Hartshorn Maxson, The Great Awakening in the Middle Colonies (1920); William G. McLoughlin, Isaac Backus and the American Pietistic Tradition (1967), New England Dissent, 1630–1833: The Baptists and the Separation of Church and State, 2 vols. (1971), and Revivals, Awakenings, and Reform (1978).

Elizabeth I. Nyvakken, "New Light on the Old Side: Irish Influence on Colonial Presbyterianism," in Journal of American History, 68 (1982); F. Ernest Stoeffler, ed., Continental Pietism and Early American Christianity (1976); Harry S. Stout, "The Great Awakening in New England Reconsidered: The New England Clergy as a Case Study," in Journal of Social History, 8 (1974), and The New England Soul: Preaching and Religious Culture in Colonial New England (1986); William Warren Sweet, Religion in Colonial America (1942); Joseph Tracy, The Great Awakening: A History of the Revival of Religion in the Time of Edwards and Whitefield (1841); Patricia J. Tracy, Jonathan Edwards, Pastor: Religion and Society in Eighteenth-Century Northampton (1980); Leonard J. Trinterud, The Forming of an American Tradition: A Re-examination of Colonial Presbyterianism (1949); George Whitefield, George Whitefield's Journals: A New Edition Containing Fuller Material (1960); Ola Elizabeth Winslow, Jonathan Edwards, 1703–1758: A Biography (1940).

[See also CHURCH AND STATE; CONGREGATIONALISM FROM INDEPENDENCE TO THE PRESENT; NEW ENGLAND PURITANISM; and REVIVALISM.]

REVIVALISM

Stuart C. Henry

R EVIVALISM, not to be confused with revival, is a distinctively American phenomenon, dating from the mid-eighteenth century
and relating to one or a series of services, often
highly emotional, designed to stimulate renewed
interest in religion. It is intended for persons
formerly identified with but now apathetic to religious life and organization, or to awaken in
those indifferent or even hostile toward religion
a sensitivity and commitment to a particular religious form or community. In America revivalism
has been largely, though not exclusively, a Protestant phenomenon.

The forces that led ultimately to distinctive
American revivalism began with the activity of
Theodore J. Frelinghuysen. German born, educated at the University of Lingen, but strongly
influenced by Dutch Calvinism, he came to
America to accept the pastorate of three small
churches in New Jersey three years after his ordination in the Dutch Reformed Church in 1717.
Alarmed and challenged by the lax state of religion he found in the colonies, he launched a
campaign of intensely evangelistic preaching and
a call for personal conviction of sin and conversion. "Alas!" he cried, "how far have we departed from the purity of the primitive churches.
Oh! how far do we yet daily depart!" Deploring
those in the churches who bore "the name of
members, though often as ignorant as heathen,
openly living in gross sins, and not marked by
the least morality," Frelinghuysen indicted the
apathy of alleged Christians. "With what reason
may we exclaim, with the holy Polycarp: O good
God! To what evil times hast thou preserved
me!" (*Sermons*, 1856, p. 65).

Frelinghuysen's preaching initiated a movement that lasted from 1720 until well past
mid-century in which colonists from Maine to
Georgia were aroused with such zeal and in such
numbers to return to the commitments of their
forefathers or to make them anew for themselves
that their activity thereafter was called the Great
Awakening. Actually there were many religious
awakenings during the period, and all were characterized by a revival of religion.

Frelinghuysen's transparent sincerity attracted popular sympathy and at the same time
occasioned controversy and objection from
other clergymen. His zeal, however, operated
effectively to secure his acceptance and success;
and his reputation, his message, and his methods
spread to adjoining areas where, among others,
William Tennent and his two sons, Gilbert and
William, Jr., labored after the same manner and
with the reassuring results that attended Frelinghuysen's efforts. At Neshaminy, Pennsylvania, in
a modest building contemptuously styled the
Log College by detractors of the Awakening, the
elder Tennent established a school for training
ministers, and in one generation educated a
number of young men, among them his son Gilbert, later celebrated as an impressive evangelist.
Gilbert's 1740 sermon "The Danger of an Unconverted Ministry" excoriated orthodox ministers, who were increasingly out of sympathy with
the Awakening and contributed to the eventual
split of Scotch-Irish Presbyterianism into Old
Side (anti-emotionalism) and New Side (pro-
Awakening) over the question of revivalism. Although Gilbert Tennent subsequently became a
leader in the reconciliation of the opposing parties, he had, nevertheless, expressed the laity's
distrust of an entrenched ecclesiastical authority,
which outlived temporary and partial harmony
between the factions.

Meanwhile in Northampton, Massachusetts,
Jonathan Edwards, restrained and disciplined in

delivery of intellectually sophisticated sermons, began unexpectedly to elicit intense and enthusiastic response to his preaching. Congregations were eager to experience the delights of redemption, frantic to escape the vividly depicted hell. Three hundred persons were converted within six months. In *A Faithful Narrative of the Surprising Work of God,* Edwards described the excitement of 1735 in his own parish:

> But though the people did not ordinarily neglect their worldly business, yet there then was the reverse of what commonly is: religion was with all classes the great concern, and the world was a thing only by the by. The only thing in their view was to get the kingdom of heaven, and everyone appeared pressing into it: the engagedness of their hearts in this great concern could not be hid; it appeared in their very countenances. It then was a dreadful thing amongst us to lie out of Christ, in danger every day of dropping into hell; and what persons' minds were intent upon was to escape for their lives, and to fly from the wrath to come. All would eagerly lay hold of opportunities for their souls; and were wont very often to meet together in private houses for religious purposes; and such meetings, when appointed were wont greatly to be thronged.
>
> There was scarcely a single person in the town, either old or young, that was left unconcerned about the great things of the eternal world.
>
> (*The Works of Jonathan Edwards,* C. C. Goen, ed., 1972, vol. 4, p. 150)

The spirit and the message of the revival at Northampton spread first to neighboring communities and then steadily through the Connecticut Valley, gaining momentum and popular acceptance. A significant shift of emphasis, however, was increasingly manifest both in the emotional proclamation of the "hot-gospelers" of the Log College perspective and in the controlled philosophical presentation of the good news by Edwards. Thereafter the change of focus was persistent, though not always consciously so, in revivalistic preaching in America. Whereas ministers earlier spoke of the gracious work of God's redemption, they now pointed to the significance of the human response to the divine mercy. The new focus both acknowledged and nourished a pietistic dissatisfaction with the standing order. (*Pietistic* here refers to the devotional or emotional dimension of religion as opposed to the intellectual.) The awakened understanding of the relevance of the Gospel to the human condition was balanced by the doubt that the unalloyed good news might at least as well—if not better—be found through individual and independent pilgrimage.

In October 1740 George Whitefield, already famous in England as evangelist without peer in persuasive eloquence, and already popular with colonists to whom he had preached on his first visit to the New World in 1738, arrived to visit Edwards in Northampton. Whitefield's charisma was as appealing as Edwards' philosophy and, as on all of his seven visits to America, he awakened thousands, speaking to and, according to contemporary records, being heard by as many as 12,000 people at a time, up and down the Atlantic seaboard. In America, as in England, his success as revivalist rested not only upon the interpretation of the Gospel in terms understandable to the masses, but on the masterfully dramatic manner of its presentation by his stirring voice.

The populace was intoxicated by Whitefield's message as well as by his manner. The idea of a God who arbitrarily elected some to salvation and some to damnation, thereby eliminating all possibility of human choice, was ill received by descendants of pioneers who had subdued Indians, cleared forests, established themselves in a wilderness, wrested a living from stony New England soil, and were soon to declare their political independence. They found it unfair that they should have no say in their souls' salvation. In typical American fashion they rooted their faith in experience, defined in terms of their ability no less than their memory. This position, styled *Arminian* since Jacob Arminius had given it formal statement in the early seventeenth century, had many ramifications; but the specific claim of the Arminians that one's ultimate fate was determined by human decision was in sharp conflict with the traditional Calvinistic stance. In his zeal to guard against a doctrine of the efficacy of good works, to say nothing of protecting the sovereignty of God, Calvin seemed to Arminians to replace the experimental dimension of faith with one that was deterministic. Neither Arminian nor Calvinist doubted that salvation was of God. Both saw faith as decision. The difficulty lay in knowing who made the decision. Whitefield insisted that he was a Calvinist. The crowds who listened to him, however, often heard him, as they heard revivalists after him, affirming human ability.

By the end of Whitefield's career in 1770, the original verve of the revival had diminished, although certain characteristic features of revivalism, which in time became indelible marks of the phenomenon, were firm: a strong and uncritical orientation to the Bible with an implied non-intellectualism, perhaps even anti-intellectualism; the possibility of every individual to convert the will toward God; the respectability, even adequacy, of emotion in and as religion; and the relation of revival and reform. Eventually each feature became a pivot of controversy, but concern and conflict over such matters—as revivalism itself—ran an undulating course. The religious fervor that accompanied the Great Awakening, in time, was displaced, and often replaced, by the zeal of patriotism.

During the procession of the Revolutionary War, French rationalism, introduced to the colonial aristocracy by European allies, began to spread through all classes. Eventually college youth adopted, or at least affected, infidelity, choosing for themselves such nicknames as Voltaire, Rousseau, and d'Alembert. Timothy Dwight, on assuming the presidency of Yale, found students who were eager to debate the question, "Are the Scriptures of the Old and New Testaments the Word of God?" Yet Dwight's devastating victory in debate with them indicated more than a new turn that the Second Awakening would take. It spoke also to a generation in terms of its own experience and its hope.

Before the end of the eighteenth century much of the enthusiasm for French philosophy in America had been dissipated by revulsion at the Reign of Terror. The disposition to reason, however, remained. Dwight did not answer the students' questions with the pronouncement of revelation that had characterized Whitefield's preaching, but with sound logic. It was practical to be Christian. Dwight fought reason with reason. And thereafter in America revivalism has had a strong strain of common sense in its appeal to the unconverted. The urge to religious apathy in the early nineteenth century retreated before the drive that prompted revival. The idealism regarding human nature and the egalitarianism that the American Revolution inevitably produced found religious expression in impassioned argument over theological anthropology. The orthodox tenet of human inability and the consequent doctrine of election were in process of being replaced by an optimistic belief in free agency. Two individuals who were prominent and influential in achieving the transition were Nathaniel Taylor and Lyman Beecher, both of whom had come under the influence of Dwight and admired him extravagantly.

During the colonial period Protestant Christianity in America was strongly Calvinistic. Edwards' reputation did not rest solely upon the brilliance of his metaphysical perception, but equally upon his fidelity to the tradition of Reformation theology. His logically irrefutable demonstration of individual responsibility in the inevitable choice of evil validated the justice of God to the popular religious mind. The doctrine of personal responsibility, however, was interpreted by Taylor and Beecher to imply the sufficiency of human ability: if the creature is responsible for personal choice, God is just in damning the creature throughout eternity; but a just God does not damn the creature, however responsible, for failure to achieve that which is beyond human ability. Taylor explicitly taxed the creature with responsibility for sin: "The question then still recurs, what is this moral depravity for which man deserves the wrath of God? I answer—it is man's own act, consisting in a free choice of some object rather than God, as his chief good;—or a free preference of the world and of worldly good, to the will and glory of God. . . ." He was equally blunt in insistence that all will sin. "What then are we to understand, when it is said that mankind are depraved by nature?—I answer—that such is their nature, that they will sin and only sin in all the appropriate circumstances of their being." Taylor altered the situation, however, by the addition of the qualification "with power to the contrary" (*Concio ad Clerum. A Sermon . . .*, 1828, pp. 8, 13). Less blatantly, but no less obviously, Beecher expressed the same sentiment. He contended that "men are free agents, in possession of such faculties, and placed in such circumstances, as render it practicable for them to do whatever God requires" ("The Faith Once Delivered to the Saints," *Sermons*, 1828, p. 218). This theological assumption is basic to practical revivalism.

Taylor taught the doctrine to divinity students at Yale. Through them his teaching pervaded the

East. Beecher in 1832 became first president of Lane Seminary in Cincinnati, Ohio, and thus in similar fashion instructed the frontier. As early as 1807 he had begun the practice of preaching human ability in evangelistic sermons that were presented in series, developing a position designed to revive an indifferent constituency to religious activity and to convert non-believers. Both Taylor and Beecher strove for a practical and systematic solution to the human predicament. The goal, if not the pattern, that Beecher adopted in his first parish at East Hampton, New York, was repeated throughout his career. He described his planning with an associate the strategy that would ensure results:

> We conferred together, and resolved to . . . labor for a revival in our churches. We went home with fire in our hearts . . . but we felt like Elijah on Carmel, when there was no cloud nor sign of rain. . . . I felt the revival in myself, but it was long, long before it came. . . . I began to predict . . . that a great work was at hand. . . . the good people wondered. They made me think of hens in the night, when you carry a candle into the henroost, how they open first one eye and then the other, half asleep. So they . . . wondered what I could see to make me think there was to be a revival.
>
> (*Autobiography,* 1865, vol. I, pp. 161–162)

Beecher persisted. Revival came. There were, Beecher reported, a "hundred converts, nearly."

Significantly, for revivalism in America there was evidence that the right procedure produced the right results. The Great Awakening had been a source of wonderment to all, not least to those who were (in their opinion) God's instruments in its accomplishment. Edwards found the work of the Holy Spirit "surprising." Nineteenth-century evangelists were increasingly committed to the confidence that by proper planning and precaution they could ensure revival. Proof of the thesis appears in the career of one of Beecher's contemporaries, Charles Grandison Finney, the first modern revivalist.

Finney was born in Connecticut in 1792, but when he was two years old his parents, following the westward migration, moved to Oneida County, New York, where he grew up exposed to the frontier environment. His personal perspective and his subsequent career in evangelism reflect a combination of the New England piety that he inherited from his parents and the pioneer spirit he absorbed in his youth. Prepared for Yale, he declined to go on the advice of his schoolmaster, who insisted that he could accomplish his own education, a project he prosecuted so successfully that when he was but twenty-two years of age he joined a law firm in Adams, New York, and shortly thereafter was admitted to the bar. Lacking clear understanding of the term "Mosaic law," which he encountered in research preparation of a brief, he bought a Bible and privately began a careful and systematic study of the Scripture, as a result of which he began to consider whether he could accept the Christ whom he found presented in the Gospels and if he would himself be acceptable to Christ. Accepting Christ offered little difficulty. As for being accepted by Christ, Finney concluded that the outcome rested upon his own decision and that the Bible plainly taught that if he decided to accept Christ's salvation, God would accept and save him. This legal analysis of the matter in terms of contractual agreement was fundamental to his later evangelizing. Finney's own decision was accompanied by a spiritual experience in which he believed himself to have seen the Lord standing before him face to face and to have received a "mighty baptism of the Holy Ghost":

> The Holy Spirit descended upon me in a manner that seemed to go through me body and soul. I could feel the impression, like a wave of electricity going through and through me. Indeed it seemed to come in waves and waves of liquid love; for I could not express it in any other way. It seemed like the very breath of God. I can recollect that it seemed to fan me, like immense wings.
>
> No words can express the wonderful love. . . . These waves came over me and over me. . . . I cried out, "I shall die if these waves continue to pass over me." I said, "Lord, I cannot bear any more."
>
> (*Memoirs,* 1876, pp. 20–21)

Finney began his work as an evangelist the following day, first retiring from a case for which he had been employed by announcing to his client, "I have a retainer from the Lord Jesus Christ to plead his cause, and I cannot plead yours" (*Memoirs,* p. 24), and then rushing out onto the street to engage all he met in conversation regarding the state of their souls.

Thereafter religion was his profession. Placed in the care of the presbytery he refused the suggestion that he go to Princeton, choosing rather to study independently, because he disapproved of and disagreed with what he knew of the theology being taught at Princeton, especially as he had seen it evidenced in some of the members of the presbytery. Nevertheless, he was ordained in 1824 and for almost a decade conducted revivals with success that brought him national celebrity. His lack of convention and his novel introduction of "new measures" became the foci of bitter conflict, especially with seminary-trained ministers, but he was successful from the first day with lay folk and eventually with clergy as well.

The measures that Finney styled "new" were less innovative than the objection to them suggests. Many of his revival techniques represented the adaptation to an urban environment of practices that had emerged in the frontier camp meetings. Their novelty lay in the ardor and efficiency with which Finney organized them into a system. The conventional religionists, even those who favored the revival, were offended, perhaps threatened, by Finney's organized and extensive use of techniques that earlier had appeared singly and sporadically. He held his services at "unseasonable hours"; that is, on days of the week and at times of day when the community was unaccustomed to assembling for divine service. He even extended the services occasionally over a period of days so that he achieved cumulative force in "breaking down" congregations, his term for reducing his hearers to a state of emotional distress and utter despair over their sinful condition and certain doom. In his sermons he used direct and forceful language, frequently more suited to the courtroom than the pulpit. His illustrations were commonplace and plain, his language blunt and expressive. He gave women the opportunity to pray in public. In his own prayers as well as in his sermons he mentioned individuals by name, often to their embarrassment, if not shame. His assistants were adept at urging folk to respond to the preacher's altar calls, and there was, finally, the "anxious bench" where sinners were invited, encouraged, and almost forced to sit, directly under the watchful eye of the preacher as he piloted or prodded them into the Kingdom. These measures occasioned violent physical manifestations. People wept without control, cried out, fainted, fell into trances. Finney's methods effected numerous conversions, many of them, reportedly, permanent; they also sparked severe criticism, especially from clergymen.

In July 1827, eighteen Presbyterian and Congregational ministers—representatives from East and West—met at New Lebanon, New York, to reach some compromise in matters of faith and practice in revivalism. Easterners were eager to preserve the growing sentiment for revival; but they were uneasy over the unconventional style that Finney was popularizing. Western ministers were insistent that the new vitality of religion was expressly due to the revival meetings, which were carefully planned and guaranteed of success in part through the use of new measures. There was little conclusive action or resolution at the conference. What victory there was seemed to belong to Finney. Certainly the new measures for which he contended were neither effectively indicted nor abandoned. Rather they tended to become the norm. Years later Beecher, reporting the matter to his adoring children, who were compiling material for a biography of their father, remembered his role as braver and more definitive than the recorded history of revivalism in America sustains. He had, he said, minced no words with Finney:

> I know your plan, and you know I do; you mean to come to Connecticut and carry a streak of fire to Boston. But if you attempt it, as the Lord liveth, I'll meet you at the State line, and call out all the artillerymen, and fight every inch of the way to Boston, and then I'll fight you there.
> (*Autobiography*, vol. 2, p. 101)

Yet four years after the New Lebanon conference Beecher invited Finney to Boston. He came.

More basic than the Beecher-Finney quarrel over the new measures was their substantial agreement regarding human ability. Each in his way affirmed not simply the right, but the ability, of the human will to turn itself to God. When the two ministers later parted company it was not in conflict over revivalistic innovations, but concerning the theology known as Oberlin Perfectionism, by which Finney simply meant that an individual committed to Christ could, by discipline and effort, come to the point that he could obey the law of God. Meanwhile Finney, who had sustained no formal censure, nor retreated from his position, continued to refine his techniques for controlling the Holy Spirit and thus, in effect, bringing about a revival by following a reasonable procedure. In his *Lectures on Revivals of Religion,* published in 1835, he contended that a revival "is not a miracle, or dependent on a miracle, in any sense. It is a purely philosophical result of the right use of the constituted means —as much so as any other effect produced by the application of means." Finney further argued that a revival was to be expected "when the attention of ministers is especially directed to this *particular object,* and when their preaching and other efforts are aimed particularly for the conversion of sinners." He says quite baldly, "You see why you have not a revival. It is only because you don't want one. Because you are not praying for it, nor anxious for it, nor putting forth effort for it" (William G. McLoughlin, ed., 1960, pp. 13, 325).

Finney's position was completely different from that of Jonathan Edwards and from the typical Calvinist of the Old School. Ironically, both Finney and Beecher claimed allegiance to the Westminster orthodoxy of Calvinism, but they insisted that their own interpretation was a more faithful statement of the tradition than that of those whose theology practically denied freedom of will. After Finney, American revivalism was oriented not to the inscrutable will of God but to human effort which, if fervent and faithful, would surely achieve salvation. Calvinism's concept of the sovereignty of God was supplemented now by a strong doctrine of human ability.

Especially did the emerging American character of revivalism flourish in the West. Following the Revolution a steady stream of pioneers, traveling by the Wilderness Road, through Maryland or southern Pennsylvania, or floating on flat boats down the Monongahela and Ohio rivers, poured westward in such numbers that by the third decade of the nineteenth century more than a third of the nation's population was west of the Allegheny mountains. In the frontier situation, however, there was limited opportunity for re-creating or preserving the ecclesiastical forms of the Eastern Seaboard. Religion—especially in its revivalistic manifestation—tended to be more, rather than less, emotional. Theology was often reduced to the bare-bones essentials. And in this connection, folk who braved the dangers of the wilderness and survived through coura-

geous spirit, indomitable will, and physical strength were understandably ill-disposed to hear of their inability to effect any positive contribution toward their own salvation. They rejected the theology of "cannotism"—an expression used by Finney to indicate and deplore belief in humans' inability to turn to God by their own power—and welcomed the egalitarian and essentially optimistic spirit of revivalists, who offered salvation freely to all who would accept. Their distinctive pioneer expressions of religion were not only contributions to the national tradition but developments, as well, in the revival phenomenon. Subtly dominant in the story of American religion, western revivalism was recognizably influential at some specific points.

The camp meeting was a natural outgrowth of frontier conditions. It originated in Kentucky, where as early as 1797 there was spontaneous revival in Logan County. The Cane Ridge camp meeting in 1801 proved to be both inspiration and model for meetings that followed in Kentucky and elsewhere, without diminished popularity until the 1840s. Set at a time that did not interfere with the farmer's calendar, and conveniently located near a water supply, these outdoor religious meetings often brought together thousands for four days or longer. Services were conducted throughout the day and into the night, frequently with several ministers preaching simultaneously in different parts of the camp ground, though not out of earshot of each other. Emotional irregularities abounded. Worshipers not uncommonly suffered attacks of the "jerks" or the "barks," lapsed into trancelike states, or danced wildly. Routinely the high point of the camp meeting was the sacramental service. The coalescing features of the camp meeting underscored the importance of human response to the divine redemption, strengthened the commitment to the potential of human ability, and by the democratic association in common celebration of the sacrament of a variety of denominational representatives (to say nothing of those who were formal members of no religious group) liberated a nascent ecumenism and indirectly discredited the necessity of church membership for salvation. The most famous of the early camp meetings, which in somewhat altered form have continued into the twentieth century, was that at Cane Ridge, Kentucky, in the summer of 1801. For emotionalism, informality, and lack of inhibition, this event, which brought together perhaps 20,000 people, has not been surpassed.

The circuit rider was not an innovation of western revivalism, although he was singularly adaptable to the peculiar conditions of the frontier. Almost a hundred itinerant preachers were laboring in America by the end of the Revolution. As pioneers pushed farther into the wilderness, their number increased to serve the growing number of settlements. Although education was not necessarily frowned upon, it was by no means regarded as necessary for the circuit rider. His authority lay in physical endurance (it was not unusual for a rider to need as much as six weeks to complete a circuit) and in his identification with the people to whom he ministered. His creed was sparse but strong, his orthodoxy unquestioned, and his patriotism often enough so bound up with theology that Americanism was at times represented as an expression of Christianity.

Peter Cartwright was a Titan among the itinerants. He won converts both by the power of his testimony and by his skill as a wrestler, depending upon the appeal to which some potential convert was most susceptible. By his unerring instinct of the proprieties of the wilderness Cartwright achieved deservedly the reputation of being a man of the frontier. The identification of the revivalist—and for that matter of the Christian—with the figure of the scout, a developing national ideal, is plain in Cartwright's own description of the challenge to the revivalist:

> A Methodist preacher in those days, when he felt that God had called him to preach, instead of hunting up a college or Biblical institute, hunted up a hardy pony or a horse, and some traveling apparatus, and with his library always at hand, namely, Bible, Hymn Book, and Discipline, he started, and with a text that never wore out nor grew stale, he cried, "Behold the Lamb of God, that taketh away the sin of the world!" In this way he went through storms of wind, hail, snow, and rain; climbed hills and mountains, traversed valleys, plunged through swamps, swam swollen streams, lay out all night, wet, weary, and hungry, held his horse by the bridle all night, or tied him to a limb, slept with his saddle blanket for a bed, his saddle or saddle-bags for his pillow, and his old big coat or blanket, if he had any, for a covering. Often he slept in dirty cabins, on earthen floors, before the fire; ate roasting ears for bread, drank butter-milk for coffee, or sage tea for imperial; took, with a hearty zest, deer or bear meat, or wild turkey, for breakfast, dinner, and supper, if he could get it.
>
> (*Autobiography*, 1956, p. 164)

The externalization of religion, transforming the inward and mysterious experience of God's grace of the colonial Puritans into a visible pattern of outward behavior, owed much to the influence of circuit rider and camp meeting. The frontier was not the only force in the metamorphosis, nor always the strongest, but it was significant. Revivalism in its camp-meeting manifestation encouraged the notion that one must know with specificity the exact time and place of conversion; and the pragmatic concept of religion that saw orthodoxy measured, at least partially, with reference to a quasi-ascetic Spartan life-style was strengthened by the figure of the circuit rider–revivalist, whose strength was great because his creed was true, and whose rejection of strong drink, cardplaying, theater, and dancing both demonstrated and commended his interpretation of religion.

The recurring waves of religious awakening that since the colonial period had galvanized the interest of Americans and directed them toward the practical expression of orthodoxy in everyday life was always concerned with reform. Edwards had deplored the "dullness" of religion among his parishioners, where "Licentiousness for some years greatly prevailed among the youth of the town; they were many of them very much addicted to night walking, and frequenting the tavern, and lewd practices . . ." (*A Faithful Narrative . . .*, p. 146). Lyman Beecher preached a bloodcurdling series of sermons on intemperance. The goals and the technique of reform, however, varied greatly. No revivalist doubted, and no convert questioned, that reform naturally followed conversion; but the resulting program was often without organization, lacking in clarity as to whether it should appropriately be personal or social, and inexpressible in neat and succinct summaries and reports. The principle was constant, but the manifestation was protean. Generally, the interest in reform divided along two lines: there were those who thought that individuals, redeemed and reformed, would automatically and irresistibly transform the social order. Others believed that only through broad attack on social problems could the Kingdom be forced. There were, nevertheless, certain problems—especially after 1830—that continually plagued religionists, regardless of whether the awakened spirit was temporarily active or dormant: temperance, Sabbath observance, prison reform, prostitution, and poverty.

Characteristically, the early-nineteenth-century reformers (honest though ill-advised) tended to direct their efforts toward effecting superficial change. They attacked alcoholism as a bad habit, they saw poverty as the result of laziness, and they conceived proper Sabbath observance as quiet inactivity undisturbed by such distractions as the dispatch and delivery of mail or any unnecessary physical exercise. As revivalism was for the most part a phenomenon of Protestantism, the matter of reform was further complicated by disparity between the Roman Catholic and the Calvinistic traditions. During the early nineteenth century the American concept of Christian reform was confronted by growing numbers of European emigrants, Catholic for the most part, who brought with them a standard of acceptable behavior as different from that of the normative Calvinistic colonial tradition as Reformed theology was different from that of Thomas Aquinas. Moreover, within the ranks of American Protestants various movements—some sporadic and short-lived, some hardy and widespread—veered enough from the norm in matters of theory and practice to complicate further the philosophy of reform. One of the more important of these was that of perfectionism, often styled holiness. The women's rights movement, working for social equality and liberation, was still strongly allied with and supportive of the prohibition movement. Eventually the Chatauqua movement sought reform through education and wholesome entertainment.

Early-nineteenth-century utopianism fostered many and varied programs and platforms of perfectionism. Finney, who taught theology at Oberlin College, espoused and extolled his own version of the doctrine, by which he meant that a sanctified Christian could by self-discipline achieve perfect obedience to God's law. Optimistic anthropology—which believed in the intrinsic value, ability, and potential (in some cases even the perfectability) of the human race—though less glowing, had been pointed in the thought of

Beecher and Taylor, but it was also enthusiastically held by many untutored lay folk. Principal commitment to and confidence in free will and its outcome was found with Methodists, who derived their theology from a combination of John Wesley's concept of sanctification and the belief in free agency and human ability common to the times. In the period immediately before the Civil War, and indeed during and beyond it, church members generally accepted the obligation of individual holiness that Christianity laid upon its followers, and, given a belief that ability is commensurate with command, there was no logical escape from perfectionism. No revivalist was plainer than Finney: converts "should always look at Christ as their model. . . . they should aim at being holy, and not rest satisfied till they are as perfect as God." The implied prospect of such a future made millennialism more than a theological term. Some of the faithful, the Millerites, for example, set an exact time and place for the coming of the millennium. Many who claimed no clairvoyance were confident of the coming Kingdom, and, though uncertain of its calendar, were unshaken in their faith that those who moved toward perfection were hastening the date. "If the church will do all her duty," said Finney, "the millennium may come in this country in three years" (*Lectures on Revivals of Religion*, pp. 403, 306). At a practical level perfectionism and millennialism informed the activity of the religious abolitionists, who condemned slavery not because it was economically unwise, or politically hazardous, but because it was sinful. Although the problem of slavery was predominant in the religious effort to narrow the gap between professed creed and actual behavior, the relation between revival and reform was already evidenced in city missions, industrial schools, charity hospitals, the YM and YWCA's. That disposition to social reform continued and widened after Appomattox, and, although concern was often greater than correction, the Christian community acknowledged the problem of social as well as personal morality.

Until almost the beginning of the Civil War revivalism in America had, in one respect, remained unchanged from the eighteenth century: it was still the province of ordained clergymen. Moreover, before that time, revivalists, for the most part, had been educated men. Whatever quarrel the community or church had with them arose not from the inadequacy of their credentials, but primarily from objections to their irregular behavior, conduct not normally to be expected from an ordained, educated ministry. Frelinghuysen was a maverick, but he had been educated at the University of Lingen and ordained by the Dutch Reformed Church. Edwards, so unacceptable to his generation that he was expelled from his pulpit, had received a stunning classical education and was not only ordained but descended from Protestant ministers as far back as the time of Queen Elizabeth I. Whitefield lacked distinction as a scholar; nevertheless he was a graduate of Pembroke College, Oxford, and had been ordained by the bishop of Gloucester. His offense lay in his innovative style as a priest. Taylor was educator as well as educated, and Beecher qualified as alumnus of Yale and ordained clergyman, however controversial his revival tactics.

Even Finney, who rejected and denounced the conventional courses in divinity available to him, became professor of theology and, finally, president of Oberlin. Finney's work evolved from random revival programs to carefully planned series of services with teams of workers who laid their plans and followed through with scientific care procedures that—as he pointed out in *Lectures on Revivals*—would ensure success. In this respect he is indeed the father of modern revivalism. Yet the person who actually converted revivalism into a business, who demonstrated that it could be conducted as a business, was Dwight Lyman Moody. But the significant metamorphosis was not essentially one from small to large, an inevitable transition in the days when the young America was breaking out of the chrysalis of adolescence. The revolutionary transition was to the acceptance of an unordained and uneducated layman as an appropriate interpreter of the tradition, spokesman for the church, and shepherd of souls.

Born in Northfield, Massachusetts, in 1837, Moody was one of nine children of a widowed mother whose straitened circumstances dictated an arduous existence that would have crushed a lesser spirit. Denied an education but resolute, resourceful, and optimistic, the energetic Moody worked on nearby farms until the age of seventeen, when he went to Boston to seek a better life. A maternal uncle employed him in his shoe store, a situation in which young Moody at once proved himself a natural salesman, a tireless worker, and an ambitious lad with much common sense and an unbelievable tenacity of purpose. Plainly he was on the way to financial success and security. Meanwhile he had maintained and multiplied his natural and genuine concern for the church, although he was far from considering religion as a profession. As a child he had been baptized in the Unitarian church. In Boston he went regularly to a Congregational church, because his uncle had made his attendance (along with prohibition of drink and gambling) a condition of employment. These "good habits" continued after he moved to Chicago in 1856, where he began almost immediately moving up the ladder of affluence. Moody's conversion experience and his testimony regarding it had been so understated that the elders of the Mount Vernon Church in Boston had kept him on probationary status for a year before accepting him into full membership. The conversion had been genuine, however, and in Chicago he joined the Plymouth Congregational Church, where soon he was renting four pews that he filled with young men whom he knew and acquaintances solicited from neighboring shops or even strangers invited from the casual crowd of passersby on Sunday mornings. On Sunday afternoons he went into poor sections of the city and distributed religious tracts to sailors, saloon habitués, and slum dwellers. Moody's strong personality and aggressive manner operated as successfully in his religion as in his business career. His shrewd common sense and his ability to define a goal and concentrate on its accomplishment were combined with a personality that was dominant rather than domineering. His ability to enlist others in his own program was at times described as bullyragging, an indictment that would perhaps have surprised but certainly not have distressed him. As he sold people shoes that they needed rather than shoes that they wanted, so he introduced them to the Gospel, which, whether they knew it or not, was the prize they sought. But the twin success in business and religion intensified a personal problem. Early on he became involved in mission classes, organized the North Market Sabbath School, and persuaded a prominent Chicago merchant to become superintendent. Along with the classes in Bible study and meetings for prayer there were substantial philanthropic programs of relief and recreation. He was doing equally well in business. By the time he was twenty-three his income was more than $5,000 a year. Increasingly he felt the pressure to choose between a career in commerce or a commitment to service of the church. The decision when it came was characteristic: he would be a full-time city missionary without any assured salary or income.

Under Moody's guidance the Sunday school prospered. So also did the new YMCA of which he became president. He organized a non-denominational church and secured the construction of an adequate sanctuary for it. In 1867 he sailed, a nobody, for the first of three early visits to Great Britain; and when, after a two-year stay, he returned from his third visit to England, he was a celebrity. His steadily growing power as a revivalist had overcome the frostiness of the English and the uncertainty of the Scots. American response was equally enthusiastic. Thereafter he continued with impressive results to conduct his campaigns in America. Brooklyn, Philadelphia, New York, Chicago, Boston, Baltimore, St. Louis, San Francisco—one by one they fell before him. His revivals were organized to the last detail. Publicity was distributed weeks before a campaign began. Supervised teams of dedicated workers assisted during services and in guiding converts to permanent church homes after the revivals were closed.

When crowds outgrew church sanctuaries, Moody moved to tabernacles, often specially constructed for his revivals. The expense involved was considerable—as much as $42,000 for a fourteen-week series—and, as there was usually no collection taken at his services, the revivals were supported by private gifts, special drives, the sale of gospel songbooks, occasional auctions of materials and effects associated with Moody, the generosity and cooperation of such men as Cyrus McCormick, George Armour, John Wanamaker, Cornelius Vanderbilt II, and J. P. Morgan, and contributions of main-line Protestant churches whose support of Moody correctly recognized his efforts as ecumenical and welcomed his presence.

Under Moody, revivalism became big business. He continued to make periodic visits to Great Britain, but it was in America that he stamped revivalism with his character and his creed. Most immediately apparent was Moody's effective use of music. Tone deaf himself and completely unable to sing, he recognized the power of music to dispose people to hear the Gospel and to pressure them to accept. Accordingly, when Moody met Ira D. Sankey he immediately recognized, and almost as immediately commandeered, his genius. Sankey had nothing to commend him except for an affecting (if untrained) voice, sincere emotion, and an unerring dramatic instinct for choosing the right hymn for the right occasion. Overweight, bewhiskered, and unctuous, he could move vast audiences. He sang and also composed hymns that, in spite of indifferent aesthetic merit, spoke to the needs and tastes of Moody's audiences. None was more characteristic or more effective than his famous "Ninety and Nine," a simple, melodic setting for Elizabeth Clephane's poem of Christ the good shepherd who forsakes the flock in shelter of the fold to search for the one who was lost "on the hills away, / Far off from the gates of gold." Introduced in Scotland, where conservative Scots had at first condemned Sankey for his portable organ, the ballad swept Britain and later America.

Music was a telling device for Moody, not alone because it stirred audiences to emotional response, but because the hymns Sankey sang struck the note that characterized Moody's preaching more surely than any other; namely, that God is love. The Great Awakening had appealed to people's fear; they often were warned to flee from the wrath to come and were consequently actually frightened into conversion. Edwards had so vividly represented hell to his congregations that they were known on at least one occasion to lay hold of the backs of the pews in front of them lest they slide then and there into the yawning abyss of perdition opening at their feet, the sulfurous fumes of which already seemed to be stifling them. Moody, who surely believed in a literal hell the heat of which could be measured in degrees Fahrenheit, snared converts in what he called the "gospel net" by his compassionate picture of the loving, searching, long-suffering Father God. Though he continually offered people the choice between heaven and hell, it was upon the joys of heaven that he dwelt. The hymns with which Sankey melted congregations were sentimental, yet filled with hope for all, hope even at the last minute, hope beyond human expectation or deserving. Sankey simply sang what Moody preached.

Moody died in 1899, following a brief illness that struck him during a revival in Kansas City. He had changed the lives of literally hundreds of thousands and had established the Chicago Bible Institute, later the Moody Bible Institute, so those without college education might prepare themselves for foreign or home missionary careers.

This man, essentially an unsophisticated rustic who had brought revivalism to the cities—and changed an informal, often casual approach to evangelism into a business that flourished in the marketplace—had not come alone from village to metropolis. He had moved with the population, and the urbanization of the country was but another side of the metamorphosis from agriculture to industry. At the end of the Civil War scarcely a fifth of America's population lived in cities. When Moody died, 40 percent of the nation lived in urban areas. With the growth of the city, however, there surfaced new or at least intensified forms of sin that became the object of special attacks by the evangelists. Overcrowding of people in substandard housing led to the formation of slums with the concomitant breeding of crime and disease.

A substantial percentage of the rapidly developing labor population was made up of recently arrived European immigrants. The growth of industry, which was dependent on the labor of slum dwellers, concentrated enormous wealth in the hands of a relatively few powerful and often unscrupulous individuals. The church, accordingly, was faced with the urgent necessity of decisions that the urbanization-industrialization of the country demanded: What is the Christian's responsibility to social ills? What is the proper relation between business and the Gospel? The questions were not new, but their form and the urgency with which they were asked made them appear so. The Social Gospel sought to meet the challenge by calling for a complete reorganization of society—industry, politics, education, religion—on what seemed then and seems now to some a genuinely sincere but naive assumption that the Kingdom of God can be taken by force and actualized on earth. The revivalists, for the most part, held to a traditional approach. To the downtrodden they preached the virtue and joy of accepting one's lot, even if it were poverty, and of serving God in whatever situation one happened to be. To the wealthy they commended charity. All, of course, were admonished to resist sin, usually perceived as personal immorality.

Following Moody, chronologically if not ideologically, there were many revivalistic evangelists in America, resembling each other in essence of concern, even in technique, without sacrificing their idiosyncrasies or individuality. Their appeals, emotional or not, evoked emotional response from their hearers. All of them sought to elicit personal and definite commitments from their audience, whether indicated by a walk down the center aisle, a grasp of the preacher's hand, or signing a covenant card. Their appeals were non-sectarian, though they encouraged their "converts" to associate themselves with a church, but, above all else, to "lead a better life." Sam P. Jones, for example, using crude language and coarse humor, attracted huge crowds. So also did his contemporary B. Fay Mills, considerably more refined and destined for the Unitarian church. Both commended the good life; that is, a practical relation of creed to personal behavior. The appeal of such evangelists was primarily to middle-class church people. It is possible to see revivalism as an effort to preserve the status quo, for such preachers as Jones and Mills offered an essentially priestly, rather than a prophetic and self-critical, religion. It was one means of preserving the tradition that for them represented security.

Concurrently, two persisting notions, always latent in the national tradition, flourished in the revivalist phenomenon as they were increasingly articulated by the itinerant gospelers: the equation of Christianity with Americanism, and an understanding of prosperity as a natural and inevitable consequence of true faith.

The patriotic revivalist without peer in his generation—perhaps in the history of the nation—was William Ashley (Billy) Sunday, born in Ames, Iowa, in 1862. Sunday was a devout prophet of America as God's millennial agent and a highly successful vendor of war bonds. Sunday's nativism, more frequently voiced in religious rather than ethnic idiom, attacked Roman Catholicism as a threat to the free expression of Protestantism and the unfettered practice of democracy.

Many Americans' anxiety over the wave of immigration that flooded the country in the 1820s spawned anti-Catholic periodicals, books, and organizations. An angry mob destroyed the Ursuline convent in Charlestown, Massachusetts, in 1834. Until diverted by disputes over slavery, nativism in mid-century seemed a formidable political factor. The Civil War, however, distracted the popular mind, and the problems of Reconstruction temporarily occupied public attention after Appomattox. But the continuing arrival of German and Irish workers, most of whom were Catholics, revitalized dormant prejudices. America's involvement in World War I prevented the mounting intolerance toward Catholics and a union of that prejudice with jingoism from reaching political influence. Coincidental with the outbreak of the war, and skillfully combining professional Americanism, anti-Catholicism, and old-time religion, was the burgeoning career of Billy Sunday.

When Sunday was converted in 1887 he had been for four years on the team of the Chicago Whitestockings and was thereafter known as a Christian ballplayer. He came to his career of evangelist by way of the YMCA, and as a quasi-apprentice-associate of J. Wilbur Chapman, the professional evangelist whose unexpected acceptance of a pastorate in Philadelphia catapulted the hesitant Sunday toward a course of independent revivalism. A small Iowa settlement of hardly a thousand inhabitants invited Sunday in 1895 to conduct a series of services in their town. Presbyterian ordination in 1903 enhanced his modest status and he quickly progressed from villages and tents to cities and churches, steadily gaining reputation and confidence until, at the height of his career, having already succeeded in Washington, Philadelphia, and Boston, he appeared in New York on the eve of America's entry into World War I, speaking in a specially constructed tabernacle that accommodated 20,000 people.

Sunday commanded attention and respect abroad, while at home he was endorsed by such tycoons as John D. Rockefeller and Henry Clay Frick and such political celebrities as Woodrow Wilson and Theodore Roosevelt. Wide acceptance of his pietistic theology and biblical literalism ensured popular support at the outset of his career, but his brand of Fundamentalism temporarily lost considerable credibility after the Scopes trial in 1925 in Dayton, Tennessee. An implication of Sunday's laissez-faire benediction on the world of big business was a resultant unwillingness (save in the case of prohibition,

where his word was effective in more than one state election that resulted in the outlawing of alcohol) to consider socioeconomic problems (especially those of labor) in theological perspective. By definition, of course, "atheistic communism" was beyond the pale of orthodoxy.

Until after the war, Sunday's own career was attended by material success and sympathetic acclaim. He was by some reputed to have accumulated a fortune through his career as an evangelist. Compared to the contemporary financial barons, he was not a man of great wealth. He did, however, come from poverty to an impressive degree of material comfort and security. He did not remain firmly on the dizzy height of celebrity to his life's end, but he did rise from obscurity to national celebrity. Much of his story is like that of the rags-to-riches heroes in the novels of his contemporary Horatio Alger, Jr. Billy Sunday, though, was no mythological figure. He was real. What happened to him was what many Americans were longing to have happen to themselves. Sunday assured them that it was no idle dream, but an actual possibility for the redeemed in Christ. His story was their story, or, more correctly, his dream was their dream.

There is reason to believe that the enormous response of those who accepted the invitation to take the sawdust trail—a phrase originated in the description of those who walked down the wood-shaving-covered aisles of the roughly constructed tabernacles to grasp the hand of Billy Sunday (equivalent to a "decision for Christ")—was for the most part from people already identified with and even active in church life. As many as 300,000 are said to have answered the revivalist's call. With the commonality, however, whether secular or sympathetic to the church, professional revivalism lost much of its appeal before Sunday's career was finished. His last years were without the approval he had known at the apex of his fame. A more sophisticated intelligentsia, a less naive populace rejected Sunday's teaching, though they still turned out to hear him. He outlived his vogue rather than his capital. During his latter years revivalism became dormant (some said moribund) and remained so for almost a generation after Sunday's death in 1935, until the appearance of a new generation of conservative evangelists, whose work was exemplified by none more typical (or more successful) than Billy Graham.

REVIVALISM

Not since the days of George Whitefield has an American evangelist achieved the enthusiastic acclaim that has increasingly followed William Franklin Graham in his spectacular career of revivalism. The evangelist was born near Charlotte, North Carolina, in 1918, approximately a year-and-a-half after Billy Sunday's stunning conquest of New York City, the apex of an impressive career. That Graham followed Sunday in prophetic succession is more easily established in chronological sequence than in identical particulars, although in various ways Sunday's mantle appears to have fallen upon the younger man. From the first the southern evangelist was known—as was his athletic revivalist-ancestor—as Billy rather than as William. He, too, employs common speech; but his words are plain rather than colloquial. The slang of his early sermons, like the flamboyance of his youthful dress, has virtually disappeared.

Graham, like Sunday, is a biblicist, and though his interpretation is often similar to Sunday's, his knowledge is doubtless more extensive. Theologically, however, the two are in agreement that it is a simple matter to explain or to accept the Christian tradition. Both preachers not only have attracted crowds of middle-class Americans (the sustaining element of their popularity) but have engaged the attention, and the loyalty as well, of celebrities from Hollywood to the White House, although Graham has been more consistently accepted by young people.

Reared in the Associate Reformed Presbyterian church (a body of Calvinists so conservative that until lately they allowed only psalms to be sung in church), Graham was from childhood considered a Christian, early a member of the church, and after a conversion experience a tardy, if reluctant, candidate for ordination. Following courses at Bob Jones College (then in Cleveland, Tennessee) and Florida Bible Institute and ordination as a Baptist minister, he entered Wheaton College (Illinois), from which he earned a degree in 1943. Having worked for several years with various church and educational organizations, he came by 1950 to a disciplined focus on evangelistic crusade. In that year he inaugurated a radio program, *The Hour of Decision*. Though he was not even then without recognition, from that point on he was, thanks to the media, familiar to all who could see or hear. William Randolph Hearst, it is said, had advised his papers to "puff Graham." Radio first and later television brought his voice and face to folk who might never have sought him out or met him otherwise. His crusades have taken him literally around the world, and listeners in many countries have taken him to themselves as arbiter of religion. Graham's preaching is simple: he does not shout (any longer), his speech is conversational, and there is a measure of restraint in his presentation.

The ultimate value of Graham's preaching cannot be any more accurately reckoned during his lifetime than could that of Edwards have been in his day. Graham has achieved wide recognition, and, by conventional standards, great success. He preaches regularly to thousands who, through television and radio, are multiplied to millions. His audiences respond to music as did those of Moody and Sankey. And his hearers are invited to come forward and publicly declare themselves for Christ much as those who listened to Finney and Sunday were urged to make the decision. Through the response of these congregations he has extended his ministry to global dimensions. Like revivalists before him he has projected individuality, yet, like them he documents certain characteristics of revivalism constant enough in essence to suggest the meaning intrinsic in the protean form of the phenomenon.

The church is neither enemy nor guarantor of salvation. To be sure, evangelists urge church membership, and revivalists in America have consistently preferred to work with and through the established clergy, but they have not been unduly frustrated because it has not always been necessary (and sometimes not possible) for them to do so. The validity of religion, in revivalism, does not finally depend upon church affiliation or creed. Again, the tendency of revivalism is ever to return to the old, the pure, the original, rather than to reach out for the new, the evolving, and the experimental. New measures and procedures are inaugurated, when they are, only to achieve old ends. Moreover, a pronounced bent to pietistic ethics has tended to equate true religion with a particular external pattern of behavior. Nevertheless, at the basic level, revivals and the revivalism that they foster have been and are (whether misguided or temporary) genuine expressions of faith-renewal. It has been estimated that Graham has reached as many as 90 million people through his crusades and television appearances.

While some revivalists have claimed that all classes and conditions are appealed to by revivalist preachers, others have insisted that the appeal of revivals has been restricted to the middle class. It is insisted by advocates of revivals that the lost are saved, but skeptics reply that those who make decisions are already associated, even formally, with the church. Revivals have been extolled by some as the rejuvenating force of the church and dismissed by others as little more than temporary diversions for the populace that leave no lasting change in the communities where they are held.

BIBLIOGRAPHY

Sydney E. Ahlstrom, *A Religious History of the American People* (1972); David Bohr, *Evangelization in America: Proclamation, Way of Life, and the Catholic Church in the United States* (1977); Jerry D. Cardwell, *Mass Media Christianity: Televangelism and the Great Commission* (1984); Richard K. Curtis, *They Called Him Mister Moody* (1962); Melvin Easterday Dieter, *Revivalism and Holiness* (1973); James F. Findlay, *Dwight L. Moody: American Evangelist 1837–1899* (1961); Charles Grandison Finney, *Charles G. Finney: An Autobiography* (1892); Carol Flake, *Redemptorama: Culture, Politics, and the New Evangelicalism* (1984); Norman F. Furniss, *The Fundamentalist Controversy, 1918–1931* (1954).

Edwin S. Gaustad, *The Great Awakening in New England* (1957); Wesley M. Gewehr, *The Great Awakening in Virginia, 1740–1790* (1930); C. C. Goen, *Revivalism and Separatism in New England, 1740–1800* (1962); Andrew M. Greeley and Mary Greely Durkin, *How to Save the Catholic Church* (1977); Jeffrey K. Hadden and Charles E. Swann, *Prime Time Preachers: The Rising Power of Televangelism* (1981); Stuart C. Henry, *George Whitefield* (1957) and *Unvanquished Puritan: A Portrait of Lyman Beecher* (1973); Peter G. Horsfield, *Religious Television: The American Experience* (1984); Laura McElwain Jones, *The Life and Sayings of Sam P. Jones* (1907); David S. Lovejoy, *Religious Enthusiasm and the Great Awakening* (1969).

William Gerald McLoughlin, *Billy Sunday Was His Real Name* (1955), *Modern Revivalism: Charles Grandison Finney to Billy Graham* (1959), *Isaac Backus and the American Pietistic Tradition* (1970), *Revivals, Awakenings, and Reform: An Essay on Religion and Social Change in America, 1607–1977* (1978), and, as ed., *The American Evangelicals, 1800–1900* (1968); Martin E. Marty, *Pilgrims in Their Own Land: Five Hundred Years of Religion in America* (1985); Charles H. Maxson, *The Great Awakening in the Middle Colonies* (1968); Clifton E. Olmstead, *History of Religion in the United States* (1960); John Pollock, *Billy Graham: The Authorized Biography* (1966); Liston Pope, *Millhands and Preachers* (1954); Timothy L. Smith, *Revivalism and Social Reform in Mid-Nineteenth-Century America* (1957).

[See also FUNDAMENTALISM; GREAT AWAKENING; NINETEENTH-CENTURY EVANGELICALISM; and SOCIAL REFORM FROM THE COLONIAL PERIOD THROUGH THE CIVIL WAR.]

HOLINESS AND PERFECTION

Jean Miller Schmidt

THE nineteenth-century holiness movement in America developed out of the "new measures" revivalism of Charles Grandison Finney and the attempts of American Methodists to revive the Wesleyan teaching and experience of Christian perfection. Its beginnings can be traced to several events of the 1830s, including the Oberlin perfectionism of Finney and Asa Mahan and the special efforts to promote holiness by members of the Methodist Episcopal Church, such as the Tuesday Meeting begun by sisters Sarah Lankford and Phoebe Palmer and the *Guide to Christian Perfection,* founded and edited by the Rev. Timothy Merritt. Beginning in the eastern metropolitan areas, the holiness revival within the Methodist church can be understood as part of that church's adjustment to the transition from a predominantly rural to an increasingly urban and middle-class denomination. This revival reached its peak with the holiness camp meetings sponsored by the National Camp Meeting Association for the Promotion of Holiness beginning in 1867 and evoking a strong positive response through the 1870s.

During the 1880s, however, regional associations were organized in the Midwest, South, and Southwest that developed leadership and structures independent of the church and less willing to compromise; increasingly these associations exerted pressure toward separate holiness bodies. At the same time, Methodist bishops tightened the disciplinary line on independent agencies. The result was the gradual evolution after 1890 of numerous separate holiness denominations. The movement continues to the present in the form of groups affiliated with the Christian Holiness Association.

THE WESLEYAN DOCTRINE

From the time of his Oxford conversion in 1725, John Wesley was a seeker after holiness. In his work of 1766 entitled *A Plain Account of Christian Perfection,* he attempted to demonstrate that he had taught the same doctrine of Christian perfection and made it central to his understanding of the Christian life for forty years. This leader of the Methodist revival in the Church of England said about the teaching of perfection: "This doctrine is the grand depositum which God has lodged with the people called Methodists; and for the sake of propagating this chiefly He appeared to have raised us up" (J. Telford, ed., *Letters,* 1931, vol. 8, p. 238).

In his 1733 sermon "The Circumcision of the Heart," Wesley described the goal of the Christian life as "that habitual disposition of soul which, in the sacred writings, is termed holiness; and which directly implies, the being cleansed from sin, . . . the being so 'renewed in the spirit of our mind,' as to be 'perfect as our Father in heaven is perfect.' " The essence of Christian perfection, as Wesley understood it, was perfect love of God and neighbor.

There was some development in Wesley's view of the way such perfection was to be attained. Here he learned not only from his own search for it, but also from studying the religious experience of other Christians. By 1763 he was ready to affirm, on the basis of the testimony of many witnesses, that Christian perfection was a second, definite, instantaneous work of grace receivable now and by faith. He believed, however, that the gift was both preceded and followed by gradual sanctification, or growth in holiness.

Wesley understood sanctification as a process,

generally long, that begins with the real, inward change of regeneration and continues to and beyond the instantaneous experience of entire sanctification. (*Entire sanctification,* then, was a more technical theological term, a synonym for Christian perfection, perfect love, or holiness, and to be distinguished from the process of sanctification.) In one of his most balanced sermons on this subject, published as "The Scripture Way of Salvation" (1765), Wesley explained that salvation consists of two stages or levels in the Christian life, justification and sanctification. Justification is pardon, our acceptance of God.

> And at the same time that we are justified—yea, in that very moment—*sanctification* begins. In that instant we are "born again, born from above, born of the Spirit." There is a *real* as well as a *relative* change. We are inwardly renewed by the power of God. We feel "the love of God shed abroad in our heart by the Holy Ghost." (Outler, 1964, p. 274)

We at first imagine that all sin is gone, but we soon realize that sin is only suspended, not destroyed. We now feel two principles in ourselves, and as the gradual work of sanctification takes place in us, we are enabled by the Spirit to become "more and more dead to sin," and "more and more alive to God"; thus we wait for entire sanctification, "for a full salvation from all our sins. . . . or . . . . perfect love" (Outler, p. 275).

The Christian perfection that Wesley taught was a limited perfection; it did not exclude ignorance, error, infirmities, or temptation. It was sinless only in Wesley's sense of sin as a voluntary transgression of a known law of God. In other words, it was perfection of intention and motive, "the fulfillment of faith's desire to love God above all else and all else in God, *so far as conscious will and deliberate action* are concerned" (Outler, p. 32). It was deliverance from inbred sin, from that universal diseased human condition from which sins as voluntary transgressions spring. It was spiritual health fully restored. Yet it was not a finished state, but rather a moment-by-moment reliance on God's grace so that love filled the heart and the life.

In Wesley's view, perfection or holiness was a practical way of life available to and necessary for all regenerate Christians. He did not insist on an "orthodoxy of method" nor on a particular terminology. He was cautious about testimony to the experience, urging those who had attained it to avoid all appearance of boasting, and telling his preachers to "lead" persons to it rather than to "drive" them. The pursuit of holiness was to take place within the nurture and discipline of the Wesleyan societies and within the sacramental context of the church. As with assurance of justification, Wesley believed that assurance of entire sanctification derived both from the witness of the Spirit and from the fruits of the Spirit. Among the latter he included love, joy, peace; patience, gentleness, goodness; tenderness of spirit, calmness; fidelity, simplicity, and godly sincerity. He taught that the blessing should not be claimed without the witness of the Spirit and warned that one could fall from it.

TUESDAY MEETINGS

In 1835 Mrs. Sarah Lankford professed the experience of entire sanctification and began at her home in New York City a weekly afternoon prayer meeting for women of the Allen Street and Mulberry Street Methodist Episcopal churches. This meeting soon became known as the "Tuesday Meeting for the Promotion of Holiness." In the beginning the leadership of this Tuesday Meeting was shared by Mrs. Lankford and her sister Phoebe Worrall Palmer, wife of a young physician and Methodist layman, Walter C. Palmer. Later Phoebe Palmer assumed the leadership of the group (having experienced entire sanctification on what she always called the "day of days," 26 July 1837). This Tuesday Meeting was to become the center of the holiness movement in the Methodist Episcopal Church.

At first the Tuesday Meetings were open only to women. In 1839 Prof. Thomas C. Upham of Bowdoin College, a Congregational minister whose wife had been a member, asked to attend and experienced entire sanctification under Phoebe Palmer's guidance. From that time on, the meeting included men as well as women, and attracted prominent Methodist figures as well as leaders of other denominations. Editors Nathan Bangs and George O. Peck, bishops Edmund Janes and Leonidas L. Hamline, and educators Stephen Olin and John Dempster were among the Methodists who attended and endorsed the movement. Others included Asa Mahan (president of Oberlin College and a colleague of evangelist Charles Grandison Finney), Baptist evangelist A. B. Earle, Presbyterian William E. Boardman, and Quakers Hannah Whitall Smith and David B. Updegraff. Both Phoebe Palmer's teachings about holiness and the methods used in her Tuesday Meeting were to be powerful factors in shaping the holiness revival and institutions that followed the Civil War.

In Phoebe Palmer's first, and probably most influential, book, *The Way of Holiness* (1843)—it had its fiftieth American edition by 1867—she addressed the question "Is there not a shorter way?" Claiming to be faithful to John Wesley's teaching, her message contained some emphases, particularly concerning the timing and method of attaining perfect love, that tended to deviate from his. She spoke of entire sanctification as presently available to all regenerate Christians who were ready to meet the scriptural requirements of consecrating all to God and believing God's promises. Urging that holiness was "a state of grace in which every one of the Lord's redeemed ones should live" (p. 33), she employed an "altar" terminology, declaring that Christ was the altar that sanctified, or made acceptable, the Christian's total consecration of self. She described such consecration in this way: "O, Lord, I call heaven and earth to witness that I *now lay body, soul,* and *spirit . . . upon thine altar, to be for ever* THINE! 'TIS DONE! Thou hast promised to receive me! . . . *Thou dost receive me now!* From this time henceforth I *am* thine—*wholly thine!*" (p. 41).

Once this consecration was complete, she taught that the seeker should exercise faith and lay claim to the promise of entire sanctification. "Just so soon as you come believingly, and make the required sacrifice, it will *be done* unto you *according to your faith*" (1849, p. 53). Unlike John Wesley, who believed that the seeker would be made conscious of the attainment of perfect love through the witness of the Holy Spirit, Phoebe Palmer taught that the scriptural promises were sufficient witness for faith, whether or not there was an accompanying emotional experience. Another distinctive emphasis of her teaching was that public testimony to the experience of holiness was necessary to the retention of that experience. These emphases generally became characteristic of the holiness movement that ensued.

Likewise, the practices of the Tuesday Meet-

ing were influential in the entire subsequent movement. Phoebe Palmer hoped that her meetings, like the Wesleyan class meetings, would be a source of spiritual awakening for the whole church. These meetings were interdenominational and did much to foster the growing sense of unity among promoters of holiness. Although numbers of clergy were always present, lay men and women were treated with equal respect as recipients of the gifts of the Holy Spirit. This theology, and the place of public testimony, gave women a prominent leadership role in the holiness movement.

In answer to inquiries about how the Tuesday Meeting was conducted, Mrs. Palmer gave the following account:

> After the opening exercises, any one is at liberty to speak, sing, or propose united prayer. . . . Testimony follows testimony in quick succession, interspersed with occasional singing and prayer, as the circumstances may seem to demand. . . . In these meetings the utmost freedom prevails. The ministry does not wait for the laity, neither does the laity wait for the ministry. . . . How small do all merely earthly distinctions appear, when brought under the equalizing influences of pure, perfect love! And it is this equalizing process, that, to our mind, forms one of the most important characteristics of this meeting.
>
> (1859, pp. 229–234)

Home meetings patterned after the Tuesday Meeting began to be organized in various parts of the Northeast and, later, throughout the country. By 1886 some 200 such meetings were operating in the United States and abroad. The Tuesday Meeting itself was so popular that it continued for over sixty years, even after Phoebe Palmer's death in 1874. (Sarah Lankford became the second Mrs. Walter C. Palmer after her sister's death.)

In addition to the Tuesday Meeting, Phoebe Palmer promoted holiness through a vigorous publishing program and through evangelism. In 1858 Walter Palmer purchased the already popular journal *Guide to Holiness* (begun in Boston in 1839 as the *Guide to Christian Perfection* and published as the *Guide to Holiness* from about 1845 to 1901), moved its offices to New York, and secured the services of his wife as editor. Under her direction it reached the height of its circulation (some 30,000). After 1850 both Palmers became increasingly involved in evangelistic efforts, particularly camp meeting revivals in the late 1860s. By the time of Phoebe Palmer's death, 25,000 souls were said to have been saved under her instrumentality.

Sandra Sizer's analysis in *Gospel Hymns and Social Religion* (1978) of "social religious meetings" in nineteenth-century revivalism suggests that prayer, testimony, and exhortation by lay people in a communal context were effective in creating a community of shared emotions and controlled feeling. She explores the use of such gatherings in Finney's revivals. Although early Methodist class meetings were a forerunner, clearly Phoebe Palmer's Tuesday Meetings are an intriguing illustration of this kind of social religion.

As a popular religious movement, the holiness revival developed its characteristic literature: the edifying theological biographies that were to create in the reader a thirst for holiness and give instruction on how to obtain the blessing; collections of testimonies like the best-selling *Pioneer Experiences* (1868), edited by Phoebe Palmer; and periodicals like the *Guide to Holiness* and the later *Christian Standard and Home Journal*, which helped to create a supportive network and a spirit of contagious enthusiasm.

HOLINESS AND ABOLITIONISM

Following the example of John Wesley, early American Methodism had been vigorous in its opposition to slavery. The founding conference of the Methodist Episcopal Church in 1784 stipulated that Methodists who did not free their slaves would be expelled from membership. By 1816, however, this rapidly growing church had retreated from an antislavery norm because of strong southern opposition and the concern of Methodist preachers to have access to the souls of slaves. By its 1840 General Conference, southerners and northern anti-abolitionists succeeded in silencing the abolitionist minority and declared that slaveholding was no barrier to the ordination of ministers.

Orange Scott and Luther Lee were born into impoverished homes in New England and upper New York State, became Methodist ministers, and rose to prominence in their annual conferences because of their preaching and leadership abilities. In the 1830s both became converted to abolitionism and worked as antislavery agents (part of the band of antislavery workers led by Finney convert Theodore Dwight Weld). In the 1836 and 1840 General Conferences, they fought a losing battle to persuade the church to take action against slavery. Discouraged by the bishops' suppression of antislavery discussion within the church, and convinced that there were no prospects that "this church will ever be reformed, so long as slavery exists in this country," Scott and Lee reluctantly led a secession from the Methodist Episcopal Church in 1842. "We wish it to be distinctly understood," Scott explained, "that we do not withdraw from any thing essential to pure Wesleyan Methodism. We only dissolve our connection with Episcopacy and Slavery. These we believe to be anti-scriptural, and well calculated to sustain each other" (1848, pp. 8, 14).

Other antislavery secessions had already occurred in Ohio, Utica (New York), and Michigan. At a convention in Utica in May 1843, the Wesleyan Methodist Connection was organized as a protest against Methodist compromise on slavery. An abolitionist church, it was committed to the conjunction of piety and radicalism. In the pastoral address at the convention, Lee urged the members to make holiness their motto: "It is holiness of heart and life that will . . . give you moral power to oppose the evils and corruption in the world, against which we have lifted up a standard." The address closed with the prayer, "The very God of peace sanctify you wholly. . . ." (Matlack, 1849, pp. 343–344). An article on sanctification was inserted in the first *Book of Discipline* (the official book of doctrine, discipline, and church law of religious bodies with Methodist polity), thus early identifying the Wesleyan Methodists as a holiness church.

After Scott's early death in 1847, Lee assumed the leadership of the new denomination. When the Methodist Episcopal Church in 1864 at last took a clear antislavery stand, Lee and some other Wesleyan Methodist ministers and clergy returned to that church, significantly strengthening the holiness presence within it.

REVIVALISM AND PERFECTIONISM

In 1835 Asa Mahan moved to Oberlin, Ohio, to become president of Oberlin College, and evangelist Charles Grandison Finney gave up his

HOLINESS AND PERFECTION

New York City church to become professor of theology there. Mahan was in many ways the major architect of Oberlin perfectionism, and the closer of the two men to Wesleyan holiness. Born in Vernon, New York, Mahan was a graduate of Andover Theological Seminary and served his first church at Pittsford (seven miles east of Rochester) at the time of Finney's famous Rochester revival of 1830–1831. From there he moved to the Sixth Presbyterian (later Vine Street Congregational) Church in Cincinnati, becoming a member of the board of trustees of Lane Seminary. A strong abolitionist, Mahan supported the Lane rebels who left the school under the leadership of Theodore Weld when President Lyman Beecher and a trustee committee prohibited discussion of the slavery issue. No doubt it was Mahan's staunch support of these abolitionist students that led to his invitation to become president of Oberlin when the students decided to move there. Arthur and Lewis Tappan, Finney's New York philanthropist friends, agreed to provide financial support. Soon higher education at Oberlin was open to both black and female students.

In 1836 both Mahan and Finney began to explore the doctrine of Christian perfection. Mahan's sanctification experience occurred that year after long searching for the "all-constraining" love of Christ that was the secret of St. Paul's piety. When an Oberlin student asked Mahan and Finney at a public meeting whether a Christian might hope for entire sanctification in this life, the two men resolved to search for the answer. Both read John Wesley's *Plain Account of Christian Perfection* at this time. In his *Lectures to Professing Christians,* delivered in New York City during the winter off-term (1836–1837), Finney spoke on "Sanctification by Faith" and "Christian Perfection." Basically he agreed with Wesley that the great design of the Gospel was deliverance of human beings from sin. Defining Christian perfection as perfect obedience to the law of God—that is, disinterested benevolence to God and neighbor—Finney was convinced that since God commanded us to be perfect, such perfection must be possible in this life.

This was the beginning of Oberlin perfectionism, which Finney and Mahan were at pains to distinguish from the antinomian perfectionism of John Humphrey Noyes. (Noyes's view that perfection, once attained, could never be lost led him to reject conventional mores and institute the socialism and complex marriage practices of the Oneida Community, founded in 1848.) In 1839 Mahan's *Scripture Doctrine of Christian Perfection* was published, in which he described victory over sin through the indwelling Christ. The Oberlin community in general was caught up by the holiness viewpoint. The *Oberlin Evangelist* was founded in 1838 (and published continuously until 1862) to promote and extend the doctrine. After leaving Oberlin in 1850, Mahan was president of Adrian College in Michigan from 1859 to 1872. (A Wesleyan Methodist school, it was taken over by the Methodist Protestant Church in 1868.) Mahan's wife, Mary, died in 1863; he married again three years later and moved to London with his second wife, also named Mary, in 1874. Soon after his arrival he became involved in holiness circles there.

In *Revivalism and Social Reform* (1957), Timothy L. Smith argued that American revivalism and perfectionism were not declining influences by 1850, but rather that "revival measures and perfectionist aspiration flourished increasingly between 1840 and 1865 in all the major denominations—particularly in the cities" (p. 8). Smith went on to make the still controversial claim that these very influences prepared the way for the later Social Gospel. The 1857–1858 revival, characterized by its daily noontime prayer meetings, quest for practical holiness, and interdenominational lay leadership, effectively spread perfectionist ideals. Social and intellectual factors also contributed to the perfectionist climate. As Smith later put it, "entire sanctification was a kind of evangelical transcendentalism which thrived amid the optimism, the idealism, and the moral earnestness which were so much a part of the nineteenth-century American character" (1964, p. 610).

In 1858 Presbyterian minister William E. Boardman published *The Higher Christian Life.* His intention was to present the idea of holiness in a terminology that would be acceptable to non-Methodists. The following year the well-known Baptist evangelist A. B. Earle had the sanctification experience he later described in *The Rest of Faith* (1871) and began to preach it in his revivals.

As mentioned earlier, during the 1850s Phoebe Palmer's writings attracted widespread attention and went through numerous editions. Some Methodist leaders expressed reservations about aspects of her teachings. For example, Nathan Bangs (a firm believer in entire sanctification and a longtime friend of the Palmers and their Tuesday Meeting) was concerned that her stress on laying claim to the experience by faith threatened the importance of the witness of the Spirit. The Palmers were, nonetheless, strongly supported by the official leadership in the Methodist Episcopal Church, who encouraged the holiness awakening. Two men who would become bishops in 1872 wrote works on holiness in the 1850s, and both had come under the influence of Phoebe Palmer. One was Randolph S. Foster, whose *Christian Purity, Its Nature and Blessedness* was published in 1851; the other was Jesse T. Peck, whose popular volume of 1856 claimed that entire sanctification was *The Central Idea of Christianity*. In Timothy Smith's words, "the gospel of Christian holiness thus became a chief strain in the melody of mid-century Methodism. But precise orchestration of the theme produced occasional discords" (1957, pp. 124–125). The Free Methodist schism of 1860 is the best illustration of the latter.

Benjamin Titus Roberts, a Methodist minister in Buffalo, became the leader of a reforming party in the Genesee Conference in western New York (part of the "burned-over" district, so called because it had been so often swept by revival fires). Especially after receiving "the blessing of holiness" at a camp meeting at which the Palmers were present in the early 1850s, Roberts began to be outspoken in his criticism of the worldliness of the Methodist Episcopal Church. Referring to the majority in the conference as "New School Methodism," he attacked their drift from holiness and consequent lax discipline, their toleration of slavery, their loss of simplicity in worship, their system of pew rents, and their membership in secret societies. Soon the minority and majority parties began to be known derisively by the epithets Nazarite and Regency, signifying the uncompromising simplicity of the former and status of the latter. The publication of Roberts' accusations in *The Northern Independent* (edited by William Hosmer, a radical abolitionist sympathetic to the Nazarite protests), precipitated the crisis leading to the formation of the Free Methodist Church. Key Nazarite leaders, including Roberts, were quickly punished by the Regency majority, assigned to poor charges and apparently deprived of the opportunity for a fair hearing. Roberts was expelled from the conference in 1858 and his

appeal to the General Conference in 1860 failed. His major fault in the church's eyes was disobedience to discipline. The bishops' address at this General Conference is revealing. Responding to the Nazarite views on Christian perfection, they said:

> These individuals claim to be strictly Wesleyan in their views of the doctrine, and probably are so substantially. Nor do we impugn their motives. But in our judgment, in denouncing those in the ministry and laity who do not sympathize with them and adopt their measures . . . by employing and encouraging erratic and irresponsible persons to conduct religious services, they have erred, and unhappily agitated some of our societies, and in a few instances caused secessions. It is our opinion there was no occasion for these specialties. Our ministers are generally Wesleyan in their faith and preaching on this subject.
>
> (Benjamin, 1964, pp. 354–355)

In August 1860 the Free Methodist Church was formally organized, affirming that it would be free from slavery, secret societies, and rented pews, and would have the freedom of the Spirit in its worship. Added to the Articles of Religion was a statement on sanctification, interpreting it as an instantaneous work of God in the consecrated, believing soul. Roberts was "not an irresponsible schismatic" nor were the holiness advocates in the Genesee Conference the only Methodists who saw the revival of this aspect of Wesleyan doctrine as a possible antidote to the growing worldliness of the church. Personal and sociological factors in this situation appear to have exacerbated the religious issues. The slavery question was also a crucial issue at a time when the northern Methodists feared the loss of the border conferences. Discussion and advocacy of holiness, at any rate, continued unabated.

HOLINESS CAMP MEETINGS

After the Civil War, Methodist pastor John S. Inskip was instrumental in the organization of the first camp meeting "for the promotion of holiness." Ordained an elder in 1840, Inskip had served appointments in Pennsylvania and Ohio before moving to New York City in 1852.

Inskip owed his mature experience of entire sanctification and his entrance into a larger leadership role among the holiness ranks of Methodism to his wife's influence. In August 1864 Martha Inskip claimed the blessing of perfect love at a camp meeting and subsequently testified to her experience at a public prayer meeting in her husband's South Third Street Church in Brooklyn. The following Sunday, Inskip preached on the present attainability of entire sanctification and urged his congregation to consecrate themselves to God at once. Setting the example himself, he said, "Come, brethren, follow your pastor. I call Heaven and earth to witness that I now declare I will be henceforth wholly and forever the Lord's." According to his biographers, "he was then and there divinely assured of its consummation. . . . It was to him a new life" (McDonald and Searles, 1885, p. 152).

Soon after, Inskip attended the Palmers' Tuesday Meeting for the first time and engaged them to come and hold meetings in his church for the promotion of holiness. He established a holiness meeting in his church and began to feel called to "arouse the church" on the subject of holiness. His views on the doctrine of full salvation show the influence of Phoebe Palmer's teachings, especially regarding the "way of faith" and the necessity to testify in order to retain the experience. In 1866 Inskip was appointed to Green Street Church, in downtown New York City, where he continued to emphasize the availability of entire sanctification. Under his preaching, the famous black holiness evangelist Amanda Smith "was brought into the experience of perfect love" (McDonald and Searles, p. 183).

In the spring of 1867, William B. Osborn, a Methodist minister from the New Jersey Conference, pressed upon Inskip his conviction that "God would have us hold a holiness camp meeting." At a formal meeting in Philadelphia on 13 June, it was decided to issue a call for such a camp meeting at Vineland, New Jersey, in July. That Vineland camp meeting is generally regarded as the beginning of the postwar holiness revival in the United States.

At Vineland in 1867, the National Camp Meeting Association for the Promotion of Holiness (hereafter, National Association) was formed. Inskip was chosen its first president (a position he held until his death in 1884). Other active members of the organization were John A. Wood and W. B. Osborn, Alfred Cookman, George Hughes, William McDonald, Charles J. Fowler, and Bishop Matthew Simpson. The next two camp meetings were at Manheim in Lancaster County, Pennsylvania, in July 1868, and Round Lake, New York, in July 1869.

In the spring of 1871 Inskip left the pastorate to devote himself to full-time holiness evangelism. He began by accompanying Bishop Edward Ames as preacher on the round of annual conferences that spring. He then traveled with other National Association evangelists to California and on to Salt Lake City. Together with his wife, Martha, who led the testimony meetings, sang Gospel hymns in the regular services, and pioneered in children's work, Inskip spent the remaining years of his life as a holiness evangelist. By the time of his death, there had been fifty-two national camp meetings, at forty-eight of which he had presided. From 1876 until his death in 1884, he also edited the *Christian Standard,* a publication of the National Publishing Association for the Promotion of Holiness from 1867 to 1913.

Although the Vineland and Manheim camp meetings were advertised as interdenominational, camp meeting evangelism was seen by the leaders of the National Association primarily as an instrument to bring the Methodist Episcopal Church back to holiness. After 1868 the leaders decided to take their evangelistic ministry only to Methodist camp meeting grounds and on invitation from local camp meeting administrators. Most of the preachers were Methodist Episcopal pastors under regular appointment who were traveling evangelists only for this summer camp meeting circuit.

Like the earlier frontier camp meetings, which became a Methodist institution, holiness camp meetings among the Methodists were carefully controlled. The day's schedule was filled with religious activities, behavior on the camp meeting grounds was carefully regulated, and sites like Ocean Grove, New Jersey, soon developed into wholesome resort communities where middle-class, newly urban churchgoers could find both rest and "the great salvation."

The Gospel songs that became popular for use in these camp meetings reveal the development of a whole terminology of holiness, in which the Wesleyan theology of salvation was compared to Israel's journey from Egypt to Canaan, and the experience of entire sanctification was referred to as Canaan, or Beulah land. (For example, "I have found the land of Beulah/The blessed land of perfect rest.") The connection between the promised land, the holiness experience, and camp meetings themselves is evident in Edgar Page Stites's popular Gospel song "Beulah Land" (1875), part of which goes as follows:

> I've reached the land of corn and wine,
> And all its riches freely mine,
> Here shines undimm'd one blissful day,
> For all my night has pass'd away.
> [Refrain:] O Beulah Land, sweet Beulah Land,
> As on thy highest mount I stand,
> I look away across the sea,
> Where mansions are prepared for me,
> And view the shining glory shore,
> My heav'n, my home, for evermore!

Martin Wells Knapp, Methodist Episcopal minister and later a preacher and leader in the Pilgrim Holiness Church, wrote a book entitled *Out of Egypt into Canaan; or, Lessons in Spiritual Geography* (1887), which elaborated on these metaphors connecting the Wesleyan pilgrimage from sin to sanctification with the Exodus from Egypt to the Promised Land of Canaan. Perhaps the most striking feature of the book was the elaborate map that served as the frontispiece, depicting the personal journey from spiritual night and bondage to the sunshine, purity, and power of perfect love. The title "Out of Darkness into His marvelous Light" also bore the subtitle "Where Art Thou?"

HIGHER LIFE MOVEMENTS

The holiness movement in American Methodism was not the only expression of perfectionism and the call to a "higher Christian life." Quakers, Congregationalists, Baptists, and Presbyterians were influenced by the holiness movement and also made a major impact on the Keswick movement that arose in England as a series of conventions in the 1870s. This movement had its context in Reformed theology and emphasized gradual, rather than instantaneous, sanctification.

In the years immediately following the 1857–1858 revival, both Finney and the Palmers had conducted evangelistic meetings in the British Isles. Another husband and wife team, Robert Pearsall and Hannah Whitall Smith, also lay people, were instrumental in the holiness revival that

became the Keswick movement. Both had experienced sanctification under Methodist auspices in holiness meetings in Philadelphia and southern New Jersey in the late 1860s.

Hannah Whitall Smith described her spiritual pilgrimage in two very popular books: *The Christian's Secret of a Happy Life* (1875), which was intended to help others to experience sanctification, and *The Unselfishness of God and How I Discovered It* (1903). Born into a family of Philadelphia Quakers, Hannah claimed to have had her first real experience of God during the 1858 revival (shortly after the death of her first child), when she came to know God's love and forgiveness. Not long after, she was riding on a tram one day when she had a sudden realization of the "unselfishness" or "mother heart" of God, which for her meant universal salvation. In 1865 she was led by her dressmaker in Millville, New Jersey, to a holiness meeting attended mostly by "poor ignorant factory people." For some time she had been seeking a fuller Christian experience. "To be a child of God," she said, "and yet to be unable to act like one, made me wonder whether I could have missed something in religion which could have given me victory, and I determined to find out if possible what that something was." Becoming a regular attender of that Methodist holiness meeting, she soon experienced this victory for herself.

Her husband, Robert, claimed the blessing of holiness in an emotional experience at the Vineland camp meeting in July 1867. On a trip to England in 1872–1873 the Smiths both testified to their holiness experiences, and invitations soon multiplied within English evangelical circles. As it happened, W. E. Boardman was also in England that spring and he was warmly received. By this time the works of holiness advocates Mahan and Upham were well known in England, as well as Boardman's *The Higher Christian Life* (1859) and Robert Pearsall Smith's *Holiness Through Faith* (1870). The highly successful evangelistic campaign of Dwight L. Moody and Ira D. Sankey in Great Britain in 1873–1874 awakened many more to the possibilities of a new Christian life.

The first convention to promote scriptural holiness was held in Oxford in late summer 1874. Mahan preached the opening sermon, and Boardman and the Smiths were principal speakers. One of those present at the convention was the Rev. T. D. Harford Battersby, vicar of St.

John's Keswick, who would become one of the founders of the Keswick movement.

The next June, some 8,000 persons gathered at Brighton, on the southern coast of England. Again the Smiths and Mahan were prominent speakers. While at Brighton, Canon Battersby announced a similar convention to be held just three weeks later in his parish at Keswick, a small town in northwest England, and invited some of the leading speakers at Brighton to take part.

A few days before the opening of the Keswick Convention it was suddenly announced that Pearsall Smith's speaking engagements had been canceled and that he had returned to America because of failing health. Rumors of sexual indiscretions were never completely put to rest, and Smith did not resume his speaking career. The annual Keswick conventions remained a permanent tribute, however, to the effectiveness of the Smiths' evangelism.

Rev. H. W. Webb-Peploe, a distinguished Anglican clergyman, replaced Smith in that first Keswick Convention and became a dominant figure in the movement. He particularly helped to shape Keswick teaching, which stressed the "suppression" of sin rather than its eradication, and spoke in terms of "yielding" (consecration) and the counteracting grace of being filled with the Holy Spirit. Aiming at practical holiness, the Keswick (or Reformed holiness) movement has never consisted of separate denominations but is rather a conglomerate of individuals and groups who are in sympathy with its teachings and life-style. After the mid-1870s this Keswick holiness influence, including an emphasis on premillennialism (the expectation that Jesus Christ would personally return to earth before establishing his thousand-year kingdom) and faith healing, returned to America through the work (and Northfield conferences) of Dwight L. Moody. The concept of "power for service" became especially important to Moody and his co-workers and followers.

HOLINESS ASSOCIATIONS AND "COME-OUTISM"

In his 1962 history of the Church of the Nazarene, Timothy L. Smith suggested that there were four factors after 1880 that helped to determine whether Methodist holiness leaders stayed in the church or decided to leave:

(1) the persistent opposition of ecclesiastical officials to independent holiness associations and publishing agencies; (2) the recurrent outbursts of fanaticism among persons who were members of the associations but not of the churches; (3) the outbreak in the 1890's of strenuous attacks upon the doctrine of sanctification itself; and (4) the increasing activity of urban holiness preachers in city mission and social work.

(*Called Unto Holiness*, p. 27)

After 1875 there was a growing division between Methodist officials and those who "made a specialty of the second blessing." Initially organized around major eastern metropolitan areas, the National Camp Meeting Association for the Promotion of Holiness began in the 1870s and 1880s to expand into other parts of the country. Eventually this expansion into the Midwest, South, and Southwest gave rise to a rural and more radical phase of the holiness revival. These evangelists placed more stress on standards of dress and behavior and were far less attached to Wesleyan tradition and discipline.

Gradually the regional holiness associations became less concerned about the revival of holiness in Methodism and more committed to an inclusive membership on the basis of (Wesleyan) holiness doctrine. The changing emphasis is reflected in the name of the organization: by 1894 it had dropped "Camp Meeting" from its title and until 1971 it was officially called the National Association for the Promotion of Holiness, usually referred to as the National Holiness Association. (In 1971 it was changed to its present name, the Christian Holiness Association.)

Among these new radical leaders was John P. Brooks, editor of *The Banner of Holiness* (Bloomington, Illinois), who left the Methodist Episcopal Church about 1885. His 1887 work, *The Divine Church*, became the textbook of "come-outism," the call to withdraw from denominations that were opposed or indifferent to holiness in order to create new believers' fellowships in which holiness doctrine and life-style could be nurtured and promoted. This was the radical application of perfectionism to the nature and organization of the church itself. Another such leader was Daniel S. Warner, founder in 1880 of the Church of God (Anderson, Indiana) on an antidenominational platform. Warner had been a member of the Indiana branch of the General Eldership of the Churches of God, in North

America, a German Pietist group founded by John Winebrenner, and was sanctified under the ministry of National Association workers. He broke, however, with both his denomination and the holiness association, believing that membership in denominational churches was antithetical to true Christianity. He and other early Church of God leaders claimed that holiness and unity were the essential qualities of their community of faith. Hardin Wallace, an Illinois Methodist evangelist, began the holiness revival in rural east Texas in 1877, set up interdenominational holiness "bands," and then moved to southern California to work with what later became the Holiness Church.

These early secessions were a considerable embarrassment to the more conservative holiness leaders, who always insisted on loyalty to Methodism. When Brooks and others convened the General Holiness Assembly in Chicago in May 1885, National Association leaders saw that George Hughes (editor of the *Guide to Holiness*) was elected chairman, and barred from consideration a letter from B. A. Washburn of the Southern California and Arizona Holiness Association calling for the assembly's endorsement of separate and independent churches.

In 1881 some of the most prominent defenders of the holiness awakening in Methodism, including scholars John Miley, Daniel Steele, Asbury Lowrey, and Milton S. Terry, urged the leaders of the Methodist Episcopal Church to call a great national convention for the promotion of holiness. In a public letter the bishops bluntly rejected the proposal. "It is our solemn conviction that the whole subject of personal experience . . . can be best maintained and enforced in connection with the established usages of the church" (Smith, 1964, p. 619). J. E. Searles replied in defense of the National Association that such an organization was still needed to encourage the experience of sanctification in a time of growing worldliness and to shield state and local associations from fanaticism.

The holiness crusade came later to the Methodist Episcopal Church, South (which separated from the Methodist Episcopal Church in 1844 over the issues of slavery and the power of the episcopacy). Although the perfectionist revival was originally regarded by the new denomination as abolitionist and a tool of the northern church, by the 1880s it was highly successful

there as well. In response to the separatism of this more radical brand of holiness, however, the leadership of the church felt called to take firm action. The bishops' address to the Methodist Episcopal Church, South, in 1894 was a strong denunciation of independent holiness associations. The bishops rebuked the party that had sprung up "with holiness as a watchword" and that maintained

> holiness associations, holiness meetings, holiness preachers, holiness evangelists, and holiness property. . . . We do not question the sincerity and zeal of these brethren; we desire the church to profit by their earnest preaching and godly example; but we deplore their teaching and methods insofar as they claim a monopoly of the experience, practice, and advocacy of holiness, and separate themselves from the body of ministers and disciples.
>
> (Smith, 1962, p. 41)

A final factor that alienated many holiness leaders from Methodism was their participation in rescue mission and social service work that their bishops refused to approve. By the 1890s urban holiness preachers were active in hundreds of missions to the poor, some serving families who had recently moved from the country into the cities. Such missions inevitably produced converts who did not feel at home in stylish Methodist churches. The result was the organization of scores of independent holiness congregations in cities where holiness believers sought the company of like-minded people. The earliest Church of the Nazarene congregations all originated in this way.

HOLINESS DENOMINATIONS

Two of the largest holiness bodies, the Church of the Nazarene and the Pilgrim Holiness Church, developed in very similar stages: pressure on a strong leader to withdraw from the Methodist Episcopal Church, the formation of an independent holiness church, and mergers resulting in a fully organized holiness denomination.

Phineas F. Bresee, a Methodist pastor who served churches in Iowa, eventually became a presiding elder and editor of the conference paper. In 1883 he moved to California after an unfortunate investment in Mexican iron mines left him bankrupt. Invited at once to fill prominent pulpits in Los Angeles, he became a member of the Southern California Conference and was offered the pastorate of First Methodist Church in Los Angeles. While a Methodist minister in Los Angeles, Bresee first encountered the holiness movement. Within the membership of his church there was a minority who were "fully sanctified." They persuaded their pastor to call evangelists from the National Holiness Association to lead a meeting. During that revival, but while alone in his parsonage, Bresee had an emotional experience of sanctification. Appointed presiding elder of the Los Angeles district in 1891, he began conducting revivals in churches in his charge, enlisting the assistance of National Association evangelists. Bresee's perfectionism was not appreciated by John H. Vincent, the new bishop in the Southern California Conference, who relieved him of the presiding eldership and appointed him pastor of two debt-ridden churches in succession. In 1894 Bresee decided to seek supernumerary status (relief of regular pastoral duties to pursue other religious work, but retaining ministerial relationship in the annual conference) to go into mission work. This request having been denied by the bishop, Bresee withdrew from the Methodist ministry after thirty-seven years.

Once out of the Methodist church, holiness leaders like Bresee attempted to create a pure church, often beginning their revival of primitive Wesleyanism by ministering to the poor. At first Bresee joined forces with T. P. and Manie Ferguson at the Peniel Mission in Los Angeles. When their visions for the mission proved incompatible, Bresee announced services in Los Angeles in 1895. Three weeks later, the Church of the Nazarene was organized by 135 charter members. It was committed to city missions, evangelistic services, and house-to-house visitations in order to convert sinners, sanctify believers, and care for the poor. In 1896 a simple board tabernacle was built (later nicknamed by worshipers the Glory Barn). Describing itself as a church with a mission, the Church of the Nazarene was enormously successful. Prominent evangelists preached in the tabernacle, a periodical was begun in 1898, and the organization expanded not only in California, but into the Northwest

and Midwest as well, concentrating its efforts on urban areas.

The eastern branch of what was to become in 1907 the Pentecostal Church of the Nazarene began with the joining of a significant number of independent holiness congregations into the Association of Pentecostal Churches of America in 1896–1897. Some of these congregations were led by strong individualists favoring "independency, congregationalism, and perfectionism" (Smith, 1962, p. 59). Others were headed by ex-Methodist preachers who left the church because of increased opposition to those professing sanctification. Three of these, H. N. Brown, A. B. Riggs, and John N. Short (pastors of independent holiness congregations in Brooklyn and Massachusetts), were the "three wise men from the East" who would go to Los Angeles to initiate union with Bresee's Nazarenes there (Smith, 1962, p. 81). By 1915 additional mergers had resulted in a Pentecostal Church of the Nazarene numbering 178 congregations and nearly 35,000 members.

The origin and development of the Pilgrim Holiness Church followed a very similar pattern. Martin Wells Knapp, a member of the Michigan Conference of the Methodist Episcopal Church, also got in trouble for taking part in a holiness evangelistic program. Knapp became a Methodist pastor after graduating from Albion College and apparently early earned the reputation both for mercilessly attacking worldliness and for successful evangelism. In 1886 he withdrew from the conference to devote himself full-time to revivalism and was sanctified in 1889 while reading his Bible. In 1888 he started a journal devoted to the renewal of holiness teaching in the church and began publishing a series of books that brought him into prominence in the midwestern holiness movement.

In 1892 Knapp moved to Cincinnati, where he began an aggressive holiness evangelistic program and continued his editorial work. In 1893 the Central Holiness League was organized. Loyal to the Methodist Episcopal Church until this time, Knapp became interested in mission work in Cincinnati with Appalachian mountain people. He not only withdrew from the conference in 1901 but also found the Central Holiness League too restrictive as he increasingly stressed divine healing and the second coming of Christ. In September 1897, Knapp and about a dozen followers formed the International Holiness Union and Prayer League. Interdenominational in scope, the group included among others George B. Kulp, a Methodist minister of the Michigan Conference, and Seth C. Rees, an Indiana-born Quaker evangelist.

While the Church of the Nazarene was expanding in the West, the International Holiness Union experienced the same pressures to become a church rather than simply an interdenominational association. Although early projects of the union such as homes for unwed mothers, God's Bible School and the Missionary Training Home, and the Revivalist publishing enterprises were protected from church control, "expansion and institutional development combined to promote denominational order" (Jones, *Perfectionist Persuasion*, 1974, p. 115). Reflecting these changes, the name of the group was altered in 1905 to the International Apostolic Holiness Union and Churches, and in 1913 to the International Apostolic Holiness Church. Again like the Church of the Nazarene, the International Apostolic Holiness Church would participate in mergers between 1919 and 1925 resulting in a large national holiness church, the Pilgrim Holiness Church. In 1926 it had over 15,000 members in 441 congregations.

HOLINESS AND SOCIAL WITNESS

The quest for holiness was by no means limited to matters of personal piety and morals. John Wesley believed that human life can be transformed; his teaching that Christian perfection was, above all, love of God and neighbor encouraged a remarkable spirit of mutual helpfulness and service in the early Methodist societies. Converts of Finney's revivals constituted a major force behind the evangelical antislavery movement of the 1830s. As mentioned earlier, both the Wesleyan Methodists and the Free Methodists began as abolitionist churches committed to the conjunction of holiness and uncompromising opposition to slavery. In 1850 Phoebe Palmer founded the Five Points Mission in one of the worst slum areas of New York City. It was a pioneering effort in urban social welfare work. These and many other holiness leaders found a natural connection between perfectionist aspiration and a profound reforming impulse.

In at least three areas, holiness groups related perfectionism to an often radical critique of existing society: abolitionism, feminism, and a commitment to the poor. Timothy L. Smith's research on revivalism and the quest for Christian perfection between 1840 and 1865 led him to claim the "evangelical origins of social Christianity." However one evaluates his thesis, it must be said that holiness people did not forget the special Christian responsibility to the poor and the oppressed. They were also increasingly critical of middle-class church life and its accommodation to the world. During the 1880s, when the Social Gospel movement began to address the problems of laboring people and the urban poor, holiness groups were also active in the urban slums. In pursuit of evangelism, holiness workers gained an intimate knowledge of slum conditions that sometimes led to more basic involvement in reforming social structures. At the very least, they were diligent in social service and welfare work among the very poor.

We have already referred to the city mission efforts of the independent holiness denominations. The Church of the Nazarene founders saw themselves as called to labor in the neglected areas of the cities and chose the group's name to symbolize the lowly, serving mission of Christ. Other groups that identified themselves with the poor in the 1880s were influenced by or in some way related to the holiness movement. The Christian and Missionary Alliance began with the work of A. B. Simpson, a Presbyterian minister, who left his denomination in 1881 to labor among the poor and neglected who were outside established churches. Formed in 1887, the alliance was closer to Keswick than to Wesleyan holiness beliefs. The Salvation Army, widely known for its urban evangelistic and social service work among the very poor, was founded by British Methodist William Booth as a London mission in 1865 and with its present name and organization in 1879. Booth had been influenced by American holiness evangelist James Caughey. The movement came to the United States in the early 1880s.

Holiness groups that emerged in the late nineteenth century and subsequently were typically sectarian in terms of their opposition to and refusal to compromise with the world around them. As we have seen, they were critical of established denominations such as the Methodist Episcopal Church for their "worldliness." For most holiness people, social service was secondary to evangelistic and personal moral concerns. It is clear, however, that for some, faith in the transforming Holy Spirit led to genuinely radical commitments to social reform.

Social concern seems to have been typical of holiness evangelicalism (in both its Wesleyan and Keswick forms) through the 1890s. The relevant factors are complex, but most scholars agree that between 1900 and 1930 a "great reversal" occurred, in which social concern became suspect among evangelicals. Part of this so-called reversal involved distancing themselves from a liberal Social Gospel. After the Fundamentalist controversy of the 1920s (a struggle between "fundamentalists" and "modernists" for control of the Presbyterian, Baptist, and other denominations), evangelical Protestantism was characteristically lacking in social concern until the 1970s. Recently evangelicals have been rediscovering a nineteenth-century perfectionist heritage in which revivalism and social witness were familiar allies.

HOLINESS AND WOMEN

Although he refused to sanction women preachers in general, John Wesley gradually admitted that there might be some exceptions. By 1771 he was convinced that female as well as male lay preachers might have an "extraordinary" call to preach. With Wesley's blessing then, women like Sarah Crosby, Mary Fletcher, and Sarah Mallett were accepted into the traveling ministry along with lay men, preaching to large crowds and holding class meetings. When asked why he encouraged certain females to preach, Wesley replied: "Because God owns them in the conversion of sinners, and who am I that I should withstand God?" (Earl Kent Brown, *Women of Mr. Wesley's Methodism*, 1983, p. 30).

In spite of this prominent early role, women were excluded from leadership positions in the Methodist Episcopal Church after its organization in America in 1784, largely because of the change to an ordained clergy. During the nine-

teenth century, it was primarily the holiness movement that kept alive the earlier Methodist tradition of religious leadership for women.

In the Wesleyan understanding of holiness, power and authority were conferred on women as well as men through the gifts of the Holy Spirit, quite apart from traditional sources of ecclesiastical authority. In *Promise of the Father*, Phoebe Palmer defended women's right to preach on the basis of the gift of the Spirit to the church at Pentecost, with its promise that "your sons and your daughters shall prophesy." Mrs. Palmer did not press for ordination for women, since she viewed the whole system of ordination as unscriptural. She deplored the trend in her day to discourage women from speaking in public, insisting that women be permitted to pray and testify in the churches and even to preach Christ for the conversion of sinners. Her teaching that the experience of entire sanctification must be professed in public to be retained gave considerable weight to this issue during the holiness awakening. (One of the "new measures" for which Finney had been so severely criticized, especially during the early years of his revivals, was his requirement that women were to pray and to testify in religious meetings.)

Among the women empowered by the experience of holiness and encouraged by the example of Phoebe Palmer were Catherine Booth, wife of Salvation Army founder William Booth, who began to preach and conduct revivals with her husband all over England; Frances E. Willard, leader of the Women's Christian Temperance Union, who professed entire sanctification at a holiness revival conducted by the Palmers in Evanston, Illinois, in 1866; and Jennie Fowler Willing, Methodist local preacher and tireless worker for temperance, woman's suffrage, and missions, who declared Pentecost as "Woman's Emancipation Day."

In 1853 Wesleyan Methodist pastor Luther Lee preached the ordination sermon for Congregationalist Antoinette L. Brown, graduate of Oberlin College and probably the first woman to be fully ordained to the Christian ministry in an American denomination. Lee's sermon, entitled "Woman's Right to Preach the Gospel," interpreted Galatians 3:28 to mean that men and women are equal in rights, privileges, and responsibilities in the church. He went beyond

Phoebe Palmer in claiming that prophecy and preaching were the same and that women therefore had the same right as men both to preach and to be ordained.

B. T. Roberts, founder of the Free Methodist Church, likewise defended the right of women to be ordained. Women held major leadership roles in the Pilgrim Holiness Church, the Church of God (Anderson, Indiana), the Church of the Nazarene, and the Pillar of Fire, a small holiness body founded in Denver, Colorado, in 1901 as the Pentecostal Union and officially renamed Pillar of Fire in 1917. The founder and first bishop of the Pillar of Fire was Alma White, wife of a former Methodist pastor, who had a sanctification experience in 1893 and immediately began to do evangelistic preaching and organize holiness meetings. She was ordained in 1902 and constantly promoted women's equality in church, home, and state, both in her sermons and in *Woman's Chains,* the journal she began in 1923. The original feminist impulse of the holiness movement was weakened by the biblical literalism of Fundamentalism and by the rising social status of holiness denominations and their consequent socialization to the dominant society.

HOLINESS AND PENTECOSTALISM

The immediate origins of the early-twentieth-century Pentecostal movement are to be found in the holiness movement. According to the dominant (Wesleyan) view, holiness was a second definite work of grace ("second blessing") after justification. By the end of the nineteenth century, this work was frequently equated with the baptism of the Holy Spirit. The most distinctive characteristic of Pentecostalism was its conviction that speaking in tongues was the outward sign of a Spirit baptism. Some Pentecostal groups retained the holiness view of sanctification as a second work of grace and regarded the baptism with the Holy Spirit as a third blessing, with speaking in tongues as evidence. Particularly in the South there were significant shifts of holiness groups to this new movement after 1900. Other holiness groups like the Pentecostal Church of the Nazarene deleted the word "Pentecostal" from their official title in order not to be confused with the "tongues" movement. A number of scholars have suggested that the Pentecostal understanding of baptism in the Spirit as a separate "enduement of power" is closer to the Keswick than to the Wesleyan holiness view.

Some Pentecostals date their origins from the New Year's Eve service at Charles F. Parham's Bethel Bible College in Topeka, Kansas, in 1900, when a student named Agnes Ozman received the baptism of the Holy Spirit and spoke in other tongues.

The Azusa Street revival in Los Angeles in 1906 is, however, generally regarded as the beginning of the modern Pentecostal movement. The leader of that revival was the southern black holiness preacher William J. Seymour. Convinced by Lucy Farrow, a black woman, and Charles Parham, a white man, that sanctification and the baptism of the Holy Ghost were separate experiences and that tongues was the first evidence of the Spirit baptism, Seymour began to preach the new Pentecostal doctrine in the old abandoned Azusa Street Mission. There for many years blacks and whites alike experienced the Holy Spirit baptism and went home to organize Pentecostal churches. Two of the most influential of these were G. B. Cashwell and Charles H. Mason. It was at Cashwell's revival meetings in Tennessee and North Carolina that Ambrose Jessup Tomlinson, founder of the Tomlinson Church of God in Cleveland, Tennessee, and J. H. King, later bishop of the Pentecostal Holiness Church, received their Spirit baptism. Mason founded the Church of God in Christ, one of the largest black Pentecostal bodies.

Interpreters of Pentecostalism have generally stressed its compensatory function as a religion of the disinherited. Recent writings by such black scholars as James S. Tinney, Leonard Lovett, James A. Forbes, and Cheryl Townsend Gilkes have argued that black Holiness-Pentecostalism (what Gilkes refers to as "the Sanctified Church") provides effective empowerment for liberation and should be studied in its own right rather than as a variant of white Pentecostalism.

HOLINESS AND METHODISM

After the exodus of the most outspoken advocates of holiness from the Methodist Episcopal churches (North and South) between 1880 and 1900, sanctification generally became a neglected emphasis in Methodism. Concomitant with this development and at least partly responsible for it were the rise of liberal theology and the Social Gospel and their widespread appeal among university-educated Methodist clergy and college and theological school faculty. Where a doctrine of holiness was retained, its gradual rather than instantaneous nature was stressed (in obvious reaction against what were perceived to be extreme and divisive aspects of the "second-blessing" view). To advocates of a Social Gospel, much of the stress on the old Methodist doctrines of experience appeared to be too individual and pietistic. Bishop Francis McConnell was unwilling to give up the ideal of entire sanctification, but he interpreted it in a social sense as "bringing all of life into subjection to God's Kingdom" (*The Essentials of Methodism*, 1916, p. 22). Many were simply weary of the controversy over holiness. Referring to these conflicts as "the greatest tragedy in Methodist history," Albert Outler aptly described what was lost: "The ironic outcome of this process was that the keystone in the arch of Wesley's own theological 'system' came to be a pebble in the shoes of standard-brand Methodists" (*Theology in the Wesleyan Spirit*, 1975, p. 67).

Candidates for ordination as elder and for acceptance into membership in full connection in an annual conference in the United Methodist Church are still asked the series of questions formulated by John Wesley (and asked of his lay preachers): "Have you faith in Christ? Are you going on to perfection? Do you expect to be made perfect in love in this life? Are you earnestly striving after it?" In the first half of the twentieth century these questions were often the source of considerable embarrassment and uneasiness among Methodists. Asbury Theological Seminary (founded in 1923) represented a self-conscious holiness wing within Methodism, while a number of holiness bodies, Methodist in derivation, claimed to be faithful to the Wesleyan heritage. (The United Methodist Church referred to above represents the reunion of the Methodist Episcopal Church, the Methodist Episcopal Church, South, and the Methodist Protestant Church in 1939 to form the Methodist Church; in 1968 this body merged

with the Evangelical United Brethren Church, resulting in the present United Methodist Church.)

Since midcentury, however, there has been increasing evidence that Methodist theologians from various points on the theological spectrum are exploring in fresh ways what this Wesleyan doctrine of holiness of heart and life might mean in the modern world. (In addition to the Outler book cited above, a recent example is Theodore Runyon, ed., *Sanctification and Liberation*, 1981. This work illustrates another fairly new development, the fruitful dialogue between holiness and United Methodist scholars on sanctification and related issues.)

HOLINESS AND AMERICAN CULTURE AND RELIGION

The evangelicalism that became pervasive and dominant by the mid-nineteenth century has been characterized by historians as Arminian, revivalistic, romantic, perfectionistic, and millennial. So widespread were these developments that the period has been spoken of as "the Methodist age" in America. The 1857–1858 revival is often taken to illustrate how thoroughly normative Methodist piety had become within American Protestantism. Combined with a democratic optimism from the Jacksonian era, this evangelical consensus persisted into the last quarter of the nineteenth century, when it began to disintegrate under the pressures of external challenges and competing world views.

After the Civil War the holiness movement attempted to respond to the growing worldliness of the Methodist churches and people. Formerly a plain and "peculiar" people in dress, behavior, and worship, Methodists (particularly in the cities) began to reflect their rise to middle-class social status. First from within Methodism and later through the formation of sect groups, holiness people protested Methodism's loss of identification with the poor.

Arising originally in the cities of the Northeast, the holiness movement helped newcomers to the city to cope with the impersonal, strange, and pluralistic society they found by offering familiar preaching and worship, and countering the corrupting threat of the city by defining the bounds of appropriate Christian conduct. Gospel hymns and witnessing were important in creating and reinforcing the community of intense feeling to sustain these commitments. The holiness movement, then, in many ways succeeded Methodism as a popular religious movement.

RECENT TRENDS

Two excellent works for understanding both the historic and contemporary forms of the holiness movement are Charles Edwin Jones, *A Guide to the Study of the Holiness Movement* (1974) and Donald W. Dayton's 1971 essay "The American Holiness Movement: A Bibliographical Introduction" (*"The Higher Christian Life"* series, vol. 1, 1984).

Both authors consider affiliation or a cooperating relationship with the Christian Holiness Association (1971; successor to the National Holiness Association) as a rough guide to the contemporary contours of the holiness movement. Membership includes Mennonite bodies like the Missionary Church and the Brethren in Christ (products of the impact of holiness revivalism on German Pietist groups); Friends Yearly Meetings like the Ohio and Rocky Mountain (part of the Evangelical Friends Alliance), influenced by revivalistic and perfectionistic evangelicalism in the nineteenth century; and small twentieth-century offshoots of Methodism, such as the Evangelical Methodist Church (1946) and the Evangelical Church of North America (1968). Dayton estimated the membership of the Christian Holiness Association at about 1 million in 1970 (with an even greater number in terms of actual constituency).

There are three theological seminaries associated with the movement: Asbury Theological Seminary in Wilmore, Kentucky (founded 1923), the Nazarene Theological Seminary in Kansas City (1945), and Western Evangelical Seminary in Portland, Oregon (1945). A Wesley Theological Society holds annual meetings and publishes the *Wesleyan Theological Journal* (begun in 1966).

Most of the holiness groups have experienced numerical growth and material prosperity in the post–World War II years. It would be accurate to describe the majority of them as still in the process of transition from sect to church. The following figures give some indication of recent membership (they are taken from the 1985 *Yearbook of American and Canadian Churches*): Church of the Nazarene: 507,574; The Wesleyan Church (product of the merger in 1968 of the Wesleyan Methodist Church and the Pilgrim Holiness Church): 107,672; Church of God (Anderson, Indiana): 182,190; Free Methodist Church of North America: 70,657; Salvation Army: 428,046.

All indications are that holiness groups are flourishing. Dayton describes them as "fiercely ecumenical within their own circle," encouraging historical and biblical studies, and increasingly open to exploring Christian experience in the light of modern psychology. Holiness scholarship has in many ways come into its own since the 1970s, manifesting a new interest in and commitment to the study and reinterpretation of this holiness tradition. Part of the "evangelical renaissance" of the 1970s and 1980s, the holiness movement has produced some highly articulate and respected leaders who are convinced that characteristic Wesleyan holiness emphases —such as resistance to dispensational premillennialism, a nondogmatic style of life in the Spirit, and renewed emphasis on sanctification in the search for a Christian life-style and a recovery of social witness—have much to offer contemporary evangelicalism.

BIBLIOGRAPHY

General

Donald W. Dayton, *Discovering an Evangelical Heritage* (1976) and, as ed., *"The Higher Christian Life": Sources for the Study of the Holiness, Pentecostal and Keswick Movements*, 48 vols. (1984–1985); Melvin E. Dieter, *The Holiness Revival of the Nineteenth Century* (1980); Charles E. Jones, *A Guide to the Study of the Holiness Movement* (1974) and *Perfectionist Persuasion: The Holiness Movement and American Methodism, 1867–1936* (1974); Timothy L. Smith, *Revivalism and Social Reform in Mid-Nineteenth-Century America* (1957) and "The Holiness Crusade," in Emory S. Bucke, ed., *The History of American Methodism*, vol. 2 (1964).

John Wesley's Doctrine of Christian Perfection

Harald Lindström, *Wesley and Sanctification* (1946; repr. 1984); Albert C. Outler, ed., *John Wesley* (1964); Phoebe

Palmer, *The Way of Holiness* (1843; repr. 1985), *Faith and Its Effects* (1849; repr. 1985), and *Promise of the Father* (1859; repr. 1985); John Leland Peters, *Christian Perfection and American Methodism* (1956); Richard Wheatley, *The Life and Letters of Mrs. Phoebe Palmer* (1876; repr. 1984).

Wesley and Free Methodists

Walter W. Benjamin, "The Free Methodists," in Emory S. Bucke, ed., *The History of American Methodism*, vol. 2 (1964); Donald G. Mathews, *Slavery and Methodism* (1965); Lucius C. Matlack, *The History of American Slavery and Methodism, from 1780 to 1849, and History of the Wesleyan Methodist Connection of America* (1849; repr. 1971); Orange Scott, *The Grounds of Secession from the M.E. Church* (1848; repr. 1969).

Holiness Camp Meetings

Martin Wells Knapp, *Out of Egypt into Canaan* (1887); William McDonald and John E. Searles, *The Life of Rev. John S. Inskip* (1885; repr. 1985); Alexander McLean and J. W. Eaton, eds., *Penuel: or, Face to Face with God* (1869; repr. 1985).

Perfectionism and Higher Life Movements

Steven Barabas, *So Great Salvation: The History and Message of the Keswick Convention* (1952); J. B. Figgis, *Keswick from Within* (1914; repr. 1985); Edward H. Madden and James E. Hamilton, *Freedom and Grace: The Life of Asa Mahan* (1982); George M. Marsden, *Fundamentalism and American Culture: 1870–1925* (1980); Hannah Whitall Smith, *The Unselfishness of God and How I Discovered It* (1903; repr. 1985).

Holiness Denominations

John W. V. Smith, *The Quest for Holiness and Unity* (1980); Timothy L. Smith, *Called Unto Holiness* (1962).

Holiness and Women

Lucille Sider Dayton and Donald W. Dayton, " 'Your Daughters Shall Prophesy': Feminism in the Holiness Movement," in *Methodist History*, 14 (1976), and, with Nancy Hardesty, "Women in the Holiness Movement," in Rosemary Ruether and Eleanor McLaughlin, eds., *Women of Spirit* (1979).

Holiness and Pentecostalism

John T. Nichol, *Pentecostalism* (1966); Vinson Synan, *The Holiness-Pentecostal Movement in the United States* (1971) and, as ed., *Aspects of Pentecostal-Charismatic Origins* (1975).

Black Holiness-Pentecostalism

Cheryl Townsend Gilkes, "Together and in Harness: Women's Traditions in the Sanctified Church," in *Signs: Journal of Women in Culture and Society*, 10 (1985); Leonard Lovett, "Black Holiness-Pentecostalism: Implications for Ethics and Social Transformation," Ph.D. diss., Emory Univ., 1978; James S. Tinney, "William J. Seymour: Father of Modern-Day Pentecostalism," in Randall Burkett and Richard Newman, eds., *Black Apostles: Afro-American Clergy Confront the Twentieth Century* (1978).

[*See also* FUNDAMENTALISM; PENTECOSTALISM; *and* UNITED METHODISM.]

MILLENNIALISM AND ADVENTISM

Charles H. Lippy

FROM seventeenth-century New England Puritans to contemporary students of biblical prophecy, the fascination with millennialism—correlating current events with a presumed timetable for the end of history and the return of Christ—has been a vital current in American religion. Within the Christian tradition, the millennium refers to a thousand-year period associated with the final defeat of sin and Satan; the Second Coming, or *Parousia* (Second Advent), of Christ; the last judgment of humanity; and the glory of the redeemed.

Over the centuries, the Christian faithful have developed many conflicting interpretations of the millennium. One long-standing view, known as *premillennialism,* argues that the return of Christ will precede a thousand-year reign on earth that will end in the ultimate battle between good and evil at Armageddon. Thereafter the rapturous believers of all generations will share in the triumph and glory of Christ in heaven, the world will be transformed again into an Edenic paradise, and sinners will reap everlasting punishment. Another perspective with a long heritage has been labeled *postmillennialism.* Generally described as more optimistic than premillennialism, this position claims that humanity will gradually progress toward goodness and righteousness, slowly conquering the forces of evil in preparation for Christ's return in glory following a thousand years of peace.

The basis for Christian millennialism is found in the apocalyptic literature of the Bible, particularly the books of Daniel and Revelation. Indeed millennialism and apocalypticism are often linked together, though they are technically distinct. Apocalypticism deals with revelations or prophecies about the end of chronological time and the inauguration of a new age, usually conveyed in highly esoteric symbolism. Millennialism becomes connected with the apocalypse, since the millennium itself is generally seen as part of the complex of events associated with the end time.

Millennialism has spawned its own technical vocabulary. Some writers, for example, speak of *millenarianism* rather than millennialism. Though in a narrow sense the terms are synonymous, millenarianism sometimes refers to belief in a future salvation from present turmoil, a salvation involving the cataclysmic destruction of the powers of evil, but such a belief is not necessarily identified with the Christian expectation of the Second Advent of Christ. Some variants of millennialism are clustered under the rubric of *adventism* because here the crux of speculation centers around the expected literal return of Christ more than around the details of Christ's anticipated thousand-year reign. Another term in the millennial lexicon is *chiliasm.* Chiliasm derives from the Greek word for "one thousand," rather than from a Latin one (as do both millennialism and millenarianism), and simply refers to the Second Coming of Christ and the expected thousand-year reign of Christ on earth.

Many analysts of American millennialism have emphasized the different consequences seen to result from premillennialism and postmillennialism. Premillennialism, because of its belief in a thousand years of tribulation before the final triumph of Christ, was regarded as essentially pessimistic. Premillennialists, it was claimed, had little interest in the social order and eschewed social reform since the world itself was thought to be the arena of Satan and would be subject to destruction when Christ returned. Furthermore,

831

any effort to allay sinfulness would lead only to greater despair because of the realization of sin's pervasiveness. The task of the zealous premillennialist was simply to proclaim the gospel of the coming of Christ and rescue a righteous remnant from the clutches of a sinful world. Premillennialists, however, were and still are not cut from a single cloth. Some have indeed been concerned with social issues, though more with an eye to protect the righteous remnant from contamination than to transform the very fabric of society. There have been numerous divisions among premillennialists over whether the end was near at hand or at some indefinite point in the future. Some have been obsessed with pinpointing the precise date for Christ's return, assiduously appraising the events of world history and correlating them with biblical references to signs of the apocalypse. Others have been wary of fixing a schedule of events leading to the Second Advent, aware that the disappointment that would follow could lead many to forsake the faith.

By contrast, postmillennialists have usually been classified as more liberal and more involved in seeking social change because of their conviction that humanity must progressively eliminate evil to set the stage for the millennium's dawning. As a rule, postmillennialists have been less prone to set dates for the return of Christ, though many have overoptimistically viewed events in their own times as clues that society was evolving toward the millennium.

While these distinctions are real, they have been eclipsed in current scholarship by the contention that it is the strident espousal of any form of millennialism that sets adherents apart from others. It matters little whether one expects the return of Christ to initiate or terminate the millennium. What is important, however, is that any variant of millennial expectation values the future and sees the present from the vantage point of an expected time when the shape of society, of human relationships, indeed of the whole of reality, is transformed into the ideal. The future becomes the genuine level of reality by which the present is interpreted and evaluated. But present time gains a fresh value as well, for whether it is a time dominated by satanic forces or marked by evolution toward a divine goal, it is nevertheless leading to the culmination of history.

What has led scholars in the last three decades to regard millennial affirmation as significant in itself is their increasing awareness that Christian millennialism is part of a larger genre. Millennial currents may be found in many traditions. Christian millennial expectation, for example, is akin to Jewish messianism, which likewise looks to a coming Edenic age when the Lord will reign supreme. Within the Zoroastrian tradition one finds a firm belief in a final cosmic conflict between the forces of good and evil in which the ultimate triumph of good will transform the present reality. The Cargo Cults of Melanesia have affinities as well in anticipating the destruction of the forces of oppression and the restoration of life as it should be at a time near at hand. Strands of both the Hindu and Buddhist traditions have interpreted history in cycles of creation, annihilation, and re-creation, claiming that the present age is on the brink of destruction because it has abandoned true devotion for false concerns.

Hence American millennialism is now seen as part of a larger phenomenon in human religious experience, one that appreciates and anticipates the power of the future in present affairs; thus, millennialism and adventism in American religion cannot be understood exclusively from the vantage point of the Christian theological tradition or restricted to movements within Christian groups and denominations. Looking to the future in order to understand the present is a continuous strand undergirding the American religious experience; it also links American religious life to the religious life of humanity.

The image of a millennial age in which God's elect will share in the divine glory and in which judgment will be the lot of the wicked has penetrated the American religious mind from the arrival of the first European invaders of the New World to the present. At times its influence has been overt; at other times, subtle. It is as if there were a millennialist/adventist stratum in the self-consciousness of those who have shaped American life, a stratum that sometimes rises to the surface and at other times quietly weaves in and out of the fabric of common life. The Puritans who settled in New England, for example, were acutely conscious that theirs was an enterprise with a special destiny. In the words of John Winthrop, the Puritan experiment was to create "a city upon a hill" that would be the model for the world and a prototype of the millennial kingdom. Influenced by the various strands of millennialism that erupted with new force during the era of the English Civil War, the Puritans looked to the day when, under the sovereign power of God, they would share in the inauguration of Christ's reign on earth. But this vision entailed a great responsibility, one that Puritan preachers and poets often felt was being abandoned by those who strayed from the theocratic ideal. Countless jeremiads warned of impending judgment and urged hearers to recommit themselves to the ways of God. Michael Wigglesworth's famous *The Day of Doom* (1662) issued in verse a similar message: the coming judgment that will usher in the rule of Christ will fall heaviest on those who wander from the path of the elect.

When the revivals of the Great Awakening swept the English colonies in North America in the eighteenth century, many were convinced that in the new religious enthusiasm were clear signs of the coming millennial kingdom. Jonathan Edwards, the fomenter of revivals in Northampton, Massachusetts, came to believe that the Awakening was itself the inbreaking of the millennium and that America had been chosen by God as the place where the reign of Christ would begin. But the millennialist undercurrents of the revivals had a political cast as well. As the era of the American Revolution drew near, many regarded the moves toward independence as omens of the future glory destined for the American nation. Religion and the public order fused in a "civil millennialism" that imbued the cause of liberty with such a sacrality that Congregationist clergyman Ezra Stiles, president of Yale College, could speak of "the United States elevated to glory and honor." And when revolutionary fervor spread in Europe, many eagerly found signals of the biblical prophecies of the end of the age and the dawn of the millennium; those who viewed the papacy as Antichrist were particularly taken when Napoleon extended his power over the papacy. The so-called democratic revolutions that rocked Europe in the 1840s were likewise seen as signs that the millennial reign of Christ was at hand.

During the early nineteenth century, the idea of the millennium remained a part of the ideological reservoir that shaped American public consciousness. The camp meetings of the frontier and the revivals that cascaded across upstate New York and into urban centers betokened the start of what Robert T. Handy has called the "quest for a Christian America" that would cast American society in a millennial mold. The exuberance of conversion led to the establishment of voluntary societies so numerous that they have been labeled a benevolent empire. But the rationale in part was to root out social evils and prepare the nation for its destiny as God's kingdom. Hand in hand with revivals and social reform went the formation of hundreds of utopian communitarian ventures that frequently saw in withdrawal from the mainstream the opportunity to create on earth the life of the millennial age. Those who gathered at Oneida, at Amana, at Zoar, at Harmony and Economy, or in the numerous Shaker enclaves all believed that they had established the millennial order here and now. The revivals likewise gave birth to restorationism, the attempt to reinstate the practices of early Christianity in religious life in the conviction that by so doing the world would move closer to the millennial age. That impulse prompted Alexander Campbell, for example, to dub his restorationist paper the *Millennial Harbinger* (founded in 1830), and while the expectation of an imminent millennium may be more muted today in his Disciples of Christ heirs, it lives on in sober, but strident fashion in groups such as the Christadelphians, who owe their genesis to the primitivism of Campbell and his associates.

The era of the camp meeting and the revivals was also the time of large-scale westward movement. For many, westward expansion itself was infused with millennialist meaning. The Mormons may be simply the most conspicuous example of a people who moved westward to raise a new civilization in the wilderness structured in anticipation of the heavenly kingdom's coming to earth. In a more subtle fashion, millennial notions fed into the idea of Manifest Destiny. The sense that God had ordained the expansion of the United States from the Atlantic to the Pacific was but a prelude to the future reign of Christ.

In time, many came to view slavery as the major force impeding the establishment of the millennial order in the United States. A passion for creating the conditions conducive to the arrival of the millennium motivated the abolitionism and other social reform activities of many, such as Theodore Dwight Weld. Dissenting voices, among them that of James Henley Thornwell, argued that expectation of a millennial age actually gave sanction to the maintenance of a slave labor system. When the Civil War erupted, numerous preachers and layfolk understood the struggle as an "American apocalypse," to use James H. Moorhead's apt phrase, a struggle that would cleanse the nation in preparation for the advent of the millennium. Later wars likewise spurred millennialist speculation and anticipation; millennialist images, for example, infected Woodrow Wilson's vision of the war to make the world "safe for democracy" and for the irenic age that could ensue with a League of Nations dedicated to peace.

Millennialist symbols provided support as well for the optimistic program for social reform known as Social Christianity, or the Social Gospel, which peaked around the time of World War I. Walter Rauschenbusch, for one, was convinced that humanity possessed the knowledge and skills to Christianize the social order to such an extent that it would evolve into the coming kingdom of God. But during the same era that Rauschenbusch and others were calling for the transformation of American society into the divine kingdom, others had a more pessimistic view of the age. As Ernest Sandeen and others have demonstrated, British and American millenarianism fused with certain strands of dispensationalist thought in an emergent Fundamentalism that regarded history as divided into periods (dispensations) leading up to the dawn of the millennium. Expecting a time of turmoil when evil would be ascendant, these dispensationalists-Fundamentalists, who gathered at the Niagara Bible Conferences starting in 1875 and at other similar meetings, were inclined to see signs of doom and despair where Rauschenbusch saw signs of hope and progress. But they also believed that the seeming omnipresence of evil had brought civilization into the "shadow of the Second Coming" (to use Timothy Weber's phrase) and that the end was near and judgment at hand. Similar strains of millennialism echo through the Pentecostal movement, which gained ground in the opening years of the twentieth century and continues to surge as the century draws to a close.

Another manifestation of the penetration of millennialism into the religious subconscious is the multifaceted missionary movement generated by the American experience. The millennialist undercurrent may be most obvious in the foreign missions movement, which got under way in the early nineteenth century and experienced great growth in the age of optimism that marked the closing years of the nineteenth century. The clarion call to "win the world for Christ" stemmed in part from the belief that the global proclamation of the Gospel was a prerequisite to bringing in the millennium. But millennialist symbols occurred in other facets of the missionary thrust in American religion. A vision of the millennial age was already there, for example, among the Franciscans, who had come to evangelize the native Indian population in the wake of the Spanish conquest, and it also linked the "home missions" movement with the social reform endeavors of the nineteenth and twentieth centuries.

Millennial imagery has also taken institutional roots in several organized religious groups, sects, and denominations. This more formal strain of millennialism stretches back to the age of revivals in the early nineteenth century, when the evangelical zeal for conversion, the enthusiasm for social reform, and the excitement of molding the shape of the new republic went hand in hand with adventist expectation.

Much of the early story revolves around William Miller and the following he ultimately attracted. Miller, of sturdy Vermont frontier stock and a veteran of the War of 1812, dabbled with religious radicalism in the form of deism in his early years, but underwent a dramatic change when struck by an experience of conversion in a local revival. Affiliated with a Baptist congregation, Miller became an avid student of Scripture; he was increasingly taken by the chronology advanced by Archbishop James Ussher (which was later to play a prominent role in dispensationalism and to guide Cyrus I. Scofield in preparing his *Reference Bible* geared to adventist thinking). The apocalyptic portions of the Bible, particularly the book of Daniel, intrigued Miller as he attempted to decode prophecy and determine when the millennium would begin. Around 1818 he became convinced that a mere quarter-century remained until the return of the Lord. Overcoming an initial reluctance to proclaim his views publicly, Miller soon became a well-known regional revivalist.

In the 1830s Miller gained a wider hearing. Ordained as a Baptist in 1833, two years later he published a series of lectures on the return of

Christ, based on his interpretation of chronological symbols in biblical apocalyptic literature. Referring to the 2,300 days mentioned in Daniel 8:14 as the time to pass before the final cleansing of the earth as years and dating the original prophecy to 457 B.C., Miller insisted that the apocalypse would come in 1843. But it was not publication of his millennial speculation that brought him national prominence. Rather, it was his association with Joshua V. Himes, a Boston pastor who was a genius at public relations as well as a skilled organizer. Under Himes's tutelage, Miller was launched onto the revival and camp meeting preaching circuit and soon attracted large audiences eager to learn the timetable for the Lord's coming. In the early 1840s, Miller toured the nation, convincing thousands of the urgent need to prepare for the millennium. His work was buttressed by the publication of adventist papers and a hymnal, all edited by Himes.

When the millennium did not commence in March 1843, Miller's initial prediction, he redid his arithmetic, first fixing March 1844 as the expected time and finally staking all on 22 October 1844. While earlier tradition held that Millerites "ran riot, went crazy, committed suicide, gave up their jobs and their property, made white robes, and gathered in cemeteries or on hilltops to await the Lord at the appointed time" (Brown), evidence suggests the contrary; namely, that Miller's followers gathered at their usual meeting places to worship and pray as the end approached. However, again the Lord failed to appear on schedule. Miller and his devotees had to face what has been called the "great disappointment."

As might be expected, many deserted the adventist movement. But Miller himself and a faithful remnant refused to accept defeat. In April 1845 a number of these steadfast adventists met in Albany, and plans for a congregational structure began to take shape. This preliminary effort at a separate organization marked a decided shift in the character of the adventist movement. Prior to the Albany gathering, most of Miller's followers had remained within their own churches, for a degree of interest in the millennium was fairly widespread at the time. A few churches had closed their doors to Miller as the date of the Lord's expected return drew nigh, for millennialist thinking in the mainstream shied away from

setting a strict timetable and Miller's approach seemed rash. And some of the denominations had previously dismissed clergy who espoused strident millennialist views. So although only a few Millerites had withdrawn from their churches earlier, more did so once the Albany gathering had formulated elemental proposals for a congregational structure, continuing Bible instruction, the establishment of Sunday schools, and a statement of doctrine drafted by a committee that Miller chaired. In 1858 a second gathering in Boston continued on the route to a more definite structure by adopting the name American Millennial Association, which was changed a few years later to the Evangelical Adventist Association. By then Miller himself was dead, and the movement eroded in the absence of his leadership, with the result that by the mid-1920s, the Evangelical Adventists had ceased to exist as a discrete entity.

Part of the difficulty stemmed from dissension among those who were still convinced that the Second Advent was imminent. Some followed the lead of Joseph Turner, a Maine resident who refused to perform manual labor in the belief that it would lead to judgment since the Great Sabbath must have already arrived, though in ways not yet clear to mortals. When that view gradually dissipated, Turner advanced the hypothesis that adventists should cease all evangelistic activity, announcing that Christ had indeed returned and that consequently no new souls could be saved; the door had been shut to unbelievers. For a time, this "shut door" perspective gained general acceptance among adventists but was gradually replaced by the view that only those who had heard the adventist gospel and had refused to accept its validity were beyond the pale. Hence there was still a need to bring the truth to those who had not yet heard it.

Yet another faction adhered to the teaching of Hiram Edson, a farmer from New York who, following a vision in a cornfield, reinterpreted Miller's teaching to argue that Christ had cleansed a heavenly temple rather than an earthly one on the expected day. Others sought association with kindred spirits, particularly Seventh-Day Baptists, after an ongoing study of Scripture had convinced them that Sunday worship was a sign of the Antichrist, since it had been sanctioned by the Pope, and that the commandment to "remember the Sabbath day" required literal adherence. Disputes over relatively minor points of adventist belief caused further divisions. By the time the Civil War erupted, adventism was in disarray and had generated numerous sectarian bodies, some of which have endured to the present: the Advent Christian Church, the Church of God (Adventist), the Church of God (Oregon, Illinois), the Church of God (Seventh Day), the Fort Wayne Gospel Temple, the Life and Advent Union, and the Primitive Advent Church. In 1980, the combined membership of these groups totaled fewer than 10,000.

Of the Millerite offshoots, the most significant in terms of size and impact on American religion is the group that formed around the teaching of Ellen G. (Harmon) White: the Seventh-Day Adventists. She had been converted to Miller's millennialist doctrines in 1842 and came to be known as an adventist prophetess within a few years. Her position within the movement was strengthened by her marriage in 1846 to the Rev. James White, a confirmed adventist and owner of the adventist Review and Herald Publishing House. Subject to frequent ecstatic experiences, Mrs. White embraced adherence to the fourth commandment, insisting on Saturday Sabbath observance, after a vision in which an angel had told her that failure to keep the Ten Commandments had delayed Christ's return. Absorbing many of the disillusioned Millerites who were attracted to Sabbatarianism (observing Saturday as the Christian day of worship), Mrs. White's group was centered in Battle Creek, Michigan, after 1855. Another vision soon augmented the brand of adventism taught by Mrs. White. Long subject to ill health, Mrs. White received word in June 1863, while in a trance, that change of diet and health reform were as central to the holy life as keeping the Sabbath. Advocating vegetarianism, calling for avoidance of alcohol and tobacco, condemning masturbation, and criticizing reliance on medical science and drugs during illness, Mrs. White linked adventism to the broader cultural fascination with diet promoted as early as the 1830s by onetime Presbyterian evangelist Sylvester Graham, now associated primarily with his crackers. While rigid adherence to these dietary and related hygienic precepts had a checkered history in the first decades of the Seventh-Day Adventist movement, they did bestow an ongoing concern for health-related issues in Mrs. White's followers, a concern that endures today. Perhaps the most well-known results of this conviction that the elect must pay heed to diet are the invention of peanut butter and numerous cereal products. Dr. John Harvey Kellogg, a devotee of Mrs. White, not only transformed the adventist water cure center in Battle Creek into a renowned sanitarium, but he also invented corn flakes.

Early Seventh-Day Adventism had a distinctive political flavor as well. Convinced that American Protestantism had long ago lost God's favor through Sunday worship, the Adventists worked assiduously against "blue laws" and similar phenomena that were part of mainstream evangelical Protestantism's effort to create a Christian nation in the mid-nineteenth century. In addition, Adventists believed that the nation as a whole had forfeited God's favor by maintaining a slave labor system, which contradicted the republican principles presumably integral to national identity. Mrs. White became an outspoken abolitionist, but she and her followers were in a quandary when the Civil War broke out. Simply put, the dilemma was whether Adventists should participate in the war and thereby lend tacit support to a government that no longer had God's blessing. In some cases, Adventists' refusal to take up arms led to civil recrimination, but Mrs. White herself waffled on whether pacifism was essential to true belief, proclaiming that while a true believer should have nothing to do with the war effort (despite its being seen as a war that would end the evil of slavery), Christians were nonetheless obligated to honor both God and country. Once hostilities ceased, Adventist criticism of the nation became more muted, and primary attention was given to evangelism both at home and abroad. Particular success came in making converts outside the United States.

As might be expected, over the years Seventh-Day Adventism has taken on more of the appearance of conservative Protestantism, although some distinctive beliefs and practices are maintained. Biblical prophecies, especially those in Daniel and Revelation, remain central, and there continues to be a lively sense that history has witnessed the fulfillment of all the prophecies except for the full gathering of a "prepared people." In addition, the writings of Ellen White continue to be held in high regard and have assumed a near-sacred status. Baptism by immersion is the mode of entry into the fellowship of the redeemed. Following Mrs. White, Adventist doctrine continues to assert that immortality is not the reward of the faithful at death, but rather a status that will be conferred on believers when the Second Advent does transpire. Death for believers and unbelievers alike is akin to a deep, dreamless sleep. When the Lord returns, resurrection for the redeemed will occur; those who fail to accept the Adventist truth will be raised at the close of Christ's millennial reign for judgment and destruction. During the millennium itself, the resurrected redeemed will reside in heaven while the earth will remain the uninhabited abode of Satan. The final defeat of Satan and the destruction of the unredeemed will allow the elect to return to the earth for eternity. Mrs. White's doctrine does not consign unbelievers to an eternity in hell, but rather to a final destruction. In 1982, the Seventh-Day Adventists numbered some 588,536 in the United States, an increase of 35 percent since 1972.

Ranking among the fastest-growing religious bodies in the United States in the last quarter of the twentieth century is another millennialist group, which developed around the teachings of Charles Taze Russell. Russell, a haberdasher by profession, was a Congregationalist layman from Allegheny, Pennsylvania, who embarked on a private program of Bible study following a time of religious doubt and uncertainty. In 1872 he began to organize his followers under the rubric of the International Bible Students' Association. Russell's perspective, while often confusing and lacking tidy coherence, represents perhaps the most radical millennialism to emerge from the adventist undercurrents in American religion. According to Russell, the millennium has already dawned, but in a fashion quite different from what other adventists have expected. In *The Plan of the Ages,* first published in 1881 as *Food for Thinking Christians* and reprinted many times since, Russell asserted that the "Millennial Dawn" commenced in 1874 with a spiritual return of Christ to the "upper air" and that the Lord's reign would begin in heaven in 1914. Hence, the millennium is already under way in one sense, although incomplete at present. The final consummation of the millennium, which Russell expected at any moment, would await the annihilation of all associated with the reign of Satan. In that category, Russell included the

churches and denominations, the nations of the world, and, of course, both political and religious leaders. Asserting that "millions now living will never die," Russell supplied his followers with a vast array of writings on the Bible to enable them to study Scripture with an eye to preparing for the Second Advent.

Russell diverged from standard adventist approaches as well as from orthodox Protestant thought in the sharp distinction he drew between Jehovah and Jesus Christ, arguing that they are two separate individuals. In Russell's scheme, Christ is a created spirit, although a perfect man while living. After the crucifixion, Christ again became a spirit whose body might be produced sometime in the future, should God so desire. This dyad denies any role for the Holy Spirit, central to orthodox Christian trinitarianism. In addition, Russell did away with any notion of hell. In its place, he developed a rather elaborate doctrine of resurrection and "second probation." Those who die before the final consummation of the millennium, whether believers or unbelievers, experience total annihilation. When the Lord does return to earth, all the dead will be re-created rather than resurrected and then returned to earth for the thousand-year reign of Christ. During this period, those who earlier refused to accept Russell's version of the Gospel will be offered fresh opportunities to repent. Russell anticipated that millions of sinners would avail themselves of this chance, for if they did not, at the close of Christ's reign they would again be exterminated, though without suffering. Those who repented during the millennial age would be granted "eternal life," although in a fashion different from that of those who had believed the truth during their lifetimes. The former would still require food for nourishment, while the latter would enjoy a totally spiritual life.

While Russell attracted a large following in his own lifetime, his successor, "Judge" Joseph F. Rutherford, had the promotional skills necessary to spur rapid growth. While Rutherford did not abandon the basics of Russell's perspective, he was more cautious in fixing a precise chronology for the Second Advent on earth. Rutherford organized the Jehovah's Witnesses—the designation he gave the unincorporated group in 1931 —into groups similar to churches, though called Kingdom Halls because of the conviction that the churches were of Satan. He structured a program of door-to-door evangelism. The designation of adherents as Witnesses stemmed in part from the assertion that because ministers in the established churches were part of the rule of Satan, the group had to eschew having a clergy and regard each member as a witness to the truth. The only formal organization that the Jehovah's Witnesses have maintained, one whose operations expanded greatly under the guidance of Rutherford and then Nathan A. Knorr, is the Watchtower Bible and Tract Society, a publishing operation headquartered in Brooklyn, New York. In addition to publishing *The Watchtower,* the Witnesses' widely circulated magazine, the society prepares materials for use in evangelistic activity, prints Russell's volumes of biblical exegesis, and at one time produced record albums, which were played by visiting Witnesses in the homes of prospective converts.

The Witnesses' insistence that they are living in the Theocracy, Christ's kingdom, and that human governments are enemies of the truth has brought them into sharp conflict with the federal government from time to time. During World War I, for example, Witnesses refused to accept conscription in the armed forces, claiming that to do so would be to endorse the legitimacy of the government and that since all Witnesses are "ministers," all merit clerical exemption. Hundreds were arrested and imprisoned. During World War II, at least 2,000 Witnesses served prison terms in the United States for refusing to enter the military or perform alternative service. A similar fate met Jehovah's Witnesses in Canada, Britain, Germany, and elsewhere.

Accusations of disloyalty to the United States and of fostering unpatriotic activity also stemmed from the Witnesses' prohibiting members, children and adults alike, from joining in the Pledge of Allegiance to the flag. While in some instances Witnesses formed their own schools for children ostracized or expelled from the public schools for adherence to this prohibition, the real test came in the courts. In the early 1940s several cases reached the Supreme Court. In a 1940 ruling, the court insisted that the Witnesses' children had to salute the flag, but a 1943 ruling, still in effect, finally upheld their right to such refusal on religious grounds.

Another source of external conflict stemmed from the virulent anti-Catholicism that was particularly characteristic of many of Rutherford's public statements. In the 1930s, Rutherford had launched an extensive campaign on commercial radio to propagate the Witnesses' belief that Catholicism was to be identified with the forces of Antichrist. In 1937 Rutherford finally yielded to Catholic protests and voluntarily abandoned commercial radio. In Quebec, conflict between Witnesses and Catholics came to a head in the 1940s: several Witnesses were attacked because of objections to their aggressive door-to-door proselytizing. In 1950, after a bitter struggle, Canadian courts did guarantee certain protection to the Witnesses.

In recent years public controversy has centered around their beliefs regarding certain forms of health care, particularly their refusal to accept blood transfusions. While the resolution of this problem has varied from country to country, in the United States there have been conflicting court decisions. In 1958, for example, the Supreme Court ruled that the constitutional rights of a Witness had been abridged when a circuit court judge ordered a blood transfusion, while a decade later the Supreme Court twice denied Witnesses the right of appeal in similar cases.

The net result of this conflict in the public arena has been twofold. On the one hand, the constant sense of persecution by an alien world has nurtured solidarity and cohesion within the movement, thus strengthening the conviction that the Witnesses alone are the elect of God. On the other hand, the notion that the Witnesses maintain socially aberrant beliefs and practices has hindered acceptance of the group within a religiously pluralistic culture and impeded establishment of a good working relationship with other Protestant bodies. Nevertheless, the Witnesses continue to grow at an astonishing rate, both within the United States and elsewhere. In recent years, missionary endeavors have expanded globally, with work in Africa consuming much energy. In the United States in 1982, some 588,503 persons counted themselves as Witnesses, a growth rate of 41 percent over a decade.

Millennialist impulses have not been restricted to whites in the American religious experience. Apocalyptic visions have from time to time nurtured religious life among both American blacks and native American Indians, but in forms and ways different from those that produced the Millerites, the Seventh-Day Adventists, the Jehovah's Witnesses, and other such groups. In the black experience, for example, the sense of an imminent millennium has rarely surfaced with the intensity that it has in white experience, perhaps because the oppression wrought by slavery snuffed out most remnants of the African tribal religious traditions that might have been recast in a millennial form and because the absence of effective power under slavery muted visions of an immediate overturning of the present order with the dawning of a millennial age. Even when blacks have clustered in Pentecostal and Holiness groups, which are sustained in part by millennial undercurrents, they have tended to emphasize conversion, sanctification, and a rigid ethical morality more than millennial expectations. But to deny the millennial dimension in black religion is to gloss over an important element in the overall story. As Donald G. Mathews wrote in his careful study *Religion in the Old South* (1977):

> It is the Apocalypse which is missing from most evaluations of black Christianity. The issues of accommodation, compensation, and survival, like the figure of Uncle Tom, ignore the fact that the chosen community of love and forbearance is also that of hope, but not a flaccid expectation that everything will turn out right in the end. The hope is Apocalyptic; that is, it is based on the vision of a future, violent struggle in which Evil is destroyed.

And as I have noted in "Waiting for the End":

> The references to freedom in many slave spirituals, for example, pointed to release from slavery within historical time as well as to release from spiritual bondage to sin. Those which spoke of future rewards in heaven likewise had a double meaning: it was necessary to prepare not only for heavenly existence after death, but also for a future on earth when the oppression of slavery would cease.

These visions of the future are millennialist in that they project a time when the vagaries of the present age are replaced by the ideals of what life should be. As such, they serve as ongoing forces imbuing black religious life with fresh vitality. One could argue as well that the civil rights movement and black militancy of recent decades are simply the transmutation of this millennialism into the secular realm. At least in the public discourse of a figure such as Martin Luther King, Jr., the fusion of the religious and the secular was obvious. His well-known "I Have a Dream" speech, for example, clearly projected a coming age when the ideals of the civil rights movement would be attained for all, and it drew heavily on biblical symbols to make its point.

Another sort of millennial variant has emerged from time to time among various native American Indian groups, serving as well to revitalize the integrity of a tribal life threatened with extinction by pressures from the dominant white culture. No discussion of the broad contours of millennialism in American religion would be complete without mention of the milleniarian movement known as the Ghost Dance, which arose primarily among California tribes in 1870 and again in 1890 among groups (mostly Sioux) to the east. In both surges of millennial expectation, charismatic leaders (Tavibo in 1870 and Wovoka in 1890) cried out for their followers to recapture their own history and traditions following ecstatic experiences of an apocalyptic nature. Both movements came at times of marked stress within native American Indian culture, stemming from increased conflict with government and military personnel and culminating in the disastrous massacre at Wounded Knee, South Dakota, in 1890.

The Ghost Dance centered around formalized rituals of song and dance, which were seen as signals that the dead would return to usher in an age of glory in which the now powerless Indians would again receive power. Indeed, the ecstatic dances—and there were numerous tribal variants—not only accented the imminence of a new age's dawning, but were in a sense catalysts to spur its arrival. The second outbreak of the Ghost Dance predicated as well the cataclysmic destruction of white Americans and their culture. While the millennialism of the Ghost Dance differed from that nurtured within white Christianity by viewing the coming age of glory as a restoration of a past golden age rather than as a radically new age, it did infuse tribal life with such vitality that the federal government believed its control over the tribes was threatened. The response was even more repression, evidenced in Wounded Knee, which "not only obliterated the internal integrity of tribal cultures for generations, but also destroyed the apocalyptic hopes kindled anew by the Ghost Dance" (Lippy).

Millennialist dreams of yet another sort permeate the so-called new religions, many of which have their roots in non-Western traditions. The Unification Church of Sun Myung Moon, for example, grafts Christian apocalyptic ideas onto Korean roots and claims that the present age provides humanity with the final opportunity for repentance before the millennium arrives. Only in turning from the crass materialism of the consumer society and embracing the teaching of Moon can humanity hope to share in the glory to come. Devotees of Krishna eschew the present because it is the last stage of the Kali Yuga, a time likewise characterized by materialism. In humble worship of the Lord Krishna, they await the dawning of a new day when peace and happiness will reign supreme.

Adventism also marked the many groups identified with the "Jesus Movement" of the early 1970s. Charismatic leaders such as David Berg of the Children of God and "Daddy" Jack Sparks of the Christian World Liberation Front, to name only two, proclaimed a simple gospel of salvation and apocalypse, painting the world as an arena fraught with danger on all sides, with escape from impending destruction to be found only in tight control of behavior within the confines of group membership.

The subtle ways millennialism and adventism have been part of the national religious consciousness as well as the presence of organized religious groups and churches such as the Seventh-Day Adventists and Jehovah's Witnesses are only part of the story of the millennialist imprint on American religion. There are many other avenues by which millennialist and adventist ideas and symbols have been kept alive, perhaps unwittingly, in popular religion and popular culture.

Cyrus I. Scofield, an adherent of John Nelson Darby's dispensationalism, prepared the *Reference Bible* (using the King James Version), correlating the biblical text with premillennialist dating of prophetic fulfillment. While Scofield's edition was widely used in explicitly adventist circles after its appearance in 1909, it also gained considerable popular usage. Many rank-and-file

Protestants who would not have identified themselves as ardent millennialists or adventists nevertheless became exposed to dispensationalist ideas and have taken that interpretation of Scripture as normative. In contemporary circles in which there is a decided preference for the King James Version, the Scofield reference edition is frequently used for corporate and private Bible study.

In addition, a network of educational institutions, many not directly affiliated with an adventist group, has provided training for generations of pastors, teachers, and other church workers. Of those associated with recognized denominations, the Seventh-Day Adventists' Loma Linda University in California may be the most widely known. Among the independent schools that perpetuate a millennialist ideology are such institutions as Bob Jones University ("The World's Most Unusual University") in Greenville, South Carolina; Chicago's Moody Bible Institute; the Dallas Theological Seminary in Texas; and the Practical Bible Training School, with its own post office in Bible School Park, New York. Many, but not all, of these schools have eschewed seeking routine academic accreditation on the grounds that their work is to be judged only by God and not by human standards. Most owe their genesis to the fascination with biblical prophecy and dispensationalism that marked late-nineteenth- and early-twentieth-century millennialism as well as to the enduring presence of Fundamentalism as a force within American Protestantism.

A number of journals, magazines, and other periodical literature, again often published independently of any adventist denomination, have served to keep belief in the imminent return of Christ before the devout. The more intellectually oriented have the *Adventist Heritage* to peruse, while the *Moody Monthly* presents millennialist fare for a mass readership hovering near one-quarter of a million. To these may be added materials prepared for use in Sunday schools and other religious educational activities by publishers such as the Scripture Press. In addition, there are scores of pamphlets, Bible study guides, and booklets hawked by television evangelists, all of which are predicated on the assumption that the Lord is soon to return.

Popular hymnody, standard fare in many

mainline Protestant churches as well as among the explicitly adventist and millennialist groups, continues to reinforce millennialist precepts. Many of the hymns stem from the adventist fervor of the nineteenth century, but are now regarded as "old favorites." Note the way millennialist and/or apocalyptic imagery marks the following:

Jesus may come today.
　Glad day, Glad day!
And I would see my Friend;
　Dangers and troubles would end
If Jesus should come today.
　Glad day, Glad day!
Is it the crowning day?
　I'll live for today, nor anxious be;
Jesus, my Lord, I soon shall see.
　Glad day, Glad day!
Is it the crowning day?

Stand up, stand up for Jesus,
　Ye soldiers of the cross.
Lift high his royal banner;
　It must not suffer loss.
From victory unto victory
　His army shall he lead.
Till every foe is vanquished,
　And Christ is Lord indeed.

And, Lord, haste the day when the faith shall be sight,
The clouds be rolled back as a scroll,
The trump shall resound and the Lord shall descend,
"Even so"—it is well with my soul.

One day He's coming, for Him I am longing;
One day the skies with his glory will shine;
Wonderful day, my beloved ones bringing;
Hope of the hopeless, this Jesus is mine.
Living, He loved me; dying, He saved me;
Buried, He carried my sins far away;
Rising, He justified, freely forever;
One day He's coming—O glorious day!

In recent years, popular millennialism has been buttressed by the appearance of several books by Hal Lindsey, all pitched to a mass audience, marketed through television commercials, and sold in book racks everywhere from supermarkets to airports. *The Late Great Planet Earth* (1970) has sold more than 9 million copies, while both *Satan Is Alive and Well on Planet Earth* (1972) and *The Terminal Generation* (1976) have had several printings. Finding fulfillment of biblical prophecy in everything from the establishment of Israel as a nation state to the rise of the Unification Church of Sun Myung Moon, Lindsey trumpets the nearness of Armageddon, the millennial reign of Christ, the triumph of Christ over evil, and the eternal bliss of believers in heaven. As did millennialists and adventists in previous generations, Lindsey's swift reading of contemporary history through prophetic lenses lends an excitement to his proclamations, while his charismatic earnestness grants his interpretations plausibility. Lindsey's audience has not formed itself into a denomination or other identifiable religious group, but what is important is the way in which his readers have absorbed the millennialist-adventist scheme and bring it to their involvement in already established churches.

Lindsey's approach is one shared by the popular evangelists of the "electronic church"—Fundamentalists such as Pat Robertson, Jim Bakker, and Jerry Falwell—whose presence has marked the rise of the so-called new religious right. While their message is not exclusively millennialist, it is permeated with images of the stark contrast between good and evil, the need to shun evil to prepare for the Lord's return, and the lively expectation that the millennial age with both its judgment and its glory will soon begin. While scholars have challenged these televangelists' reports regarding the size of their audience and the numbers of their followers, none can deny that they have helped perpetuate a millennialist subconscious among the American laity.

Of course, popular evangelists for decades have used the adventist lexicon to dramatize the urgency of religious commitment. While now more comfortably in the conservative center, Billy Graham lent credulity to this form of popular millennialism in his early evangelistic crusades. As historian William G. McLoughlin reported in his study of revivalism, *Modern Revivalism: Charles Grandison Finney to Billy Graham* (1959), in 1950 Billy Graham boldly proclaimed, "I sincerely believe that the Lord draweth nigh." Graham told his crusade audience, "We may have another year, maybe two years to work for Jesus Christ, and [then], ladies and gentlemen, I believe it is all going to be over. . . . Two years, and it's all going to be over." But as with many of his predecessors, and Hal Lindsey currently, when the millennium did not begin on schedule, Graham did not, in his early years at least, abandon his conviction that the end was at hand. Two years after he made the previous remarks, he somberly pronounced impending judgment: "Unless this nation turns to Christ within the next few months, I despair of its future."

Popular millennialism has likewise captivated the masses in a more secular form. The threat of nuclear holocaust resulting from conflict among world powers continues to generate images of a cataclysmic end for millions. Then, too, the enthusiasm of the American public for films such as *Star Wars, The Empire Strikes Back, The Return of the Jedi,* and others of that genre betokens a continuing fascination with the ultimate confrontation between the forces of good and evil, a pregnant hope that the good will triumph, and a simple expectation that an Edenic age will someday return to the earth. The *Star Trek* films, which proclaim that a new world of peace and joy has already been established though the forces of evil await final defeat, are also obvious examples of the secularization of a latent millennialism.

In popular literature, a secularized millennialism has also gained currency, though frequently without offering the hope of salvation from destruction, which most religious versions share. Charles Reich's best-selling *The Greening of America,* along with novels such as *1984, On the Beach,* and *Fail Safe,* for example, envision a new day coming, but one of gloom more than of glory. Television presentations such as *The Day After* and *The Fate of the Earth* also suggest that the "Age of Aquarius" will end in less than utopia. While such films, television shows, and literary works do not use explicitly religious images of apocalypse and millennium, they do draw from the same ideological pool that sustains the writing of a Hal Lindsey as well as the proselytizing of the Jehovah's Witnesses. They reveal the depth of the millennialist consciousness among all Americans, not just those who are part of an adventist religious body.

But what gives millennialism and adventism, whether as a continuing substratum of American self-identity, as institutionalized in a denomination or movement, or a dimension of popular culture, their plausibility? At one time it was fashionable in scholarly circles to explain es-

pousal of millennialist and adventist ideas in terms of deprivation. Individuals were thought to be drawn to visions of an ideal future age whose irruption in human affairs was imminent because they were in some sense excluded from full participation in the religious and/or cultural life of the day and sought fulfillment in some "other" realm in which the benefits denied in the present would be bestowed in abundance. By regarding the coming age as the only genuine level of reality, the oppression experienced in this age (whether presumed or actual) could be denied any ultimate reality, its effects mitigated and understood, and its unpleasantness endured. History was but an interim whose end was drawing nigh, to be replaced by a more equitable if not ideal plane of existence. The dynamism of millennialist religion came in its offering a due inheritance to whose who were, in H. Richard Niebuhr's term, the "disinherited."

In recent years, however, the viability of this interpretation has been challenged on many grounds. It has become increasingly clear that appraisal of deprivation comes only from the vantage point of the "undeprived." That is, those who are part of adventist groups would not themselves argue that their belief emerges from their having a presumably lower status in the social order than that of the mainstream. Deprivation is instead imputed to them by the majority. Then, too, the continuing presence of millennialist ideas, particularly in notions of the role of the American people, would suggest that millennialism is an ongoing dimension of American life rather than an aberration that bursts into public view from time to time to offer solace to the deprived. In addition, as mentioned earlier, recent comparative studies of millennialism broadly construed have revealed that some form of adventism, some expectation of a future ideal age, is far from limited to Western religions or Western culture, but a widespread phenomenon that permeates human consciousness. It is not simply an overemphasis on one theological aspect of Christian doctrine that emerges under conditions of repression; it is part of the way human beings in many cultures at many times make sense of the world they inhabit. Finally, current investigations of the development of the Christian tradition itself have shown that millennialism was far more central to early Christian affirmation than had been generally understood and to a large extent owes its being shunted to the periphery to the early medieval identification of Christendom with the kingdom of God on earth. Considered together, these perspectives mean that associating millennialism with deprivation, however defined, will simply not do.

Norman Cohn has argued persuasively that millennial ideas flourish during times of social transition, periods when an old order is passing, but a new one has not yet emerged in any cohesive fashion. While Cohn's work concerned medieval millenarian movements, it is instructive for understanding the pervasiveness of millennial constructs in the American context. The transit of the Puritans from Old World to New brought tremendous dislocation and hence a tendency to interpret their experience in millennial terms. The era of the Great Awakening and the impetus it gave to replacing a British colonial identity with an American one, as well as to reviving interest in things religious, was likewise a time of transition. Hence millennial symbols assumed peculiar power both in the thinking of a Jonathan Edwards and in that of those who helped develop the civil millennialism of the revolutionary generation. National growth plus the intricacies of implementing the ideals of American democracy in the age of Jefferson and Jackson helped grant credence to such diverse millennial expectations as those associated with revivals and camp meetings, communitarian experiments such as those of the Shakers and the Oneida Perfectionists, the ideology of Manifest Destiny, and the teaching of William Miller. The turmoil of war always brings a certain amount of social unsettledness, hence the appropriateness of interpreting the Civil War in apocalpytic terms.

The late nineteenth century was also a time of transition and dislocation for many as the nation came to grips with the closing of the western frontier, rapid industrialization and urbanization, massive immigration and in-migration, the emergence of the United States as a world power, and the intellectual challenges of Darwinism, positivism, and biblical criticism. This milieu likewise saw the birth of such diverse strains of millennialism as the facile, optimistic progressivism of Social Christianity, the unique adventism of Charles Taze Russell and the Jeho-

vah's Witnesses, the dispensationalism that nurtured early Fundamentalism, and the Sioux Ghost Dance. And the uncertainties of the atomic age in the twentieth century have spawned renewed interest in millennialism, as evidenced in the continuing growth of the Witnesses, the allure of groups such as the Moonies and Krishna Consciousness, and the prevalence of millennial and apocalpytic themes in popular literature, television, and films. While transition may be a constant in American life, those who feel its effects most acutely may be more explicitly drawn to millennialism as a way of making sense out of the present and finding hope for the future, whether in this world or a world to come.

Much of American millennialism, of course, lies beneath the surface in an inchoate substratum of ideological constructs on which people draw individually or collectively to lend meaning to their experience. What brings this constellation of ideas and symbols together into identifiable religious or social movements? Here discussions of the charismatic figure advanced by such thinkers as Max Weber and Edward Shils is to the point, for in the American setting at least the coalescence of millennial images in a coherent ideology for a group or movement may be correlated with the teaching, preaching, or oratory of charismatic individuals. William Miller, Ellen G. White, Charles Taze Russell, Wovoka, Sun Myung Moon, Jerry Falwell—all exemplify the characteristics associated with possession of charismatic power.

Weber argued that the "charismatic prophet" had an authority derived from personal gifts (traditionally such abilities as divination and healing, but also including ecstatic experience and direct revelation). At least initially operating outside established institutions, charismatic figures gain a following because they are able to capture the inarticulated discontent and frustration of persons ill at ease with empirical reality (those perhaps most cast about by the forces of social transition and change) and place them into an interpretive framework in which a sublime future beyond chronological history or somehow removed from history becomes a convincing alternative to the unsettledness of the present age. In turn, adherents' belief in charismatic figures' proclamations and acceptance of their leadership reinforce the sense of authority that accom-

843

panies possession of unique personal gifts. Without a charismatic leader to bring together both a negative appraisal of the present order and the hope for a positive future, millennial notions lose potency, though they do not disappear. Under the guidance of a charismatic leader, they become forces that propel the development of recognizable groups and movements such as the Ghost Dance, the Seventh-Day Adventists, the Jehovah's Witnesses, and the new religious right.

Since John Winthrop and the band of Puritans began to build their "city on a hill," Americans have nurtured millennial hopes. The awaited return of Christ or the dawn of an ideal age has sometimes fostered despair at the trials to be endured until the glory beyond becomes real. The conviction that a new day will come has led many to search for signs to determine when Christ would come or when the forces of oppression would be defeated. Some have concluded that the United States itself was chosen by God to be the site of Christ's millennial reign. Others, such as the Shakers and Oneida Perfectionists, believed that they were already living in the millennial age, even if it had not come in all its fullness. Some individuals, such as William Miller, developed a sense of urgency to complete work on earth, convinced that they had unraveled the timetable announcing the Second Advent. Contemporary groups such as the Seventh-Day Adventists and the Jehovah's Witnesses owe their genesis and sustenance to millennial fervor. The same fervor has at times revitalized a sense of peoplehood and integrity among the oppressed, as the Ghost Dance did among many native American Indian tribes, or created a new identity, as among the devotees of Krishna and the Moonies. While millennial flames may burn most brightly during times of rapid social transition, they have also been quietly fanned by an ongoing conviction that the American nation and the American people have a special destiny in human affairs. Among the masses a more amorphous millennialism endures in the hymns of popular religion, the preaching of television evangelists, and the work of authors such as Hal Lindsey. But millennial expectation has its secular buttresses as well in popular literature and film. To appreciate the dynamism of American religion, one must listen for the echoes of a millennialism that trumpets the advent of a new age and yearns for its arrival.

BIBLIOGRAPHY

James A. Beckford, *The Trumpet of Prophecy: A Sociological Study of Jehovah's Witnesses* (1975); Charles S. Braden, *These Also Believe: A Study of Modern American Cults and Minority Religious Movements* (1949); Ira V. Brown, "Watchers for the Second Coming: The Millenarian Tradition in America," in *The Mississippi Valley Historical Review,* 39 (1952); Kenelm Burridge, *New Heaven, New Earth: A Study of Millenarian Activities* (1969); Elmer T. Clark, *The Small Sects in America* (1949; rev. 1965); Norman Cohn, *The Pursuit of the Millennium* (1957; rev. 1970); Marley Cole, *Jehovah's Witnesses: The New World Society* (1955).

James W. Davidson, *The Logic of Millennial Thought: Eighteenth-Century New England* (1977); Leon Festinger et al., *When Prophecy Fails* (1956; rev. 1969); Edwin S. Gaustad, ed., *The Rise of Adventism: Religion and Society in Mid-Nineteenth-Century America* (1974); C. C. Goen, "Jonathan Edwards: A New Departure in Eschatology," in *Church History,* 28 (1959); Nathan O. Hatch, *The Sacred Cause of Liberty: Republican Thought and the Millennium in revolutionary New England* (1977); A. Leland Jamison, "Religions on the Christian Perimeter," in *The Shaping of American Religion,* James Ward Smith and A. Leland Jamison, eds. (1961); Charles H. Lippy, "Waiting for the End: The Social Context of American Apocalyptic Religion," in *The Apocalyptic Vision in America: Interdisciplinary Essays on Myth and Culture,* Lois P. Zamora, ed. (1982).

James H. Moorhead, *American Apocalypse: Yankee Protestants and the Civil War, 1860–1869* (1978); Francis D. Nichol, *The Midnight Cry: A Defense of the Character and Conduct of William Miller and the Millerites* (1944); H. Richard Niebuhr, *The Kingdom of God in America* (1937); Ernest R. Sandeen, *The Roots of Fundamentalism: British and American Millenarianism, 1800–1930* (1970); Hillel Schwartz, "The End of the Beginning: Millenarian Studies, 1961–1975," in *Religious Studies Review,* 2 (July 1976); David E. Smith, "Millenarian Scholarship in America," in *American Quarterly,* 17 (1965); Cushing Strout, *The New Heavens and New Earth: Political Religion in America* (1974); Leonard I. Sweet, "Millennialism in America: Recent Studies," in *Theological Studies,* 40 (1979).

Sylvia L. Thrupp, ed., *Millennial Dreams in Action: Essays in Comparative Study, Comparative Studies in Society and History,* supp. 2 (1962); Ernest L. Tuveson, *Redeemer Nation: The Idea of America's Millennial Role* (1968); Timothy P. Weber, *Living in the Shadow of the Second Coming: American Premillennialism, 1875–1982* (enl. ed., 1983); Bryan Wilson, "Millennialism in Comparative Perpective," in *Comparative Studies in Society and History,* 6 (1963–1964); Joseph F. Zygunt, "Prophetic Failure and Chiliastic Identity: The Case of the Jehovah's Witnesses," in *American Journal of Sociology,* 75 (1970).

[See also CHURCH AND STATE; HOLINESS AND PERFECTION; NEW ENGLAND PURITANISM; NINETEENTH-CENTURY EVANGELICALISM; *and* REVIVALISM.]

RESTORATIONISM AND THE STONE-CAMPBELL TRADITION

David Edwin Harrell, Jr.

THE leaders of the varied nineteenth-century restoration movements in American Christianity generally believed that they were a part of the quest for religious reform that began with the Reformation. They often called themselves reformers and set out to strip the church of the unscriptural additions of the centuries. They generally believed that the reformers of the past had gone as far as their insight would take them, and they honored them for their contributions, but they saw in the Protestant churches of their day countless perversions that had destroyed the unity of the Christian church. Successful reformation would have to be based on a return to the pattern of New Testament Christianity.

Some early American restorationists were aware of similar movements in the British Isles in the eighteenth and nineteenth centuries. Two movements that played direct roles in the formation of the largest restorationist group in America, the Disciples of Christ, were schisms in the Church of Scotland led by John Glas and Robert Sandeman and by James and Robert Haldane. The movement begun by Glas and carried forward by Sandeman elaborated many of the ideas adopted later by American reformers. Sandeman came to America in 1763 and established a congregation in Danbury, Connecticut, that later became a Disciples church. The Haldanes were important leaders of the small Scottish independent churches of the early nineteenth century and they had direct contact with several American restoration leaders. Their ideas were widely known in America as well as in Scotland.

The flourishing of restorationist thinking in America contributed to the establishment of a number of new sects and influenced the thought of others. The idea of restoring New Testament Christianity to its original purity seemed a perfect corollary to the secular understanding of the meaning of the new nation. As American democratic society represented a stripping away of the unjust and unreasonable restraints of feudalism and monarchy, so the return to simple New Testament Christianity was an attack on religious privilege and ecclesiastical tradition. As the post-revolutionary generation of Americans lionized reason as the divine path to the discovery of natural law, so restorationists believed that man's reason would reveal the primal truth in divine law. The secret in both cases was honest investigation and an open mind. As the political democratization of the nation challenged the remaining remnants of privilege and class distinction and claimed a symbolic victory with the election of Andrew Jackson in 1828, so the restoration movements of the early nineteenth century were religious challenges to the churches of the elite —bold assertions by the common people that they were able to construct and manage their own religious affairs. Finally, the idea of religious restoration fit well with the optimistic mood of early America. The political vision of a just and rational society meshed with and promoted an ebullient postmillennialism in nineteenth-century American religion. Most early restorationist leaders shared in that optimistic vision and saw their work as the key to inauguration of God's millennium in the nation He had prepared for that task.

Many contemporary American churches shared to some extent the restorationist ideology. Several frontier Baptist churches held ideas similar to those of the restoration leaders—frequently they were called Churches of Christ— and scores of them ultimately joined the Disciples of Christ with virtually no change in organization or belief. Several of the other native American churches of the period, such as the Cumberland Presbyterian Church and the Mormons, had strong restorationist motifs in their thought. John Winebrenner lead a restorationist movement within the German Reformed Church beginning in 1825, which resulted in the formation of the Church of God in North America. The Disciples of Christ and other restorationist groups were conscious of the restorationist emphasis in these churches, but they never viewed them as part of the amorphous network of churches and leaders that prior to 1830 tentatively discussed with one another their ideal of re-creating New Testament Christianity.

The American restoration movement began in four widely scattered centers around the turn of the nineteenth century. The earliest stream was a division in the young American Methodist Church in the 1790s. Francis Asbury's appointment as bishop was greeted with democratic indignation by many of the American Methodist preachers. Having worked without denominational control during the American Revolution, American ministers saw episcopal government as a serious threat to their freedom. At the church's first general conference in 1792, James O'Kelly introduced a resolution granting the right of appeal to any minister who objected to his assignment by the bishop. When his motion failed, he and a number of preachers from Virginia and North Carolina left the church. Asbury's attempts to placate the protesters were successful: most rejoined the church, but O'Kelly and about thirty other ministers formed the Republican Methodist Church in 1793.

In a conference the following year, the new denomination adopted the name Christian Church and announced that the Bible would be its only creed. The name for the new group had been suggested by Rice Haggard, a Methodist lay preacher and supporter of O'Kelly, who was to take his suggestion west to a second restoration movement a decade later. The new group was strongly congregational, providing that conferences would be strictly advisory. Although the church's early doctrinal argument with Methodism appeared to be entirely organizational, its independence, according to Charles Franklin Kilgore, soon left it "so divided and subdivided that it was hard to find two of one opinion." Nonetheless, the Christian movement had an estimated membership of over 6,000 in 1795 and

fifteen years later that number had grown to about 20,000.

A second restorationist stream began among New England Baptists; it was associated largely with the work of two young ministers, Elias Smith and Abner Jones. They protested against the staunch Calvinism of the New England Baptist churches and, shortly after the turn of the century, founded independent Christian churches and continued to do so for over forty years. In 1808, Smith published the first American religious newspaper, the *Herald of Gospel Liberty*, a venture that continued uninterrupted until the Christian churches united with the Congregationalists in the twentieth century. According to Kilgore (1963), one supporter of the Christian movement in New England reported in 1827 that he had found

> nearly one hundred companies of free brethren that meet together to worship God in the name of Christ without any sectarian name connected with it, without any sectarian creeds, articles, or confessions, or discipline to illuminate the Scriptures. . . . It is our design to remain free from all human laws, confederations and unscriptural combinations; and to stand fast in the liberty wherewith Christ has made us free.

By 1830 the independent congregations could be found as far west as Ohio.

More influential in the long run were two restorationist movements led by Barton Warren Stone and Alexander Campbell. Stone was a fifth-generation American. Born in southern Maryland, he migrated with his family to the Virginia–North Carolina border while still a youngster and in 1790 enrolled in an academy operated by David Caldwell, a Presbyterian minister who had been trained in William Tennent's "log college" (later Princeton). There he came into contact with the fervent preaching of Presbyterian leaders of the Great Revival in the West, especially James McGready. He was converted and, after several years of teaching in academies as far south as Georgia, in 1796 was ordained by the Orange Presbytery of North Carolina. Later that year he settled near Paris, Kentucky, where he became the minister of two congregations, Cane Ridge and Concord.

Stone's religious pilgrimage had taken place entirely in the free religious environment of the postrevolutionary American frontier. The Presbyterian ministers who had influenced him most were fervent supporters of religious revival and readily confessed admiration for the zeal of their Baptist and Methodist competitors for the affections of the common people. During his stay in Georgia, Stone had taught in a Methodist academy and had shared the pulpit with Methodist ministers. By the time he moved to Kentucky, he had reservations about Presbyterian theology. At his ordination by the Transylvania Presbytery in 1798 he was asked: "Do you receive and adopt the Confession of Faith, as containing the system of doctrine taught in the Bible?" He replied: "I do, as far as I see it consistent with the word of God" (McAllister and Tucker, 1975, p. 68).

The immediate impetus for Stone's departure from the Presbyterian Church was the outbreak of the Great Revival in the West, which spread rapidly after 1800 through a series of spontaneous camp meetings. Perhaps the most famous was held at Cane Ridge, Kentucky, in August 1801, when thousands of westerners flocked to hear the preaching of Presbyterian, Methodist, and Baptist evangelists. The meetings were marked by enthusiastic and emotional outbursts, but Stone believed that the hundreds of conversions and the ecumenical cooperation of the ministers marked them as the work of God. Just a few months after the close of the Cane Ridge revival, however, one of the Presbyterian ministers who had participated, Richard McNemar, was called into question by his presbytery for teaching doctrines that contradicted the Bible and the Westminster confession of faith. In 1803 the Synod of Kentucky suspended five of the leading participants in the revival: Robert Marshall, John Dunlavy, Richard McNemar, John Thompson, and Barton Stone.

The rebellious ministers formed the Springfield Presbytery, still claiming to be Presbyterians, and in 1804 were supported by fifteen congregations, including Cane Ridge and Concord. Less than ten months after forming the presbytery, they dissolved it in one of the most famous documents in restoration history, "The Last Will and Testament of the Springfield Presbytery." An ironic and sometimes caustic attack on the movement's critics, the most succinct item in the "Will" stated:

> We *will*, that the people henceforth take the Bible as the only sure guide to heaven; and as many as are offended with other books, which

stand in competition with it, may cast them into the fire if they choose; for it is better to enter into life having one book, than having many to be cast into hell.

(Garrison and De Groot, 1948, pp. 109–110)

Rice Haggard, who had recently joined the movement, suggested that they call themselves Christians (as he had suggested ten years earlier to the Republican Methodists), and another Christian church was born.

The Christian movement was seriously threatened in 1805 when three missionaries representing the United Society of Believers in Christ's Second Appearing (Shakers) appeared in Kentucky; among their converts were Richard McNemar and John Dunlavy. A second setback came in 1811, when Robert Marshall and John Thompson returned to the Presbyterian Church. Of the original five architects of the Springfield Presbytery, only Stone remained. Nonetheless, the Christian movement grew steadily and probably numbered more than 10,000 members by 1830. In 1826 Stone began publishing a monthly magazine, the *Christian Messenger,* that gave some cohesion to the movement. Still a critic of creeds and ecclesiastical hierarchies, Stone increasingly became a proponent of Christian union—basing his appeals on his respect for biblical authority.

When the Kentucky Christians wrote "The Last Will and Testament of the Springfield Presbytery" in 1804, Thomas Campbell was still a minister in the strict Antiburgher, Seceder Presbyterian church in Ulster, having just moved his family to Rich Hill, where he both ministered to the church and conducted an academy. A student at the University of Glasgow from 1783 to 1786, Campbell was a man of irenic nature and independent thought; during his years of ministering in northern Ireland he developed a distaste for sectarian bickering and a personal acquaintance with such Scottish independents as James Haldane. In 1807 Campbell determined to become a part of the exodus of settlers who were leaving Ulster for America, going ahead to select a place to live before being joined by his family two years later.

Upon his arrival in America, Campbell presented his credentials to the synod that was meeting in Philadelphia, requested assignment to the Chartiers Presbytery, which included Washington, Pennsylvania, where many of his acquaintances had settled. He was immediately accepted by the Seceder church there as its pastor. Campbell was distressed by the sectarian division he found in the area, particularly by the treatment accorded to the scattered settlers whose denominations had established no presence in the area. When Campbell conducted a communion service allowing all Presbyterians in a community to participate just five months after he arrived in America, he was charged by the presbytery with heresy. After months of charges and appeals Campbell was formally suspended by the Associate Synod of North America in May 1809.

Immediately after his troubles with the synod, Campbell and a few of his friends in Washington began meeting as a "Christian Association." In an address before the first meeting Campbell summed up the basis of their association: "That rule, my highly respected hearers, is this, that where the Scriptures speak, we speak; and where the Scriptures are silent, we are silent" (McAlister and Tucker, 1975, p. 110). In the fall of 1809 the association published a fifty-six-page booklet, written by Campbell, entitled *Declaration and Address of the Christian Association of Washington.* The booklet decried creeds and ecclesiastical authority and appealed to the New Testament as the sole religious guide. It was also a fervent appeal for Christian union. Perhaps the most famous single sentence in the booklet affirmed

> that the church of Christ upon earth is essentially, intentionally, and constitutionally one; consisting of all those in every place that profess their faith in Christ and give obedience to him in all things according to the scriptures, and that manifest the same by their tempers and conduct, and none else, as none else can be truly and properly called christians.

While he was still in the midst of editing the *Declaration and Address,* Thomas Campbell's family arrived in America. Campbell learned that his twenty-one-year-old son, Alexander, had studied for a semester in Glasgow while waiting to depart for America and had fallen under the influence of Greville Ewing, a disciple of the Haldanes. Alexander excitedly read the booklet written by his father and pronounced himself heartily in sympathy with its content. While Thomas Campbell remained the leader of the small group of dissidents for several years, when an independent congregation, the Brush Run Church, was formally organized in 1812, Alexander was named its minister and he quickly became the spokesman and moving force behind a widening movement.

The next two decades were years of study and transition for the Campbells; Alexander Campbell first, and later his father, became convinced that New Testament baptism was immersion and in 1812 they asked a Baptist minister to baptize them. This decision opened to them a new circle of acquaintances among the Baptists of the region. The Brush Run Church was invited to join the Redstone Baptist Association and did so in 1815, although some of its members had serious reservations about the union and the church submitted a long statement of its beliefs when it applied for membership. The union was never regarded as perfect by either side and the Campbells continued to view themselves as reformers.

Alexander Campbell's influence grew slowly; by 1820 he had earned a reputation as one of the most skilled religious debaters in the West. In 1820 he debated the Presbyterian minister John Walker in Mt. Pleasant, Ohio, on the question of the proper subjects and means of baptism. During the next twenty-three years, Campbell conducted four additional debates (including a discussion with renowned freethinker Robert Owen and the Roman Catholic archbishop of Cincinnati, John Purcell), ending with a two-week discussion with another Presbyterian minister, Nathan L. Rice, in Lexington, Kentucky, in 1843, that was moderated by Henry Clay. All of the debates were published, and they not only broadened Campbell's influence but they also led many to regard him as the foremost defender of Christianity against atheism and Protestantism against Catholicism.

More important in spreading Campbell's influence was his decision to begin publishing a monthly magazine in 1823, the *Christian Baptist.* The journal was barbed and iconoclastic; its attacks on ecclesiastical institutions caused Campbell to be identified with the growing Baptist antimission movement, a strongly Calvinistic protest that led to the establishment of scores of Primitive Baptist Associations in the Midwest and South. It greatly expanded Campbell's influence among Baptist churches in the West and the South, until his relationship with the Baptists was formally ended in 1830—as was the *Christian Bap-*

tist. By that time, the views of Campbell on such subjects as the abolition of the Old Testament law and the necessity of baptism for the remission of sins thoroughly estranged him from most Baptists. Baptist associations either expelled the "Campbellite" churches or, as in the case of the Mahoning Baptist Association in Ohio, where the reformers were in a majority, disbanded. By 1830 the rapidly growing movement probably included about 12,000 people.

Another Presbyterian minister who was generally regarded as a founding father of the Disciples of Christ movement was Walter Scott, apparently a graduate of the University of Edinburgh who migrated to America in 1818. Already influenced by Scottish independent ideas, in 1821 he met Alexander Campbell and became his most visible lieutenant. As the two young men struggled to find a formula for the restoration of New Testament Christianity, Scott became the chief architect of the movement's "plan of salvation"—a five-finger summary of the Gospel that included believing, repenting, and being baptized to receive the forgiveness of sins and eternal life. Scott also became the movement's first highly successful evangelist, attracting hundreds of new converts in the late 1820s in the Western Reserve area of Ohio.

All of these restorationist groups had some knowledge of the others, though most remained primarily isolated in the areas where they began. While the Stone and Campbell movements were still in their early stages of development, however, the Christian groups of New England and North Carolina effected a loose union in 1820, though a general conference was not formed until the early 1830s. When the conference was formed in 1831 it also included a large number of Christian churches from the Stone movement, particularly in Ohio and Indiana. The church had distinctive northern and southern wings and divided in 1854 because of the passage of anti-slavery resolutions by the general conference. Two central commitments held the Christian churches together—a belief in the total independence of the local congregation and a respect for diversity of belief. In New England the churches continued the Baptist tradition of baptism by immersion while in the South and Midwest both sprinkling and immersion were practiced.

This loose fellowship of Christian churches, generally called the Christian Connection

Church in the nineteenth century, grew slowly; the church healed the sectional schism in 1890 but remained strong mostly in the areas where the original movements had begun. By about 1900 the church (renamed the General Convention of the Christian Church) listed 1,379 congregations with 110,117 members. It was strongest in its original centers of strength—Ohio and Indiana listed over 20,000 members, North Carolina nearly 16,000, and Virginia over 8,000. More than 900 of the church's congregations were rural, and in the early decades of the twentieth century it declined in membership.

More auspicious was the union of the Stone and Campbell movements in the early 1830s. The two movements had been flourishing in the Upper South and the Midwest in the 1820s and they increasingly found themselves to be friendly competitors. Campbell toured Kentucky in 1824 and met Stone and other leaders of the Christian movement; they recognized the general similarities between their pleas. Once the Campbell "reformers" began more and more to distance themselves from the Baptists, leaders in both groups began exploring the possibilities of union. Both groups advocated restoring primitive Christianity on the basis of New Testament authority and a hope for Christian union. They also found that many of their specific practices were similar. Both were congregational in organization, rejected creeds and non-biblical titles and names, and insisted on liberty of opinion in all matters not scripturally bound. The Stone movement had long used the name Christian as a designation; once Campbell severed all connections with the Baptists, he favored the name Disciples of Christ. While the issue of designation was the cause of some friction, it was not a serious obstacle to union. Local churches in both movements were often called Church of Christ.

There were several fairly serious differences, however, that required patience and compromise. While immersion was widely practiced in the Christian movement, it was not universal or required as in the Disciples movement, nor had Stone and other Christian leaders arrived at the conclusion of Scott and Campbell that baptism preceded the remission of sins—though most seemed open to the idea. There probably continued to be some diversity within the movement on those questions for a generation, although the Disciples' view of baptism soon came to be the dominant (and distinctive) one within the church.

The Disciples also represented a more rationalistic approach to Christianity and conversion than did the Christians, many of whom, in common with Barton Stone, had begun their religious experiences amid the enthusiasm of the Great Revival in the West. In general, the united church again drifted toward the Disciples' rejection of revivalism and crisis conversion. Finally, from the beginning of the Brush Run Church, the Campbells had followed the Haldanian practice of the weekly observance of the Lord's Supper. By 1830 Stone had also reached the conclusion that such was the apostolic practice, but it had taken him many years to reach that conclusion, and he insisted that liberty should be allowed in each local church. Once again, in the long run, the weekly observance of the Lord's Supper not only became the common practice of the movement, it became one of its distinctive marks.

The union of the two groups was consummated during a four-day meeting in Lexington, Kentucky, beginning on Christmas Day 1831. The key figure in arranging the union talks was John T. Johnson. Johnson was a member of a distinguished Kentucky family (his brother Richard was elected vice president in 1836). He served as a member of the Kentucky legislature and the U.S. House of Representatives before accepting Campbell's view of restoration in 1831 and becoming the minister of a Disciples congregation. Also a close friend to Stone, he came to be regarded as a member of both groups and was the personal link that led to the union meeting. Although Campbell was not present, several widely known Disciples preachers were. Barton Stone was the chief spokesman for the Christians, John Smith for the Disciples. All agreed that they should unite their efforts. Two evangelists—John Smith (Disciple) and John Rogers (Christian)—were dispatched to ride together throughout the country informing the churches of their meeting. Smith and Rogers also wrote articles appealing to their respective brethren. Since there were no societies or denominational organizations to merge, the union of Christians and Disciples amounted primarily to encouraging a sense of fellowship among the scattered local churches. Both groups were jealous of the local autonomy of the local churches; the merg-

ing of specific churches in the same community proceeded slowly and imperfectly.

Although the union was gradual, in many areas it was virtually complete. Some of the Christian churches of the South and Midwest rejected the union, choosing rather to unite with the Christian Connection movement. The Disciples probably outnumbered the Christians at the time of the union by several thousand and the personality of Alexander Campbell came to dominate the united movement long before the death of Barton Stone in 1844. Nonetheless, many of the most visible leaders began as a part of the Christian movement and the two groups showed little residual loyalty to their distinctive pasts after the passing of a few decades.

While there was never perfect uniformity of practice among the churches of the restoration movement, by mid-century most of the central beliefs had been worked out. Perhaps most important was the emphasis on New Testament precedent for everything practiced by local churches. Alexander Campbell explored that subject in a long series of articles in his magazine entitled "The Restoration of the Ancient Order of Things" and in 1835 summarized his thinking in a book entitled *The Christian System.* Organizationally, the churches were autonomous, presided over by elders and deacons. In worship, they differed little from their evangelical neighbors other than in the weekly observance of the Lord's Supper. Doctrinally, the movement's most distinctive teaching was its insistence that baptism preceded the remission of sins and admission into the church.

For many years the leaders of the restoration movement were influenced by the millennialistic ideas current in the 1830s and 1840s. A few supported the premillennialist speculations of William Miller, but much more common was an optimistic postmillennialism that envisioned the gradual appearance of peace on earth, triggered by the introduction of the restored Gospel. In 1830 Alexander Campbell renamed his monthly publication the *Millennial Harbinger* and for two decades he heralded the hope that all Christians would use their God-given reason to unite on the clear revelation of the New Testament, as he and other Americans believed man could learn to live in harmony with God's natural law. The early optimism began to fade in the 1850s, when it became more and more obvious that denominational religious structures would not vanish with ease—that Christian union was not a realistic goal—and as the slavery issue led the nation inexorably toward a national holocaust rather than a millennium. Second-generation Disciples of Christ leaders inherited a badly battered hope for Christian union.

Another important motif in early Disciples history was a commitment to liberty of opinion. The leaders of the restoration movement allowed and demanded freedom of conscience in all questions that were not "essential." The definition of "essentials" has never been clear-cut in the movement's history and has been a constant source of friction and schism, but it has also provided a canopy for a wide variety of beliefs on theological questions and matters of personal conduct. To some extent, the movement also accommodated considerable variation in the practice of local churches.

A generation of farmer-preachers spread the restoration message west from its centers in Ohio, Virginia, and Kentucky in the decades from 1830 to 1860, and on the eve of the Civil War the Disciples of Christ reported around 200,000 members. Like most of the frontier evangelical churches, the Disciples did not have much success in the East, but rather moved with the frontier population, becoming strong in the tier of midwestern states that included Ohio, Illinois, Indiana, and Iowa. The church was strongest in the Upper South states of Kentucky and Missouri, but it was also established early in Tennessee and spread from there as settlers moved into Arkansas and Texas.

Disciples of Christ churches competed with the Baptists and Methodists for the religious allegiance of the common people during the first half of the nineteenth century. They inherited from Alexander Campbell a reputation as debaters and engaged readily in the doctrinal argument so common on the religious frontier. While many Disciples preachers were farmers, others combined an educational career with preaching and they frequently established academies and short-lived colleges.

The most important school founded by first-generation Disciples leaders was Bethany College, which was established by Alexander Campbell near his farm in western Virginia in 1840. The Disciples also created the movement's first quasi-official organization in 1849, the American

Christian Missionary Society. Both Campbell and Stone had been critical of missionary societies in their early years, but their objections had been largely practical rather than doctrinal. When the society was formed in 1849, it met some opposition but for the most part went unchallenged. However, the society remained weak in its early years and was ignored by the vast majority of the churches.

While the Disciples movement grew rapidly during these years, there was also a constant attrition of the discontented—frequently preachers whose novel ideas were squelched by Alexander Campbell. Among the early defectors were McNemar and Dunlavy, who joined the Shakers, and Sidney Rigdon, who in the 1830s worked with Walter Scott in Ohio before defecting to become Joseph Smith's most important early convert to Mormonism.

The most visible dissenter in the 1840s was John Thomas, who had come to America from England in 1832 and began publishing a paper, the *Apostolic Advocate,* in Philadelphia. A man of considerable ability, he soon became minister of the Sycamore Church in Richmond, Virginia, the first Disciples congregation in that city, and built a large following in the area. While generally sympathetic with the views of Campbell, Thomas pressed a number of novel and divisive teachings. Perhaps most troublesome was his insistence on the reimmersion of all who did not have a proper understanding of New Testament teaching at the time of their baptism. He attacked the older denominations much more vehemently than many Disciples believed necessary. Campbell and Thomas maintained an uncomfortable truce for about a decade—including a meeting in 1838 designed to halt the growing disharmony. But all efforts failed and in 1844 Thomas led a few congregations out of the Disciples movement.

Even before his open break with the Disciples, Thomas had formulated most of the distinctive doctrines that marked his group, the Christadelphians. His Christology resembled that of the early Unitarians and he taught a version of soul sleeping, which questioned the natural immortality of man. Thomas also formulated an elaborate premillennial theory. Christadelphians refused to vote, serve in the military, or hold political office; they adopted the name Christadelphian (friend of Christ) only because some

851

designation was required in order to apply for exemption from military service during the Civil War. While all of these views would have been unusual in early Disciples churches, it is probable that all of them were openly discussed by the restorers. Thomas, however, tested the Disciples commitment to liberty of conscience, elevating his teachings to matters of faith. In addition, he challenged the leadership of Alexander Campbell. Division was the inevitable result.

The growth of the Christadelphians was slow in the United States; the church had its greatest success in England. By 1900 the church listed only 70 congregations with 1,412 members in America. They were scattered throughout the country but the nucleus remained in Virginia, whose churches claimed 650 members. The group suffered a major schism in the 1890s because of a controversy over "resurrectional responsibility" that left groups known as the Amended Christadelphians and Unamended Christadelphians. The question of whether both the faithful and the unfaithful will be raised to be judged by Christ has remained of sufficient import in the movement to keep it divided into two relatively equal segments.

Otherwise, the nineteenth-century restoration movement escaped serious division. The slavery question created tensions, but church leaders were overwhelmingly border state moderates and they resisted extremist positions in the 1850s. Campbell decried slavery but dismissed abolitionism as irrational and unscriptural. By the middle of the 1850s the church included a group of disgruntled abolitionist leaders in Indiana and Illinois, and in 1859 they formed a competing missionary society, but their efforts constituted little threat to the unity of the movement. Congregational autonomy did much to defuse sectional tensions; local churches were free to follow independent courses. In the absence of authoritative national organizations, the Disciples survived the slavery controversy and the Civil War without formal division. However, in the postwar years sectional bitterness rose to the surface and contributed to division. That sectional resentment began during the debate over slavery; it deepened during the war when many church members served in the armies of the North and South. Particularly galling to postwar southern church leaders was the fact that in 1863 and 1864 the American Christian Missionary Society, meeting without representatives from southern churches, passed resolutions supporting the Union cause.

In the years after the Civil War, the Disciples of Christ movement entered a second phase of its history—an era marked by the emergence of a new generation of leaders, continued growth, increasing sociological diversity, growing sectional tension, new doctrinal disputes, and schism. At the time of the publication of the U.S. Census Bureau's survey of religious bodies in 1906 the movement counted a total membership of about 1 million, but it also had completed a division that separated a little over 10 percent of the most conservative churches from the remainder of the movement.

In the absence of official organizations, the most powerful centers of influence among the Disciples were religious papers; their editors have been compared to bishops by the movement's historians. In the post–Civil War years a new generation of papers was established that would exercise dominating influences for the next hundred years. Their editors filled the leadership vacuum left by the passing of the first-generation restorers; Alexander Campbell, the last, died in 1866.

Actually, before Campbell's death other editors had come to exercise considerable influence in the loose-knit movement. For a time, the most important was probably Benjamin Franklin, who in 1856 began editing the *American Christian Review* in Indianapolis. In the late 1880s the influence of the *Review* was eclipsed by that of three other journals that came to be symbols of the theological and sociological partitioning of the movement. In the South, the most influential paper was the *Gospel Advocate,* founded in 1855 by Tolbert Fanning, one of the patriarchs of the church in Tennessee. Its publication was interrupted by the war, but in 1866 it was revived by Fanning and young Tennessee preacher David Lipscomb. Lipscomb edited the paper for over fifty years; he brought to it a stolid, conservative character that captured the mood of the Disciples churches in the South of the time. By the 1880s the most widely circulated paper in the movement was the *Christian Standard,* published in Cincinnati beginning in 1866 and edited by Isaac Errett. Errett came to be viewed as the voice of moderation within the church. By the end of the century the *Christian Standard* had probably been supplanted as the leading journal by the more liberal *Christian-Evangelist,* which for many years was edited by James H. Garrison in St. Louis.

The three periodicals illustrated the three paths that were to separate the movement into three distinct churches in the early twentieth century. By the end of the nineteenth century, a majority of the southern churches were separated into a small, extremely conservative sect. In the 1920s a larger group of congregations withdrew support from the major Disciples institutions and formed a second independent church. The third wing of the movement moved steadily toward becoming a mainstream American denomination.

The most conservative churches clung tenaciously to the restoration plea and increasingly objected to the "digression" of more liberal churches. The specific issues that became most divisive were conservative objections to the introduction of instrumental music in the worship, new attacks on the missionary society and other church organizations as unscriptural, and opposition to the growing power of "pastors" in local churches as opposed to congregational elders. The rejection of organs and support for the missionary society provided convenient methods of marking the dissenting congregations. In 1906, Lipscomb insisted that the conservative churches should be listed separately in the census, and they were identified as the Churches of Christ.

The Disciples churches that remained united after the conservative defection were by no means united in belief. While all still paid lip service to the old slogans of restoration, many of the leaders of the denomination—particularly a group of young men associated with the University of Chicago—embraced liberal theology at the end of the nineteenth century. In the twentieth century, the *Christian Century,* a Disciples journal that had begun as the *Christian Oracle* in Chicago in 1884, became the foremost organ of liberal Christianity in America. Charles Clayton Morrison was the first of a distinguished group of churchmen who edited the magazine. The rise of this outspoken and talented liberal leadership disturbed many of the conservative Disciples; they came to view the *Christian Standard* as their voice. The *Christian-Evangelist,* on the other hand, became the organ of the more liberal element of the church. After decades of debate over Higher Criticism, Darwinism, other intellectual issues that threatened all American evangelical churches in the 1920s, and such practical issues

as the reception of unbaptized members, in 1927 several hundred of the more conservative Disciples churches withdrew their support from the church's agencies and founded a competing convention, the North American Christian Convention. The boundary between the two groups remained obscure for years, many congregations passing easily back and forth between support of the two conventions. Not until the 1970s, after the liberal Disciples had restructured into a representative denomination, did the lines become rigid and the picture clear.

These divisions seemed to mark the failure of the optimistic dreams of early restoration leaders. It had become clear by 1865 that the Disciples formula for restoring New Testament Christianity was not going to result in an immediate end to religious strife and division, introducing a millennium of Christian union. In a sense, second-generation Disciples were forced to choose between restoration and Christian union. Conservatives clung to the hope for restoration, in spite of the fact that it proved divisive rather than ameliorative. More liberal thinkers, on the other hand, increasingly sought to extend the area of religious liberty, keeping alive the hope for Christian union. All Disciples tried to retain some allegiance to all of the original pleas of the first generation, but it was clear that they increasingly emphasized one plank or the other.

The division in the restoration movement had clear sociological parameters as well as theological explanations. The separation of the Churches of Christ had strong sectional underpinnings. The census of 1906 reported that about 100,000 of the group's 159,000 members lived in the former states of the Confederacy. The more liberal Disciples had about 138,000 members in the South, but that represented a small proportion of the church's total membership of nearly 1 million. Southern church leaders frequently rallied sectional prejudice against the North to accompany their theological attacks on northern liberals.

Even more marked, however, was the economic nature of the division. The U.S. Bureau of the Census survey in 1936 highlighted the urban-rural disparity of the two groups. In the northern-dominated Disciples of Christ nearly 750,000 of the group's 1,196,315 members were classified as urban. On the other hand, over 175,000 of the Churches of Christ's 309,551 members were affiliated with rural churches, making it one of the most rural religious bodies in the nation. Still more impressive were the census estimates of the value of church edifices in each state. For the Churches of Christ the total value of church edifices divided by the total number of congregations amounted to less than $3,000; the comparable figure for the Disciples of Christ was nearly $16,000. In Texas the average for the Disciples of Christ was $20,000 and for the Churches of Christ $3,500; in Tennessee, $14,000 to $3,000; and in Indiana, $13,000 to $2,300. David Lipscomb surmised that the "fundamental difference between the Disciples of Christ [i.e., Churches of Christ] and the society folks" was that the conservatives wanted people "to come to Christ," while the liberals wanted to build "a strong and respectable denomination" based on "moneyed societies, fine houses, fashionable music, and eloquent speeches" (Harrell, 1973, p. 344).

In the twentieth century, then, a variety of American churches traced their origins to the early-nineteenth-century efforts to restore New Testament Christianity. Some of these groups—most notably the Christadelphians—developed enough doctrinal eccentricities to make it difficult for them to make peace with mainstream Christianity. But for the most part, the restoration movement has accommodated easily to the religious and secular society surrounding it. The movement's basic ideas have not been so extreme as to alienate it from the mainstream, and as the church came to include diverse sociological classes, it spread quickly across the scale of religious types spanning from sect to denomination.

The twentieth-century history of the movement has thus become the story of very diverse religious bodies—all sharing a common heritage but radically dissimilar in belief and practice. The General Convention of the Christian Church remained a relatively small denomination with most of its churches located in the Midwest and the South; in the religious census of 1926 its membership was 112,795. The church developed a full body of boards, headquartered in Dayton, Ohio, and operated a number of colleges, including Defiance College in Ohio and Elon College in North Carolina. The group retained a strong emphasis on Christian union and in 1924 began a dialogue with the National Council of Congregational Churches. Five years later a plan of union was adopted by both

churches and in 1931 the General Council of Congregational and Christian Churches was formed. The plan of union reflected many of the old restorationist beliefs of the Christian Connection Church, including celebrating the Bible as the only rule for religious faith and life, an emphasis on congregational independence, and the insistence that liberty of opinion be preserved in most matters of belief. In 1955 the Congregational and Christian Churches united with the Evangelical and Reformed Churches to form the United Church of Christ. Generally regarded as among the more liberal American denominations, the United Church of Christ congregations retain much of the flavor of nineteenth-century New Testament restorationism.

The liberal orientation of some Congregationalists and concern over the union with the Evangelical and Reformed churches resulted in two minor schisms. The Conservative Congregational Conference was organized in 1948 in Chicago to uphold biblical conservatism and congregational independence; in the 1980s the conference claimed 138 churches and around 25,000 members. More substantial was the National Association of Congregational Christian Churches, formed in 1955. Headquartered in Lansing, Michigan, the group was made up of churches that refused to compromise their congregational independence by joining the United Church of Christ. In 1980 the group claimed 107,300 members, mostly in the Midwest.

The Christadelphians in the twentieth century remained a small and isolated sect. In 1936 the group claimed 109 churches with 2,755 members in the United States. As opposed to most of the other restorationist churches, the Christadelphian membership, in both England and America, was overwhelmingly urban and working-class at one time. Seemingly dormant in the early twentieth century when the church membership dwindled slightly, the church has shown a new vitality since World War II and in 1984 its estimated American membership was 6,000. Evangelization is carried on entirely at the initiative of each local congregation (*ecclesia*), but the group has always published and circulated generous amounts of promotional literature.

The history of the Churches of Christ in the twentieth century seems in many ways to mirror nineteenth-century Disciples history. The conservative wing of the Disciples movement listed only about 160,000 members in the religious census of 1906 but it became one of the fastest-growing religious bodies in the nation, claiming 317,937 in 1923 and 682,172 in 1947; and in the 1960s its membership was estimated at over 2 million. These statistics were little more than rough estimates since the independent local churches kept few records; more conservative surveys in the 1980s have judged the Churches of Christ to have about 1.5 million members. Under any circumstances, the growth of the Churches of Christ is remarkable, and it probably had become the largest of the wings of the restoration movement by 1985. The church remains particularly strong in the South; in some states, most notably Tennessee and Texas, it rivals the Baptists and Methodists in size and influence. But the church also spread by migration and evangelization and has become a minor presence in most sections of the country. Local Churches of Christ also sponsor active mission programs in a large number of foreign nations and count thousands of members in such places as the Philippines and Nigeria.

The growth of the Churches of Christ must be attributed largely to their evangelical fervor for their restorationist plea. It took place in the almost total absence of denominational organization. The message was spread by evangelists, many of whom were only partially supported by individual churches. The independent local churches did begin supporting a variety of small institutions in the twentieth century, including orphan homes and colleges. While the institutions had no formal identification with the churches, they became centers of influence and gave a certain cohesion to the movement. Colleges begun by members of the Churches of Christ include David Lipscomb College (Nashville, Tennessee); Harding College (Searcy, Arkansas); Abilene Christian University (Abilene, Texas); Pepperdine University (Los Angeles, California); and Freed-Hardeman Junior College (Henderson, Tennessee).

The chief unifying force in the church continues to be religious periodicals. Unquestionably the most important is the *Gospel Advocate*. After a series of relatively short-term successors to David Lipscomb, in 1938 Benton C. Goodpasture became editor of the magazine and continued in that post until his death in 1977, exercising a powerful influence over the course of the church's history. A Texas journal that rivals the power of the *Gospel Advocate* in some sections is the *Firm Foundation*, long under the editorial leadership of Reuel Lemmons.

While the fervent, sectarian dedication of the Churches of Christ to the principles of restoring New Testament Christianity gave impetus to the movement, it also held the seeds of ceaseless difficulties. The demand of the Churches of Christ for biblical precedent for all modern church practices (the basis upon which they had rejected instrumental music and the missionary society) essentially killed the hope for Christian union. The Churches of Christ came to be identified as legalistic and pugnacious. They conducted countless debates with Fundamentalist Baptists and Pentecostals in a war for the loyalty of the common people of the nation. But the spirit also led to endless internal debate and bickering, resulting in several splits and countless temporary estrangements between congregations and individuals.

In the years before World War II several small groups of churches severed relations with the majority of the Churches of Christ and have remained separate ever since. In the 1920s some congregations objected to the introduction of individual containers for serving the Lord's Supper. These "one cup" churches have maintained a distinct identity, mostly in Oklahoma and Texas. In the 1930s a Louisville preacher, R. H. Boll, took a strong premillennialist stand that was rejected by the majority of the church and led to the estrangement of perhaps 100 congregations. Other church leaders in the 1930s objected to Sunday schools as an unscriptural innovation, and perhaps as many as 35,000 modern members of Churches of Christ have founded papers and schools to support that distinctive restoration teaching. Countless other issues interfered with the fellowship of local congregations—including conflicting views on marriage and divorce, the covering of women's heads in worship, kneeling in prayer, and whether the Lord's Supper could be observed twice in one day. The twentieth-century Churches of Christ have driven the search for the ancient order to its troublesome and schismatic end.

More important than the minor splinterings of the pre–World War II years, however, was a larger and more sociologically provocative division that began in the 1950s and isolated between 10 and 15 percent of the churches by the 1980s. The doctrinal issues that once again separated the most conservative churches from the remainder of the movement had largely to do with the support of the institutions that had developed in the movement in the early twentieth century. Conservatives opposed church contributions to orphan homes, but found even more objectionable the support for such institutions as colleges and hospitals. In addition, they were offended by the growing social activities of many churches and the building of recreational facilities in some church buildings. While all of the older papers and institutions supported these practices, the most important "anti" paper of the 1950s was the *Gospel Guardian,* edited by Yater Tant. A small junior college, Florida Christian College, supported the conservative position, refusing to take contributions from churches. By the 1980s the anti-institutional Churches of Christ included perhaps 150,000 members scattered throughout the country and were growing rapidly. While the movement was strongest in such old strongholds as northern Alabama and Florida, it also had considerable success in California and in the Midwest.

While the doctrinal issues dividing the Churches of Christ were once again thoroughly explored in the light of restoration principles both in the journals and in scores of debates, it is also clear that the division has a sociological base much like that of the dividing of the Disciples of Christ in the nineteenth century. In the course of the twentieth century, and particularly in the post–World War II period, many of the Churches of Christ had grown into large middle-class congregations filled with members who were successful professionals. Although economic statistics have not been collected, it is clear that the conservative division of the 1950s was a rebellion of the less affluent in the church against the leadership of a new sophisticated elite. The restoration movement had once again shown itself particularly subject to spanning the sect-to-denomination spectrum; the Churches of Christ had come to include a diverse sampling of the nation's population.

The mainstream Churches of Christ remained a theological and sociological mixture after the shedding of the most conservative churches. Many remained militant restorationists who justified the church's institutions with biblical arguments. They remained strongly sectarian and refused any association with other denominations. On the other hand, by the 1980s the group's colleges and larger churches were filled with graduates of the nation's best universities and many of them were open to friendly discussions with the broader Christian community. The tensions between these elements in the Churches of Christ seem to point to another inevitable division in the future. At the local level, many of the more conservative churches balked at supporting the colleges and institutions that increasingly fell under the influence of the liberals. The old traditional papers such as the *Gospel Advocate* supported more conservative views, while the most outspoken voice of the new liberalism was the *Mission Journal,* whose first editor was Roy Bowen Ward. Accompanying the appearance of a more moderate leadership in the Churches of Christ has been an apparent slowing in its rate of growth.

The Christian churches associated with the North American Christian Convention also prospered in the twentieth century. Generally known as "independent" or "conservative" Christian churches, their fellowship has been only slightly more structured than that of the Churches of Christ and it has been difficult to pinpoint the exact size of the group until recent years. Dissatisfaction with the drift of the Disciples toward a more liberal theology and the church's association with the Federal and National Churches Council of Christ coalesced around the *Christian Standard* and the North American Christian Convention. While the convention was only an informal meeting for fellowship and worship, it has become a means of identifying dissatisfied congregations and led to the establishment of a cluster of competing mission organizations and Bible colleges. Virtually all of the historic institutions within the Disciples movement were controlled by the more liberal element, including Bethany College and Butler, Drake, and Texas Christian universities.

For many years, a large number of Disciples congregations vacillated about whether to identify with the liberal or conservative conventions and their institutions—some supported both. Not until 1955 did the conservative churches publish *A Directory of the Ministry of the Undenominated Fellowship of the Christian Churches and Churches of Christ,* an act that has been regarded as the official symbol of division. The fellowship was drastically changed in 1968 when the more liberal Disciples of Christ restructured into a representative denomination. An estimated 2,000 congregations refused to participate in the change and they flooded into the ranks of the conservative fellowship. By the 1980s, the conservatives claimed a membership of over 1 million in more than 5,000 churches and supported over 40 colleges and about 60 benevolent institutions. The independent Christian churches range from strongly sectarian congregations that have little association with other denominations to groups that associate easily with other evangelicals. James DeForest Murch, one of the church's most influential leaders, was one of the early promoters of the National Association of Evangelicals.

The division between the Undenominated Fellowship of Christian Churches and the more liberal Disciples church, now officially named the Christian Church (Disciples of Christ) again appeared to have sociological dimensions. In the 1970s the two groups listed nearly the same number of members, but the conservative fellowship included over 1,000 more congregations. The average size of a conservative church was considerably smaller than that of its liberal counterpart. The independent Christian Church cut most heavily into Disciples strength in the rural midwestern heartland of the restoration movement. In 1971, Illinois listed 489 conservative churches and 244 liberal congregations with memberships of 101,316 and 69,170; in Indiana the ratios were 621 to 293 churches and 157,753 to 98,975 members. The Disciples, on the other hand, fared better in those areas where churches had been planted more recently, frequently in urban areas, such as California and Texas.

Probably the most visible remnant of the nineteenth-century restoration movement, though no longer the largest, is the Disciples of Christ. After the formation of the American Christian Missionary Society in 1849, the Disciples of Christ movement went through decades of haphazard institutional expansion that in the early twentieth century ended with scores of agencies and boards making independent appeals to the churches. In 1917 an international convention was formed to coordinate this institutional work. The convention was voluntary and the churches remained totally independent. Much more controversial was the step taken in 1968 to restructure the church into a representative denomination with a powerful national organization elected by delegates at biannual conventions. The restructuring seemed imperative to many of the group's ecumenical-minded leaders, who

chafed about the inability of the church to act as a unit. While the loss of congregational autonomy was unacceptable to hundreds of congregations, and they refused to join the denomination, in 1971 the church listed 4,835 congregations with 1,158,855 members. The *Christian* (formerly the *Christian-Evangelist*) is the most widely circulated paper. The denomination supports a wide variety of mission and social agencies and the location of most of them in Indianapolis and St. Louis fittingly symbolizes the continued centers of the church's membership.

In the twentieth century Disciples leaders have been among the most outspoken liberal theologians in the nation and also among the staunchest advocates of ecumenism. The *Christian Century* was headed by a series of Disciples editors, including Herbert L. Willett and Harold Fey. While liberal Disciples continue to honor the nineteenth-century practice of adult baptism, they generally practice "open membership," accepting members into local churches on the basis of their membership in other denominations. Disciples churches also continue to practice the weekly observance of the Lord's Supper but would be strangers to the legalistic arguments made for the practice by more conservative restorationists.

More than any other descendants of the nineteenth-century restorers, however, the Disciples pursue the ideal of Christian union. They held dialogues with several churches looking toward union and were among the first participants in the Consultation on Church Union (COCU) in the 1960s. Disciple Paul A. Crow, Jr., was general secretary of COCU during its early years and became an important spokesman for the union.

Like most mainstream churches, the Disciples has suffered from declining membership in recent years, the losses being exacerbated by the exodus of congregations during restructure. But the problem was a pervasive one and by 1981 the number of congregations in the denomination had diminished to 4,296. In the 1970s the church spotlighted the need for renewed zeal for church building in the midst of its ecumenical quest. Although denominational leaders have tried to make more palatable to the mass of the church's members the stream of liberal social pronouncements passed by the general assembly, it is clear that they have frequently moved to the left more rapidly than the constituency.

Taken together the groups descended from

the nineteenth-century restoration movements in America include probably 4 million persons in the 1980s. The groups range from extremely legalistic and sectarian churches still intent on restoring the pattern of New Testament worship, organization, and practice to one of the most ecumenical denominations in the nation. There are common threads of doctrine still visible in all of the groups, which betray their common origin, but theologically and sociologically they are vastly different. The central themes of the restoration movement—restoration, unity, and liberty—no longer seemed plausible in the late nineteenth and twentieth centuries. The descendants of the original reformers were compelled to choose which of the planks they would emphasize. The choices they made were no doubt influenced by the fact that the descendants of the pioneer settlers who accepted the early restoration plea included both those who lingered to farm the homestead and those who became doctors, merchants, and college professors. In the restoration heritage each sought a usable past.

BIBLIOGRAPHY

Alexander Campbell, *The Christian System* (1835) and *Popular Lectures and Addresses* (1861); Paul A. Crow, Jr., *A Bibliography of the Consultation on Church Union* (1967); Winfred Ernest Garrison and Alfred T. De Groot, *The Disciples of Christ: A History* (1948); Colby D. Hall, *The "New Light" Christians: Initiators of the Nineteenth-Century Reformation* (1959); David Edwin Harrell, Jr., "The Sectional Origins of the Churches of Christ," in *Journal of Southern History*, 30 (1964), *Quest for a Christian America: The Disciples of Christ and American Society to 1866* (1966), and *The Social Sources of Division in the Disciples of Christ, 1856–1900* (1973); Nathan O. Hatch, "The Christian Movement and the Demand for a Theology of the People," in *Journal of American History*, 67 (1980); Richard T. Hughes, "From Primitive Church to Civil Religion: The Millennial Odyssey of Alexander Campbell," in *Journal of the American Academy of Religion*, 44 (1976).

Charles Franklin Kilgore, *The James O'Kelly Schism in the Methodist Episcopal Church* (1963); John Leslie Lobingier, *Pilgrims and Pioneers in the Congregational Christian Tradition* (1965); Lester G. McAllister and William E. Tucker, *Journey in Faith: A History of the Christian Church (Disciples of Christ)* (1975); Milo T. Morrill, *A History of the Christian Denomination in America, 1794–1911* (1912); James DeForest Murch, *Christians Only: A History of the Restoration Movement* (1962); Thomas H. Olbricht, "Christian Connection and Unitarian Relations," in *Restoration Quarterly*, 9 (1966); Robert Richardson, ed., *Memoirs of Alexander Campbell*, 2 vols. (1868–1870).

Claude Spencer, *Periodicals of the Disciples of Christ and Related Religious Groups* (1943), *An Author Catalog of Disciples of Christ and Related Religious Groups* (1946), and *Theses Concerning the Disciples of Christ and Related Religious Groups* (1964); Durward T. Stokes and William T. Scott, *A History of the Christian Church in the South* (1973); William E. Tucker, *J. H. Garrison and Disciples of Christ* (1964); Earl Irvin West, *The Search for the Ancient Order*, 3 vols. (1964–1980); William Garrett West, *Barton Warren Stone: Early American Advocate of Christian Liberty* (1954); Bryan R. Wilson, *Sects and Society: A Sociological Study of Elim Tabernacle, Christian Science, and Christadelphians* (1961). [See also NINETEENTH-CENTURY EVANGELICALISM; and REVIVALISM.]

COMMUNITARIANISM

Charles H. Lippy

THE image of utopia (derived from Greek, literally "no place"), the ideal society, has enchanted men and women in the Western religious traditions at least since the time when accounts of Eden circulated in ancient Israel. Within the Judeo-Christian heritage, the impulse to live in utopia now, to form the perfect social order in which one could live in spiritual purity, has long been associated with communitarianism; that is, the committed withdraw from the mainstream of society to establish a community of the faithful who, in relative isolation from worldly contamination, pursue the quest of the ideal life. As Benjamin Zablocki (*Joyful Community,* 1971, p. 19) has noted, an intentional community is nothing less than an attempt to create a "whole way of life" molded by a vision of the ideal. Such efforts in Western religious history are legion.

The Essenes, for example, withdrew to Qumran along the shores of the Dead Sea in the years just prior to the dawn of the Christian era to follow the path of righteousness, which they believed most of the Hebrews had long forgotten. In the early centuries of Christianity, individuals withdrew first to the deserts of Egypt and then to cloistered monasteries scattered throughout Christendom to devote themselves to the religious life, to revitalize the whole of Christianity by recalling the church to its spiritual aspects, to reform a religion that had become too caught up in the ways of a secular world. The Christian tradition is replete with attempts, some enduring but most short-lived, to gather the devout into communities totally committed to God's way. Always a minority effort, such groups at times have been regarded as heretical, for they held up to the tradition a vision of what the Christian life ought to be and contrasted it with what the Christian life had become in ordinary society.

The Albigenses (Cathari) of medieval France and the Waldenses, also of the twelfth century, were but two of a host of cadres willing to risk persecution and death to remain faithful to their version of true Christianity. The Reformation, likewise, spawned numerous communitarian groups, including the ancestors of the present-day Hutterites, who pushed for the restoration of primal Christianity in the midst of religious and social upheaval. The American religious landscape also has been dotted by hundreds of communities of a similar ilk over the years, generating an unusually large number of utopian experiments perhaps because of the multifaceted pluralism that has characterized American culture at least from the midcolonial period on.

American communitarian groups share several features with similar societies from other times and places. All such groups come into being because of a perception that religion has lost its authentic spiritual base; all are convinced that spiritual purity may be attained only by separating from the rest of a polluted society. In many cases this separation has meant physical withdrawal into enclaves removed as much as possible from contact with a corrupt world and a corrupted religion. All are predicated on the assumption that recovery of spiritual purity is possible, that the authentic truth of the religion has been realized in the peculiar constellation of beliefs and practices to which the group is committed. All share the hope that by living the pure life now, they will provide an example for the masses, who will in time bring about reform of the mainstream once the truth is witnessed. Occasionally, some have been as concerned with perpetuating a particular ethnic identity as a religious ideology, largely because the two are seen as indistinguishable.

In her provocative 1972 study *Commitment and*

859

Community, Rosabeth Moss Kanter suggested other features that mark utopian experiments. Underlying the quest for the ideal society, Kanter noted, is the conviction that human nature and human institutions are indeed perfectible. Hence a sense of optimism pervades communitarianism, optimism that the vision can indeed become empirical reality. Kanter also has called attention to the sense of order that pervades intentional communities. No aspect of life is too trivial to escape recasting, for all must be brought into the realm of the sacred and the pure. In addition, as Kanter and numerous others have noted, the communitarian passion for order corresponds to a perception that the external society is a place of chaos, of disorder, of good intentions gone astray. Only within the community can true order prevail.

As highlighted by Kanter, this penchant for order often results in strong fraternal bonds—one might speak of kinship bonds—that community members see both as a value of their association and as a reality experienced by the committed. Parallel with this bonding is a willingness to experiment with social forms. Kanter perceptively argues that because intentional communities regard themselves as deviating from social norms (and also are regarded as deviant by the larger society), they dare to be deviant in the creation of internal social institutions and patterns. The result of this openness to doing things differently, when taken together with the inherent optimism in the communitarian approach, is a sense of uniqueness that brings a high degree of coherence and solidarity to a community. Because the group believes that it alone possesses the blueprints for the perfect society, it justifies its concern for order and cements the sense of kinship in the conviction of its own rightness and righteousness.

Communities past and present, long-lived and short-lived, also have had to address a common set of problems. The longevity and/or success of an individual group depends on its ability to resolve these problems. For example, all groups must determine standards for admitting new members, such as ethnic identity, acceptance of an ideology, or radical inclusiveness. All must create structures to provide for leadership and decision making. In other words, any intentional community must deal with practical matters of organization if it hopes to endure. Every utopian endeavor must develop procedures for distributing work, for determining ownership of property, and for disciplining those who fail to live up to the community's standards. Each group must deal with those loyalties that compete with an individual's pledge to the community—loyalty to a biological family, to a spouse, to offspring, to others within the community itself. Any loyalty that intrudes on one's commitment to the ideals and practices of the community must be eliminated or strictly regulated, lest the very foundation of the community collapse.

Thus, all communities develop mechanisms that will strengthen the commitment of the individual to the group and concomitantly erode attachment to alternative ideologies or social structures. Kanter has written of the need for an intentional community to demand sacrifice, investment (physical, psychological, and/or economic), renunciation (of one's past as well as of other ways of living), and mortification (abandonment of any self-interest). At the same time an intentional community provides a high degree of communion and a sense of the transcendent nature of communal aims. These benefits, Kanter claims, will allow a community to maintain the devotion of members even in the face of opposition, competing world views, occasional personal dissatisfaction with communal life, or even defections from the group's ranks. Zablocki has likened entrance into an intentional community to brainwashing in the sense that individuals must receive all meaning and purpose in life, their entire identity as human beings, from the community itself. Again, the degree to which any group is able to develop mechanisms of commitment, to render individual identity wholly dependent on dedication to the community, will determine the community's ability to translate its vision from dream to reality.

While our concern here is primarily with those communitarian ventures that have an explicitly religious focus, other forces have prompted an interest in establishing intentional communities. In the mid-nineteenth century, for example, as the effects of the industrial revolution were beginning to be felt in Europe, particularly in areas such as Great Britain and France, several individuals proposed a reordering of society along communitarian lines to avoid the competition and division into class groupings that industrialization seemed to foster. A Welshman, Robert

Owen, for example, sought to establish socialistic experiments on both sides of the Atlantic that would be models of the ideal factory community. Altogether some two dozen Owenite communities were set up, but all were dissolved by 1830. Other economically oriented communities were organized by followers of Charles Fourier. Fourierist economic socialism attracted several leading Americans, including Albert Brisbane, newspaper editor Horace Greeley, and William Henry Channing, and for a time even the intellectually oriented transcendentalist commune at Brook Farm became a Fourierist phalanx. Even if one argues that these socialistic experiments had at least an implicit religious quality in their efforts to institutionalize a total world view, their obvious secular basis may have lessened their possibilities for success. As chroniclers of the American religious past such as Sydney E. Ahlstrom and Robert T. Handy have noted, the absence of the depth of commitment to an ideal that religion inspires may well have eroded the intensity of loyalty to an economic ideology.

Both religious and socialistic communitarian efforts require a particular conjunction of social conditions in order to provide plausible alternatives to dominant cultural patterns. On the one hand, a radical reshaping of society has greater appeal during times of social transition, when even established institutions no longer seem to be functioning. Certainly the transition that came to Europe with the beginnings of the industrial revolution threatened to undercut entrenched patterns. In the United States, the period from the Revolution to at least the Civil War was an era of great social fluidity. It was a time when a distinctly American self-consciousness was replacing an outmoded colonial identity, when friend and foe alike wondered whether the democratic ideology embedded in the Constitution could be translated from theory to practice, when the start of westward expansion brought, as Whitney R. Cross demonstrated, not only the contagious excitement of constructing a society from raw materials (human and otherwise) but also an incalculable degree of social dislocation.

American communitarianism in the nineteenth century flourished not only in the frontier regions of the nation, where one might escape from the patent contradictions of American society—for example, the discrepancy between democratic ideology and the perpetuation of a slave labor system—but also in regions where perceived social dislocation was most acute. On the frontier, which in the early nineteenth century meant much of upstate New York, the old Western Reserve, Kentucky, and the like, ties were severed with family and friends whose parents and grandparents may have lived in the same small geographic area, prompting the loss of both tribal or community identity and the sense of a personal past. Gone too were the amenities of civilization, such as they were: educational institutions, developing medical assistance, and the like. Frontier people were without roots, striving to carve civilization out of wilderness. Thrust into an ethos where the struggle to survive was more fact than fiction, the support provided by a tightly knit intentional community whose corporate gaze was fixed on things eternal struck many as a viable alternative to the vagaries of empirical reality. Life in such a community brought not only a modicum of economic security but also freedom from association with a world where institutions such as slavery threatened to pollute, if not destroy, the soul of society.

On the other hand, the frontier also provided space for experimentation with alternate modes of living in society. As Sidney E. Mead convincingly argued in *The Lively Experiment* (1963), one factor that has shaped all of American religious history is the presence of space in both geographical and psychological senses. There was enough geographic space available in the formative years of the nation for those who did not fit in simply to go elsewhere and set up the kind of life they wanted. But that same expanse of geographical space also provided a psychological space: persons had space to develop and implement alternative visions of what society should be. Frontier conditions in the nineteenth century thus were ripe for the eruption of an interest in communitarian ventures.

Another condition conducive to communitarian experimentation is the presence of charismatic leaders who are able to articulate both the aspirations and fears of men and women who feel out of place in the world around them. As Max Weber, Edward A. Shils, and others have demonstrated, the charismatic leader is able to impose another vision of reality on the inchoate world views of others. Virtually every intentional community has developed around the teachings and leadership of charismatic figures; most nineteenth-century leaders assumed an active role in forming the ideologies behind a particular community, and many offered near dictatorial guidance in community organization. Intentional communities of the twentieth century have not lacked charismatic leaders, although their role has tended to be more implicit than explicit.

Two particular components of American Christianity have reinforced the social conditions that have provided such fertile ground in the United States for communitarianism. One is the technique of revivalism as a means to promote allegiance to Christianity. Revivalism has been central to American religion since the Great Awakening of the eighteenth century. Until the late nineteenth century, revivalism found its most comfortable home on the frontier or in rapidly developing areas of the nation. Revivalism's call for an inner experience of conversion stresses the affective side of religious life. By painting a vivid portrait of the contrast between human sinfulness and divine goodness, it both exposes the shortcomings of human life as it is and offers a vision of what life ordered according to the will of God might be.

Along with revivalism frequently has come a resurgence of belief in millennialism. While the expectation that the kingdom of God is about to come to fruition is an important ingredient in the historical Christian theological tradition, it has been particularly prominent in American Christianity. From the time that Jonathan Edwards proclaimed that the revivals of the Great Awakening heralded the future coming of the kingdom in America, millennialism has infused revivalism with a peculiar hope that bringing human life into harmony with God's will would create a social order in which the members of American society would function as the agents to usher in the divine kingdom. A corollary to millennialism in Christian theology is belief in perfection, an idea that permeates communitarian thinking but has roots in Greek philosophy as well. The kingdom of God represented perfection itself, and if conversion could transform American society into the perfect social order, then America would be the locus of the coming kingdom. The same contagious excitement and anxious dislocation of frontier life that made communitarianism plausible also made revivalism a workable vehicle for the propagation of the faith, inspired a rebirth of interest in millennialism and its belief that the perfect social order could be realized, and produced charismatic preachers who could implant their own dreams of the kingdom in the minds of their hearers in the call for conversion. Where revivalism and millennialism flourished, there too communitarianism found a welcome.

Historians of American communitarianism have recognized that, with a few scattered exceptions (such as the first intentional community established by a group of Dutch Mennonites in 1663), most communities have been formed in one of three waves of communitarian interest. Kanter, for example, noted that the bulk of the religious communities—such as those of the Shakers, Oneida, Amana, Zoar, and the Harmony Rappites—were founded and/or reached their numerical zenith prior to 1845. (These groups will be discussed in greater detail below.) Secular communities such as those of Owen and Fourier and similar economic experiments tended to come into existence between 1820 and 1930, with most in the early years of that period, when the same matrix of social conditions that spurred religious communitarianism also fed into economic communitarianism. The third wave, Kanter claims, came in the years following World War II, peaking in the late 1960s and early 1970s.

Kanter argues that the most recent intentional communities are distinctive in that they stem from a psychological critique of American culture rather than from a religious or economic critique. More diffuse in geographical distribution, more difficult to sustain because of the increasing interdependence of social institutions in the twentieth century, and generally more short-lived because of the problem in developing workable mechanisms to enhance commitment, these later communal experiments nevertheless may have emerged from contemporary counterparts to the conditions that proved so hospitable to groups such as the Shakers and Oneida Perfectionists. The global civilization that resulted from World War II, the threat of nuclear annihilation, and the emergence of an international economy perceived by many to be tied to the military-industrial complex combined to create another epoch of transition, another age in which the old ways no longer seemed viable and values were again rapidly changing. Hence it should have come as no surprise that a longing for a more perfect society—some would label it a nostalgia for a past social order—would have prompted thousands of rural and urban communitarian experiments in the postwar decades.

Among indigenous American religious communitarian efforts, the earliest revolved around the charismatic Jemima Wilkinson. Supportive of the emotion-charged revivalism of the late eighteenth century, Wilkinson experienced a series of visions that not only resulted in her expulsion from Quaker circles, but also left her convinced that she, while ill, had died in her former self and been reborn as what she called the "Publick Universal Friend." Becoming an itinerant preacher, Wilkinson traveled throughout much of New England and part of Pennsylvania calling for conversion, as did other evangelicals, but also exhorting her hearers to adopt celibacy as the avenue to spiritual purity. By 1789, the year George Washington was inaugurated as president under the Constitution, Wilkinson had gathered enclaves of followers in several towns and begun to envision the establishment of a permanent community.

Coming to the Finger Lakes region of western New York, then basically wilderness yet to be conquered by white Americans, Wilkinson set up a community of the faithful first on Lake Seneca and then on Keuka Lake, when the presence of uncommitted outsiders and legal difficulties threatened the demise of the first settlement. After establishing her Jerusalem on Keuka Lake, Wilkinson ceased her itinerant preaching but continued to offer guidance and counsel to the few hundred who gathered around her until her death.

All along, however, the Universal Friend was plagued with difficulties. There were always ongoing problems over ownership of the land that formed the nucleus of Jerusalem. In addition, Wilkinson never created carefully considered standards for admission to the Jerusalem community, nor did she develop permanent mechanisms to ensure continued commitment to her evangelical/millennialist/Quaker ideology. While the devout continued to worship together for a time after her death in 1819 and to maintain a modicum of communal identity until the time

of the Civil War, this early communitarian experiment was too bound to the personal charisma of the Universal Friend to endure as a cohesive community in her absence.

More enduring and perhaps the model par excellence for other religious communitarian ventures was a group that also had roots in a dissident evangelical Quakerism, espousal of celibacy, and the charisma of a woman. In 1774 a small band of persecuted men and women arrived in America with their leader, "Mother" Ann Lee. From their inception the Shakers, as Ann Lee's followers popularly have been known, believed that theirs was a religious enterprise, an invitation to men and women to leave the life of this world and enter the millennial kingdom now. Before coming to New York, Ann Lee already had been the subject of several ecstatic experiences. These times of revelation, while accenting the chasm between the human and the divine, provided her with a glimpse of the spiritual realm and convinced her that it was accessible to men and women here and now.

Pressured by her father into what became an unhappy marriage, Ann Lee watched her four children die in infancy or early childhood. Consequently she came to believe that the human sexual impulse and the marriage relationship that carnally bound woman to man represented the source of human sin. Confirmation of this belief came in a moment of rapture when Ann Lee was imprisoned for disturbing the peace. There she beheld Adam and Eve alone in Eden. Contrary to biblical mythology, her vision did not picture the ingestion of forbidden fruit as the act that necessitated expulsion from the purity of the Garden. Rather Adam and Eve's lustful intercourse had thrust humanity into the abyss of sin. Accompanying the vision was the revelation that Ann herself was Christ come again as Holy Mother Wisdom destined to inaugurate the millennial kingdom on earth.

The notion that physical expression of sexuality brought evil into the world and the concept of a masculine-feminine deity provided the framework for the structures of Shaker belief and practice; they also offered clues for the attainment of a wholly pure life. On the one hand, adoption of celibacy was the logical corollary to Mother Ann's vision of the cause of sin. When sexual relations were prohibited, not only were community members free from human entanglements that thwarted the search for Edenic innocence, but also women were released from the burden of family and home to devote themselves to God's work. In addition, the ascription of divine status to Ann Lee fostered the belief, more radical then than now, that men and women were equal in God's eyes and must become so in the world.

The first Shaker community was "ordered" at New Lebanon, New York, in 1785, one year after Ann Lee's death. The dilemma that confronted the Shakers centered on how to develop institutions that would maintain commitment among members, facilitate their pursuit of the millennial life, and allow transmission of their ideology to converts. The most obvious structure designed to protect the purity of the Shaker adventure was the insistence on physical separation from the world. By withdrawing into their own economically self-supporting communities, the Shakers were able to delineate a geographic boundary between themselves and a sinful world. Psychological boundaries were also constructed. During the early years, for example, novices were forbidden to maintain contact with their families or former friends unless they were potential converts. Instead, members accepted their sisters and brothers within the community as surrogates for family and friends left behind. Persons seeking to join the Shakers presented themselves to their spiritual superiors in the community, women to the eldresses and men to the elders, to make private confession of the evils of their past lives. As a ritual form, confession allowed one to reformulate past experiences by identifying them as evil and to state one's intent to adopt the goal of purity in this life by submitting to Shaker structures.

Within the community, internal structures were devised to bolster and protect the separation of the sexes and the ideology of sexual equality. To a certain extent, celibacy and equality were two sides of the same coin. Celibacy not only enhanced the status of women by providing a set of values in which women may be free and equal, but also offered a means to challenge and perhaps change societal gender roles. By sacralizing celibacy, the Shakers were providing a virginal source of redemption, untainted and pure, for a polluted world. Leadership and work patterns likewise reinforced the celibacy/equality matrix. Each Shaker family had two male and two female leaders charged with both the spiritual nurture of members and the economic operation of the community. The latter task involved developing a job rotation system, which offered numerous advantages: several persons could be trained with the skills needed for efficient management of any communal task, members had variety in their work, and none could develop an "impure" pride in his or her performance of a given job. While in theory every job was considered of equal value and importance, in the assignment of specific tasks the Shakers were wedded to cultural stereotypes: women engaged in cooking, cleaning, laundering, and the like; men, in carpentry, agricultural activity, and other "male" tasks. But men and women did have equal leadership roles, although men assumed the responsibility for dealing with "the world." In the early years especially, many of the female leaders, such as Lucy Wright, exercised a stronger impact on the ethos of the group than did the male leaders.

Within a Shaker settlement additional boundaries between men and women were drawn, further reinforcing the sense of isolation from the world and the ideology of equality in celibacy. Men and women had separate entrances to buildings and used separate staircases. At meals, eaten in silence, they sat at separate tables. At work, they labored silently in separate quarters or in separate areas of the estate. At worship, men and women formed separate ranks on opposite sides of the room. Even in the famous ritual dances, they moved in separate lines. Any contact was strictly controlled. "Union meetings," held for a few hours each week, found men and women, usually in groups of four, sitting across the room from each other; each Shaker spoke only to the person directly opposite. But a spirit of oneness in separation and isolation was created.

All these mechanisms required the kind of sacrifice of which Kanter spoke. An element of sacrifice entered the picture when one signed over his or her material possessions to the common or joint trust. Entrance into the fold also brought an end to following the fashions of the world, for Shakers had uniform clothing for members, a powerful symbol of internal equality and a visible sign of distinction from outsiders. Daily life followed a ritualized order designed to bolster commitment and identification with the community. Insistence on celibacy is the most obvious example of sacrifice, for the Shakers in effect sacrificed individual control over sexuality to the pursuit of purity. But the Shaker message resounded in areas where revivalism flourished. At their peak in the 1840s, the Shakers numbered some 6,000 adherents living in nineteen separate settlements.

From the Shaker perspective, their withdrawal from the world into celibate enclaves received justification in their conviction that the second coming of Christ had transpired in Ann Lee. With the advent of Christ's return, a new age had dawned: the millennial kingdom had been inaugurated. Shakers believed they were living in the heavenly sphere now. Hence firm lines were needed to demarcate the millennial society from the outside world. Adoption of practices and structures that reversed patterns prevalent in a polluted world signaled a reversal of direction, the exchanging of sin and evil for purity and holy simplicity. The religious rationale for the Shaker position is evident: life in the millennial kingdom entailed forsaking what the world held dear. All the devices that buttressed renunciation of worldly ways operated to transmit a qualitatively superior status to the devotee. Shaker belief and practice represented a continuing pilgrimage on a path perceived as higher and better than anything mundane because it was the road ordained by God Almighty and Holy Mother Wisdom.

The complementary functions of reversal and status elevation come to light in the religious rituals of the Shakers, the translation into song and dance of Shaker ideology. Physical manifestations of the divine presence were hardly unknown in frontier revivals, where individuals frequently were seized by "exercises" and lost physical control. But the ecstatic Shaker dancing, while a physical manifestation of the spirit, was different from the chaotic frenzy of the revival. Rather, the Shakers practiced structured dances with uniform, precise patterns of movement each week in preparation for the Sunday worship celebration. Participation in ritual activities strengthened identification with the community since all were involved. It also broke the rhythm of silence and controlled emotion in an acceptable form of release. Only during the late 1830s and 1840s, the era called in Shaker history "Mother Ann's Work," did the mechanisms for commitment and control threaten to collapse, for then many brothers and sisters fell into fits of individual religious ecstasy. Recognizing the dangers to structure, the Shaker hierarchy closed services to outsiders until order had returned.

Today the Shakers are nearly extinct, their once flourishing communities sold or converted to museums. Yet their survival for more than two centuries makes their experiment the longest-lived communitarian venture in American religious history. Decline resulted from many factors. The rise of mass production and the rapid industrialization of American society sounded the death knell to the basically agrarian Shaker communities and their small industries. Celibacy also contributed to decline, for growth depended exclusively on conversions rather than on internal propagation. Also, as the growing pains of the new nation gave way to stability and the chaos of the frontier gave way to order, the need for the kind of security provided by the Shaker corporate quest for purity dwindled. Simply put, the Shaker vision could not be adapted to keep pace with the presumed progress of an increasingly complex, highly interdependent, urbanized, and industrialized society. Now the Shakers are remembered more for their folk art and furniture, their hymnody and dance than for the intricate structures created to guide and sustain commitment to the pure life in the millennial kingdom.

The quest for perfection took a very different shape in the community centered at Oneida, New York, after John Humphrey Noyes and a handful of followers moved there from Putney, Vermont, in 1848, when the Shakers were at their zenith. Noyes, converted in a revival in 1831, had studied for the ministry first at Andover and then at Yale. While a student at Yale, he adopted a Perfectionist ideology. Believing that the second coming of Christ had transpired in A.D. 70, Noyes became convinced that believers could achieve salvation from sin, that they could lead lives of perfection by replicating the ideals and practices of the apostolic church. This restoration of pure primitive Christianity involved sharp breaks with prevailing social structures and patterns for Noyes, as had the pursuit of purity for the Shakers.

Noyes promoted what he called Bible communism, a form of socialism that involved common ownership of property and material possessions.

This belief derived from his reading of the Book of Acts, which describes the early church as holding all things in common. As had the Shakers, Noyes regarded marriage as an unholy institution that made the wife the slave of her husband. Within the ranks of the perfected, love could not be exclusive. Rather, each man should regard each woman within the community as a wife, and each woman should regard each man as a husband. Noyes dubbed his alternative "complex marriage," and as with Ann Lee's espousal of celibacy, Noyes's position stemmed as much from personal experience as from ideological conviction. Married in 1838, Noyes had a wife who had difficulties with childbearing. He also developed an amative attraction to Mary Cragin, the wife of one of his followers. His wife's situation and his involvement with Mrs. Cragin combined with Noyes's conviction that exclusive marriage did not exist in the heavenly kingdom to produce his doctrine of complex marriage. To those in Putney who did not subscribe to Noyes's teaching, complex marriage seemed an immoral scandal. Hence Noyes and his converts, many initially drawn from his family, retreated to Oneida, where, in an isolated community, they could live the perfect life now.

Settled at Oneida, the Perfectionists sought to implement their ideology. While outsiders continued to condemn complex marriage as "free love," within the community relations between the sexes were carefully regulated. Indeed, complex marriage was more a mechanism to maintain social control than it was an invitation to license. Men were expected to approach women through a third party, usually an older woman, and in theory any woman could decline to have sexual relations with any individual man. At the same time, older persons were expected to initiate younger persons into the procedures of complex marriage, which for many years involved a form of birth control that Noyes called "male continence" (coitus reservatus). The community recognized that the birth of children needed to wait until Bible communism was securely established and the group had a firm economic base. Complex marriage was as much a form of sacrifice as celibacy was for the Shakers, since individuals had to submit to a set structure rather than yield to personal whim in arranging sexual liaisons. Only after a generation did the Oneida Community embark on a carefully structured program of internal propagation called stirpiculture, a form of eugenics in which a committee, in consultation with Noyes, authorized specific couples to have a child. The intent was to match men and women in such a way as to produce children who would be the most spiritual and thereby more prone to the perfect life. Even before the stirpiculture experiment, couples who showed signs of developing an exclusive attraction would be separated, and after children were born, contact with parents was regulated in order to prevent an attachment that would possibly weaken attachment to the community as a whole.

Under Noyes's charismatic and often authoritarian leadership, Oneida developed many structures that enhanced commitment to the Perfectionist ideal. New members were required to sign over personal property to the group, a practice that required sacrifice of control over one's possessions and gave individuals a stake in the success of the community. Clothing styles were also uniform within the community, with the pantaloons worn by women regarded as scandalous by outsiders in an age before bloomers became popular. Work assignments at Oneida were set up on a rotational basis, though persons who had particular skills would generally be allowed to stay with one job.

Oneida also from time to time sent members outside the community to gain an education in areas in which the group needed expertise. Encouraged by Sewell Newhouse and John R. Miller, two devotees, Oneida embarked on a program of manufacturing steel animal traps, a venture whose success secured the financial base of the community. In time, Oneida and its colony at Wallingford, Connecticut, expanded the economic foundations of the community to include the manufacture of traveling bags, the sale of preserved fruit, the production of silk thread, and eventually the manufacture of high-quality silver plate.

Two features of life at Oneida probably were the most effective in promoting total commitment to the community—"home talks" and "mutual criticism." While the group did not hold regular religious services in the traditional sense, it did gather for a period each evening for general discussion of communal affairs. While Noyes himself did not always preside at these meetings —theoretically a central committee was responsible for the overall Oneida operation—he generally did make short presentations, or "home talks," in which he expounded his Perfectionist theology and socialistic views. There was thus a regular, ritualized form in which devotion to the communal ideology was reinforced and members were encouraged to continue on the path of perfect righteousness. Many of the home talks were published in periodicals that the community circulated among outsiders as a means both to proclaim the Oneida message and to respond to criticism of the Perfectionists' beliefs and practices.

The most powerful mechanism for sustaining commitment, however, was the practice of what Noyes called "mutual criticism." In one sense, mutual criticism stemmed from Noyes's notion of Perfectionism. Perfection for him and his followers did not denote an absence of faults or flaws in personality and behavior. Perfection was concerned more with intent than with deed and in time became viewed as a process rather than as a fait accompli. Hence individuals were expected to be constantly seeking improvement and working to eliminate from their lives attitudes and actions that impeded the full realization of perfection. In mutual criticism, persons offered themselves to others in the group for comments on their own shortcomings. While there was no regular schedule for this criticism, no one was exempt and everyone was expected to participate. Accounts of these sessions reveal that critiques were often thorough and devastating, although positive comments were included so that an individual might not become overly discouraged. Mutual criticism, from the perspective of communal structure, was vital in breaking the kind of individualism that would inhibit total commitment to the community and in reminding persons that their whole identity revolved around the extent to which they were willing to submit to and accept the will of the community.

Oneida and its associated community at Wallingford (a few other satellite communities were abandoned shortly after founding) peaked at a combined membership of about 300. After a generation, problems emerged that ultimately brought an end to the Perfectionist experiment as a communitarian endeavor. Over the years, the Perfectionist impulse became muted as Noyes himself gradually became more concerned with the socialist economic system that undergirded the community than with the pure ideology of Perfectionism. The ascendancy of secular communitarianism within Oneida brought a concomitant erosion of the religious dimension so important to community continuity and commitment. The material success of the community also created its own dilemmas. As with the Shakers, Oneida's openness to efficiency in work brought an interest in labor-saving devices, which gradually resulted in a subtle shift of values to the standards of the world and a privatization of needs that undercut the sense of community.

Complex marriage and stirpiculture, always the major focuses of external hostility, likewise contributed to Oneida's decline. Over the long haul, it proved impossible to thwart incidences of "exclusive attraction" among couples and parent-child bonding once the stirpiculture program was introduced. Consequently, despite mutual criticism and an ideology that advocated an inclusive love, individual personal relationships assumed greater importance than communal ones. Finally, Noyes's near dictatorial leadership style provoked such resentment, particularly among younger and newer members, that Noyes himself was forced to flee to Canada in 1879 at a time when Oneida faced unusually strong external opposition because of complex marriage. Still the titular leader, Noyes wrote home advising that complex marriage be abandoned, and although the community acquiesced in his advice, the difficulties proved insurmountable. Within a brief period, a large number of the Perfectionists entered into legal marriages, thus ending any pretense of totally inclusive love. Noyes never returned to Oneida, and in 1881 the communitarian experiment dissolved, being replaced by a joint-stock corporation, Oneida, Ltd., which continues to prosper as a major producer of silver plate. Many of the Oneida communitarians continued to reside in the area, but their quest for millennial perfection in community had ended.

A group that combined ethnic, religious, and socialistic principles in a utopian endeavor was the Community of True Inspiration, more commonly known as the Amana Society. Amana's roots lay in the quietistic pietism and mysticism of Rhineland Protestantism. Even before migrating to the United States from Germany in 1842 under the leadership of Christian Metz and Barbara Heinemann, the group had embarked on a communal venture in Europe. Coming to New York State, the scene of so much religious experimentation in the first half of the nineteenth century, the Inspirationists made their first American home at Ebenezer, near Buffalo. Within a decade, the rapid population growth of the area had brought the temptations of the world too close, spurring the group to push westward to east-central Iowa, where relative isolation in a frontier region was still possible. There ultimately some seven villages with a total population of 1,800 persons sought to live out the Inspirationist message, first formulated by Eberhard Ludwig Gruber and Johann Frederick Rock in 1714, to serve God, in the words of the Amana Society's constitution,

> according to His laws and His requirements in our own consciences, and thus to work out the salvation of our souls, through the redeeming grace of Jesus Christ, in self-denial, in the obedience to our faith, and in the demonstration of our faithfulness in the inward and outward service of the Community by the power of grace which God presents us with.

While Metz continued to provide strong leadership to the Amana colonies until his death in 1867—at which time Heinemann became the acknowledged leader, until her death sixteen years later—control of the enterprise was vested in thirteen elected elders who formed a board of trustees. The same individuals comprised the Great Council of the Brethren, responsible for the spiritual nurture of adherents. The separate villages had their own elected boards to oversee day-to-day affairs, following the general principles and policies set forth by the board and Great Council. Most property was communally owned, although Amana never espoused the brand of socialism that lay behind Oneida, and individuals were permitted to keep a few personal possessions acquired with token allowances provided from the general treasury. The Inspirationists attempted to fuse loyalty to the community with maintenance of nuclear family relationships by assigning each family its own living quarters while having kitchens, bakeries, dairies, and dining halls in common. Inspirationists also adopted the familiar communitarian practice of having clothing tailored in the same simple style, one reflective of German folk culture at the be-

ginning of the century. While the Oneida Perfectionists found a secure economic base in the manufacture of steel traps, Amana found a secure base in a prosperous woolens industry, although the community also sought to be self-sufficient in the production of its own food products. Amana's textile endeavors did not result from adopting the profit motive, but from the simple desire to provide for daily needs and have a small reserve on hand for difficult times.

Central to the Amana colonies were religious services, generally eleven per week. In keeping with the emphasis on simplicity, the meetinghouses were unadorned and without pulpits. Men and women sat separately during the services of silent prayer, Bible readings, discourses by the elders, and the chanting of unaccompanied hymns. The frequency of religious services was one potent mechanism for buttressing commitment to the simplicity and pietism of the Inspirationists' ideal. Then, too, members were expected to present themselves annually before the elders for a spiritual examination. While these sessions lacked the severity of Oneida's mutual criticism, they nevertheless also reminded the colonists of the primacy of the community over individual interests and strengthened the ways in which identity was tied to the group itself.

For more than a generation Amana flourished, growing with the arrival of fellow Inspirationists from Germany as well as from within. But seeds of erosion were planted early. After Metz's and Heinemann's deaths, no single individual provided the kind of unofficial but vibrant leadership they had offered Amana. The succeeding generations found government by committee increasingly ineffective in offering firm guidance. Then, too, the world came ever nearer as westward migration, an expanding rail system, and a growing volume of tourists made Amana less a haven for the holy and more an anachronistic curiosity to behold. By the early twentieth century it was clear that the younger generation had lost the commitment to the simple piety of their elders. In addition, financial problems came to Amana; some members objected that others were not contributing their share to the community's labor. Finally, a special committee proposed a drastic reorganization of the Inspirationists. Spiritual and temporal concerns were to be separated and the Amana industries were to be restructured as a joint-stock corporation, with individuals receiving shares in proportion to their longevity in the community. Endorsed by some 90 percent of the members, the proposal was adopted, and on 1 June 1932 the communitarian adventure of the Amana experience formally ended.

But the dissolution of the community did not bring an end to the religious side of the Inspirationist movement, nor did it bring an end to economic association. While communal kitchens and dining arrangements were discontinued and the nuclear family became the basic social unit within the old colonies, the cooperative business venture guaranteed employment to all members at the time of dissolution and offered a dazzling array of fringe benefits, such as free medical and dental care and a generous retirement plan. In the midst of the Depression, Amana remained an oasis of economic prosperity, a prosperity that has continued to the present as Amana industries expanded beyond textiles and the curing of meats to include, for example, the manufacture of food freezers. The Amana Church Society, the specifically religious organization formed in 1932, continues to keep alive the pietism and aspirations of Gruber, Rock, Metz, and Heinemann.

The Inspirationists were not the only group that attempted to fuse ethnic, religious, and socialistic dimensions in a communitarian experiment. Lutheran dissident and separatist George Rapp, also strongly influenced by the pietistic strand of Protestantism and anticipating the imminent arrival of the millennium, arrived in the United States from Württemberg in 1804. Like the Shakers, the Rappites espoused a radical doctrine of purity that, after 1807, involved strict celibacy, opposition to marriage, and consequently no internal propagation. In addition, the Rappites showed little inclination to seek converts.

Rapp and some 600 followers migrated to Pennsylvania, where they set up their first community, Harmony, based on common ownership of property and acceptance of Rapp's near dictatorial leadership. So adamant was Rapp in his insistence on common ownership that in 1818, with the community's consent, he personally burned the list of original contributions so that there would be no record of individual shares in the enterprise should someone seek to defect

and request compensation for property signed over. Indeed, Rapp's preoccupation with common ownership and its economic implications led Arthur Bestor, in *Backwoods Utopias* (1950), to claim that Harmony quickly became more absorbed in its communitarian economy than in its sectarian religious ideology, a claim that receives some validation when one recalls that the Rappites named their final and presumably permanent settlement Economy.

Harmony quickly became widely known and an economic success. At Rapp's insistence, the group practiced rigid self-discipline with an aim similar to that of the Shakers. Simply put, the Rappites viewed themselves as the righteous remnant that would be judged as pure and holy when the Lord returned and humanity was required to make a final accounting before God. Within the community, this discipline involved much more than mere common ownership of property. Members were divided into six groups, based on age and gender, that met weekly for "mutual improvement," a mechanism of oral confession that worked much the same way that the Oneidans' mutual criticism did. Rapp also kept a watchful eye on his devotees, periodically appearing unannounced to make sure that all were adhering to the community's regimen. (These strange appearances were aided by a series of secret passages that Rapp is reported to have had constructed so that he could move with ease from one part of the community to another without being observed.) Like other successful groups, the Rappites also abandoned worldly fashion in clothing and had all their attire made in a uniform style.

The structural organization of Harmony and the later Rappite settlements also promoted total commitment to the community. Members were divided into families consisting of from two to eight persons. While the village remained the center of communal activity, each family was responsible for preparing its own meals, providing much of its own food, and caring for other domestic concerns. While persons were theoretically equal within the group and families were assigned housing that was fairly uniform, it is clear that Rapp was "first among equals," having the largest residence by virtue of his unquestioned dominance in the community. As was the case with John Humphrey Noyes at Oneida, Rapp enjoyed a position of privilege in the community, though there can be no doubt that his personal charisma was foremost in promoting cohesion and commitment to Harmony's vision of the pure life.

In 1815 the Rappites left Pennsylvania, joined in the general westward migration, and set up a settlement named New Harmony Colony in Indiana. There the group remained as a prosperous venture for nearly a decade before it was determined to return to the area around Pittsburgh. In 1824 Harmony's property was put on the market and eventually sold to Robert Owen, who christened the place New Harmony and set up his first American socialist Eden there.

The Rappites built their new community, where they expected to remain until the millennium dawned, at Economy, located in Ohio and fairly close to Pittsburgh. But by the time of the move to Economy, there were already subtle signs of dissatisfaction with the Harmony operation, most of which revolved around Rapp's authoritarian and sometimes bizarre leadership. In 1832 there was an internal rebellion against Rapp led by Bernhard Müller, who called himself Count Leon. Before the turmoil subsided, Count Leon had defected with nearly one-third of the Rappite membership of 800. Although Rapp retained control of the community, which remained at Economy until his death some fifteen years later, and the community itself did not dissolve formally until 1905, the schism marked the beginning of a slow decline.

The Rappites would not have remained intact as long as they did had there not been such strong mechanisms for commitment operating. Yielding one's property to the community enhanced the dimension of sacrifice requisite to communal success, as did the practice of celibacy. Mutual improvement served as a vehicle to remind members of the supremacy of the group over the individual. The family system provided daily reinforcement of identification with the community, while the conviction that the disciplined communal life offered the only path to millennial purity granted an aura of transcendence. If Rapp's domination of the community and his personal charisma were the major forces holding the Harmonites together in the early years, they were also major factors in the group's decline. The Rappites provide a classic example of the dangers of overreliance on the guidance of a single individual and the failure to provide for

transmission of authority to other persons and structures once the leader dies. Although the Rappites were subject to the same tensions and pressures from external social forces that challenged the communal ideal for other groups, their internal problems with authority may have been more significant in accounting for their gradual erosion. Nonetheless, had the other mechanisms been less effective, the community would have disintegrated sooner. Survival for a century marks the Rappites as one of the more successful communitarian endeavors in American religious history.

One other group with roots in Württemberg merits mention. In 1817 some 300 quietistic pietists ended a migration that had taken them from Bavaria to Württemberg and Baden and finally to Zoar, Ohio. Under the leadership of Joseph Michael Bimeler (originally Baumeler), the Zoarites hoped to lead a simple life of religious devotion in community. Initially not committed in principle to the common ownership of property, poverty forced the Zoarites to pool their resources, a practice that continued until the community broke up in 1898. But common ownership did not immediately alleviate the dire financial situation of the group. What finally brought relief and a modicum of economic success was the opening of the network of canals linked to the Erie Canal, which introduced greater opportunities for commercial activity. Poverty as well as conviction also lay behind the adoption of a uniform style of clothing.

Like several other groups, the Zoarites also adopted the practice of celibacy both because they were at first simply unable to support children and because without routine family responsibilities they could focus all attention on things divine. The practice finally proved unworkable. Bimeler, like Rapp, enjoyed a position of unusual privilege—he, too, was provided with a large and elegantly appointed home—and chose to marry in 1828. Consequently, others ended the practice of celibacy, though many at the time doubted the wisdom of doing so. However, any spiritual advantage thought to accrue to a celibate status vanished in 1834, when the Zoarite ranks were decimated because a cholera epidemic wiped out about one-third of the faithful.

The end of celibacy, a powerful mechanism for social control and commitment, did not at first mean an end to the primacy of the community as the basic social unit. Children born at Zoar were raised communally in order that devotion to the community took precedence over attachment to the biological family. But just as Oneida encountered difficulties when family attachments emerged during the stirpiculture experiment, Zoar found that the ideal of communal parenting worked only for one generation. Along with the failure to provide for effective transmission of authority after Bimeler's death in 1853, the generational conflict that emerged as family commitments took precedence over communal devotion contributed greatly to Zoar's demise as a communitarian venture. Numbering around 500 adherents at its zenith, Zoar counted only 222 when it disbanded.

Other communities of Germanic heritage also have been part of the story of American religious communitarianism. The Mennonites, the Amish, the Hutterites, and in recent decades the Bruderhof all have made important contributions. Those of ethnic communities of quite a different sort are less well known and usually omitted from analyses of American communitarian experiments; namely, those ventures made up primarily or exclusively of black Americans. "Black utopias" established during the nineteenth-century wave of communitarian experiments emerged largely from the discrimination encountered by free blacks, although religious elements were also involved. The communities drew from a diverse cross section of the black population. Generally they mixed together fugitive slaves (mostly from the upper South) and northern free blacks who resisted such movements as the African resettlement endeavors of the American Colonization Society. Some of the black communities depended on white leadership and attracted not so much those whites who guided the antislavery movement as those who either espoused racial equality in principle or who saw in communitarian experiments a vehicle for improving the lot of black Americans in the larger society.

Of the early black communitarian efforts, the best known is Nashoba, established by Fanny Wright in western Tennessee in 1826, although there were a few other scattered settlements organized by slaveholders for manumitted slaves both before and after Nashoba. Intending to base Nashoba on cooperative principles modeled after those of the Rappites, Wright's goal was to train and educate blacks for recolonization in Africa. Although a cooperative in structure, Nashoba expected blacks to earn enough money through work in community enterprises to finance their own support, purchase their freedom, pay for their resettlement in Africa, and reimburse the community for whatever had been received from communal funds. Within a year, illness forced Wright to turn over direction to a board of trustees, which effected some minor changes in policy, such as encouraging whites and free blacks to become members and declining to admit slaves unless their owners were members.

As William and Jane Pease have noted, the situation at Nashoba was an anomaly. It offered few advantages to free blacks, went against popular sentiment by downplaying the role of religion in communal life, and defied public opinion in bringing blacks and whites together. Within the community, slaves were still regarded as inferior. Wright eventually joined the Owenites at New Harmony in 1828, and within two years the Nashoba settlement was abandoned. While the vocational and educational aims of Wright reflected the idealism common to utopian movements, her failure to develop mechanisms for commitment, her sense of racial superiority, her lack of a vision for a total society, and her disregard for the religious element doomed Nashoba from the start.

Plans for several black communities focused on acquiring land in Canada on the mistaken assumption that the absence of slavery in Canada had created a social order more racially inclusive than that in the United States. As with Nashoba, most reflected a paternalistic idealism that simply did not take adequate account of the depth of racism. Among these, one of the earliest was Wilberforce, planned in Cincinnati but planted in Ontario. Blacks from Cincinnati began to settle there in 1829. In comparison with groups such as the Shakers and the Oneida Perfectionists, Wilberforce lacked many structures that might have fostered success. Predominantly agrarian, Wilberforce perpetuated the individualism that pervaded white culture, though it was cooperative in principle. In looking back at the extravagant educational programs envisioned for the community, it is obvious that Wilberforce was designed to inculcate the values of white capitalistic society in its black members. Few if any of the blacks who came to Wilberforce had money or other property to donate to the venture; consequently the settlement remained dependent on contributions from outsiders, its residents consigned to poverty. Its demise, difficult to date but for all practical purposes effected by 1836, soured many potential benefactors of similar proposals for at least a decade.

Other black communities in Canada included the British-American Institute at Dawn, Elgin in Ontario, and the Refugee Home Society established in Windsor, close to Detroit. Their primary aims were educational and vocational, not strictly communitarian, and all the efforts foundered. Similarly, the Port Royal experiment on South Carolina's Sea Islands during the Civil War years was more concerned with demonstrating that blacks were worthy of economic acceptance in white society than with communitarian ideals.

Although America's most well-known religious utopias emerged in the nineteenth century, the communitarian impulse was by no means confined to that epoch. Indeed, as many analysts of contemporary culture have pointed out, the period after World War II, particularly the late 1960s and early 1970s, also saw a boom in community establishment. While some have estimated that the number of contemporary communes has reached at least 30,000, few are on a par with their earlier cousins, for most lack a clear ideology, defined mechanisms for maintenance of commitment, and carefully prescribed standards for admission. Kanter has distinguished between two types of modern communities, those she calls retreat communes and those she labels communities with a mission. The former, whether rural or urban, are basically collectives of persons seeking to escape or at least to mitigate the depersonalization of a highly differentiated technological society. The latter, communities with a mission, include countless examples of associations with a single purpose: promotion of ecology, women's liberation, macrobiotic diets, and the like. However, at least two deserve mention, for they are groups that have a comprehensive vision of a new social order predicated on religious and ethical values: Koinonia, near Americus, Georgia, and the Sojourners Fellowship, headquartered in Washington, D.C.

Koinonia dates back to the 1930s, when Clar-

ence Jordan and a handful of associates sought to implement Christian ideals of racial justice and racial inclusiveness by forming what was hoped would be a self-sufficient biracial community. Suffering much persecution at the hands of those opposed to racial inclusiveness, the community faltered for many years. Based on common ownership, democratic decision-making processes, and shared labor, Koinonia nevertheless depended heavily on Jordan for leadership and the securing of outside financial support to help sustain the community. Koinonia's vision was rooted in southern evangelical religion insofar as it attempted to take seriously the implications of the ethics of Jesus and love for humanity. However, Koinonia also had internal difficulties in its early decades, in part because of its dependence on (and occasional resentment of) Jordan's charismatic presence. Reorganized on cooperative more than communitarian principles, Koinonia survived Jordan's death in 1969 and has continued to be a witness to what its members regard as the simple life of love.

The Sojourners Fellowship is more recent in origin, tracing its roots to a group of students at Trinity Evangelical Divinity School near Chicago who were discontent with evangelicalism's response to such issues as poverty, the Vietnam conflict, and the other social concerns of the 1960s. Initially known as the People's Christian Coalition of Deerfield, Illinois, these students sought to promote their vision of an evangelical social ethic (what they called "Christian radicalism") in the pages of a periodical known at its founding in 1971 as the *Post-American*. The guiding force behind the movement is Jim Wallis, who was drawn to rethink the social implications of Christian belief when he became an antiwar activist while a student at Michigan State University in the late 1960s. In the fall of 1975, under Wallis' leadership, the community responsible for the *Post-American* moved to Washington, renaming itself the Sojourners Fellowship and the journal *Sojourners*.

Convinced that Christians who take biblical mandates seriously always will identify with the poor and dispossessed, the Sojourners Fellowship has organized itself as a community with common ownership of property, but committed to living near the poverty level. Individuals who work outside the community donate salaries, and wages paid to those who produce the journal and carry out other formal activities are kept low. Not necessarily seeing itself as a model for society at large, the Sojourners Fellowship regards itself more as a prophetic leaven to keep before the churches a vision of a religious style and pattern of living thought consonant with Scripture. Two forces provide what cohesion the Fellowship has: Wallis' charisma and the publication of *Sojourners*. Otherwise the only mechanism for enhancing commitment is a shared evangelical social ethic. Should either be removed, the future of the Sojourners Fellowship would be tenuous at best.

The panorama of utopian communities includes numerous additional experiments, many discussed in other essays. Early Mormonism, for example, had a distinctive communitarian cast that for a time involved sharing of property, while the move to Utah under Brigham Young's leadership bore many characteristics of communitarianism. In the twentieth century the Catholic Worker movement spearheaded by Dorothy Day fused aspects of Marxism, utopianism, and communitarianism with the tradition of Catholic social action in its urban ministry. As well, one should note the enclaves of Hasidic Jews, particularly in Brooklyn and elsewhere in the New York metropolitan area, who maintain a highly communitarian style with strong mechanisms to promote commitment in the midst of alien cultural and religious forces. A complete list of religious utopian and communitarian endeavors would seem endless, but the point is clear. American religious life has long included communities committed to a vision of life as it should be and can be.

From the Shakers to the Sojourners, one can trace a continuing conviction that the shared life offers opportunities not only for attaining personal spiritual purity but also for promoting social change in the anticipation that someday purity will prevail throughout the social order. With ties to revivalism, millennialism, and economic socialism, religious communitarianism in the United States has tended to flourish when society itself was undergoing transition, offering both security and challenge to thousands who felt out of place in a corrupt world. Often overdependent on the dreams and ideologies of individual leaders and constantly struggling to balance individual identity with commitment to the community, hundreds of ventures have experimented with new forms of social organization, economic association, and interpersonal relationships as they developed different mechanisms to enhance devotion to the ideal life. While always a minority strand in American religion, communitarianism nonetheless has served as an ongoing reminder to the majority that there is hope of bringing empirical reality into harmony with religious visions of the perfect society.

BIBLIOGRAPHY

Edward Deming Andrews, *The People Called Shakers* (1963); Karl J. R. Arndt, *George Rapp's Harmony Society, 1785–1847* (1965) and *George Rapp's Successors and Material Heirs, 1847–1916* (1971); Arthur F. Bestor, *Backwoods Utopias: The Sectarian Origins and the Owenite Phase of Communitarian Socialism in America, 1663–1829* (1950; 2nd ed., 1970); Maren Lockwood Carden, *Oneida: Utopian Community to Modern Corporation* (1969); Henri Desroche, *The American Shakers: From Neo-Christianity to Presocialism* (1971); Catherine R. Dobbs, *Freedom's Will: The Society of the Separatists of Zoar* (1947); James E. Ernst, *Ephrata: A History* (1963).

Michael Fellman, *The Unbounded Frame: Freedom and Community in Nineteenth Century American Utopianism* (1973); Lawrence Foster, *Religion and Sexuality: Three American Communal Experiments of the Nineteenth Century* (1981); Joyce O. Hertzler, *The History of Utopian Thought* (1923); Morris Hillquit, *History of Socialism in the United States* (1903; rev. 1910; repr. 1965); William A. Hinds, *American Communities and Co-operative Colonies* (2nd ed., 1908); Mark Holloway, *Heavens on Earth: Utopian Communities in America, 1680–1880* (1951; rev. 1966); John A. Hostetler, *Communitarian Societies* (1974); Robert Houriet, *Getting Back Together* (1971); Judson Jerome, *Families of Eden: Communes and the New Anarchism* (1974); Rosabeth Moss Kanter, *Commitment and Community: Communes and Utopias in Sociological Perspective* (1972) and, as ed., *Communes: Creating and Managing the Collective Life* (1973); Keith Melville, *Communes in the Counter Culture: Origins, Theories, Styles of Life* (1972).

Charles Nordhoff, *The Communistic Societies of the United States* (1875; repr. 1965); John Humphrey Noyes, *History of American Socialisms* (1870; repr. 1966); Pierrepont B. Noyes, *My Father's House: An Oneida Boyhood* (1937) and *A Goodly Heritage* (1958); Robert A. Parker, *A Yankee Saint: John Humphrey Noyes and the Oneida Community* (1935); William H. Pease and Jane H. Pease, *Black Utopia: Negro Communal Experiments in America* (1963); Bertha M. H. Shambaugh, *Amana That Was and Amana That Is* (1932); Robert David Thomas, *The Man Who Would Be Perfect: John Humphrey Noyes and the Utopian Impulse* (1977); John M. Whitworth, *God's Blueprints: A Sociological Study of Three Utopian Sects* (1975); Barbara S. Yambura, *A Change and a Parting: My Story of Amana* (1960).

[*See also* ETHNICITY AND RELIGION; HOLINESS AND PERFECTION; NEW ENGLAND PURITANISM; *and* RELIGIOUS ARCHITECTURE AND LANDSCAPE.]

NINETEENTH-CENTURY EVANGELICALISM

Leonard I. Sweet

EVANGELICALISM stands as the most powerful social and religious movement of nineteenth-century America. It was a time when evangelicals had things mostly their own way, a time when someone like the hapless John Danforth could be arrested and convicted of the crime of blasphemy for shouting angrily on a New York City street in 1825, "Jesus Christ is a bastard, his mother a whore, and God a damned old whoremaster." A rich and changing phenomenon of many contradictions and conflicts, evangelicalism proved to be the dominant expression of Protestant faith in nineteenth-century America. Evangelicalism's stage is spacious, covering every conceivable corner of American life; its cast of characters colorful, including a good assortment of some of the most important and eccentric figures in American history; its script dramatic, one of bold designs and sly attempts to conquer an entire culture; and its story epic, one of the most successful penetrations of a culture by religious faith.

The term "evangelicalism" eludes definition, but then words like "evangelical" are in any case crude instruments for an understanding of nineteenth-century mainstream religion and its innumerable rivulets. Robert Baird, an influential early historian of religion in America, divides religion in America into the evangelical and unevangelical denominations. He defines evangelical churches as those that "hold the great doctrines of the Reformation" and "whose religion is the Bible, the whole Bible and nothing but the Bible" (*Religion in America,* 1844). An exploration of evangelicalism and its creation of a new cultural consensus in nineteenth-century America must begin with an understanding of the movement's theological life and lexicon. The urgent, confident, aggressive, and practical spirit of evangelical theology can be traced to the ensemble of attitudes found in its doctrines of conversion, usefulness, commonsense realism, and millennialism.

Those "great doctrines of the Reformation" Baird alludes to were largely what evangelicals took for granted. The evangelical credo was summarized succinctly in the constitution of the American Missionary Association, founded in 1846:

> A belief in the guilty and lost condition of all men without a Savior; the Supreme Deity, incarnation and atoning sacrifice of Jesus Christ, the only Savior of the world; the necessity of regeneration by the Holy Spirit; repentance, faith and holy obedience, in order to [achieve] salvation; the immortality of the soul; and the retributions of the judgment in the eternal punishment of the wicked, and salvation of the righteous.
>
> (*Proceedings of the Second Convention for Bible Missions, Held in Albany September Second and Third . . . ,* 1846, pp. 4–5)

While such doctrines formed the heart of the tradition, what they did not take for granted gave intellectual vigor to evangelical theology. Evangelicalism's reigning theological temper was Arminian, a liberal reaction to the determinist logic of Calvinist doctrines such as Total depravity, Unconditional election, Limited atonement, Irresistible grace, and Perseverance of the Saints (TULIP). Calvinism, which had absorbed the shocks of New World existence for such a long time, could no longer adequately meet the spiritual needs of people with republican and romanticist sensibilities. A widespread religious revival known as the Second Great Awakening, which occurred from about 1795 to 1835, when evangelicalism defined itself, achieved self-consciousness, and institutionalized its identity, drained the dregs of Calvinism out of evangelicalism through its stress on moral ability over moral depravity and a definition of sin as volitional, not constitutional. The premier revivalist of antebellum America, Charles G. Finney, both reflected the cultural distaste of rationalistic formalism and positioned a major social transition on a high moral plane. Finney's dyadic doctrine of human freedom and self-determination, in which sin was something one did, not something one was, broke the back of Calvinism by 1830 and proved the perfect theological scaffolding for the emergence and espousal of a free-labor, free-market economy. Sometimes the "new measures" of Finneyite revivalism were picked up by other evangelists, penetrating even into the South through the ministries of Daniel Baker, Isaac Jones, and William Claybourne Walton of Virginia. Sometimes they were shunned. But the Arminianized evangelicalism of New Haven theology that Finney represented, where soteriology made Christ human and anthropology made humans Christlike, became the common coin of the evangelical realm. Even when Calvinist terminology endured, with the architect of "New Divinity" and Yale theology professor Nathaniel Taylor refusing to jettison it while making freedom of the will and God's moral government the new workhorses of theology, Calvinist doctrine had been transformed into a practical Arminianism. What disparagers called the "cannotism" of Calvinism increasingly found itself in an inhospitable theological and social climate. Don't wait for feeling, Finney said. "DO IT."

CONVERSION

What sinners were supposed to do, whether they felt like it or not, was get converted. Nothing was dearer to the evangelical heart than conversion; it was both coat of arms and call to arms for evangelicalism. As coat of arms, conversion was what the many and various evangelical denominations had most in common. Evangelicals could argue and fight over many things, but they were united in seeing nothing more important than saving lost sinners, reproducing the new birth, and promoting the life of holiness.

This manifested itself in nearly everything, from denominational structures geared for missions and revivals to a new conception of the ministry in which the major function of the pastor was to win souls to Jesus.

Evangelicals divided life into three stages: preconversion, conversion, and postconversion. With Finney the nature of preconversion changed. The heart was now made a person's spiritual center, and a change in heart could be effected by a change of purpose or will. The title of Billy Graham's magazine *Decision* sums up the inheritance of this theological revolution that removed conversion from the realm of destiny. Conversion was not something one awaited but rather what one worked for. Conversion was in one's own hands, as the title of one of Finney's most famous sermons suggests: "Sinners Bound to Change Their Own Hearts." Tracts filled with the sound of crackling flames and sinners screaming or techniques of self-control (especially in the sexual realm) were designed to show people "How to Change Your Heart" (another Finney sermon) and prevent those moral and spiritual slipups that might diminish the desire for change. Finney's handbook on how to mass-produce religious experiences, *Lectures on Revivals of Religion* (1835), which within three years went through seven editions in England, is a masterful textbook in marketing and techniques of mass persuasion. In the words of Tyler Owen Hendricks, "religious experience became one of the first products of American technology" ("Charles Finney and the Utica Revivals of 1826: The Social Effect of a New Religious Paradigm," Ph.d. diss., Vanderbilt Univ., 1983).

The conversion stage was marked by a period of "conviction," during which an unbeliever became conscious of the sinfulness of the soul, and a moment of conversion, both the heartbeat and headache of evangelical piety. By midcentury new models of piety had emerged whereby conversion was fast becoming less a convulsive, emotional crisis than a simple acceptance of Christ or a steady socialization of children and teenagers in the evangelical ethos. In fact, the distinction between crisis and gradual conversions dissolved in the catachetics of conversion taught by evangelical parents, churches, and societies, whose efforts reaped such rich harvests during revivals. Horace Bushnell's famous 1846 dictum "that the child is to grow up a Christian" and, as he later added in other editions, " never know himself as being otherwise" (*Views of Christian Nurture,* 1847), can be found operating early in the century through the Sunday school movement and later in the century in the Young Men's and Young Women's Christian Associations, where as late as 1890, 77 percent of the men's branches were holding prayer meetings or Bible classes.

A sizable segment of the evangelical community saw the quest for a second conversion as the dominant characteristic of the postconversion life. In general this meant, as Finney was one of the first to see, that one conversion was not enough and that Christians needed to be "frequently converted, and humbled, and broken down before God, and reconverted" if what had been obtained was to be retained. But technically a second conversion meant a tearing at the roots of sin in a believer's life, or what evangelicals variously called sanctification, going on to perfection, or the quest for holiness. The convert's desire to pass through the well-visited regions of sin and into the neighborhood of holiness were the rails on which evangelicalism ran. In the idiom of the nineteenth century, if conversion is getting a drowning person out of the water, sanctification is getting the water out of the person. Evangelicals were not of one mind as to how much water could be removed through the resuscitation of the Spirit, but they all believed that to love God was to hate sin.

The religious and cultural currents of Methodism, pragmatism, revivalism, romanticism, and realism flowed together into a sort of tide, floating perfectionist sentiments up in the evangelical mind until the pinnacle of the holiness movement was reached from 1840 to 1870. Phoebe Palmer, who along with Finney and Asa Mahan was a primary theologian of this movement, saw holiness as the "great doctrine of the Bible" around which all evangelicals might gather (Palmer, *Present to My Christian Friend, or Entire Devotion to God,* 1858). One cannot set limits on God, the argument went, or stand in the way of what God can do. "There is a shorter way," Palmer proclaimed in her best-selling *The Way of Holiness* (1850), a shortcut to sanctification that would make Christian perfection not a pilgrimage, or a process, but a present possession. In-

troducing "altar theology" into the argot of American evangelicalism, Palmer contended that whatever was placed on God's altar, God would sanctify. The divine will is for holiness; the only question is whether it is a human's will. Significantly, the visible expression of holiness supposedly manifested itself in labors toward the moral perfection of society. To be sanctified, Palmer said, is to be "set apart for holy service" (1850).

By midcentury a holiness emphasis asserted itself among American evangelicals that led to a reform-minded call for an alignment of personal morality with social and political purity. The way in which evangelicals related holiness doctrine to social currents can be seen in the life of Asa Mahan, the first president of Oberlin College, who was at the center of all the major reforms of his day: abolition, peace, women's rights, temperance, education. Women especially found their role in church and society expanded in the liberating wake of holiness teaching. Just as speaking in tongues certified the baptism of the Spirit for the twentieth-century charismatic movement, so speaking in public certified Pentecostal power for Palmer's followers. While later in the century holiness doctrines and ethical concerns retreated from the social arena and were evident only in individual conduct, the effect of the holiness movement on evangelicalism was to give it an attentiveness to everything (perhaps its most overlooked strength), an uncompromising spirit, and a rather difficult temperament. The enabling factor in the case of much evangelical social reform was perfectionism, and its uncompromising standards and unyielding disposition meant that evangelicalism did not suffer sin gladly, or passively. In the words of *Zion's Herald,* an unofficial New England Methodist weekly (1823–1955), about Phoebe Palmer's theology, "Her books make working Christians."

Whatever the reaction to the holiness movement, however, evangelicals were in agreement that there was life after conversion. Evangelicalism marched its newly converted recruits through postconversion paces, insisting on devotional disciplines and revival regimens that left evangelicals with a vast spiritual repertoire and a range of interior resources available for the ailments and agonies of human existence. Evangelicalism's postconversion stage also entailed certain action drills, which raises the issue of conversion's call to arms, its doctrines of usefulness.

USEFULNESS

More than an initiatory rite into the adult religious community, more than a means of resolving the conflict between personal anxieties and religious passions, and more than a plugging up of leaking doubts, conversion was most importantly a symbolic ritual by which one became deaf to the sirens of self and alive to vocational goals. Self-interest was replaced by "usefulness," the evangelical expression of the Protestant work ethic. The Puritan ethic of duty, its values of sobriety, frugality, and industry shattered by industrial morality, was rebuilt into an evangelical ethic of usefulness, with virtues of self-control, deferred gratification, and self-improvement that stand as the foundation of the modern work ethic. Asked if it were wrong to pray for happiness, Finney replied that even the devil could pray that prayer. After quoting a verse from the Psalms (51:13), Finney exclaimed: "See! The Psalmist did not pray for the Holy Spirit that he might be happy, but that he might be useful" (*Memoirs of Rev. Charles G. Finney,* 1876). Evangelicals immediately put the newly converted to work in a host of benevolent pursuits and viewed usefulness as a primary proof of conversion. Disinterested benevolence became the sum of Christian duty.

COMMONSENSE REALISM

What enabled Robert Baird to talk about evangelicalism as a religion of the book was the perception that the Bible was readily accessible to the study and exposition of individual Christians and that no aids or authorities other than common sense were necessary for admittance. Faith in the common person's ability to expose humbug and search out truth and a commonsense approach to theological matters were the hallmarks of the Scottish school of commonsense realism, which supplied the philosophical presuppositions for evangelical theology. The soil of Lockean epistemology, lumpy with ab-

stractive, hypothetical deposits, proved too rocky for evangelical theology to express itself and develop. Instead, for most of the nineteenth century the flower of evangelicalism grew in Scottish realism's rich soil of Baconian inductive methodologies, which proved to have such fertilizing properties in American religious life. The Baconian commonsense system united with the compatible doctrines of Arminianism and a popularized Enlightenment "rhetoric of rights" to overthrow the reigning Calvinist academic orthodoxy and to become the new foundation of evangelicalism.

Scottish realism proved so attractive in America because its instincts were toward egalitarianism, voluntarism, and pragmatism. It claimed that the mind could actually grasp what it perceives and that awareness of God can be direct and immediate. The dictates of common sense, self-evident truths, and obvious intuitions verified right and wrong, God's existence, and the hereafter. As Alexander Campbell proclaimed in his famous 1828 debate with Robert Owen, skepticism rests on speculation and hypotheses, but the Christian faith is built on facts and experience. Evangelicals could now profess to be in touch with both the commonsense assumptions of American society and with the day's most advanced scientific method of empirical investigation. In fact, commonsense realism and moral philosophy, which was the application of inductive scientific reasoning to the intellectual, social, and moral universe and was a required course in almost every seminary and college in nineteenth-century America, were largely one and the same. The psychology taught by such courses and by the commonsense method itself stressed the importance of introspection and led to the ceaseless scrutiny of motives and self-administered spiritual autopsies so characteristic of evangelical piety.

MILLENNIALISM

The construction of the millennium was the evangelicals' dream, and its deconstruction their nightmare. Millennialism is the belief in a future, thousand-year period of blessedness based on ideas popular in Jewish apocalyptic literature, the teachings of Jesus about the coming "kingdom of God," and the Book of Revelation, especially chapter 20. To look at evangelicalism's millennial ideology, then, is to look at the myths and monsters with which it lived.

Ever since postmillennialism made its triumphal entry into American religion with Jonathan Edwards, evangelicals drew from a common pool of millennial ideas, which gave evangelicalism its peculiar velocity, valor, and intellect. Briefly stated, postmillennialism was an attempt to slip the restraints of history and to erase the boundaries between heaven and earth. The millennium would not only be followed by the Second Coming of Christ, which advocates of premillennialism worked hard to prove was putting first things last, but could actually be ushered in by human initiative and industry in spreading righteousness over the earth. It stands as one of the most potent mythologies in all of American history.

The memory nineteenth-century evangelicals invoked was a richly apocalyptic and dramatic one—the Puritan errand into the wilderness, the First Great Awakening, the rise of the new nation —and the events they were living through seemed no less eschatological in significance. The early Methodist leaders Francis Asbury and Jesse Lee both interpreted the revivals of the Second Great Awakening as heralding the dawning "glories of the millennium" in which "the kingdoms of this world would soon become the kingdoms of the Lord and of his Christ" (William B. Bennett, *Memorials of Methodism in Virginia*, 1871; Jesse Lee, *Short History of the Methodists*, 1810). Finney's dizzy decree that the millennium could come in America in three years if the church got busy exists against this mythic background that reduced peaks to hillocks. A plethora of activities radiated from this central belief. Indeed, postmillennialism became a primary mechanism for translating evangelical goals into social and political realities. Building a millennium became the international industry of the evangelical empire.

The evangelical era was one of millennial ambition. The coincidence of biblical prophecies with the stirrings of the Spirit in the new nation was so striking that evangelicals came to believe that America was chosen to be God's crucible from which would emerge the millennium. When evangelicals believed not only that millennialism was to mold the values of the American republic but that the American republic itself was a value that would mold the millennium, a dis-

tinct "civil millennialism" was introduced to transform America from a nation that would be redeemed into a "redeemer nation." The compelling entirety of this vision was difficult to resist. Alexander Campbell, the founder of the Disciples of Christ, initially opposed to any means other than a united church in bringing about the millennial restoration of apostolic purity, changed his mind by the 1840s to allow for the use of voluntary societies in building the kingdom of God. It was but a short step from there for Campbell to embrace the ideal of a "Christian America" as the primary instrument of millennial regeneration. The degree to which the concept of a redeemer nation took hold can also be seen during the Civil War, when both sides defined their purpose and mission in the civil millennialist terms memorialized in the Great Seal of the United States, in which the watchful eye of God (the eye above the pyramid surrounded by rays of light) conveys both the joy of *Annuit Coeptis* ("He has favored [our] undertaking") and the judgment of how well we are doing at creating this *Novus Ordo Seclorum* ("A New Order of the Ages") and in which the eagle holds in its talons the two ways in which the millennial vision of *E Pluribus Unum* ("From Many, One"), which the eagle holds in its beak, is to be established: through conquest (arrows of war) or the contagion of its example (olive branch of peace).

A subtle shift also began in the nineteenth century that altered the definition of American destiny from the expansion of evangelical values in the creation of a "righteous empire" into the notion of an American "manifest destiny," a concept that was widespread long before it became a slogan in 1845. Evangelicals replaced the theological doctrine of predestination with a political doctrine of predestination—the evangelical empire was predestined and thus had a natural right to expand to its geographical boundaries, which were across the continent, and to its religious boundaries, which were across the globe. By becoming "manifest" American destiny departed in a significant way from the Puritan portrayal of the destiny of the chosen people, which held that the ultimate reason for God's selection of Israel was hidden in mystery and the inscrutability of the divine will. But when postmillennialism was yoked with manifest destiny, God's election of the New Israel was for clear, manifest reasons: a superior form of government, geographical location, benevolence of the people, mastery of nature, the utilization of natural resources, religious ideals, and similar progressive virtues. Just how far such ideas spread can be seen in the words of Herman Melville, far from a conventional evangelical Christian: "We Americans are the peculiar, chosen people—the Israel of our time: we bear the ark of the liberties of the world."

Evangelicalism's rather rarefied view of its mission and its obstinate refusal to scale itself down to lifesize were the by-products of postmillennial theology. Postmillennialism did, however, cast two shadows, one of evolutionary progress and the other of apocalyptic regress, perfectionism, and primitivism. The nineteenth-century mood was an odd amalgam of the sense of great promise and great peril. Postmillennialism provided evangelicals with a vehicle for expressing this double vision and for endorsing a new social order while keeping alive the memory and imagery of the old. Evangelicalism reflected the breakdown of traditional New England social structure by sharpening divisions between converted and nonconverted, God and the world, home and business, work and leisure, reason and emotion, private and public. But postmillennialism functioned as the pivot which saw to it that both blades of the scissors did the cutting, as biblical symbols were used to invest the rise of a modern society and its attendant sphere of differentiation and function-specialization with eschatological meaning and legitimacy.

Not until the last decades of the nineteenth century were postmillennial beliefs seriously challenged. They began to come apart after the Civil War because the props that supported them were weakened. De-emphasis on conversion meant that evangelicals were no longer forced to rehearse personally the apocalyptic drama. Biblical criticism eroded the apocalyptic imagery and symbols that maintained postmillennialism's stability. Heaven was domesticated and made more an extension of ordinary life, and hell increasingly was dismissed—like death, people preferred not to talk about it. Premillennial notions of the Second Coming, the Great Tribulation, and the Last Judgment, which had been present throughout the century as a subdominant theme, now began to take over. But for one group of evangelicalism's descendants, the Social Gospelers, the nineteenth century ended where it had

begun, with the attempt to build the kingdom of God on earth.

There was another side to millennialism, however, that revealed evangelicalism's darker desperations. The millennial destiny of the American nation called for expansion, but it was an expansion by extension, not integration. Furthermore, whenever there is the concept of a chosen people, there is always the implicit, and commonly explicit, notion that some people are not chosen, and therein the seeds of nativism find soil for growth. The cultural score and high-fever pitch of postmillennialism made it difficult for a residual nativism not to sound throughout virtually all of nineteenth-century evangelicalism. At various times Freemasons, Mormons, Roman Catholics, and others found themselves labeled a sinister force, and the public sentiment lashed into a state of fury against them. At first nativism played itself out largely in the religious arena, but after 1835 evangelicals increasingly expressed their nativist sentiments through political channels. A good example of this is the anti-Masonic movement, which thrived along with revivalism in the flourishing townships of the so-called burned-over district of western New York in the late 1820s and 1830s. Beginning as a highly motivated evangelical crusade against what was perceived as an occult conspiracy and rival to the church, by the mid-1830s evangelical ultra anti-Masonry had been joined by political anti-Masonry bent on party-building. The latter group was successful in establishing the first effective third party in American history and pioneered in the development of the modern party system through the innovative use of the party platform and the nominating convention. Although political anti-Masonry was no longer a potent force after 1840, evangelical anti-Masonic excitement was not spent until the 1880s, and even then it was perpetuated by holiness groups, some of which based their opposition to labor unions on the same principles.

What frightened evangelicals most, however, were Roman Catholics. Two sermons by two of evangelicalism's most respected leaders, Lyman Beecher and Horace Bushnell, reveal more than any other sources evangelicalism's acute fears and spleen. Beecher's *Plea for the West* (1835) and Bushnell's *Barbarism: The First Danger* (1847) only were models for increased intensity in scores of other anti-Catholic sermons preached by evangelicals in isolating infidelity, popery, and slavery as the triple threat to America's millennial destiny. By 1850 the ethnic identity of most state populations had been severely scrambled. Confronted by a growing Roman Catholic electorate, evangelicalism closed ranks in defense of its hegemony. Evangelicals feared conspiracies against republican institutions amid the social and political crises of the antebellum decades, and they linked despotism with popery, based on Roman Catholic views on popular education and church government. Evangelicalism's increasingly denunciatory style, fueled by the public naming of and praying for unconverted sinners in "new-measures revivalism" and the abolitionist controversy, provided the flammable conditions that could ignite nativist flareups.

But most important was evangelicalism's sensitivity about Roman Catholic inroads in the West, where the population was sparse, where Catholic presence was noticeable, and where missionary endeavors and millennial hopes were high. The belief that the Pope had designs on the Mississippi Valley as a future site for the Vatican was widely accepted by evangelical leaders and associations, and they organized to prevent the Roman Catholic Church from wresting the West out of their control. Anti-Catholic voluntary associations such as the short-lived Christian Alliance, formed in 1843, were founded with the contradictory goals of the "promotion of religious freedom" and the destruction of Roman Catholicism. Its officers included such evangelical luminaries as Lyman Beecher, Nathaniel W. Taylor, Leonard Bacon, and Horace Bushnell. The successor body was the American and Foreign Christian Union, a merger of the Christian Alliance, the Foreign Evangelical Society, and the most important of the anti-Rome groups, the American Protestant Society. The religious press and church organizations fell in with this anti-Catholic crusade, and all too many evangelicals were more than eager to be conscripted into the ugly war against Rome by the Native American Party (1845) and the Know-Nothing Party of the 1850s.

Historians must be careful, however, not to overstate this nativist phenomenon of bullying piety. Evangelicals drew from an abundant tradition of antipopery, and the closer assessments of nativism get to popular sources, the more it appears that nativism was less severe or deep than many have supposed. Even evangelical leaders who enjoyed their role in stirring up nativist feelings could give public recognition and praise to the Roman Catholic clergy's leadership in charitable and public health activities. Evangelical strategists also saw in anti-Catholic rhetoric a financial ploy. By pointing to a competitor in the race to conquer the West, fund-raising appeals carried more urgency and weight. Finally, the immense popularity of nativist literature like Maria Monk's salacious *Awful Disclosures of the Hotel Dieu Nunnery of Montreal* (1836) may be less a reflection of common values than the nineteenth-century equivalent of pornography interpreted as having a redeeming social value.

METHODS AND TACTICS OF EVANGELICALISM

Evangelicalism was a faith that knew its business. Its tactics for the transformation of American culture were sophisticated and smart, involving some of the newest techniques in communications, fund-raising, promotions, entertainment, education, organization, and evangelism. To explore such subjects as evangelical publications, play, worship, revivalism, camp meetings, voluntary societies, seminaries, and colleges is to look at the center of American social and religious life.

Evangelical presses produced an extensive offering of popular literature, and the most modern methods of communication were expertly used to manufacture and manipulate symbols. Evangelicalism both catered to America's enormous religious appetite for devotional, educational, editorial, hagiographical, and homiletical literature and created on its own a love for books. A tremendous flow of literature was channeled in the direction of every conceivable age, interest, and denominational group. Evangelicals not only skillfully used the printing press to create a pantheon of heroes like those in Protestant missions, for example, but evangelical missionary heroes such as the Judsons wrote books targeted and retailed to markets like female piety and youthful sensibilities, which they also helped to shape. Adoniram Judson, known as the "Apostle of Burma," was one of the first foreign missionaries of the American churches. Two early biographies illustrate his influence on popular missionary literature: Francis Wayland's *A Memoir of the Life and Labors of the Rev. Adoniram Judson* (1854) and Robert Middleditch's *Burmah's Great Missionary* (1854). Of even greater influence in shaping the popular missionary literature market were the three wives of Judson. Ann Hasseltine Judson's *A Particular Relation of the American Mission to the Burman Empire* (1823) stimulated enthusiasm and involvement on the part of American Baptists for the missionary enterprise. Sarah Hall Boardman Judson expressed her missionary zeal in poetry that frequently found its way into religious publications. Emily Chubbuck had established herself as a popular fiction writer under the pen name of "Fanny Forester." After her marriage to Judson in 1846 such publications as *An Olio of Domestic Verse* (1852), *Memoir of Sarah B. Judson* (1848), and *The Kathayan Slave and Other Papers Connected with Missionary Life* (1853) helped shape this new market.

The autobiographical genre of pious memoirs was a staple of the evangelical diet. Voluntary societies and denominations alike made use of the printed word, developing their own periodicals, tracts, and volumes, with annual reports even designed to be distributed as popular documents. In its first five years (1833–1838) the American Antislavery Society put out three-quarters of a million pieces of propaganda. By the time the evangelical industry swung into full production, the American Sunday School Union and the American Tract Society sold thousands of tracts, pamphlets, and books, distributing in 1836 a total of seventy-three million pages of printed material. To look at it from the standpoint of mass marketing, the American Tract Society developed a distribution system whereby a new tract a month could be personally delivered to every household in New York City.

Falsely caricatured by contemporaries as having fire in their bellies and ice in their veins, American evangelicals could be grim and determined in their opposition to any form of literature or amusement in which God was not to be found. But evangelicals did not simply cast an unsmiling eye over entertainments they found loathsome; they also worked to put something wholesome in their place. During the nineteenth century the most significant form of popular culture was the theater, which was dominated by melodrama. To a group trying to get people to listen to the latest word from heaven, melodrama's fairground of frivolity, seduction, and sentimentalism seemed to convey the latest word from the pit. With furrowed brows and cross tones evangelicals were quick to pounce on dancing, theaters, taverns, circuses, novel reading, card playing, and cockfighting as unholy pursuits. But at the same time evangelicals generated their own solemn thrills and created a host of what they called "moral" or "reform" entertainments such as mass meetings, lectures, concerts, exhibitions, public debates, and traveling museums with moral dramas and religious art. Holidays like the Fourth of July were turned into evangelical rituals, replete with Sunday school parades, picnics, readings, and orations. In the period 1845–1855 numerous temperance and abolitionist dramas were introduced specifically to be the evangelical counterparts of popular, "immoral" theater presentations. The most popular of these were the reform dramas *The Drunkard; or, The Fallen Saved* by William H. Smith and George L. Aiken's adaptation of Harriet Beecher Stowe's *Uncle Tom's Cabin*, both plays breaking every existing performance record and attracting evangelicals into the theater for the first time.

MUSIC AND EVANGELICALISM

Evangelical worship habits had an important role to play in the Christianization of popular culture. Evangelicals transformed the order, conduct, and liturgical setting of worship to make it more accessible. Preaching, praying, and singing now carried most of the weight of worship. Worship revolved around plentiful preaching, mostly extempore, and homespun homilies that moved people to action, giving each listener something to do. Prayer was the liturgical spur of evangelical worship, and in its various forms (private prayer, social prayer, family prayer, prevailing prayer, and others) was the very lifeblood of evangelicalism itself. But it was in the realm of music that evangelicals made some of the most far-reaching changes.

Evangelicalism popularized hymns as an important component of the worship life of the American people. By introducing and experimenting with a wide variety of hymn styles such as camp-meeting spirituals, slave spirituals, Sunday school songs, revival songs, and devotional hymns, evangelicals spurred the development of new forms of hymnody while spurning conservative forces like those that resisted congregational hymn singing or the trend for American churches to install organs during the first half of the nineteenth century. In the amalgam of revival songs and devotional hymns (plus white minstrel songs) that combined in the 1850s and 1860s to form the gospel music tradition, evangelicalism gave America its own distinctive hymn style. Evangelicalism increased the role of music in worship throughout the nineteenth century with more hymn-singing, special music, and instrumental accompaniments until by the time of Dwight L. Moody and Ira D. Sankey the hymn was almost equal to the sermon in importance. By 1880 the pattern that obtains today was set: evangelists have music professionals on their staff, and in evangelical worship music takes up as much time as anything else.

Unfortunately, the significance of the hymn in evangelical culture has been more affirmed than explored. One evangelical pastor in 1889 looked back over his shoulder at American religious life and concluded that "the hymnbook is next to the Bible among religious books in its influence over mind and heart" (Robert S. MacArthur, *Baptist Quarterly Review,* 11, 1889). Evangelicals memorized hymns and sang them everywhere. Hundreds of hymnbooks sold millions of copies. The power of the sung text was felt from the fire altars of rural Cane Ridge, Kentucky, to the fancy platforms of Billy Sunday's metropolitan campaigns. Hymns helped to draw people together ("praise songs"), melt the hardened heart ("experience" and "burden" songs), entice the sinner to the altar ("mourner" and "invitation" songs), set the newly converted to work ("martial songs"), help the community say good bye to each other ("farewell songs"), and do all of the above ("slave spirituals"). The evangelical worship style required and relied heavily upon the emotional involvement of the participants garnered through the catchy choruses, repetitive refrains, and haunting melodies of the hymns. In the words of the widely used *Sabbath Hymn and Tune Book* (1859), an evangelical worshipper was supposed to "make the song his own, assuming the words are real expressions of the inward sense of his own soul."

Hymns were a primary means of building community, creating moods, and releasing pent-up emotions. While evangelical hymnody was not written to teach theology or to confess beliefs, these "sermons in song" did help evangelicals to believe their confessions in God's love, grace, and forgiveness, thereby giving primary expression to American evangelical theology. In their Christocentric focus on the sacrifice Jesus made on the cross (of the more than eight thousand hymns she wrote, perhaps Fanny Crosby's "Jesus Keep Me Near the Cross" best exemplifies this evangelical theology), the hymns paradoxically pointed to the depth of human sinfulness while at the same time lifting up the height of human worth and value.

Rural revivals led the way in fusing music and message in the revival ritual. Why urban revivalists did not integrate hymns more fully into their services is still unclear. Finney used hymnals especially published for his meetings, and to direct his choirs he employed the noted hymnist and sacred music teacher Thomas Hastings, who along with Lowell Mason dominated church music for half a century from 1825 and published in 1831 *Spiritual Songs for Social Worship,* a dignified alternative to the popular collections of texts set to the tunes of love songs, circus music, and street songs that were widely used at camp meetings. But Finney believed that singing could injure a prayer meeting, for it was the "agonizing spirit" produced by prayer that brought people to the point of conversion, not the "spirit of joy" created by music. Throughout the Second Great Awakening and up until the Union Prayer Meeting Revival, which most historians date from 1857 to 1860 but which is best interpreted as America's Third Great Awakening, lasting until about 1870 and part of a great worldwide evangelical revival, music was less important to evangelicals in the North than in the South, where plain folk first added choruses to Wesleyan hymns, speeding them up, and where popular collections like the shape-note songster *The Sacred Harp* (1844) were first published and are still in use today in some rural areas. The prominence of music in evangelical worship in 1876 was illustrated in the emergence of a new class of professionals—gospel song composers like Fanny Crosby, one of the most important figures in the gospel music tradition, not just because she wrote thousands of hymn texts, but because she proved conclusively that Isaac Watts was right in claiming that people would remember a song far more easily than a sermon, and musical evangelists like Philip Paul Bliss, Philip Phillips, John R. Sweney, and Crosby's close friend and promoter Ira D. Sankey.

THE SUNDAY SCHOOL

Evangelicals exerted a tremendous educational force in nineteenth-century America. In their infant schools and Sunday schools evangelicals proved that they knew how to reach the children of America and educate them in the rudiments of learning, piety, and citizenship. Infant schools functioned as both day-care facilities for working-class mothers with children in the two-to-six age bracket and as nurseries for future Sunday school pupils. Like infant school, Sunday school began as a mission to the children of the urban poor and unchurched working classes. Many evangelical clergy at first were reluctant to embrace Sunday school education, primarily because it originated outside the church and was dominated by laity (many of whom were women), but they quickly saw the potential in the movement and transformed it in the evangelical image. Although educational attention was refocused to give pride of place to the children of the church, evangelicals first used Sunday schools as another device along with picnics, even fishing trips (and later "inquiry meetings" and moral dramas), to draw converts from the working classes and urban dispossessed. By 1828 one-seventh of the nation's children ranging in age from five to fifteen were attending Sunday schools. More than a few early labor leaders testified to having had their thinking and action shaped by religious rhetoric and Sunday school piety learned while they sat in classrooms for two-and-a-half hours of instruction each Sunday, and then marched to sit with their teachers in church during the morning worship.

Sunday schools were of critical importance to American evangelicalism for three reasons. First, through the Sunday school movement laity achieved outstanding success independent of clergy, thereby elevating their confidence as evangelical leaders and giving them a sense of ownership of the movement. Too much ownership, some clergy felt. The revivalist Asahel Nettleton complained to Lyman Beecher about the new power of the laity whereby "it is much easier now to 'shake off' a minister that is disliked" (*Letters of the Rev. Dr. Beecher and Mr. Nettleton*, 1828). In particular, Sunday schools provided an opportunity for women to enter new fields of endeavor like social work, classroom teaching, personnel supervision and organizational management, theological study, and librarianship. Women gave the earliest impetus for founding Sunday schools, and the majority established in this country were like the one founded in Utica, New York, in 1816, when five young women labored to organize the city's first Sunday school, facing the scowls of their pastor and the indifference of their church. Some clergy at first saw the interdenominational, lay-controlled Sunday school movement as presenting a direct threat to their leadership by taking on the moral and religious education of the young. As if to have their worst fears confirmed, juvenile literature presented the Sunday school teacher, not the pastor, as the person dying children most likely called to witness their last words and receive their final expressions of gratitude before sinking back into the eternal arms of Jesus. Clergy were actually barred from holding office or being managers of the most aggressive of the voluntary societies, the American Sunday School Union, which was founded in 1824 by Joanna and Divie Bethune with the intent of uniting Sunday schools into a uniform, structured, assertive, propagandist body. Other clergy welcomed the Sunday school as an auxiliary to the ministry of the church.

What none could do was ignore it. By the 1820s, a concentrated effort by American denominations to make Sunday schools into the church's institution began. The general conference of the Methodist Episcopal Church in 1824, for example, made it "the duty of each traveling preacher in our connexion to encourage the establishment and progress of Sunday schools." When Presbyterian ministers vacillated in their support of Sunday schools, they were admonished with the reminder from the Princeton Sunday School Union that "the period of the world in which our brief space for action is assigned us, though marked by many important characteristics, is peculiarly distinguished by the influence it will probably have on the coming of the millennium" (*Plans and Motives for the Extension of Sabbath Schools, Addressed to Clergymen*, 1829).

NINETEENTH-CENTURY EVANGELICALISM

The second point marking the critical importance of Sunday schools is that as the century progressed, Sunday schools increasingly carried the weight of being the primary vehicle for evangelism, especially among the children of the faithful but also as a means toward the end of evangelical world conquest. Sunday school books and ditties functioned as a motherland of myth whereby the epic stories, heroes, and spiritual sureties were passed on to succeeding generations, who were thereby tutored to think in biblical clichés. Evangelicalism's story literature was enormous, and the Sunday school library was often the only source available for reading material, especially volumes suitable for young children. Through Sunday school libraries evangelicals could penetrate even the most inhospitable households, as every week a child could take home a tiny "children's Bible," with illustrative engravings, or a catechism book, or any number of devotional tear-jerkers, most likely stories about some child "ripening early for heaven" with the obligatory deathbed scenes that sold books in nineteenth-century America. Sunday school literature taught that children are sinful and in dire need of their Savior's redeeming love, but at the same time never chronicled a child's actual descent into hell at death. At the moment of truth it was the child's innocence that evangelicals extolled, and the specter of eternal damnation was washed away by the tears of a grieving mother or dedicated Sunday school teacher. Significantly, the books in Sunday school libraries, which were replaced toward the end of the nineteenth century by Sunday school handouts, championed few social reforms other than temperance.

As the revival spirit eventually settled in the Sunday school, the church's emphasis on conversion as an agent of church growth diminished. The centralized, bureaucratic character of public education, which was in place by 1880, was paralleled by developments in the Sunday school movement. "Uniform" was now the magic word, as evangelical leaders sought to replace revivalism with the Sunday school as the major unifying force in American religious life. The Uniform International Lesson Plan, which was pushed through the National Sunday-school Convention by Methodist John H. Vincent and Baptist Benjamin F. Jacobs in 1872 over the opposition of denominational boards, replaced biblical memorization with a systematized curriculum based on the quarter system and a carefully plotted journey through the Old and New Testaments in a seven-year cycle replete with familiar features such as a weekly "Golden Text." The disciplined, ordered, and efficient pattern to evangelicalism's new approach to evangelism found economic equivalents in American industrial life, with in many cases the same names—the Colgates, H. J. Heinz, John Wanamaker—leaders in both.

The third point of importance is that from the very beginning evangelicals used the Sunday school both for conversion toward church membership and for moral instruction toward American citizenship. The Sunday school, it was believed, could produce moral character for democracy, build a Christian America, and provide America with a constantly renewed soul. The 1828 charter of the American Sunday School Union defined the Sunday school as an institution "eminently adapted to promote the intellectual and moral culture of the nation, to perpetuate our republican and religious institutions, and to reconcile eminent and national prosperity with moral purity and future blessedness" (*The Charter: Being a Plain Statement of Facts . . .*). At first Sunday schools worked in partnership with the public schools, with the American Sunday School Union attempting to place its books in elementary schools. But eventually evangelicals were willing to turn over to the state the education of their children because it was essentially an evangelical parochial education that was being carried on. The public school system had become the unofficial educational wing of evangelical Protestantism. Roman Catholics opposed public schools precisely because of the evangelical Protestant tenor of their teaching, and this became one of the major factors promoting the development of an extensive parochial school system throughout the country.

In one sense the Sunday school and its successor, the common school, were an extension of a number of child-rearing concerns of the family. Lessons found in *The Union Spelling Book* and *The Sunday School Spelling Book,* not to mention the *McGuffey Readers* (which were textbooks for 75 percent of the nation's children for most of the nineteenth century), centered on moral issues such as lying, temperance, and honesty and provided catechetical training in republican values,

NINETEENTH-CENTURY EVANGELICALISM

including those that portrayed America as a midwife to the millennium. The biblical content of the public school curriculum diminished until by 1900 it was virtually nonexistent. But there was a similar loss within evangelicalism itself, with personal conduct increasingly guided in the North by guilt and conscience. Southern conduct seemingly held more tenaciously to old patterns based on the Bible, home, and honor.

Evangelical initiatives in higher education were ambitious and highly successful. Evangelicalism regained control over educational institutions in the 1830s and 1840s and became the dominant force on most college campuses by 1850. The American Education Society (1826) and the Society for the Promotion of Collegiate and Theological Education in the West (1843) made the nineteenth century into an era of educational experimentation and college building. Baptists and Methodists founded colleges in western states—Ohio, Indiana, and Illinois by the early 1840s, Michigan by the 1850s. And through the hundreds of female seminaries established by evangelicals across the country women were provided an education that approached, if not rivaled, that of men.

REVIVALISM

The main ritual of evangelical Protestantism and the fundamental armature that held up evangelicalism's complex structure in widely different settings was revivalism. Perry Miller called revivals "the defining factor" of nineteenth-century American life, and credited Finney, the founder of modern revivalism, with leading America out of the eighteenth century (*Life of the Mind in America*, 1965). Revivalism proved so successful that by 1830 in the South, where skepticism had been the intellectual and genteel fashion during the eighteenth century, evangelicalism became the convention.

Revivalism was, first and foremost, evangelicalism's chief instrument of evangelism, giving way to Sunday schools as the century progressed. The four to six days of virtually nonstop preaching, praying, singing, testifying, and visiting had as their uppermost goal the salvation of sinners. Preaching was directed at turning attention to human sinfulness and the need for divine grace, overturning whatever blockages prevented the will from making a decision. Prayer

meetings were designed to meet the needs of almost every type of sinner, with "inquiry meetings" scheduled just for those who had reached the stage of conviction but had not yet experienced the moment of conversion. Sinners were visited house-to-house at the request of family and friends. And songs were sung that made strangers feel less estranged from God and from each other.

Revivalism also shows most clearly the ecumenical, transatlantic cast to the movement. Primitivist tendencies helped give revivalism its ecumenical complexion, as all traditions found their bloodlines in the early church, away from creedal and clerical encrustations. Revivalism not only gained the confidence of and created a common ritual for members of popular denominations but in the process prodded ecumenical initiatives of major importance. The symbiotic, transatlantic character of English and American revivalism is illustrated in the 1846 meeting of the Evangelical Alliance in London, gathered to rally around a common core of beliefs only to fall apart within a few days over slavery issues. Evangelicals helped to stir up urban revivalism in America, while American evangelists such as Finney, Moody, and James Caughey raked up the ashes of religious fervor once again in England, Scotland, and Wales.

Revivalism also proved flexible enough to accommodate various styles and strategies. The one hundred fifty different revivalists who labored in Rochester, New York, between 1825 and 1835 represented one of three basic types of antebellum revivalism. First, there was the new-measures revivalism of Finney, for whom revivals were not "showers" sent from heaven, as the Puritans had likened them, but socially engineered structures that resulted from "the right use of the appropriate means." Second, there was the predominant alternative to new measures misleadingly called "reasonable revivalism" or more accurately "respectable revivalism," which characterized the evangelistic outreach to the more educated and aristocratic sectors of American society. It was this more orderly and subdued approach that appealed to the "gentlemen theologians" of the South, such as John Adger, Robert J. Breckenridge, John England, Richard Channing Moore, Thomas O. Summers, and John Holt Rice, who took the offensive against deists and skeptics, and which had such marked success in seminaries and colleges, especially in the South. Finally, there was the "camp-meeting revivalism" that did so much to shape and solidify patterns of popular and folk culture. Regardless of the differences over the means of promoting revivals (the respectable revivalist from Connecticut Asahel Nettleton snubbed Finney's western new-measures revivalists as "ragamuffins"), it was rare to find evangelicals attacking revivals themselves. The famous week of debates among clergy representatives from the East and West that took place in New Lebanon in 1827 and put new-measures revivalism on trial was really a family dispute, since all who attended supported revivalistic evangelicalism.

Revivalism also proved to be an integrative, transitional social process that pushed a premodern society toward consensus around the values of a modern social state. As an "organizing process" revivalism gave moral direction and a unifying ideology to a young nation uncertain of its identity and legitimated new political and economic energies while preserving enough inherited norms to stabilize the social order.

COMMUNITY VS. INDIVIDUALISM IN REVIVALISM

Revivalism was a primary agent for creating a new sense of community based more on shared faith and feeling than on inherited social status. One of the most appealing features of evangelicalism was its offer of community, especially to persons who lived on the ground floor of a multistoried, hierarchical society. Initially, evangelicalism had a democratic, egalitarian spirit that ignored the steepness of the social hierarchy. The poem "Saturday Night" by a "Journeyman Mechanic" reveled in the republican significance of the Sabbath:

> Of rich and poor the difference what?—
> In working or in working not
> Why then on Sunday we're as great
> As those who own some vast estate.
> (Quoted in Sean Wilentz, *Chants Democratic: New York City and the Life of the American Working Class, 1788–1850,* 1984)

Revivalism cut across racial, class, and educational lines, creating unity and community out of diverse and sometimes antagonistic social groups. The intimate fellowships engendered by evangelicalism's communal democratic character go a long way in explaining the social interaction and close spiritual ties that often developed between blacks and whites, especially in the old South. Early-nineteenth-century evangelical culture was biracial; up until 1820 almost everything was shared in common. Whites testified without embarrassment to having learned to kneel through blacks. George Brown attended a camp meeting in 1813 outside Baltimore and heard his first black preacher: "The sermon revealed some things to me, first, that he was a capital preacher; and second, that I was a poor sinner in great danger of losing my soul" (*Recollection of Itinerant Life,* 1866). Evangelical religion is central to understanding the slave experience. It gave blacks meaning and purpose, a countervalue system to white racism, and the psychological strength to resist dehumanization.

As organic communities decomposed in American life, evangelicalism created voluntarist modes of social organization with standards of self-worth based not on deferential patterns or establishment definitions but on new distinctions that revolved around religious and communal values validated by the group itself. At a time when American society was becoming increasingly individualistic, evangelicalism provided individuals with a deeply social, republican religion where community life could be lived from a new center. In welcoming new converts who stepped from a cold, chaotic world into the warmth of a caring, intimate, disciplined, and orderly environment, evangelicals demonstrated that individuality and community need not be mutually exclusive.

The way in which evangelicalism addressed human impulses toward both individuality and community, while keeping the dialectic in balance, is manifested in the relationship of conversion to revivalism. Conversion was a profoundly individual experience, but because of the structures of revivalism it took place within the connectedness of community. Evangelical congregations summoned new converts and surrounded them with soul mates. People with shared experiences and ambitions held out the "right hand of fellowship"—they hugged, kissed, shouted for joy, and called each other "brother" and "sister." Even church discipline, which was intended to protect the community and ensure its purity, acknowledged the individual and aimed at restorative resolutions. The rich variety of translocal community life that evangelicalism offered its members—the denominations, the local, regional, and national benevolent societies, and the network of publications advocating evangelical values and causes—gave organizational witness to this preoccupation with community-building that nevertheless did not absorb the individual into a collective.

To be sure, the community-building features of evangelicalism suffered as the creed of individualism became more dominant, leaving Horace Bushnell to worry about revivalism's "fictitious and mischievous individualism" (*Views on Christian Nurture,* 1861). In fact, the uniting of individuals through a complex of small group support systems, gatherings, and associations (prayer meetings, class meetings, love feasts, camp meetings, voluntary societies, etc.) could actually lead to an attenuation of community ties, since the new communities thus formed, in their mobile, egalitarian, segmented, and utilitarian character, eroded more traditional understandings of "community" based on geography and authority. The trend for evangelicalism to lose its democratic passions and give in to American society's individualistic bent and middle-class bias became more pronounced as the Civil War approached. An underdeveloped sense of community can be seen, for example, in an evangelical biblicalism that was in place by the 1840s, where the right of private judgment reigned supreme over mediated authority. As middle-class values became the ultimate arbiters, the individual assumed greater importance than the community, and the gap between private interest and communal benefit became more severe. This can be seen in conceptions of the church's mission and social ethic, the opting for individualistic "romantic love" as a basis for marriage, and the loosening of the community's hold over individual conscience. But until the Civil War the ecology of evangelical religious life demonstrated a remarkable resistance to unbonded souls.

THE CAMP MEETING

The intensity and inclusiveness of evangelical community life is reflected sharply in one of the most remarkable phenomena of American history, camp-meeting revivalism. Going to camp meeting for evangelicals was like, as the hymn put it, "marching to Zion." A foretaste of the messianic banquet and the heavenly community, camp meetings were replete with invitatory symbols, rituals, and songs. One of the most frequent ways for a camp-meeting chorus or hymn to begin was with a hearty "Come": "Come to Jesus, come and welcome . . . "; "Come, ye sinners poor and needy . . . "; "Come, friends and relations, let's join heart and hand . . . "; "Come, sisters and brothers . . . "; "Come, all ye young people . . . "; "Come, thou fount of every blessing." The camp meeting was an earnest of eternity, a sacred space where heaven was home, the world was a place to pass through, and frontier disorder was rebuked by the settled order of sanctified community life. It was a community where all barriers were broken—physical, emotional, spiritual, and social. As one critic observed, camp meetings were "generally composed of a mixed multitude of all colors, nations and languages; and of the fanatics of all religious denominations. They encamp in the woods; and, after camping on for the space of three, four, five or six days and nights, in a manner which no tongue nor pen can describe, the actors become quite exhausted, and return home to recruit their strength and spirits for the next campaign" (*The Camp-Meeting, With a Variety of Songs, Poetry, Prose, Anecdotes, Riddles, etc.,* 1819; the book survives in a single copy only). Black and white, native Americans and immigrants, women and men, youth and aged, evangelicals and nonevangelicals, "professors" and "believers," were told to "Come" and imagine for a while what it would be like to live in the New Jerusalem:

> On Jordan's stormy banks I stand
> And cast a wishful eye
> To Canaan's fair and happy land
> Where my possessions lie.
>
> I am bound for the promised land,
> I'm bound for the promised land.
> O, who will come and go with me?
> I am bound for the promised land.

Camp meetings arose among plain folk on the southwestern frontier, the territory of Kentucky and Tennessee, where eye-gouging was a sport and slave-whipping a form of exercise. There is little wonder, then, that camp meetings from the very beginning exhibited physical piety and high-strung rituals. Virginia Baptists held overnight outdoor meetings as early as 1767, but camp meetings were not brought to the evangelical world's attention until a spiritual volcano erupted on the Kentucky frontier around 1800. Known as the Great Revival of 1800, it was these series of religious awakenings that established the South as the place of evangelical dominance. Legendary meetings at Red River in 1799, Gaspar River in 1800, and, most famous, Cane Ridge in 1801, under Methodist, Presbyterian, and Baptist auspices, brought camp meetings to the forefront of America's religious consciousness, where they remained as expressions of popular evangelical piety until the mid-1840s. At these gatherings unprecedented crowds from hundreds to thirty thousand were matched by spectacular conversions of notorious drunkards, criminals, prostitutes, and disbelievers. The emotional spectacles of the "exercises" (falling, jerking, barking, dancing, laughing, and other physical reactions) and the "impressions" (divine directions on problems in life such as marriage, business, and health) gave rise to the charge that people were being swooned into salvation.

Evangelicals sensed the psychological importance of large groups, but such goings-on scared many away. By 1805 the Baptists and Presbyterians had drawn back from sponsoring camp meetings, leaving them to the Methodists both to defend, as Lorenzo Dow (who introduced camp meetings in England in 1807) did so systematically in his *History of Cosmopolite* (1814), and to develop, which they did with great success, holding four hundred camp meetings by 1811, six hundred by 1816, and one thousand by 1820. The first Methodist bishop, Francis Asbury, demonstrated his enthusiasm for camp meetings when he chronicled the numbers saved and sanctified at an 1806 camp meeting in a letter to one of his presiding elders. Asbury concluded with the remark "Oh, my brother, when all our quarterly meetings become camp meetings, our American millennium will begin" (*The Journal and Letters of Francis Asbury,* 1958). But not until Methodists demonstrated that camp meetings could be wiped clean of impure emotions did other evangelical denominations begin to participate in them again.

Camp meetings were a favorite target for pop-

ular literature, especially novels, where sarcasm and criticism of camp meetings often came to a head. Critics did not lack material to work with. Apart from what contemporaries called the "religious catalepsy," camp meetings attracted to the grounds the evil as well as the good, the "Sabbath-breakers, rum-selling, tippling folk, infidels, and ruff-scruff generally" that Lyman Beecher associated with democratic gatherings (*Autobiography and Correspondence of Lyman Beecher,* 1865). Often people came to camp meetings with mixed motives: some women came for what amounted to a dress parade and cooking contests; some wealthy came to parade their power; some politicians came to seek votes; some merchants came to hawk wares, including a few with more than cider in their canteens; some town rowdies came to stir up trouble; and some young people came for reasons that are best not scrutinized too closely. In 1807 a not uncommon camp-meeting brawl occurred on the Wyoming-New York circuit after local ruffians had infiltrated the women's side of the camp-meeting tent and the men rushed to their aid. The result was a free-for-all and numerous arrests, including that of a presiding elder who struck someone with a hard right and landed in jail for assault; he was joined a little later by a red-faced Methodist bishop, who had also been arrested for fighting. The ignorant, indecorous, gullible features of those who attended an Arkansas camp meeting in the 1830s were satirized in a famous passage in Mark Twain's *The Adventures of Huckleberry Finn* (1884). Catharine Read Williams' *Fall River* (1834) allegedly documented the gross immorality promoted by camp meetings, and a popular anthology of poems, the first of which was entitled "The Camp-Meeting" (1819), was sexually explicit in describing how such events led to more souls being made than saved.

Perhaps camp meetings fell under the greatest suspicion, however, for their mixing of business with pleasure. In the words of a character in Mary Clemmer Ames's *Eirene* (1871), "The whole scene bore witness to what it was—a great religious picnic, in which material pleasure and human happiness blended very largely with spiritual experience." The camp meeting was a profoundly sensuous experience. For its defenders this was a source of its power, and for its detractors its peril. At camp meetings evangelicals enjoyed God, battled Satan, and consecrated the commonplace. They sensed the presence of God through smell, in the fragrance of nature's incense: the clean scent of the sawdust trail, the sweet odor of sap from the pine trees, the breath of smoke from the fire altars. While "tenting on the old campground," they sensed the presence of God through sight: in the beauty of nature and in the graceful arcs of a theologically-based elliptical layout of tents. Camp meetings were first called "open forest cathedrals" because they were held in nature's temple under the canopy of clouds by day and the chandelier of stars by night, when torches would cast their eerie shadows across the brush arbor and tents.

They sensed the presence of God through touch: through the feeling of the earth as a mattress and splintery logs as a pew; through the touching of each other in forgiving embrace at the mourner's bench, in the kiss of peace at the "glory pen," and in the handclasping ceremony at the speaker's platform.

They sensed the presence of God through sound: with the voice of singing, praying, and preaching. Evangelicals pined for upcoming camp meetings for they knew that "great shouters" would be there, as well as "plain preachers" who pioneered in the use of anecdotes and illustrations. The poetry of camp meetings' spiritual ballads, praise hymns, and revival spirituals was not among the finest of American literature, but in the words of Washington Irving, "The psalms thus chanted in the open air, by voices of great power and sweetness, had a solemn and a thrilling effect" (*The Life and Letters of Washington Irving*, 1864). The camp meeting's emotionalized theology was straight from the heart of experience and was bold in expressing the freedom, joy, and forgiveness evangelicals found in the Christian life.

There are some reports that the preaching got so intense at camp meetings that people forgot to eat. More often God was sensed through taste: people looked forward to camp meetings as a yearly oasis of hospitality in a wilderness of frontier loneliness and isolation—hospitality shown through sumptuous meals and cookouts. One report even suggests that the Cane Ridge camp meeting finally dispersed only because the food ran out.

The camp meeting may have been the product of the Kentucky-Tennessee southwestern frontier, but it did not stay there. It moved into the northwestern frontier of Illinois, Indiana, and Michigan, and from there into America's northern urban areas as part of "new measures" revivalism. Called "protracted meetings" by northern revivalists like Finney, these annual gatherings were held indoors in churches, public buildings, barns, anywhere that weather could not discourage the Spirit. Protracted meetings were held at all times of the year, including the winter months when industrially employed families could more easily fit spiritual activities into their crowded schedules. By allowing people to attend with minimal infringement upon work patterns or interference with daily routines, the protracted meeting proved to be a very versatile and popular form for releasing evangelistic energies. In some cases its adoption had the ironic effect of extending the duration of revival services, although increasingly the commitments people were asked to make were confined to the evening hours. The protracted meeting, or what eventually became known simply as the revival meeting, had been so successfully employed in the North that southern evangelicals began to drop the camp meeting in favor of the protracted meeting in the 1830s and 1840s. It was in the South that the protracted-meeting format achieved its greatest development.

By the time northern urban areas got around to adopting the camp-meeting model, it had been scrubbed free of frontier associations. The two-story gingerbread cottages, graveled avenues, showcasing of the arts and "higher" culture, and spacious resort atmosphere that one finds at an Ocean Grove, New Jersey (1869), or a Chautauqua, New York (1874), testifies to the attraction of the camp-meeting design for evangelicalism's newly attained middle-class respectability.

The most lasting effect of the camp meeting, however, was not on evangelical denominations like the Methodists, Baptists, or Presbyterians, or even on those holiness groups in the last third of the nineteenth century that particularized for their own purposes a repristinated camp-meeting tradition through the National Camp Meeting Association for the Promotion of Holiness (1867). The most enduring legacy of the camp meeting was in the realm of politics. The political rally was more than a secular counterpart to camp meetings. It was an actual borrowing of camp-meeting methods by American political party structures, and the nominating convention of today is probably the closest thing to an evangelical nineteenth-century camp meeting that most Americans experience.

VOLUNTARY AND MISSIONARY ACTIVITIES

Perhaps the most revealing frame in which the hopes and fears of evangelicalism were observable was the system of voluntary societies, known collectively as the Evangelical United Front or the "benevolent empire," which Alexis de Tocqueville esteemed the key to the vitality of American democracy. The first half of the nineteenth century witnessed the formation of hundreds of single-issue, lay-led, national, interdenominational voluntary associations aimed at making the identification of America and evangelicalism complete. When the Evangelical Alliance was formed in London in 1846, Americans could not get as excited as the British, who already had one. Such alliances of voluntary societies proved to be a potent means of social organization; they structured an integrative, disciplined, stable social existence for a dynamic, rapidly expanding society and supplied late-nineteenth-century corporate society with organizational models and precedents.

"Our age is singular and remarkable for its disposition to associate in action," Rufus Anderson of the American Board of Commissioners for Foreign Missions declared as he observed the multiplication of associations. The nineteenth century as an "Age of Action" was in large part another assertion of evangelical power and prestige and strong testimony to the vital social life of evangelical doctrines. The fundamental premise of these associations, which were modeled after older British societies, was that a nation could be conquered for Christ just as readily by collective action as by political coup. Millennial excitement gave unity and motivation to the multitudes of associations characterized by various degrees of political activism, social-class mix, and geographical identity and having as their goal almost every reform imaginable. "We are doing a work of patriotism, no less than that of Christianity," read the Constitution of the American Home Missionary Society (1826). The range of concerns represented in these societies reveals, more than any other source, the fact that evangelicalism would brook no boundaries, that it was willing to wander along paths on which it had no right of way, and that it was on the offensive against anything that endangered the planting of the kingdom of God on American soil.

Early evangelical action in the benevolent empire had worked diligently on two fronts, through multidenominational and denominational structure. By 1828 the federal government had spent for internal improvements from its foundation only seven hundred thousand dollars more than the combined revenues of the thirteen largest benevolent societies, and by 1840 the combined budgets of all voluntary societies probably exceeded that of the federal government. In 1860 one-third of the adult population of New York City belonged to at least one of the scores of church-related associations. And by that time a strong denominational self-consciousness had emerged, which threw the multidenominational agencies into disarray. Other forces besides denominational rivalry that worked toward the collapse of the evangelical united front were a shattering of Presbyterian unity in 1837, sectional rivalry, tension over slavery, and inadequate personnel. Some found the aggressive, confident, militant spirit of evangelical voluntarism a little too hectoring. John Leland retranslated Matthew 10:7 to fit in with this organized quest for evangelical dominion that evaporated so much of evangelicalism's energies during the antebellum period: "And as you go, preach to the people, your money is essential to the salvation of sinners, and therefore form into societies, and use all desirable means to collect money for the Lord's treasuries; for the millennium is at hand," (L. F. Greene, *The Writings of the Late Elder John Leland,* 1845). While many of the passions that animated evangelical organizational life in the antebellum period still burned strongly, a bureaucratic network of denominational structures had taken over by 1900.

There was general agreement that the evangelical united front stood for action; there was widespread disagreement about what action meant. For some action meant a vigorous evangelistic witness, which gave rise to the nineteenth century as "The Missionary Century." Virtually every missionary sermon and missionary society report sounds the millennial summons to make the "kingdom of grace," as one missionary preacher phrased it, coincident with the "kingdom of glory." The missionary character of evangelicalism can be seen in the way revivals sent the converted to the "Indian of the wilderness, to the depressed African, to the remote settler of the frontier, and to the poor in many other parts" (*General Assembly's Missionary Magazine,* I, January, 1805). At first evangelicals' preoccupation was with planting churches in the West, as the eschatological implications of western migration excited the missionary spirit. It seemed to many, as one concerned easterner said in 1800, that "all America seems to be breaking up and moving westward." But by 1830 the dream of world conquest became the *cause célèbre* of evangelicalism.

In the early national period evangelicals made no distinction between home-country and foreign missions. The fact that the founder and organizer of the American Board of Commissioners for Foreign Missions (*ca.* 1810), Samuel John Mills, Jr., spent most of his life working in home missions indicates the way most evangelicals saw both endeavors as partners in building the kingdom, although interest in overseas missions increased from various sources—the student revivals on college campuses as part of the Second Great Awakening, the drama and adventure associated with going to other lands that attended the growth of foreign trade and the development of international commerce, and the understanding of America as a "redeemer nation" chosen above other nations for a redemptive purpose. In a missionary sermon of 1824 Francis Wayland, the educational reformer and president of Brown University, asked, "What object ever undertaken by man can compare with this same design of evangelizing the world? Patriotism itself fades away before it" (*Moral Dignity of the Missionary Enterprise,* 1824). Evangelicals, who did nothing on a miniature scale, sincerely believed that the entire world could be converted. If mobilized to the missionary purpose, evangelicalism could convert the whole world in only twenty years, according to two members of the American Board of Commissioners for Foreign Missions (Gordon Hall and Samuel Newell, *The Conversion of the World,* 1818).

For others action meant moral suasion and social activism, which gave rise to the nineteenth century as "The Woman's Century." The dream of a Christian America inspired unprecedented numbers to come alive to their individual and social responsibilities. Just when the stride of aggregate action would seem to be checked by the realities of American life, an antebellum movement like new-measures revivalism would make evangelicalism a mighty social force by leading societies from benevolence to reform. Or crusades like antislavery, moral reform, or temperance would release new energies, zeal, liberal longings, and fresh recruits into associational ranks. Or a postbellum attempt to establish the kingdom in America—for example, the Social Gospel movement, which refocused attention away from the moral dilemmas of the poor and remedial social service to the culture of poverty and preventive social action—would resurrect memories of evangelicalism's working to make over the world.

By the 1850s, however, evangelicals began to reflect the sociological maxim that the more social integration of a group, the less able it is to criticize the normative assumptions of the larger society. Revivalism began to ignore social issues in favor of enhancing social stability. One of the major exceptions to this trend, however, was the reform of temperance, which by the 1840s had moved from moral suasion into legislative reform. Temperance enjoyed the greatest intensity and longevity of any reform movement in American history, and evangelicals were zealous in promoting it. Ten years after it was founded in 1826, the American Society for the Promotion of Temperance had eight thousand auxiliaries and over one and a half million practicing members. It is possible to link evangelicals and temperance too tightly, but the creation of cold-water or "dry" communities and the defeat of Demon Rum were the primary reform agendas of evangelicals in both North and South. Temperance reform has often been seen as an exercise in economic self-interest by masters and entrepreneurs who discovered that the traditional labor disciplines failed in a capitalist society. While the temperance crusade did have the effect of buttressing a capitalist system with an individualist ethic of self-discipline, self-improvement, and responsibility, evangelicals justified their temperance action as a religious and patriotic duty to build a sober and energetic republic of good rather than a drunken and lazy republic of evil.

WOMEN AS EVANGELISTIC FORCE

The fact that a substantial majority of temperance society members were women illustrates a larger truth about voluntary societies in particular, and evangelicalism in general: women were involved as both leaders and followers in disproportionate numbers. Throughout the century between two-thirds and three-quarters of evangelical church members were women. By 1840 there were over sixteen hundred women's missionary auxiliaries in existence, and while only one-quarter of the men's associations were actively raising money for missionary causes, two-thirds of the women's associations were making monetary contributions. Women's missionary societies of the last three decades of the century departed from earlier patterns in making "woman's work for woman" their dominant focus. But the entire system of voluntary societies throughout the century was largely a debt owed to evangelical women.

Evangelicalism afforded many satisfactions for women. Conversion offered women a higher allegiance; worship encouraged public speaking (praying, exhorting, testifying); reform commitments sanctioned public activities outside the home; voluntary societies gave women feminist solidarity as well as leadership training in a variety of skills; and the church itself afforded expansive and rewarding career advancements as the wife of a minister, missionary, or later in the century as a missionary or minister herself. Evangelicalism involved for women a continuous call to meetings, many of them conducted in homes where women were the keepers. It would be too much to call evangelicalism a "household religion," but as the family began to take on the nurturing, fulfilling function earlier associated with the "church" and "community," the importance of women to American society was enhanced. To be sure, there was often a high psychological cost to these evangelical women activists who challenged socially determined patterns of behavior. But in evangelicalism's legitimation of cultural changes that introduced new

roles and responsibilities some women found the strength to step forward.

EVANGELICALISM AND SLAVERY

Evangelical theology offered a critique of the social order and a heightened moral sensibility that spawned movements for social reform. Even evangelicals who persisted in defining sin in terms of personal morality nevertheless insisted that personal morality had an inevitable social dimension. In 1841 Finney listed "Abolition of Slavery, Temperance, Moral Reform, Politics, Business Principles, Physiological and Dietetic Reform" as political issues the church must address, and he himself led the way in making the walk to the "mourner's bench" a signal of both a decision *for* God and *against* intemperance, slavery, prostitution, and an ornate, ostentatious life-style. So many revivalists intended it. Southern evangelicals were no less socially conscious than northerners, but their approach to reform was less one of moral suasion or social activism than one of individual reformation and personal piety, which they believed would indirectly elevate the moral well-being of society.

For most white evangelicals during the revolutionary era slavery stank of hell. Some eighteenth-century evangelicals literally wept over slavery, a phenomenon called "moral weeping" that shucked chains as it shed old life-styles. Abolitionism, in fact sprang directly from the thoughts and experiences of evangelicals. There are at least two reasons why eighteenth-century evangelicalism bred a hostility to slavery as a social evil. First, the social experience of poor white evangelicals reinforced an identification with the black slave. Both were numbered by the gentry establishment among the outcasts, and white evangelicals' experience of oppression heightened their sensitivity to the truly oppressed. Second, the countercultural aspect of evangelical spirituality melded with republican notions of public virtue, resulting in an ethic of simplicity and an attack on the "greed" and "luxury" of a compromising worldliness. Slavery took a rather severe pummelling by eighteenth-century evangelicals because it stood as a symbol of a corrupt way of life.

With the outlawing of the importation of

slaves in 1808, however, the social experience of southern evangelicals changed radically. Bitten by the bug of prosperity and smitten by social respectability, southern evangelicalism went from defining itself vis-à-vis establishment culture to defending establishment culture. The convenience of its eighteenth-century calling to conduct the affairs of the church against the grain of the time was now made apparent. As the estates of southern evangelicalism began to swell, the state of its soul grew lean. When the spiritual ground evangelicals occupied was no longer unfashionable, southern evangelicalism abandoned emancipationism and settled for a more complacent, compliant conception of slavery reform.

Evangelicalism in the South capitulated to the power structure when it began to place success in society above faithfulness to the gospel. As long as evangelicalism retained a kind of counterculture identity, attempts to bring down slavery did not shake its foundations. But when southern evangelicalism discarded its cell-group mentality and adopted a main-street, conquest-through-compliance religiosity, evangelicals found antislavery sentiments an obstacle to evangelism, for they drove away precisely those converts evangelicals coveted most. In other words, evangelicalism threatened to come to grief on its own premises. Made corrigible by the prospect of a spurned gospel, evangelicals reduced their reform expectations, became shy about mixing politics and religion, and retreated into an enclosed world. There the eternal destinies of souls (black and white) assumed far greater importance than the temporal state of slaves, and the primacy of the spiritual and the aristocracy of the afterlife conspired to muffle the sounds of clanking chains. The South's struggle with slavery gave to southern evangelicalism a distinctive slant—an enhanced sense of divine sovereignty, a diminished sense of human ability to set things right. The southern spiritual ethos was not without a social ethic, but southern evangelicalism never managed to produce a compelling religious critique of the social order.

Southern evangelicalism's antislavery commitment was not entirely perishable. The social conscience of most southern evangelicals still deemed slavery to be a pernicious force. But the redefinition of the spiritual life inherent in the newly devised doctrine of the "spirituality of the church" said that the church must confine itself to spiritual matters and leave political and economic issues like slavery to politicians. This provided evangelical churches with a way out of their moral dilemma and a way into a new moral posture. Through "spiritual" renewal they could at the same time opt for order, preserve their social position, and pursue slavery reform. Evangelical spirituality went from being a source from which flowed opposition to slavery to being a stream on which opposition to slavery was carried. Southern evangelicals now spent their energies on Christianizing the slaves and humanizing the master-slave relationship rather than on emancipation.

Religious instruction and slave missions were instituted as more than benign interferences in the "peculiar institution." Southern evangelicals felt a religious obligation to protect the humanity of slaves, care for their moral and physical well-being, and stress the duties and responsibilities of their masters—inhospitable moral territory when occupied by racist ideology. The reformist slave-holding ethic, which one historian has called "the white South's unique contribution to Christian social ethics" (Mathews, *Religion in the Old South*), was an ironic outcome of southern evangelicalism's concern for discipline and obedience. Evangelicalism disciplined itself to obey the prevailing social order rather than discipline its members to obey what it perceived to be biblical injunctions against slavery.

In the North evangelicalism was pivotal in producing the complex movement fostering social change known as abolition. Not only were religious arguments critical in undermining black slavery, as both slaves and planters attested, but the early abolitionist movement was dominated by evangelicals. Evangelicals initiated one of the first national petition campaigns against slavery. Northern evangelicals contributed a disproportionate number of leaders to the abolitionists' ranks, and those areas swept by religious revivals in the 1820s and 1830s infused the abolitionist movement with its largest number of recruits. Liturgical traditions such as Roman Catholicism, Episcopalianism, and Old School Presbyterianism showed significantly less interest in abolitionist activism than did evangelicals. Evangelical denominations ultimately rejected abolitionism, but evangelicalism as a movement embodied the theological impulses such as conversion and sanctification that, properly nourished, were breeding grounds for abolitionist sentiment. Indeed, the antislavery movement in many ways resembled an evangelical movement. It assumed the form of a millennial crusade and even a "sacred vocation" for many who joined its ranks, taking from revivalism many of its techniques, grammar, rhetoric, and moralistic imagery. The majority of evangelicals saw slavery as an obstacle to an emerging millennium and wanted it removed. There could be a conservative cast, however, to what appeared to be progressive attacks on an entrenched social institution. Evangelicals hoped that Christianity would be restored to a more apostolic state through the battle against slavery. In other words, they backed into the future.

A theological consensus existed among northern evangelicals that deplored slavery as a political and social evil. The question became whether slavery by its very nature was a sin in itself, a position that became known as the *malum in se* argument. If slave-holding were a "personal sin" rather than simply "evil," immediate repentance would be required and church discipline exercised on all members who owned slaves. Beginning in 1831 the imputation of slavery as sinful nursed notions of immediate emancipation, and indeed William Lloyd Garrison is reported to have derived his doctrine of "immediatism" from sermons delivered by Lyman Beecher. The first "immediatist" organization was the New England Anti-Slavery Society (1832), but the American Anti-Slavery Society, founded in late 1833 and guided by the skilled and affluent evangelical Lewis Tappan, spread abolitionism throughout the North, claiming a quarter of a million membership and over thirteen hundred auxiliaries by 1838. Evangelical immediatists accused gradualists of dreaming of incremental progress toward emancipation while the slave population quadrupled.

To be sure, not all northern evangelicals were immediate abolitionists; most were not. But most of the early immediate abolitionist leaders were evangelicals. Abolitionist lecturer and agent Theodore Dwight Weld, converted under the revivalism of Finney, presented the evangelical argument for immediatism in *The Bible Against Slavery* (1837). To evangelicals (especially those using the "grammatical-historical" method of biblical study) whose exegetical theories denied that the objective text revealed that slavery was a sin, Weld argued that the problem was not exegetical at all, but moral and biblical. The Bible was not the "sanctuary" of slavery but its "sepulchre." It was to protect themselves against northern evangelicals like Tappan and Weld and immediatist abolitionist societies like the American Anti-Slavery Society that southern evangelicals, including Methodists, Baptists, and Presbyterians, opted to establish their own ecclesiastical organizations by 1845. Evangelicalism found the coils of the slavery controversy impossible to get out of. Its strategies proved inadequate to eradicate America's greatest evil and instead ended up rending divisions, splitting denominations, enraging religious friends, and alienating social institutions and political parties.

IMPACT ON POLITICS

Evangelicals enjoyed a love-hate relationship with the "world," rebuking the world not so much to repudiate it as to convert and control it. The ambiguity of evangelicalism's relationship with American culture makes it extremely difficult to measure evangelical influence over the whole of American society. On the one hand, evangelicals were remarkably watchful about social and political developments and were constantly sticking their noses into the public arena. The dream of an evangelical imperium meant that evangelicals tended to be uncomfortable around a plurality of social practices, and they worked diligently to provide America with a national self-definition and to help American culture get a grip on itself by defining and refining the nation's morals. As a result, the evangelical community wielded enormous social and political power, and although there is no secure way to quantify it, the evangelical ethos was so pervasive in nineteenth-century American culture that it helped to shape the political life of the country.

Indeed, all parties picked up evangelical themes and techniques, with the Democratic party leading the way in adapting the camp-meeting model for political rallies. In fact, beginning in the 1840s many elections can be understood best as a form of "political revivalism." Evangelical piety could infuse passion into a campaign, as it did, for example, when evangelical hopes to jerk the world out of its indifference on issues related to temperance, Freemasonry, the Sabbath, native Americans, and Roman Catholics came together in the election of 1840 and resulted in William Henry Harrison's being, as one historian has put it, "sung into the Presidency." Less commonly, the relationship of evangelicalism to politics could also take the form of Ezra Stiles Ely's "Christian party" in 1828 or the "Anti-Masonic party" of 1836, both short-lived attempts at organizing evangelicals for political ends, or a close alliance between a denomination and a party, as was the case between the Liberty party and the Wesleyan Methodists.

Party alignments and political alliances were more likely split along ethnoreligious than ethnocultural lines, and evangelicals often made different political choices in the voting booths than others. Politics in the nineteenth century was more constructed around religious issues than around socioeconomic ones. Down through the Populist and Progressive eras, political debate was not fashioned so much around national controversies like trusts and tariffs, taxes and internal improvements as around evangelical issues like temperance, Sabbath observance, public schools, nativism, and similar matters. Even though evangelicals were most tied in the popular mind with the Whigs and Republicans (the new Republican party in the 1850s became a major magnet for evangelicals), many evangelical reforms had social and political ramifications that led to the Jacksonian Democrats.

On the other hand, evangelicalism was so encompassing a religious tradition that it cannot be hitched to a simple political persuasion. Even though something of an evangelical consensus eventually gathered around a political philosophy that was positively predisposed to political intervention which promoted religion and morality, there was significant sectional difference over what was to be included under the rubric of "religion." Not everyone who was nurtured by evangelical doctrines became socially or politically active or even joined voluntary societies. No architect of evangelical political thought emerged to present a unifying vision. Evangelicalism's attempts to join hands with culture made it extremely difficult to disentangle itself from the wider culture; as a consequence, evangelicalism consolidated the power of the culture it also criticized and sought to reform.

By the 1830s Americans had succeeded in creating a legal, *de jure* disestablishment of religion. But they also created a *de facto* establishment of evangelicalism whose security lay in a common ethos, a common outlook on life and history, a common piety, and common patterns of worship and devotion. Even the Civil War only strengthened the hold of evangelicalism on American life. Behind both lines army revivals continued the Union Prayer Meeting Revival that had begun in 1857. In the aftermath of the war southern evangelicalism meshed with a "lost cause" civil religion to embed itself in southern culture as never before, further reinforcing the distinctiveness of southern religious identity. In the North evangelicals, many of whom genuinely believed emancipation would inaugurate the millennium, emerged from the war with millennial aspirations for a reconstructed South, and northern evangelists, teachers, and church planters followed in the wake of Union troops to set up ambitious educational programs that would make blacks into republican citizens through free labor and freedmen's schools.

DIVISIVE FORCES

The last three decades of the nineteenth century saw evangelicalism battered by a number of crosswinds. Issues raised by the study of comparative religions were exciting, but disorienting. Evangelical religion found itself constantly battling a growing secular, entrepreneurial spirit, and the tradition of Christian reform-minded industrialists such as Arthur and Lewis Tappan gave way to a tradition of Christian robber-baron industrialists such as John D. Rockefeller and J. P. Morgan. In an era of efficiency evangelicalism's earlier balancing act between piety and technique tilted in the direction of technique, and evangelicals began to lose their eye for the unseen, their ear for the unheard. The kingdom was now to be brought in more by scientific planning and a rationalized church than by converted individuals and consecrated associations. The bureaucratization of church life accelerated, spurred on by scientific management, progressivism, and industrialism's mocking of inefficient and antiquated functions marking the church. Bureaucratic authority structures increasingly were controlled by national boards composed of trained specialist professionals in various fields. Evangelical pastors felt squeezed into giving up their role as program innovators and community builders in favor of becoming brokers and implementers of national plans and policies. The maturation of evangelical denominations led to a revolt against all this formalization and routinization, with subsequent new groups constantly being formed. Voluntary societies and educational institutions, once happily under the wing of evangelicals, now began to break free and fly off in their own independent directions.

Evangelicalism also smuggled concerns into theology that threatened, if not subverted, the supernatural character of the evangelical Christian faith. A scientific and historical spirit worked to flatten the landscape of the spiritual life. It was still on an upward path, but without the sharp and unexpected intrusions of mountains and valleys that had once characterized the evangelical souls' ascent to heaven, which now was different only in degree, not kind, from earth. A parallel development led to postmillennialism being stripped of its apocalyptic content and being replaced by a natural, organic evolutionism on the one hand and apocalyptic premillennial ideology on the other. Evangelicals first worked together on the exploding challenges of new forms of scholarship—biblical criticism, evolution, Marxism, historicism—only to emerge in the early twentieth century as foes on different ends of a battlefield. But more than any other, it was the challenge to biblical authority presented by higher criticism that struck at evangelicalism's core and led to divisions within the evangelical body along conservative and liberal lines. Biblical criticism threatened the basic assumption of commonsense realism and popular piety—that the Bible was open to the average person. A series of heresy trials revealed that evangelicals were no longer moving in the same direction. A liberal element embraced modern forces, refusing to be nudged off those scholarly and cultural fronts now advancing away from religion. Three parallel movements—holiness and Pentecostal denominations, which shunned any changes that garbed (or as they saw it, garbled) the gospel in modern dress, and a conservative group within denominations that resisted accommodation to the immanentist, progressivist, and naturalist tendencies of modern thought—provided the foundation for twentieth-century fundamentalism. Surprisingly, the banner of evangelical reform still was unfurled, however limply at times, over all segments of the evangelical world, even those segments that were breaking off and coming apart. An active social consciousness was still strong among conservatives from 1870 to 1900. If anything, the Social Gospel was a unifying force that drove the controversies over higher criticism and evolution underground until social concern was popularly identified with liberal theology in the early twentieth century.

Josiah Strong, Dwight L. Moody, and Henry Ward Beecher, three of the most prominent evangelical leaders of the Gilded Age, respectively illustrate the sociological, theological, and cultural ways in which the strands making up the mesh of evangelical culture were being ripped apart. The year after Strong published *Our Country* (1885), there were over sixteen hundred strikes, the Knights of Labor claimed over one million members, a dominant Protestant numerical majority dissolved in waves of immigration, the Haymarket Square riot and Ku Klux Klan midnight rides focused the fears of segments of Americans, restrictive labor laws and a crop lien system throttled economic growth, and the American middle class was triple the size it had been in 1850. Surveying America's cities, Strong lambasted an evangelical empire on the defensive and in retreat. He called for it to go on the offensive. But it was an evangelical offensive inspired by fear, not hope—fear of immigration, intemperance, wealth, Romanism, and socialism. When evangelicals found themselves living in a pluralist society with alien values, foreign faiths, and creeping irreligion, they could no longer sustain the cultural tension between innovation and tradition, and they failed the test of skill and will presented by unsettling cultural changes.

The revivalist Dwight L. Moody symbolizes the extent to which evangelicalism, as a theological movement, was deteriorating and was even in shambles. In Moody's sermons sin now became social improprieties; grace was equated with a blessing-prone life; conversion was little more than a refreshing spiritual bath; and the goal of sanctification was to become one's best self. To shepherd the flock was now to feed them in greened glades and peaceful meadows rather than to walk them safely through valleys and over cliffs. An anecdotal theology replaced doctrinal theology, as evangelical theology began thinning out into a tepid moralism. Once steeped in post-millennialism, evangelical theology was now dipped in premillennialism. The most popular hymns sung in the Moody revivals—Fanny Crosby's "Safe in the Arms of Jesus," "He Hideth My Soul," "Pass Me Not, O Gentle Savior," "Rescue the Perishing"—reveal a sovereign God domesticated into a personal counselor, an identification of Jesus less with salvation and regeneration than with comfort and protection, and a yearning for refuge and safety amid crumbling social values and intellectual disorder.

In Henry Ward Beecher can be seen a remarkable refraction of evangelical predicaments and compromises into flesh, blood, and bone. On virtually every issue from evolution to ethics Beecher attempted to bring Christ and culture together, sprinkling religiosity on whatever culture brought out. Buried under the crush of blessings brought by success, evangelicalism could no longer act as an arbiter of cultural values. It had become too accustomed to rowing with the wind and tide. With the fundamental assumptions of their belief taken for granted and their stamp set distinctly on all sectors of American life, many evangelicals settled snugly in a society that seemed comfortably Christian, equating liberty with loyalty and finding patriotism in piety, treason in heresy, and disloyalty in dissent. Trimming itself to culture's expectations and tending to make culture-bound decisions, Gilded Age evangelicalism found it hard to resist any cultural temptation, and it no longer insisted on those moral distinctions that had differentiated it from popular culture. Success had siphoned away evangelicalism's energy, self-confidence, resourcefulness, and ambition. It no no longer aspired to shoulder the responsibilities of the universe.

BIBLIOGRAPHY

Anne M. Boylan, "Evangelical Womanhood in the Nineteenth Century: The Role of Women in Sunday Schools," in *Feminist Studies* 4 (1978), "Sunday Schools and Changing Evangelical Views of Children in the 1820's," in *Church History*, 48 (1979); Dickson D. Bruce, Jr., *And They All Sang Hallelujah: Plainfolk Camp-Meeting Religion, 1800–1845* (1974); Joan Jacobs Brumberg, *Mission for Life: The Story of the Family of Adoniram Judson, the Dramatic Event of the First American Foreign Mission, and the Course of Evangelical Religion in the Nineteenth Century* (1980); Donald E. Byrne, Jr., *No Foot of Land: Folklore of American Methodist Itinerants* (1975); Richard Carwardine, *Transatlantic Revivalism: Popular Evangelicalism in Britain and America, 1790–1865* (1978); Marie Caskey, *Chariot of Fire: Religion and the Beecher Family* (1978); Whitney R. Cross, *The Burned-Over District: The Social and Intellectual History of Enthusiastic Religion in Western New York, 1800–1850* (1950; repr. 1982); James Findlay, "Agency, Denominations and the Western Colleges, 1830–1860: Some Connections Between Evangelicalism and American Higher Education," in *Church History* 50 (1981).

Herbert S. Gutman, "Protestantism and the American Labor Movement: The Christian Spirit in the Golden Age," in *Work, Culture, and Society in Industrializing America: Essays in American Working-Class and Social History* (1976); Nathan O. Hatch and Mark A. Noll, eds., *The Bible in America: Essays in Cultural History* (1982); E. Brooks Holifield, *The Gentlemen Theologians: American Theology in Southern Culture, 1795–1860* (1978); Winthrop S. Hudson, "The Methodist Age in America," in *Methodist History* 12 (April, 1974), "Walter Rauschenbusch and the New Evangelism," in *Religion in Life* 30 (1961); Paul E. Johnson, *A Shopkeeper's Millennium: Society and Revivals in Rochester, New York, 1815–1837* (1978); Joe L. Kincheloe, Jr., "Similarities in Crowd Control Techniques of the Camp Meeting and Political Rally: The Pioneer Role of Tennessee," in *Tennessee Historical Quarterly* 37 (1978), "Transcending Role Restrictions: Women at Camp Meetings and Political Rallies," in *Tennessee Historical Quarterly* 40 (1981); Anne C. Loveland, *Southern Evangelicals and the Social Order, 1800–1860* (1980); Robert W. Lynn and Elliott Wright, *The Big Little School: 200 Years of the Sunday School* (1980).

George M. Marsden, *The Evangelical Mind and the New School Presbyterian Experience: A Case Study of Thought and Theology in the Nineteenth-Century Mind* (1970), *Fundamentalism and American Culture: The Shaping of Twentieth Century Evangelicalism, 1870–1925* (1980); Donald G. Mathews, *Religion in the Old South* (1977); William G. McLoughlin, *Revivals, Awakenings and Reform: An Essay in Religion and Social Change in America, 1607–1977* (1978); Glenn T. Miller, "Trying the Spirits: The Heresy Trials of the Nineteenth Century as Cultural Events," in *Perspectives in Religious Studies* 9 (1982); James H. Moorhead, *American Apocalypse: Yankee Protestants and the Civil War, 1860–1869* (1978), "Social Reform and the Divided Conscience of Antebellum Protestantism," in *Church History* 48 (1979); Mark A. Noll, "Common Sense Traditions and American Evangelical Thought," in *American Quarterly* 37 (1985).

Lewis O. Saum, *The Popular Mood of Pre–Civil War America* (1980); Milton C. Sernett, *Black Religion and American Evangelicalism: White Protestants, Plantation Missions and the Flowering of Negro Christianity, 1787–1865* (1975); Gregory H. Singleton, "Protestant Voluntary Organizations and the Shaping of Victorian America," in *American Quarterly* 27 (1975); Sandra S. Sizer, *Gospel Hymns and Social Religion: The Rhetoric of Nineteenth-Century Revivalism* (1978); Timothy L. Smith, *Revivalism and Social Reform: American Protestantism on the Eve of the Civil War* (1957, repr. 1980); Leonard I. Sweet, "Millennialism in America: Recent Studies," in *Theological Studies*, 40 (1979), "'A Nation Born in a Day'": The Union Prayer Meeting Revival and Cultural Revitalization," in *In The Great Tradition: Essays in Honor of Winthrop S. Hudson*, Joseph Ban and Paul R. Dekar, eds. (1982), *The Minister's Wife: Her Role in Nineteenth-Century American Evangelicalism* (1983), "The Female Seminary Movement and Woman's Mission in Antebellum America," in *Church History* 54 (1985), ed., *The Evangelical Tradition in America* (1984); Ferenc Morton Szasz, *The Divided Mind of Protestant America, 1880–1930* (1982); Timothy P. Weber, *Living in the Shadow of the Second Coming: American Premillennialism, 1875–1982* (1983).

[*See also* CALVINIST HERITAGE; FUNDAMENTALISM; GREAT AWAKENING; HOLINESS AND PERFECTION; NEW ENGLAND PURITANISM; REVIVALISM; SOCIAL CHRISTIANITY; SOCIAL REFORM AFTER THE CIVIL WAR TO THE GREAT DEPRESSION; *and* SOCIAL REFORM FROM THE COLONIAL PERIOD THROUGH THE CIVIL WAR.]

CHRISTIAN SCIENCE
AND HARMONIALISM

Stephen Gottschalk

CHRISTIAN Science is one of several indigenous American religious denominations. It was founded in 1879 by Mary Baker Eddy, who gave definitive expression to its teachings in her book *Science and Health with Key to the Scriptures*, first published in 1875. Harmonialism, however, does not denote a specific church or a well-defined theology. Rather, it is a term coined by religious historian Sydney E. Ahlstrom and epitomizes a broad religious attitude characteristic mainly of New Thought groups and writers. According to Ahlstrom, harmonialism "encompasses those forms of piety and belief in which spiritual composure, physical health, and even economic well-being are understood to flow from a person's rapport with the cosmos" (1972).

Strictly speaking, the aims and theological standpoint of Christian Science and of harmonialism differ so markedly that the two cannot be assumed to represent the same tendency. Yet their histories intertwine in complex and fascinating ways that help to explain why they have so often misleadingly been identified with one another. Probably the most historically significant example of how this has happened is the assessment of Christian Science and harmonialism by William James, the foremost American intellectual contemporary with the rise of both. In 1901–1902, at the height of his fame and powers, James delivered the Gifford Lectures on natural religion at the University of Edinburgh. The lectures were published in 1902 under the title *The Varieties of Religious Experience* and rapidly became a classic. In them he described what he called "the religion of healthy-mindedness," which he saw as best illustrated in "mind-cure"—or as it was then coming to be called, New Thought.

Although the term "harmonialism" was not coined till some years later, James's portrayal of the "religion of healthy-mindedness" remains perhaps the clearest delineation of its spirit. He described it as a view congenial to temperaments "organically weighted on the side of cheer and fatally forbidden to linger . . . over the darker aspects of the universe." James's own guarded sympathy for the religion of healthy-mindedness has been taken by some historians to reflect harmonial tendencies in his own thought. Yet he could not but feel that there was a fundamental deficiency in any religious philosophy that "deliberately excludes evil from its field of vision." Mind-cure, he wrote, was so "wholly and exclusively compacted of optimism" that its adherents never crossed that threshold of human pain and despair which great religious innovators must pass. The true religious genius, James observed, was always "twice born" because of radical experiences that brought about the creation of a new inner person.

To the healthy-minded or "once born," however, religion consists more of exploring the potentialities of the self as it exists. Mind-curers feel that through "systematic exercise and passive relaxation, concentration, and meditation," or even hypnotism, they can tap a subconscious self without undergoing this new or second birth. By way of contrast to such adherents of "the sky-blue optimistic gospel," James spoke of those "sick souls" for whom "pity, pain, and fear, and the sentiment of human helplessness," open a deeper view of the meaning of life.

The founder of Christian Science, Eddy, has sometimes been seen as an exponent of harmonialism. Yet her life shows her to have been one of the most conspicuous examples of the "twice born" in religious history. Born in rural New Hampshire in 1821, she suffered from nervous instability and a variety of physical illnesses. The deaths of her favorite brother, first husband, and mother were followed by enforced separation from her only son (due to her ill health), an unhappy second marriage ending eventually in divorce, and the further deterioration of her health. During a low point in her life in the 1850s, she anticipated James's phrase the "sick soul" by asking in a poem, "Knowest Thou not my pain and agony?/For my sick soul is darkened unto death . . ." (Manuscript Copybook 2, Archives of The Mother Church).

What she came to call her "discovery" of Christian Science marked the abrupt transition from the natural to the spiritual life characteristic of the "twice born." That the unaided human mind has within itself no resources by which to achieve physical or spiritual well being became a central point of her theology. As she put it in *Science and Health*, the "erring, finite, human mind has an absolute need of something beyond itself for its redemption and healing." According to Eddy, this mind needs a spiritual rebirth out of the sense of sinful separateness from God, which she saw as at the root of the mortal condition.

Neither this sinfulness nor mortality itself, she held, has objective existence as a God-permitted part of reality. Ontologically they must be understood as "nothingness." This, however, is no warrant for ignoring or minimizing evil but rather for uncovering its nature and effects, which can be eradicated only through the recognition of their nothingness before God. In her *Message to The Mother Church* written the first year that James's Gifford Lectures were delivered, Eddy inveighed against sin in words that would be difficult to find in the whole literature of harmonialism: "The most deplorable sight is to contemplate the infinite blessings that divine Love bestows on mortals, and their ingratitude and hate, filling up the measure of wickedness against all light." Far from an isolated instance, this statement is characteristic of her whole view of human existence.

How, then, could a thinker so acute as James speak of Christian Science as an example of "the religion of healthy-mindedness" that determinedly ignores evil, or write that from its standpoint duty forbids us to pay evil "the compliment even of explicit attention"? A crucial historical fact helps to answer this question. James's attitude toward both Christian Science and mind-cure was strongly shaped by his former graduate student Horatio Dresser, who was a deeply interested party to a long-standing dispute about the origins and nature of Christian Science. Dresser had a strong personal interest in linking Christian Science with mind-cure and in denying that it must be understood as a distinct religious teaching.

Dresser's influence on James in this respect is instructive, but not only for what it reveals about the background of the philosopher's views. It illustrates that the confusion that has plagued academic discussion of Christian Science and mind-cure since the beginning of the twentieth century can be traced back to controversies arising from the interaction of these two forms of belief during the period in which both arose. Historical perspective and advancing scholarship, however, now make it possible to clarify essential facts about the two movements and their relationship as linked but disparate phenomena on the American religious scene.

THE ROOTS OF HARMONIALISM

Harmonialism, especially in its mid-twentieth-century incarnation in the gospel of positive thinking, has often been viewed as the quintessential expression of the American ethos of optimism and success. So it is ironic that its first expressions did not reflect native influences but were strongly conditioned by the theory and practice of mesmerism, which first attracted attention in late-eighteenth-century France. It is even more ironic that the religion of harmonial "healthy-mindedness" should have owed so much to a tradition rooted in occultism. Mesmerism—or animal magnetism—represented far more than a faddish interest in the experiments and theories of the Austrian showman-scientist Franz Anton Mesmer. It was really a latter-day outcropping of an esoteric and subterranean stream that has flowed alongside and occasionally joined with most major religious traditions, especially in their more primitive forms.

The excitement over mesmerism in French intellectual circles reflected both an extension of Enlightenment rationality to the investigation of the occult and an incipient reaction against that spirit of rationality itself. But the fact that by the mid-nineteenth century mesmerism in America had become something between a fad and a folk movement needs to be explained differently. First popularized through the lectures of the French mesmerist Charles Poyen in 1836, the news of animal magnetism was spread both by a flood of books and articles and by traveling mesmerists anxious to provide a hungry public with convincing exhibitions of clairvoyant healing and hypnotic control. Significantly, the circuits these mesmerists traveled were parallel to those frequented by itinerant revivalists. As the historian Robert C. Fuller has observed, "Mesmerism, no less than revivalism, provided confused individuals with an intense experience thought to bring them into an interior harmony with unseen spiritual forces" (1982).

This process depended upon the substitution of the "inner" forces of the human psyche for the soul that Christian orthodoxy sought to save and, in a certain sense, for the saving power itself. Theoreticians of mesmerism, such as ex-Universalist minister John Bovee Dods, might have seen what he called "electrical psychology" as the key to an understanding of Jesus' healings. Yet they offered what amounted to secular salvation on the basis of principles precisely the reverse of Christian orthodoxy, stressing the adequacy of the human mind as a source of power and meaning rather than the necessity for the radical salvation of mankind through an agency outside of itself. If revivalism fostered the emotional climate in which mesmerism temporarily flourished, there could be no effective fusion between basic mesmerist assumptions and traditional Christian doctrine.

The visionary writings of the eighteenth-century Swedish thinker Emanuel Swedenborg, however, provided a channel through which mesmerism could be assimilated into an alternative religious framework loosely associated with Christianity. Swedenborg's vast corpus of writings purported to represent his illumined understanding of Scripture gained through contact with angelic spheres, which in his grand scheme interpenetrated with the physical and mental orders. His vision of the human and spiritual realms as congruent, together with his method of searching for the hidden symbolic meaning of Scripture, made him a seminal figure in the development of nineteenth-century alternative religion. It provided basic working principles for such figures as James's father, Henry James, Sr., William Blake, and Ralph Waldo Emerson. And it gave mesmerist metapsychologists a concep-

tual framework within which to adduce religious significance from their practices, viewing the mesmerized trance state as a means of access to perception of the higher spiritual spheres of which Swedenborg had spoken. In some cases Swedenborgians embraced mesmerism; in other cases mesmerists embraced Swedenborgianism. Both elaborated the same message: the human and divine orders are potentially congruent, and the human psyche is itself the medium through which divine currents flow.

It is not too much to say that harmonialism as an identifiable tendency came into being as mesmerism and Swedenborgianism were conjoined and popularized, especially through the agency of early American spiritualism. After the "rappings" of the young Fox sisters, Kate and Maggie, attracted widespread attention in 1848, spiritualism became progressively associated with parlor tricks and medium-induced spirit manifestations. But its earlier expressions in the writings of the ex–Universalist minister Thomas Lake Harris and the "seer of Poughkeepsie," Andrew Jackson Davis, revolved around a broader idea basic to harmonialism: the capacity of the mind to achieve harmonious rapport with beneficent cosmic powers, latent in its own nature, through which personal power could be expanded and enhanced. This power might be used in a number of ways, one of which is to contact the spirits of the departed. But it could also be directed toward the renovation of the social order and the healing of disease.

The first figures to focus exclusively on the implications of this essential harmonial idea for healing were Warren Felt Evans and Phineas P. Quimby. Of the two, Evans deserves prior consideration as the earliest, most wide-ranging, and most broadly influential theoretician of mental healing. Born in Vermont, he had a rather rocky career as a Methodist minister for some twenty years before becoming an ardent Swedenborgian in the early 1860s. Possibly as a result of the breakdown of his health, he developed a strong interest in mental healing, publishing three books on the subject (*The Mental Cure*, 1869; *Mental Medicine*, 1872; and *The Divine Law of Cure*, 1881) well before mind-cure became an identifiable movement in Boston during the 1880s.

Evans' role in the development of harmonialism has been to some extent eclipsed by Quimby, who, though by far the more arresting figure, had virtually no direct influence on its development. Indeed, few of Quimby's writings had been published until 1921, by which time the major ideas of New Thought had long been fully formed and widely disseminated. Yet historians have generally portrayed Evans as a Quimby disciple whose own work in mental healing was launched after he was supposedly cured by Quimby of a long-standing ailment in 1863. The only direct evidence bearing on the question, however, leads to no such conclusion. In fact, it fully supports Evans' view formed after two brief visits with Quimby and reported by mind-curer A. J. Swartz in 1888, that Quimby's methods were "like those he [Evans] had employed for some years, which was a mental process of changing the patient's thinking about disease" (1888).

As Evans described them, his methods were an extension of the practice of mesmerism or animal magnetism, from which he—unlike Quimby—made no effort to disassociate himself. Evans spoke repeatedly of putting patients into the "impressionable magnetic state" in which they were subject to the influence of "suggestion." And although he elaborated his basic Swedenborgian and mesmeric concepts in a variety of intellectual contexts, including German philosophic idealism, Eastern thought, and ultimately in what he called "esoteric Christianity," he never abandoned or seriously modified the fundamental view expressed in his first book, *The Mental Cure,* that there are

> . . . a variety of phenomena, passing under the names of Mesmerism, Psychology, Biology, Animal Magnetism, Pantheism, Hypnotism, and even Psychometry, that are reducible to one general principle,—the influence or action of mind upon mind, and the communication of spiritual life from one person to another, who is negatively receptive of it.
>
> (p. 252)

Quimby's writings have none of Evans' religious and philosophic range of reference but are richer and more original. Temperamentally he was not so much a theoretician as a Yankee empiricist with touches of both the genius and the crank. Born in New Hampshire, Quimby worked as a clockmaker before becoming so entranced with Charles Poyen's exhibitions of mesmerism in 1838 that he became a practicing mesmerist himself, with increasing success in healing.

In the early years of his practice Quimby used hypnosis in his healing work. By the late 1840s, however, he no longer put his patients or an intermediary into an induced trance state, claiming that healing could be effected through suggestion alone, and to the end of his days he maintained that he had broken with mesmerism. Even so, he continued to employ the magnetic "rubbing" or manipulating of patients in his practice as well as concepts derived from mesmerism to explain his cures, especially the view that health was regulated by a subtle yet material magnetic "fluid." Most important, Quimby retained and expanded the principle of healing through suggestion or through what could be called hypnotism in a larger sense—perhaps his most original and practical conclusion being his analysis of how disease can originate through suggestion. He came to see disease as caused by negative opinions or "errors" that the patient entertained and healing as the result of the "explanation" through which the patient was delivered from the effects of this ignorance.

At the urging of friends, Quimby began in the late 1850s to attempt explaining in writing his curative methods, which on more than one occasion he frankly admitted he scarcely understood himself. It is virtually impossible to impose theoretical consistency on the miscellaneous notes and articles that comprise the Quimby manuscripts, the vast majority of which are not in his own hand but were copied and sometimes recopied by associates. Some of his working ideas were adapted from the available stockpile of Swedenborgian and mesmeric concepts. Swedenborg, for example, had written of God as "wisdom," a term that Quimby adapted to refer to the clairvoyant powers through which he healed. Again, mesmerists had seen their cures as reproducing the healing works of Jesus; and it was a short step for Quimby to identify the practical use of his own "wisdom" with Christ.

If any claim for conceptual originality can be made for Quimby, it should probably be on behalf of his belief that there is an empirically verifiable science of mental healing. He never claimed to have explained this science to his own satisfaction; indeed, his manuscripts show him constantly struggling to articulate points that seemed to elude him. Yet his writings have an authenticity, daring, and crude force that surpass anything in Evans or other writers in the harmonial tradition, the reason being that they were the direct outgrowth of his own intense involvement in healing. In Quimby's own words, "All my writings are the effect of impressions made on me while sitting with the sick . . . of the lives and sufferings of my patients, their trials and sorrows, and my arguments are in their behalf" (1921). For this reason, too, Quimby's conclusion as to the mental origin of disease has the force of empirical observation and experiment behind it. And it can no less readily be understood as an antecedent of developments in psychotherapy, placebos, and psychosomatic medicine than as a rudimentary form of harmonialism in religion.

Quimby's religious interests, however, were entirely secondary to his practical healing concerns, which served the end of human health and happiness rather than salvation in any acceptable Christian sense. Although familiar with Scripture, especially the Gospels, he was militantly anticlerical, inveighing in typically rationalist tones against religious "superstition" and humanity's "bondage to priests" and writing that Jesus' disciples stole his body "to establish their belief that it rose again." Actually, Quimby drew from the Bible only what could be used to confirm or amplify his own views on healing. As Robert C. Fuller puts it, he psychologized theological doctrines "so as to better square with the phenomenon of mental cure" (1982).

In some of his writings Quimby haltingly begins to explore a few of the larger implications of his belief that "opinion" rather than physical conditions determines health, at points verging on a crude idealism expressed in Swedenborgian terms. Yet as even Dresser had acknowledged, Quimby's primary interest did not lie in exploring things of the spirit. His reason for incorporating religious subjects into his writing was entirely secondary to his primary interest, which lay in therapeutic technique. He explains that some of his patients "are continually dwelling . . . on the Bible. So to cure I have to show by the Bible that they have been made to believe a false construction. My arguments change their minds and the cure comes. This is my excuse for what I have said upon the Scriptures" (1921).

EDDY AND QUIMBY

An essential starting point for an understanding of Eddy's relation to Quimby is that her primary interest lay in the Scriptures all along. Through her contact with Quimby in the early 1860s she touched the cultural milieu that nourished the development of harmonialism in America. This milieu might be described in the theologian Henry P. Van Dusen's phrase as an example of a "third force" in American Christendom—that is, an alternative source of religious interest outside mainstream Protestantism and Catholicism. Yet her own religious sensibility had already been molded by the much older and very different tradition of American Puritanism, the embers of which still glowed brightly in the rural New Hampshire in which Eddy was born in 1821. And it bore the clear imprint of that Puritan longing for the divine that historian Perry Miller called "the Augustinian strain of piety" and identified as the decisive factor in the shaping of the New England mind (*The New England Mind: The Seventeenth Century*, 1939).

Eddy's autobiography—which bears the characteristically Puritan title *Retrospection and Introspection* (1891)—includes a passage unconsciously reminiscent of both Saint Augustine and the theologian Jonathan Edwards: "From my very childhood I was impelled, by a hunger and thirst after divine things,—a desire for something higher and better than matter, and apart from it,—to seek diligently for the knowledge of God, as the one great and ever-present relief from human woe." Such words came naturally to one who had been reared on a steady diet of sermons delivered by ministers schooled in Edwards' New Light theology. And when she wrote in 1901 of the religious teachers of her youth that "their piety was the all-important consideration of their being, the original beauty of holiness that to-day seems to be fading so sensibly from our sight" (1901), she was speaking from the heart.

Yet like many other sensitive souls in early-nineteenth-century America, Eddy reacted with all her strength against the Calvinist conception of a God of wrath capable of damning the vast majority of mankind to hell. Through the increasingly bitter experiences of her middle years, she found the problem of evil ramified from theology into life. Recourse to the Bible was a constant in her experience through this period. According to the British historian H. A. L. Fisher, who in most respects was highly critical of her, "Prayer, meditation, eager and puzzled interrogation of the Bible, had claimed from childhood much of her energy. . . . The great ideas of God, of immortality, of the soul, of a life penetrated by Christianity, were never far from her mind" (1929). Yet Eddy's piety could not flow freely in orthodox channels. Surviving letters and poems, especially from the 1850s when her life reached its lowest ebb, show her grappling with the question of theodicy for which orthodox theology held, for her as for so many others, no satisfying answer. As she asked in a poem written in 1859, is "This crushing out of life, of hope, or love/Thy *will* O God?"—a question followed by the revealing lines "the strong foundations of my early faith/Shrink from beneath me . . ." (Manuscript Copybook 2, Archives of The Mother Church).

Eddy broke drastically from the Calvinist faith of her early years. Yet she remained among those for whom the problem of being was always acutely real and for whom it could be solved only in terms that admitted the primacy of what she called "one supreme and infinite God" (1875). How, then, is one to explain the enormous enthusiasm for Quimby and his ideas that Eddy, then Mrs. Patterson, displayed after she first appealed to him for aid in October 1862? For she not only spoke and wrote publicly in his praise, but also spent many hours in the last three months of 1862 and for several more months in 1863–1864 in intensive discussions with him. The most obvious answer is her understandable gratitude for her rapid physical improvement at his hands—improvement that, though not lasting, was dramatic. But her persistence in trying to absorb Quimby's therapeutics into her own religious frame of reference shows that something deeper was involved.

Well before meeting him, she had reached conclusions of her own as to the mental causation of disease through experiments with homeopathy, a medical system that holds that a patient's ability to fight an illness is stimulated by the administration of minute doses of a drug that, in healthy persons, produces symptoms of the disease being treated. While some mid-nineteenth-century advocates of homeopathy had strong affinities with Swedenborgianism, the system's significance to Eddy lay in its empirical bearing on the mental origin of disease. Sometime during the 1850s she concluded that it was the patient's faith in the drug rather than the drug itself that was responsible for the substance's apparent effects. This conviction, which was in consonance with Quimby's own views on the role of belief and "explanation" in causing and curing disease, helps explain why on first writing to him Eddy professed "entire confidence" in his philosophy—which she soon came to see had even greater religious implications than she had thought.

Eddy's contact with Quimby appears to have been one of those moments, apparent in other careers as well, in which previously disparate elements are drawn into sudden unity, opening further channels for investigation. Specifically, her encounter with Quimby related her medical experiments and her Christian preoccupations by suggesting that the mental basis of disease pointed to a science underlying Jesus' healing works. On the specific nature of this science Eddy's ultimate thinking differed radically from anything Quimby wrote. But the idea that there could be such a science operated as a catalyst in her experience, giving specific focus to her nascent desire for a more spiritually and physically liberating Christianity.

From the first Eddy projected onto Quimby an intensity of religious interest that was as native to her as it was foreign to him. Whereas he connected his healing technique only intermittently with religion, she did so consistently, referring to it in her first newspaper tribute to him as "a very spiritual doctrine" and praising him publicly upon his death in a poem on "Dr. P. P. Quimby, Who Healed with the Truth that Christ Taught." As Fisher wrote, Quimby "held that religious beliefs were founded in deception. Mrs. Patterson was an earnest advocate of the view that religion was all in all." The assessment of the matter by the eminent German church historian Karl Holl is hard to fault:

> That which connected her with Quimby was her conviction that all disease in the last analysis has its roots in the mind, and that healing therefore must be effected through mental influence. But it was her earnest Puritan faith in God that separated her from Quimby from the beginning.
> (1921–1928, pp. 463–464)

That Eddy may have had an inkling of this disparity is suggested by her question in a letter to Quimby in 1864, "What is your truth if it applies only to the evil diseases which show themselves?'' (Archives of The Mother Church, letter of 24 April 1864), implying a far broader vision of the religious implications of his therapeutics than he entertained. This prodding question addressed to Quimby when his influence on her was supposedly at its height tends to confirm her later claim that the influence ran both ways. Horatio Dresser's mother, Annetta, recalled well after the controversy over Quimby's influence on Eddy had erupted that "those interested would in turn write articles about his 'theory' or 'the Truth,' as he called it, then bring them to him for criticism" (Peel, 1966). But as Eddy's biographer, Robert Peel, notes, Quimby's son George's recollection of Mrs. Patterson "talking with [Quimby], reading his Mss., copying some of them, writing some herself and reading them to him for his criticism" is the only record of anyone's having done this.

Certainly the basic principle—or Principle as Eddy would have it—of Christian Science cannot be traced to Quimby's writings, nor is there any evidence that he would have agreed with it. The testimony of George Quimby is relevant on this point. He insisted that Eddy got "her inspiration and idea"—that is the concept "that disease was a mental condition"—from Quimby. But he also stated categorically, "The *religion* which she teaches certainly *is hers,* for which I cannot be too thankful; for I should be loath to go down to my grave feeling that my father was in any way connected with 'Christian Science'" (1921). If Eddy's "inspiration and idea" was simply "that disease was a mental condition," she might well have owed this to Quimby—though her own experience had already led her toward this conclusion. But the "inspiration and idea" of Christian Science as a theology and a metaphysic was something far different—so different that George Quimby was exceedingly anxious to dissociate himself and his father from it. To what, then, did she owe the "inspiration and idea" of Christian Science itself?

"A WOMAN OF ONE IDEA"

To Eddy this "inspiration and idea" was in one sense the fruit of the many years of struggle and searching through which, as she put it, God had been "graciously preparing" her to receive Christian Science. Specifically, she associated its

"discovery" with a moment of spiritual illumination gained while reading a Gospel account of one of Jesus' healings. That illumination, she claimed, brought about her immediate recovery from the severe effects of a fall in February 1866, less than three weeks after Quimby's death. The details of the incident have been much disputed, the crux of the matter being the conflict between what the attending physician was reported by a newspaper at the time as saying about the gravity of her injuries and his downplaying of the incident years later. Eddy's turning to the Bible for healing, however, fits well with the pattern suggested by other evidence and in the long run is more historically significant than the degree of her injuries.

Abundant evidence of her activities over the next several years shows her deeply preoccupied with exploring the Scriptures, in which she believed she was discovering the science underlying Christian healing. By the autumn of 1866 she was deeply immersed in an intensive analysis of Genesis intended to be the first volume of an ambitious but uncompleted work to be called "The Bible in Its Spiritual Meaning." Other contemporary testimony leaves no doubt of her increasing conviction, in the words of one who knew her at the time, that she "had cognition of certain great principles in the life and teachings of Christ which were not well understood or properly set forth by religious teachers" (Peel, 1966).

What Eddy felt she had discovered through her exploration of Scripture was a radically new and enlarged concept of God that correlated with her own deepest religious experience. In this respect the numinous quality of the language in which she describes her healing is itself revealing. "That short experience," she wrote in 1896, "included a glimpse of the great fact that I have since tried to make plain to others, namely, Life in and of Spirit; this Life being the sole reality of existence" (1896).

For her this true sense of Spirit meant that God was real, sovereign, and absolute in a way that contradicted materialistic assumptions far more radically than traditional Christian theology had ever conceived. Given Eddy's strong religious background, it would simply never have occurred to her to question that God was the intelligent, loving Father to whom Christians prayed. But she held too that the full promise of

Christianity could not be realized until God was seen as the Life, Soul, and ordering Principle of all being, which must like him be spiritual—until it was understood that there could be no actual life, substance, or intelligence apart from him.

This was the fundamental idea that Eddy fleshed out over the nine years after 1866 into the theology and metaphysics of Christian Science. It was basic to both that one infinite God must be unconfinable in the forms he creates. In the chapter "Recapitulation" from *Science and Health,* which she had adapted from a series of questions and answers originally prepared for classroom use in 1870, she wrote: "This is a leading point in the Science of Soul, that Principle is not in its idea. Spirit, Soul, is not confined in man, and is never in matter." Mortality itself, she contended, proceeded from and operated within the sinful sense of the one Soul or Life as fragmented and divided into a multiplicity of human personalities, each with a finite mentality and body expressing it. She used the terms "personal sense" and later "mortal mind" as shorthand for this false sense or basic error, eventually adopting the phrase "animal magnetism" to indicate the hypnotic nature of its operation.

The whole meaning of Jesus' saving mission, she contended, lay in the fact that his healing works and overcoming of death broke through the false concept of existence built up by mortal mind on its mistaken premise of life apart from God. The virgin birth of Jesus, Eddy held, enabled him to live man's spiritual sonship with God in the midst of human experience. She believed that this sonship, or true status of man in Christ, was uniquely embodied in the life and person of Jesus yet not confined to him. For her Jesus' healing as well as his crucifixion and resurrection were historical events of supreme importance, revealing that authentic spiritual being is inseparable from God and therefore triumphant over suffering and mortality.

It was to open the possibility of achieving this authentic spiritual being to all men that Jesus struggled and sacrificed on humanity's behalf. As Eddy wrote in her short work *No and Yes* (1891):

> The glory of human life is in overcoming sickness, sin, and death. Jesus suffered for all mortals to bring in this glory; and his purpose was to show them that the way out of the flesh, out of the delusion of all human error, must be through the baptism of suffering, leading up to health, harmony, and heaven. . . .
>
> Love bruised and bleeding, yet mounting to the throne of glory in purity and peace, over the steps of uplifted humanity—this is the deep significance of the blood of Christ. Nameless woe, everlasting victories, are the blood, the vital currents of Christ Jesus' life, purchasing the freedom of mortals from sin and death.
>
> (pp. 33–34)

In contradistinction to the theory of the substitutionary atonement, Eddy maintained that "Jesus spares us not one individual experience, if we follow his commands faithfully; and all have the cup of sorrowful effort to drink in proportion to their demonstration of his love, till all are redeemed through divine Love" (1875). This true Christian discipleship, she insisted, must include Christian healing if it is to make good on the meaning of Jesus' mission. Her discovery of Christian Science, she felt, had elucidated this healing and the science that made it possible; and its conscientious practice had resulted empirically in the radical healing of both sickness and sin. But the purpose of physical healing for her was entirely secondary to the healing of sin. Far from merely improving human existence, it was intended to prove that spiritual being was not, as Christian orthodoxy would have it, a condition belonging to some heavenly realm in the beyond. Rather, it was the Kingdom of God to which ordinary material sense is blind but which is nevertheless present to be brought to light. From this standpoint the materiality that appears so palpable to the senses really represents only a limited or uninspired grasp of spiritual reality. In the Christian terms that came so naturally to her, Eddy saw matter as "the flesh" opposed to "the Spirit" and the belief in its reality as a denial of her basic conviction of "Life in and of Spirit, this Life being the sole reality of existence."

As a Unitarian minister who interviewed Eddy just after she moved to Boston observed, ". . . she is a woman of one idea, almost to the point of wearisomeness" (Gottschalk, 1973). This conviction of "Life in and of Spirit" well expresses that "one idea." Eddy's contact with Quimby was an important aspect of the process whereby she arrived at it and provided her with some working concepts and useful language to define the operation and effects of "mortal mind." But nothing in Quimby accounts for the idea itself. It was not Quimby adapted or Quimby Christianized; it was simply a different idea. And it was her one great theme from 1866 onward.

CHRISTIAN SCIENCE AND MIND-CURE IN BOSTON

From 1866 until the publication of *Science and Health* in 1875 Eddy, separated from her second husband and with scant means of support, lived an obscure and sometimes friendless existence, moving about from one living situation to another in the suburbs of Boston. Yet she was increasingly emboldened by a new sense of mission and absorbed in developing her ideas, pursuing the healing work that she felt confirmed their truth, and teaching the handful of students, mostly of working-class background, who showed interest in her ideas. In 1879 she and a small group of students formed the Church of Christ, Scientist. After her move from Lynn, Massachusetts, to Boston in 1882 a growing number of followers from mainstream Protestant denominations were attracted to the rapidly growing movement, to the consternation of an increasingly aroused clergy.

The growth of Christian Science in the early 1880s in Boston triggered the emergence of mind-cure, through which harmonial ideas first apparent in the work of Evans and Quimby reappeared in new and expanded form. Indeed, one can hardly speak of harmonialism as a continuously developing American religious tradition in view of the fact that for sixteen years after Quimby's death in 1866, Evans' activities as a writer and healer constituted virtually all there was to it. His books sold fairly well, and he continued to practice and teach mental healing until his death in 1889. But there is no evidence of his arousing a substantial following, much less anything that could be described as a movement.

Nor was Quimby a factor at this point. Eddy had written to Julius Dresser in 1866 asking him to take up the healer's work. In reply Dresser, then a newspaperman, declared forthrightly that he had neither the disposition nor the ability to teach much less practice Quimby's theory. Some sixteen years later, however, having heard of Eddy's success in Boston, Dresser and his wife

returned there, took a class in Christian Science from a renegade follower of Eddy's, and charged in a series of newspaper articles that her teaching was no more than a mixture of Eddy's "chaff" with Quimby's "wheat." Dresser then joined the growing ranks of mental healers, almost all of whom were apostates from the Christian Science movement who had found Eddy's leadership too rigid and her doctrine too confining.

Names such as A. J. Swartz, Mary Plunkett, Ursula N. Gestefeld, and Luther Marston—all among prominent mind-cure leaders of the time—are largely forgettable today. Yet one name stands out, that of Emma Hopkins, who, after a brief stint in 1884–1885 as editor of the *Christian Science Journal,* broke off from Eddy to pursue an independent and long-lasting career as a teacher of New Thought. Among the future leaders of the movement she taught were Malinda Cramer, co-founder of Divine Science; Charles and Myrtle Fillmore, founders of the Unity School of Christianity; Dr. H. Emilie Cady, whose writings became a staple of Unity literature; and much later Ernest Holmes, founder of the Church of Religious Science, the last formed of the larger New Thought groups. Mrs. Hopkins' influence on these mind-curers illustrates the continuity between mind-cure and New Thought, so assessing the close and competitive interaction of mind-cure and Christian Science in the 1880s makes it possible to see also the relation of New Thought to Eddy's teaching.

The sometimes acrimonious literature of the period shows that whatever personal feelings may have been involved, matters of principle were at the heart of the dispute. Mrs. Hopkins' free-roving eclecticism, rejecting not only Eddy's teaching but the normative authority of the Bible, gives a good idea of what was at stake. Along with most mind-curers of the time, she was hospitable to any mystical and metaphysical literature, Christian or otherwise, that appeared to expand on the central theme of "the God within." As the basic principle of mind-cure literature, this idea represented a restatement of the fundamental harmonial concept that the human mind is in harmonious rapport with the divine. But it did so in language that was to a large degree adapted from Christian Science, with the notable and revealing exception of those terms in Eddy's teaching that revolve around the Christian concept of sin and make evident her basic insistence that the unregenerate human or mortal mind is not natively congruent with but in fundamental opposition to the Mind that is God.

"The human mind," Eddy wrote, "is opposed to God and must be put off, as St. Paul declares" (1875). That man's original "scientific" being is in harmony with God as his reflection or manifestation is basic to her teaching, as is her insistence that this authentic selfhood comes to light only as material selfhood is put off through repentance and purification. "Without a knowledge of his sins, and repentance so severe that it destroys them," she wrote, "no person is or can be a Christian Scientist" (1896). Indeed, no words better epitomize her strong statements on the need for Christian rebirth than James's own explanation of what it means to be "twice-born": ". . . the man must die to an unreal life before he can be born into the real life" (1902).

This Christian rebirth and the healing effects that follow it, Eddy maintained, come about through the power of Christ acting on the human mentality and its bodily expression, not through any power resident in that mentality itself. "Christian Science," she insisted, "demands as did Paul's Christianity that we look outward for divine power, and away from human consciousness. St. Paul argues against introspection whereby to work out the salvation of man" (1886). The human mind, which virtually every figure in the harmonial tradition saw as an ameliorative agent through which divine power was channeled, was to her the fundamental cause of what the one divine Mind alone could cure. This "mortal 'mind-cure,' " she said, "produces the effect of mesmerism. It is using the power of human will, instead of the divine power understood, as in Christian Science; and without this Science there had better be no 'mind-cure,'—in which the last state of patients is worse than the first" (1896).

Mind-curers were explicit in their opposition to Eddy on this point. Commenting on her use of the term "mortal mind," a writer for the mind-cure periodical *Mental Healing Monthly* declared, "If the mind be the thinking principle of spirit, it must necessarily be *immortal* and the term is not only a misnomer but is self-contradictory" (Gottschalk, 1973). No element in her writings did they find more objectionable than her contention that the human mind, which they thought to be inherently benign, was capable of con-

sciously injuring others through what she called "mental malpractice." Indeed, she felt that the death of her third husband, Asa Gilbert Eddy, had been effected through just such means.

As mind-curers saw it, both her views as to the dangers of mental malpractice and the larger concept of animal magnetism of which it was an aspect were aberrations that Eddy would have done well to eliminate from her teaching. Yet her emphasis upon specifically recognizing and dealing with evil in all its phases was no mere adjunct to Christian Science but deeply integral to it. Since evil for her had no actual and objective existence as a power apart from God, it could appear real and powerful through hypnotic action alone. Animal magnetism, therefore, did not refer in her teaching merely to specific forms of evil but to the underlying source of all of its manifestations.

Hence her extreme reaction to Dresser's attempt to portray Christian Science as merely an outgrowth of Quimbyism. For some six years after her "discovery" of Christian Science she had continued intermittently to link her teaching with Quimby. Yet in 1872, a full decade before the Quimby controversy began, even while cherishing his memory, she felt compelled to acknowledge that his thinking still belonged in the orbit of mesmerism. To identify Christian Science with Quimby's thinking was, therefore, virtually the same as seeing it as just another form of mind-cure—but with one important difference. Where mind-curers secularized terms and concepts derived from Christian Science, Julius Dresser and his son Horatio spiritualized Quimby's beliefs in such a way as to make them appear more consonant with Christian Science. Indeed, when Horatio Dresser edited the Quimby manuscripts for publication in 1921, his selection of materials (about 40 percent of the entire corpus), editorial insertions, and frequent capitalization of terms whose deific reference was at best ambiguous in the originals had the effect of giving a religious cast to Quimby's thinking that differs markedly from the impression given by his manuscripts as a whole.

Penetrating through the haze of language that has obscured these questions, it is not difficult to see that the issues involved relate to far more than an arcane dispute over words. The harmonial concept of "the God within" represents an extreme and at points pantheistic form of the belief in divine immanence characteristic of liberal Protestantism. Mind-curers differ from liberal Protestants in that they see matter as subject to the control of thought. But unlike Christian Scientists they see it as having actual if relative existence. It is not surprising, then, that New Thought has sometimes been seen—for example, by Charles Braden, who wrote a detailed and sympathetic account of the movement—as belonging in a broad sense to the liberal Protestant tradition.

Christian Science does depart in some essential respects from Protestant orthodoxy. Yet Eddy's central contention that God in no sense inhabits finite forms and her explicit repudiation of pantheism are really far closer than mind-cure to the traditional view of his absolute sovereignty and transcendence—a view that, given her Calvinist roots, she naturally saw as basic to Christianity. Indeed, her strong condemnation of mind-cure was impelled by her belief that it had borrowed the language of Christian Science while totally rejecting the Christianity so essential to Christian Science's theology. Hence her terse statement to a class that ". . . a [Christian] Scientist can be a Christian and a mind-curer could not" (Janet Colman Reminiscences, Archives of The Mother Church).

CHRISTIAN SCIENCE AND HARMONIALISM: ORGANIZATION AND DIFFUSION

For Eddy's followers the rise of mind-cure meant more than a challenge to her theology: it raised a serious question about the continued existence of the Christian Science movement. One informed observer estimated that of the approximately five thousand nominal Christian Scientists in Boston by 1889 only one thousand followed her. By the next decade, however, mind-cure and Christian Science were developing along distinct lines, though they continued to be confused in the public mind. Mind-curers had largely ceased referring to themselves as Christian Scientists—or even for that matter as mind-curers. The broader term "New Thought" began to gain currency in 1895, the year in which the Christian Scientists dedicated the original building of the "mother church" in Boston.

The growth patterns of both movements initially ran parallel, though the relation between their development becomes increasingly difficult to trace. In the 1880s mind-cure in Boston had sprung up in the wake of interest already aroused in Christian Science. During the same decade mind-cure "institutes" in New York, Chicago, Denver, and San Francisco, largely under the tutelage of Mrs. Hopkins and her pupils, helped spark the formation of other groups. Past this point it is difficult to trace the development of mind-cure and New Thought with any exactitude, though that of Christian Science is comparatively easy to follow.

By 1890 there were twenty-five local Christian Science congregations, by 1900 nearly five hundred, and by 1920 slightly over sixteen hundred. The increase in the number of practitioners was similarly steep, jumping from 262 in 1890 to 2,564 in 1900 and 4,350 in 1920. The distribution of both in the United States indicates that by 1910 the movement had its strongest representation in the Midwest, the Northeast, the West, and the South, respectively, though it was growing faster in the West than in any other section. Contrary to the conventional wisdom that Christian Science was largely a big-city phenomenon, most of its adherents were in cities and towns of less than one hundred thousand. While a large proportion of Christian Scientists were women, the proportion of men in the movement as a whole was considerably greater than their representation among the ranks of practitioners, which after 1910 was never greater than 13.4 percent.

It is probably a safe generalization that Christian Science and New Thought had about the same regional distribution and sexual ratios. It is also clear, however, that their institutional character—indeed, their whole approach to the question of church organization—differed radically. Eddy never lost the suspicion of organization to which she gave clear expression in the first edition of *Science and Health* and intermittently in later years as well. At the same time the pressure of events—including the rise of mind-cure, internal divisiveness within the Christian Science movement itself, and mounting opposition from the clergy—convinced her that a more disciplined and effective form of church government than the congregationally organized church she had founded in 1879 was essential for the perpetuation and protection of Christian Science. The result was the reorganization in 1892 of the church into its present form as the First Church of Christ, Scientist—The Mother Church—in Boston with branches around the world.

As has sometimes been observed, Eddy's structuring of the reorganized church resembles the relation of the American federal government and states under the Constitution. Under the *Manual of the Mother Church,* a skeletal body of church rules that she published in 1895 and continued to revise until her death, The Mother Church was given responsibility for the overall affairs of the movement. While basic decisions about church affairs lay with Eddy while she was alive, ongoing responsibility for the execution of the provisions of the *Manual* and for day-to-day conduct of church affairs is vested in a self-perpetuating five-member Board of Directors. The *Manual* also spells out the form of worship followed in the branch churches for both Sunday services, which revolve around a Bible lesson studied daily by Christian Scientists, and Wednesday meetings, which include testimony of healings. These branches are otherwise self-governing. Since by Eddy's designation the Bible and *Science and Health* constitute the only "pastor" of the denomination, which has no ordained clergy, services are conducted by lay readers elected from the congregation.

The shaping of the Christian Science church in the 1890s fully bore out the title by which Eddy wished to be known: "the Discoverer and Founder of Christian Science." From the point of view of her detractors her determining role in this process was clear evidence of her desire for unchecked power and authoritarian control. From her own standpoint each of her steps was necessary to bring the structure and functions of the church she was founding into accord with the spiritual authority of the science she had discovered. The former was certainly the predominant view of those within New Thought, for whom a native bias against all religious authority was intensified by Eddy's outspoken claim that Christian Science had the authority of revelation. Indeed, one of the cardinal principles of the "new" as opposed to the "old" thought was an extremely liberal attitude toward church organization, a view that sprang from the conviction that since the human soul is natively receptive to divine influence, tides of revelation and inspiration can flow into it from virtually any source.

This outspokenly antinomian claim, more than any other factor, accounts for the appeal of New Thought. It has become something of a historical commonplace to speak of it as supplying a kind of spiritual narcotic to help soothe the "troubled souls of females" (Meyer, 1980) in a period when social and economic change was as unsettling to individual lives as to the society as a whole. Yet tens of thousands of Americans found not only emotional and physical healing through the ministrations of its healers and literature but also a sense of spiritual liberation and exhilaration difficult to recapture at this date. Something of this spirit is conveyed by the titles of such New Thought periodicals as *The Coming Light, Eternal Progress, New Man, Practical Ideals,* and *Radiant Center* and of such widely read books as Elizabeth Towne's *The Life Power and How to Use It* (1906), Henry Wood's *Ideal Suggestion Through Mental Photography* (1893), Horatio Dresser's *Living by the Spirit* (1900), and the most popular of all harmonial texts, Ralph Waldo Trine's *In Tune with the Infinite* (1897), which has sold over one and a half million copies in English and has been translated into some twenty languages.

The movement had far greater impact on American life through the circulation of such literature than through organized religious channels, which many in the movement felt were inimical to its spirit. W. W. Atkinson, a prominent New Thought leader, spoke for others when he pointed out that trying to give organizational shape to the movement would "result merely in dwarfing and stultifying it, and in a denial of its essential substance and thought" (Braden, 1963). Mind-cure institutes had flourished in the 1880s, and New Thought leaders made sporadic efforts to found functioning churches. But informal conference and discussion groups proved more congenial to the spirit of the movement— for example the Greenacre Conference in Eliot, Maine, which in 1894 brought together a number of New Thought advocates for a summer gathering that proved to be prototypical of other such conferences and retreats. Similarly, a Metaphysical Club formed in 1895 provided a lecture forum for New Thought leaders on the Boston scene, becoming a model for similar clubs scattered throughout the country.

This Metaphysical Club also proved a springboard for attempts to organize New Thought groups into a larger umbrella organization. A rather bewildering variety of conferences, conventions, and federations beginning in the earlier mind-cure phase preceeded the formation in 1908 of the National New Thought Alliance, modified in 1914 to become the International New Thought Alliance (INTA) as the movement gained modest overseas representation, particularly in Great Britain. The INTA, however, was intended from the first to be a loose federation of genuinely autonomous groups. Although exerting no power over its members, it has continued to sponsor a variety of conventions, congresses, and retreats.

Joining the INTA in 1919 were two groups that, though broadly New Thought in outlook, maintained distinct identities within the movement. The earlier of them, Divine Science, was founded in Denver in 1889. While there have never been more than two dozen Divine Science churches, the group's teaching activities and publications have largely accounted for the interest aroused by New Thought in the West prior to the rise of the Church of Religious Science in California in the 1920s.

Publication on a grander scale has accounted for the widespread influence of the Unity School of Christianity, founded in Kansas City, Missouri, in 1889 by Charles and Myrtle Fillmore, who, like so many other New Thought leaders, had studied with Mrs. Hopkins. The Fillmores insisted, however, as most New Thought leaders did not, that their teachings be explicitly associated with Christianity. The key emphasis of these teachings is on meditation and prayer that allow one to attain unity with God, outwardly manifested in greater peace, health, and abundance in daily life. While Unity holds conventions and organizes small centers in which various church services are held, the most vital part of its operation is the Silent Unity, which began in 1891 as a prayer group offering round-the-clock spiritual help to those in need and by mid-century was responding to more than a half-million telephone and mail requests for help yearly.

CHRISTIAN SCIENCE, HARMONIALISM, AND AMERICAN CULTURE

The fact that Unity, the largest and most popular of the harmonial groups, is centered in the midwestern American heartland and diffuses its message throughout the United States symbolizes the consanguinity of harmonialism with an important strain in American popular culture. Affirmative in general attitude, antiformalist in organization, loosely Christian in religious orientation, espousing both altruism and the gospel of success, Unity has attained a warm place in the hearts of thousands whose needs it has met over the years—if not a very elevated place in the annals of American theology.

Although Charles Fillmore insisted—without rancor—that Unity should be distinguished from New Thought and withdrew it from the INTA in 1922, its affirmations fit in comfortably with the Declaration of Principles adopted by the INTA in 1919 and retained until mid-century as the basic statement of New Thought principles:

> We affirm the freedom of each soul as to choice and as to belief . . . each individual must be loyal to the Truth he sees.
> We affirm the good. . . . Man is made in the image of the Good, and evil and pain are but the tests and correctives that appear when his thought does not reflect the full glory of this image.
> We affirm health. . . . Man's body is his holy temple. Every function of it, every cell of it, is intelligent and is shaped, ruled, repaired, and controlled by mind.
> We affirm the divine supply. . . . He who gives himself . . . he who trusts in the divine return, has learned the law of success.
> We affirm the New Thought of God as Universal Love, Life, Truth . . . that His mind is our mind now.
> We affirm Heaven here and now . . . and the quickened realization of the indwelling God in each soul.
>
> (Braden, 1963, pp. 195–196)

In his book *A History of the New Thought Movement* (1919) Horatio Dresser pointed out that this platform showed New Thought broadening its outlook and emerging from its earlier preoccupation with mental therapeutics. New Thought writers had long sought to relate the movement to the larger stream of American culture by speaking of the venerable Ralph Waldo Emerson as one of its patron saints, though his philosophy had no direct bearing on the formation of New Thought ideas. From the mid 1890s on, they also stressed the applicability of New Thought concepts to economic life by emphasizing that right thinking—for example, holding the "prosperity thought"—brought "supply" and even "abundance."

As the range of New Thought concerns broadened, however, the roots of the movement in the very earliest phase of harmonialism became more evident through the increasing emphasis in its literature on the role of mental suggestion. Dresser noted that "suggestion or affirmation came to be recognized as the common factor in all types of mental healing." It became the crucial element relating the broadening ideals of New Thought to conduct and so making its affirmations a practical force in daily life. At the same time, as Dresser also observed, the rising interest in psychology was helping to make the role of suggestion more intelligible to the general public.

Just what the role of suggestion meant in the practical application of New Thought principles can be seen in a passage from Trine's *In Tune with the Infinite.* Although Trine's words apply specifically to the attainment of "prosperity," they give a clear idea of the New Thought approach to the healing of disease:

> Suggest prosperity to your self. See yourself in a prosperous condition. Affirm that you will before long be in a prosperous condition. Affirm it calmly and quietly, but strongly and confidently. Believe it, believe it absolutely. Expect it, —keep it continually watered with expectation. You thus make yourself a magnet to attract the things that you desire. Don't be afraid to suggest, to affirm these things, for by so doing you put forth an ideal which will begin to clothe itself in material form. In this way you are utilizing agents among the most subtle and powerful in the universe.

> (p. 181)

There is nothing in Eddy's writings that bears directly on the attainment of prosperity as does the foregoing text from Trine. But her explanation of the process of physical healing from the preface to *Science and Health* does provide a pertinent contrast to the role of suggestion in the New Thought approach to healing in general:

> The physical healing of Christian Science results now, as in Jesus' time, from the operation of divine Principle, before which sin and disease lose their reality in human consciousness and disappear as naturally and as necessarily as darkness gives place to light and sin to reformation. Now, as then, these mighty works are not supernatural, but supremely natural. They are the sign of Immanuel, or "God with us,"—a divine influence ever present in human consciousness and repeating itself, coming now as was promised aforetime,
>
> To preach deliverance to the captives [of sense],
> And recovering of sight to the blind,
> To set at liberty them that are bruised.

> (p. xi)

As the biblical tenor of this passage indicates, Eddy and her followers saw her teaching as opening a new stage for Christian experience, restoring "primitive Christianity and its lost element of healing." This healing, she further insisted, must eventually extend to the "healing of the nations." And it was partly to lift her followers' sights to the larger demands of Christian regeneration on the world scene that in 1908 she founded the *Christian Science Monitor,* an international daily newspaper of widely recognized excellence. Adherents of New Thought often spoke of their movement as marking the dawning of a new spiritual age in which people would more confidently learn to direct their own destinies. But given the liberal eclecticism as well as the individualism of their approach, they conceived of this process in broad evolutionary terms which by no means required enlistment in a particular cause or membership in a specific church.

Harmonialism, therefore, can be viewed in broad terms as a religious tendency consistent with and to a large degree expressive of one dimension of the American cultural ethos. This explains why its influence in American life as a whole is so greatly disproportionate to its numbers and strength as an organized religious movement. Indeed, it is difficult to tell just where harmonialism breaks off and the general American ethos of optimism begins. For this reason Franklin Roosevelt's declaration in 1933 that "The only thing we have to fear is fear itself" may be considered more a triumph for the spirit of harmonialism than any of the usual evidences by which the influence of religious movements and ideas is measured.

Christian Science, on the other hand, stands

CHRISTIAN SCIENCE AND HARMONIALISM

in a very different relation to American culture as a whole. The values that stem from its practice cannot be said to support the American ethos of optimism with which harmonialism agrees so well. In fact, Eddy uses the word "optimism" only once in all her writings and then not in an approving sense. She did teach that true Christians can have increasing spiritual light and peace regardless of disruptive exterior circumstances. But far from seeing human experience in optimistic terms, she maintained that general dislocation and suffering would continue and even increase until humanity awakened from the fundamental error of belief in existence separate from God. For her this error has no ontological existence and so can be defeated. But doing so requires, she insisted, a determined confrontation with its consequences in human experience.

It is therefore understandable that New Thought was not only more "harmonial" than Christian Science in its teachings but also in its relation to the American social environment. Many of those who embraced New Thought remained within established churches, quietly reading and practicing its precepts on the side. Those who left their churches might associate with one of many loosely organized harmonial groups but could hardly be identified as members of a threatening new denomination or sect.

Given its clear-cut identity and rapid growth, however, Christian Science posed a very distinct threat to many orthodox clergymen who saw it as a dangerously attractive heresy. In addition, Christian Scientists believed that although reliance on spiritual means for healing must be voluntary, the premises of spiritual healing were so opposed to those underlying medical treatment that they could not be combined. This conviction, which adherents of New Thought did not share, brought the movement into open conflict with the medical profession, which at the turn of the century initiated a widespread though unsuccessful campaign legally to prohibit the practice of Christian Science healing.

While Christian Scientists generally rely on spiritual means for healing, they respect the rights of all individuals and in no way seek to force their choice on others. They do view their healing practice as a religious discipline that is at the same time an effective therapy. But they do not denigrate the sincere efforts of others dedicated to healing. As Thomas C. Johnsen has noted, "Eddy's own attitude toward the medical community belied the 'faith healer' image. . . . In spite of—or perhaps because of—her strong views on healing, she respected the humanitarianism of physicians and seemed to identify with the motives if not the methods of the profession" (1986).

Whatever the rigorous demands of Eddy's teaching and the conflict it engendered with the religious and medical establishments, there is clear evidence that Christian Science was sometimes distorted in practice into a means for attaining the middle-class values of respectability, comfort, and success. It is not difficult to find a strain of secularism in some of the testimonies and articles published in Christian Science periodicals whereby the distinction between Eddy's teaching and harmonialism is blurred—a point that helps to account for the confusion between the two among historians and in the public mind. One example is the emphasis in the movement during the first two decades of the twentieth century particularly on "using" Christian Science to achieve success in business life through "applying" spiritual power to the solution of business problems. This tendency prompted Alfred Farlow, an early spokesman for the church, to observe, "It seems to us that a Christian Scientist can judge better as to his real advancement by noting how many of his pet sins he is escaping, rather than by counting the amount of money he is gaining" (Gottschalk, 1973).

What Farlow was really criticizing in this statement, at least by implication, was the acculturization of Christian Science, a process that has increased its public identification with harmonial movements. Yet when Christian Science is practiced as a mental technique for the realization of essentially secular ends and when its metaphysics are used as a pretext for avoiding a confrontation with evil, there is no valid basis for distinguishing it from harmonialism in terms of its practical outcome. The crucial distinction between the two lies in the fact that this more secularized practice of Christian Science represents a distortion of its basic purpose, whereas harmonialism was essentially more secular to begin with and openly advocates the technique of mental suggestion that Eddy's teaching explicitly repudiates. Indeed, most forms of harmonialism with the exception of Unity have not considered themselves specifically Christian at all.

CHRISTIAN SCIENCE AND HARMONIALISM

These points help to locate Christian Science within the spectrum of American Christianity as one of those groups in the radical Reformed Protestant tradition that insists upon going back to pure and normative Christian beginnings. While the Christian Science movement in practice has to some degree compromised the religious purpose of Eddy's teaching, these purposes have never really been shared by the advocates of harmonialism at all. Because the aims of harmonialism are far more congruent with the culture in which both movements arose, it has been a significant influence strengthening tendencies that already existed in that culture. The impact of Christian Scientists' commitment to healing through spiritual means, however, has been an important factor in the broad reawakening of interest in spiritual healing in modern Christianity. Both Christian Science and harmonialism are phases of the American experience that need to be more discriminatingly analyzed in relation to each other, to the culture in which they emerged, and to the Christian tradition as a whole.

BIBLIOGRAPHY

Sydney E. Ahlstrom, "Harmonial Religion Since the Later Nineteenth Century," in *A Religious History of the American People* (1972); Ernest Sutherland Bates and John V. Dittemore, *Mary Baker Eddy: The Truth and the Tradition* (1932); Charles Braden, *Spirits in Rebellion: The Rise and Development of New Thought* (1963); Emilie Cady, *Lessons in Truth* (1894); *A Century of Christian Science Healing* (1966); *Christian Science Journal;* Malinda E. Cramer, *Divine Science and Healing* (1905); Horatio W. Dresser, *A History of the New Thought Movement* (1919); Mary Baker Eddy, *Science and Health with Key to the Scriptures* (1875), "Questions Answered," in *Christian Science Journal* 1 (October 1886), *Retrospection and Introspection* (1891), *No and Yes* (1891), *Miscellaneous Writings, 1883–1896* (1896), *Message to The Mother Church, Boston, Mass., June 1901* (1901); Warren Felt Evans, *The Mental Cure: Illustrating the Influence of the Mind on the Body, Both in Health and Disease, and the Psychological Method of Treatment* (1869), *Mental Medicine: A Theoretical and Practical Treatise on Medical Psychology* (1872).

Charles Fillmore, *Prosperity* (1907); H. A. L. Fisher, *Our New Religion* (1929); Robert C. Fuller, *Mesmerism and the American Cure of Souls* (1982); Stephen Gottschalk, *The Emergence of Christian Science in American Religious Life* (1973); Karl Holl, "Der Szientismus," reprinted in *Gesammelte Aufsätze Zur Kirchengeschichte* III (1921–1928); William James, *The Varieties of Religious Experience* (1902); Dewitt John, *The Christian Science Way of Life* (1962); Thomas C. Johnsen, *Christian Science and the Puritan Tradition*, Ph.d. diss., Johns Hopkins Univ. (1983), "Christian Scientists and the Medical Profession: A Historical Perspective," in *Medical Heritage* (1986); J. Stillson Judah, *The History and Philosophy of the Metaphysical Movements in America* (1967); Jean A. McDonald, "Mary Baker Eddy and the Nineteenth-Century 'Public' Woman: A Feminist Reappraisal," in *Journal of Feminist Studies in Religion* (1986); Donald Meyer, *The Positive Thinkers: Religion as Popular Psychology from Mary Baker Eddy to Oral Roberts* (1980).

Gail Thain Parker, *Mind Cure in New England: From the Civil War to World War I* (1973); Charles Brodie Patterson, *The Will to be Well* (1901); Robert Peel, *Christian Science: Its Encounter with American Culture* (1958), *Mary Baker Eddy: The Years of Discovery* (1966), *Mary Baker Eddy: The Years of Trial* (1971), *Mary Baker Eddy: The Years of Authority* (1977), *Spiritual Healing in a Scientific Age: A Christian Science Perspective* (1987); Phineas Parkhurst Quimby, *The Quimby Manuscripts*, Horatio W. Dresser, ed. (1921); Israel Regardie, *The Romance of Metaphysics: An Introduction to the History, Theory, and Psychology of Modern Metaphysics* (1947); A. J. Swartz, "Editorial Reports," in *Mental Science Magazine* (March 1888); John F. Teahan, "Warren Felt Evans and Mental Healing: Romantic Idealism and Practical Mysticism in Nineteenth-Century America," in *Church History* 48 (March 1979); Ralph Waldo Trine, *In Tune with the Infinite* (1897); Henry Wood, *Ideal Suggestion Through Mental Photography* (1893).

[*See also* MEDICINE AND MEDICAL ETHICS.]

SOCIAL CHRISTIANITY

Charles H. Lippy

The social gospel is the brotherhood of man and the fatherhood of God. It is the old gospel of peace on earth among men of good will. It is the proclamation of the kingdom of heaven, a divinely ordered society, to be realized on earth. It is the application of Christ's Golden Rule and Law of Love to all the business and affairs of life. It is the glad tidings of peace and purity and plenty.

(White and Hopkins, 1976, p. 151)

THUS declared the Christian Commonwealth Colony, a short-lived communal experiment in Georgia, in the opening pages of its journal, the *Social Gospel,* in 1898. Unwittingly the journal's name became attached to a movement in American Protestantism committed to the development of a social order grounded in principles believed to be those taught by Jesus. Before the label *Social Gospel* became generally accepted, the same spirit of reform was known variously as Social Christianity, the gospel of the kingdom, Christian Sociology, or, following its Anglo-European parallel, Christian Socialism.

While the Social Gospel usually refers to a Protestant trend between the Civil War and World War I, the interest in revamping society to reflect religious values was limited neither to this epoch nor to Protestantism. American Catholics devoted much discussion to "the social question," particularly after the promulgation in 1891 of Pope Leo XIII's encyclical *Rerum Novarum.* And, as Timothy Smith has demonstrated, American religion's dedication to social reform had roots in the antebellum revivals associated with Charles Grandison Finney, the numerous voluntary societies designed to create a Christian America, and the Holiness awakening that erupted on the eve of the Civil War. Social Chris-

tianity broadly construed had a well-established heritage when individuals as diverse as Josiah Strong and John A. Ryan, Washington Gladden, and George Herron called for a fresh application of Christian precepts to social problems in the closing decades of the nineteenth century.

Social Christianity was as varied in the forms it took as it was in the sorts of individuals who promoted it. It encompassed reasoned, systematic theological statements such as Walter Rauschenbusch's *A Theology for the Social Gospel* (1917) and polemical tirades such as Josiah Strong's *Our Country* (1885). Social Christianity denoted carefully thought-out, comprehensive programs for social change, such as those advanced in the *Dawn,* the periodical of the Society of Christian Socialists, as well as much more ad hoc proposals set forth by scattered thinkers for remedying particular social ills at particular times. It may be understood as the personal agenda for social change of an array of individuals as much as it may be seen as the corporate call for an ethical order in the social creeds of the denominations. Social Christianity took shape in ecumenical ventures as assorted as the Evangelical Alliance, the Federal Council of Churches, and the United Church of Canada, in institutions and agencies as different in style as the Salvation Army and the Society of St. Vincent de Paul, in organizations for trade union leaders, clergy, and female temperance advocates. Although it reached millions via popular, sometimes best-selling novels, it did not win to its ranks the masses of people either within or outside of the churches. Hence it is difficult for the analyst of American religion to identify and analyze Social Christianity neatly. Whatever the name, though, and whatever the manifestation, the movement was concerned with redirecting the course of

American life by bringing the ethical principles of Christianity to bear on the social conditions of the day.

Martin E. Marty, in his *Righteous Empire* (1970), identified two basic models in American religion's response to social conditions, that of the rescuer and that of the reformer. The first regards society as evil and corrupt by nature and sees the role of religion as rescuing individuals from its influences through the experience of salvation; society itself will change only when all the individuals who comprise it have been saved. The latter, while not necessarily denying the need for individual salvation, sees religion's task as reforming the social order to render it a fit habitation for the righteous. It assumes that an evil environment may generate sin as much as a fallen nature may. To these models should be added a third: the revolutionary or the radical. For the revolutionary or the radical, because society has strayed so far from the ideals advocated by religion, neither rescuing individuals nor reforming institutions is satisfactory. Rather, the social order must be revolutionized or reconstructed from the bottom up.

In looking at northern Protestantism in the post–Civil War years, Henry F. May called the manifestations of these three types conservative Social Christianity, progressive Social Christianity, and radical Social Christianity. Regardless of designation, all three models commingled but offered different programs for change. All were attempts to respond to the "new civilization," to use Josiah Strong's description, wrought by urbanization and industrialization. All three drew from the same ideological repository and were stimulated by the same forces.

Some of the impetus for a new Social Christianity derived from analogous movements in Europe, particularly in Great Britain and Germany. The ideas of British thinkers such as Thomas Chalmers, Henry Scott Holland, Charles Kingsley, Frederick Denison Maurice, and John R. Seeley had especial impact, though more on expressions of Social Christianity in Canada than in the United States. In Britain, Christian Socialism developed largely as a reaction to the utilitarianism and laissez-faire philosophy of Jeremy Bentham, John Stuart Mill, and others. Promulgating its programs for social change in a series of tracts that appeared beginning in 1850 and in agencies such as the Working Men's College in London, Christian Socialism in Britain called for greater educational opportunities for the working class, support for trade unions, and the passing of cooperative legislation. In Germany, Christian Socialism took on a more political cast and led to attempts to form a political party to promote its agenda in the public sector. Christian Socialism in Europe received a psychological boost in the democratic revolutions of 1848, which many saw as the last gasp of the old order and the dawn of a new day for the working people.

More immediately in the background of American Social Christianity, as noted above, was the metamorphosis that transformed rural, agrarian America into an urban, industrialized nation. Between 1870 and 1920, the age of the Social Gospel, the rise of the city and the growth of industry were the two distinguishing characteristics of American common life. Thousands left rural and small-town America to seek a better life in the city through jobs in the rapidly growing factory system and other forms of businesses associated with industrialization. Indeed the fruits of the urban working class rendered the United States the major industrial power in the world by the opening of the twentieth century. But for Americans accustomed to an agrarian culture, the industrialized city brought forever to an end what Josiah Strong heralded as "the simple, homespun individualistic life of the world's past." In the industrial city, division of labor and specialization created a dependence on the work of others for survival. The close-knit rural community gave way to intricate webs of secondary relationships in the ongoing desire to find meaning in human association and interaction.

Along with this in-migration to industrial centers came massive immigration. In the half-century leading up to 1920, when the Bureau of the Census noted that for the first time in the nation's history a majority of Americans lived in urban communities, more than 26 million immigrants entered the United States, most often clustering in ethnic ghettos in the cities and accepting jobs at whatever wages business and industry would pay. By the 1890s, immigrants coming from southern and eastern Europe outnumbered those from northwestern Europe, which had provided the basic stock that engineered the European invasion of North America in the seventeenth century. The dilemma of housing these millions, incorporating them into American society, and providing for their spiritual nurture was a major problem that the United States and its people had to confront.

For those who imbibed the heady wines of Social Darwinism, the new interest in scientific method, and the wonders of the machine, the emergence of an industrialized urban society signaled proof that limitless progress toward national greatness had become a reality. But while pulpiteers preached a "gospel of wealth" to businessmen counting their profits, others gradually recognized that the urban working class knew only poverty. While capitalists celebrated unprecedented industrial growth, laborers lamented low wages, long hours, and unsafe working conditions. It was not long before the monumental growth of business and industry generated ever-increasing conflict between employers and employees.

As the labor union movement gained ground, workers' strikes began to shatter the illusion that growth was synonymous with progress. From the railroad strike of 1877, the Haymarket Affair (1886), and the Pullman strike (1893) to the devastating coal strike of 1905, labor strife was basic to the age. In addition, the swelling population of the cities had produced the slum and the tenement. Some astutely recognized that the evangelical Protestantism which had captured the American mind and spirit in the antebellum period seemed in retreat. Once-fashionable downtown churches watched congregations dwindle as the affluent moved to suburbs, while the Protestant working class remained alienated and the newer immigrants retained allegiance—perhaps somewhat tenuous at times—to the Roman Catholic, Jewish, and Eastern Orthodox traditions of their native lands. Was religion irrelevant to industrial life in the city? Or, put another way, how could the evangelical message of salvation make sense to the urban masses?

The struggle to respond to such questions was one force that gave birth to Social Christianity. For example, these issues prompted Congregationalist Josiah Strong to publish extensively on his appraisal of the Protestant situation. Convinced that the city provided the opportunity to develop communities where selfless love and service could be controlling principles of individual and corporate life, Strong urged Protestants to recommit themselves to evangelism in the cities. As a conservative rescuer, Strong believed that it was only through the experience of salvation that persons could reap the benefits that urban life offered.

Suspicious of Roman Catholicism, socialism, and the growing concentration of wealth in the hands of a few, Strong lent support to the more conservative approaches to revitalizing religion, such as the institutional church, city mission work, and the like. His conviction that it was America's and the Anglo-Saxon race's destiny to lift humanity to its full potential has often led later critics to condemn him as a racist and imperialist, but the charge is only partially warranted. The racist and imperialist tone particularly apparent in *Our Country* (1885) stemmed not from a sense of superiority but from the belief that industrialization and urbanization had bestowed a greatness on the United States that mandated implementation of the Christian ideals of the kingdom. After leaving the staff of the Evangelical Alliance, Strong for a time edited *Social Service,* which sought to demonstrate how the churches could use the techniques and theories of the social sciences to further the coming of the kingdom.

Washington Gladden, a progressive reformer, was drawn to rethink his notion of Christianity's meaning when, as a Congregationalist pastor in North Adams (1866–1871) and Springfield (1875–1882), Massachusetts, and then in Columbus, Ohio, he witnessed the labor-capital conflict at first hand. While ministering to employer and employee alike, he became sensitized to the justice of the laboring class's complaints. Consequently he became the "Father of the Social Gospel," as he relentlessly argued the need for both individual and social salvation. Persons still needed to experience salvation from sin, but in his mind social institutions, particularly economic ones, also needed redemption. For Gladden, cooperation had to replace capitalistic competition as the basic operating principle of industry before social salvation could become a reality.

Gladden produced nearly three dozen books derived from his sermons and lectures, popularizing themes in the new liberal theology that undergirded Social Christianity and showing how the cause of labor advanced the cause of the kingdom. It was Gladden's critique of capitalism and his insistence that adherence to the social principles of Jesus required cooperation to supersede the competition fostered by capitalism that targeted the capital-labor conflict as one primary arena for change in Social Gospel circles. In time Gladden became one of the few theorists of Social Christianity who recognized the injustices that American society perpetrated on its black citizens and summoned Americans to ensure that blacks secured at least the right to vote and the right of access to opportunities for higher education.

In 1885 Walter Rauschenbusch, grounded in German evangelical piety, became pastor of the Second German Baptist Church on the edge of New York City's infamous Hell's Kitchen. His direct experience and deepened awareness of the situation of the neighborhood's laboring class and the city's immigrant population brought about his conversion to Social Christianity of the progressive reform type. While a pastor, Rauschenbusch helped form the Brotherhood of the Kingdom, a group composed initially of Baptist clergy but soon ecumenical in character that sought to develop styles of ministry responsive to human need in the city.

After a decade in the pastorate, Rauschenbusch became a professor of church history at what later became the Colgate-Rochester Divinity School in New York. During his years as a professor he wrote the major theoretical works of the Social Gospel movement: *Christianity and the Social Crisis* (1907), *Christianizing the Social Order* (1912), and *A Theology for the Social Gospel* (1917). Also for several years a popular lecturer, particularly in the Northeast, Rauschenbusch drafted a volume of prayers, translating many themes of Social Christianity into popular language for ordinary men and women. In an article published the year he died, Rauschenbusch reflected on his personal transformation:

> When I had begun to apply my previous religious ideas to the conditions I found, I discovered they didn't fit. . . . All my scientific studying of the Bible was undertaken to find a basis for the Christian teaching of a social gospel.

If urbanization and industrialization were the primary catalysts that spurred the birth of Social Christianity, other forces also lay in the background. On an intellectual plane, as Rauschenbusch implied, the appropriation of scientific approaches to the study of Scripture had significant impact on the way Protestants especially interpreted biblical texts. Pioneered largely in Germany, the new understanding of Scripture known as the Higher Criticism involved the use of literary critical constructs to probe issues such as authorship, dates of composition, audience, and setting of the books of the Bible. In the hands of Social Gospel advocates, the scientific method became a means primarily to determine the original meaning and intent of the message of the Hebrew prophets and the teachings of Jesus recorded in the New Testament gospels.

Parallel to the rise of biblical criticism were new currents in theology that ultimately became labeled as liberal. Again German thinkers such as Albrecht Ritschl and Adolf von Harnack, influenced by the ramifications of evolutionary theory in the sciences, led the liberal quest to peel away the accretions of time from the Christian theological tradition to expose the original core of Christian proclamation. The essence of Christianity, liberal thinkers concluded, lay in the simple affirmation of "the fatherhood of God and the brotherhood of man" realized in the teaching of Jesus about the kingdom of God. These ideas in turn became the central components of Social Christianity's theological program.

Rauschenbusch, who studied in Germany, drew much from the liberal school in constructing his theology for the Social Gospel. Within American Protestantism, the work of Horace Bushnell, particularly his writings on the doctrine of the atonement and on Christian nurture, helped pave the way for liberal currents to gain a hearing. Washington Gladden, for example, acknowledged his own debt to Bushnell as he moved into the forefront of American Social Christianity. Other American theologians whose liberal focus provided an ideological reservoir for ideas articulated by champions of Social Christianity included, among others, Theodore Thornton Munger, William Adams Brown, Henry Churchill King, and William Newton Clark.

In other intellectual circles, the emergence of the social sciences as accepted disciplines within the academic curriculum lured some into the orbit of Social Christianity. The experience of Richard T. Ely, one of the founders of the American Economic Association (1885) and the American Institute of Christian Sociology (1893), is representative. Ely was a prominent spokesman for Social Christianity from about 1885 to 1895. As a student in Germany and then as a professor of economics at the University of Wisconsin, Ely became convinced of the relativity of economic theory. Simply put, economic theories reflected the social context of their own day; as society evolved, so, too, did economic theory and economic institutions.

Ely sought to use social science methodology to explain the dynamics of society, in particular the interrelatedness of all social institutions. His *Social Aspects of Christianity* (1889) and *Social Law of Service* (1896) attempted to show why human solidarity demanded progressive reform to render the institutions of society fit expressions of humanity's love of God and love of one's fellow creatures. He was particularly concerned with economic disparities that impeded society from becoming the human replica of the divine kingdom and hoped they could be eliminated. After a decade, though, Ely began to give greater attention to the demands of his academic career and withdrew from the front ranks of Social Christianity.

The social sciences, however, remained for Ely and for others mechanisms that would show how to apply Social Christianity's affirmation of human solidarity and mutual love to the concrete institutions that made up the social order. Academically, the impact of the social sciences became secure, for example, with the introduction into both the secular and theological curricula of courses in social ethics, Christian sociology, and the like. Practically it came in such ways as the adoption of neighborhood survey techniques by local churches in various urban centers to ascertain the religious composition of the population.

Schools where liberal theology and the social sciences took hold tended to be concentrated in the North and Northeast, but Social Christianity was neither exclusively a northern phenomenon nor limited to the United States. As Kenneth Bailey, J. Wayne Flynt, John Eighmy, and others have shown, industrialization and urbanization were likewise hallmarks of the New South, which combined with more distinctively regional problems (farm tenancy, illiteracy, and racial discrimination) to bring a heightened social consciousness to southern Protestantism; by the outbreak of World War I, it had also given birth to a southern Social Christianity. While surely not as pervasive as northern Social Christianity in penetrating the denominations' organizational structures, southern Social Christianity left its own enduring legacy.

Across the border in Canada, as John Webster Grant has argued, the Social Gospel of American Protestantism and "the constant fertilization of British ideas as well" brought Social Christianity to the Canadian churches as they, too, responded to the economic transformations of the late nineteenth century and more especially to the rapid growth of the Canadian population in the early twentieth century. But precisely what did Social Christianity hope to accomplish?

Unfortunately, advocates of Social Christianity, whether conservative rescuers, progressive reformers, or radical revolutionaries, did not offer a single program for revamping social institutions. Individuals promulgated their own prescriptions to cure society's ills, though there was substantial agreement on some points. For example, while nearly all voices calling for Social Christianity supported arbitration in labor disputes, higher wages for workers, and some sort of cooperative principle in organizing business and industry, they sharply disagreed over whether to endorse unions and such tactics as strikes. The more conservative Joseph Cook, a Boston orthodox Congregationalist pastor and lecturer who was convinced that unions fostered atheistic socialism and anarchy, nonetheless called for arbitration, better wages, and legislation to regulate child labor and women's labor. Gladden, representative of the moderate progressive reformer, defended labor's pleas for profit sharing, demanded control of trusts and monopolies, called for inspection of factories to ensure safe working conditions, and supported shorter working hours. But his views on unions were not uniform. At first wary of unions because tactics such as strikes seemed to engender violence as management and government took steps to quash them, Gladden more and more saw unions as the only effective countermeasure to the power of capital and the direct and indirect ways in which government aided capitalism. Rauschenbusch, in addition to calling for decent wages and more humane working conditions in *Christianity and the Social Crisis,* cried out for public ownership of utilities and other industries essential to the commonweal. Public ownership, presumably, would obviate the need for unions.

921

SOCIAL CHRISTIANITY

Within Protestantism, support for labor's cause was institutionalized in organizations such as the Episcopalian Church Association for the Advancement of the Interests of Labor, established in 1887, the Christian Social Union (1890), and the Christian Labor Union, founded in Boston in 1872. Many Unitarians were also involved in these organizations to promote labor's cause. More radical thinkers were not content even with these outlets and moved toward espousal of some form of socialism. W. D. P. Bliss, for example, helped organize the Society of Christian Socialists in Boston in 1889; Vida Scudder was a founder of the Christian Socialist Fellowship; George Herron for a time became active in the politics of the Socialist party. Even Rauschenbusch, the epitome of the progressive reformer, referred to himself as a socialist. Yet neither radical revolutionary nor progressive reformer defined socialism in terms of the dialectical materialism of Karl Marx.

Although most leaders of Social Christianity were familiar with Marx's writings and aware of the influence of Marx's teaching on European socialism, both religious and secular, they tended to view socialism in more evolutionary terms. For them socialism described the order that would result when human beings acknowledged their interdependence and created institutions based on common good rather than on private gain. Socialism denoted an educational process by which men and women would come to realize the gains that would emerge in a cooperative commonwealth based on love of God and love of neighbor. In Canada, however, Social Christianity in time became more directly involved in politics and in the 1930s, while Social Christianity was on the wane elsewhere, it was a major factor contributing to the founding of the New Democratic party.

While eschewing any form of socialism, the Catholic church likewise had to deal with the concerns of labor. Catholic leaders also wavered in their support for unions although Catholics accounted for a large proportion of union membership. Unions' open hostility to the church in much of Europe had bred a deep fear of the labor movement, while the Marxist socialism that undergirded labor's cause in parts of Europe was generally antagonistic to religion. Indeed, Catholic authorities repeatedly condemned socialism of all kinds on the grounds that it was fundamentally anarchistic in its attacks on the sanctity of private ownership of property. Then, too, in both Europe and America, Roman Catholicism had long been wary of both secret societies not under the church's beneficent control and secular organizations that might compete with the church for loyalty. Many saw unions as both.

Only gradually and with much internal dissent did the American church hierarchy, at the prodding of James Cardinal Gibbons of Baltimore, convince Rome that unions were beneficial to the welfare of the Catholic masses. Gibbons also was largely responsible for preventing the papacy from condemning the Knights of Labor in 1886 and for thwarting moves to place Henry George's *Progress and Poverty* (1879) on the *Index of Forbidden Books*. Gibbons' sympathy for the plight of the working class stemmed from both a personal commitment to the democratic process and a shrewd recognition that were the church to appear hostile to labor's cause it would alienate the base of its constituency. Another voice in the hierarchy that lent support to labor was Archbishop John Ireland of St. Paul, Minnesota. Ireland's endorsement of arbitration was most visibly seen in his mediatory role in two serious railroad strikes in the Northwest in 1894. But Gibbons and Ireland for a time were a minority presence in the hierarchy as the Catholic church in the United States struggled to come to grips with the religious pluralism characteristic of the culture, the pressures brought on the church by massive immigration, and the need to convince Rome that the tides of modernity in America were fundamentally different from those in Europe, where there was often open hostility to religion in general and Catholicism in particular.

The Columbian/Catholic Congress, held in Chicago in 1893, lent support to workers' demands for compulsory arbitration in labor disputes, while the Social Service Commission set up by the American Federation of Catholic Societies in 1911 also endorsed much of labor's program. It called for the elimination of unnecessary Sunday labor, compensation for injuries on the job, reasonable hours, safe and sanitary working conditions, the elimination of child labor, and a guaranteed living wage.

No Catholic was more outspoken on the issue of wages than John A. Ryan from St. Paul. His *A Living Wage* appeared in 1906 with an introduction by Richard T. Ely. According to Aaron

Abell, the book quickly became the *Uncle Tom's Cabin* of the minimum wage movement. Later Ryan became professor of moral theology and industrial ethics at the Catholic University of America in Washington, D.C., where he sensitized countless students to the need to relate religious principles to business and industry. As a professor, Ryan continued his public efforts to secure the eight-hour day, restrict child labor, regulate women's labor, promote compulsory arbitration, and establish such benefits for workers as accident, disability, and retirement insurance.

In Canada, Catholics in some cases formed their own unions as a means to advance labor's cause while maintaining church support, but these unions quickly became involved in collective bargaining, much to the chagrin of the church hierarchy, which at one point had condemned the Knights of Labor. Clearly support for labor's pleas to share in the prosperity that industrialization had brought to the capitalist class was central to Social Christianity's vision of a new order. While in time much of labor's agenda became not only recognized as legitimate but also common practice, in the era of Social Christianity it appeared extreme.

Social Christianity's response to the crisis of urbanization was even more diffuse. The most familiar type of response to urban America, common among both Protestants and Catholics and reflective of the conservative rescue approach, was the social service agency. The various types of organizations in this category had one general goal: providing relief from presumably corrupting influences of the city that resulted from inadequate and/or overcrowded housing, lack of recreational facilities, unemployment, crime, and the like. Rarely did social service institutions deal with the causes that created such conditions. Rather, they sought to alleviate their effects. The assumption behind this approach was both simple and simplistic: show individuals how to order their lives in a socially acceptable manner and they will automatically change the way they live.

Among Protestants, the city mission represents one type of social service institution, popular among conservative rescuers, that tried to assist individuals in improving their lot. City missions such as the Pacific Garden Mission in Chicago, while unabashedly seeking to save souls, in many cases offered lodging, occasional meals,

and perhaps assistance in finding employment. The settlement house, of which the most well known is Jane Addams' Hull House in Chicago, provided a broader array of services, many of which were oriented toward children, youth, young adults, and adult women. Instruction in arts and crafts, physical fitness, and domestic arts was a staple of settlement house fare. In some cases, the settlement house was a precursor of modern day-care centers in providing programs for children while parents labored in the burgeoning factories.

The operations of both the rescue mission and the settlement house merged to some extent in two other agencies that marked Social Christianity's urban program. More on the conservative end of the spectrum, the Salvation Army, transplanted from England shortly after its founding there in 1878, adapted the style of the street in bringing both a message of salvation and practical assistance to thousands of city dwellers. Although its style offended many entrenched in the staid ethos of "establishment Protestantism," the Salvation Army and its schismatic offshoot, the Volunteers of America, gradually won the respect of former detractors because of their ability to meet the poor, the homeless, and the unemployed on their own terms.

More in keeping with mainline Protestantism's ethos was the "institutional church," a phenomenon endorsed by conservative rescuers and progressive reformers alike. The institutional church, in addition to the usual array of religious services, frequently offered extensive educational and recreational programs in gymnasia and other buildings attached to the church structure. The goal was to respond to the needs, spiritual and otherwise, of urban residents. Episcopalians especially led the way in organizing institutional churches, St. Bartholomew's and St. George's in New York City being two prominent examples. Some institutional churches emerged from the need to provide aid to recent immigrants as well as a program for neighborhood residents. For instance, the Jan Hus Bohemian Brethren (now Presbyterian) Church, also in New York City, maintained rooms that newly arrived Czech immigrants could rent at low cost while adjusting to the American scene.

Akin to the institutional church in program format were the YMCA and YWCA. While the Y's go back to the antebellum period, they experienced their greatest growth as the United States became urbanized. Their aim was to offer educational and recreational opportunities and often low-cost housing in a Christian setting to the thousands of young men and young women who flocked to the cities hoping for employment in business and industry. The Y's attempted particularly to reach those who were unaffiliated with local churches, in the anticipation that the religious orientation of the Y's would reinforce moral values and lessen the likelihood that young workers would abandon religion entirely for the secular ways of the city. Within the churches, youth were drawn into the orbit of Social Christianity by the Christian Endeavor Society, the Epworth League of the Methodists, and their parallel groups in other denominations, as well as by the expanding Sunday school movement.

If, as Janet Forsythe Fishburn has charged, Social Christianity perpetuated a Victorian view of women, it did include many women among its supporters and workers. Much of the day-to-day work in settlement houses, the institutional churches, the Salvation Army "slum brigades," and the YWCA's was carried out by women. Among Protestants, Social Christianity was a catalyst in nurturing many women's groups that had earlier origins—the ladies' aid society, the home missionary society, and the like—and in giving birth to new ones such as the King's Daughters, which coordinated efforts of women to provide religious instruction and other educational activities for laboring women and other women in the growing cities. Women offered their most conspicuous leadership, however, in the temperance movement.

All these Protestant endeavors had parallels within American Catholicism. Indeed the bulk of Social Christianity's urban work rested on Roman Catholicism, whose constituency was drawn largely from the immigrant laborers who flooded the cities. Many Roman Catholic parishes became social centers as immigrants sought the familiar in the midst of a new and alien environment. Many offered help in finding housing and employment in addition to instruction in the English language, the American political system, the "American way of life," and sometimes basic health care. The Central Verein, for example, under the leadership of Frederick Kenkel and, briefly, Peter Dietz, devel-

oped a wide range of programs, mostly of the conservative rescue type, to minister particularly to German Catholics. The verein, based in St. Louis, was also an early supporter of the labor union movement within Catholic circles as well as a potent force in Catholicism's urban ministry.

After Dietz left the Central Verein, he remained for a brief time a potent voice for Catholic Social Christianity, concerned with the consequences of both industrialization and urbanization. In Aaron Abell's words (1960), "Just as John A. Ryan was the academician, so Peter E. Dietz was the organizer of the American Catholic social movement." Dietz, however, hoped too optimistically that the Central Verein's benevolent societies, its educational programs, and its support for the labor union movement would form the foundation for a nationally coordinated Catholic social reform endeavor. This hope motivated him to help found the American Federation of Catholic Societies in 1901, as well as the Militia of Christ for Social Service, an organization of Catholic trade union officials. Although the verein's more conservative stance gradually became adopted by most Catholic societies, Dietz's federation never had the impact he anticipated because it suffered from internal dissension. By the time of World War I, the National Catholic War Council came to dominate organized programs of social action, and Dietz retreated from the public eye, pursuing his vocation as a parish priest.

Perhaps the most controversial Catholic spokesman for Social Christianity was Edward McGlynn, who became pastor of St. Stephen's Church in New York City in 1866. McGlynn's conviction that the fundamental social problem was economic led him to embrace Henry George's single-tax proposal, voice support for the Irish Land League, and call for a thorough rethinking of how property was distributed. Because his views seemed to contradict official church teaching on the sanctity of private property, McGlynn was for a time forbidden by his superiors to speak and at one point briefly excommunicated. Nonetheless, his presence did much to spur American Catholicism to confront the implications of Social Christianity.

Much of the social service work of American Catholicism had pre–Civil War roots, and much of it paralleled the kind of work done by Protestant agencies. The Society of St. Vincent de Paul, established in France in 1833 and first organized in the United States in St. Louis in 1845, in time provided services to the urban Catholic population similar to those offered by the Salvation Army. Many Catholic orders ran boarding houses for young men and women working in the cities and/or set up educational ventures (often called industrial schools or manual labor schools) that sought to train orphans and other children for the new kinds of jobs that came with industrial expansion. The Brothers and Sisters of Holy Cross, the Sisters of Mercy, the Sisters of Charity, and other groups all enlarged programs begun in the antebellum epoch to meet the pressing needs of the Catholic working class. Catholic women could volunteer for social service work in the cities under the aegis of organizations such as the Queen's Daughters (the Catholic counterpart to the Protestant King's Daughters) and the National League of Catholic Women. Increasingly, though, the task of coping with the rapid rise of the urban Catholic population fell to local parishes, often organized along ethnic lines, which did a great deal in helping immigrants to find a niche in American society and migrants to the cities to adjust to the urban environment.

One of the few areas that found Protestants and Catholics working together in the cause of Social Christianity was the temperance movement. Some Protestants, such as Josiah Strong, regarded increasing consumption of alcoholic beverages, the saloon, and the growing liquor industry as results of Catholic immigration (results that would be mitigated, Strong thought, if Catholics converted to evangelical Protestantism). In time many Protestant and some Catholic leaders came to believe that abuse of alcohol accompanied labor unrest, urban congestion, and alienation from society, though the rank and file, particularly in Catholic parishes, remained divided on this issue. While temperance and/or prohibition would not eradicate the plight of the urban working class, it would, in the minds of the movement's supporters, allow men and women to devote what resources they had to improving their situation. One could argue that in some ways the temperance movement, which resulted in the brief experiment in national prohibition, was the most obvious success story of Social Christianity; but one could also argue that it was a dubious success at best. As noted earlier, the temperance movement did draw many women into the front ranks of Social Christianity, and many found their efforts in this arena a prelude to greater social reform activity. The case of Frances Willard is instructive.

Known best for her work in helping found the Women's Christian Temperance Union in 1874, Willard gradually came to see the broader dimensions of Social Christianity. She lent support to the labor cause, becoming a member of the Knights of Labor, and also joined the ranks of the women's suffrage movement. Firm in her evangelical faith, Willard moved to an ever more liberal position on social issues because she recognized the futility of proffering salvation to individuals who would remain debased and dehumanized by oppressive social structures.

There were as well many mechanisms by which the spirit of Social Christianity filtered down to ordinary men and women (layfolk, rural, and urban), who alike had to confront the realities of life in an industrialized age. One way was through a spate of periodicals. The Philadelphia *Catholic Standard*, the *Catholic Columbian* in Columbus, Ohio, and the New York *Catholic Herald* and *Catholic World*, for example, regularly brought social issues to the attention of lay subscribers. George Herron's *The Kingdom*, published in Minneapolis in 1894–1895, fused the more revolutionary Social Christianity with agrarian populism for a general readership. *Equity* (1874–1875) highlighted labor concerns from a Christian perspective, and the *Dawn* popularized the program of the Society of Christian Socialists. *Social Service*, under the editorial direction of Josiah Strong, represented a major endeavor to educate the Protestant public on social issues. The *Andover Review*, somewhat more academically directed, helped carry the message of Social Christianity and liberal theology to pastors.

Even more important in reaching ordinary folk was the Social Gospel novel, including, among many others, *The Silent Partner* by Elizabeth S. Phelps (1871), *Dollars and Duty* by Emory J. Haymes (1887), *How They Lived at Hampton* by Edward E. Hale (1888), *If Christ Came to Chicago* by William T. Stead (1894), and the best-selling *In His Steps* (1896) by Charles M. Sheldon. These works are fictional portrayals of what might result if Christians put ethical principles into practice in daily living; they imply that social transformation would ensue. Social Christianity also generated a hymnody that carried its message to Protestants as part of regular Sunday worship. Washington Gladden's well-known text "O Master, Let Me Walk with Thee" stressed Social Christianity's notion of selfless service; Frank Mason North's poem "Where Cross the Crowded Ways of Life," which when set to music became the most well-known Social Gospel hymn of the day, brought attention to the urban situation. Laity also imbibed the ideology of Social Christianity through public lectures and the programs and courses of study developed by the Chautauqua Institute in upstate New York.

Social Christianity's concerns, as noted elsewhere, also led to the formation of important ecumenical institutions. For example, the Social Service Council of Canada came into being as a direct result of the Social Christianity movement, and when the United Church of Canada was organized in 1925, its Department of Evangelism and Social Service ensured that attention to social problems would continue. As well, the formation of the Federal Council of Churches in the United States in 1908 stemmed in large measure from the desire of denominational leaders to work together in promoting action on social problems, a policy continued by the council's successor, the National Council of Churches (founded in 1950).

Behind the myriad institutions, organizations, proposals, and popular phenomena that comprised Social Christianity's eclectic program for injecting a Christian character into American common life lay several ideological constructs. Some reveal that Social Christianity was a creature of its age, while others represent a recasting of motifs long a part of the Christian theological tradition. Some demonstrate that American religious thought shared in currents that had come to the fore in European Christianity, while others were attempts to come to grips with what was seen to be the unique shape American culture was assuming. Proponents of Social Christianity, whether Protestant or Catholic, conservative rescuers, progressive reformers, or radical revolutionaries, held some ideological perspectives in common, though the particular configuration of these views differed from person to person.

In varying ways, each approach imbibed the spirit of optimism characteristic of the age. Con-

servative rescuers were optimistic because the churches had the means to create a Christian society by developing new forms of evangelism appropriate to the unchurched masses of the cities. They included not only the familiar technique of revivalism as practiced by evangelists such as Dwight L. Moody, but also city missions, settlement houses, self-help lectures, and the like. Through these, conservatives such as Joseph Cook believed that souls would be saved, and as a consequence they confidently thought the condition of the urban working class would automatically improve.

Progressive reformers drew on a different strand of optimism in their facile belief that advances in science and technology provided the knowledge necessary to reshape the social environment to the extent that both individuals and the institutions of society might be redeemed. Proponents of Social Christianity of this stripe developed an organic concept of society that challenged laissez-faire economic theory as it affirmed the interconnectedness of all social institutions and hence the need for cooperative endeavors as society gradually progressed toward perfection.

Radical revolutionaries shared the optimism that creation of the ideal social order was a realizable goal, though they were less sanguine about the possibility of achieving it through reform. Rather, radicals such as W. D. P. Bliss, though frequently designated anarchists by detractors, argued for educating the public in the ethical implications entailed in espousing the vision of a Christian commonwealth, convinced that once people recognized the advantages of cooperation over capitalistic competition, they would reject capitalism's structures.

Particularly in Protestant Social Christianity, and more obviously in the thought of the progressive reformers, optimism was fused with an emphasis on the immanence rather than the transcendence of God. To take seriously the long-standing Christian affirmation of "the fatherhood of God" was to stress the continuities, the points of contact, between the human and the divine, between reason and revelation, between the coming kingdom and the present age. Here the Christocentrism of much Protestant Social Gospel thought becomes evident, for men such as Gladden and Rauschenbusch found in

Jesus' relationship with God as father the archetype for all humanity's relationship with God. It was Jesus' demonstration in his teachings and his actions of what "the fatherhood of God" meant —namely the life of love for neighbor—that made belief in "the brotherhood of man" its logical corollary. The incarnation ceased to be an abstract notion, but instead signaled the potential within all humanity for love of God and love of one's fellow human being.

For the progressive reformers, Jesus' example meant discarding competition and espousing cooperation, rejecting rigid social class distinctions, accepting at least in theory the equality of all as children of one God, and affirming (in Rauschenbusch's words) the "latent perfectibility" of humankind and society through God's grace. The writings of the Hebrew prophets concerning social justice provided progressive reformers with additional guides for describing the authentic community ("brotherhood") that came in adopting the life of love. Conservative rescuers did not deny belief in "the fatherhood of God and the brotherhood of man," but felt that the progressives obscured the infinite qualitative distinction between the divine and the human, which could not be closed through evolutionary growth but only through the individual experience of salvation. Radical revolutionaries, in contrast, were impatient with the progressives' assertion that growth toward perfection came gradually and hoped instead for what George Herron called a "social conversion" in which the ideal would be attained now, though even Herron admitted that a process of education would have to precede such a social conversion.

For many Protestant advocates of Social Christianity, the model for a new society was the kingdom of God about which Jesus taught and about which the Hebrew prophets wrote in their descriptions of the true Israel. While for conservative rescuers the kingdom remained a possibility beyond time, which would be realized only when the eschaton came, and while for radical revolutionaries it was a blueprint for an order that could become empirical reality now, for Rauschenbusch and the progressive reformers it was a most effective symbol. Rauschenbusch did not deny the apocalyptic dimension of the kingdom, nor did he regard the kingdom as a utopia that would readily be constructed here and now. Rather, in keeping with the liberal appropriation of evolutionary models, Rauschenbusch saw the kingdom's coming in terms of process and progress toward the ultimate triumph over the kingdom of evil. It was more a gradual growth toward the ideal society than a cataclysmic phenomenon that would accompany the end or be brought into being in the present. What was vital to Rauschenbusch and those who adopted his views was the conviction that humanity had the skills and knowledge to Christianize the social order; only the impetus to use them to reform urban, industrialized America was lacking. Failure to strive toward the kingdom ideal was the most grievous sin.

What would the kingdom be like? In January 1913, Rauschenbusch described his own developing notion of the kingdom in an address at the Cleveland, Ohio, Central YMCA. The kingdom of God, he said,

> was a religious conception that embraced it all. Here was something so big that absolutely nothing that interested me was excluded from it. Was it a matter of personal religion? Why, the kingdom of God begins with that! The powers of the kingdom of God well up in the individual soul; that is where they are born, and that is where the starting point necessarily must be. Was it a matter of world-wide missions? Why, that is the kingdom of God, isn't it—carrying it to the boundaries of the earth. Was it a matter of getting justice for the workingman? Is not justice part of the kingdom of God? Does not the kingdom of God simply consist in this—that God's will shall be done on earth even as it is now in heaven? . . . The kingdom of God . . . is a social conception. It is a conception for this life here of ours because Jesus says: "Thy kingdom come, thy will be done" here. . . . It is a matter of community life. The perfect community of men —that would be the kingdom of God! With God above them; with their brother next to them— clasping hands in fraternity, doing the work of justice—that is the kingdom of God!

Here, too, may be seen the subtle millennialist dimension of Social Christianity's ideology, for it was the arrival of the kingdom that would bring in the millennial age.

Roman Catholic Social Christianity was less

obviously influenced by the ideological triad of "the fatherhood of God," "the brotherhood of man," and the kingdom of God, though the values implicit in them did undergird Catholic social thought. *Rerum Novarum,* issued by Pope Leo XIII in May 1891, provided the more direct ideological supports for Catholic Social Christianity. The encyclical addressed the condition of labor, calling for economic reform that embraced neither laissez-faire nor socialism per se. Upholding the sanctity of private property over against what he termed "the main tenet of Socialism, the community of goods," Leo argued that there could be no resolution of social problems "without the assistance of Religion and the Church." Christian teaching about justice and charity meant that labor and capital should cooperate, since each needed the other, and that those who possessed wealth should give to the needy.

Leo encouraged the expansion of Catholic benevolent agencies as one means to deal with labor's dilemma, but he also gave support to certain types of workmen's associations (though only obliquely to the labor unions emerging in Britain and the United States). More important for American Catholic advocates of Social Christianity, the encyclical called for government to eliminate Sunday labor, regulate child and women's labor, guarantee decent wages, and the like because it was the duty of government to advance human welfare when established social institutions refused to do so on their own. As John Lancaster Spalding, the bishop of Peoria whose personal position was somewhat more conservative than that taken by the encyclical, noted in an article in the influential *Catholic World* (September 1891), the pope made it plain that "the mission of the Church is not only to save souls, but also to save society." With that sentiment, Protestants—particularly of the progressive reform and radical revolutionary sort— would have readily concurred.

Social Christianity's influence, however, was not as extensive or as enduring as its visionaries hoped. As Henry F. May noted, Protestant Social Christianity must be judged a failure insofar as through persuasion and rational argument it never succeeded in winning over its opposition to its point of view. Capitalism remained the basis of the American economic system. Then, too, the social service agencies associated with

Social Christianity did not eliminate the plight of the urban masses, though they did mitigate it for many, at least temporarily. Nor did they bring large numbers into the membership of the mainline Protestant denominations.

In terms of influencing the public mind, Social Christianity's effect was largely limited to the emerging urban middle class, already inclined to support reform in part, at least, because of its own lack of status in the social structure. Many later critics in both the United States and Canada have castigated Social Christianity as a middle-class phenomenon and a reflection of middle-class values rather than viewing it as a challenge to conventional patterns.

To a large extent, the parallel rise of populism and Progressivism, both intertwined with the rise of the new middle class, brought political leaders into office who had the power to effect some of Social Christianity's program of change that religious agencies and spokesmen lacked. As Aaron Abell (1943) pointed out,

> From a religious viewpoint, Progressivism marked the triumph of the social gospel: if the Protestant social reformers of the 1880's and 1890's had failed to draw the working people into their churches, they had succeeded in predisposing their vast middle-class constituency to social reform.

Of course, Progressivism also encompassed much of the Roman Catholic concern for social justice. When men such as Theodore Roosevelt and Woodrow Wilson used the powers of the presidency to promote Progressivism's platform, there was an end to uncontrolled laissez-faire and a beginning of concern for the regulation of business and industry, which aided the cause of labor. It has also been argued, though, that Progressivism was a means to perpetuate established power blocs rather than redistribute power and national wealth on any significant scale.

Ultimately more of Social Christianity's agenda was reflected in the New Deal of Franklin Delano Roosevelt than in Progressivism, but by the 1930s, Social Christianity itself had lost much of its vitality and was hardly a spur to the economic legislation of the New Deal. Nevertheless, one cannot deny that the movement to implement the coming kingdom of God within the industrial order did at least help create the ethos in which some reform did occur, particularly in the areas of better wages, a shorter work week, the breaking up of some trusts and monopolies, regulation of child labor and women's labor (the latter perhaps ironic in an age that was concerned about the equality of women), the introduction of factory safety standards, and related concerns.

Within the churches, Social Christianity had a more lasting effect through ecumenical and/or denominational institutions. The Federal Council of Churches remained committed to social justice. The Federal and then (after 1950) the National Council of Churches have prodded member denominations to pay heed to social concerns through adoption of "social creeds" and cooperative social action programs. Virtually every Protestant denomination maintains some official position statement on social issues, encompassing an even broader array of interests than Social Christianity addressed (among them, ecology, civil rights, nuclear power, arms race), and boards or agencies to promote its perspective. The United Church of Canada, a direct outgrowth of Social Christianity, remains a vital part of Canadian religious life with its own social action organizations.

By the second decade of the twentieth century, "the social question" had also become institutionalized in American Catholicism, though it had by and large come under the control of the hierarchy. The National Catholic War Council, formed to coordinate Catholic support for the American effort in World War I, was reorganized as the National Catholic Welfare Conference and, although restructured again in the wake of Vatican II (1962–1965), perpetuates official Catholic attention to social matters. Even the interests of the old Central Verein are maintained in the pages of *Social Justice Review*.

By the time World War I broke out, however, Social Christianity had lost much of its steam, more because of events than because of its shortcomings. The horrors of the war years demolished Social Christianity's optimism and the expectation that the ideals of the kingdom could readily be made empirical reality. The war and events in the decade before the Great Depression seriously undercut the currents of Social Christianity. As men and women confronted the vagaries of the twentieth century, it no longer

seemed easy to blueprint a way to implant the social principles of Jesus on American life. Optimistic belief in steady progress nearly vanished, for it did not prepare adherents for a different "new world civilization" than that anticipated by Josiah Strong. The foundation of Protestant Social Christianity in the new liberal theology also crumbled as thinkers such as Karl Barth in Europe and Reinhold Niebuhr in the United States articulated a new orthodoxy that abandoned the liberal emphasis on human potential, progress toward the kingdom, and the immanence of God and again stressed the extent and effects of human sin, the transcendence of God, and the limits of human ability.

Other flaws in the fabric of Social Christianity are readily discernible in hindsight. So engrossed were Social Christianity's leaders in the dilemma of labor and the urban situation that they failed to address other problems that impeded society's evolution into the kingdom of God. For example, racial discrimination and racial injustice were virtually ignored by Social Christianity's advocates. Among northern leaders, only Washington Gladden gradually came to incorporate some concern for black Americans in his vision of a new age, while in the South, F. D. Weatherford was one of a very few who recognized that so long as racial injustice permeated the culture it would never be Christianized. The maltreatment of Native Americans and the poverty that demolished whatever integrity remained in tribal life on the reservations received even less attention. In addition, while many advocates lent support to the women's suffrage movement, few departed from a Victorian paternalism whose images of the family and gender roles kept women from attaining effective power and perpetuated an outmoded and unjust sense of women as the "weaker" sex. The coming kingdom remained a white male hope.

Then, too, the failure of Social Christianity to embrace a coherent program of social change and the continuing animosity between Protestants and Catholics that generally prohibited effective cooperation or coordination of reform efforts dissipated the power of the movement to alter the character of American life. Here the links of Social Christianity to the emerging urban middle class are important, for although Social Christianity may have assisted the new middle class in gaining a sense of identity and a viable world view, its middle-class orientation weakened its ability to change the attitudes or situation of either the urban working class or the affluent capitalist class. Perhaps Social Christianity was too wedded to an image of the nation predicated primarily on evangelical Protestant ideals to recognize that the American way of life itself, ever more tied to an industrial economy, was part of the problem. In this vein, Social Christianity's espousal of much of populism and Progressivism may also be construed as a weakness, for it meant that Social Christianity tied its fortunes to political movements that were themselves culture bound. Social Christianity's inability to see beyond Progressivism, to appreciate other secular currents dedicated to reform, lessened its potency to accomplish its aims.

Finally, as Egal Feldman has pointed out, a subtle anti-Semitism in Social Christianity prohibited any real association with America's Jews in promoting social reform, though many of the humanitarian precepts integral to Social Christianity were and are basic to Jewish social ethics. Even in Reform Judaism there was not a movement analogous to Social Christianity, although the Pittsburgh Platform (1885) did emphasize the need to "solve on the basis of justice and righteousness the problems presented by the contrasts and evils of the present organization of society." Among leaders within American Judaism, Rabbi Stephen S. Wise, influenced by Josiah Strong, Washington Gladden, and other advocates of Social Christianity, supported numerous reform efforts. Perhaps the most important attempt at interfaith social reform came in the 1920s, as Social Christianity was fading, when the Federal Council of Churches, the National Catholic Welfare Conference, and the Central Conference of American Rabbis jointly investigated several strikes and also jointly urged the steel industry to abandon the twelve-hour day and seven-day work week.

Nevertheless, if Social Christianity lost much of its force by the 1920s as external events and internal weaknesses rendered it anachronistic, its spirit has left a rich legacy. As already noted, much of its agenda became government policy in the era of the New Deal. The "Christian Realism" of Reinhold Niebuhr, John C. Bennett, and others, while critical of the liberal theological basis of Social Christianity, nonetheless sought to apply Christian ethical principles to social

situations, but with a less optimistic expectation for permanent change and a greater sensitivity to the complexities of social dilemmas.

The civil rights movement of the 1950s and 1960s also owed much to the ethos of Social Christianity. Martin Luther King, Jr., for example, acknowledged his own debt to Rauschenbusch's vision of the just society as he led the cry for America to end practices and to restructure institutions that perpetuated racial discrimination. The same spirit lives on in other contemporary movements for human liberation; for example, in the religious dimensions of the women's movement and in the organization of the Universal Fellowship of Metropolitan Community Churches by Troy Perry in 1968, with its ministry to homosexuals. Many have gay/lesbian groups or caucuses, but none has actively embraced ministry with gays and lesbians as has UFMCC. It is there also to a lesser extent in the ideologies associated with the "theology of hope" and "liberation theology." Theology of hope points to the role of Providence in ultimately transforming human life and society. Liberation theology has been primarily concerned with the ways in which economic and social systems are unjust, especially to the poor and those without political or economic power. Social Christianity, as an historical phenomenon, may be inextricably bound to the middle-class ethos of late-nineteenth- and early-twentieth-century America. But its conviction that religion provides both resources to guide social change and models of what society could and should be is a vital strand weaving in and out of the story of religion in America.

BIBLIOGRAPHY

Aaron Abell, *The Urban Impact on American Protestantism, 1865–1900* (1943), *American Catholicism and Social Action: A Search for Social Justice, 1865–1950* (1960), ed., *American Catholic Thought on Social Questions* (1968); Richard Allen, *The Social Passion: Religion and Social Reform in Canada, 1914–1928* (1971); Paul Carter, *The Decline and Revival of the Social Gospel: Social and Political Liberalism in American Protestant Churches, 1920–1940* (1956; rev. ed., 1971); Robert D. Cross, ed., *The Church and the City* (1967); Stewart Crysdale, *The Industrial Struggle and Protestant Ethics in Canada* (1961); Horton Davies, "The Expression of the Social Gospel in Worship," in *Studia Liturgica*, 2 (1963); James Dombrowski, *The Early Days of Christian Socialism in America* (1936); Jacob Dorn, *Washington Gladden: Prophet of the Social Gospel* (1967); John Eighmy, "Religious Liberalism in the South During the Progressive Era," in *Church History,* 38 (1969).

Egal Feldman, "The Social Gospel and the Jews," in *American Jewish Historical Quarterly,* 58 (1969); Janet Forsythe Fishburn, *The Fatherhood of God and the Victorian Family: The Social Gospel in America* (1981); Philip Gleason, *The Conservative Reformers: German-American Catholics and the Social Order* (1968); Robert T. Handy, *A Christian America: Protestant Hopes and Historical Realities* (1971) and, as ed., *The Social Gospel in America, 1870–1920: Gladden, Ely, Rauschenbusch* (1966); C. Howard Hopkins, *The Rise of the Social Gospel in American Protestantism, 1865–1915* (1940); Jean Hulliger, *L'Enseignement social des évêques canadiens de 1891 á 1950* (1958); William R. Hutchison, "The Americanness of the Social Gospel: An Inquiry in Comparative History," in *Church History* 44 (1975); Philip D. Jordan, *The Evangelical Alliance for the United States of America, 1847–1900: Ecumenism, Identity, and the Religion of the Republic* (1983).

John Patrick McDowell, *The Social Gospel in the South: The Woman's Home Mission Movement in the Methodist Episcopal Church South, 1886–1939* (1982); Norris Magnuson, *Salvation in the Slums: Evangelical Social Work, 1865–1920* (1977); Henry F. May, *Protestant Churches and Industrial America* (1949); Donald B. Meyer, *The Protestant Search for Political Realism, 1919–1941* (1960); Robert M. Miller, *American Protestantism and Social Issues, 1919–1939* (1958); Dores R. Sharpe, *Walter Rauschenbusch* (1942); Timothy L. Smith, *Revivalism and Social Reform in Mid-Nineteenth-Century America* (1957); W. A. Visser't Hooft, *The Background of the Social Gospel in America* (1928); Francis P. Weisenburger, *Ordeal of Faith: The Crisis of Church-going America, 1865–1900* (1959); Ronald C. White, Jr., and C. Howard Hopkins, *The Social Gospel: Religion and Reform in Changing America* (1976).

[*See also* LIBERALISM; RELIGIOUS THOUGHT SINCE WORLD WAR II; SOCIAL REFORM AFTER THE CIVIL WAR TO THE GREAT DEPRESSION; SOCIAL REFORM FROM THE COLONIAL PERIOD THROUGH THE CIVIL WAR; *and* SOCIAL REFORM SINCE THE GREAT DEPRESSION.]

PENTECOSTALISM

Grant Wacker

ON a foggy evening in the spring of 1906, nine days before the San Francisco earthquake, several black "saints" gathered in a small house in Los Angeles to seek baptism in the Holy Spirit. Before the evening was over, a frightened child ran from the house to tell a neighbor that the people inside were singing and shouting in strange languages. Several days later the group moved to an abandoned warehouse on Azusa Street in a run-down section of the city. Soon they were discovered by a *Los Angeles Times* reporter. The "night is made hideous . . . by the howlings of the worshippers," he wrote. "The devotees of the weird doctrine practice the most fanatical rites, preach the wildest theories and work themselves into a state of mad excitement."

The Azusa Street revival is commonly considered the cradle of modern Pentecostalism, the beginning of what Peter Williams has aptly called "*the* popular religious movement" of the twentieth century. No one knows how big the movement really is, but studies show that there are several million adherents in the United States and perhaps a hundred million worldwide. In the United States alone there are more than three hundred Pentecostal denominations. Most are quite small, but the two largest, the Assemblies of God and the Church of God in Christ, each claim more than two million American followers and additional millions in other parts of the world. Nor has respectability lagged far behind. The *Christian Century* has judged the Pentecostal minister Oral Roberts one of the ten most influential religious leaders in America, and Pentecostal statesman David J. Du Plessis clearly has become a star in international ecumenical circles.

Contemporary Pentecostalism is so vast and sprawling, it is sometimes difficult for an outsider to know exactly what it is. Like the animals in Noah's ark, Pentecostals come in a bewildering variety of species. Protestant, Catholic, Reformed, Wesleyan, Trinitarian, Unitarian, mainline, sectarian, white, black, Hispanic—the list of adjectives that describes one group or another could be extended indefinitely. Perhaps more than in any other segment of Christendom, the boundaries of modern Pentecostalism seem hopelessly tangled in crisscrossing beliefs and practices.

There is, however, one conviction that pervades all parts of the movement: conversion must be followed by another life-transforming event known as baptism in the Holy Spirit. Pentecostals believe that a person who has been baptized in the Holy Spirit will normally manifest one or more of the nine gifts of the Spirit described in 1 Corinthians 12 and 14: wisdom, knowledge, faith, healing, miracles, prophecy, discernment of false spirits, unknown tongues, and interpretation of tongues. Although other Christians sometimes share this interest in the gifts of the Spirit, Pentecostals are distinguished by the emphasis they place upon one of them, the gift of unknown tongues, technically called glossolalia. (Pentecostals believe that a glossolalic utterance may be a "divine language," intelligible only to God, or it may be an actual foreign language that the speaker has not learned but is enabled to utter by the inspiration of the Holy Spirit. The latter is sometimes called xenoglossolalia.)

Virtually all of the older Pentecostal denominations insist that there are two kinds of glossolalia: the *gift* of tongues and the *sign* of tongues. The two forms sound alike but differ in function. The former is intended for most but not necessarily all Christians. Its purpose is to express the longings of the heart when utterance is made in private prayer or to edify the church when it is made in a public setting and interpreted by one

933

who has the gift of interpretation. The sign of tongues, on the other hand, is considered normative for all Christians. Its purpose is to serve as a supernatural sign or witness that the believer has been baptized in the Holy Spirit. Traditional Pentecostals are convinced that all instances of baptism in the Holy Spirit explicitly referred to in the Acts of the Apostles were accompanied by the sign of tongues. Since this pattern appears to them to have been normative for the early church, they believe it is normative for the modern church as well. Thus the hallmark of traditional Pentecostalism is the conviction that all Christians who are truly baptized in the Spirit will speak in tongues at the moment of baptism (although some may never do so again). While the movement's theologians are careful to say that believers should seek the living Holy Spirit rather than the experience of tongues, in reality the gift of tongues is highly prized, and the sign of tongues is deemed essential. Indeed, in most of the older denominations ordination applicants are required to affirm, among other things, that they have experienced the sign of tongues as the "initial physical evidence" of baptism in the Holy Spirit.

It should be noted that this description of Pentecostalism focuses upon a cluster of doctrines that distinguish Pentecostals from other evangelical Protestants. This is to say that the movement is better defined by its beliefs than by its practices. Contrary to the stereotype, Pentecostals are extremely serious about doctrine. They habitually define themselves in these terms, and some of the deepest wounds they have inflicted upon their movement have come from brawls over technicalities of doctrine. Nonetheless, a purely ideational definition of the movement is too thin. For many years—perhaps through the second generation—Pentecostalism was a total style of life, a way of seeing and feeling and experiencing reality. The driving force was, as the historian Perry Miller once said of the Puritans, not in the movement's doctrines but behind them, in the spirituality that sparked the movement and the certitude that sustained it.

THE EMERGENCE OF PENTECOSTALISM

It is difficult to know where the story of Pentecostalism begins. Pentecostals, like many sectarians, tend to think of their origins as miraculous, and thus they have never shown much interest in a critical reconstruction of their own history. But this is beginning to change. In the last twenty years several third-generation Pentecostals have written doctoral dissertations on different aspects of their tradition. Most trace the movement's roots to the economic, social, and cultural crises of the late nineteenth century. As the stable structures of small-town America gave way and established Protestantism grew soft and fat, the argument runs, Pentecostalism came into existence as a plain-folks religion in which simple virtues and the old-fashioned Gospel could still be found.

There is merit in this view, for it is true that the movement initially flourished in regions suffering severe disruption of traditional ways. The cradle of the Church of God, for example, was in the southern Appalachians, where timeless patterns of farming, hunting, and fishing were rapidly displaced at the turn of the century by industrialization and the commercialization of agriculture in the new South. The dusty little town of Dunn, North Carolina, became an epicenter of Populist agitation and, soon thereafter, of fiery holiness preaching that soon led to the formation of the Pentecostal Holiness Church. The Apostolic Faith, a precursor of the Assemblies of God, erupted in the midst of a lead-mining boom in the region where Kansas, Oklahoma, and Missouri intersect. By the same token, Los Angeles was the most rapidly growing city in the nation at the time of the Azusa Street revival, jostling thousands of uprooted midwesterners with blacks, Mexicans, and Orientals. And of course the tensions of the era were cultural as well as social. Evangelical Protestants were increasingly alarmed by the growth of theological liberalism, the apparent crumbling of traditional standards of morality, and the insurgence of Catholicism and of unfamiliar sects such as Theosophy and Christian Science.

Nonetheless, interpretations that depict Pentecostalism as a direct response to social and cultural stress are inadequate, partly because it is risky to explain any religious movement in strictly functional terms, and partly because this approach fails to account for significant data. Why did Pentecostalism grow so quickly and luxuriantly in Oregon, which was not an area of exceptional turmoil? Why did it fail to take root in the restive Dakotas or in the turbid cities of the

Northeast? Or why did Pentecostal literature before the 1920s show virtually no awareness of—not to mention confrontation with—the modernist impulse in American Protestantism?

These and other considerations suggest that the forces that gave rise to Pentecostalism were broader and deeper than the social and cultural shock waves of the 1890s. To a great extent the movement was the product of trends that had been developing for many decades. These included a growing fascination with miracles, millennialism, physical health, the activities of the Holy Spirit, and the meaning of obscure passages in Scripture. Reaction to the vigorous expansion of the Churches of Christ across the upper South and the persistence of the problem of certainty in the realm of religious experience are also parts of the story. But above all, Pentecostalism was the product of clashing forces within the vast and amorphous holiness movement that had swept across evangelical Protestantism in the last third of the nineteenth century.

A comprehensive history of the holiness movement has not yet been written, but it is clear that in the United States it embraced at least four traditions that eventually molded the shape of Pentecostalism: the Wesleyan idea of entire sanctification, the Reformed idea of power for Christian service, the Plymouth Brethren idea of dispensational premillennialism, and a highly protean theology of faith healing.

The Wesleyan idea of sanctification was rooted in John Wesley's conviction that conversion is the beginning of a lifelong process of moral perfection. In the new birth, sin is forgiven and the will is regenerated, but not wholly; the corrupting influence of original sin persists. This "inbred sin" must be eradicated in a definable second blessing, or second moment of grace, which signifies the entire sanctification of the heart. "Be of sin the double cure," it is phrased in a hymn long cherished by Methodists; "save from wrath and make me pure." Wesley's theology of Christian perfection crossed the Atlantic early in the nineteenth century, but it underwent a partial sea change. Although Wesley never doubted that the sanctification experience was instantaneous, he ordinarily stressed the progressiveness of the sanctification process, a development that began with the "first dawning of grace in the soul" and deepened until it was "consummated in glory." In the work of Ameri-

can Methodists such as Phoebe Palmer, however, spiritual growth increasingly came to resemble distinct stages: unconverted, converted, entirely sanctified. By the time of the Civil War there was also a shift in popular terminology. The phrase "baptism in the Holy Spirit," which had been used in various ways since the mid-eighteenth century, now became synonymous with the second blessing. Most important, near the end of the century a lay Baptist preacher in Nebraska named Benjamin Hardin Irwin, came to the conclusion that there was a third experience, beyond the experience of entire sanctification, which he called the baptism of the Holy Spirit and fire. Irwin later added fourth, fifth, and sixth experiences to the sequence, but it was the idea of a third experience, an event that decisively fulfilled a person's spiritual hunger, that captured the popular imagination and became crucial to the formation of Pentecostalism.

The second major tradition that influenced Pentecostalism was the Reformed emphasis upon power for service. This tradition flowed from two sources: a broad "higher-life" impulse that had permeated Baptist, Congregational, and Presbyterian churches since the middle of the nineteenth century, and a similar movement in England associated with an annual summer conference at Keswick. Central to both traditions was a conviction that conversion was only the first step, the bare beginning of a vigorous Christian life. Recent scholarship has shown that higher-life teachings originated early in the century and ranged widely—touching persons as different as William Ellery Channing, Nathaniel W. Taylor, Charles G. Finney, Asa Mahan, and William E. Boardman. In the 1880s and 1890s the various streams of this impulse merged in the work of several men who constituted an "establishment" of sorts on the Reformed side of the holiness movement. The most important were A. J. Gordon, Dwight L. Moody, A. B. Simpson, Arthur T. Pierson, and, above all, Reuben A. Torrey. Like the Wesleyan holiness leaders, these men believed that the higher life began at conversion, but they differed from the Wesleyans in two respects. First, they thought that inbred sin was progressively subjugated, yet never eradicated. Second, they agreed that there was a second experience known as baptism in the Holy Spirit, but they insisted that its primary effect was an endowment of power that enabled a Christian to witness, sacrifice, and serve. "Baptism with the Spirit," Torrey testily remarked, "is not primarily intended to make believers happy nor holy, but to make them useful."

The third and fourth traditions that led to Pentecostalism were dispensational premillennialism and a new theology of faith healing. The former, contributed by the Plymouth Brethren and promoted especially through the Niagara Bible and Prophecy Conferences in the 1880s and 1890s, entailed the idea of an imminent secret rapture of the saints, immediately followed by seven years of Great Tribulation, the Second Coming of the Lord, and the Millennium. A new theology of faith healing also gained wide acceptance during these years. It departed from historic Christian belief, which enjoined elders to anoint and pray for the sick, by insisting that Christ's atonement provided for physical healing just as it provided for spiritual healing. Both dispensational premillennialism and the theology of healing through the atonement spread rapidly in the half-dozen years preceding the turn of the century. A large minority of Wesleyans and probably a majority of believers in the Reformed wing of the holiness movement readily accepted both notions. By the close of the century Moody, Pierson, and Torrey had become the most prominent American spokesmen for dispensational premillennialism (although Moody was vague on the details), and Gordon and Simpson had become the principal architects of the new theology of healing.

It is important to remember that each of these theological traditions or movements—namely, entire sanctification, empowerment for service, dispensational premillennialism, and faith healing—was supported by an extensive institutional network. The first three were sustained by conferences, summer camps, books, magazines, colleges, Bible institutes, and a web of national, regional, and local associations. The theology and practice of faith healing were also maintained through a chain of "faith homes" established throughout the Northeast and Midwest in the 1880s and 1890s. The better known included Episcopalian Charles Cullis' Faith Cure House in Boston, Presbyterian A. B. Simpson's Berachah House in New York City, and, most notably, Zion City (later Zion), Illinois. This town of five thousand was organized by John Alexander Dowie in 1900 as a communitarian theocracy devoted to personal asceticism and faith healing. Spectacu-

lar healing rallies also started in the late 1880s and 1890s as Dowie and Maria B. Woodworth (later Woodworth-Etter) separately crisscrossed the country with their independent healing meetings.

As the century drew to a close these various traditions collided, broke apart, and reassembled in unpredictable ways. But there was a common denominator. Virtually everyone associated with the holiness movement was deeply committed to the doctrine and the experience of baptism in the Holy Spirit—whether it was defined as entire sanctification or empowerment or both. Many believed that the growing hunger for the Holy Spirit, reinforced by miracles of faith healing, proved that the end was near. Not everyone who believed these things became Pentecostal, but all who became Pentecostal shared these beliefs. And then there was the revival setting. In B. H. Irwin's fire-baptism meetings, one leader remembered, the "people screamed until you could hear them for three miles on a clear night, and until the blood vessels stood out like whip cords." A newspaper reporter who visited Maria Woodworth-Etter's meetings similarly recalled that one could not

> . . . imagine the . . . confusion. . . . Dozens lying around pale and unconscious, rigid and lifeless as though in death. Strong men shouting till they were hoarse, then falling down in a swoon. Women falling over benches and trampled under foot. . . . Aged women gesticulating and hysterically sobbing. . . . Men shouting with a devilish, unearthly laugh.
> (*Muncie Daily News,* 21 September 1885)

In contexts of this sort it was only a matter of time until some would begin to look for proof—preferably palpable proof—that they had been baptized in the Holy Spirit and thus were ready for the Lord's return.

No one knows when the phenomenon of tongues first occurred. After the Pentecostal movement was well under way many claimed to have spoken in tongues in holiness meetings in the 1880s and 1890s. But there is reason for skepticism, for none of these events was reported at the time they ostensibly occurred. It is possible, of course, that glossolalic outbursts took place but were not reported because the religious culture had not yet invested the experience with clear theological meaning. And there is a venerable popular tradition that tongues had become regular occurrences in holiness meetings everywhere by the end of the century, especially in the Southeast, where B. H. Irwin frequently preached about baptism by fire. Moreover, it is undeniable that Pentecostalism first took root in areas systematically prepared by white-hot holiness revivals. These included the coastal plains and Piedmont of the Carolinas and Georgia, the southern Appalachians, southeastern Kansas, southeastern Texas, Los Angeles, northern Illinois, and an arc stretching across northern Ohio and Pennsylvania where outposts of Simpson's Christian and Missionary Alliance had been established.

Whether glossolalia did or did not precede the birth of Pentecostalism is less significant than the theological meaning it soon acquired. To link tongues with baptism in the Holy Spirit was natural enough; in the Acts of the Apostles aberrant or enigmatic language was clearly associated with the presence of the Holy Spirit. But to say that tongues *invariably* accompanied baptism and to insist that this was a *third* distinct experience following conversion and the second blessing were much bigger claims. Yet this complex linkage was forged no later than the fall of 1900 in the healing revivals of Charles Fox Parham.

Parham is one figure modern Pentecostals would just as soon forget. Sickly, physically deformed, and ultimately disgraced by rumors of sexual misconduct, Parham advanced ideas that exemplified many of the most eccentric political and religious notions circulating through the radical fringe of popular evangelicalism. Like many come-outers who were, as Timothy Smith has said, "unable to accept much real discipline save their own," he drifted from the Congregationalists to the Methodists to Irwin's Fire-Baptized Holiness Association. He met and seems to have been influenced by notable faith healers such as Dowie and Frank W. Sandford, founder of the Shiloh movement in Maine. Like many of the early Pentecostal leaders, Parham had experienced stunning healings in his own body and was able to heal many of the sick who flocked to him. It is easy to believe that in a non-Western culture he would have been considered a shaman.

By Christmas of 1900, as Parham tells the story, he had come to the conclusion that the clear import of Acts 2:4 was that baptism in the Holy Spirit was always marked by the "initial physical evidence" of speaking in tongues. Parham believed that glossolalia was an unlearned foreign language, whose purpose was to enable believers to preach the Gospel in foreign lands. For most Pentecostals this conviction soon shrank to the more prudent view that glossolalia was sometimes an actual foreign language, but usually it was a "divine language" intelligible only to God or to other believers when it was interpreted by one who had the gift of interpretation. Nonetheless, Parham's main contention—namely, that speaking in tongues always accompanied baptism in the Holy Spirit—gradually became universal among Pentecostals. At first there was much confusion about the necessity of tongues, but by 1915—or 1920 at the latest—acceptance of this point had become the test of orthodoxy among all of the white and some of the black Pentecostal denominations. Indeed, it was their adamance on this matter that, more than anything else, irrevocably split Pentecostals from the main body of the holiness movement.

The setting in which Parham's ideas sprouted was a tiny Bible institute he founded in Topeka, Kansas, in the fall of 1900. Parham claimed that the "fire fell" New Year's Day 1901 after he had taught the students to seek baptism with the expectation of tongues. However, the first student to speak in tongues, Agnes N. Ozman, later claimed that after days of fasting and seeking baptism, she suddenly and unexpectedly broke into tongues—and no one, including Parham, knew what to make of it. In the following months, in any event, the revival raced across southeastern Kansas, then sputtered and nearly died. The message was saved by Parham's decision in 1903 to return to a faith-healing ministry. This time his success as a healer was rewarded with a measure of regional prominence. In the summer of 1905 the Apostolic Faith, as he called it, reached Houston, Texas, where his growing healing ministry thrilled believers and reportedly awed the skeptical.

At this point William J. Seymour, the most enigmatic major figure in the early history of Pentecostalism, entered the picture. Seymour was a black itinerant preacher associated with the Evening Light Saints, a radical Wesleyan sect that espoused entire sanctification, faith healing, and restoration of the gifts of the Spirit as a prelude to the Lord's return. For several weeks in the fall of 1905 Seymour attended a makeshift Bible school that Parham had set up in Houston. In January 1906 Seymour carried Parham's teachings to a black holiness group in Los Angeles, where the events described at the beginning of this essay took place in April of that year.

The recollection of Jennie Moore, who was the first woman to receive the baptism experience in the Azusa revival, is typical of hundreds, if not thousands, of testimonials in the early periodicals. "When the evening came," she wrote, "we attended the meeting [and] the power of God fell and I was baptized in the Holy Ghost and fire."

> It seemed as if a vessel broke within me and water surged up through my being, which when it reached my mouth came out in a torrent of speech in the languages which God had given me. . . . I sang under the power of the Spirit in many languages. . . . The Spirit led me to the piano, where I played and sang under inspiration, although I had not learned to play.
> (*Apostolic Faith,* May 1907, p. 3)

Given the legendary stature the Azusa revival has acquired, it may be useful to pause a moment to examine it. The meetings started at mid-morning and lasted past midnight, seven days a week, for the greater part of three years. Participants perceived the meetings in different ways. One recalled that "when someone would begin to pound the seat . . . Brother Seymour would go to them and tap them on the shoulder and say, 'Brother that is the flesh,' and a holy hush and quietness would settle down." Others remembered a different scene. One witness, who later became a patriarch of the movement, described the meetings as "Holy Ghost bedlam." Parham visited in November and said it reminded him of a "Holy Roller" revival where the worshipers "pulled all of the stunts common in old camp meetings among colored folks." Alma White, founder of the ardently anti-Pentecostal Pillar of Fire mission, charged that many "lost control of themselves and went under a hypnotic spell."

Descriptions of Seymour himself vary as much as the descriptions of the revival. In some accounts he is depicted as an unlettered bumpkin; in others, as a leader with astute theological insight. In any event, the Azusa Mission soon became exclusively black. Despite a serious schism in 1908, it prospered in a modest way until Seymour's death in 1922. Nine years later the building was torn down and the site is now occupied by a Japanese trade center.

In the intervening years the Azusa revival has become all things to all people. Several historians have said that it exploded like a bomb upon the city. Others, anxious to establish the black origins of the movement, have insisted that it was composed mostly of blacks. Indeed, some of the most able historians of Pentecostalism have suggested that the movement is best defined as an ecstatic religious revival that largely started in and grew from the 1906 Azusa meetings.

Actually, none of these claims is entirely supportable. In the first place, the revival did not flourish until four or five months had gone by and neighboring holiness missions started to force Pentecostal worshipers out of their midst. Second, after the first week or so the meetings were thoroughly interracial, including native whites, blacks, Mexicans, Orientals, and eastern Europeans. Third, Azusa understandably appears to have sparked the Pentecostal movement because so many travelers who visited in 1906 and 1907 took its message home with them. Most, however, ignited fires at home that were already near flash point or added fuel to ones that had been burning for some time.

The Church of God in Christ, the Church of God (Cleveland, Tennessee), and the Pentecostal Holiness Church fit the first category—groups that needed only a spark. At the time, all were small but solidly established holiness sects. All were characterized by a belief in the necessity of entire sanctification (conceived as a second distinct work of grace), acceptance of the theology and practice of faith healing, and a fervent desire for restoration of all of the gifts of the Spirit in anticipation of the Lord's return. In the meetings of these groups trances, visions, and other forms of ecstatic behavior were common occurrences. Thus it is not surprising that within three or four years all adopted the doctrinal hallmark of early Pentecostalism: that salvation, entire sanctification, and baptism in the Holy Spirit, with the "initial physical evidence" of speaking in tongues, were normative for all Christians.

The oldest and largest of these bodies is the Church of God in Christ, with headquarters in

Memphis, Tennessee. This mostly black group was founded in Mississippi in 1897 by Charles Price Jones and Charles H. Mason. Jones and Mason were Baptist ministers who had accepted the Wesleyan view of entire sanctification. In March 1907 Mason, who by then had become pastor of a congregation in Memphis, traveled to Azusa, where he experienced baptism with the evidence of tongues. When he returned he found a Pentecostal revival surging at full steam. He also found that Jones had determined to stop it. The group split, with Mason's faction keeping the original name and securing a charter of incorporation in Memphis in the fall of that year.

The second oldest Pentecostal denomination is the Church of God in Cleveland, Tennessee. This group sometimes traces its roots to a revival among Baptists in the eastern Tennessee mountains in 1886, and sometimes to an 1896 revival, also among Baptists, just over the state line in the hamlet of Camp Creek, North Carolina. The mountain folk who participated in the latter revival had at some point adopted the Wesleyan view of entire sanctification, along with faith healing and the expectation of the Second Coming. They may have had contact with Irwin's fire-baptized followers as well. Although proof is elusive, it was later said that this 1896 revival was punctuated with tongues and miraculous healings. The most reliable starting date for the Church of God is, however, 1902, when these men and women organized themselves more formally as the Holiness Church of Camp Creek. This tiny band might well have disappeared into the mists of history if they had not been discovered by an itinerant Bible salesman named Ambrose Jessup Tomlinson. Unquestionably pious, Tomlinson was also complicated, egotistical, and, above all, a born leader. He had traveled in the same circles Parham had frequented, and it is possible that they knew each other. In any event, Tomlinson quickly assumed control of the budding denomination. In 1907 he renamed it the Church of God and moved its headquarters to Cleveland, Tennessee. Speaking in tongues probably became a regular feature of Church of God meetings in 1907 or 1908, but the group did not officially place itself in the Pentecostal camp until it published its first doctrinal statement in 1910.

The Pentecostal Holiness Church is the third oldest Pentecostal denomination. It resulted from the merger in 1911 of two Wesleyan holiness sects: the Fire-Baptized Holiness Church, founded in South Carolina in 1898 by B. H. Irwin, and the Pentecostal Holiness Church, founded in North Carolina in 1900 (before the word *Pentecostal* was associated with tongues). Both of these groups had been drawn into the Pentecostal orbit by a notable evangelist named Gaston Barnabus Cashwell. Originally a Methodist minister, he had joined the Pentecostal Holiness Church in 1903 and journeyed to Azusa in the fall of 1906 to receive baptism in the Holy Spirit. For the next three years Cashwell became a one-man fireworks show blazing across the South with the Pentecostal message. In the wake of his preaching, the majority of ministers in both groups soon adopted the view that baptism in the Holy Spirit was invariably signified by speaking in tongues. Because these originally Wesleyan bodies held virtually identical doctrines, and because they occupied pretty much the same territory in Georgia and the Carolinas, it was deemed prudent to unite. The composition of the (present) Pentecostal Holiness Church was completed in 1915 when it absorbed several Presbyterian churches in South Carolina that had become Pentecostal five years earlier, apparently without direct influence from Azusa. For many years the Pentecostal Holiness Church was centered in Franklin Springs, Georgia, but in 1973 moved its headquarters to Oklahoma City.

The Church of God in Christ, the Church of God, and the Pentecostal Holiness Church, all in the Southeast, were thus nudged into Pentecostalism by news and travelers from Azusa. The process that led to the formation of the Assemblies of God in the lower Midwest was, however, only tangentially related to the California revival.

The Assemblies of God represents the amalgamation of four distinct groups. The most substantial was the core of Parham's followers in southeastern Texas known as the Apostolic Faith. A second cluster, which called itself the Church of God, grew up in Alabama between 1907 and 1910. These bodies struck an alliance in 1912 and received permission from C. H. Mason's Church of God in Christ to use its name in order to gain the benefits of legal incorporation and railroad clergy discounts. The third group in the amalgamation was centered in northern Illinois. Parham's disciples had penetrated Dowie's stronghold in Zion City in 1904, and by 1906 many of the latter's followers had converted to Pentecostalism. The message soon spread to Chicago, where it was heralded by two extraordinary preachers, William H. Durham at the North Avenue Mission and William H. Piper at the Stone Church. It is true that Durham traveled to Azusa in 1907, where he received the baptism experience, but he and Piper first learned about it from Pentecostals in Zion City. The fourth group consisted of persons who had been forced to withdraw from Simpson's Christian and Missionary Alliance between 1907 and 1911, as Simpson grew increasingly hostile to Pentecostalism. Clergymen from this group were probably the best-educated ministers in the Assemblies of God.

These four bodies were drawn together partly by necessity and partly by theological affinity. The necessity was created by doctrinal irregularities, emotional excess, organizational chaos, and financial fraud. Early leaders were understandably reluctant to say much about these problems in print, but stray comments leave no doubt that the movement was bedeviled by cranks, charlatans, and religious fanatics. Thus by 1912 many thoughtful men and women had become fearful that the infant movement would be dashed against the rocks if it were not brought within the protective discipline of a formal organization.

The theological affinity stemmed from disenchantment with the Wesleyan emphases inherited from Irwin, Parham, Seymour, and Tomlinson. All of these men insisted upon three distinct steps in the order of salvation: conversion, entire sanctification, and baptism in the Holy Spirit. The dissidents, largely drawn from Baptist, Presbyterian, and other non-Wesleyan traditions, especially disliked the Wesleyan idea that "inbred sin" was eradicated in the sanctification experience. They were certain that this notion fostered antinomian excesses, undercut confidence in Christ's atonement, and, above all, had no biblical warrant. Thus they wanted to return to a position more characteristic of the Reformed tradition, in which sanctification was understood as a process that commenced at conversion but was not perfected or completed until death. Indeed, William H. Durham, the most articulate spokesman for the non-Wesleyan Pentecostals, espoused a view of sanctification more characteristic of the Moravian tradition: namely, that God did not literally implant new spiritual life in believers but ascribed it to them, for Christ's sake, at the moment of rebirth. Like many non-Wesleyan converts to the movement, Durham was particularly concerned that the distinctively Wesleyan-holiness emphasis upon the work of the Holy Spirit might overshadow the centrality of Christ's atonement on the cross. Thus this Finished Work faction, as it came to be called, insisted that conversion and sanctification constituted a single experience. That meant that the order of salvation entailed only two steps: new birth and baptism in the Holy Spirit with the evidence of tongues.

Beyond these practical and theological considerations, a measure of simple self-interest—including new opportunities to exert leadership and exercise power—undoubtedly was mixed into the decision to form a new denomination. Whatever the exact blend of motives, representatives of these four groups met in Arkansas in 1914, where they formed the General Council of the Assemblies of God. Shortly afterward its headquarters was permanently located in Springfield, Missouri. This overwhelmingly white, non-Wesleyan denomination soon became the largest, strongest, and most acculturated of the Pentecostal denominations in the United States.

In summary, then, four of the six largest Pentecostal denominations, representing the great majority of denominationally affiliated American Pentecostals, were organized shortly before World War I. The other two, the International Church of the Foursquare Gospel and the United Pentecostal Church International, also have their roots in this period.

The Foursquare, as it is commonly called, was incorporated in Los Angeles in 1927. The only significant difference between this group and the Assemblies of God is that it is still strongly influenced by the memory of its flamboyant founder, Aimee Semple McPherson, whose barnstorming faith-healing tours before and after the war had led to the founding of Angelus Temple in Los Angeles in 1923. Always glamorous, occasionally indiscreet, Sister Aimee single-handedly led the Foursquare until her death by barbiturate overdose in 1944.

The United Pentecostal Church traces its

roots to a doctrinal controversy that erupted in the Assemblies of God in 1913. The dispute started as a disagreement about whether believers should be baptized in the name of the Father, Son, and Holy Ghost, as recorded in Matthew 28:19, or in the name of "Jesus only," as recorded in Acts 2:38. Debate about the proper baptismal formula quickly escalated into a confrontation about the nature of the Godhead. By 1916 the "Jesus only" advocates had become, in effect, Jesus Unitarians, for they now insisted that the names of the members of the Trinity were only different names for the one true God, who had been wholly incarnated in Jesus Christ. After a bitter power struggle, which nearly wrecked the infant denomination, the "Jesus only" faction was thrown out. In the succeeding decades Oneness Pentecostals (as they prefer to be called) were rocked by a succession of doctrinal controversies that had racial and rural-urban overtones, but substantial stability was achieved with the formation of the United Pentecostal Church in St. Louis in 1945.

Many of the smaller Pentecostal denominations also trace their roots to the decade preceding World War I. The Church of God of the Mountain Assembly, centered in eastern Tennessee, the Pentecostal Free-Will Baptist Church, rooted in the eastern coastal counties of the Carolinas, and the black United Holy Church, also rooted in the Carolinas, were tiny but well-established Wesleyan sects that turned to Pentecostalism in 1906 and 1907. Tensions resulting from interracial worship in the Fire-Baptized Holiness Church (before it merged with the Pentecostal Holiness Church in 1911) prompted William E. Fuller to leave that body and establish the black Fire-Baptized Church of God of the Americas in 1908. Charles Fox Parham was "disfellowshiped" by a majority of his followers in Texas in 1907, but he continued to lead another faction until his death in 1929. This group, known simply as Apostolic Faith, still thrives in Kansas, Missouri, and Oklahoma. In 1908 Florence Crawford, a disgruntled disciple of William J. Seymour, established an extremely rigorous offshoot in Portland, Oregon, known as The Apostolic Faith. A substantial minority of black Pentecostals adopted the Oneness position between 1913 and 1916 and eventually formed a score of denominations. The largest of these include the Pentecostal Assemblies of the World, incorporated in Indianapolis in 1919, and the Apostolic Overcoming Holy Church of God, incorporated in Mobile, Alabama, in 1920.

Several numerically significant denominations were formed between the world wars. All but one resulted from doctrinal or personality conflicts in the older groups. In the Church of God a persistent determination to enforce the New Testament blueprint for church government was the source of endless polity fights and three major schisms: the Original Church of God in 1919, the Tomlinson Church of God in 1923 (renamed the Church of God of Prophecy in 1952), and the Church of God World Headquarters in 1943. Disputes about polity and mores in the Pentecostal Holiness Church prompted the Pentecostal Fire-Baptized Holiness Church and the Congregational Holiness Church to break away in 1916 and 1921, respectively. Similar controversies in Aimee McPherson's Foursquare and in Florence Crawford's The Apostolic Faith produced schismatic factions. Two of these united in 1935 in Des Moines, Iowa, taking the name Open Bible Standard Churches, Incorporated. The only one of the post–World War I denominations that grew from a coalescence of previously unaffiliated believers is the Pentecostal Church of God in America, which was founded by John C. Sinclair in Chicago in 1919. This group's headquarters is now located in Joplin, Missouri.

In summary, all of these bodies were to some extent products of social and cultural strain. But primarily they were brought into existence by the fusion of religious and theological traditions that had been developing for many decades: a desire for baptism in the Holy Spirit, conceived, more often than not, as both a purifying and empowering experience; a new theology of faith healing; and expectation of the imminent Second Coming of the Lord. When these currents coalesced in a setting of turbid revivalism, people started to believe that speaking in tongues was palpable proof of baptism and, along with faith healing, a tocsin of the end of time. The process was well under way by 1890, and by 1914 it was largely complete.

Understanding why Pentecostalism emerged is one thing, understanding why it survived is another. Historians have discerned several factors. One of the more important was that Pentecostals inherited from the nineteenth-century holiness movement an elaborate network of publications, conferences, Bible schools, and foreign missions. Another factor was opposition. At different times and places converts were harassed with peltings, beatings, arson, ridicule in the press, and merciless excoriation by their evangelical rivals. One prominent holiness speaker's judgment that Pentecostalism was the "last vomit of Satan" was more graphic than most, but in substance not unusual. Even so, it is important to remember that the persecution Pentecostals suffered was enough to toughen yet not enough really to harm them. While Fundamentalists and other sectarians fought Pentecostals at every turn in the road, the established denominations and the civil courts of law seemed scarcely to notice their existence. All things considered, however, the secret of the movement's success was rooted deep within the religious life of Pentecostalism itself. It met the needs of ordinary people with an ecstatic, ahistorical, and millenarian faith that was largely impervious to the acids of modern criticism. The movement flourished, in short, not in spite of the fact that it was out of step with the times, but precisely because it was.

RECENT PENTECOSTALISM

In the early years Pentecostal churches often called themselves Full Gospel Tabernacles. By this they meant to assert that the full Gospel entails a fourfold affirmation that Christ is "Savior, Baptizer, Healer, and Soon Coming King." Over the years this "foursquare" Gospel has been the uniform hallmark of American and, for that matter, worldwide Pentecostalism. Nonetheless, throughout most of its history the movement has been riven with doctrinal, cultural, and sociological fractures.

One serious doctrinal division has been that between the Wesleyan Second Blessing and the non-Wesleyan Finished Work Pentecostals. Before the founding of the World Pentecostal Conference in 1947 and the Pentecostal Fellowship of North America in the following year, there was virtually no communication between, on the one side, Wesleyan denominations such as the Church of God in Christ, the Church of God (Cleveland, Tennessee), and the Pentecostal Holiness Church, and, on the other, non-Wesleyan groups such as the Assemblies of God, Church of the Foursquare Gospel, and Open Bible Standard Churches. Another persistent division, especially before mid-century, has been that between the various Church of God groups in the southern Appalachians and virtually all other Pentecostals. The overwhelming pressure of the restorationist impulse prompted the former to remain rigidly exclusive, punctilious about polity, and singularly autocratic in administration. But by far the deepest division has been that separating Trinitarian and Oneness Pentecostals. A conviction prevalent in both camps that the other is unchristian has blocked virtually all communication to this day.

Pentecostals have also been divided by cultural and sociological differences. The most visible is, predictably, racial. Although a few denominations, such as the Church of God (Cleveland, Tennessee) and the Church of God of Prophecy, are discernibly interracial, most are predominantly, and a few are exclusively, black or white. The same is true of English-speaking and Spanish- or Italian-speaking denominations. Differences of social class have also divided denominations and, especially, congregations within denominations. In the early years these disparities probably were not as apparent as they are now. The social homogeneity of early Pentecostalism stemmed from the movement's common origins in the lower sector of the social system. (While it is commonly believed that first-generation Pentecostals were drawn from the most impoverished stratum of society, close scrutiny of the evidence suggests, rather, that they ordinarily came from the ranks of the stable working class.) But things have changed to a degree. Working-class Pentecostalism still flourishes in inner-city missions, Appalachian hollows, and small-town revival centers. At the same time, a glance at the parking lot of a typical suburban Assemblies of God church leaves little doubt that since World War II growing affluence has markedly changed the face of some parts of the movement.

Even so, the divisions and variations in the topography of American Pentecostalism should not obscure the fact that, as a whole, the movement has undergone a slow but remarkably uniform acculturation toward the values of middle-class, mainstream Protestantism. Initially, this may be difficult to see. The official doctrinal position of the major denominations has changed little, and their worldview continues to be nearly as supernaturalistic as it was in 1900. Compared with the earliest years, tongues and healing are more circumscribed, but compared with other evangelical Protestants, Pentecostals are still remarkable in the extent to which they cultivate the miracles of the Spirit.

Nonetheless, appearances can be deceiving. The little-studied role of faith healing is a good indicator of what has taken place. Although in the beginning millenarian expectation probably was dominant, the four facets of the "foursquare Gospel"—salvation, baptism, healing, and the Second Coming—were inseparable components of the movement's life. Very soon, however, healing tended to be relegated to an elite body of shaman-like specialists. From the time of their emergence as a distinct group around 1910, and lasting until about 1950, these specially gifted individuals were highly respected as leaders within the denominations. Then, in the late 1940s and early 1950s, for reasons that are not wholly clear, the healers rocketed into national prominence and acquired extraordinary influence among rank-and-file members. Most were promptly squeezed out of their denominations by leaders dismayed at the fraudulence of some of the healing claims and at persistent rumors of financial irregularities. But the attempt to ostracize celebrities such as A. A. Allen, William Branham, and Oral Roberts predictably backfired. Unfettered by denominational constraints, many soon established private empires of seemingly boundless power and financial support.

The crisis provoked by the sudden prominence of the independent faith healers is extremely interesting. It suggests that at mid-century, American Pentecostalism was torn between a traditional, primitivizing impulse on one hand, and a modernizing, acculturative impulse on the other. For the former, it was a last gasp. By the end of the 1960s the big tents were gone, and the stars were dead or disgraced or, like Roberts, grown prudently modern in their methods and diversified in their interests. In retrospect, the rise and fall of the faith healers appears to have

been a final outburst that marked the exhaustion of the old Pentecostalism and the beginning of a new style of life and worship in the established denominations.

Scanning the literature from 1900 to 1980 one gains the impression that this acculturative process started after World War I, sharply accelerated after World War II, and has continued unabated into the mid-1980s. Tents and wood-frame tabernacles have been displaced by architecturally stylish churches; boisterous hand-clapping, shouting, and dancing in the Spirit have given way to robed choirs and restrained (though nonliturgical) worship. Changes in the strategy of evangelism further illustrate the shift. In the early years Pentecostals invariably sought the lowest common denominator, following, as it were, Billy Sunday's advice always to keep "the cookies on the bottom shelf." Sister Aimee's opening worship in Angelus Temple by riding a motorcycle onto the platform, and her proclaiming that for "sheer, breathtaking 1000 percent thrills" there is nothing like watching sinners "run down the aisle," are elements of the heritage most Pentecostal leaders would prefer to bury.

Acculturation is particularly evident in Pentecostal attitudes toward government and society. Pacifism, nearly universal among Pentecostals during World War I, turned into a reluctant willingness to fight during World War II, and then into strident superpatriotism during the cold war and Vietnam eras. Similarly, a genuine lack of interest in the affairs of secular society in the early years evolved after World War II into a studied disinterest in "purely political" concerns such as the civil rights movement. Since the mid-1970s most white and many black Pentecostal leaders have shed the pretense of political noninvolvement and openly endorsed the candidates and aims of the most conservative wings of the Democratic and (more often) Republican parties.

Many of the changes evident in contemporary Pentecostalism have resulted not from drifting with the culture, but from deliberate decisions to use modern means to achieve traditional ends. Street-corner evangelism has mushroomed into a billion-dollar television ministry. Tiny Bible institutes have grown into fully accredited colleges, seminaries, and professional graduate schools. Once plagued by zealots and crackpots, the larger denominations have developed strongly centralized administrations with a reputation for financial sobriety and rigorous internal discipline. Interminable wrangling between factions generally has been replaced by a disposition to cooperate with other Pentecostals, non-Pentecostal Evangelicals, and "charismatics" in the Roman Catholic church and in the mainstream Protestant denominations. In the local community the typical Pentecostal minister has become more respected for his daily pastoral skills than for his charismatic gifts. Sinclair Lewis' Elmer Gantry always was a caricature, but in the context of most Pentecostal churches he is now scarcely imaginable.

The transition from embattled sect to comfortably established religion is well illustrated by the career of Oral Roberts, who started as a country pastor in the Pentecostal Holiness Church. After turning to a full-time healing ministry in 1948, Roberts' ability to cure the sick and reputation for financial honesty quickly propelled him to the forefront of the faith-healing movement. A portent of things to come was his decision in 1954 to have his outdoor healing services carried live on network television. But in the 1960s, again displaying the keen sense of timing that marked his career, he concluded that the day of the tent revivals had passed.

Roberts' desire to proclaim the Pentecostal message in more up-to-date ways led, first, to the establishment of Oral Roberts University in Tulsa, Oklahoma, in 1965. Best known perhaps for its nationally ranked basketball team and spectacular $250 million campus, the university was by 1985 enrolling five thousand students in a fully accredited college and in six professional graduate schools. In 1968 Roberts—almost predictably—left the Pentecostal Holiness Church to join the United Methodist Church. He also launched a nationally syndicated newspaper column, a weekly television program, and a series of quarterly network television specials. The latter featured the interracial and conspicuously attractive World Action Singers as well as a constant stream of Hollywood celebrities. Roberts' doctrinal ideas were evolving, too. Having come to believe that prayer and scalpels were equally God's instruments for healing, he determined to build a hospital and medical research facility that would rival the Mayo Clinic. Started in 1978, the

$150 million City of Faith Medical and Research Center now includes graduate schools of medicine, dentistry, and nursing, a sixty-story clinic, a thirty-story hospital, and a twenty-story laboratory specializing in aging, cancer, and heart disease. Roberts' holistic view of health care is reflected in the university's motto: "To educate the whole man in spirit, mind and body." It is also reflected in the school's requirement that all students and faculty meet exacting physical fitness tests or be dismissed. One Oral Roberts University official may have said more about the acculturation of modern Pentecostalism than he intended when he explained, "You can't be much of a witness [for Christ] if you are a loser."

Pentecostalism has paid a steep price for having moved into the mainstream. The movement's uncritical identification with the values of Middle America—indeed, its apparent inability even to suspect that the faith of the fathers has become entangled with the class and status interests of its upwardly mobile constituency—represents a measurable loss of prophetic vision. In 1976 Martin E. Marty perceptively noted that in times past Pentecostalism "was 'true' because it was small and pure, but now it is 'true' because so many are drawn to it" (*A Nation of Behavers*).

Still, the story of the American Pentecostal movement is not adequately grasped if we think of it only in sociological terms as a sect struggling to become a church, or as a refuge for the disinherited quietly drifting back into the mainstream of respectable Protestantism. While that may be an accurate depiction of post–World War II and, especially, post-1960s Pentecostalism, it was not true of the first and second generations. For one thing, primitive Pentecostalism harbored a regressive and disruptive strain that was, by any reasonable measure, socially dysfunctional. Its defiance of social conventions, its bellicosity and zealotry, its ecstatic excess and deliberate scrambling of the human language surely reflected a primordial urge toward disorder. This is to say, in short, that first- and second-generation Pentecostalism is best understood not simply as a response to social marginality, but also as a burst of radical perfectionism; not as an effort to escape life's difficulties, but as a sustained attempt to transcend them. Like all true perfectionist movements, primitive Pentecostalism tried to cope with life's perennial dilemmas by forging a new vision of reality. It promised meaning for this life and salvation for the next. It was a faith to live by, not because it told the truth about this thing or that, but because for the true believer it proved to be, as G. K. Chesterton said of Christianity itself, a "truth-telling thing."

BIBLIOGRAPHY

For a comprehensive bibliography of primary and secondary materials pertaining to American and, to some extent, world Pentecostalism, see Charles Edwin Jones, *A Guide to the Study of the Pentecostal Movement*, 2 vols. (1983). A smaller yet handier guide is David W. Faupel, *The American Pentecostal Movement* (1972).

For a historical survey of Pentecostalism worldwide, see Walter J. Hollenweger, *The Pentecostals*, trans. R. A. Wilson (1972 [Ger. orig. 1969]). The best general study of early Pentecostalism in the United States is Robert Mapes Anderson, *Vision of the Disinherited: The Making of American Pentecostalism* (1979). Another valuable survey, though less critical, is Vinson Synan, *The Holiness-Pentecostal Movement in the United States* (1971).

Particular aspects of Pentecostalism have been ably studied. For the rise and partial demise of independent deliverance evangelism in the mid-twentieth century, see David Edwin Harrell, Jr., *All Things Are Possible: The Healing and Charismatic Revivals in Modern America* (1976). One of the virtues of this exceptionally interesting book is its extensive bibliographic guide to the primary and secondary literature pertaining to Pentecostal faith healing. The definitive biography of the world's most prominent Pentecostal leader is David Edwin Harrell, Jr., *Oral Roberts: An American Life* (1985).

Pentecostal theology has been surveyed in numerous doctoral dissertations. Two of the best include Donald W. Dayton, "Theological Roots of Pentecostalism," Ph.D. dissertation, University of Chicago, 1983; and Edith L. Waldvogel, "The 'Overcoming Life': A Study in the Reformed Evangelical Origins of Pentecostalism," Ph.D. dissertation, Harvard University, 1977. Pentecostal biblical scholarship is discussed in Russell P. Spittler, "Scripture and the Theological Enterprise," in Robert K. Johnston, ed., *The Use of the Bible in Theology: Evangelical Options* (1985). For black Pentecostalism, see Arthur E. Paris, *Black Pentecostalism: Southern Religion in an Urban World* (1982); and Douglas J. Nelson, "For Such a Time as This: The Story of Bishop William J. Seymour and the Azusa Street Revival: A Search for Pentecostal/Charismatic Roots," Ph.D. dissertation, University of Birmingham (UK), 1981.

Not surprisingly, Pentecostalism has attracted the interests of numerous social scientists. Much of this literature is surveyed in Killian McDonnell, *Charismatic Renewal and the Churches* (1976). For an especially provocative study of the social and cultural texture of the movement, see Luther P. Gerlach and Virginia H. Hine, *People, Power, Change: Movements of Social Transformation* (1970). For analyses of glossolalia see William J. Samarin, *Tongues of Men and Angels: The Religious Language of Pentecostalism* (1972); and H. Newton Maloney and A. Adams Lovekin, *Glossolalia: Behavioral Science Perspectives on Speaking in Tongues* (1985).

Nothing like a comprehensive collection of Pentecostal primary materials exists. However a revealing assortment of autobiographical accounts from the early years has been collected in Wayne Warner, ed., *Touched by the Fire: Patriarchs of Pentecost* (1978). A fascinating book-length account of the emergence and tempestuous early history of the revival by an eyewitness is Frank Bartleman, *How "Pentecost" Came to Los Angeles—How It Was in the Beginning* (1925), reprinted in unabridged form as *Azusa Street: The Roots of Modern-Day Pentecost* (1980). The first years of the Azusa Mission's newspaper have been photographically reprinted; see Fred T. Corum, collector, *Like as of Fire: A Reprint of the Azusa Street Documents* (1981), available from the Gospel Publishing House, Springfield, Missouri.

For classic statements of the main themes of Pentecostal doctrine, see Ralph M. Riggs, *The Spirit Himself* (1949); and Charles W. Conn, *Pillars of Pentecost* (1956). For a critique of Pentecostal theology by an empathetic outsider, see Frederick Dale Bruner, *A Theology of the Holy Spirit: The Pentecostal Experience and the New Testament Witness* (1970).

Finally, it should be noted that the Society for Pentecostal Studies, an association of men and women with graduate degrees who are sympathetic to the aims of the World Pentecostal Conference, publishes a semiannual journal called *Pneuma: The Journal of the Society for Pentecostal Studies*. This journal presents a Pentecostal point of view on a variety of historical, biblical, and theological subjects, yet it is relatively free of the sectarian defensiveness still evident in most Pentecostal publications.

[*See also* CONSERVATIVE AND CHARISMATIC DEVELOPMENTS OF THE LATER TWENTIETH CENTURY; FUNDAMENTALISM; HOLINESS AND PERFECTION; MASS COMMUNICATIONS; *and* MEDICINE AND MEDICAL ETHICS.]

FUNDAMENTALISM

George M. Marsden

FUNDAMENTALISTS are first of all aggressively "evangelical" Christians. They are Bible-believers who take absolutely seriously the understanding of the Gospel message that proclaims that God sent his son into the world to die for sinners and that the only hope for eternal salvation, and to avoid an eternity in Hell, is to believe that Jesus died for one's sins and to make him the Lord of one's life. The only ultimately important question for humans is "What must I do to be saved?" A whole eternity hangs on knowing, believing, and acting on the correct answer to this question. Accordingly, no kinder act can be done for another person than to tell him or her of the Gospel promise of salvation. No cause is more worthy of support than missions that will bring this message to the whole world.

What distinguishes Fundamentalists from many other evangelical Christians who believe this Gospel message with similar passion are a set of nineteenth- and twentieth-century historical circumstances that have led Fundamentalists to adopt certain characteristic traits. The most widespread of these distinctive traits is a conspicuous militancy in defending what is regarded as the traditional Protestant Gospel against its major twentieth-century competitors, especially modernism or liberalism in theology, secularism or "secular humanism" in cultural values, evolutionary naturalism, Marxism, Socialism, Roman Catholicism, and religious cults. Bible-believers with these militant emphases have come from many evangelical traditions, so Fundamentalism has always been a coalition of militants, partly organized at its center but always with many loose ends and many parallels.

Fundamentalism can be distinguished from the Holiness movement and Pentecostalism, two similar and closely related movements that emerged in America at nearly the same time. All three grew out of nineteenth-century revivalism and provided distinct alternatives to secularizing trends that were developing both outside and within the major denominations. The Holiness movement, arising first in the mid-nineteenth century as a renewal movement within Methodism and then in separate denominations, responded to modernity with a heightened emphasis on the power of the Holy Spirit to transform one's moral life. Pentecostalism, leading to separate denominations after the turn of the century, countered modern secularism with intense emphasis on the experiential side of spirituality, manifested in ecstatic speech, healing powers, and other spiritual gifts. Fundamentalism arose in the early decades of the twentieth century but developed a distinct identity and separate organizations only later. Fundamentalism's most distinguishing trait emphasized the necessity of fighting secularizing forces at the level of ideology. Christians should fight for the fundamentals of the faith against doctrinal erosions and compromises. They should not allow their culture to turn from the God of the Bible. These cognitive and cultural emphases reflected the influence of broadly Calvinist traditions in America. Fundamentalists were largely Baptist or Presbyterian. Despite their differing key emphases, the Holiness movement, Pentecostalism, and Fundamentalism shared many traits.

Fundamentalism, in its original meaning, designated a trend, found in many denominations, of militant opposition to erosions of traditional Protestant faith in American churches and culture. The word "Fundamentalist" was invented in 1920 by a conservative Baptist editor, Curtis Lee Laws, to designate those ready "to do

947

battle royal for the Fundamentals." Soon "Fundamentalist" was being used to designate any Protestant conservative who was willing to affirm certain "Fundamental" doctrines and to fight against the spread of modernist theology in the major denominations or against some secularizing trends, such as the teaching of biological evolution in public schools. In this broad sense "Fundamentalism" refers to a certain religious type and is more a widespread tendency than an organized movement. By extension, the term sometimes has been used to designate militant traditionalists beyond evangelical Protestantism, such as Mormon "fundamentalists" or Islamic "fundamentalists."

At the core of Protestant Fundamentalism in this broad sense, however, is a much more distinct and unified movement. Although organizationally diverse, and sometimes sharply divided, "Fundamentalism" in this core meaning has been almost a denomination, at least in the sense of being a term by which interrelated religious groups denominate themselves. This informal denomination has built up an infrastructure of Fundamentalist organizations and an elaborate network of personal connections. So some groups that might be generically Fundamentalist in attitudes and might fully assent to the fundamental doctrines of the core Fundamentalist movement might not be directly connected with that movement nor think of themselves as "Fundamentalists." For instance, many black churches might be Fundamentalist in the broad sense but not be directly connected to the distinct Fundamentalist movement. Although it is legitimate to use "Fundamentalist" generically (meaning militant conservative religionist) or doctrinally (one who insists on the traditional "Fundamental" doctrines), Fundamentalism is best understood as a historical movement if the term is used to refer primarily to the distinct coalition of those who have called themselves "Fundamentalists."

BACKGROUND

This distinct Fundamentalist movement has a history that goes back beyond the coining of the term "Fundamentalist" in 1920. The Fundamentalist movement that took clear shape in America during the 1920s and the 1930s was, in fact, the amalgamation in the heat of controversy of at least five major traditions. Each of these gave the emergent movement some of its most important traits.

Revivalist Evangelicalism. More than by any other tradition, the conspicuous traits of Fundamentalists have been shaped by American revivalist evangelicalism. The conservativism of Fundamentalists has been directed largely toward maintaining the major emphases of this nineteenth-century movement, which had dominated American religious life.

Especially important among the revivalist evangelical traits that have been conserved in Fundamentalism are the emphases on proclaiming the Gospel message of salvation of souls only by faith in Christ, the importance of conversion, and hence of evangelism, witnessing, and missions. Prayer and Bible study loom large in both traditions, both as the core of private devotions and public worship. Catchy Gospel hymns are a nineteenth-century revivalist tool, developed avidly by Fundamentalists. Both movements place tremendous rhetorical stress on getting back to the Bible alone as the only legitimate religious authority. Hence both have been suspicious of churchly traditions, and both have thought of themselves as restoring the practices of the New Testament church. Correspondingly, each movement has lacked a strong doctrine of the church. Denominations have been regarded as essentially convenient associations of like-minded Christians. Independent agencies are considered just as legitimate as denominations for carrying on the work of Christ. Local churches in nineteenth-century evangelicalism and in twentieth-century Fundamentalism have offered strong communities even though they are individualistic in theory. Salvation was basically a matter between oneself and the Lord, individual choice was crucial to conversion, spiritual power came directly from the Holy Spirit, and an individual conscience informed by Scripture could in principle override any church group.

The nineteenth-century American revivalist movement and its twentieth-century Fundamentalist heirs have shared many similar views on ethical questions. Fundamentalist personal ethics, like those preached by earlier revivalists, often have centered on avoiding the vices of the barroom. Hence a test of commitment has been whether one totally avoids drinking, smoking, dancing, card playing, and theater or movie attendance. These themes are strong in the Methodist tradition and the prohibitions of dancing, cards, and theater suggest continuing Puritan traditions. Oddly, one of the most distinctive traits of all these traditions, strict Sabbath observance, disappeared in most Fundamentalism. Fundamentalist ethics have also reflected the middle-class Victorian outlooks of their revivalist predecessors. They have had strict views regarding sexual behavior and have put strong emphasis on the patriarchal family.

The free-enterprise liberalism characteristic of nineteenth-century America also dominates Fundamentalist economic and social thought. Most social problems can be solved by individual effort and hard work. The less government interference the better, except in dealing with specifically ethical issues, as defined above. Fundamentalists again follow their revivalist predecessors in ambivalence concerning the question of a Christian's obligations toward social reform. Some, in the tradition of Dwight L. Moody, have viewed the Christian's chief duty of rescuing lost souls from hell as so overriding as to render social concerns relatively inconsequential. In reaction to the liberal Social Gospel of the early twentieth century, some Fundamentalists have elevated this attitude to a principle, maintaining that it is wrong for Christian groups to engage in social reforms. Such positions have rarely been consistently maintained. Fundamentalists are also heirs to another tradition, prominent in the era of Charles G. Finney, when abolitionism and other evangelical-supported reform movements were popular, that emphasizes that evangelical Christians have a deep responsibility for the American social order. In this tradition, which goes back to the Puritans, America is viewed as a nation especially chosen by God to carry forward the banners of Protestant civilization. The United States, accordingly, is blessed or punished according to how true it has been to this covenantal birthright; that is, how well it has kept God's moral law. Social questions, viewed in their moral dimensions, are therefore of great concern to Christians. The fate of the nation hinges on its moral behavior. Taking this outlook seriously, revivalists and later Fundamentalists have worked avidly for social-moral reforms. In the twentieth century Fundamentalist reform

and political efforts have been conservative relative to the rest of the culture, based largely on dominant nineteenth-century values and ideologies. Sometimes twentieth-century liberal critics have spoken of Fundamentalists, who might support such causes as prohibition, antievolution, antipornography, or antiabortion, as though they preached an otherworldly religion with no social conscience or concern. More accurately, Fundamentalists have often expressed social-political concerns—but of an almost uniformly conservative sort. Furthermore, while they have opposed many twentieth-century governmental efforts to solve social problems, Fundamentalists have acted with the sincere (though inconsistently applied) belief that the best way to change society is to change individual lives.

Hand in hand with Fundamentalists' concern for the moral welfare of the nation has been their characteristic American nationalism. Again, nineteenth-century patriotism is the precedent. America, Fundamentalist preachers have proclaimed, is in grave danger of judgment if it does not repent. Nonetheless, such preachers also leave no doubt that America is God's chosen nation, the greatest nation on earth.

Dispensational Premillennialism. The ambiguities regarding social and nationalist questions are accentuated by the influences of the most distinctive of the traditions shaping the core Fundamentalist movement. This tradition, dispensational premillennialism (or dispensationalism) teaches that according to the Bible all history is divided into seven dispensations. Each of these dispensations, such as the era in the Garden of Eden, the era that ended with the Genesis flood, the historical period that ended with the dispersion at Babel, and so forth, is a time when God tests mankind. Mankind fails each test and is punished with a judgment that ends the era. Currently we are in the sixth dispensation, or the "church age." This age is also rapidly drawing to a close as modern civilization, even the so-called Christian civilization, has failed another divine test. Even the churches, rife with paganism and apostasy, are ripe for God's judgment. In the meantime, however, God is preparing for the advent of the last dispensation, or the millennial age. The clearest evidence of this preparation is the rebirth of the state of Israel, predicted in Scripture and foretold by nineteenth-century dispensationalists. Israel will be the site of the political kingdom in which Jesus, having returned to earth, will reign for the last thousand years of the planet's history. After the millennium will be the final judgment and a "new heavens and a new earth."

If dispensationalist teachings are taken completely literally, as they are by a few Fundamentalist groups, modern politics is a hopeless enterprise, and believers should concentrate their energies on preparing for the coming kingdom. The only chosen nation is Israel. Viewing America as virtually the chosen nation would be inconsistent with the dispensationalist reading of the Bible, which maintains that the biblical promises to Israel will be fulfilled literally in the nation of Israel and do not apply to anyone else. All the other nations in this dispensation are condemned. Most American Fundamentalists, however, have not given up their concerns about American political and social questions and their hope that America will be blessed by God, even though the end of the dispensation may come any day. In fact, the Puritan-evangelical tradition of America as Israel and the dispensationalist tradition that only Israel is Israel exist side by side. Fundamentalists sometimes explain this anomaly by citing God's promise to Abraham in Genesis 12:3 that "I will bless those who bless you." America's treatment of the Jews and the state of Israel is, then, especially important to its prosperity.

Dispensationalism first took distinct shape in Great Britain during the 1820s and 1830s. At that time a number of British prophetic interpreters, of whom Edward Irving was the best known, were teaching that if biblical prophecies were interpreted literally, instead of figuratively as they usually were, we would learn the essentials of the impending judgment on this dispensation, the promised return of the Jews to Palestine, and the coming millennial reign of Christ on earth. John Nelson Darby, the major figure in the new Plymouth Brethren movement, developed further distinctive teachings. Darby was primarily concerned with corruption of the organized churches. He proclaimed the churches and Christendom were in ruin and that the only true church was a spiritual fellowship. The Plymouth Brethren movement was an attempt to restore New Testament practice while avoiding the corruptions of institutionalization that had intervened. Darby advocated ecclesiastical separation

from all unbelief and saw the true church as a spiritual haven from a hopelessly corrupt world. His unique doctrinal contribution to later Fundamentalism was consistent with such motifs. The return of Christ would actually take place in two stages. First would be the "secret rapture" of the saints, who would suddenly disappear from earth to meet Christ in the air. Then would be a seven-year series of cataclysmic events, known as the tribulation, involving the rise of the military empire of the Antichrist, the conversion of many Jews and their persecution, and a series of wars culminating in the return of Christ with his saints, victory at the battle of Armageddon, and the establishment of the millennial kingdom. This scenario, the details of which were often disputed, was based on Darby's novel interpretation of a prophecy in the book of Daniel. Many interpreters saw this prophecy as referring to a 490-year period from the Old Testament rebuilding of Jerusalem to the coming of Christ. Darby argued that this and other prophecies concerning the Jews could be interpreted literally if 483 of the years referred to the point in the New Testament when the church was founded. Then, Darby asserted in his crucial innovation, there has been a "parentheses" of the unforetold "church age," after which the last seven years of the prophecy will commence. This era, he said, will end when the remnant of the true church is raptured. After that come the events of the last seven years foretold in the prophecy.

Darby traveled widely, and in America around the Civil War era he found some receptiveness for his prophetic interpretations. Very few of his American followers, however, fully accepted Darby's views of the ruin of the church and the necessity of separating from their denominations and becoming part of a separate fellowship such as the Plymouth Brethren. In the 1870s some American prophetic interpreters, mostly Presbyterians and Baptists, established their own dispensationalist movement with the founding of the annual Niagara Bible Conferences in 1876. They also instituted a series of International Prophecy Conferences every decade or so beginning in 1878. Some of the best-known leaders of this movement were James H. Brookes, William E. Blackstone, Adoniram J. Gordon, Arthur T. Pierson, James M. Gray, Amzi C. Dixon, and Reuben A. Torrey. Cyrus I. Scofield aided the wide dissemination of classic dispensationalist teaching with the publication of the *Scofield Reference Bible* in 1909.

Many of the early leaders of the dispensationalist movement in America were close associates of the leading evangelist of the day, Dwight L. Moody. Moody himself was not a strict dispensationalist, but he did emphasize the premillennial return of Christ to set up an earthly kingdom. The connection with Moody exemplified that the first interest of the organizers of the movement was evangelism. Working largely independently, with only loose connections to their denominations, these evangelists placed tremendous stress on the sole authority of the Bible. The dispensationalist prophetic movement was thus an important auxiliary movement to promote better Bible study and clearer understanding of the evangelical mission in the latter days.

The same combination of motives was evident in the main institutional development of the movement, the founding of Bible institutes. Moody Bible Institute in Chicago, founded in 1886, was the best-known model for a score of other institutes established in major American cities by 1910. These were training schools for evangelists and Christian workers that could get people into the field without the delays and barriers of college and seminary. Biblical study was at the heart of the curriculum, and most of the schools taught the Bible according to the dispensationalist system. Such schools became the heart of the emerging Fundamentalist movement. Often interconnected through summer Bible conferences that employed their faculties, the Bible schools nourished informal networks of like-minded dispensationalists into a formidable movement.

Contrary to some popular images of Fundamentalism, this early dispensationalism movement was not entirely anti-intellectual. Bible institutes indeed were an overtly pragmatic effort to circumvent what remained of the tradition that the church should be led by a learned clergy. Dispensationalism itself was a shortcut to biblical scholarship. Any reasonably intelligent person could become an expert in it with only a short course of study. Moreover, especially after the turn of the century, in the era of the evangelism of Billy Sunday, revivalists were relying on hoopla to attract people to the Gospel message. Nonetheless, it was characteristic of evangelists in the dispensational movement to take the intellectual content of their message very seriously and to avoid sheer emotionalism. One of the reasons they were so ready to battle modernism was that they were so insistent on the importance of sound doctrine.

Dispensationalism appealed to a distinctly scientific bent in the evangelical movement and in popular American thought generally. Nineteenth-century Americans often believed that the most rational method of discovering the truth was through the scientific method that they associated with Francis Bacon. One should collect hard facts, carefully divide and classify them, and build nonspeculative scientific conclusions. Nineteenth-century evangelical Americans often combined high regard for this method of discerning truth with their reverence for the Bible as the surest source for truth. Dispensationalism combined and accentuated these themes in the late nineteenth century, just at a time when the intellectual foundations of the old Protestant evangelical establishment were being shaken by new historical consciousness and biblical criticism. Dispensationalists insisted that theirs was the only truly scientific method of Bible interpretation. Moreover, true to the Baconian tradition, they were fascinated with dividing and classifying, as the sharp distinctions among the dispensations themselves exemplify.

Most important for the long run was that dispensationalists insisted that the biblical data itself be treated as hard, exact facts. The Bible, they said, was filled with propositions, and its statements must be interpreted literally, that is as referring to literal historical events, whenever such an interpretation made sense. The guarantee of the exactness of the biblical statements, dispensationalists insisted strongly, was that the Bible was authored by God, even though written by human agents in their own idiom. Every word was from God. Hence, the Bible was without error in any of its statements, including statements on historical and scientific matters. This doctrine of the "inerrancy" (as it became known) of Scripture had been loosely presumed by many spokespersons in the history of the church and emphasized in some scholastic Lutheran and Reformed traditions since the seventeenth century. For dispensationalists the inerrancy of scripture, used in the sense of its historical exactitude, was a crucial doctrine. For their scientific interpretations of prophecies to work convincingly, the prophetic numbers of Scripture had to be exact. The number 483, for example, had to mean exactly 483. For this reason, combined with their strong emphasis on the totally supernatural character of the divine record, dispensationalists were the chief instruments in making inerrancy a central dogma of twentieth-century Fundamentalism.

The Victorious Life. The new movement that was emerging in the late nineteenth century had many sides. Despite their conservatism on traditional fundamental doctrines concerning the supernatural origins of Christianity, the enthusiastic evangelizers were themselves open to doctrinal innovation. Often working in quasi-independent local churches and founding their own network of institutions, including missions organizations, evangelistic agencies, magazines, publishing houses, Bible institutes, and summer Bible conferences, the leaders of the movement were effectively free from ecclesiastical control. For getting new teachings off the ground, the summer Bible conference was probably the most effective institution of the movement. Capitalizing on the new transportation possibilities and the popularity of rustic vacations, the Bible conference offered both relaxation and spiritual growth. In this context Victorious Life teaching developed, alongside dispensationalism, as another important innovation of the emerging Fundamentalist outlook.

The Victorious Life teachings that eventually spread through much of American Fundamentalism first took shape, beginning in 1875, at summer Bible conferences held at Keswick, England, and so are often known as "Keswick Holiness" teachings. The evangelical movement of which Fundamentalism became a part had long been a transatlantic movement. In 1875 Dwight L. Moody was just completing his first spectacularly successful tour of Great Britain, thus continuing transatlantic revivalist connections that went back to Charles Finney's tours of Britain in the earlier nineteenth century and George Whitefield's key role in the American Great Awakening of the eighteenth century. The original Keswick conferences themselves included a strong American element and were part of a wider Holiness movement that was growing on both sides of the Atlantic. John Wesley had taught a doctrine of Christian perfection, and in the nineteenth century various American Methodists had revived that perfectionist Holiness teaching, leading to the founding of the various separate Holiness denominations. In the meantime similar doctrines were being disseminated within the Reformed tradition, notably by the Oberlin Perfectionists such as Asa Mahan, and popular Holiness teachers such as William E. Boardman and Hannah Whitall Smith. All these persons were involved in the founding of the Keswick Conference in England, but the Keswick teaching itself quickly developed some unique emphases. As was common in much of the Holiness teaching of the era, the key to the holy life was a second intense spiritual experience, subsequent to conversion in which one "yielded" or surrendered everything in one's life to God. But while in most Holiness teaching such a yielding would lead to a "Baptism of the Holy Ghost" that would result in sinless perfection, Keswick teaching was more modest as to the result. The yielding or emptying of oneself, if accompanied by trust in God to do what one could not do for oneself, would lead to an experience of being filled with the Holy Spirit and a life of a closer walk with Christ and constant victory over sin. As long as Christ, through his Spirit, filled one's life, sin would not triumph. Lapses, however, were possible, even if not to be expected. As in most Holiness teaching, the symptoms of the victory could be seen best by a life of avoidance of specific vices or pleasures, such as drinking, smoking, dancing, and so forth, no doubt accentuating the importance of these sins, relative to more subtle and intangible vices, in the ethical emphases of the movement. Positively, victorious spirit-filled people would be "empowered for service," especially the service of evangelism and missions, central imperatives proclaimed by the Keswick movement.

These views were adopted by most of Moody's American associates. They were generally the same evangelists and Bible teachers who promoted dispensationalism, although the two submovements were typically promoted at separate conferences. The Keswick doctrine gained an important boost in 1910 with the conversion to that doctrine of Charles G. Trumbull, editor of the influential *Sunday School Times.* Under Trumbull's editorship the *Sunday School Times* became a powerful influence in Fundamentalist circles. In 1913 Trumbull and others founded an American Keswick conference. A prominent figure in the early organization was a transplanted British Bible teacher, W. H. Griffith Thomas, a founder in 1924 of what became Dallas Theological Seminary, a leading center for dispensationalism. In contrast, early American Keswick leader Robert C. McQuilkin in 1923 founded Columbia Bible College, which became a major center for Keswick Victorious Life teaching, but without dispensationalism. Since Keswick teachings had to do mainly with deepening personal religious experiences, it was less divisive than dispensationalism and its influences harder to measure. After the mid-twentieth century it declined as an organized movement, but continued to have wide influence among Fundamentalists and closely related Evangelicals.

Presbyterian Conservatism. While Fundamentalism was primarily a nondenominational coalition, almost all of its early adherents had traditional denominational affiliation. Conservative parties in such denominations, while not identifying with the emerging Fundamentalist distinctives, nonetheless had some impact in shaping the movement. Among these, Presbyterian and Baptist traditions were by far the most influential.

In the era when Fundamentalism was emerging before World War I, its closest parallel and allies were found among conservative Presbyterians. This was because many of the early dispensationalist leaders were Presbyterians. Moreover, the two movements had some important points in common. Conservative Presbyterians in America inherited a long tradition of militancy against modern doctrinal deviations. This "Old School" Presbyterian tradition had very influential and talented intellectual spokespersons at Princeton Theological Seminary. The Princetonians also held the view of the historical and scientific reliability of Scripture that in the late nineteenth century became known as "inerrancy," and the Princeton theologians promoted this view vigorously against any concessions to higher criticism of the Bible. Their views paralleled and reinforced those of dispensationalists, although the two traditions had developed more or less independently, and the dispensationalist version of inerrancy was tied to a more thoroughly literalistic biblical hermeneutics than that taught at Princeton. The Princetonians, being strict confessionalists, were not happy with the dispensationalist and Keswick doctrinal innovations, but they usually tolerated these because of their common unwillingness to compromise in the larger fight against theological liberalism.

The underlying philosophical assumptions of the two movements were also similar. Like that of their dispensationalist allies, the Princeton theology was deeply committed to a scientific, "Baconian" approach to Scripture, which they regarded as revealing a set of fixed facts or propositions. Underlying each outlook, moreover, was the philosophy of Scottish Common Sense Realism, which had been the dominant academic philosophy throughout America through the Civil War era. The pervasiveness of the assumptions of this tradition, which helped shape popular American conceptions of truth, fostered wide Fundamentalist support in communities not infected by more modern philosophies. Common Sense philosophy affirmed the essential reliability of our common basic belief-producing mechanisms. People can get at the essential truth of things through commonsense procedures. These assumptions, combined with Baconian ideas of induction, led to a confidence that biblical truth was straightforward and could be discovered by simple analysis. Problems of historical and cultural relativism, which created such havoc among Christians who accepted the dominant late-nineteenth- and twentieth-century intellectual fashions, interfered little with the process of discovering truth according to the commonsense assumptions. Princeton theologians, notably Benjamin B. Warfield and J. Gresham Machen, made the strongest arguments for the superiority of the commonsense approach versus its historicist rivals. Probably more important, the popular versions of the commonsense assumptions meshed with anti-elitism and resentment of experts that were important to the twentieth-century Fundamentalist appeal. Although Fundamentalists were always more than happy to point to some highly trained experts on their side, they also insisted that common sense was better than a Ph.D. as a guide to understanding the fundamental truths of the Bible.

Because of their affinities in the battle against modern thought, dispensationalists and Presbyterian conservatives were loosely allied, and in the decades around World War I they also developed a common strategy of emphasizing certain fundamentals of the faith. From 1909 to 1915 dispensationalists, supported financially by California oil magnates Lyman and Milton Stewart, published a series of twelve substantial booklets, entitled *The Fundamentals.* These were sent free to pastors and church workers and intended as a great "Testimony to the Truth." Leading conservative scholars were enlisted for this work, and some confessionalist Presbyterians contributed to it.

Meanwhile, within the Presbyterian Church (U.S.A.), the major northern Presbyterian church, conservatives successfully persuaded the General Assembly to adopt a five-point declaration of "essential" doctrines of the faith as an attempt to halt the spread of liberalism in the denomination. These doctrines were: the inerrancy of Scripture, the Virgin Birth of Christ, his substitutionary atonement, his bodily resurrection, and the authenticity of the miracles. These five points were reaffirmed by the General Assembly in 1916 and 1923 and may have been the basis for what came to be known as "the five points of Fundamentalism." The most typical form of these "five points" was the inerrancy of Scripture, the deity of Christ, his Virgin Birth, his substitutionary atonement, and his physical resurrection and coming bodily return to earth. These five points have been widely and informally used by Fundamentalists to describe their own stance especially during the 1950s and 1960s, although the exact formula seems to have been based on a confused summary by historian Stewart G. Cole in 1931. Like the Presbyterian conservatives, early Fundamentalists did have various lists of fundamental doctrines, but seldom had lists of five.

Baptist Traditions and Polity. While emerging Fundamentalism at first had the most affinities with conservative Presbyterian, it had increasing connections with Baptist traditions after it became a distinct movement in the 1920s. Baptist polity, more congregational and less centralized than Presbyterian, was better suited to militant conservatives in the era when they no longer had much hope of controlling the major denominations. The formation of independent churches, for instance, which became a major trend in Fundamentalism after the 1920s, was much better suited to Baptist than to Presbyterian polity. Moreover, the evangelists' emphasis on dramatic

conversion experiences was better suited to adult baptism to symbolize such conversion, rather than to infant baptism that was based on the premise that Christian children could be gradually nurtured into church membership. Baptists emphasized strongly the individual's standing alone before God as did Fundamentalists. The antielitist and antiecclesiastical sentiments of the Baptist heritage also made it congenial to the outlook of much of twentieth-century Fundamentalism.

THE DEVELOPMENT OF FUNDAMENTALISM

The Formative Era: To 1918. Fundamentalism, a blend of these and other traditions, reshaped by its own experiences, has gone through several stages involving changes in character and emphasis.

In the era before World War I, what became Fundamentalism was a very loosely connected series of tendencies, involving the traditions already discussed. The movement during this period was less militantly controversialist than later, a key feature separating this proto-Fundamentalism from Fundamentalism as such. The positive evangelism of Dwight L. Moody, connected with nearly everyone who was part of these proto-Fundamentalist developments, fostered this positive outlook. Dispensationalist and Keswick teachings arose primarily as renewal movements. While alarms about the rise of theological liberalism were being sounded, even *The Fundamentals,* the chief symbol of the rising new militancy was relatively mild by comparison with later Fundamentalist attitudes. Moderate conservatives, such as those who did not take hard-line stands for the inerrancy of Scripture or against all biological evolution, were included among the contributors. The importance of separation from apostasy was suggested only by the most extreme dispensationalists. Dispensationalism itself was not taught in the volumes.

During this era American Protestants on the whole were facing the new century with optimism and activism and were not altogether aware of the degree to which their philosophical and theological differences would eventually separate them. For the time being there might be ominous rumblings in the distance, but in general a Sunday school–picnic atmosphere prevailed. Conservatives, moderates, and liberals in the old evangelical tradition could still have fellowship and sometimes cooperate.

The Era of Controversy: 1918–1925. World War I was the catalyst that precipitated the growing differences between the two parties, and in the crucible of the ensuing controversies Fundamentalism assumed its classic shape. On the one side were militant conservatives and aggressive dispensationalists; on the other side were theological modernists, moderates, and tolerant conservatives who wished to avoid controversy.

The war heightened American feelings on public issues and especially aroused intense concerns about the future of civilization. The cataclysmic international struggle increased interest in prophecy and premillennialism so that dispensational ideas gained wide attention. Moreover, the British capture of Jerusalem in 1918 and the possibility of a restored Jewish state added immensely to the credibility of dispensationalist predictions. Modernists, especially those at the divinity school of the University of Chicago, launched an attack on premillennialism, saying it was an inherently pessimistic doctrine that would undermine the war effort to make the world safe for democracy. Premillennialists responded that modernist theology came from the same barbarous German civilization that Americans were now fighting and that both modernism and the "might is right" attitudes of the Germans were based on evolutionary philosophy.

The end of the war only intensified such disputes. Modernists and their allies hoped for a great Protestant church union movement that would provide a base for social progress. Dispensationalists and militant conservatives were afraid that the spread of sub-Christian philosophies in the name of Christianity would lead American civilization to the same demise that they saw in Germany. In 1919 dispensationalist Baptist William B. Riley founded the World's Christian Fundamentals Association to raise the banner against false doctrine and the trend of America away from the Bible.

A similar controversial spirit erupted in some of the largest Protestant denominations, especially in those where the two parties were of comparable strength. First recognized in 1906, the Disciples of Christ, who had already experienced a gradual exodus of the strict Churches of Christ, continued to suffer major controversies between liberals and Disciples traditionalists, eventually leading to an informal separation of competing fellowships in 1927. More directly connected with interdenominational Fundamentalism were the severe controversies within the major Baptist and Presbyterian denominations in the North. "Fundamentalism" was first applied in 1920 to a coalition of militant conservatives who were trying to stop the spread of liberalism in the Northern Baptist Convention, especially in its educational and missions agencies. Baptist dispensationalists, led by William B. Riley, were part of this original Fundamentalist effort. Within two years, however, it having become apparent that the dispensationalists were more radical in their demands for doctrinal purity than were other Baptist Fundamentalists, Riley formed the Baptist Bible Union to represent the demands of the more divisive of the militants.

Meanwhile, the Baptist controversies sparked a similar blowup in the northern Presbyterian Church (U.S.A.). In the spring of 1922 Harry Emerson Fosdick, a modernist Baptist preacher with a New York Presbyterian pastorate, threw down the gauntlet with a widely publicized sermon, "Shall the Fundamentalists Win?" Strict confessionalist Presbyterians, with support from a contingent of Presbyterian dispensationalists, counterattacked, reaffirming their essential "five points" at the General Assembly of 1923. Fosdick left his Presbyterian pastorate to avoid controversy; but Presbyterian liberals and moderates issued the "Auburn Affirmation" in 1924, which affirmed the importance of doctrinal latitude. In both the Presbyterian Church (U.S.A.) and in the Northern Baptist Convention most of the ministers and even more of the constituents were conservative theologically. Many conservatives, however, did not approve of theological fights. So in these denominations the Fundamentalists seldom could enlist majority votes for their views even at the height of their power. Episcopalians and Methodists had small Fundamentalist wrangles during this era also. But Fundamentalism as such was confined largely to white Presbyterians and Baptists, whose traditions had Calvinist roots in which the content of doctrinal assent was emphasized. Among both

FUNDAMENTALISM

Southern Baptists and Southern Presbyterians the doctrinal conservatives, who were sympathetic to Fundamentalism, though not much connected with the national movement, controlled the denominations.

Canadian churches during this era also experienced Fundamentalist controversies paralleling and often connected with those in the United States. In Great Britain, on the other hand, despite many North American connections and parallels, this era was not marked by unusual controversy, and militant Fundamentalism never had the wide impact it had in America.

In the meantime in the United States Fundamentalism had emerged as a highly publicized national movement on another front, in efforts to stop the teaching of biological evolution in public schools. This campaign, led by three-time presidential candidate William Jennings Bryan, broadened the Fundamentalist coalition and hence blurred the definition of the movement. Many of the dispensationalist Fundamentalists, such as those in William B. Riley's World's Christian Fundamentals Association, were active in the antievolution crusade. But these campaigns also helped create a Fundamentalism that was a sort of religious-cultural, antimodernist attitude more than a clearly delineated movement. Antievolution efforts signaled the rise of a cultural-political Fundamentalism, distinguishable from the theological-ecclesiastical Fundamentalism that originally provided most of the leadership for the movement. Both groups were made up of militant evangelical Protestants angry about modern trends. One branch focused on modernism in the churches and the other on certain modern trends in the culture. Fundamentalists might be involved in either or both of these concerns.

The culturally and politically oriented side of Fundamentalism was built on the premise that the United States was a Protestant nation founded upon biblical principles. This outlook had a long heritage and broad support in popular belief. What turned this belief into Fundamentalism was the conviction that America was losing this heritage and that strong action must be taken to reverse the trend. This belief became widespread rather suddenly after World War I. The success of the Prohibition movement was one evidence of wide national sentiment on such points; but Prohibition was not primarily a Fundamentalist accomplishment, since it had large support from moderate and liberal church people. Nonetheless, World War I greatly aroused fears that America would lose its heritage. The Red Scare after the war exemplified this mood. Again, this anticommunist fear was not initially much connected with Fundamentalism. Fundamentalists, however, pointed to the dangers of Marxism in America as one reason for alarm lest the nation lose its moorings. Changes in public behavior in the "jazz age" also fomented such fears.

For Fundamentalists, biological evolution became the chief symbol for these fears. Darwinism could be tied to both theological modernism and the threat to civilization by pointing to the destructive influences of the spread of evolutionary views in German theology and culture. William Jennings Bryan and his Fundamentalist supporters also emphasized that evolutionary doctrines undermined faith in absolutes and therefore morality. They focused, however, on biological evolution where the new philosophy claimed the prestige of science. Basing their outlook on the old Baconian views of science as properly nonspeculative, they argued that Darwinism was an unproven hypothesis. "It is millions of guesses strung together," said Bryan.

In the South biological evolution had long been anathema to many church people, symbolizing northern trends that were threatening to corrupt the region. Resisting such modern thought was implicitly part of remaining loyal to the true American heritage as represented in the pre–Civil War, largely evangelical, South. By the mid-1920s a substantial number of southern states had passed or were considering legislation banning the teaching of biological evolution in public schools.

Fundamentalism became a worldwide media sensation as these issues were debated at the trial of John T. Scopes in Dayton, Tennessee, in July 1925. Scopes, a young high school teacher, had defied the new Tennessee antievolution law. The American Civil Liberties Union supported Scopes with a team of lawyers led by the famed Clarence Darrow. William Jennings Bryan volunteered his services for the state. Amid the ballyhoo characteristic of the era, Bryan and Darrow debated the merits of modern biology and literal interpretations of the Bible. Scopes was judged guilty; but Bryan got the worst of it in the press.

956

His death five days after the trial signaled the passing of the peak for Fundamentalism as a powerful national movement. In fact, Fundamentalism held substantial ground in American churches and culture, but after 1925 it seldom could command the headlines or the intimidating support it had during this formative era of controversy.

Building an Independent Movement: 1920s–1940s. Despite defeats in efforts to control the major northern denominations, ridicule, and fading interest in the movement as a national sensation, Fundamentalism was not in retreat. Defeat and ridicule only fueled Fundamentalist arguments for a need for strenuous efforts to fight the enemies of the truth. Moreover, revivalist evangelicalism had a long history of working virtually independently of denominations. So the Fundamentalist version of that movement was not much slowed by failing to control the traditional centers of power in American Protestantism. Decentralization was in fact an advantage. Enterprising Fundamentalist leaders could establish new institutions quickly as opportunities arose. They could build personal loyalties that were more solid than those to an abstraction such as a denomination. No one measured Fundamentalist growth in the era before World War II, since the parameters of the movement were difficult to define. Nonetheless, every indication is that during this time of "the American religious depression" in the mainline denominations Fundamentalism was growing in countless local churches and agencies.

The base of the movement was the local congregation, characteristically with Calvary or Bible in its name, usually pastored by a Bible institute graduate. Such congregations might or might not be affiliated with a major denomination; but increasingly during the 1920s and 1930s a major trend was developing toward establishing independent Fundamental churches.

The network of Bible institutes gave the movement its unity. By 1930 the number of Fundamentalist institutes had increased to about fifty. These taught similar, usually dispensationalist, curricula, hence providing some uniformity in a movement that looked anarchical. The institutes took on quasi-denominational functions, organizing many local Bible conferences and becoming clearing houses for independent missions. The larger institutes published influential magazines and had publishing houses that controlled Fundamentalist book publications. During the 1930s Moody Bible Institute in Chicago expanded vastly in such activities, far surpassing the other institutes. Such influence led to the only half-facetious definition that "Fundamentalism is all those churches or persons in communion with the Moody Bible Institute."

In addition to the Bible institute were the traditional foci of American revivalist evangelicalism, the empires built around individual leaders. William B. Riley, the principle organizer of militant Fundamentalism in the 1920s, built such an empire around his large Baptist church in downtown Minneapolis. Although Riley remained technically in the Northern Baptist Convention until his death in 1947, he worked virtually independently. In addition to his national activities in the World's Christian Fundamentals Association, the Baptist Bible Union, and many publications, Riley had immense influence on Baptists throughout Minnesota. By the 1940s most of the Baptist churches in the state were served by graduates of his Northwestern Schools, including a Bible institute, a college, and a theological seminary. At the end of his career Riley chose Billy Graham to be his successor, designating the young evangelist as president of the Northwestern Schools. Graham, however, eventually made Minneapolis headquarters for his own, less combative empire.

In the South the closest counterpart to Riley was J. Frank Norris, long the pastor of the large First Baptist Church in Fort Worth. Norris was a sometimes volatile controversialist who in 1926 even shot a man to death, apparently in self-defense, in an argument over Norris' attacks on the Roman Catholic mayor of Fort Worth. Anti-Catholicism was a prominent feature of Norris' Fundamentalism, especially in his opposition to Al Smith for president in 1928. Norris also kept up a steady attack on the Southern Baptist Convention, which he considered soft on modernism. In 1931 he organized his own fellowship, which became known as the World Baptist Fellowship. Norris, an effective evangelist, helped spread separatist Fundamentalism in the South. Especially influential in the 1940s was his Bible Baptist Seminary, founded in 1939. A split in this institution and the World Baptist Fellowship in 1950 led to the formation of the Baptist Bible Fellowship and its school, Baptist Bible College of Springfield, Missouri. These institutions carried on much of the Norris heritage in several huge independent Fundamentalist churches of the next decades and also provided training for Jerry Falwell, who later organized the Moral Majority.

T. T. Shields was another of the original Fundamentalists who perpetuated controversialism in a long urban ministry. Shields was pastor of the Jarvis Street Church in Toronto, Canada, from 1910 until his death. During the 1920s he was prominent in organized Fundamentalism in the States, joining Riley and Norris in early efforts of the World's Christian Fundamentals Association and the Baptist Bible Union. Shields was aggressively anti-Catholic. During the 1920s he also led a major effort to purge Ontario's McMaster University, a Baptist institution, of modernism. From 1927 to 1929 he headed Des Moines University, which the Baptist Bible Union had made into its school; but he was driven from the position by a student riot that led to the school's closing.

More successful as a college builder was Bob Jones, Sr. A Southerner with a Methodist background, Jones became a successful evangelist and in 1924 founded his own college, which eventually became Bob Jones University, located in Greenville, South Carolina. Bob Jones combined southern conservatism with northern Fundamentalist dispensationalism and militancy. Although the early Fundamentalism of Jones himself was not much different from that of its counterparts elsewhere, the school that bore his name and was headed by two namesakes, Bob Jones, Jr., and Bob Jones III, later became renowned for its strict separatism and its avowal of racial segregation as a religious principle. Perhaps reflecting its Methodist background, the school enforced extremely strict Fundamentalist mores.

Another leader of monumental importance in spreading Fundamentalism in the South as well as the North was Baptist evangelist John R. Rice. Originally a protégé of Frank Norris, Rice built a large church in Dallas during the 1930s. A prolific writer, he was author of an immense number of books, often widely circulated. He also developed an effective radio ministry. His most influential work, however, was through his newspaper, *The Sword of the Lord,* founded in 1934, which by the 1970s had reached a circulation of a quarter of a million.

The classic Fundamentalism that emerged in the 1930s at many such centers typically put evangelism first. While its adherents were usually very conservative on most political issues, politics was not usually the most prominent concern, except when issues like Catholicism or prohibition were being publicly debated. Some held that Christians' meddling in politics smacked of the modernist Social Gospel, but this position was never consistently maintained throughout the movement. A few Fundamentalists put far-right politics in the forefront of their ministries. Most notable was Gerald B. Winrod, a Fundamentalist evangelist who in the 1930s became convinced of the connections among an international Jewish conspiracy, Communism, and the New Deal. His *Defender* magazine had over one hundred thousand subscribers by the late 1930s. William B. Riley held similar views, although politics was never his all-consuming interest. However, because of the importance of the Jews in dispensationalism, probably most Fundamentalists either eschewed or, like Frank Norris, explicitly repudiated anti-Semitism.

In evangelism, which stood at center of the movement, the 1930s and 1940s were periods of growth and success. Radio proved an especially useful means for extending the ministries of the many independent branches of the movement. Bible institutes could serve widespread regions through regular religious broadcasts on their own radio stations. Preeminent among these was WMBI of the Moody Bible Institute, which came to be an influential Fundamentalist voice throughout the Chicago area. Even before 1930 many of the major Bible institutes and evangelists had founded their own radio stations. Evangelist Paul Radar in Chicago, fiery controversialist John Roach Straton in New York City, the Bible Institute of Los Angeles, and Frank Norris in Texas were among the early broadcasters. Donald Grey Barnhouse of the Tenth Presbyterian Church in Philadelphia was broadcasting nationwide on CBS in the early 1930s, and many hundreds of other Fundamentalists were on the air locally or regionally. The most successful of the broadcasters was Charles E. Fuller, whose programs were carried nationwide on the Mutual network by the late thirties. During the war years Fuller's "Old-Fashioned Revival Hour" was reputed to have the largest audience of any program on the air.

While such activities were seldom given much

notice in the secular press, many signs of Fundamentalist growth and influence throughout American evangelicalism were present during the 1930s and 1940s. Wheaton College was the fastest-growing college in the nation during the middle years of the depression and became an important center for training a new generation of Fundamentalist leadership. Gordon College of Theology and Missions similarly was having a large influence in New England. Fundamentalist foreign missions were also growing during the depression years. By the late 1930s some important efforts were being made in youth work. Percy Crawford, founder of King's College outside New York in 1938, preached to young people by radio and sponsored well-attended youth rallies. His protégé Jack Wyrtzen led a number of spectacularly successful youth rallies in New York City during the war years and helped inspire Fundamentalist youth rallies throughout the nation. In 1945 the youth rally movement was organized into Youth for Christ International, which hired Billy Graham to be its first full-time evangelist.

Separatist Fundamentalism and New Evangelicalism: 1940s to 1970s. While these positive activities were going on, the Fundamentalist movement was beginning to split over an issue that proved irresolvable. If Fundamentalists failed to throw modernists out of their church councils, was it then necessary to separate entirely from churches and their members that tolerated such unbelief? By the 1930s important persons who had separated were saying that separation from unbelief should be an article of faith. Frank Norris, for instance, could not continue fellowship with so conservative an evangelical denomination as the Southern Baptist Convention. In the North the two major denominational controversies led to several small divisions that nonetheless sparked large intra-Fundamentalist debates about the merits of separation. In 1932 the Baptist Bible Union organized the General Association of Regular Baptists among those who had left the Northern Baptist Convention. In 1947 another small group of Northern Baptists left their denomination in protest against modernism in Baptist missions and founded the Conservative Baptist Association of America. Among the Presbyterians, Princeton Seminary professor J. Gresham Machen led protests that brought the establishment of his independent Westminster Theological Seminary in 1929 and the founding

in 1936 of what became the small Orthodox Presbyterian Church. One of Machen's allies in these splits was Carl McIntire, who in 1937 broke away from Machen's closest followers to found his own, even smaller, Bible Presbyterian Church. McIntire, however, proved an effective publicist for Fundamentalist separatism, first in his weekly newspaper, *The Christian Beacon,* and later also in widely heard radio broadcasts.

By far the larger part of the Fundamentalist coalition, including such important dispensationalist centers as the Moody Bible Institute and Dallas Theological Seminary, were nonseparatist. In 1942 a coalition of leaders attempted to bring some federated cooperation to the movement with the formation of the National Association of Evangelicals. This effort at unity had been inspired by the successful efforts of J. Elwin Wright in New England to establish cooperation and communication among over a thousand local Fundamentalist churches in New England. The National Association of Evangelicals similarly represented an emphasis on positive outreach rather than separatism and even included some Pentecostal denominations in its numbers, an affiliation that was anathema to the stricter Fundamentalists. The NAE included only between one and two million members in its first decade, since some of the largest evangelical denominations, such as the Southern Baptist Convention, put denominational distinctives first. But the NAE leadership, drawn from the nonseparating Fundamentalist axis of the Moody Bible Institute, Wheaton College, Dallas Seminary, Gordon College, and the like, brought together a core of interdenominationalists who had some claim to represent a considerably larger movement.

In the meantime Carl McIntire started a smaller rival organization, the American Council of Christian Churches, founded in 1941. This organization was designed to be the counterpart and opponent of the Federal Council of Churches, an organization that all Fundamentalists considered too liberal. McIntire demanded strict separation from denominations that belonged to the World Council.

The broad Fundamentalist coalitions that had taken shape by the end of World War II changed character with the emergence of a new generation of leadership in the postwar era. At first calling themselves "neo-Evangelicals," these leaders pushed to move the NAE type of interdenominational Fundamentalism away from some of the newer and harsher aspects of the heritage. Not only did this group condemn strict separatism, they abandoned or de-emphasized dispensationalism, urged Fundamentalists to appropriate sophisticated learning and culture, and called for conservative concern for the whole direction of civilization, including social, political, and economic relationships. Among the leaders of this group were Harold John Ockenga, Carl F. H. Henry, and Edward John Carnell, all of whom were associated with Fuller Theological Seminary in California, founded in 1947. In 1956 Henry became the first editor of *Christianity Today,* which he developed into an important voice of this new evangelical movement.

Most important, however, this group was closely allied with Billy Graham. Graham's rise to international prominence after 1949 was at first applauded by most Fundamentalists, and Graham identified himself with that movement. In 1957, however, in planning a New York City crusade, Graham accepted the sponsorship of the ecumenical Protestant Council. This move precipitated a decisive split in Fundamentalism, with the more separatist leaders such as Bob Jones, Jr., John R. Rice, Carl McIntire, and others bitterly and tirelessly condemning Graham as a traitor to Fundamentalism and as dangerous as the modernists themselves. This schism led to a narrowing in the use of the term "Fundamentalist," so that by the end of the 1960s it was seldom used as a self-description except by strict separatists. Such groups included a membership of perhaps four million by the 1970s. The nonseparatists, in turn, came more and more to call themselves simply "Evangelicals." Evangelicalism included a core of ex-Fundamentalist interdenominationalists who attempted to speak for the whole movement; but as the movement gained national prominence by the 1970s, it was apparent that it was much larger (often estimated at forty million or more) and much more diverse than the groups immediately represented by this prominent ex-Fundamentalist "evangelical" leadership. A substantial number of nonseparatists, who had been Fundamentalists but now accepted the new name "Evangelical," in fact remained Fundamentalist in everything but name. Other Evangelicals, often from non-Fundamentalist backgrounds, were considerably broader in their views.

In the meantime, militant Fundamentalists who were still proud of the designation were entrenched in their own organizations. Most such Fundamentalists were independent Baptists and dispensationalists, typically associated in federations, the largest of which was the Baptist Bible Fellowship. The major institutional motif of the movement, however, remained the local church, sometimes built into a complex empire of supporting agencies and schools by enterprising and successful evangelists. The Highland Park Baptist Church in Chattanooga, pastored by Lee Roberson since 1942, became a model of such enterprise. By the 1980s the church claimed a total membership of 33,000 and average attendance of 11,000 per Sunday. Moreover, its influence is as great as that of many denominations, through its complex of the Tennessee Temple Schools, radio and television broadcasts, publication work, and missions. Similarly, large churches and empires include those built by Jack Hyles in Hammond, Indiana, John W. Rawlings in Cincinnati, and Jerry Falwell in Lynchburg, Virginia.

Many of the most successful pastors regarded each other as allies, but within the movement were bitter controversies as well. The sharpest were those that developed in the 1960s and 1970s over how far to go with the doctrine of separation. Some Fundamentalists, most notably those in the orbit of Bob Jones University, insisted on "secondary separation." This meant that one must separate not only from apostate liberal Christians but also from conservative Evangelicals who associated with such apostates. These issues led to a bitter war of words during the 1970s between Bob Jones, Jr., and John R. Rice, arising from the fact that Rice, despite his own separatism, remained in fellowship with Fundamentalist Christians who remained in the Southern Baptist Convention. Such combatants agreed, however, on issues of personal separation, that is, insisting that Christians should be strictly conservative not only in behavior but also in appearance. They condemned, for instance, hair over the ears for men and slacks for women.

Despite strongly conservative political views, most strict Fundamentalists in the era from the 1950s to the 1970s kept a low profile concerning public issues. The exceptions were vocal anti-communist preachers, most notably Billy James Hargis and Carl McIntire. Such preachers claimed that the international communist conspiracy was well advanced in taking over American government and media. It was, they said, a major force in the National Council of Churches and World Council of Churches. Such Fundamentalist anticommunism was particularly apparent at the time of Barry Goldwater's presidential campaign in 1964.

Resurgent Fundamentalism: 1970s and 1980s. Two factors seem to have contributed most forcefully to the resurgence and return to national prominence of Fundamentalism in the later 1970s and 1980s. First was the new public acceptance of diversities of religious commitments during the 1960s and 1970s. Intense spirituality of almost every sort was much more in vogue by the 1970s than it had been in the 1950s. Among conservative Christians the emergence of the new charismatic movement and the greater openness to Pentecostalism was one manifestation of this trend. Fundamentalists, despite their condemnations of charismatics and Pentecostals, had many of the same traits and styles and flourished in such an atmosphere. In the 1970s and 1980s large and profitable television ministries supported such trends.

The other major factor in the Fundamentalist resurgence was the national social-political mood that had emerged from the Vietnam-Watergate era. Groups such as Fundamentalists, whose political instincts were highly patriotic and conservative, were politicized and polarized during this era, as were almost all Americans. Patriotism and conservative politics were matters of high passion, and such passions could easily be wedded to old-time Gospel preaching. The American heritage, now threatened by the "secular humanism" (defined as godless man-centeredness) of the liberals and radicals, was viewed as having been based on conservative biblical principles. The Gospel message could thus blend easily into militancy for reversing the trends and restoring America as a Christian nation.

By far the most prominent manifestation of this political impulse was the emergence of the Moral Majority in 1979, organized under the leadership of Jerry Falwell. While strictly a political agency, rather than an ecclesiastical one, the Moral Majority had largely Fundamentalist leadership. Capitalizing on a growing conservative mood in the nation and good press coverage, the Moral Majority emphasized several key types of issues. These included those having to do with family and sexuality, such as opposition to abortion on demand, the Equal Rights Amendment for women, and pornography; putting Christian symbolism back into public life, as in urging prayers in public schools or requiring the teaching of "creation science" to balance evolutionary teachings in public schools; tax support for establishing private Christian schools and freedom of such schools from government regulation; conservative free-enterprise economics and opposition to the welfare state; anticommunism; strong American patriotism and militarism; and support for the state of Israel.

The Moral Majority, involving a wide political coalition, broadened Fundamentalism and blurred the line between Fundamentalists and the more conservative or Fundamentalistic wing of evangelicalism. Strict Fundamentalists accordingly tagged Falwell a traitor to their cause. Meanwhile the rising conservative reaction since the early seventies brought a resurgence of Fundamentalistic tendencies within evangelicalism itself. The inerrancy of Scripture, a doctrinal test that was the focus of sharp internal controversies among Missouri Synod Lutherans and Southern Baptists, became increasingly used by Fundamentalistic Evangelicals as the key test of whether one was within the pale. Such resurgent militance, combined with conservative politics directed toward restoring a "Christian America," brought the right wing of evangelicalism into close proximity with the type of Fundamentalism represented by Falwell. This was a coalition of groups that had many common origins.

BIBLIOGRAPHY

James Barr, *Fundamentalism* (1977); Stewart G. Cole, *The History of Fundamentalism* (1931); George W. Dollar, *A History of Fundamentalism in America* (1973); Gabriel Fackre, *The Religious Right and Christian Faith* (1982); Norman K. Furniss, *The Fundamentalist Controversy* (1954); Louis Gasper, *The Fundamentalist Movement* (1963); Willard B. Gatewood, Jr., ed., *Controversy in the Twenties: Fundamentalism, Modernism, and Evolution* (1969); Richard Hofstadter, *Anti-Intellectualism in American Life* (1962), *The Paranoid Style in American Politics and Other Essays* (1963); James Hunter, *American Evangelicalism: Conservative Religion and the Quandary of Modernity* (1983); Robert C. Liebman and Robert Wuthnow, eds., *The New Christian Right: Mobilization and Legitimation* (1983).

George M. Marsden, ed., *Fundamentalism and American Cul-*

ture: The Shaping of Twentieth-Century Evangelicalism, 1870–1925 (1980), ed., *Evangelicalism and Modern America* (1984); William G. McLoughlin, *Billy Sunday Was His Real Name* (1955), *Modern Revivalism* (1959); Richard V. Pierard, "American Evangelicals in Politics: The Roots of the New Christian Right," in *Evangelicalism and Modern America*, George Marsden, ed. (1984); C. Allyn Russell, *Voices of American Fundamentalism: Seven Biographical Studies* (1976); Ernest R. Sandeen, *The Roots of Fundamentalism: British and American Millenarianism 1800–1930* (1970); Ferenc Morton Szasz, *The Divided Mind of Protestant America 1880–1930* (1982); Timothy P. Webber, *Living in the Shadow of the Second Coming: American Premillennialism 1875–1982* (enlarged ed., 1982).

[*See also* Conservative and Charismatic Developments of the Later Twentieth Century; Holiness and Perfection; Millennialism and Adventism; Mass Communications; Nineteenth-Century Evangelicalism; Pentecostalism; Popular Culture; *and* Revivalism.]

CONSERVATIVE AND CHARISMATIC DEVELOPMENTS OF THE LATER TWENTIETH CENTURY

Richard Quebedeaux

IN this essay, *conservatism* in modern North American Christianity refers specifically to the Neoevangelical movement that emerged out of sectarian Fundamentalism in the early 1940s, gained visibility and a measure of stature by the late 1950s, and broadened to become the virtual Christian mainstream by the late 1970s. *Charismatic* refers to the Neopentecostal or charismatic renewal movement—closely akin to Neoevangelicalism—that was born out of sectarian Pentecostalism in 1960, peaked in 1977, and finally became an acceptable minority variant within the Christian mainstream by the early 1980s.

Led by a small group of young intellectuals who had been reared in Fundamentalism—including Harold John Ockenga, Edward John Carnell, and Carl F. H. Henry—the Neoevangelical movement of the 1940s saw itself as a revival of Reformed Protestant orthodoxy without the "extremes" of sectarianism and culture rejection, anti-intellectualism, and scholastic dogmatism that had come to characterize Fundamentalism by that time. The very word *neoevangelical*, coined by Ockenga in the late 1940s, signified a renewal of the spirit of the eighteenth- and nineteenth-century evangelical awakenings that had helped transform the wider society and a repudiation of later Fundamentalist revivalism that sought, rather, to separate itself from that sin-infested society. Nevertheless, until the late 1970s the Neoevangelical movement did retain the major theological distinctives of Fundamentalism and was marked by a vocal adherence to them. Foremost among these was a strong belief in the efficacy of an instant, historically identifiable moment of conversion to Christ (the "born again" experience), occurring as often as not during a planned revival; the absolute authority of the Bible alone—not personal experience, church councils, or "manmade" theology—to define the character of the Christian faith; and the efficacy of propositional doctrine, meaning that the Bible teaches clear, logical, defensible doctrines that, when properly organized, constitute the essence of the Christian faith.

Neoevangelicalism was "transdenominational" from the beginning, in that it was willing to recognize as fellow believers all Christians who held to these distinctives, regardless of denominational affiliation. Nevertheless, its characteristic way of thinking and its religious style of life appealed mainly to white Baptists or Presbyterians, Calvinists, ardent premillennialists, and upwardly mobile cultural conservatives.

1956–1959: NEOEVANGELICALISM

During the Eisenhower administration, there was a major resurgence of religiosity in public life. The president composed a prayer for his inauguration, was baptized and became a member of Washington's National Presbyterian Church, appointed a staff assistant as a liaison on religious matters, declared a National Day of Prayer each year (required by a law passed in 1952), and appeared regularly at the Presidential Prayer Breakfasts beginning in 1953. The most significant acts of official religiosity during these years were the addition of the words "under God" to the Pledge of Allegiance in 1954 and the adoption of "In God We Trust" as the national motto in 1956.

Neoevangelicals, of course, welcomed the new respectability of religion in government circles. Indeed, it was in the 1950s that Billy Graham established a working relationship with the White House that was to become a characteristic of his career as an evangelist. (This, together with the appointment of Eisenhower's pastor, Edward R. Elson, as Senate chaplain—himself a Neoevangelical like Graham—demonstrated how Neoevangelicals were gradually coming to acceptance in high places.) Graham was called upon by the president to help him relax racial tensions generated by civil rights measures, and the evangelist offered the president advice on spiritual and political matters. He became close friends with Vice President Richard Nixon, who addressed his New York crusade in 1957, and he functioned in 1960 as an unofficial adviser on religious questions to the Nixon presidential campaign.

The Neoevangelical movement itself took on additional visibility as the result of two important events—the founding of *Christianity Today* in 1956 and the Billy Graham crusade in New York City in 1957. *Christianity Today,* the first really sophisticated Neoevangelical journal, was established specifically to give theological substance and direction to the wider religious revival of the 1950s, which was heralded not only by the emergence of Christian celebrities like Eisenhower and Graham, but also by increasing church membership, weekly attendance at services, financial support, and church construction. Edited by Carl F. H. Henry and supported by Billy Graham himself, *Christianity Today* emerged as a major non-denominational magazine for clergy that would provide them with the best Neoevangelical thought and information and would soon rival the liberal *Christian Century,* the venerable mainline Protestant journal. Heretofore, Neoevangelical revivalists had too often been regarded by mainstream clergy as fanatics or money-grubbers. The highly literate editors and contributors to *Christianity Today* did much to counteract those damaging stereotypes by giving a sophisticated theological rationale for revivalism in general and Graham's crusades in particular. Considerable financial support for the magazine came from business people, the most substantial being an ongoing grant from J. Howard Pew of Sun Oil Company that allowed virtually every ordained Protestant minister in the nation to receive a free subscription during the journal's early years of publication. With *Christianity Today,* Neoevangelicalism began to take on respectability, even in the mainstream theological academy.

Then came the Billy Graham crusade in 1957. After months of extensive and energetic planning, the revival began in Madison Square Garden on May 15. The directors had left little undone, having utilized fully the most current media equipment and promotional advertising. And they hoped that somehow this crusade would not be limited, as were Graham's earlier ones, to revival and mass conversion in just one specific city or region, but that what was started in Manhattan would eventually envelop the whole nation. In fact, early accounts sent to crusade leaders talked of a substantial increase in weekly congregational services in the area and of a marked renewal of interest in evangelistic preaching and witnessing, enhanced by the impressive nightly tally of those who had "come forward" at the altar call. And for a few brief weeks, the leaders did feel a national revival was imminent. But spring became summer in what Graham had termed America's most sinful city; and, despite a flurry of enthusiasm for the Labor Day finale, observers and friends alike realized that the revival was not going national.

Billy Graham's crusade not only failed to spread across the nation; it also failed to have a major impact in the city itself, among those important "secular" New Yorkers whom Graham and his team wanted desperately to reach. Most of the 20,000 persons who recorded "decisions for Christ" at Madison Square Garden were actually young suburbanites who already had a religious identification and were attending church regularly at the time of their decision. *Christianity Today* blamed the crusade's "failure" on "an enormous increase in pure selfishness" in which Americans considered the highest good for themselves to be indulging in personal pursuits rather than the evangelization and consequent improvement of society. Although the revival may not have lived up to its planners' expectations, it was one of Billy Graham's most important campaigns, giving him and the whole Neoevangelical movement he represented more national visibility.

1960–1972: THE NEOEVANGELICAL ESTABLISHMENT AND THE BEGINNINGS OF DISSENT

The period from 1960 to 1972 witnessed further gains by Neoevangelicals in the public sector of American life. Several of their number had been elected to Congress in the 1950s and more were in the early and mid-1960s. Active prayer groups existed in both houses of Congress and in various governmental units around the capital. "Christian anticommunism," with its Fundamentalist and Neoevangelical leaders, became popular in conservative political circles. And Billy Graham was welcomed by presidents Johnson and Nixon into the circle of their advisers.

By far the best-known Neoevangelical lawmakers appeared on the scene during this era: Rep. John B. Anderson of Illinois and Sen. Mark O. Hatfield of Oregon, both Republicans. Anderson, a member of the Evangelical Free Church, became notorious among conservatives in his party when he cast the decisive vote for the open housing bill in 1968. While governor of Oregon, Hatfield, a conservative Baptist, delivered the keynote address at the 1964 Republican convention and was widely considered as a vice presidential possibility, but he strayed from the party line by opposing the Vietnam War.

As to the public role of Billy Graham himself, Lyndon Johnson kept him from backing Barry Goldwater in 1964 and obtained the evangelist's endorsement of his civil rights program and war on poverty. But Richard Nixon was able to woo Graham back to the conservative camp by the late 1960s, and with him the vast majority of Neoevangelicals, all of whom admired his close ties with the evangelist and frequent expressions of public religiosity, such as the White House church services. Most Neoevangelical leaders supported Nixon's reelection in 1972.

At the same time that the presence of Neoevangelicals was increasingly being felt in the wider public arena, there emerged within the movement itself a group of institutions that gave it identity as a religious force and provided it with symbolic unity. In fact, by the early 1970s, four of these institutions and their leaders had become the core of the Neoevangelical establishment. The first two have already been mentioned —Billy Graham and his evangelistic association and the journal *Christianity Today*. Graham himself continued to represent all that was good in the American way to Neoevangelicals, while his televised crusades and the organization that ran them kept evangelism—the conversion of sinners to Christ—at the forefront of Neoevangelical priorities. During this period *Christianity Today* became the most important apologetic

medium within the movement. Its first two editors, Carl F. H. Henry and Harold Lindsell, who succeeded Henry in 1968, had created a magazine that provided Neoevangelicalism with its primary theological (and cultural) identity. The journal not only articulated the character, goals, and strategies of the movement; it also defined who and whose concerns could be legitimately accepted under the Neoevangelical umbrella. In so doing, *Christianity Today* tried to chart a Christian course midway between liberalism on the left and Fundamentalism on the right.

The third institution that came to make up the core of the Neoevangelical establishment during this period was the Evangelical Theological Society (ETS). In 1949, a group of sixty Neoevangelical academicians had met in Cincinnati to draft a constitution that brought the ETS into being. These scholars represented a wide variety of schools and affiliations, but there was no disposition to compromise on the one matter all the delegates considered pivotal in importance—the "inerrancy of the Scriptures." Thus the creedal statement, signed by every member of the society and made a nonnegotiable condition for membership, was narrowed to this single fundamental: "The Bible alone and the Bible in its entirety is the word of God written, and therefore inerrant in the autographs."

Like those of other professional societies in religion, the national and regional gatherings of the ETS are characterized by the reading of prepared papers, by addresses, and by panel discussions to stimulate further research and debate by the theologians. Some of the papers read at the annual meetings are published together with book reviews and announcements in the quarterly *Journal of the Evangelical Theological Society*. The ETS grew in the 1950s, gained stature in the 1960s, and reached the high point of its influence within the Neoevangelical movement by the early 1970s. By asserting the Fundamentalist doctrine of inerrancy, it sought to defend the authority—the absolute authority—of the Bible against its liberal critics, and in so doing identified the central task of Neoevangelical theology as apologetics. The mark of a good theologian in the ETS was his vocal belief in "God's inerrant word" and his ability to defend that belief in any forum.

The fourth major institution in the emerging Neoevangelical establishment was the National Association of Evangelicals (NAE) itself, the organization founded in 1942 as a conservative but nonsectarian alternative to the predominantly liberal Federal (now National) Council of Churches. With headquarters in Wheaton, Illinois, the NAE was founded as a voluntary association of Neoevangelical, Holiness, and Pentecostal denominations, churches, schools, other organizations, and individuals, all of which affirmed belief in its strong creedal statement, beginning with the clause "We believe the Bible to be the inspired, the only infallible, authoritative word of God."

By 1977 the NEA provided a Neoevangelical identification for 30,000 congregations and 3½ million Christians, and represented 35 complete denominations. Like the National Council of Churches, the NAE meets regularly and passes resolutions in its plenary assemblies. Furthermore, to carry on its work it has a number of task-oriented commissions and affiliates that serve Neoevangelical interests in the larger society. Very important among them are the office of Public Affairs in Washington, D.C., the Evangelical Foreign Missions Association, the National Association of Christian Schools, and the National Religious Broadcasters, which focus, respectively, on the areas of public policy regarding religion, evangelism in the Third World, private Christian education, and Christian radio and television operations. All of these concerns took on major proportions by the 1970s.

Although a host of other institutions—colleges, seminaries, magazines, book publishers, and associations—identified with Neoevangelical beliefs and goals in the period between 1960 and 1972, it was Billy Graham and his evangelistic organization, *Christianity Today,* the ETS, and the NAE that together became the principal guardians of the movement's identity and the symbols of its unity. They emerged as the core of the Neoevangelical establishment and characterized it by a strong commitment not only to biblical inerrancy and aggressive evangelism, but also to cultural and political conservatism.

In these same years, the Neoevangelical movement grew and pressed on with its critique of theological and political liberalism. Liberalism itself, in both its "conservative" form as Neo-orthodoxy and its radical form as "secular Christianity," did pose a challenge to Neoevangelical leaders. But so did stirrings from within. There arose side by side with Neoevangelicalism, and

within its own ranks, two strong new Christian movements that at first bolstered its visibility in the public eye, but later seemed to challenge the very core of its distinctives. The first and earlier of these was charismatic renewal or Neopentecostalism, the emergence of the Pentecostal movement within the historic, mainline denominations beginning in 1960.

Named in memory of the occurrences on the Day of Pentecost described in the Acts of the Apostles, Pentecostalism was born in Topeka, Kansas, in 1901, among a small group of working-class Bible students who experienced what they later identified as the biblical "baptism in the Holy Spirit." Central to this experience were the practices of speaking in tongues (glossolalia), divine healing, and prophecy—outlined by St. Paul as "spiritual gifts" (Greek, *charismata*) in I Corinthians 12–14—that had all but died out in the ensuing 1,800 years of church history. The leader of this group, Charles Parham, and his students took the message and experience of Spirit baptism from Topeka to various other places in the Midwest and South, where it took root among conservative Christians. The movement captured the attention of the mass media in Los Angeles; from there it spread throughout the United States and the world.

Founded and led by William Seymour, a former slave, the Azusa Street Mission in Los Angeles was the focal point of the movement from its beginnings in 1906. Here and elsewhere Pentecostalism developed a distinct religious style and an oral liturgy derived largely from African rhythms, movement, and vocalization that would characterize it during most of its development. This liturgical style was supplemented by the practice of spiritual gifts during worship—speaking in tongues, healing, "possession" by spirits, and prophetic utterances, all of which had also been common in the shamanistic traditions of Africa long before they were Christianized in the Pentecostal movement.

Within a few years Pentecostalism became diffused, and Azusa Street lost its visibility as the movement's center. The black and white leaders of early Pentecostalism intended their movement to be racially integrated and nonsectarian, a renewal force for Christianity as a whole that would bring back Spirit baptism and even the most "spectacular" *charismata* to the life of the churches. But the churches, liberal and conservative, wanted nothing to do with these phenomena and their not very sophisticated proponents. The spontaneity of Pentecostal worship and its "crude negroisms" were simply not acceptable in the Christian mainstream of that era, so the Pentecostals were forced to establish their own separate denominations, which also became racially segregated. Like Fundamentalism, this movement became a sectarian entity of marginalized believers completely outside mainline Christianity by the 1920s.

After World War II, upward mobility emerged within the Pentecostal movement—a force that led, ultimately, to the rise of a "new Pentecostalism" within the Christian mainstream itself by 1960. The beginnings of this charismatic renewal can be traced to isolated incidents of Pentecostal phenomena among clergy and laity of the historic denominations in the mid-1950s. In addition, substantial groundwork for the movement was also accomplished during the 1950s through the activities of the Full Gospel Businessmen's Fellowship International (FGBMFI) and the ecumenical ministry of David du Plessis.

The FGBMFI was born in Los Angeles in 1951 as a nondenominational fellowship of "full gospel" (i.e., Pentecostal) businessmen and professionals who were reacting against the increasing clerical dominance within the Assemblies of God, the largest white Pentecostal denomination. Supported initially by Demos Shakarian, a wealthy California dairyman, and Oral Roberts, the faith-healing evangelist, local chapters of the FGBMFI were formed throughout America. In 1953 the organization began publishing its monthly "testimony" magazine, *Voice*. Beginning in 1960, meetings of the local chapters and large interchapter conventions attracted mainline clergy and laity who had received the Pentecostal experience or who were merely interested in finding out more about it. Such gatherings provided an opportunity for fellowship with now "respectable" Pentecostals (i.e., businessmen and professionals) without the explicit or even implicit demand for affiliation with any particular Pentecostal denomination or church. And copies of *Voice* magazine, featuring testimonies of mainline Christians who had been baptized in the Spirit, were circulated increasingly among lay people and ministers of the historic denominations. Thus the FGBMFI became the chief cornerstone in the foundation for charismatic renewal.

Another part of the groundwork for charismatic renewal was fashioned by David du Plessis, a leading minister of the Assemblies of God, who spent much of the 1950s participating as a Pentecostal "observer" in the emerging ecumenical movement. His own dialogical and irenic stance as a Pentecostal spokesperson in ecumenical circles did much to dignify the Pentecostal experience and message among non-Pentecostal clergy and laity. By the mid-1950s, some mainline church leaders had even come to regard Pentecostalism as a "third force" in world Christianity—with Protestantism and Catholicism—and du Plessis himself can be credited with the slow growth.

As a movement, charismatic renewal began in 1960, when, on Easter Sunday, the rector of fashionable St. Mark's Episcopal Church in Van Nuys, California, made a public issue of his Pentecostal experience. Father Dennis Bennett had spoken in tongues in a private prayer meeting. But when he reported it to his congregation from the pulpit, the church divided. Bennett was forced to resign his pastorate, but he refused to leave the Episcopal Church, insisting that he could be a good Episcopal priest and a Pentecostal at the same time. His bishop sent him away to serve a dying inner-city parish in Seattle, where he promoted the *charismata*, and the church grew rapidly because of it. In the wake of Bennett's experience—reported in both *Time* and *Newsweek*—hundreds of mainline ministers and priests gave public support during the ensuing years to what would soon be dubbed Neopentecostalism. And the mass media would also give it considerable attention.

Suddenly the new Pentecostal movement became a *cause célèbre* among many Protestants and posed a conservative theological challenge to the liberal schools of religious thought that had dominated the major denominations for decades. Surprisingly, the movement quickly attracted intellectuals and theologians of even the sacramental churches, and by 1963 speaking in tongues had broken out even at Yale University—among students in the neoevangelical Inter-Varsity Christian Fellowship.

Then, in 1967, the movement penetrated Catholicism for the first time, when two professors of theology led about twenty students and faculty at Duquesne University into the Pentecostal experience. From there it spread to the Catholic student populations at Notre Dame and the University of Michigan, and by the end of the decade Catholic Pentecostalism, which had started among intellectuals, had filtered down to the masses. In the years to follow, hundreds of Catholic charismatic prayer groups would arise throughout America, and conferences would be held with tens of thousands of participants.

As more and more Catholics and Protestants became part of the burgeoning charismatic renewal, theologians began to reflect on the movement's theology and ecclesiology. In the mainline churches, the Pentecostal experience had been subdued—accommodated to white, middle-class styles of worship. Gone were the familiar black rhythms, movement, and vocalization—the oral liturgy—and much of the spontaneity that had characterized sectarian Pentecostalism. Furthermore, the practice of charismata—glossolalia, healing, and prophecy—was generally removed from public services of worship and made, rather, the central feature of private prayer meetings. Thus the formal liturgies of churches in the movement were affected hardly at all.

Theologically, charismatic renewal was close to Neoevangelicalism and included many Neoevangelicals within its ranks. It too emphasized the authority of the Bible, the need for personal conversion to Christ, and the mandate for evangelism. But, unlike Neoevangelicalism, it did not insist on doctrinal agreement as the precondition for Christian unity. Rather, the movement saw Spirit baptism—the Pentecostal experience —as the unifying principle that could bring separated believers and denominations together. In Pentecostalism, experience and testimony always took precedence over correct doctrinal formulation.

Charismatic renewal accomplished a lot in the course of its development. First of all, by the early 1970s it had achieved objective recognition by mental health professionals, who, in the past, had viewed the practice of speaking in tongues as, at least, evidence of a subnormal psychological state. Thus, Pentecostalism as a whole received the "legitimacy" denied it by the mental health community for seven decades. Secondly,

in its stress on the recovery of the New Testament charismata, Neopentecostalism accomplished a surprising restoration of an emphasis on experiential religion within middle-class, Western Christianity of the modern period. Both Protestant Neoevangelicalism, centered on a reverence for "propositional revelation" and Baconian inductive logic in its doctrine of biblical inerrancy, and Protestant and Catholic liberalism, with its rational and "demythologized" theology, had lost the sense of mystery in the cosmos. But Spirit baptism—within charismatic renewal—made it possible once again for even sophisticated theologians to have a direct experience of God. And that was a surprise. Finally, Neopentecostalism earned respectability within the historic denominations themselves and, thus, a place for the Pentecostal experience in the Christian mainstream. Practitioners of the charismata gained an intractable foothold in those churches and helped Protestantism into a new age of pluralism by their charismatic spirituality, which rivaled, and sometimes relativized, doctrinal diversities systemic to Christianity since the time of the Reformation.

The second major challenge to Neoevangelical distinctives in the period between 1960 and 1972 emerged among conservative Christian young people themselves. Influenced both by the student protest movement and by the counterculture of the 1960s, these Neoevangelical and Pentecostal youth were joined by other young people who became converts to a new style of conservative Christianity. The Jesus People, as they were called, tried to Christianize the counterculture by living within it and urging their fellows to "get high on Jesus" rather than on drugs; by creating a whole new genre of worship and religious music—"gospel rock"—and by observing an "authentic Christian life-style" in an emerging counterculture that repudiated traditional religiosity as blatantly hypocritical.

Although there were spontaneous beginnings elsewhere, the Jesus People movement first gained public notice in California. An early group in the Haight-Ashbury district of San Francisco was related to Ted Wise, a sail-maker from Sausalito, who had been deeply involved in drug use. Late in 1967 he established a coffee house known as the Living Room, forerunner of a commune called the House of Acts. Then Lonnie Frisbee founded a similar commune in southern California, the House of Miracles. In 1969, Campus Crusade for Christ, the nation's largest Neoevangelical campus ministry organization, established the Christian World Liberation Front in Berkeley, led by Jack Sparks. And so the pattern continued.

By 1970 there were Jesus People groups everywhere; *Time* gave the movement a cover story in 1971. The appeal of "Jesus alone" to disillusioned youth who had found organized religion apathetic was not unlike the appeal of Oriental religious traditions to their friends. Many found in simple Gospel texts meaning and direction—unhampered by the doctrinal and life-style requirements imposed by organized religion—that released them from drug-oriented escapes. And their new commitment, while not changing the life-style represented by countercultural dress and communes, did result in a shift to sober, disciplined living coupled with new excitement and purpose.

While very diverse, the Jesus People shared certain common emphases. These included a nonintellectual insistence on the simple Gospel message without culturally conditioned doctrinal accoutrements and a belief that they were living in the biblical "end times" (Jesus People were the first to gravitate around Hal Lindsey's bestseller *The Late Great Planet Earth,* published in 1970). Also included was a widespread use of the *charismata,* a strong tendency toward some kind of communal living, a bias against organized Christianity—conservative and liberal—and a utilization of the dress, music, and vocabulary of the counterculture in their evangelism.

By 1972, however, the Jesus People movement, no less than the wider counterculture, was on the wane. But its impact on Neoevangelicalism, in particular, had already been felt. Like charismatic renewal, this movement attracted widespread media coverage, a fact that greatly enhanced the public visibility of conservative Christianity. In addition, it also had a profound and creative effect on conservative Christian music and styles of worship. But most important, the Jesus People movement legitimated "protest" by the young against the rising authority of the Neoevangelical establishment. This new dissent—in theology, politics, and life-style—would grow and mature in the years between 1973 and 1977 and would shake the foundations of Neoevangelicalism in the process.

1973–1977: THE YOUNG EVANGELICALS

As the result of the combined impact of charismatic renewal, the Jesus People movement, and trends in the wider society more generally, there occurred from 1973 to 1977 deep changes—in political and social philosophy, theology, and day-to-day life-style—within the (mainly younger) intellectual leadership of the Neoevangelical community, which became noticeably more "liberal" during this period. The leftward trend in political commitment and social perspective came first and was the most visible.

Already in 1947, Carl F. H. Henry had published his groundbreaking book, *The Uneasy Conscience of Modern Fundamentalism,* which castigated the Fundamentalist movement for its sometimes blatant lack of "social concern." But the Neoevangelicalism of the ensuing years posed no real alternative, since its leaders remained overwhelmingly conservative and laissez-faire when it came to political and social change. Throughout the 1960s Neoevangelical opinion makers were hardly less conservative than their Fundamentalist counterparts. On civil rights they generally counseled a moderate course of working for improving the attitudes of individual whites and blacks toward each other rather than support for national legislation such as the civil rights acts of 1964 and 1965, which they felt were too coercive and demanded integration too rapidly. And they viewed the civil disobedience of Martin Luther King, Jr., with suspicion, to say the least. When it came to the war in Vietnam, these leaders strongly supported the U.S. military presence and the defeat of Communism there. They were prime backers of Richard Nixon's bids for the presidency in both 1968 and 1972.

Nevertheless, during the same period increasingly loud dissident voices came to be heard within the wider Neoevangelical community. Senator Hatfield and Representative Anderson broke from their religiously nurtured conservative political backgrounds at this time and began acquiring a liberal voting record on legislation. In 1965 the first Neoevangelical magazine oriented toward the left was published. Now *The Other Side*, it was originally named *Freedom Now*, symbolizing its goal of raising issues of racial injustice among Neoevangelicals and Fundamentalists. At the 1966 Wheaton Congress on the Church's Worldwide Mission, the Neoevangelical establishment itself took up the call for renewed Christian social awareness and action. Then in 1969, at the United States Congress on Evangelism, even Leighton Ford, Billy Graham's brother-in-law, challenged conservative Christians to match their profession of faith with good works in a new social activism.

But perhaps the biggest surprise within Neoevangelicalism came in 1970, at the triennial world missionary convention of Inter-Varsity Christian Fellowship, held in Urbana, Illinois. For the first time, Billy Graham was not invited to speak—because of his "hand-holding" with President Nixon. And the 12,000 college and university students in attendance—most from solid Neoevangelical backgrounds, but deeply influenced by the counterculture—heard black evangelist Tom Skinner, a former Harlem gang leader, attack the hypocrisy of conservative Christians and churches for their major contributions to institutionalized racism and poverty. They stood and cheered when he lashed out at Wall Street, big business, "suburban bliss," and the "myth of democracy." Because of the speeches of Skinner and other plenary lecturers —and the warm response given them by the students—Urbana demonstrated to the Neoevangelical establishment that the social radicalism of the counterculture had caught up with even *its* young people in a big way.

During the early 1970s there emerged a number of prominent individuals and groups that professed allegiance to Neoevangelical theology but were also politically and socially radical in the sense that characterized the New Left. These people were most often highly educated idealists, mainly young and white, who shared a common conservative Christian background, yet saw in that faith commitment a good ideological basis for Christianizing, as it were, the core values of the New Left. The "radical evangelicals," as they came to be known, were centered in those years in Berkeley, Philadelphia, and Chicago; the most important group was the People's Christian Coalition, made up of students at Trinity Evangelical Divinity School in

Deerfield, Illinois, a suburb of Chicago. In 1971 the coalition began publishing the *Post-American* (now *Sojourners*), edited by Jim Wallis; it rapidly became the prime vehicle in transmitting the message of Christian radicalism to the larger Neoevangelical community. The *Post-American* joined company with *The Other Side* in Philadelphia and *Right On* (later *Radix*), published since 1969 by the Christian World Liberation Front in Berkeley, to provide that community with a socially and politically liberal alternative to *Christianity Today* and other media of the Neoevangelical establishment.

In 1972 representatives of the People's Christian Coalition and some of their sympathizers in the theological academy proposed a gathering of moderate to radical Neoevangelical leaders who would work out a new confession of faith that would affirm their commitment to social justice and change. About fifty of them, led by individuals in their twenties—writers, editors, activists, church officials, and professors—met in November 1973 at the Wabash YMCA in downtown Chicago to formulate the much publicized Declaration of Evangelical Social Concern, a document that received far more media attention and a more favorable reception than its framers expected. The Chicago declaration accused Neoevangelicals of complicity with militarism, racism, and the maldistribution of the world's goods and resources—to the neglect of the poor. And it denounced sexism, at least in general terms, criticizing the "prideful domination of men" and the "irresponsible passivity of women" its framers felt were encouraged by most conservative churches and other organizations. Because its formulators and early signers included Neoevangelical leaders whose credentials could not be questioned—Carl F. H. Henry, Mark O. Hatfield, and Leighton Ford among them—the Chicago declaration for the first time really legitimated the new leftward trend among the younger conservative Christian intelligentsia.

Theological changes in Neoevangelical academic circles during this period were subtle and less visible than those occurring in the realm of politics. But they too were highly significant. The increasing acceptance and use of the Higher Criticism of the Bible had become widely apparent in the movement's centers of theological education in the 1960s, most notably at Fuller Theological Seminary in Pasadena, California. This trend continued and became fully developed in the 1970s.

In 1972 the clause affirming complete biblical inerrancy was removed from Fuller's statement of faith. And by 1975 one of its prominent faculty members, Paul K. Jewett, dared to say in his book *Man as Male and Female* that St. Paul was wrong in at least some of his teaching on women. Although Fuller Seminary no longer subscribed to total inerrancy, it still retained belief in limited inerrancy, the absolute truth of the Bible in matters of faith and conduct, but not in all its statements about history and the cosmos. Yet Jewett went beyond even this by challenging the veracity of St. Paul's instructions about the role of women in church and society, thus questioning heretofore infallible biblical doctrine affecting Christian faith and practice. Needless to say, this development did not please the Neoevangelical establishment; it was opposed by some of the movement's most notable theologians, among them Francis A. Schaeffer, one of the most articulate Neoevangelical apologists, and Harold Lindsell, editor of *Christianity Today.* Lindsell responded to Jewett's liberalized hermeneutic—and that of his like-minded colleagues at Fuller and elsewhere—with his highly controversial book *The Battle for the Bible,* published in 1976 to expose the new critical scholarship being produced in conservative institutions. He was sure that, if left unchecked, it would undermine Neoevangelical integrity and ultimately destroy its authority.

Lindsell's work, supplemented by the speeches and writings of Schaeffer and others, did attract a lot of media attention, and the resulting controversy regarding biblical inerrancy split one denomination, the Lutheran Church–Missouri Synod, and caused the heads of a few Neoevangelical theologians to roll. But, by and large, it had little real effect, because the historical-critical method of studying the Scriptures was by now deeply embedded in the curricula of the movement's leading theological seminaries and college religion departments. It didn't go away.

Neoevangelical theologians continued their use of traditional religious symbolism, but much of it lost its transcendent character and took on an existential dimension, focusing more on this world and its future than on heaven, hell, and the life to come. Ardent premillennialism (the scho-lastic and "magical" dispensationalism of the Scofield Reference Bible)—questioned already for decades by the Neoevangelical intelligentsia—was now widely repudiated. In 1979, Charles H. Kraft, also of Fuller Seminary, published *Christianity in Culture,* an anthropological work that introduced broad cultural analysis into the study of Neoevangelical mission and evangelism methods. Kraft not only urged conservative missionaries and evangelists to "contextualize" their message within the culture they hoped to reach; he also encouraged an attitude of dialogue and mutual respect between Christians and others that seemed to relativize the once certain and non-negotiable requirements for salvation.

During this period, Neoevangelical theology often looked very much like the Continental Neoorthodoxy of the 1950s and early 1960s. Karl Barth, once the whipping boy of the movement's theologians, gradually became a hero, as did Dietrich Bonhoeffer. Beginning with the work of David O. Moberg, a prominent American sociologist, there also emerged a growing interest in the social-scientific study of religion and in psychology—as a friend, rather than a "tool of Satan." Thus, Neoevangelical intellectuals were slowly but surely catching up with "respectable" mainline Christian theologians in the production of critical scholarship that, by the late 1970s, came to be assigned and read even in long-time liberal seminaries.

In terms of life-style, Neoevangelical young people, especially, had begun experimenting with new ways of living "the Christian life" during the Jesus People movement, and this continued throughout the 1970s. Their politics ranged from moderate Republicanism to democratic socialism, and more than a few accepted the Marxian class analysis of society. Most still affirmed the nuclear family, but they were also open to alternative life-styles, from extended families to communes. Just about all of them became feminists to one degree or another, supporting the ordination of women to the ministry, egalitarian marriage, and the use of inclusive language. Divorce and remarriage became acceptable, while sexual permissiveness increased. And the old Fundamentalist taboos against alcohol, tobacco, and social dancing were almost completely discarded.

New organizations came into being to promote the interests of these "young evangelicals" by the mid-1970s, associations that challenged the authority of the Neoevangelical establishment. They included the Theological Students' Fellowship, in Madison, Wisconsin, which fostered critical biblical and religious studies in its highly sophisticated *TSF Bulletin.* Evangelicals for Social Action (based in Philadelphia) emerged as a result of the Chicago Declaration, as did the Evangelical Women's Caucus, a fellowship of conservative Christian feminists in West Newton, Massachusetts. And there even arose an association of gay and lesbian conservative Christians named Evangelicals Concerned (with headquarters in New York City).

As the ideological and behavioral boundaries of Neoevangelicalism and Pentecostalism widened, the very word *neoevangelical* became too limiting. It had already fallen into disuse by the 1960s and was generally replaced by the simpler designation *evangelical.* But this was now a broader label that came to include a much wider spectrum of believers than the old Neoevangelical designation encompassed. In the 1970s, there were conservative evangelicals (the old neoevangelicals), Reformed evangelicals (Calvinists with an emphatic "covenant theology" and hermeneutics), Lutheran evangelicals (the "original" evangelicals of the Reformation), Anabaptist evangelicals (emphasizing pacifism and "simple life-styles"), Wesleyan evangelicals (stressing "sanctification" and Arminian principles), charismatic evangelicals (focusing on the spiritual gifts), even black evangelicals (accommodating the core of Neoevangelical theology to the new black consciousness), to name just a few. By 1978, Robert Webber of Wheaton College, Illinois, could identify at least fourteen different evangelical subcultures.

The upward mobility of contemporary evangelicals and their increasing cultural sophistication formed the groundwork for the evangelical revival of the mid-1970s, heralded by the mass media. Evangelicals became a talking point everywhere, warranting a *Newsweek* cover story in 1976 ("the year of the evangelical") and a *Time* cover story in 1977. Their growing churches, highly visible youth and student ministries, phenomenally successful publishing and other media efforts, and unlikely twice-born celebrities such as Charles Colson, Jeb Magruder, and Eldridge Cleaver attracted public attention as

never before. And the election of Jimmy Carter, a born-again southern Baptist, to the presidency in 1976 seemed to legitimate the whole evangelical movement. In that same year George Gallup discovered that fully one-third of all American adults had been born again, and magazine writer Garry Wills insisted that "evangelical chic" was impending. Thus, evangelical Christianity, in its broadened form, seemed to become the new religious mainstream in the United States, and its leaders—young and old—gloried in the movement's triumph.

1978 TO THE LATE 1980S: THE WORLDLY EVANGELICALS

The years from 1978 to 1987 have been marked by increasing heterogeneity among evangelicals, symbolized best by the 1980 presidential election, in which all three major candidates—Ronald Reagan, Jimmy Carter, and John B. Anderson—identified themselves as born-again Christians. The campaign itself demonstrated to Americans that modern evangelicals could just as easily be politically liberal as conservative. And the old stereotype equating evangelical Christianity with the Republican party "at prayer" might have fit the winner, Reagan, but it certainly didn't apply either to Carter or to Anderson, who was even endorsed by New York's venerable Liberal party.

If evangelicals lacked respectability in previous generations, such was clearly no longer the case by the late 1970s. In the theological academy, evangelical scholarship finally came to be recognized. The American Academy of Religion itself organized a well-attended section on evangelical theology at its annual conventions, and the prestigious American Theological Society elected Carl F. H. Henry to a term as president (he succeeded Gordon Kaufman of Harvard). Union Theological Seminary in New York City, that great bastion of liberalism, hired two Pentecostal professors, and Harvard Divinity School announced that it was seeking endowment for a professorship of evangelical Christianity. Established ecumenical conferences, which had repudiated the born again in a previous era, now welcomed evangelical scholars, pastors, and activists as featured speakers.

With all this respect coming from its old archenemy, liberalism, the evangelical movement as a whole no longer saw the Antichrist behind such "modernist" organizations as the National Council of Churches and the World Council of Churches. (Indeed, there was a vocal contingent of especially positive evangelical leaders at the 1983 General Assembly of the World Council of Churches.) And thanks to charismatic renewal, the wall between Catholics and evangelicals has broken down as well. No longer were mainline Protestant and Catholic liberals consigned to hell, as in the past. Rather, "dialogue" became an increasingly popular activity for evangelicals —with Catholics, Protestant liberals, members of other religions, and even outright secularists. In 1975 a major dialogue between evangelicals and Jews took place under the sponsorship of the American Jewish Committee. And in 1978 a similar dialogue occurred between a number of evangelical leaders and members of the Unification Church, the "Moonies." Then, in 1977, the very secular publisher of *Penthouse* magazine convened a symposium on "the new evangelicalism" with liberals and evangelicals in conversation. The transcript of that dialogue was published in the April 1978 issue of the magazine.

Charismatic renewal also received added legitimacy with the election of Jimmy Carter to the presidency in 1976. His sister, Ruth Carter Stapleton, was a prominent charismatic healer featured in a *Newsweek* cover story in 1978. Actually, the new charismatics had been so successful in gaining acceptance for the Pentecostal experience in mainline Christendom that the movement as such was no longer necessary. Already by 1977 it had achieved its basic goal and began losing its visibility and distinctiveness, coalescing, finally, into the larger evangelical mainstream. Furthermore, with continuing upward mobility, even the once sectarian Pentecostal denominations had "opened up" to the point that they were often scarcely distinguishable from the nonsectarian charismatic renewal.

During this period, doctrinal purity had been replaced by church growth as the principal aim of mainstream evangelicals. The "umbrella ministry" of television evangelist Robert H. Schuller, encompassing both conservatives and liberals, became very appealing, as did the church growth conferences held several times on the campus of his Crystal Cathedral in Garden Grove, California. Schuller's positive thinking approach (he calls it "possibility thinking") was derived from the theology of Norman Vincent Peale, and it integrates the major themes of evangelical revivalism with the liberal New Thought tradition of mind over matter into a new synthesis that attracted even nonreligious media celebrities. There was no hellfire and brimstone for sinners in Schuller's message ("Jesus never called anyone a sinner"), just self-esteem and success ("Tough times don't last, but tough people do"). And it became the premier theology for the upwardly mobile of whatever religious persuasion, or none—"the new reformation," as Schuller termed it.

Further accommodation of the evangelicals to the wider culture occurred in the 1980s. Organizations such as Evangelicals for Social Action, Evangelicals Concerned, and the Evangelical Women's Caucus attracted more and more attention from mainline clergy and laity, Protestant and Catholic. And magazines like *The Wittenburg Door* (the evangelical *National Lampoon*), *Daughters of Sarah* (a feminist journal), *Radix, The Other Side,* and *Sojourners* took on typographical and editorial sophistication, thus appealing increasingly to the Christian mainstream. The activism of the young evangelicals moderated as they became older, got married, and started their own families; but some of the leaders of the minuscule Evangelicals for McGovern coalition in 1972 were now prominent in the antinuclear movement, the focal point of mainline religious social concern in the early 1980s. Billy Graham even came out on the side of nuclear disarmament during these years. But most of this escaped public notice with the vast amount of media attention given to the rise of the so-called New Christian Right, the surge to prominence of Fundamentalism in the late 1970s.

As the mass media were focusing on the emerging "evangelical left" during the Carter administration, the Fundamentalists and a host of conservative evangelicals also began to take on public visibility as opponents of this trend. Their popular television evangelists—including Pat Robertson, Jim Bakker, Jimmy Lee Swaggart, and Jerry Falwell—suddenly became famous even in the secular media as viewership and financial intake increased dramatically. Aided by the arrival of effective business computers to correspond "personally" with their contributors, to process donations, and to develop highly selective mailing lists for their solicitations, these television evangelists of the "electronic church" were each bringing in as much as $60 million or more per year. And from whom? Gallup discovered that the persons most likely to watch religious television in general and the conservative evangelists in particular were nonwhite, older adults, widowed individuals, Protestants, regular churchgoers, and people with no more than a grade school education. Viewers and contributors were concentrated in the rural areas and small towns of the South, West Central, and Mid-Atlantic regions, and in the mid-sized cities of the South and Midwest. Underrepresented in the large cities, they were most likely to be found in the lower echelons of educational achievement, income level, and occupational status—that is, within the lower-middle and working classes. As a whole, these persons lived and worked in an environment isolated from the secularizing forces of modernity and pluralism and the high culture of urban American elites.

The New Christian Right, then, was made up almost entirely of individuals who believed in traditional Judeo-Christian values and thus looked askance at evolution, sexual permissiveness, "value-free" public education, abortion, and accommodation to communism, all associated in their minds with secularization and the rise of "secular humanism." With significantly increased visibility, Jerry Falwell was able to found the Moral Majority in the late 1970s as a lobbying effort for the restoration of conservative values, and he became the foremost spokesperson for this movement. The Fundamentalists were now using the same kind of sophisticated political lobbying that liberal religious groups had used in the past, and the predominantly liberal mass media worried about the New Christian Right's impact on social and political legislation. But their fears were generally groundless. Gallup discovered in late 1980 that only 40 percent of all Americans polled had even heard of the Moral Majority, while even fewer—only 26 percent—were familiar with the objectives and goals of the organization. And among the latter informed group, disapproval outweighed approval 13 percent to 8 percent, with 5 percent undecided.

Of course, the Fundamentalists' favorite, Ronald Reagan, did become president in 1980. But survey researchers have shown that this victory was due far more to widespread public dissatisfaction over high inflation and unemployment than to the efforts of the New Christian Right and the evangelists of the electronic church who worked so hard on his behalf. Only a few of their people received appointments in the administration, and most of their primary concerns—other than a "pro-life" stance on abortion—were put on the back burner. Although the 1982 midterm and 1984 general elections demonstrated that the Moral Majority and its kin did not have the clout they claimed, they have remained a force to reckon with.

Furthermore, the prepluralistic vision of a Bible-based "Christian America" that Jerry Falwell and the New Christian Right seemed to have had in the beginning was quickly transformed when they realized that without pluralism *their* rights as conservatives might be threatened by an adversary liberal administration and Congress. And it was put aside when they saw that even President Reagan had to compromise at times and work with people of differing beliefs to achieve his main political and economic objectives.

Falwell himself already began accommodating to the wider culture when he repudiated the old Fundamentalist doctrine of total separation from "the world" by creating the Moral Majority, in which *all* his sympathizers—including Mormons, Orthodox Jews, and secular conservatives—could work together with him, regardless of religious profession or lack thereof. As a result of his visibility, the television evangelist began lecturing and debating on secular television shows and on college and university campuses, Harvard among them.

Further accommodation to mainstream values became apparent in Falwell's book *The Fundamentalist Phenomenon,* published in 1981. This is a sophisticated and scholarly treatment of the history and character of modern Fundamentalism (it was actually written by two professors at his Liberty University in Lynchburg, Virginia). Here he identified and critiqued dominant elements of his own Fundamentalist tradition—intolerance, absolutism, inflexibility, and lack of social concern—much as Carl F. H. Henry had done in 1947; termed those who practice such things "hyper-fundamentalists," a perverse deviation from the true spirit of the movement; and called, rather, for an alignment of Fundamentalists with conservative evangelicals.

Finally, by 1984, the television evangelist had even accepted the principle of dialogue. He demonstrated this vividly by inviting his ideological archenemy Sen. Edward Kennedy to speak at Liberty University and have dinner with him and his family, despite their many disagreements. In all of this, it was clear that upward mobility and a measure of acceptance by the wider culture because of it had brought Falwell, the most prominent Fundamentalist of them all, to the place where many Neoevangelicals were in the 1960s.

Evangelicalism accommodated to modernity faster than Fundamentalism, but slower than mainline Protestantism and Catholicism. None except the most marginalized sectarian religious groupings could resist modernity's impact, and even some of them began to show evidence of secularization, a concomitant of modernity, to one degree or another. Secularization may be understood to include two related transformations in the way people think. First, there is an increasing worldliness in the attitude toward persons and things. What is fundamentally involved here is the abandonment of emotional commitment found in the religious response, the response to the sacred and holy. Second, there is a rationalization of thought, the repression of emotional involvement in thinking about the world. Rationalization suggests a manner of thought that is comparatively free of emotion and in which logic replaces emotional symbolism in organizing reflection and speculation.

The secularization of culture, epitomized in the technological revolution, indicates that a religious world view is no longer dominant as the frame of reference for thought (this despite the continued high percentage of Americans who attend church regularly). And the rational methodology inherent in modernity requires that social phenomena of all kinds, including religion, be interpreted less and less in theological and moral terms and more by reference to empirical evidence about society itself. Thus, a Gallup poll on religious attitudes attracts far more public interest than does the latest genre of academic theology.

As Neoevangelicalism accommodated to modernity and became the more inclusive and heterogeneous evangelical Christianity of the late 1970s and 1980s, it lost much of its distinctiveness and identity. It became worldly. Unlike liberalism, however, the movement insisted on the centrality of biblical authority for faith and conduct, and continued to employ orthodox Christian symbolism in its increasingly diverse theologies. But at the same time modern evangelicals came to share a traditionally liberal critical methodology in dealing with that authority. They emphasized the relativity of orthodox doctrinal formulations, believed that personal experience (as well as "propositional truths" in Scripture) can inform Christian ethics, and held that appropriate Christian behavior ("orthopraxis," a word they borrowed from "liberation theology") can be learned from the world as well as from the Bible and the church.

The two major theological concerns of Western Christianity as a whole during the modern era have been ecumenism and Christian social ethics. And theological conservatives have contributed to these concerns in the later twentieth century. The new charismatics greatly enhanced the grassroots unity between Protestants and Catholics in an increasingly autonomous and anonymous postindustrial society. They were the major evangelical ecumenists. And it was the young evangelicals who actually replaced the liberals as the vanguard of Christian social concern in the 1970s. In their social ethics, the Neoevangelicals had already affirmed in the 1940s that God requires justice and that conservative Christians should promote the creation of a just society. But the new evangelicals of the 1970s insisted that all Christians must work for that society, the very Kingdom of God itself. The Chicago declaration confessed: "God requires justice. But we have not proclaimed or demonstrated his justice to an unjust American society." Without God, a just and righteous society was impossible. But without God's people working together for social change—in the world—it was just as impossible.

The thinking, writing, and action of the young evangelicals surely strengthened the larger Christian concern for the creation of a more just American society. Yet, by the 1980s, it was manifestly clear that mere moral pronouncements, statements of Christian social concern, and calls to action—made by the Moral Majority (renamed the Liberty Federation in 1986) on the right or the radical evangelicals on the left—did not, of themselves, motivate many American Christians or others to actually do something tangible to promote change. Religion had become privatized, and its moral teachings had lost their normative character and application.

The present era is a time in which the authority of all religious traditions and their leaders in the West has waned considerably, and religion has lost much of its public character, except, perhaps, as a "show," a form of entertainment. The privatization of religion and the loss of its social impact are major problems in the 1980s for all those who still see in the Christian faith the means to change the world. Modernity, shaped so much by Darwin, Marx, and Freud, has no need for faith in God, and religion has yet to cope adequately with its secularizing force. If Christians ever hope to correct this situation, they—with all their differences—will have to get together in order to meet such a powerful onslaught. In the past, the conservatives among them would have repudiated such a call for unity. Now, however, many of them agree.

BIBLIOGRAPHY

Robert Mapes Anderson, *Vision of the Disinherited: The Making of American Pentecostalism* (1979); James Barr, *Fundamentalism* (1977; rev. 1978); Donald G. Bloesch, *Essentials of Evangelical Theology*, 2 vols. (1978–1979) and *The Future of Evangelical Christianity* (1983); Mark Lau Branson, ed., *The Reader's Guide to the Best Evangelical Books* (1982); Richard J. Coleman, *Issues of Theological Conflict: Evangelicals and Liberals* (1972; rev. 1980); Donald W. Dayton, " 'The Battle for the Bible': Renewing the Inerrancy Debate," in *The Christian Century* (10 November 1976); Jerry Falwell, *The Fundamentalist Phenomenon* (1981); Carol Flake, *Redemptorama: Culture, Politics, and the New Evangelicalism* (1984); Ronald B. Flowers, *Religion in Strange Times: The 1960s and 1970s* (1984); Robert Booth Fowler, *A New Engagement: Evangelical Political Thought, 1966–1976* (1983); Marshall Frady, *Billy Graham: A Biography of American Righteousness* (1979); J. L. Garrett, E. G. Hinson, and J. E. Tull, *Are Southern Baptists "Evangelicals"?* (1983).

Jeffrey K. Hadden and Charles E. Swann, *Prime Time Preachers* (1981); David E. Harrell, Jr., *Oral Roberts: An American Life* (1985) and as ed., *Varieties of Southern Evangelicalism* (1981); Carl F. H. Henry, *The Uneasy Conscience of Modern Fundamentalism* (1947), "Revolt on Evangelical Frontiers," in *Christianity Today* (26 April 1974), and *God, Revelation and Authority*, 6 vols. (1976–1983); James Davison Hunter, *American Evangelicalism: Conservative Religion and the Quandary of Modernity* (1983); Paul K. Jewett, *Man as Male and Female* (1975); Dean M. Kelley, *Why Conservative Churches Are Growing* (1972; rev. 1977); Charles H. Kraft, *Christianity in Culture* (1979).

Robert C. Liebman and Robert Wuthnow, eds., *The New Christian Right: Mobilization and Legitimation* (1983); Robert P. Lightner, *Neoevangelicalism Today* (1965; rev. 1978); Harold Lindsell, *The Battle for the Bible* (1976); Hal Lindsey, *The Late Great Planet Earth* (1970); George M. Marsden, ed., *Fundamentalism and American Culture* (1980) and *Evangelicalism and Modern America* (1984); Martin E. Marty, "A Taxonomy of the Born-Again," in *The Christian Century* (4 October 1978); David O. Moberg, *The Great Reversal: Evangelism and Social Concern* (1972; rev. 1977); Bob E. Patterson, *Carl F. H. Henry* (1983); Arthur C. Piepkorn, *Profiles in Belief: The Religious Bodies of the United States and Canada*, vols. 3 and 4 (1979); Richard Quebedeaux, *The Young Evangelicals* (1974), *The Worldly Evangelicals* (1978), *I Found It!: The Story of Bill Bright and Campus Crusade* (1979), *By What Authority: The Rise of Personality Cults in American Christianity* (1982), *The New Charismatics II* (1983), "We're on Our Way, Lord!: The Rise of 'Evangelical Feminism' in Modern American Christianity," in Ursula King, ed., *Women in World Religions Past and Present* (1986), and with Rodney Sawatsky, eds., *Evangelical-Unification Dialogue* (1979); Bernard L. Ramm, *After Fundamentalism: The Future of Evangelical Theology* (1983).

Ernest R. Sandeen, *The Roots of Fundamentalism: British and American Millenarianism, 1800–1930* (1970); Francis A. Schaeffer, *The Complete Works of Francis A. Schaeffer*, 5 vols. (1982) and *The Great Evangelical Disaster* (1984); Anson Shupe and William A. Stacey, *Born Again Politics and the Moral Majority: What Social Surveys Really Show* (1982); Ronald J. Sider, ed., *The Chicago Declaration* (1974); John R. W. Stott and Basil Meeking, eds., *The Evangelical-Roman Catholic Dialogue on Mission, 1977–1984* (1986); Leonard I. Sweet, ed., *The Evangelical Tradition in America* (1984); Marc H. Tanenbaum, Marvin R. Wilson, and A. James Rudin, eds., *Evangelicals and Jews in an Age of Pluralism* (1984); Donald Tinder, "Are We Worldly?" in *Christianity Today* (19 May 1978); Marlin J. Van Elderen, "Evangelicals and Liberals: Is There a Common Ground?" in *Christianity and Crisis* (8 July 1974); Dennis Voskuil, *Mountains into Goldmines: Robert Schuller and the Gospel of Success* (1983); Jim Wallis, "Revolt on Evangelical Frontiers: A Response," in *Christianity Today* (21 June 1974); Timothy P. Weber, *Living in the Shadow of the Second Coming* (1979; rev. 1983); David F. Wells, and John D. Woodbridge, eds., *The Evangelicals: What They Believe, Who They Are, Where They Are Changing* (1975; rev. 1977); "Worldly Evangelicals," in *The Wittenburg Door* (June–July 1978).

[*See also* FUNDAMENTALISM; MASS COMMUNICATIONS; *and* PENTECOSTALISM.]

THE ECUMENICAL MOVEMENT

Paul A. Crow, Jr.

THE word *ecumenical* is derived from a family of words in classical Greek: *oikos,* meaning a house, family, people, nation; *oikoumene,* meaning "the whole inhabited world," or "the world community"; *oikoumenikos,* implying "related," or "open to the whole world." Like most Christian words, *ecumenical* was first a secular word that came to be invested with Christian meanings. In the Gospel of Matthew the *oikoumene* is the object of God's mission: "And this gospel of the kingdom will be preached throughout the whole world [*oikoumene*] as a testimony to all nations" (24:14). For the author of Hebrews the *oikoumene* is the world destined "to be redeemed by Christ" (2:5). Luke used *oikoumene* to refer to the unity expressed throughout the Roman Empire (2:1). In Acts 17:6 Paul and Silas are described as "These men who have turned the *oikoumene* upside down."

Over the course of centuries this classical, theologically neutral word took on other particular meanings and passed through several mutations. The church in the New Testament is presented as the community that manifests an all-embracing wholeness, a fullness in Christ that unites all people and all things (*ta panta*) in all ages—past, present, and future. *Ecumenical* in this sense speaks of the universal church, the one people of God. The second-century church father Polycarp prayed "by day and by night" for the unity of the churches of the *oikoumene,* that is, the universal church; and, also in the second century, Irenaeus wrote of "the church dispersed throughout the *oikoumene* to the ends of the earth." The church was envisaged as coextensive with the *oikoumene.*

Later *ecumenical* was used to distinguish those councils (e.g., Nicaea, Chalcedon) that were representative of the universal church in contrast to other councils that had only limited participation and reception. The Eastern Orthodox Patriarch of Constantinople was given the honorary title of Ecumenical Patriarch, since for many centuries his see was located in the capital of the *oikoumene,* and since as *primus inter pares* (first among equals) among the other patriarchs, he was the convenor of ecumenical councils that made decisions about the faith and mission of the universal church. *Ecumenical* also was applied to any teachings that were universally accepted; certain teachers were called "ecumenical doctors." In the sixteenth century three creeds (the Apostles', the Nicene, and the Athanasian) were termed ecumenical because they witness to the faith of the universal church.

In the nineteenth and twentieth centuries— after centuries of divisions—the term *ecumenical movement* took on a modern meaning, namely, the pursuit of visible unity or union of Christians and churches of different traditions or denominations. The unity of the church is understood as a sign of the unity of the human family. In this light the ecumenical movement has been variously defined as the "spiritual traffic between the churches which draws them out of their isolation and into a fellowship (*koinonia*) of conversation, mutual enrichment, common witness and common action" (Visser't Hooft); the "growing consciousness of all churches of the Church universal conceived as a missionary community" (Hogg); "the total effort of Christians of varied traditions and loyalties to join forces, in order to more adequately discharge their total task and fulfill their total responsibility throughout the whole world" (Van Dusen); and "the whole historical experience of the Church as the pilgrim people of God, in whose midst Christ is continuously present through the indwelling of the Spirit . . . [and whose mission derives from] its essential unity and universality in Christ, in realizing the unity of humankind as the one redeemed and sanctified people of God, the kingdom of heaven upon earth'' (Torrance). In its broadest sense, the ecumenical movement describes "everything that relates to the whole task of the whole Church to bring the Gospel to the whole world" (Central Committee of the World Council of Churches, Rolle, Switzerland, 1951).

To speak of an ecumenical *movement* is to describe many immensely varied activities undertaken by all sorts of persons and organizations. It is certainly not a single organization, not a single world communion or concept. Individual voices, cooperative action in mission and service, prayer and common worship, Bible study, and international conferences, theological dialogues, church union consultations—all represent a dynamic and developing process aimed at drawing Christians together and reconciling them, healing their divisions, renewing the churches and the human community, so making a common witness in the world. The terms *ecumenicity* and *ecumenism* convey the essence of this movement.

In its methods and goal the ecumenical movement is marked by a spiritual ecumenism that seeks a unity with diversity as well as a communion based on faith. There is no place for spiritual coercion, strategies of dominance or superiority, calls to return to the "mother church," expectations of monolithic uniformity or a super-church. Nor is the solution to the divisions among the churches to be found in a least common denominator theology. Ecumenism is a transforming movement of theological integrity, spiritual openness, struggle against divisive powers, acknowledgment of Christian truth in other traditions, mutual acceptance, and searching for spiritual and visible communion. The ecumenical movement points to the essential oneness of the people of God, derived from their unity and universality in Christ. It seeks to overcome all things that divide the church as well as the human community; that isolate people, nations, and cultures; that break fellowship or separate persons from God and from each other.

UNITY IN THE BIBLICAL PERSPECTIVE

The biblical witness to Christian unity begins not in the New Testament but in the Old Testament, or Hebrew Scriptures. The tradition of ancient Judaism was based on the concept of the one people of God. This unity was an expression of monotheism, the oneness of God (Yahweh). As Genesis portrays, Yahweh created the world as one cosmos, an ordered unity determined by one single will where all creatures are responsive to the purposes of the Creator. Yahweh chose Israel from all the nations of the world and entered into a covenant with it. The sacred mission of Israel was to preserve the unity of God's people and to prepare for its final realization. But generation after generation of God's people broke the covenant, rebelled against God's love. The Hebrew Scriptures from beginning to end, therefore, tell of alienation and reconciliation, brokenness and restored unity. The prophets and pastors of Israel called the people back from humiliation and division to their vocation of unity and mission to society and the nations.

This vision of unity dominates the self-understanding of the church of the New Testament. The most constant motif in the life of the community is that of it being one church, a unique society constituted by the act of God through Jesus Christ in history. The yearning for oneness among all Christians was dramatically articulated in the high-priestly prayer that Jesus offered at the Last Supper: "That they may all be one; even as thou, Father, art in me, and I in thee, that they also may be in us, so that the world may believe that thou hast sent me" (John 17:21). The Apostle Paul summed up God's "plan for the fulness of time" as "to unite all things in him [Christ], things in heaven and things on earth" (Ephesians 1:10). Throughout his epistles this apostle to the Gentiles gave pastoral counsel to those earliest Christians at Corinth and Ephesus by exhorting them to value and preserve the unity of Christ's body. The church is one, all the writers of the New Testament confess, because to be "in Christ" is to belong to the one fellowship (*koinonia*) composed by all who believe in him. The biblical writers use a number of colorful metaphors to describe the church: the Body of Christ (I Corinthians 12:17–20; Ephesians 4:11–15); the household of God (Ephesians 2:19); the temple of God (Ephesians 2:21; I Corinthians 3:16–17); God's building and the Bride of Christ (Ephesians 5:22–32; Revelation 21:9). All portray the church's unity. The church is a visible community and its unity is of the *esse* (being) of the church. Division in the church is far more damaging than might be assumed. The loss of visible unity is tantamount to the loss of something essential for the church. Division means Christ himself is divided, an unthinkable distortion of the reality of the church (I Corinthians 1:10–17).

Christianity assumed diverse forms throughout the known world of the first century A.D. The church in Jerusalem, Antioch, Corinth, Ephesus, or wherever had different ways of worship, social practices, food laws, views of membership, offices of ministry, even viewpoints on Christology. Biblical scholars refer to Jewish Christianity, Hellenistic Christianity, apocalyptic Christianity, early Catholicism—all illustrative of a creative diversity. The early church was also plagued by tensions that threatened disunity. Personality conflicts were severe in Corinth, revealing a schismatic loyalty to such leaders as Paul, Apollos, and Cephas/Peter (I Corinthians 1:10–16). Paul and Peter strongly disagreed over whether Gentile Christians had to fulfill the Jewish requirements in order to be welcome at the Lord's Supper. Theological aberrations were throughout: Colossians refuted gnosticism, the Johannine Epistles warned of docetism, II Peter and Revelation attacked false prophets.

Yet this panorama of theological, social, racial, and geographical diversity did not create schism in the New Testament community. There were certainly no denominations or divided communities as were to develop later in church history. The earliest Christians remained of "one accord," visibly together. Their unity was "a solidarity of differences," to use Ernst Käsemann's phrase. The nature of this unity was at least fourfold: there was a free exchange of members among the various congregations; the ministers of the various churches were mutually accepted and received as ministers of the whole church; believers from other places were welcomed at the Lord's Supper; and unity reached beyond the local congregation and brought all Christians together in the church universal. The biblical community was a portrait of unity with diversity.

DIVISION AND UNITY IN THE CHURCH'S HISTORY

The church's history is marked by two drives: one toward sectarianism and division, the other toward catholicity and unity. After the first century the dark shadows of conflicting movements gathered. Some were foreshadows of theological conflicts that threatened the apostolic message and how it was to be handed down to later generations; others were internal quarrels related to liturgical differences, to power politics between different patriarchates or church centers (Alexandria and Antioch, Constantinople and Rome), or to social and cultural conflicts. Beyond this sad story of schism, however, there were men and women who continuously struggled to restore the vision of the one, worldwide Christian church, the single *oikoumene* in Christ.

Divisiveness in the second century A.D. took place over Quartodecimanism, a dispute between Christians from Asia Minor and Rome over the date of Easter, and over Montanism, a revivalist movement that taught an enthusiastic faith prompted by the Holy Spirit, the imminent Second Coming of Christ, and a perfection marked by regular fasting and abstinence from marriage. During the Roman persecutions by the emperor Decius in A.D. 250, the Novatians broke fellowship with those Christians who lapsed, that is, offered sacrifices under pressure to pagan gods. Another schism came in North Africa during the Diocletian persecutions of the fourth century over those who acted unfaithfully by handing over copies of the Scriptures to the Roman authorities for destruction. The Donatists were rural North African Christians who would not share communion with the lapsed. This schism also reflected regional and national, cultural and economic differences between the poor North Africans and the sophisticated, urban Romans who were their neighbors. These early schisms were mostly regional in their effect and were later resolved or disappeared.

The severe breaks in the unity of the church began to take place within Eastern Christianity in the fifth century. Technically they were doctrinal divisions and those who left were labeled heretics. Yet, in fact, the underlying causes of division were also political and cultural, and the instruments of debate were differences of philosophy and linguistics. The controversy first centered around the relationship between God the Father and God the Son, and later upon the relation of the divine and the human elements in the nature and person of Jesus Christ. The first four "ecumenical" councils at Nicaea (A.D. 325), Constantinople (A.D. 381), Ephesus (A.D. 431), and Chalcedon (A.D. 451) defined the consensus to be taught in the Nicene Creed and the Chalcedonian Formula. As a result, those who did not agree with the official definitions of faith—the Arians, the Nestorians, and the Monophysites —separated themselves from the Catholic/Orthodox Church, and the unity of the Eastern Christian world was shattered. Since these non-Chalcedonian Christians were great missionaries, their churches spread through Asia and the Middle East—Armenia, Egypt, Ethiopia, Syria, and the Malabar coast of India. These churches, which separated from the Eastern Orthodox Church, are known as the Oriental Orthodox.

The greatest schism came between the Eastern patriarch of Constantinople and the Western pope (patriarch) of Rome. While A.D. 1054 is the official date of the separation, this agonizing division had been six centuries in the making. The friction was ignited by several matters: the Orthodox disagreed when the Western church introduced into the Nicene Creed the doctrine that the Holy Spirit proceeds not from the Father alone—as earlier church fathers taught—but from the Father *and the Son* (Latin, *filioque*); the Western church, following the demarcation of the Roman Empire into two zones, began to claim the superiority of Rome over Constantinople; in their missionary efforts, especially the conversion of the Slavs in Bulgaria, the East and West were placed in competition. Lesser matters of worship and church discipline—for example, married clergy and rules of fasting—also strained relations. The tensions became a schism in A.D. 1054 when an uncompromising patriarch of Constantinople and an uncompromising pope of Rome excommunicated each other. This separation was, however, neither widespread nor final until the nominally Christian crusaders, some half a century later, made their military campaigns to save Jerusalem and the Holy Land from the Muslims and en route ravaged Orthodox territories. When, in 1204, the crusaders of the Fourth Crusade sacked Constantinople, murdering thousands of Orthodox Christians and desecrating churches and icons, the schism became definitive.

Two important attempts were made at reunion between Christians in the East and the West. The Second Council of Lyons (France) in 1274 tried to reunite the church, even to the point of securing the agreement of the Orthodox delegates to recognize the papal claims to primacy and to receive the Nicene Creed with the *filioque*.

But the agreement was only a paper act, politically motivated, that was fiercely rejected by the clergy and laity in Constantinople and other Orthodox provinces. The second attempt at reunion came at a council that met at Ferrara (Italy) in 1438 and at Florence in 1439. The Greeks were then militarily threatened by the approaching Turks. Eventually these councils approved a formula of union that offered a new model of doctrinal dialogue and collegiality in relation to the two different teachings about the Holy Spirit as an expression of the one and the same faith. While approved by the delegates, the consensus was short-lived, however, because it was not acceptable to the rank and file Eastern Christians. One Byzantine duke in Constantinople remarked, "I would rather see the Moslem turban in the midst of the city than the Latin miter." Both of these reunion councils failed primarily because they were politically motivated and involved only bishops and not the people.

The next dramatic Christian division came in the sixteenth-century Reformation led by Martin Luther, John Calvin, and others. In one sense the Protestant Reformation created a separation, especially as a reaction against the rigid juridical structure of the medieval Roman Catholic Church and its claim to universal jurisdiction. It was a crisis "between theological catholicity and institutional universality" (Torrance). But in another sense the Reformation was a form of inward, evangelical renewal of the church as the one Body of Christ, an attempt through a recovery of the apostolic and patristic sources "to recover the face of the ancient Catholic Church" (Calvin). Indeed, as John T. McNeill showed, "The ideal of Christian Unity was a pronounced original characteristic of Protestantism"; the restoration of catholicity, the wholeness and fullness of the church, was "among their [the reformers'] deepest convictions." Any divisions or disruptions that followed were against the principles of the leading reformers. Luther and Calvin both, aided by the irenic spirits of Martin Bucer and others, held various conferences on unity, such as the one at Marburg (Germany) in 1529, where Luther and Ulrich Zwingli considered the presence of Christ in the Lord's Supper. In 1541 Calvin, Bucer, and Melanchthon met at Ratisbon (Regensburg, Germany) with Roman Catholic representatives seeking to reconcile their differences on justification by faith, the Lord's Supper or Mass, and the papacy. A historic correspondence begun in 1555 between Melanchthon and the patriarch of Constantinople used the Augsburg Confession as a point of dialogue between Orthodox and Lutherans. These efforts were made irrelevant, however, when the Roman Catholic Council of Trent (Italy) in 1545 defined Christian teaching in such a way that Protestantism was excluded. The Counter-Reformation erased even the faint hopes for unity.

In the seventeenth and eighteenth centuries, plagued by storms of contention and division among Protestants, a band of individuals in different parts of Great Britain and continental Europe proclaimed the ecumenical vision through conferences and treatises proposing church union, mutual recognition, and intercommunion. Among the German Lutherans, George Calixtus called for a united church between Lutherans and Reformed by a return to the Apostles' Creed and the patristic agreements of the first five centuries. Hugo Grotius, a Dutch philosopher and international lawyer, held that "since all Christians are baptized into the same name, therefore, there ought to be no sects or divisions among them." John Amos Comenius, the great seventeenth-century Czech educator and union advocate, lamented the disunity of the church and produced a plan for world education based upon the common knowledge of God and the integration of all human culture. Such, he believed, would unite the churches. The most widely traveled ecumenist of the seventeenth century was John Dury, a Scots Presbyterian minister who journeyed to Sweden, Holland, Germany, and England, attempting to negotiate "ecclesiastical pacification" based on the simplicity of the early Christian life and faith, the Apostles' Creed, and the theological principles of the church fathers. Richard Baxter, a Presbyterian Puritan minister and a colleague of Dury, made many proposals for union in England, including his Worcestershire Association, a local ecumenical venture for Presbyterians, Independents, and Anglicans. William Wake, archbishop of Canterbury, maintained a long correspondence proposing union with Swiss Protestant theologians and French Roman Catholic divines, especially Dr. Louis Ellies Du Pin, at the Sorbonne. The great philosopher Gottfried Wilhelm Leibniz worked tirelessly for union between Protestants and Roman Catholics, by writing an apologia for Roman Catholic doctrines, thus hoping to make them acceptable to Protestants. Leibniz also engaged in (unfruitful) correspondence with Jacques Bossuet, the Gallican (French) leader who became the Roman Catholic bishop of Meaux. Bossuet made considerable efforts toward Roman Catholic–Protestant reunion. Daniel Ernst Jablonski of the Church of the Bohemian Brethren proposed a plan of union for all Protestant churches in Prussia and England of which the cornerstones were biblical orthodoxy and episcopacy. Friedrich Schleiermacher, the father of modern theology, forcefully promoted unity negotiations that gave birth in 1817 to King Frederick William III's dream of the union of Lutheran and Reformed churches in Prussia. Among Roman Catholic theologians, Johann Adam Möhjer and other scholars at Tübingen (Germany) represented an irenic Catholic approach to Protestant churches. In Russia, Metropolitan Philaret and theologian Alexis S. Khomiakov addressed the problem of church unity in its broadest sense. Disunity was rampant in these times, but these voices courageously spoke of the vision of visible unity from different countries, traditions, and walks of life.

In the nineteenth century the impetus toward Christian unity shifted to the United States. Ironically the young nation's religious life was shaped by the church divisions of Europe that had taken hold in the new land. New conflicts and a bewildering variety of sects and denominations developed in a religious atmosphere tempered by radical individualism, religious freedom, and competitive evangelism. The established churches of the old countries and the free churches of the new nation were molded into a new pattern of ecclesial community called denominationalism.

This early ecumenism in the United States assumed three forms. The first was cooperation by individuals in nondenominational bodies. In response to the revivalism of the Second Great Awakening, a flock of voluntary societies arose that were committed to evangelism, religious education, and social witness. Among them were the American Board of Commissioners for Foreign Missions (1810), the American Home Missionary Society (1826), the American Bible Society (1816), the Sunday School Union (1824), the American Peace Society (1828), and two Christian youth movements, the Young Men's Christian Association (England, 1844; United States, 1852) and the Young Women's Christian Association (England, 1854; United States, 1872). The impact of these voluntary societies was so forceful that historians speak of them as the Evangelical Empire.

Holding a unique place among these voluntary associations of individuals was the World Evangelical Alliance, the most significant organization in the nineteenth century with Christian unity as its primary purpose. Founded in London in 1846, its purpose was "simply to bring individual Christians into closer fellowship and cooperation on the basis of the spiritual union which already exists in the vital relation of Christ to the members of His body in all ages and all countries" (Philip D. Jordan, *The Evangelical Alliance for the U.S.A.,* 1982). The alliance adopted a doctrinal basis of nine "great evangelical principles," fairly representative of the conservative theology of the era. Its programs encouraged an annual Week of Prayer for Christian Unity, religious liberty, international Christian education, and worldwide missions. Americans made up 10 percent of the participants at the inaugural conference, but an American branch was not organized until 1867—two years after the Civil War—since the alliance did not admit members who owned slaves. Once launched, the American Evangelical Alliance was a powerful ecumenical presence that attracted such leaders as the layman William E. Dodge, church historian Philip Schaff, and social activist Josiah Strong.

The second approach to Christian unity in nineteenth-century America was federative action by denominational bodies. In this model the relationships were not those of individuals but of churches engaged in official relations of cooperative witness. Two German-American theologians—Lutheran Samuel Simon Schmucker and Reformed Philip Schaff—were the most articulate proponents of federation.

In 1838 and 1870 Schmucker issued his "fraternal appeal to the American churches" to confederate in an alliance through which they would cooperate, mutually recognize each other's ministries, and practice intercommunion, all without affecting the authority, polity, worship, or discipline of the denominations. A similar vision was advocated by Schaff, the renowned historian and theologian whose *Creeds of Christdom* and multivolume history of Christianity influenced the

ecumenical movement. In 1893, just before his death, he delivered a paper to a meeting of the World's Parliament of Religions, held in connection with the Chicago World's Fair. Schaff called for "federal or confederate union," which he defined as

a voluntary association of different churches in their official capacity, each retaining its freedom and independence in the management of its internal affairs, but all recognizing one another as sisters with equal rights and cooperating in general enterprises such as the spread of the gospel at home and abroad, the defense of the faith against infidelity, the elevation of the poor and neglected classes of society, works of philanthropy and charity and moral reform.

(*The Reunion of Christianity,* 1893)

While lonely prophets in the nineteenth century, Schmucker and Schaff offered a vision that was partially fulfilled in the next century.

The third type of unity proposed in nineteenth-century America was organic or corporate union. In union the traditions and practices of two or more divided churches are blended into a common identity, bringing about a common ecclesial life marked by diversity. Two churches, from different venues on the ecclesiological spectrum, that gave particular impetus toward a united church were the Episcopal Church and the Disciples of Christ. Drawing on the ecumenical legacy of the Anglican tradition, three American Episcopal ministers were visionaries for visible unity: Thomas Hubbard Vail, William Augustus Muhlenburg, and William Reed Huntington. In 1870 Huntington's notable essay about unity, *The Church Idea,* offered the Episcopal Church as "the Church of the Reconciliation," and proposed a four-point platform as the basis for all future church union attempts. His intent was not "to absorb other communions, but rather cooperating with them . . . to discountenance schism." His "Quadrilateral" was the Holy Scriptures as the Word of God, the Apostles' and Nicene creeds as the sufficient statement of the Christian faith, the two sacraments of baptism and the Lord's Supper, and the historic episcopate as "the keystone of governmental unity." This formula was approved by the 1886 Chicago General Convention of the Episcopal Church and in 1888 by the Lambeth Conference of Anglican bishops. The Chicago-Lambeth Quadrilateral, as it came to be known, was until recently the basis for any organic union conversations involving Anglicans.

The Disciples of Christ, a nineteenth-century church, was born in Great Britain and the American frontier. Their study of the New Testament gave them an abhorrence of sectarianism and disunity and a passion for the visible unity of all Christians. Barton Warren Stone, a Presbyterian minister born in America and later one of the founders of the Disciples of Christ, was one of the chief actors in the Cane Ridge Revival in Kentucky (1801). This mass revival was an ecumenical "sacramental meeting" that brought Presbyterians, Methodists, Baptists, and others together on the divided frontier to celebrate the Lord's Supper. This event convinced Stone and his followers to decry divisive "partyism" and to seek true unity, taking "the Bible alone as the only true standard of faith, practice and discipline." Stone's plea for union was contained in *The Last Will and Testament of the Springfield Presbytery* (1804), whose first item declared: "We will that this body die, be dissolved, and sink into union with the Body of Christ at large, for there is one Body and one Spirit, even as we are called in one hope of our calling." Preceding Schmucker, Schaff, and others, Stone in 1836 proposed an American conference at which the various denominations would "consult upon some general points respecting the union of Christians."

The other Disciples' movement was led by Thomas Campbell and his brilliant son Alexander Campbell, both Scots-Irish immigrants to the United States and ministers of the Seceder strain of Presbyterianism. The Campbells found the anti-ecumenical practices of nineteenth-century Presbyterianism unbearable. Thomas Campbell's apologia for Christian unity, *Declaration and Address* (1809), is heralded as one of the classic ecumenical documents. It pleads for the unity of all Christians based on the simplicity of the biblical faith and the denial of the divisive use of creeds. The mandate for Christian unity was eloquently declared: "The Church of Christ upon earth is essentially, intentionally, and constitutionally one." Alexander Campbell shared the vision of his father and became a leading ecumenical theologian, denouncing the evil of church division and affirming that church union

is essential for the conversion of the world. The Disciples (Campbell) and Christians (Stone) united in 1832 at Lexington, Kentucky. The Disciples of Christ's plea for unity was uniquely American and constituted an important voice in the irenic chorus foretelling the modern ecumenical movement.

THE MODERN ECUMENICAL MOVEMENT

In the twentieth century the dreams and struggles to draw the churches together on a world scale reached their fruition. The scandal of disunity had been felt, as we have seen, in all ages by dedicated Christians of many churches. But the experience of a new era gave the ecumenical movement dynamic momentum and comprehensiveness through hundreds of organizations and institutions. Four particular movements coalesced to give shape and spiritual energy to the wholeness of the church: the student Christian movement, the International Missionary Council, the Life and Work movement, and the Faith and Order movement—the latter three giving birth to the World Council of Churches (1948). In all four tributaries American Protestantism made important contributions to world Christianity.

A worldwide Christian movement among university students began in 1886 at a student conference planned by Dwight L. Moody at his conference center in Mount Hermon, Massachusetts. One hundred students made decisions to become overseas missionaries. John R. Mott, a young American Methodist layman and administrative genius, organized this evangelical enthusiasm into the Student Volunteer Movement for Foreign Missions. Nearly a decade later, in 1895, at Vadstena, Sweden, Mott, Luther D. Wishard of the American YMCA, and representatives from Great Britain, Germany, and Scandinavia founded the World Student Christian Federation (WSCF). Immediately messages were sent to Asia and other places to begin to make the WSCF a global movement, under their self-proclaimed mandate: "the evangelization of the world in our generation." Its purpose, as outlined at Vadstena, was "to lead students to become disciples of Jesus Christ as only Saviour and as God; to deepen the spiritual life of students; and to enlist students in the work of extending the Kingdom of Christ throughout the whole world." The pioneering role of the WSCF for the whole ecumenical movement is seen in the fact that it was "a laboratory of ecumenism" (Rouse) that trained many of the future leaders for ecumenical organizations. It wrestled with issues—reconciliation of war's hostility, evangelization in a truly global world, the challenges of social crisis—that later were placed on the agenda of the churches and that became "the first fruit of Christian unity among men and women, among theologians and ordinary lay people, among various Christian confessions and among people of different nations and races" (Weber). This universal company of students was extended under the leadership of a French electrical engineering student turned biblical scholar, Suzanne de Diétrich, and Willem Adolph Visser't Hooft, a Dutch theologian who succeeded Mott as the second general secretary of the WSCF. Throughout its history the WSCF has been and continues to be an ecumenical crucible in which university students look for ways to express the Christian faith in the context of the human dilemma and the missionary vocation in a changing world.

A second impulse in the modern ecumenical movement came through missionary cooperation. The last half of the nineteenth century had seen the growth of missionary societies and their phenomenal record of missionary expansion, especially in Asia and Africa, admittedly often with colonialistic implications. In a relatively brief time those Western missionaries felt the disgrace of disunity in their efforts; the divided churches of Europe and North America were a hindrance to the faith and mission of the church. The result was a series of missionary assemblies that climaxed at a strategy conference of official representatives of the missionary societies of the main Protestant churches in the West held at Edinburgh in 1910. With some 1,200 delegates gathered for the purpose of research and dialogue about missionary work and problems, Edinburgh 1910 was transformed into an assembly where "the theme of Christian unity is running through the whole conference like a subterranean stream" (Morrison). Two of the principal architects were John R. Mott and Joseph H. Oldham, an Anglican layman from Scotland whose leadership in the ecumenical movement for the coming decades would be unparalleled. Edinburgh was prophetic about the ecumenical future. It was also quite Western in its perspectives and spoke out of a pre–World War I optimism bubbling with the Enlightenment's faith in human progress. Even with these limitations the conference gave organizational focus to the ecumenical movement.

In 1921 at Lake Mohonk, New York, the missionary vocation created the International Missionary Council (IMC), through which the missionary societies and the new Christian councils in Asia, Africa, and Latin America were brought into continuous consultation and planning. The IMC's history has been punctuated with a series of international conferences that reflect the emerging agenda of world mission. The first conference at Jerusalem (1928) was sensitive, on the one hand, to the threat of secularism and, on the other hand, to the importance given in mission to the spiritual values of other world religions. William Temple drafted the conference's message, entitled "Our Message Is Jesus Christ." Racism, industrialization, and rural development were mission issues identified, but Christians at Jerusalem differed on the relation of these issues to the message of the Kingdom of God. The 1938 conference at Tambaram, near Madras, India, considered the centrality of the church and the authority of faith. The relation of the Christian faith to other world religions was the heart of a major theological debate between Dutch missionary theologian Hendrik Kraemer and William Ernest Hocking of Harvard University. The witness to Christian unity was seen as a sign of hope.

At Whitby, Canada (1947), the missionary enterprise began to replace the colonialism of the past with a partnership between the sending and receiving churches; the indigenization of the church in the places where people live and witness was thought essential for mission. Willingen, Germany (1952), faced head-on the inevitable and inseparable relation between mission and Christian unity, although the centrality of the church as the agent of mission was called into question. The understanding of mission as a sign of the presence of God in the secular world was strongly affirmed. The conference at Accra, Ghana (1957), struggled with the "lost direction" of mission prompted by a changing world and affirmed the integration of the IMC into the

World Council of Churches (WCC) in order that mission and unity could be effectively pursued together. At the New Delhi Assembly in 1961 the IMC became the Commission on World Mission and Evangelism (CWME) of the WCC. The pattern of international conferences continued at Mexico City (1963), emphasizing that all six continents need to receive the Good News and come to terms with its demands and promises; for the first time both Orthodox churches and Roman Catholic observers participated fully in a world missionary conference. At Bangkok, Thailand (1972–1973), under the theme "Salvation Today," the CWME affirmed the indissoluble relation between the individual and social expression of salvation. The Melbourne Conference (1980) on "Your Kingdom Come" confirmed a strategy of mission that accepted the particular gifts and initiatives from the churches of the oppressed and identified with the poor. Melbourne underlined that evangelism takes place in the midst of human struggles.

Before World War I there developed among many leaders a concern for cooperation in moral and ethical issues facing the church. The churches must, they confessed, witness to the Gospel in all realms of life, acting together "as if they were one body, in one visible fellowship." This movement, called Life and Work, was largely the vision of Nathan Söderblom, the Lutheran archbishop of the Church of Sweden, who believed a truly united church would enable Christians to confront the urgent problems of practical social Christianity. Life and Work received the benefit of work by various agencies dealing with social and ethical matters. The Federal Council of Churches in America was formed in 1908 by twenty-nine churches with the goal "to express the fellowship and catholic unity of the Christian Church" and "to secure a larger combined influence for the churches of Christ in all matters affecting the moral and social condition of the people." Momentum came, also, from the heroic work of the World Alliance for Promoting International Friendship through the Churches, formed at Constance, Germany, in 1914, largely at the initiative of the American Peace Union. Its conviction was that if Christians of all communions in all parts of the world would unite in promoting international goodwill and peace a great step could be taken to rid the world of war. The third Life and Work initiative came

at Birmingham, England, in 1924 when the British churches held a Conference on Christian Politics, Economics, and Citizenship (COPEC). The conference, chaired by William Temple, then the Anglican bishop of Manchester, brought clear formulation of the social significance of the Gospel.

All these efforts led in 1925 to the Universal Christian Conference on Life and Work at Stockholm, chaired by the persuasive and inspiring Söderblom. J. H. Oldham guided the conference from its early planning to the end. A major American leader was William Adams Brown, professor at Union Theological Seminary, who gave leadership in countless ecumenical ventures. Under the rubric "doctrine divides, service unites," Stockholm dealt ecumenically with international relations as well as social, economic, and industrial life. Afterward a continuation committee was appointed that five years later became the permanent agency known as the Universal Christian Council for Life and Work.

The second Life and Work Conference, the World Conference on Church, Community and State, was held at Oxford, England, in 1937. Alarming clouds of war were on the horizon in the 1930s when National Socialism came to power in Hitler's Germany. The issue of the times was the relation of the church to the state; namely, the question of the church's allegiance to any secular, political authority. Oxford defined, said Oldham, "the life and death struggle between the Christian faith and the secular and pagan tendencies of our time." Probing the meaning of ecclesiology, Oxford erupted in defense of the integrity of the church: "Let the Church be the Church!" Life and Work clearly saw the task of the church to be in acts of Christian witness in the social, political, and international arenas of God's world. The conference announced the recovery of the prophetic function of the Church.

Later, within the World Council of Churches, the witness of Life and Work was dramatically made in two world conferences. In 1966 the Church and Society unit, Life and Work's successor, held a landmark ecumenical conference at Geneva under the theme "Christians in the Technical and Social Revolutions of Our Time." It clearly identified the new Christian sensitivity to the harmful effects of the phenomenal achievements in science and technology; e.g., world economic development and the nonviolent approaches to social justice. In 1979 a World Conference on Faith, Science, and the Future brought scientists, technologists, and theologians together on the campus of the Massachusetts Institute of Technology (Cambridge, Massachusetts). This conference confronted four critical ecumenical concerns: the ethical issues arising from high technological development, such as the biological manipulation of life; justice in the sharing of technology between developed and developing countries; Christian social responsibility in the use of science and technology in terms of their impact on the earth's resources, the environment, and the well-being of peoples; and the encounter between faith and the contemporary technological world view. These two conferences signaled a new era for ecumenism in which the problems of science and technology are at the forefront.

An American Episcopal bishop who attended Edinburgh 1910, Charles H. Brent, returned home convinced that "a similar conference on matters of Faith and Order might be productive of good." Under Brent's influence, the General Convention of the Protestant Episcopal Church meeting at Cincinnati in October 1910 adopted a resolution calling for a world conference "to be participated in by representatives of all Christian bodies throughout the world which accept our Lord Jesus Christ as God and Saviour, for the consideration of questions pertaining to the Faith and Order of the Church of Christ." In one of those coordinated ironies of church history, a similar action was taken by the General Convention of the Disciples of Christ at Topeka, Kansas, on the same day (19 October 1910) as the Episcopal action. Peter Ainslie III, minister of the Disciples' congregation in Baltimore and an unwearied worker for the union of the church, led the Disciples to call for a world conference "with other bodies relative to Christian union." A seconding action came a few days later at the National Council of Congregational Churches gathered at Boston. While the histories of Faith and Order have given primary attention to Bishop Brent, it is important to acknowledge that the origins of this movement toward catholicity were rooted in two diverse American churches, Episcopal and Disciples.

The infant theological movement had several decades of preparation. Beyond Brent and Ainslie, Faith and Order was guided by an Episcopal lawyer from Boston, Robert H. Gardiner, whose administrative skills and dedication communicated the goals of the new movement. Deputations were sent to England to visit Anglican and Free churches, to Constantinople and Athens to invite Eastern Orthodox participation, and to Rome to converse with Vatican leaders. In a dramatic moment of ecumenical history the first World Conference on Faith and Order was held in 1927 at Lausanne, Switzerland. Representatives from 108 churches, including full participation by the Eastern Orthodox, discussed the Gospel, the nature of the church, a common confession of faith, the ministry, and sacraments. The greatest achievement of Lausanne was a statement on "The Call to Unity," unanimously approved, that sounded the call to unity and alerted the churches to its significance. The purpose of Lausanne was to draw the divided churches "from isolation into conference." The methodology came to be called *comparative ecclesiology,* whereby each church would state its teachings in comparison to other traditions, thus identifying the areas of agreement and disagreement.

Ten years after Lausanne the second Faith and Order Conference was held at Edinburgh, Scotland, in 1937. Bishop Brent's successor as chairman was Archbishop of Canterbury William Temple, whose gifts of conciliation, consensus drafting, and humor greatly influenced the ecumenical movement. The Edinburgh conference marked a definite advance over those of the preceding decade. The theological homework done produced richer reports and deeper consensus; for example, the reports on the doctrine of grace as well as the ministry and the sacraments. The most memorable was an affirmation that told of the firm commitments now present in Faith and Order:

> We are one in faith in our Lord Jesus Christ. . . . This unity does not consist in the agreement of our minds or the consent of our wills. It is founded in Jesus Christ Himself. . . . We humbly acknowledge that our divisions are contrary to the will of Christ, and we pray God in His mercy to shorten the days of our separation and to guide us by His Spirit into fullness of unity.

Later this movement also continued its witness within the World Council of Churches. The third World Conference on Faith and Order at Lund, Sweden, in 1952 was largely concerned with clarifying the differences about the church, worship, and intercommunion, and with comparing the ecclesial traditions out of which these differences had come. Special attention was also given to the so-called non-theological (i.e., social, political, cultural, and personal) factors that divide the churches. Very powerful was a statement from the younger churches in those countries where united churches had been achieved or were in progress. They appealed to the Westerners "to encourage similar schemes of union among yourselves and your kindred overseas." At Lund a dramatic shift in the methodology toward unity took place. The delegates confessed that it is not effective enough to bring visible unity for the churches to explain and compare themselves to each other; they must "penetrate behind . . . divisions to a deeper and richer understanding of the mystery of the God-given union of Christ and his Church."

The fourth World Conference at Montreal in 1963 devoted attention to the themes of Christ and the church, tradition and traditions, worship, and institutionalism, but its historic breakthrough centered around the matter of the authority of the church. Montreal affirmed Scripture and tradition ("the Gospel itself, transmitted from generation to generation in and by the Church, Christ himself present in the life of the Church") as authoritative. This awareness of a common tradition made it possible to begin to bridge the gulf between Catholic and Protestant understandings of the church and its unity, which have divided Christians for centuries.

Proposals for a new world organization of the churches came sporadically before the twentieth century from such persons as William Carey, Jonathan Edwards, and Alexander Campbell. Two later proposals, inspired by the prospects of a League of Nations, came first from the ecumenical patriarchate of Constantinople and from Archbishop Nathan Söderblom, and gave momentum to the concept. In 1919 the Holy Synod of the Church of Constantinople felt that "a League of Churches" composed of the different Christian traditions could give "the impetus for the union of all churches in Christian love." An encyclical of 1920 drafted by Germanos Strenopoulos, Metropolitan of Selenkia and dean of the Orthodox Theological School of Halki, Turkey, made the proposal official. Unfortunately, in the midst of all the problems after World War I, the proposal did not receive wide circulation.

Almost at the same time Nathan Söderblom called for "an Ecumenical Council of Churches" that could manifest the universal character of the church, "representing Christendom in a spiritual way." During the summer of 1920 the continuation committees of the IMC, Life and Work, and Faith and Order met in and near Geneva; among other agenda items they heard proposals for a world organization of the churches. Favorable response in these meetings set in motion a series of dynamics. A meeting of representatives of the primary ecumenical bodies took place in 1933 at the initiative of William Adams Brown. In 1937 world conferences of Life and Work at Oxford and Faith and Order at Edinburgh voted to accept the idea of a world council. In 1938 at Utrecht, Holland, a provisional committee of "the World Council of Churches in Process of Formation" was established. (The name World Council of Churches [WCC] was proposed by American ecumenist Samuel McCrea Cavert.) William Temple was the unanimous choice to be chairperson, a position he held until his sudden death six years later. W. A. Visser't Hooft, formerly the general secretary of the WSCF, was elected to be the WCC's first general secretary and, until his retirement in 1966, offered the churches a model of intellectual excellence and diplomatic genius. Henry Smith Leiper, an American Congregationalist, served as the executive secretary of the New York office.

Hardly had the constitutional ink dried and the provisional committee begun its work when World War II began. The World Council of Churches' formation in the midst of wartime was to shape it in a definitive way. First, since Christians who gave birth to the dream were separated by the suspicions and rages of war, this fragile fellowship of the official ecumenical movement was severely tested. The consequence was a deeper spiritual awareness and caring among the churches, a fact that gave a spirituality to the emerging WCC. Second, from its beginning the WCC was engaged in practical tasks, such as helping with prisoners of war and refugees uprooted from their homes and countries, and the postwar reconstruction of churches in Europe. The WCC's Commission on Inter-church Aid, Refugee and World Service remains one of its most significant programs, constituting nearly 85 percent of its budget. Third, the rationale of the new ecumenical body was tested under fire and validated before the eyes of the churches and the world. By the end of the war the churches had an existential conviction about the sacred tasks of the WCC.

The first assembly, originally planned for 1941, met at Amsterdam in 1948. One hundred and forty-seven Protestant and Orthodox churches representing all major Christian traditions except the Roman Catholic Church constituted the WCC, under the theme, obviously related to the war and the postwar situation, "Man's Disorder and God's Design." Theologians of the stature of Karl Barth (Switzerland), Reinhold Niebuhr (United States), and Josef Hromadka (Czechoslovakia), and politicians such as John Foster Dulles (United States), led the debate and dialogue. Leaders of a new generation were chosen as officers of the central committee; namely, the moderator George K. A. Bell, Anglican bishop of Chichester, and vice-moderator Franklin Clark Fry, president of the Lutheran Church in America. Considerable time was given to explanations about the nature of the WCC. Critical was the original basis, adapted slightly from the World YMCA: "The World Council of Churches is a fellowship of Churches which accept our Lord Jesus as God and Saviour." At the third assembly at New Delhi (1961) the basis was expanded to its present form:

> The World Council of Churches is a fellowship of churches which confess the Lord Jesus Christ as God and Saviour according to the Scriptures, and, therefore, seek to fulfill their common calling to the glory of the one God, Father, Son, and Holy Spirit.

The fellowship is that of churches, not individuals or councils; the content of that fellowship is Christological and Trinitarian.

The nature of the WCC's authority was articulated in the letter of invitation sent by William Temple to the churches. The council has no constitutional authority whatsoever over its constituent churches. "Any authority that it may have will consist in the weight which it carries with the churches by its own wisdom." In short, the WCC has no authority to speak on behalf of

the churches and it is in no sense a super-church. After Amsterdam further reflection on the critical question of the WCC's nature and its relationship to the member churches required the central committee, meeting at Toronto (1950), to prepare a landmark statement on "The Church, The Churches and the World Council of Churches." The statement first indicated that the WCC does *not* seek to become a super-church, negotiate church unions, presuppose a specific doctrine of church unity, or imply that a church relativizes its own doctrines when it participates in the WCC. Such a provisional neutrality was essential in order for the divided churches to begin to experience truly this dynamic fellowship. Since Toronto, the matter of the ecclesiological significance of councils of churches continues to require further reflection.

As with the first, all the assemblies of the WCC have reflected upon Christological themes. The second assembly at Evanston, Illinois (1954), proclaimed "Jesus Christ, the Hope of the World" while struggling with the cold war. In the WCC's first assembly in an Asian context, the third assembly gathered at New Delhi, India (1961), under the theme "Jesus Christ, the Light of the World." New Delhi etched a special place in ecumenical history by ratifying a major statement that describes the future goal of the ecumenical movement as the visible unity of "all in each place"; voting into membership the Orthodox churches from the Eastern-bloc countries of the U.S.S.R., Bulgaria, Rumania, and Poland as well as two Pentecostal churches from Chile; and approving the integration of the IMC into the WCC. The theme of the fourth assembly at Uppsala, Sweden (1968), "Behold I Make All Things New," provided the context for a stark sensitivity to a changing world order marked by racism, student riots, the growing gap between the rich and the poor, and ambiguity toward the new scientific technology. The preacher at the opening service was to have been Martin Luther King, Jr., who was assassinated shortly before. He was replaced by D. T. Niles, the dynamic Methodist leader from Sri Lanka who had spoken as a youth at Amsterdam and in the intervening years had stretched the ecumenical movement's understanding of mission and unity.

At Nairobi, Kenya (1975), the fifth assembly experienced Africa and the situation of the Third World under the theme "Jesus Christ Frees and

Unites." Nairobi offered a new vision of the goal of Christian unity; namely, the one church that is envisioned as "a conciliar fellowship of local churches which are themselves truly united." Such a unity would address the divisions caused by racism, sexism, and the political struggles for liberation. The sixth assembly at Vancouver, British Columbia (1983), confessing "Jesus Christ, the Life of the World," gave clues to visible unity in the historic theological convergence text on *Baptism, Eucharist and Ministry* and identified threats to peace and survival, justice and human dignity.

In 1986 the WCC represented an incredible diversity: 304 member churches from more than 100 countries, six continents, and the three geopolitical worlds, First, Second, and Third. Even its general secretaries reflected this diversity: Visser't Hooft (Holland, 1948–1966), Eugene Carson Blake (United States, 1966–1972), Philip Potter (Dominica, 1972–1984), and Emilio Castro (Uruguay, 1985–). This diversity is both the gift of grace and a source of struggle to the ecumenical movement. The shared life between the Western churches and the churches of the Third World is a sign of hope. The relationship between Protestants and Orthodox in the WCC means that for the first time each has a permanent forum for dialogue, consultation, and cooperation toward *koinonia* (deep fellowship) with one another.

Beyond the WCC, we should mention numerous councils or conferences of churches at national and regional levels, many of which are associated with it. In the United States there is the National Council of Churches in the U.S.A. (NCC), constituted at Cleveland, Ohio, in 1950, when twelve cooperative agencies (including the Federal Council of Churches) and twenty-nine churches (twenty-five Protestant and four Eastern Orthodox) formed a cooperative relation. The NCC's program includes evangelism, Christian education, translation of the Bible, overseas ministries, ministries of compassion and development through Church World Service, and international affairs; yet it receives media attention primarily for its public witness against racial and economic injustice and the lack of community between men and women. Only in 1959 did the council create a department on Faith and Order. Like any religious body, the NCC has gone through several structural revisions. The latest,

presenting a major commitment to the goal of visible unity, restated in 1982 the nature of the NCC as

> a community of Christian communions which in response to the gospel as revealed in the Scriptures, confess Jesus Christ, the incarnate Word of God, as Savior and Lord. These communions covenant with one another to manifest ever more fully the unity of the Church. Relying upon the transforming power of the Holy Spirit, the Council brings these communions into common mission, serving in all creation to the glory of God.

An alternative ecumenical organization in the United States is the National Association of Evangelicals. Founded in 1942, the NAE is a body for common witness and action among congregations and associations of a theologically conservative perspective. The NAE's basis is a seven-point statement requiring agreement on the Bible as the only infallible, authoritative word of God; the Trinity, the virgin birth of Jesus Christ, substitutionary atonement, and "spiritual" unity of all believers in Christ. The NAE maintains its original sharply critical position toward mainline ecumenical bodies and attitudes.

From a global perspective, other national and regional bodies have given significant leadership. Now there are nearly ninety national and seven regional councils, including the British Council of Churches (1942), the National Christian Council of India (1947), the Christian Conference of Asia (1959), the All-Africa Conference of Churches (1963), the Pacific Conference of Churches (1966), the Caribbean Conference of Churches (1973), the Middle East Council of Churches (1974), and the Latin American Council of Churches (1982), all of which have similar aims and work in partnership with the WCC. Since Vatican II, the Roman Catholic Church through its National Conferences of Bishops has become a full member in more than twenty-five national and regional councils (eleven in the United States). The increasing importance of these councils is a part of the new reality of the ecumenical movement.

A unique chapter in the quest for visible unity is the formation of united churches in different parts of the world. Indeed, in reviewing the plans of union Anglican Bishop Stephen Neill declared, "The forty years between 1910 and 1950 have achieved more toward the overcoming of differences between Christians, and towards the recovery of the lost unity of the Body of Christ, than any period of equal length in the previous history of the Christian Churches." A united church exists when two or more churches, usually from different Christian traditions, become visibly, organically one; their life is marked by common theological affirmations of the apostolic faith, mutual sharing in the sacraments and ministry, and common decision-making about mission. Church union is inevitably a long and arduous process, and is expressed in a great variety of forms and places. It is conditioned by the issues and context of a particular country or culture. In recent years negotiations for union have been hampered by divisiveness over such matters as racism, sexism, tribalism, and institutional loyalties.

The earliest and most frequent church unions during the first half of the twentieth century were among churches of the same family tradition. In the United States, for example, a large proportion of Presbyterians, Methodists, and Lutherans, so fragmented internally by the forces of the post-Reformation era, came together in worship and witness in united churches. The more dramatic attempts at union, however, have been those that bring together churches from different family traditions. It is no secret that most of these trans-denominational unions took place in countries and continents outside the West. At the Willingen Conference (1952) of the International Missionary Council the delegates from the younger churches said: "We believe that unity of the churches is an essential condition of effective witness and advance. . . . While unity may be desirable in the lands of the older churches, it is imperative in those of the younger churches."

In Asia and Africa the churches are more sensitive to the missionary situation that Christianity confronts and less inclined to accept the divided practices and traditions of Europe and North America. In India, the South India United Church was formed in 1908 by Congregational, Presbyterian, and Reformed churches. In 1927 the Church of Christ in China embraced Presbyterians, Congregationalists, Methodists, Disciples of Christ, Baptists, and others. The Kyodan, the Church of Christ in Japan, was constituted in 1941, primarily under government pressure, but

since World War II it has held together fifteen churches representing half of all Protestants in that country. United churches of similar constituencies appeared in the Philippines and Thailand. The first multilateral union in North America came in 1925, when Presbyterians, Congregationalists, and Methodists became the United Church of Canada.

The rapidity of these developments can be seen in the fact that between 1948 (when the WCC was founded) and 1965, twenty-three united churches were formed; in the brief period 1965 to 1970 united churches were born in Jamaica, Ecuador, Zambia, Zaire, North India, Pakistan, Madagascar, Papua–New Guinea and the Solomon Islands, and Belgium. Later unions have been constituted in Australia, England, and the United States. Several united churches have achieved distinct historic reconciliation. The widely heralded Church of South India, which in 1947 brought together Anglicans, Methodists, Presbyterians, and Congregationalists, is unique because for the first time in history a church reconciled episcopal and non-episcopal ministries. With less fanfare and on a smaller scale, the United Reformed Church of the United Kingdom reconciled believer's and infant baptism into one ecclesial fellowship.

Church union has had a distinctive although largely unsuccessful witness in the United States, where the pragmatic approach of councils of churches has been the main ecumenical mold. In the first half of this century three plans were proposed. Between 1918 and 1920 representatives from nineteen communions met regularly in Philadelphia under the aegis of the Conference on Organic Union. The vision of "the United Churches of Christ in America" was unfulfilled when the Presbyterians, who initiated the plan, withdrew. From the late 1930s to the early 1940s Methodist evangelist E. Stanley Jones unveiled his plan for "union with a federal structure" modeled after the federal-state structure of the United States. The charismatic preaching and travels of Dr. Jones gave his proposal great attention especially among lay people, but it was never officially claimed by the churches. From 1946 to 1957 the Conference on Church Union gathered nine churches for serious dialogue toward "an organic union, a fellowship and organization of the churches which will enable it to act as one body under Jesus Christ."

A Plan for a United Church in the United States (1951), whose primary drafter was Charles Clayton Morrison, was studied but never voted upon by the churches. One positive contribution of the Greenwich Plan (so called because the delegates usually met in Greenwich, Connecticut) was that it served as the context for the uniting of the Congregational Christian and the Evangelical and Reformed Churches in 1957 to become the United Church of Christ.

The most historic and dramatic American union effort is the Consultation on Church Union (COCU). Prompted by a sermon by Eugene Carson Blake, the stated clerk of the United Presbyterian Church in the United States, at Grace Cathedral (Episcopal) at San Francisco in 1960, COCU involves nine churches: African Methodist Episcopal, African Methodist Episcopal Zion, Christian Methodist Episcopal, Christian Church (Disciples of Christ), Episcopal, National Council of Community Churches, Presbyterian (U.S.A.), United Church of Christ, and United Methodist Church. By 1984, at its sixteenth plenary at Baltimore, COCU had reached unparalleled theological consensus and proposed a step toward unity called "covenanting." This venture is offering significant prospects for a united church in the United States involving predominantly black and predominantly white communions that reflect a broad ecclesiological spectrum. In separate actions, other unions mark progress in the ecumenical movement: Unitarian-Universalist (1961), United Methodist Church (1968), Presbyterian Church, U.S.A. (1986), and the Evangelical Lutheran Church in America (1988).

Church union negotiations have also experienced failures. In the decade 1975 to 1985 conversations encountered major obstacles in Canada, New Zealand, Ghana, Sri Lanka, Great Britain, and South Africa. Many are due to the withdrawal of Anglicans who now look toward the Roman Catholic Church as their normative partner. Other reasons are related to racial, cultural, and political differences that divide the local societies. Despite these difficulties the church union movement constitutes one of the pivotal frontiers in the modern ecumenical movement.

A recent phenomenon in the ecumenical movement is the unfolding of bilateral dialogues; that is, official theological conversations toward unity between two families of Christian world communions. Held on national and international levels, the bilaterals are particularly concerned about consensus on doctrinal matters and its prospect of achieving visible unity. While they existed before, bilateral dialogues intensified after the Second Vatican Council (1962–1965). Although there are a variety of partners and goals, the majority of present dialogues involve the Roman Catholic Church as one of the two partners with different traditions—Protestant, Anglican, Orthodox, and Old Catholic.

In Europe a bilateral dialogue between the World Alliance of Reformed Churches and the Lutheran World Federation (1964–1973), meeting in Leuenberg, Switzerland, reached a theological consensus on the faith, sacraments, and ministry that led them to declare that their divisions "had been rendered obsolete by theological developments and the remaining differences in ecclesiastical doctrines, order, and style of life possess no church-separating significance." In 1982 in the United States, Lutherans and Episcopalians entered into a covenant relation leading toward intercommunion and shared ministry.

Between Roman Catholics and other churches a wide variety of bilaterals exists. In the United States official dialogues are being pursued, for example, between the Episcopal and Roman Catholic churches (begun in 1965), the Lutheran–RC (1965), the Presbyterian–RC (1965), the Disciples of Christ–RC (1965), and the Southern Baptist Convention–RC. At the international level dialogues with the Roman Catholic Church include Orthodox and Anglicans (1967), Lutherans (1965), Methodists (1967), Reformed (1970), Pentecostals (1970), and Disciples of Christ (1977). Already in a brief time the theologians of these churches are reaching dramatic agreement about the nature of the church, authority, Baptism, Eucharist, and ministry. The test of the bilaterals as instruments of visible unity will come, however, not merely from the reaching of theological consensus. Their contribution to visible unity will be judged by the degree to which these agreements are "received"; that is, claimed as teaching documents of a tradition and translated into practice in the living fellowship of the partner churches.

In the early years of the modern ecumenical movement the Roman Catholic Church reacted with suspicion and harsh critique. Twice (1914 and 1919) Pope Benedict XV refused invitations to join the Faith and Order movement. The Holy Office gave instructions that precluded Roman Catholic participation in the conferences of Life and Work. In 1928 Pope Pius XI reiterated the negative assessment of the ecumenical movement in his encyclical *Mortalium Animos,* in which he said unity must be based on the acceptance of Christ's entire revelation and a willingness to submit to the magisterium and the pastoral office of the pope as the Vicar of Christ. At the Amsterdam assembly of the WCC the Holy Office warned Roman Catholics not to attend. One year later (1949) the encyclical *Ecclesia Catholica* warned Catholics of the dangers of irenicism and indifference, but allowed mixed conferences only if they promised the possibility of the return of the separated brethren to the Roman Catholic Church. Despite this spirit of rejection, certain Roman Catholic theologians—among them, Max Pribilla, S.J., Yves Congar, O.P., Max Josef Metzger, Bernard Leeming, S.J., and Gustave Weigel, S.J.—began to interpret the ecumenical movement and the Roman Catholic Church to each other. Also, while official Roman Catholic intransigence was disappointing, it was received by the officials of the ecumenical movement as a challenge to be resolved.

The dramatic turning point came in 1959, when Pope John XXIII called for the Second Vatican Council, thus initiating an ecumenical spirit and policy in Rome. He also created a Secretariat for Promoting Christian Unity, under the leadership of Cardinal Augustus Bea and Bishop (later Cardinal) Jan Willebrands, that gave official status to ecumenism in the Vatican's policies. Protestant and Orthodox churches were invited as observers to the forthcoming council. In 1961 four Roman Catholic observers were sent to the New Delhi Assembly of the WCC, establishing the principle of official observers in the various assemblies and commissions (especially Faith and Order). Eventually a Joint Working Group was set up as a permanent commission for dialogue and joint action between the Roman Catholic Church and the World Council of Churches.

The substance of the Roman Catholic ecumenism is articulated in the documents of Vatican II. The *Dogmatic Constitution on the Church,* the *Declaration on Religious Freedom,* the *Constitution on the Sacred Liturgy,* and the *Pastoral Constitution on the Church in the Modern World* all articulate pro-

found ecumenical implications about the unity of all baptized Christians as well as the Roman Catholic Church's role in the *oikoumene.* The *Decree on Ecumenism* (promulgated on 21 November 1964) is the charter and mandate for Roman Catholic involvement in the ecumenical movement. It claims Roman Catholic responsibility for the schisms throughout the centuries; acknowledges the unity that already exists between Orthodox, Protestants, and Roman Catholics; recognizes other churches as ecclesial communities; and calls upon all Catholics to work for ecumenism and the renewal of the church, saying, "There can be no ecumenism worthy of the name without a change of heart." As we have seen earlier, this ecumenical vocation led to an expansive set of relations through bilateral dialogues and councils of churches. Full unity has a long way to go; hesitancies and frustrations continue to mark ecumenical relations, but now the frustrations are shared within the one ecumenical movement.

The ecumenical movement has always had a concern for the relation between Christianity and other living faiths and ideologies. In the last decades of the twentieth century this interfaith dialogue has become more genuine and substantial. Protestants, Orthodox, and Roman Catholics have been brought into communication and dialogue with their Jewish, Buddhist, Hindu, and Muslim neighbors. The Nairobi (1975) and Vancouver (1983) assemblies of the World Council of Churches gave evidence of this new era by their programs on "Seeking World Community —The Common Search of People of Various Faiths, Cultures, and Ideologies." Since World War II, the Christian-Marxist dialogue has brought church leaders together across the geopolitical walls that divide the people of the West and the East, and helped them analyze and evaluate the ideological systems and convictions that divide the human race. The interfaith dialogue does not replace ecumenism, the search for visible Christian unity, but it does accentuate the pluralistic world community that forms the context.

BIBLIOGRAPHY

Robert McAfee Brown, *The Ecumenical Revolution* (1967); William A. Brown, *Toward A United Church: Three Decades of*

Ecumenical Christianity (1946); Samuel M. Cavert, The American Churches in the Ecumenical Movement, 1900–1968 (1968) and Church Cooperation and Unity in America: A Historical Review (1970); Paul A. Crow, Jr., Christian Unity: Matrix for Mission (1982); Harold E. Fey, ed., A History of the Ecumenical Movement, 1948–1968, vol. 2 (1970); Austin Flannery, ed., Vatican Council II: The Conciliar and Post-Conciliar Documents (1975); Norman Goodall, The Ecumenical Movement (1961) and Ecumenical Progress, 1961–71 (1972); William Richey Hogg, Ecumenical Foundations (1952); Ernst Lange, And Yet It Moves: Dream and Reality of the Ecumenical Movement (1979).

John T. McNeill, Unitive Protestantism (1964); Harding Meyer and Lukas Vischer, eds., Growth in Agreement: Reports and Agreed Statements of Ecumenical Conversations on a World Level (1984); Charles Clayton Morrison, The Unfinished Reformation (1953); Constantin G. Patelos, ed., The Orthodox Church in the Ecumenical Movement, 1902–1975 (1978); Ruth Rouse and Stephen C. Neill, eds., A History of the Ecumenical Movement, 1517–1948 (1954); Barry Till, The Churches Search for Unity (1972); Thomas F. Torrance, "Ecumenism: A Reappraisal of Its Significance, Past, Present and Future" in his Theology in Reconciliation (1975); Henry P. Van Dusen, One Great Ground of Hope: Christian Mission and Christian Unity (1961); Maurice Villain, Unity: A History and Some Reflections (1963); W. A. Visser't Hooft, Memoirs (1973); Hans-Ruedi Weber, Asia and the Ecumenical Movement, 1895–1961 (1966).

[See also CATHOLICISM SINCE WORLD WAR I; LIBERALISM; and SOCIAL CHRISTIANITY.]

Part VI
AMERICAN RELIGIOUS THOUGHT AND LITERATURE

AMERICAN CATHOLIC THOUGHT

Robert Emmett Curran

AN offshoot of English Catholicism, the American Catholic community developed its intellectual life during the colonial and early national periods very much within the former's cultural orbit. Given the alien status of that community during the colonial period it is not surprising that it produced little intellectual coin in the public realm. For nearly 150 years no Catholic in British America published a book or significant writing. In one area only, that regarding religious liberty, did Catholics make an intellectual contribution.

Maryland, the center of the Catholic community in British America, was the first colony to practice religious toleration. Notably unsuccessful in attracting the Catholic gentry to his colony, despite the neofeudal privileges he offered, and sensitive to the very large Protestant majority among the first settlers, Cecilius Calvert, the second Lord Baltimore, pursued a policy of toleration as a prudent entrepreneur's way of protecting his investment in the New World. As an early pamphlet ("Objections Answered Touching Mariland," 1649) defending the religious toleration of the colony put it, to force allegiance to a particular religion was to undermine the state itself since those who feign religious beliefs for political or social ends cannot in the end be trusted.

But more than prudence seems to have fostered liberty in Maryland. As the first assembly in 1639 made clear, there was to be no established religion in Maryland. For almost a century before the *Ark* and the *Dove* left Cowes for Maryland, English Catholics had been dissidents. They could not remember the time when Catholicism was the established religion of the realm. They had long since known a de facto separation of church and state. For Catholics in England and Maryland, practice would precede theory. During the 1639 assembly the Catholic-dominated legislature declared that "the inhabitants of this Province shall have all their rights and liberties according to the great charter of England." Lord Baltimore in his code had restricted such rights, including religious liberty, to Christians. This act in effect extended them to all, regardless of belief. It indeed went further than the more renowned act of 1649, which was drawn up under Puritan pressure and restricted religious freedom to those who professed the Trinity.

When Coode's Rebellion drove the Calverts from power in 1689 and penal laws were subsequently imposed on Maryland's Catholics, the latter were forced to reflect on the meaning of the original experiment in religious freedom, including its theoretical implications. In 1720 a Maryland Jesuit, Peter Attwood, wrote a long treatise entitled *Liberty and Property; or, The Beauty of Maryland Displayed in a Brief and Candid Search into Her Charter, Fundamental Laws & Constitution.* To Attwood "the Law of Liberty of Conscience . . . [was] the chief and fundamental part of" the Maryland constitution. He contended that this liberty had been religiously observed for the first sixty years of the settlement and that it had been esteemed by the inhabitants "as their birth-Right." A person's religion, according to Attwood, "was neither a help nor a hindrance and nothing came under a consideration but his integrity, parts and Capacity." Attwood argued that religious freedom was the fundamental right upon which rested the enjoyment of all other rights and privileges, including the right to property. He underscored the intrinsic connection between liberty and property that was a prominent feature of the revolutionary ideology of the next generation of Americans.

Catholics played a minor but significant role in the constitutional debate that led to revolution, independence, and the formation of the federal government. Most prominent was Charles Carroll of Carrollton, whose controversy with fellow Marylander Daniel Dulany was his major contribution to the evolution of the argument for self-government. Two other Maryland Catholics, Thomas Attwood Digges and Charles Wharton, aided the revolutionary cause as propagandists, publishing a political novel and patriotic poetry respectively.

Carroll, Digges, and Wharton had been educated in Europe, in schools that English Catholics had established in the Low Countries. There they had been exposed to currents of the Enlightenment mediated by French Catholic intellectuals in the eighteenth century. This enlightened Catholicism stressed the reasonable person, the intelligibility of Christianity, the continuity between nature and grace, and the communal nature of the church. No Maryland Catholic was more influenced by this moderate form of the Enlightenment than John Carroll, Charles Carroll's schoolmate at St. Omer's and his distant cousin. John Carroll, like Wharton, had joined the Society of Jesus in Europe. With the suppression of the order in 1773, he returned to America, where he wholeheartedly supported the Revolution and championed as a model for the world the civil and religious liberties that followed. In 1789 his fellow clergy elected him bishop of the newly created see of Baltimore, the first American Catholic prelate.

As an overburdened bishop whose diocese stretched from Vermont to Louisiana, Carroll had little time for reflection. Still his correspondence and pastoral letters reveal a distinct vision of an American Catholicism for a republic born in the noontime of the Enlightenment. As he reflected in his most widely read publication, *An Address to the Roman Catholics of the United States of America by a Catholic Clergyman* (1784), ". . . the ministers of religion should always remember, that it is their duty as well to enlighten the understanding, as improve morals of mankind." Drawing heavily upon the ideas of English Catholics such as Joseph Berington and John Fletcher, Carroll stressed the complementarity of Scrip-

ture and tradition, both emanating from the apostles and their successors. The church, for Carroll, was the community of those who believe in Christ. His ecclesiology distinguished carefully between those who were members of the church (believers) and those in communion with her (professing Catholics). The Holy Spirit dwelled in all members but infallibility was given only to the community as such, represented by the pope in union with his fellow bishops. The Spirit thus enhanced the natural dignity of the individual and ensured institutional fidelity to revelation.

In the tradition of his Maryland ancestors, Carroll vigorously championed religious liberty as the prerequisite for the enlightened inquiry and discussion that were the best hope for Christian reunification. In the denominational competition to represent Christianity, Carroll saw the vital necessity for the use of the vernacular in the church's liturgy. Conversely he saw two great threats to the church in America: the undue extension of the Holy See's jurisdiction and trusteeism, and the claim of lay Catholics to exercise authority in the churches in which they served as trustees, including the right to control the finances as well as the appointment and removal of pastors.

Carroll wholeheartedly supported the separation of church and state in America. To Carroll government was essentially secular in nature; the success of republican government rested on its preservation of the liberty and property of its citizens, not on its promotion of the religious doctrines of churches. As the church was to be independent of state control in America, so too, in Carroll's vision, was it to be relatively independent of control from Rome, subject to the spiritual authority of the pope only. He thought it particularly appropriate that bishops be elected by their peers in this country, not appointed by a papal congregation.

If Carroll feared the harmful overextensions of papal jurisdiction (the suppression of the Society of Jesus was a favorite example for him), he also was concerned about the possibility in a republican church of disunion with Rome. The cultural distance of America from Rome, he once remarked, was much greater than that counted by geographers. Thus the importance of uniformity in discipline within the American church became a special concern of Carroll's in his later years as trusteeism asserted itself in New York, Philadelphia, and other cities in his diocese. He saw in the claims of trustees an "ecclesiastical democracy" that, if successful, would reduce the church in America to atoms of independent pious societies. Given the traditional polity of Roman Catholicism in which bishops exercised not only spiritual but temporal authority over local congregations, such a concern was natural.

Education was crucial to Carroll's vision of a republican church. Regretting his own "cramped" education at Liège, Carroll labored to found educational institutions that would "widen the circle of knowledge" as well as promote religion and build character. Georgetown, Georgetown Visitation Academy, Mount St. Mary's College, and St. Joseph's College were the results of his efforts.

This Enlightenment Catholicism was promulgated in the late eighteenth and early nineteenth centuries through manuals, catechisms, and apologetic works of American and European Catholics. Fletcher's *Reflections on the Spirit of Religious Controversy* (1804) and Jacques Bénigne Bossuet's *Exposition of the Doctrine of the Catholic Church in Matters of Controversy* (1685, 1808) were two influential works by foreign authors. A work by former Jesuits, the *Pious Guide to Prayer and Devotion* (1792), and Roger Baxter's *The Most Important Tenets of the Roman Catholic Church Fairly Explained* (1820), were early products of native or immigrant American Catholics.

If American Catholic intellectual life, such as it was, centered about the clergy, the French émigrés, as a body, were the most learned. Although most of the French bishops and priests accommodated themselves remarkably well to America, it was an Irish immigrant bishop, John England, who continued Carroll's attempt to adapt Catholicism to a republican society. A child of the Enlightenment, like Carroll, England in his prolific writings labored to demonstrate to Americans the reasonableness of Catholicism. Man, England taught, had the responsibility to believe and act according to the light of his reason, not only in the natural order but in that area of knowing which the rational creature could not discover without revelation. The test for revelation, like the truths of natural religion, was its authority, or compelling power to convince the inquiring person of its authenticity. Such revelation took place in history, leaving evidence that

could be scrutinized by inquirers according to general laws.

Miracles, prophecies, and other evidence that could be historically verified demonstrated the authority of the church in teaching and judging. Central to this process were the miracles and prophecies of Jesus and the apostolic age but these confirming phenomena could be found in the present age as well. The continuation of miracles and prophecies in enlightened times was but proof of the superiority of Catholicism's claim to the mantle of Christianity. Thus England studied for six years a miraculous cure that occurred in Washington in 1824. Ann Mattingly, the sister of the mayor of the city, was instantly healed of a breast tumor that over the course of seven years had brought her to death's door. Witnesses claimed that her health was restored at the very moment she received the eucharistic bread at the conclusion of a novena performed in conjunction with the European priest healer Prince Alexander Hohenlohe. Scores of persons were familiar with her history; a roomful of relatives and friends witnessed the event; hundreds visited her immediately following the cure. Because of the open character of the event and the availability of the evidence to public examination, England professed it a reasonable phenomenon that pointed to "the immediate and miraculous interference of the Creator himself" (Messmer, ed., 1908, vol. 6, p. 156).

In this understanding of revelation, faith for the individual becomes primarily an intellectual assent to doctrinal propositions that the magisterium (the teaching authority, primarily comprising the bishops in union with the people) of the church articulates as the authentic interpreter of God's action in history.

England's ecclesiology was very republican, the outgrowth of his Irish experience as a young clerical polemicist. He once wrote: "I profess in America what I professed in Ireland . . . I have not changed . . . a single principle, either political or religious, which I have cherished" (Carey, 1982, frontispiece). Voluntarism was a key to both political and ecclesiastical structures. The church itself in England's view was a contractual body whose members (pope, bishops, clergy, and laity) all had rights and limited power. He made his own diocese of Charleston a model of the local church as "constitutional communion" in which bishops, priests, and laity worked together within the framework of a basic body of law that they had commonly adopted.

The constitution that England drew up for his diocese was unique in the history of American Catholicism. It established vestries composed of elected laity and resident clergy for the governance of parishes and annual conventions of representatives from the clergy and laity (males) for the governance of the diocese itself. It reflected England's conviction that the church in America would flourish if its character was truly republican. As he once said in reference to the diocesan constitution, "by confirming the rights of all . . . [it] has insured the support of all" (Messmer, ed., 1908, vol. 6, p. 156).

Education was the key to self-governance for England. So in 1822 he established the first Catholic newspaper in the United States, the *United States Catholic Miscellany,* set up schools, and began a seminary to train an indigenous clergy. He was not looking for state support. England, like John Carroll, believed in a free church in a free society. He thought it healthy for the hierarchy to be dependent upon the laity, not the state, for its financial support. He was optimistic that if the laity's rights were respected, their financial support would follow.

England was sure that not only would such a republican structure allow the church to flourish, but it would deflate nativist charges that the church was a cancerous presence within American culture. England was walking a middle road between trusteeism, or local lay autonomy, and episcopal autocracy. But his fellow bishops found even his limited republicanism threatening. He did manage to persuade his peers to meet regularly, beginning in 1829, to act in concert about common issues (a tradition Carroll had begun with his fellow clergy in the 1780s). Such collegial action, England felt, was essential in promoting the republican character of the church across diocesan lines. The more the American hierarchy acted in common the less danger he thought there would be of episcopal autocracy within individual dioceses and the less reason Rome would have to intervene in American Catholic affairs. Despite England's hopes, the episcopal councils fueled nativist suspicions about Catholic power in America by increasing the authority of the bishops. Autocracy rather than republicanism became the organizing principle as ecclesiastical bosses like John Hughes increasingly dominated an immigrant church that put a premium on unity, discipline, and authority.

The collegial tradition that England revived in the United States did promote the intellectual life of the American Catholic community insofar as the councils encouraged the development of the Catholic press and related publishing ventures to defend Catholicism against the increasing hostility the church encountered in the antebellum period. Such apologetic and didactic goals in the long run worked against the flowering of an American Catholic literature. By the end of the conciliar period the American Catholic subculture was rather barren soil for writers. (The last council of bishops was held in 1884. The subsequent appointment in 1893 of a permanent apostolic delegate from the pope essentially changed the relationship of the national episcopacy to Rome and reduced its authority as a body.) Other intellectuals fared better until the turn of the century.

The most elementary needs of immigrants and the hostile climate retarded the intellectual life of the church in America in the nineteenth century. Native converts provided much of the strength in the intellectual community that survived the passing of the old Catholic minority. America's counterpart of the Oxford movement produced a remarkable group of converts from the Episcopal Church, including William Henry Anderson, Jedediah Huntington, James A. McMaster, Levi Silliman Ives, and Augustine Hewit. Although affected by this movement, the two most influential converts in shaping the intellectual life of the church, Orestes Brownson and Isaac Hecker, came through the way stations of evangelical Protestantism, radical social reform, and Transcendentalism.

Brownson at first glance seems a bull in the china shop of American ideas, now going on one polemical rampage, now on another, and all in the name of logic. But there was more consistency to his thought than appears on the surface of his intellectual pilgrimage. Long before his entry into the church in 1844 he was searching for something that would transcend the self, that would reconcile faith and reason by ascertaining "a solid ground for faith in the reality of the spiritual world" (Perry Miller, ed., *The Transcendentalists,* 1950, p. 243). As a Transcendentalist, he rejected the epistemological tyranny of empiricism (the theory that the source of all knowledge is sensory experience) and affirmed the universal possession of "spontaneous reason" or intuition by which everyone had the capacity to have a direct and immediate knowledge of God and spiritual truths. But he became disillusioned with the Transcendentalists' identification of God with nature. To "sink God in nature," he told William Henry Channing in 1842, is "to lose him entirely" because it meant eliminating providence from reality and reducing divinity to the maintenance of the cosmos.

> Nature, when there is no God seen behind it, to control it, to do with it as he will, in fact, that wills to overrule its seeming evil for real good, is a mere fate, an inexorable destiny, a dark, inscrutable, resistless necessity. It has no freedom, no justice.
>
> (*Works,* 1882–1887, vol. 4, p. 148)

God, to be sovereign, had to be free.

By 1844 Brownson had come to see that Transcendentalism was the ultimate consequence of the Protestant impulse that made the individual the measure of truth and goodness. To Brownson such a solipsistic philosophy was lethal to the human quest for community and fulfillment. For the very progress of the race, mankind needed an institution that could meet its social needs. It needed a church. Brownson was attracted to the corporate vision of Saint-Simon (Claude Henri de Rouvroy, Comte de Saint-Simon), the French social philosopher and reformer, in which a cooperatively producing society constituted a new Christianity for the industrial age.

The election of 1840, in which the Whigs out-Jacksoned the Jacksonians in their manipulation of political symbols (Tippecanoe and Tyler too), produced grave second thoughts in Brownson about the spontaneous reason of the masses and the likelihood of mankind redeeming itself. He began to appreciate the need for authority in government so it could govern wisely and justly. This political swing to the right hastened his movement toward religious conservatism. His search for religious certainty and social order ended in his conversion to Roman Catholicism.

He wrote in his autobiography, *The Convert:*

> It is necessary to show, not merely assert that the two orders [of faith and reason] are not mu-

tually antagonistic; that one and the same principle of life runs through them both; that they correspond one to the other, and really constitute but two parts of one comprehensive whole. . . . man was intended from the beginning to live simultaneously in two orders, the one natural and the other supernatural.
>
> (*Works,* vol. 5, pp. 174–175)

Brownson failed to find such a reconciliation in standard Catholic philosophy. Instead he had typically found his own way to the church. In this journey two European philosophers were particularly influential: Pierre Leroux and Vincenzo Gioberti.

Brownson attributed to Leroux a large role in revolutionizing his views from the eclectic romanticism of Victor Cousin (the nineteenth-century French philosopher who taught that truth is found in the four major forms of knowledge: idealism, materialism, skepticism, and mysticism) to a more realistic ontology. To live, Leroux taught, it is not enough to feel; one has to realize oneself in passing from the state of mere being to life. For everyone except God, this process requires an other, an object. The human person realizes himself in three possible ways: through the mediation of God, nature, and fellow humans. Thus life comes through communion. And only religion could build this social bond among persons. Brownson, unlike Leroux, saw in Christianity the perfect expression of religion as social bond. At its core was a social gospel. The individual was redeemed only through his participation in society. Christ's teaching proclaimed the ideal vision of humanity's unity. For Brownson, following Leroux, the concept of life through community consisted of three dimensions; continuity, progress, and solidarity. In the context of Christianity, this meant tradition, perfectibility, and unity.

Vincenzo Gioberti gave Brownson the key to his epistemology through his reversal of the dominant view of the post-Cartesian age—that method precedes principles. The knowing subject cannot establish principles through any reflective act. Contrary to Kant, who presupposed that the true objects of knowledge are dependent upon and formulated through mental constructs, Gioberti contended that principles themselves are constitutive of mind, known through intuition, not apperception. In these principles man encounters actual and transcendent being within which he knows himself as real. Thus even before experience the knower grasps real, objective being. The person in such an act intuits that God, existences, and the creative act are related to each other by a bond that is real and necessary. Such an epistemology allowed Brownson to escape the pantheism into which he felt his fellow Transcendentalists had fallen. It also gave him a firm ontological base for faith, since in this process all being is intelligible in itself. It is only from the human standpoint that some reality is supraintelligible. Thus revelation is needed to render this reality intelligible to the believer. For the believer, revelation is the understanding that faith seeks; it is reasonable, even if its reasonableness cannot be measured by any criteria outside of faith itself.

God, then, is immanent in human knowing, the light by which we see all existence. This immanent God enables us both to know and to love. But to commune directly with God, to share his divine life, is beyond the finite and sinful person. The only apt mediator to bridge the gap between finite and infinite, sinful and holy, is the God-man, Jesus. Without the historical Jesus there is no Christianity. Jesus is the quintessential "providential man" who exhibits to the world a higher order of spiritual and moral life than it could discover on its own. Through the possession of Jesus' Spirit in the shared life that the organic church embodies, men and women become capable of communicating it to others. Brownson had no sympathy for the ecclesiological views of Carroll and England because such semi-independent regional churches undercut the internal unity of the church, epitomized by papal infallibility.

"I sought the truth," Brownson noted in *The Convert,* "in order to know what I ought to do, and as the means of realizing some moral or practical end. I wanted it that I might use it" (*Works,* vol. 5, pp. 39–40). In 1840, as a member of the Workingmen's party, Brownson penned one of the most radical critiques of American society in the antebellum period, attributing the rapidly deteriorating position of workers to the capitalistic economy and predicting class warfare as the price of justice. In his Catholic period Brownson's views on government became more authoritarian and conservative under the influence of Joseph-Marie de Maistre, the French counterrevolutionary philosopher who found in tradition the supreme revelation of truth, but he did not waver in his view of capitalism. In 1857 he still found the great mass of workers "virtually slaves." Capitalists everywhere, he wrote in *The American Republic* in 1866, used their power over government in the worst possible way, to advance their own selfish interests. " 'Let government take care of the rich, [they say] and the rich will take care of the poor,' instead of the far safer maxim, 'Let government take care of the weak, the strong can take care of themselves.' "

Unlike most Catholic intellectuals, Brownson denounced slavery but opposed abolition as a threat to the Union and the Constitution. Once the war began he became an early advocate of immediate emancipation, now convinced that slavery was the greatest threat to the providential republic that preserved liberty through order. Like Lincoln and other abolitionists, he could see no other solution to the dilemma of a biracial society than the colonization of blacks. In the postwar period he became very pessimistic about the compatibility of democracy and Catholicism as his views became increasingly ultramontane, centralizing authority in the church, both in ecclesiastical government and doctrine, in Rome and the pope. His fear was no longer that Catholicism would fail to conquer America but that American ideals and values would conquer the faith of Catholics.

Isaac Hecker referred to the older Brownson as his "spiritual Parent." He had looked to Brownson to lead the crusade that would convince American Protestants that Catholicism was the religion most appropriate to a democratic people. But Brownson lacked the temperament and eventually the democratic convictions for such a role. The mystical Hecker paradoxically proved to be the pivotal figure in the efforts of liberal Catholics in both America and Europe to unite the church and the modern age.

The son of German immigrants, Hecker, like Brownson, was drawn to many of the most distinctive religious movements in the antebellum period: Methodism, Unitarianism, Mormonism, and Transcendentalism. He was also for a short time active in the Locofocos, the radical faction of the New York Democratic party. Each left its mark on his mind. The Methodist doctrines of providence, free will, and perfection; the Unitarian stress on the goodness of human nature; the

Mormon goal of a radical reordering of society; the Transcendentalist stress on divine immanence; the social and millennial Christianity of Locofocoism—all resonated with his experience of God.

As with Brownson, 1840 was a crucial year. For Hecker, however, the decisive event was internal, a religious awakening of his spirit that drove him to seek something that would satisfy the powerful stirrings he was experiencing. Brownson became a mentor; German romantics like Friedrich von Schelling and Jean Paul Richter legitimated his affective quest. Stays at the utopian communities Brook Farm and Fruitlands failed to provide the life of contemplation and social purpose he was seeking. Brownson advised that he had to choose between Catholicism and mysticism. Hecker, having already discovered Catholic mystics like Catherine of Siena, knew better. His entrance into the Roman Catholic community in 1844 (some two months before Brownson's) brought immediate peace but only further stimulated his search for the mission he was convinced God had planned for him.

The vision that gradually evolved within Hecker following his conversion grew out of his synthesis of the formative ideas that had brought him to seek baptism as a Catholic. Hecker appropriated the myth of America's millennial character but asserted that Catholicism, not Protestantism, was the spiritual dynamo that could effect such a special destiny. To Hecker there was an affinity between American culture and Catholicism that Protestantism could not match. Identifying Protestantism with Calvinism, Hecker contended that its denial of freedom, universal salvation, and goodness of human nature put it at permanent odds with the values and beliefs of a democratic people. Catholicism, on the other hand, with its positive doctrines of justification and grace, affirmed the basic convictions of the American character. Its natural law philosophy provided a secure foundation for American institutions that proclaimed natural rights. For its part, Catholicism was advancing in America because of the freedom and openness of American society, which gave full vent to intelligence and the spirit. What continued to hamper Catholicism was its failure to fully identify with the positive elements of that society, its refusal to be "entirely at home in it." Should that occur, Hecker was convinced, not only would America become Catholic but a higher civilization would be the result of the union. It would also make America a leaven for the transformation and renewal of the church and society throughout the world.

Whereas Carroll and England had labored to show that Catholicism was compatible with republicanism, Hecker gave a radically new meaning to the equation. He tended to read his own experience as a paradigmatic one for his generation. Few exceeded him in optimism. He was sure that countless persons, like himself, were searching under the pressure of the Spirit for the light and peace that Catholicism alone could give. His two books written in the 1850s, *Questions of the Soul* (1855) and *Aspirations of Nature* (1857), were attempts to begin the process of showing that Catholicism met the needs of both heart and head. The former work was an unprecedented form of Catholic apologetics inasmuch as it had a psychological starting point. The latter showed that reason as well as the affections would find satisfaction in embracing the church.

Hecker's Missionary Society of St. Paul the Apostle, established in 1858, was a corporate means to pursue the mission of converting America. The *Catholic World* (1865) and the Catholic Publication Society (1866) were further steps to carrying the message to Catholic and non-Catholics alike. But the mass conversions did not follow. Both the American Catholic community and the Holy See in the late nineteenth century were preoccupied with consolidation and survival rather than the incorporation of an alien, if not hostile, Western society, as Vatican I clearly showed, with its definition of papal infallibility and curbing of intellectual freedom.

Within Catholic America there were stirrings of a liberalism coming to terms with the culture and the age. A group of New York City priests, known as the Accademia and partly influenced by Hecker, was one manifestation. Edward McGlynn, a member of the group, was a very vocal proponent for the theories of Henry George who, in *Progress and Poverty* (1879) and other tracts, identified land monopolization as the enemy of economic democracy. In 1887 McGlynn was excommunicated for his failure to go to Rome to explain his denial of private ownership of property, but was restored to the church five years later when the pope's special delegate ruled that his views were compatible with church teaching.

Lay Catholic congresses in 1889 and 1893 in Baltimore and Chicago, respectively, were another sign of intellectual ferment as lay speakers addressed questions regarding religion and society. Hecker had been urging such meetings of the laity since 1867 as a way of promoting lay leadership in building bridges between the church and the culture. The emergence of such progressive prelates as James Gibbons, John Ireland, John Keane, and John Lancaster Spalding was a further encouraging development. The creation of the Catholic University of America in 1887, with Keane as rector, was still another indication of an American Catholic flowering that would result from the cross-fertilization of the best of America and Catholicism. Implicit was the recognition of the pluralistic character, not only of American society in general, but of the American Catholic community in particular.

Under the leadership of Ireland, Keane, and the rector of the American College in Rome, Denis O'Connell, these progressives began to work to accommodate the American church to its host society through a program of ecumenism, Americanization of immigrants, "public" Catholic schools (funded and supervised by the state but taught by Catholics in church-owned buildings), and related matters. With the aid of the newly appointed apostolic delegate, or representative of the pope to the national hierarchy, Archbishop Francesco Satolli, they won significant victories in the early 1890s regarding the legitimacy of public education and the rights of priests (McGlynn was one of the dissidents restored to the church by Satolli in 1892). Catholics, led by Keane, took part in the World's Parliament of Religions in Chicago in 1893.

Archbishop Ireland, the chief spokesman for this liberal party, stressed the divine cause of the accelerating progress in both "Church and age." America, he insisted, was the ideal environment for realizing this union of church and age worldwide. Ireland and O'Connell were particularly active in exporting this "Americanism" to Europe. At the International Catholic Scientific Congress in 1897, O'Connell delivered an address entitled "A New Idea in the Life of Father Hecker" in which he distinguished between political and ecclesiastical Americanism. Political Americanism he identified with "the first principles of the law of nature," which the Declaration of Independence had proclaimed and American common law and the Constitution codified. In O'Connell's reading of Hecker the common law tradition as it had evolved under the pressure of American experience was much more compatible with the church's teaching on the nature of man than was church law itself, which recognized no God-given rights. Ecclesiastical Americanism, O'Connell argued, was the separation of church and state in America, which allowed the church more freedom and the pope more real authority than they knew anywhere else.

Two months before O'Connell's address, a French translation of a biography of Hecker (who had died in 1888) introduced the Paulist founder to European Catholics as a model of the modern Christian, an American whose independence, initiative, inner direction, and aptitude for change held the key to the democratization of the church. The book quickly became a tract for liberal Catholics throughout Europe. Conservatives denounced it as a canonization of a semi-Pelagian (one who attributes to the human will partial efficacy in the work of salvation), subjectivist (one who makes the norm of morality individual experience), and rationalist. The outbreak of war between Spain and the United States less than a year later seemed to provide a dramatic testing ground for the comparative values of American and European civilization.

American Catholic liberals saw themselves in league with Pope Leo XIII in their attempts to bring the church into the modern world. The pontiff's recognition of the republican government of France had been a major cause of the liberals' conclusion about Leo's intentions. But they had badly misread the pope's mind, despite the clear warnings. (Ironically Leo's French strategy was part of his effort to secure the republic's support for the restoration of the papal states.) A papal letter (*Longuinqua oceani*) to the American church in 1895 had been one. Leo had cautioned there that the separation of church and state in America constituted no ideal for the universal church. The removal of O'Connell and Keane from the rectorships of the American College and the Catholic University of America in 1895 and 1896, respectively, were others.

The next encyclical that addressed the American church left no doubt about the pope's intentions. *Testem Benevolentiae* (1899) condemned a "religious Americanism" that rendered external authority superfluous and extolled natural virtues over supernatural ones. The prominent episcopal supporters of Americanism duly denied that they had ever advocated the ideas denounced by the pope. In fact, the pope and the American liberals were operating out of the fundamentally different intellectual contexts of neo-Thomism (the revival of the philosophical system of Thomas Aquinas in the nineteenth and twentieth centuries) and progressivism, respectively, in which words like nature and liberty had radically different meanings. For their part the Americanists had appropriated part of Hecker's vision but gave little, if any, attention to such a crucial matter as his trust in the Spirit's power to change consciousness and thus reform society. Much more the children of their age of consolidation than the unworldly Hecker, Americanists like O'Connell and Ireland were attempting to make the American church a partner with the United States in the international world. Interest group politics had replaced national conversion. If Hecker had no intention of making American culture normative for the world, nonetheless, given the unique role he saw American Catholicism playing in the advancement of the church throughout the world, it is hardly surprising that his thought should have nurtured an uncritical affirmation of American society and cultural imperialism among the Americanists.

Testem Benevolentiae made liberal American Catholics cautious about their premises, but in the very first years of the new century there was a flowering of American Catholic thought. An ambitious plan to publish a multivolume *Catholic Encyclopedia* was initiated and brought to completion. New journals were begun, including the *New York Review,* the first scientific Catholic theological review in America. According to its editor, James F. Driscoll, its purpose was "to interpret with becoming care and reverence the old truths in the light of the new science" (Gannon, 1971, p. 334). Dunwoodie Seminary, which housed the *Review,* was the major institution for the training of priests for the archdiocese of New York. At Dunwoodie, in Yonkers, the archdiocese had assembled an outstanding faculty. Most notable were three members of the Society of the Priests of St. Sulpice, a congregation dedicated to the formation of seminarians: Francis E. Gigot, the leading Catholic Scripture scholar in

the American church; Joseph Bruneau, professor of dogmatic theology; and Driscoll, professor of Semitic languages. In 1905, the year the *Review* was started, Gigot, Driscoll, and three other Sulpicians resigned from the society in order to escape an authority they found suspicious, if not repressive, of scholarship. Cardinal John M. Farley immediately accepted them as diocesan priests.

His protection, however, did not reach to Rome. In the summer of 1907 appeared a new syllabus, detailing the errors of Modernism, and an encyclical of Pope Pius X, *Pascendi Dominici Gregis,* formally condemning them. Most historians have minimized the connection between the Americanist and Modernist movements. Modernism was a European Catholic movement to incorporate modern historical criticism, evolutionary philosophy, and literary exegesis into theology and Scripture studies. The defections from the church in America because of the condemnation were minimal. American Catholic scholarship, in its infancy in these fields, was highly dependent on its European counterpart, as the articles in the *New York Review* made plain. But the Americanist movement, in urging that the church engage the modern world at its cutting edges, was at the very least encouraging that scholarship, derivative as it might necessarily have been. What is beyond question is the devastating impact of the double condemnation of Americanism and Modernism. In the words of the historian Michael V. Gannon:

> Free intellectual inquiry in ecclesiastical circles came to a virtual standstill. The nascent intellectual movement went underground or died. Contacts with Protestant and secular thinkers were broken off. It was as though someone had pulled a switch and the lights had failed all across the American Catholic landscape.
>
> (p. 341)

Even before the condemnation of Modernism, Catholic intellectuals had been dealt a serious blow in the area of science. Catholic scientists had been slow to respond to the Darwinian challenge. Those who did tended to act as though there need be no conflict between the principles of evolution and essential Catholic doctrines about the origin of species, including man. In his book *Evolution and Dogma* (1896), John A. Zahm,

C.S.C., a scientist at the University of Notre Dame, attempted to make the case for evolution. Two years later the Sacred Congregation of the Index censured the book and forced its withdrawal. Zahm, in effect, was silenced and American Catholic support for evolution, much less for natural selection, was also virtually silenced for the next half century.

In the wake of *Pascendi,* intellectual repression quickly set in. One of the first victims was the *New York Review,* discontinued in 1908 apparently in response to pressure from Rome through the apostolic delegate. Other reviews confined their attention to pastoral issues, literature, and other safe topics. James Driscoll, the progressive rector at Dunwoodie, was transferred to a parish. There were attempted purges, including the successful one at the Catholic University of America in 1910, when Henry Poels, a professor of Scripture, was dismissed for his questioning of the Mosaic authorship of the Pentateuch. In 1910 the Oath Against Modernism was instituted for all candidates to the priesthood and those teaching in seminaries.

In 1913 papal decree established Thomism (the body of thought derived from the writings of the thirteenth-century Dominican philosopher Thomas Aquinas) as the normative system of philosophy for Catholic institutions of higher learning. Inertia, isolation, complacency, the climate of fear that followed the condemnations of Americanism and Modernism—all tended to produce a certain intellectual rigor mortis within the American Catholic institutional landscape. There was little interest in becoming part of the larger community of scholarship, much less in promoting it. As William L. Sullivan, one of the American Modernists, commented, "Over the schools and sanctuaries of Catholicism broods in Buddhistic calm the new Pax Romana" (Reher, 1981, p. 100).

If intellectual inquiry in Catholic America went into a long slumber after the double condemnation, ideological ambition did not. In the wake of the decline of Protestant liberalism and the disillusionment of American intellectuals with an objective reality that reason could not only discern but shape, Catholics saw the opportunity to be the new cultural guardians of America. As Henry Adams had found in the Middle Ages the high-water mark of the human attempt to find unity and meaning in experience, so

Catholics in the 1920s and 1930s focused on medieval culture as a model for a unified culture, a monolithic world in which faith and reason walked hand in hand. As Catholic intellectuals reclaimed their past, they found there the roots of the American political tradition as well, the genius of Aquinas and the seventeenth-century Jesuit Robert Bellarmine lying behind that of Thomas Jefferson and James Madison. In this reconstruction of American ideology Thomism became the twentieth-century equivalent of the Scottish commonsense philosophy that had undergirded American culture in the previous century. Its confident Catholic expositors celebrated Thomism as "the crystallized common sense of the ages." Mindless of its pluralistic character, American Catholic interpreters such as the historian Ross Hoffman and the writer James J. Walsh made Thomism a brick and mortar philosophy that reduced reality to manageable proportions and molded a secure belief structure within which an upwardly mobile Catholic community could safely make its way into the American mainstream. Such enlightened reason could also fulfill the American promise that American liberalism had failed to deliver.

Despite the heady ambitions of American Catholic thinkers in the 1920s and 1930s, their influence upon the general culture proved to be insubstantial. Their major concern was more internal than external: the articulation of the unity of Catholic thought to the Catholic masses and the creation of a network of Catholic professional societies to work out applications in the various areas of social and cultural life. The National Catholic Educational Association (1904), the American Catholic Historical Association (1919), and the American Catholic Philosophical Association (1926) were major components of this professionalization of Catholic thought that eventually affected, among other areas, literature, sociology, economics, poetry, and art.

The journals *Commonweal* (1924), *Thought* (1926), and the *Review of Politics* (1939) made significant contributions to the vitality of Catholic intellectual life during this period. George Shuster, the managing editor of *Commonweal* from 1928 to 1937, promoted a wisdom that combined conventional scholarship, a liberal education, practical experience, theology, prayer, and liturgy. In an age in which philosophy dominated the marketplace of Catholic knowledge,

Shuster insisted on the importance of theology, which he regarded as "God's greatest gift to man," in its ability to see the "glory of the supernatural . . . in a glass darkly" (Blantz, 1985, p. 361).

Another intellectual who promoted Catholic thought in the interwar years was the historian Peter Guilday. Monsignor Guilday, as professor of church history at the Catholic University of America, began the *Catholic Historical Review* in 1915 to bring professional history to a broad audience. For Guilday, documents, properly prepared by the historian, had an almost inherent power to reveal truth. Four years later he organized the American Catholic Historical Association in an effort to build an intellectual community among historians. Constrained by the intellectual chill, Guilday's public vision of America's Catholic past tended to be more defensive and triumphalistic than his private appraisal.

The collapse of the economy in 1929 produced a spectrum of responses from Catholics. Charles E. Coughlin, the prominent Michigan priest and founder of the National Union for Social Justice, blended elements of populism, corporatism (the organization of the economy by means of occupational associations or corporations), anticommunism, and anti-Semitism to explain the international crisis to his weekly radio audiences. An effective outlet for Catholic frustration and legitimizer of positive government in the early days of the Depression, Coughlin saw his popularity wane in the latter part of the decade as he became increasingly pro-Fascist and anti-Semitic in his public attacks.

Occupying the center ground in Catholic social thought was Monsignor John A. Ryan of the Catholic University of America and the Social Action Department of the National Catholic Welfare Conference. Ryan, the author of *A Living Wage* (1906) and of the "Bishops' Program" for reconstructing the public order in 1919, was the foremost theorist of Catholic liberalism in the 1920s and 1930s as he applied the social teaching of the church to the economy of the United States. Articulating from a different perspective many of the concerns of the Social Gospel movement, Ryan was an effective supporter of the New Deal and industrial democracy.

The most radical Catholic critique of the socioeconomic order came from those who espoused personalism, or a voluntary reconstruction of apostolic community through radical personal reform and example. The Benedictine priest Dom Virgil Michel, O.S.B., at St. John's College in Minnesota, promoted liturgical renewal as the key to such reform through his journal *Orate Fratres.* For Michel the major evil afflicting Catholics was their internalization of bourgeois values. He called for heroic perfectionism as the only antidote to the materialism and individualism plaguing American society.

A kindred spirit was Dorothy Day, a founder of the Catholic Worker movement in 1933. Day's co-founder, Peter Maurin, and Father Paul Hanley Furfey, a sociologist at the Catholic University of America, were the theoreticians of this experiment in Christian anarchy. Furfey had become disillusioned with the capacity of the behavioral sciences to redeem the world. While not abandoning that methodology, he began to elaborate a social philosophy of separatism that involved nonparticipation with "the modern world" and witness bearing against the evils of racism, militarism, and the success ideal.

The intellectual sources of Maurin's personalism were many, from Léon Bloy and Emmanuel Mourier to Leo XIII and G. K. Chesterton. Introduced to Dorothy Day in New York City by George Shuster, the itinerant Frenchman had persuaded her to collaborate in the founding of the Catholic Worker movement. A paper of the same title was begun in 1933 as the first step of Maurin's program of promoting a Christian communism based on voluntary poverty. Through the paper and its hospices, the Catholic Worker movement served as an important clearinghouse for social theorists, both Catholic and non-Catholic, radical and mainstream. Much less successful were the agrarian communes that Maurin designed as the alternative to capitalistic society. The most profound instance of utopianism in American Catholic history, the movement was a radical model of the integration of religion and politics, spirituality and social concern that was possible for individual Catholics banding together with those who shared their heritage and convictions.

In the postwar period another Catholic cleric commanded a national audience, first through "The Catholic Hour" on radio and then through his long-running series on television, "Life Is Worth Living." In the 1950s and early 1960s

Bishop Fulton J. Sheen was to millions of Americans the voice of the church in the United States, a Catholic itinerant preacher in the electronic age spreading the good news of God in an austerely pleasant manner. But Sheen was more than a Billy Graham with miter. In his talks and writings he was presenting in popular form the social teaching of Catholicism as the middle way between communism and corporate capitalism. The peace of mind that he offered was the product of a social consciousness keyed by religious renewal. Most television viewers, however, appeared to miss the social message.

In higher education Thomism was still regnant. Neo-Thomism itself had benefited greatly from the arrival of Jacques Maritain in 1940, one of the few Catholics involved in "the intellectual migration" from Fascist Europe. A convert of Léon Bloy's, Maritain through his prolific writings and lectures applying Aquinas to the modern age played a large role in raising Scholastic philosophy above the level of the manuals. Unfortunately the philosophy in the curriculum of American Catholic colleges and universities was still being taught mainly for its apologetic value, and, as James Collins, a Scholastic philosopher, admitted in the 1950s, failing to confront the complexities of the modern world, including the diversity of its types of knowledge. Through his teaching at St. Louis University and his prolific scholarship (including *The Existentialists*, 1952; *A History of Modern European Philosophy*, 1954; *Three Paths in Philosophy*, 1962; *The Emergence of the Philosophy of Religion*, 1967; and *Interpreting Modern Philosophy*, 1972), Collins himself proved a significant countercurrent to the prevailing complacency and insularity of American Catholic philosophy by his engagement of modern philosophy on its own ground, as pluralistic as that might be. By his brilliant interpretation of European philosophy, he worked out a Catholic vision that drew from as well as responded to modern philosophical thought. Robert Pollack of Fordham University attempted a similar synthesis through his examination of American philosophical traditions.

In 1955 the leading American Catholic historian, John Tracy Ellis, created a stir when he charged that American Catholics were failing to exercise a role in the intellectual life of the nation proportionate to their numbers and resources. This was not the first such charge. In 1925 George Shuster had lamented the Catholic wasteland in scholarship and pleaded for lay vocations to the life of intellectual husbandry, but he was virtually ignored. That Ellis' remarks thirty years later touched off the controversy they did was a testament to Catholic mobility in the interval. Assimilation of the Catholic community had progressed to the point in the 1950s where "its intellectual status and prestige had become a matter of sufficiently wide interest to become the central issue in American Catholic life" (Gleason, 1969, p. 19). Ellis singled out several reasons for this, including a residual anti-Catholic prejudice among intellectuals, but asserted that the principal cause was the "self-imposed ghetto mentality" of American Catholics.

Thomas O'Dea, a Catholic lay sociologist, reenforced Ellis' attack through a more extensive analysis of his own. O'Dea noted that Catholics in America had failed to develop an intellectual life because they had been unwilling to take the inevitable risks that such a life entails. The catechetical nature of theology on most Catholic campuses was symptomatic to O'Dea of the general condition of the American Catholic intellectual body. "If we fail to engage our students in such a central intellectual quest as religion," O'Dea wrote, "how can they develop a genuinely open intellectual attitude toward other fields of knowledge?" (1958, p. 64).

Although it had barely reached the colleges by the late 1950s, a revival of theological studies was already well under way. In 1936 the Catholic Biblical Association of America was founded, and three years later the *Catholic Biblical Quarterly*. In 1940 *Theological Studies* was started at Woodstock College, the Jesuit seminary in Maryland, with John Courtney Murray, S.J., as editor after its first year. Murray, who had joined the Woodstock faculty after obtaining his doctorate in dogmatic theology at the Gregorian University in Rome, had challenged his colleagues at a national meeting in 1939 to develop a theology "wholly orientated toward life," one that would help the laity relate their faith to the secular world they inhabited" (Gleason, 1979, p. 200). A series of lectures that Murray later delivered at Yale University, "The Problem of God," was published in 1964 and used widely as a college textbook in the 1960s and 1970s.

Murray's major contribution was in the field of religious liberty. Creatively adapting the thought of classical Catholic theorists to the American context, Murray endeavored to show that the American experience of religious freedom and of the separation of church and state was the concrete fulfillment of the spirit of Catholic doctrine. His two major sources were Gelasius I, the fifth-century pope who enunciated the doctrine of the two distinct societies (church and state), and Jean de Paris, the thirteenth-century Dominican theologian who delineated the limits of civil and papal authority. Murray's distinctive approach was that of a historically conscious world view in which permanent principles had carefully to be distinguished from historical circumstances. The failure to do so, Murray implied, had resulted in the promulgation of certain de facto arrangements as universal and permanent ideals.

In tracing the organic development of the church-state relationship, Murray, following Gelasius, propounded a political theory that respected both the spiritual autonomy of the church and the secular autonomy of the state. The church, in order to be true to its transcendent character, cannot identify with any historical political form, although its rootedness in history requires that it adapt its thought and conduct according to varying rational political exigencies. The neutrality of a modern secular state toward religion is a recognition of the autonomy of the church and of its own limited power. Society thus encompasses both church and state, which are distinct from each other. In pursuing Jean de Paris's notion of indirect power, Murray argued that the church confronts the state only through the individual. It recognizes the dualism inherent in the human person, simultaneously subject to civil authority and to conscience within the two realms of state and church. In grounding rights in persons and not in abstract principles, Murray escaped the traditional trap of conventional Catholic church-state theory that error has no rights. He traced the emergence of a papal teaching, culminating with Leo XIII, centered on human dignity and its concomitant rights.

In America the political maturity of the people was a key factor in the full incarnation of both these theories. Here, too, pluralism had been a fact of life from the very beginning. Here one encountered "a pattern of interacting conspiracies," in which the faiths, including secularism, struggled for dominance. The American political tradition had made dialogue possible and contained the ideological warfare, the most one could expect.

Murray concluded that America, in first desacralizing the state and conserving the natural law tradition at a time when Europe was capitulating to totalitarianism, had founded a republic on the key principles of the Western Christian political tradition. Murray had thus finally made explicit what earlier American Catholic thinkers had sensed about the American experience. He also had achieved this legitimation of the American Catholic situation without submerging the cross beneath the flag.

Murray's explanation of religious liberty as a tradition consistent with the fundamental principles of Catholicism encountered opposition in both America and Rome from those who regarded the recognition of religious liberty as an approval of religious indifference. At the opening of the first session of the Second Vatican Council in 1962 he was still under suspicion. But an invitation from Cardinal Francis Spellman to serve as his adviser at the council led to Murray's playing a key role in drafting the Declaration on Religious Liberty in 1965. As one American bishop observed, "The voices are the voices of United States bishops; but the thoughts are the thoughts of John Courtney Murray" (Gannon, p. 362).

Another Jesuit whose influence went far beyond Woodstock during the Vatican II era was Gustave Weigel. Weigel lectured and wrote textbooks on a vast array of topics, from the psychology of religion to the Orthodox churches. His major contributions were to the fields of ecclesiology and ecumenism. His eleven years as a professor in Chile had profoundly broadened his understanding of the church. Returning to Woodstock in 1948 as professor of ecclesiology, Weigel became increasingly convinced that the church needed a more adequate explanation of itself in the modern world, one that would focus more on its necessary involvement in the world and the role of the laity in that involvement. He also was concerned about the recovery of the collegial tradition within the church, a tradition that had been prominent in the American church, in the nineteenth century. *Lumen Gentium,* the Vatican Council's document on the church, summed up much of what Weigel had been articulating as its nature and functions.

A broker of ideas rather than an originator, Weigel nowhere manifested this more than in his work to promote ecumenism. While on a speaking tour of West Germany in the summer of 1953, he was asked what American Catholics were doing about ecumenism. He had to answer that they were not doing much, if anything. The following year he published a slim monograph entitled *Survey of Protestant Theology in Our Day.* From this modest start he proceeded to become the outstanding American Catholic spokesman for ecumenism. Other books followed, most notably *An American Dialogue,* with Robert McAfee Brown, in 1960. At the Vatican Council he served as a consultant to the Secretariat for Promoting Christian Unity.

Weigel was an early participant in the controversy over Catholic intellectual life. He was particularly concerned about the tendency within Catholic institutions of higher learning to subordinate intellectual inquiry to the preservation of religion. Intellectual excellence, he insisted, had to be the main criterion of a school's purpose and worth. At the university level, scholarship was primary. By the late 1960s there had been considerable improvement, not only in the quality of education within Catholic colleges and seminaries but in the emergence of a generation of Catholic scholars who were entering the intellectual mainstream. Theology and biblical studies, which had earlier languished, boasted eminent scholars by the 1970s: Charles Curran, Avery Dulles, S.J., Richard McCormick, S.J., and David Tracy in theology; Raymond Brown, S.S., Joseph Fitzmeyer, S.J., George MacRae, S.J., and Roland Murphy, O. Carm., in biblical studies.

Ironically, just as this coming of age was occurring, Catholics were caught up in the turmoil of the 1960s. Some repudiated the very notion of the intellectual life; others pressed for the ideal of the activist intellectual who, like the Jesuit Daniel Berrigan, would seek not to be part of the mainstream but to subvert it. If consensus was a casualty of the decade, nowhere did it come apart more noisily than in the American Catholic community under the twin pressures of the reforms connected with Vatican II and the sociocultural disruptions of the larger society. Pluralism manifested itself in ways that John Courtney Murray had not anticipated, although his own church-state theory presupposed a pluralistic theology.

No Catholic intellectual has better captured the dimensions of that unraveling than Gary Wills, who was himself profoundly affected by it. A classicist and journalist who cut his ideological teeth as a staff writer for William Buckley's *National Review* in the 1950s and functioned as the house conservative for the liberal *National Catholic Reporter* in the 1960s, Wills found his orthodoxy shaken by events in the streets of Chicago and elsewhere, culminating in the apocalypse of 1968. Not only did Wills break company with his fellow conservatives by denouncing the Vietnam War; he virtually ostracized himself by identifying the practitioners of civil disobedience in the civil rights and antiwar movements as the soul of church and nation. "Change," he had come to conclude, "is initiated by the principled few, not the compromising many; by the 'crazies' in the streets, not by politicians on the hustings" (1979, p. 162). "The best things in the church," he wrote in 1972, "as in a nation, or in individuals, are hidden and partially disowned, the vital impulse buried under all our cowardly misuses of it—as the life of a nation lies under and is oppressed by its crude governing machinery. . . . It is time to join the underground" (*Bare Ruined Choirs: Doubt, Prophecy, and Radical Religion,* 1972, p. 272).

For Wills the crisis confronting the church in the wake of the Second Vatican Council was due not to the aberrations of radicals and/or liberals, but to its own fatally flawed system of authority and relationship with the state. Reform for the church, like the state, tends to come from the stirrings below, from those lacking official power. One obstacle to reformation lay in the official church's captivity by the state. Religious liberty is largely irrelevant in such a situation. Murray and other liberals erred in assuming a benign neutrality as the normal relationship between church and state in a secular age.

Wills's own political theology is a Catholic version of neo-orthodoxy. Augustine provides him with his model of the secular state, radically unable to know ultimate ends and hence extremely limited in its ability to achieve justice. Its fundamental purpose accordingly is not the pursuit of justice but the holding together of people in peace, a pragmatic accommodation of multiple interests. Whereas the Wills of the early 1970s tended to view the political structure of the United States as an oppressive and crude piece of machinery, a decade later he had come to appreciate the genius of a system in which people *"agree to agree to as much as we can* without doing positive violation to our soul's higher destiny" (1979, p. 214). The American political landscape allows citizens to find common ground short of deepest commitments. It is a system that makes for inertia, continuity, and contentment, in short, for a peaceful society in which justice at least remains possible for the prophetic outsiders to initiate. By the end of the 1970s Wills was engaged in an attempt to recover the intellectual sources of this system rooted in the common good with books dissecting such key documents as the Declaration of Independence (*Inventing America,* 1978) and the Federalist Papers (*Explaining America,* 1981). His is a theory of society very compatible with the Catholic social tradition.

In Catholic universities and colleges the pursuit of excellence seemed to be related to growing secularization. By the mid-1970s the institutions were belatedly engaging in self-reflection about their identity and purpose. Theology was regarded as a key to the uniqueness of Catholic institutions of higher learning but within theology by the 1980s pluralism in methodology and presuppositions seemed as much challenge as path to that goal.

What it meant to be a Catholic intellectual in the 1980s could no longer be answered in the terms of the 1950s. Assimilation had heavily eroded the distinctiveness that identified Catholics in the preconciliar period. If Catholics were at last beginning to carry their weight in the intellectual world of America, there was little evidence that their faith was affecting the thought of most of them. The fragmentation and bureaucratization of knowledge in the modern world was one problem. If the affections are the source of religious activity, including thought, the endemic lack of passion among intellectuals was another.

There is no doubt that there has been a certain loss of confidence among those who profess to bring the Catholic intellectual heritage to bear upon the disciplined perspectives of the intellectual community in America. A group of neoconservative intellectuals, led by a philosopher, Michael Novak, and a historian, James Hitchcock, argue that the resolution of the crisis lies in a recovery of the tradition that liberal and radical Catholics of the 1960s and 1970s had repudiated for the porridge of respectability and self-gratifi-

cation. The journal *Catholicism in Crisis* (1983) was founded to represent that tradition, as the neoconservatives understand it, to a new generation.

Novak is an intellectual refugee from the liberal ranks of the 1960s. Milestones of his odyssey can be found in his *A Theology for Radical Politics* (1969) and *Toward a Theology of the Corporation* (1981). As with Wills, the traumatic period from 1968 to 1972 proved a watershed for his thought. For Novak it was the culmination of a bitter experience that shook him out of his liberal assumptions and radical sympathies. An early proponent of the reforms of the Second Vatican Council, Novak now confesses that his expectations were too conditioned by a romantic liberalism that failed to consider that once the windows of the church were opened, spirits other than that of the Third Person of the Trinity could make their way in to wreak destruction.

Part of that destruction, albeit unintended, has been the abandonment of Thomism and the death of the Catholic renaissance associated with Étienne Gilson and Jacques Maritain, among others. For Novak this has accelerated a tragic loss of intellectual coherence in the postconciliar church. In its place he sees a theological anarchy in which the church has become a voluntary association with no special claim on conscience. At the same time he sees a growing clericalism in which priests and bishops, succumbing in varying degrees to utopian ideology, attempt to craft policy on nuclear war, the economy, and other areas in which they have, at best, marginal competence.

Novak considers himself now a neoliberal or biblical realist, standing between traditionalists and the Catholic left, in the struggle to preserve the integrity of the faith. Neither individual conscience nor institutional authority is absolute for him. He insists there must be an interplay between the two. Being Catholic, he contends, means being faithful not only to conscience but even more, to a community of conscience. Having come to realize that democracy and democratic capitalism are the best protectors of "the productivity, liberty, creativity, dignity, community and individuality both of human persons and human societies" (*Confessions of a Catholic,* 1983, p. 204), he has increasingly been drawn to the task of forging a vision that blends the best of the Catholic and liberal traditions.

Andrew Greeley, the sociologist who has perceptively studied the American Catholic community since the 1950s, agrees with much of this indictment of the Catholic liberal elite. Greeley, however, has little faith in professional Catholic intellectuals in general, whom he sees lagging behind their secular counterparts, including those Catholics who have made it into the intellectual mainstream but have little concern for matters that tend to preoccupy the professional Catholics. The polymathic Greeley looks to "communal Catholics," those formed by Catholic education but free of the ideological blinders of left and right, to "save the Catholic Church" by nurturing in their experience the distinctive sacramental sensibility and analogical imagination (emphasizing the similarity between God and the phenomena of his creation) of the Catholic tradition.

The feminist theology that has sprung up within American Catholic circles in the past two decades has challenged the church to reconstruct not only its language and polity but even its self-understanding of its history, to truly claim the mark of catholic in its character. Rosemary Radford Reuther has been the leading voice in this movement whose goals are to liberate the church from its patriarchy and fashion a theology from a feminine perspective. Nothing inside or outside of the church that "diminishes or denies the full humanity of women," she argues, can be considered redemptive or of God (*Sexism and God Talk: Toward a Feminist Theology,* 1983, p. 19). She proposes a theology that incorporates the wisdom of pre-Christian religions, biblical prophetism, Christian theology, and modern Western cultures. Elizabeth Schüssler Fiorenza, a Scripture scholar, has used the New Testament itself to attempt to show that Jesus was egalitarian in his attitudes and behavior toward women, but his words and deeds were distorted by patriarchal elements who selected and interpreted the texts that became the Scripture of God's revelation through Christ. The equality of women within the church, according to Fiorenza, is part of its authentic tradition (*In Memory of Her: A Feminist Theological Reconstruction of Christian Origins,* 1983).

As feminist theologians sought to reshape the church's consciousness about women, there were disturbing signs of a Roman movement to restore intellectual conformity within the church. The Vatican's withdrawal in the summer of 1986 of Charles Curran's commission to teach on the theological faculty of the Catholic University of America for his dissent from church teachings on several issues related to sexual morality raised serious questions about the extent of religious liberty *within* the church. What are the boundaries there of intellectual freedom and authority? This is a matter that Vatican II did not resolve in its historic Declaration on Religious Freedom. In prohibiting public dissent from authoritative but noninfallible teachings of the magisterium, ecclesiastical authorities seemed to be setting ominous limits to theological inquiry and discussion among Catholic scholars. It suggested a desire to restore a confessional church in which noninfallible and infallible teaching converge to protect a laity that cannot cope with complexity and uncertainty.

Ironically, the American bishops, *pace* Greeley, increasingly turned in recent years to Catholic intellectuals in universities and research institutes for instruction and advice in their public role of teaching through pastoral letters on such major moral issues as nuclear armament and the economy. In this development there was a growing involvement of lay Catholic thinkers. In American Catholic thought the clergy had continued to dominate the field well into this century. Given the immigrant character of the Catholic community, that was probably inevitable. Given, too, the greater vulnerability of the clergy to hierarchical discipline, the emergence of lay theologians seemed especially fortuitous. It was clear by the mid-1980s that the future of American Catholic thought lay largely with the nurturing of a body of lay Catholic intellectuals who would care enough to continue the dialogue that John Carroll had begun and John Courtney Murray legitimized. Such a group would not so much seek a new synthesis of Catholic knowledge with which to engage American culture but rather work under the liberating pressure of faith within diverse traditions of thought that can relate to the tangled web of the modern world.

BIBLIOGRAPHY

Thomas E. Blantz, "George N. Shuster and American Catholic Intellectual Life," in Nelson H. Minnich et al., eds.,

AMERICAN CATHOLIC THOUGHT

Studies in Catholic History in Honor of John Tracy Ellis (1985); Henry F. Brownson, ed., *The Works of Orestes A. Brownson,* 20 vols. (1882–1887; repr. 1966); Patrick Carey, *An Immigrant Bishop: John England's Adaptation of Irish Catholicism to American Republicanism* (1982); Mary Peter Carthy, *English Influences on Early American Catholicism* (1959); Joseph P. Chinnici, *The English Catholic Enlightenment: John Lingard and the Cisalpine Movement, 1780–1850* (1980); James D. Collins, *Crossroads in Philosophy: Existentialism, Naturalism, Theistic Realism* (1969); Michael J. DeVito, *The New York Review, 1905–1908* (1977).

John Tracy Ellis, "American Catholics and the Intellectual Life," in *Thought* (1955); John Whitney Evans, "American Catholics and the Intellectual Life: Thirty Years Later," in Nelson H. Minnich et al., eds., *Studies in Catholic History* (1985); John Farina, ed., *Hecker Studies: Essays on the Thought of Isaac Hecker* (1983); Michael V. Gannon, "Before and After Modernism: The Intellectual Isolation of the American Priest," in John Tracy Ellis, ed., *The Catholic Priest in the United States: Historical Investigations* (1971); Leonard Gilhooley, ed., *No Divided Allegiance: Essays in Brownson's Thought* (1980); Philip Gleason, "The Crisis of Americanization," in Gleason, ed., *Contemporary Catholicism in the United States* (1969) and "In Search of Unity: American Catholic Thought, 1920–1960," in *Catholic Historical Review* (1979).

William M. Halsey, *The Survival of American Innocence: Catholicism in an Era of Disillusionment, 1920–1940* (1980); Thomas O'Brien Hanley, ed., *The John Carroll Papers,* 3 vols.

(1976); Isaac Thomas Hecker, *The Church and the Age: An Exposition of the Catholic Church in View of the Needs and Aspirations of the Present Age* (1887); Christopher J. Kauffmann, ed., "Catholics and the Intellectual Life," in *U.S. Catholic Historian,* 4 (1985); Thomas T. McAvoy, *The Great Crisis in American Catholic History, 1895–1900* (1957); Donna Merwick, *Boston Priests, 1848–1910: A Study of Social and Intellectual Change* (1973); Sebastian G. Messmer, ed., *The Works of the Right Reverend John England,* 7 vols. (1908); John Courtney Murray, *We Hold These Truths: Catholic Reflections on the American Proposition* (1960).

Michael Novak, *Confessions of a Catholic* (1983); C. J. Nuesse, *The Social Thought of American Catholics, 1634–1829* (1945); David O'Brien, *American Catholics and Social Reform* (1968) and "Peter Guilday: The Catholic Intellectual in the Post-Modernist Church," in Nelson H. Minnich et al., eds., *Studies in Catholic History* (1985); Thomas O'Dea, *American Catholic Dilemma: An Inquiry into the Intellectual Life* (1958); Donald E. Pelotte, *John Courtney Murray: Theologian in Conflict* (1976); Mel Piehl, *Breaking Bread: The Catholic Worker and the Origin of Catholic Radicalism in America* (1982); Margaret Mary Reher, "Americanism and Modernism—Continuity or Discontinuity?" in *U.S. Catholic Historian* (1981); Gary Wills, *Confessions of a Conservative* (1979).

[*See also* CATHOLICISM FROM INDEPENDENCE TO WORLD WAR I; CATHOLICISM IN THE ENGLISH COLONIES; CATHOLICISM SINCE WORLD WAR I; *and* RELIGIOUS AUTOBIOGRAPHY.]

JEWISH LITERATURE AND RELIGIOUS THOUGHT

*Deborah B. Karp and Abraham J. Karp**

JUDAISM is a literature-centered faith, as well as a civilization in which religion plays a central but not all-encompassing role. In considering the American Jewish cultural scene, it is appropriate to present first a description of Jewish literary and scholarly activity to convey their scope and variety and then a sampler of Jewish religious thought to permit the reader to "hear" representative thinkers express their responses to the central concerns of their time.

JEWISH LITERATURE

Jews brought to America their tradition as a People of the Book. Far from ancestral influence, in a land where community institutions such as schools and synagogues had to be fashioned anew, most Jews sought to maintain their religious and group identity. They were helped toward this goal by a continuous flow of translations and adaptations of the Bible, prayer books, and religious texts; a large number of popular journals in English, Hebrew, German, and Yiddish; and scholarly publications as well as belles lettres in all four languages.

Prayer Books. Both the freedom afforded by the new country and the bonds with Jewish tradition were indicated by the publication in New York City in 1766 of the first English translation of the Hebrew prayer book. As Isaac Pinto explained in his introduction to *Prayers for Shabbath, Rosh Hashanah, and Kippur, According to the Order of the Spanish and Portuguese Jews,* "Hebrew being imperfectly understood by many, by some not at all, it has been necessary to translate our Prayers

in the language of the Country wherein it hath pleased the divine Providence to appoint our Lot."

Peculiarly American needs came into consideration in later editions of prayer books. The desire of native-born Jews for a briefer, more understandable service was the basis for *The Sabbath Service and Miscellaneous Prayers, Adopted by the Reformed Society of Israelites* (Charleston, South Carolina, 1830). Editor Isaac Harby included English renditions of prayers and instructions for Jewish ceremonies. In 1826 Solomon Henry Jackson printed on his own press in New York City *The Form of Daily Prayers, According to the Custom of the Spanish and Portuguese Jews,* with the Hebrew text revised by E. S. Lazarus and with translations into English by the publisher. In his notes Jackson explained that in keeping with "our republican institutions" the traditional prayer for the welfare of the reigning monarch of the land had been changed to one for elected officials.

The Spanish and Portuguese, or Sephardic, tradition had been the first to take root in the New World, the still-flourishing Shearith Israel congregation having been established in New Amsterdam (now New York City) shortly after the arrival of twenty-three Jewish refugees from Dutch Brazil in 1654. However, Ashkenazic Jews from Central and Eastern Europe quickly outnumbered Sephardic Jews, with immigrants from German-speaking areas accounting for a large proportion of the newcomers who raised the Jewish population to 15,000 in 1840 and to 150,000 in 1860.

The Reverend Isaac Leeser, minister of the Mikveh Israel congregation in Philadelphia, succeeded in meeting the religious needs of Jews of varying levels of knowledge who had brought with them the slightly differing religious rites, or *minhagim,* of their places of origin. In 1836 and

---

*Deborah B. Karp wrote the section on Jewish Literature and Abraham J. Karp wrote the section on Jewish Religious Thought.

1015

1837 he produced a six-volume Sephardic-rite prayer book in Hebrew and English, a masterwork of translation as well as of the bookmaking art. A dozen years later he published *Sidur Divrei Tsadikim: The Book of Daily Prayers for Every Day of the Year According to the Custom of the German and Polish Jews.* While his Sephardic prayer book had included a choice between "A Prayer for a Royal Government" and "A Prayer for a Republican Government" in deference to the needs of Jews of England and of the West Indies, the Ashkenazic prayer book spoke only to citizens of a democracy.

The many versions of the prayer book that followed these early editions further reflected differing rites and congregational goals and the diverse religious outlooks of their composers. They reflected also the freedom of thought encouraged in an American society growing in numbers and diversity.

Reform-oriented prayer books, with either German or English translations and with abridgment of the traditional Hebrew texts, appeared in numbers after 1850. They usually shared a rational, "modern" outlook, eliminating references to resurrection of the dead and the coming of a personal Messiah. Prayers for the return to Zion, the rebuilding of the Temple in Jerusalem, and the reestablishment of the Davidic dynasty were replaced by prayers for universal salvation. America was now to be considered the Promised Land and Judaism one of its many religious denominations.

The Order of Prayers for Divine Service, prepared by Rabbi Leo Merzbacher of Temple Emanu-El in New York City in 1855, was a moderate abridgment of traditional Hebrew texts with an English translation. It was followed by the milestone publication of Isaac Mayer Wise's *Minhag Amerika,* which appeared in both English and German versions in Cincinnati in 1857. Rabbi Wise, later to found the Hebrew Union College and other institutions that made Reform Judaism an organized religious movement, viewed his prayer book as a force for "Americanization" and modernization of thought and ritual in conformity to the "refinements" of the age, as well as a common form that would unify the various streams of American Jewry into one rite, or *minhag.* In 1858, in Baltimore, the more radical Reform ideologist David Einhorn issued his *Olat Tamid: Gebetbuch für israelitische Reform-Gemeinden,* a largely German-language prayer book that spoke of the mission of the Jews to be a prophet-people.

A prayer book specifically for women, *Roochamah: Devotional Exercises for the Use of the Daughters of Israel,* was prepared by the Reverend Morris J. Raphall of New York City in 1852. He argues the need for such a work in America, "where Hebrew educational institutions for both sexes are in their infancy and girls' schools can scarcely be said to exist." The first prayer book for children, *Orders of Prayers for Hefzi-Bah Hebrew School, Temporarily Compiled for the Devotion of the Solemn Holidays of the Year 5621 (1860),* was a small pamphlet of 114 pages of English text interspersed with brief Hebrew sections, compiled by the Reverend Julius Eckman, rabbi, educator, and editor in San Francisco.

The development of an indigenous, highly Americanized Judaism was challenged by the influx into America of almost two-and-a-half million Jews from Eastern Europe between 1880 and 1925. In response to the growing needs of the burgeoning Jewish community, Jewish publishing houses sprang up, mainly in New York City, to turn out traditional daily, Sabbath, and holiday prayer books. Many included Yiddish-language notations as well as English headings and translations. Besides liturgical works, there appeared books of Talmudic commentary, codes (compilations of Jewish law), and responsa (questions and answers on problems occurring in Jewish religious life).

Each of the three major movements in Jewish religious life—Orthodox, Conservative, and Reform—has sponsored prayer books as well as other publications to meet the ritual and educational needs of its own constituency. The Union Prayer Book used by Reform congregations has now been superseded by the more traditionally oriented *Gates of Prayer.* The Conservative Rabbinical Assembly has kept in its prayer books the basic traditional liturgy, with small changes such as the substitution for the blessing thanking God "Who has not made me a woman" of the formula "Who has made me in His image."

Bible Translations. The need for a translation of the Hebrew Scriptures into English was apparent to Isaac Leeser when, arriving from Germany in Richmond, Virginia, in 1824, he found his fellow Jews scantily educated in the Hebrew language and forced to turn to English Bibles that cited

Old Testament passages to prove the truth of Christianity. In 1853, in addition to writing textbooks, catechisms, and volumes of sermons, he became the first Jew to produce a complete English translation of the Hebrew Bible. Leeser was founder in 1845 of the first Jewish Publication Society, which produced eleven small instructive volumes that he called the Jewish Miscellany series. The currently active Jewish Publication Society of America, a later institution founded in 1888, produced in 1917 an authoritative Jewish translation of the Bible into English, edited by the scholar Max L. Margolis. In 1955 a revised translation was undertaken to reflect recent scholarly findings and new insights into biblical language. Under the direction of Harry M. Orlinsky the new version aimed to be both more accurate and more intelligible. With literal and traditional English translations included in marginal notes, this version, published in 1985, eschewed the use of "thou" and found modern equivalents for Hebrew idioms.

Scholarship. Early creative Jewish scholarship in America included Benjamin Szold's commentary on the *Book of Job* in Hebrew (1888) and Marcus Jastrow's two-volume *Dictionary of the Targumim, the Talmud Babli and Yerushalmi, and the Midrashic Literature* (1886–1903). The first Hebrew book written and printed in America was Joshua Falk's *Avney Yehoshua* (1860), a homiletical commentary on the Mishnaic tractate *Ethics of the Fathers.*

The landmark publication of the twelve-volume *Jewish Encyclopedia* in New York City (1901–1906) established the importance of Jewish scholarship in America. Among the American scholars, some European-trained, whom the publisher Funk and Wagnalls named as editors were Cyrus Adler, first recipient of a doctorate in Semitics in America, a founder of the Jewish Publication Society and the American Jewish Historical Society, and president both of Dropsie College and of the Jewish Theological Seminary of America; Richard Gottheil, professor of Semitic Languages at Columbia University; Kaufmann Kohler, later president of Hebrew Union College, and the author of seminal works on Jewish thought and theology; and Louis Ginzberg, professor of Talmud at the Jewish Theological Seminary.

In 1902 Solomon Schechter was brought from Cambridge University to head the Jewish Theological Seminary, founded in 1886 as a Conservative institution of higher learning. Himself a scholar in theology and liturgy, he brought to the faculty an unparalleled body of scholars. Louis Ginzberg, trained in the *yeshivot* (institutions for advanced Talmud study) of Eastern Europe and in German universities, became the acknowledged leader for half a century of American Jewish scholarship. His multivolume *The Legends of the Jews* was a rich collation of ancient rabbinic lore on biblical personalities and incidents. His Hebrew commentary on the first four chapters of the tractate *Berakhot* of the Jerusalem Talmud constitutes a work on Jewish law, theology, history, and culture. Colleagues at the Seminary included Alexander Marx, historian and bibliographer, who made the Seminary library the greatest repository of Jewish books and manuscripts ever assembled; Israel Friedlaender, scholar of the Bible and of Judeo-Arabic language and literature, whose career was cut short when he met a martyr's death while on a mission of mercy to the Ukraine after World War I; Israel Davidson, whose *Thesaurus of Medieval Hebrew Poetry* stands as the basic collection in the field; and Mordecai M. Kaplan, American-trained rabbi, educator, theologian, and religious leader, who has been among the most influential of American Jewish religious thinkers.

The faculty of the Seminary continued the scholarly tradition. Louis Finkelstein, professor and president, made distinguished contributions to the field of Rabbinics. Professors H. L. Ginsberg and Robert Gordis brought modern approaches to biblical scholarship, while Shalom Spiegel provided new insights into medieval Hebrew literature. Abraham Joshua Heschel, scion of a Hasidic line, became the most widely read and highly regarded Jewish theologian in America. Professor Saul Lieberman was head of the faculty for many years; his works on the Palestinian Talmud and the influence of Hellenism on Judaism marked him as the preeminent modern scholar of Rabbinics.

Scholars at the Hebrew Union College in Cincinnati, the Reform rabbinical seminary founded by Isaac Mayer Wise in 1875 and the first such institution to endure in America, have excelled in biblical and historical studies. Bible study and translation have been enriched by Max L. Margolis, Julian Morgenstern, and Harry M. Orlinsky. Jacob Z. Lauterbach wrote on the Talmudic age, and David Neumark on the history of Jewish philosophy. Nelson Glueck, president of the college, was a distinguished biblical archaeologist. Jacob R. Marcus, dean of historians of the American Jewish experience, founded and heads the American Jewish Archives.

Talmudic study and scholarship in the Eastern European tradition has been carried on in the third great institution of higher Jewish learning, Yeshiva University, which began in New York in 1886 as a Talmudic institute and grew to become a comprehensive university, with an undergraduate college and graduate schools offering programs of both secular and religious studies. Its most influential faculty member has been Dr. Joseph D. Soloveitchik, who comes from a distinguished family of Talmudic scholars and is a world-renowned authority on Jewish law and philosophy. Dr. Bernard Revel, its first president, and Dr. Samuel Belkin, his successor, have gained esteem both as scholars and as educational administrators.

The variety of Jewish scholarship in America embraces thorough and insightful research, often strikingly original, as in such works as Arnold Ehrlich's *Mikra ki-Peshuto* (The Bible in Its Plain Meaning); Meyer Waxman's multivolume *A History of Jewish Literature from the Close of the Bible to Our Own Days;* Menahem M. Kasher's twenty-volume compendium of *midrashim* on the Bible, *Torah Shelemah;* and the ten-volume *Universal Jewish Encyclopedia* published in 1940 under the editorship of Isaac Landman.

Much Hebrew religious scholarship in the traditional forms has been produced in America: books of responsa, volumes of sermons, works of Jewish philosophy and theology. In 1903 Rabbi Dov Ber Abramowitz began the monthly *Bet Vaad Lachachamim,* with articles on Jewish law and the modern religious scene by Orthodox scholars. Rabbi Moses Benjamin Tomashoff transferred the publication of his periodical *Yagdil Torah,* devoted to traditional rabbinic scholarship, from Russia to the United States in 1916.

Among American universities, Harvard and Columbia appointed professors of Jewish studies who made monumental contributions to the study of philosophy and history. Russian-born Harry Austryn Wolfson became professor of Hebrew literature and philosophy at Harvard in 1925 and wrote extensively on Philo, the Church Fathers, and Baruch Spinoza, synthesizing the structure and growth of philosophic systems from Plato to Spinoza.

Salo Baron, born in Tarnow, Poland, studied at both the University of Vienna and the Jewish Theological Seminary of that city. Coming to New York in 1926, he taught at the Jewish Institute of Religion and in 1930 was appointed to the Miller Chair for Jewish History, Literature, and Institutions at Columbia University. Professor Baron drew on his magisterial knowledge of many languages and cultures to present Jewish history in the context of world history. His masterwork, *A Social and Religious History of the Jews,* comprised nearly a score of volumes by the time of his ninetieth birthday in 1985, with his studies of the modern age expected to fill several more.

The post–World War II years saw the establishment of courses of Jewish studies in most American universities. A majority of current professors of Jewish studies, whether at universities or at seminaries, received their education in American institutions. Destruction of the Jewish communities of Europe, with their *yeshivot,* seminaries, and study houses, made necessary the establishment of America as a new major center of Jewish scholarship, rivaled only by Israel.

Periodicals. From the mid-nineteenth century on, the printed word brought culture and unity to the scattered Jewish communities, which, accompanying the general migration, soon reached from coast to coast. Periodicals appeared with a variety of religious and polemical goals, filled with literature and editorial comment as well as with news and instructive articles.

The first Jewish periodical in America appeared from March 1823 to March 1825. In response to strong missionary efforts directed toward the Jews, Solomon Henry Jackson of New York published a vigorous defense of his faith in this monthly, *The Jew: Being a Defence of Judaism Against All Adversaries and Particularly Against the Insidious Attacks of Israel's Advocate.*

American Jewish journalism began in earnest with the appearance in Philadelphia in April 1843 of Isaac Leeser's *The Occident and American Jewish Advocate,* with the purpose of spreading "whatever can advance the cause of our religion, and of promoting the true interest of that people descended from the stock of Abraham." Over the next quarter-century, the editor published correspondence expressing the varying viewpoints of American Jews and his own editorial attacks on bigots and missionaries without, reformers and assimilationists within. Reports on conditions of Jewish life ranged from descriptions of small Sunday schools in frontier cities to appeals for funds for children's schools in Alexandria and Cairo. Worldwide reports of Jewish life and problems, as well as literary excerpts teaching Jewish tradition, were brought to widely dispersed subscribers.

In 1854 Isaac Mayer Wise began the publication in Cincinnati of a weekly, *The Israelite,* expressing his philosophy of American Judaism, engaging in polemical exchange with Leeser, and continuing to speak for Reform Judaism for almost fifty years. His advocacy of the American *minhag,* a style of Judaism suitable for all residents of the land, was voiced also in *Deborah,* his German-language monthly.

Other Jewish periodicals established in the 1850s included the traditionalist *Jewish Messenger* (1857) in New York City, David Einhorn's radical Reform *Sinai* (1856) in Baltimore, and *The Hebrew Observer* (1856) and Julius Eckmann's *The Gleaner* (1856) in San Francisco. By 1905, 140 English-language journals had been established, as well as 18 in German, 8 in both English and German, 25 in Hebrew, and 104 in Yiddish.

Nationally circulated journals of news and opinion, which included comments and often controversy on questions of social and religious consequence in the Jewish community, were best typified by *The American Hebrew,* which began publication in 1879 in New York City. In its pages appeared Emma Lazarus' "Epistle to the Hebrews," proclaiming her hope for reeducation and revitalization of the Jewish people, and thoughtful discussions by the editors on such topics as Americanization of the Russian immigrants and support of political Zionism. *The Maccabean,* a Zionist monthly, was started in 1901 in New York City under the editorship of Louis Lipsky.

An outstanding contribution to the literary and cultural scene was the *Menorah Journal* (1915–1962). Edited by Henry Hurwitz with the aid of Elliot E. Cohen, it included articles on Jewish life and thought by such writers as Salo Baron, Israel Friedlaender, Mordecai M. Kaplan, Horace Kallen, Marvin Lowenthal, Maurice Samuel, Harry A. Wolfson, Clifton Fadiman, Irwin Edman, and Lionel Trilling.

Commentary, published since 1945 by the American Jewish Committee and edited by Norman Podhoretz, publishes articles on the Bible, Zionism, and Jewish religious questions side by side with general social and literary criticism and articles advocating a conservative domestic and foreign policy. *Midstream,* a Zionist monthly presenting views on Israel, also contains literature and cultural analysis. Since 1935 *Jewish Spectator* has been the voice of its editor, Trude Weiss-Rosmarin, who demands of Judaism and its followers rationality and justice. Organizations such as Hadassah and other Zionist and communal groups and the congregational unions of the three major branches of Judaism put out their own publications. Summer retreats and forums such as those sponsored by B'nai B'rith and by the American Jewish Congress help to stimulate literary and cultural interest among the laity.

Internationally read scholarly journals published in the United States include the *Jewish Quarterly Review* (1910), the *Hebrew Union College Annual* (1924), the *Proceedings of the American Academy for Jewish Research* (1936), *Jewish Social Studies* (1934), and *American Jewish History* (begun in 1893 as *Publication of the American Jewish Historical Society*).

The Yiddish Press. The Yiddish press in America served the primary purpose of the daily newspaper, providing news of the neighborhood and the world, but because it was directed to a specific immigrant group it served specific religious and cultural purposes, too. Each newspaper favored a certain religious or political point of view, whether Orthodox or secular, moderate or leftist. All contained news, articles, stories, and information about the Jews and Jewish tradition. All served as Americanizing agents, informing the newcomers about the requirements and the opportunities of citizenship in the new country.

After some failed attempts to establish Yiddish newspapers in the 1870s, the *Yiddisches Tageblatt* published by Kasriel Zvi Sarasohn gained a widespread readership after its founding in 1885. It represented the Orthodox religious viewpoint, as did the equally popular *Morgen-Journal,* founded after the turn of the century, with which it merged in 1928. The *Forverts,* or *Jewish Daily Forward,* under the editorship of the highly literate Abraham Cahan, became the largest Yiddish newspaper ever published. It advocated universal socialism and labor unionism as primary ideals but with the rise of Nazism dealt with Zionism favorably. Nobel laureate Isaac Bashevis Singer, who wrote all his works first in Yiddish, provided stories and serial romances for the *Forverts*.

The outstanding Yiddish journal of literature and thought was the *Zukunft* (1892), which for twenty-five years was under the editorship of the poet Abraham Liessin.

Belles Lettres. American Jews entered the fields of journalism and belles lettres early, showing their interest in Jewish tradition and Jewish concerns in many of their writings. In the first half of the nineteenth century, Mordecai Manual Noah, playwright, editor, and public figure, devoted his literary skill to Jewish interests and appeals for the restoration of the Jews to their ancient homeland. Isaac Harby, initiator of the Charleston prayer book of 1830, was a well-known playwright and journalist.

Of lasting literary merit are the poems produced by two women, one in the early and one in the latter part of the nineteenth century. Penina Moise conducted a Sunday school and aided communal causes in the Jewish community of Charleston. Moise published her poems as *Fancy's Sketch Book* in 1833 and wrote pious lyrics and hymns collected in *Hymns Written for the Use of Hebrew Congregations* (1856). Addressing the Jews of Central Europe, who were suffering from oppression in their home communities, she offered a welcome:

> If thou art one of that oppressed race,
> Whose pilgrimage from Palestine we trace,
> Brave the Atlantic—Hope's broad anchor weigh,
> A Western Sun will gild your future days.

Similarly concerned with the plight of fellow Jews, in this case those driven in the 1880s from Eastern Europe, Emma Lazarus had at first devoted her talents to poems, such as *Admetus*, on mythological and romantic themes. Her fervor for Judaism was kindled not by her family's participation in services at Shearith Israel, the Spanish and Portuguese congregation of New York, but by her first view, at Ward's Island, of Russian Jews who had fled from the pogroms of 1881. From then on she associated herself and her gifts with her people, studying Hebrew, reading the literature, and publishing in the *Century* magazine defenses of Judaism and proposals for the rebuilding of national vigor, evincing Zionist as

well as American loyalties. In "The Banner of the Jew," she wrote:

> With Moses' law and David's lyre,
> Your ancient strength remains unbent.
> Let but an Ezra rise anew
> To lift the banner of the Jew!

Lazarus' poem "The New Colossus" is inscribed on the base of the Statue of Liberty, where it has greeted immigrants since 1886.

Hebrew and Yiddish Literature. Although the reading and writing of Hebrew as a modern language was limited to a small number of educated Eastern European immigrants, before World War I several Hebrew weeklies and even a Hebrew daily, *Ha-Yom* (Today), had appeared for brief periods. The literary magazine *Ha-Toren* (The Mast) fostered original creative Hebrew writing from 1913 to 1925.

Bitzaron (Stronghold), a monthly journal edited for nine years by the scholar Chaym Tchernowitz, and the quarterly *Talpiot* (Turrets), edited by Rabbi Samuel K. Mirsky, have each enjoyed high-quality writing and a long publication history. The major organ of American Hebrew literature, the weekly *Hadoar* (The Post), edited for many years by the late Menahem Ribalow, offers news of interest to Hebrew educators and scholars as well as contributions by them.

Hebrew poetry appeared with the first Eastern European immigrants. Some of the poets, such as Menahem Mendel Dolitsky, who published *Shirai Menahem* (Poems of Menahem) in 1900, had already been recognized in Russia. Naphtali Herz Imber's wandering life brought him in the early part of the century to New York, where he composed the Zionist anthem *Ha-Tikvah* (The Hope), later adopted by the State of Israel. A manifestation of the acculturation of the younger Hebrew poets to life in the new country was their frequent choice of peculiarly American themes. Benjamin N. Silkiner in 1910 published an epic poem in Hebrew about American Indian life, *Mul Ohel Timorah* (Facing Timorah's Tent). Another tragedy about Indian life is Ephraim E. Lisitzky's *Medurot Do'akhot* (Dying Campfires, 1937). Lisitzky, who lived in New Orleans, also wrote about black folklore and suffering in *B'Oholei Kush* (In the Tents of Kush, 1953). The Hebrew poets, facing their own crisis of spiritual survival in America, sympathized with the Indians' struggle to maintain life on their ancestral soil and the black endeavor to achieve a sense of worthwhile identity.

As examples of Jewish use of American and English literary themes, Hillel Bavli wrote about Mormons and New Englanders, Simon Ginzburg wrote about New York, Simon Halkin translated Walt Whitman's *Leaves of Grass,* and Israel Efros, Bavli, Lisitzky, and Silkiner all translated plays by Shakespeare.

Novels as well as poetry appeared in Hebrew. Halkin wrote novels as well as poems about American Jewish conflict between spiritual goals and earthly desires, as in *Yehiel Ha-Hagri* (1928). Reuben Wallenrod wrote on one family's disappointment in its effort to realize the American dream; in *Ki Fanah Yom* (The Day Wanes, 1965) idealistic Jewish farmers in the Catskills are forced to turn to hotel-keeping.

The Yiddish language also became the vehicle for popular literature. Poets and novelists of the first decades of the twentieth century depicted the cultural and social conditions under which the Jews lived both in Europe and in America, often touching upon the religious and spiritual components of Jewish life.

Morris Rosenfeld, a poet of the ghetto, expressed the plight of the poor, exploited immigrant clothing worker in bitter, sentimental poems such as "I Am a Millionaire of Tears" and the well-known "My Little Boy." The folk poet Eliakum Zunser wrote of the immigrant's disillusionment with the "Golden Land" that he had been promised. He also wrote of spiritual and Zionist yearnings and of the necessity for the Jews to become citizens of the new land, which would eventually be a "secure, serene place." David Edelstadt and Morris Winchevsky cried out in protest against social conditions, the latter proclaiming, "You can kill only our body, our flesh, but not our holy spirit." The most gifted American Yiddish poet was Yehoash (Solomon Bloomgarden), whose poetry draws upon biblical sources and imagery. His major work was the translation of the Bible into Yiddish.

In an "art for art's sake" movement a group of poets calling themselves Di Yunge (The Young) began to write in Yiddish in 1907. The poetry of Joseph Opatoshu, Moshe Leib Halpern, Halper Leivick, I. J. Schwartz, and Menahem Boraisha, whose epic poem *Der Geher* (The Wanderer, 1943) speaks of mankind's quest for salvation, was supposed to be individual, imagist, and impressionist; however, the poets turned to biblical, historical, and mystical themes that reflected their heritage.

Prose writers in Yiddish who continued their work after emigrating from eastern Europe included Sholem Aleichem, who incorporated the immigrant experience in his last stories; Israel Joshua Singer, who wrote a family and community history of rare power in *The Brothers Ashkenazi* (1936); and Sholem Asch, who in *East River* (1946) spoke of the immigrant family facing the social problems of isolation and integration. All gained acclaim through English translations of their works.

First-Generation Writers in English. An editorial in *Harper's Weekly* stated in 1916: "It is from the Russian Jews, who are the mass of poor Jews in America, that the real contribution to American life is likely to come, because their aspirations are spiritual, their imagination alive." Out of the intellectual and cultural ferment of the Eastern European immigrant generation and that of their children came much literary creativity in novels, memoirs, and polemics.

The Promised Land was the title chosen by Mary Antin for her autobiographical paean to America, published in 1912. Public school was paradise, and she found it not only necessary but also praiseworthy to discard all ties to Jewish religion and the Jewish past in order to become one with the new society.

The classic story of immigrant life, *The Rise of David Levinsky,* by Abraham Cahan, editor of the influential *Jewish Daily Forward,* appeared in 1917. The novel concerns a penniless *yeshiva bachur* (Talmudic student) who escapes oppression and comes to New York in the 1880s, as Cahan himself had come. The protagonist becomes a multimillionaire clothing manufacturer, sacrificing along the way the piety, the love of learning, the ideals of social justice, and even the hope of simple family joys that might have been his heritage as a Jew.

Anzia Yezierska, unlike Mary Antin, found poverty and frustration in her search for education and assimilation, problems described in *Hungry Hearts* (1920). The struggle to earn a living and retain one's self-respect in the majority society and the heartbreak of defection from the faith by the second generation were among the themes related to Jewish life treated by Myron

Brinig in his Montana saga *Singermann* (1929), by David Pinsky in *The Generations of Noah Edon* (1931), by Charles Reznikoff in *By the Waters of Manhattan* (1930), and by Louis Zara in *Blessed Is the Man* (1935). Negative aspects of ghetto life, its narrowness and ugliness, and the purported avarice of its children were made much of by writers such as Ben Hecht, Samuel Ornitz, Budd Schulberg, and Jerome Weidman and by leftist writers of "proletarian" literature like Michael Gold in the 1930s.

Henry Roth, in a masterly portrayal of a Jewish immigrant child's world at the start of the century, shows the terror and confusion faced by the child at home and in the unfriendly streets of New York. Assailed by things sordid and strange, he gains a momentary vision of bright glory in a prophetic Bible passage that he hears an older boy reciting at Hebrew school and almost meets death while striving to re-create lightning at the electrified third rail of the trolley tracks. *Call It Sleep* (1935) has been called the best literary evocation of Jewish childhood and of the religious seeking and misunderstanding that may be every child's portion.

Second-generation Jews grown to young adulthood in Chicago are the subject of *The Old Bunch*, a panoramic novel by Meyer Levin published in 1937. The relationship of the child to foreign-born parents, the conflict of traditional ideals with youthful drives for success or freedom, the corruption of hopes by social unrest, crime, depression, and poverty, and the love of learning and desire to serve humanity that characterize some of the "bunch"—all ring true in this superb picture of American life. Levin was an original in writing of a young Jew whose Zionist ideals took him to a kibbutz (Jewish collective farm) in Palestine in the 1920s, and among the first to retell Hasidic lore in English. (Hasidism was founded in Eastern Europe in the eighteenth century as a movement of religious enthusiasm.) Works dealing with such subjects were rarely published before World War II.

The barring of Jews from most of American intellectual and academic life in the first half of the century was evident in the experience of Ludwig Lewisohn. A brilliant German-born graduate student of English literature at Columbia, he was told by his professors that a Jew had no chance of becoming part of any English department fac-ulty. Raised in the South without any Jewish contacts, he turned in bitterness to a new self-awareness as a Jew. His novel *The Island Within* (1928) and autobiographical works such as *Up Stream* (1922) tell of the hopelessness of trying to find fulfillment through intermarriage and assimilation. "To rise from my lack and confusion into a truly human life," he concluded in *Up Stream*, "it was necessary for me to affirm the reintegration of my entire consciousness with the historic and ethnic tradition of which I was a part." A champion of Zionism and intensive Hebrew education, Lewisohn wrote authoritatively on American culture and finally became professor of comparative literature at Brandeis University.

Most brilliant of the analysts of the Jews' place in history and the modern world was Maurice Samuel, who came to the United States after graduating from the University of Manchester. Upholding the special virtues of his people, he answered historian Arnold Toynbee, who had called Judaism "a fossil civilization," by citing the tremendous range of literature, thought, and cultural creativity that Judaism had contributed to the world since Christianity had supposedly superseded it. Samuel taught himself Yiddish and became the great popularizer of Yiddish writers I. L. Peretz in *Prince of the Ghetto* (1948) and Sholem Aleichem in *The World of Sholem Aleichem* (1943). He later learned Russian in order to write on the Mendel Beilis blood-libel case (which had shocked Moscow in 1911) in *Blood Accusation* (1966). He put forth challenging hypotheses, such as that locating the basis for anti-Semitism in amoral man's rage against the group for imposing moral restraints on his passions in *The Great Hatred* (1940). *The Gentleman and the Jew* (1950) argues that the world suffers by its idealization of the gentleman who fights and kills for honor; while the Jewish ideal, also held up by Christianity, of the peace-loving, cooperative, moral person is the one the world needs.

Playwrights and Poets. Socially conscious Jewish playwrights of the 1920s and 1930s, such as Clifford Odets in *Awake and Sing* (1935) and Elmer Rice in *Street Scene* (1929), showed through Jewish characters the conflict between social and family pressures on the one hand and the needs of the young on the other. In both light and serious drama and in musical comedy, motion pictures, radio, and television, Jews were prominent in numbers far beyond their percentage of the population, but although one finds in their productions what has been called a biblical-utopian picture of America, where right prevails and wrong is punished, it is hard to find Jewish content in their work.

Since the 1950s Arthur Miller has been considered a foremost American playwright. His works, such as *Death of a Salesman* (1949), *All My Sons* (1947), *The Crucible* (1953), and *A View from the Bridge* (1955), do not necessarily deal with Jewish characters but with Judeo-Christian ethical questions of conscience and of duty to family, self, and society. Paddy Chayevsky in *The Tenth Man* (1959) utilized the Jewish mystical theme of the *dybbuk*, a human soul, seeking justice, that occupies another body.

In poetry Jews have also often chosen to deal with Jewish themes such as the relationship to God, exile and alienation, Zion and Sinai. Louis Untermeyer and Babette Deutsch, both known also as critics and anthologizers, made their contributions. Untermeyer used biblical themes in his collections *Roast Leviathan* (1923) and *Burning Bush* (1928) and in his novel *Moses* (1928); so also did Deutsch in *Honey Out of the Rock* (1925).

The explosion of Jewish writers into print after World War II brought forth poets of prominence. Karl Shapiro, champion of more expressiveness of feeling as against the leading school of "cerebral" (and often anti-Semitic) poets led by Ezra Pound and T. S. Eliot, gathered his best early works into *Poems of a Jew* (1958). In it he speaks of the Jew as "man essentially himself, the primitive ego of the human race . . . absolutely committed to the world." On the founding of Israel, he wrote, echoing the medieval poet Judah Halevi:

> When I think of the battle for Zion I hear
> The drop of chains, the starting forth of feet,
> And I remain chained in a Western chair.

Others whose Jewishness added depth to their poetry included Howard Nemerov, Delmore Schwartz, and Hyam Plutzik. Muriel Rukeyser wrote:

> To be a Jew in the twentieth century
> Is to be offered a gift. If you refuse,

> Wishing to be invisible, you choose
> Death of the spirit, the stone insanity.

Charles Reznikoff wrote lovingly of Judaism in such lines as these in praise of Hebrew:

> Like Solomon,
> I have married and married the speech of
> strangers;
> None are like you, Shulamite.

The most haunting evocation of Jewish tradition is that of A. M. Klein, a Canadian, whose masterpiece of prose-poetry, *The Second Scroll* (1951), sums up the range of Jewish history, wandering, suffering, longing, and glory. The narrator seeks in the countries of Jewish dispersion and in Israel for his uncle Melech Davidson, whose name signifies King David and the Messiah.

The leader of a cult of outspoken, free-living "beat" poets of the 1950s and 1960s was Allen Ginsberg, who combined a Whitmanesque line with a Jewish sensitivity. His howls against society's infringement on the individual soul include *Kaddish* (1961), an unmodulated lament for his youthful years ruined by the need to care for his psychotic mother.

Novelists. After World War II, moved by both the revelation of the Holocaust and the founding of the State of Israel, the American press and public became widely hospitable to Jewish writing about Jewish characters. The second generation, now college-educated, created what critics of the 1960s called the "new dominant school in American fiction"—the Jewish school.

First to appear in the new wave of best-sellers on Jewish themes were a number of books depicting the Jew as victim of anti-Semitism. Arthur Miller's *Focus* (1945) and Laura Hobson's *Gentleman's Agreement* (1947) each presents a Christian protagonist who is mistakenly regarded as a Jew and thus has his eyes opened to injustice. Two of the three young men in Irwin Shaw's *The Young Lions* (1948) are Jews: Noah, the victim of barracks anti-Semitism, and Michael, the intellectual who learns to care for others during the war against the Nazis. Norman Mailer's *The Naked and the Dead* (1948) has two Jewish soldiers, Goldstein and Roth, who are marked respectively by their "authentic" acceptance and "inauthentic" rejection of the predicament of being Jewish. Arthur Koestler's statement that Jewishness is only an unwelcome burden—"an empty knapsack"—was a theme of many writers of the 1940s and 1950s. *Wasteland* (1946), by Jo Sinclair, concerns a self-hating protagonist learning through psychoanalysis to accept his Jewish background.

Other novelists, more sympathetic to Jewish experience, used Jewish characters and themes in books in which the particular experience may have universal application. Edward Lewis Wallant in *The Human Season* (1960) shows a bereaved widower questioning God's justice; *The Pawnbroker* (1961) describes the blunting of human sensitivity and the possibility of its reawakening after the Nazi Holocaust. Something similar to Herbert Gold's *Fathers* (1966) might have been written by the son of many an immigrant family.

Several writers have produced works dealing with characters who are conscious participants in Jewish history. Herman Wouk in *Marjorie Morningstar* (1955) shows a college girl of the late 1930s pursuing the American dream of romance and stardom, with no thought of social responsibility. She eventually becomes a respectable matron who sends her children to a Hebrew day school. A devout Jew, Wouk describes his religious way of life in *This Is My God* (1959). His earlier book, *The City Boy* (1948), has been called a "Jewish *Tom Sawyer*."

Charles Angoff's multivolume saga of a literate, sensitive American Jew, David Polonsky, reflects the author's own experiences of going from Harvard to the heady atmosphere of American intellectual life (Angoff was an editor of *American Mercury*). The story, beginning with *Journey to the Dawn* (1956), is, as he described it, "multi-generation in structure and takes in every aspect of Jewish life in the United States: Americanization, assimilation, Zionism, secularism, the various religious denominations, Jews in industry and the professions, anti-Semitism and intermarriage" (*Jewish Book Annual,* vol. 25, 1967–1968).

The Holocaust and the founding of the State of Israel were reflected in books by popular authors as well as in personal memoirs. Leon Uris' *Exodus* (1958) became a best-selling source of fictionalized information about the establishment of the state. *Mila 18* (1961), Uris' novel on

the Warsaw Ghetto uprising of 1943, followed *The Wall* (1950), by John Hersey, who, though not Jewish, made full use of authentic literary source materials.

Most authoritative of the Holocaust memoir-novels are those of Elie Wiesel. His stark account in *Night* (1960) of the dehumanization of victim and captor and the questioning of God in the death camps and other novels like *The Gates of the Forest* (1966) address the survivor's need to go on living and to tell the tale. In other works Wiesel has retold Hasidic lore and has championed the right of Soviet Jews to emigrate as well as the importance of the survival of the State of Israel.

Saul Bellow, called by many critics the leading contemporary novelist, was awarded the Nobel Prize for literature in 1976. Well-versed in Jewish as well as in general culture, he has introduced intellectual discontent and spiritual striving as literary themes in his novels of modern urban men, their tangled family relationships, and their irksome daily adventures. *The Adventures of Augie March* (1953), set in Chicago, echoes in its title the prototypical American quest novel, *The Adventures of Huckleberry Finn.* Its amiable protagonist, adopted in turn by a variety of American types for a series of outlandish adventures, seeks some sort of salvation, hoping ultimately to serve and help people. The roaring millionaire in *Henderson the Rain King* (1959) is driven to seek in Africa the answer to his soul's persistent call of "I want, I want, I want." *Herzog* (1964) tells of a neurotic, twice-divorced academic as he relives his failures and composes letters, never sent, about improving the world. When there is nothing left to say, he decides literally to try to set his own house in order. *Mr. Sammler's Planet* (1970) presents the distilled essence of Jewish, European, and Bloomsbury intellectual elegance in the character of the Polish- and British-educated Holocaust survivor Artur Sammler, who is forced to face vulgarity and violence on the West Side of Manhattan.

The suffering of thinking, feeling urban man in the contemporary world is a popular theme among Jewish writers. The New York—read "Jewish"—school of literary critics, including Leslie Fiedler, Irving Howe, Alfred Kazin, Norman Podhoretz, and Theodore Solotaroff, speak of the sensitivity of the Jewish writer and his preoccupation with modern man's alienation and feeling of exile as creating a new theme in American literature. "Bellow's heroes are more often conscious seekers of fulfillment, in essence intellectuals," writes Joseph C. Landis in the *Jewish Book Annual* of 1967–1968. In the works of Bernard Malamud "reluctant, less-than-ordinary men, seeking only to survive, unlikely candidates for moral greatness, grow into heroes that illustrate his theme of the ability of any man to redeem himself by acquiring moral identity."

In Malamud's *The Assistant* (1957) the orphaned, rootless Frank Alpine, through his association with a saintly Jewish grocer, rises to the discipline of moral law and becomes a Jew. In *A New Life* (1961) the New York *schlemihl* (hapless blunderer) exposed to the wide vistas as well as the mental narrowness of the Pacific Northwest gains a kind of nobility in failure. *The Fixer* (1966) again reveals the pattern: a Jewish laborer in Moscow in 1911 gains greatness of soul as he endures imprisonment under sentence of death for a murder he did not commit. Malamud began his oeuvre with *The Natural* (1952), on the most American of themes, baseball, with the most English of myths, that of King Arthur, as its framework. He went on to develop in his work a peculiarly Jewish mythology—encompassing the irony of fate and the closeness of angels and the divine to lowly people, with the Jew standing for the fool, the victim, and ultimately the partner of God—that echoes Hasidic mysticism and the work of I. L. Peretz.

Philip Roth in his incisive short stories comments on the bourgeois failings, spiritual insufficiency, and loss of identity of American Jews. "Goodbye Columbus" shows the philistinism of the new Jewish rich; "Eli, the Fanatic" shows the embarrassment of suburban Jews when Holocaust survivors in old European garb open a yeshiva for the Gentiles to see. The criticism Roth received from Jewish sources for his self-ridiculing, raunchy *Portnoy's Complaint* (1969) is echoed and answered in Roth's books on the character Zuckerman, a similarly criticized writer. In *The Ghost Writer* (1979), Zuckerman imagines himself engaged to Anne Frank, who has miraculously survived the Holocaust, to prove to his father that he has Jewish loyalties.

Beyond using aspects of the Jewish experience as part of the framework of their stories, some Jewish writers have made the Jewishness of their characters the central element in their lives and the primary basis for their actions. Chaim Potok's *The Chosen* (1967) is a tale of two boys growing up in neighboring Orthodox communities in Brooklyn, one Hasidic, where the son of the *rebbe* (spiritual leader) is supposed to eschew secular studies and prepare to take over his father's dynasty, the other rationally traditional, where all learning is valued for enabling a better life.

Cynthia Ozick has brought a new element into American Jewish writing, stories in which philosophical outlook and religious unease are the center. Her novel *Trust* (1966) deals in part with the differing American traditions, including the moral Jewish one. In "The Pagan Rabbi" (1971) she presents graphically the painful theme of the split in peoples and in individuals between the Greek way of freedom and creativity and the Jewish way of moral responsibility. Her other themes have included Yiddish writers in America, Hasidic towns in New York State, Jewish day schools of dual English and Hebrew curriculum, and resurrected Jewish loyalties among assimilated modern Jews.

In an older Jewish tradition are the writings, translated from Yiddish, of Isaac Bashevis Singer. He presents mainly tales of the Eastern European *shtetl* (small Jewish town) in all its exoticism; but even his stories set in America deal with Jews of strong passions and a mystical bent, bothered by angels and demons, daring God's wrath as they lead eventful lives. Love continuing after death, violence, and the incursion of the supernatural in the lives of ordinary people—Singer's themes are foreign to America's prevailing idea of the cerebral Jew, but all continue an ancient tradition of the folktale. Bellow was the one who introduced Singer to the American public through his translation in *Partisan Review* of "Gimpel the Fool" (1953), a story whose protagonist gains wisdom and a form of sainthood through decades of ridicule and suffering as the town simpleton. Two years after Bellow received the Nobel Prize in literature, the 1978 award was given to Singer, an American Jewish writer in the Yiddish language, who celebrates the Eastern European Jewish community that is gone.

American culture has been enriched by Jewish writers and the themes, styles, and questionings they have brought into the mainstream of American literature.

JEWISH RELIGIOUS THOUGHT

The Jews of Europe entered the modern world through the twin experiences of emancipation and enlightenment. It was a long process extending from the French Revolution to the post–World War II era. Emancipation, granting to Jews civic and political rights, began in France; enlightenment, participation in the cultural life of the larger community, was first experienced in Germany. The goal was the full integration of the Jews into the political, social, and cultural life of the nation. The first Jews to experience political participation and cultural integration quickly perceived that both the society opening its doors and the state granting rights were demanding accommodation on the part of the Jews through an alteration of their corporate status, their way of life, and their purpose in life.

Long looked upon as a foreign element to the body politic, "a nation within a nation," the Jews were quick to alter their corporate status from a nation with its own distinctive political and cultural identity to a "religious community" separated from their fellow citizens by religious persuasion alone. They confidently expected that the new identity would ease and hasten their integration and acceptance. Some, concluding that full acceptance would come only with the eradication of all differences, the religious included, entered the larger society by way of the baptismal font. The overwhelming majority, while laboring for greater emancipation and fuller integration, were determined to retain their Jewish identity. The accommodation they were ready to make to modernity and for integration was a change in their way of life, removing from it those aspects that visibly separated them from their neighbors: language, ritual, dress, diet, rites of worship. Determined to remain within the faith, they nevertheless asked themselves—or heard their neighbors ask—why they continued Jewish corporate existence. Of what value was it to the larger society or to the individual Jew?

Ideological justification for continuing Jewish corporate existence in the modern world was formulated by Rabbis Abraham Geiger and Samuel Holdheim, leaders of Reform Judaism in Germany in the mid-nineteenth century. Seizing upon the then popular theory—which romantic nationalism made emotionally acceptable and intellectually respectable—that a people is endowed with a unique native genius that it should use in service to humanity, Geiger applied it to the Jews. "In the Greek nation we observe a national genius that enabled it to produce masters in every art and science," he wrote. "Is not the Jewish people endowed with such a genius, with a religious genius?" Geiger's colleague Holdheim turned observation to mandate: "It is the Messianic task of Israel to make the pure law of morality of Judaism the common possession and blessing of all peoples on earth." The "mission idea," as it came to be known, declared that the Jewish people is a religious community dispersed by God throughout his world, and charged by him to bring to humankind the teachings of ethical monotheism. This never-ending mission demands that Israel, God's priest-people, live on in obedience to him and in service to humanity. A "religious community" was the appropriate status for Jews in the modern national state granting emancipation; a "divine mission" was adequate justification for their continued distinctive identity and fullest integration in a society espousing enlightenment.

The challenge of modernity confronted the Jew in the New World as in the Old. The earliest Jewish religious ideologists, all European born and trained, saw America through European spectacles. At first they perceived the confrontation to be the same that they had experienced in Europe and responded with the ideological formulations fashioned there. Later they saw that America was different. In Europe emancipation was a gift granted at the end of a long struggle; in America it was an "inalienable right." In Europe enlightenment—i.e., participation in the larger culture—was grudgingly granted; in "melting-pot" America it was readily extended. The American Jew quickly learned that the same America that urged cultural assimilation, accepted religious differentiation. Here no justification was demanded of him for his persistence in corporate identity. But he just as quickly perceived that the identity which was most readily acceptable, and which helped his integration into America, was a religious identity. So, as in nineteenth-century Western Europe, the American Jews adopted the posture of a "religious community."

Later, in the twentieth century, when the American Jews felt more at home in America, they discarded the melting-pot image of America for that of cultural pluralism, which permitted the free expression of ethno-national sentiments and the retention of a creative ethnic culture. In post–World War II America, the American Jew welcomed sociologist Will Herberg's description of America as the "Land of the Three Great Faiths," for it lifted Judaism to equal partnership in the American triad of—in Herberg's title—*Catholic, Protestant, Jew.* Feeling fully at home in America, Jewish religious leaders could now turn from formulations of justification to theological consideration of God, man, and the world they shared. Among the theological concerns they addressed were the God in and of history in the post-Holocaust world, and the covenantal relationship of God and man as seen from an existentialist perspective. At home in America, Jewish religious thinkers turned from the *why* of continued Jewish existence to the *how* of creative Jewish living.

David Einhorn. Identity as a religious community established the appropriate status for Jewish survival in America, but what of the religious content? What kind of Judaism was appropriate for that community? During the mid-nineteenth century the community was well enough established to begin to invite spiritual leaders from Europe. Foremost among them was Rabbi David Einhorn, who arrived in 1855 to serve the Reform congregation Har Sinai in Baltimore. Later he served synagogues in Philadelphia and New York and became the ideological leader of Reform Judaism in America. In his inaugural sermon at Har Sinai he offered his definition and description of Judaism:

> We must turn our entire attention to our system of belief. The more the ceremonial laws lose of importance and dominion, the more necessary is a comprehension of the Jewish faith . . . the fountain of our strength, the cause of endurance. . . . Ours is the belief in God, the only one, who reveals himself particularly in man as the

all-pervading immanent Spirit. . . . Ours is the belief in one human family, whose members, all being made alike and endowed with the same claim and title to happiness will all participate in the bliss of that glorious time when . . . God alone will rule as King over all the nations who will become the one people of God.
> (Kohler, ed., *David Einhorn,* p. 437)

As a Reform spokesman, he draws a contrast between the perishable body and the imperishable spirit of divine law:

> The former consists of forms intended to serve as signs and symbols, or as an armor of protection for the eternal truth, which must constantly differ. . . . The other is the religious and moral truth as expressed in its fundamentals in the decalogue of Sinai, destined to become through Israel the common possession of mankind. Our pious fathers . . . clung to lifeless customs which dulled their religious and moral sense. . . . Judaism must be reformed from within. . . . Lest our children emancipate themselves from Judaism altogether, we must emancipate Judaism from such shackles.
> (*David Einhorn,* p. 436)

Einhorn's emphasis on the mission idea was constant and pervasive. He had preached it in Europe:

> Israel was chosen by the Lord to be the receptacle for the balm of Sinaitic doctrine; predestined to cause all parts of the earth to become suffused with [its] fragrance. . . . In obedience to the Lord it has come forth from isolation [in Palestine] . . . to permit the pleasing aroma of its precious balm to penetrate everywhere.
> (*David Einhorn,* p. 321)

He made the mission idea the focal message of a special service he created for the traditional day of mourning for the destroyed Temple and the exile of the Jewish people from its ancestral homeland, transforming *Tisha B'Av* from a day of mourning into a day of thanksgiving and consecration:

> Not as a disowned son thy first born went into strange lands, but as an emissary to all the families of man. The one temple in Jerusalem sank into the dust, in order that countless temples

might arise to thy honor and glory all over the wide surface of the globe.

(Einhorn, p. 331)

Einhorn also made this doctrine of a divine mission the central point of the platform adopted by the first conference of Reform rabbis held in America, which he convened in Philadelphia in 1869 and which he dominated. The first two platforms proclaim:

> The Messianic goal of Israel . . . [is] the union of all men as children of God. . . . The fall of the second Jewish commonwealth [is] not punishment . . . [but] divine purpose. . . . The dispersion of the Jews to all parts of the earth, for the realization of their highly priestly mission, to lead the nations to the true knowledge and worship of God.
>
> (Plaut, p. 30)

Kaufmann Kohler. In 1885 Einhorn's disciple and son-in-law, Kaufmann Kohler, convened another Reform conference in Pittsburgh at which Isaac Mayer Wise—founder of Reform Judaism's rabbinical seminary, Hebrew Union College, and architect of Reform Judaism in America—presided. The mission idea appears as a "given" in the platform adopted but does not receive central emphasis. Centrality is accorded to another idea: "We consider ourselves no longer a nation, but a religious community and therefore expect neither a return to Palestine . . . nor the restoration of any laws concerning the Jewish state." The platform offers a definition of Judaism that conforms to its posture as a *religious* community: "Judaism presents the highest conception of the God idea as taught in our Holy Scriptures and developed and spiritualized by the Jewish teachers, in accordance with the moral and philosophical progress of their respective ages" (Plaut, pp. 33–34).

Christianity and Islam share with Judaism in the "providential mission in the spreading of the monotheistic truth." In America the Jewish religious community continues to preserve "this central religious truth" in cooperation with its fellow religious denominations. Here also "the spirit of broad humanity of our age is our ally in the fulfillment of our mission." This turning to liberal America was influenced by Wise, who espoused an *American* Judaism, moderately Reform

in practice, moderately liberal in theology. He viewed America, as Edward McNall Burns described it, as "a unique place [which] has a special destiny among the nations of the earth" (p. 5). Wise wed Judaism's to America's sense of mission: "And America is THE COUNTRY where universal religion will celebrate its first and glorious triumphs" (Heller, p. 561). His patriotic spirit led him to proclaim that "here in America the salvation of mankind must originate," and his ebullient nature led him to predict that *"before this century will close,* the essence of Judaism will be the religion of the great majority of intelligent men of this country."

Kohler, Wise's successor to the presidency of Hebrew Union College, was American Reform Judaism's premier theologian. He was fully at home in the classic texts of Judaism and in contemporary world philosophies, and used traditional sources to which he brought a modernist interpretation in order to express an optimistic faith. Unlike Wise, who saw Darwin's theory of evolution as giving a negative and brutal picture of man, Kohler hailed the theory, for, he said, "it offers a religion of hope, of life grander than any system. It accounts better for all our errors and failings, for the shortcomings of our morals and religious life, for the very evils which surround us from within and from without." His bold theological revisionism led him to choose the Darwinian account of man's creation as superior to the biblical one:

> . . . which of the two is the higher conception of God: the one which has man fashioned by God of a piece of clay . . . equipped with all the faculties of heart and mind befitting the Divine Mould, and then allowing him from his high station to fall so low in intellect and manners? . . . Or the one [in] which man . . . the highest and most fitted in the scale of beings, at last emerges . . . to grope and work his way up into an ever nobler and finer stature?
>
> (Noveck, p. 299)

The religious soul in man demands to know what God is to him. The God of Judaism, says Kohler, is neither the

> lifeless powers of nature and destiny, which were worshipped by the ancient pagans, nor the God of modern paganism, a God divested of all personality and self-consciousness, [but] the liv-

ing Fountain of all that knowledge and spirituality for which men long, and in which alone they may find contentment and bliss. . . . He reveals Himself in self-conscious activity, determining all that happens by His absolutely free will. . . . Beside the all-encompassing Deity no other divine power or personality can find a place. God is in all; He is overall; He is both immanent and transcendent.

Kohler addressed himself to the apparent conflict between religion and science. "The Biblical account," he writes, "is not intended to depreciate or supersede the facts established by natural science, but solely to accentuate those religious truths which the latter disregards."

Central to Kohler's conception of Judaism is its ethical system: "Divinity is mirrored in the virtues of justice, mercy, purity and holiness, which man strives for . . . and Ethical Theism [which] gave humanity its vigorous idealism." The emphasis of this conception on community keeps it from the "two false notes sounded in the New Testament ethics . . . [which] cares only for the individual soul and overlooks the greater task of social justice . . . and has the character of other-worldliness."

Even stronger is his critique of the Christian church itself, which "in her efforts to conquer the heathen world was to a large extent conquered herself by the heathen view." The Jew, on the other hand, according to Kohler,

> excelled everywhere by his zeal for truth, his love of knowledge and wisdom. . . . In the midst of a world full of profanity and vulgarity . . . he displayed the virtues of chastity and modesty in his domestic and social sphere. . . . Each Jew was a living protest against the dogma of the Church which placed a man born of woman on God's throne, and defied human reason in order to save a soul. He was God's priest and prophet pointing to a better day, to God's kingdom on earth.
>
> (pp. 188, 190–191)

Kohler reaffirmed the mission idea fashioned in the Old World but with a boldness more suitable to the New. In part the boldness was due to the freedom felt by the Jew in America; in part it was also due to the desperate situation of American Judaism at the turn of the century. But Kohler's was a marshalling cry that seemed to fall on deaf ears. Few if any American Jews could take seriously a missionary role. There was little in their lives that made them more pious, more religious than their neighbors. To the contrary, a Judaism stripped of its national character, devoid of ritual and ceremony, language and culture, could neither evoke enthusiasm nor even sustain commitment. The past was stripped away and with it the future. Among the first to perceive this and to raise the alarm was Reform Rabbi Bernhard Felsenthal.

Bernhard Felsenthal. Felsenthal argued that a Judaism professing merely an exalted God concept, some universal ideals, and a lofty ethic, all of which it shared with other faiths, would not long survive. Survival demanded the acceptance by the Jews of their distinctiveness and the fostering of those elements of culture and nationality that constitute the "Jewish national religion."

> "Judaism" and "Jewish religion" are not synonymous terms . . . "Jewish religion" is only part of "Judaism" . . . [which] is the sum total of all the ethnological characteristics which have their roots in the distinctively Jewish national spirit. . . . The Jewish people, is the fixed, the permanent, the necessary substratum, the essential nucleus. The Jewish religion is that which inheres in and qualifies this nucleus. Judaism is not a universal religion. There would be no Judaism without Jews.
>
> (pp. 66–67)

Yet this national Jewish religion would serve humanity in general, for as "each national religion . . . beneficially exerts an influence on a particular nation, it also adds to the adornment of all humanity." Felsenthal urged a definition of Judaism that "brings together under a common denominator both the most fundamentalist, excessively pious, mystical, wonder-working rabbi [of Russia]" and the most religiously liberal, ritually lax, ultra-rationalistic American Reform rabbi, but which at "the same time excludes the non-Semitic Unitarian." In practical terms Felsenthal intended a definition of Judaism that would place great emphasis on all facets of Jewish culture—language, literature, traditions—and on Zionism.

Kohler warned against any support for Zionism, for he saw it as opposed to the "mission of Israel," which demanded the dispersal of the

Jews and implied "that we have for us and for our children a land dearer and holier to us" than the land Jews live in. Wise voiced his opposition to Zionism in 1899, because, as he said, "We are American citizens, who will never violate our allegiance to our country. . . . Judaism is to us a system of religion and ethics, with a mission to mankind, entirely independent of nationality, politics . . ." (*Hebrew Union College Journal,* vol. 4, no. 3 [1899]). Felsenthal answered Wise, saying that

> it is "mean and base" for American Jews to oppose the endeavors of liberty-loving, philanthropic, and especially philosemitic fellow-Israelites, who ardently wish that for their suffering brethren such secure homes may be established, in which they can enjoy as much freedom and independence as is granted to the inhabitants of a village in a backwoods county in an American state or territory.

Solomon Schechter. In 1906 Solomon Schechter, president of the Jewish Theological Seminary, the training school for Conservative rabbis, hailed Zionism "as the great bulwark against assimilation," which he defined as the "loss of identity; or that process of disintegration which, passing through various degrees of defiance of all Jewish thought and of disloyalty to Israel's history and its mission, . . . is consummated by a final, though imperceptible, absorption in the great majority." The issue concerned the survival of the Jewish people, especially so in American society. What threatened survival was "a sort of 'eclectic religiosity' that coquettes with the various churches"—i.e., the definition of Judaism as a universal religion, stripped of its own unique culture, language, literature, and the sense of its historic national identity. In response, Schechter claimed that

> Zionism declares boldly to the world that Judaism means to preserve its life by *not* losing its life. It shall be a true and healthy life, with a policy of its own, a religion wholly its own, invigorated by sacred memories and sacred environments, and proving a tower of strength and of unity not only for the remnants gathered within the borders of the Holy Land, but also for those who shall, by choice or necessity, prefer what now constitutes the Galuth [Diaspora]. It has enriched our literature . . . [and labors] to

make the sacred tongue a living language. . . . Zionism has succeeded in bringing back into the fold many men and women, who otherwise would have been lost to Judaism. It has given them a new interest in the synagogue and everything Jewish.

> (pp. 95, 101)

Schechter espoused Zionism not only because a return to the Holy Land would be the fulfillment of biblical prophecy and the establishment of a Jewish commonwealth would be a mandate of Jewish history, but also because the Zionists' program of cultural revival and national regeneration was in accord with a definition of Judaism and Jewish identity that alone would assure Jewish survival. Zacharias Frankel formulated such a definition in mid-nineteenth century in Germany and called it "positive historical Judaism." It describes Judaism as the product of historical development. It demands a positive attitude toward traditional Judaism—namely, that the complex of Jewish values, practices, and ideals is not lightly to be surrendered. The specifically Jewish elements in Judaism—such as the Hebrew language—are essential to the preservation of its character and vitality. The Jews, to be sure, are a religious community, and more, they are a *people,* with a history, a way of life, and a national destiny.

Israel Friedlaender. Among the co-workers of Schechter who best expressed this view was Israel Friedlaender, a professor at the Jewish Theological Seminary and founder of the Young Israel movement in Orthodoxy. He introduced to American Jewry the cultural Zionism of Zionist ideologist Ahad Ha-am and the Diaspora nationalism of historian Simon Dubnow. He was thus devoted both to the establishment of a Jewish community in Palestine and to the fashioning of a vital Jewish community in America.

Friedlaender emphasized the need for a national identity and a cultural renaissance for the American Jewish community. He found American Jewry at the beginning of the twentieth century wanting in both ideology and practice. Religion divorced from nationality and culture could neither save nor survive. He noted that "the theory of a Jewish Mission" does not "exert the slightest influence upon the life and activity of the individual Jew or of the Jews as a whole." If Judaism would survive in America, he argued, then "it must break the narrow frame of a creed and resume its original function as a culture" (p. 267).

The emancipated Jews of Western Europe adopted the thesis "Judaism *qua* Religion"; their brethren in Eastern Europe, seeking emancipation, countered with the antithesis "Judaism *qua* nationalism." The American Jews were working out the synthesis "Religion *plus* Nationalism"—a development that "nowhere assumed such huge proportions and such striking development as it did in America." This, Friedlaender maintained, was the true and authentic description of Judaism, for "Judaism was essentially a *national* religion . . . [and] the Jewish people was, first and foremost, a *religious* nation." A community living in response to the mandates of such an identity, religious and national, "deeply rooted on its national soil, clinging to the traditions of a great past," not only would be true to itself, but would become "a most valuable and stimulating factor in the public and civic life of any country." In America only "a sharply marked community, distinct and distinguished," would add "a new note to the richness of American life, leading a new current into the stream of American civilization." In service to America and to mankind the American Jew would have to demonstrate "the courage to be different, to think his own thoughts, to feel his own feelings, to live his own life . . . but with the lofty consciousness that only in this way does he fulfill his destiny—for the benefit of mankind" (pp. 253–278).

Friedlaender called for the assumption of a religious and national identity expressed through a life of broad Jewish culture—language, literature, art, music, folkways, and national memories and aspirations. He recognized that the American scene made religious identity readily acceptable and the synagogue functionally useful. He called on organized religion to frame a wider and more inclusive definition of Judaism and on the synagogue to fashion its program in accordance with such a national, religious, and cultural concept.

The narrower creedal definition of Judaism formulated in the nineteenth century had been in response to the perception of America as a "melting pot" (though the term was first used in the twentieth century), which demanded ethnic and cultural assimilation, accepting only religious differentiation. The climate in twentieth-century America that Friedlaender found hospitable to his broader national and cultural definition was due to a changing image of America, early perceived and advocated by two secular ideologists of Jewish life, Chaim Zhitlowsky and Horace M. Kallen. Each attacked the "melting-pot" image from his own background and stance, calling the concept inimical to American culture and civilization, urging a new view that would foster the cultural pluralism that would in turn preserve democracy and contribute to a vibrant culture. Not incidentally, according to these thinkers, Jewish survival would be greatly enhanced by the acceptance of the legitimacy and worth of cultural pluralism.

Cultural Pluralism. Dr. Chaim Zhitlowsky came to America in 1904 and was for the next forty years the chief advocate and architect of Yiddish cultural nationalism. In 1911 he advocated an image of America as a "nation of united nationalities . . . where each national individuality unfolds and brings into the open all the richness with which its soul may be blessed by nature." Such an America could act as an example of different nationalities living in peace and cooperative harmony: "This nation can become a light unto the nations, a model of how they should live with each other." Such a peaceful creative unity of national cultures would lead to mutual enrichment, to the benefit of American civilization. For the Jews he advocated a national culture to be expressed in the Yiddish language, which he called "a colossal national preservation force." Yiddish cultural nationalism did not last beyond the immigrant generation, but Zhitlowsky's vision of a nation of nationalities helped the European immigrant Jew feel more at home in America, provided justification for ethno-cultural identity and cultural creativity, and urged acceptance of cultural pluralism upon a large segment of the American Jewish community.

It was Horace M. Kallen, Harvard-educated student and disciple of William James, who gave currency to the concept of cultural pluralism. "Democracy *versus* the Melting Pot" appeared in *The Nation* in February 1915. True democracy, Kallen argued, demands an imaging of America other than as a "melting pot." His seminal essay concludes with "the outlines of a possibly great and truly democratic commonwealth": "Its form would be that of a federal republic; its substance a democracy of nationalities, cooperating voluntarily and autonomously. . . . The common language . . . would be English, but each nationality would have . . . its own individual and inevitable esthetic and intellectual forms."

Five years earlier Kallen had been critical of those who erase Jewish group identity and uniqueness: "What really destroys the Jews is what 'universalizes' them, what empties their lives of distinctive content and substitutes void phrases to be filled with any meaning the social and religious fashion of the day casts up" (p. 28). He called for "the persistence of a 'Jewish separation' that shall be national, positive, dynamic and adequate." His friend and disciple, Milton R. Konvitz, claims that Kallen "arrived at Cultural Pluralism through his thinking about himself as a Jew and the meaning and significance that his Jewishness should have for him" (p. 76).

Mordecai M. Kaplan. In American Jewish life the period between World Wars I and II was the era of cultural pluralism—an era in which Jewish religious, cultural, and institutional life underwent significant change. The chief figure in the redefinition of Judaism and the reconstitution of Jewish life was Mordecai M. Kaplan.

Kaplan's definition of Judaism is distilled from those of Felsenthal and Friedlaender with their emphasis on a broad definition that included the cultural and national elements as well as the religious. His advocacy of Jewish corporate existence in America as an "organic community" echoes the emphases of Zhitlowsky and Kallen. The title of his magnum opus, *Judaism as a Civilization* (1934), presents his definition: Judaism is the evolving religious civilization of the Jewish people. Civilization includes "peoplehood, history, language, music, literature and art" in which the Jewish people is the enduring, creative constant. The motive force of this civilization is religion. Like the civilization itself, religion is evolving, growing, changing, yet basic forms persist. "The conservation of form with the reconstruction of meaning has been the history of the Jewish civilization." The citizen of a modern state, Kaplan argues, "is not only permitted but encouraged to give allegiance to two civilizations; one, the secular civilization of the country in which he lives, and the other the Christian which he has inherited from the past."

The American Jew lives at one and the same time in two civilizations, that of America and that of his group. The distinction would suggest "his *religious* group," but for historical and ideological reasons Kaplan would not use the phrase. It would conjure up memories of the narrowly defined "religious communalism" of classic Reform; it would tempt one to conclude that American Jewry is a religious "community" rather than a "civilization"; and it would suggest organization along religious rather than communal lines. "Jewish communal life," he continues, "is the *sine qua non* of cooperation among Jews. In America, particularly, Jews will need a measure of communal autonomy if American-Jewish life is to develop along broad inclusive lines." And, he says, "Congregations will be units in these communities. . . . The community, however, is larger than its congregations" (*Judaism,* pp. 516–517).

Kaplan's definition of Judaism as a religious civilization was accepted as normative in Conservative Judaism, and he directly influenced Reform in its redefinition. The Pittsburgh Conference of 1885 defined Judaism as "the highest conception of the God idea." In 1937 the Central Conference of American Rabbis redefined it as "the historical religious experience of the Jewish people."

"To survive the present crisis," Kaplan argued, "the Jewish religion will have to transform itself from an other-worldly religion offering to conduct the individual to life eternal through the agency of the traditional Torah, which is regarded as supernaturally revealed, into a religion which can help Jews attain this-worldly salvation." The issue is survival, as it had been for the earlier American ideologists of Judaism. Modernity and freedom made Jewish survival problematical, the former challenging the traditional tenets of the faith, the latter affording easy access into the dominant host society. Kaplan undertook the task of the "modernization" of the ancient faith, attempting to make it accord with the "truths" revealed about man and his world by modern advances in the natural and social sciences. The focus of religion was turned from supernaturalism and otherworldliness, from a personal God and man in service of him, to acceptance of the natural order of being as man perceives it and science presents it, to the world as man observes it and experiences it, and to the concept of a deity that man comes to know "only as a member of society" and that is the "cosmic process that makes for man's life abundant, or salvation."

Kaplan's is a radical revaluation of Jewish tradition and even more so of God. He argues that "traditional Jewish religion belongs to an altogether different universe of discourse from that of modern man. . . . The traditional concept of God is challenged by history, anthropology and psychology. . . . As long as Jews adhere to the traditional conception of Torah as supernaturally revealed, they would not be amenable to any constructive adjustment of Judaism that [is] needed to render it viable." There is need then for a *new* concept, a new understanding of God and of the source of religious truth. The ancients looked to a "God of miracles," the theologians to a "God of metaphysics," Kaplan to a "God of experience"—not a God of individual experience but a God of group experience. For Kaplan, "it is only as a member of society that man comes to know God at all."

How does man become aware of God and what is God? Kaplan claims that the objective study of religion proves beyond a doubt that "belief in God originated neither in speculative reasoning nor in any supernatural revelation." How then did it come to be?

> *By the same token that man becomes aware of himself as a person engaged in a struggle against dangers and difficulties, he also becomes cognizant of the help of a power or powers to conquer obstacles.*

What is most distinctive about himself as a person is termed "soul," and what is most distinctive about the power or powers upon whom he depends is termed God.

> *We suggest that God be thought of as the cosmic process that makes for man's life abundant or salvation.*
>
> (*Future*, pp. 171, 183)

"Salvation," according to Kaplan, is "when our mind functions in such a way that we feel that all our powers are actively employed in the achievement of desirable ends."

Revelation is not a historic event but a theological concept. The Bible is not the source of religious truth but a source of religious instruction if its contents are revaluated by "disengaging from the traditional content those elements in it which answer permanent postulates of human nature, and . . . integrating them into our own ideology." The same is to be done with the entire Jewish religious tradition. The traditions of a group or a people are sacred because they have become the *Sancta*, the sacred objects of the group, and they are therefore retained, but in

order for them to maintain vitality their meaning or message often needs reinterpretation.

Kaplan's theology has been subjected to serious criticism. His most gifted disciple, Milton Steinberg, raises these questions:

> Because Kaplan has refused any description of his God . . . because he speaks so generally of the God-idea rather than of God; because he shrinks God to those aspects of reality which enhance man's life . . . [the] actuality of God is brought under question. . . . Does God exist or is He only man's notion? The universe is left unexplained . . . The need arises for another God . . . who shall account for the world. . . . Something alarmingly close to tribalism is revived.
>
> (p. 183)

Others would question Kaplan's continuous insistence on placing "survival" at the center of the enterprise of Judaism, questioning the religious validity of statements such as that "Judaism, to evoke American Jews' loyalty, must be not only compatible with their loyalty to America but also corroborative of it." But in spite of these criticisms there is wide agreement that no American Jewish religious thinker has subjected Judaism to so comprehensive and searching an analysis as has Kaplan and that no one has put forth a more authentic and useful definition of Judaism.

In the Postwar World: Existentialism. The post–World War II decades saw the entry of American Jews into areas of American economic, social, and cultural life that had previously been largely closed to them. American Jewry partook of the religious revival of the time. Whether it was a social or theological phenomenon may still be debated, but it clearly gave the American Jew a sense of well-being and a feeling of being at home in America, invigorated organized religious life, placed synagogue and rabbi at the center of Jewish activity, and brought on interest—even a spurt of theological creativity—in Jewish religious thought. It also brought on a confrontation with the meaning of the Holocaust and served as the arena for the most creative and influential American Jewish theologian, Abraham Joshua Heschel. Survival in the post-Holocaust world seemed not so much a problem to be dealt with by the best minds as a challenge to be confronted by communal enterprise. Freed of the need to justify Jewish survival or to fashion strategies for it, intellectual energies could now turn to theology. It became the fashion to read and quote the works of Martin Buber, but his influence was far greater on Christian thought than on Jewish. His books on Hasidism received a respectable readership, but his opposition to Jewish law, ritual, and ceremonies, which he saw as roadblocks on man's way to God, vitiated whatever influence he might have had. Far more influential were the life and thought of Buber's friend and co-worker, Franz Rosenzweig.

First introduced to the English-speaking reader in 1941 by Jacob B. Agus in his *Modern Philosophies of Judaism,* Rosenzweig became a dominant force in American Jewish religious thought with the publication of Nahum N. Glatzer's *Franz Rosenzweig: His Life and Thought* a dozen years later. In his introduction to a symposium on Jewish thought by American Jewish rabbis that appeared in *Commentary* (published in book form as *The Condition of Jewish Belief,* 1966), Milton Himmelfarb notes that almost half the participants, "mostly youngish," could be called disciples of Rosenzweig and states that "the single greatest influence on the religious thought of North American Jewry, therefore, is a German Jew—a layman, not a rabbi—who died before Hitler took power and who came to Judaism from the very portals of the Church."

No doubt his rejection of Christianity (which some of his Jewish-born friends had embraced) and his zealous turning to Judaism with an ever-growing allegiance to the Law evoked the enthusiastic approval of rabbis ever concerned with Jewish survival, but they were also taken with his espousal and presentation of an existentialist expression of Judaism. Agus wrote in 1955 that Rosenzweig's genius

> is felt as a living influence in the intellectual circles that incline toward the impassioned decisiveness of existentialism. . . . Our soul [Rosenzweig declared] is unhappy when left alone in isolation from the universe. It finds the meaning of its life . . . in the message of love that is directed to it from [God] . . . and seeks to unfold the infinite implications of the assurance of divine love. . . . The Jewish people owes its character and destiny to an act of Divine love—revelation, which the Jewish people translated into a host of sacred books and a Law.

The living God who calls in love and awaits response in deeds, a sacred literature ever unfolding truths that instruct life, and an all-encompassing legal system as the Jewish vocabulary of response have been the three intertwined themes of contemporary Jewish thought.

In America, too, it was Will Herberg, a layman and not a rabbi, who, "converting" from Marxism to Judaism, was the first to expound the philosophy of existentialism to the American Jew and did so in dramatic and challenging language:

> We must dare the leap [of faith] . . . but once the decision . . . has been made, it is seen that the leap was possible only because the gulf had already been bridged from the other side. [Man's] capacity for good, though grounded in his nature, needs the grace of God for its realization. [Israel] is a supernatural community, called into being by God to serve his eternal purposes in history . . . a community created by God's special act of covenant.
>
> (pp. 39, 76)

For the Jew, Herberg states, the authentic response to the divine call is to live a life of holiness through the wholehearted acceptance of the Law, the content of which is provided by "the historical belief and practice of the community of Israel."

Two decades later, in 1972, *Time* magazine, in a cover essay on "What It Means to Be Jewish," noted:

> Among the most influential Jewish thinkers is a cross-denominational group of theologians and philosophers who have become known as the "Covenant theologians." What they try to promote, explains theologian Seymour Siegel, is the idea that Jews "are *not* a people like other people, nor a religious society promoting certain metaphysical principles and ideas, but a group joined together in relation to God." The Covenant theologians . . . generally agree that the Jews' special relationship with God demands some kind of loyalty to traditional Jewish law. "Without law the Covenant is empty and even meaningless," says Siegel. "There can be no Covenant without observance."

The Holocaust: Challenge and Response. The greatest challenge to the traditional Jewish belief in an omnipotent and good God was presented by the Holocaust. Most Jewish thinkers, stunned and perplexed by so shattering and traumatic an event, found themselves unable to address its theological meaning. Others strode boldly forward, aware of the painful task of the revision or the affirmation of long-held theological positions.

Richard Rubenstein's *After Auschwitz* (1968) was a radical revision. He could admire Pastor Heinrich Grüber's heroic resistance to Nazism, but he had to reject his theological view.

> If I believed in God as the omnipotent author of the historical drama and Israel as His Chosen People, I had to accept Dean Grueber's conclusion that it was God's will that Hitler committed six million Jews to slaughter. I could not possibly believe in such a God nor could I believe in Israel as the Chosen People of God after Auschwitz.

"We live in a time of the death of God," said Rubenstein, which meant that human existence was perceived as neither planned nor purposeful, God was no longer the guarantor of morality, the cosmos was indifferent to the human situation, which was devoid of any transcendental purpose, and the covenant between God and his people of Israel was sundered. Said Rubenstein:

> My own way of facing the question of God and the deathcamps has been to regard life as arriving out of God's Nothingness and ultimately returning to that same Nothingness. . . . The ironies and tragedies of life can only be overcome by a return to God's Nothingness. Auschwitz is part of the terrible price we have to pay for the human condition.

It was because of the new perception of the human condition and Jewish situation that Jews should have felt all the more the need for Jewish community and Jewish ritual, according to Rubenstein: "It is precisely the ultimate hopelessness and gratuity of our human situation which calls forth our strongest need for religious community. If all we have is one another, then assuredly we need one another more than ever."

No longer a community of faith, but a "community of shared predicament and ultimate concern," Jews needed to mark decisive events in life —birth, adulthood, marriage, death—in the company of the community, which through participation reveals and expresses its ultimate concerns. Jews turned from the God of history, whom they could no longer affirm, to the God of nature, to the "ancient earth gods and the realities to which they point."

Eliezer Berkowitz's *Faith After the Holocaust*

(1973) is an affirmation of the manner in which Judaism has viewed its history and its God. The Holocaust is an event in history; it is only its magnitude that gives it the aspect of uniqueness. As Berkowitz notes, "Without the insults, humiliations, and degradations heaped by Christianity upon Judaism . . . without the ceaseless oppression, discrimination, expulsions, pogroms, massacres practiced in Christian lands on the Jews, the Holocaust would not have been possible." The problem of theodicy has long confronted the Jewish people, and an adequate explanation has been available to the faithful as well. The very survival of the Jewish people points to a living God who has chosen them to be his people. But he is a God of the hidden face: "I will surely hide my Face" (Deut. 31:18). Why the hiding of the face? Berkowitz's answer is not "punishment" but "human freedom." For man to be fully man, he must have the freedom of moral choice. To grant man this freedom, God turns his face, absents himself from history:

> Justice, love, peace, mercy are ideals for man only. They are values that may be realized by man alone. God is perfection. Yet because of His very perfection, He is lacking—as it were—one type of value; the one which is the result of striving for that value. . . . He who demands justice of God must give up man; He who asks for God's love and mercy beyond justice must accept suffering [for God's love and mercy would extend to the evildoers as well].

And yet, Berkowitz affirms, God of the hiding face does not withdraw his presence from the world, his providential concern from history. It is his providential presence that keeps man from ultimate folly. He points to the establishment of the State of Israel and its victory in the Six-Day War (1967) as "positive proof of God's presence in history." He posits the continued existence of the State of Israel as a theological imperative, for it is an indication of God's presence after the Holocaust.

Existentialist philosopher Hans Jonas' argument in his *The Phenomenon of Life: Toward a Philosophical Biology* (1966) expresses a concept of God that gained considerable acceptance after the Holocaust:

> The *Deus absconditus*, the hidden God, is a profoundly un-Jewish conception. Our teaching

holds that we can understand God, not completely, to be sure, but something of Him—of His will, intentions, and even, nature, because he has told us. There has been revelation. . . . After Auschwitz . . . an omnipotent deity would have to be either not good or totally unintelligible. But if God is to be intelligible . . . (and to this we most hold), then his goodness must be compatible with the existence of evil, and this it is only if He is not *all*-powerful.

He is a suffering, becoming, caring God, but a "God who for a time—the time of the ongoing world process—has divested himself of any power to interfere with the physical course of things." Yet, because he is caring, God "responds to the impact on His being of worldly events . . . with the mutely insistent appeal of His unfulfilled aim."

Elie Wiesel, an Auschwitz survivor, spoke to the post-Holocaust generation through autobiographical novels, each more mystical and profound. He experienced the death of God in Auschwitz, saw him hanging on the gallows that had taken the life of a boy, "the little servant, the sad-eyed angel." He called this first of his works *Night* (1960). Five novels later, in *The Gates of the Forest* (1966), the survivor, Gregor, as if in response to his own question, "After what has happened to us, how can you believe in God?" speaks to Clara, a survivor who has become his wife:

> "Whether the Messiah comes doesn't matter; we'll manage without him. It is because it is too late that we are commanded to hope. . . . The Messiah isn't one man, Clara, he's all men. As long as there are men there will be a Messiah." Gregor recited the *Kaddish*, that solemn affirmation, filled with grandeur and serenity, by which man returns to God his crown and sceptre.

Abraham Joshua Heschel, the most gifted Jewish theologian in the postwar age, turned from theological speculation to prophetic exhortation in *Man's Quest for God* (1954).

> At no time has the earth been so soaked with blood. Fellowmen turned out to be evil ghosts, monstrous and weird. Ashamed and dismayed we ask: Who is responsible? We have called for the Lord. He came. And was ignored. We have preached but eluded him. We have praised but defied him. Now we reap the fruits of our failure. . . . We have failed to fight *for* right, *for* jus-

tice, *for* goodness. . . . Where were we when men learned to hate in the days of starvation? . . . The conscience of the world was destroyed by those who were waiting to blame others rather than themselves. . . . Our martyred brothers . . . died with disdain and scorn for a civilization in which the killing of civilians could become a carnival of fun. . . . The greatest task of our time is to take the souls of men out of the pit. . . . God is involved . . . God will return to us when we shall be willing to let Him in—into our banks and factories, into our Congress and clubs . . . into our homes. . . . For God is everywhere, or nowhere, the Father of all men or women. . . . The apostles of force have shown us that they are great in evil. Let us reveal that we can be as great in goodness. . . . There can be no neutrality.

Abraham Joshua Heschel. Scion of an aristocratic Hasidic family of scholars, educated in Poland and Germany, Heschel became in America what Reinhold Niebuhr predicted for him on the publication of his first work, *Man Is Not Alone: A Philosophy of Religion* (1951): "a commanding and authoritative voice not only in the Jewish community but in the religious life of America." His was a commanding and demanding voice at the White House Conference on Aging (1961), at the National Conference on Religion and Race (1963) during the civil rights movement, and among the advocates of peace during the Vietnam War. He marched with Martin Luther King, Jr., in Selma, Alabama, and was the Jewish theological expert at Vatican II. His voice was heard in the classrooms of the Jüdische Lehrhaus in Frankfurt, the Institute for Jewish Studies in Warsaw, the Hebrew Union College in Cincinnati, and the Jewish Theological Seminary in New York, as well as on campuses, at conventions and conferences, and from pulpits throughout the United States. He reached, and continues to reach, his widest audience through a series of books written in a poetic, epigrammatic style urging and instructing man how to attain "a vision of the sacred."

> Technical civilization is man's conquest of space. . . . But time is the heart of existence. . . . [In the] realm of time, the goal is not to have but to be, not to own but to give, not to control but to share, not to subdue but to be in accord. . . .
>
> Every one of us occupies a portion of space. . . . No one possesses space. . . . Through ownership of space, I am a rival of all other

beings; through my living in time, I am a contemporary of all other beings. . . .

Time is the presence of God in the world of space . . . in the dimension of time man meets God.

(*The Sabbath*, pp. 3, 99, 100)

Heschel's is the existentialist approach. He begins not with systems, philosophical or theological, but with man as he is. *Man Is Not Alone* opens with the idea that "there are three aspects of nature which command man's attention: power, loveliness, grandeur. Power, he exploits, loveliness he enjoys, grandeur fills him with awe" (p. 3). Modern man, according to Heschel, needs no instruction in how to exploit power, nor direction in how to enjoy loveliness; but how to stand in awe of grandeur is a lost art that man must recover.

Awareness of grandeur brings no physical or aesthetic reward, serves no social purpose, and it may even fill us with fright or resignation. "Still we insist that it is unworthy of man not to take notice of the sublime." Man does look beyond himself, seemingly impelled to transcend himself by reaching out to mystery in awe and to grandeur in radical amazement. He seeks to live in a partnership with him who is beyond the mystery and grandeur of the universe, a presence that he cannot express, the ineffable, which he senses, feels, and knows is *all*. "God in the universe is a spirit of concern for life. What is a thing to us is a concern to God." God is a God of pathos. Although inexpressible, God is reachable because he cares.

In the relationship between God and man, God is the subject, man the object. Man seeks God, and "God [is] in search of man" (the title Heschel gives to his book on his philosophy of Judaism [1956]):

There is only one way to define Jewish religion. It is the awareness of God's interest in man, the awareness of a covenant, of a responsibility that lies on Him as well as on us. . . . God is in need of man for the attainment of His ends, and religion . . . is a way of serving these ends, of which we are in need . . . ends which we must learn to feel the need of.

"Jewish faith," says Heschel, "is an attitude, the joy of living a life in which God has a stake . . . of being needed, of having a vocation, of being commanded." A pious Jew, Heschel sees

"genuine history enshrined in our rituals," yet, he warns, "ritual loyalty, theology, remain deficient unless there is an on-going responsiveness . . . to the demands of immediate history, of our own situation." The most authentic spokesmen of Judaism have not been its theologians who speak *about* God, but its prophets, who speak *for* God. Heschel is a theologian, but in the prophetic tradition.

As American Jewry became ever more integrated into the social, cultural, and spiritual fabric of America, the central concerns of its religious thinkers intensified to concern for the quality of the inner life of the individual and expanded to encompass concern for the survival of the human race. The form of expression changed as well, from theological thinking to existentialist involvement. Einhorn, in concern for the Jewish situation in his time, expounded the mission idea; Heschel, in response to the human condition in his time, lived a life of social concern. Spiritual spokesmen express in an intense and articulate manner the central concerns of their people.

BIBLIOGRAPHY

Jewish Literature

Abraham Chapman, ed., *Jewish-American Literature: An Anthology* (1974); Theodore Gross, ed., *The Literature of American Jews* (1973); Louis Harap, *The Image of the Jew in American Literature: From Early Republic to Mass Immigration* (1974); Abraham J. Karp, *Haven and Home: A History of the Jews in America* (1985); Charles A. Madison, *Yiddish Literature: Its Scope and Major Writers* (1968); Irving Malin and Irwin Stark, *Breakthrough: A Treasury of Contemporary American-Jewish Literature* (1964); J. K. Miklizanski, *A History of Hebrew Literature in America* (1967; in Hebrew); Daniel Walden, ed., *On Being Jewish: American Jewish Writers from Cahan to Bellow* (1974).

Jewish Religious Thought

Edward McNall Burns, *The American Idea of Mission* (1957); David Einhorn, *Olat Tamid: Book of Prayers for Israelitish Congregations* (English tr. 1872); Bernhard Felsenthal, "Fundamental Principles of Judaism," in *The Maccabean*, vol. 1, no. 2 (1901); Israel Friedlaender, *Past and Present: A Collection of Jewish Essays* (1919); Albert H. Friedlander, ed., *Out of the Whirlwind: A Reader of Holocaust Literature* (1968); James G. Heller, *Isaac M. Wise: His Life, Work, and Thought* (1965); Will Herberg, *Judaism and Modern Man: An Interpretation of Jewish Religion* (1952); Abraham Joshua Heschel, *Between God and Man: An Interpretation of Judaism*, ed. Fritz A. Rothschild (1959), and *The Sabbath: Its Meaning for Modern Man* (1951).

Horace Kallen, *Judaism at Bay: Essays Toward the Adjustment of Judaism to Modernity* (1932); Mordecai M. Kaplan, *Judaism as a Civilization: Toward a Reconstruction of American-Jewish Life* (1934) and *The Future of the American Jew* (1948); Kaufmann Kohler, *Studies, Addresses, and Personal Papers* (1931) and, as ed., *David Einhorn, Memorial Volume: Selected Sermons and Addresses* (1911); Milton R. Konvitz, "Horace Mayer Kallen," in *American Jewish Yearbook, 1974–75;* Simon Noveck, ed., *Contemporary Jewish Thought: A Reader* (1963); W. Gunther Plaut, *The Growth of Reform Judaism: American and European Sources Until 1948* (1965).

Solomon Schechter, *Seminary Addresses, and Other Papers* (1915); Joseph D. Soloveitchik, *On Repentance,* tr. Pinchas H. Peli (1980); Milton Steinberg, *Anatomy of Faith* (1960); Mordecai Waxman, *Tradition and Change: The Development of Conservative Judaism* (1958).

[*See also* JUDAISM IN CONTEMPORARY AMERICA; RELIGION AND LITERATURE; *and* SOCIAL HISTORY OF AMERICAN JUDAISM.]

THE CALVINIST THEOLOGICAL TRADITION

William K. B. Stoever

TOWARD the end of the seventeenth century, *Calvinist* came to designate the theological tradition of Reformed Protestantism deriving from the Swiss and Southwest German Reformers. Reformed theology was not John Calvin's sole creation, nor was it dependent on his personal authority, though his *Institutes of the Christian Religion* (1559) was a forceful statement of Reformed views and long served as a source of theological instruction in Reformed churches. At the same time, Reformed thinkers turned as readily to other "standard Reformed divines" as they did to Calvin.

CALVINIST DOCTRINE

Reformed doctrine achieved fullest formal expression in the Heidelberg Catechism (1563), the Canons of the Synod of Dort (1619), and the Confession and Catechisms of the Westminster Assembly (1647), the principal dogmatic statements, respectively, of German, Dutch, and English Reformed Protestantism. The Westminster Confession was affirmed variously by the Congregationalist Puritans of Massachusetts Bay (1648, 1680) and of Connecticut (1708); by the Philadelphia Association of Baptists (1707); and by American Presbyterians (1729). Scottish Presbyterians and Dutch and German Reformed brought their appropriations of the tradition to North America. The Anglican Thirty-nine Articles of Religion (1563) were Reformed in theology; later Anglicanism and its Wesleyan derivative manifested the tradition in its "Arminian" variant. A majority of the people who "declared their independence in 1776" thus bore the imprint of Reformed Protestantism, which continued to inform the religious and moral aspirations of Americans, in varying degree, into the twentieth century.

The Calvinist tradition shared with the Lutheran the characteristic Protestant doctrines of salvation by grace alone, freely given by God, and by faith alone, understood as trust in God's intent to save in one's own case; of the Bible as the sole repository of Christian truth; and of the church as the company of the faithful, taught by the Holy Spirit in the biblical word. The Reformed distinguished themselves in their emphasis on the sovereignty of God as an organizing principal in theology and as the ground of confidence of salvation; in their understanding of the Lord's Supper as a spiritual communion of the living substance and life-giving power of the exalted Christ; and in their comprehensive sense of Christian obligation to organize earthly life, civil and ecclesiastical, in conformity with God's revealed will.

Central to Reformed thought was the affirmation of God's sovereign freedom. The being, particular condition, and destiny of all creatures depend upon God's determination concerning them, concluded in eternity before time, solely according to his "free good pleasure." Crucial also was affirmation of the catastrophic consequences of Adam's disobedience to the divine command. From this original apostasy, man is guilty before God and corrupted in his nature, incapable of knowing God as he is or of loving him as his highest good, and mankind is justly condemned to eternal punishment. Further, all human action is vitiated by sin, understood as deliberate disobedience to God's law, and the sinner, seeking his own ends in preference to God's, is at enmity with his creator.

From this situation, only a new creative act on God's part can save, an act restoring corrupt human nature, illuminating the darkened mind, reordering the perverse will. Such an act is made possible through the work of Christ, the god-man, who in his life and death satisfied divine justice respecting the punishment due to sin and fulfilled in all particulars the requirements of the divine law. Redemption thus obtained is sufficient for all mankind, but is effective only for those whom God has chosen for it. To these, redemption is "applied" through the ministry of law and Gospel, awakening sinners to their need for grace and their utter inability to attain it, and declaring to them God's offer of pardon to all who believe. Faith, as trusting God and relying on Christ for salvation, alone justifies in God's sight, not as a human act meriting pardon, but as the instrument ordained by God for joining the benefits of Christ's work and sinners' necessity. That a particular individual believes is due solely to God's eternal determination to save him, and the act of faith is the effect of supernatural grace freely given, apart from any natural ability to believe or other qualification in the individual. The same supernatural grace enables the believer, willingly though imperfectly, to obey the moral law, God's rule for the conduct of human life, of which the Decalogue is the summation.

Godly works manifest divine grace to and in the worker, and diligence in them affects God's proximate, though not his ultimate, treatment of the Christian. The sacrament of the Lord's Supper seals and sustains the life of grace, in union and communion with Christ, of which relationship faith is both medium and first fruit. The absolute sovereignty of God's will in election, and the entire sufficiency of God's power to accomplish what he wills, are together the foundation of Christians' assurance of salvation, and of their sure continuance in the life of grace until it is perfected in heaven. The object of this entire transaction, encompassing the work of creation, mankind's fall, Christ's sacrifice, the glorification of the elect, and the perdition of the nonelect, is "the manifestation of [God's] glory in a way of justice upon the reprobate, [and] in a way of justice tempered with mercy upon the elect" (John Norton, *The Orthodox Evangelist,* 1654, pp. 55–56).

The foregoing is, in outline, the sum of Reformed teaching as received in New England in the middle third of the seventeenth century.

Thereafter, its history in America was one of gradual erosion in the face of social and intellectual conditions uncongenial to it, punctuated by defenses of varying potency. It was also in significant part the history of the adaptation of Reformed theology to the experiential piety distinctive of English and New England Puritans, which, via a succession of "awakenings," became the dominant force in American Protestantism. Determined to create churches of the truly godly, Puritans made experience of grace in conversion the definitive event in a Christian's life, and they made the manner in which God translates individuals from bondage in sin to union with Christ the principal interest in theology. Unlike revivalists of a later era, Puritans viewed conversion as unfolding gradually under the ministry of preaching and instruction, not as instantaneous or primarily emotional. By focusing on conversion, however, they shaped the issues that dominated American Calvinism until they were eclipsed in the late nineteenth century by different concerns.

NEW ENGLAND PURITANS

The Puritan clergy who settled New England, trained largely at Cambridge, belonged to the generation of Protestants who systematized Reformation doctrine in the idiom of late scholasticism. They read Calvin, but cited Theodore Beza and David Pareus more often, and, in their formal divinity, drew upon medieval and contemporary scholastics and upon a multitude of Protestant divines, English and Continental. In logic and rhetoric they tended to follow the French philosopher Petrus Ramus (Pierre de la Ramée). In psychology, physics, metaphysics, and cosmology, and in their sense of the unity of knowledge, of which theology is the crown and God the end, they were Protestant schoolmen. Like their mentor William Ames, whose divinity handbooks *Medulla Theologica* (1623; Eng. tr., 1642) and *De Conscientiae* (1630; Eng. tr., 1643) were standard reading in New England, they considered theology a practical rather than a speculative discipline. Theology is "the doctrine of living to God." It comprises faith, the heart's resting on God for salvation, and "observance," willing performance of what God commands.

THE CALVINIST THEOLOGICAL TRADITION

Like all arts, theology's end is *eupraxia,* good practice. It is the noblest art, for it consists in enjoyment of God and obedience that aims at God's glory. Theology is thus the guide to living well in an ultimate sense, and as such there is no realm of human activity, including "domestic economy, morality, political life, or lawmaking" (Eusden, ed. 1968, bk. II, i), to which it is not pertinent. Central to theology is the application of redemption to the elect, in effectual calling, which comprises union and communion with Christ, which together encompass the act of faith, justification before God, adoption as God's child, infusion of sanctifying grace, and perfection of holiness in heaven. Collectively, these topics define the character and prospects of Christian existence.

In New England, theological exposition was essentially pastoral, and its form predominantly sermonic. The bulk of it dealt with calling. Thomas Hooker, minister at Hartford, Connecticut, during a long career in England and America preached exhaustively on the topic, and died while reworking his material for publication. An extensive fragment of it appeared posthumously as *The Application of Redemption* (1656). *The Sound Believer; or, A Treatise of Evangelicall Conversion* (1645), by Thomas Shepard, minister at Newtown (Cambridge), Massachusetts, was also a sermon cycle. In it, Shepard carefully reviewed the stages of conversion, ranging from initial conviction of sin, through the work of faith, to glorification, and concluded with a meditation on the obedience that the faithful are to render to God, according to the moral law. Published in London, it became part of the standard Puritan literature of practical divinity. The characteristic literary form of Protestant scholasticism was the *loci communes,* or common places, of divinity, methodically arranged. New England's representation of the form was John Norton's *The Orthodox Evangelist* (1654). Norton, minister at Ipswich, began with the divine essence, progressed to the divine subsistence, Christ and his work, the divine decree, and the divine efficiency, and ended with the estate of the blessed. The heart of his treatise was devoted to conversion. All three men gave extended attention to the "antecedents" of conversion, in which, by the ministry of the law, sinners are made conscious of their sin and sorrowful for it, and are brought to recognize their need of Christ as savior. Such "preparations" are part of the order by which God brings the elect to Christ and are the Holy Spirit's work. They are the effect of "common" grace and are qualitatively distinct from vocation itself, the work of "special, saving" grace. In both preparation and vocation the soul is passive.

COVENANT THEOLOGY

Toward the end of the sixteenth century, Reformed divines began to formulate God's salvific relation to mankind in conventional terms. English Puritans contributed significantly to this development, and New England Puritans assumed it. According to this "covenant theology," the external decree of election encompasses the means of its execution in time, which takes the form of a covenant with Adam, in two dispensations. Initially, God made a "covenant of works" with Adam, promising him eternal felicity on condition of perfect obedience to the moral law, and gave him power to obey. God dealt in this manner out of consideration for Adam's nature as a rational being, capable of deliberate choice. After the fall, God offered Adam a "covenant of grace," which became effective when Christ fulfilled the law's requirements. Under this covenant, salvation is offered on condition of sincere faith, and God himself undertakes to enable the elect to believe, the elect being powerless in themselves to do so. Like the covenant of works, that of grace is conditional, in view of man's nature as a "cause by counsel," although neither covenant is between equals, and both are "of grace" in respect of man's ability to perform the required conditions. After Christ, the covenant of grace is dispensed through the medium of preaching, whereby grace is conveyed to the soul, enlightening intellect and empowering will, so that the individual actually believes.

Puritan covenant theology fostered a strenuous, introspective piety. It made the sermon the primary means of grace and it assumed an understanding of mind in which will, as the seat of action, is the crucial faculty. Will follows intellect's valuation of an object, but will moves the soul toward the valued object. The character of the will, respecting the sorts of objects that it is able to choose, determines the character of the individual. The sermon, rationally developing doctrines from Scripture and applying them affectingly to the hearer's spiritual situation, propounds arguments to intellect and motives to will. By the Holy Spirit's power, intellect is enabled to accept the first and will to act upon the second; the individual is thus persuaded to "close with Christ" in the covenant. The act of faith is the person's act, but the power of it is God's. The freeness of justification, under the covenant, is secured by the absoluteness of the divine decree and by the gratuity of regenerating grace, and is supported by the scholastic theory of multiple causation. The "efficient cause" of justification, according to Norton, is "God the Father, Son, and Holy Ghost" operating on the soul of the believer; the "material cause" is Christ's active and passive obedience; and the "formal cause" is God's free imputation of Christ's obedience to the believer. The "instrumental cause" applying this imputation, relatively but not properly, is the believer's faith. The "final cause" is declaration of "the glory of God in a way of mercy, mixt with righteousness" (Norton, *The Doctrine of Godliness; or, Living Unto God,* 1658, pp. 40–41).

New England Puritans were firmly committed to the institution of a learned ministry and established Harvard College to equip the young for godly service in church and, congruent with their comprehensive sense of "living to God," in civil state. They regarded grammar, rhetoric, and logic as instruments for expounding Scripture's true sense, for which the biblical languages are prerequisite. History and natural philosophy are important adjuncts in the same enterprise. Systematic divinity provides the methodical frame for such exposition, and casuistry for the practical application of it to individuals' spiritual and ethical circumstances. For the clergy, the end of learning was the sermon, and the public and private work of instruction, as the means of redemption's application. One monument to their educational success was New England's theological summa, the folio *Compleat Body of Divinity* (1726) of Samuel Willard, minister of Boston's Third Church and a graduate and vice president of Harvard. Typically, it was a practical work, comprising 250 public lectures on the Westminster Shorter Catechism. In substance it was a comprehensive exposition of the principal themes and presuppositions of Puritan divinity, in the tradition of William Ames.

COTTON MATHER

Another monument to Puritan education was Cotton Mather. The son and grandson of leading Boston ministers, precocious in piety and learning, Mather graduated from Harvard in 1678, began preaching in Boston's Second church in 1680, and was ordained there in 1685 as his father's colleague. He early conceived a personal responsibility for maintaining New England's Reformed heritage in an increasingly commercial society subject to royal intervention, encroaching Anglicanism, religious toleration, and changing religious fashion. He made his career, as conscientious pastor, organizer, and tireless, voluble publicist, in the service of this task. Widely read in ancient and modern authors, cognizant of contemporary European intellectual and religious developments, interested in medicine and natural science as well as pastoral care and formal divinity, Mather at once exemplified the intellectual world of his ancestors and the expanding cultural horizon of New England's provincial metropolis.

Mather's literary output was enormous. His views may be traced partially in four works treating, respectively, history, ethics, natural theology, and ministerial training. In *Magnalia Christi Americana; or, The Ecclesiastical History of New England* (1702), the largest single publication of his lifetime, Mather assembled and celebrated the history of New England's settlement, the biographies of its magistrates and ministers, the history of its college and its ecclesiastical organization, and the divine providences visited upon it; and he reviewed the disruptions that it suffered after 1688. In memorializing the founders, he established the image of early New England as a heroic, disciplined, divinely directed enterprise and also marked the distance between its exemplary circumstances and those of his own day. *Magnalia* was at once a work of filial piety and a moral mirror, reflecting the relative poverty of his generation.

Mather suggested that exemplary New England might live only in its history; and later he severely qualified the notion of Puritan New England's distinctive mission. He persisted, however, in the doctrinal convictions and experiential, activist piety of his forebears. Conversion, as the infusion of saving grace into the soul, is the foundation of the Christian life, which is manifest in works of holiness. Partly stimulated by his reading of contemporary German pietists, and partly as an application of the familiar doctrine of sanctification, he elaborated a program of systematic benevolence toward people within his care and reach, in Boston and the world. He published it as *Bonifacius: An Essay Upon the Good That Is to Be Desired* (1710; republished as *Essays to Do Good*). The good to be done consists in spreading the Gospel, reforming evil manners that inhibit conversion, and relieving the miseries of the afflicted. In his development of these *desiderata*, enlightened progressive motifs combined with traditional themes of Puritan civic responsibility and piety. The latter dominated: one is to "do good" for the benefit of humanity, but primarily for the glory of God, in imitation of Christ.

On several occasions in his career, Mather investigated spiritual manifestations, both divine and diabolical. He also studied natural science and medicine, and later systematically collected natural "curiosities," communicating them to the Royal Society in London, to which he was elected in 1713. As a "good deed," against fierce opposition, he promoted inoculation during Boston's smallpox epidemic in 1721; and at his death he left the manuscript of a comprehensive treatise on practical medicine. He followed the development of the new science intently, and the natural theology that it generated, reading Robert Boyle and Robert Hooke and pious Newtonians like William Whiston.

In *The Christian Philosopher: A Collection of the Best Discoveries in Nature, with Religious Improvements* (1721), Mather produced his own review, based on English sources, of recent findings by European scientists. He covered the natural world, from light and heavenly bodies through atmosphere, earth, the orders of animals, to man, the crown of creation and the subject of redemption. Each topic concluded in an appropriate spiritualizing meditation, and all appeared as exemplifying the ancient affirmation that God's glory is displayed in his created handiwork. The Christian philosopher, exercising his rational faculty upon the order and regularity

elucidated by natural science, cannot but recognize the presence of an omnipotent, benevolent, ceaselessly active architect. God's "Book of the Creatures" complements his "Book of the Scriptures," and contemplation of the former is an incentive to faith, an expression of piety, and glorifies God as creator and provident governor. Elsewhere, Mather speculated that gravitation, which Isaac Newton insisted could not inhere in matter, is the effect of God's continuous activity, sustaining the universe in all its parts.

Manuductio ad Ministerium: Directions for a Candidate of the Ministry (1726) was Mather's professional testament. He restated the characteristic themes of his ministry: experience of grace, doing good, study of nature, obeying and glorifying God in all things. The end of man, in this life and the next, recalling the Westminster Shorter Catechism, is "to glorify God and enjoy him forever." A minister is both an example of this condition and an instrument of its achievement in others. On this ground, Mather offered "a plan of real and regular living, . . . [a] method of living unto God," in which all intention, action, and enjoyment are referred to God as creator, redeemer, sustainer, and judge. He reiterated the doctrinal motifs that informed his preaching: necessity of regeneration by the Holy Spirit, redemption through Christ's sacrifice, sovereignty of saving grace and man's utter dependence upon it, "eternal election and . . . ensured perseverance," obedience to the moral law "upon the principles of the Gospel," application of the covenant of grace. To these Reformed affirmations he assimilated three universal maxims of piety that, he maintained, unite all Christians beyond the particularities of party, including the Calvinist party: affirmation of the one, triune God, service and obedience to whom is "the main intention of my life"; affirmation of Christ the eternal Son, upon whom I rely for reconciliation to God, and by whose "living in me" I may "live unto God"; and "out of respect unto God and His Christ" to "heartily love my neighbor."

The core of the tract comprised a comprehensive program of ministerial study. Mather emphasized ancient languages, history, natural philosophy and its pious interpretation. He subordinated formal logic to unencumbered exercise of natural reason, and formal rhetoric to study of God's rhetoric in Scripture. Study of formal divinity is to begin with standard compendiums like Ames's, and to embrace selected continental Reformed scholastics and English Puritan divines from the middle and latter seventeenth century, the church fathers, and German and Dutch Pietists. He concluded with maxims conducive to personal health and prudent conduct. Mather's work, in effect, was to transmute the religious and intellectual values of early Puritan New England into an energetic, intellectually alert, tolerant, philanthropic piety commensurate with the developing sensibilities of his own era.

JONATHAN EDWARDS

The outstanding figure in the American Calvinist tradition, and one of America's leading theological minds, was Jonathan Edwards, minister at Northampton, Massachusetts, and at his death in 1758 president of the College of New Jersey. He entered Yale College in 1716, remaining, with interruptions, until 1726, when he joined his grandfather, Solomon Stoddard, at Northampton. When Edwards went to Yale, "enlightened Christianity," with its sensitivity to the canons of humane reasonableness, had already taken root in New England culture, including Harvard. Its effect on Reformed theology was to diminish divine sovereignty in respect of creation, providence, and redemption and to enhance human independence, producing by degrees an estimate of mankind more morally capable and of God more benevolent. In and around Boston, this interest was prominently represented by Charles Chauncy, minister at the First Church, Jonathan Mayhew at the West Church, and Ebenezer Gay, minister at the First Church in Hingham. In the name of freedom, justice, and reason they abandoned, variously, characteristic Calvinist doctrines and some traditional Christian ones. Samuel Johnson, sometime tutor at Yale and eventual president of King's College in New York, traveled partway on the same path.

The presence of rationalizing tendencies in the Connecticut Valley prompted Edwards, in the winter of 1734–1735, to preach on justification by faith and election, provoking an upwelling of religious earnestness that quickly spread through the region. In 1740 the American colonies were caught up in a "great and general awakening," and by 1743 Edwards was busy defending the revival as a divine work against rationalists and conservatives alienated by its emotion and tumult, and against enthusiasts who celebrated both. As a student, Edwards assimilated the Newtonian view of the natural world and eagerly read John Locke's *Essay Concerning Human Understanding* (1690). To elements of Lockean psychology and epistemology he joined a theological idealism reminiscent of Augustine, employing both in defense of high Calvinism and of vital, "experimental religion." The frame and much of the substance of his thought derived from the Puritan divinity of the generations between Ames and Willard. His views are most directly expressed in four major treatises, respectively on religious affections, freedom of will, original sin, and true virtue.

Edwards' defense of the Great Awakening, *A Treatise Concerning Religious Affections* (1746), was an elaboration of the "distinguishing qualifications" of the truly converted. It reflected a century and a half of Puritan discussion about evidences of regeneration, to which Edwards gave characteristic formulation. He defined "true religion" as chiefly a matter of "holy affections," or "lively . . . inclinations," respecting divine things, and he identified twelve "signs" that are not in themselves conclusive evidence of true piety, and twelve more that are. The former, tending to be sudden, temporary, and emotive, are traceable to common grace or excited imagination; the latter, abiding and pervasive, are effects of saving grace. His analysis recapitulated the Puritan affirmation that, in calling, God works a permanent qualitative change in individuals, beyond anything of which natural faculties are capable. In this change, the mind is enlightened to apprehend God in his true being and character, and the will becomes disposed to love and seek God for his own sake. Edwards described this transformation in the traditional way, as the effect of the Holy Spirit's indwelling as an abiding principle of life and action, and as the infusing of new powers into mental faculties. By the Spirit's participation, God conveys into the soul the beauty and holiness of his own nature, whereby the saints enjoy communion with him.

Edwards also spoke of regeneration as communication of God's refulgence, which the saints do not merely reflect, but of whose "lightsome" nature they actually partake, becoming in themselves "little suns." Applying Lockean categories, he characterized regeneration as the implanting of "a principle of a new kind of perception or spiritual sensation, . . . a new spiritual sense," above and independent of all ordinary powers of the unsanctified mind. This principle is the ground of a new, distinctive apprehension of divine things, coupled with a new delight in them, the source of a "new simple idea," i.e., an underived impression of divine being upon the mind. The object of spiritual sensation is God's beauty, loveliness, and moral perfection, as perfect being and highest good. Spiritual understanding consists in such apprehension and is the source of holy affections, of which the chief, corresponding to the object of understanding, is love to God. True religion consists wholly "in this divine affection, and an habitual disposition to it, and that light which is the foundation of it, and those things which are fruits of it." All four elements are empirically discernible and are grounds for distinguishing true spiritual piety from passing religious fancy, whether intellectual or emotional.

Edwards' theological standing in his own day rested significantly on his *Careful and Strict Enquiry into . . . Freedom of Will* (1754), which was both a defense of a basic Calvinist principle and an assertion of God's sovereign freedom. In it he attacked the "Arminian" notion that he found in the works of the deist Thomas Chubb, the Anglican Daniel Whitby, and the Nonconformist Isaac Watts; namely, that absolute self-determinacy of will is necessary to human liberty and moral virtue. Edwards considered this idea an impediment to convincing sinners of their absolute need for grace and a hindrance to effective preaching; he rejected it as conceptually flawed and logically absurd. His argument comprised a double appeal: to reason, "common sense," and the "light of nature," and to the doctrines of divine sovereignty and foreknowledge, as propositions and as displayed in their effects in the Bible.

Edwards argued that moral agency pertains to the soul's ability to choose, and to execute the choice, not to the will as the soul's power of choosing. To suppose that will chooses out of absolute indifference assumes either that the will is uncaused or that its choices result from previous choices. The first puts will beyond the influence of reason (and preaching) and severs the empirical connections underlying all apprehensions. The second issues in infinite regression. "Common sense" teaches that every event outside of God has a cause, i.e., a certain connection to an antecedent. Such causal necessity obtains in the realm of motives and volitions, as in the natural realm. Will necessarily follows what, in the mind's view, is the strongest motive to action, as the "greatest apparent good," and apparent goodness is ultimately a matter of "inclination," of the soul's character. "Moral inability" is not a matter of the will's incapacity of choosing, which it is "naturally" capable of, but a failure of antecedent motivation to a particular kind of choice.

Human virtue is rooted in the soul's inclination toward virtue as such, and is reflected in acts, which are virtuous because of their nature, not because of the manner of their production. Liberty of indifference disconnects choice from inclination and makes attainment of virtue fortuitous; whereas moral necessity, which links inclination and acts, consists with exhortations to seek virtue, and with praise and blame relative to it. God's moral excellency, and Christ's, are both necessary, but nonetheless praiseworthy. So also the moral in-excellency of human beings is truly reprehensible, for they have the mental equipment to act differently but lack the underlying disposition to be otherwise.

If the Arminian view is correct, God's providential and redemptive economy is contingent on unpredictable actions of moral agents, and God is subject to frustration respecting the end for which he created the world. Such a condition contradicts the doctrine of divine foreknowledge, which Arminians share with Calvinists, and the Calvinist premise that God, as "absolute governor of the universe," orders events certainly and necessarily according to his sovereign wisdom. Absolute freedom of will, far from preserving human integrity and responsibility, casts both God and man upon a "wild contingence," leaving them "to act absolutely at random." A proper view of human freedom, Edwards concluded, is crucial to maintenance of other Calvinist fundamentals (essentially those formulated at Dort): "universal, determining providence," "total depravity . . . of man's nature," efficacious and irresistible grace, particular election, particular efficacy of Christ's death, and perseverance of the saints.

In *The . . . Doctrine of Original Sin Defended* (1758), Edwards examined the origin and nature of the human disposition that, apart from divine intervention, determines the motives that prompt volitions. He considered the doctrine to be basic to true appreciation of the significance of Christ's work, of the Gospel's content, and of the need for belief in it. His principal foil was an enlightened Nonconformist, John Taylor, who recoiled from the notion that God condemns multitudes for one person's ancient sin and brings humanity corrupted into the world so that they cannot choose freely. Edwards reiterated his view that virtue inheres in a disposition to act virtuously, and that, according to the "natural dictate of reason," observable effects imply proportionate causes. He observed that the pervasiveness and predominance of sinfulness in human behavior argue as its source a universal "innate depravity of the heart," a "propensity in all to sin immediately, as soon as they are capable of it, and to sin continuously." In his argument, he invoked familiar Reformed notions about the nature of sin and about Adam as representative human being, and a distinctive idea of identity in created being.

Edwards defined sin as transgression of divine law, whose sum is the command to love God for himself, according to his excellency. As created, Adam possessed, in addition to natural principles of self-love, a "virtuous and holy disposition of heart," and was capable of such love. When he broke God's covenant and fell under its curse, God withdrew the communion of his Spirit on which indwelling spiritual principles depend, resulting in thorough disruption of man's moral being. Whereupon, man "immediately set up himself and the objects of his private affections and appetites, as supreme," in the place of God. Self-interest came wholly to possess the soul and to dominate all human action, in despite of God's law, so that human beings are continually at enmity with God. In this situation Adam and his posterity are united. God imputes Adam's sin to mankind as his offspring, because they are one with him and are "disposed to approve of" and consent entirely with his sin, "as fully as he himself approved of it when he committed it." Adam's sin is their sin.

In the covenant, God dealt with Adam, respecting both blessing and curse, as a "public person" and "head of the human species," and with his posterity in him. This relationship is not merely representative, but an actual continuity of being. Adam's children were in him and belonged to him, "as much as the branches of a tree . . . are in the tree." This continuity is not simply organic, either, but a function of the exercise of God's power. Edwards maintained that all continuity of "all created substance . . . , in the different moments of its duration," depends upon "a divine constitution, or law of nature" that God has established. At each successive moment, by immediate exercise of his creative power, God produces out of nothing the properties, relations, and circumstances of created being. The inference of continuity rests on God's determination to maintain the sameness of successive properties and relations. This "constitution" operates in moral as in physical nature. Permission of Adam's sin, and its propagation in his offspring, are referrable solely to God's sovereign will, guided by his wisdom. Human beings may wonder and cavil at this way of proceeding, but they cannot alter the fact of it.

In *The Nature of True Virtue* (1765), Edwards defined the disposition that distinguishes the godly. His formulation united a neoclassical esteem for order and proportion and a Platonic conception of the universe as a hierarchy of being. His subject, although he did not say so, was Puritan divinity comprehended under "sanctification."

Virtue is a kind of beauty, in the sense of "consent" and harmony of mutually related elements, and is proportionate to the extent of relatedness encompassed. In moral beings, virtuous beauty pertains to disposition of heart and exercises of will. It is "that consent, propensity, and union of heart to being in general, which is immediately exercised in a general good will." Such benevolence seeks the "highest good of being in general" and of individual beings in relation to general good. True virtue is love, of which there are two kinds: "benevolence," which is primary and whose object is being as such, and "complacence," whose object is benevolence in another. True spiritual beauty combines both, and exercise of spiritual beauty and recognition of it in another both depend upon inherent "taste" for it, arising from a benevolent disposition. Love directed to being in general is equivalent to love directed to God; for "pure benevolence" is proportionate to the degree of existence and benevolence of an object, and God has "infinitely the greatest share of existence" and is the perfection of spiritual beauty.

True virtue in creatures appears in the degree to which their love to objects coincides with God's love to the objects and agrees with the end that he intends for them. God created moral agents for his own glory, and a "truly virtuous mind," accordingly, is one that makes the divine glory, under the "dominion of love to God," his "supreme, governing and ultimate end." Love to creatures, which is not primarily love to God and which is indifferent to God's hierarchy of ends, is not virtue. All self-love is characterized by restriction of benevolence to some particular segment of being. It is in tension with being in general and hostile to the supreme regard that God, "as all-comprehending Being," commands. It exalts the "private object" above the universal and subordinates the "infinitely supreme interest" to the "infinitely inferior."

In Edwards' characterization of virtue as beauty and benevolence, and in his association of benevolence with inherent "virtuous taste," there was an echo of the moral philosophy of Francis Hutcheson. Edwards criticized Hutcheson, however, for restricting benevolence to creatures and refused to admit his innate "moral sense" as a ground of true virtue. He identified a "natural beauty," or quasi virtue, consisting in consent and agreement of different elements respecting form, arrangement, quantity, and design, but one that does not involve will or disposition and is not specific to spiritual beings. God renders the mind appreciative of such natural beauty, in architecture, machinery, and in social, intellectual, and judicial matters. "Taste" for such harmony coincides with "moral sense" and with "natural conscience." The latter, however, is informed by self-love, and the former by concern for personal equity; both are qualitatively distinct from "truly virtuous taste, . . . arising from virtuous benevolence of heart." Or, in Westminster's idiom (though Edwards did not invoke it here), the good deeds of the unregenerate are sinful.

Edwards' thought was marked by a philosophical idealism that, while not foreign to earlier Puritans, was distinctive in its thoroughness and explicitness. The fundamental quality of mate-

rial being is power of resistance, which is "a mode of an idea." Its existence depends upon its being thought, so that intelligent beings are the only real substances, "inasmuch as the being of other things is only by these." Ultimately, the contents and laws of operation of the created world, physical and mental, derive from the agency of God, who is directed by his wisdom. The whole system of being, and our apprehension of it, depends on God's thinking of both; truth lies in "consistence and agreement of our ideas" with God's. Continuity in the course of nature depends moment by moment on God's immanent activity, "ever passing and returning, as colors of bodies are every moment renewed by the light that shines upon them, and all is constantly proceeding from God, as light from the sun." The physical world is the type and image of the spiritual; physical bodies are "but the shadow of being" and, in their consent and harmony, the shadow of divine excellency. The whole creation is the overflowing of divine being, whence metaphor and metaphysics coincide.

This perspective is strikingly expressed in Edwards' *Dissertation Concerning the End for Which God Created the World* (1765). God's internal glory consists in his knowledge, resident in his understanding, and his holiness and happiness, seated in his will, which glory is "enlarged" by communication *ad extra*. God extends his image, comprising understanding and will, to moral beings, and gives them knowledge of, love to, and happiness in himself. The "great and last end" of all God's works is manifestation of his glory, as "the effulgence . . . of light from a luminary." In the creature's knowing, loving, and rejoicing, God's glory is both "acknowledged [and] returned." "Here is both an emanation and a remanation. . . . The beams of glory come from God, and are something of God, and are refunded back again to their original" (Faust and Johnson, 1935, pp. 343–344).

THE NEW DIVINITY

Edwards' followers, who created the tradition in New England theology known as the New Divinity, failed to grasp the depth of his thought and tended to alter it even as they perpetuated it. Like their mentor, they sought to defend Calvinism from rationalist attack and to focus it upon experience of grace as the definitive religious event. They were more remote than Edwards from the intellectual culture of seventeenth-century Puritanism and more closely engaged by the voluntarist, constitutionalist, and humanitarian impulses of the late eighteenth century; and they were more sensitive than Edwards to issues raised by enlightened critics, whose perspective they shared. They sought to maintain Calvinist assumptions about divine sovereignty and human dependence and depravity, while simultaneously asserting the individual's personal accountability for his spiritual estate and his capability as a rational agent. They shared Edwards' respect for common sense and took up elements of his theory of moral agency, his notion of God's constitution in the moral realm, his definition of sin as selfishness and of holiness as benevolence, and his insistence that God's permission of sin is subject to his beneficent wisdom. They abandoned his idealistic ontology, his theory of identity, and his theocentrism.

Samuel Hopkins, Edwards' pupil, friend, and biographer, and minister at Newport, Rhode Island (1770), was representative of the conservative wing of the school. His *System of Doctrines* (1793) was the first systematic elaboration of New Divinity motifs. Hopkins was committed to the divine sovereignty, but he represented God chiefly as a universal moral governor, whose principal attribute is benevolence, and he grounded the divine decrees in God's love. God delights in the display of his moral perfection in the communication of his goodness to creatures, which communication entails their greatest possible happiness. In his infinite wisdom, God permits sin as a necessary means to the greatest moral good in the best possible world, though sin is nonetheless evil and the individual sinner is without excuse. Adam's children are sinful, according to the divine constitution, but are not guilty of Adam's sin, or punished for it, save as they approve it by sinning as Adam did. Their corruption and guilt are as much their own as if Adam had not sinned, and their sin begins as soon as they are capable of a moral exercise contrary to God's law. Hopkins exploited Edwards' distinction between natural and moral ability to maintain that individuals are not physically hindered from obeying God's law or from respond-

ing to the Gospel's command to believe and repent. The natural powers of will and understanding are not affected by Adam's act, although in consequence of it heart and inclination are opposed to such obedience.

Hopkins distinguished "regeneration," as God's renovation of the heart, in which the individual is passive, from "active conversion" deriving from it, comprising "holy exercises" of faith and repentance. The first is instantaneous, complete, and imperceptible; the second is perceptible and the object of God's promise of salvation. Regeneration frees the heart from selfishness and forms it to "disinterested benevolence" toward being in general, though primarily toward fellow "intelligent beings." Such disinterestedness is manifest in willingness to be damned for the glory of God, if God's grand scheme should require it. Chiefly, however, benevolence appears as obedience to God's law in the performance of appropriate moral duties. In this respect, the New Divinity tended significantly toward moralism and humanitarianism.

With his fellow Edwardsean Joseph Bellamy, Hopkins held a "governmental" theory of the atonement. Christ's death does not so much satisfy God, who is offended by sin, as vindicate the divine law and uphold the dignity of God's government, of which law is the foundation. In this context, atonement is chiefly exemplary of God's hatred of sin, although Christ's active obedience, in fulfilling the law's requirements, obtains salvation for human beings who are incapable of such fulfillment. The atonement's efficacy is sufficient for all mankind, although God renders it effective for less than all. This "universalism," together with emphasis on conversion as a personal act rooted in natural ability to believe and repent, formed the basis of the New Divinity's conversionist homiletics. Hopkins' insistence that prior to regeneration every effort at holiness is vitiated by self-love and is wholly evil served to emphasize the hearer's desperate condition and urgent need for the Spirit's work.

NEW HAVEN THEOLOGY: NATHANIEL WILLIAM TAYLOR

The radical wing of the New Divinity was personified in Nathaniel William Taylor, minister at Center Church, New Haven (1812), and professor of didactic theology (1822) at the newly founded Yale Divinity School. The pupil and friend of Timothy Dwight, Edwards' grandson, Taylor came to prominence as a successful revival preacher in the Connecticut phase of the Second Great Awakening, and he entered his professorship during the heat of the Unitarian controversy. He sought simultaneously to defend Calvinism from the charge that it made God the author of sin and unjust in his treatment of human beings, and to provide a homiletically effective theology in support of the Awakening. To both ends he contended against the notion that God brings individuals into the world with corrupt natures and condemns most of them for actions that, in consequence, they cannot help. The New Haven Theology that he articulated had enormous influence, providing legitimation for a multitude of Congregational and Presbyterian revivalists and inciting intense controversy in both denominations. His views appeared most directly in *Concio ad Clerum: A Sermon on Human Nature, Sin, and Freedom* (1828) and at greater length in *Lectures on the Moral Government of God* (1859) and *Essays . . . Upon . . . Revealed Theology* (1859).

Taylor assumed the New Divinity view of God's government, the atonement, selfishness and benevolence, and imputation. He felt, however, that some Edwardseans were insufficiently precise respecting moral agency and the moral character of God's rule, and he objected to the view of more traditional Calvinists that a prior, hereditary sinful disposition underlies sinful acts, as promoting indifference to the pursuit of grace and inhibiting conversion. Sin and guilt, he insisted, pertain only to free voluntary actions in respect of known law; only sins are sinful. Responsible agency, moreover, requires a real "power to the contrary" in every choice, whether or not the individual actually chooses otherwise. At the same time, it is entirely certain that, apart from the Holy Spirit's intervention, all mankind will choose their own interest as their highest good, in preference to God. This certainty is assured by a bias, not itself sinful, rooted in mankind's propensity to "natural" good. In this sense, human beings are "by nature" morally depraved, "such . . . that they will sin and only sin in all the appropriate circumstances of their being" (Ahlstrom, 1967, p. 222), immediately they become moral agents.

Taylor rejected the notion that God ordains sin as a necessary means to the greatest good as both unprovable and as compromising the divine goodness. He preferred to say that the non-prevention of sin, in a world of free agents, may be better than God's direct overruling of it at the expense of free agency. He treated election in governmental terms, as the working out of a system of benevolent "influences" upon intelligent beings, under the direction of a wise governor. These influences impinge in varying degree upon different people, according as God foresees that it will produce holiness in his kingdom as a whole; with some people they issue in conversion. Election is not so much the consequence of God's good pleasure, and regeneration of his sovereign power, as the natural product of his benevolent administration.

Taylor treated regeneration as a voluntary act, from which individuals are not prevented by any "physical" inability, but for which they have in fact a "constituted" propensity. Human beings are naturally motivated by a desire for happiness, by a "self-love" that is neither sinful nor holy, and to this disposition the Gospel appeals. Regeneration consists in displacement of exclusive self-interest by love to God as highest good. Although the effect of the Holy Spirit, regeneration is the act of the individual, who repents, believes, and loves through the exercise of his natural powers. This view of sin and agency bears directly on preaching as the instrument of regeneration, for it is preaching's function, in God's system of influences, to fasten upon moral agents the urgent conviction that their sin and guilt are their own, that they merit their own damnation, and that it is their duty to comply with the Gospel's terms, "as a point-blank direction to business now on hand and now to be done" (Ahlstrom, 1967, p. 241).

Integral to the New Haven Theology was the commonsense realism developed during the Scottish Enlightenment by Thomas Reid and Dugald Stewart. Reid aimed to counter Humean skepticism with a realistic theory of perception that gave assured access to truth about material and moral worlds. The common sense of intelligent men is to be trusted above purely "speculative" philosophy, respecting the principles governing belief and practice in the "common concerns of life." The primary datum of philosophy is self-consciousness, observation of which yields the conclusions that the external world exists as it appears, that fundamental moral principles are self-evident intuitions of the moral sense, that individuals are moral agents capable of free choice, and that only intelligent being can be a true efficient cause. In the *Concio,* Taylor appealed, after invoking the "ablest divines" and the apostles, to "common sense" and "human consciousness" to demonstrate that sin is universally held to reside in "private selfish interest" and voluntary preference of the world over God (Ahlstrom, 1967, pp. 217, 220, 229). Likewise, it is contrary to the common sense of ordinary people to believe that they are accountable for any but their own freely chosen acts or that they are really one with Adam and share his guilt. Taylor's "power to the contrary" came from Reid.

Until after the Civil War, Scottish realism was the dominant philosophical element in American Calvinism. It provided a powerful constructive and apologetic instrument to direct against received theological tradition or to defend it and a means of assimilating the encouraging elements of Enlightenment rationalism, while resisting its disquieting elements. Coupled with popular Baconianism, it provided a means of integrating natural, moral, and theological "sciences," all operating inductively upon assured truths of common sense, and therein free from "speculation" and forming together a grand system, all in the self-evident consciousness that only a supreme intelligence can be an adequate cause of their several phenomena. This perspective effectively insulated a significant proportion of American Calvinists from the implications of Immanuel Kant's critique, G. W. F. Hegel's dialectic, and Friedrich Schleiermacher's reformulation of Reformed doctrine in terms of self-conscious feeling.

PRINCETON THEOLOGY: CHARLES HODGE

The chief representative of Reformed scholasticism in nineteenth-century America was Charles Hodge, from 1822 professor successively of biblical, didactic, and polemic theology at Princeton Theological Seminary. Founded in 1812, partly out of concern for the influence of Connecticut Congregationalism on Presbyterian theology and polity, Princeton became the intellectual center for Old School Presbyterians, as against the revivalist, Taylorite New School. The seminary was established on a combination of confessional strictness and erudite, academic divinity, which Hodge developed and which his successors maintained into the next century. Hodge learned commonsense philosophy at the College of New Jersey and from 1826 to 1828 studied in Germany, whence he returned with a keen sense of the dangers of "speculation" as applied to theology. He campaigned against New School "Arminianism," Mercersburg idealism, Oberlin perfectionism, and other instances of what he considered theological innovation and error. In later controversies over creedal reform and doctrinal fundamentals, the Princeton Theology guided conservative Presbyterians; it was read selectively, into the late twentieth century, by conservative Protestants, not all of whom were self-conscious Calvinists. Hodge's principal works were *Essays and Reviews* (1857), *Discussions in Church Polity* (1878), and *Discourses Doctrinal and Practical* (1879). The summation of his reflection appeared as *Systematic Theology* (3 vols., 1872–1873).

The *Theology* was a complete divinity course, embracing the chief heads, though not the order, of the Westminster Standards, a discourse on theological method, and commentary on current philosophical, scientific, and theological issues. By midcentury apologetics had become, almost, an American theologian's chief task. Hodge conducted a running skirmish with "rationalism" from Hume to Mansel, "pantheism" from ancient Brahmans to Schleiermacher, and "materialism" from Epicurus to Darwin, as well as with Arminian, Lutheran, and Catholic mistakes. In construction, certain doctrinal emphases, and its assumption that theology is essentially propositional, Hodge's work followed the Genevan theologian François Turretin, whose *Institutio Theologiae Elencticae* (1688) served the seminary initially as a textbook. Hodge's method combined old scholastic orthodoxy and "new" Scottish philosophy. For Turretin, theology depended on "indubitable principles and self-evident truths," independent of methods of reasoning necessary in natural and philosophical matters. Hodge concurred, invoking the perspective of common sense. Theology is a "science," like all others the classification and articulation of "facts," in this case "facts" infallibly revealed in Scripture. Since the same God who authored the Bible authored mankind's moral "constitution," the "facts" entailed in the latter are congruent with those of the former, and both are self-evident to ordinary people. In places, notably with respect to the nature of God, man, sin, and free agency, Hodge appealed nearly as often to the "common consciousness of men" as to "authenticated" biblical "revelations." As the science of divinely authored facts, theology differs qualitatively from "merely" human speculation in philosophy and natural science.

Hodge retained the covenantal conception of God's salvific relationship with mankind, comprising covenants of works and grace. Following Turretin, he maintained that Adam in the original covenant acted as the "head and representative" of the human race, in virtue of which his sin, though not his posterity's act, is "immediately" imputed to them, as the ground of their liability to the same punishment that befell Adam. Hodge regarded Edwards' theory of identity as an idiosyncrasy, and he rejected the notion that punishing one individual for another's sin is unjust, as contrary to the biblical norm. He regarded the view that moral agents are responsible only for their own acts as beside the point. Acts, as expressive of character, are rooted in prior dispositions that, if sinful, are so however they are acquired.

Invoking Westminster, Hodge insisted that the supreme end of all God's action is manifestation of his glory, in the display of his perfections. God permits sin as a means of manifesting his justice, which is not to be subsumed into his benevolence. To make production of happiness God's chief end is to confuse happiness and holiness. God seeks creatures' happiness, but as a subordinate end. God's character as moral governor comprises his justice, internally as his moral perfection, externally in the prescription of moral obligation upon rational creatures and in the rectitude of his dealing with them regarding that obligation. The central fact of theology is the divine sovereignty. All laws, moral and physical, the orders of created beings, the status and lot of nations and individuals, in all particulars, are referable solely to God's "good pleasure." The decrees underlying creation and providence are entirely free, comprehensive, eternal, "certainly efficacious," and uniformly directed by God's determination to manifest his glory.

Certainty issuing from divine sovereignty, Hodge maintained, also invoking Westminster, is consistent with liberty of moral agents. God exercises his efficiency so as to secure the certainty of the intended event, while permitting second causes and moral agents to operate according to their natures. Moral agents are said to be free insofar as their volitions are determined by nothing outside of themselves, but proceed from their own "views, feelings, and immanent dispositions," so that they are deliberate, conscious expressions of "character." The New England distinction between natural and moral necessity is improper and misleading. An agent is free as long as it is able to control its volitions. The real issue is not "necessity," nor "freedom of the will" as an entity distinct from the rest of the soul, but the liberty of the agent altogether. Ultimately, the issue is "ability," in the sense of power to make oneself holy. "Free agency is the power to decide according to our character; ability is the power to change our character by a volition." The former belongs to human beings as such; the latter does not belong to fallen human beings at all. Liberty and responsibility are consistent with certainty, but not with "power to the contrary," which, if genuine, renders the event uncertain. Hodge's argument on this point was essentially that of Edwards. Contrary to the New School view, the doctrine of divine sovereignty does not impede use of the means of grace, but is the ground of hope in their efficacy, and the doctrine of inability stimulates the sensible to seek aid in God's grace, where alone aid can be had.

Hodge considered the definition of sin as selfishness to be a correlate of the mistaken notion that benevolence to creatures is God's chief end. Sin is the opposite of holiness, in the sense of conformity to the divine law as expressing God's moral excellence and as the standard of excellence for rational creatures; it is not reducible to a single principle such as love to creatures or self. It is "want of congeniality of one moral nature to another." Sin resides not in weakness of the soul's faculties, nor in want of free agency, nor in inherent disinclination, but in failure of "spiritual discernment" and perversion of "taste" and feelings, i.e., in pervasive corruption "below" the faculties and controlling them. As a result, human beings "universally in all the circumstances of their existence in the world" do not merely sin but "are sinful." Given the nature of God's law and of his justice, Christ's work is necessarily satisfactory, respecting the obedience required and the punishment incurred under the law. The theory that the atonement serves to exert a moral influence on mankind eliminates justice from the divine attributes; the governmental theory that the atonement exhibits God's dislike of sin resolves justice into benevolence.

Hodge criticized the tendency of revivalists to resolve regeneration, as God's act upon the passive soul, into conversion as man's act, in order to increase their hearers' sense of personal responsibility for their own estate. Theologians may convince themselves by verbal agility that men have all the "natural" ability necessary to love God, but the hearers know better. Regeneration is new life, the effect of God's almighty power, affecting the whole soul, beyond anything of which second causes are capable. It is manifest in "new views" of God, Christ, sin, and holiness, and in "spiritual illumination," which issues necessarily in "delight in the things . . . revealed." Christ appears as "the one altogether lovely," and the soul responds in faith. In his understanding of vocation and of regeneration that renders it effectual, Hodge reflected the views of his seventeenth-century theological forebears. In his language of illumination and delight, and his notion of holiness as congeniality to the divine nature, he echoed Edwards, although distantly.

INFLUENCE OF GERMAN THOUGHT

American Calvinist theology, whether in the New England or the Princeton vein, was formulated in individualistic, voluntaristic terms. Faith and obedience are personal obligations, and revelation's claims, expressed in theological formulas, impinge directly on individuals. Salvation is a forensic transaction, and the church provides occasion for confrontation between God and sinners. By the mid-nineteenth century, however, interest began to appear in a more organic conception of religious life, stimulated in part by discovery of German philosophy, theology, and historical scholarship. This discovery was mediated partly by the writings of Samuel Taylor Coleridge and by a handful of Americans who studied in Germany. Theologians of the German "mediating" school, chiefly at the universities of Halle and Berlin, were particularly important for American Calvinists. These men sought to combine a resurgent experiential piety and a religious idealism shaped by Hegel and Schleiermacher. They regarded Christology as the dominant element in theology, and the church as the historical embodiment of the principle of the Incarnation. During the decade after 1844, efforts to recast American Calvinism along similar lines appeared in the work of John W. Nevin and Phillip Schaff at the German Reformed seminary at Mercersburg, Pennsylvania, and of Henry B. Smith at Union, the New School Presbyterian seminary in New York City.

Nevin, an Old School Presbyterian and Hodge's pupil, had begun to rethink his theological orientation when he went to Mercersburg in 1839, where Schaff joined him five years later, fresh from graduate study with leading mediating theologians. The Mercersburg Theology that they articulated was informed by a new sense of the Reformed tradition's historicity and of its relationship to the church catholic, together with an ecclesiology that Nevin discovered in the Heidelberg Catechism and interpreted in idealistic, Christological terms. In *The Anxious Bench* (1843), Nevin criticized the atomistic, legalistic spirit of revivalistic American Calvinism. The church is not a mechanical aggregate of individuals, nor is Christian life defined by the transient enthusiasm of revivals. Rather, the church is an "organic life," the embodiment of Christ's life as an organizing power in the world. Subjectively, the Christian life is participation in Christ's life; objectively, it is participation in the environing community of the church, which is prior to the individual and his private emotional experience. The church, properly, is shaped by the "system of the catechism," that is, by ongoing instruction, discipline, and worship, in which the Eucharist is central.

Nevin's *The Mystical Presence* (1846) was a historical and theological reappropriation of the eucharistic doctrine of the spiritual real presence, as held by Calvin and the Continental Reformed confessions. The Eucharist, as a specific, distinctive communion of the believer with Christ, is the church's most characteristic activity. It is mystery and miracle, participation in Christ's person, the flowing together of his life and the believer's. In a single visible transaction, the sacrament concentrates the presence and power of Christianity as the supernatural order of life flowing from the Incarnation, the central fact of Christian and of human existence. The Incarnation unlocks all of God's revelations and discloses the meaning of all his created work. Theology, accordingly, unfolds from the Apostles' Creed as the definitive expression of the Gospel and the fundamental symbol of the whole church, and all doctrines are ultimately and organically Christological.

Smith, a Hopkinsian Congregationalist turned New School Presbyterian, left the chair of moral and mental philosophy at Amherst to teach church history (1850) and systematic theology (1855) at Union. From 1837 to 1840 he had studied at Halle and Berlin, returning to become an authority on contemporary German theology and historical scholarship. He concluded that New England theology was limited by its preoccupation with divine sovereignty and human agency, isolated from the developing intellectual situation, in which the truth of Christianity altogether had replaced freedom of will as the urgent issue, and in need of a new apologetic. He did not share Nevin's sacramentalism and objective ecclesiology, and he retained the presuppositions and the substance of New England theology; but he found in the Christocentric theology and historical idealism of his German teachers resources for addressing the new apologetic situation. At Union he offered a vision of Christianity as a progressive force, flowing from Christ as the manifestation of God in the world, shaping the course of universal history. Christianity's true character and significance are objectified in the church's institutional history, and its inner principle in the history of doctrine. Both together provide factual confirmation of the faith and of American Calvinism's penultimate place in God's providential scheme, and they provide solid defense against philosophical speculation. In Christ, who is the center of history, all the religious aspirations and philosophical musings of mankind are satisfied. Theology is essentially Christology, and the content of church history, understood as the history of redemption, is the basis for theology. Smith's addresses and essays appeared as *Faith and Philosophy* (1877).

Nevin's and Smith's efforts were transient and of limited impact. They indicated, however, a shifting of the center of intellectual stimulation in American theology from Great Britain to Germany, the emergence of a sense of the historical character of Christian experience, and a weakening of the appeal of commonsense philosophy. Concurrently, the Congregationalist Horace Bushnell, minister at Hartford's North Church from 1833 to 1859, articulated an indigenous religious romanticism of direct importance for the Christocentric liberal theology that developed among Congregationalists and others after the Civil War. Bushnell studied under Taylor and was unimpressed by his method and matter. Early in his pastorate he rejected the strategy and presuppositions of revivalistic experientialism, in favor of a program of unbroken nurture from infancy in a Christian community of which the family is a redemptive extension. He also expressed serious doubt about the ability of theological language to convey adequately the substance of religious feeling. In *Christian Nurture* (1847), *God in Christ* (1849), *Nature and the Supernatural* (1858), and other works, he reflected suggestively upon the organic character of Christian life, the social nature of language, the symbolic function of religious expression, and the interpenetration of nature and spirit, and he conducted a sustained meditation on the divinity of Christ and the atonement, in relation to love, sacrifice, and forgiveness. His work marked a substantive break in the New England theological tradition.

THEOLOGICAL TRANSITION

The transitional character of the later 1880s, when theological liberalism began to provoke controversy, appears variously in William G. T. Shedd's *Dogmatic Theology* (3 vols., 1888–1894) and Augustus H. Strong's *Systematic Theology* (3 vols., 1886; rev. 1890). Shedd, an Old School Presbyterian, taught church history (1854) at Andover Seminary and systematics (1874) at Union. He published an American edition of Coleridge (1853). His pioneering *History of Christian Doctrine* (1863) was developmental and idealistic in conception and marked by a sense of historical particularity and of the influence of philosophy in doctrinal construction. He did not equate development with progress, and the *Theology* articulated his preference for sixteenth- and early-seventeenth-century Calvinism as the fullest expression of Christian truth, as distinct from later scholastic modifications, which he associated with Turretin, and modern American so-called improvements. In structure his work resembled Hodge's, shorn of commonsense apologetics, though not of commonsense principles, and was nearly as critical of Princeton theology as of Taylorite.

An infralapsarian, Shedd made the decree of election follow the fall, and grounded it in God's compassion rather than his justice; and he claimed early Calvinist support for the position. He regarded Hodge's covenantal theory of the imputation of Adam's sin to his posterity as a speculative intrusion into the implicitly Augustinian conception of Westminster. He asserted a traducian view of Adam's moral relation to his issue, namely that original sin is conveyed by "natural generation," human nature having sinned in Adam "before it was individualized by propagation." Shedd considered Hodge's creationist view, whereby God brings into being individual souls that are sinful in virtue of their contractual relationship with Adam, an offense against the divine goodness. Shedd sided with Edwards on the fact of inability to choose holiness, but criticized his conceptualizing of the problem. His historical sense indicated that however useful to the times contemporary versions of Calvinism, liberal or conservative, might be, they were not wholly genuine, and on this ground he pointedly defended Westminster faith in the controversy then shaping among Presbyterians.

Strong graduated from Yale in 1857 and from Rochester Seminary, where he later became president and professor of biblical theology (1872). His *Theology* was a distant, American recension of Reformed orthodoxy in the Puritan vein. In construction it was both a theological handbook, reminiscent of Ames's, and a commonplace book, in the spirit though not the form that Willard enjoined on his students. In its expository sections, comprising the bulk of the work, nineteenth-century figures—theologians, exegetes, philosophers, and writers, religious and secular, from America, Germany, and Britain—predominated, followed by Puritans. Strong's tone throughout was moderate and his spirit edificatory, and his canvassing of controversy was fuller and more balanced than Hodge's. He agreed with Shedd on imputation and the order of the decree of election, but with Taylor on activity in conversion and the role of preaching. He followed Hodge partway on the nature of theology and the sources of the idea of God, but he abandoned the covenantal scheme entirely.

Strong represented the dogmatic emphasis from which Baptists like Walter Rauschenbusch revolted. At the same time, his temperate cognizance of a broad range of contemporary thought was part of the context whence individual Baptists emerged to become leading theological liberals. Strong professed to find no incompatibility between evolutionary theory and Higher Criticism and the "old doctrines," on the ground of his personal experience of union with Christ, recognized, by the light of Paul and John, as the universal revealer of God, in nature, history, and Scripture. His profession echoed the Puritan commonplace that God is disclosed in the structure of the universe, the course of human events, and the hearts of the faithful, who, enlightened by grace, are able to behold his glory in all his works.

In 1865 the Congregational churches reaffirmed the Savoy version of the Westminster Confession as the substantial embodiment of their historic faith, though they refrained from identifying that faith as Calvinistic and there was uncertainty about the real meaning of their declaration with respect to distinctive Calvinist doctrines. In 1883 they adopted a new creed, in modern idiom, that reflected classic Reformed themes but marked the end of the Westminster tradition in the denomination. Concurrently, at Andover Seminary, founded in 1808 in opposition to Unitarian Harvard and sustained in tension with Taylorite Yale, the last Hopkinsian, Edwards A. Park, was being overwhelmed by a new faculty committed to a self-consciously modernizing "progressive orthodoxy." Their orthodoxy was broadly Christian and nominally Reformed Protestant, but their interest in human growth, social justice, religious intuition, and historical change carried them progressively away from the historic formularies. Other Congregationalists participated with equal readiness in the intellectual movement that, between about 1870 and 1920, brought modern historical, scientific, philosophical, social, and psychological thinking into the circle of Christian reflection. By 1931, when the denomination was joined by a group of Christian Churches born in the Second Great

Awakening, there was scarcely any doctrinal Calvinism left in it.

In 1869 Old and New School Presbyterians reunited on the basis of the Westminster Confession, as "containing the system of doctrine taught in the Holy Scriptures," allowing to stand a qualification that had obtained since 1729 to the effect that the affirmation applied to "essential and necessary articles of faith" (Loetscher, 1954, pp. 2, 4). This qualification had allowed the New School to interpret doctrine progressively and functioned similarly as Presbyterians became engaged, in the 1880s, with issues of biblical and historical scholarship, natural science, and modern philosophy. In the ensuing controversy Princeton Seminary served as the chief center of resistance, and Union the center of affirmation. In 1892 the General Assembly of the Presbyterian Church declared the Princeton theory of biblical inerrancy and verbal inspiration a necessary article of faith. Eleven years later, partly in deference to the modern temper, the assembly adopted modest but significant creedal revisions, interpreting divine sovereignty in terms of God's universal love, offering hope to nonelect infants dying in infancy, and clearing the good deeds of the unregenerate from the taint of sinfulness. In the contention about Christianity's essential content, which gripped the church until the late 1920s, a quite different set of doctrinal "fundamentals" was at issue than the Dortian ones that Edwards had defended. The death in 1921 of Benjamin Warfield, Hodge's great successor, left Princeton largely isolated in a church that was taking a different direction. At the general assembly of 1927, moderate theological liberalism gained a legitimate place in the denomination. When, in 1967, northern Presbyterians at length undertook thorough creedal revision, they included the Westminster Confession and Shorter Catechism with six other historic statements of Christian and Reformed faith, which they affirmed as their heritage; but they formulated their own contemporary belief in quite different terms.

Viewed broadly, by about 1910 it appeared that the Calvinist theological tradition in America had dissolved or was dissolving into nontheological experientialism, modernist progressivism, combative biblicism, and premillennialism; however, this was not wholly the case. Historic confessional and nineteenth-century scholastic Calvinism persisted, in varying degree, in the smaller, conservative Presbyterian and Reformed denominations into the middle of the twentieth century, and the major denominations did not altogether abandon the tradition, even as they transformed it. When, in the middle third of the century, American Protestants were inspired to recover elements of the Reformation heritage, the Calvinist tradition became an object of renewed study and, selectively, a source of inspiration, although it did not appear to furnish a frame, as it had previously, for sustained theological construction.

BIBLIOGRAPHY

Puritanism

John D. Eusden, tr. and ed., *The Marrow of Theology: William Ames, 1576–1633* (1968); Ernest B. Lowrie, *The Shape of the Puritan Mind: The Thought of Samuel Willard* (1974); Robert Middlekauff, *The Mathers: Three Generations of Puritan Intellectuals, 1596–1728* (1971; repr. 1976); Perry Miller, *The New England Mind: The Seventeenth Century* (1939; repr. 1961) and *From Colony to Province* (1953; rep. 1961); Samuel E. Morison, *The Intellectual Life of Colonial New England* (1956); Kenneth Silverman, *The Life and Times of Cotton Mather* (1984); William K. B. Stoever, *"A Faire and Easie Way to Heaven": Covenant Theology and Antinomianism in Early Massachusetts* (1978).

Edwards

C. Conrad Cherry, *The Theology of Jonathan Edwards: A Reappraisal* (1966); Douglas J. Elwood, *The Philosophical Theology of Jonathan Edwards* (1960); Clarence H. Faust and Thomas H. Johnson, eds., *Jonathan Edwards: Representative Selections* (1935; rev. 1962); Norman Fiering, *Jonathan Edwards's Moral Thought and Its British Context* (1981); Perry Miller and John E. Smith, eds., *The Works of Jonathan Edwards* (1957–); Harvey G. Townsend, ed., *The Philosophy of Jonathan Edwards from His Private Notebooks* (1955).

Nineteenth Century

Sydney E. Ahlstrom, "The Scottish Philosophy and American Theology," in *Church History*, 24 (1955); William Breitenbach, "The Consistent Calvinism of the New Divinity Movement," in *William and Mary Quarterly*, 41 (1984); Ralph J. Danhof, *Charles Hodge as a Dogmatician* (1929); Frank H. Foster, *A Genetic History of the New England Theology* (1907; repr. 1963); Bruce Kuklick, *Churchmen and Philosophers: From Jonathan Edwards to John Dewey* (1985); Lefferts A. Loetscher, *The Broadening Church: A Study of Theological Issues in the Presbyterian Church Since 1869* (1954); George M. Marsden, *The Evangelical Mind and the New School Presbyterian Experience* (1970); Sidney E. Mead, *Nathaniel William Taylor, 1786–1858: A Connecticut Liberal* (1942); James H. Nichols, *Romanticism in American Theology: Nevin and Schaff at Mercersburg* (1961); Mark A. Noll, ed., *The Princeton Theology, 1812–1921* (1983); H. Shelton Smith, *Changing Conceptions of Original Sin: A Study in American Theology Since 1750* (1955) and, as ed., *Horace Bushnell* (1965); William K. B. Stoever, "Henry Boynton Smith and the German Theology of History," in *Union Seminary Quarterly Review,* 24 (1968).

General

Sydney E. Ahlstrom, *Theology in America: The Major Protestant Voices from Puritanism to Neo-Orthodoxy* (1967); John T. McNeill, *The History and Character of Calvinism* (1954; repr. 1973); Thomas F. Torrance, tr. and ed., *The School of Faith: The Catechisms of the Reformed Church* (1959); Williston Walker, *The Creeds and Platforms of Congregationalism* (1893, 1960).

[*See also* CALVINIST HERITAGE; IMPACT OF PURITANISM ON AMERICAN CULTURE; NEW ENGLAND PURITANISM; *and* PRESBYTERIANISM.]

THE IMPACT OF PURITANISM ON AMERICAN CULTURE

Daniel Walker Howe

THE Puritans of colonial America are among the most-studied people in all history. Even more has been written about them than they wrote themselves—which was a lot. Probably the most important reason for this concentrated attention is that scholars have an invincible sense that in studying Puritanism they are uncovering the roots of American culture, "the origins of the American self." Any sound description of seventeenth-century Puritans would have to be careful to emphasize the many ways in which they were not like us. This article, however, is concerned with the aspects of Puritanism that have survived to help shape the culture of America.

Puritanism is so important that some scholars have treated it as a "consensus" within which all American civilization has taken shape. Puritanism, however, has always had to struggle to impose its cultural standards. At all times in American history there have been many who have considered themselves non-Puritans or anti-Puritans. Instead of constituting an all-pervading consensus, American Puritanism has typically been engaged in dialogue with one or more adversaries, such as Anglicanism, the Enlightenment, or southern slave power. Puritanism is not responsible for everything about America, but it was certainly one of the seminal cultural impulses from which America historically derived.

Americans of the nineteenth and twentieth centuries have looked back upon the Puritans in a variety of ways, frequently projecting their own positive and negative feelings onto them. The Puritans have been Pilgrim Fathers to patriotic schoolteachers, courageous rebels to radical abolitionists, and prudish villains to H. L. Mencken and Hugh Hefner. Modern scholars have shown that many commonly received notions of the Puritans are misconceptions: they did not dress all in black or wear cone-shaped hats; they were not teetotalers; they were not especially repressive toward children or criminals by the standards of their age. Yet the scholars too have sometimes projected their own hopes, fears, aspirations, and aversions onto the Puritans. Sometimes they have treated them as defenders of an idealized premodern social order, sometimes as alienated intellectuals. Sometimes they have used Puritanism as a whipping boy and sometimes as a stick with which to beat the America of their own day. The emotion-charged quality of American attitudes toward Puritanism is, of course, testimony to its continuing cultural relevance.

Originally, Puritanism was a call for the reform (or "purifying") of Christianity in Tudor-Stuart England. An outlook on life rather than a united movement, Puritanism may be considered a religious revival. It addressed the individual lay believer and demanded his or her commitment to Christ through a conversion experience, without which a person was irretrievably lost in sin. The emphasis was on a reawakening of personal piety through private devotional practices, primarily Bible reading, and on the sermon in public worship. Sacraments and sacerdotalism were downgraded, liturgical formalism and ceremonies discouraged. The theology was in the Reformed, or Calvinistic, tradition, affirming predestination. Puritans espoused a wide variety of ecclesiological positions, reflecting disagreement among them on how much institutional restructuring would be necessary to accomplish the desired revival of piety; but the most characteristically Puritan polity, and the one that has been most influential in America, was Congregationalism.

As a means to the implementation of its religious program, English Puritanism became committed to political reforms as well. For some purposes of analysis one may consider the political dimension of Puritanism secondary to the religious, although church and state were so closely intertwined at the time that the distinction is not altogether meaningful. None of the English monarchs of the period was disposed to undertake a thoroughgoing reform of the church, and the Puritans remained dissatisfied with the Elizabethan ecclesiastical settlement. Consequently the Puritans came to look for support in centers of power other than the royal court, among them the country gentry, the courts of common law, and Parliament. As the decades passed under Elizabeth I and then James I, the Puritans became gradually more restless. The colonization of New England by Puritan migrants reflected their growing disenchantment with Puritan prospects in the old country. Charles I pursued religious and political policies that were positively reactionary and drove the Puritans to take up arms in rebellion. When matters came to a head, religious issues were inextricably bound up with constitutional and financial ones. The experience of the English Puritans as political dissidents was critical in shaping their outlook and the legacy they passed on to America.

An examination of the Puritan impact on American culture is for the most part a story of secularization. Attitudes and practices that for the Puritans had religious motives and meaning have outlived this original frame of reference and taken on a life of their own. Whether, in doing so, they have been debased or dignified is for the reader to decide.

PURITANISM AND AMERICAN DEMOCRACY

American democracy can trace many of its distinctive characteristics, including its reliance on written constitutions, to origins in Puritanism. It is important to state at the outset, however, that this does not imply that other democratic forms could not have evolved without Puritanism, much less that religion is in general a precondition for democracy. What the historian can conclude is that political democracy first appeared in those countries, among them the United States, where there were features of the religious situation encouraging it.

The English Puritans who established the colony of Massachusetts Bay in 1630 avowed not the slightest fondness for democracy. John Winthrop, their leading magistrate, called it "the meanest and worst of all forms of government." Yet their way of life contained the seeds of democracy despite their disavowals. The Puritans lived in a transitional world between medieval and modern times. Their outlook was both authoritarian and individualistic, traditional and rational, tribal and cosmopolitan. The side of Puritanism that has been most important for American political life, however, has been the individualistic, rational, and cosmopolitan. The political goal of the Puritans was the dictatorship of God's elect, but among the means by which they sought that end were constitutional government, a considerable dismantling of hierarchy in church and state, and a franchise open to any godly man. In America these means have proved much more durable than the Puritans' end, and over the years they have taken on a different claim to legitimacy. It is worth noting that the democratic implications of Puritanism became apparent in England, too, after the Puritans had overthrown Charles I, but there they were undone by counterrevolution and the restoration of the monarchy in 1660.

Limited Government. English Puritans had much in common with Calvinist Reformers elsewhere, and like their counterparts in the Low Countries, France, and the Holy Roman Empire they found themselves in a position of political opposition to the monarch. The veneration of the Reformers for Scripture provided them with a source of authority independent not only of pope but also of king. Politically disaffected social groups in parts of Europe—including nobles, gentry, and burghers—adopted the Calvinist religious agenda. In it they found legitimacy for both opposition to absolutism and political action of their own. If Calvinism was the religion of the rising middle classes, as is often said, it was so not just because they were middle class but also because they were rising. All over Europe, monarchs typically identified Calvinism with insubordination and dissent.

In England the Puritans declared Scripture to be a law higher than ecclesiastical tradition, legal prescription, or the divine right of kings. "It is against reason," wrote the Puritan theologian William Perkins, "that human laws, being subject to defects, faults, errors, and manifold imperfections, should truly bind conscience as God's laws do.'' The Church of England, on the other hand, maintained the more conventional position that the laws of the state embodied God's will and were morally binding. The great Anglican thinker Richard Hooker believed the Bible left many things "indifferent" with regard to religious and social practice. His position sounds very tolerant until we notice that he assigns to the king authority to decide whatever the Bible leaves indifferent. The Puritans, with their "precise" biblical literalism, were limiting royal discretion. When some of them decided that episcopacy had no warrant in the New Testament, they were threatening the king's greatest source of patronage and influence. "No bishop, no king," was James I's apt comment.

It was the Puritans who confirmed in Anglo-American tradition the principle that the king is not above the law but is responsible to it. They also firmly established the right of revolution against the king when he failed to abide by the law. In this regard the American Revolution represents no advance over Puritan principles. In fact, the Roundheads who rebelled against the king in the 1640s went much further than the Glorious Revolutionaries of 1688 or the American Patriots of the 1770s had any need to go, for they put Charles I on trial and executed him. (After the Restoration, Puritans in New Haven, Connecticut, sheltered three of his judges from Charles II's retaliation.) When the New England clergyman Jonathan Mayhew delivered his famous sermon against the doctrine of unlimited submission to royal authority in 1750, he was vindicating the Revolution of 1641 as well as anticipating that of 1776.

Probably any tradition of religious dissent, whether Calvinist Puritan or not, could have helped to establish a right of resistance. After all, Catholic theologians justified disobedience and tyrannicide in places where they were cast in opposition to the ruler. The distinctively Puritan contribution to the American tradition of limited government lies in the strong Calvinist emphasis on the sovereignty of God and the sufficiency of his revelation in Scripture, which implies that no earthly power can be absolute. The equally strong Calvinist emphasis on the sinfulness of man implies that even rulers cannot be altogether trusted. A good Calvinist would be suspicious of government not only when it was run by infidels, but even when it was in the hands of his fellows.

Individualism. At the time of America's colonization what Protestants did not believe was every bit as important as what they believed. They did not believe in the ecclesiastical traditions that had grown up justifying sacerdotalism in all its ramifications: purgatory and indulgences; the invocation of saints and cults of relics; the sacrament of penance and absolution; the authority of the pope and his cardinals, the right of the church to interpret and supplement Scripture. By getting rid of this overlay of clericalism, Protestantism empowered the common lay person to assume control over his or her destiny in the next world—and eventually in this world as well. The name for this personal authority in Protestant theology was "the priesthood of all believers." One of its important facets was the right of private judgment in the interpretation of Scripture. What this meant in the early modern world is well described by William Haller: "Without benefit of clergy, without the aid of scholastic logic, every man could find in the poetry of Scripture the mirror of his own thoughts and spiritual strivings, could talk, argue, preach, and write about what he found there, could concoct his own Utopia by its aid" ("The Puritan Background of the First Amendment," in Conyers Read, ed., *The Constitution Reconsidered*, 1938).

All Protestants accepted the right of the laity to read, study, and interpret the Bible for themselves. The Puritans who settled New England added another important aspect to this individualism. They admitted as members of their churches only those men and women who could testify to their firsthand experience of saving grace. In other words, they called upon each person not only to think for himself but also to feel for himself. Before the Reformation the ordinary Christian believer had all too often been merely a nonparticipant witness at a weekly miracle; Puritanism made him an activist. Since the conversion experience was open to everyone, regardless of social rank, sex, or even age, it served as a prototype of the merit-based egalitarianism that later came to characterize secular institutions.

To be sure, the conversion experience was caused by God's grace, his reaching out to sinful humanity; according to Puritan theology it was never earned. Yet, once the saint had been thus mysteriously elected, the emphasis in Puritanism was on his freedom. The individual freely chose to enter into a covenant relationship with God and his fellow church members. Blessed by the assurance that he was justified in the sight of God, he voluntarily embraced sanctification and a righteous life. Predestined to eternal joy, he volunteered for Christ's army anyway. Paradoxically, Calvinist determinism had the effect of strengthening the wills of its adherents and encouraging them in voluntary activity. Ralph Barton Perry has appropriately named these Puritans "moral athletes."

Furthermore, although the church members were set apart from the rest of society, within their own group a high degree of equality existed. Puritan clergy did not have the "keys to the kingdom," the power to admit and excommunicate church members; this power was wielded by the laity themselves. One gained admission to the church and presumptive membership in the communion of saints by convincing a jury of one's peers. The measure of equality that was enjoyed by Puritan laity included women to an unprecedented extent. Marriage, for the Puritans, was a civil institution and not a sacrament; being a covenant or contract, it could be undone through divorce in a way that neither the Anglican nor Catholic church permitted. As a partner to the marriage contract a Puritan wife enjoyed certain legal rights even within a position of general subordination to her husband. Women also read the Bible and experienced conversion; they had study groups and church activities of their own. It is not surprising that the first major religious revival in Puritan America, the "antinomian controversy" of 1636–38, was led by a woman—Anne Hutchinson, one of the founders of Rhode Island.

Anne Hutchinson was condemned by the Puritan authorities of Massachusetts as a heretic and exiled. Their action illustrates the typical unwillingness of most seventeenth-century Puritans to recognize all the libertarian and democratic implications in their doctrine. Yet, precisely because Puritan theology taught that God revealed himself through his word to the minds of individual believers and by his grace to their hearts, some measure of free discussion was essential if this revelation was to be understood and interpreted by the group. God was no re-specter of persons, and even the most eminent Puritan divine had to be prepared to rely on persuasive arguments rather than authority. Thus the seeds of toleration were planted even in the intolerance of Puritanism, and they produced great writings on behalf of liberty as early as 1644, the year of both John Milton's *Areopagitica* and Roger Williams' condemnation of *The Bloudy Tenent of Persecution*. The individual rights that the Puritans endorsed as a means to moral and religious goals have become for most Americans today a value in themselves.

Government by Consent. Participation is the corollary of individualism; people who think for themselves will want to be consulted and have their cooperation elicited in group endeavors. The history of Calvinism illustrates this: Calvinism spread across Europe chiefly through "conventicles," voluntary societies of believers, in contrast to Lutheranism and Anglicanism, which staked their fortunes on Protestant rulers. Within England some Puritans were willing to operate through Episcopal or Presbyterian structures, but the founders of New England espoused the ecclesiastical organization known as Congregationalism. In this church polity each congregation of believers covenanted together to worship and serve the Lord, called their own minister(s), admitted members, and exercised "watch and ward" over their conduct. All this was done independently of outside authority, although Congregational churches could meet together in synods to address common problems. Unquestionably, Congregationalism proved to be a training ground for government by compact and consent.

In colonial New England the political consequences of Congregationalism had a chance to unfold in relative isolation from Old World constraints. The settlers extended their experience with local self-government from their churches to their towns. Each town had a meetinghouse, used for worship and all other town business, secular as well as religious. Town meetings usually operated by consensus rather than formal voting, and the opinions of prominent citizens carried great weight, but even a man who was not a member of the church could be heard.

Massachusetts Bay, the largest of the New England colonies, was settled in 1630. Beginning in 1634, the freemen of the colony possessed the right to elect deputies for each town to the General Court; they came to function as the lower house of a colonial legislature. Any adult male church member was qualified for freemanship, a status that conferred certain responsibilities like jury duty in addition to the right to vote. In the early days of the colony a majority of men probably met the qualification of church membership; by the 1660s probably less than half. By seventeenth-century standards this was an extraordinarily broad franchise. Representative government in New England was abolished by the British Crown in 1684; when it was reinstituted after the Glorious Revolution, the new Massachusetts charter provided for a property-based suffrage rather than a religiously based one. The Puritan experiment in government by the saints had come to an end, but its legacy proved very durable.

A Written Constitution. God had dealt with mankind through a series of covenants with Adam, Abraham, and Christ, according to the covenant (or "federal") theologians whom the New England Puritans revered. And when they set up their churches in the wilderness, the Puritans did so through covenants with each other, according to terms they believed were prescribed in the Bible. The natural law of reason, Puritans felt, taught them the same respect for covenants in secular affairs. "It is evident by the light of nature that all civil relations are founded in covenant," declared Boston's leading minister, John Cotton. Some of the written agreements on which New England government was based were charters granted by the king. Even more interesting, however, were the ones drawn up among the colonists themselves, such as the Mayflower Compact of Plymouth Colony (1620), Connecticut's Fundamental Orders (1638), or the Massachusetts Body of Liberties (1641). Most remarkable of all from the viewpoint of later America is the constitution for Providence Plantations drawn up in 1647, which took the radical step of calling its form of government *democratical.*

The Puritan practice of ordering all relationships, human and divine, through covenants formed the intellectual background for the political thought of John Locke in England. Locke, the son of a Puritan revolutionary army officer, became the key figure in the secularizing of social-compact theory. An analogous role was played on a smaller scale in the colonies by John Wise, minister of the little town of Ipswich, Mas-

sachusetts. In *A Vindication of the Government of New England Churches* (1717) Wise defended the Congregational polity by arguments drawn from the natural rights of man, relegating biblical arguments to a subordinate role. In the 1770s Wise's work was reprinted by revolutionary patriots.

The Founding Fathers who met at Philadelphia in the summer of 1787 to write the Constitution of the United States included few men who could be called Puritans but many who were influenced by Puritan and Calvinist political thought. James Madison, the most influential of them, had received an orthodox Calvinist education at Princeton. Like almost all of the Puritans the Founding Fathers believed classical "mixed government," that is, a balance among monarchical, aristocratic, and democratic elements, preferable to pure democracy. As John Winthrop had tried to balance these elements for Massachusetts Bay under the old charter, they carefully constructed their new constitution, in which only the House of Representatives was elected directly by the people. They relied on checks and balances to limit the amount of evil any one person could do, for they retained a Puritan sense of human selfishness, even though many of them no longer called it "original sin." Horace White observed that the Constitution of the United States is "based upon the philosophy of Hobbes and the theology of Calvin" (quoted in Richard Hofstadter, *The American Political Tradition,* 1948; repr. 1958). Neither Hobbes nor Calvin believed the individual naturally virtuous, but both believed in the value of covenants to discipline and control him.

Separation of Church and State. The New England Puritans endorsed what they called separation of church and state, although outside Rhode Island it existed only in limited form. By this separation the Puritans meant that church and state would cooperate within their separate spheres, temporal and spiritual. The church was restricted to the spiritual sphere much more than in either Catholic or Anglican practice. New England churches owned no property (even the meetinghouses belonged to the towns), and their clergy were ineligible for political office—in contrast to Europe, where bishops sat in parliaments and prelates often became prime ministers. In England ecclesiastical courts had jurisdiction over probate, contract, and family law; in New

England these were matters for the civil courts. What we would call a religious establishment still existed, however, because the Puritan churches received tax support in most towns to help pay the minister's salary. The Bible, especially the Old Testament, was used as a law book alongside English common law authorities.

Rhode Island, under the leadership of the Puritan Separatist Roger Williams, carried separation further than any other colony. There, no tax moneys went to the churches, and no requirement that voters be church members existed. Williams insisted on this extraordinary degree of separation because he wanted to keep the church uncontaminated by the world. When the First Amendment to the United States Constitution forbade any establishment of religion by the new federal government, it was adopted through an alliance between Protestant Pietists working in the tradition of Williams and eighteenth-century deists like Thomas Jefferson who wanted to keep secular politics uncontaminated by the church. The amendment applied only at the federal level; the New England states were free to retain their own tax-supported religious establishments. Disestablishment occurred by state action in New Hampshire (1817), Connecticut (1819), and Massachusetts (1833).

Pluralism. There was no possibility of a national established church in the European sense within the newly independent United States even without the First Amendment, simply because no one religion had the power to force all the rest into subordinate positions. Religious diversity was thus an important guarantor of religious freedom. But among the different religious traditions in early America Puritanism was the most important; and Puritanism itself fostered religious diversity, even if no non-Puritan religions had been transplanted to the New World.

During the Puritan Commonwealth in England there was an unprecedented proliferation of sects, halted by the restoration of Anglicanism and the monarchy. In America Puritanism also gave birth to a multitude of daughter sects, and the process never stopped. Baptists, Presbyterians, Congregationalists, Quakers, Unitarians— all can trace their lineage to Puritanism, and many other bodies of later origin like Latter-day Saints and Christian Scientists drew their first followers primarily from Puritan descendants and show affinities with the Puritan tradition.

Unlike the separation of church and state, however, pluralism must be accounted an entirely unintentional by-product of Puritanism. The early Puritan settlers believed that they had discovered the one true way of interpreting the Scriptures, which all other people of good will should acknowledge. They established their colonies as an example of purity to the world, and they regarded the coming of religious diversity as an embarrassment.

PURITANISM AS AN INTELLECTUAL INFLUENCE

Puritanism was a religion of a book. It was also a religion centered on hearing the Word contained in that book preached from a pulpit. To practice the religion one had to be able to read the book as well as to follow and ponder the exposition of the Word. To a remarkable extent Puritan devotions took the form of reading, memorizing, analyzing, and applying passages from the Bible. Puritan piety was thus predicated on a measure of literacy and verbal aptitude. Insofar as historians can reconstruct the statistics, colonial New England had a significantly higher rate of literacy than either Quaker-founded Pennsylvania or Anglican-founded Virginia. The only other parts of the world with literacy comparable to New England at that time were Scotland and Sweden; all three were places where Protestant churches enforced mass education.

Of all the legacies Puritanism has left for American civilization, its contribution to education is perhaps the clearest and the most benign. It has proved a continuing influence. The roster of great American educational leaders and reformers in every period is to a surprising extent a list of New Englanders of Puritan extraction, among them Benjamin Franklin, Horace Mann, Catharine Beecher, Charles W. Eliot, and John Dewey.

Schools. Massachusetts enacted the first provision for free public schools in this country in 1647; "it being one chief project of that old deluder Satan, to keep men from the knowledge of the Scriptures," explained the lawmakers. Connecticut followed suit in 1650. Several New England towns had organized public schools even before these laws. The Massachusetts and Connecticut educational systems required each town of fifty families or more to support a teacher and each town of a hundred families or more to maintain a grammar school where Latin would be taught; even where no teachers or schools existed, parents were legally responsible for the education of their children. Originally elementary schools, many of these grammar schools evolved into secondary schools. Several of the earliest have survived to the present day: Boston Latin, Cambridge Latin, Roxbury Latin, and the Hopkins Latin School of New Haven. Although the Puritan public school system was created for religious reasons, it was under the control of the secular authorities, and schoolteachers could not be ministers.

The Puritans included some provision for girls as well as boys within their program of primary education, for females also needed to read the Bible; however, further formal education was restricted to males. In the nineteenth century, when women gained access first to secondary and then to higher education, they did so initially in those parts of the country that had felt the strongest impact of the Puritan tradition. The United States has been a leader among the nations of the world in women's education.

After independence New England continued its role of schoolmaster to America. Horace Mann established the first statewide system of administrative supervision over local school districts while secretary of the Massachusetts Board of Education (1837–1848) as well as the first teachers' college, at Lexington in 1839. New England was a leader in private education, too. The two Phillips academies had been founded at Andover, Massachusetts (1778), and Exeter, New Hampshire (1781); originally they did not have dormitories, and the students boarded in town. The private boarding school was pioneered by Joseph G. Cogswell at Northampton, Massachusetts, in the 1820s. Examples such as these were critically important in shaping both public and private education elsewhere in America. Public school systems did not become standard throughout the northern states until the mid-nineteenth century; they were not extended to the South (where segregated dual systems were created) until after the Civil War.

Higher Education. "After God had carried us safe to New England, one of the next things we longed and looked after, was to advance learning and perpetuate it to posterity, dreading to leave an illiterate ministry to the churches when our present ministers shall lie in the dust" (*New England's First Fruits,* 1643). The New England Puritans created their educational system from the top down. After founding a college in 1636, subsequently named Harvard, they established schools to prepare students for it. The college took priority because it was essential for the training of clergy, though from the start the curriculum was much broader than theology, and even in the seventeenth century only a minority of the graduates entered the ministry. First-generation Massachusetts Bay Colony had perhaps the highest educational level of any community in the world because it included so many English university graduates. Within a few years Harvard College achieved high academic standards, and its degrees were being accepted by Oxford and Cambridge as the equivalent of their own.

Today an impressive array of American colleges and universities are tangible precipitates of the Puritan tradition. Colleges proliferated not only in New England (which still has the highest proportion of college students of any region), but also wherever New Englanders settled. Yale (1701), Dartmouth (1769), Williams (1785), Bowdoin (1794), Middlebury (1800), and Amherst (1821) all were founded to suit special geographical and religious needs of New England Congregationalists. By the time Brown was founded (1764), the Rhode Island heirs of Roger Williams and Anne Hutchinson called themselves Baptists. Princeton (1746), though its Calvinism was Presbyterian, had Puritan ties, illustrated by the (tragically brief) presidency of Jonathan Edwards. Union College (1795) in Schenectady, New York, was founded, as the name indicated, by Congregationalists and Presbyterians jointly. Rutgers (1766) was Calvinist too, but Dutch rather than English. In the nineteenth century New Englanders moving across the continent founded in their wake a broad band of liberal arts colleges, among them Oberlin, Antioch, and Western Reserve in Ohio, Rockford and Illinois colleges in Illinois, Beloit in Wisconsin, Grinnell in Iowa, Carleton in Minnesota, Yankton in South Dakota, all the way to Colorado College in Colorado Springs and Pomona in Claremont, California. Some of these institutions resulted from the academic missionary efforts of the neo-Puritan Society for the Promotion of Collegiate and Theological Education at the West. So many of them were founded by Yale graduates and looked to Yale as their model that Yale became a veritable mother of colleges.

The Puritan-Congregationalist influence in higher education has not by any means been confined to Americans who are descended from the Puritans, either physically or religiously. Among the institutions deriving from the Congregationalist tradition are black colleges in the South founded after the Civil War, including Hampton Institute in Virginia, Fisk University in Tennessee, and Tougaloo College in Mississippi. Sometimes Yankee-Congregationalist initiatives created secular state universities, as happened with the University of Illinois at Urbana and the University of California at Berkeley. Anglicans and Roman Catholics early developed their own academic networks, and in 1765 the first secular college in the world was founded at Philadelphia, later to be named the University of Pennsylvania (though it was and is a private institution, not a state university). Yet the largest and most important institutional "family tree" among American colleges remains the one planted by the Puritans.

The Life of the Mind. There was nothing anti-intellectual about Puritanism. In addition to theology early Harvard taught classics, rhetoric and oratory, mathematics, and natural and moral philosophy. As the years passed moral philosophy occupied an increasingly important place in the curriculum, largely displacing systematic theology by the late eighteenth century.

From Puritan origins three durable traditions in American philosophy can be traced; the greatest of colonial Puritan thinkers, Jonathan Edwards, made a contribution to all of them. The first is a Platonic tradition emphasizing ethical rationalism and including Francis Bowen and Josiah Royce. The second is a pietistic tradition concerned with the nature of religious experience. It begins with John Cotton and Anne Hutchinson and continues through Edwards and his New Divinity followers; unorthodox products include Ralph Waldo Emerson's *Nature* (1836) and William James's *The Varieties of Religious Experience* (1902). The third mediates between the first two; we may call it the Connecticut Valley tradition because it has been so often centered at Yale. It seeks to balance "head" and "heart," or more accurately, to take into account both logical rationality and the needs of human nature. It

can be traced from Edwards through Nathaniel William Taylor to Horace Bushnell and (in secularized form) John Dewey.

The suspicion of science that Charles Darwin later engendered in some evangelical Protestants was not typical of the early Puritans. In fact, seventeenth-century Puritans were among the most hospitable people of their age to science. Historians have long wondered whether there was anything especially favorable to the scientific world view in Calvinist religion, but the evidence is inconclusive. As late as the nineteenth century scientific research was often encouraged by natural theology, the religious appreciation of God through his works in nature; however, natural theology was not peculiar to Puritanism, and Anglicans in particular had their own strong tradition of natural theology and science.

The impact of Puritanism on American literature is incalculable. Seventeenth-century New Englanders read not only the Bible and devotional works but also romances, ballads, almanacs, technical books, and popular histories. The first printing press in North America was set up at Cambridge in 1638 to publish *The Bay Psalm Book* (1640) for use as a hymnal. Until the rise of New York City in the mid-nineteenth century Boston remained the literary and publishing capital of America.

What seventeenth-century New Englanders wrote best, other than sermons, was history and poetry. In both genres they founded long traditions of excellence that have continued in New England throughout the nineteenth and twentieth centuries. The Puritan sermon exerted a powerful force through a third genre: oratory. Blending with classical forms of declamation, the New England sermon started a tradition of oratory and elocution in America that remained strong until the end of the nineteenth century. The Puritans also have been credited with a distinctive literary aesthetic (the "plain style") and symbolism ("typology").

The Puritans' influence in American literature, however, has been exerted not only by their example but even more through the frame of mind that they passed on to later generations. Together with their fellow Calvinists in the Middle Colonies (especially the Dutch) and the South (especially the Scots-Irish) they provided the ingredients for a somber Calvinist tradition in American literature. Typical themes in this

THE IMPACT OF PURITANISM ON AMERICAN CULTURE

literary tradition are introspection, predestination, guilt, pride, and theodicy (the problem of evil). It is impossible to understand such nineteenth-century authors as Nathaniel Hawthorne, Herman Melville, and Harriet Beecher Stowe without reference to this Calvinist heritage, though all rejected as formal theology what they practiced as literary artists.

The power of Puritanism in American literary history is evident not only in overt celebrations like Henry Wadsworth Longfellow's "The Courtship of Miles Standish" (1858). Much of American literature can be interpreted as dialogue with Puritanism. Emerson and Henry David Thoreau repudiated human depravity and revealed religion but retained a strong consciousness of their Puritan inheritance and displayed it in their style and in their sense that both nature and art were fundamentally moral. Some American writers defined themselves as anti-Puritan, like Washington Irving, Edgar Allan Poe, and George Santayana. Mark Twain hated and fought against Calvinist religion but could not rid himself of its influence. T. S. Eliot turned his back on America and his Puritan family lineage to embrace Britain and High Anglicanism. But even in the twentieth century Calvinist literary themes have remained prominent, especially in the writings of southerners like Robert Penn Warren, William Faulkner, and Tennessee Williams. A more distinctively New England version of the Puritan tradition is clearly relevant to the poetry of Robert Lowell and Robert Frost.

While Puritanism fostered strong traditions in such verbal activities as philosophy, literature, and oratory, it did little to encourage music or the fine arts. Puritans generally tolerated or even appreciated these arts in a secular context, but not in a religious one—and religion has frequently given decisive impetus to art forms. If there was little difference between Puritans and other English people in their everyday material culture, there was a significant difference in their modes of worship. There, Puritans relied almost exclusively on the written and spoken Word, in contrast to Roman Catholics and Anglicans, who employed many media of religious communication: liturgy, drama, music, architecture, sculpture, and decorative arts. The attitude of the Puritans was summed up in their preface to the *Bay Psalm Book:* "God's altar needs not our polishing." Puritans expected art to be functional, which usually meant didactic; they disliked the "merely" ornamental. (One of their principal controversies with the Anglicans concerned vestments.) An art form actively discouraged by Puritans and their evangelical heirs was drama, which they disliked chiefly because of the immoral associations of the theater as a place of assignation. The Puritans' preference for verbal expression and their commitment to didacticism and plain style shaped American high culture for a long time. Artists who rejected these standards often came from outside the Puritan tradition; for example, when a distinctive American contribution to music appeared, it came largely from Afro-Americans. The American poet Mather Byles, an Anglican, satirized the prevailing Puritan aesthetic in 1744: "Solid, and grave, and plain the country stood,/Inelegant, and rigorously good."

PURITANISM AND ECONOMIC ACTIVITY

Puritanism in Stuart England was strongest in the South and East, which were the most economically developed parts of the country, and among social groups touched by commercial or (in the case of woolens) industrial innovation. The possibility of a connection between Puritanism and nascent capitalism has long tantalized researchers. In 1904 the German sociologist Max Weber published one of the most famous books in social science, *The Protestant Ethic and the Spirit of Capitalism.* Although he undertook to treat European Calvinism in general, Weber drew most of his evidence from Anglo-American Puritanism. He argued that Calvinism had promoted a life-style encouraging sustained systematic economic activity and reinvestment of profits. Eventually this "Protestant ethic" became divorced from its religious motivation; in its secularized form he called it "the spirit of capitalism." This "spirit" was not the same as capitalism itself; but, when widely diffused among the population, it explained why people were willing to labor conscientiously and save money instead of working according to natural rhythms and consuming any surpluses.

It might have been better if Weber had used the term "work ethic" instead of "spirit of capitalism," for the way of life he described is not confined to capitalists or even to people living in capitalist societies; wage earners and socialists can and do manifest the work ethic. The work ethic is logically linked with a stage in economic development when a country is trying to accumulate capital by encouraging production and discouraging consumption. This was done in the United States and other Western nations through capitalism, but it can be accomplished under other economic systems. Wherever it is done, however, be it Cuba under Castro or China under Mao, some functional equivalent of the work ethic is invariably introduced to replace the habits of a premodern economy.

Some of the same cautions expressed at the beginning of the section on democracy are relevant here, too. The Puritans no more desired to promote modern capitalism than they intended to practice democracy. Early Puritans, like good traditional Christians, condemned extortion and mercenary motives and endorsed sumptuary laws and a "just price" for everything. And if Puritanism inadvertently fostered capitalism in certain ways, we should remember that Puritanism was not essential to capitalism, any more than capitalism is essential to modernization.

Puritanism and Modernization: The Work Ethic. Weber described the evolution of the work ethic in three stages: monasticism, Calvinism, and the secular spirit of capitalism. During the Middle Ages some people felt a "calling" (or vocation) to serve God through a religious life of prayer and work; they took vows and lived in celibate monastic communities apart from the world under the discipline of the rule of their order. Typically this rule required conscientious labor and ascetic self-denial; many communities became well organized bureaucracies that kept records and operated large-scale economic activities. After the Reformation Protestants rejected the monastic ideal. Among the Calvinists, however, a "worldly asceticism" developed, analogous to the monastic way of life. All elect men and women now had "callings" to both prayer and work; each should serve God in a useful occupation, be it weaver, cooper, housewife, or magistrate. Work became a form of self-discipline and a religious regimen for all, as it had once been only for monastics. The Calvinist saint was no more self-indulgent than the monk, so he did not squander his earnings. In Weber's third stage faith in God disappeared. The profits resulting from diligent labor and thrift became an end in themselves—but the compulsive sense of duty to work for them remained.

Weber's thesis has never lacked critics, but there is much evidence in its support. The innovative economic role of the monasteries is well attested. And European Calvinists often played a commercial role typical of certain religious minorities the world over; compare the Armenians in the Ottoman Empire, the Parsees in India, the Bahai in Iran, or the Jews. Anglo-American Puritans taught that "for a man to rise early and go to bed late, and eat the bread of carefulness, not a sinful, but a provident care," was a mark of a holy life. The great preacher John Cotton declared that a man should "lose no opportunity to bestir himself for profit"—yet he must do so for the glory of God and remain "deadhearted to the world" (*Christ the Fountaine of Life,* 1651). A difficult balancing act! In the absence of sacraments the Puritan had to look for other visible signs that he enjoyed God's grace. Diligence in one's calling was such a sign, said Puritan theologians like William Perkins. Although he did not earn salvation by his works, the Puritan was forever working, proving to himself that God had indeed chosen him for salvation.

The religious origins of the American work ethic concern more than New England only and involve several varieties of Puritanism. In Pennsylvania the Quakers, an offshoot of Puritanism even more radical than the antinomians, shared the ethic of steady work and asceticism, though since they did not consider theology worthwhile they did not develop such an elaborate rationale for it. Early Virginia tried to enforce a work ethic but with little success, and the introduction of slavery undercut efforts to dignify labor. Then in the eighteenth century the Great Awakening brought an upsurge of popular piety in Virginia and the rest of the South, precipitated by Calvinist revivalists from old and New England. The itinerant evangelists preached a life not only godly but also disciplined. They challenged ideals of the plantation gentry that accepted pride, violence, and conspicuous consumption. For generations the South was to be a cultural battleground between a hedonistic, premodern, "lazy" way of life and an austere Protestant one with historic ties to Puritanism.

To some extent the Puritan work ethic was a middle-class one. Seventeenth-century Puritans deplored lower-class "vagabonds" and "sturdy beggars'' who refused to work, but they also attacked the idle rich, the fawning courtiers, and the hordes of servants with little to do but display their masters' livery. Among the social evils the Puritans criticized in England, unemployment and conspicuous consumption were prominent. Within the middle ranks of society the lower middle class of artisans and small farmers had more reason to endorse the Puritan social ethic than the upper middle class, for the activities of merchants were dangerously close to the vices of "speculation" and "usury." In its purest form the Puritan work ethic was really an independent craftsman's ethic, a value system that made good sense out of his life and enabled him to disapprove of others. After large-scale industrialization in the nineteenth century it became necessary to adapt the work ethic to an emergent proletariat. Employers spared no pains to instill in their wage earners, who were often former peasants without a Puritan heritage, habits of punctuality and factory discipline. This new industrial work ethic could be either secular or religious. The appearance of an evangelical temperance movement in the nineteenth century, for the first time in the long history of Christianity, is often explained in terms of industry's need for a sober work force.

A characteristic of the work ethic in the forms we have been discussing is a preoccupation with the long term rather than the short term. This emphasis is related to a shift to urban living, for there are few ways in which a traditional peasant can plan beyond the next harvest. The "worldly ascetic" way of life was socially functional in a phase of modernization demanding great sacrifices and deferring gratification to future generations. But as wealth accumulated, Puritanism adapted.

Puritanism and Capitalism: The Gospel of Wealth. Before capitalism could become the dominant economic system of Western civilization, economic activity had to achieve autonomy from many traditional restraints, ranging from the low prestige of earning money to restrictions on lending at interest. Puritanism helped it attain this autonomy, partly as a result of the individualism it encouraged in intellectual and political matters. The early Puritans were, of course, emphatic in their denunciations of selfish and mercenary behavior. However, they did seek to emancipate lay people from certain kinds of clerical control, including the jurisdiction of ecclesiastical courts over probate and contract law. They also objected to many religious festivals (including Christmas) observed by Catholics and Anglicans, complaining that these interfered with business. We have already discussed the importance the Puritans attached to covenants in religious relationships, and how it carried over into their political compacts. The covenant must have helped legitimate contractualism in economic life as well, though historians have investigated this implication much less. Whatever the intentions of the Puritans, the pluralism that came into English and (even more) American life as a result of the multiplication of sects weakened the ability of any religious group to control economic action. While this chain of events was preparing the way for capitalism, things were very different in many Catholic countries, where absolutist monarchies allied with the Counter-Reformation put down individualism and new ideas, in the process severely restricting not only heresy and dissent, but also science and economic progress.

Once economic activity had achieved autonomy, what capitalism most needed from religion was legitimation for financial gain. This, too, Puritanism was prepared to grant, though grudgingly. The early Puritans had been generally suspicious of too much money because it offered so many temptations. As time went by, however, Puritan spokesmen made their peace with prosperity. Other sins—mainly sins of the flesh—largely replaced avarice in their catalog of warnings, except during revivals and times of crisis. Leading Puritans of the late seventeenth century, like Richard Baxter in England and Cotton Mather in America, showed an increasing appreciation of business virtues like prudence and the welcome opportunities for philanthropy that come with profits. (Benjamin Franklin's famous list of business virtues grew out of his satire of Mather.) Using the concept of Christian stewardship, Puritans like Mather justified wealth that was consecrated to God and the community through generous charity.

Still another rationalization for prosperity connected it with the doctrine of election. A person whose honest toil had turned a profit must have been blessed by God; if one enjoyed God's favor in this life, was it not logical to suppose him among those elected for eternal life? This line of reasoning was never official; strictly speaking, there were only three indications of saving grace: correct belief, a conversion experience, and a godly, moral life. But as an informal assumption rather than an authentic doctrine, a connection between worldly success and heavenly success seemed more and more plausible as the generations passed—at least to those descendants of lower-middle-class Puritans who became upper-middle- and upper-class Yankees.

During the nineteenth century several conflicting tendencies could be observed. Secularization proceeded apace, in the sense that economic theory and action were emancipated from religious control (and, to a great extent, from government control as well). However, most of the "captains of industry" remained at least nominal Protestants, and some were quite fervent, like the Presbyterian Cyrus McCormick (inventor of the reaper and patron of McCormick Theological Seminary in Chicago), or the Baptist John D. Rockefeller (founder of Standard Oil Company, the University of Chicago, and Riverside Church in New York), two perfect exemplars of worldly asceticism. The "Protestant ethic" did not simply give way to the "spirit of capitalism," but coexisted with it for a very long time. Within the churches, there were clergymen who celebrated capitalism and the dream of success, as Henry Ward Beecher and Russell Conwell did through their sermons or Horatio Alger through his children's books. But there also appeared Christians who espoused the Social Gospel, which was critical of capitalism and its abuses. There is a cyclical pattern to the history of Christianity, and it is not unreasonable to see in a reforming Congregationalist minister like Washington Gladden a renewal of the spirit of early Puritan protest.

The most famous documents of the capitalist ethos in American culture are Benjamin Franklin's *Autobiography* (first full edition 1868) and Andrew Carnegie's essay "The Gospel of Wealth" (1889). Although both Franklin and Carnegie were self-made men, neither was the simple apologist for success that is usually supposed. Franklin was raised a Puritan in Boston but became a utilitarian man of the Enlightenment in Philadelphia; his account of his youth as an apprentice is detached, ironic, witty. Insofar as it can be taken as serious advice, it is as much a lesson in public relations as in sheer hard work.

Carnegie was a Scottish-born immigrant with a family tradition of artisan radicalism who amassed one of the greatest fortunes of all time in the steel industry. Like Franklin he is remembered even more as a philanthropist than as a businessman. Carnegie's essay on wealth is primarily a discussion of the responsibility to administer a great fortune in the public interest; although he dismisses socialism as unworkable, he favors confiscatory estate taxes, so as not to deprive the rich man's heirs of the salutary chance to work for a living. Together, Franklin's and Carnegie's writings demonstrate two attitudes typical of Americans, both of which have origins in the Puritan milieu and were more or less successfully secularized: one is the sense that working for a living is a moral arena in which the individual proves his worth; the other is a sense that success is validated through public service.

PURITANISM WITHOUT CALVINISM

The term *Puritan* drops out of English history in 1662, the year when those Protestants who remained dissatisfied with the Church of England were ejected from it by the restored Stuart government. From then on there was no more hope of their "purifying" the national church; they reconciled themselves to the role of "Dissenters." In American history no such neat chronological division exists, but the word "Puritan" is seldom applied to people after the death of Jonathan Edwards in 1758, except metaphorically; instead one speaks of Yankees or Congregationalists. What changed, gradually and almost imperceptibly, was mainly the theological component of American Puritanism. Calvinism went into a long, slow decline after Edwards; the process took until the early twentieth century to run its course. The rest of Puritanism, however, persisted and continues to influence American culture. In colonial America there were more Calvinists than Puritans, since so many Dutch, German, French, Scottish, and even Anglican colonists accounted themselves disciples of the Genevan Reformer. By the nineteenth century, however, it would be fair to say that Puritanism as a generalized cultural force was stronger than the theology of Calvin. Hence it is appropriate to discuss Puritanism without Calvinism.

Why Calvinist theology gradually lost its appeal is an elusive question, since it was not forcibly repressed in America as it was in so many parts of Europe. The answer would not seem to lie in any inadequacy on its part to answer the fundamental questions it addressed, but rather in long-range changes in its environment. Ironically, these were often changes that Calvinism itself had originally promoted. Calvinism helped win political rights, and when they got them, people felt more secure and less in need of assurance of God's election. Calvinism fostered intellectual activity, and beginning with the Enlightenment, intellectuals in Western civilization have tended to lose interest in systematic theologies such as Calvinism. Calvinism fostered economic development, and as people became more prosperous they often found the ascetic way of life irksome. Calvinism fostered individualism, and eventually people found more persuasive the Arminian doctrine that individuals could respond to God's grace of their own free will. A faith well suited to a particular historical phase, Calvinism gradually came to seem old-fashioned. On both sides of the Atlantic it lost adherents first among the urban, the prosperous, the cosmopolitan; it held on to them longest among the provincial lower middle class. The most persistent American defenders of Calvinist theology during its long slow decline were not Yankee Congregationalists but Scots-Irish Presbyterians, whose intellectual capital was Princeton but whose geographical distribution was chiefly in the hinterlands of the South and West.

Nationalism. The political dimension of Puritanism survived in the eighteenth century, carried on by a group of Dissenting intellectuals in Britain called the commonwealthmen. Their ideas were very influential in the colonies and in the young United States. This political Puritanism (if we may call it that) was marked by moral disapproval of aristocracy, suspicion of government, and a persistent fear of collusion between government and special interests at the expense of the ordinary person's rights. The commonwealthmen called this collusion "corruption" or "conspiracy." Given the prevailing practices of aristocratic government in eighteenth-century Britain, such attitudes were often quite justified. They provided a suitable climate of opinion for the growth of colonial dissatisfaction with British rule and continued to influence American forms of government set up after independence. The

fullest American expression of this point of view is found in the writings of John Adams, but most of the colonial pamphleteers and protesters shared it in one way or another.

During the agitation leading up to the American Revolution the precepts of the Puritan rebels of 1641 were often invoked. Patriot leaders appealed not only to the political predispositions inherited from Puritanism but to Puritan economic prejudices as well. Programs to boycott British imports were justified as restoring America's hardy virtue and discouraging the growth of "luxury." In Britain commonwealthmen like Richard Price and Joseph Priestley sympathized with American grievances. When war came, the New England Congregational clergy was among its most enthusiastic supporters, nicknamed "the black regiment." They had been accustomed during the recurrent wars with the French to identifying the cause of Protestantism with that of political liberty and readily substituted an American for a British patriotism. Of course, once independence was declared the Enlightenment ideology of natural rights to a large extent subsumed the more limited Puritan political ideology.

The early Puritan settlers had a strong sense of mission, which has carried over to color American nationalism even after independence. They did not carry out their "errand in the wilderness" simply to put the true model of Christianity into practice, but also to demonstrate it for the benefit of the rest of Christendom and the English church in particular. The classic expression of this sense of mission was given in a speech by John Winthrop called "A Model of Christian Charity," delivered aboard the ship *Arbella* en route to the New World, in which he told his fellow passengers to remember that "we shall be as a city upon a hill; the eyes of all people are upon us." Even after the ideals that America was demonstrating changed from congregational purity to democracy and human rights, the sense of mission, of being an example, remained. Abraham Lincoln expressed it well when he called America "the last best hope of earth." This sense of mission, originally Puritan, has helped infuse American patriotism with a loyalty to ideals transcending the nation-state itself. An example of these ideals—which the world has not lived up to—would be the Covenant of the League of Nations, drawn up by a devout Presbyterian of Calvinist heritage, Woodrow Wilson.

THE IMPACT OF PURITANISM ON AMERICAN CULTURE

The claim that the United States possesses the "manifest destiny" to conquer and rule other peoples, such as Indians, Mexicans, and Filipinos, has represented a historic negation of the Puritan sense of mission. These endeavors have always provoked bitter debate among the American public between the imperialists and those who maintain the traditional Puritan position that America should spread its ideals and institutions through example, not conquest.

A more authentic expression of the Puritan sense of mission is provided in the jeremiad. The American jeremiad is a literary form in which society is criticized for not living up to the ideals of the founders. It was begun by Puritan preachers, who took as their model the stern challenge of the biblical prophet Jeremiah to his people, Israel, warning them that if they did not keep their covenant, the divine wrath would fall upon them. Because the preachers set impossibly high standards and then lamented a "decline" from them, the jeremiads cannot be taken literally as evidence that Puritanism started declining as soon as it arrived in America; insofar as they illustrate the continuing relevance of Puritan standards, they indicate just the opposite. The convention of the jeremiad has been prominent in American social criticism, though the founders who have been invoked for the past two centuries are typically the authors of the Constitution, not the first settlers of New England. In this secularized form the jeremiad has provided Americans both a reproach to current performance and a reaffirmation of basic ideals. Political speeches as far separated in time as Abraham Lincoln's "Cooper Institute Address" (1860) and George McGovern's "Come Home, America" (1972) are examples of secularized jeremiads.

Many early Puritans were chiliasts; that is, they believed the end of the world was coming soon and looked for signs of how and when it would occur. The Great Awakening seemed to some, for a time, to herald it. Jonathan Edwards studied eschatology deeply and speculated, briefly, on the possibility that Christ's second coming might occur in America, a recurrent idea in American religion that also appears in Mormonism. Over the years millennial hopes became fused with American patriotism in many ways. Nineteenth-century evangelists like Lyman Beecher believed that the moral reformation of America would provide Christ a beachhead for his return. The development of a "postmillennial" school of thought by Edwards and others, teaching that the Second Coming would occur only after a thousand years of peace and justice, encouraged faith in progress, hope for social reform, and a patriotic conviction that America would have a special role to play in the divine dispensation.

Liberals and Evangelicals. Since the Great Awakening of the 1740s the Puritan religious tradition has bifurcated into liberal and evangelical wings. The cultural history of early liberalism is to a large extent the history of Unitarianism. Small and marginal as a religious denomination, Unitarianism has loomed large and central in its cultural impact. It originated in eastern Massachusetts among the oldest Puritan-founded churches in the country, reflecting the growing preference for Arminianism over Calvinism and the increasing distrust of the methods of revivalists in eliciting conversions. These attitudes were developing throughout the Calvinist world, but among the Massachusetts Unitarians they appeared early, explicitly, and in extreme form. As a result, the Unitarian denomination acted as a prototype for the development of liberal Protestantism as a whole. The denomination takes 1819, the date of William Ellery Channing's sermon *Unitarian Christianity*, as its landmark date, but the division among Congregationalists between the liberals and those who remained orthodox had been slowly building up ever since the Great Awakening had disenchanted many people with emotional revivalism.

Dispensing with both Calvinist theology and the necessity for an identifiable conversion experience, the nineteenth-century Unitarians preserved and reinvigorated Puritan culture in other ways. Under the auspices of their Christian humanism the Puritan tradition of literacy flourished. Public school systems were extended to meet the needs of the nineteenth century, Harvard transformed into a great research university, a model for others around the country. Philosophy, science, and scholarship were encouraged more than ever. Literature flowered in what has become known as the New England Renaissance. Traditional Puritan modes of expression remained important for the Unitarians: their poet/moralists include Emerson and James Russell Lowell, their historians George Bancroft and John L. Motley, their communal orators

THE IMPACT OF PURITANISM ON AMERICAN CULTURE

Daniel Webster and Charles Sumner. Some of the Unitarian authors wrote within conventions we now term "Brahmin" or "genteel"; the Transcendentalists, however, were heterodox in lifestyle, opinions, and even in their version of Unitarian religion itself. Women took up a new collective self-consciousness; many of them attained prominence, including Margaret Fuller, journalist and feminist; Dorothea Dix, mental health reformer; and Louisa May Alcott, novelist. Together with the Quakers, the Unitarians supplied a disproportionate number of leaders in the movement for women's rights.

While liberals were emphasizing the religion of the "head," the Evangelical heirs of the Puritans were emphasizing the religion of the "heart." Like the liberal Unitarians the Evangelicals tended to give up Calvinist theology—though more slowly and less explicitly—in favor of belief in free will. Unlike them they enjoyed wide popularity and have retained a large following in the twentieth century. The conversion experience has remained central to the Evangelical conception of Christianity, and a proud tradition of American revivalists, including Lyman Beecher, Charles G. Finney, Dwight Moody, William Jennings Bryan, and Billy Graham, has carried on the work of John Cotton and Jonathan Edwards in bringing souls to Christ. Many of these Evangelical leaders have been courageous crusaders for social justice, as have black Evangelicals like Martin Luther King, Jr., who operate out of a proud tradition of their own. Although the Evangelicals have been staunch supporters of public education and have founded many colleges and universities, such as Wheaton College in Illinois, Temple University in Philadelphia, and Texas Christian University in Fort Worth, they have not had an impact on literature and learning equivalent to that of the nineteenth-century Unitarians. Those Fundamentalists among them who have insisted on a literal and inerrant interpretation of the Bible have cut themselves off from much of modern science and scholarship.

Together, liberal and Evangelical Protestants set the tone for a culture we may term American Victorianism, because another version of it prevailed in Britain, and its hegemony in both countries roughly coincided with the reign of that British monarch (1837–1901). Victorian culture was descended from Puritanism but by no means identical with it, and some Victorians moved outside Christianity altogether to adopt a secular world view. The Victorians intensified the work ethic, carrying worldly asceticism to extremes that would have astonished the Puritans, such as total abstention from alcohol and a prudish aversion to any mention of sex. American Victorians were also more individualistic than the Puritans, who retained a strong sense of community. They were sentimental in ways that the Puritans were not (about the virtues of children, for example) and substituted for the Puritans' grim pessimism about human affairs an unrealistic optimism. In spite of these differences Americans in the twentieth century have tended to identify Puritanism with Victorianism and in rebelling against the latter to suppose that they were repudiating the former as well.

Essays to Do Good. The Puritans of Tudor-Stuart times were noteworthy for their innovations in philanthropy. Not only did they seek to relieve suffering, they also began to inquire into its causes, such as poverty. By the time the American Puritan Cotton Mather wrote his *Bonifacius; or, Essays to Do Good* in 1710, he was already working in a Puritan tradition of philanthropy (and using the word "essay" to mean both a literary and a practical endeavor). Mather encouraged the establishment of voluntary organizations to address specific community needs. This became a pattern typical of American Protestantism, though not peculiar to it, for American philanthropists often followed examples of their British counterparts. By the nineteenth century a network of Protestant voluntary organizations operated domestic and foreign missions and offered relief to innumerable people in need, including battered wives and children, convicts, alcoholics, and prostitutes. In an overwhelmingly Protestant nation they provided many services performed in Catholic countries by the religious orders or in twentieth-century societies by the welfare state.

The activities of the "Evangelical united front," as the interdenominational network of Protestant organizations was called, have a certain moral ambiguity from our point of view. They often seem condescending and paternalistic as well as constructive. The missions, for example, were sometimes a thinly disguised form of imperialism. Yet, when white settlers demanded the expulsion of Indians, it was some-

THE IMPACT OF PURITANISM ON AMERICAN CULTURE

times missionaries who defended the treaty rights of the natives, as in the famous confrontation between the Cherokee Nation and the state of Georgia. At their best the missionaries could provide occasions for two-way cultural interaction and a legacy of democratic ideals, as did the American University in Beirut until the devastations of the 1980s.

The Puritan social conscience as carried to America addressed not only what we would define as charitable and missionary activity but also politics. Intending, as they did, to make the visible church correspond as closely as possible to the invisible one and the secular power cooperate with the true church, the early Puritans were not content to leave this world in the hands of evildoers but labored that righteousness might prevail here and now. Of the many crusades for justice that this demand for righteousness has initiated throughout American history, the greatest was the one against slavery. It involved Protestants of a variety of views, especially Quakers, Unitarians, and New School Evangelicals—for Puritanism without Calvinism proved to have an even stronger social conscience than Puritanism with Calvinism. Among the white population religion seems to have been a necessary force in motivating abolitionist sentiment; in nineteenth-century America only blacks could formulate an antislavery position without its aid. In the West the abolitionist movement was predominantly Evangelical, under the leadership of Theodore Dwight Weld and the Tappan brothers, two Christian businessmen who illustrate the Puritan work ethic quite as well as the Puritan social conscience. In the East its religious character was more diverse, with radicals like William Lloyd Garrison, Quakers like Lucretia Mott, and Transcendentalist-Unitarians like Theodore Parker. Everywhere it operated much as a religious sect, calling for a revival of morals, purity of motive, and a decision for Christ. Even the more moderate Free-Soil position, which became prominent after the abolitionists had succeeded in raising the national consciousness on the moral issue of slavery, shows the influence of Puritan culture; Lincoln's Cooper Union speech, calling for a reaffirmation of the principles of the Founding Fathers regarding the nonextension of slavery, is a secular jeremiad, warning of the corruption of liberty in the fashion of the commonwealthmen.

But antislavery was only one of many neo-Puritan or Victorian reform movements that affected American political life during the nineteenth and early twentieth centuries. Typically, these movements were didactic and redemptive in purpose, like temperance and sabbatarianism. Sometimes particular groups were singled out as the objects of reformers' concern: asylums addressed the insane, penitentiaries criminals, and schools the young. As these examples indicate, the reformers showed considerable institutional creativity. More often than not they worked through the Whig and Republican political parties, where their supporting constituencies were found, and they were often opposed by the Democrats, who disliked their paternalism. After the Civil War the movement to reform politics itself, which we usually call by the unfairly disparaging term "mugwump" and which sought to limit corruption and establish a federal civil service, continued this moral concern. In some ways the "progressive" reformers of the early twentieth century carried on this tradition, exemplified magnificently in Theodore Roosevelt's peroration upon being nominated for president by the Progressive party in 1912: "We stand at Armageddon, and do battle for the Lord."

One of the important legacies of Puritanism in America has been a tendency to politicize personal morality. Matters like prostitution and gambling, which are often left to the individual's moral choice in other countries, have been legally banned in this country. The Puritans of colonial New England had strong reasons for applying strict moral standards to their communities. They wished their churches to consist only of true saints, whose members were responsible to one another for leading an upright life and who maintained corresponding watch over each other's conduct. They also believed that God punished his people collectively whenever the community did not live up to the standards demanded by their covenanted relationship, just as he was on record as doing with ancient Israel. Even a secret and individual sin could bring the wrath of God upon the community. For these reasons the church, through its power to admonish and excommunicate members, and the state, through its criminal law, sought out private sins. Throughout American history this preoccupation with maintaining moral standards has brought matters of private conduct into the public arena of law enforcement. The Victorians were even more determined to politicize morality than the Puritans had been, although by the nineteenth century the original theological rationale was largely superseded. Under the Victorians laws prohibiting contraception were enacted; at first demanded by Protestants, these laws ironically found their chief twentieth-century defenders among Catholics. The Puritan tradition of identifying political and personal morality has been interpreted by some cultural historians as the origin of American social conformity. Yet, paradoxically, the Puritan sense of moral responsibility has also inspired courageous dissenters to demand, in the spirit of the prophet Amos, that society repent and return to the ways of the Lord. Finally, the tradition has also inspired such classics of moral individualism as Thoreau's essay on the duty of civil disobedience. All these cultural legacies may seem admirable or not, depending on one's point of view; but for good or ill they have contributed to making America what it is today.

POST-PURITAN AMERICA

The late Sydney Ahlstrom observed that "a great Puritan Epoch can be seen as beginning in 1558 with the death of Mary Tudor, the last monarch to rule over an officially Roman Catholic England, and as ending in 1960 with the election of John Fitzgerald Kennedy, the first Roman Catholic president of the United States" (*A Religious History of the American People,* 1972). In the four hundred years between those dates there is no doubt that the causes of patriotism and liberty were, to a very large extent, identified with Protestantism by public opinion in both Great Britain and the United States. The contribution of Anglo-American Puritanism during those centuries to shaping the culture of the two countries was immense. Will it be so important to the next epoch?

To begin with, we should not exaggerate the extent of the power Puritanism enjoyed even in its prime. There were always non-Puritans with rival value systems, representing other religions, ethnic minorities, nonbourgeois social classes, premodern traditions, and secular ideologies to compete against Puritanism and its nineteenth-century daughter culture, Victorianism. To suppose that American history has taken place under the secure umbrella of a single culture not only is unfair to these rival traditions, it is to rob the

Puritans themselves of credit for waging their struggle and to deprive American history of much of its drama. There has been a cultural change in twentieth-century America, to be sure, but it is not a change from unity to multiplicity —the multiplicity has been present all along. Rather, the change that has occurred in this century is from a situation in which the cultural tradition descended from Puritanism often enjoyed a kind of hegemony over others to a situation in which it does not. Even before the twentieth century, however, the power of the Puritan/Victorian tradition was by no means uniform: it was weaker on the frontier and in the old South, for example. In the course of the nineteenth century evangelical religion finally established its hegemony in the South, and that region—ironically—became its strongest bastion in the twentieth century.

Much of twentieth-century American history has concerned struggles over the perpetuation of aspects of the Victorian culture of the nineteenth century. The great controversies over Prohibition, the teaching of evolution in the schools, sexual morality and birth control, the fundamentalist/modernist split in the churches —all must be seen in this light. So must subtler trends like the increasing use of leisure, the rise of new art forms, and the decline of didactic paternalism in all its manifestations. We must not assume, however, that the Puritan cultural tradition is defeated and dead; rather, it has been transformed and broken asunder. The work ethic, which by now derives from other sources as well as Puritan culture, survives not only in the form of a secular "spirit of capitalism" but also in the career orientation of the employees of large corporations. Where Puritanism has had its greatest impact on American life, in constitutional and intellectual affairs, that influence is so secularized and blended with non-Puritan contributions that most people are no longer conscious of this Puritanism as such. The greatest division within the Puritan/Victorian cultural tradition today exists between those who accept its secularization and those who do not.

If we look for the people within American society who carry on the Puritan cultural tradition in the most identifiable ways, two very different groups can be identified. One of them is the evangelical Christians, whose religion is the most Puritan of any, some of whom are even Calvinists in theology. The other group, less obviously, is the liberal reformers, whose desire to reshape society along morally defensible lines is partly a continuation of the political dimension of old-time Puritanism and its successors like the commonwealthmen and the abolitionists. Many reformers of our times have been religious people (especially in the civil rights and peace movements), although they are by no means necessarily in the tradition of Puritan religion; many are Catholics and Jews. A way of conceptualizing the split in the Puritan tradition is to say that since the time of Woodrow Wilson its religious thrust and its reform thrust have tended to go their separate ways. Only among blacks have evangelical religion and reform politics continued their historic close association. (Former president Jimmy Carter, a devout Evangelical, is a humanitarian rather than a reformer.)

We can say that postindustrial America is largely post-Puritan, if we mean that Puritanism is no longer an ideal consciously followed by many people; the Puritan legacy, however, has been built into our institutions and culture. In some ways we are emancipating ourselves from that legacy (as in our new emphasis on leisure and play), but in others we have secularized and firmly retained it (as in our tradition of individual rights). As our population becomes more and more ethnically diverse, the number of people who identify themselves with non-Puritan traditions will increase, and the likelihood of any one tradition attaining the kind of hegemony enjoyed by Victorian neo-Puritanism is minimized. It would appear that Puritan religion (as distinct from its secularized legacy) has already exerted its principal cultural influences and that it will not be a major factor in shaping the future in new ways. Evangelical Protestantism, which has exercised such a creative influence in earlier generations, now plays mainly a conservative role, preserving rather than innovating. Liberal Protestantism, the heir of nineteenth-century Unitarianism, has turned over its most important social and intellectual functions to secular control.

The original Puritanism was appropriate to an early modern society, one undergoing the discipline of modernization. Today America is a different kind of society. The only circumstances under which some value system similar to early Puritanism might recover active cultural leadership would be if the United States should un-dergo terrible reverses, such as those inflicted by a nuclear war, provoking widespread hardship and a need for nerves of steel. If this happens, the survivors may then be grateful for whatever memory remains of the Puritans' stern courage, sense of responsibility, and faith in the ultimate justice of the universe.

BIBLIOGRAPHY

E. Digby Baltzell, *Puritan Boston and Quaker Philadelphia* (1979); Lee Benson, *The Concept of Jacksonian Democracy* (1961); Sacvan Bercovitch, *The Puritan Origins of the American Self* (1975) and *The American Jeremiad* (1978); Paul Boyer, *Urban Masses and Moral Order in America* (1978); Lawrence Buell, *New England Literary Culture from Revolution Through Renaissance* (1986); William Clebsch, *From Sacred to Profane America* (1968); Paul Conkin, *Puritans and Pragmatists: Eight Eminent American Thinkers* (1968); S. N. Eisenstadt, ed., *The Protestant Ethic and Modernization* (1968); Stephen Foster, *Their Solitary Way: The Puritan Social Ethic* (1971); Robert W. Green, ed., *Protestantism, Capitalism, and Social Science* (1959; 2nd ed., 1973); Philip Greven, *The Protestant Temperament* (1977); William Haller, *Liberty and Reformation in the Puritan Revolution* (1955); John L. Hammond, *The Politics of Benevolence: Revival Religion and American Voting Behavior* (1979); Daniel W. Howe, "The Decline of Calvinism," in *Comparative Studies in Society and History*, 14 (1972), and, as ed., *Victorian America* (1976); George L. Hunt, ed., *Calvinism and the Political Order* (1965); John Owen King, *The Iron of Melancholy: Structures of Spiritual Conversion in America from the Puritan Conscience to Victorian Neurosis* (1983); Bruce Kuklick, *Churchmen and Philosophers from Jonathan Edwards to John Dewey* (1985); David Little, *Religion, Order, and Law: A Study in Pre-Revolutionary England* (1969).

Henry May, *Protestant Churches and Industrial America* (1949; rev. 1967); Michael McGiffert, ed., *Puritanism and the American Experience* (1969); William G. McLoughlin, *Revivals, Awakenings, and Reform* (1978); Perry Miller, *Errand into the Wilderness* (1956) and *Nature's Nation* (1967); Edmund Morgan, ed., *Puritan Political Ideas, 1558–1794* (1965); Samuel Eliot Morison, *The Intellectual Life of Colonial New England* (1936; rev. 1956); James H. Nichols, *Democracy and the Churches* (1951); Ralph Barton Perry, *Puritanism and Democracy* (1944); Clinton Rossiter, *Seedtime of the Republic* (1953); William H. Shurr, *Rappaccini's Children: American Writers in a Calvinist World* (1981); Alan Simpson, *Puritanism in Old and New England* (1955); Chard Powers Smith, *Yankees and God* (1954); Marion Starkey, *The Congregational Way* (1966); George M. Stephenson, *The Puritan Heritage* (1952); Cushing Strout, *The New Heavens and New Earth: Political Religion in America* (1974); Michael Walzer, *The Revolution of the Saints* (1965); Austin Warren, *The New England Conscience* (1966); Max Weber, *The Protestant Ethic and the Spirit of Capitalism* (1930; 1958; 2nd ed., 1976); Larzer Ziff, *Puritanism in America: New Culture in a New World* (1973).

[See also CALVINIST HERITAGE; CALVINIST THEOLOGICAL TRADITION; NEW ENGLAND PURITANISM; and RELIGION AND LITERATURE.]

THE BIBLE IN AMERICAN CULTURE

Mark A. Noll

THE study of American civilization is in no small part the study of the Bible. For almost all Americans the Judeo-Christian Scriptures have provided a vast reservoir of themes, phrases, meanings, and habits of thought. Public surveys testify to the Bible's continuing resiliency: 42 percent of the population, as polled by George Gallup in 1978, professed to believe that "the Bible is the word of God and is not mistaken in its statements and teachings." Belief can come cheap, so it is even more impressive that Gallup found 30 percent of the population actually reading the Bible at least once a week (12 percent at least once a day).

The names given by early settlers to their communities, particularly in the eastern half of the country, offer further testimony to the pervasive presence of Scripture: Zoar in Ohio, from Genesis 13:10; Ruma in Illinois, from II Kings 23:36; Mount Tirzah in North Carolina, from Joshua 12:24; Zela in West Virginia, from Joshua 18:28; and also forty-seven variations on Bethel, sixty-one on Eden, and ninety-five on Salem. Of the nation's first seventeen presidents, twelve possessed biblical first names. About half of those who published books in the early years of the country were also similarly named.

The Bible has appealed to both the masses and the elite in America. William Bradford, the early Pilgrim governor, wrote his *History of Plymouth Plantation* (ca. 1630–1647) in a biblical idiom as pronounced as that which his near contemporary John Bunyan employed in *The Pilgrim's Progress* (1678). Noah Webster, creator of the American dictionary, thought he could teach the children of the new United States to read and write by giving them a distinctly American translation of the Bible (1833). The Scriptures have been the constant companion of many presi-

dents: the great (Abraham Lincoln), the near great (Woodrow Wilson), the forgotten (Grover Cleveland), and the yet to be judged (Jimmy Carter). The Bible has colored the imaginative universes of some of America's best writers, from Herman Melville, who wrote of Ishmael, Ahab, and Leviathan in *Moby-Dick* (1851), to William Faulkner, whose very titles—*Absalom, Absalom!* (1936) or *Go Down, Moses* (1942)—reflect a biblical presence. Even those who abandoned conventional religion sometimes retained a loyalty to Scripture. Thomas Jefferson, who thought the supernatural stories of the Bible were merely legends that inflamed the childish longings of immature people, was nonetheless a consistent reader of the Bible. On two occasions he even prepared abridged editions of the New Testament to rescue the wise sayings of Jesus from the contagion of the miraculous.

It is easy to establish the omnipresence of Scripture in American life; it is much harder to say what that omnipresence means. Is the Bible still a genuinely moving book, with its own center of values and its own ability to influence individuals and groups? Or is it merely a rhetorical artifact, with no power in its own right and no function except to stimulate public nostalgia for a mythical golden age of social harmony and religious unity? Has the Bible in America ever been anything more than a tool of the upper classes, who exploited its language and stories as religious sanction for their hegemony? If so, why have alienated groups, especially blacks, been able to counter white oppression by appealing to Scripture? Why have different groups used different parts of the Bible to interpret the rest of the sacred book? Why do some biblical themes appear prominently in the public use of Scripture, and others almost not at all? Answers to these questions, and many more that could be asked, are not simple, nor do they emerge from merely observing the great numbers of Americans who have put the Bible to use in their lives.

A survey of the Bible and American civilization may properly begin with a brief examination of the translation, publication, and distribution of the Scriptures. It is then appropriate to look at the Bible's central position in the history of American churches. This, in turn, provides an appropriate place for considering briefly the academic study of the Bible. Finally, some consideration is necessary of the role of Scripture in the history of American social, intellectual, and political life.

PUBLISHING THE BIBLE

The publishing history of the Bible in America extends back to the earliest Spanish explorers and continues to the present, when the sale of Bibles represents at least a $150 million annual business. Throughout their history Americans have sustained an enormous rate of Bible publication and an even more stupendous appetite for literature about the Bible. The definitive bibliography of the Bible in America lists more than 2,500 different English-language editions published between 1777 and 1957. In this same period at least 1,324 different publishers or printers brought out texts of the Bible (including 35 firms in Baltimore, 39 in Chicago, 41 in Hartford, 42 in Cincinnati, 157 in Boston, 224 in Philadelphia, and 371 in New York City).

The Authorized, or King James, Version (AV) has always been the best-selling Bible in America. But since World War II modern translations have also appeared in breathtaking numbers, several of which are revisions of the AV based upon improved Greek and Hebrew texts. The Revised Standard Version (RSV), with well over 50 million copies in circulation since its publication in 1952, has been the most widely used. The New American Standard Bible, a recent recasting of the 1901 American revision of the AV, has also sold very well (14 million copies as of 1981). And in 1982 America's largest Bible publisher (and the largest producer of Bibles in the world), Thomas Nelson of Nashville, Tennessee, released a modernized version of the AV called the New King James Version.

Still other versions have involved completely new translations from the Hebrew and Greek. The Good News Bible, sponsored by the American Bible Society, is a translation with basic vocabulary—a boon for children and new readers of English. In 1978 the New York International Bible Society published the New International Version, prepared by a large team of theologically conservative scholars; it has received favorable critical reception and may replace the AV among more traditional Protestant groups. A popular paraphrase known as the Living Bible has been the inspiration for worldwide efforts at putting Scripture into more colloquial speech. In 1982 *The Reader's Digest Bible,* an abridged version of the RSV (300,000 words deleted), was published. This effort to capitalize on the nation's penchant for distillations of serious reading is selling well. Between 1961 and 1981, Americans also purchased over 12 million copies of the New English Bible, a translation from Great Britain.

Most of the best-selling Bibles have been produced under Protestant auspices, but Catholics and Jews have also been active in promoting the Scriptures. The RSV has been adopted for use by Catholics, and Catholics sit on the continuing review committees for this translation. American Catholics also sponsored the New American Bible (1970) and promoted distribution of the Jerusalem Bible (1966), which came from the labors of British Catholics and the inspiration of a noteworthy French translation. And in 1979 and 1983 the Sacred Heart League established new marks in quantities of Scriptures ordered at one time by requisitioning first 775,000 New Testaments and then 800,000 from the American Bible Society. In 1982 the Jewish Publication Society completed a new translation of the Hebrew Scriptures.

Publication of the Bible has been a flourishing business in America. Mason Weems, the biographer of President George Washington, earned his living during the early years of the United States as a Bible salesman in Virginia. From there he once made a rhapsodic report of business:

> I tell you this is the very season and age of the Bible. Bible Dictionaries, Bible tales, Bible stories—Bibles plain or paraphrased, Carey's Bibles, Collin's Bibles, Clarke's Bibles, Kimptor's

Bibles, no matter what or whose, all, all will go down—so wide is the crater of public appetite at this time. God be thanked for it.

(Wills, p. 68)

Earlier, in 1743, the first European-language Scriptures published in America (an edition of Martin Luther's Bible, with Apocrypha, on type carried from Frankfurt) had established the family of Christopher Sower as America's leading printer of German books.

Yet the publishing results have not always been so lucrative. During the American Revolution, a Philadelphia printer, Robert Aitken, petitioned Congress for permission to bring out the Bible in America. (American access to English-language Scriptures had been limited to exports from British printers, who enjoyed a royal monopoly for printing the AV.) In spite of protests from a few Congregationalists and Baptists, who feared that a Bible printed in America could not measure up to acceptable standards of accuracy, Congress allowed Aitken to proceed. A New Testament appeared in 1777, and the entire Bible in 1782. Unfortunately for Aitken, the end of hostilities with Great Britain in 1783 reopened the American market to British publishers. The imports undersold Aitken and left him with a stagnating inventory.

Nineteenth-century publishers who underwrote efforts to produce a Bible specifically for their countrymen found considerable market resistance to any version that departed from the AV. In 1833 Webster published his translation of a Bible shorn of British spellings and archaic usages, and his contemporary Andrew Comstock devised a phonetic "purfekt alfabet" for his "Filadelphia" New Testament of 1848. But these and similar efforts met with little success. Only with the production of the American Standard Version in 1901 did publishers begin to enjoy the market for newer versions that has burgeoned in recent years.

By that time, however, enthusiasm for the production of Scripture was a well-established part of American life. It had been an especially vital aspect of missionary work to, from, and within America. During the late sixteenth century Spanish Franciscans were translating biblical liturgies and other Catholic literature for the Rimucuan Indians of Florida, even before the English began their permanent colonies in New England.

The Massachusetts Puritan minister John Eliot exercised herculean efforts in translating the Bible into Algonquian (New Testament 1661; entire Bible 1663), fully expecting it to provide the foundation for the Christianization of the native Americans. In spite of failure on that score, other laborers since Eliot have translated parts of the Bible into a whole series of Indian languages, including Apache, Cherokee, Cheyenne, Choctaw, Dakota, Hopi, Inupiat, Kuskokwim, Muskogee, Navajo, and Ojibwa.

In the early nineteenth century Bible societies arose as a part of a great effort in "home missions" associated with the national revival known as the Second Great Awakening. This effort enlisted the support of many, like the first president of Congress (Elias Boudinot of New Jersey) and the first chief justice of the Supreme Court (John Jay of New York), who believed in Scripture as a supernatural source of spiritual new life. But it also was aided by rationalists like Jefferson, who was impressed enough with the Bible's civilizing effects to contribute money to these ventures.

Since its founding in 1816, the American Bible Society, the largest organization remaining from that period, has distributed over 3 billion complete Bibles, testaments, scriptural portions, and selections. The society has also distributed over 100 million different pieces of the Bible, from verses to the entire book, each year in the United States alone. And it maintains an even larger program of Scripture translation and distribution overseas in association with the international United Bible societies.

Other groups, such as the Wycliffe Bible Translators/Summer Institute of Linguistics, have been nearly as active in the effort to promote Christianity through dissemination of the Bible. Since its founding in 1934, workers with Wycliffe have translated at least a portion of the Scriptures into nearly 1,000 languages. Other groups have channeled their evangelistic efforts through the distribution of Scriptures in already written languages. Prominent among these has been the Gideons International, an organization of Christian laypeople founded in 1899. Since its inception the Gideons have distributed over 10 million copies of the Bible and over 100 million copies of the New Testament, primarily in the United States but also in more than 130 other countries.

As great as the quantity of Bibles printed in America has been, even greater has been the quantity of literature about the Bible. Statistics alone can suggest the merest outline of a literary mountain. The 1982–1983 subject guide to *Books in Print* from American publishers contains fifty-six tightly packed pages of titles concerning the Bible. The Library of Congress's National Union Catalog of books held by American libraries before 1956 includes four large volumes on the Bible, with 63,000 entries in 700 languages.

It is not always clear how often Americans read the Bible or literature about it, both of which exist in such profusion, nor is it always clear how such reading affects their lives. It is clear, however, that Bible publication has not only constituted a very large business but also reflected a major commitment to the importance of Scripture. And this great outpouring of publication has had its most obvious impact in the churches.

THE BIBLE IN THE CHURCHES

It is not an exaggeration to say that the Bible has been of crucial importance for virtually every variety of Christianity in America. Leaders of Protestant denominations, for whom the ability to expound the Scriptures is a prerequisite for employment, have been most conspicuous in the use of the Bible. Yet a great deal of evidence also exists that the American laity has been almost as deeply involved with the Scriptures. Inventories of wills from the colonial period show that if common people possessed any books at all, the Bible was sure to be among them. Records left by wealthy Virginians also reveal a general familiarity with Scripture. William Byrd II, planter, author, and colonial official, normally read a biblical passage—in Greek or Hebrew—at the start of each day. Where schools existed in the colonies, the Bible was regularly used as a text to teach reading. In seventeenth-century New England and the eighteenth-century South, it was common for individuals to meet in private homes for Bible reading, particularly when bad weather or long distances made it difficult to attend formal church services. One well-known laywoman who led such a Bible study, Anne Hutchinson, was able to quote lengthy portions of Scripture at her trial in 1637 before the Massachusetts magis-

trates. They felt her interpretation of the Bible's teaching on grace undercut the good works necessary to sustain the commonwealth, and so they banished her into the wilderness.

In the democratic age that followed the Revolutionary War, a thorough acquaintance with the Bible was the one characteristic shared by founders of religious bodies. Leaders of these groups —Disciples of Christ, Christian Methodists, Cumberland Presbyterians, Free-Will Baptists, Shakers, Universalists, and those who desired no name but Christian—usually began their organizational activities as laymen after prolonged personal immersion in Scripture and, in turn, urged their followers to become conversant with the Bible.

The experience of an early leader of the Universalists, Elhanan Winchester of Philadelphia, illustrates this implicit trust in Scripture. Winchester was pastor of a Baptist church until he began to have doubts about traditional teachings on the eternal punishment of the lost. The way he resolved his difficulties stamped him as a steadfast biblicist and a democratic individualist: "I shut myself up chiefly in my chamber and read the Scriptures, and prayed to God to lead me into all truth" (*The Universalist Restoration,* 1788).

That some of this intense involvement with Scripture remains an important part of American civilization is the testimony of recent polling. In a 1978 survey 40 percent of those polled said that they would turn first to "what the Bible says" in order to test their religious beliefs. This was also the response of 25 percent of the Catholics, whose official dogma continues to uphold the church as the designated interpreter of Scripture.

A number of circumstances have contributed to the central place of Scripture. First in time was the fact that America's earliest settlers, who set a course that survived long after their passing, were not only Protestants but also Puritan and Pietistic Protestants. Since their origin in the Reformation, Protestants have considered the Bible their final religious authority. But for Puritans and Pietists, Scripture was also often proclaimed as the only religious authority.

Churches in seventeenth-century America were normally the product of English Puritanism. Unlike their Anglican contemporaries in England, who felt that reason and tradition were important secondary authorities in religion next to Scripture, Puritans insisted on setting everything aside in favor of the Bible. The English Puritan William Bradshaw spoke for his fellows who emigrated to America when he said in 1605 that "the word of God contained in the writings of the Prophets and Apostles, is of absolute perfection, given by Christ the head of the Churche, to bee unto the same, the sole Canon and rule of all matters of Religion, and the worship and service of God whatsoever" (*English Puritanisme*).

During the eighteenth century many of those who emigrated to America had been touched by the Pietistic revivals in England, Germany, and Holland. The general spirit of Pietism was established in Germany by Philipp Jacob Spener, who called for Christians to study the Bible intensely in small groups, and in England by John Wesley, who so emphasized the importance of Scripture that he came to be known as "a man of one book." Immigrants under Pietistic influences much preferred simple scriptural instruction to the formalized liturgies of the established churches. Even where they remained faithful to a distinctive theological tradition, they subjected it to the sovereignty of the Bible. The pledge of Peter Brunholtz in 1744, when he was ordained for Lutheran service in Pennsylvania, illustrates this hierarchy of authority. He swore

> to be faithful to the Word of God, pure and incorrupt, as this is contained according to the mind of the Spirit in the Scriptures of the holy prophets and apostles and as this was afterward repeated and clearly set forth in the three chief Creeds and especially in the confession of the Lutheran Church . . . all of which have been drawn with great diligence out of the Holy Scriptures.

Whether a Presbyterian or Congregationalist under Puritan influence, or a Lutheran, Dutch Reformed, Moravian, Mennonite, Methodist, or Brethren in the Pietist tradition, these early Americans found a common point of reference in the exaltation of Scripture as the sole guide for ecclesiastical life.

The very presence of so many different Protestant groups also contributed to the expanded importance of the Bible. Representatives of the different Protestant traditions had many more occasions for contact with those of other groups in the New World than had been the case in the Old. It quickly became apparent that the only hope for consensus and for a common religious influence on public life lay in emphasizing a conviction shared by all Protestants—the centrality of the Bible—at the expense of the particular distinctiveness of each group.

The developing American civilization also added considerably to the prominence of Scripture within the churches. America was the world's "first new nation," according to President John Adams. "We have it in our power," wrote Tom Paine in 1776, "to begin the world over again." The American Revolution was not revolutionary in its attack on property or religion, but it was revolutionary in its disdain for the past, its dismissal of tradition, and its distrust of authority. American government, so the Constitution asserted, arose when "We the People of the United States" decided it was necessary. Hereditary influence, established tradition, deference to an aristocracy—all became suspect.

The result was a culture whose people spoke, wrote, and organized on a number of fronts against the authority of mediating elites, of social distinctions, and of any tie that did not spring from volitional allegiance. The only traditional authority that democratic America did not jettison was the Bible. The sacred book was simply too much a part of the Protestant, Puritan, and Pietistic heritage. Yet if respect for Scripture survived the onslaught of democracy, the Bible now emerged as a religious force by itself. Much weakened in post-Revolutionary America were the ecclesiastical, theological, social, and intellectual traditions that before the Revolution had accompanied traditional deference to the Bible.

In this way the Bible maintained its place in American culture. Noting in 1840 that the United States appeared to be more religious than European nations, Alexis de Tocqueville reasoned that in Europe the spirit of liberty and the spirit of religion had marched in opposite directions. In America, by contrast, the two had become "one undivided current," so much so that people had trouble distinguishing between them. It was particularly the Second Great Awakening, a vast series of religious revivals that swept across New England and New York as well as Tennessee, Kentucky, and the western territories during the first two decades of the nineteenth century, that solidified the new United States as a Christian country. Yet this outpouring of religious concern led to no alteration in the culture's antitraditional, antiestablishment character. It was still the will of the people that held the key to religious life, to Christian evangelism, and to social service. Again as de Tocqueville noted, religion in America had aligned itself with democracy and therefore flourished, while the Christianity of Europe languished in its alliance with conservative traditions. Unlike Europe, where people rejected religion and the clergy "because they are the friends of authority," Americans adapted religion to the forms of democracy. And this meant specifically that Americans read the Bible for themselves.

The Scriptures remained the principal religious authority in America. But in becoming the people's Book—with everyone free to construe its message as he would—the Bible lost the cohesiveness that it had enjoyed in earlier Protestant traditions. Few Americans before the Civil War questioned the sacredness of Scripture. And many could agree that its message of salvation, freedom, and hope bore surprising similarities to national ideals. Yet the danger of fragmenting and trivializing the Bible had also appeared. In the face of egalitarianism, ecclesiastical bodies had largely abandoned the conviction that they could tell their own members what the Bible meant. And as a result of democratization any person's reading of the Bible was in principle as acceptable as anyone else's.

One other important development also encouraged American Protestants to give the Bible prominence as an unmediated source of authority in their churches. This was the importation by the country's leading intellectuals of Scottish commonsense philosophy. Francis Hutcheson and Thomas Reid had developed this perspective in Scotland during the eighteenth century. It exerted a brief influence also in Europe but was accepted most broadly in the United States. Against the skeptical conclusions of David Hume and the radical proposals of the Continental Enlightenment, Scottish philosophers argued that people possessed an innate sense for both the realities of the physical world and the norms of morality. In America this philosophy rapidly became an intellectual byword. The effort to ground epistemological certainty on the common sense of the people at large accorded well with the ideology of democracy. The effort to

base moral values on the sense of the heart reinforced the peculiarly American distrust of inherited ethical authorities. Under these convictions Christian faith and practice remained important, but in no small part because they seemed to be the final products of common sense.

The commonsense tradition, especially in its popularized forms, encouraged Christians to appropriate without delay the whole Scriptures for themselves. Meanings that seemed to lie on the surface were the ones that counted. Since the common people did not have to defer to scholars or external authorities, they could interpret the Bible for themselves. Such reading often led to intense convictions about the need for spreading Christianity and working for justice. The great currents of nineteenth-century social reform owed much to this impulse. Less propitiously, a commonsense approach to Scripture also led to ethnocentric and ahistorical distortions in understanding the world of the Bible and many distinctive features of its teaching.

The combination of these influences—a revolution against history, an intense democratization, a commitment to common sense—pushed European-based denominations closer to the more democratic patterns of the Anglo-American churches. For example, the American-born Lutheran leader Samuel Schmucker was leading his denomination toward a more ostensibly Bible-centered, democratic faith until the great waves of immigration from Germany and Scandinavia in the mid-nineteenth century pulled Lutheran attitudes back toward a confessional stance.

For Americans without such close ties to European traditions the intensely Protestant heritage and the distinctly antitraditional tendencies of the new United States led to the conviction that Christians could establish and maintain churches on the basis of the Bible alone. "No Creed But the Bible" became the rallying cry for many such groups that longed for a re-pristinated New Testament Christianity freed of the corrupting influences of history. It did not dampen their enthusiasm to discover that others who were attempting the same feat on the basis of the same Bible were coming to different conclusions about doctrine, church order, and social practice. It was the Bible and the Bible only that they desired. Ironically, the self-consciously antitraditional thrust of these convictions soon developed into its own powerful tradition. And it became especially difficult for many believers to distinguish what they perceived as the message of Scripture from the values promoted by American democratic ideology.

The major exception to this generalization was provided by the experience of American blacks. Democratic ideology had a very different place in their experience with Scripture. In the days of slavery, blacks often went to extreme lengths to learn to read the Bible and to possess the Scriptures for themselves. Albert Raboteau, author of the distinguished history *Slave Religion* (1978), describes slaves as "distrustful of the white folks' interpretation of the Scriptures" and eager "to be able to search them for themselves." Slaves also sought diligently for opportunities to hear unrestricted expositions from Scripture. As one former slave recorded: "A yellow [light-complexioned Negro] man preached to us. She [the slave owner] had him preach how we ought to obey our master and missy if we want to go to heaven, but when she wasn't there, he came out with straight preachin' from the Bible."

Because of these experiences, American blacks developed just as much of a fixation on Scripture as did whites. But the Bible spoke much more about unjust oppression and a hope for those in bondage than it did for whites. To this day preaching in black churches is intensely biblical, but it also continues to stress themes of liberation, of spiritual promise, and of all-encompassing social harmony. It could hardly be otherwise in a civilization that for whites represented an exodus from Egypt but that for blacks was an Egypt from which to await an exodus.

The great interdenominational Bible societies that sprang up early in the nineteenth century reinforced the centrality of the Bible among Protestants. These societies proposed to place a Bible in the hands of every American, especially those on the frontier. They enlisted support from all the major English-speaking denominations as well as from some foreign-language bodies.

Late in the nineteenth century, controversy over the Higher Criticism (or naturalistic study) of Scripture further solidified the Bible as the central religious concern of American Protes-

tants. Fundamentalists, theological conservatives who supported traditional positions militantly, were arrayed against modernists, who felt that the progress of the modern world called for a reinterpretation of traditional Christian doctrines. First among the five points of "essential" doctrine reaffirmed by the Presbyterian General Assembly in 1910 was the "inerrancy," or infallibility, of Scripture. The twelve-volume series *The Fundamentals: A Testimony to the Truth,* published from 1910 to 1915, presented article after article reaffirming the reliability of the Bible. In those combative days one's stance concerning the Bible was far more important than one's traditional ecclesiastical allegiance, for Presbyterians, Episcopalians, Methodists, and Baptists could be found on both sides of the debate. The result, which continues to the present, is that convictions about Scripture regularly count for more than loyalty to a denomination when it comes to creating new ecclesiastical structures, selecting allies for Christian work, or certifying already existing institutions.

It is possible to view these Fundamentalist-modernist battles as a singularly American debate over secularization. For American Protestants the continuing validity of the Bible was the crucial issue thrown up by the general currents of modernity as well as by the specific proposals of Europe's great thinkers of the nineteenth century, like Charles Darwin, Karl Marx, and Sigmund Freud.

Self-consciousness about the Bible continues to characterize many Protestant denominations. More theologically conservative bodies stress their fidelity to the older view of the Bible as God's infallible revelation to mankind. More liberal theological bodies attempt to demythologize the antique message of Scripture for the needs of the twentieth century. Within the Southern Baptist Convention, America's largest Protestant denomination, and the Lutheran Church–Missouri Synod, one of the nation's largest Lutheran denominations, debate over the character and authority of Scripture during the 1970s led to acrimony, ecclesiastical strife, and even schism.

Concentration upon the Bible has also had an effect on Catholics, who by virtue of the international character of their faith, are often resistant to some of the more strictly local fashions in

America. Publication of the Catholic Douay-Rheims translation of the Bible first took place in America in 1790, as a result of the cooperation between an Irish Catholic printer, Mathew Carey, and the first American Catholic bishop, John Carroll. Bishop Carroll enthusiastically supported the effort to place this version "in the hands of our people, instead of those [Protestant] translations, which they purchase in stores and from Booksellers in the Country." The pastoral letter from the first council of American bishops in 1829 urged Catholics to recognize that "one of the most precious legacies bequeathed to us by the Apostles and Evangelists is the sacred volume of Holy Scriptures," which were "profitable to the pastor" and "when used with due care, and an humble and docile spirit, for the edification and instruction of the faithful." Similar letters from subsequent councils repeated the same message. Since the early 1960s and the lowering of barriers between Catholics and Protestants as a result of the Second Vatican Council, American Catholics have been among the leaders in promoting neighborhood studies in which members of various religious groups gather to read and discuss the Scriptures with each other. Catholic emphasis on the Bible has never been as consistent as that of the Protestants, but it has been an important part of American Catholic history from its earliest days.

THE BIBLE IN THE ACADEMY

Given the prominence of Protestants in nineteenth-century society, it is no surprise that they pioneered in the "scientific" study of the Bible. Although there was no necessary connection, scientific approaches were linked with efforts to regard Scripture as a human rather than a divine book that appeared during the first half of the century. This, however, was mostly limited to New England and to religious bodies furthest removed from the evangelicalism then dominating religious life. Thus, the Transcendentalist Theodore Parker accepted many of the then radical conclusions about the human origins of Scripture and popularized German views about the mythological character of biblical stories.

More typical in the first wave of Bible scholars were Harvard professors like Andrews Norton, who also read the newer biblical criticism from the Continent but only to buttress Unitarian views of the Bible's divine character and its recital of supernatural events. Moses Stuart of Andover Theological Seminary was a rare conservative who also appropriated current scholarship from Europe. But he did so out of the conviction that such research made it possible to discern more accurately the actual messages of the Bible, which to him was still very much a supernatural revelation. Even Stuart's cautious approach, however, could arouse suspicion. As he put it once himself, "No sooner had I begun to speak of some of the varieties of German criticism, than some of my best friends began to feel a degree of alarm" (Brown, 1969, p. 49). As his complaint suggests, most Americans read the Bible during the antebellum period with little interest in the criticism of Scripture that was going on in Europe.

Reluctance to use biblical criticism ceased in academic circles during the last third of the nineteenth century. A number of factors contributed to the willingness to imitate Europe. The first of these was the growing influence of new ideas. Americans learned from G. W. F. Hegel about the evolution of consciousness from the primitive past to the enlightened present; from Friedrich Schleiermacher they discovered that religion consisted not in hard and cold facts but in feelings of dependence; from Albrecht Ritschl they learned that religious propositions were functions of a community social experience. Those who were convinced by these ideas found it much easier to treat the Bible as a book arising within history and subject to regular human verification or explanation than as a revelation coming from outside the historical process.

The appearance of these ideas coincided with the restructuring of higher education in America. When impartial scientific inquiry became the key to reforming the university, a premium was placed upon meticulous research and value-free scholarship. One of the by-products of this spirit was a great increase in the number of professional academic organizations. Students of Scripture moved with the times by forming the Society of Biblical Literature and Exegesis (SBL) in 1880 and by launching the *Journal of Biblical Literature* the following year. At the start this organization was small (forty-five members at the end of the first year), its constituency came largely from the Northeast, and the influence of continental scholarship was obvious (half of the charter members had received some training at European, mostly German, universities).

From the first, the SBL reflected the tension between the study of Scripture as a supernatural book and as simply an important artifact of human culture. Although theological conservatives, who questioned many attitudes of modern scholarship, have never been prominent in the organization, they have regularly taken part in its activities. Their presence, and even more the deeply ingrained assumptions about the uniqueness of the Bible that are shared almost without reference to theological persuasion, kept this tension alive. Nonetheless, in the SBL and the academic world at large it has long been the custom to present research on the Bible strictly in terms of its mundane contexts. The SBL soon became a large, diversified, and successful forum for the promotion of biblical scholarship. It also branched out quite early to promote research in cognate subjects related to Near Eastern history and languages more generally.

Many other groups also promote the study of Scripture. Some date from even before the SBL; others are very recent. Some are strictly academic; others are connected to denominations or linked to theological positions. One of the most important of the latter is the Catholic Biblical Association, whose members, in the wake of the Second Vatican Council (1962–1965), seek much broader contacts in their work. Official delegates were first exchanged between the Catholic Biblical Association and the SBL in 1959, but by 1966 a Catholic had been elected president of the SBL.

Even these few words about the roles of Scripture in American churches and institutions of higher learning should make it obvious that the Bible has always been used in many different ways in American culture. Some treat Scripture as a compendium of doctrine and use it to construct elaborate theological systems. Others read it as a source of piety, as a means of awakening emotions and the heart to communion with God. Still others have treated the Bible as a guidebook for morality, laying greatest emphasis on its rules for daily living. And a few Christians, represented by Reformed groups from the Continent, have looked upon the Bible as a source of cultural reconstruction, believing that Scripture provides specific clues to the organization of

schools, the functions of government, the structures of business and labor, and the like. With these varied ways of using the Bible, the concentration upon Scripture has taken many forms. But what Americans have shared in common, probably as much as any other people in the world, is the conviction that the Bible belongs at the heart of their civilization.

THE BIBLE AND AMERICAN CIVILIZATION

The story of the Bible and American civilization has begun, however, only when we have examined Scripture's publishing history and its place in the churches and the academy. Alongside this internal and religious history—which has been the focus of much of the literature on the topic—stands also an external and cultural history. Much less attention has been paid to the way in which the Bible has played a role in the broader story of America. When Americans who derive their values from Scripture, or who think they do, have participated in public life, the Bible has entered into a complex set of relationships. Sometimes biblical values have shaped the course of national history. Sometimes national values have determined the way in which citizens understand the Bible. And on many occasions the network of influences between the Bible and American culture is so dense that it becomes impossible to unravel. Perry Miller's observation about the Scriptures in the nineteenth century pertains to almost the whole of American history: "The Old Testament is truly so omnipresent in the American culture of 1800 or 1820 that historians have as much difficulty taking cognizance of it as of the air people breathed" (1955, p. 54).

It is nonetheless possible to sketch broadly some facets of the history of the Bible as a force in American civilization. To do this, however, moves us from settled religious convictions to complex cultural ambiguities.

Within American social history the Bible has acted as both a conservative and a radical force. It has provided a vocabulary for both traditional deference and innovative egalitarianism. It has been a source for both stability in the face of anarchy and freedom in the face of tyranny. The clearest example of Scripture's deep penetration into American social consciousness involves its use at the time of the Civil War. Before that conflict proponents of abolition and defenders of slavery both claimed the Bible as the source of their own positions. From abolitionist Theodore Dwight Weld one could hear this statement about the Bible:

> The spirit of slavery never seeks refuge in the Bible of its own accord. . . . Goaded to phrenzy in its conflicts with conscience and common sense, denied all quarter, and hunted from every covert, it vaults over the sacred inclosure and courses up and down the Bible, "seeking rest, and finding none." . . . At last, it slides away under the types of the Mosaic system, and seeks to burrow out of sight among their shadows. Vain hope!
> (*The Bible Against Slavery,* 1838, p. 5)

From a southerner, Howell Cobb, it was a different story: "We assert . . . that the system of slavery in the United States, in every feature and in every particular of every feature, is essentially the same as the system authorized by the Bible, and introduced into the church at the time of its organization, and continued to the present day" (*A Scriptural Examination . . . ,* 1856, p. 9). Until the triumph of Union arms made further debate pointless, Americans continued to assault each other with texts from the book they both revered, using, for example, Exodus 21:16 ("He that stealeth a man, and selleth him, or if he be found in his hand, he shall surely be put to death") and Leviticus 25:45 ("Moreover of the children of the strangers that do sojourn among you, of them shall ye buy, and of their families that are with you, which they begat in your land: and they shall be your possession").

During the Civil War, northern Presbyterians employed Scripture to define the magnitude of southern evil: "Rebellion against such a government as ours . . . can find no parallel, except in the first two great rebellions, that which assailed the throne of heaven directly [Satan], and that which peopled our world with miserable apostates [Adam and Eve]." Southerners responded by calling Lincoln pharaoh; they praised their own president, Jefferson Davis, as Moses; and they likened the northern recourse to arms as the work of Judas.

From the underside of American civilization came yet another biblical interpretation of affairs. A Union chaplain in the army that occupied the South commented on the beliefs of the freed slaves in 1864:

> There is no part of the Bible with which they are so familiar as the story of the deliverance of the children of Israel. Moses is their *ideal* of all that is high, and noble, and perfect, in man. I think they have been accustomed to regard Christ not so much in the light of a *spiritual* Deliverer, as that of a second Moses who could eventually lead *them* out of their prison-house of bondage.
> (Raboteau, 1978, pp. 311–312)

A modern student of slave society, Eugene Genovese, has provided a more balanced explanation of this slave expectation: "Moses had become Jesus, and Jesus, Moses; and with their union the two aspects of the slaves' religious quest—collective deliverance as a people and redemption from their terrible personal sufferings—had become one through the mediation of that imaginative power so beautifully manifested in the spirituals" (*Roll Jordan Roll: The World the Slaves Made,* 1972, p. 253).

The profound, but also profoundly varied, penetration of biblical themes into social consciousness continues into the present. Particularly among politically active Christian groups, it may be seen, for example, in rightist defenses of private property (Gary North, *An Introduction to Christian Economics,* 1973) and leftist advocacy for redistribution of wealth (Ronald Sider, ed., *Cry Justice! The Bible Speaks on Hunger and Poverty,* 1980).

The Bible's place in the rhetoric of social values testifies to its power to shape and express different cultural attitudes that have flourished in America. More than a century before the Civil War, for example, scriptural phraseology could inform a very traditional picture of society from William Byrd II: "Like one of the Patriarchs, I have my Flocks and my Herds, my Bond-men and Bond-women, and every Sort of Trade amongst my own Servants, so that I live in a kind of Independence on every one but Providence." It could also inspire an attack on the socially stabilizing hierarchies of the church from the Presbyterian minister Gilbert Tennent: "We should mourn over those that are destitute of faithful Ministers . . . *as Sheep having no Shepherd.*

. . . And let those who live under the Ministry of dead Men, whether they have got the Form of Religion or not, repair to the Living, where they may be edified."

In the twentieth century the fund of such rhetoric is not yet exhausted. In 1963, for example, Martin Luther King, Jr., expressed his dream for social transformation with the language of Scripture:

> I have a dream today! I have a dream that one day "every valley shall be exalted and every hill and mountain shall be made low. The rough places will be made plain and the crooked places will be made straight, and the glory of the Lord shall be revealed, and all flesh shall see it together" [Isaiah 40:4–5]. This is our hope. This is the faith that I go back to the South with. With this faith we shall be able to transform the jangling discords of our nation into a beautiful symphony of brotherhood.

And President Ronald Reagan in 1982 employed it in an effort to buttress received American institutions: "I have always believed that this anointed land was set apart in an uncommon way, that a divine plan placed this great continent here between the oceans to be found by people from every corner of the Earth who had a special love of faith and freedom."

The Bible has also been a charter of social liberty for many who have felt constrained by traditional rigidities or even dominating cultural fashion. Some of the favorite texts of the slaves were verses that heralded the universality of the Gospel's message: Acts 10:34 ("Of a truth I perceive that God is no respecter of persons") or Acts 17:26 ("And [God] hath made of one blood all nations of men"). Early in the twentieth century, Fundamentalists could stand against the tide of secularization because they were secure in their convictions about what the Bible taught.

But in other situations the Bible has fulfilled quite a different role by serving as a means to enforce social conformity. When the bishop of Philadelphia, Francis Patrick Kenrick, petitioned city officials in 1842 to allow Catholic schoolchildren to hear readings from the Douay version of the Bible instead of the King James Version sacred to Protestants, strong protest followed. Evangelical ministers formed national anti-Catholic organizations and, eventually, Protestant laymen vented their spite by rioting against Philadelphia's Catholic churches. In the late twentieth century the appeal to "biblical values" may often express only a desire to uphold the status quo.

If the Bible deserves special attention for its presence in American society, it should receive no less when considering the life of the mind. The celebrated debate over evolution between William Jennings Bryan and Clarence Darrow at Dayton, Tennessee, in 1925 represents only the most extravagant instance of an ongoing effort to forge a unified field of knowledge with both Scripture and human learning in their proper places. It is possible to dismiss the acrimony between these forms of knowledge as the result of badly posed questions, as G. K. Chesterton did in 1933 with savage delight:

> Private theories about what the Bible ought to mean, and premature theories about what the world ought to mean, have met in loud and widely advertised controversy, especially in the Victorian time; and this clumsy collision of two very impatient forms of ignorance was known as the quarrel of Science and Religion.

In the contingencies of actual history, however, the issue will not go away.

During most of the nineteenth century, American Christians confidently acted as if the study of Scripture and the study of the natural world could proceed side by side with ever-increasing harmony. The rise of Darwinism seemed to call this assumption into question, so much so that by the early twentieth century a belief in the Bible was thought in many cultivated circles to preclude an appreciation of science. More recently, American scholars have made genuine advances in clarifying the different nature of scientific and religious discourse and in showing how artificial the so-called warfare between science and Scripture really is. On the basis of works by Michael Polanyi, Ian Barbour, and others it has become clear that scientific and religious languages, while overlapping, make use of different conceptions of correspondence between observation and reality and different ways of linking metaphor and the world as it exists. Yet outside of a few enlightened academic circles the battle goes on. Popularizers of modern science continue to trumpet the latest scientific eurekas as the refutation of the Bible; determined Christian pulpiteers continue to rail at what they consider the godless presumptions of science.

General reflections on American intellectual history serve only to heighten the complexity of the relationship between scriptural and other forms of knowledge. The Bible provided the staple intellectual diet for Jonathan Edwards, one of America's authentic geniuses, and for many of its organizational prodigies, such as Alexander Campbell, founder of the Disciples of Christ, but also for more than a handful of its eccentrics, freaks, and psychopaths. In addition, the history of American formal public education could itself almost be written as a function of efforts to come to terms with the Bible. From the early seventeenth to the late nineteenth century faculty and students labored to integrate scriptural and other forms of truth; since then one concern of many American educators has been to overcome the effects of scriptural training.

The Bible has also played an important role in efforts to define the character of the nation. Books by Sacvan Bercovitch, including *The Puritan Origins of the American Self,* have shown the extent to which stories from from the Bible have defined Americans' images of themselves—from Cotton Mather's description of John Winthrop constructing a "New Jerusalem" in Massachusetts to later proclamations that America represented "the chosen people." Particularly at moments of crisis, the themes of Scripture have become themes of national identity. During the Revolutionary and Civil wars an apocalyptic note was often in the air. In 1776, for example, the antirevivalist Samuel West of Dartmouth, Massachusetts, and the pro-revivalist Samuel Sherwood of Weston, Connecticut, both described British "oppression" as the activity of the "beast" from the thirteenth chapter of St. John's apocalyptic Revelation. From the seventeenth century to the late twentieth century, times of natural disaster have elicited repeated appeals for Americans to repent and reaffirm their covenant with God. As the North moved toward victory at the end of the Civil War, some in that part of the country began to talk boldly of national redemption and of their leader as Father Abraham. "Mine eyes have seen the glory of the coming of the Lord," Julia Ward Howe wrote in the most famous hymn of the Civil War. "We have seen Him in the watchfires of a hundred circling camps . . . His truth is marching on." During World War I a Presbyterian minister's son, Woodrow Wilson, attempted to realize his vision of divine order in making the world safe for democracy, first on the field of battle and then through the League of Nations.

It could be argued that the Bible's presence in political history has been more superficial than in social or intellectual history, since politicians have rarely been able to resist the temptation to employ scriptural rhetoric for shortsighted partisanship. One of the results of this process has been to reduce the Bible to a kind of cracker barrel filled with aphorisms into which one dips when a widely recognized saying is required. This is very much how Sen. Sam Ervin, chairman of the committee that investigated President Richard Nixon and the Watergate scandal of 1972–1974, put the Bible to use, peppering his remarks with snippets of biblical "wisdom" interspersed with quotations from Shakespeare and the Declaration of Independence.

Yet it cannot be denied that themes in American politics have frequently depended upon the meanings of Scripture. The very construction of the Puritan commonwealths in the colonial period was modeled upon an understanding of ancient Israel. William Penn's vision, which created Pennsylvania as a haven for Quakers, Mennonites, Moravians, and other peace seekers, depended in part on Jesus' beatitude concerning the "peacemakers" (Matthew 5:9). And throughout the great age of social reform before the Civil War, visions of social righteousness and millennial hope were taken directly from the Acts of the Apostles or the Apocalypse of St. John into the thick of the political process. These influences have become more diffuse in the twentieth century, but they linger as a persistent rhetorical presence. On occasion, as in the political career of Sen. Mark Hatfield of Oregon, a Baptist who has been in the forefront of efforts to curb international warfare and feed the world's hungry, words from the prophets Amos and Micah about "doing justice" or from Jesus about "feeding the hungry" assume a more distinct shape. An active concern to reflect Jesus' love for "the least of these my brethren" (Matthew 25:40) also appears among some who attack nuclear arms and among some who oppose the liberalization of abortion laws.

It is difficult to make conclusions about the relationship between Scripture and American politics, partly because that relationship has existed on so many levels and partly because it has been a part of so many contradictory political positions. Yet the Bible has been everywhere present as a backdrop in the history of American politics. To be sure, Scripture has often suffered grievous exploitation at the hands of politicians, but on occasion it has exerted a greater influence on them than they have on it.

In conclusion, the importance of the Bible in American civilization, yet also the ambiguity of that importance, can be illustrated by incidents involving two well-known American leaders. When President John F. Kennedy, the first Roman Catholic president of the United States, was assassinated in Dallas, Texas, on November 22, 1963, his assistants made a special effort to secure the slain president's own leather-bound Bible for the swearing-in of Lyndon Johnson as his successor. Somehow the continuous use of that one Bible spoke of larger American continuities. Yet these efforts almost came to naught when the staunchly Protestant judge responsible for the ceremony hesitated momentarily at using Kennedy's Bible, worrying that it might be a "Catholic Bible" with suspect alterations from the Authorized Version.

A hundred years earlier, in another poignant ceremony involving the Scriptures, a group of blacks from Baltimore, Maryland, presented President Abraham Lincoln in September 1864 with a token of their appreciation for his emancipation of the slaves. The gift was a pulpit Bible bound in violet-tinted velvet, furnished in gold, with a raised design depicting the release of the captive. It cost $580.75, more than the average white American of that day earned in an entire year. In response, Lincoln called the Bible "God's best gift to man."

Six months later, and only six weeks before his assassination, Lincoln pronounced the address for his second inauguration as president. In what remains one of the most profound theological statements ever made by an American, he reflected on the turmoil and grief that the Civil War had brought to both North and South. He concentrated his remarks on the issue of slavery and on how difficult it had proved to end this form of oppression. Yet the speech was neither vindictive nor vituperative. And it dwelt at length on the ironies that had attended the struggle and that, *mutatis mutandis,* have attended so much of America's entire history:

Neither party expected for the war, the magnitude or the duration, which it has already attained. . . . Each looked for an easier triumph, and a result less fundamental and astounding. Both read the same Bible and pray to the same God; and each invokes His aid against the other. . . . The prayers of both could not be answered. That of neither has been answered fully. The Almighty has His own purposes.

BIBLIOGRAPHY

Dickinson W. Adams, ed., *Jefferson's Extracts from the Gospels* (1983); Lloyd R. Bailey, ed., *The Word of God: A Guide to English Versions of the Bible* (1982); Carlos Baker, "The Place of the Bible in American Fiction," in James Ward Smith and A. Leland Jamison, eds., *Religion in American Life,* vol. 2 (1961); David L. Barr and Nicholas Piediscalzi, eds., *The Bible in American Education* (1982); Sacvan Bercovitch, *The Puritan Origins of the American Self* (1975); Donald E. Boles, *The Bible, Religion, and the Public Schools* (1961, 1963); Ruth M. Brend and Kenneth L. Pike, eds., *The Summer Institute of Linguistics: Its Works and Contribution* (1977); Ira V. Brown, "The Higher Criticism Comes to America, 1800–1900," in *Journal of the Presbyterian Historical Society,* 38 (1960); Jerry Wayne Brown, *The Rise of Biblical Criticism in America, 1800–1870: The New England Scholars* (1969); Frederick F. Bruce, *The English Bible: A History of Translations from the Earliest English Versions to the New English Bible* (1961, 1978).

C. Conrad Cherry, ed., *God's New Israel: Religious Interpretations of American Destiny* (1971); S. L. Greenslade, ed., *The Cambridge History of the Bible* (1963); Giles Gunn, ed., *The Bible in American Arts and Letters* (1983); Nathan O. Hatch and Mark A. Noll, eds., *The Bible in America: Essays in Cultural History* (1982); Margaret T. Hills, ed., *The English Bible in America: A Bibliography of Editions of the Bible and the New Testament Published in America 1777–1957* (1961); James T. Johnson, ed., *The Bible in American Law, Politics, and Political Rhetoric* (1984); Abraham I. Katsh, *The Biblical Heritage of American Democracy* (1977); David H. Kelsey, *The Uses of Scripture in Recent Theology* (1975); John Leighly, "Biblical Place-Names in the United States," in *Names,* 27 (1979).

Norman Maring, "Baptists and Changing Views of the Bible, 1865–1918," in *Foundations,* 1 (1958); Perry Miller, "The Garden of Eden and the Deacon's Meadow," in *American Heritage,* 7 (1955); Robert A. Rees, "Toward a Bibliography of the Bible in American Literature," in *Bulletin of Bibliography,* 29 (1972); Ernest R. Sandeen, ed., *The Bible and Social Reform* (1982); Ernest W. Saunders, *Searching the Scriptures: A History of the Society of Biblical Literature, 1880–1980* (1982); Timothy L. Smith, "Righteousness and Hope: Christian Holiness and the Millennial Vision in America, 1800–1900," in *American Quarterly,* 31 (1979); Elizabeth Cady Stanton et al., eds., *The Woman's Bible* (1895–1898); Ernest Lee Tuveson, *Redeemer Nation: The Idea of America's Millennial Role* (1968); Gary Wills, "Mason Weems, Bibliopolist," in *American Heritage,* 32 (1981).

[*See also* CIVIL AND PUBLIC RELIGION; IMPACT OF PURITANISM ON AMERICAN CULTURE; *and* NEW ENGLAND PURITANISM.]

THE ENLIGHTENMENT

John Corrigan

THE word *Enlightenment (l'âge de lumière* in French; *Aufklärung* in German; *Illuminismo* in Italian) identifies the historical period of profound intellectual and social change that extended approximately from the Glorious Revolution of 1688 in England to the overthrow of Napoleon in 1815. The Enlightenment emerged as the culmination of Renaissance individualism (in particular, its elevated view of human capability), the promotion of religious diversity that came with the Reformation, and the new empiricistic, inductive science of the seventeenth century. The Enlightenment as a self-conscious movement based its criticism of philosophy, religion, and government on the historical study of the ideas and institutions of Greco-Roman antiquity. Such criticism was characterized in general by a metaphysics that emphasized the authority of human reason, the necessity for political and intellectual liberty, the perfectibility of the individual, and the human capability to shape history. The Enlightenment originated in England in the philosophy of John Locke, the science of Isaac Newton, and the political commentary of Thomas Hobbes, and it reached its peak in the mid-eighteenth century in the writings of Voltaire and Jean-Jacques Rousseau (and in the French Revolution), and in Scotland, in the philosophies of David Hume and Francis Hutcheson. In Germany and Italy, Immanuel Kant, Gotthold Lessing, and Cesare Beccaria followed the lead of the English and French philosophes. In the early eighteenth century, Americans learned of these developments in European thought from *History of the Works of the Learned* (a monthly English review periodical), from *Nouvelles de la République des Lettres* (a favorite journal of the young Jonathan Edwards), from the lectures of emigré scholars, from correspondences, and from American collections of European books.

The English Puritan thought to which Americans were indebted had prepared colonial intellectual soil for the reception of the ideas of the European Enlightenment. Englishmen such as Alexander Richardson and William Ames, drawing on the writings of Dutch logician Petrus Ramus (Pierre de La Ramée), had fashioned a theory of knowledge which held that the rules of the arts, such as grammar, mathematics, and physics, could be discovered through sense perception and induction. Ames, in fact, explicitly recommended the experimental method of Francis Bacon as "of the greatest use not only for constituting the disciplines, but also for understanding and correcting them." Once the rules of the individual arts were understood, the relations between the arts, or "technometry," the circle of the arts, could be discerned.

This seed of empiricism in Puritan thought blossomed in America in spite of the fact that Ames and other European writers condemned metaphysics as pagan profanity and insisted that conduct be guided by Scripture, not moral philosophy. No Puritan would deny the necessity of religious conversion nor the proposition that knowledge of God came from revelation. As much as the new science might attract them, Puritans desired more than anything the knowledge of God that came from the experience of a mysterious and powerful stirring of the religious affections. Religious conversion was the root of Puritanism.

The typical Puritan was introspective, kept a diary, and scrutinized the quality of his religious affections at least as much as he endeavored to

1089

learn the rules of the arts. Much Puritan theological writing was concerned with dissecting and analyzing the passions and the stages of conversion, so that Puritan preaching in the "plain style" might be better directed toward awakening and enlivening the religious affections. Puritanism, particularly as it developed in America in the seventeenth century, therefore, was a mixture of practicality and mystery, of Aristotelianism and Neoplatonism.

The first of several waves of ideas from Europe that transformed American theological and philosophical thought was Cartesianism. In 1649 René Descartes published *Les Passions de l'âme,* a treatise that classified the passions, related them to the soul and the body, and argued for their value as authentic guides to moral conduct. The influence of Descartes was felt in America primarily through the works of other Continental and English writers. (An exception is Solomon Stoddard, who owned Descartes' works while a student at Harvard in 1664.) Henry More of Cambridge University published his Cartesian ethics text *Enchiridion Ethicum* in 1667, and the book was introduced into the Harvard curriculum late in the seventeenth century. Other Cartesian works that found their way to America at about the same time include Nicolas de Malebranche's *De la recherche de la verité* (1674–1678), translated into English as *Search after Truth* and published in London (2 vols., 1694–1695); Port-Royalists Antoine Arnauld's and Pierre Nicole's *Logique,* published in English translation in 1685; and the works of Leiden professor Adrian Heereboord. Such writings mixed well with American interest in the affections and bred philosophical rationalism in the American mind without undermining the empirical strand of thought that was included within Puritan technometry.

Among those responsible for encouraging the study of European writers in America was John Leverett, a Harvard graduate and grandson of the former governor of Massachusetts, who was appointed tutor at Harvard in 1685 and served as its president from 1707 to 1724. With his colleagues William Brattle and Charles Morton (who emigrated from England in 1686), Leverett dismantled the scholastic curriculum at Harvard and fashioned an intellectual climate in which the American Enlightenment could grow. Leverett and Brattle were also instrumental in forming in 1699 the Brattle Street Church, which provided a pulpit for theological liberalism in New England.

Leverett's pupil Benjamin Colman, the first pastor of the Brattle Street Church, turned for inspiration for his sermons to the writings of John Tillotson, archbishop of Canterbury and a leader of philosophical Anglicanism beginning in the 1670s. Primarily a moralist, Tillotson held that faith consisted in rational assent to the truth of religious propositions, that revelation gave authoritative confirmation to rational choice, and that true religion was always in harmony with human nature. Immensely popular in both the northern and southern colonies, Tillotson's ideas placed Puritan concern for the analysis of human nature alongside arguments for natural religion and thus functioned for Americans as a bridge from Cartesian influence to English empiricism. Indeed, it was through such works as the Englishman John Ray's *Wisdom of God Manifested in the Works of Creation* (1691), a work dedicated to Tillotson, that some Americans acquainted themselves with the groundwork for a natural theology.

It was against this background of ideas that Americans read Newton and Locke, but in the first third of the eighteenth century, only certain writings of these two men exercised an influence on the American mind (with a few exceptions). The *Principia* was published in 1687, but instruction in Newtonian mechanics was unavailable at Harvard until midcentury. Cotton Mather was familiar with Newton and the "new science," but he was more attracted to Newton's argument for an orderly, connected, whole universe than to any evidence the new science offered specifically in support of a natural theology. Mather's *Reasonable Religion,* published in 1700, shows the influence of Tillotson, not Newton, and Mather felt compelled that same year to supplement the book with another treatise, *The Everlasting Gospel,* which stated in no uncertain terms that reason without revelation was incapable of comprehending the divine. Even *The Christian Philosopher* (1721), Mather's mature Newtonian work, was an attempt to explain that the laws of nature were in fact the laws by which God governed the world. Other writings of the early eighteenth century that emphasized order and reason in the universe were Colman's *God Deals with Us as Rational Creatures* (1723) and a treatise by Martha's

Vineyard pastor Experience Mayhew entitled *A Discourse Shewing that God Dealeth with Men as Reasonable Creatures* (1720). The latter work exemplifies the concern of the time for moral behavior rooted in rationality—as God deals with humanity rationally, so must humans deal with each other—but proves as well the persistence of Puritan beliefs in its claim for the necessity of conversion through supernatural means.

When American writers began drawing upon Locke, generally it was less for his empiricism and skepticism than for his thoughts on the reasonableness of Christianity or on society and government. Rev. Ebenezer Pemberton, a student of Leverett and a Harvard tutor at the turn of the century, upon his death in 1717 left a personal library of over 700 titles, including works by More, Malebranche, Descartes, Boyle, and Arnauld, and Locke's *Reasonableness of Christianity* and *Thoughts on Education* (both 1695). A copy of the *Essay Concerning Human Understanding* (1690) was not in his possession. Rev. John Bulkley of Connecticut, author of *The Necessity of Religion in Societies* (1713), was one of the first Americans to rest an argument upon foundations provided by Locke, but he drew from Locke's teachings about property, not from his epistemology.

Yale College was founded in 1701, partly as a conservative response to Harvard liberalism. Ramist logic, the Westminster Confession, and English Puritan writings such as Ames's *Medulla Theologiae* (1623; translated into English as *The Marrow of Sacred Divinity,* 1643), formed the core of the curriculum. The character of a Yale education, however, was broadened, if not transformed, as a result of the donation made by Jeremiah Dummer to the college's library in 1714. Included in the nearly 500 European titles were most of the writings of Locke, Newton, and the English scientist Robert Boyle.

The first person to make use of this collection was Samuel Johnson, the son of a Congregational deacon, who after graduating from the college in 1714 returned the following year to tutor and to pursue his master's degree. Johnson's writings as an undergraduate mimicked the technometry of Ames, but a reading of Bacon's *Advancement of Learning* (1605) and Locke's *Essay* subtly altered his thinking. In "Introduction unto Sophia" (1716) Johnson departed from the Amesian classification of knowledge, in which ethics had no legitimate place apart from revealed theology, and formulated a scheme in which ethics could be included under the category of natural theology as well. Moreover, Johnson elevated the Aristotelian side of Puritan technometry, claiming that metaphysics was necessary as a prologue to theology. It was a theme he would take up again a decade later, but in the interim, he defected from his Congregational ministry at West Haven, took orders in the Anglican church, and, returning to America in 1723, settled in Stratford, Connecticut.

Johnson developed a close friendship with Bishop George Berkeley during the latter's stay in Rhode Island, from 1729 to 1731, and before Berkeley returned to England, Johnson produced the *Introduction to the Study of Philosophy.* In this essay he declared that the goal of all learning was happiness and, drawing on Locke, proposed that knowledge be ordered under three headings: rational philosophy, natural philosophy, and moral philosophy. By including God and the religious affections within the domain of the last category, Johnson placed moral philosophy before theology, thus departing from Amesian tradition. The break was by no means complete, however—as Jonathan Edwards would later demonstrate—as long as the affections, God, and moral conduct were understood to be intimately related. Johnson stopped short of positing a "moral sense," though his theories anticipated those of Bishop Joseph Butler, Francis Hutcheson, and the third earl of Shaftesbury, whose writings were just coming to the attention of colonists and would exercise a considerable influence over American thought by midcentury. Johnson, who served as the first president of King's (now Columbia) College, argued that "intellectual light," or divine illumination, made possible the knowledge of "archetypes." In his *Elementa Philosophica,* published by Benjamin Franklin in 1752, he explained that "archetypes" were standards of truth that were identical with God. This theory, parts of which were available to Johnson from Cambridge Platonists such as John Norris and Ralph Cudworth, represents a retreat from Johnson's earlier tendencies toward a natural theology to the Platonic side of Puritan thought.

Jonathan Edwards, who for a short time was Johnson's student at Yale, came closer than his teacher to integrating Puritan tradition with

European science and moral philosophy. Edwards read Locke's *Essay* as an undergraduate, probably in 1717; this evidently whetted his appetite for the Dummer collection, for he remained at Yale for four out of the five years after his graduation, first as a master's student, then as a tutor. In 1723, the year he spent away from Yale as minister to a Presbyterian congregation in New York, he experienced a religious conversion. In 1727 Edwards left New Haven for Northampton, Massachusetts, where he was ordained by his grandfather, Solomon Stoddard. Edwards became pastor at Northampton after Stoddard's death in 1729, and endeavored, like his predecessor, to kindle the piety of the congregation. His preaching efforts were rewarded with a dramatic revival of religion in Northampton in 1734 and with a share of the religious enthusiasm that swept through the colonies in the early 1740s.

Locke's *Essay* had a profound effect upon Edwards, who agreed with Locke that it was through the operation of the senses that understanding was supplied with the raw materials of ideas. He went beyond Locke, however, in analyzing human perception of the qualities of matter. Locke had argued that secondary qualities such as taste, color, and smell were mental impressions, not inherent qualities of matter. If one viewed the world through a microscope, one would see dots, not colors. Independently of Berkeley, but influenced by Newton and More's *Immortality of the Soul* (1659), Edwards extended the analysis to include primary qualities:

> Let us suppose two globes only existing; and no mind. There is nothing there, *ex confesso,* but Resistance. That is, there is such a Law, that the space within a globular figure shall resist. Therefore, there is nothing there but a power, or an establishment. . . . The world is therefore an ideal one.
>
> ("Notes on the Mind," in Wallace F. Anderson, ed., *Works,* 1980)

For Edwards, substance was "the infinitely exact and precise and perfectly stable idea in God's mind."

Though he was in some ways philosophically more daring than Locke, Edwards was a Puritan, a believer in the Calvinist doctrine of human depravity, and he remained convinced, like Ames, that ethics must be drawn from theology. In his analysis of the affections, Edwards endeavored to bring together his idealist metaphysics, his empirical epistemology, and his Calvinism. He argued that divine grace stirred the affections and inclined the will toward certain ideas. Truth, or "Beauty," consists in the "consent" of ideas received through the affections with perceptions of existence ("the divine idea") present in the understanding. Beauty is thus the consent of being to being. "True virtue" is not the benevolence of Hutcheson, which is directed toward creatures, but rather a love of being in general.

Edwards believed that only supernatural illumination could overcome the depraved inclinations of the will, yet he also believed that preaching, particularly the emotional sort that characterized the Great Awakening, played an active role in the process of conversion. His support of the Awakening was construed by some of his fellow clergymen in New England to be an encouragement of illuminationist anarchy, which in turn would undermine the ecclesiatical order in New England. However, Edwards always held that religious passion which did not result in the practice of virtue was merely a delusion. Religion was a matter of both head and heart. His work constitutes the most ambitious attempt made by any American in the eighteenth century to reconcile traditional Puritan doctrines with European science and philosophy.

Edwards' chief critic was Boston Congregationalist minister Charles Chauncy, who condemned the *"Groanings, Quakings, Foamings, . . . and Faintings"* of the revival and argued for the value of moral conduct over religious enthusiasm. Together with Jonathan Mayhew, pastor of Boston's West Church, and Rev. Ebenezer Gay of nearby Hingham, Chauncy engineered the transition in New England religion from orthodox Calvinism to rational religion. At Harvard, Chauncy studied under Thomas Robie, a scientifically minded tutor whose reports on astronomical phenomena played down the theological significance of celestial events and emphasized instead natural explanations. Chauncy also became close friends with Professor John Winthrop, a popularizer of Newton's ideas in the colonies. Like Edwards, Chauncy sought to blend his Puritan heritage with the new learning.

His synthesis differed from Edwards', however, and inclined toward Arminianism rather than Calvinist orthodoxy.

Chauncy's opposition to the Great Awakening stemmed from a larger concern for the social order, which he inherited from his Puritan forebears and which he enlarged upon throughout his life. One of the most energetic defenders of the New England tradition of ministerial authority, he upheld the place of the minister as a spiritual guide, morals teacher, and community leader. In *Seasonable Thoughts* (1743) and other works he argued that persons must not attempt to act above their "station" nor interfere in the "business of others." Chauncy condemned those "who keep not within *their own Bounds,* but go over into *other Men's Labours:* They herein intermeddle in what does not belong to them, and are properly Busie-bodies." He initially directed such rhetoric at revivalists who were claiming that conversion, not education, ought to be the prime qualification for the ministry. He eventually invoked the deep-rooted Anglo-American tradition of deference to one's social superiors to extend his argument to include the order of civil society as a whole. In writings such as *Enthusiasm Described and Caution'd Against* (1742) Chauncy expressed his belief that the smooth functioning of society required that persons know their "rank" and that they defer to those in higher ranks.

Nevertheless Chauncy, like Edwards, was not an uncritical advocate of Puritan ideas. Influenced by English Whig writers such as Robert Molesworth, Sidney, Benjamin Hoadly, and Locke, Chauncy held that the social order was not inviolate. As one of the Boston leaders of the rebellion against England, he accepted the necessity of resistance to corrupted authority. He also accepted the fact of social mobility in the colonies: indeed, he encouraged persons to work hard so that they might advance through the ranks of society to become part of the "better sort." Chauncy thus blended a defense of fixed social order with advocacy of resistance (of one sort or another) to that order. He supposed that these seemingly opposite purposes were dialectically related in the smooth functioning of society as a whole.

Chauncy's theological ideas developed alongside his social theories. As protector of Puritan ecclesiastical tradition, he resisted any infringements upon the authority of the clergy. He was convinced not only that the universe was perfect in its Newtonian order and connectedness but that humans were endowed with faculties which allowed them to reason to an understanding of that perfection. Chauncy argued that by carefully cultivating one's implanted powers, one both fulfills one's moral obligation and advances toward perfection and happiness. Persons were ultimately capable of "resembling the Deity in knowledge, holiness and happiness" by "the right use of their implanted powers" (*Five Dissertations,* 1758). As it was later developed, this rationalist doctrine undercut clerical authority because it made religion essentially a private matter, a process of self-improvement and the cultivation of reason. Chauncy thus contributed to the demise of the institutions he hoped to preserve.

Chauncy was not thoroughly rationalist, however, just as he was not unqualifiedly revolutionary in his social theories. Influenced by the "supernatural rationalism" of English writers such as Samuel Clarke, and still loosely bound to the side of Puritan thought that stressed mystery and the affections, he admitted that the affections "have their Use in Religion, and it may serve a great many good Purposes to excite and warm them" (*Ministers Cautioned Against Occasions of Contempt,* 1744). Chauncy affirmed the importance of divine grace and of participation in church sacramental life as a means of grace, but he cautioned that it was only through a "balance" of the affections with reason that spiritual progress could be made. In *Salvation for All Men* (1782), a Universalist treatise published late in his life, he struck directly at the heart of Calvinism, arguing that the "benevolent Governor of the world" would not consign the soul of a finite creature to infinite suffering, no matter how grievously that person had sinned.

A transitional figure in eighteenth-century American religious thought, Chauncy endeavored to combine the New England theological tradition with the philosophy, theology, and social theories of the Enlightenment. His synthesis was neither as sophisticated as that of Edwards nor as successful a defense of Puritan ideas. Though conservative in many of his ideas, Chauncy's inclination toward rational religion ultimately made his theology subversive not only of Puritan religious ideas but of New England church order as well.

Jonathan Mayhew was more active in his defense of the political rights of Americans and was a bolder advocate of rationalist religious ideas than was his close friend Chauncy. Like Chauncy, Mayhew often argued in support of the authority of the clergy but, also like Chauncy, his thinking tended toward religious individualism that was opposed to clerical authority. Mayhew's rationalism was, moreover, all the more powerful because it was linked with criticism of royal authority in the colonies. One of his sermons against the British so inflamed a Boston crowd that they looted the residence of the royal governor of the province. Mayhew's rhetoric urging resistance to the establishment in America of an Anglican bishopric—on the grounds that it was the first stage in a British conspiracy to deprive the colonies of their religious and political rights—formed a point of departure for colonial thinking about the logic of rebellion in the years leading up to the Revolution. Such a defense of the political liberties of individuals blended well with Mayhew's ideas about the role of reason in religion, especially as these ideas were expressed in *Seven Sermons* (1749). In a sermon from this volume entitled "The Difference Betwixt Truth and Falsehood," he argued three points: there is a difference between truth and falsehood; humans are endowed with faculties to discern the difference; and persons are therefore under an obligation "to judge for themselves in things of a religious concern." Mayhew stated this principle in the title of another of the seven sermons, "The Right and Duty of Private Judgement."

Mayhew, who was influenced by Newton, Boyle, Tillotson, and Ray, believed in an ordered universe governed by regular laws, and he extended this understanding to the realm of morality. So sure was he of the availability of "moral law" to reason that he cautioned his congregation that "to speak reproachfully of reason in general, is nothing less than blasphemy against God." Like Chauncy, Mayhew believed that reason ought to be balanced by the affections and that faith together with works was necessary for spiritual growth.

Mayhew's most daring theological statement came in his *Sermons upon the Following Subjects* (1755). In a note to this volume, he undermined the doctrine of the Trinity, writing that "scrip-

ture informs us that the *Logos* had a *body* prepared for him, and that he partook of *flesh* and *blood*. . . . But that he took into *personal union* with himself, an human *soul,* my Bible saith not." Mayhew's succesor at West Church, Simeon Howard, argued Mayhew's anti-Trinitarianism more forcefully in the late 1760s, disclaiming belief not only in the Trinity, but explicitly rejecting the doctrines of human depravity and predestination as well.

A close friend of Mayhew and Chauncy and the senior spokesman for rationalistic, Arminian theology in Massachusetts was Ebenezer Gay. Gay interpreted the Great Awakening as a dangerous disruption of the social and ecclesiastical order. Wary of any sort of social change, he remained loyal to the Crown during the Revolution. Gay was nevertheless liberal, even radical, in his theological ideas. As Dudleian lecturer at Harvard in 1759, he addressed his audience on the topic *Natural Religion, as Distinguish'd from Revealed* (1759). He argued that revealed religion, "that which God hath made known to Men by the immediate Inspiration of his Spirit," and natural religion, "that which bare Reason discovers and dictates," were complementary ways to knowledge of God. Since "Absurdities and Contradictions" did not belong to true religion, "no Pretence of Revelation can be sufficient for the Admission of them." Gay accepted the authority of the Bible but insisted that reason must confirm what Scripture reveals. Like Chauncy and Mayhew, he used the phrase "benevolent deity" to describe a compassionate God who rewards the practice of virtue and whose glory lies in his plan for the ultimate happiness of all humanity.

Together with his fellow Boston liberals, Gay also incorporated into his thinking the notion of the Great Chain of Being, of an interconnected universe that was nevertheless clearly divided into separate links, or "ranks." Popular in Europe in the seventeenth and eighteenth centuries, this concept suggested how unity was related to diversity and how change was related to permanence. It served as an excellent organizing metaphor for liberal thought, a model for a system in which natural theology complemented revelation, reason mixed with the affections, and social stasis was balanced by individual advancement through the ranks of the social order.

The beginnings of Unitarianism in America

are directly related to the liberalism of Chauncy, Mayhew, Gay, and Lemuel Briant of Braintree, Massachusetts. The first congregation to systematically purge its services of references to the Trinity, however, was an Episcopal church in Boston, King's Chapel, under the guidance of Rev. James Freeman, a Harvard graduate and leading liberal. Influenced by the English Unitarian William Hazlitt, whom he met at Chauncy's house, Freeman in 1785 revised the liturgy and in 1787 accepted lay ordination at King's Chapel. Freeman's Harvard classmate and ally Rev. William Bentley, a more aggressive advocate of Unitarianism, argued in 1791 that salvation was attainable through the cultivation of one's implanted faculties and that "personal virtue alone secures heaven." Bentley believed that revelation was useful as a guide to moral conduct, but that it taught nothing which was not in accord with "natural religion." His rationalism was similar to Mayhew's in that it stressed free inquiry, private judgment, and education. An admirer of Thomas Jefferson (Bentley declined Jefferson's offer of the presidency of the University of Virginia), he supported republicanism, which earned him the scorn of Salem's conservatives.

Criticism of Berkeley's idealism and of David Hume's skepticism took place in Scotland in the mid-eighteenth century and resulted in the commonsense philosophy, which became influential in England, France, and America. The failure of the Presbyterian Synod in 1738 to convict Francis Hutcheson of heresy—the charge being Hutcheson's alleged separation of morals from revelation—signaled the beginning of a period of moderate control of the Scottish Kirk and of intellectual creativity in the Scottish universities. Steeped in the inductive method of Bacon and Newton, Scottish commonsense philosophers claimed that persons perceive the world directly, not through "impressions" or "ideas." Led by Thomas Reid of Aberdeen and Dugald Stewart of Edinburgh, they criticized Locke's notion of the mind as a tabula rasa, arguing that the operations by which the mind structures knowledge are innate and that "common sense" in persons includes a capability for making moral judgments whose truth is self-evident.

Commonsense philosophy came to America with John Witherspoon, a conservative evangelical who had studied the new philosophy and science at Edinburgh and Glasgow. This combination of learning and conservatism led to his appointment as president of the College of New Jersey (now Princeton) in 1768. Witherspoon's conservatism softened in America, and the Princeton curriculum took shape along new lines, with Hume, Thomas Reid, Hutcheson, Lord Kames (Henry Home), and Adam Smith on the reading list, alongside scientific writings on "natural philosophy." Witherspoon did not think that the problem of free will was a key theological issue, arguing that moral choices must be made regardless of the metaphysics within which such choices are set. He thus launched Princeton theology on a course significantly different from that envisaged by Jonathan Edwards, a former president, and from the New Divinity of Edwards' followers. Witherspoon actively opposed the New Divinity equation of virtue with the love of being, and he revised Edwards' theory of the religious affections as conduits of divine guidance, accepting their role in moral choice, but adding that the natural affections, even feelings of anger and malice, were valuable influences on human conduct.

Witherspoon's *Lectures,* a volume of notes from his Princeton classes, was published posthumously in 1795, but his influence was considerable during his lifetime, owing partly to the fact that notes taken in his classes were circulated widely in the middle and southern colonies. The spirit of the *Lectures* is a promise that both moral philosophy and natural philosophy will yield their truths to reason when investigated according to the inductive method. Witherspoon was confident that the universe was orderly and harmonious, that science and theology were compatible, and that human biology was a necessary influence upon human nature and moral conduct. Though he was particularly interested in the role of the affections in human life, he was little concerned with religious conversion. His realist philosophy was introspective without being mysterious. He studied the "science of human nature."

Witherspoon resisted idealism, but, like many of his contemporaries, he placed the pursuit of happiness at the center of his moral philosophy. Civil liberty, the product of a contract among members of a society to surrender some privileges so that the rights of the whole are protected, contributes to human happiness. Liberty is not valuable in and of itself, but, rather, more concretely, because it allows for an environment compatible with human nature, within which human potential can develop. Witherspoon combined his interest in liberty and the affections in a sermon preached to Princeton students on 17 May 1776. He argued that God himself was arousing the "disorderly passions" of Americans against the English and that rebellion would fulfill God's will.

Witherspoon's son-in-law S. Stanhope Smith, a Presbyterian minister, succeeded him as president of the college in 1795. Converted by Witherspoon from idealism to commonsense realism, Smith advocated an enlarged science curriculum and was a key supporter of science in general in the colonies. Elected in 1786 to the American Philosophical Society, an organization that his close friend Benjamin Rush had co-founded, Smith worked to enlarge the domain of psychology to include the findings of biology, climatology, chemistry, and so on. He hoped to discover the factors responsible for differentiation in humankind, and, in so doing, to discover the original common nature of humans. Smith's *Essay on the Causes of the Variety of Complexion and Figure in the Human Species* (1787), one product of his investigations in this area, proposed that Negroes should not be considered innately inferior to whites, because their dark skin whitened as they lived outside their native climate.

Smith's efforts, however flawed by bias, were important in establishing a context for cooperation between science and religion. Like his American forebears the Puritans, Smith recognized the fundamental role of the affections in religious life. Following Witherspoon and the Scottish Enlightenment, Smith enlarged this concern to include human nature as a whole, in its natural as well as its religious aspects. His *Lectures on Moral and Political Philosophy* (1812), popular through much of the nineteenth century, was an outgrowth of his faith in the inductive method, the observation of effects, and Newtonian order, and it had little place for Puritan mystery or a priori knowledge of God.

The center of the Enlightenment in America was Philadelphia, and the central figure among Philadelphia philosophes was Benjamin Franklin. Raised in a devout Puritan family in Boston, Franklin was apprenticed to his brother, a printer, at the age of twelve. Embarking on a program of self-education, Franklin read widely, studying Locke, Shaftesbury, and the English deist Anthony Collins alongside Plutarch and the *Spectator*. At the age of thirteen Franklin read William Derham's Boyle lectures refuting deism, *Physico-Theology* (1713), and became a deist. A few years later he published under the pseudonym Silence Dogood a series of letters attacking Cotton Mather's moralistic *Essays to Do Good* (1710). In 1724, while working as a printer on a visit to London, he helped set type for a revised edition of William Wollaston's *Religion of Nature Delineated* (1722), and the next year he published his criticisms of it in *A Dissertation on Liberty and Necessity, Pleasure and Pain*. Franklin argued that human acts cannot conflict with God's will if God is omnipotent, and therefore, "If there is no such Thing as Free-Will in Creatures, there can be neither Merit nor Demerit in Creatures." He rejected Wollaston's claim that a benevolent God will balance the pain of human life with pleasure in an afterlife. Franklin proposed that since all desire is an attempt to escape pain, and since pleasure is the fulfillment of desire, then pain and pleasure always balance, and an afterlife is unnecessary.

Franklin's early writings on religion and morality show no concern for the affections, religious or natural. Franklin rejected outright the side of his Puritan heritage that stressed the supernatural, conversion, and the infusion of divine grace into human souls, replacing it with a model of the universe and human action more plainly mechanistic than even the "clockmaker" cosmos proposed by the English philosopher William Paley.

Though he traveled widely in the colonies and in Europe, on official and unofficial business, Franklin was a Philadelphian from 1723 onward. As he became more seriously involved with scientific experimentation—the reports of his experiments with electricity were published in 1751—he retreated from his radical deism. Though he continued to reject original sin, the divinity of Jesus, and irresistible conversion, he accepted the doctrine of an afterlife of rewards and punishments and allowed for the possibility of divine intervention in human affairs. He did not propose a theory of the affections, as did Edwards, to account for divine providence. Franklin valued practicality over metaphysical speculation, and therefore set out not to determine the "nature of true virtue," but rather to discover which specific virtues produced favorable consequences when practiced. In a well-known passage from his *Autobiography* (1791) Franklin listed thirteen virtues, the practice of which he thought ought to be made a habit: temperance, silence, order, resolution, frugality, industry, sincerity, justice, moderation, cleanliness, tranquillity, chastity, humility.

This scientific spirit and practical approach to the investigation of virtue set the tone for the Enlightenment in Philadelphia. Philadelphia physician Benjamin Rush experienced a religious conversion during the Great Awakening and attended Princeton during the presidency of Samuel Davies, who had left his labors in the revival in Hanover County, Virginia, in order to succeed Jonathan Edwards. Rush studied medicine in Edinburgh, where he became friends with Stewart and Witherspoon, persuading the latter to come to America. Rush believed in original sin, but he believed as well that through divine grace the effects of sin would be overcome in all men. Perhaps partly because his thinking was so practically oriented, his theology remained somewhat disconnected and incomplete. He did not explain, for instance, how his Calvinism was related to his apparent Universalism. Rush generally considered life to be a trial, even a misery, that would eventually lead to spiritual purification and an eternal reward. The practical side of Calvinism appealed to him, but the harshness of its eschatology did not.

Believing that social reform was a Christian duty, Rush, like Franklin, was active in forming voluntary societies for the improvement of government, education, medicine, and the general morality. A signer of the Declaration of Independence and a member of the convention that ratified the Constitution, Rush viewed the establishment of republicanism as the turning point in the march of reason and history toward a Christian millennium.

Rush's medical science was an attempt to demonstrate the interconnectedness of body and mind, an endeavor that one of his patients, S. Stanhope Smith, no doubt encouraged. Rush's *Inquiry into the Influence of Physical Causes upon the Moral Faculty* (1786) examined the relation between sickness and human temperament, arguing not only that bodily infirmities affected moral judgment, but suggesting as well that dis-

turbances in the moral faculty might lead to physical symptoms. In his notes a few years later, "On the Influence of Different Religions on the Health of the Body," he extended his theory to include organized religion alongside the moral faculty as a probable source of certain bodily conditions.

Rush was indebted for some of his key ideas to the materialism and associationism of English philosophes David Hartley and Joseph Priestley. Hartley's *Observations on Man, His Frame, His Duty, and His Expectations* (1749), an attempt to rescue Locke's psychological associationism and doctrine of the experiential source of knowledge from Hume's skepticism, proposed "vibration" as the physical principle upon which sensations and ideas are based. Drawing on Newton's *Opticks* (1704), Hartley suggested that classes of sensations are transmitted through the nerves and brain by the vibration of corpuscles. He argued that after a class of sensations is thus experienced repeatedly, habits of thought develop in the mind that can be triggered by the experience of any sensation of that class. An admitted mechanist, Hartley partially offset his determinism with arguments for the existence of God and for a moral sense shaped by Christian doctrine, education, self-interest, and sympathy.

Hartley's theories were widely influential in America, particularly as they were preached by his follower Priestley. An accomplished scientist —his achievements include the discovery of oxygen ("dephlogisticated air") and experiments with electricity—Priestley left England after his house and chapel were destroyed by a mob that disapproved of his pro-French and republican sentiments. In 1794 he settled in Pennsylvania, and his influence on American thought, already considerable, was compounded through his frequent associations with Jefferson, Rush, David Rittenhouse, and other members of the American Philosophical Society in Philadelphia.

Priestley clarified Hartley's materialism and addressed the deterministic implications of Hartley's ideas. He endeavored to remove the dualisms that remained in Hartley's theories, just as Hartley had attempted the same of Locke. Priestley attempted to overcome the mind/body dualism by arguing that matter was capable of mental activity. In *Disquisitions Relating to Matter and Spirit* (1777) he rejected the notion of matter as inert, arguing that it was active, the locus of powers of attraction and repulsion. Thought is thus always associated with some order of matter—the spinal cord, the brain, and so forth. A thoroughgoing empiricist and materialist, Priestley nevertheless found himself in agreement with Edwards on the matter of free will. In *The Doctrine of Philosophical Necessity Illustrated* (1777) he claimed that the doctrine of free will could not be reconciled with belief in an omnipotent God, and that it was unnecessary as a metaphysical basis for evaluating human actions. He argued that "voluntary" acts were governed by past experiences of pleasure and pain, and that choice eventually became habitual according to associationist laws. Voluntarism and necessity are therefore not incompatible.

Priestley played a key role in the establishment of Unitarianism in Philadelphia and in its growth throughout the states. James Freeman promoted his ideas in New England by sponsoring the publication of Priestley's *Discourses Relating to the Evidences of Revealed Religion* (1796) and his *Socrates and Jesus Compared* (1803), which had a strong influence on Jefferson's ideas about religion. Because of its materialist context, Priestley's religion was more radical than the Unitarianism of New England liberals. Such a materialist viewpoint was especially radical as it was developed by Priestley's English son-in-law, Thomas Cooper, who had emigrated in 1793.

Cooper lived with Priestley for a time in Pennsylvania and taught medicine and chemistry at Carlisle (now Dickinson) College and at the University of Pennsylvania. Cooper campaigned vigorously against clerical control of education, charging that the Calvinist clergy, in particular, "are united in persecuting every man who calls in question any of their metaphysical opinions." Drawing on the thought of French philosopher-physicians such as François Broussais and Julien de La Mettrie, he extended the materialism of Priestley and Hartley to the brink of a rejection of metaphysics altogether. Cooper considered consciousness as an aspect of physiology, alongside sensation and feeling, arguing that "we may, without difficulty, and assuredly without hypothesis, reduce all abstract substances, or entities, to functional phenomena." Human behavior could be understood without recourse to a theory of the soul. Jailed for six months in 1800 under the Sedition Act for his criticism of John Adams, and rejected by Virginia Presbyterians for a professorship at the University of Virginia—despite Jefferson's belief that he was "the greatest man in America, in the powers of mind and in acquired information"—Cooper eventually became president of South Carolina College (now the University of South Carolina) but was forced out even from that position because of his anticlericalism.

Anticlericalism was a serious problem in the South well before Cooper. In Virginia, hostility toward the Anglican clergy surfaced in the Parson's Cause case (1755–1758) over the payment of church taxes, a dispute that prompted even Patrick Henry, an Anglican, to attack the clergy violently in the course of the trial. Resentment of the Anglican clergy sprang from a conception of them as worldly, lax, and politically conniving. The post-Awakening disturbances in the South focused these sentiments even more sharply. Before the American Revolution, however, there was little developed thinking of a liberal or deistic nature. The College of William and Mary, struggling to survive through much of the eighteenth century, became a center of Enlightenment learning in America only after disestablishment and the installation of Rev. James Madison as its president in 1777. Its most distinguished alumnus, Thomas Jefferson, attended the college prior to that, however, from 1760 to 1762. Jefferson was tutored in mathematics, science, and moral philosophy by William Small of Aberdeen, a representative of the Scottish Enlightenment who later joined the scientific circle of Joseph Priestley and Erasmus Darwin in England. He also read law with George Wythe, an admirer of classical authors and of Locke.

Having rejected orthodox Christianity early in his life, Jefferson settled upon a materialist epistemology that left room for an omnipotent and benevolent God. Drawing on the ideas of Locke, Stewart, and Priestley as well as those of the French ideologues Pierre Cabanis and Antoine Destutt de Tracy (who argued that human psychology was best understood in biological/zoological terms), Jefferson took a practical approach to religion. The order of the cosmos pointed to the existence of a material God who created it and to the existence of an immortal, material human soul. There was no mystery in Jefferson's religion, no place whatsoever for revelation or the authority of Scripture, no need for faith beyond faith in reason. Jefferson participated in the Anglicanism of the Virginia gentry, but his interest was in the value of the moral teachings of Jesus, not his divinity. In *The Life and Morals of Jesus* (ca. 1819) Jefferson strung together excerpts from the Gospels that he considered to be accurate records of the life and words of Jesus, omitting those parts that he thought were corruptions and embellishments (such as the miracles and resurrection stories) of history. Influenced by English deist writers and by the Unitarianism of Joseph Priestley, Jefferson believed that religion was essentially a private matter whose value rested upon its rationality and usefulness as a guide to human conduct.

Jefferson believed in an innate moral sense that directs human action toward what is virtuous; however, "virtue does not consist in the act we do, but in the end it is to effect. If it is to effect the happiness of him to whom it is directed, it is virtuous." The same act performed in two differing contexts might be virtuous in one and vicious in the other. Moreover, there is something of a reciprocal relationship between culture and the moral sense. The moral sense helps to shape a culture, and this culture will, in turn, allow for greater development of the moral sense. The exercise of human reason—in science, government, literature, history, the arts—adds to human knowledge and therefore also contributes to the improvement of human culture and to the development of morality.

Jefferson's campaign for religious liberty grew from his confidence in the capability of reason and the moral sense to guide human conduct. The duty of the state to foster morality could thus be best discharged by its support for an environment of free inquiry and the unhindered development of human potential. In 1776 Virginia ended the compulsory financial support of the establishment, but it was not until 1786 that Jefferson's landmark "Virginia Statute of Religious Liberty," which completely divorced church and state, was put into effect. Jefferson considered its enactment one of his three greatest accomplishments, alongside his authorship of the Declaration of Independence and his founding of the University of Virginia.

Jefferson was actively aided in his campaign for religious liberty by James Madison. Madison had been raised an Anglican in Virginia, but he chose to attend the College of New Jersey rather than William and Mary. A student of Wither-

spoon, he did not become as much of a rationalist in his religious views as did Jefferson. He was also less optimistic than Jefferson about the possibilities for human perfectibility through the cultivation of implanted faculties. Accordingly, he viewed the separation of church and state as a necessary protection of organized religion as much as a guarantee for the free exercise of reason.

John Adams, like Jefferson, conceived of his religion essentially as a body of principles of human conduct. Adams' views of religion began to take shape in his hometown, Braintree (now Quincy), Massachusetts, under the influence of Lemuel Briant, a close friend of Mayhew and an outspoken opponent of the Calvinist doctrine of predestination. Before graduating from Harvard in 1755, Adams read widely in English deistical literature and rejected the doctrines of the Trinity and the Incarnation. He did not replace these doctrines with a philosophy of self-improvement, however. Revelation was a necessary part of his religion. Like Madison, he could not be as optimistic about human nature as was Jefferson, and his theory of government was based on belief in the necessity of controlling human passion, not on the triumph of reason and the moral sense. Adams also differed from Jefferson in his view of the French Revolution, eventually denouncing it violently; he was suspicious of it as early as 1790, when he wrote to English Unitarian clergyman Richard Price: "I know not what to make of a republic of thirty million atheists."

The influence of Enlightenment rationalism (particularly the ideas of English deists John Toland and Matthew Tindal) reached its peak in the decade after the French Revolution. Deism grew among the Virginia aristocracy partly as a result of the morbid state of Anglicanism after disestablishment, and also because of Jefferson's reconstitution of the curriculum at William and Mary (divinity chairs were abolished) and the presence there of deist faculty members such as St. George Tucker. In Charleston deism was also present, but it competed with evangelical religion among the planters. In New England and the middle colonies deistic ideas found a receptive audience outside of the upper class. Americans were also exposed to French freethinking and anticlericalism through contact with French military personnel during the Revolutionary War.

THE ENLIGHTENMENT

Ethan Allen, the Vermont patriot and militia officer known for his capture of Fort Ticonderoga, grew up on the frontier and did not attend college. Having rejected the doctrine of original sin in his boyhood, he studied grammar and philosophy under the guidance of Connecticut physician Thomas Young, who was acquainted with Charles Blount and the ideas of other English deists. In 1784 Allen published *Reason the Only Oracle of Man,* a work that President Timothy Dwight of Yale called "the first formal publication in the United States, openly directed against the Christian Religion." Dwight's predecessor at Yale, Ezra Stiles, commented more passionately on Allen's ideas, remarking on Allen's death: "And in Hell he lift up his Eyes being in Torments." Though most copies of Allen's book were destroyed in a fire at the printer's shop, the few that remained circulated throughout New England, passed from hand to hand by persons such as William Bentley, who loaned his copy to friends in Massachusetts. Allen's book consisted of vitriolic attacks upon the Great Awakening Calvinism of his youth, mixed with unoriginal defenses of natural religion. He rejected the authority of the Bible and the clergy, miracles, and the doctrines of the Trinity and original sin. Allen believed in an immaterial God, known to reason through the evidences of nature, in human immortality, and in an afterlife of rewards and punishments, although the punishments will not be eternal. It was the duty of humans to worship God and to live virtuously, according to reason.

A more attractive case for deism was made by Thomas Paine, eloquent author of *Common Sense* (1776) and *The American Crisis* (1776–1783). An English Quaker, Paine came to America in 1774 and served the American Revolution first as a soldier and then as a member of the foreign affairs committee of Congress. Part of the reason for the popularity of *The Age of Reason* (1794–1796)—beyond its attractive literary style—was that Paine, like Allen, was himself popular for his role in the American Revolution. Paine wrote *The Age of Reason* to counter the influence of the Catholic clergy in France, whose alliance with the monarchy threatened republicanism there.

By debunking revealed religion in general, and biblical revelation in particular, Paine hoped to undercut the basis for clerical authority. He argued that the Old Testament writings ascribed to David (Psalms), Solomon (Proverbs), Joshua, and Samuel were in fact not written by them. The Pentateuch was not written by Moses but by "very ignorant and stupid pretenders" centuries after Moses. The Hebrew prophets were either impostors or overrated eccentrics. The life of Jesus that appeared in the Gospels was a fiction invented many generations after Jesus' death. Jesus was a great man, not a redeemer. Though Paine condemned atheism and upheld belief in God, virtue, and an afterlife, his reputation suffered at the hands of his Christian and Federalist opponents. Even the open-minded Benjamin Rush terminated his friendship with Paine over *The Age of Reason.* If the book's impact on American religious thinking can be gauged by the depth and breadth of attacks upon Paine, then it is clear that it is one of the two or three key documents of American deism.

A popular companion volume to *The Age of Reason* was Constantin-François Chasseboeuf, Comte de Volney's *Les Ruines: Ou méditations sur les révolutions des empires* (1791), translated into English as *Ruins: Or a Survey of the Revolutions of Empires* (1799). Volney fled Jacobin France and settled in Philadelphia, where he became a member of the American Philosophical Society. *Ruins* addressed the topic of divine revelation within the context of a discussion of the decline of ancient civilizations. Volney traced the fall of ancient empires to the tyranny of priests, who manipulated superstition in order to gain power and riches. Opposed to supernaturalism of any sort, Volney explicitly rejected original sin and the divinity of Jesus.

Joel Barlow translated *Ruins* from the French, dedicating it to scientist and boat builder Robert Fulton. He also arranged for the publication of Paine's *The Age of Reason.* A Yale graduate and the most productive American poet of his day, Barlow served as a chaplain in the Revolutionary War. He spent the years from 1788 to 1805 in Europe, exchanging ideas with Priestley, Paine, and Price in England and working for the French Revolution in Paris as associate of the Marquis de Condorcet and the Girondins. Barlow believed that virtue springs from habit, rather than from any innate faculty, and that it could be nurtured in a carefully designed social environment. His faith in a science of morality was apparent in his *Advice to the Privileged Orders* (1792) and in his massive epic poem of the American Enlightenment, the *Columbiad* (1807), where he wrote: "Mold a fair model for the realms of earth,/Call moral nature to a second birth,/Reach, renovate the world's great social plan/And here commence the sober sense of man."

The guiding spirit of deism in America was Elihu Palmer, and the core of Palmer's message was human perfectibility. Palmer was born in Connecticut, graduated from Dartmouth, and entered upon a career as a Presbyterian minister in Massachusetts and New York. He was sufficiently outspoken in his repudiation of Calvinist doctrines to earn the dislike of his Presbyterian congregations, and after a short term in a Baptist pulpit in Philadelphia, he founded a "Universal Society" in that city in 1791. In 1794, after losing his wife and his sight to yellow fever, he founded the Deistical Society of New York on the following principles, which, taken together, constitute a fairly accurate representation of the ideas common to Americans of the time who were called "deists," "infidels," or "freethinkers":

1. That the universe proclaims the existence of one Supreme Deity, worthy of the adoration of intelligent beings.

2. That man is possessed of moral and intellectual faculties sufficient for the improvement of his nature, and the acquisition of happiness.

3. That the religion of nature is the only universal religion; that it grows out of the moral relations of intelligent beings, and that it stands connected with the progressive improvement and common welfare of the human race.

4. That it is essential to the true interest of man, that he love truth and practise virtue.

5. That vice is everywhere ruinous and destructive to the happiness of the individual and of society.

6. That a benevolent disposition, and beneficent actions, are fundamental duties of rational beings.

7. That a religion mingled with persecution and malice cannot be of divine origin.

8. That education and science are essential to the happiness of man.

9. That civil and religious liberty is equally essential to his true interests.

10. That there can be no human authority to which man ought to be amenable for his religious opinions.

11. That science and truth, virtue and happiness, are the great objects to which the activity and energy of the human faculties ought to be directed.

In 1800, inspired by the apparent victory of the Enlightenment in America (as symbolized by Jefferson's election to the presidency), Palmer redoubled his efforts to organize deism. Intermittently from 1800 to 1803 he published a deist weekly paper, the *Temple of Reason,* and in 1801 he published *Principles of Nature,* a collection of his lectures. Paine's return to America in 1803 breathed new life into organized deism, and Palmer enlisted his help for *Prospect, or View of the Moral World,* a monthly publication that appeared from 1803 to 1805. Palmer was also aided in his efforts by Universalist preacher John Foster in New York and by English emigré John Stewart in Philadelphia. Stewart's *Opus Maximum,* a treatise on the perfectibility of the individual (though not fixed within a social context, as Palmer conceived of the process), combined the concept of karma and other Oriental ideas with a quasi-utilitarian analysis of morality and happiness.

Organized deism lost momentum after 1811, when the *Theophilanthropist,* a deistic periodical begun by friends of Paine, ceased publication after only one year. Part of the reason for the loss of interest was the considerable public opposition to Paine for his anti-Christian views and his radical republicanism. In addition, enthusiastic Christianity was experiencing a revival that would soon reach its peak in the Second Great Awakening.

The Enlightenment was characterized generally by hope for the perfectibility of humankind, and more specifically by the belief that the cultivation of innate human faculties would result in that perfection. Some aspects of the Enlightenment challenged religion; others, such as the emphasis on human rights and liberties, advanced religion. Oddly, the Enlightenment had much in common with the Great Awakening, for both movements emphasized the individual and undermined the authority of the clergy.

The Enlightenment in America, which began by compromising with Puritanism, did not end with the decline of deism. After a century of experimentation with metaphysics, rationalism, moral philosophy, common sense, materialism, anticlericalism, and republican enthusiasm, some Americans discovered that conversion, piety, and mystery were still central to their religion. Other Americans accepted the importance of the affections, but found that logic, rationality, and education were necessary to keep them in check. Still other Americans were drawn to a religious viewpoint that allowed for mystery but broke with Christian traditions. All of these groups, inasmuch as they made room for some measure of individual initiative, assimilated the Enlightenment to a greater or lesser extent.

The Enlightenment has had other long-range effects on religion in America. First, the meeting of European empiricistic philosophies with Puritan theology, which emphasized religious experience, formed the basis for American religious empiricisms that emerged in the nineteenth and twentieth centuries, especially in the work of William James and in Process theology, such as that of Bernard Meland and Bernard Loomer. Second, the characteristic Enlightenment belief in human capability to live morally through the cultivation and exercise of reason served as a foundation upon which the argument for the separation of church and state was constructed: since religion was not the only basis for moral life, withdrawal of state support would not result in the moral decay of society. Third, the Enlightenment belief in human perfectibility blended with the spirit of personal independence that came with westward movement to produce the Perfectionist revivalist theology of the nineteenth and twentieth centuries, a theology apparent as early as the 1830s, when Charles Grandison Finney introduced the "anxious bench" and urged his congregation to "grasp" conversion. Fourth, the Enlightenment emphasis upon the moral necessity for the reformation of society has influenced the development of religion in America toward various "social gospels," from Lyman Beecher, through Washington Gladden and Walter Rauschenbusch, to the Niebuhrs. Fifth, the reaction against Enlightenment rationalism contributed to the emergence in America of various forms of religious romanticism, particularly in the nineteenth century. Finally, the Enlightenment optimism with regard to individual and social possibilities reinforced the already hopeful American religious self-understanding of "promised land" and "chosen people" and, more specifically, it has helped to shape the vision of America as a "redeemer nation," a savior to the world.

BIBLIOGRAPHY

Alfred O. Aldridge, *Man of Reason: The Life of Thomas Paine* (1959) and *Benjamin Franklin and Nature's God* (1967); Bernard Bailyn, *The Ideological Origins of the American Revolution* (1967); Daniel J. Boorstin, *The Lost World of Thomas Jefferson* (1960); Ernest Cassara, *The Enlightenment in America* (1975); H. Trevor Colbourn, *The Lamp of Experience: Whig History and the Intellectual Origins of the American Revolution* (1965); Henry Steele Commager, *The Empire of Reason* (1977); Joseph Ellis, *The New England Mind in Transition: Samuel Johnson of Connecticut, 1696–1772* (1973); Norman Fiering, *Jonathan Edwards's Moral Thought and Its British Context* (1981) and *Moral Thought at Seventeenth-Century Harvard* (1981); Elizabeth Flower and Murray G. Murphey, *A History of Philosophy in America*, vol. 1 (1977).

Peter Gay, *The Enlightenment: An Interpretation*, vol. 1 (1966); Lee J. Gibbs, ed., *William Ames: Technometry* (1979); G. Adolph Koch, *Religion of the American Enlightenment* (1933); Henry May, *The Enlightenment in America* (1976); Donald H. Meyer, *The Democratic Enlightenment* (1976); Perry Miller, *Jonathan Edwards* (1949; repr. 1981); Herbert M. Morais, *Deism in Eighteenth Century America* (1934); Stow Persons, *American Minds: A History of Ideas* (1958; rev. 1975); Woodbridge Riley, *American Thought from Puritanism to Pragmatism* (1915); Herbert W. Schneider, *A History of American Philosophy* (1946; 2nd ed. 1963); Morton White, *Science and Sentiment in America: Philosophical Thought From Jonathan Edwards to John Dewey* (1972); Conrad Wright, *The Beginnings of Unitarianism in America* (1955; repr. 1976).

[*See also* LIBERALISM *and* UNITARIANISM AND UNIVERSALISM.]

ROMANTIC RELIGION

George H. Shriver

IN Western general history, as well as Western religious history, perhaps no words are more shop-soiled than *romantic* and *romanticism.* Both have been abused, misused, confused, and suffered multiple definitions. That may be the invariable destiny of "watershed" words that have to do with epochal historical movements. T. S. Eliot once said that "romanticism is a term which is constantly changing in differing contexts." He is correct in the sense that the wide variety of themes and persons in the movement left virtually no area of life untouched. Romanticism is to be found in artistic, literary, political, philosophical, and religious realms of activity. This essay is primarily concerned with the religious sphere, especially the American religious sphere.

The best definitions of romanticism advanced through the years have taken a holistic approach and have emphasized a constellation of themes and subjects to be found in this new mood of Western man. Romanticism revolted from reason and preferred emotion and nature to science; it stressed individual accomplishment and a liberation of the unconscious; it revived pantheism, idealism, and Catholicism; and it reveled in things medieval and exotic. No one definition is satisfactory, for too many human traits and a unique mood defy a simplistic approach.

Rather than attempt to add a new definition to the already overflowing store, it is more useful to locate the period and the leading European figures of this new frame of mind that followed the Enlightenment and then trace the major influences on the American religious scene. Although there are ragged edges and numerous overlappings, the most notable European figures in this movement were born between 1770 and 1815 and achieved distinction in the first half of the nineteenth century. Their mood and traits

had to do with literally everything that touches the human spirit. The suggestion that the Renaissance, with its similar mood and traits, was the original period of romanticism is worthy of consideration.

Nineteenth-century romantics wanted to create a brave new world on the ruins of the old, and due to different temperaments, geographical situations, and special interests they pursued different ways to this end. Romantic man was overwhelmed with the abundance of life, and no one member of the movement can be palmed off as representing the whole. This, in part, accounts for the wide diversity. A new freedom to experience life in all its completeness and complexity was illustrated by the leaders and followers of the movement.

By 1850 in Europe all the major themes of romanticism had been sounded and most of the greatest notables were dead, among them Edmund Burke, Robert Burns, Lord Byron, Percy Bysshe Shelley, William Blake, William Wordsworth, Samuel Taylor Coleridge, Friedrich von Schiller, G. W. F. Hegel, Friedrich von Schelling, Friedrich Schleiermacher, Novalis, and the brothers Schlegel. During this period and beyond, the works of these writers were being read in the United States, and the new romantic mood was becoming a reality in the New World in numerous bold and exciting ways. From Germany, France, and England the ideas of this many-sided movement made inroads on religious thinking in the United States, with broad and creative consequences even beyond the century. The works of Jean-Jacques Rousseau, Immanuel Kant, Schleiermacher, Hegel, Ferdinand Baur, Johann Neander, Coleridge, Wordsworth, and the leaders of the Oxford movement were being read and appreciated in a wide variety of places in the

United States. European romanticism was thus having a direct influence on such persons as Horace Bushnell, John W. Nevin, and Philip Schaff and on such movements as Transcendentalism, liberalism, and ecumenism.

This essay will attempt to identify and briefly describe a select number of the leading European proponents of these new traits and this unique mood and then locate the more important figures and movements in the United States that were directly affected and influenced by European romanticism. Again, it must be noted that romanticism did not begin de novo; its roots extended into earlier epochs and included persons who are usually identified with the eighteenth-century Enlightenment and its major emphasis on the powers of the human reason.

Certain sons and daughters of the Enlightenment and Age of Reason often dealt with themes generally associated with romanticism. The Enlightenment did not suddenly end, just as romanticism did not suddenly begin.

Jean-Jacques Rousseau, a pilgrim *genevois* and Enlightenment notable, early dealt with subjects having to do with true religion, nature, and individuality. In *Émile* (1762), *Confessions* (1781–1788), and *Rêveries* (1782) he wrestled with these themes and became a veritable pastor to his century, calling mankind to new values and larger visions. Almost a motto for later figures was his observation: "If it is by reason that man is made, it is feeling that guides him."

The German Immanuel Kant was both a son and a critic of the Enlightenment and opened the way to fresh approaches in philosophy. His *Critique of Pure Reason* (1781) was a "Copernican revolution" in the field of philosophy; in it he distinguished between the phenomenal and the noumenal, between what man experiences and the thing-in-itself. Man's knowledge is limited to the phenomenal world, and he cannot arrive at the noumenal mysteries of God with either proof or disproof. Natural theology is thus rendered useless. In his *Critique of Practical Reason* (1788) Kant found his "moral imperative," which made testimonies about human freedom, moral law, and divine reality. Though he later wrote *Die Religion innerhalb der Grenzen der blossen Vernunft* (1793; varying in translation but simply rendered as *Religion Within the Bounds of Reason Only*), a group of younger thinkers including Johann Gottlieb Fichte, Schelling, and Hegel were already building philosophical idealism by drawing upon certain romantic ideas in his work and other sources.

It has often been observed that, religiously speaking, the nineteenth century must be conceded to Friedrich Schleiermacher. Often called the "father of modern theology," he was certainly the most influential theologian of his time and one of the notables of romanticism. This "Herrnhuter of a higher order" (influenced early by Pietistic Moravians) was a little-known chaplain in a Berlin hospital in 1799, when he gave early notice of himself in his now famous but then anonymous *Reden über die Religion* (1799; *Speeches on Religion to Its Cultured Despisers*). Thoughts deeply influenced by romantic currents were expressed here as he tried to show his young cultured friends in Berlin that true piety was actually culture-affirming and that the nurture and development of religious self-consciousness were absolutely necessary to the complete development of the human spirit. Otherwise life was actually empty and devoid of meaning. True religion or piety, he urged, is not first to be identified with institutions or dogma, with doing or morality, or with knowing or science. It is an original form of self-consciousness that he called feeling (*Gefühl*) and intuition (*Anschauung*).

From Berlin Schleiermacher moved to Halle as a professor of theology (1804–1807) and then back to Berlin, where he was for three years a most successful pastor at Trinity Church. Upon the founding in 1810 of the University of Berlin, he was appointed professor of theology, a post he retained until his death in 1834.

His mature thought was elaborated in his magnum opus, *Der christliche Glaube nach den Grundsätzen der evangelischen Kirche* (1821–1822; *The Christian Faith According to the Principles of the Evangelical Church*). Here he repeats his belief that true religion involves an immediate awareness of God and a feeling of absolute dependence on God, but he goes on to distinguish the Christian religion from all others on the basis of the absolute consciousness of God observed in the person of Jesus Christ. He it is who illustrates the absolute experience and who would awaken in man a similar experience. With this central Christological motif Schleiermacher reinterpreted Christian doctrine and set forth his understanding of the Christian community as one of persons with such awareness. Such awareness gives identity to the person as well as a kinship of the self with all other beings. It would be difficult to overestimate the important role he played in the later development of American religious thinking. He was certainly *the* theologian of romantic religion.

Romantic motifs also resulted in new emphases in the study of history. Johann Gottfried von Herder, Fichte, Schelling, and especially Hegel made major contributions to the new romantic understanding of history. If Schleiermacher was the theologian of the new romantic spirit, Hegel was its philosopher. He is to be seen in this role especially during his tenure at the University of Berlin (1818–1831). Hegel turned all his philosophical powers to the elaboration of a dialectical view of all of reality—natural, human, and divine. Everything had its history and might be seen through the Hegelian triad of thesis, antithesis, and synthesis. This construct had implications for everything from an explanation of the Trinity to an ecumenical vision of the future unity of Christianity.

In the same period, Ferdinand Baur expounded the idea of historical progress at Tübingen in his New Testament classes, and Friedrich Schelling gave lectures at the University of Berlin that projected a grand and ecumenical vision of all church history. Romanticism thus nourished an intense interest in the past and suggested options for the future within the construct of evolutionary development.

Though applicable to other disciplines as well, key terms relating especially to the new understanding of history were *historicism, organicism,* and *developmentalism.* Historical scholarship as well as historical imagination responded creatively to the new stimulus. Historicism urged that all things are historical, cultivated a genuine respect for the past, and taught that all sociocultural phenomena are historically determined. Organicism compared history to a biological organism in its being subject in an analogous way to the stages of birth, maturity, and death. Events of history are then due to a more or less concealed organic process. Developmentalism stressed the gradual unfolding of history and an evolution by change from a less perfect or organized point in time to a more perfect one. Historical reality is an organic whole evolving toward perfection. Hegel, Baur, and Schelling cultivated

substantive scholarship as well as giving glorious dreams and visions of the past, present, and future. Man and his world were in an upward spiral, toward point omega.

A "mediating" school of theologians deeply influenced by Schleiermacher was also prominent in Germany in the nineteenth century. Perhaps the most influential figure was Johann Neander, church historian at the University of Berlin (1813–1850). He saw the life of the church as dynamically manifested in individuals and therefore wrote his histories by means of biographical portraits. The motto of his life seemed to be expressed in the words "The heart makes the theologian," and by no means his least contribution was his personal impact on students. Few professors have been so personally loved by their students.

Though a *genevois,* Rousseau could well be claimed by France. The French Revolution can be called *the* historical background event of romanticism with its emotion, idealism, break with the past, and emphasis on the individual. Following the French Revolution and its aftermath, France also began to feel the full impact of the new romantic mood in Germany. Madame de Staël's affirmations of the new spirit in *De l'Allemagne* (1810) began to be widely influential in France. Other elaborations of romantic motifs were projected from the likes of Chateaubriand, Constant, Lamennais, and Cousin—each to have an effect on New World thinking.

As there were points of contact between Pietism and romanticism in Germany, so there were numerous similar motifs shared by Methodism and romanticism in England. For several decades in the late eighteenth century, Methodism and the more general evangelical movement had been marked by themes found in romantic circles later—emotion, emphasis on the individual, challenges to old religion, and humanitarian impulses. There were numerous points of contact.

The ground was fertile for Coleridge, Wordsworth, Thomas Carlyle, and others to pursue romantic lines of thinking. Coleridge and Wordsworth's *Lyrical Ballads* (1798) reflected their emphasis on feeling and antagonism to science, with numerous implications for Christian theology, later spelled out by Coleridge. Wordsworth defined the poet as one who "rejoices more than other men in the spirit of life that is in him," and in "Tintern Abbey" he affirmed that "Nature never did betray / The heart that loved her . . . / for she can so inform / The mind that is within us. . . ." Though thinking of himself in earlier years as unorthodox, Wordsworth later lapsed into a rather conservative orthodoxy.

It was Coleridge, sometimes referred to as the English Schleiermacher, who made an impact on the religious thought of the century. Son of a clergyman and addicted to opium used as a pain-killer, he studied in Germany in 1798–1799 and was especially taken with Kant, Fichte, and Schelling. His varied spiritual pilgrimage also identified him with earlier "Platonizing divines" of England. By far his best-known work was *Aids to Reflexion and Confessions of an Inquiring Spirit* (1825). Here he sharply distinguished between "reason" and "understanding." Understanding was related to mundane, everyday matters of life. Reason related to man's divinity, his *imago dei*, his intuitive knowledge of religious truths. Using Kant, this "moral reason" also has its unconditional command, its moral imperative. The mysteries of God were then seen as based not on any external proofs but on religious consciousness. In this respect Coleridge could be said to be a forerunner of the Broad Church way of thinking.

There are many other aspects and figures in this romantic revolution that have not or barely been mentioned. The popular blending of romance and history in Walter Scott's novels and poems, the massive poetic achievements of John Keats, Shelley, Byron, and Burns, and the vast amount of scholarly works by continental biblical critics, among other matters, have not been touched. But at least enough suggestive remarks have been made to underscore the majestic breadth and power of romanticism in Europe. From the European scene America was flooded with the ideas of romanticism, and the responses in the New World were as diverse and unique as the themes themselves. The very mood and spirit of the new nation perfectly coincided with romanticism—revolution, emotion, unspoiled nature, individualism, and plenty of space for exploration and travel.

Of course those themes more descriptive of the "darker" side of romanticism would also enter the warp and woof of the new nation and would be illustrated in bizarre and often negative ways. Excessive emphasis on the subjective self, ego assertion, unrestrained freedom, and uncontrolled passion had the potential of unleashing seemingly demonic forces. Positive ecumenism would be countered by negative sectarianism, for example—both in their own way emerging from romanticism, illustrating the irony of history. The animating forces of man and nature might also be marked by unrestraint and wildness. This "underside" of romanticism could be labeled inauthentic, perverted, bastardized. All the same, it has its own dark history that is yet another story.

The new United States was fertile soil for the ideas of romanticism. "Nature's nation," as Perry Miller has so aptly called it, had just been through its own revolution and break with the past, and now turned toward the development of a continent with an idealistic and optimistic outlook. The new nation was a paradise made to order for a fresh resurgence of the romantic spirit. The American scene was charged through and through with individualism, optimism, hope, spontaneity, naturalness, simplicity, and, in the main, unspoiled nature.

Henry David Thoreau's *Walden* (1854), with its appreciation of nature, would become one of the supreme literary achievements of romanticism in the United States. Elaborating on this appreciation, Ralph Waldo Emerson almost prayed in hushed tones:

> The air is fanned by innumerable wings, the green woods are vocal with the song of the insect and the bird; the beasts of the field fill all the land untenanted by man, and beneath the sod the mole and worm take their pleasure. All this vast mass of animated matter is moving and basking under the broad orb of the sun,—is drinking in the sweetness of the air, is feeding on the fruits of nature,—is pleased with life, and loth to lose it. All this pleasure flows from a source. That source is the Benevolence of God.
> (Miller, 1967, p. 283)

The delicate children of life would, in this new and fresh context, reflect, respond, and uniquely contribute to romanticism in its religious dimensions. The earliest of these were the Transcendentalists.

The Transcendentalist movement was itself an early and major force in shaping American religious thought in its liberal expression. In the first four decades of the nineteenth century, immigrants were entering the country in vast numbers; German, French, and English ideas were flooding the marketplace by means of the printed word; American professors were spending time abroad; and Europeans were coming to the New World to teach and write. All the major figures of European romanticism were being avidly read. Fully one-third of Theodore Parker's 13,000-volume library was in French and German. The presses were also kept busy with fresh translations. Among the early leaders in mediating and modifying the ideas of European romantics were the Transcendentalists:

> a number of young Americans, most of them born into the Unitarianism of New England . . . who in the 1830's became excited, or rather intoxicated, by the new literature of England and of the Continent (and also by a cursory introduction to that of the Orient), and who thereupon revolted against the rationalism of their fathers.
>
> (Miller, 1957, p. ix)

Relevant even today, they were reformers in relation to slavery, education, and women's rights; they were ecological prophets; they had sound dietetics; and they exuded boundless enthusiasm and hope with an ardor of feeling and a glow of language. Their works contained verses and phrases that would become memory work for every public school student in the United States. Indeed, Emerson was correct: "No truer American existed than Thoreau." The trinity of the movement was Emerson, Parker, and Thoreau—father, son, and holy spirit.

The most important year for Transcendentalism was 1836, with Emerson's *Nature* appearing and the Transcendental Club being founded at Willard's Hotel in Cambridge, Massachusetts —a lively group reveling in dissent and adopting only one rule: "no man should be admitted whose presence excluded any one topic." The manifesto of Transcendentalism, however, and the finest summary of ideas, early and late, was Emerson's Harvard Divinity School address in 1838, a charge given to a whole class of future ministers that included the nodding head of Theodore Parker. The introductory appreciation of nature is worthy of presentation:

> In this refulgent summer, it has been a luxury to draw the breath of life. The grass grows, the buds burst, the meadow is spotted with fire and gold in the tint of flowers. The air is full of birds, and sweet with the breath of the pine, the balm-of-Gilead, and the new hay. Night brings no gloom to the heart with its welcome shade. Through the transparent darkness the stars pour their almost spiritual rays. Man under them seems a young child, and his huge globe a toy. The cool night bathes the world as with a river, and prepares his eyes again for the crimson dawn. The mystery of nature was never displayed more happily.
>
> (Ahlstrom, 1967, p. 296)

Beyond this poetic opening, Emerson cast down the gauntlet to what he considered to be a defective Christianity and a decaying church. In this address and elsewhere, he seemed to have absorbed the complete impact of romanticism and with American enthusiasm urged almost revolutionary ideas for religious circles. He bitterly opposed religious tradition and urged his listeners toward continuing revelation and inspiration of the theonomous self. Self-reliance was his cardinal virtue—but the self only as submissive to the oversoul. Each is taken up in the All, and in final analysis self-reliance is really God-reliance. Emerson would completely recast religious life and thought.

Theodore Parker elaborated on these themes, even adopting the conclusions of German critical studies in their various lives of the historical Jesus. Parker packed the halls of Boston with his lectures. With his liberal theistic thinking, he was at the center of a tempest within Unitarianism, with many of the younger men rallying around him, certainly, in part, due to his stand against slavery. In this regard he may be said to have been a major force upon the conscience of America.

Henry David Thoreau perhaps carried Emerson's ideas on self-reliance to the greatest extreme of individualism, and *Walden* was certainly a "peak experience" for Transcendentalism and romanticism. In his essays "Civil Disobedience" (1849) and "Life Without Principle" (1863), one finds the essence of this supreme individualist. He urges, "Get out of the way with your cobwebs; wash your windows." He tersely observed that very few moral teachers could be found among preachers in America and that so-called prophets were more involved in excusing the sins of man than in exposing them. At Thoreau's funeral, Emerson summed up his younger colleague's forty-four years: "The country knows not yet, or in the least part, how great a son it has lost."

Transcendentalism involved many other brilliant persons who spelled out romantic themes in so many new ways. George Ripley, Orestes Brownson, Amos Bronson Alcott, James Freeman Clarke, and Frederic Henry Hedge were among numerous others. Clarke's *Ten Great Religions* (1871–1883) should be noted as an illustration of the romantic interest in other world religions, certainly inspired by Emerson and others.

Playing a unique role, though, was Margaret Fuller, the only woman to take a major part in Transcendentalism. The main literary expression of this movement, the *Dial,* was edited by her for two of its four years. By the early 1830s she was already wrestling with German idealist literature and even translating some of the material. Her own place in American intellectual history was won by her *Woman in the Nineteenth Century* (1845). It holds the distinction of being the first major literary effort in this country on feminism and sexual equality.

Though always a minority, the Transcendentalists made early and major contributions to a translation of romanticism on the American scene and to a unique adaptation of its many motifs to American religion. Soon enough, the Transcendentalists were joined by others who adopted and adapted romantic ideas. Some of these were ministers, and the greatest of them was Horace Bushnell.

Bushnell has often been referred to as the American Schleiermacher as well as the "father of American religious liberalism." Bushnell himself, many years later, reflected by dim pencil on a stray sheet of paper about his obscure beginnings: "Take the report of my doings on the platform of the world's business, and it is naught. I have filled no place at all" (Cheney, 1880). The judgment of later interpreters would hardly agree.

Born in Bantam, Connecticut, of farming parents with Episcopal and Methodist backgrounds (though both were Congregationalists), in 1821 Bushnell, in a gesture to the tradition, "owned the covenant." After completing his basic degree

at Yale in 1827, he tried teaching and then journalism, deciding at that juncture to return to Yale and study law. About the time that he was looking forward to being admitted to the bar, a revival came to the Yale campus, and he had a deep emotional experience. A rather skeptical tutor at the time but aware of younger students who were looking to him for guidance, Bushnell reflected:

> What shall I do with these arrant doubts I have been nursing for years? When the preacher touches the Trinity and when logic shatters it all to pieces, I am all at the four winds. But I am glad I have a heart as well as a head. My heart wants the Father; my heart wants the Son; my heart wants the Holy Ghost.
> (Cheney, p. 56)

Interestingly, he became a product of a kind of revivalism that he would oppose in later years.

After this conversion, the law student transferred to the Yale Divinity School and his unique pilgrimage continued. The major theological voice of the Divinity School at this time was Nathaniel William Taylor, considered a liberal by conservative orthodoxy in New England in his numerous challenges to old Edwardeanism. Bushnell admired his challenging spirit, but actually Taylor's Scottish commonsense philosophy and abstract logic had little appeal. Rather, during these years an exciting and new theological world was opened up for him by Coleridge's *Aids to Reflection* and Schleiermacher's writings. Romantic motifs would from this point on be dominant in his thinking. Perhaps illustrative of his spirit is his own love of nature as reported by his daughter:

> Never was there such a companion for a walk or a drive. . . . He saw twice as much as most people do out-of-doors, took a mental survey of all land surfaces, and kept in his head a complete map of the physical geography of every place with which he was acquainted. He knew the leaf and bark of every tree and shrub that grows in New England . . . —nothing escaped him.
> (Cheney, p. 456)

Following his graduation from the Yale Divinity School in 1833, Bushnell accepted the pastorate of North Church in Hartford and remained there until an early retirement in 1859 due to ill health. He remained in ill health in Hartford until his death in 1886. At Hartford he became one of the nation's greatest scholar-theologian-pastors. He began almost immediately his method of comprehensiveness, for he had inherited a church rent by the controversy over old orthodoxy and new Taylorism as well as that over revivalism. In this strife-torn parish he tried to show appreciation of roots of the past as well as sensitivity to the new winds of thinking and action. In Hartford he developed a religious romanticism indigenous to the American scene.

Reflecting on his Hartford beginnings, Bushnell put his finger on a critical aspect of his methodology in formal as well as practical theology:

> I was just then passing into the vein of comprehensiveness, questioning whether all parties were not in reality standing for some one side or article of the truth. . . . My position among you kept me always in living contact with the opposite poles to be comprehended . . . and I rested in the conviction that the comprehensive method is, in general, a possible, and, so far, the only Christian method of adjusting theologic differences.
>
> (Cheney, p. 280)

Hegel, and Cousin's eclecticism, certainly influenced Bushnell in his method of comprehensiveness. One must attempt to comprehend the truth contended for on both sides of a controversy and rise to a higher synthesis of positions. Bushnell was opposed to ironclad reasoning in theology. One does not arrive at reality brick by brick. The bricks may fit together but be lifeless. He also applied this to church polity and for that reason was not so disparaging of sectarianism, but was hopeful that a new unity might follow such challenges of the old traditions.

His first and probably most famous work was *Christian Nurture* (1847; rewritten and enlarged in 1861), in which he suggested that through such nurture, a person need never remember a time when he was not Christian. This idea certainly struck out at fabricated revivalism, to say nothing of the Puritan idea of original sin and Calvin's view of total depravity. Indeed, this book would become a bible for religious educators who stressed the redemptive role of the family as well as that of the church in the evolving life of the individual from infancy to adulthood.

In 1848 Bushnell had yet another major religious experience. His wife referred to it as "the central point in the life of Horace Bushnell." As late as 1871 he himself commented on the crisis moment of that early morning in February when his wife awoke to face an almost new husband:

> I seemed to pass a boundary. I had never been very legal in my Christian life, but now I passed from those partial seeings, glimpses and doubts, into a clearer knowledge of God and into his inspirations, which I have never wholly lost. The change was into faith,—a sense of the freeness of God and the ease of approach to him.
>
> (Cheney, p. 192)

He went on to describe this new "faith" as "the trusting of one's being to *a being,* there to be rested, guided, moulded, governed, and possessed forever." Faith brought "God in immediate, experimental knowledge" to Bushnell. Among other sources, Coleridge and Schleiermacher now made good evangelical sense to him. It cannot be stressed too strongly that hereafter Christology was the driving force of his thought and ministry. In 1849 his magnificent *God in Christ,* with its important preface on the nature of religious language, was published.

In large part his theory of religious knowledge came from Coleridge and Cousin. Before Bushnell left Yale, he had his copy of *Aids to Reflection* and what at first "seemed foggy" eventually became "lucid and instructive." Coleridge showed Bushnell how one might know God intuitively. As early as 1839 he had rejected natural religion in favor of intuition. The Transcendentalists had already accepted Cousin's "spontaneous intuition" with its implications for self-knowledge, knowledge of the world, and knowledge of God. To this idea Bushnell was also receptive. Kant, Hegel, Schelling, and especially Friedrich Heinrich Jacobi also had their influence on his understanding of religious knowledge being primarily intuitive. Often he defined his theory as "the doctrine of the heart" or "the new inner sense" and defined doctrine as "formulated Christian experience."

In his epochal discussion of religious language in *God in Christ,* he insisted that verbal communication was not an exact science, especially in the religious realm. Words thus used are evocative and symbolic but not exact and literal.

Religious language is profoundly allied with poetry. This approach of course ruled out of hand any literalistic appeal to Scripture and creed alike. Heresy hunters and dogmaticians were thus bastardized—they had no legitimate place in religious life. Christianity had been impoverished by strict logic-chopping systems. One does not arrive at religious truth by mere syllogism. In part, the Gospel is a gift to the imagination, and words can never completely capture in any equivalent way this gift. This could issue in humble theologians. "Whoever attempts," suggested Bushnell, "to bring any truth out of form, into an exact, literal, abstractive language clear of form, begins in a delusion at the outset, and is very certain to be deeper in delusion at the end." (Smith, 1965, p. 37).

Bushnell was of course not suggesting that one give up the theological task; he was simply attacking certain methodologies that insisted on their truth being *the whole* and exact truth. By forsaking infallible claims to truth, theology might itself be brought along to become a more adequate discipline. Here, again, his method of comprehensiveness comes into play. One must attempt in his pursuit of religious truth to see clearly the insights of the various positions and bring them into some kind of higher synthesis. Bushnell himself entered into the dialogue by further defending and amplifying his own views in such volumes as *Christ in Theology* (1851), *Nature and the Supernatural* (1858), *The Vicarious Sacrifice* (1866), and *Forgiveness and Law* (1874).

His revival of the moral-influence theory of the atonement, first championed by Peter Abelard in the twelfth century, with its emphasis on man's response, and his rejection of the penal theory aroused even more opposition from traditionalists. His whole approach was almost a threat to their understanding of their very raison d'être. In fact, opposition was so strong that North Church pulled out of the consociation in 1852 to stop the machinery of a heresy trial for Bushnell that appeared to be imminent.

Opposed to slavery from the start, Bushnell became one of the most creative interpreters of the Civil War. He found wrong on both sides as well as national chastisement. But the tragedy of war was seen to have opened up the tremendous possibility of rebirth and rededication of a *nation* where before there had only been a group of states. The nation as a holy commonwealth might now evolve from the rubble of war.

Horace Bushnell transcended his own time and context to produce a body of work that would endure and influence other generations in their thinking about educational theory, analysis of theological language, and religious thought in church and society. Romantic religion entered the pulpits and seminaries of America through Bushnell in more ways than can be counted. For years to come, Bushnell's theology would prove itself to be useful "in the battle . . . for a humane, enlightened, viable Christianity" (Cross, 1958, p. 168). In the centennial year, American religious liberalism was given its patron saint. Bushnell was certainly a watershed thinker in relation to American religious liberalism, and his numerous ideas would be expanded in many different directions. To say the least, liberalism would express itself in a variety of ways.

Liberalism is a difficult term to define, especially because of the wide variety of individuals who call themselves liberal. Broadly, liberalism urges greater freedom of thinking and liberation from orthodox church, doctrinal, and social shackles. It urges awareness of one's own contemporary time and therefore is committed to the principles of contextuality and relativity in religious matters. Theology in a new key is needed in every generation, in other words. At the same time, Bushnellian liberalism was also insistent that the essence of the Gospel (the genuine *traditio*) be retained—the *evangelical* nature of faith.

With this understanding, liberalism in the modern period stretches from Schleiermacher to Bushnell and back again full circle. After Bushnell, however, American religious thought had to wrestle with the implications of two new intellectual developments: Darwinian science and European biblical criticism, especially that coming from Germany. As scholars of a liberal mind grappled with stating theology in a contemporary key in light of these two developments, traditionalists rejected both Darwin and the new biblical criticism, urging conservatism in religious matters. The country experienced intellectual, social, and religious turbulence. Liberal pastors and professors were often subjected to heresy trials in all the major American denominations. The two-party system of liberalism and conservatism in American Protestantism, as Martin Marty describes it, was developing its root system. The twentieth century would witness the continuing struggle for denominational authority between the conservatives and the liberals.

As has been noted, the specifics of liberalism in the post-Bushnellian age deal with an amazing variety. But that strain of liberalism most identified by the same principles and motifs to which Bushnell was committed can best be designated as "evangelical liberalism." Major figures in this line include Henry P. Smith, William A. Brown, Newman Smyth, William N. Clarke, and Lewis F. Stearns. Each figure was unique but as a group there were common commitments that were impressive and revealing of liberal spirit similar to that of Bushnell. Christology, ethics, moral education, the Christian conscience, and the kingdom of God were among their common interests. It is obvious, then, that certain roots of the later Social Gospel movement are to be found among the evangelical liberals. Many other liberals reflect the spirit of Bushnell but the evangelical liberals are those who bear closest kinship to him and his major interests. They exuded spiritual energy and vitality, and their works continue to have applicability in today's world. If liberals produced their own literature, they were influenced by as well as having an influence upon the major poets and novelists of the century.

If Emerson was read and memorized in the public classrooms of America and Bushnell was required reading in the seminaries and divinity schools, other romantic literature with religious themes was being read in the parlors and bedrooms of America. Elsewhere in these volumes these writers merit specific and detailed attention, but it would be an error not to mention their enormous influence here.

Reference is obviously made to the poets and novelists of the nineteenth century who reflected in one way or another all of the grand motifs of romantic religion. The entire list would be long indeed, but would certainly include William Cullen Bryant, Oliver Wendell Holmes, James Russell Lowell, John Greenleaf Whittier, Henry Wadsworth Longfellow, and especially Emily Dickinson, Nathaniel Hawthorne, and Herman Melville. Their multifaceted symbols, their depth of interest in perennial human problems, and their occasional attacks on old forms of or-

thodoxy, doctrine, and viewpoints have been dealt with in numerous literary works. Some of their fictional persons have become a part of American history—Captain Ahab, Hester Prynne, Evangeline, Billy Budd. Some of these writers were and are heard in many of their religious observations as veritable lay preachers. Romantic religious themes were expressed in brief and light poems as well as in heavy, classical novels. Their ideas and sometimes their memorized words were woven into the warp and woof of American religion in general. Historical novels themselves underscored yet another romantic theme—a new awareness and appreciation of history in a nation that had been preoccupied in making history at the expense of contemplating it.

The single most important movement related to historical awareness was found in perhaps the most unlikely of places—the sleepy Pennsylvania village of Mercersburg. The young and struggling seminary of the German Reformed Church in the United States had moved there in 1836 from York. It joined Marshall College, which had been founded as an academy in 1831. In this struggling academic setting of a terribly small denomination appeared two of the most creative and productive thinkers in American religious history—both strongly influenced by continental romanticism. They would have been joined in their fame by a third except for his early death. F. A. Rauch, German immigrant and Heidelberg graduate, introduced Hegelian thinking to America in his *Psychology; or, A View of the Human Soul* (1840) while at Mercersburg, but an untimely death ended a most promising career. John Williamson Nevin and Philip Schaff lived to complete long, productive, and creative careers.

Nevin experienced a twisting and turning pilgrimage in his religious outlook, for he grew up in "Puritanism" and at Mercersburg reacted against it or what might be more correctly called "low evangelicalism." Born near Upper Strasburg, Pennsylvania, Nevin attended Union College in New York. There he was introduced not only to the liberal arts but also to a restrained revivalism. During his junior year he was converted. After graduation he went home in a sick and depressed mood. In 1823 he commenced his formal theological education at Princeton and, according to Charles Hodge, became the most brilliant student Hodge ever taught. Upon graduation Nevin was honored by being asked to teach for Hodge while he studied abroad in a European setting. After briefly teaching at Princeton, Nevin received an appointment to Western Theological Seminary in Pittsburgh, where he taught for a decade in a Presbyterian setting. In Pittsburgh he witnessed the "new measures" revivalism against which he reacted so strongly later in his writings. He also began to read and appreciate a wide array of German theologians and historians, including Schleiermacher and Neander.

In 1840 Nevin accepted an invitation to join Rauch on the faculty of the German Reformed Seminary at Mercersburg. When Rauch died unexpectedly the next year, Nevin was the only theological professor there for several years. Continuing his wide reading, he moved on to the positions that would become hallmarks of the "Mercersburg theology."

In part as a reaction to "anxious bench" revivalism in Mercersburg, he published *The Anxious Bench* (1844), which attacked this type of revivalism as sheer quackery. Nevin urged the "system of the catechism" as opposed to the "system of the bench" as the legitimate church approach of Christian nurture. Expanding Reformation themes a few years later, he published a far deeper work, *The Mystical Presence: A Vindication of the Reformed or Calvinistic Doctrine of the Holy Eucharist* (1846). In this critical work he charged that virtually all the Calvinistic churches of America had fallen away from the authentic sixteenth-century position on the Eucharist. He wrote on behalf of the restoration of genuine Reformed Catholicism to replace in America what he considered to be a deteriorated Zwinglianism. He aimed salvos in many directions, including some of the Puritan divines and even his former professor at Princeton, Charles Hodge. In 1847 he published *The History and Genius of the Heidelberg Catechism,* calling his adopted communion to historical and doctrinal awareness of its long and rich Reformation heritage. At this juncture began the lengthy and heated eucharistic and liturgical controversy within the German Reformed Church, with repercussions in many other communions.

Rauch was finally replaced in 1844, when Philip Schaff joined Nevin on the faculty of the seminary. Born in 1819 in the mountains of German-speaking Switzerland, Schaff absorbed Pietism along with his mother's milk. In his midteens he even experienced an emotional "conversion experience" while meditating and praying in the woods. His university years were spent in three of the finest German universities—centers of academic excellence and new and creative theological ideas. He was exposed to the best German theological minds of the century at Tübingen, Halle, and Berlin. Theologians of the school of mediation were Schaff's favorites—Christian F. Schmid, J. A. Dorner, Friedrich A. Tholuck, Julius Müller, and Johann Neander. But he listened carefully to other positions and professors, especially to Ferdinand C. Baur at Tübingen. Baur first introduced Schaff to the idea of organic and progressive development in history, a central motif of all his later historiographical efforts. In Berlin he absorbed the historical method of Neander, as well as sowing the seeds of what would steadily grow into his understanding of "evangelical Catholicism"—a new age in the future to replace the Catholic and Protestant positions (Hegel, Baur, Schelling synthesized).

Shortly after his arrival in America, Schaff made the following entry in his journal:

> I feared I might not find any sympathy in [Dr. Nevin] for my views of the church; but I discover that he occupies essentially the same ground that I do and confirms me in my position. He is filled with the ideas of German theology.
> (David Schaff, *The Life of Philip Schaff,* 1897, p. 103)

And in their views of history, the church, the sacraments, and liturgy, these two men essentially agreed.

Within two years of his arrival, Schaff had undergone baptism by fire in the form of two heresy trials. The first trial (1845) was the result of ideas he expressed in the required inaugural address, later expanded in *The Principle of Protestantism,* with a strongly worded commendatory preface by Nevin. Using the developmental theory of history, Schaff presented the Reformation as having evolved naturally out of the best in medieval Catholicism—there had been no "break" in history and no "trail of blood" of true believers outside Catholicism and stretching back all the way to Jesus of Nazareth. The church had evolved with curves and turns into the sixteenth-century Protestant movement. And it would yet evolve.

Beside this work must be placed Schaff's 1846 *What Is Church History? A Vindication of the Idea of Historical Development.* Here he surveyed church historiography since the sixteenth century and identified himself with the contemporary historical school that stressed themes uniting past and present in an organic way. The principles set forth in these two works would be expanded in numerous other volumes and articles on history, doctrine, liturgy, and ecumenics.

Exonerated in the trial, Schaff continued to be pursued by conservative elements in the denomination led by Joseph Berg, a pastor in Philadelphia. The second trial of 1846 resulted from Schaff's idea of a "middle state" of the soul after death, expressed in writings done in Germany before coming to the United States. Cleared on this charge as well, Schaff made important contributions to the history of the achievement of academic freedom in America. There was never another heresy trial in this particular denomination. In 1891–1893, when he defended C. A. Briggs at Union Theological Seminary in probably the most famous heresy trial of the century, Schaff would certainly recall these early days.

One of the great theological journals of the nineteenth century saw its birth during the Nevin-Schaff years. The *Mercersburg Review* was started in 1849 with Nevin as its first editor (Schaff was a coeditor with E. V. Gerhart from 1857 to 1862). Dozens of scholarly and semischolarly articles and reviews filled the early volumes of the *Review* planned by Nevin and Schaff, and every one of them illustrated in one way or another the major themes of the Mercersburg theology. Some articles drew more fire than others. "Romanism" was an oft-heard criticism in the context of anti-Catholicism in the United States and among conservative Protestants. Nevin attacked "low evangelicalism," especially in his "True and False Protestantism," "Early Christianity," and "Cyprian." Though assailed for Romanism, he actually presented the theory of historical development in this series of articles. Both he and Schaff called their own denomination as well as the entire American religious scene to historical awareness and consciousness. They paid attention to liturgies and creeds in such essays as "The Athanasian Creed," "The New Liturgy," "The Holy Eucharist," and "The Anti-Creed Heresy." Liturgical reform within the German Reformed Church was urged and nurtured by both.

Ecumenism was a theme that also crisscrossed many articles in the *Review.* As James H. Nichols wrote, "On all the contemporary themes of ecumenical study, Nevin and Schaff speak with startling actuality" (1961, p. 310). An additional contribution to theological science was made by them in the *Review.* Their articles, especially Schaff's, served as bridge builders between the United States and Europe—acquainting American scholars with the major figures as well as the most current theological scholarship in Europe.

In 1851 Nevin left the seminary and for a year served as president of Marshall College. Due to sickness, in part emotional because of the years of denominational turmoil, he left this post in 1852. After recovery in 1857 he spent the balance of his life in writing and retirement. Teetering on the edge of Roman Catholicism, he wrote Schaff in 1854 of his "some-time desire" that his life had been cast in the thirteenth century—the glorious age of Innocent III. He may at times have longed for such a romanticized age, but he remained committed to the truth of historical development and Protestantism.

Schaff continued teaching at the seminary until 1862 and during his second decade there became an international figure in church history. He interpreted America to the Germans and Germany to the Americans in numerous ways. Perry Miller has judged Schaff's *America* (1855), written for a German audience, to be as "fine a tribute to America as any immigrant has ever paid." Then in 1857 his *Germany: Its Universities, Theology, and Religion* brought eyewitness and firsthand accounts of academe in Germany to American readers. Contributing to liturgical renewal in the German Reformed Church in so many ways, he also published his *Christian Catechism* (1861). His heavier scholarship appeared in his *Geschichte der apostolischen Kirche* (1851; *Apostolic Christianity*) and the first of his seven-volume *History of the Christian Church* (1858–1892).

In 1862 Schaff secured a leave of absence and by 1864 was living in New York City. He resigned in 1865 while in Germany, during one of his fourteen trips to Europe.

Schaff's first five years in New York were spent in numerous lecture stints as well as serving as secretary of the New York Sabbath Committee.

In 1870 he accepted an appointment as professor at Union Theological Seminary and served there until his death in 1893. The number of his publications both popular and scholarly during this period is astonishing. But perhaps all that he did touched in one way or another upon his romantic dream of an age of "evangelical Catholicism" when Protestants and Catholics would be united in a synthesis of the best of the two traditions (Hegel, Schelling, Baur again) and own a common creed of Christ (Schleiermacher's Christological motif). His energies toward this dream were limitless, but some highlights deserve mention.

He was active in the Evangelical Alliance and was actually the driving force behind the 1873 international meeting of the alliance in New York City. This was the major organized ecumenical voice of the nineteenth century. Between 1870 and 1885 he served as president of the Bible translation project that produced one of the most scholarly translations of the Bible in English literary history (the English Revised Version). On behalf of the project he traveled thousands of miles raising funds and attending project meetings. Among dozens of books and articles as well as numerous translation projects, perhaps his three-volume *Creeds of Christendom* (1877) stands out as a classic, in which he hoped a future creed of Christ might unite all Christians.

The union he sought was one in which scholars of different denominational backgrounds could stand and view history free from a sectarian bias. And so, he invited scholars from numerous traditions to his home in New York City on March 23, 1888, and founded the American Society of Church History. Thus would be brought together on a catholic and irenic basis a wide array of scholars, and this would "indirectly aid the cause of Christian union."

One month before his death in 1893, Schaff participated in meetings unlike any ever held—the World's Parliament of Religions in Chicago—with leading figures from all the major religions in the world. Schaff spoke appropriately on "The Reunion of Christendom." With his romantic, idealistic vision, he foresaw a peaceful end to all sectarian wars "when all the churches shall be thoroughly Christianized and all the creeds of Christendom united in the creed of Christ." This ideal American scholar perhaps summarized romantic religion in his person and formal contributions better than any other in the nineteenth century.

The "church question" was an important issue in other circles than Mercersburg, of course. The Oxford movement had reached America, with its own kind of historical awareness and understanding of the church.

The Oxford, or Tractarian, movement in England was uniquely marked by its interest in history and the nature of the church. In fact, the Anglo-Catholic party, founded by such figures as R. H. Froude, J. H. Newman, E. B. Pusey, and John Keble, resulted from this movement. These writers and their movement urged that the church must be restored to the purity of the ancient apostolic period in all its practices and beliefs. They located the "true Church" in the ancient period of church history with its truly ecumenical councils, the literature of the great church fathers, and in the historic episcopate. This further led to an emphasis on the liturgy, ritual, and practice of that period rather than the contemporary. The leaders of the movement produced ninety tracts (thus, Tractarianism), and no parish was immune to its influence. At Cambridge another "church movement" was born, the Cambridge movement. The romantic interest in the pristine purity of past ages was in this case focalized in the Middle Ages. It revived Gothic architecture and championed the restoration of medieval ways of worship, its emphasis being more aesthetic but, due to its popularity, probably wider ranging in the long run than that of the Oxford movement.

These two movements had their general impact on Nevin, Schaff, Orestes Brownson, and others who were keenly aware of the role history and tradition should play in one's view of the church. More specifically, in the Protestant Episcopal church in the United States there were points of contact and signal developments. One of the most important was at the General Seminary in New York City, which became, as it were, a "little Oxford" where the works of the Tractarians inspired a number of priestly candidates with concerns about the church, its ministry, and its sacraments. As had John Henry Newman in England, some even became converts to Roman Catholicism.

The General Seminary continued to be a center of Tractarian emphases. From such roots a church attitude known as "Anglo-Catholic" eventually emerged, with numerous aesthetic points of contact with Roman Catholicism. W. A. Mühlenberg was a major spokesman for many motifs of Tractarianism and from the Church of the Holy Communion in New York City (a Gothic structure) he introduced liturgical and other practices that were hallmarks of Oxford. He also agitated on behalf of the romantic idea of "evangelical Catholicism" and saw the Episcopal church as a possible via media between Protestants and Catholics. In several important ways Mühlenberg summarized in his person how romantic religion would play a longer role in the Episcopal communion.

Romantic impulses of the nineteenth century continue to be critical parts of contemporary American religious history. Works of the Transcendentalists and poems and novels of romantic writers exploring religious themes are required reading from grade school through college. Their works as well as those of Bushnell, Nevin, and Schaff are on required and suggested reading lists in seminaries and divinity schools all across America. The influence of liberalism has been felt directly or indirectly in nearly every denomination and pulpit in the United States. By some in religious circles, the ecumenical movement has been called the "great new fact" of the twentieth century. It is also, in a unique way, the last great outburst of romantic religion in the century, with its idealism, historic awareness, hope, sensitivity to man and nature, and dream of world unity. Practically every major motif of romanticism is illustrated in the history of the ecumenical movement. It is not surprising, then, that its patron saints and prophets are to be found among those influenced most by romantic religion.

BIBLIOGRAPHY

Sydney E. Ahlstrom, *A Religious History of the American People* (1972) and, as ed., *Theology in America* (1967); Jacques Barzun, *Classic, Romantic and Modern* (1943; rev. 1961); Mary B. Cheney, *Life and Letters of Horace Bushnell* (1880; repr. 1969); Barbara M. Cross, *Horace Bushnell* (1958); John Killinger, *The Failure of Theology in Modern Literature* (1963); Kenneth S. Latourette, *The Nineteenth Century in Europe: The Protestant and Eastern Churches* (1959).

Perry Miller, ed., *The American Transcendentalists* (1957) and *Nature's Nation* (1967); James H. Nichols, *Romanticism in American Theology* (1961); Philip Schaff, *America* (1855; rev. 1961); Friedrich Schleiermacher, *Speeches in Religion* (1892; 1955); George H. Shriver, *Philip Schaff* (1987) and, as ed., *American Religious Heretics* (1966); Hilrie S. Smith, ed., *Horace Bushnell* (1965) and, with Robert T. Handy and L. A. Loetscher, eds., *American Christianity*, vol. 2 (1963).

[See also HISTORIOGRAPHY OF AMERICAN RELIGION; LIBERALISM; RELIGION AND LITERATURE; *and* TRANSCENDENTALISM.]

TRANSCENDENTALISM

Catherine L. Albanese

TRANSCENDENTALISM arose in the 1830s in New England as a religious, literary, and, in the loose sense, philosophical movement. The movement and its followers received their name first in derision. In their enthusiasm for German and Kantian philosophical idealism, critics claimed, members of the "new school" walked with their heads in the clouds, out of touch with the common ground. The young people who bore the brunt of the criticism were mostly Unitarian in background, middle-class, and educated at Harvard. Their movement was based in or near Boston and at its center was a group of roughly thirty. Some were identified with Transcendentalism from its beginning, most notably Ralph Waldo Emerson, its acknowledged leader. Others, like Henry David Thoreau, involved themselves later.

Definitions of what constituted Transcendentalism or a Transcendentalist have generated much heat and little final resolution. Unlike a church or sect, Transcendentalists kept no membership rolls and exacted no financial or doctrinal fees. Perhaps it is best to understand their movement as a collection of friends and fellow travelers who shared certain fundamental ideas and outlooks, oriented their lives around common rituals, and, important among them, liked to meet together for conversation.

Indeed, the group and the movement acquired some definition with the meetings of the so-called Transcendental Club. Beginning on 19 September 1836 with six or seven present, the Transcendentalists met from time to time for an evening's conversation on topics of mutual concern. Often prompted by the arrival of Frederic Henry Hedge from Bangor, Maine, where he ministered to a church, these meetings attracted many of Boston's liberal elite. Their discussions ranged over such themes as the problems of "American genius," the "education of humanity," Harvard College, law, truth, Emerson's journals, property, and worship. By 1839 club members were actively planning a periodical to give expression to their views, and by July 1840 the first number of the *Dial* was sounding a new era in American literature. Club members, however, understood their movement as, first and foremost, spiritual.

In addition to Emerson and Hedge, the others present at the first meeting of the club were Amos Bronson Alcott, an innovative young educator, among the most mystical in the group, and best-known later as the father of Louisa May Alcott; George Ripley, by 1841 the founder of the well-remembered communitarian experiment Brook Farm; James Freeman Clarke, Unitarian editor of the *Western Messenger* in Cincinnati and later the founder of a new religious society; Convers Francis, a conservative Transcendentalist and eventually a professor at Harvard; and probably Orestes Brownson, like Clarke, the founder of a new religious society, then an editor preoccupied with social reform, and later a prominent Roman Catholic convert.

Others who appeared at meetings or were associated with the movement included Henry Thoreau, who was to be remembered as a giant of American literature; Margaret Fuller, first and chief editor of the *Dial* and an early feminist; Theodore Parker, religious innovator and fiery antislavery preacher; William Henry Channing, ecclesiastical and social reformer and editor; the younger William Ellery Channing, poet and close friend of Henry Thoreau; Elizabeth Palmer Peabody, owner of a bookstore that became a Transcendental gathering place and publisher of the *Dial;* Jones Very, mystic and poet; and William Henry Furness, author of *Remarks on the Four Gospels* (1836) and another Transcendental conservative.

The looseness of the movement was no accident. Rather, it mirrored the common core of commitments that Transcendentalists were likely to share. Among these, the primacy of inward experience and intuition was key, and an impatience with inherited external forms provided strong accompaniment. With each person listening to inner voices and scorning the formalism of traditional outward organization, Transcendentalists could never make the transition from movement to institution. Moreover, for all of the ideological shifts that their movement represented, and for all of its self-consciousness about breaking with the past, Transcendentalists were in many ways children of the past and, especially, of the collision of past with present.

First, the Transcendentalists were children of the Puritans, who had early exhibited a mystical strain and an ability to find God in nature. The Puritan practice of keeping intimate journals revealed an introspective concern for the condition of the soul and the presence or absence of grace. Even more, Puritan "heresies," such as the Quaker doctrine of the inner light and the antinomian teaching of Anne Hutchinson, expressed in pronounced form the interiorizing dynamic in Puritan culture. From a rationalistic perspective, Cotton Mather in *The Christian Philosopher* (1721) extolled the revelation of God in nature with its abiding order and harmony. And Jonathan Edwards, the great latter-day Puritan theologian, found nature an occasion for meeting God. Whether inwardly in the self or outwardly in nature, the Puritans were sensitive to the God who was immanent as well as transcendent. They gave to their Transcendentalist heirs a religious culture in which nature and the interior life were respected in the light of divinity, and they encouraged a seriousness and intensity of purpose in the pursuit of spiritual things.

Beyond that, Puritan philosophical thinking had favored the Platonic tradition with its idealism and its system of analogy between material world and spiritual realm. Yet Puritan inwardness and idealism were woven into the fabric of a culture that also emphasized the world. Imbued with a sense of high morality and divine calling in every profession, Puritans moved with confidence and ability—a pragmatic, efficient, and industrious people.

The Transcendentalists continued to embody these Puritan tendencies and qualities even as they rebelled against the past. Like their ancestors, the Transcendentalists wrote footnotes to Plato as they fashioned a spirituality that spoke to the condition of their times. Like their ancestors, too, they were impelled by their sense of the moral law and regarded the task of spreading their gospel as a vocation. And like their ancestors, they preached with a confidence that betokened their sense of intimacy with God. Meanwhile, that sense of intimacy was reflected in a predilection for the interior life and a cultivation of mystical themes. The intimacy was also reflected in a celebration of nature as the abode of spirit, when Transcendentalists, in a form of spiritual pragmatism, pointed to nature's religious usefulness. While these qualities in many cases went further than earlier Puritan expressions, the seed of Transcendentalist religious culture could still be found in Puritanism.

Second, the Transcendentalists were children of the Unitarians who had emerged from the liberal wing of Puritanism. Developing the rationalism that was already a part of Puritanism, these Unitarians embraced the Enlightenment philosophy of John Locke. With its doctrine of epistemological materialism, Lockean philosophy had rejected the traditional theory of knowledge through innate ideas. It argued instead for the mind as a tabula rasa, a clean slate on which knowledge was recorded through the impression of the senses and then subjected to reflection to give rise to ideas. For the Unitarians, this sensationalist philosophy had religious consequences, and in their theological quest for certainty they found evidence for the truth of Christianity in the miracles to which the Gospels witnessed. Here was proof through the senses of the authenticity of the character of Jesus and of the message that he preached; and so, here was a rational argument for the faith of a liberal nineteenth-century person.

By emphasizing rationalism in their liberal quest, Unitarians had created a theological milieu free from dogma, making space for an intellectual and spiritual freedom that the Transcendentalists would harvest anew. Moreover, freedom from dogma was related to the further

TRANSCENDENTALISM

Unitarian emphasis on individual responsibility. With their cultivation of morality, Unitarians, perforce, turned to the individual who carried on the struggle for righteousness, a person, Unitarians thought, intrinsically capable of acting responsibly and, thus, innately good. In a related intellectual move, Unitarians turned from the trinity to the unity of God. For the individual who lived out the moral life as a single self, the unity of God and the earnest and exemplary character of Jesus seemed compelling symbols, and the divine community of a trinity appeared not nearly so meaningful.

Finally, Unitarians refined their moral theology through their appropriation of Scottish commonsense philosophy. As expounded by Thomas Reid and his followers, among them Dugald Stewart and Thomas Brown, Scottish common sense adhered to much of Locke's empiricism but argued for the self-evidence of fundamental rational principles ("common sense") as grounds for knowledge of the objective world. It argued, too, for a moral sense, a basic intuitive understanding by means of which people distinguished between good and evil.

The Transcendentalists came to regard Lockean sensationalism as the enemy to be destroyed in the service of the Spirit. Indeed, the case can be made that without the goad of Locke their movement might not have arisen. However, it was Locke as mediated through the rationalism of Unitarian preaching that most disturbed the Transcendentalists, with their revolt, as in Emerson's Divinity School address (1838), time and again witnessing to the barrenness and coldness that they found in the doctrinal message of their church. Moreover, their self-consciousness as a separate movement grew in the context of the miracles controversy that pitted Transcendentalists like Ripley and Parker against Unitarian "pope" Andrews Norton and others. Rejecting Lockean sensationalism for an intuitional philosophy, the Transcendentalist repudiated miracles as Christian evidence, arguing that the truth of the Gospels was confirmed by the moral character of Christ there revealed and intuitively grasped.

Yet in the climate of freedom that the Unitarians had provided, the Transcendentalists continued to uphold much of the older vision. Unitarian stress on individual responsibility and optimism regarding human goodness became also the Transcendentalist gospel. Unitarian rejection of the orthodox trinity cleared the ground for the mystical unitarianism of Transcendentalists who spoke of the divine Mind and Reason and the Oversoul. Unitarian-bequeathed Scottish commonsense philosophy, with its teaching of the moral sense, blended with new sources of Transcendentalist thinking to support the spirituality based on the primacy of intuition. Unitarian self-culture, the active flowering of its individualism, was appropriated by the Transcendentalists and, as will be seen, developed even further.

Children of Puritans and Unitarians, the Transcendentalists found many of the new sources for their thought and spirituality in Europe. For they were, third, children of the Europeans, especially in their romantic phase. Members of the "new school" grew enthusiastic about the philosophy of Immanuel Kant, which challenged the epistemological doctrine of Locke and the British empiricists. For Kant, knowledge was mediated through a series of mental categories that shaped the raw data of experience. Thus, knowledge was partly ideal (the product of the mind) and partly empirical (the product of the senses). The Transcendentalists turned eagerly as well to Friedrich Jacobi, another German thinker, who countered the Kantian philosophy to argue for the direct and immediate knowledge of intuition. A third German hero for the Transcendentalists was Johann Fichte, who exalted the human mind as the ultimate reality, going beyond Kantian idealism by denying the existence of an objective, external world. Other Germans, too, drew Transcendentalist approval and enthusiasm, among them Friedrich Schleiermacher, the theologian of Pietism who identified religion with feeling.

German influences reached the Transcendentalists in various ways. In 1819 the return of two New Englanders—Edward Everett and George Ticknor—from studies in Göttingen and then in 1822 the return of a third—George Bancroft—excited interest in German literature. Later, from 1825, Charles T. C. Follen taught German at Harvard; and, among the founding members of the Transcendental Club, Hedge spent four years studying in Germany. However, the Transcendentalists got much of their German secondhand. In the final analysis, it was the work of Samuel Taylor Coleridge and, in some measure, of other English romantics like Thomas Carlyle and William Wordsworth that influenced them more.

Coleridge had been introduced to an American audience in 1829, when James Marsh, a Calvinist cleric and professor of philosophy at the University of Vermont, produced an American edition of Coleridge's *Aids to Reflection.* In a preliminary essay and notes Marsh stressed Coleridge's distinction between Reason and Understanding, a distinction that was based on Kantian terms but was also a simplification and transformation of them. Moreover, for Coleridge as interpreted by Marsh, Reason was the high faculty of intuition that could have direct and positive knowledge of spiritual things, while Understanding was the lesser faculty that dealt with the material world. The American Transcendentalists made this distinction basic to their religious understanding. A number of them never came to terms with the original philosophy of Kant, although they thought that through Coleridge and Marsh they had done so.

If German and English romantics made their mark, so to some extent did the French. Eclecticism, especially in the work of Victor Cousin, found a congenial audience among Transcendentalists like Ripley and Brownson. Cousin, along with Théodore-Simon Jouffroy, combined Scottish common sense with German idealism and other sources, arguing that each possessed truths that could be understood intuitively. Meanwhile, the Neoplatonic and metaphysical tradition of Europe—with its long history preceding the rise of romanticism—had been discovered by many of the Transcendentalists. New spiritual heroes were found in men like Emanuel Swedenborg and Jakob Böhme.

The Transcendentalists absorbed Neoplatonism with their Platonism, for they read Plato with the aid of the introductions and translations of Thomas Taylor, a British scholar who gave his readings a Neoplatonic and mystical cast. Emerson was also greatly affected by his discovery of Sampson Reed, a young Swedenborgian whose speaking and writing introduced the Transcendentalist leader to the prolific Swedish mystic. When, in 1826, Reed published *Observations on the Growth of the Mind,* Emerson could not praise it enough in his journal. Still more, Emerson studied Swedenborg's own works in which the doctrine of correspondences between earth and various spiritual spheres was developed. Although in later life Emerson qualified some of his earlier enthusiasm, the effect of Swedenborg's teachings proved to be profound and lasting.

Emerson's close friend Bronson Alcott was deeply drawn to Neoplatonism; and later the *Harbinger,* a periodical begun at Brook Farm in 1845, strongly reflected Swedenborgian teaching. Various other Transcendentalists spoke with approval and admiration of Swedenborg and Böhme and of general Neoplatonic teaching. But the ecumenism of the Transcendentalists extended beyond the esoteric tradition of Europe to embrace, in time, the spirituality of the East.

Here, with the movement already in its heyday, the Orient acted not as a first teacher but as a corroborator of what the Transcendentalists already knew. The excitement of discovering insights and experiences similar to their own among strange and distant peoples was strong, and both Emerson and Thoreau have left literary records of their encounters with the East. From India the Bhagavad Gita, certain texts of the Vedas, and the *Laws of Manu,* and from China even the sayings of Confucius, whetted Transcendentalist appetites for the East. Read in inaccurate translations and mingled eclectically with other sources, the Eastern works proved malleable to Transcendentalist reconstruction. The union of Brahman with Atman, the forms of yoga, the harmonial disciplines of spiritual paths, all found new reincarnations in the "new school" synthesis. Thus, from one perspective, because the reconstructed Orient told the Transcendentalists what they already believed, they read the Eastern classics simply for support and confirmation. But from another, their gesture of openness toward religious paths totally "other" was a testimony to the romantic spirit of expansiveness. In the end, that romantic spirit had been kindled in the Transcendentalists by the gift of Europe.

Whatever the largesse of the European gift, however, the Transcendentalists were, fourth and finally, children of their contemporary America. Outside the Brahmin enclaves of Boston, a new nation was living through an era of material and mental ferment. The industrial revolution was bringing the factory system of collective manufacturing and, with it, the dislocation of many farm people who settled in company towns. A transportation revolution was introducing canals and steamboats and, most important, railroads. Cities grew, swelled by the arrival of rural migrants and foreign immigrants. The frontier was being pushed farther and farther west. In 1828 Andrew Jackson, to the horror of conservative Whigs, was elected president, inaugurating a new age of popular democracy. The economy alternately boomed on a tide of speculation and crashed with its own weight.

Like their economy, Americans were strained by the pressures of the times, and many were drawn to a subculture of ultraism. Some immersed themselves in reform movements for causes like temperance, antislavery, peace, and women's rights. Others turned to revivals and new religious movements, while a few experimented with more radical ways of living, often in nontraditional sexual or communitarian contexts or both.

In the midst of this world of rapid change and continuing social upheaval, the Transcendentalists responded in complex and ambiguous fashion. Conceptually, they were often ambivalent about a culture so mindlessly on the move, fearing for the materialism of the era and the absence of more lasting values. Yet their ambivalence did not prevent them from throwing themselves into various reform movements or experimenting with different ways of life. In truth, at a deeper level the Transcendentalists shared the excitement of their times and held to a vision in which flux was at the heart of things, a vision reflected in the language of motion they preferred when speaking of religious truth.

Inheritors of a complex past, the Transcendentalists moved beyond their legacy to think, write, and act in ways they made their own. They were protagonists in an equally complex present that they succeeded in meeting with a distinctive spirituality, the lived expression of their religious vision. Like Swedenborgians and Neoplatonists in general, the Transcendentalists grounded their thought in the ancient world view of correspondence, seeing the relationship of human life to what lay beyond it as that of microcosm to macrocosm. The realm of divinity and spirit, or the domain of nature, the macrocosm was the fathomless source of human things, transcendent and ultimate in its greatness. Still more, the macrocosm manifested the lawfulness of all creation, the controlling providence that unfolded in the order of the universe.

For the Transcendentalists, as for others, there were practical religious consequences deriving from this world view. First, the theory of correspondence made the universe and spiritual order clearly prior, so that respect and reverence for nature and spirit became cardinal moral requirements. Second, the structural description of correspondence suggested that the way to learn the truth about human life was to look at the universe, taking note of what it was and what rhythms it kept. Third, human life also acquired greater "reality" when grounded on the larger pattern of the cosmos. And fourth, since correspondence taught that the microcosm was simply a small-scale replica of the macrocosm, there could be no radical break between the sacred and profane. All of human life was religious.

These insights yielded directives both for communities and for individuals. Harmony with cosmic law became the great canon for both; mysticism, the aspiration for the individual. Measured against the pattern, the Transcendentalists, even with their individualism, were seekers after communal harmony. Their words and deeds testified to their regard for nature and, beyond it, the moral law and spiritual sources of life. With their rebellion against the traditional ritual forms of Unitarian Christianity, the Transcendentalists were expressing their sense that the sacred could not be cordoned off. Harmony with the cosmos led ultimately, for them, to the world.

Seen in terms of the individual, Transcendentalist religion did not necessarily enjoin public worship in the church. For some Transcendentalists, it seemed nearer the mark to contemplate nature, catching there a glimpse of the spirit that animated all things. It also seemed pointless to struggle against faults and blemishes according to memorable Puritan rule. Rather, one should seek the moral expression that arose from a rightly ordered life without artificial thought or effort. Disorder would always be evident in the lack of mental peace, in the failure of health, in the frenetic quest after fortune, in stepping out of place.

On the other hand, real religion meant living in tune with the divinity within oneself, listening for the answering divinity in nature and spirit. It meant openness to intuitive knowledge, awareness that intuition corresponded to reality outside the self. In short, living in harmony with cosmic law meant cultivating the ground for mysticism. Indeed, the possibility for mystical experience was contained in the idea of correspondence, since correspondence made it possible to collapse space, time, self, and world. For the Transcendentalists, human beings empowered by their divinity could live expansively, learning to control and order their lives and environments.

However, if the world view at the basis of Transcendental harmony and mysticism was correspondence, the kind of correspondence admitted of an important qualification. Unlike a more traditional cosmos, the universe to which the Transcendentalists sought attunement was a world set in motion to a degree and with an intensity that offered a marked contrast to quiet, more contemplative rhythms. Mirroring the rapidity of pace in the nineteenth-century United States, this kinetic vision of correspondence, as articulated by the Transcendentalists, was the new American twist on an old idea. Thus, the Transcendentalist appropriation of correspondence reveals elements taken from each of the sources of Transcendental thought. Puritan and Unitarian concern for moral law; Puritan Platonism, mysticism, and love for introspection; European romanticism; Neoplatonism and the metaphysical movement, especially as mediated in the work of Swedenborg; Eastern religious classics; and American "effervescence" in a frenetic age—all found their place in the understanding of correspondence that the Transcendentalists reflected.

Beyond that, distinctive thought meant distinctive writing. Hence, the Transcendentalists refined for themselves a romantic literary theory, viewing symbol as the revelation of artistic and, ultimately, spiritual vision. As Emerson taught in *Nature,* in a literary version of correspondence, words were signs of natural facts, and natural facts in turn were the emblems of spirit. The full list of Transcendentalist publications would be impossible to discuss here, but it is worth noting at least a few of the contributions.

In fact, the year in which the Transcendental Club first met has been called the annus mirabilis of the movement because, in that remarkable year, so many Transcendentalist writings made their way into print. In 1836 Emerson's *Nature* authoritatively proclaimed the revolution and gospel of the new school; and Alcott published the first volume of his *Conversations with Children on the Gospels,* an account of his experiment in education at the Temple School in Boston. In that year, too, Ripley reviewed James Martineau's *Rationale of Religious Inquiry* in the pages of the Unitarian *Christian Examiner,* creating a controversy because the outspoken reviewer disparaged the usefulness of miracles as Christian evidence. Likewise, Furness published *Remarks on the Four Gospels,* in which he challenged the miraculousness of the resurrection of Jesus, arguing that the supernatural was contained in the natural world. Orestes Brownson published *New Views of Christianity, Society, and the Church,* locating Unitarian history in the context of two warring social systems, the material and the spiritual, with Unitarianism a case of the victory of materialism. Meanwhile, a tract written by Convers Francis, *Christianity as a Purely Internal Principle,* also appeared as a Transcendentalist Christian testament.

The collective character of the Transcendentalist enterprise was apparent in a series of periodicals published by members of the group. The earliest of these, the *Western Messenger,* appeared in Cincinnati in 1835, ostensibly devoted to Unitarian Christianity. With James Freeman Clarke and, later, William Henry Channing among its editors, however, the *Messenger* occupied a central place in the evolution of the Transcendentalist movement until the periodical's demise in 1841. But the *Messenger* was eclipsed in its role as vehicle for Transcendentalist ideas by the *Dial,* which appeared for a four-year span, beginning just nine months before the *Messenger* ended. "Dial" meant a sundial, assuming for the Transcendentalists symbolic and spiritual proportions. Ideas of nature, progress, and correspondence were joined in the title, a hermetic sign for the initiated and a clue to the spiritual reformation that the *Dial* sought to accomplish.

The new periodical published poetry, articles on religious, literary, and social issues, excerpts from spiritual classics, book reviews, and other critical commentaries. Some of Emerson's best poems and lectures were printed there. So, too, was Fuller's article "The Great Lawsuit," which she later developed into *Woman in the Nineteenth Century* (1845). Alcott contributed many of his "Orphic Sayings," while Ripley, Clarke, Parker,

Thoreau, and both Channings also offered material for the journal. Although often condemned or ridiculed, the *Dial* did succeed in mirroring Transcendentalist views and applying them broadly to literature and culture. It is the most enduring collective legacy of Transcendentalism.

Other Transcendentalist periodicals came and went, most of them shorter-lived than the *Dial*. Brownson's *Boston Quarterly Review* (1838–1842) was among them, vocal in its social emphasis and growing further from Transcendentalism with each year of publication. Likewise, Brook Farm's *Harbinger,* originally more or less associated with the movement, became Fourierist, and its links to Transcendentalism grew tenuous at best. An assistant editor of the Fourierist *Harbinger,* the reform-minded William Henry Channing earlier edited the *Present* in New York City from September 1843 to April 1844, while in 1849 Elizabeth Peabody succeeded in producing one number of a periodical she titled *Aesthetic Papers,* and from 1847 to 1850 Parker edited the *Massachusetts Quarterly Review.*

Outside the pages of these periodicals, the Transcendentalists proved to be prolific authors, contributing to other journals and publishing independently. After the appearance of *Nature,* Emerson wrote voluminously, mostly essays and lectures. Alcott, too, continued to publish into his old age, offering collections of aphorisms and conversations. Parker's writings comprised some fifteen volumes in the American Unitarian Association edition (1907–1911), best-known among them his ringing declaration of faith in the sermon "The Transient and Permanent in Christianity" (1841). More slowly and quietly, Thoreau produced expressions of his inner and outer life, his *Walden* (1854), "Civil Disobedience" ("Resistance to Civil Government," 1849), and *A Week on the Concord and Merrimack Rivers* (1849), justly numbered among the classics of American literature. The ambitious Ripley enlisted the aid of his friends for the fourteen-volume *Specimens of Foreign Standard Literature* (1838–1842), a series of translations of French and German works. Fuller, Ellery Channing, Furness, and Very (with Emerson's help), as already noted, published their works; and other Transcendentalists likewise found their way into print.

If the Transcendentalists thought and wrote in distinctive ways, most significant in revealing the extent of their commitment was the fact that they also acted distinctively. First, they experimented with new life-styles and their symbolic encodement in ceremonial forms. Second (and here the record is mixed), they devoted themselves to contemporary efforts for social reform.

The two new life-styles that attracted the Transcendentalists were self-culture and communitarianism. Of the two, self-culture remained the more basic, the fundamental requirement for all. Inherited from the Unitarians but developed further, self-culture, with its emphasis on education, moral development, and creative expression, was predicated on a sense of private integrity. Different from traditional forms of Western mysticism, it shared the mystics' introspectiveness and need for centering. Like the mystics, too, the Transcendentalists sought divinity within themselves, and they understood intimacy with divinity as a radical force revising their lives. Yet, different from traditional mysticism, revision was built on the notion that the God who dwelled within was the God who empowered the ego-directed self to fulfill its capacities and goals.

From this perspective, the experiments with communal living that engaged some of the Transcendentalists were one way to implement the basic task of self-culture. Utopian communities were attractive because they might foster the social conditions in which each reconstituted self would grow in an atmosphere of freedom, support, and trust. Thus it was that George Ripley and those who joined him from 1841 created Brook Farm, while Bronson Alcott and others, on a smaller scale, in 1843 initiated Fruitlands.

The more celebrated and successful Brook Farm began with Ripley's discomfort in his Unitarian ministry. His concern for the people in the deteriorating neighborhood that surrounded his parish blended with his Transcendentalist idealism to suggest an experiment in economic and social democracy. The community that he proposed would support the efforts of its members to engage in reform projects. With these ends in mind, Brook Farm was organized as a joint stock company in which members held the shares and so some proprietary interest. Ripley, who resigned from the ministry, led the community on a farm of 160 acres in West Roxbury, Massachusetts, and to it flocked a series of Transcendentalist notables, most of them frequent visitors rather than members.

With freedom the cardinal rule of the community, members of Brook Farm worked at agriculture, crafts, and light industries and established a highly regarded school. Although some, like Nathaniel Hawthorne, grew less enthusiastic for manual labor as the months passed, for the most part morale was high, with theater and concerts, games and dances, and long conversations. Members endorsed an impressive list of social reforms; speakers addressed the group on a spectrum of issues; and women's rights thrived as female members voted and held office. By 1844, the web of reform activities led the community to become Fourierist, since Ripley had been convinced by the socialist ideas of Charles Fourier through his American disciple Albert Brisbane. Two years later, however, a fire destroyed the nearly completed central "phalanstery," and the community ended in a matter of months.

Despite Ripley's efforts, Emerson had refused to become involved in the community, thinking that the demands of solitary self-culture were too compelling to admit of communal endeavor. Thoreau, likewise, preferred the solitude of Walden Pond (1845–1847). But Parker was close to being a member, visiting several times a week and being visited by a group of Brook Farmers at his regular Sunday services. Fuller, too, liked to hold conversations at the farm; and Alcott visited and spoke but instead of staying founded his own community at Fruitlands, near the town of Harvard, thirty miles from Boston.

During a trip to England in 1842, Alcott had conceived the vision of his community in the context of his growing friendship with the Englishman Charles Lane. It was, indeed, Lane who financed the venture, purchasing the ninety-acre farm where his and Alcott's Transcendentalist ideas of community might be tested. Lane and his young son joined the five members of the Alcott family and a few others for the experiment. As at Brook Farm, individualism was valued, but Alcott in his zeal enacted a series of sweeping prohibitions. The use of meat, alcohol, tea, coffee, and milk was forbidden, as were carrots and potatoes, which did not grow toward the sun. So, too, were the wearing of cotton and woolen garments, both the products of slavery and exploitation: cotton, the slavery of black people, and wool, the slavery of sheep. Coldwater bathing was the rule for the community, which arose and retired with the sun. Meanwhile, Lane tried to introduce celibacy, thus separating Bronson and Abigail Alcott, and this—combined with the poor farm productivity of the community—brought Fruitlands to a swift conclusion.

The experiment had lasted seven months, for that short time a testimony to the absoluteness with which Transcendentalist ideals could be upheld as well as their sometime impracticality. But the enthusiasm and commitment that flowered in the everyday practice of self-culture and communitarian experiment were nourished in more intense moments that, through formal and repeated enactments, ritualized Transcendentalist beliefs. Such ritual moments took a variety of forms: the keeping of private journals (often to be shared), stylized modes of communing with nature, and equally stylized "conversations."

As inheritors of the Puritan tradition of spiritual autobiography and self-examination, the Transcendentalists frequently kept journals, or commonplace books. Emerson, Alcott, Parker, Thoreau, and Fuller all followed the custom, considering journal-keeping a solemn and serious matter. However, unlike their Puritan ancestors, the Transcendentalists distrusted any set pattern for their spiritual development and expected, instead, that their journals would assist in the free unfolding of their inner natures in self-culture. Moreover, the etiquette of sharing private journals suggested the communal dimension of the introspection that the Transcendentalists sought. Paradoxically, though committed to individual freedom, they aimed for meditative community.

Community with nature, too, came through the morning walks in which Emerson, Alcott, and other Transcendentalists delighted. It came through bathing in Walden Pond, as Thoreau did, with studied spiritual discipline. Or it came, as in the case of Parker, through the bouquet of flowers placed in his pulpit by friends when he preached.

Conversation, however, provided the communal act that most clearly fulfilled the conditions for ritual with its public and collective character. In his journal, Emerson confided his religious ideal of conversation as the Pentecostal coming of the spirit, an ideal that apparently took flesh in the meetings of the Transcendental Club. But formal conversations were also conducted by individual Transcendentalists. In 1833 Peabody had offered a series of conversations for the public, repeating the gesture several times in later years. Fuller, too, initiated conversations in Boston from 1839 to 1844. Alcott made conversation the basis of his career as an educator and, as he grew older, traveled extensively to lead discourses.

Although what the Transcendentalists approved most about their conversations was their openness to spontaneity, in fact, the act of coming together to await the spirit was a ritual performance. By means of the rite of conversation, Transcendentalists could attune themselves to one another and to the world. Empowered by their conversations, they could live out their creed in chance and regular everyday encounters. Hence, for the Transcendentalists and for others, ritual led naturally to moral concerns. Already the life-styles of self-culture and communitarianism expressed a moral sensitivity consonant with Transcendentalist belief and ritual practice. But self-actualized persons could not stop with themselves, and so the reform activity of different Transcendentalists unfolded from their religious commitments. Brook Farm, founded in the context of Ripley's social concern, had already signaled the Transcendentalist understanding. Similarly, in their revolt against Unitarianism, the Transcendentalists were taking a stand regarding an established order that, for them, required correction.

Thus, the need to reform the church yielded a series of experimental ministries at the margin of the Unitarian establishment and outside it. In 1836 Brownson had formed the experimental Society for Christian Union and Progress, abolishing pew ownership to further his ministry to the working class and preaching social reform and progress. Clarke founded the Church of the Disciples in 1841 with a broad doctrinal statement, flexible ritual arrangements, and, again, a system of free pews. Parker, after a formal "tea" that verged on a heresy trial and then ostracism by other Unitarians, became, in 1845, the leader of the Twenty-eighth Congregational Society. His preaching at the Boston Melodeon and later the Music Hall drew crowds; and, abolishing the proprietary pew system as well as the regular collection, he eventually presided over the largest congregation in Boston.

William Henry Channing, after a youthful experiment in 1837 as minister to New York City's poor, returned to Brooklyn in 1842 and then, in 1843, to the Christian Union he established in New York City on principles of "Humanity, Wisdom, and Holiness." Later, in Boston in 1846, Channing again worked to apply his principles of church reform in the Religious Union of Associationists, a Fourierist "church" including members from various denominations who all subscribed to the associationist gospel of Universal Unity.

Channing's linkage of Christianity with Fourierist social reform pointed toward the larger focus of Transcendentalist moral effort. Government, economy, education, and the dynamics of the social process all were objects of concern, as different events brought various problems to the fore. The ideals of the Transcendentalists were equality and justice for all; and even the less socially involved among them, like Emerson, were quick to notice when justice had been violated and equality ignored. Emerson, it was true, provided the rationale for the more hesitant who did not plunge headlong into reform activity, arguing that each person must accomplish self-reform before society could be changed. Yet Emerson, the accepted leader of the others, also thought that the reform impulse was intrinsic to human nature. Reluctant though he was, he spoke out on slavery, on Indian removal, on temperance, and on peace.

Similarly, although Thoreau militantly defended the individual against the encroachments of society, his well-known literary exposition of civil disobedience (1849) was preceded by a four-year period during which he abstained from paying his poll tax to the Massachusetts government, which implicitly supported slaveholding. When, in 1846, the Mexican War augured more territory for slaveholders and, at the same time, Massachusetts grew less lenient in its tax collecting, Thoreau spent one memorable night in jail. Perhaps less known, he also worked to help slaves escape to freedom in Canada and in 1859, after John Brown's raid on Harpers Ferry, supported the abolitionist publicly.

Even more active in the antislavery effort and other reform causes was Parker. The Peace Society of Massachusetts, the work of Dorothea Dix for the insane, penal reform, the abolition of capital punishment, the common-school movement of Horace Mann—all received his active endorsement. But Parker's greatest concern was antislavery, and his sermons on the subject were renowned. Like Thoreau, he worked to conceal fugitive slaves and to help them reach Canada. A member of the Vigilance Committee to safeguard fugitives from arrest and return to the South, he roused fellow citizens against the Fugitive Slave Act of 1850. Parker even participated in an abortive effort, in 1854, to free the fugitive Virginia slave Anthony Burns from the courthouse in Boston where he was being held.

In the group that mobbed the courthouse was also Bronson Alcott. An early abolitionist, Alcott was a charter member of the Preliminary Anti-Slavery Society (1830), which two years later became the New England Anti-Slavery Society. And like Thoreau, Alcott was arrested (although never jailed) for refusing to pay his town tax to a slaveholding government. Like Parker, too, enthusiastic for universal reform, Alcott attended meetings of the Convention of Non-resistants, the Convention of the Friends of Universal Reform, the Come-outer Convention, the Groton Convention, and the Chardon Street Convention. In England, he was present at anti–Corn Law conferences, met with Chartists, and mingled with other zealots of reform. Indeed, for Alcott, Fruitlands was an enacted plan for social reform that began with individuals. And Alcott's educational efforts in nontraditional schools challenged the educational establishment of his day, moving beyond Transcendentalism in their social significance.

Ripley's experiments at Brook Farm have already been noted; and even after the community's failure Ripley, who became a writer for Horace Greeley's *New York Tribune,* continued to affirm the values of association on Fourierist principles. Likewise, William Henry Channing, who worked to reform the church, embedded his efforts in his larger concern for the Fourierist reform of society. Meanwhile, Brownson linked himself with Jacksonian democracy, at the same time seeing the main theme of history as the struggle between the classes. His two-part article "The Laboring Classes" (*Boston Quarterly Review,* 1840), a thoroughgoing critique of the social system based on wages, included a call for economic and social equality. Fuller, too, made lasting contributions to reform, mostly in the field of women's rights. Her already noted *Woman in the Nineteenth Century* taught that freedom for women would enable the divine energy to fill nature as

never before. Fuller later traveled to Italy, most probably married the marquese Giovanni Angelo Ossoli, and participated with him in the Italian revolution of 1848–1849.

Hence, these Transcendentalists and others who counted themselves among them moved with the reformers of their times. If human beings possessed divinity within themselves, the Transcendentalists thought that divinity ought to grow unimpeded by external forces. Both the more mystical, like Alcott, and the less mystical, like Parker, could find a connection between their ideals and earnest social action. Emphasizing individual integrity and human freedom, they still found in their beliefs the impetus for action on behalf of society.

An active expression of Transcendentalist beliefs was integral to the movement, as these social-reform efforts and experimental life-styles and rituals suggest. Yet, measured against their evangelical contemporaries, the Transcendentalists were decidedly subdued in proclaiming their gospel. True, their writings were prolific; and Emerson's two volumes of *Essays* (1841 and 1844), including in the first series such classics as "Self-Reliance" and "The Over-Soul," were much admired and loved. But, except for the work of Emerson, the writings of the Transcendentalists never attained a wide circulation in their time. In fact, perhaps the chief means for the contemporary dissemination of their teaching was the lyceum circuit and, especially, the reports of lyceum speeches in local and, sometimes, national newspapers. By the 1840s, some 3,500 to 4,000 communities were participating in the lyceum movement, in a network of town halls where educational lectures were held. A lecturer on the circuit could count on speaking to about 50,000 people in one season, and most of the audience was made up of middle-class people aspiring to learn. In this midcentury precursor of the Chautauqua movement, Emerson became a popular institution. He traveled widely and regularly, often to the Midwest; his lectures attracted admiring crowds; and newspapers duly summarized his speeches.

Other Transcendentalists also used the lyceum to share their views. Parker addressed audiences in Massachusetts, Rhode Island, Maine, Ohio, and even Indianapolis and Chicago. Thoreau, an officer in the Concord lyceum, spoke in Concord and in other New England towns.

Hedge spoke at least in Bangor, Maine, and Francis in Salem, Massachusetts. In a related effort, Alcott from 1848 increasingly offered formal conversations in Boston and, from 1853 to 1882, launched ten conversational tours of the Midwest.

However, because of the nature of the movement, the extent of Transcendentalist influence is difficult to measure. Conversions to Transcendentalism, in the evangelical sense, were impossible, while protestations of freedom and divinity of the self led in centrifugal directions. The pioneering efforts of some Transcendentalists in church reform did point the way for others. Similarly, the Transcendentalists who joined cause with social reformers of their time helped to write an important page in American social history.

In a much more diffuse—and, finally, more effective and lasting—fashion, the Transcendentalists helped sow the ground for a series of other movements in religion and thought. Later nineteenth-century theological liberalism was surely in their debt, as the Transcendentalist remnant gathered in the Free Religious Association (1867) especially testifies. So, too, was the empirical tradition, as evidenced particularly in the religious reflections of William James. Probably most notable, however, was the relationship of Transcendentalism to the metaphysical and meditative traditions. Popularizations of Platonism, Neoplatonism, and Swedenborgianism, as filtered through Transcendentalist rhetoric, helped create the climate that made Christian Science and New Thought attractive religious options. Thus, mental healing became one expression of a divine power latent within each individual. For many who followed harmonial religion in the late nineteenth century and thereafter, material prosperity, with God as all-generous Supply, became another. Indeed, the pursuit of positive thinking and the New Age religions of the late twentieth century are also a heritage of Transcendentalism.

From another perspective, the birth of the conservation movement late in the nineteenth century owed a good deal to the Transcendentalists. John Muir, whose nature writing acquired evangelical and political overtones in a battle to preserve the valley of the Yosemite—launching, in effect, the national park movement—regarded Emerson and Thoreau as mentors. His written response to the Yosemite was filled with the language of religious exaltation, and, like the Transcendentalists, he regarded nature as the emblem of spirit. Hence, the theory of correspondence was given substance outside the metaphysical tradition in his work. In this context, the twentieth-century ecological movement is one more expression of a nature religion that received its first cogent articulation in Transcendentalism.

In sum, the refusal of Transcendentalism to institutionalize itself did not bring about its demise. Rather, it encouraged so widespread a diffusion of Transcendentalist thought and values that they became virtually identical with American culture. In the end, Transcendentalism—despite its pilgrimage to European and Eastern traditions—was an American product. What it took from American culture it gave back in abundance. Twentieth-century American religion is still indebted to its legacy.

BIBLIOGRAPHY

Major works by the Transcendentalists have already been cited in the essay above and are readily available. The following bibliography includes useful contemporary anthologies of Transcendentalist writings, important secondary studies of Transcendentalism pertinent to its religious dimension, and key studies of individual Transcendentalists.

Anthologies

George Hochfield, ed., *Selected Writings of the American Transcendentalists* (1966); Perry Miller, ed., *The Transcendentalists: An Anthology* (1950) and *The American Transcendentalists: Their Prose and Poetry* (1957).

Transcendentalism

Catherine L. Albanese, *Corresponding Motion: Transcendental Religion and the New America* (1977); Paul F. Boller, Jr., *American Transcendentalism, 1830–1860: An Intellectual Inquiry* (1974); Arthur E. Christy, *The Orient in American Transcendentalism: A Study of Emerson, Thoreau, and Alcott* (1932; repr. 1978); George Willis Cooke, *An Historical and Biographical Introduction to Accompany the "Dial,"* 2 vols. (1902; repr. 1961); Octavius Brooks Frothingham, *Transcendentalism in New England: A History* (1876; repr. 1965); Philip F. Gura, *The Wisdom of Words: Language, Theology, and Literature in the New England Renaissance* (1981).

William R. Hutchison, *The Transcendentalist Ministers: Church Reform in the New England Renaissance* (1959; repr. 1965); Nathaniel Kaplan and Thomas Katsaros, *The Origins of American Transcendentalism in Philosophy and Mysticism* (1975);

Alexander Kern, "The Rise of Transcendentalism, 1815–1860," in *Transitions in American Literary History,* Harry Hayden Clark, ed. (1954; repr. 1967); Anne C. Rose, *Transcendentalism as a Social Movement, 1830–1850* (1981); Herbert W. Schneider, "The Transcendental Temper," in *A History of American Philosophy* (1946; 1963).

Transcendentalists

Gay Wilson Allen, *Waldo Emerson: A Biography* (1981); Bell Gale Chevigny, *The Woman and the Myth: Margaret Fuller's Life and Writings* (1976); Henry Steele Commager, *Theodore Parker* (1936; 1947; repr., with new introduction, 1960); Charles Crowe, *George Ripley: Transcendentalist and Utopian Socialist* (1967); Frederick C. Dahlstrand, *Amos Bronson Alcott: An Intellectual Biography* (1982); Walter Harding, *The Days of Henry Thoreau* (1965; rev. 1982).

Ralph L. Rusk, *The Life of Ralph Waldo Emerson* (1949; repr. 1967); Odell Shepard, *Pedlar's Progress: The Life of Bronson Alcott* (1937; repr. 1968); Ronald Vale Wells, "Frederic Henry Hedge, 'Prophet of Liberal Christianity,' " in *Three Christian Transcendentalists: James Marsh, Caleb Sprague Henry, Frederic Henry Hedge* (1943; repr. 1972); William J. Wolf, *Thoreau: Mystic, Prophet, Ecologist* (1974).

[*See also* BUDDHISM; HINDUISM; *and* UNITARIANISM AND UNIVERSALISM.]

LIBERALISM

William McGuire King

THE defining mark of liberalism in the "liberal era" of American Protestantism (1875–1935) was neither creed nor precept. Its most pronounced feature was a spirit of intellectual adventurousness. At the height of his distinguished preaching career, George A. Gordon (1853–1929) explained to divinity students at Yale the theological situation they would face in their ministry. "There is still only the promise of a theology to replace that which has gone," he remarked. But they should grasp that promise, for it was "fitted to gladden the Christian heart and to stimulate able and honest men everywhere to do what may be done to carry the prophecy to fulfillment" (*Ultimate Conceptions of Faith,* p. 75). What made such liberal hope modern was its conviction that religious truth "can only be attained through a never-ending process of criticism and experiment" (D. D. Williams, *The Andover Liberals,* p. 64). What made it religious was its confidence that such truth existed.

By the beginning of the twentieth century the liberal spirit of criticism and experiment had permeated all the traditional centers of American Protestantism and almost half the Protestant seminaries in the country (W. R. Hutchison, ed., *American Protestant Thought: The Liberal Era,* p. 11). Rather than spawning new denominational alignments, modern liberalism fostered an ecumenical community of preachers, scholars, and churchmen intent on working within traditional structures. Congregationalists, Presbyterians, Baptists, Methodists, Episcopalians, Unitarians, and Disciples were all well represented in liberal ranks. The popularity of the liberal style within traditionally evangelical denominations may seem surprising, but it reflected in part the experiential bent of American piety, in part the imposing intellectual issues confronting urban America's new middle class, and in part the religious yearnings of the age.

These factors shaped the liberal conception of theology and gave liberal theologians a common intellectual perspective, despite intramural squabbles over method. Victorian Americans characteristically sought truths that seemed grounded in everyday realities—in the decisions, experiences, and commitments of strenuous living. Religious liberals accepted the principle that theological truths must also emanate from the common realities of human existence and religious commitment. "A religion that is not passionate is simply not worth considering," wrote Henry Nelson Wieman during the later era of Babe Ruth and Lou Gehrig. "Therefore, I say, we need more sandlot religion" (in R. C. Miller, *The American Spirit in Theology,* p. 92). Theology's task was to unpack and clarify the data of sandlot religion. Liberals agreed that shoring up traditional doctrines and theological propositions through appeals to religious authority or abstract argumentation no longer sufficed. Not only had such methods lost their hold on the modern mind, but they severed theology from its roots—personal encounter with the present reality of God.

In modern liberal theology, therefore, the starting point for theological reflection had shifted. Knowledge of God was no longer to be found in doctrinal systems per se, but in the concrete experience of God's reality to which all doctrine should point. Liberals seldom bothered with rational proofs for God's existence, although they often provided rational grounds for such belief. Their starting point was rather the liberal religious spirit itself: the conviction that God's creative power and potency manifest themselves in human experience and become known in the enhancement and transformation of life. The liberals' God revealed himself as "immanent presence and palpitating power in the universe" (*Andover Review*, 1890, p. 300). Although liberals tended to explicate such power in ethical terms, their understanding of "ethical" was existential rather than narrowly moralistic. "Faith," maintained Newman Smyth, is "a relation of the whole man . . . to the whole God" (*Princeton Review*, 1882, p. 299). Knowledge of God emerged from encounter with the ultimate power at work in the universe, from encounter bringing new self-understanding, reconciliation, recuperation, and moral freedom. Such knowledge was not an intellectual or abstract matter, but an experience triggering human capacities for renewal and love.

The liberal view of revelation had both universal and specifically Christian components. Liberals wanted to correlate the two sources of knowledge without reducing one to the other. How to do so was one of the difficult methodological issues in liberalism, yet liberal theologians were convinced that theology could discover and articulate the nature of this experience of God. In the minds of liberal theologians, theology represented a form of power—dispelling the mists of theological rationalism, illuminating the deepest dimensions of human experience, and ushering humanity again into the presence of the living God. Theology had a mission. Perhaps that was why liberal theologians of this generation spoke so ebulliently of "the theological renaissance of the nineteenth century" and pursued so earnestly the intellectual beckonings of the coming age.

THE DEVELOPMENT OF EVANGELICAL LIBERALISM, 1875–1900

Despite the temptation today to accuse liberalism of remoteness from popular concerns, the first stirrings of modern liberalism actually came from the pulpit, not the academy. Liberalism did not arise primarily as a response to the intellectual challenges of modern science; it began as a working out of the changing forms of piety and religious sentiment of the Victorian era. The origins of liberal theology, Henry Churchill King explained, "are to be found in a deepening of the Christian spirit itself, and the *influence of the new intellectual, moral, and spiritual* world in which we live and upon which this spirit has been working" (in W. R. Miller, ed., *Contemporary American Protestant Thought, 1900–1970*, p. 8). Theological liberalism expressed one facet of the Victorian generation's search for a broader insight into Christianity. It was a generation for whom "religious experience of a different type emerged, and liberal theology was its interpretation" (Williams, p. 156).

In the 1870s sensitivity to "this new atmosphere, this new world," as King called it, was most acutely felt by the younger group of preachers. Many experienced a sense of urgency about adapting Christian theology to the changing religious needs of their congregations, composed of the new Protestant middle class—affluent and earnest. The outstanding liberals of this period were preachers: Henry Ward Beecher, Phillips Brooks, David Swing, Theodore Munger, Newman Smyth, George A. Gordon, Washington Gladden, Lyman Abbott, and William Newton Clarke.

Not until the 1880s did the liberal spirit begin penetrating existing evangelical seminaries, and then it did so largely under pressure from restless divinity students and from faculty recruited out of liberal pulpits. John Wright Buckham recalled his student years at the Andover Theological Seminary as "a shrine in which to gain the historic sense and feel the spirit of the staunch New England Puritanism, about to pass away." The young seminarians rallied around the newer, more liberal members of the faculty, knowing "that these men were fighting for liberty, not for themselves alone, but for the ministry. They assumed heroic proportions to us" (in V. Ferm, ed., *Contemporary American Theology*, vol. 1, p. 87).

Perhaps the first major achievement of liberalism was the creation of a new style of parish ministry. Liberalism was preeminently a pastoral theology. Liberal preachers emphasized Christianity's support for the welfare and aspirations of the total human community:

> The great task of the minister is to give the people an abiding sense of moral and spiritual values, to make them realize what is worth while. It is to give them some dominating conception of life and its meaning. It is to furnish some gen-

eral standards that may reconcile and unify the scattered and conflicting insights of our complex and hurried civilization.

(W. H. P. Faunce, *The Educational Ideal in the Ministry*, p. 24)

As counselor and friend, theological seer and social critic, the liberal preacher found a new role for the pulpit in American culture.

The popularity of the liberal pulpit demonstrated the changing religious sentiments of middle-class evangelical Americans, a change representing something broader and more pervasive in scope than a "revolt against Calvinism." It was a reaction against the increasingly rationalistic spirit of orthodoxy and the increasingly formalistic spirit of revivalism. For many Americans both had become remote from the practical affairs of life, and each seemed unduly legalistic in its view of God. According to Henry Ward Beecher, the old theology had not died; it was simply ebbing with the tides of the times. "If I thought God stood at the door where men go out of life," he exclaimed, "ready to see them down to eternal punishment, my soul would cry out: 'Let there be no God.' My instincts would say: 'Annihilate him!' " (in W. Hudson, *The Great Tradition of the American Churches*, p. 171).

Liberalism was thus the offspring of the changed religious imagination of the age. The liberal spirit emphasized the everyday reality of God's grace. It felt "at home" in the universe, as the Christian spirit had seldom felt before. Instead of sharp lines between the sacred and the secular, between the realms of grace and nature, the liberal imagination perceived continuity. It enlarged the idea of the sacred until the most commonplace dimensions of experience had been embraced. "Utterly swept out of our thought must be any old contradiction between the graces of the gospel and the natural affections," declared Phillips Brooks. "The natural affections reach upward and when they find the God who has been in them from the beginning, then they are the Christian graces" (Hudson, p. 164). Rather than being secularists and theological minimalists, the evangelical liberals were theological maximalists and expansionists.

Theologically, the liberal emphasis on continuity represented a repudiation of supernaturalism. God was not to be found where natural explanations and mundane experience left off.

Such a doctrine of God, liberals believed, merely pushed God farther and farther into the woodwork of modern life. The theology of the day, remarked Henry Churchill King, "is quite unwilling to take its stand on gaps." Theology must "trace the process of God's working" in everyday life, thus replacing the God of the gaps with "the enlarged conception of God in his immanence in the world" (in W. R. Miller, ed., pp. 20–21).

The liberal insistence on continuity and immanence appealed to the sentimental longings of Victorian America. The popular Chautauqua Institute in southwestern New York State, for example, was founded in 1874 by Evangelicals dissatisfied with the prevailing camp-meeting piety of revivalism. Although originally founded as a summer institute for the training of Sunday school teachers, the Chautauqua Institute quickly developed into a national forum for educating the public on trends in the sciences and the humanities, for advancing the fine arts, and for airing issues of immediate political and social concern. It soon became a home for budding religious liberals (including several leaders, like William Rainey Harper and George Edgar Vincent, later associated with the reorganization of the University of Chicago). The Chautauqua spirit emphasized education, inspiration, fellowship, and social service, believing that "things secular are under God's governance and are full of divine meanings" (T. Morrison, *Chautauqua*, p. 47). This attitude did not express complacency so much as a desire to see all of life, in George Gordon's phrase, "under the shadow of an Infinite Name." It expressed the conviction of a generation that viewed itself "living and dying in the heart of an enfolding presence," certain that the mind of Christ was "the secret moulding energy of our entire civilization" (*The Christ of To-Day*, pp. 50–51).

As for theological orthodoxy, liberal attacks on its rationalistic methods reflected the legacy of Horace Bushnell and Ralph Waldo Emerson, as well as Friedrich Schleiermacher, Samuel Taylor Coleridge, Frederick Denison Maurice, and Frederick William Robertson. Liberal attacks were based on a critical view of religious language, a kind of linguistic relativism that was dubious about the capacity of language to express religious experience. For Bushnell language was at best a pointer to the truths of experience, for language always distorted the reality to which it referred ("Preliminary Dissertation on the Nature of Language," in *God in Christ*, 1849). "The Gospel," explained Bushnell at the installation of Washington Gladden at North Adams, Massachusetts, "must get expression not through tongues and propositional wisdom, and the clatter of much argument, but through living persons, seen in all the phases of the better life they live" (in F. H. Foster, *The Modern Movement in American Theology*, p. 60). Poetic statements and paradoxical forms of expression might be more accurate barometers of truth than literal propositions. Theological rationalism restricted truth by abstracting from experience, whereas poetry drove the mind back to the heart of experience. Therefore, not only were systems of doctrine irrelevant to genuine religious knowledge, they possibly obscured and falsified the finespun quality of reality. "The present restlessness in the world of theological thought," wrote Theodore Munger, "is due largely to the fact that the teachings of literature have prevailed over the teachings of the systems of theology. One covers the breadth of human life, the others travel a dull round in a small world of their own creation; they no longer interest men" (*The Freedom of Faith*, p. 30).

Carried to extremes, such linguistic relativism could undermine all confidence in the theological enterprise and vitiate theological discourse altogether. But that was not the liberal intent, though the history of liberalism could be written in terms of a response to the trammels of relativism. The liberal intent was to restore experience to a place of priority in theological reflection and to gain for theology a flexibility and freedom of expression against the rigors of theological rationalism. "Each age," claimed Henry Churchill King, "must be its own interpreter in spiritual things" (in W. Miller, ed., p. 15). Theology was not to build for itself an intellectual empire but to direct attention away from itself to the reality of God known in the processes of everyday living. Theology, wrote Newman Smyth, is "to seek and to find reality" (in J. W. Buckham, *Progressive Religious Thought in America*, p. 262). It was shaped by "the logic of life," determined by the premises and syllogisms found "in daily existence, in the struggles and conflicts and contradictions of this struggling and contradictory world," explained Theodore Munger. The workshop of theology must be the "actual life of men in the world" (*The Freedom of Faith*, pp. 28, 34–35). It was there that God's "moulding energy" revealed itself.

FIRST STIRRINGS

The first rumblings of controversy in the evangelical churches came early in the 1870s, and centered on the demand for greater pulpit freedom. As early as 1871 Henry Ward Beecher was warning future preachers to "make their theological systems conform to facts as they are" and to "recognize what men are studying" if they wished to retain the respect of moderns. "The providence of God," he proclaimed, "is rolling forward in a spirit of investigation that Christian ministers must meet and join. . . . You cannot go back and become apostles of the dead past, drivelling after ceremonies, and letting the world do the thinking and studying" (in Hutchison, ed., pp. 43–44).

The 1874 trial of David Swing, a popular Presbyterian preacher in Chicago, demonstrated the growing candor and strength of the liberal movement. Swing was charged with violating the standards of the Westminster Confession, but the fundamental issue was Swing's attack on traditional modes of theological thinking. His acceptance of the relativity of creedal statements angered defenders of orthodoxy. At the peak of tensions Swing delivered a counterblow in a sermon entitled "A Religion of Words." The corruption of Christianity began, he asserted, when Christianity was equated with "the propositions to which one was willing to subscribe." In every theological dark age "it was words, words, words, and death everywhere" (Hutchison, p. 48). Although acquitted by the local presbytery, Swing chose to leave his denomination and preach to even larger interdenominational audiences.

Swing's trial differed from previous ones in that Swing declined to defend himself on orthodox grounds. He explicitly scorned the rationalistic methods of orthodoxy, asserted the autonomy of modern theology, and even resorted to ridicule. "To the teachings of Calvin and Luther," he remarked, Christianity "adds the teachings of the Saviour as an important supplement" (Hutchison, pp. 53–54). The Swing trial indicated just how far public opinion had shifted in liberal favor and showed that a bond of solidarity had been forged among liberal advocates. A new party had emerged. Both Washington Gladden, editor of the *Independent,* and Beecher, editor of the *Christian Union,* rallied to Swing's defense. During Swing's trial, Beecher roared from his pulpit that preachers must have "liberty of judgment, liberty of interpretation, and liberty of action, within the sphere of Christ-likeness or of the Christ-spirit; and no man has a right to judge another in regard to his usages, his ordinances, his forms of church organization, and his methods of instruction" (*Plymouth Pulpit: Sermons,* vol. 2, p. 196).

Shortly thereafter, a storm brewed in Congregationalist circles over the doctrine of eternal punishment. In 1876 the Reverend James Whiton published a book claiming that the Bible "does not assert the absolute endlessness of [God's] punishment." The following year a Congregational church refused to install James Merriam because he had denied the eternal punishment of the wicked. An even greater furor arose when Theodore Munger was installed at North Adams, Massachusetts, despite stating that "I utterly reject the opinion that the great masses of mankind are subjected to endless pains in the future world" (in Foster, p 24). Munger's personal beliefs outraged critics less than his claim that the doctrine of hell was an "opinion." The entire controversy revealed the strong influence of English liberalism, for Frederick Denison Maurice had already reinterpreted the Christian doctrine of hell in largely existential terms. The debate culminated in the refusal of the Board of Visitors of the Andover Theological Seminary to approve the appointment of Newman Smyth as Abbott Professor of Christian Theology because Smyth countenanced the possibility of salvation after death for those not saved in this life.

The argument over Christian eschatology continued for many years, especially in the context of Protestant missionary work (see Hutchison, *The Modernist Impulse in American Protestantism,* pp. 136–137). Yet liberals preferred not to dwell on it. Smyth got some measure of satisfaction by publishing a translation of Isaac Dorner's universalistic reformulation of Christian eschatology (*Dorner on the Future State,* 1883), but in general the liberals seemed somewhat embarrassed by the indelicacy of the issue. They should not have been, for the debate concerning the doctrine of

hell was hardly a peripheral one. "It strikes right into the heart of the question of man's freedom and responsibility, his awareness of good and evil and the perilousness of his choosing between them, and it inevitably reflects on the nature and character of God" (Geoffrey Rowell, *Hell and the Victorians,* pp. 216–17). The doctrine of endless punishment, so critical to orthodox Christianity, stood at loggerheads with the liberal doctrine of God as parental, forgiving spirit and as creative energy working for the fulfillment of the divine purpose for humanity. Rather than fight over traditional doctrines, however, American liberals decided to move boldly in new directions.

By the end of the 1870s liberals were ready to begin a broader reconstruction of Christian theology in the light of the intellectual currents of the age. Newman Smyth published three seminal statements of the "New Theology": *The Religious Feeling* (1877), *Old Faiths in New Light* (1879), and *The Orthodox Theology of Today* (1881), each reflecting Smyth's thorough familiarity with the German liberal theology of Schleiermacher, Dorner, and Rudolf Hermann Lotze. Shortly thereafter, two excellent summaries appeared: Theodore Munger's essay "The New Theology," in *The Freedom of Faith* (1883), and A. V. G. Allen's article "The Theological Renaissance of the Nineteenth Century," in the *Princeton Review* (November 1882 and January 1883). In *The Continuity of Christian Thought* (1884) Allen tried to put the New Theology into the context of church history and to show its correlation with patristic thought. Various specialized aspects of the New Theology, including questions of eschatology, were covered with the publication of *Progressive Orthodoxy* (1885) by members of the faculty at the Andover Theological Seminary, for which five of them were brought to trial by Andover's Board of Visitors (the suit was eventually withdrawn after considerable controversy).

By the turn of the century more mature statements appeared. Lewis Stearns reviewed the entire theological situation in *Present-Day Theology* (1893), as did Henry Churchill King in "Reconstruction in Theology" (reprinted in W. Miller, ed., *Contemporary American Protestant Thought, 1900–1970,* pp. 7–36). William Newton Clarke presented the first systematic statement of liberal theology in *An Outline of Christian Theology* (1898). This became a standard textbook in liberal seminaries until it was supplemented by William Adams Brown's *Christian Theology in Outline* (1906). Brown's *The Essence of Christianity* (1902) explained the European roots of liberal theology, and Arthur Cushman McGiffert's *The Rise of Modern Religious Ideas* (1915) traced the entire development of the liberal movement in the nineteenth century. Finally, Shailer Mathews made an important restatement of liberal principles from the point of view of the "socio-historical" method in *The Faith of Modernism* (1924).

THEOLOGY, BIBLICAL CRITICISM, AND SCIENCE

The events of the 1870s suggest that liberalism did not simply arise as a response to the challenge of modern science. To be sure, such a challenge was never far in the background, but in general the liberals did not give extensive attention to the relationship of theology and science until after the initial statements of the New Theology had appeared. By that time liberals had become confident in their ability to assimilate the findings of natural science and historical criticism.

Somewhat naively, perhaps, American liberals viewed the development of the sciences as a theological boon. Liberals did not perceive a tension between science and religion but saw instead an opportunity for Christian theology to assume a place alongside modern science in reconstructing the story of human development. Rather than blaming modern science for endangering the credibility of Christianity, liberals tended to blame conservatives. The literalism, supernatural rationalism, and authoritarianism of conservative theology seemed on trial, and liberals could welcome science as an ally in its apologetical arsenal.

By the 1880s a tradition of spending at least a year or two in German universities had become customary among American liberal scholars. While American liberals felt a strong sense of kinship with English liberals (like Frederick Denison Maurice, Frederick William Robertson, and Andrew M. Fairbairn), they seemed to turn to Germany when the theological going got really tough (see Hutchison, *The Modernist Impulse in American Protestantism*, pp. 84–87, 122–132). In late nineteenth-century German theology Fried-

rich Schleiermacher's emphasis on religious experience was being supplemented by the metaphysics of Rudolf Lotze, the Christology of Isaac Dorner, the ethics of Richard Rothe, the method of Albrecht Ritschl, and the historical scholarship of Adolf von Harnack.

Of the two primary challenges to traditional theology—Darwinism and the historical criticism of the Bible—the latter demanded more urgent consideration than did Darwinism. Liberals devoted far more attention to the problem of interpreting biblical history than they did to the problem of natural history. Indeed, when liberals spoke of the challenge of modern science to theology, they were speaking as much of historical science as of Darwinism. Newman Smyth's *Old Faiths in New Light* (1879), one of the earliest and most significant attempts to establish a rapprochement between science and theology, devoted four to five times as much space to historical issues as it did to natural science—despite Smyth's keen personal interest in biology. William Jewett Tucker, president of Dartmouth College, testified in his autobiography that the application of scientific standards to biblical history "awakened more concern, and stirred more bitterness, than the new hypothesis regarding the origin of man" (*My Generation*, p. 6).

As early as 1878 Phillips Brooks dared to defend from his pulpit the methods of the New Theology, especially "the growing freedom of thought about the Bible." "The world," he declared, "will never go back again to the old ideas of verbal inspiration" (in A. V. G. Allen, *Life and Letters of Phillips Brooks*, p. 503). As Theodore Munger put it, the Bible had become for liberals "an ever-opening book" (*The Freedom of Faith*, p. 21). Liberal repudiation of orthodox biblical hermeneutics thus preceded the introduction of critical methods, rather than vice versa. Thank goodness, exclaimed Smyth, "that with us the Word of God is not bound" (in Foster, *The Modern Movement in American Theology*, p. 35).

During the 1880s Smyth and the Union Theological Seminary biblical scholar Charles Briggs led the public defense of the new methods of biblical study. Neither was particularly restrained in his attack upon "the theological demagogue," as Smyth called him, who "passes through the Bible and history in the same blind, partisan way" and "casts his drag-net over the Scriptures, to gather—it matters not from what part—proof-texts for his favorite dogma" (*Old Faiths in New Light*, p. 23). The authority of the Bible is actually weakened, he thought, if it is defended "as an infallible treatise of morals and divinity, of equal inspiration and authority throughout, finished and accurate in every sentence and part." To put the matter bluntly, "the Bible is not the Koran" and Christians had better know the difference. Charles Briggs was even more outspoken than Smyth in asserting the cultural relativity of biblical language and concepts. This relativity made scientific, historical criticism all the more necessary. "Every catechism and confession of faith," wrote Briggs in his first major work, *Biblical Study* (1883), "will in time become obsolete and powerless.... Each age has its own peculiar work and needs." For Briggs, theology could be satisfied with a Bible that "gives us the *material* for all ages, and leaves to man the noble task of shaping the material so as to meet the wants of his own time" (in Hutchison, *The Modernist Impulse*, p. 92).

Such statements did not sound so relativistic to the liberals of the late nineteenth century as they sound today. While using the scientific methods of research and reconstruction, liberals also read into their historical materials a philosophy of development that restored meaning and order to historical data. The "historicism" that characterized theological liberalism was not an all-out relativism but a belief that "historical process has its own meaning," discoverable through the joint efforts of science and theology (Hutchison, ed., *American Protestant Thought: The Liberal Era*, p. 69). Liberals thus viewed history as if it were personal experience writ large and found in it "a complex pattern with unique meaning." Apparently they had replaced the teleological argument based on the design of nature with one drawn from historical design. This shift in paradigm, as Stow Persons has pointed out, was distinctively modern in outlook, a product of "transferring the source of religious authority from nature to history" ("Religion and Modernity," in J. W. Smith and A. L. Jamison, eds., *The Shaping of American Religion*, p. 383).

Historical science seemed to promise a way to unravel the complexities of religious experience and explicate the meaning of revelation. Historical reconstruction could disclose the pattern of meaning hidden in events, which in turn would reveal the gradual unfolding of religious revelation, showing how God adapted and accommodated himself to the developing intellectual and ethical capacities of human cultures. The key was the evolutionary model (see Smyth, *Old Faiths in New Light*, p. 16). Liberals regarded evolution not as random variation but as purposive adaptation in accordance with strict sets of laws and principles of design. Smyth and the Andover liberals used the term "progressive orthodoxy" to refer to this developmental model of revelation. It seemed to enable them to avoid the perils of cultural relativism and interpretive subjectivism without returning to the rigid theological schemes of orthodoxy. Historical science thus seemed to come to theology's aid by disclosing the abiding truths of experience veiled behind ever-changing cultural forms.

Use of the developmental model of knowledge clearly implied a changed understanding of the meaning of revelation in liberal thought. The Bible became a record of revelatory experiences whose authority lay in its ability to direct human attention to the personal experience of God in this age. Knowledge of God was experiential, not propositional; thus the Bible was merely a tool—an instrument or means making the revelatory event possible—not a substitute for revelation. "The Bible itself is an expression of experience," wrote William Newton Clarke. "The value of the Scriptures in keeping the experience true is beyond all estimation; and yet to think that Christianity would have perished from the world if there had been no Scriptures is to overlook its living power, as well as the teaching of its early history." The authority of Scripture was not monolithic and infallible. It did not reside in "minute accuracy of statement," but in "the living and effective conveyance of truth concerning God and Man" (*Outline of Christian Theology*, pp. 18, 36; see also Washington Gladden, "How Much is the Bible Worth?" in *Who Wrote the Bible?*, pp. 351–381).

Liberals carried into the debate over Darwinism the same developmental model used to justify the progressive interpretation of the Bible. Having already abandoned biblical literalism and the conservative view of revelation, liberals were not so obviously threatened by the new findings of natural science as were the defenders of Christian orthodoxy. Perhaps that was why liberals did not feel any great sense of urgency about coming to terms with Darwin. At the end of the century, Henry Churchill King could remark that in treating the influence of natural science on theology, "it is easy to overestimate the importance of this relation and the extent of this influence; and both are often overestimated, I believe" (in W. Miller, ed., p. 17). While embracing the concept of evolution, liberals neither wholeheartedly accepted nor rejected the specific theories of Darwin. Evolutionary thought seemed to support the liberal rejection of supernaturalism. It was not natural evolution per se, but rather Darwin's theory of natural selection that caused some consternation in the liberal camp (see J. Moore, *The Post-Darwinian Controversies,* pp. 217–251). Natural selection undercut the teleological explanation of nature, permitted a purely naturalistic worldview, and raised doubts about the credibility of liberal faith in the beneficence of the natural order.

Rather than meeting the challenge of Darwinism head on, liberals tried to assimilate Darwin's findings to their own developmental model. In essence they tried to read historical design into the natural history of the world. For some—like Henry Ward Beecher, Lyman Abbott, John Bascom, Joseph LeConte, John Fiske, Minot Savage, and Henry Drummond—Herbert Spencer's cosmic philosophy of development provided the key to assimilation.

Many important theological liberals, however —like Newman Smyth, Borden Bowne, and Henry Churchill King—turned away from Spencer and his theories of the universal reign of impersonal law. German idealism, especially as modified by the teleological metaphysics of Rudolf Hermann Lotze, provided liberals with a way to accept naturalistic hypotheses while modifying their implications. Lotze recognized the validity of naturalistic descriptions of phenomena, but he also denied that such descriptions sufficed as causal explanations. Naturalistic descriptions had a residue of incompleteness that failed to explain the inner relatedness of phenomena. According to Lotze, the laws governing natural phenomena, which the theologian must respect as much as the scientist, were not to be interpreted in purely impersonal and mechanistic terms. They were rather the aggregate or abstract result of concrete purpose, directions, and creative interactions present in every natural event, which together pointed toward an ultimate harmony in the order of events. In Lot-

zean terms evolution disclosed a dual principle of causation in the natural world, events being determined in terms of both external and internal relations. Even natural law was not absolute in its operation, thought Lotze, for science itself revealed elements of natural spontaneity and freedom, suggesting a dimension of creativity and novelty in the evolutionary process. One was thus entitled to speak of purpose and direction in nature. Indeed, the duality between naturalism and religion was only apparent; philosophy (or theology) also reflected upon the data of experience and entered into a dialogue with the natural scientist (see P. Kuntz, ed., *Lotze's System of Philosophy*).

DISTINCTIVE THEOLOGICAL EMPHASES

How did theological liberals interpret the meaning of the Christian tradition and its relation to religious experience? In negative terms they explicitly rejected the Augustinian presuppositions that had dominated Western theology. "It is not Christianity in itself which is today obnoxious to serious men," wrote A. V. G. Allen, "but a Latinized Christianity" (in Hutchison, ed., *American Protestant Thought: The Liberal Era,* p. 62). In the liberal view this Latinized Christianity was guilty of metaphysical dualism, contrasting natural grace with supernatural, the created world with the reality of God. The result, liberals believed, was a doctrine of God in which God transcended the temporality of existence and a doctrine of salvation in which the total depravity of human nature could be remedied only by the "alien" character of divine intervention. Liberals found it easy to dismiss such views as part of the pessimistic cultural baggage of late antiquity, which the West had been toting around for too long. The doctrines of Augustine and Western orthodoxy, claimed Theodore Munger, "are the reflections of the social conditions in which they were formulated" (*The Freedom of Faith,* p. 21). Since liberals were quite explicit in their repudiation of Augustinianism, it probably begs the question to accuse them of ignoring the doctrine of original sin. They did not so much ignore it as question whether it must be integral to Christian theology.

Believing that Augustinianism need not be

normative for theology, liberals looked to the incarnational theology of the ancient Greek fathers for precedents to support their own claims. "The Greek theologians may be to us," thought Allen, "our emancipators from false conceptions, our guides to a more spiritual, more intellectual, more comprehensive interpretation of the Christian faith, than the church has known since the German races . . . accepted a Latinized Christianity in place of the original divine revelation" (in Hutchison, ed., *American Protestant Thought: The Liberal Era*, p. 67). What appealed to Allen and his cohorts was a synergistic understanding of grace in Greek theology, in which the human and divine wills worked together freely, and a patristic conception of salvation as the restoration and fulfillment of created nature.

Even more important, however, was the ancient conception of Christ as the *Logos*, the principle of intelligibility embedded within nature and universal experience. In Christian experience, explained Newman Smyth, "we find that there are facts and laws of nature, as well as groupings of events in history, of which Jesus Christ is the centre and harmony" (*Old Faiths in New Light*, p. 287). Liberals spoke of the cosmic Christ, in whom the rationality and meaning of the world cohere. "Our whole thought of God and man," proclaimed George Gordon, "our entire working philosophy of life; our modes of intellectual vision, types of feeling, habits of will; our instinctive, customary, rational, emotional, institutional, and social existence,—is everywhere encompassed and interpenetrated by Christ" (in Foster, p. 114). Liberals therefore viewed the doctrine of salvation in patristic terms as the restoration and fulfillment of nature. That restoration was accomplished in the revelation of "the second Man, the Lord from heaven," wrote Smyth. "The Word made flesh," he insisted, "is the utmost gift of God in the creation." Christ, the *Logos*, is "the last conceivable, perfect, and final self-impartation of God"; he is "the divine creative process, ever advancing to more perfect work" (*Old Faiths in New Light*, p. 279). For Theodore Munger, too, human life made little sense unless it was apprehended in the light of Christ's victorious cosmic rulership. "If it is a fallen world, it is also a redeemed world; if it is a lost world, it is also a saved world; the Christ is no less to it than Adam; the divine humanity is no smaller than the Adamic humanity; the Spirit is

as powerful and as universal as sin" (*The Freedom of Faith*, p. 23).

These liberal motifs are often characterized as Christocentric. The term "Christomorphic" may, however, be slightly more accurate, Christ being the form in which God makes himself known in human experience (see B. Gerrish, *A Prince of the Church: Schleiermacher and the Beginnings of Modern Theology*, pp. 53–54). Technically speaking, liberal theology did not take Christology as its exclusive starting point. Universal religious experience was also an essential element in the knowledge of God; science and history in their own ways testified to the reality of God; and even the biblical proclamation of Christ had to be placed within the parameters established by historical methods of interpretation. Christ represented the principle of coherence that unified and rendered intelligible these disparate experiences and fields of knowledge. Christ was the form by which the reality of God and the nature of human experience could be identified. The most systematic exposition of this Christomorphic method was made by the Oxford don A. M. Fairbairn, whose *The Place of Jesus Christ in Modern Theology* (1893) became a classic in American liberal circles.

According to liberalism, Christ and his kingdom of sacrificial love formed the *telos* of all creation. The first cause of creation, declared Smyth, was "the self-imparting energy of love . . . by which [God] really gives of his own life, places something over against himself with which he enters into relations" (*Old Faiths in New Light*, pp. 278–79). Had there been no Fall, had sin not spoiled the creation, suggested Smyth, the incarnation of Christ would have occurred anyway, for "the whole creation is first for Christ, who is then for the whole world" and "God's love would still have finished its perfect work" (pp. 284–85).

Sin, in liberal thought, represented one's estrangement from Christ, from the purpose and end of one's created nature. Liberals viewed the human will, not human creatureliness, as the source of this estrangement. "Sin cannot be adequately explained as the dominion of the body over the spirit," wrote William Newton Clarke in his profoundly influential *Outline of Christian Theology*. Neither could sin be explained "as a mere incident of growth." Sin resided "in the spirit of man," and "the deepest sin is not sin of passion, but sin of will." Such sins of the spirit, emphasized Clarke, were far more insidious than sins of the flesh; "for the spirit has subtle and dangerous sins of its own, in the life that lies above the realm of the brute. The higher part of man has capabilities of moral evil far greater than the brute element ever possessed." It was this wrong spirit, this misdirection of will, and not human passion that "instantly alienates a man from God and from humanity, and places him in a false position toward both, and toward himself" (pp. 231–36).

According to Clarke, sin "is in the human race" and "has tainted that continuous stream of life we call humanity," despite Christ's presence in nature and history. Depravity persists "through transmission and social influences," and "it is the nature of this process to continue indefinitely." Rather than being wide-eyed optimists, most liberals would have agreed with Clarke that the "double flow of good and evil in the common stream of life . . . casts no doubt upon the persistence of evil in the race." Moral progress was certainly possible, given Christ's rulership; but even moral progress was circumscribed by inherent limitations. Old evils might fade, "but the new and better conditions that follow develop new evils of their own." All human history testified to "that central alienation of man from God and from his brothers in which sin consists" (pp. 239–45). The persistence of evil, Smyth maintained, indicated that Christ's world was an "unfinished world," and "the evidences are daily pressed home to our hearts of the incompleteness of the present visible order of existence." Indeed, it was the nature of Christianity "to cherish the hope that the process of God's creative work is not ended, its promise and potency not exhausted in the present visible system of things" (*Old Faiths in New Light,* pp. 291–93).

Liberals thus insisted that the Christian doctrine of salvation was "not veiled legalism." It was "from first to last a gospel of grace," wrote Clarke. "Paul's noble doctrine of free grace is but the amplification of Christ's own teaching." Salvation lay in experiencing that grace, experiencing Christ as the true form and *telos* of creation, including one's own created nature. And the demonstration of this reality was "the life and cross of Christ," which expressed "not what God appointed Christ to feel, but what God felt." The cross revealed the suffering at the heart of God. "He is the God that he is" because "love suffers in saving" (*Outline of Christian Theology,* pp. 336–47). God's ongoing participation in human suffering, noted Henry Churchill King, meant that modern theology should modify the classical theistic emphasis on God's immutability and changelessness and make "the frank admission of the passibility of God, whether it has the look of an ancient heresy or not" (*Theology and the Social Consciousness,* p. 221). The incarnation and the crucifixion thus stood together, explained Smyth, as inseparable elements of the one Christian revelation of God. Both revealed that "the first element, or energy, of God's love" was "the giving of self to the utmost" (*Old Faiths in New Light,* p. 278).

Self-giving love was the first principle of creation, as it was of redemption; it expressed the *Logos.* Personal regeneration must therefore consist in re-creation or restoration, in a union with Christ expressed in a life of self-giving love. "The act of faith is an act of moral unity and fellowship with Christ." One "identifies himself with Christ for the future; he joins himself to Christ in reliance upon saving grace for his own soul, and in fellowship with Christ's saving love and service toward other souls" (Clarke, pp. 356–57).

The oft-repeated quip that in liberalism "a God without wrath brought men without sin into a kingdom without judgment through the ministrations of a Christ without a Cross" is an unfortunate misreading of the Christian spirit of liberal theology (H. R. Niebuhr, *The Kingdom of God in America,* p. 193). How did liberals view the question of salvation? "The same love that endured the cross," wrote Clarke, "now calls men to Christ, and seeks to transform them into his likeness by joining them to him in spiritual union. Union with Christ is salvation" (Clarke, p. 356).

MODERN CRITICAL LIBERALISM, 1900–1935

As liberalism matured, it began to demonstrate a more self-critical spirit. The result was an increasing methodological self-consciousness and a greater theological diversity within the movement. This critical spirit owed its existence to the extension of liberal thought beyond the confines of pulpit and seminary. The liberal point of view soon pervaded the intellectual atmosphere of colleges and universities and shaped graduate education in the fields of religion and philosophy. One sign of liberal expansion, for example, was the number of college and university administrators drawn from liberal ranks at the turn of the century. This new intellectual environment naturally altered the questions that liberalism asked. Liberals could no longer simply be concerned with the relevance of Christian thought, but also had to address the role of religion itself in the modern world.

Liberal theology thus focused more explicitly on the universal dimensions of liberal claims. This change of focus has led recent commentators to draw a distinction between "evangelical" liberals and later "modernist" liberals—the former working within the parameters of Christian revelation, the latter turning to modern science for the data of theological reflection (K. Cauthen, *The Impact of American Religious Liberalism*, pp. 26–30). Although this distinction has some usefulness, it is too sharp, because it obscures the continuity of the liberal tradition in America and is therefore historically misleading (Hutchison, *The Modernist Impulse in American Protestantism*, pp. 7–9). All liberals intended to correlate the twin poles of Christian knowledge of God and universal knowledge. Individual theologians might emphasize one aspect rather than the other, but it was characteristic of liberal thought that both constituted the data for theological reflection. Liberal theology had never posited only one starting point for theological reconstruction, but had always assumed the compatibility of multiple starting points. As Theodore Munger had emphasized early in the liberal movement, liberals looked for knowledge of God "in the Bible, in history, in the nation, in the family, in the material creation, and in the whole length and breadth of human life" (*The Freedom of Faith*, p. 8).

Twentieth-century liberal theologians were merely extending the principles of liberalism articulated in the 1870s and 1880s. In essence these principles were two: modernism and empiricism. Modernism was more an attitude of mind than a set of doctrines. It was the self-conscious acknowledgment of the historical tentativeness of all theological formulations, thus freeing modern theology from the grip of tradi-

tion. Since current human experience formed the subject matter of reflection, theology could not be restricted to a closed body of previously formulated truths. Modernists assumed a posture of intellectual openness to the discovery of new truths and accepted the principle that theology must adjust itself to whatever truths emerged in modern culture (Hutchison, *The Modernist Impulse in American Protestantism*, pp. 1–11).

Empiricism represented the liberal conviction that the truth of religious statements could be verified by examining the human experience to which they refer, rather than by appeals to traditional authority. As D. D. Williams has pointed out, the appeal to experience had been a central feature of the American theological spectrum since the days of Jonathan Edwards. It had been a typically American way of vindicating the objectivity of Christian claims ("Tradition and Experience in American Theology," in Smith and Jamison, eds.). Nevertheless, the nature of that appeal had usually been intuitive and ad hoc. Experience had seldom functioned as an independent principle of theological reason. What modern theological liberalism did was to intensify the analysis of experience so that the argument from experience could become a primary principle for authenticating theological claims. The liberal understanding of experience was broad enough to encompass scientific research and functional theories of the effects of religious commitments.

Such radical empiricism was an element in liberalism from the beginning. Munger maintained that liberal theology could establish its truth "on scientific grounds and as inductions from phenomena, and therefore claims for itself the possession of knowledge that is such in reality" (*The Freedom of Faith*, p. 27). The Andover liberals agreed that theological claims were "susceptible of verification" and subject to "all the tests of the understanding, of logic, of experience, of history, of life" (in Foster, p. 199). Clarke likewise insisted that "experience has its rights in theology"—so much so that it would be naive to assert "that the facts of religion are incapable of scientific treatment" (*Outline of Christian Theology*, pp. 5, 19).

Twentieth-century liberals did, however, give greater attention to the issue of empirical verification than had the earlier generation. American liberals had become increasingly sensitive to charges of theological subjectivism. Critical liberals were convinced that their nineteenth-century predecessors had relied too heavily on intuitive knowledge derived from a special "religious consciousness." Critical liberals were no longer completely at ease with the tradition of Schleiermacher and wanted to escape the dilemma of subjectivism by empirically grounding theological claims in universal human experience. Their motive was not to substitute rational certitude for religious faith. By "verification" they did not mean absolute intellectual certainty; in fact, they expressed doubts that even modern science would want to make that claim. What they meant was that certain types of religious belief contributed to the coherence, intelligibility, and meaningfulness of human experience. Such beliefs were a "live option," in William James's words, fulfilling the demands of experience for an ultimate reality that would give value to human destiny and enhance the process of living.

PERSONALISM, RITSCHLIANISM, AND PRAGMATISM

Philosophical idealism provided many American liberals with a method for defending the New Theology. One of the most popular forms of this defense was theological personalism, reflected in the work of Henry Churchill King at Oberlin, and Borden Parker Bowne, Albert Knudson, and Edgar Brightman in Boston. In many respects theological personalism represented an important transitional mode of thought, at least in terms of the history of modern liberalism. Based on the teleological idealism of Rudolf Hermann Lotze, personalism took seriously the data both of personal experience and of scientific research, trying to show how they together point to a cosmic purpose as the ground of reality. As King put it, theology "is not at all against law, against mechanism"; it simply insists that "we are not to make a god of mechanism" (in W. Miller, ed., p. 19). According to the personalists, science could only describe external relationships among things, but human reason was concerned with the fullness of immediate, lived experience and the internal relationships that gave meaning and structure to experience. Personalists thus strove to reconcile empiricism and idealism by appealing to a broader analysis of human experience than had been customary.

One of Lotze's favorite expressions was "experience is richer than thought." Lived experience was not passive or static but alive with moral feelings and changing possibilities. The mind was not merely a mirror of some changeless, external reality; rather, it could genuinely penetrate reality only by means of moral participation in life's ongoing demands. "The nature of things does not consist in thoughts," King quoted Lotze as saying; "the whole mind experiences in other forms of its action and passion the essential meaning of all being and action, thought subsequently serving it as an instrument by which that which is thus experienced is brought into the connection which its nature requires" (W. Miller, ed., p. 27). Thought was an instrument to illuminate and give coherence to the raw structures of lived experience. Borden Parker Bowne agreed with Lotze's assessment of this "richer experience," stressing that knowledge was never a product of abstract reasoning but emerged from reflection only on the interaction of the self with its environment. "Will," Bowne wrote, "is an important and essential function in what we call intellect" (Personalism, p. 200). Moral value and purpose was not subjectively imposed on experience; it was an ineluctable part of having any experience at all.

Personalists anticipated the empirical school of liberal theology in its view of experience as a field of relationships and meanings. The field of lived experience included not only sense data but also the persistence of value structures. The Lotzean philosophy diverged from the closely related Ritschlian movement at just this point: in refusing to separate judgments of fact from value judgments. For the personalists value was part of the sheer facticity of experience itself. As a result they believed that careful attention to the pull of lived experience would disclose the operation of moral purpose in nature as well as in human history. The cosmos was an expression of personal life inhering in autonomous centers of moral will, freedom, and spontaneity. The goal of all experience was the fulfillment of value through the moral integration of each self with other selves. Personal life was therefore more than individual life; it represented a way of relating to others and to the moral pull of existence.

This was the direction, or *telos,* manifest in universal human experience. In speaking so frequently of "the infinite worth of the person," personalists were not at all echoing a purely individualistic ethic. In fact, personalists were strong advocates of social reform and cooperation. "The infinite worth of the person" was the personalists' way of indicating that God, or the ultimate ground of value, did not run roughshod over the particular needs of the individual but was serving those needs by preserving whatever was worthwhile in personal life. The significance of the personalist position was that it attempted to establish a rational basis for belief in the objectivity of moral value and an experiential basis for faith in the world's moral integrity.

Closely allied with the personalists were the "Ritschlians": William Adams Brown and Arthur Cushman McGiffert at Union, Walter Rauschenbusch in Rochester, George Burman Foster in Chicago, and Harris Franklin Rall at Garrett. They were indebted to the theological work of Albrecht Ritschl, who was influenced by Lotze. The Ritschlians were primarily interested in drawing out the implications of Christian experience, in which they resembled the liberals of the nineteenth century. With the personalists they interpreted Christian experience in terms of purpose and direction—namely, the realization of the socioethical unity of mankind in the kingdom of God. The realization of this kingdom, they believed, formed the center of Jesus' proclamation. In the light of the principle of the kingdom of God all human experience needed to be revalued. However, Ritschl himself had drawn such a sharp distinction between factual and value judgments (with a corresponding disdain for metaphysics and natural theology) that it was difficult for Ritschlians to explain how Christian experience was related to universal human experience. American Ritschlians tended to diverge from Ritschl on precisely this point; they continued the American quest for experiential grounds to verify religious value judgments (see Cauthen's remarks on Brown, pp. 41–60). Indeed, American Ritschlianism remained a somewhat unstable synthesis of liberal ideas, and most American Ritschlians eventually wandered into other theological camps.

The philosophies of pragmatism and instrumentalism were additional sources for critical liberal apologetics in the early twentieth century, and many liberals welcomed the fresh perspectives of William James and John Dewey. It was James's contribution to show that religious faith could be a "live option" in modern life whenever religious belief was consistent with the demands of living. Both Eugene Lyman at Union and Gerald Birney Smith at Chicago were influenced by James. In *Theology and Human Problems* (1910) Lyman found the meaning of religion to reside in the moral struggles of human existence, in the kind of life that must "grapple with moral evil in the world" in both its individual and corporate dimensions (p. 213). The truth of religious faith was demonstrated by its ability to release the creative freedom for participating in the cosmic struggle against all that threatened to destroy human values. G. B. Smith found the meaning of religion to reside in the creative power that enabled individuals to respond most freely and effectively to their environment. Religious truth was located in felt experience, in "the possibility of feeling the reality of what has not been precisely formulated by science." Theological doctrines did not exist to express abstract truths but "to enable man to realize the best possibilities by relating himself to all the resources of the actual environment from which life must be nourished" (in R. C. Miller, p. 61). Theological reflection disclosed those beliefs and experiences that made such nourishment most likely.

THE EMPIRICAL SCHOOL OF THEOLOGY

G. B. Smith was part of an empirical school of theology that developed at the University of Chicago, where he was joined by Shailer Mathews, Edward Ames, and, after 1927, Henry Nelson Wieman. The empirical school expressed considerable dislike of the philosophical idealism that seemed to prevail in much liberal theology and was equally dissatisfied with the restrictive epistemology of the Ritschlians. Ames and Mathews, in particular, were indebted to John Dewey's functional interpretation of knowledge and attempted to utilize the methodologies of the historical and social sciences as a way to unravel the problem of religious knowledge. Ames explicitly approached religion from the standpoint of human social psychology. Religious symbols expressed a devotion to human values arising from "the deep instinctive historical and social consciousness of the race" (*The Psychology of Religious Experience*, p. 318). The concept of God was man's way of articulating the fact that "the order of nature including man and all the processes of social life" seem to support moral endeavor (*Religion*, p. 177).

Shailer Mathews—New Testament scholar, historian, and theologian—took a similarly functional approach to religious knowledge, but Mathews was also sensitive to the reductionistic tendencies of the functional approach. His position might be labeled "functional realism." While the nature of theological language was purely instrumental, the underlying experience it pointed to was objectively real. In *The Spiritual Interpretation of History* (1916) and later works Mathews used a "socio-historical" method to show how all theological language reflected the "patterns of thought" and symbolic structures of particular cultures. All thought and action, even in the contemporary world, were governed by analogies drawn from social life and action. Religious belief emerged from the social processes of life, and the task of theology was to illuminate the paradigms that give religious meaning to human experience. This held true for speech about God. Mathews defined his own theological position as "conceptual theism"—that God was "our conception, born of social experience, of the personality evolving and personally responsive elements of our cosmic environment with which we are organically related" (*The Growth of the Idea of God*, p. 226). We can respond to this "cosmic environment" only in the terms set by our own cultural situation. For Mathews the universality of this process in human culture—revealed through detailed historical and sociological investigation—permitted one to assume the empirical reality of that which had produced such a response in the first place. "There must be personality-evolving activities in the cosmos," he argued. "We can no more escape the influence of these personality-evolving activities than we can escape the influence of those impersonal forces with which chemistry and physics deal" (p. 214). Mathews thus believed that the unity, coherence, and purposefulness of human experience could be uncovered by the socio-historical study of human behavior, and he assumed that the source of this coherence was "the experience of God which comes when men accept Jesus as Lord" (*The Faith of Modernism*, p. 143).

The "empirical" approach became increasingly popular in liberal Protestant seminaries after World War I, reaching its apogee in the work of Douglas Clyde Macintosh at Yale and Henry Nelson Wieman at Chicago. The term "empiricism" can be misleading, for the theological empiricists did not construe experience solely in terms of sense data. They fundamentally agreed with the personalists, pragmatists, and functionalists in regarding experience as a field of relationships needing reflective clarification. Reflection on this field disclosed the structures in reality that regulate how we know and relate to the world. Truth was verified by its practical congruity with the structures of lived experience.

Macintosh was more traditionally Christian in his understanding of the task of theology than was Wieman. For Macintosh a sense of awe and wonder in the face of our own existence was the starting point of all religious experience. This experience did not become fully realized, however, until it eventuated in personal transformation and in the affirmation of moral value. Reflection on this moral response to existence led to an awareness of a sacred structure in experience that had elicited such a response. What "verified" the objective reality of that structure, according to Macintosh, was the fact that the active moral life seemed to encourage and support such religious transformation of character. No other conclusion was reasonable, he believed, than that an objective factor produced this overpowering transformation and moral commitment. This "divine-value-producing factor" was God, and it could be the subject of universal investigation and corroboration. "Revelation of the reality of God in the religious experience of moral salvation is as normal and natural as any other process of cognition. It is the discovery of reality through experience" (*The Reasonableness of Christianity*, p. 126).

Macintosh qualified this strong claim in only one respect. The experience of the sacred dimension of the moral life itself depended upon "the right religious adjustment." Those who stubbornly resisted the value-producing, wonder-producing quality of life would certainly remain as ignorant in religious matters as an uninquisitive person could remain in the fields of mathematics, history, and science. Yet, assuming the right religious adjustment or disposition, any person would be able to attain "verified religious knowledge and reasonable religious belief" ("Experimental Realism in Religion" in D. C. Macintosh, ed., *Religious Realism,* pp. 328–29). In addition to such "verified" beliefs Macintosh tried to establish a realm of permissible over-beliefs in which the distinctive Christian elements in the doctrine of God could be accepted as the most coherent and intelligible expression of universal religious knowledge.

Henry Nelson Wieman was uncomfortable with the implicit evangelicalism and ethical intuitionism of Macintosh's position. Wieman desired a more naturalistic description of religious knowledge. Wieman too spoke of the transformative and renewing dimension of experience, but his conception was broader and more pluralistic than Macintosh's. For Wieman transformation was marked by creative growth and value enhancement. This growth was not always experienced as ecstatic wonder or moral affirmation but was more often known as something painful and contrary to personal designs. Wieman liked to emphasize that "God is not a nice God" and that genuine moral creativity and transformation included an awareness of moral condemnation and crisis (*The Source of Human Good,* pp. 49–50). It was the recalcitrant and painful dimension of creative growth that seemed to Wieman to guarantee the objective reality of the moral demand. Human life came up against a personality-transforming structure in experience in spite of itself. This structure was known in every experience, rather than limited to a special sort of religious experience. "The ultimate constitutive structure of reality," wrote Wieman, "is creativity itself because the order of creativity is the only order necessarily present in all knowledge and in all forms of experience and changelessly present through all changes which human experience can undergo" (*Man's Ultimate Commitment,* p. 91).

God was not the experience of creativity itself, according to Wieman; least of all was God simply another name for the particular moral ideals that such creative experience produced. God was rather the changeless cause or ground of all such experience. Men might therefore abuse and distort this creative factor, and no human ideal or expression of value could possibly exhaust the meaning of the structure of the creative event. God was the source of human values, the source of human good, without being reduced to their particular human expressions. In this sense God

remained more than we could ever think; he was neither personal nor impersonal, but suprapersonal. For Wieman God was the structure of creativity that shaped human destiny even when individuals and cultures rebelled against the creative good, distorting and abusing it for destructive ends. The heart of Wieman's "theological realism" lay in his assertion that the structure of creative energy "is coercive, determinative, and antecedent to all that man may do or seek or know, setting limits to knowledge, to truth, and to all that may happen" (*The Source of Human Good,* p. 198).

THEOLOGICAL REALISM AND NEO-ORTHODOXY

In the 1930s a group of self-critical liberals joined Wieman in suggesting that God was something more than human values, ideals, and aspirations. Included in this group of "theological realists" were Walter Marshall Horton at Oberlin and Robert Lowry Calhoun and H. Richard Niebuhr at Yale. The theological realists insisted that God must not be a mere projection of human wishes, supportive of whatever moral ambitions and dreams persons might fancy. Experience disclosed a power with which humans must wrestle and struggle, a power that stood in judgment on human actions and schemes. This power often resisted human aspirations in order to enable the human spirit to deepen its vision of reality. In particular, the realists emphasized that theology could no longer avoid facing the tragedies of human experience but had to address the problem of evil in experience. The human struggle with evil, they believed, pointed to a transcendent dimension in experience that permitted one to speak of the presence of God (see D. C. Macintosh, ed., *Religious Realism,* and W. M. Horton, *Realistic Theology*).

By the end of the decade the cohesiveness of the liberal movement had ended. The liberal spirit in religion remained, but liberals no longer spoke with a unified voice. Further advances in scholarship seemed to undermine confidence in liberal claims of universality. Biblical scholarship raised doubts about the developmental model of history that liberals had used in interpreting Scripture. The newer social sciences raised doubts about the objective reality of the structures that liberals claimed to have found in experience. A pervasive sense of epistemological relativism and skepticism overtook liberal self-confidence. Furthermore, world events generated a mood of moral pessimism that debilitated any appeal to human experience as a criterion of ultimate truth.

This loss of confidence in the testimony of experience gave rise to American theological interest in the European Neo-Orthodox movement. Yet American Neo-Orthodoxy remained essentially liberal in outlook, sensitive to the ambiguities of theological language and to the continuing need for experiential relevance. By and large, Neo-Orthodox critics took liberalism to task for faults that liberals themselves had long been concerned about. According to these criticisms, liberalism had been too subjective, too much a projection of self-justifying moral fancies, too insensitive to the problem of evil, and too unaware of the depth of perversion in the human will. The critics also charged that liberalism had neglected to apply the lessons of cultural relativism to its own claims. Liberalism had failed to recognize that experience was much too ambiguous and limited by sin and finitude to render definitive knowledge of God. No wonder many liberals felt chastened, for these were precisely the areas that had long haunted liberal apologetics. The Neo-Orthodox correction in liberalism was a refreshing one, reminding liberals of the neglected resources of the Christian tradition, of the collective dimension of religious knowledge, and of the inescapability of historical experience and testimony. In the end, however, Neo-Orthodoxy did not eliminate the need for further reconsideration of liberal questions regarding the nature of theology and the relationship between Christian faith and universal human experience.

CULTURAL IMPACT

The cultural impact of liberalism has been enormous in modern American Christianity in spite of the vicissitudes of liberal theology in the twentieth century. The liberal movement created a distinctive style of "churchmanship" that has endured in mainline Protestantism, especially in its view of the ministry, religious education, social activism, and missions.

Liberals were strong exponents of professionalism in the Christian ministry. During the liberal era many works appeared redefining the professional obligations of the parish minister. Washington Gladden's *The Christian Pastor* (1898), George Gordon's *Ultimate Conceptions of Faith* (1903), Lyman Abbott's *The Christian Ministry* (1905), W. H. P. Faunce's *The Educational Ideal in the Ministry* (1908), Francis McConnell's *The Prophetic Ministry* (1930), and William Adams Brown's *The Minister: His World and His Work* (1937) were all part of this genre. Not any less important were popular, inspirational novels about the ministry, such as Charles Sheldon's *In His Steps* (1897). Each described the minister as a religious professional—compassionate but skilled in human relations. He/she was to be an intellectual guide through the perplexities of faith and an interpreter of the moral complexities of modern civilization. The minister must be the complete pastor—counselor and advocate, friend and supporter, moral educator and social prophet. Much of the cultural popularity of liberalism lay less in its erudition and intellectual claims than in its sensitivity to the problems of everyday life. However, a side-effect of the liberal conception of the ministry may have been the tremendous institutional burdens that it placed on the minister. It may also have helped to increase the distance between clergy and laity by enveloping the ministry in a cult of professionalism.

Liberalism was also largely responsible for the creation of the modern religious education movement. George Coe, Henry Churchill King, Shailer Mathews, and others led the way with the founding of the Religious Education Association in 1903. Liberal religious education stressed the developmental character of religious faith, showing how religious faith contributed to the process of value formation and aided children in developing a sense of moral autonomy and social responsibility.

Furthermore, many twentieth-century liberals were in the forefront of movements advocating social change and reform. The liberal Social Gospel insisted that institutional Christianity needed to respond intelligently and sympathetically to the new demands for a more humane and just social order. Since liberal theology interpreted experience as a field of relationships and social interactions, the social aspirations and struggles of humanity took on a new significance as the place to discover God's present power and potency. The Social Gospel helped to change the attitudes of American Protestants toward urban life, toward the role of government, toward the role of the church in supporting those without power or privilege. If it was not completely successful in this endeavor, it still left an indelible mark on American attitudes toward labor, pacifism, civil rights, and international cooperation. It gave rise to the expectation that modern Christianity would be culturally discerning and socially alive.

Finally, liberalism helped to shape the missionary policies and ecumenical perspective of modern Protestantism. Liberals believed that Christianity had a message of reconciliation and healing to share with other cultures. They assumed that other societies would experience the same disrupting effect of industrial modernization as had America and would therefore face the same need for religious reconstruction as had liberalism. Missionary work was in a sense an outgrowth of the social thrust of liberalism, both of which were to be pursued in the context of ecumenical cooperation. The creation of the Federal Council of Churches (1908), the National Council of Churches (1950), and the World Council of Churches (1948) would hardly have been possible without the liberal spirit that underwrote such ventures.

In conclusion it should be noted that liberalism has always been susceptible to accusations of accommodating too much to modern culture. Sociological critics have described it as capitulating to the middle-class values of "the American way of life." Neo-Orthodox theological critics have indicted it for promoting a "culture religion" deficient in Christian insight. And Fundamentalists have attacked it as "secular humanism," as nothing more than veiled atheism.

Whatever degree of truth may reside in these accusations, the fact remains that no modern religious movement can long evade the necessity of adjusting to the demands of contemporary life —intellectual, social, and moral. The virtue of liberalism was that it made explicit the dilemmas of modern religious life and thought. Whatever theological weaknesses or cultural biases may have plagued the history of the liberal movement, what should not be forgotten is that liberals themselves never promised to deliver all the answers; they only pledged to help set the agenda. "The process cannot be forced," wrote George Gordon. But if that process "is real and living, the hope thus inspired is sufficient to make every thinker do his best to contribute something toward the final grand result" (*Ultimate Conceptions of Faith,* p. 76). That sense of hope was the hallmark of the liberal spirit.

BIBLIOGRAPHY

Sydney Ahlstrom, ed., *Theology in America* (1967) and *A Religious History of the American People* (1972); Harvey Arnold, *Near the Edge of the Battle* (1966); Lloyd Averill, *American Theology in the Liberal Tradition* (1967); Henry Bowden, *Church History in the Age of Science* (1971); Robert Bretall, ed., *The Empirical Theology of Henry Nelson Wieman* (1963); Ira Brown, *Lyman Abbott, Christian Evolutionist* (1953); John Buckham, *Progressive Religious Thought in America* (1919); Kenneth Cauthen, "The Life and Thought of Shailer Mathews," in Shailer Mathews, *Jesus on Social Institutions* (1928; repr. 1971), and *The Impact of American Religious Liberalism* (1962); Clifford Clark, Jr., *Henry Ward Beecher* (1978); William Newton Clarke, *Outline of Christian Theology* (1898); John B. Cobb, *Living Options in Protestant Theology* (1962); Donald Crosby, *Horace Bushnell's Theory of Language* (1975); Merle Curti, *Human Nature in American Thought* (1980); Jacob Dorn, *Washington Gladden* (1966); Vergilius Ferm, ed., *Contemporary American Theology,* 2 vols. (1932, 1933); Frank Foster, *The Modern Movement in American Theology* (1939).

George A. Gordon, *Ultimate Conceptions of Faith* (1903); Robert T. Handy, ed., *The Social Gospel in America* (1966); J. David Hoeveler, Jr., *James McCosh and the Scottish Intellectual Tradition* (1981); William Hutchison, ed., *American Protestant Thought: The Liberal Era* (1968), "The Americanness of the Social Gospel: An Inquiry in Comparative History," in *Church History* 44 (1975), and *The Modernist Impulse in American Protestantism* (1976); Francis McConnell, *Borden Parker Bowne* (1929); William McLoughlin, *The Meaning of Henry Ward Beecher* (1970); Bernard Meland, ed., *The Future of Empirical Theology* (1969); Randolph Crump Miller, *The American Spirit in Theology* (1974); William Miller, ed., *Contemporary American Protestant Thought, 1900–1970* (1973); James R. Moore, *The Post-Darwinian Controversies* (1979); Arnold Nash, ed., *Protestant Thought in the Twentieth Century* (1951).

Schubert Ogden, "Sources of Religious Authority in Liberal Protestantism," in *Journal of the American Academy of Religion* 44 (1976); Stow Persons, "Religion and Modernity, 1865–1914," in James Ward Smith and A. Leland Jamison, eds., *The Shaping of American Religion* (1961); Darnell Rucker, *The Chicago Pragmatists* (1969); George Shriver, ed., *American Religious Heretics* (1966); David L. Smith, *Symbolism and Growth: The Religious Thought of Horace Bushnell* (1981); John Edwin Smith, *The Spirit of American Philosophy* (1963); Ferenc Szaz, *The Divided Mind of Protestant America, 1880–1930* (1982); Morton White, *Science and Sentiment in America* (1972); Henry Nelson Wieman and Bernard Meland, *American Philosophies of Religion* (1936); Daniel Day Williams, *The Andover Liberals* (1941; repr. 1970) and "Tradition and Experience in American Theology," in James Ward Smith and A. Leland Jamison, eds., *The Shaping of American Religion* (1961).

[See also ECUMENICAL MOVEMENT; ENLIGHTENMENT; ROMANTIC RELIGION; SOCIAL CHRISTIANITY; *and* UNITARIANISM AND UNIVERSALISM.]

NEO-ORTHODOXY

Dennis N. Voskuil

A significant shift occurred in American religious thought between 1925 and 1935. During this period liberal Protestantism, the dominant theological system in the United States for more than twenty-five years, underwent a process of disintegration and was succeeded by a movement that has come to be known as American Neo-Orthodoxy.

Because it suggests a wholesale return to traditional theology, the term Neo-Orthodoxy is somewhat misleading. Actually, the nascent movement had been nurtured within the liberal system, one that stressed the continuities between God and humanity, between revelation and reason, between faith and culture. The formulators of Neo-Orthodoxy were self-conscious liberals who, under the sway of a world war, economic depression, and European crisis theology (or Barthianism, the European form of Neo-Orthodoxy), became increasingly disenchanted with the reigning assumptions of liberal thought. In reacting against liberalism, the converts to the emerging movement appropriated a number of preliberal concepts, such as the belief that God is transcendent and humans are inherently evil, but in biblical scholarship, scriptural interpretation, and social ethics the Neo-Orthodox were deeply influenced by their liberal predecessors. Accordingly, the movement might have been labeled "Neo-Liberalism" rather than "Neo-Orthodoxy," for it could be argued that it more accurately represented a new form of liberalism than a repristination of orthodoxy. Such questions of terminology have become moot, however, for interpreters of American religion have given much wider currency to "Neo-Orthodoxy." Invested with historical significance, it is used to denote the postliberal theological movement that burgeoned during the 1930s and continued to influence American religious thought during the two succeeding decades.

Like most intellectual movements, Neo-Orthodoxy was diffuse and diverse and therefore difficult to circumscribe. While certain institutions such as Union Theological Seminary in New York City and Yale Divinity School tended to be centers of Neo-Orthodox influence, there was no self-conscious school of Neo-Orthodox thought. Reinhold Niebuhr and H. Richard Niebuhr, those remarkable brothers who were the most popular and important early formulators of Neo-Orthodoxy, were such independent thinkers that it cannot even be said that there was a coterie of Niebuhrians. Other exponents of Neo-Orthodoxy such as Walter Marshall Horton, Edwin Lewis, and George W. Richards constructed their own brands of theology quite apart from those of the Niebuhrs and of the Swiss theologian Karl Barth and other representatives of European Neo-Orthodoxy. If those who have been designated as Neo-Orthodox constituted no formal school or party, they did share a common core of postliberal theological assumptions and an awareness that they were in the vanguard of a new era of religious thought.

THE LIBERAL HERITAGE

Liberalism did not emerge as a strong and cohesive religious movement until the last quarter of the nineteenth century, when, battered by challenges of Darwinism, historicism, and higher criticism, the long-standing evangelical consensus became frayed and fragmented. Two strains of theologians arose in response to this crisis of modernity. On the one hand were the staunch conservatives who strengthened their theological barricades and prepared to do battle with the modern world. Later they became identified as Fundamentalists. On the other hand were those who were eager to forge a truce with the new sciences and work at mediating the modern world view and the Christian faith. These mediators were the religious liberals. Emergent during an era of industrial growth, military strength, and national self-confidence, liberalism quickly gained adherents, initially in the lecterns and pulpits, but eventually in the pews as well. By the 1920s liberalism was deeply entrenched in most of the large Protestant denominations and was strong enough to ward off Fundamentalists who were battling to gain control of the churches.

By nature inclusive and comprehensive, liberalism naturally spawned divergent theologies. All, however, were informed and undergirded by what historian William R. Hutchison has described as "the modernist impulse"—a willingness not only to embrace modern culture but also to accommodate the Christian faith to it. The major tenets of liberal thought reflect this pervasive spirit of modernism. Building upon the philosophical base of idealism, the liberals understood God, or the God-idea, to be immanent in the world, a notion that engendered a spirit of optimism and progress. While the liberals were not as naive about human nature as their Neo-Orthodox critics charged, it is certainly true that liberals tended to play down the doctrine of human depravity. It simply did not square with a pervasive modernism that tended to interpret human nature as essentially good and altruistic. The liberal Social Gospel was likewise predicated on the essential altruism of humans and upon the inevitability of moral reform. In general, the liberals put great stress on the person of Jesus, in part because he was the unique God-man but also because he was the singular example of moral perfection, the model for all humans. Finally, in their embrace of higher criticism, the liberals moved away from literal interpretations of the Bible. Certain that the Scriptures must be viewed in the light of historical development, liberals accepted as abiding truth that which confirmed the immanent presence of God revealed in and through contemporary culture.

THE INTERNAL CRITIQUE

While Neo-Orthodoxy crystallized as a distinctive theological movement during the early 1930s, its critique of liberal thought was forged a decade earlier, when liberals themselves began to question some of the essential tenets of liberalism. On the surface liberalism appeared strong and confident during the 1920s, successfully protecting its flanks against the attacks of Fundamentalists on the right and humanists on the left (humanists emphasized human values and rationality and often had an antisupernatural bias). Beneath the surface, however, liberalism was drained of much prewar idealism and optimism. Lacking in resilience and vitality, the liberal movement began to fracture as it absorbed stinging blows of self-criticism that burgeoned into a full-fledged theological revolt. While few disenchanted liberals were emotionally and intellectually prepared to abandon the liberal banner, those who did became the standard-bearers of Neo-Orthodoxy.

Certainly the most devastating internal critic of liberalism was Reinhold Niebuhr, an activist pastor of Bethel Evangelical Church in Detroit for thirteen years before his appointment to the faculty of New York City's Union Theological Seminary in 1928. A prolific contributor to liberal journals and a popular conference speaker, he had a decisive impact upon the younger liberals during this era. In the years following World War I, however, Niebuhr became disenchanted with liberalism's inability to sustain moral potency during times of trial and tragedy. His first book, *Does Civilization Need Religion?* (1927), included a wide-ranging critique of liberalism for its facile analysis of human nature, for identifying God too closely with contemporary culture, and for easy optimism regarding the social efficacy of the Christian faith.

While Niebuhr was the most persistent liberal critic during the late 1920s, he was by no means alone. Others—including Walter Marshall Horton and Edwin Lewis—were beginning to forge the postliberal theology that emerged during the 1930s. Horton, a professor at Oberlin Seminary, argued that the liberal concept of God had failed the test of reality, and that it did not appear to have a realistic understanding of human nature or social conditions, and Lewis, a former spokesman for liberalism who taught at Drew University, contended that the modern church was apostate, having sacrificed the essentials of Christian faith upon the altar of modernity.

Under the weight of mounting internal criticism, the foundations of liberalism began to crumble. Ironically, most of the theologians who effected the dissolution were themselves liberals who sincerely mourned the passing of a theological system that had once nurtured them. In August 1931, Henry P. Van Dusen of the Union Theological Seminary wrote an article for *World Tomorrow* entitled "The Sickness of Liberal Religion," in which he observed that "possibly the most certain fact in the present baffling religious situation" was "the ill-health of liberal Christianity." Van Dusen cited the falling off of missionary support, losses in church enrollment, a decline of religious certainty among the rank and file, and a mood of desperation among the liberal ministry. During the next four years other articles appeared echoing Van Dusen's pronouncement of the collapse of liberalism. But the demise of the movement was not officially ritualized until December 1935, when Harry Emerson Fosdick, the pastor of Riverside Church in New York City and the most popular liberal preacher in America, submitted his sermon "Beyond Modernism" to the *Christian Century,* a nondenominational religious journal that has long been the standard-bearer of American religious liberalism. Defining modernism as "an adaptation, an adjustment, an accommodation of Christian faith to contemporary scientific thinking," Fosdick was careful to defend those who initiated the modernist movement in religion, but he proceeded to criticize modernism for excessive intellectualism, dangerous sentimentalism, and impotent theism. He concluded with an emotional plea:

> We must go beyond modernism! And in that new enterprise the watchword will be not, Accommodate yourself to the prevailing culture! but Stand out from it and challenge it! For this inescapable fact, which again and again in Christian history has called modernism to its senses, we face: we cannot harmonize Christ himself with modern culture. What Christ does to modern culture is to challenge it.

THE THEOLOGICAL TRANSITION: HOW MINDS CHANGED

During the fall of 1938, the *Christian Century* asked a number of prominent church leaders and theologians to contribute to a series of autobiographical articles that would explore changes in religious thought during the previous decade. In the covering letter that he sent to prospective contributors, editor Charles Clayton Morrison explained that the liberal weekly had decided to undertake such an ambitious project because of the general conviction that "a radical and significant change" had occurred "in the thinking of Christian scholarship and leadership. . . . All of us are aware that ours is a period of intensive and profound transition." In response, Morrison received a number of revealing statements from some of the most important leaders of the church, especially liberal leaders. These autobiographical essays seemed to substantiate his contention that a significant transition had occurred in American religious thought. Upon completion of the "How My Mind Has Changed" series, which ran throughout 1939, Morrison concluded that as many as twenty-six of the thirty-four contributors had experienced at least a "considerable change" in their thinking and eleven of these had experienced a "radical change." In a summary statement Morrison noted that "hitherto dominant liberalism" had been put on the defensive by "a highly sophisticated attack on the foundations of liberal theology." America had just passed through a crucial decade in its religious development. Liberalism had waned while "a whole new theological outlook had emerged."

Although the 1930s saw a significant change in the tone and temper of religious thought, there had not yet been a wholesale adoption of the doctrine that came to be known as Neo-Orthodoxy. In fact, while a number of liberals did become formulators of Neo-Orthodox theology, most simply considered themselves changed liberals—but still liberals. Chastened by economic disaster and social malaise, nearly all of the contributors to Morrison's series spoke of a renewed interest in the doctrine of moral evil and a God-centered faith that could stand up to the real world of crisis and misery. While most liberals admitted that their faith had been chastened, some confessed that they had experienced intellectual conversions. These were the liberals who became early formulators of Neo-Orthodoxy.

In his contribution to the mind-change series, for instance, Reinhold Niebuhr revealed that he had undergone a "conversion of thought which involved the rejection of almost all the liberal theological ideals and ideas" that had dominated his early career. Walter Marshall Horton indicated that when he wrote *Realistic Theology* in 1934 he was not conscious of a sharp break with his past, only an increasing appreciation of the growing trend to rid liberal theology of its idealistic illusions. "But beneath this peaceful evolutionary development," he noted, ". . . there was evidently the groundswell of a more revolutionary unconscious change." The most dramatic theological conversion was documented by Edwin Lewis, who revealed that he "discovered the Bible" while editing *The Abingdon Bible Commentary* during the late 1920s. Thereafter he perceived with "devastating clarity" that divine revelation rather than speculative philosophy must provide the foundation for Christian theology. Other early exponents of Neo-Orthodoxy, such as H. Richard Niebuhr, Walter Lowrie, and George W. Richards, seem to have experienced similar patterns of ideological change during the pivotal 1930s.

THE BARTHIAN INFLUENCE

The transition from liberalism to Neo-Orthodoxy had been stimulated, at least in part, by the crisis events of the 1930s. The Depression, of course, had the most profound effect upon the thinking of American religionists, but other events, such as the failure of disarmament efforts and the emergence of totalitarian regimes in Europe, also contributed to a mood of despair. Nearly all the contributors to the *Christian Century* mind-change series took note of the "multiplying social catastrophes" that had driven most of them toward a more realistic faith. But the transition was also conditioned by the new theological currents that began flowing across the Atlantic after World War I. Among them were a renewed interest in the thought of Søren Kierkegaard; New Testament scholarship that, after Albert Schweitzer's futile quest for the

historical Jesus, began to interpret the Gospel in eschatological and apocalyptic terms; a "Luther renaissance," in which theologians such as Karl Höll and Werner Elert published works that gave contemporary relevance to the doctrines espoused by Martin Luther; the view of Anders Nygren and Gustav Aulén, of the Lundesian school in Sweden, that Christian theology must be grounded in an understanding of God's love and Christ's victory over sin and death; and the theology of crisis (also identified as Neo-Orthodoxy, dialectical theology, and theology of the Word) that, although associated primarily with Karl Barth, was also represented in the works of Emil Brunner, Eduard Thurneysen, Friedrich Gogarten, and Georg Merz. All of these schools of thought eventually affected the direction of religious scholarship, but it was the massive and dynamic dialectical movement that most directly influenced the postliberal theology developments in America.

Like most of his contemporaries, Barth had embraced liberal Protestantism, the idealistic and optimistic theological tradition that was shattered by the devastating impact of World War I and its aftermath. In 1919 Barth produced *Der Römerbrief*, Europe's first great postliberal work, a commentary on Saint Paul's Epistle to the Romans that set forth the essential features of crisis theology: the transcendence of God, the feebleness of humanity, and the "infinite distinction" between time and eternity. Forcefully advocating a "theology of the pure Word of God," *Der Römerbrief*, in the words of Roman Catholic theologian Karl Adam, "fell like a bombshell on the playground of the theologians."

It took nearly a decade for the shockwaves that Barth ignited in Europe to reach America. After 1926 a number of articles on Barthianism began to appear in the United States, but it was not until 1928 that Pilgrim Press of Boston published *The Word of God and the Word of Man*, a collection of Barth's important early addresses translated into English by Douglas Horton. The book was widely read and reviewed but did not create a mass market for Barth's works. Five years passed before an English translation of *Der Römerbrief* was published. By this time the theology of crisis was being discussed in America, but neither liberals nor conservatives wholeheartedly endorsed Barth's philosophy.

The first book-length American interpretation of Barth was written by an orthodox Calvinist, Alvin Sylvester Zerbe, professor emeritus of Central Theological Seminary in Dayton, Ohio. In 1930 Zerbe produced *The Karl Barth Theology; or, The New Transcendentalism,* an acerbic assessment of the philosophical pinions of Barth's thought. Refusing to embrace Barth as a legitimate child of the Reformation, Zerbe concluded that such theology was "but a cosmic philosophy in which the fundamental doctrines of God, man, sin, redemption, the Bible, time and eternity are in a new setting and have a meaning entirely different from the old creeds and confessions."

A far more substantial study was Wilhelm Pauck's *Karl Barth: Prophet of a New Christianity?* published in 1931. Pauck, a church historian at Chicago Theological Seminary, had been reared and educated in Germany before emigrating to America in 1925. A student of Adolf von Harnack and Ernst Troeltsch (leading German theologians generally associated with European religious liberalism), as well as Barth, Pauck betrayed a certain ambivalence about the new movement. In the first half of his book Pauck portrayed Barth as a prophet who might bridge the gap between modernism and orthodoxy and bring about a new consciousness of God's revelation. At the midpoint, however, Pauck abruptly shifted his sympathies. Concluding that Barth was not the prophet of a new theology, he criticized Barth's radical dualism and doctrine of Scripture as evidence of a return to "ecclesiastical scholasticism."

A year after Pauck's assessment appeared, Walter Lowrie produced *Our Concern with the Theology of Crisis,* a favorable assessment of Barthian thought. An Episcopal clergyman who later became better known as a translator of Kierkegaard, Lowrie served as an unabashed evangelist for the Barthian gospel.

Other interpretations of Barth followed, but the first three clearly represented the broad spectrum of the American critique. It is significant that thirty-two of the thirty-four contributors to the *Christian Century* mind-change series of 1939 took note of the Barthian movement. Most, however, rejected his method and message. To the liberal mind the philosophical constructs of paradox and dialectic, involving Barth's claim that the truth must be found outside or above pure rationality, made his writings seem opaque, convoluted, and irrational. Frederick C. Kershner, a frustrated and disapproving liberal, concluded that most of Barth's writings were nothing but "exaggerated piffle."

Predictably, those who emerged as the early exponents of American Neo-Orthodoxy acknowledged a debt to Barth. Despite his highly publicized disagreements with Barth over social issues, such as the relative importance of a Christian position vis-à-vis communism and capitalism, Reinhold Niebuhr considered himself a spiritual son of the Swiss rebel against religious liberalism. H. Richard Niebuhr described Barth as a teacher who played a pivotal role in his theological development. Edwin Lewis and George W. Richards admitted even greater intellectual debts to Barthianism. Still, even these proponents of American Neo-Orthodoxy were cautious in their embrace of European crisis theology. In fact, none comfortably claimed the Barthian label. They maintained a "yes . . . but" attitude with respect to his thought. Yes, they said, there is much that we can learn from Barth's critique of liberalism, but we do not fully accept his radical dualism, dialectical method, or biblical traditionalism. So the American movement was influenced but not definitively shaped by its European counterpart. Despite obvious connections between these postliberal theologies, American Neo-Orthodoxy was not simply a backwater variety of the European original, but a genuinely indigenous form of religious thought.

THE NEO-ORTHODOX ERA

As we have noted, the ideological lineaments of Neo-Orthodoxy were already evident during the late 1920s, when criticism of liberalism became more strident and awareness of Barthianism increased. Yet the movement did not coalesce until the early 1930s, when a series of writings were published that reflected a significant change in religious thought.

Douglas Horton's translation of Barth's essays in 1928 and the assessments of Barthian theology produced by Pauck and Lowrie in 1931 and 1932 certainly helped to introduce American theologians to the European "bomb-thrower," but the most important early treatise was Reinhold Niebuhr's *Moral Man and Immoral Society* (1932). Described by historian Sydney E. Ahlstrom as the "most disruptive religio-ethical bombshell of domestic construction to be dropped during the entire interwar period," Niebuhr's treatise took direct aim at those liberals who seemed oblivious to the basic difference between the morality of individuals and the morality of organized groups. Niebuhr disdained the ameliorative prescriptions of liberal moralists, who believed that social injustice could be resolved through moral or rational suasion. According to Niebuhr, those who did not come to grips with the inherent immorality of "collective egoism" were simply naive and softheaded. Since power respected power alone, no justice would come to minority groups unless demands were accompanied by collective power. In setting forth the principles of ethical realism, Niebuhr did not mean to glorify individual morality. The title of the book was misleading, for the theological foundation of his social theory was that individual egoism is exacerbated in group situations. Individual sin begets social sin. A more accurate title would have been "Immoral Man and Even More Immoral Society." While the book was more concerned with ethics than theology, it did set forth a social hypothesis that was founded upon a postliberal assessment of human nature.

Another important book issued in 1932 was Paul Tillich's *The Religious Situation,* translated and introduced by H. Richard Niebuhr. While the German-born theologian and philosopher wandered in and out of the Neo-Orthodox orbit during his distinguished career in America, this short book provided a somber Marxist analysis of bourgeois Western culture, one that matched the tone and temper of *Moral Man and Immoral Society.*

The new direction in American theology became evident in 1934 when a number of books appeared that celebrated Neo-Orthodoxy. As evidence of the breadth of the movement, the three most significant treatises were not produced by either of the Niebuhr brothers. To be sure Reinhold issued his *Reflections on the End of an Era* that year, but it broke little new ground. On the other hand, Walter Marshall Horton's *Realistic Theology* was a significant book that included not only a devastating critique of liberalism, but the outline of a radical Christian realism that moved him

beyond the empirical theology often associated with Douglas Clyde Macintosh and Henry Nelson Wieman. In a brilliant first chapter Horton described the collapse of liberalism as the inevitable result of its endeavor to modernize the Gospel, thereby forging an accommodating alliance with the presuppositions, prejudices, and illusions of bourgeois Western thought. With a change of the intellectual climate liberalism had been rendered impotent and outmoded. The concluding chapters proposed a realistic theology based upon the recognition of the deeply rooted nature of human sin.

In *A Christian Manifesto* Edwin Lewis expanded an attack upon liberal thought that he had outlined a year before in "The Fatal Apostasy of the Modern Church." The essay had brought reproof from those who feared that he had "gone Barthian," "sold out to the Fundamentalists," or "slipped back into orthodoxy," but *A Christian Manifesto* is evidence that Lewis refused to back away from his vigorous attack on liberalism. Blasting the liberals for rejecting or reinterpreting essential Christian doctrines, such as divine transcendence, special revelation, incarnation, and atonement, Lewis proposed that the necessary theological correction be built upon a strong doctrine of divine transcendence and a revitalized doctrine of sin.

The other important Neo-Orthodox book to appear in 1934 was George W. Richards' *Beyond Fundamentalism and Modernism: The Gospel of God.* A church historian who served as president of Lancaster Seminary (the Reformed Church in the United States), Richards was a highly respected member of the theological-ecclesiastical community. Although he was influenced by liberalism when he came in contact with the renowned church historian Adolf von Harnack while studying in Germany, Richards was one of the first Americans to commend European crisis theology. The title of his work is significant, as it indicates that Richards was convinced that his Barthian-flavored theology provided an alternative to both Fundamentalism and modernism. Richards applauded liberal efforts to modernize dogmas and institutions, but concluded that the noble desire to "humanize Christianity and Christianize humanity" had resulted in an enlightened self-reliant humanism "with a thin veneer or a faint tinge of Christian theism, parading as liberal and refined Christianity."

In 1935 two more significant books strengthened the Neo-Orthodox critique. Reinhold Niebuhr published his Rauschenbusch lectures (delivered at Colgate-Rochester Divinity School in Rochester, N.Y., during the spring of 1934) as *An Interpretation of Christian Ethics.* While it contained polemical overtones, this work was more positive and constructive than his previous treatises. He did condemn liberalism for adjusting so thoroughly to the ethos of modern culture that it had obscured that which was "distinctive in the Christian message and creative in Christian morality." Going beyond the critique, however, Niebuhr proposed an independent Christian ethic that took into account the tension between the historical and the transcendent, the real and the ideal, the relative and the absolute.

Also during 1935 H. Richard Niebuhr, Wilhelm Pauck, and Francis P. Miller collaborated to produce what Ahlstrom has called "a Neo-orthodox manifesto to the churches": *The Church Against the World.* Stressing that the crisis of the church was the result of an all too eager adjustment to the world, the contributors recommended that the church disentangle itself from corrupting alliances with contemporary culture, be these ties naturalism, nationalism, capitalism, or any other form of idolatrous anthropocentricity. In a trenchant concluding essay Niebuhr emphasized that the church must be captured by God and not by culture; the church must be separated from the world in order to serve the world.

THE NIEBUHRIAN FLAVOR

By 1935 the essential features of Neo-Orthodox thought had been consistently elaborated. This does not mean that Neo-Orthodoxy remained static from that point; nor does it mean that important writings ceased to be produced by early exponents. The Niebuhr brothers, especially, continued to issue dynamic ethical and theological treatises as their thought broadened and matured over the next three decades.

As children of a pastor in the Evangelical Synod of North America (now part of the United Church of Christ), the Niebuhrs were nurtured in the cradle of German-Lutheran piety. While their father introduced his sons to the thought of Harnack, he did not share Harnack's liberal perspective. Before they entered Yale for graduate studies, both sons were trained at a denominational college and seminary. After serving the Evangelical Synod in various ministries, Reinhold began his long career at Union Theological Seminary and Richard at Yale Divinity School.

By the mid 1930s, when he contributed to *The Church Against the World,* H. Richard Niebuhr had become a caustic critic of liberalism. His first book, *The Social Sources of Denominationalism* (1929), revealed that he had been deeply influenced by the German theologian Ernst Troeltsch as well as Barth. Using Troeltschian perspectives in *Social Sources,* H. Richard Niebuhr demonstrated that religious thought and institutions are directly shaped by social conditions and historical circumstances. While it took different forms, this interest in the relationship between social history and theology can be detected in nearly all of his later writings. His next important book, *The Kingdom of God in America* (1937), was a poignant critique of liberalism, one that contains his epigrammatic caricature of liberal faith: "A God without wrath brought men without sin into a kingdom without judgment through the ministrations of Christ without a cross." While he dealt explicitly with the relationship between faith and culture in *The Church Against the World,* H. Richard Niebuhr's brilliant *Christ and Culture* (1951) was a more dispassionate study of an issue that has long engaged Christian thinkers. Another important theme for H. Richard Niebuhr, the church as a confessing community, was developed in *The Meaning of Revelation* (1941). His last great work before his death, *Radical Monotheism and Western Culture* (1960), is a very suggestive treatise that explores the relationship between the relative and the absolute and between God and the self. Each of these works, along with *The Responsible Self* (published posthumously in 1963), reveals careful scholarship and penetrating thought. H. Richard Niebuhr has left us with some of the religious classics of the twentieth century.

By nature a polemicist, Reinhold Niebuhr was a more prolific writer than his brother, producing books that served as important tracts for the times. One exception to this might be his two-volume classic, *The Nature and Destiny of Man* (1941), which marked him as a true heir of the leaders of the Protestant Reformation. Yet even this important work was not a systematic treatment of theology, at least by traditional standards, but a vibrant and dynamic postliberal interpretation of Christian faith. In addition to *Moral Man and Immoral Society* and *An Interpretation of Christian Ethics,* produced during the heyday of Neo-Orthodoxy, some of his other important titles are *The Children of Light and the Children of Darkness* (1944), *Faith and History* (1949), and *The Irony of American History* (1952).

During the middle of the twentieth century, Reinhold Niebuhr was America's public theologian. He is best known as a social ethicist whose views on love and justice were derived from Augustinian doctrines of sin and grace. Influenced by Kierkegaard and Barth, Niebuhr employed a dialectical manner of thought that frequently confounded his readers. He was often saying "yes-and-no" or "both-and." Mankind, in Niebuhr's view, was both creator and creature, free and constrained, involved in history and transcending history. In the public arena, Niebuhr provided a philosophical framework based on the relationship between love and justice that influenced economists, politicians, and foreign-policy experts. In the arena of religious thought he did more than any other Neo-Orthodox figure to reintroduce and reinvigorate traditional Christian concepts of sin and evil.

Because of the pervasive influence and popularity of the Niebuhr brothers, it is tempting simply to define Neo-Orthodoxy as Niebuhrianism. That would be a mistake, however, for the movement was even broader in scope than the expansive minds of the Niebuhrs represented. Some of the early exponents of Neo-Orthodoxy continued to publish noteworthy books, and even those who might not be counted as bona-fide Neo-Orthodox thinkers produced writings that reflected Neo-Orthodox concerns. Such persons include John C. Bennett, John Mackay, Paul Minear, Paul Lehmann, and W. Norman Pittenger, and historians like Joseph Haroutunian and Perry Miller, who during the 1930s inaugurated fruitful reevaluations of the traditions of Puritanism and Edwardianism.

THE ESSENCE OF NEO-ORTHODOXY

Any attempt to identify the genius of American Neo-Orthodoxy must be prefaced by a reminder that it was a theological corrective, a shift in the temper of religious thought, rather than a systematic attempt to redefine doctrinal positions. To be sure the members of the movement tended to take the content and vocabulary of the historic Christian faith more seriously than they assumed their liberal predecessors had, but their "new" perspective was always shaped more by what they considered to be the weaknesses of liberalism than by a conscious effort to conform to a set of traditional doctrines.

Before summarizing some of the crucial emphases of Neo-Orthodox thought, it is helpful to examine the philosophical approaches that most influenced the movement. Certainly Neo-Orthodoxy should be identified as a variant religious strain of the broad-based movement of philosophical realism that was becoming dominant in America during the early decades of the twentieth century. Associated with such diverse figures as William James, George Santayana, George Herbert Mead, Douglas Clyde Macintosh, and Henry Nelson Wieman, philosophical realism was characterized by the proposition that there is an objective character of reality which can be known through observation. It would be misleading to contend that the proponents of American Neo-Orthodoxy built their thought directly upon the foundations of philosophical realism, but they did find some of its emphases amenable to their own religious perspectives. Certainly figures like H. Richard Niebuhr and Walter Marshall Horton, both of whom contributed articles to the important volume *Religious Realism* (1931), a symposium edited by Macintosh, were drawn to the larger movement because it provided a counterweight to the idealism of the liberals. Most often, however, the Neo-Orthodox identified themselves as realists in their basic analysis of the human condition. Horton's book *Realistic Theology* was less a religious version of philosophical realism than an attempt to construct a postliberal theology that could stand up in a world of human misery and corporate evil. The Christian realism of the Neo-Orthodox thinkers drew more from Saint Paul and Martin Luther than from William James and George Herbert Mead.

Neo-Orthodoxy was also influenced by existentialism, a movement in Western thought that has been associated with Friedrich Nietzsche, Jean-Paul Sartre, and Albert Camus, but in its Christian form owes most to Søren Kierkegaard, especially after Walter Lowrie began to translate his writings into English (the first translation appeared in 1939). Kierkegaard's emphasis upon a leap of faith, his insistence upon the importance of personal and responsible decision, and his formulation of the qualitative distinction between the divine and the human were incorporated into many Neo-Orthodox writings.

Finally, Neo-Orthodoxy was affected by the modern dialectical movement. Based on the philosophies of G. W. F. Hegel and Karl Marx, dialectics—a process of reasoning that juxtaposes contrary ideas and seeks to resolve their conflict—was put to Christian use by Kierkegaard and Barth. American Neo-Orthodox thinkers tended to resist the wholesale retreat to dialectics that characterized much of Barth's thought, but in addressing the issues of existence and faith, Reinhold Niebuhr and other American Neo-Orthodox thinkers spoke of paradoxes, contradictions, and impossible possibilities.

From its beginnings as a reassessment of liberal tradition, Neo-Orthodoxy expanded into a constructive and self-sustaining theological position. Against a liberal doctrine that seemed naively to assume the essential goodness of individuals and the essential altruism of society, the exponents of Neo-Orthodoxy reappropriated a doctrine of sin that was rooted in the thought of Saint Augustine, Martin Luther, and John Calvin. In his *Nature and Destiny of Man* Reinhold Niebuhr reintroduced the notion of original sin and stated that in mankind's pride and willfulness the human race had severed a right relationship with God. Niebuhr believed that mankind could do nothing about its sinful condition except, through a sheer act of faith, to throw itself upon God's grace made available through Jesus Christ.

Against the liberal emphasis upon divine immanence, the Neo-Orthodox affirmed the transcendent and sovereign nature of God. Concerned that liberalism had embraced a form of philosophical monism which rendered an immanent God a captive to contemporary culture, the Neo-Orthodox insisted that while God became immanent in the Incarnation, there is a qualitative distinction between creator and creature. Only as a transcendent being can God redeem and restore humanity.

The Neo-Orthodox theologians also demonstrated a renewed interest in the Bible as revelation. While they embraced most of modern biblical criticism and rejected literal interpretations of Scripture, they understood the Bible to be God's Word in a way that they believed set them apart from most liberals. Certainly, the Neo-Orthodox era stimulated new schools of biblical scholarship and interpretation in America. Old Testament scholars such as G. Ernest Wright, John Bright, and Bernhard Anderson adapted a "salvation history" approach—the conviction that Scripture reveals a dynamic God who breaks into history to redeem humanity. While New Testament scholarship did not follow this "salvation history" emphasis, it did reflect renewed interest in the writings of Saint Paul, a favorite of many Neo-Orthodox theologians.

The Neo-Orthodox thinkers posited a new version of the Social Gospel. Convinced that the liberal attempts to Christianize culture had been idealistic and individualistic, Reinhold Niebuhr and other ethicists and theologians put forth a social vision that rested upon a realistic analysis of individual and collective egoism, a commitment to serving love within the context of justice, a realization that social change depends upon the exertion of collective power, and an awareness that perfection will never be attained in a finite world.

Finally, the exponents of Neo-Orthodoxy, having denounced the liberals for wholesale accommodation of the Gospel to Western values, insisted that the church stand firm against modern culture. While they were not opposed to modern science and scholarship, the Neo-Orthodox did resist the "modernist impulse," the tendency to embrace the modern world view and adapt the Christian faith accordingly.

THE CONSERVATIVE REACTION

Despite the fact that the formulators of Neo-Orthodoxy reacted against liberalism and reappropriated some of the traditional doctrines of Christianity, American religious conservatives did not generally embrace them as allies in the long-standing battle with the liberals. While confirmed liberals tended to view Neo-Orthodoxy as a new form of Fundamentalism, inveterate conservatives tended to view it as another breed of modernism. In *The Karl Barth Theology* (1930), the first American book-length treatment of Barthianism, Alvin Sylvester Zerbe, a religious conservative, complained that the Swiss theologian had given radical new meaning to the historic doctrines of revelation, sin, and salvation. This criticism became the standard conservative reaction to nearly all forms of Neo-Orthodoxy during the succeeding three decades. The Neo-Orthodox were considered wolves in sheep's clothing, for, while they employed traditional terminology and explicated traditional doctrines, they were still liberals at heart.

The conservative theologian most assiduously devoted to the task of unmasking Neo-Orthodoxy was Cornelius Van Til, professor of theology at Westminster Theological Seminary in Chestnut Hill, Pennsylvania. He produced numerous articles and two comprehensive books on Neo-Orthodox thought, *The New Modernism* (1946) and *Christianity and Barthianism* (1962). Concentrating upon European crisis theology, Van Til systematically dismantled Barth's dialectical methodology as well as his interpretation of Scripture, history, redemption, eschatology, and sin. Van Til concluded that Neo-Orthodox thought was even more dangerous than liberalism.

Van Til wrote specifically about the Barthians, but other conservatives leveled similar criticisms at the Niebuhrians as well. In *Neo-Orthodoxy: What It Is and What It Does* (1956), Charles Ryrie, a prominent Fundamentalist scholar, lumped Barth, Barth's associate Emil Brunner, and Reinhold Niebuhr together and proceeded to condemn their views as inconsistent, illogical, and unbiblical. Charging that the Neo-Orthodox had perpetuated a "theological hoax," Ryrie insisted that their doctrines included orthodox terminology built upon liberal exegesis; Neo-Orthodoxy, according to Ryrie, "attempts to have inspiration without infallibility, and authority without actuality."

Ryrie feared that conservatives might be attracted to Neo-Orthodoxy because it allowed one to be intellectually respectable (by accepting the theories of evolution and higher criticism) while at the same time sounding like a conservative Evangelical. In some respects such fears were justified. There certainly were a number of conservatives who became Neo-Orthodox because it was a bridge into the mainstream of religious thought in America that helped to preserve the "faith" of conservatives who could not square orthodoxy with reality. Interestingly, the neo-evangelicalism that burgeoned in the 1970s and 1980s tended to view the Neo-Orthodox less suspiciously. Barth and Reinhold Niebuhr became objects of study in the Evangelical community, and in certain conservative circles Neo-Orthodoxy has been considered a new orthodoxy rather than a new modernism.

THE LEGACY OF NEO-ORTHODOXY

In most respects the 1930s must be considered the heyday of American Neo-Orthodoxy. Initially coalescing around a common critique of liberalism, the movement became increasingly diffused and diluted following World War II, when a second generation of Neo-Orthodox thinkers directed its energies toward concerns more directly related to biblical and historical studies, church school curricula, preaching, and liturgies. Neo-Orthodoxy was less "pure" after the war but began to have a wider impact upon American religious life. In fact, it was not until the late 1940s that certain Neo-Orthodox ideas, such as notions of human depravity, collective evil, divine transcendence, and resistance to modernity, began to work their way down to the grass roots of church life.

Increasingly trained by seminary professors who had absorbed Neo-Orthodox thought, some pastors of mainline Protestant churches began to preach in Barthian or Niebuhrian phrases about divine sovereignty, human sinfulness, and the need for a realistic Social Gospel. It is difficult to assess how effectively these notions were transmitted from the pulpit to the pews, but the new theological temper was certainly communicated. In addition, the educational programs of some denominations were rewritten along the ideological lines of Neo-Orthodoxy. This was certainly true of the northern Presbyterians, who not only developed their "Christian Faith and Life" curriculum but revamped their entire approach to religious education. Moreover, apart from new curricula there was a general renewal of interest in Bible study that reflected not only the general Neo-Orthodox reverence for Scripture but the "salvation history" method of biblical interpretation. Neo-Orthodoxy also stimulated a revitalized doctrine of the church, liturgical renewal, ecumenism, and, of course, a postliberal version of the Social Gospel.

While Neo-Orthodoxy did eventually reach the broad popular base of American religious life, its primary legacy remains on the level of theological development. In its critique of liberalism, Neo-Orthodoxy signaled a shift in religious thought that to some degree is still evident in the late 1980s. Certainly American theology has not returned to a pre–Neo-Orthodox understanding of human nature. A series of wars, economic recessions, and nuclear crises have reinforced and perpetuated Neo-Orthodoxy's sober assessment of the human condition. Similarly, the Neo-Orthodox doctrine of divine transcendence continues to influence American theologies, even those so-called secular ones that have emerged in recent decades, such as death-of-God theology, liberation theology, and Christian Marxism. In fact, H. Richard Niebuhr could be considered the prophet of post–Neo-Orthodox radical theologies. In 1960 he published *Radical Monotheism and Western Culture,* described by Ahlstrom as "a requiem for the Neo-Orthodox period." In his summary to this suggestive treatise, Niebuhr brought American theology to a crossroads: "Radical monotheism dethrones all absolute, short of the principle of being itself. At the same time, it reverences every relative existent."

American theologies have moved beyond Neo-Orthodoxy and its postliberal critique. They have moved from Niebuhr's crossroads down the separate paths of radicalism and neo-evangelicalism. Both, however, have been influenced by some of the more trenchant Neo-Orthodox perspectives.

BIBLIOGRAPHY

Sydney E. Ahlstrom, "Neo-Orthodoxy Demythologized," in *Christian Century,* 74 (1957), "Continental Influence on American Christian Thought Since World War I," in *Church History,* 27 (1958), "Theology in America: A Historical Survey," in James Ward Smith and A. Leland Jamison, eds., *The Shaping of American Religion* (1961), and *A Religious History of the American People* (1972); June Bingham, *Courage to Change: An Introduction to the Life and Thought of Reinhold Niebuhr* (1961); Paul A. Carter, *The Decline and Revival of the Social Gospel: Social and Political Liberalism in American Protestant Churches, 1920–1940* (1954; rev. 1956); Deane William Ferm, *Contemporary American Theologies: A Critical Survey* (1981); Richard Fox, *Reinhold Niebuhr: A Biography* (1985); Robert T. Handy, "The American Religious Depression, 1925–1935," in *Church History,* 29 (1960); William Hordern, *A Case for a New Reformation Theology* (1959); William R. Hutchison, *The Modernist Impulse in American Protestantism* (1976).

Jerry A. Irish, *The Religious Thought of H. Richard Niebuhr* (1983); Walter Kaufman, "The Reception of Existentialism in the United States," in *Midway,* 9 (1968); Charles W. Kegley and Robert W. Bretall, eds., *Reinhold Niebuhr: His Religious, Social and Political Thought* (1956); William B. Kennedy, "Neo-Orthodoxy Goes to Sunday School: The Christian Faith and Life Curriculum," in *Journal of Presbyterian History,* 8 (Spring 1980); Donald B. Meyer, *The Protestant Search for Political Realism, 1919–1941* (1960); Randolph Crump Miller, *Biblical Theology and Christian Education* (1956); Charles Clayton Morrison, "How Their Minds Have Changed," in *Christian Century,* 56 (1939), and "The Liberalism of Neo-Orthodoxy," in *Christian Century,* 67 (1950).

Paul Ramsey, ed., *Faith and Ethics: The Theology of H. Richard Niebuhr* (1959); Charles Caldwell Ryrie, *Neo-Orthodoxy: What It Is and What It Does* (1956); Herbert W. Schneider, *Sources of Contemporary Philosophical Realism in America* (1964); Nathan A. Scott, Jr., ed., *The Legacy of Reinhold Niebuhr* (1975); James D. Smart, *The Interpretation of Scripture* (1961); H. Shelton Smith, *Changing Conceptions of Original Sin* (1955); Mary Frances Thelen, *Man as Sinner in Contemporary American Realistic Theology* (1946); Cornelius Van Til, *The New Modernism* (1946) and *Christianity and Barthianism* (1962); Dennis N. Voskuil, "American Encounters with Karl Barth, 1919–1939," in *Fides et Historia,* 8 (Spring 1981), and "Neo-Orthodoxy," in David F. Wells, ed., *Reformed Theology in America: A History of Its Modern Development* (1985); G. Ernest Wright, "Neo-Orthodoxy and the Bible," in *Journal of Bible and Religion,* 14 (1946).

[*See also* CALVINIST HERITAGE; ECUMENICAL MOVEMENT; FUNDAMENTALISM; *and* LIBERALISM.]

RELIGIOUS THOUGHT
SINCE WORLD WAR II

Deane William Ferm

THE structure of American religious thought appeared solid and unshakable as World War II came to an end. The cracks in the foundations of American theology that would become so apparent within two decades had yet to reveal themselves. The old threefold Protestant classification dating back to earlier encounters with the scientific revolution remained in place: liberalism sought to come to positive terms with the modern world, harmonizing faith and reason, church and society; conservatism (and its right-wing counterpart, Fundamentalism) opposed new ways of thinking and reaffirmed certain revealed doctrines—the deity of Christ, the virgin birth, the bodily resurrection, and the second coming; and Neo-Orthodoxy, largely a protest against liberalism, remained dominant in the seminaries, where proponents simultaneously sought to uphold the sovereignty of God and the uniqueness of the Christian faith and to take seriously the conclusions of current biblical and historical research. So, too, the three branches of Judaism—Orthodox, Conservative, and Reform—retained the strength of their prewar years.

American Roman Catholic theology appeared as wedded to the past as ever. Official Protestant and Catholic relations remained intransigent. When, for example, the growing Protestant ecumenical movement resulted in the establishment of the World Council of Churches at Amsterdam in 1948, Catholic church authorities refused to send observers and reaffirmed that the Church of Rome was the one true church. A year later Francis Cardinal Spellman of New York City lambasted Eleanor Roosevelt for her opposition to federal aid to parochial schools and announced that he would no longer publicly acknowledge her. Paul Blanshard's hard-hitting best-seller *American Freedom and Catholic Power* (1949), which stressed the incompatibility of Roman and American Catholicism, showed that intolerance went both ways.

But during the later 1940s and throughout the 1950s a religious revival gained momentum, drawing upon the strength of an emerging American civil religion that had begun to erode the old religious particularities that had been so much a part of Protestantism, Catholicism, and Judaism. The wartime cry "There are no atheists in foxholes" gained further support with the statement widely attributed—though some say inaccurately—to President Dwight Eisenhower that "our government makes no sense unless it is founded on a deeply felt religious faith—and I don't care what it is."

Americans flocked to the churches as never before. Whereas in 1940 49 percent of the total population was church-affiliated, by 1950 this figure had increased to 55 percent, and by the end of the decade it had reached an all-time high of 69 percent. The building of new churches accelerated to keep pace with increasing church attendance. In 1954 the words "under God" were officially incorporated into the Pledge of Allegiance, and two years later "In God We Trust" became the official American motto. But such a revival of interest in religion turned out to be a mixed blessing. Norman Vincent Peale, Billy Graham, Bishop Fulton Sheen, and Joshua Liebman all urged Americans to return to the old-fashioned virtues, but the resultant blending of patriotism and piety intensified the erosion of the historical distinctions within the Judeo-Christian faith, leading to the triumph of the God-in-general—a victory suggested by Will Herberg's description of American religion as

1159

the "triple melting pot." The henotheistic God of American religion reigned over the gods of the particular faiths.

But it would be a mistake to categorize the period between 1945 and 1960 solely as an age of increasing popular piety. The escalating pressures of many different cultural forces—pluralism, urbanization, increased mobility, technology (including the communications revolution) —were not only reshaping American culture, but also widening the cracks in the theological structure. Consequently American religious thought had to contend not only with the growing strength of a civil religion that transcended denominationalism, but also with a tangled skein of convulsive cultural and social changes. So although some commentators have denigrated this period of American history as bland and uncreative—christening the youth "the beat generation" or "the silent generation"—Jeffrey Hart seems closer to the mark when he calls this period "a golden era," an extraordinary epoch in American life.

Protestant theologians Reinhold Niebuhr and Paul Tillich were at the height of their influence. Niebuhr had previously presented a powerful critique of liberalism and its utopianism, contending that the best of human motives are infected with pride and that sin is inevitable but not necessary. But by 1949 Niebuhr's mind had changed considerably. That year he publicly repudiated Neo-Orthodoxy's major European advocate, Karl Barth, because of Barth's charge that the Anglo-Saxon world did not take the Bible seriously enough. He also castigated Barth for allowing no positive relationship between the Christian faith and other ethical and philosophical disciplines. During the 1950s Niebuhr admitted that he was becoming less polemical, and by the end of the decade he was affirming that secular humanists may be more realistic than church people in facing forthrightly the large ethical problems of the day. By this time Niebuhr could confess that Barth no longer affected his thinking and that Barth had indeed become irrelevant to Christians in the Western world.

During this same period Paul Tillich published *The Courage to Be* (1952) and completed his three-volume *Systematic Theology.* He continued to explore the relationship between Christianity and the modern world, fulfilling his lifelong intention to remain on the boundary line between faith and culture. His conviction that God is the "being beyond being" who transcends all human manifestations implied a dissatisfaction with traditional forms of theism—a view that became the forerunner of the radical theologies of the 1960s.

Reinhold Niebuhr's brother, Richard, more a "theologian's theologian" than Reinhold, who made his major contribution as a social critic, became disturbed during the 1950s by what he termed "a new unitarianism of the second person of the Trinity" (the *Christian Century,* 2 March 1960) to be found in American forms of Neo-Orthodoxy. He admitted that he himself could no longer maintain that faith in God can be found only in Christ. Nels Ferré noted that many seminarians of the 1950s had become agnostics who no longer accepted many of the traditional beliefs of the Christian faith, and Episcopal bishop James A. Pike insisted that there had to be a large dose of agnosticism in true religion. Conservative theologian Edward Carnell pleaded for Fundamentalists to end their separatist tendencies, as did Carl Henry, whose book *Evangelical Responsibility in Contemporary Theology* (1957) had as its main thesis that Evangelicals should renounce their theological isolationism and adopt a less defensive approach to philosophy and the sciences. Even evangelist Billy Graham, who had catapulted to national prominence during his California crusades of 1949, noted ten years later that he had become far less provincial theologically and now believed that within Christianity there was a mysterious oneness that overrides all separatist features.

Perhaps the clearest manifestation of the theological and ecclesiastical winds of change sweeping through American theology in the 1950s was the emergence of a cadre of younger theologians who had been captivated by the teachings of Dietrich Bonhoeffer. Bonhoeffer had taught briefly at the Union Theological Seminary in New York City in the early 1940s and then had returned to his native Germany, where he was imprisoned by the Nazis and executed in 1945, only two days before Allied soldiers liberated his prison. The name Bonhoeffer was virtually unknown in America in the decade following the war; in fact, the first systematic study of his thought did not appear in the United States until 1960 (John Godsey, *The Theology of Dietrich Bonhoeffer*). Yet by the late 1950s some of Bonhoeffer's writings—in particular, *Letters and*

Papers from Prison (1953)—had already become a popular resource for seminaries struggling with the perennial problem of determining the proper relationship between the Christian faith and the modern world. Bonhoeffer's cryptic answer rendered him the harbinger of the 1960s: "God is teaching us that we must live as men who can get along very well without him" (p. 219).

During the 1950s there were changes in the offing in Catholic and Jewish circles, albeit less dramatic ones than those American Protestants faced. John Courtney Murray stood out as a vigorous advocate of religious freedom, pluralism, and closer ties between Catholics and Protestants. His stand caused him to be censured by the Vatican, but his ringing defense of religious freedom in his book *We Hold These Truths* (1960) was reaffirmed at Vatican II in the 1960s. Other Catholic intellectuals of the 1950s, such as Gustave Weigel, John Tracy Ellis, and Thomas O'Dea, paved the way for the entry of Roman Catholic scholarship into the American theological mainstream, as well as for the appearance of a distinctively "American" Catholic theology.

Two other Catholic theologians deserve special mention here. The European Teilhard de Chardin sought to harmonize his Catholic faith with a view of life as an ever-flowing process toward greater fulfillment, culminating in the ultimate Omega of Ecstasy. Teilhard was a philosopher and paleontologist by profession, and his masterpiece, *The Phenomenon of Man*—published posthumously in 1959 because of church objections—became a best-seller in America, suggesting an optimistic Christian humanism evolving toward an irreversible perfection. Thomas Merton, a convert to Catholicism in his early years, spent twenty-seven years at the Gethsemane monastery in Kentucky, where he wrote extensively. His most famous book, *The Seven Storey Mountain* (1948), a best-seller in the 1950s and 1960s, tells of his constant struggle for solitude. Merton's later involvement in social activism and Eastern mysticism attracted wide support during the 1960s. His unfortunate death in 1968 ended what undoubtedly would have been an enormous contribution to interfaith understanding.

Judaism witnessed a postwar revival parallel to that in Christian circles, but with one major difference. Whereas in the period between the late nineteenth century and World War II American Jews had sought to be assimilated into American culture and the ideals of American democracy, after the Holocaust they showed a new and growing concern with reasserting their separate identity. Following Will Herberg's contention (borrowed from Marcus Lee Hansen) that "what the son wishes to forget, the grandson wishes to remember," more and more Jews resisted the melting pot and sought to rediscover their Jewish roots. Abraham Heschel and Martin Buber continued to play prominent roles in Jewish theology throughout the 1950s, although Buber had an even more profound impact on his Christian colleagues than on the Jewish community. But despite their determined attempt to stress their distinctive heritage and remain a small American minority group, Jews continued to be confronted by the problems posed by assimilation, including a high rate of intermarriage and a low birth rate. Unlike their Christian counterparts, American Jews have never been particularly strong in the articulation of their specifically theological beliefs; instead of doctrine they have tended to emphasize what Rabbi Eugene Borowitz has called their "passionate ethnicity."

When the 1960s exploded like a bombshell, the theological roof caved in. Commentators have offered many descriptions of the cataclysmic changes that took place at this time: "the end of ideology" (Daniel Bell); "a watershed as important as the American Revolution or the Civil War in causing changes in the United States" (Eric Goldman); the beginning of the "Fourth Great Awakening" (William McLoughlin); "a fundamental shift in American moral and religious attitudes" (Sydney Ahlstrom). Whatever captivating description one may use, it seems clear that the cultural forces referred to earlier—pluralism, urbanization, mobility, technology—coalesced in a convulsive manner that we may well term the secular style.

Here *secularism* refers to the conviction that the only real world is the here-and-now, a world known primarily through the natural and social sciences. In the 1960s many theologians shifted gears to come to terms with this secular style, which was undergirded by supreme confidence in technology and human ingenuity. Why turn to God when humans could take matters into their own hands? A widespread questioning and, for some theologians, even a disavowal of basic traditional religious beliefs seemed a natural outcome of this emphasis on human initiative in a world in which the only certainty is that there is no certainty.

Another major feature of the early 1960s, which in certain respects complemented the new secular style in American religion, was the dramatic change in the attitude of the Catholic church toward the modern world—a change epitomized by the charismatic Pope John XXIII, who convened the Second Vatican Council in 1962 and opened the door to new and refreshing ideas and reforms. The results were truly astounding, as one innovation after another shattered the old stereotypes of the church as monolithic, hierarchical, and unchanging.

Of all the statements produced by this council, none were more revolutionary than the *Declaration on Religious Freedom,* authored in large part by John Courtney Murray, and the "Decree on Ecumenism," in which Protestants were no longer labeled heretics, but were described as "separated brethren whose Churches are used by the Spirit as a means of salvation." Catholics and Protestants now combined forces in service and worship and, twenty years after refusing to participate in Amsterdam in 1948, Roman Catholic theologians were present at the meetings of the World Council of Churches in Uppsala, Sweden. A whole new era in Catholic-Protestant relations had begun, leading the prominent Catholic theologian Hans Küng to declare that any doctrinal differences between Catholics and Protestants were merely "attitudes which have developed since the Reformation," attitudes no longer worth holding (1976, p. 503).

The most visible early Protestant response to the new secularism was Anglican bishop John Robinson's *Honest to God* (1963), which was widely influential beyond the British Isles. This little book popularized the views of Tillich and Bonhoeffer, suggesting that God is not "out there" or "up there," but "within" as the ground of our being (Tillich). To speak of God is to speak of the deepest dimensions of human existence—especially love—and to be a Christian is to accept Christ as the "man for others" (Bonhoeffer), the incarnation of God's love. *Honest to God* was a huge success in America, primarily because Robinson had made the Christian faith compatible with the new secular style.

Another significant theological development of the 1960s was process theology. Following the lead of philosopher Alfred North Whitehead and theologians Henry Nelson Wieman and Charles Hartshorne, process theologians zeroed in on the distinctive features of the secular spirit—change, growth, relativity, uncertainty—and conceived of God in like fashion, holding that God is not eternal and unchangeable in substance but is the Creative Process, finite in character, that works for greater fulfillment and the higher good. The basic aim of process theology has been to make God palatable and alive for modern believers who have lost their way in the faith of their ancestors but who nevertheless seek a vision of reality and God in tune with their own world. Contemporary process theologians such as Schubert Ogden and John Cobb continue to make major contributions to American religious thought.

By far the most significant theological development of the decade was death-of-God theology, which became a major media event throughout America. In insisting on taking the implications of the secular spirit to their extreme conclusions, theologians such as William Hamilton, Paul van Buren, and Thomas Altizer made three major claims. First, they maintained that a thorough commitment to the here-and-now meant the end of belief in anything transcendent or supernatural; thus, God was dead, unreal, gone. Second, however, they affirmed that Jesus lives: Jesus as "the man for others" is the Christian's model for right living. Third, they asserted that Christians, as citizens of the planet Earth, must become fully involved in righting the wrongs of this world; this is their responsibility because there is no longer a God to whom they can turn for sustenance and direction. Death-of-God theologians explained that this emphasis on worldly witness over transcendent faith is "the secular meaning of the gospel" (van Buren).

To be sure, like any theological movement, death-of-God theology encompassed a variety of approaches. To appreciate this variety we shall focus upon four major thinkers. First, William Hamilton sensed such a growing awareness of God's absence from everyday living that for him God was no longer knowable in human experience. Yet the theologian who honestly acknowledged this loss would become a person without faith who no longer affirmed God nor bothered with preaching, worship, and prayer. What would be left to affirm? Hamilton replied that Jesus would remain as "a place to be, a standpoint''; and although affirming Jesus is an arbitrary choice, at least it compels the Christian to face courageously this world and its problems—which was all that a Christian could now really do.

Paul van Buren denied the reality of God (and transcendence) by means of the analysis of language. Language about God is not meaningful, since truth-claims concerning the existence of God are neither falsifiable nor verifiable. The statement ''God exists'' elicits no special concrete information that would make it empirically different from the statement ''God does not exist.'' God-talk no longer has any content in a secular world. The Christian faith, therefore, must deal fundamentally with human beings. But like Hamilton, van Buren still clung to Jesus even after he had abandoned God. Van Buren maintained that Jesus was still available to the Christian as that wholly free human being whose freedom was so contagious as to inspire other human beings to follow him—in short, a visible, immanent Jesus bereft of a transcendent God.

Thomas Altizer took still another approach. He asserted that the coming of Jesus coincided with the death of God—the disappearance of transcendence into immanence. To Altizer, the Christian message was that God-as-Other died in order that God-as-here-and-now could be born in the historical event of Christ's incarnation: God became Jesus, and thus the ''death of God'' represented an actual cosmic and historical event that was final and irrevocable.

The Jewish theologian Richard Rubenstein insisted that the death of six million Jews in Europe during World War II made it inconceivable that anyone could still believe in a loving and righteous God. ''After Auschwitz, what else can a Jew say about God?'' (1966, p. 152). What was left to affirm? All that one could do is return to rituals of meaning—birth, marriage, family, death—that no longer have transcendent significance but still have deep import in the sharing of critical moments in a human community.

While he was by no means a death-of-God theologian, Harvey Cox played a prominent role in the theological reconstruction begun in the 1960s. His best-seller, *The Secular City* (1965), emphasized the positive values of the process of secularization in liberating contemporary believers from outmoded supernatural views, thereby making it possible for them to find a new Chris-

tian style of living molded to the modern world. Cox analyzed the breakdown of traditional religion and the rapid growth of urban life and concluded that secularization should be considered a healthy development that would encourage individuals to build the secular city in God's image. Cox maintained that the process of secularization was in fact a consequence of biblical faith, which denies finality to all human institutions while allowing for new ways in which God's reality can be known. Cox joined with the death-of-God theologians in expressing a heady optimism about human possibilities, but differed from them in his insistence that God was very much alive in the process of secularization. Cox believed that politics had become a major arena for God's activity. One affirms God politically, Cox argued, by becoming a responsible moral agent working to bring about social change.

By the end of the 1960s death-of-God theology had virtually disappeared; most of its proponents had either modified their views or become interested in other issues. The inherent weakness of death-of-God theology was its uncritical capitulation to secularism as a world view, which led other theologians to question both the finality of the secular dogma and the assumption that God's existence depends upon the ability of human beings to conceive of him. Although it might be difficult to articulate God's reality in the modern secular world, it is even more difficult to envisage a world devoid of some intrinsic meaning, i.e., God. When the process of secularization turns into the world view of secularism, then its proponents might simply become unwitting slaves to a particular ideology. Death-of-God theology began to recede in influence as other thinkers asked, Is there more than the here-and-now? And is that ''more'' accessible to human experience? Then, too, if Jesus was to be accepted as a model, as the death-of-God theologians insisted, would not this model include faith in God, worship, and prayer—all such vital dimensions of Jesus' own faith? And how could an arbitrary emphasis on the person Jesus be maintained in a world of increasing religious pluralism?

Harvey Cox also shifted his views; indeed, perhaps the chief reason why Cox has been able to remain an influential theologian in the 1970s and 1980s is his sensitivity to currents of change and his willingness to be open to new insights.

His book *The Feast of Fools* (1969) did not glorify secularization and urbanization, but instead suggested the need for clowning and revelry in a heavily secularized world. A few years later he wrote in *The Seduction of the Spirit* (1973) about the manner in which the Spirit can easily be seduced by human manipulation and domination, and he followed that work with *Turning East* (1977), which examined what Asian religions had to offer. Finally, in *Religion in the Secular City* (1984) Cox noted the unexpected return of religion as a significant influence in a world he and many other theologians had earlier predicted would be beyond traditional religion. Cox has consistently maintained that an adequate faith for modern believers must come to terms with the secular world but, at the same time, must also judge and go beyond that world. Thus the issue is not secularism but modernity.

Another significant theological trend that came into prominence during the 1960s was the "theology of hope." Strongly influenced by the German theologians Jürgen Moltmann, Wolfhart Pannenberg, and Johannes Metz, this theological view emphasized the eschatological dimension of history—the abiding openness to new possibilities in which God becomes the One who promises a future world of fulfillment. Proponents of the theology of hope stressed the social character of the Christian faith, maintaining that authentic faith in God must involve political activity directed toward social change. God then becomes the "power of the future," leading humanity to liberation and justice.

The theology of hope has made its greatest impact in North America, not so much as a movement in its own right but as an important catalyst for parallel theological trends. For example, it has influenced American political theology, which has had as its overriding purpose the merger of the twin biblical themes of ethics and theology. Paul Lehmann, Fred Herzog, and others have contended that the only way that Christians could avoid political issues would be by resigning from the human race. The major political concerns of the 1960s—racism, the war in Vietnam, the revolution of rising expectations—required a theological undergirding that showed a clear affinity with the theology of hope, especially with regard to its focus on the social dimension of Christianity and God's own involvement in the political process.

Some Latin American theologians who studied in Europe brought the theology of hope back home with them and applied elements of it to their own historical situation. Although it would be a serious mistake to conclude that Latin American liberation theology is but a stepchild of European political theologies, a certain degree of cross-fertilization cannot be denied. Then, too, the theology of hope made a decisive contribution to black theology. A leading black theologian, Major Jones, has called attention to this connection in the title of his book *Black Awareness: A Theology of Hope* (1971). But once again, as in the case of Latin American liberation theology, the theology of hope was for black theologians a catalyst and not the final word.

The "secular sixties" had a profound impact on American theology. But by the end of that decade America's mood had shifted, requiring a different set of theological answers. The assassinations of John and Robert Kennedy, Martin Luther King, Jr., and Malcolm X, the seemingly endless Vietnam War, the apparent failure of the war on poverty, and the race riots epitomized by the burning of Watts were some of the dramatic events that took their toll on the human spirit. Euphoria turned to cynicism, action caved into introspection, and liberalism gave way to conservatism as Americans became more deeply involved in the search for "meaning and belonging" (Andrew Greeley). Thus theology in the early 1970s took new and different directions in reaction to the chaos of the preceding years.

Two major trends merit special attention, because they represent two very different responses to the turbulence of the 1960s. On the one hand, following in the footsteps of political theologies and the theology of hope, there emerged liberation theology, fueled in part by Third World theological developments and focusing on different forms of human oppression such as racism and sexism. On the other hand, and more in tune with the emerging conservatism, there appeared a new and more open breed of evangelical theologians who, while standing squarely in the biblical heritage, also sought genuine dialogue with theologians representing other world views.

Black theology was a direct response to the civil rights and black power movements of the 1960s. Martin Luther King, Jr., had captured the imagination of both black and white Americans in his role as a Christian minister and activist, insisting that the Christian faith must provide the resources whereby black and white Americans could through nonviolence march together for justice and freedom. His famous "I Have a Dream" speech during the march on Washington in the summer of 1963 expressed the hope for the dawn of a new day in race relations. But when this again became a dream deferred, many blacks turned to Malcolm X and other more strident advocates of black power and separatism.

By the late 1960s black theologians realized the need to develop a theology specifically for black people that would capitalize on the new consciousness of black power. In *The Black Messiah* (1968) Albert Cleage painted a picture of Jesus as a black revolutionary seeking to liberate his people from white oppression. A year later, in *Black Theology and Black Power,* James Cone presented the first systematic treatment of the proper relationship between black power and black religion, insisting that black power was Christ's basic message for twentieth-century America and that Christ himself must be considered black. Cone dismissed the death-of-God theology as "child's play" and discovered in the theology of hope his main contention that God is on the side of racial liberation. Cone's extreme rhetoric—"Whether whites want to hear it or not, *Christ is black, baby,* with all the features which are so detestable to white society" (p. 68) —polarized blacks and whites. Not until the end of his book, and in subsequent writings, did Cone clarify his view that blackness referred not to skin color but rather was his ontological symbol for oppression, over against whiteness as his symbol for the oppressor. Throughout the 1970s and into the 1980s James Cone has remained a leading figure both in the development of a distinctively American black theology and in the cultivation of stronger links between black and Third World liberation theology.

During the 1970s black theologians exhibited a great deal of diversity. The major issue that divided them was the question of whether blacks should go it alone or whether reconciliation between blacks and whites was an essential component of Christian liberation. James Cone, Albert Cleage, and, later, Joseph Washington led the separatist faction, contending that the Exodus motif represented a model for black people seeking to establish their own separate identity.

James Deotis Roberts became a prime advocate for reconciliation, insisting that black theology must include a thorough and positive reorientation in black-white relations, a goal that should be achieved only through nonviolence. Major Jones also opposed black separatism, asking his colleagues whether blacks with a black God would be any better than whites with their white God. In his book *Is God a White Racist?* (1973) William R. Jones faulted black theologians for not confronting adequately the problem of evil. Jones used the continuing oppression of blacks as his rationale for rejecting a God of love in much the same way that Richard Rubenstein cited the murder of six million Jews as his reason for loss of faith. Jones's criticism still has not received a complete response from other black theologians.

In the 1980s black theology began to lose its fervor as the black power movement lost its momentum. As black theologians began to seek a closer relationship with other movements for liberation, black theology itself witnessed an identity crisis, well articulated by Warner Traynham, who asked whether black theology was basically ethnic, Christian, or liberation, and whether its roots were authentically American or African. This latter question—the relationship between American black theology and African black theology—received increasing attention in the mid-1980s. Another area of dispute has been between black theology and the black churches. Black theologians were not well received in the black churches during the 1970s, and consequently a more positive and constructive attitude between themselves and the churches became a major item on their agenda. Moreover, many black theologians have become disenchanted with European political theologies, believing that the Europeans showed a white bias by refusing to confront white racism and the black tradition. Clearly the proper relationship between black theology and so-called white theology remains a troubling issue for many black theologians. If one thing has become evident, it is that black theology has become as ambiguous as white theology.

Feminist theology has as its focal point the liberation of women from all forms of human oppression and seeks to develop a fully human view of women, including their relationship to men, nature, history, and the cosmos. How these goals are to be achieved and which ones are most important is a subject for continuing debate among feminist theologians.

American feminist theology appeared in the late 1960s and early 1970s as an outcome of the larger parallel drive for women's liberation in the socioeconomic arena. To be sure, this drive for women's liberation was not entirely new. Elizabeth Cady Stanton raised many of the issues confronted by contemporary feminist theologians in *The Woman's Bible* (1895). But it was not until the 1970s that women began in large numbers to question male theological assumptions, including the beliefs that the subordination of woman has been ordained by God, that woman is evil by nature, and that God is a male.

The first major study on the role of women and the church that suggested the need for a specifically feminist theology was *The Church and the Second Sex* (1968) by Mary Daly. Daly maintained that the church had encouraged the view of women as inferior (a "defective male," as Saint Thomas Aquinas put it) and that the church had been a leading instrument in the oppression of women. In the 1970s Daly's views grew increasingly radical as she moved outside the boundaries of the Catholic church and even beyond Christianity to seek concepts and language more closely identifiable with the growing feminist movement—views that she incorporated in her next book, *Beyond God the Father* (1973). At this point Daly insisted that the liberation of women must include the eradication of language and images that perpetuate a sexist society. In her book *Gyn/Ecology: The Metaethics of Radical Feminism* (1979) she contended that men are inferior to women and that women should become "revolting hags" seeking to affirm their original birth out of the inner mystery of the Other. Daly continued to develop these views in her next book, *Pure Lust* (1984).

Mary Daly, however, represents a small segment of feminist theologians who urge a blatant reverse sexism that seems not only to be man-hating but also antagonistic to women who are not members of the radical feminist elite. A more moderate approach is taken by Rosemary Ruether, who remains a committed Roman Catholic and an equally committed feminist. In 1970 Ruether was already comparing the rise of the women's movement with that of the black liberation movement. She noted that women and

blacks originally tried to harmonize their interests with those of their oppressors but soon concluded that to achieve authentic liberation they first had to find their own distinctive identity. According to Ruether there is a common destiny for all oppressed groups: all of them must discover their own special histories and reintegrate into their lives those particular qualities that make them unique and they also must take seriously the responsibility to liberate the oppressors as well as themselves. In her book *Sexism and God-Talk* (1984) Ruether develops a specifically feminist theology, contending that the major tenet of feminist theology is the full humanity of women and that, for example, any biblical texts which do not support this tenet should be rejected as inauthentic.

Although Daly and Ruether may be the most important representatives of two foci of feminist theology today, other women are making major contributions in their own distinctive ways. Letty Russell follows Ruether in suggesting that the exploitation of women is but one significant aspect of many forms of oppression, such as racism and capitalism. She believes that a misunderstanding of the nature of biblical religion has led to a conflict with feminism and takes pains to ground her feminism in a proper view of Scripture; Russell also demonstrates an affinity with Latin American liberation theology by incorporating its terminology. Phyllis Trible examines the issue of sexist bias in Scripture in a manner similar to that of Russell, suggesting the phrase "male and female" as essential to a proper understanding of the image of God. In similar fashion Sheila Collins sees a parallel between feminist and black theologies and looks forward to the day when men discover their femininity and women their masculinity in a truly liberating partnership. She also opts for a more feminized interpretation of history, or what she has termed "herstory."

Feminist theology has branched out into biblical, historical, social, political, and economic as well as specifically theological arenas. Sometimes feminist theology has focused sharply on the issue of sexism in a manner reminiscent of the way in which some forms of black theology have placed an exclusive emphasis upon racism. At other times feminist theology encompasses a broader understanding of liberation theology and expresses concern for a variety of forms of human oppression. *Womanspirit Rising: A Feminist Reader in Religion,* edited by Carol P. Christ and Judith Plaskow, bears witness to the wide diversity among feminist theologians as early as 1979. Although the several contributors to this collection of essays agree that the "religions of the West have betrayed women," they differ significantly in the solutions they offer to the problem. They disagree on a variety of topics: the nature and importance of tradition, the role of the religious community, the place of religious symbols, the authority or expendability of Scripture, and the proper relationship of women to nature, men, and God. By and large one does not find among most feminist theologians (Daly is an obvious exception) the same bias against men that some black theologians have expressed against white theologians. In the mid-1980s feminist theology continues to be one of the most creative theological developments on the American scene. Christ and Plaskow were accurate when they suggested in 1979 that if feminists succeeded in making a major theological breakthrough, religion would never be the same again.

Third World liberation theology has had a major impact on the various forms of liberation theology in North America. Latin America, Africa, and Asia, each in its own distinctive way, have contributed to the changing character of American theology. Third World liberation theology exhibits two primary features. First, it stresses liberation from all forms of human oppression: economic, political, social, sexual, racial, religious, and so on. Whereas in Latin America the emphasis has been on political, economic, and social oppression, in South Africa the racial component has loomed large, while in Asia liberation theology, operating within a diverse religious setting, has stressed the liberation required in seeking a common ground among the major living religions.

The other major feature of liberation theology is its conviction that theology arises out of both the local setting and basic Christian communities. Because of the importance of the indigenous, liberation theology emerging from a Latin American country cannot be transported to North America any more than South African liberation theology can be transplanted to Sri Lanka. These two features have made it essential for North American liberation theologians to be selective in their adaptation of Third World lib-

eration theology, an insight overlooked by some theologians in the early 1970s who hailed the Latin American version of liberation theology as the wave of the future for North America.

Since space does not permit an extensive treatment of the extreme variety to be found in Third World liberation theology, we can give only some generalizations about its impact on North America. Until the 1980s by far the greatest influence came from Latin America, as is indicated by the popular book *Theology in a New Key* (1978) by Robert McAfee Brown. Here Brown deals solely with Latin American liberation theology and how its themes might be adapted to the North American setting. Latin American liberation theologians contend that the primary task of theology is to relate the teachings of the Christian faith to the lives of the poor and oppressed. Theology is, therefore, not so much right thinking about ultimate reality in order to convince the nonbeliever that there is a God; rather, theology's main objective is to liberate the oppressed, a process that requires changing the structures of society which keep the oppressed in submission.

North American liberation theologians saw a clear connection between this form of theology and their own specific concerns. But ironically North Americans focused on the two areas with which Latin Americans have least concerned themselves: blacks on racism and feminists on sexism. Conversely, North American liberation theologians have had the most difficulty relating liberation theology to class differences. For although most Latin American liberation theologians are not avowedly Marxist, they have used the methods of Marxist analysis in pointing to class inequalities as the primary cause of continuing oppression—a type of analysis that does not fare well in capitalist North America. In his book *Prophesy Deliverance! An Afro-American Revolutionary Christianity* (1982) black theologian Cornel West was among the first to show the importance of Marxist social analysis to Afro-American religious thought.

In the 1980s some American theologians began to turn their attention from Latin America to Africa and Asia. While in Asia there are large numbers of people suffering from oppression and severe poverty, there are also many different religions coexisting, in a manner similar to that found in American society. At this point the

Asian context has more parallels with North America than does Latin America, with its largely Catholic population. It appears likely that liberation theology in North America will increasingly take on new forms distinctive from its Third World counterpart, reflecting a variety of ethnic groups and cultural backgrounds—for example, Native Americans, Hispanics, Asian-Americans, Afro-Americans, and even, if not especially, white males. This contextualization of theology will inevitably create new problems for American theologians, for contextual theologies are by definition partial and often provincial and will, therefore, need to be continually challenged by a global world view embracing all humanity on a rapidly shrinking planet.

In contrast to the emerging liberation theology of the 1970s, the other dominant feature of American Protestant religious thought was the turn to the right, a response to a new political and economic conservatism. Many individuals yearned for the kind of secure faith that would provide them a sturdy sense of meaning and belonging in a world of conflicting values, a world that often seemed on the brink of chaos and even extinction. Beginning in the 1940s, with the founding of the National Association of Evangelicals (1942), there emerged a group of Evangelical theologians who decried the excesses of Fundamentalism yet offered a solid biblically grounded alternative to the more liberal theological mainstream. By 1956 this camp had established its own magazine, *Christianity Today*. During the 1970s this group of theologians gained in power and influence.

In his important book *Why Conservative Churches Are Growing* (1972) Dean Kelley argued persuasively that those qualities that were most often annoying to liberals—intense commitment and a high degree of community loyalty—were the very qualities that many individuals now craved. Such commitment and loyalty involved a return to the basic affirmations of the Christian faith that had been spurned by the secular theologians. The Hartford Appeal for Theological Affirmation (1975), signed by many prominent Protestant and Catholic theologians who were not considered to be in the Evangelical camp, decried the accommodation to secularism and urged a reaffirmation of the transcendent God who judges the ways of the world. Signers of the Hartford Appeal affirmed that the church

as the bearer of the Gospel should set the agenda for the world and not the other way around, as the secular theologians would have it.

To be sure, the Evangelical resurgence of the 1970s encompassed as much variety as the secular theologies of the 1960s. But what these new Evangelicals had in common, in addition to reaffirming God's transcendence and sovereignty, was the importance of the centrality of Christ, the need for a conversion to him, and the final authority of Scripture. Yet these beliefs were presented in an atmosphere of openness to critical biblical research and basic social concerns unlike earlier forms of Evangelical theology. A strong indication of a growing social conscience can be noted in the Chicago "Declaration of Evangelical Social Concern" (1973), signed by more than forty leading Evangelical theologians. It urged Evangelical Christians to take a more vigorous stand on behalf of the social and economic rights of the poor and oppressed. *Sojourners* and *The Other Side* are two magazines that have become important forums for Evangelicals who seek to relate their faith to justice issues.

Two other manifestations of the resurgence of religious conservatism in the 1970s should be mentioned here. The first is the charismatic movement, which traces its roots to the Pentecostal movement that flourished at the beginning of this century in the lower economic classes. In the 1970s this movement became more of a middle-class phenomenon, with individual piety as its trademark. Lacking social concern and showing an indifference to doctrine, the charismatics were able to attract followers from many local Christian groups, including Roman Catholics, in numbers far greater than the established ecumenical movement. But in their lack of strong institutional direction and their tendency to be attracted to a motley crew of "spirit-inspired" leaders, the charismatics have been prone to numerous schisms, and the movement seems to have peaked in the late 1970s.

Other beneficiaries of the "return to religion" of the 1970s, who have proved to be an even more serious thorn in the flesh of the new breed of Evangelicals discussed here, have been the Fundamentalists, especially television evangelists. These modern retailers of pop religion—Jerry Falwell, Oral Roberts, Jimmy Swaggart, Pat

Robertson, Jim Bakker—have, despite their naive biblicism, received a huge response from many of those who yearn for a faith that provides clear and simple answers to complex problems. Especially troubling has been the explicit identification of the Fundamentalists with conservative political issues, a connection fostered by Falwell's political action group, the Moral Majority. It seems likely that this resurgence of the extreme religious right, with its conscious use of the latest slick Madison Avenue techniques and its prepackaged words of comfort, is here to stay for the foreseeable future and will constitute a continuing embarrassment to those Evangelicals who desire intellectual credibility.

The most critical issue facing the modern Evangelicals is the age-old problem of how to remain committed to the essential proclamations of the Christian faith and yet at the same time live as a full-fledged citizen of the world. One extreme leads to an uncritical Fundamentalism that dictates its answers to the naive believer. The other extreme erodes specific historical beliefs and endangers the distinctive beliefs offered by Evangelicals. Evangelicals today are "in search of identity," as Carl Henry suggested in 1976—a quest that Henry believes must include a truly biblical ecumenism, an interest in serious theological literature, and sophisticated involvement in the political, economic, and social issues of the day.

During the late 1960s a new trend surfaced in North American Roman Catholic theology in direct response to the Second Vatican Council and its attempt to come to terms with the modern world. The spirit of Pope John XXIII provided the stimulus for American Catholic theologians to adopt a less defensive attitude and become immersed in theological and ecclesiastical renewal. To be sure, the new breed of Catholic theologians was never as radical as the Protestant death-of-God theologians but instead sought ways in which Catholics could still have faith while confronting a world of secularism and godlessness. As early as 1962 John Courtney Murray, in an address entitled "The Problem of God—Yesterday and Today," sought to convince his listeners that the transcendent God of Christianity can be a liberating dimension of their own human experience. For Murray and his colleagues theological renewal was essential, but equally important was the necessary affirmation of God's existence and transcendence. The problem was how to define God's reality for the modern believer. At the end of the 1960s American Catholic theologians Gregory Baum, Leslie Dewart, and Avery Dulles, as well as the European Hans Küng, were not asking, Is God dead? Instead they asked, In what ways can we express the presence of God both in contemporary life and in the modern church?

In his books *The Future of Belief* (1966) and *The Foundations of Belief* (1969) Leslie Dewart became a prophetic voice in shifting attention from the role of the church to the problem of God. Dewart understood the human being as a person-in-process who accepts the evolution of belief as an essential ingredient of human experience. Such an evolution today implies the "de-Hellenization of dogma" in such a way that traditional metaphysical expressions of God's attributes are transformed and reinterpreted in terms of an evolving, self-questioning "relative theism" that confronts the continually changing human experience. Faith ceases to mean assent to propositions beyond the pale of human experience and instead becomes an affirmation of the transcendent dimension of human experience. Dewart also sought to get rid of the Hellenistic categories of supernatural over against natural, which only perpetuate a false dualism, and instead to consider God as, in the Tillichean sense, being beyond being.

Like Dewart, Gregory Baum set out to refocus theology in terms of changing human experience. In his *Man Becoming* (1970) Baum suggested a divine immanence that unites the sacred and the secular. Drawing upon the work of Maurice-Édouard Blondel, he proposed a "doctrinal shift" from the external God to the internal God who is fully involved in history and the concerns of ordinary secular experience. The person of faith is not the one who accepts absolute truth, but, as Dewart proposed, the one who becomes and acts in the ongoing process of fuller humanization. This process of becoming, forever unfinished, is in fact the action of God continually seeking to transform human consciousness. Doubt now becomes a necessary ingredient of faith, for to be creative in the insecurity of unanswered questions can be more consistent with genuine faith than simply holding onto answers that no longer make sense. Baum insisted that everything there is to say about God can be translated into affirmations about human life and that the coming of Jesus truly means that the human is the locus of the divine.

Avery Dulles suggested still another human-oriented approach. He, too, wanted to realign faith with human experience, but unlike Dewart and Baum he was more interested in redefining the nature of the church than in reinterpreting the notion of God. In his *Models of the Church* (1974) he indicated how the historical expressions of Christian belief are intertwined with different forms and styles of human experience. He put forth five models of the church to suggest different ways in which the believer can relate to the Christian faith; each model points to a different emphasis in theology and exemplifies the pluralism so important to the post–Vatican II church. Briefly, these models are the church as institution, as mystical communion, as sacrament, as herald of the Word of God, and as servant. Dulles contended that the theology of the future will display a richer pluralism, a more profound ecumenism, and a greater flexibility of church structure. This pluralism and flexibility should make all Christian churches more open to the mystery and transcendence of God that Christians encounter through Christ in their everyday lives.

The Swiss theologian Hans Küng has also had a major impact on American theological development. A frequent visitor to the United States, Küng has been a visiting scholar and teacher at leading American universities. One of the most controversial Catholic thinkers, he continues to be in and out of trouble with Vatican authorities. Küng has continually called the church to task for its failure to respond decisively to the reforms mandated by Vatican II. In his challenge to church foot-dragging, Küng has not hesitated to question the nature and content of belief, the structure of the church, and the proper role of both pope and priest. He is the author of many best-sellers, and his major tome, *On Being a Christian* (1976), is considered by many to be one of the outstanding theological treatises of the decade.

It would be impossible here to give sufficient attention to the richness of Küng's theological contributions. Briefly, he denies the historicity of both Christ's resurrection and virgin birth, questions the dogmas of papal infallibility—he pre-fers the term "indefectibility"—and apostolic succession, disputes the early origin of the seven sacraments, believes that priests should be allowed to marry, maintains that women should be permitted to be ordained, asserts that ordination was not instituted by Christ, and contends that the primary reason why one should want to be a Christian in these times is to be more authentically human.

By the end of the 1970s Roman Catholic theologians were struggling with the same basic issue that their Protestant colleagues continued to face—namely, what is the proper relationship between theology and the modern world? Many theologians other than those mentioned so far have entered onto the public stage with profound and different results. We have already referred to the creative contributions of Rosemary Ruether. Equally important is Elisabeth Schussler Fiorenza, whose book *In Memory of Her: A Feminist Theological Reconstruction of Christian Origins* (1984) breaks new ground in New Testament studies. In *Blessed Rage for Order* (1975) David Tracy wrote about the new pluralism in theology and opted for a revisionist theological model that has as its main thesis that the Christian faith is in essence the basic expression of secularity itself, a position that Tracy developed further in his book *The Analogical Imagination* (1981). Then, too, Bernard Lonergan and the European Karl Rahner, both molded in the neo-Thomistic tradition, had a great influence on American Catholic thought in their scholarly concern to do for the twentieth century what Aquinas did for the thirteenth. And, of course, most of the leading Latin American liberation theologians—among them Gustavo Gutiérrez, José Miranda, John Sobrino, and Leonardo Boff —are Roman Catholic.

In the late 1980s Roman Catholic theology in America was pluralistic, flexible, and changing, grounded in human experience, yet preserving a transcendent dimension. But the pronounced conservative bent of Pope John Paul II has made the immediate prospects for American Catholic theology uncertain, to say the least. Pope John Paul II has made the task for innovative theologians much more difficult; his disciplining of Hans Küng and the continuing attempts to silence some Latin American liberation theologians portend difficult times ahead. As Richard

McBrien has indicated, American Catholicism may have to wait for another generation and another papacy before it arises out of its present winter of discontent.

Two major issues loomed large in the American Jewish community, gaining strength in the 1960s and maintaining momentum in the 1970s and 1980s: the excruciating memory of the Holocaust and the continuing crisis of the State of Israel since its establishment in 1948. We have already noted Richard Rubenstein's conclusion that the wholesale slaughter of six million Jews during the Hitler years made it impossible for him to believe any longer in a loving and just God. But other Jewish theologians refused to follow Rubenstein in affirming the death of God. They agreed with him that it was their responsibility to keep the Holocaust at the center of worldwide attention to underscore to Jews and non-Jews alike that such a heinous atrocity must never happen again. No one has done this more powerfully than Elie Wiesel, whose novels and speeches containing vivid accounts of his own survival as well as of the extinction of many of his loved ones have seared the consciences of Americans of all religious persuasions. Emil Fackenheim, like Wiesel a survivor of a Nazi death camp, has insisted that after what happened at Auschwitz, anti-Semitism to the civilized mind has become a human impossibility. But like Wiesel and unlike Rubenstein, Fackenheim believes that "the commanding voice of Auschwitz" demands that Jews keep wrestling with the question of God in new and revolutionary ways and that religious Jews must refuse to let secular Jews use the "Holocaust club" as a means of denying God.

The other rallying point for Jews during the past two decades has been support of the State of Israel. Although in years past Zionism has been a divisive issue for some American Jews, the constant struggle of Israel to survive has unified them as never before. American Jewish support of Israel reached a peak after the Six-Day War with Egypt in 1967. But this emphasis on Israel's survival, which has done so much to unite Jews, has also served to divide them from some of their Christian friends who were slow to express their support of Israel in that war and again in the Yom Kippur War of 1973.

Some of the political policies and activities of Israel have caused a strain in the interfaith cooperation of earlier decades. To many Jews the failure of certain Christian groups and individuals to express unequivocal support of Israel constitutes an inexcusable betrayal. Although some Christian leaders tried and continue to try with little success to separate their complete backing of Israel as an independent state from all of its specific policies, other Christian leaders, such as Franklin Littell and Leonard Swidler, have excoriated their Christian colleagues for their failure to stand foursquare with Israel in all respects against its Arab neighbors. Ironically, Evangelical Christians, who often carry on aggressive campaigns in America to convert Jews—the "Jews for Jesus" movement is one example— have expressed strong support for the State of Israel on the grounds that their view of biblical prophecy indicates that Israel must survive for the Second Coming of Christ to take place.

Although growing Jewish backing for Israel had no apparent visible effect on Jewish participation in synagogue life, it has done much to reestablish Jewish pride and identity. American Judaism has also profited from the "turn to the right" that acted as a stimulus to conservative Christianity in the 1970s. Indeed, this development has proved even more significant to the small Jewish minority, who themselves must continue to struggle against assimilation. The Harvard Center for Population Studies has estimated that, if the trends in Jewish affiliation continue as they have for the past two decades, there may be only 10,000 identifiable Jews in America by the year 2076 (*New York Times Magazine*, 30 September 1984). This fact in itself helps to explain why in the past few years the Orthodox movement has become the fastest-growing group and why the American Jewish community as a whole has a renewed sense of a special mission.

Irving Howe believes that American Jews have but two options if they are successfully to resist assimilation: settle in Israel or become serious participants in the Judaism of the Diaspora. But to more liberal Jews this swing to the right seems to have become excessive in some Orthodox circles, leading Reform rabbi Balfour Brickner to accuse the Orthodox of intolerable bigotry in refusing, for example, to recognize him as a legitimate rabbi "or my marriages as marriages, or my divorces as divorces, or my conversions as conversions" (*New York Times Magazine,* 30 September 1984). Rabbi Irving Greenberg, who calls himself "postmodern Orthodox," is leading an effort to liberate extreme right-wing Orthodoxy from its exclusiveness without compromising its intense Judaism.

American Jewish thought today finds itself in a swirl of creative turmoil. Rabbi Eugene Borowitz has raised the question, What will happen to American Judaism if Israel attains peace and the memory of the Holocaust dies? (the *Christian Century,* 8 November 1978). Arthur Green and Zalman Schachter urge a revival of Jewish mysticism as a way of revitalizing Jewish life. Jacob Neusner, Eugene Borowitz, and Emil Fackenheim are the forerunners of a new Jewish intellectualism. Robert Gordis, Jacob Wolf, and many others are likewise seeking to articulate a distinctive American Jewish identity that will keep central the Jewish sense of a special destiny in a world largely alien to Jewish concerns. As Rabbi Brickner has asked: "In an age when little can or does compel, how do we stay Jewish?" (*New York Times Magazine,* 30 September 1984).

It is difficult to predict the future of American religious thought. Harvey Cox believes that the basic Christian communities of the Third World may be the "germ cells" for an American postmodern theology that will manifest itself as a new and distinctive form of popular religion. Richard Neuhaus contends that it is crucial that the "naked public square"—which in reality is never naked—be reinfused with the "great story" of the classical Christian tradition. Yet such reinfusion, if it is indeed possible, will have to be tempered by religious pluralism in American society. Jews and Mormons, Hindus and Buddhists, Moslems and Native Americans, and many others also deserve to tell their story in the public square. So the issue becomes not only how the various manifestations of American religion can come to terms with modernity, but also how each religious group can deal with pluralism, both in its own constituency and in the religious diversity of a shrinking planet?

BIBLIOGRAPHY

Thomas J. Altizer, *The Gospel of Christian Atheism* (1966); Gregory Baum, *Man Becoming: God in Secular Language* (1970); Dietrich Bonhoeffer, *Letters and Papers from Prison* (1953; rev. 1971); Robert McAfee Brown, *Theology in a New Key: Responding to Liberation Themes* (1978); Carol P. Christ and Judith Plaskow, eds., *Womanspirit Rising* (1979); James H. Cone, *Black Theology and Black Power* (1969) and *For My People: Black Theology and the Black Church* (1984); Harvey Cox, *The Secular City: Secularization and Urbanization in Theological Perspective* (1965; rev. 1978) and *Religion in the Secular City: Toward a Postmodern Theology* (1984); Mary Daly, *The Church and the Second Sex* (1968; rev. 1975) and *Beyond God the Father: Toward a Philosophy of Women's Liberation* (1973); Leslie Dewart, *The Future of Belief: Theism in a World Come of Age* (1966); Avery Dulles, *Models of the Church* (1974).

Emil Fackenheim, *God's Presence in History: Jewish Affirmations and Philosophical Reflections* (1970); Deane William Ferm, *Contemporary American Theologies: A Critical Survey* (1981) and, as ed., *Contemporary American Theologies II: A Book of Readings* (1982); Carl Henry, *Evangelicals in Search of Identity* (1976); Will Herberg, *Protestant—Catholic—Jew: An Essay in American Religious Sociology* (1955; rev. 1960); Lonnie D. Kliever, *The Shattered Spectrum: A Survey of Contemporary Theology* (1981); Hans Küng, *On Being a Christian* (1976); William McLoughlin, *Revivals, Awakenings and Reform: An Essay on Religion and Social Change in America* (1978).

Richard Neuhaus, *The Naked Public Square: Religion and Democracy in America* (1984); Jacob Neusner, *American Judaism: Adventure in Modernity* (1972) and *Between Time and Eternity: The Essentials of Judaism* (1975); Reinhold Niebuhr, *Christian Realism and Political Problems* (1953); Richard Quebedeaux, *The Young Evangelicals: Revolution in Orthodoxy* (1974); James Deotis Roberts, *Liberation and Reconciliation: A Black Theology* (1971); John Arthur Thomas Robinson, *Honest to God* (1963); Richard Rubenstein, *After Auschwitz: Radical Theory and Contemporary Judaism* (1966); Rosemary Ruether, *Sexism and God-Talk: Toward a Feminist Theology* (1984); Paul Tillich, *Systematic Theology,* 3 vols. (1951–1963); David Tracy, *Blessed Rage for Order: The New Pluralism in Theology* (1975).

[*See also* BLACK RELIGIOUS THOUGHT; RELIGION IN HISPANIC AMERICA SINCE THE ERA OF INDEPENDENCE; SOCIAL REFORM SINCE THE GREAT DEPRESSION; *and* WOMEN AND RELIGION.]

BLACK RELIGIOUS THOUGHT

James H. Cone

God is not dead,—nor is he an indifferent on-looker at what is going on in this world. One day He will make restitution for blood; He will call the oppressors to account. Justice may sleep, but it never dies. The individual, race, or nation which does wrong, which sets at defiance God's great law, especially God's great law of love, of brotherhood, will be sure, sooner or later, to pay the penalty. We reap as we sow. With that measure we mete, it shall be measured to us again.

(Carter G. Woodson, ed., *The Works of Francis J. Grimke,* vol. 1, 1942, p. 354)

Francis J. Grimke's 1901 statement is an apt summary of the major themes in black religious thought from the late eighteenth century to the present day. Although primarily Christian, black religious thought has been strongly influenced by its African background and the struggle of black people to liberate themselves from slavery and second-class citizenship in North America. Because it developed in response to the involuntary servitude of Africans and the subsequent black struggle for equality, it has never been exclusively Christian or primarily concerned with the explication of creeds and doctrines as found in the dominant theologies of Europe and America. Theology as rational reflection about God was foreign to the intellectual and religious sensibilities of African slaves. Most could not read or write, and the few who could were almost always forced to apply what they believed about God to the survival and liberation of their people, rather than to reflect upon God systematically.

No theme has been more prominent in black religious thought than the justice of God. Blacks have always believed in the living presence of the God who establishes the right by punishing the wicked and liberating their victims from oppres-sion. Everyone will be rewarded and punished according to his deeds, and no one—absolutely no one—can escape the judgment of God, who alone is the sovereign of the universe. Evildoers may get by for a time, and good people may suffer unjustly under oppression, but "sooner or later . . . we reap as we sow."

The "sooner" refers to present, historically observable events: punishment of the oppres-sors and liberation of the oppressed. The "later" refers to the divine establishment of justice in the "next world" where God "gwineter rain down fire" on the wicked and where the liberated righ-teous will "walk in Jerusalem just like John." In black religious thought, God's justice is identical with the divine liberation of the weak—if not "now" then in the "not yet." Because whites continued to prosper materially as they in-creased their victimization of blacks, black reli-gious thought spoke more often of the "later" than of the "sooner."

The themes of justice and liberation are closely related to the idea of hope. The God who establishes the right and puts down the wrong, the God who liberates the oppressed is the sole basis of the hope that the suffering of the op-pressed will be eliminated. Black people's hope is based on their faith in God's promise not to "leave the little ones alone in bondage." Indeed their faith in the coming justice of God is the chief reason why blacks have been able to "hold themselves together" in their struggles for free-dom, even though the odds have been usually against them.

The ideas of justice, liberation, and hope should be seen in relation to the important theme of love. Theologically God's love is prior to the other themes. But in order to separate black reflections on love from a similar theme in

1173

white theology, it is important to emphasize that love in black religious thought is usually linked with God's justice, liberation, and hope. God's love is made known through divine righteousness, liberating the poor for a new future.

God's creation of all persons in the divine image bestows sacredness upon human beings and thus makes them the children of God. To violate any person's dignity is to transgress "God's great law of love." We must love our neighbor because God has first loved us. And because slavery and racism are blatant denials of the dignity of the human person, God's justice means that "He will call the oppressors to account."

Despite the strength of black faith, belief in God's coming justice and liberation has not been easy for black people. Their suffering created the most serious challenge to their faith. Why did God permit millions of blacks to be stolen from Africa and enslaved in a strange land? No black person has been able to escape the existential agony of that question.

Justice, liberation, hope, love, and suffering represent the major themes in the history of black religious thought. In this essay, I will examine black religious thought in the light of these themes, beginning with its origin in slavery and its subsequent development in the activity of black churches and the civil rights movement and in the recent writings on black theology from the 1960s to the present.

ORIGIN IN SLAVERY

Black religious thought in North America achieved its distinctive theological identity in the context of the European enslavement of African people. Unlike Europeans who came to North America in search of freedom in religion and other aspects of life, Africans came on slave ships and were forced to carve out some sense of meaning in an environment of the auction block and the whip. In a strange land, where they had no rights as human beings, African slaves had to develop a system of religious beliefs and practices that would affirm their humanity.

In African traditional beliefs, reality was viewed as a single system with no sharp distinction between the secular and the sacred. In some

sense everything one did should be in service to the divine. Worship consisted in giving appropriate adoration to the High God or Supreme Being, lesser divinities, and ancestors in the expectation that African slaves in the Americas would soon return to their homeland. Many Africans believed that death would be the gateway for their reincarnation in Africa. These beliefs and ideas gave structure and meaning to the captives' world, and they served as the theological starting point for Africans in the Americas.

In Latin America and the Caribbean, African retentions were visibly present in the theology and worship of black slaves. Even to this day one finds Candomblé in Brazil, Santería in Cuba, Shango in Trinidad, Obeah in Jamica, and voodoo in Haiti. Few scholars deny that the African diaspora in Latin America and the Caribbean carried to the New World African styles of worship, patterns of religious music and dance, magical and folk beliefs, and—most important for cultural continuity—religious institutions and sacred offices.

In North America, however, white slaveholders did not permit Africans to practice their religion openly. White slaveholders readily perceived the connection between African religion and slave insurrections. Conscious suppression, along with other unfavorable conditions, greatly reduced the practice and influence of the African tradition. Nevertheless African elements survived in the slaves' music, speech, and thought patterns. Africanisms were also found in the rhythm of dance and the emotional structure of the slaves' existence. When slaves were introduced to Christianity, they reinterpreted what they received in the light of their African past, their present need for dignity and worth, and their longings for a future world in which they would be recognized and treated as human beings.

Black religious thought is neither exclusively Christian (when the latter is defined by the dominant theologies of the West) nor primarily African (when compared with past or contemporary African beliefs). It is both—but reinterpreted for and adapted to the life situation of black people's struggle for justice in a nation whose social, political, and economic structures are dominated by a white racist ideology.

The tension between African and American,

which has always been associated with the public meaning of Christian, is deeply embedded in the history of black reflections and practices in religion. W.E.B. Du Bois's classic statement remains the best description of this paradox: "It is a peculiar sensation, this double-consciousness. . . . One ever feels his two-ness,—an American, a Negro; two souls, two thoughts, two unreconciled strivings; two warring ideals in one dark body, whose dogged strength alone keeps it from being torn asunder" (1903, pp. 16–17).

The "two warring ideals" that Du Bois described have been at the center of black religious thought since its origin. It is found in the heated debates about integration and nationalism and in the attempt to name the community—first the word *African* and then at different times such terms as *colored, Negro, Afro-American,* and *black.* Because it is an unresolved tension, it is the source of both the creative contribution that black religion has made toward black liberation and also a serious theological impediment in the struggle for justice. It was the African side of black religion that helped slaves to see beyond the white distortions of the Gospel and to discover its true meaning as God's liberation of the oppressed from bondage. It was the Christian element in black religion that helped slaves to reorient African religion so that it would become useful in their struggle to survive with dignity in the fight against forces of destruction in their community.

Although the African and Christian elements have been found throughout the history of black religious thought, the Christian part gradually became dominant. Though less visible, the African element continued to play an important role in defining the core of black religion, thus preventing it from becoming merely an imitation of Protestant or Catholic theologies in the West.

Of course, there are many similarities between black religious thought and white Protestant and Catholic reflections on the Christian tradition. But the differences between them are perhaps more important than the similarities. The similarities are found at the point of a common Christian identity, and the differences can best be understood in light of the differences between African and European cultures in the New World. While whites used their cultural perspective in order to dominate others, slaves used

theirs in order to affirm their dignity and to empower themselves to struggle for justice. The major reason for the differences between black and white religion is found at the point of the great differences in life. If religion is inseparably connected with life, then one must assume that slaves' and slaveholders' religious experiences did not have the same meaning because they did not share the same life. They may have used the same words in prayer, song, and testimony or even preached similar sermons. But slaves and their slaveholders could not mean the same thing in their verbal and rhythmic expressions because their social and political realities were so radically different.

Black slaves nurtured their distinctive religion in intimate communication between friends and within families, as well as in larger secret meetings. Scholars refer to this clandestine religious activity as the "invisible institution" or the secret church. The need for secret meetings was created by the restrictions against Africans assembling without the presence of whites and also by black people's dissatisfaction with the worship and preaching in white churches. While the great majority of white Christians condoned slavery, saying it was permitted or even ordained by God, blacks contended that God willed their freedom and not their servitude. Although they knew they were risking a terrible beating or perhaps even death, slaves nonetheless found it necessary to "steal away" into the woods at night in order to sing, preach, and pray for their liberation. In these secret meetings was born not only the major slave insurrections, but also a black version of the Gospel that was consistent with the search for freedom.

Even when slaves worshiped with their masters, it was usually out of a necessity to put on a "good front" so that the masters would think of them as pious and religious. The "real meetin' " and the "real preachin' " occurred in the swamp, out of the reach of the patrols. A former slave, Litt Young, tells of a black preacher who preached "obey your master" as long as her mistress was present. When the mistress was absent, "he came out with straight preachin' from the Bible" (Norman R. Yetman, ed., *Life Under the "Peculiar Institution,"* 1970, p. 337).

It was in the context of these secret meetings that the slave songs (often called Negro spirituals) were born. The slave songs, like so many black sermons and prayers, stressed the theme of God as the liberator of the oppressed:

> Go down, Moses,
> Way down in Egyptland
> Tell old Pharoah
> To let my people go.

A similar theme of liberation is found in "Joshua fit de battle of Jericho," "Oh Mary, don't you weep," and "My Lord delivered Daniel."

The slaves' religious songs also expressed the other themes of black religious thought mentioned earlier, including God's judgment against the oppressors. As one slave expressed it: "White folk's got a heap to answer for the way they've done to colored folks! So much they won't never *pray* it away!" (Henry Swint, ed., *Dear Ones at Home: Letters from Contraband Camps*, 1966, p. 124). Blacks also expressed the same point in such songs as "Dere's no hidin' place down here" and "You shall reap jes what you sow." They believed that the wicked will be punished in hell:

> Then they'll cry out for cold water
> While the Christians shout in glory
> Saying Amen to their damnation
> Fare you well, fare you well.

As there was no justice without punishment of the wicked in hell, so there was no liberation of the oppressed without the reward of heaven. Heaven was connected with the theme of hope. Though black slaves longed for God's liberation in this world, their extreme situation of suffering did not make their physical deliverance a realistic expectation in most cases. Accordingly their hope of liberation was projected into God's eschatological future.

Because many scholars have placed a misleading emphasis upon the "otherworldly" quality of black religion, it is important to point out that heaven for many slaves referred not only to a transcendent reality beyond time and space but also designated the earthly places that they regarded as lands of freedom, particularly Africa, Canada, and the northern United States. Frederick Douglass wrote about the double meanings of these songs:

A keen observer might have detected in our repeated singing of

> O Canaan, sweet Canaan,
> I am bound for the land of Canaan,

something more than a hope of reaching heaven. We meant to reach the *North*, and the North was our Canaan.
(*Life and Times*, 1962 [1892], p. 159)

However, for those slaves who had no chance of escape, heaven referred to that reality which enabled them to affirm their being somebodies even though they were treated like nobodies in this world. Heaven symbolized the slaves' hope in their future liberation, a time when their suffering would come to an end. They looked forward to the time when they would "cross the river of Jordan" and "sit down at the welcome table," "talk with the Father," "argue with the Son," "telling them about the world we just come from."

The dominant emphases of justice, liberation, and hope are closely related to the idea of love. In the religion of the slaves, love can be seen in the absence of bitterness toward whites and in references to their own accounting in the day of judgment. When the slaves talked about the accounting that whites had to give on the day of judgment, it was not because they hated whites but because they believed in the righteousness of God. When they sang "Everybody talking about heaven ain't going there," they were referring not only to whites but also to many slaves whose lives contradicted the commandments of God. According to black slaves, God is no respector of persons and loves all the same. God's love is best revealed in Jesus, whose meaning is summarized in John 3:16: "For God so loved the world, that he gave his only begotten Son, that whosoever believeth in him should not perish, but have everlasting life."

Love and suffering belong together in black religious thought. On the one hand, God loves those who suffer; but, on the other hand, if God loves black slaves, why do they suffer so much? This paradox stands at the heart of black faith. Moses and Job, liberation and slavery, cross and resurrection—these polarities are held in dialectical tension, somewhat analogous to Du Bois's analysis of black double consciousness—"an American, a Negro." But unlike the unresolved tension in black people's cultural identity, their faith in the love of God clearly outweighed the doubt created by their suffering. The reason is due to God's suffering in Jesus.

In the suffering of Jesus, black slaves experienced an existential solidarity: "Were you there when they crucified my Lord" and "he never said a mumblin' word." They also experienced Jesus' solidarity with them. Jesus was present with them as their companion in their misery and their liberator from it into a resurrected existence: "There is a balm in Gilead, to make the wounded whole." While this faith did not cancel out the pain of enslavement, it bestowed upon them a knowledge of themselves that transcended white America's definition of them as slaves. To be sure, they sang "sometimes I feel like a motherless child" and "nobody knows the trouble I've seen"; but because they were confident of God's eschatological liberation, they could add (in the same songs!), "Glory Hallelujah!" The "Glory Hallelujah!" was not a denial of trouble; it was an affirmation of faith. God is the companion and liberator of sufferers:

> Weep no more, Marta,
> Weep no more, Mary,
> Jesus rise from de dead,
> Happy Morning.

BLACK CHURCHES

In addition to creating the invisible institution among slaves in the South, blacks also founded independent churches, mainly in the North, beginning in the late eighteenth century. Like the secret meetings of slaves in the South, the independent black church movement is additional evidence of the difference between black faith and white religion. When Richard Allen and Absalom Jones walked out of St. George's Church in Philadelphia in 1787, because they refused to accept segregation and discrimination, it was the beginning of a separatist church movement among blacks of the North that led to the founding of the African Methodist Episcopal Church (AME) in 1816, African Methodist Episcopal Zion Church (AMEZ) in 1821, Colored Methodist Episcopal Church (CME) in 1870, as well as many Baptist churches in the same period.

It is unfortunate that the black separatists did not write creeds or doctrines in order to define theologically the difference between blacks' faith and the white churches from which they separated. The failure to reflect intellectually on the meaning of their faith has led many black Christians to assume that there was no theological difference between white and black views of the Gospel, as if what one does has nothing to do with the definition of faith itself.

While the absence of intellectual reflections on the faith is unfortunate, it is, however, understandable. Since most blacks in the North, like the slaves in the South, did not have the opportunity to acquire formal theological training or the time and space to develop those skills on their own, they did not comprehend fully the theological consequences of their actions for faith. What Richard Allen and others perceived and expressed emphatically with their actions was that segregation in the "Lord's House" was "very degrading and insulting" and that they were not going to accept it. Reflecting on the event, Allen said: "We all went out of the church in a body, and they were no more plagued with us in the church" (1960, pp. 24–25).

The idea of blacks separating from whites in order to do things on their own, founding independent institutions, was a revolutionary act in the minds of both blacks and whites of that time. Even many radical white abolitionists and their black supporters rejected such an idea. For blacks to do things on their own meant they could think on their own as well. Blacks began to realize that unless they could demonstrate that they were capable of operating their own churches, it would be even more difficult to make a case for black freedom in the society. White slavemasters realized how revolutionary black separatism was and therefore declared the independent black churches illegal in many parts of the South.

The independent black church movement became one of the major bearers of black religious thought. The themes of justice, liberation, hope, love, and suffering are found in the writings and preaching of northern black church persons. Blacks used their churches not only for preaching and singing about God's justice and liberation but also for coping with the social, political, and economic needs of their communities.

Their African heritage and their life situation in America prevented black ministers from making a sharp separation between the material and spiritual needs of their people. Therefore, it was not by chance that the First National Negro Convention was held at Bethel Church in Philadelphia (1830), where Richard Allen served as the pastor. The African Methodist Episcopal Zion Church was so deeply involved in the abolitionist movement that it became known as the Freedom Church. Many black churches were used as Underground Railroad stations for runaway slaves.

Not all blacks in the North separated from white churches. Some remained in order to fight racism in the "Lord's House" as well as in the society at large. They included such persons as David Walker, Henry Highland Garnet, Nathaniel Paul, Alexander Crummell, and Francis J. Grimke.

Black Christians in white churches left an important body of theological literature that shows clearly the differences between black faith and white religion, even in the same churches. Differences occur on the issue of slavery and what should be done about it. Garnet, a Presbyterian minister, and Walker, a Methodist lay person, were the most radical and best known. Walker's *Appeal* (1829) and Garnet's *Address to the Slaves of the United States* (1843) shocked even radical abolitionists like William Lloyd Garrison. Both claimed that Christianity and slavery were radically inconsistent and that the slaves themselves must strike the blow for freedom because God demanded it. Addressing slaves, Garnet wrote:

> It is as wrong for your lordly oppressors to keep you in slavery, as it was for the man thief to steal our ancestors from the coast of Africa. You should therefore now use the same manner of resistance, as would have been just in our ancestors, when the bloody foot prints of the first remorseless soul thief was placed upon the shores of our fatherland. . . . Liberty is a spirit sent out from God, and like its great Author, is no respecter of persons.
>
> (p. 93)

In addition to addressing the slaves concerning their reponsibility to resist slavery and telling whites about the terrible consequences in store for them, black preachers also put some questions to God. The central theological question was: Why did the God of liberation, justice, and love permit millions of Africans to be stolen from their African homeland and enslaved in North America? Paul framed the issue in this manner:

> Tell me, ye mighty waters, why did ye sustain the ponderous load of misery? Or speak, ye winds, and say why it was that ye executed your office to waft them onward to the still more dismal state; and ye proud waves, why did you refuse to lend your aid and to have overwhelmed them with your billows? Then should they have slept sweetly in the bosom of the great deep, and so have been hid from sorrow. And, oh thou immaculate God, be not angry with us, while we come into thy sanctuary, and make the bold inquiry in this thy temple, why it was that thou didst look on with calm indifference of an unconcerned spectator, when thy holy law was violated, thy divine authority despised and a portion of thine own creatures reduced to a state of mere vassalage and misery?
>
> (Carter G. Woodson, ed., *Negro Orators and Their Orations*, 1925, p. 69)

The question of theodicy was the dominant question not only during slavery but also throughout the nineteenth century because the exploitation of blacks did not end with emancipation and the Civil War. Indeed, after the infamous Hayes Compromise of 1877, which led to the election of Rutherford Hayes as president and the withdrawal of federal troops from the South, blacks had even less protection against the brutality of whites than they had during slavery. Not only were blacks politically disenfranchised but the violence of white hate groups was visited on any black person they perceived as asserting equality with whites. Between 1889 and 1899, 1,240 blacks were lynched. The 244 years of slavery, followed by a brutal form of legal segregation augmented by the violence of white hate groups, forced black Christians to probe deeply into why God allowed it to happen.

Two texts served as the loci for interpreting black history in the nineteenth century: Exodus and Psalms 68:31. In Exodus, blacks identified themselves with Israel, and that helped to blunt the edge of slavery since they, like Israel, would be liberated. But this answer did not satisfy all, as suggested by J. Sella Martin: "Has Providence so little care for human lives as to permit the sacrifice of over a million of them for the purpose of overthrowing the system of slavery, only that its victims may be treated worse than slaves after they are free?" (*Christian Recorder,* 26 August 1865). The continuation of black suffering pushed black religious thought beyond Exodus to Job and thus into the realm of mystery. As Job was an example of God permitting the suffering of a good person, so the exploitation of blacks was interpreted as God allowing the suffering of a righteous people. In both cases, the reason was located primarily in the mystery of God rather than in the behavior of people.

The other text blacks most often appealed to for an explication of their destiny was Psalms 68:31: "Princes shall come out of Egypt; Ethiopia shall soon stretch out her hands unto God." With this text, they believed they had the answer regarding the divine purpose of black suffering. Its obscurity enabled blacks to give it a variety of interpretations. Some used it to refute the charge of black inferiority, by identifying "the African race" with the ancient civilizations of Egypt and Ethiopia as exemplars of a glorious African past. Others used it to say that God permitted blacks to be enslaved so they could receive education, elevation, and regeneration by Europeans in order that they might not only redeem the African race but Africa itself. As early as 1808, Absalom Jones said: "Perhaps his [God's] design was that a knowledge of the gospel might be acquired by some of their descendants, in order that they might become qualified to be the messengers of it, to the land of their fathers" (Dorothy Porter, ed., *Early Negro Writing,* 1971, p. 340).

The persistence of black suffering, especially political disenfranchisement and the emergence of white vigilante violence, after Reconstruction caused the great majority of black ministers to withdraw from political engagement and to devote most of their time to strictly ecclesiastical matters. Many scholars have described this period as the "de-radicalization of the black church." The institutionalization of the church, combined with the movement of blacks in great numbers from the rural South to the cities of the North, also encouraged many ministers to concentrate on spiritual matters. The churches assumed a conservative posture, becoming closely identified with the accommodation philosophy

of Booker T. Washington and concentrating almost exclusively on internal church affairs. The themes of liberation, justice, hope, love, and suffering were interpreted to support their withdrawal from the political struggle for justice. Love became the dominant emphasis with a focus on Jesus in terms of patience, humility, meekness, peacefulness, long suffering, kindness, and charitableness. Ministers transferred those virtues to blacks, emphasizing their Christlike nature in contrast to the imperialism, racism, and materialism of whites. Levi Coppin, editor of the AME *Church Review,* said in 1890: "It is my solemn belief, that if ever the world becomes Christianized . . . it will be through the means, under God of the *Blacks,* who are now held in wretchedness, and degradation, by the white *Christians* of the world."

Among those who took exception to this conservative posture were Henry McNeal Turner, the controversial nationalist bishop of the AME Church; Reverdy C. Ransom, an early advocate of socialism and later elected a bishop in the AME Church; and George Washington Woodbey, a Baptist minister and one of the few blacks who was a dues-paying member of the Socialist party. Bishop Turner, a fierce fighter for justice, refused to accommodate himself to any form of discrimination in the churches and the society. When the Supreme Court ruled in 1883 that the Civil Rights Act of 1875 (which gave blacks "equal enjoyment of the accommodations . . . of inns, public conveyances on land or water, theaters and other places of public amusement") was unconstitutional, Turner denounced the Constitution as a "dirty rag, a cheat, a libel and ought to be spit upon by every Negro in the land" (Redkey, 1971, p. 63). He was a major opponent of the accommodationist philosophy of Booker T. Washington and urged blacks to emigrate to Africa since they could not get justice in the United States.

But these exceptions were not enough to change the dominant emphasis of black religious thought as defined by the churches. No persons were more cognizant of this than the few ministers who were seeking to address the social and political problems of the black community. "I get mad and sick," wrote Bishop Turner, "when I look at the possibilities God has placed within our reach, and to think we are such blockheads we cannot see and utilize them" (Redkey, p. 122).

THE CIVIL RIGHTS MOVEMENT AND MARTIN LUTHER KING, JR.

The withdrawal of the black church from politics created the conditions that gave rise to the civil rights movement: the National Association for the Advancement of Colored People (NAACP) was formed in 1909, the National Urban League (NUL) in 1911, and the Congress of Racial Equality (CORE) in 1942. These national organizations, and similar local and regional groups in many parts of the country, took up the cause of justice and equality of blacks in the society. They were strongly influenced by ideas and persons in the churches. Civil rights organizations not only internalized the ideas about justice, liberation, hope, love, and suffering that had been preached in the churches; they also used church property to convene their own meetings and usually made appeals for support at church conferences. The close relations between the NAACP and black churches has led some to say that "the black church is the NAACP on its knees."

Due to the de-radicalization of the black church, progressive black ministers found it difficult to remain involved in the internal affairs of their denominations. Baptist ministers, because of the autonomy of their local congregations, found it easier than the Methodist did to remain pastors while also being deeply involved in the struggle for black equality in the society. Prominent examples are Adam Clayton Powell, Sr., and Jr., both pastors of the Abyssinian Baptist Church in New York. Powell, Jr., made his entrée on the public stage by leading a four-year non-violent direct-action campaign, securing some 10,000 jobs for Harlem blacks. In 1944 he was elected to Congress. Embracing that part of the black religious tradition which refused to separate the Christian Gospel from the struggle for justice in society, he accused the white churches of turning Christianity into "churchianity," thereby distorting the essential message of the Gospel, which is "equality" and "brotherhood": "The great loving heart of God has been embalmed and laid coolly away in the tombs we call churches. Christ of the Manger, the carpenter's

bench, and the borrowed tomb has once again been crucified in stained-glass windows" (*Marching Blacks,* 1973 [1945], p. 194).

Other influential thinkers of this period included Howard Thurman and Benjamin E. Mays. Thurman served as dean of Rankin Chapel and professor of theology at Howard University, dean of Marsh Chapel and minister-at-large of Boston University, and minister and co-founder of the interdenominational Fellowship Church of San Francisco; he also lectured at more than 500 institutions. His writings and preaching influenced many, and *Life* magazine cited him as one of the twelve "Great Preachers" of this century. Of his twenty-two books, some of the most influential are *Deep River* (1945), *The Negro Spiritual Speaks of Life and Death* (1947), *Jesus and the Disinherited* (1949), and *The Search for Common Ground* (1971). Unlike most black ministers concerned about racial justice, liberation, love, suffering, and hope, Thurman did not become a political activist; he took the "inward journey" (the title of one of his books), focusing on a "spiritual quest" for liberation beyond race and ethnic origin. He was able to develop this ecumenical perspective without ignoring the urgency of the political issues involved in the black struggle for justice.

Mays, ecumenist and longtime president of Morehouse College, also made an important contribution to black religious thought through his writings and addresses on the black church and racism in America. The author (with Joseph W. Nicholson) of *The Negro's Church* (1933), *The Negro's God* (1938), *Seeking to Be Christian in Race Relations* (1946), and *Born to Rebel* (1971), he also chaired the National Conference on Religion and Race in 1963. Mays was an example of a black religious thinker who found the black church too limiting as a context for confronting the great problems of justice, liberation, love, hope, and suffering. Like Thurman and Powell, Mays regarded racism as anti-Christian, an evil that must be eliminated from the churches and the society.

No thinker has made a greater impact upon black religious thought—and perhaps even upon American society and religion as a whole—than Martin Luther King, Jr. The fact that many white theologians can write about American religion and theology with no reference to him reveals both the persistence of racism in the academy and the tendency to limit theology narrowly to the academic discourse of seminary and university professors.

Much has been written about the influence of King's graduate education upon his thinking and practice, especially his reading of George Davis, Henry David Thoreau, Mahatma Gandhi, Edgar S. Brightman, Harold DeWolf, G. W. F. Hegel, Walter Rauschenbusch, Paul Tillich, and Reinhold Niebuhr. Of course, these religious and philosophical thinkers influenced him greatly, but it is a mistake to use them as the basis of his life and thought.

Martin Luther King, Jr., was a product of the black church tradition; its faith determined the essence of his theology. He used the intellectual tools of highly recognized thinkers to explain what he believed to the white public and also to affirm the universal character of the Gospel. But he did not arrive at his convictions about God by reading white theologians. On the contrary, he derived his religious beliefs from his acceptance of black faith and his application of it to the civil rights struggle.

In moments of crisis, King turned to the God of black faith. From the beginning of his role as the leader of the Montgomery bus boycott (1955–1956) to his tragic death in Memphis in 1968, King was a public embodiment of the central ideas of black religious thought. The heart of his beliefs revolved around the ideas of love, justice, liberation, hope, and redemptive suffering. The meaning of each is mutually dependent on the others. Though love may be appropriately placed at the center of his thought, King interpreted it in the light of justice for the poor, liberation for all, and the certain hope that God has not left this world in the hands of evil men.

He often used the writings of Tillich, Niebuhr, and other white thinkers to express his own ideas about the interrelations of love and justice. But it was his internalization of their meaning in the black church tradition that helped him to see that "unmerited suffering is redemptive." While the fighters for justice must be prepared to suffer in the struggle for liberation, they must never inflict suffering on the others. That was why King described nonviolence as "the Christian way in race relations" and "the only road to freedom."

To understand his thinking, it is necessary to understand him in the context of his own religious heritage. His self-description is revealing:

I am many things to many people; Civil Rights leader, agitator, trouble-maker and orator, but in the quietness of my heart, I am fundamentally a clergyman, a Baptist preacher. This is my being and my heritage for I am also the son of a Baptist preacher, the grandson of a Baptist preacher and the great-grandson of a Baptist preacher. The Church is my life and I have given my life to the Church.

(*Ebony*, August 1965, p. 77)

The decisive impact of the black church heritage upon King can be seen in his decision to become the pastor of Dexter Avenue Baptist Church in Montgomery, Alabama (and later of Ebenezer Baptist Church in Atlanta, Georgia), rather than a professor of theology or an administrator in a college or seminary. It is also evident in his ideas about justice, liberation, love, hope, and suffering. He took the democratic tradition of freedom and combined it with the biblical tradition of justice and liberation as found in Exodus and the prophets. Then he integrated both traditions with the New Testament idea of love and suffering as disclosed in Jesus' cross, and from all three King developed a theology that was effective in challenging all Americans to create the "beloved community" in which all persons are equal. While it was the Gandhian method of nonviolence that provided the strategy for achieving justice, it was, as King said, "through the influence of the Negro church" that "the way of nonviolence became an integral part of our struggle" (*Why We Can't Wait*, 1963, p. 91).

As a Christian whose faith was derived from the cross of Jesus, King believed that there could be no true liberation without suffering. Through nonviolent suffering, he contended, blacks would not only liberate themselves from the necessity of bitterness and feelings of inferiority toward whites, but would also prick the conscience of whites and liberate them from a feeling of superiority. The mutual liberation of blacks and whites lays the foundation for both to work together toward the creation of an entirely new world.

In accordance with this theological vision, he initially rejected "black power" because of its connotations of hate, and he believed that no beloved community of blacks and whites could be created out of bitterness. King said that he would continue to preach nonviolence even if he became its only advocate. (A few months before his death, King realized that black power is not primarily defined by its connotations of violence and hate but rather as black self-esteem in culture and self-determination in politics and economic development. With these emphases, he endorsed black power and even began to speak of "the necessity for temporary segregation in order to get to the integrated society" [*Conservative Judaism,* spring 1968, p. 8].)

A similar but even more radical position was taken in regard to the Vietnam War. Because the Civil Rights Act (1964) and the Voting Rights Bill (1965) did not significantly affect the life-chances of the poor, and because of the dismal failure of President Johnson's War on Poverty, King became convinced that his earlier dream had been turned into a nightmare. Gradually he began to see the connections between the failure of the War on Poverty and the expenditures for the Vietnam War. In the tradition of the Old Testament prophets and against the advice of many of his closest associates in black and white communities, King stood before a capacity crowd at Riverside Church in New York City (4 April 1967) and condemned America as "the greatest purveyor of violence in the world today." He proclaimed God's judgment against America and insisted that God would break the backbone of its power if this nation did not bring justice to the poor and peace to the world. Vicious criticisms came from blacks and whites in government, civil rights groups, and the nation generally as he proclaimed God's righteous indignation against the three great evils of our time—war, racism, and poverty.

During the severe crises of 1966–1968, King turned, not to the theologians and philosophers of his graduate eduation but to his own religious heritage. It was the eschatological hope, derived from his slave grandparents and mediated through the black church, that sustained him in the midst of grief and disappointment. This hope also empowered him to "master [his] fears" of death and to "stand by the best in an evil time." In an unpublished sermon, preached at Ebenezer Baptist Church in Atlanta in November 1967, he said:

> I've decided what I'm going to do; I ain't going to kill nobody . . . in Mississippi . . . and . . . in Viet Nam, and I ain't going to study war no

more. And you know what? I don't care who doesn't like what I say about it. I don't care who criticizes me in an editorial; I don't care what white person or Negro criticizes me. I'm going to stick with the best. . . . Every now and then we sing about it, if you are right, God will fight your battle. I'm going to stick by the best during these evil times.

> ("Standing by the Best in an Evil Time")

It was not easy for King to "stand by the best," because he often stood alone. But he firmly believed that the God of black faith had said to him: "Martin Luther, stand up for righteousness. Stand up for justice. Stand up for truth. And lo, I will be with you, even until the end of the world" ("Thou Fool," unpublished sermon).

King combined the exodus-liberation and cross-love themes with the message of hope found in the resurrection of Jesus. Hope for him was not derived from the optimism of liberal Protestant theology but rather was based on his belief in the righteousness of God as defined by his reading of the Bible through the eyes of his slave foreparents. The result was the most powerful expression in black history of the essential themes of black religious thought from the integrationist viewpoint:

> Centuries ago Jeremiah raised a question, "Is there no balm in Gilead? Is there no physician?" He raised it because he saw the good people suffering so often and the evil people prospering. Centuries later our slave foreparents came along and they too saw the injustices of life and had nothing to look forward to morning after morning, but the rawhide whip of the overseer, long rows of cotton and the sizzling heat, but they did an amazing thing. They looked back across the centuries and they took Jeremiah's question mark and straightened it into an exclamation point. And they could sing, "There is a balm in Gilead to make the wounded whole. There is a balm in Gilead to heal the sinsick soul."

> ("Thou Fool")

BLACK POWER AND BLACK THEOLOGY

From its beginnings, black religious thought has been faced with the question of whether to advocate integration into American society or separation from it. Since the Civil War the majority of the participants in the black churches and the civil rights movement have promoted integration, and they have interpreted justice, liberation, love, suffering, and hope in light of the goal of creating a society in which blacks and whites can live together in a "beloved community."

While integrationists have emphasized the American side of the double consciousness of African-Americans, there have also been nationalists who rejected any association with the United States and instead have turned toward Africa. Nationalists contend that blacks will never be accepted as equals in a white racist church and society. Black freedom can be achieved only by black people separating themselves from whites—either by returning to Africa or by forcing the government to set aside a separate state in the United States so blacks can build their own society.

The nationalist perspective on the black struggle for freedom is deeply embedded in the history of black religious thought. Black nationalism is centered on blackness, a repudiation of any value in white culture and religion. Some of its prominent advocates included Bishop Henry McNeal Turner of the AME Church; Marcus Garvey, the founder of the Universal Negro Improvement Association; and Malcolm X of the Nation of Islam. They reversed the values of the dominant society by attributing to black history and culture what whites had said about theirs. For example, Bishop Turner claimed: "We have as much right biblically and otherwise to believe that God is a Negro, . . . as you . . . white people have to believe that God is a fine looking, symmetrical and ornamented white man" (Redkey, 1971, p. 176). Marcus Garvey held a similar view: "If the white man has the idea of a white God, let him worship his God as he desires. . . . We Negroes believe in the God of Ethiopia, the everlasting God—God the Father, God the Son and God the Holy Ghost, the One God of all ages" (Jacques-Garvey, 1968, vol. 1, p. 44).

The most persuasive interpreter of black nationalism during the 1960s was Malcolm X, who offered a challenging critique of King's philosophy of integration, nonviolence, and love. Malcolm X advocated black unity instead of the "beloved community," self-defense in lieu of nonviolence, and self-love in place of turning the other cheek to whites.

Like Turner and Garvey, Malcolm X asserted that God is black; but unlike them he rejected Christianity as the white man's religion. He became a convert initially to Elijah Muhammad's Nation of Islam and later to the worldwide Islamic community. His analysis of Christianity and of American society as white was so persuasive that many blacks converted to the religion of Islam and others accepted his criticisms even though they did not become Muslims. Malcolm pushed civil rights activists to the left and caused many black Christians to reevaluate their interpretation of Christianity:

> Brothers and sisters, the white man has brainwashed us black people to fasten our gaze upon a blond-haired, blue-eyed Jesus! We're worshiping a Jesus that doesn't even *look* like us! . . . Now, just think of this. The blond-haired, blue-eyed white man has taught you and me to worship a *white* Jesus, and to shout and sing and pray to this God that's *his* God, the white man's God. The white man has taught us to shout and sing and pray until we *die,* to wait until *death,* for some dreamy heaven-in-the-hereafter, when we're *dead,* while this white man has his milk and honey in the streets paved with golden dollars right here on *this* earth!
>
> (1965, p. 222)

During the first half of the 1960s, Martin Luther King, Jr.'s interpretation of justice as equality with whites, liberation as integration, and love as nonviolence dominated the thinking of the black religious community. However, after the August 1965 riot in Watts (Los Angeles) black clergy began to take another look at Malcolm X's philosophy, especially in regard to his criticisms of Christianity and American society. Malcolm X's contention that America was a nightmare and not a dream began to ring true to many black clergy as they watched their communities go up in flames while young blacks shouted in jubilation, "Burn, baby, burn."

It was during the June 1966 James Meredith "march against fear" in Mississippi (Malcolm X had been assassinated in February 1965) that some black clergy began to openly question King's philosophy of love, integration, and nonviolence. When Stokeley Carmichael proclaimed black power, it sounded like the voice of Malcolm X. Though committed to the Christian Gospel, black clergy found themselves moving slowly from integration to separation, from Martin Luther King, Jr., to Malcolm X.

The rise of black power created a decisive turning point in black religious thought. Black power forced black clergy to raise the theological question about the relation between black faith and white religion. Although blacks have always recognized the ethical heresy of white Christians, they have not always extended it to Euro-American theology. With its accent on the cultural heritage of Africa and political liberation "by any means necessary," black power shook black clergy out of their theological complacency.

Separating themselves from King's absolute commitment to nonviolence, a small group of black clergy, mostly from the North, could not ignore or reject black power. Like King and unlike black power advocates, they were determined to remain within the Christian community. This was their dilemma: How could they reconcile Christianity and black power, Martin Luther King, Jr., and Malcolm X?

In their attempt to resolve the dilemma, an ad hoc National Committee of Negro Churchmen, later the National Conference of Black Churchmen (NCBC), published a statement on "Black Power" in the *New York Times* on 31 July 1966. The publication was the beginning of a process in which a radical group of black clergy in both black and white denominations made a sharp separation between their understanding of the Christian Gospel and the theology of white churches. Addressing the leaders of white America (especially the churches) and the black community, black clergy endorsed the positive elements in black power, especially the right of blacks to acquire power in all areas of life. "Powerlessness," they said, "breeds a race of beggars" (Wilmore and Cone, 1979, p. 23).

In the debate that followed, the clergy of the NCBC became certain that their theological orientation in black history and culture created in them a radically different view of the Gospel from that of white Christians. The term *liberation* emerged as the dominant theme in black theology, and justice, love, hope, and suffering were interpreted in the light of the political implications of liberation. Black clergy were determined that they would not allow the theology of white racists to separate them from their solidarity with suffering blacks in the urban ghettoes. That was

why they found Malcolm X more useful than King, even though they were equally determined not to separate themselves from the latter.

Writing in the general area of black theology began with the public statements of the NCBC in which blacks attacked racism in the white church as heresy. Also important for the development of black theology was the contribution of Vincent Harding. In his essays "Black Power and the American Christ" (1967) and "The Religion of Black Power" (1968), Harding articulated the religious meaning of black power and the challenge it posed for the followers of King.

In 1968, Albert Cleage published a book of sermons with the provocative title *The Black Messiah*. The contents were as controversial as the title. Unlike Henry McNeal Turner and Marcus Garvey, Cleage argued that Jesus and God were literally black. His theological position came to be known as Black Christian Nationalism. He attempted (unsuccessfully) to convince black power advocates that they were the church (even though they were not religiously conscious of it) and he tried to make the clergy of the NCBC understand that the only true church was the black liberation struggle. Cleage interpreted the ideas of liberation, justice, and love exclusively in terms of the philosophy of black separatism.

Although the NCBC and Cleage endorsed black power, it was not until 1969 that the first book on black theology appeared: *Black Theology and Black Power* by James Cone. Cone, less radical than Cleage but somewhat to the left of the NCBC, agreed with both in his identification of the Gospel of Jesus with God's liberation of the poor and the weak. White theology, therefore, was defined as heretical, and black power's message of liberation was referred to as the true Gospel for twentieth-century America.

With the publication of Cone's second book, *A Black Theology of Liberation* (1970), the word *liberation* was made the organizing principle of an emerging black perspective on theology. On the one hand, Cone, unlike Cleage, remained in dialogue with other perspectives on the Christian faith; on the other hand, he, like Cleage, interpreted the themes of justice, love, suffering, and hope according to the political liberation of the black poor.

Other black theologians and clergy of the NCBC supported Cone in his definition of Christian theology as a theology of liberation. In June 1969, shortly after the publication of *Black Theology and Black Power,* the Theological Commission of the NCBC assembled a group of black clergy and theologians who met in Atlanta to write a statement on black theology. They defined it as "a theology of black liberation" and they also connected it with James Forman's "Black Manifesto" (which demanded $500 million in reparations from white churches). "Reparations," they said, "is a part of the Gospel message" (Wilmore and Cone, 1979, p. 101).

In 1971 two important texts on black theology appeared: J. Deotis Roberts' *Liberation and Reconciliation: A Black Theology* and Major Jones's *Black Awareness: A Theology of Hope.* Both Roberts and Jones supported the concept of black theology as liberation theology, but they felt that Cone's emphasis on liberation was too narrow and that his attack on white people was too severe. Roberts balanced the idea of liberation with reconciliation, and Jones balanced Cone's "by any means necessary" with an ethic of nonviolence. Both attempted to develop a black theology that was not dependent on black power and thus did not exclude whites from the Christian community in the struggle to build a just society. Roberts and Jones appealed to the life and writings of Martin Luther King, Jr., for their claims about the Gospel and the black struggle of freedom, while Cone turned to Malcolm X.

No issue affected the development of black theology more than the question of its relation to African history and culture. This issue had been introduced in theology in a provocative manner with the publication of Joseph R. Washington's *Black Religion* in 1964. He claimed that black religion was a unique, non-Christian folk religion derived from the African heritage and the black struggle for social and political betterment. He also deplored black people's separation from true Christianity and blamed it on white Christians. While most black theologians spoke against Washington's ideas, especially his low evaluation of black religion when compared with white Christianity, several agreed with him about the importance of the African heritage in black religious development. Charles Long, Gayraud Wilmore, Cecil Cone, and others went on to offer a related criticism of black liberation theology. Because James Cone and other radical black

theologians concentrated on liberation and did not mention the importance of the African heritage of black theology, the critics contended that the liberation theologians needed to recognize and correct their dependence upon the supposedly heretical European theologians. If black theology is to be truly black, it must derive its meaning from the history and culture of the people in whose name it claims to speak. This critique was substantially incorporated into black liberation theology, particularly in James Cone's *The Spirituals and the Blues* (1972), *God of the Oppressed* (1975), and subsequent writings. Cone began to turn away from his former use of white theologians and to rely instead on slave narratives, sermons, prayers, and songs as the chief sources for the development of the themes of justice, liberation, love, suffering, and hope in black theology.

The most challenging critique of black liberation theologians came from William R. Jones, who asked the provocative question "Is God a white racist?" In his 1973 book, with that question as its title, Jones asked: If God is liberating the black oppressed from bondage, what is the evidence for that claim? Although Jones's analysis posed a serious challenge for all religions of salvation, the way he put the question gave it a special poignancy for blacks. Black theologians could not ignore or belittle it.

Of course there was no answer to Jones's question that would meet the demands of his philosophical structure. But his critique forced black theologians to face head-on the problem of suffering. He made them realize that suffering must be the controlling category of black theology along with liberation, so that black professors could not easily identify liberation with any particular realization in history. The response of black theologians to Jones was to focus more consciously on the theme of hope, as Martin Luther King, Jr., had done earlier. Using the Scripture and the black experience, they contended that in the cross of Jesus, God takes the suffering of the victims upon God's self; and in the resurrection of Jesus, evil is overcome. The victims can now know that their humanity is not negated by their victimization.

Although black theologians debated among themselves about liberation and reconciliation, African religion and Christianity, liberation and suffering, they agreed that white religion is racist and therefore un-Christian. In black theologians' attack on white religion and in their definition of the Gospel as liberation, they moved toward solidarity with liberation theologians in Africa, Asia, and Latin America, and with other oppressed groups (Native Americans, Hispanics, Asians) in the United States. In the early 1970s the dialogues between black and Third World theologians began—first with Africans, then with Latin Americans, and lastly with Asians. The dialogues with Third World theologians on other continents created a realization of the need for dialogue between blacks and other oppressed minorities in the United States and with an emerging feminist consciousness in all Christian groups.

The dialogue with other liberation theologians has revealed both the strengths and weaknesses of black theology. For example, Africans showed the lack of knowledge black theologians had about African culture; Latin theologians revealed the lack of class analysis; Asia showed the importance of a knowledge of religions other than Christianity; feminist theology revealed the sexist orientation of black theology; and other minorities in the United States showed the necessity of a coalition in the struggle for justice in the nation and around the globe.

A black feminist theology has already begun to emerge in the work of such persons as Paula Murray, Jackie Grant, Katie Cannon, Delores Williams, and Kelly Brown. It is clear that black theology will develop radically new directions when a fully developed feminist consciousness emerges. It will deepen its analysis of racism and also protect it from the worst aspects of sexism.

The impact of Third World theologians has already pushed black theology in the direction of a consideration of Marxism and socialism. The context of this exploration has been in the Ecumenical Association of Third World Theologians (EATWOT), which held its organizing meeting in Dar es Salaam, Tanzania, in 1976. Since then meetings have been held in Ghana (1977), Sri Lanka (1979), Brazil (1980), India (1981), and Geneva (1983). Black theologians have also had a positive impact on Third World theologians in accenting the importance of the problem of racism. These dialogues have also established the category of liberation as the heart of the Gospel for many Third World theologians here and abroad.

CONCLUSION: IMPACT ON AMERICAN RELIGION

The impact of black religious thought on American religion has been significant. During the years of slavery, it challenged the white interpretation of Christianity by creating the invisible institution and separatist churches that emphasized God's justice and love as being identical with the liberation of slaves from bondage. When physical liberation seemed impossible, blacks affirmed their humanity by projecting their liberation into God's eschatological future, a time when all wrongs will be righted and evil will be completely exterminated.

From the time of its origin in slavery to its contemporary embodiment in the civil rights and black nationalist movements, black religious thought has challenged segregation and discrimination in society and in the churches. It has contended that God's justice and love cannot be reconciled with racism. Black Christians not only preached and sang about liberation in the next world; they also used their churches as instruments for the establishment of justice in this one. They created organizations that supported their churches and sometimes went beyond them in the fight for the equality of blacks in society.

Through the life and thought of Martin Luther King, Jr., and Malcolm X, black religious thought achieved national and international recognition. King is the only American, besides George Washington and Abraham Lincoln, whose birthday is a national holiday and the second black American to receive the Nobel Peace Prize. Both King and Malcolm X laid the foundation for the black liberation theology that has become widely known and taught in many parts of the world.

The significance of black theology for black religious thought was its identification of racism in white churches as a Christian heresy in contrast to the previous tendency to limit its critique to the ethical behavior of white Christians. Black theology claimed that the faith of white Christians was defective because of their indifference to and support of racism in their churches and the larger society. By identifying white faith with heresy and the Gospel of Jesus with the struggle for justice, black theology has made an important contribution to liberation theology in the churches of the United States and in the church universal. The impact of black theology among black Christians can be seen in their widespread acceptance of the cultural heritage of Africa as important in their struggle for political liberation and also in their definition of the Gospel of Jesus Christ. Black Christians have been challenged to develop their own theology and not simply accept white theological reflections as valid for their experience. Black theologians are teaching them that the black experience of suffering, struggle, and hope can make important contributions to their understanding of the Christian faith. As a result of the growing acceptance of black theology, many black Christians are openly displaying black images of biblical personalities and of the divine (i.e., Moses, prophets, angels, Jesus, and many others) in their churches. Many black heroes (like Henry H. Garnet, David Walker, Harriet Tubman, Sojourner Truth, Malcolm X, and Martin Luther King, Jr.) are also appearing in their churches and homes as prophets and prophetesses. Like other liberation theologies in Asia, Africa, and Latin America, black theology is revitalizing black churches by showing that the Gospel of Jesus is a liberating force for change in society as well as in the hearts of people.

BIBLIOGRAPHY

Richard Allen, *The Life Experience and Gospel Labors of the Rt. Rev. Richard Allen* (1960); Allan Boesak, *Farewell to Innocence* (1977); George Breitman, ed., *Malcolm X Speaks* (1965); Albert B. Cleage, *The Black Messiah* (1968); Cecil W. Cone, *The Identity Crisis in Black Theology* (1975); James H. Cone, *Black Theology and Black Power* (1969), *A Black Theology of Liberation* (1970), *The Spirituals and the Blues* (1972), *God of the Oppressed* (1975), *For My People* (1984), and "Martin Luther King, Jr.,

"Black Theology—Black Church," in *Theology Today*, 40 (1984); St. Clair Drake, *The Redemption of Africa and Black Religion* (1970); W. E. B. Du Bois, *The Souls of Black Folk* (1903); E. Franklin Frazier, *The Negro Church in America* (1963); Henry Highland Garnet, *An Address to the Slaves of the United States of America* (1843); Carol V. R. George, *Segregated Sabbaths: Richard Allen and the Rise of Independent Black Churches, 1760–1840* (1973).

Charles V. Hamilton, *The Black Preacher in America* (1972); Vincent Harding, "Black Power and the American Christ," in *The Christian Century* (4 January 1967), "The Religion of Black Power," in D. R. Cutler, ed., *The Religious Situation: 1968* (1968), "Religion and Resistance Among Antebellum Negroes, 1800–1860," in August Meier and Elliot Rudwick, eds., *The Making of Black America*, vol. 1 (1969), and *There Is a River* (1981); Amy Jacques-Garvey, ed., *Philosophy and Opinions of Marcus Garvey*, 2 vols. (1923–1925; repr. 1968–1969); Clifton H. Johnson, ed., *God Struck Me Dead* (1969); William R. Jones, *Is God a White Racist?* (1973); Martin Luther King, Jr., *Stride Toward Freedom* (1958), *Strength to Love* (1963), *Where Do We Go From Here: Chaos or Community?* (1967), *The Trumpet of Conscience* (1967), and unpublished sermons, Center for Nonviolent Change, Atlanta, Ga.; C. Eric Lincoln, *The Black Muslims in America* (1961; rev. 1973), *The Black Experience in Religion* (1974), and *The Black Church Since Frazier* (1974); Charles Long, *Significations: Experience and Images in Black American Religion* (1986); John Lovell, Jr., *Black Song* (1972); Malcolm X, with Alex Haley, *The Autobiography of Malcolm X* (1965); Benjamin E. Mays, *The Negro's God* (1938); Peter Paris, *Black Leaders in Conflict* (1978) and *The Social Teaching of the Black Churches* (1985); Alphonso Pinkney, *Red, Black, and Green: Black Nationalism in the United States* (1976).

Albert J. Raboteau, *Slave Religion* (1978); Edwin S. Redkey, ed., *Respect Black: The Writings and Speeches of Henry McNeal Turner* (1971); J. Deotis Roberts, *Liberation and Reconciliation: A Black Theology* (1971); Milton C. Sernett, ed., *Afro-American Religious History: A Documentary Witness* (1985); Howard Thurman, *The Negro Spiritual Speaks of Life and Death* (1947) and *Jesus and the Disinherited* (1949); David Walker, *Walker's Appeal in Four Articles* (1829); Joseph R. Washington, *Black Religion* (1964); Charles H. Wesley, *Richard Allen: Apostle of Freedom* (1935); Cornel West, *Prophesy Deliverance!* (1982); Gayraud S. Wilmore, *Black Religion and Black Radicalism* (1973; rev. 1983) and, with James H. Cone, as eds., *Black Theology: A Documentary History, 1966–1979* (1979); Theo Witvliet, *The Way of the Black Messiah* (1987); Carter G. Woodson, *The History of the Negro Church* (1921; 2nd ed., 1945); Josiah U. Young, *Black and African Theologies: Siblings or Distant Cousins* (1986).

[See also AFRICAN HERITAGE IN CARIBBEAN AND NORTH AMERICAN RELIGIONS; BLACK CHRISTIANITY IN NORTH AMERICA; BLACK MILITANT AND SEPARATIST MOVEMENTS; *and* RELIGIOUS THOUGHT SINCE WORLD WAR II.]

RELIGIOUS PHILOSOPHY

Henry Samuel Levinson

FROM the late 1870s through the 1930s professional philosophical communities in the United States gave serious attention to the study of religions. These were the years when the writings of Charles Sanders Peirce, William James, Josiah Royce, George Santayana, and Alfred North Whitehead commanded the attention of a broad sweep of intellectuals. Each of these philosophers identified philosophy as a civic profession, one that served the public good and concerned itself with problems that citizens faced. Each saw that profession as playing a crucial role in federal republican life. Each assumed that the distinctive social and political characteristic of federal republican life was an effort to organize diverse and conflicting interests into a harmonious community, *e pluribus unum,* or one out of many. Further, they each assumed that their nation was to be ordered from the bottom up; that its citizenry or their representatives would decide issues of policy and elect administrators to carry it out. In view of these political and social arrangements they assumed that a good outcome depended on an informed and virtuous citizenry, one that cared for and acted on behalf of the public good. They saw themselves as training people who would become citizen-leaders both to depict virtue and evoke it in others. Each investigated religious thinking, feeling, conduct, personalities, and institutions, because they assumed that without religion, or more particularly some form of Christianity, the American experiment in federal republican life would fail. They assumed that religion or religiousness underpinned federal republican life by emphasizing the commonality of diverse peoples and by authorizing strenuous moral conduct among them. Each claimed that republican life became seriously distorted without religion or religiousness.

Before the late 1870s, to be sure, philosophers in America had already identified their work as serving the public interest. Indeed, they had pictured philosophy as responsible for normalizing the social virtues requisite for Christian republican institutions to thrive. Their assumptions, unexceptionally, had been theological. But the courses that they taught, the lectures that they gave, and the essays and books that they wrote did not investigate or reflect upon religion in any scholarly way. To the contrary, these philosophers made claims about nature, morality, civil polity, and the divine ties among them without much reference to the human activities of religions.

After the 1930s the profession of philosophy and the scholarly study of religion began to part ways. Philosophy was transformed by its practitioners into a technical profession preoccupied with logical issues randomly related to the cultural support of Christian republican institutions. Studies of religion were channeled into mainly Protestant divinity schools and into new religious studies programs in colleges and universities. Prominent religious thinkers in the United States, again mainly Protestant, tended in the direction of varieties of Neo-Orthodoxy and existentialism. They wrote theologies that emphasized differences between reason and faith, world and church, the gracious nature of religion and the calculations of philosophy. Those Protestant thinkers who openly championed varieties of modernism, liberalism, and, in a few cases, naturalism challenged the hegemony of Protestant theologies that emphasized the importance or even inerrancy of Christian beliefs at odds with contemporary knowledge. But writers such as Henry Nelson Wieman, Bernard Meland, and Bernard Loomer were celebrated and followed by divinity school communities, not communities of professional philosophers.

Why did philosophers in the United States turn to religious studies in the late 1870s? What did they accomplish by doing so? And, finally, why and how did philosophy and religious studies ultimately diverge by 1940? Such are the questions that are considered in this essay on religious philosophy in the United States.

PHILOSOPHY AND RELIGION BEFORE THE 1870S

Traditionally, relations between philosophy and religion in Protestant cultures have been problematic at best. This was so because fathers of the Reformation had attempted to wean their more learned followers away from reliance on Scholastic philosophy to Scripture. For Martin Luther, Aristotle was synonymous with philosophy. Luther held that Aristotle's *Nichomachean Ethics* was directly contrary to God's will and opposed Christian virtues. He strongly advised Christians not to read philosophy. His evangelical principle and his theology of the cross made the word in Scripture, preaching, and the sacraments the vehicles of God's grace. For him biblical commandments were apposite God's revelation in Christ, but philosophy opposed Christian faith. The very idea of religious philosophy, therefore, was outlandish.

In principle John Calvin's covenantal theology rendered philosophy imperfect and supportive at best. According to the federal theology that shaped so many of the expectations of Puritan New Englanders, the Old Testament provided a full revelation of the ways in which to organize and run civil society, and the New Testament proclaimed the promise of Christian faith just as fully and finally. But Calvin, who had been a humanist before becoming a Reformed theologian, provided conceptual space for the practice of Puritan Scholasticism to emerge. He argued, on the basis of the doctrine of common grace, that God could will that Christians receive and accept assistance from ungodly sources. Christians, he argued, could learn a great deal about running a commonwealth from Greek and Roman books. This view, along with the example of Augustine as well as the widely held notion that classical philosophy had emerged from Mo-

saic sources anyhow, secured a place, no matter how problematic, for philosophy at early American institutions like Harvard.

Nevertheless, the antiphilosophical strain in the Reformation tradition received strong representation in colonial academies through the writings of William Ames and his followers. Ames made every effort to subsume philosophy under practical theology and doxology, or the principles by which to praise God. But New Englanders had strong desires to keep up with the latest academic advances in England and on the Continent. In the seventeenth and eighteenth centuries this meant paying attention to the new philosophers, for example, René Descartes, Nicolas Malebranche, Blaise Pascal, Baruch Spinoza, Thomas Hobbes, and John Locke. New Englanders squared their concern for piety with such interests by distinguishing between natural and supernatural knowledge and then by making natural knowledge an adequate guide for external (but not spiritual) conduct. This, for example, was the view voiced by Theophilus Golius, whose *Epitome Doctrinae Moralis* (1592) was used as an ethics text in the seventeenth-century Harvard curriculum. Even though imperfect, the natural knowledge of virtue provided by such classic authors as Aristotle, Plato, Cicero, Seneca, and Plutarch could and should be put into civic use.

This compartmentalization of philosophy as relevant to civic life, exclusive of spiritual matters, provided no space for the idea of religious philosophy. So long as the ancients maintained their hegemony over British and Continental scholars, reflective Protestants could assign philosophy strictly nonreligious tasks and distinguish it altogether from the purity of heart inspired by and disposed to God. Things began to change with the revolution in university curricula that occurred in the seventeenth century, a movement that displaced Aristotelianism in natural philosophy, logic, and moral philosophy. The rise, first of Cartesian rationalism, then of rival rationalisms, Lockean empiricism, and rival empiricisms led to new studies of the mind, soul, will, and passions. Such movements of thought were stimulated by Christian reform and attracted many Puritan intellects. The new emphasis on interior life overlapped with Pietist emphases on the ethics of intention, the inner experience of grace, and the importance of the heart as well as the head. If, for Aristotelians, virtue was grounded in rational deliberation, or reason in conjunction with certain natural propensities that were perfectly external, it was linked indelibly to interior life for both Puritans and the new moral philosophers.

By far the most influential books in moral philosophy found in American libraries in the eighteenth century were written by people who thought of their works as equipping Christianity with better insights about Christian virtues than more traditional sources. To be sure, both Hobbes and David Hume tended to bedevil Americans who aimed at maintaining their colleges as Christian seminaries. But the materialist Hobbes and the skeptical Hume were influential as stalking horses. Anthony Ashley Cooper, Francis Hutcheson, and then David Fordyce and George Turnbull, for example, construed their work as explicitly and self-consciously Christian. Even to their most brilliant Christian opponent, Jonathan Edwards, these moralists were Christians heretical for their moralisms. Cooper, Hutcheson, and their successors developed a benevolistic variant on Protestant themes. These thinkers were called Benevolists because they argued that, as a result of God's common grace, men had within them a moral sense or affection that rendered a life of disinterested benevolence not simply appropriate but delightful. For them virtue was not reducible to discursive knowledge or social knowhow. As Christians, they demanded an understanding of virtue that made purity of heart the linchpin for saintly life.

The thing that distinguished British Benevolism from Edwards' neo-Puritanism was the latter's commitment to an utterly theocentric Christianity. For the Benevolists religion and natural virtue were one and the same. For Edwards the saint differed from the naturally righteous person. His reflections on moral experience outside and inside the realm of grace mark the historical emergence of religious philosophy in America, the point at which religious experience was demarcated from moral experience as something that philosophers might study. The conversations and arguments constituted by Edwards and the Benevolists he opposed created the conceptual space needed for the idea of religious philosophy. As the Benevolists saw things, nothing was wanting to people as regarded true virtue if they were not wanting to themselves. As Edwards understood things, however, religious

experience made all the difference: without religion the only thing constitutive of true virtue—the Lord God—was missing.

But Edwards' religious philosophy, as distinguished from both his practical theology and metaphysics, lay fairly dormant as an influence on professional philosophical discourse until Ralph Waldo Emerson tried to wrestle cultural authority away from both nineteenth-century academic moralists and ecclesiastically based preachers. Emerson turned specifically to Edwards to emphasize the gratuitous and delightful qualities of spiritual life as distinguished from the oppressive qualities of conventional moral life.

Between Edwards and Emerson, of course, Protestant religious traditions continued to thrive; theology did, too. But philosophical study of religion, understood as a distinctive element in human experience, did not. In part this was the case because a strong tendency toward spiritual exceptionalism in the American colonies got stronger as Americans approached, fought for, and finally won their independence from Britain. "Spiritual exceptionalism" was the position that some one group, namely "ours," was different from others because "we" maintained some special or privileged relationship to God.

Spiritual exceptionalists in America were committed to the view that their forefathers had established the rudiments for a kingdom of God. In every other nation, they claimed, national conventions and the laws of God's kingdom to come were absolutely different. But not so in America. According to Protestant American exceptionalists, Christian virtue both reflected the rule of God and secured a moral basis for civic life. Holiness and moral righteousness in America, on these grounds, were virtually identical. In this view, grace and law had become one in America as nowhere else.

Within the context of this Protestant kind of exceptionalism, a sort of Scholastic moralism thrived. In other words, philosophers concerned themselves with applying unquestioned moral principles to particular cases. Philosophers paid little attention to religious, as distinguished from moral, life. After the Revolution, as Christian republicanism dominated the national period, or the era between independence and the Civil War, philosophers envisioned their task in moralistic ways. They assumed that only devotion to virtue in public life could safeguard republican liberty from the menacing clutches of coercive interests.

Philosophers during the national period identified their work as professional because it was a form of civic service. They invariably pictured the nation they served as a Christian republic, a polity that could organize itself from the bottom up, *e pluribus unum,* so long as its people maintained Christian virtues in public ways. They saw their role as both depicting and evoking these Christian virtues, conserving the truism that American polity was divinely based and sanctioned, and teaching their students how to apply the rules of Christian virtue to various personal and public predicaments they might face.

These philosophers, who have since become known as "the academic moralists," conceived of their profession as both conservative and maintaining traditional standards of thought and action. The problem facing them was not how to discriminate rules of thought and action in a critical way, nor the discovery and celebration of spirituality; their task was to demonstrate how people should apply accepted rules of thinking and acting to particular cases.

Theories of knowledge and metaphysics did play roles in the works of such academic moralists as Archibald Alexander at Princeton, Philip Linsley at Cumberland, Charles Grandison Finney at Oberlin, James Walker and Francis Bowen at Harvard, Mark Hopkins at Williams, Francis Wayland at Brown, and Noah Porter at Yale. The restrained Baconian empiricism typical of this group restricted science to an accumulation of observations (including the observations of biblical witnesses) and an articulation of laws or rules understood as generalized statements of fact. The thing that made their empiricism restrained was their distrust of "theory" and their unwillingness to make explanations on the basis of "hypothesis" rather than fact. Knowledge, for them, established what nature was, but not why nature was what it was. The metaphysical realism (often identified as Scottish commonsense philosophy) of this tradition, or the view that there is one invariant world, one Reality, and our knowledge is in correspondence with it, went hand in hand with its empiricism, establishing the objective situation corresponding to natural and moral knowledge claims. Metaphysical claims were construed as providing unshakable

intellectual foundations for the normal natural and moral sciences.

The scholars teaching moral philosophy during the national period assumed, without exception, that Christianity made the difference between a simply dutiful America and one that went beyond the call of duty for love of God and neighbor. They were typically trained for the ministry, often the presidents of their schools, and their courses in moral philosophy were at the top of hierarchical curricula that were arranged neither to question nor disturb so much as to settle disputes according to accepted norms. They wrote textbooks that were not just moral but moralistic, scientistic, legalistic, and conservative, socially, politically, and economically. They did not, however, either investigate religion or think of themselves as displacing its function. Whether moral rightarians or ethical teleologists, they scrupulously stuck to questions of moral rule, leaving reflections on grace to servants of the church.

Emerson opposed himself to Unitarianism in particular, but his writings called any sort of academic moralism into question, along with ecclesiastically based religious authority. He challenged both academy and church as backward-looking, spiritless guardians of oppressive convention. According to his view, both institutions were spiritually diseased because they generated life at second hand. They obstructed immediate encounter with the world, suppressed the possibility of inspiration, alienated people from nature—their own, the world's, and God's. Transcendental method, or the bracketing of beliefs not central to his self-understanding, was a discipline for curing the disease of spiritlessness that saturated the church and the academy. The task, he claimed, was to discipline oneself for inspiration, to embark from society and to break away from its conventions adequately enough to listen to one's own soul listening to the process of creation. That, said Emerson, amounted to living at first hand. He urged people not to rely on the conventional formulae of inherited patterns of living but to pattern their own on the basis of their close, solitary observations. He predicted that if people did this, they would find that their own patterns overlapped sufficiently with those that had come before to maintain a sense of continuity and coherence. But they would also experience loss and change and, perhaps, a kind of renewal that had made peace with the past without becoming incarcerated by it, a kind of renewal that left them open-minded about the future but not at loose ends, and finally, a kind of renewal that prepared them to decide what to do with themselves.

Reinvigorating the old grace/law rhetoric of the Puritan traditions, Emerson's variety of radical monotheism placed great emphasis on the differences that religious experience made in American lives. As Edwards had claimed nearly a century before, religious experiences made the difference between feeling at odds and at home with God's world.

By the time Emerson died in 1882, his name had become synonymous with an age of American criticism that was religious to the core. It is no coincidence that the magnificent building that Harvard built for its philosophy department, the very heart of religious philosophy in its heyday, was called Emerson Hall. Emerson would have been appalled by this identification with the academy; so too the academic moralists who stood opposed to his flights of imagination. But the young philosophers—for example, William James, Josiah Royce, and George Santayana—who canonized Emerson's work engaged in just the sort of revision and criticism of tradition that Emerson had championed.

CULTURAL CRISIS AND THE TURN TO RELIGIOUS PHILOSOPHY

Academic moral philosophy relied upon certain entrenched conceptual and practical distinctions that came loose for some influential, culturally conversant parties in the United States around 1860. Indeed, as both intellectual and social historians have shown, American culture in general underwent such massive transformations socially, politically, economically, and intellectually at this time that American self-understanding demanded revitalization.

In particular, classical Christian republican philosophy depended upon distinctions between time and eternity, prudence and virtue, the natural and the supernatural, and ecclesiastical and civic responsibilities. The task of the philosopher had been to teach Christian republican citizens the dictates of their consciences, given to them by a supernatural God for the sake of breaking through time to eternity, or, put another way, for the sake of subordinating prudential desires to

moral laws. Piercing through historical desires (typically characterized in economic and military images) to eternal virtues let a republican citizenry understand its duties. The proclamation of the Gospel message in church provoked that citizenry not only to heed the call to duty but to transcend it, gracefully inspired to go the extra mile for the love of God and neighbor.

But this whole picture began to lose its force for many participants in American high cultural conversation who began to suspect that the supernatural was illusory, that things were historical all the way along, that morality emerged out of the shared interests or desires of "the people," and that some of America's good citizens— people who went beyond the call of duty in their support of federal republican institutions—paid little if any attention to the Gospel message as articulated in Protestant churches.

Then, too, some people began to suspect that the Christian republican vision of a righteous Protestant empire might be a sad little joke as Americans butchered one another through the Civil War, as managers squashed unrest among the workers they exploited, and, finally, as it became less and less possible to tell the difference between the quest for an evangelization of the world on the one hand and the leap to military and economic power on the other.

The task confronting the younger generation of philosophers at the end of the 1870s was to maintain the continuity and coherence of their Christian republican traditions and institutions in light of the very real changes their culture was undergoing. This was no simple enterprise because some of the most entrenched or deep-seated conceptual distinctions binding that culture together were coming apart.

Here it is important to note that the resources of the Christian republican tradition were rich enough to include a mechanism for change that permitted continuity and coherence while also allowing for self-criticism. The tradition, Reformed to the core, relied upon a spirit/law distinction that, as already noted with respect to Edwards and Emerson, made possible both rhetorical strategies for criticizing worn-out rules of thought and practice as well as recommendations for developing spiritual refreshment, reawakening, or reform. The religious investigations of philosophers of the rank of Peirce, James, Royce, Santayana, John Dewey, and Whitehead, then, signaled a revisionary episode in Christian republican culture, one that left American colleges and especially universities in charge not only of conserving the normal arts and sciences but also of developing spiritual or religious criticisms of them.

To be sure, the religious philosophers had their differences. Hindsight, at least, suggests that the deepest opposition to emerge among them was metaphilosophical. In other words, they argued about the point or function of philosophy. On the one hand, Peirce had sparked interest in a back-to-Kant movement for the sake of delineating a better theory of inquiry, and Royce had followed suit. Both these thinkers were traditional. Like the academic moralists who preceded them, they conceived of philosophy as articulating a privileged language for discriminating the truly true and the really real. They demanded reform of the tradition because they had good arguments showing that the classic modern views of knowledge, Cartesian rationalism and both Lockean and Scottish empiricisms, could not deliver the conceptual tools required to safeguard the crucial distinctions on which Christian republican self-understanding depended. But their effort was to reaffirm differences between eternity and history, virtue and prudence, physics and metaphysics, civic and ecclesiastical responsibilities.

On the other hand, James, and then Santayana and Dewey, argued that the Western philosophical tradition since Socrates had been on the wrong track in its quest for ahistorical moral standards and for some special science that could discipline people to see them face to face. These radicals accepted varieties of historicism that sounded the death knell for classical Christian republicanism by showing how Abraham Lincoln's last best hope on earth—a nation constituted *e pluribus unum*—could survive the sloughing of the eternity/history and virtue/prudence distinctions. Their effort was to revitalize American self-understanding by showing how a historicized vision of both moral and religious life better suited intellectual discourse in twentieth-century America.

THE REFORMERS

Charles Sanders Peirce. Following Immanuel Kant, Charles Sanders Peirce tried to render philosophy more scientific. His superordinate concern was to develop a more rigorous set of categories than had Kant for clarifying the very possibility of experience. In the doing, Peirce developed an end-of-inquiry realism, a view that the scientific community eventually established as a true picture of reality. Employing a logic of chance, he argued that scientific opinion would inevitably, though not necessarily, converge in a true set of statements revealing the way things are, much as sixes would inevitably, though not necessarily, result from throwing dice in the long run. This sort of realism accommodated both short-run fallibility in science as well as a kind of critical, criticizable, religious belief.

According to Peirce, the thing that made science better than other methods for fixing beliefs about the ways of the world was the fact that it was self-corrective. Other traditional ways of fixing belief, including belief by governmental decree, by church authority, or by dogmatic metaphysics, stymied revision. Only the demand for open-ended experimentation in the natural sciences, the inevitable return to investigation of a changing world, made cognitive revision an assumption and goal. This was why he so eagerly defended the autonomy of pure research from religion, politics, and technology. On the other hand, and quite without self-contradiction, Peirce insisted that in practical matters of vital concern people might learn from lower animals to trust their instincts. Indeed, in Peirce's view there was no good motive for trusting reason when it conflicted with instinct on vitally important topics.

This instinctivism of Peirce's set the context for his view of religion, particularly his view of belief in deity. Religion, Peirce thought, descended from encounters with deity. People who opened their hearts instinctively to the purposive character of things in general were religious. Moreover, Peirce claimed that religiousness was universal. The members of humankind had a "sort of sentiment . . . of a something in the circumambiant All" (*Collected Papers*). Indeed, he claimed, the immediate experience of an ultimate well-being saturating the universe was so intimately related to a person's understanding of himself, his fellows, and his universe that "religion" was no mere set of beliefs but a way of living.

Peirce got very close to articulating a strong practical/theoretical dualism at this point, which threatened to undercut his commitment to the old Christian republican view that the truth is one. He hedged his distinction between religion as life and science as thought by arguing that views, originating in religious experience and maintained by religious institutions, remained subject to the tests of experience and experiment. A religiously mature person did not fear inquiry. To the contrary, he was sure that changes in knowledge would affect the expression of a religiously mature faith, not the core insight expressed.

Eventually, such views about religion and science led Peirce to place great weight on metaphysics understood as a third and privileged sort of investigation. Thinkers required a general theory of reality, he claimed, that could adequately show how religious views and science hung together. Peirce abandoned philosophical foundationalism, or the search for invariant grounds for making knowledge claims, for a metaphysics of pure process. But he did so for the sake of better fulfilling the traditional Western quest of representing reality in general. He simply came to believe that foundationalist attempts to do this were bound to fail due to certain human incapacities he tried to delineate.

As a metaphysician Peirce developed at least three distinctive doctrines. Tychism, synechism, and agapism committed him, respectively, to the claims that chance played an indelible role in a developing universe; that cosmological development was continuous, in light of chance, not despite it; and that this continuity was fundamentally teleological, aiming toward a lovely and lovable harmony of all things. Peirce construed these doctrines as the keystones of a picture of things he frankly called theistic.

Indeed, Peirce argued that love was the principle that rendered the world "one out of many" (not coincidentally, the republican motto). Relying on the traditional grace/law distinction, Peirce distinguished this divine love from morality. "God," he claimed, meant aesthetic spiritual perfection. The hanging of parts of the universe together in ways that overcame bifurcation or division and, hence, produced feelings of well-being, occurred spontaneously, not voluntarily, just as much in spite of human will as in light of it.

Because Peirce construed religion as instinctual, a sort of life, the idea of developing a positive theology made little sense. Religious thought was better off presented as a platform for ecclesiastical activities such as preaching salvation. His Kantian effort to place philosophy on the secure path of a rigorous science, together with his respect for the vagaries of human instinct about such matters as the purposive character of the universe, rendered most theologies ridiculous in his eyes, either because they displaced rigor with banality or transformed the properly vague into the clearly fictive.

So far as religion was of concern, Peirce placed far greater emphasis on ecclesiastical activities than on theology. He argued that the spontaneous expression of religious instinct would die away were it not for social institutions. Indeed, without a church, "the religion of love can have but a rudimentary existence; and a narrow, little exclusive church is almost worse than none. A great catholic church is wanted" (*Collected Writings*). Such a church should be coextensive with a civilization, saturating culture with its gospel of inclusive love. This vision, he claimed, coincided with "the Christian theory of the way in which the world is to be made better and wiser" (*Collected Writings*).

Peirce's pragmatic view of meaning served as an engine of Protestant criticism in regard to worn-out theologies as well as materialisms. Both theologies and materialisms, he thought, gave static pictures of a world that was actively in process. He argued that people should "consider what effects, that might conceivably have practical bearings, we conceive the object of our conception to have. Then, our conception of these effects is the whole of our conception of the object" (*Collected Writings*). With this instrument of criticism, Peirce said, he hoped to show that some supposed problems are not really so. The pragmatic test could be used to break through pseudoproblems in conventional thinking in order to live spiritually at first hand.

This pragmatic understanding of meaning came to have a profound effect on the Harvard philosophers constituting America's "golden age" of philosophy between 1880 and 1915. But it was not the only thing that Peirce brought to America's preeminent community of philosophers at the turn of the century. A thinker of diverse sensibilities and aspirations, he eventually became recognized as providing a precedent for conflicting parties to philosophical and metaphilosophical dispute. Thus, for example, he is recalled now as perhaps the first profound American contributor to *Erkenntnistheorie*, or the theory of knowledge understood as a systematic science grounding all claims to meaning and knowledge, sometimes in the same paragraph that he is identified as the father of American pragmatism, a movement that came to be dedicated to sweeping philosophy clean of *Erkenntnistheorie* altogether.

Josiah Royce. Peirce remained a philosopher's philosopher for many years, famous for relatively technical advances that seemed (but were not) randomly related to philosophy understood as a civic profession. Josiah Royce was the first civic philosopher in the United States to gain recognition for his efforts to make good on Kant's desire to transform philosophy into an architectonic science.

To be sure, Royce made this effort within the context of philosophical statesmanship. Like Peirce, he was drawn to reading Kant in the wake of suspicions about the breakdown of the Christian republican synthesis. Again like Peirce, Royce was critical of Kant's specification of the categories of thought but was devoted to answering Kant's questions about the conditions that rendered any experience possible. He was eager to do better what Kant had attempted for good republican reasons: he wanted to establish rules of thinking and conduct that would let people subordinate interests to duties, break through time to eternal virtue, and thereby overcome discordant divisions.

In his technical work in religious philosophy, Royce developed a systematic idealism that was geared to set absolute standards for both thought and action, to vindicate belief in the existence of the traditional Christian deity, and to make metaphysical knowledge or interpretation the keystone of rational life.

For Royce, even more clearly than for Peirce, thinking amounted to accurately representing the real. The crucial rational task was to present things as they are; the philosopher's job in particular was to represent things in general sub specie aeternitatis. Thus Royce was fully committed to the republican distinctions between time and eternity, interest and virtue, natural and supernatural.

Royce found it so very important to explore and specify "the religious aspect of philosophy" because he was haunted by the notion that, unless humankind was embedded in some reality that transcended, governed, and lent it lasting meaning, life was a painful tragicomedy. Moral rules, to be sure, organized human conduct. But if those rules did not reflect principles governing being in general, there could be no grounded hope in achieving the well-being for which people yearned. People were saved from meaninglessness by grasping the absolute truth, a truth revealing the role that the human community played in a providential economy. Humankind was revealed as the vehicle of divinity, working to transform the many sorts of things extant in the universe into a harmonious whole. Thought was teleological, militantly transforming many into one.

With this republican vision in mind Royce developed his variety of absolute idealism (something he sometimes called absolute pragmatism because of its voluntarist bent, or its emphasis on the primacy of will). He rejected common sense realism in light of skeptical problems. He argued that knowledge was a kind of judgment, a willful response to a problematic situation requiring solution for the sake of human welfare. But, Royce warned, conditions must be specified to guard against subjectivism. Loyal to the traditional claim that truth lies outside the bounds of variable convention, he insisted that true ideas were both categorical and universal in application.

This, Royce claimed, was as much the case with moral truths as with any other. No sort of truth could be specified simply in terms of the momentary satisfaction of individual needs. In each case, the question occurred whether an individual ought to satisfy the need at issue.

Following precedents in post-Kantian idealism, Royce argued that subjectivism could be overcome, but only by vindicating belief in eternal deity. Morality was not simply a matter of personal choice, because when it was proper, at least, it was generated from an eternal principle of good activity. Religion provided objective grounding for moral decision-making. Indeed, religion, which Royce defined as belief in a deity, was a necessary fact of consciousness, something on which moral life, personal identity, and claims to truth logically depended. This was the thrust of his first major book, *The Religious Aspect of Philosophy* (1885).

In that book Royce argued that in matters of truth, human solidarity or agreement was not enough; there must be some objective test that makes agreement either right or wrong, some foundation on which to secure moral life. Harking back to Cartesian methodological skepticism, Royce claimed that the key to discovering this foundation lay in reflection on doubt and error. In a chapter that Royce always considered the bedrock of his absolute idealism, "The Possibility of Error," he contended that there was at least one absolute truth, namely, "There is error." What made this absolute truth possible? Assuming a kind of phenomenalism, or the view that propositions about physical objects are actually about ideas or sense-data, he argued that two disputants are not able to make erroneous claims about each other, unless they admit that they are finite parts of an infinite and inclusive consciousness. When John makes some claim about Thomas, he is making an assertion about his idea of Thomas. The same holds for Thomas and his "John." This problem, Royce said, may be resolved only if the matter is looked at from the standpoint of a third person, who is neither John nor Thomas but who is able to see Thomas' idea of John, the real John, and so on. Error is possible because "any one finite thought, viewed in relation to its own intent, may or may not be seen by this higher thought as successful and adequate in this intent."

Certainly, Royce noted, someone might contend that the logical possibility of such an infinite all knower was the only requirement for rendering error possible. But Royce countered this by arguing that if something was truly possible, it was actual. If the absolute was truly possible, it was actual. But it must be truly possible, because error is actual. Moreover, reminding his reader that truth claims were judgments about how to resolve human problems in satisfactory ways, Royce claimed that an all knower must inevitably be utterly beneficent, so that the world, "as a whole, is and must be absolutely good, since the infinite thought must know what is desirable, and knowing it, must have present in itself the true objects of desire" (*The Religious Aspect of Philosophy*, p. 444).

In the thirty years following publication of *The Religious Aspect of Philosophy*, Royce made many philosophical advances, some very closely tied to brilliant work in mathematics, but his core epistemological and metaphysical allegiances to an eternal divine spirit grounding both truth and goodness never waivered. His Gifford Lectures, *The World and the Individual* (1900–1901), responded to the charge that his absolute idealism undercut any sense of personal identity. There he argued that individuals were constituted by the absolute system of ideas of which they were a part, but that the uniqueness of personal life was maintained through the exclusive interest that the absolute took in each and every finite being. This accounted not only for unique personal identity, but personal freedom as well.

But until the publication of such later works as *The Philosophy of Loyalty* (1908), *The Sources of Religious Insight* (1912), and *The Problem of Christianity* (1913), Royce's work constantly drew the charge that it was abstract. In *The Philosophy of Loyalty* he clarified his position on selfhood by arguing that it was an ethical concept, a notion that individuated life plans in terms of loyalty to causes or objectives. The absolute was a social whole, a community constituted one out of many by their harmonious loyalty to loyalty. In *The Sources of Religious Insight* he argued that metaphysical reflection systematized what immediate religious experiences intuited. It was reflection on life, not apart from it. Finally, in *The Problem of Christianity*, relying heavily on a doctrine of signs developed by Peirce, Royce identified "the will to interpret" as the central Christian principle of thought and action. This principle commanded people to transform opposing parties into united communities of thoughtful action dedicated to the satisfaction of their members' best interests.

The aim of the religious philosopher, Royce said, was to win the world over to this Christian (republican) doctrine of life. He argued, indeed, that this doctrine was mediatory, expansive, and inclusive. He supported this vision with a theory of interpretation that made mediation between dangerously opposed kinds of thinking and acting the keystone of human life. Personal identity, moral life, and the recognition of metaphysical truth logically depended on the notion of a divine community working to reconcile each and every opposition. In fact, he argued, the will to interpret was the essence of every historical religion; his Christian characterization of it was surely the most adequate one.

Royce thus continued to support distinctions crucial to the maintenance of classical Christian republican culture in America, arguing that eternity enveloped history, that virtue could be distinguished from interest or prudence, and that the ways of the world were divinely ordered.

RELIGIOUS PHILOSOPHY

THE RADICALS

William James. Like Royce, William James was impressed with the intensity of cultural confusion in the United States during the last quarter of the nineteenth century. He was aware that the conceptual, institutional, and psychological bases of Christian republican life had all been threatened. His work, like Royce's, attempted to revitalize American culture by recasting its self-image in ways that accommodated contemporary trends in philosophy, science, literature, politics, and economic life.

James attempted to defend the old natural/supernatural distinction, actively searching for powers at work in the world that might help to save people from calamity when they could not save themselves. But, unlike Royce, James viewed the dissolutions of old distinctions between the eternal and the historical and between virtue and prudence as more promising than problematic. James argued that, even if there were supernatural powers at work in the world, moral republics had no other choice than to get along without ahistorical standards of action and thought. In fact, none were available. But the alternative to objectivity was not moral or intellectual chaos. People were better off owning up to the fact that they were responsible to one another; that their laws and customs were, for the most part, inherited; that they were responsible for maintaining or modifying them as they saw fit; and that they were obligated to transmit them to the next generation. Moral life did not oppose desire in general; it expressed shared desires or interests. This was self-consciously and explicitly so for articulate federal republicans, or people committed to the "one out of many" principle of social and political life.

In a series of brilliant articles and books from 1878 to 1910 James developed a naturalistic and pragmatic view of rationality, morality, and knowledge. In various articles leading up to his magisterial *Principles of Psychology* (1890), he abandoned the old view of rationality as getting to the one right picture of Reality for a Darwinian rendering of intelligence that emphasized the satisfaction of interests, the management of difficulties, and the solution of problems. In James's view rationality was characterized by an ability to maintain an open mind, changing beliefs when circumstances, ideals, or both demanded it.

According to James, once philosophers abandoned the outmoded conception of rationality as representation, they could reshape their understanding of knowledge and morality. Architectural and geometric models of knowledge did not suit his view of rationality as open-mindedness. "Truths" were conceptual tools that worked well enough to help people manage relevant difficulties that stood in the way of satisfying relevant demands. Inquiry proceeded well enough without receiving foundations from epistemology. This was the message of James's *Pragmatism* (1907) and *The Meaning of Truth* (1909).

But if people were responsible to one another's claims, not to some tablet of eternal commandments, then what difference did religion make? For James religious experience transformed an otherwise oppressive and depressing human existence into something delightful, lovely, and joyous.

Recalling both Emerson and Edwards, he argued that people could live a virtuous life in or outside the context of spiritual encounter. They might be lucky enough to live a satisfactory life simply by disciplining themselves to do the right things. So long as human energies sufficed, no extraordinary help was needed; willpower was enough. But to suggest willpower to someone haunted by death, a sense of failure, or feelings of impotency was a sick joke. The achievements of the righteous lay constantly shadowed by the ultimate inability of humankind to direct its own fate.

Moreover, James argued in his Gifford Lectures, *The Varieties of Religious Experience* (1902), that people who lived moral lives outside the context of spiritual encounter typically felt exhausted by their efforts; they felt hitched to virtue the way oxen were hitched to yokes. Religious saints, to the contrary, felt transported and expressed a sense of exhilaration in the wake of their experiences of felt supernatural help. Their lives were graceful, not just moral, showing the world what it was like to overcome bifurcations between man and himself, man and his fellows, man and nature, man and his deities. Their gratuitous concern for others, often antinomian in expression, made the life of voluntary righteousness look paltry.

This sharp emphasis on the old Protestant distinction between grace and law shaped James's concerns as a religious philosopher. He pinned his defense of religion on the importance of saintliness, not on the old eternity/history and virtue/prudence distinctions. First arguing that people had the right to believe in eventual and ultimate salvation or well-being in his influential essay "The Will to Believe" (1896), he attempted to vindicate the spirit/law distinction and the supernaturalism he thought it implied in *The Varieties of Religious Experience.* He called that work his contribution to the fledgling "science of religions" that was geared to establish a consensus about supernatural powers at work in the world. He claimed, on the basis of his review of conversion and mystical literature, that it was reasonable to conclude that at least some people were "continuous with a wider self through which saving experiences come." Testimony supported his view of human-divine continuity as transactional; salvific experiences were joint ventures linking human and divine energies.

James's Gifford Lectures left him with a number of unresolved problems about religion. In particular, he needed to develop a view of experience that both accounted for the possibility of religious encounter and dispelled charges that experiences of deities were merely subjective. He also needed to elaborate a view of inquiry outside the context of "epistemological" foundationalism, or the task of giving knowledge claims unshakable rock-bottom support.

James's *Essays in Radical Empiricism* (1912) was an attempt to rectify the notion of "experience" in ways that would vindicate both his understanding of inquiry and his supernaturalism. In these essays he argued that pure experience was neither subjective nor objective, but affectional; neither inner nor outer so much as happening. "Subjectivity" and "objectivity" were second-order terms of classification, not basic "ontological" kinds of being that required linkage of some sort. Disputed experiences—for example, divine encounters—either held up as such in light of further experiences or they did not. So long as they continued to have consequential effects on the world, there were good enough reasons to hang them together with other events. In any case, religious experiences of delightful well-being could not be placed either in the mind or outside it because they saturated everything in a person's life.

But even granting that religious experiences were affectional, not subjective, traditional empirical investigators found James's supernaturalism preposterous, because it pictured humanity and divinity conjunctively. Ever since Hume empiricists had pictured experience disjunctively and, in doing so, had inaugurated the puzzles on which post-Kantian epistemologists and ontologists had worked.

The thing that made his empiricism radical, James claimed, was its realization that conjunctive relations rested at the heart of historical experience. Experienced things maintained continuity and coherence without having any essential identity making them fundamentally disjunctive from everything else. But if this were so, there was no conceptual difficulty claiming experiences of union between selves and wider selves, people and gods. Thus, there was no conceptual problem supporting the actuality of graceful saintliness.

Indeed, on the basis of his essays in radical empiricism, James was able to rework the conclusions of his Gifford lectures into a new pantheism, one that reflected a post-Christian but religious republican culture devoted to making the world one out of many. The varieties of religious experience, he thought, sufficiently confirmed the chance of salvation by showing that humanity and divinity might work together to overcome the things that impeded joy in the world. Divine encounters revealed that grace might secure what moral volunteers could never accomplish, a cooperative republican life remarkable for its selfless beauty.

James attempted to make this vision persuasive in *A Pluralistic Universe* (1909), the last major book he saw published. There, he pictured the ways of the world as analogous to a federal republic and continued to exhort his readers to take up gladly the cause of *e pluribus unum.* The book presented a pluralistic pantheism, a view that made divinity ultimate, not absolute, or some state of affairs that would come to be but was not in control of everything all the time. Divinity, James argued, was in the making. Things would become utterly divine if and when the shared interests of all of the many agents constituting the universe became satisfied in joyous ways.

George Santayana. A student of both James and Royce, George Santayana joined them as a colleague at Harvard in 1889 (the year Francis Bowen retired). He followed James's revolt against the philosophical tradition for the sake of espousing a sort of religious naturalism that he blended, at least for a time, with a devotion to republicanism. Like James, Santayana abandoned allegiance to old distinctions between "eternal" virtue and "temporal" interests, on the one hand, and knowledge and opinion, on the other. He followed James's lead in picturing humankind as plural and in voicing a natural interest theory of morality and a pragmatic understanding of knowledge. But unlike James, Santayana abandoned supernaturalism as well. He urged people to retain certain religious dispositions like piety, spirituality, and charity without mistakenly claiming that such modes of life were grounded in, or tied to, any supernatural power at work in the world. Such views received classic expression in *The Life of Reason* (1905–1906), a five-volume study of the ways in which common sense, society, religion, art, and science together constitute culture.

In that work Santayana argued that piety amounted to thanksgiving for the powers on which a person's being depended; for example, the natural environment, one's nation, cultural institutions, and parents. Spirituality was expressed in one's active allegiance to superordinate ideals. Charity was the realization of the relativity of one's own pious allegiances and spiritual goals, the ability to appreciate the innocence of the things one hated and the clearness of the things one frowned upon or denied.

So far as the quest for immortality went, Santayana challenged religiously minded people not to confuse material everlastingness, simply a wishful thought unsupported by sound observations, with ideal immortality, the ability to render one's life a transparent vehicle of qualities randomly related to time. He recommended the latter course to the spiritually minded. Such qualities as piety, spirituality, and charity were not only consonant with but partly constitutive of moral life together in his view. But there were superstitious and fanatical elements in traditional religion that could, and should, be abandoned.

Superstition, Santayana claimed, occurred whenever people confused ideals with powers. Divinity, for example, was an expression of ideal goodness, perfection, or beauty, not a power at work in the world, except as it informed human conduct. Experiences of divinity were the conse-

quences of natural events, not the result, as James had tried to show, of encountering supernatural beings. Fanaticism took place whenever people mistook their own aspirations as either inclusively or exclusively proper.

But if religions required modification away from superstition and fanaticism, they were also to be celebrated because they, more than other elements of culture, let people love life in the consciousness of impotence. Santayana argued for the dissolution of a Christianity that distinguished two worlds, natural and supernatural, two levels of truth, practical and theoretical, and two kinds of moral insight, human and divinely revealed. But he also argued repeatedly that the natural world "has a spiritual life possible in it, which looks not to another world but to the beauty and perfection that this world suggests, approaches, and misses" (*The Realm of Spirit*, 1942).

Spiritual life, including philosophical meditation, Santayana claimed, should be understood on the model of festivity. It let people embark from the constraints of their normal routines for spiritual refreshment that came from taking delight in lovely things. Rituals displaced the rules, roles, and relationships that constituted hierarchical social institutions; they highlighted conditions that bound people together in joyful ways, giving them a sense of human solidarity and leading them to an avowal of their humankindness. This was the aim of Santayana's own meditations, especially those published after he left his professorship at Harvard in 1912 to devote himself to writing full time in England and western Europe.

From Santayana's spiritual perspective the course of modern philosophy was profoundly off track. In his view the philosopher's task was to reflect on the difficulties of human finitude. But ever since Descartes philosophers had abandoned this work in order to solve something that to Santayana was a pseudoproblem—the problem of the external world. Contemporaries like Bertrand Russell and George E. Moore were, thereby, suffering from "intellectual cramp"; they were turning philosophy into a "colossal folly" because they were "keenly excited about not knowing where they are" (*Soliloquies in England*, 1967).

Santayana joined pragmatists like James and Dewey in efforts to dissolve interest in epistemology. Somewhat like Martin Heidegger in Germany, however, he maintained that pragmatists obscured the basically poetic character of discourse by picturing it as instrumental, or as a sort of practical tool, all the way down. In the doing, they collapsed spiritual quests for consummation into the tasks of social reform. The pragmatists, he claimed, wrote works that issued social imperatives. He wished them well. But he was interested in pursuing disciplines that let people sense the beauty of reflective mortal life no matter how society was composed, decomposed, or recomposed.

On the basis of this orientation Santayana wrote such works as *Scepticism and Animal Faith* (1923), *Dialogues in Limbo* (1925), *Realms of Being* (1927–1940), *The Idea of Christ in the Gospels* (1946), and *Dominations and Powers* (1951). His most sustained set of philosophical exercises, *Scepticism and Animal Faith* simultaneously sought to undo the projects of modern philosophy and to confess an understanding of the predicaments and promises of humankind. He attempted to wean philosophy from the task of mirroring nature as she understands herself, by showing that skeptical discipline resulted in intuitions randomly related to inquiry. He confessed that he could not make sense of himself as a human animal without voicing the languages of matter, spirit or consciousness, essence or the terms of discourse, and truth.

In *Realms of Being* Santayana argued that humans were thrown into material circumstances of overwhelming force that demanded accommodation for life's sake, not to mention well-being. Humans were spiritual by their ability to think about thought as such, a capacity that let them change their minds by bringing new standards or purposes into their lives. But thought as such was impotent apart from material being. Truth was morally basic, not because error was such a great problem, but because deception and self-deception (particularly about the power of thought) were the root of distinctively human misery.

In his *Soliloquies* Santayana characterized his own faith as comic, as a belief that death-haunted creatures could take joy just as seriously as meanness, hoping not for eternal bliss but for memorably delightful being. *The Idea of Christ in the Gospels* showed how meditation on Christ crucified might be taken at least as seriously by comic naturalists as by supernaturalists. If few were courageous enough to accept their mortal lot, this was possible. Those who ventured to do so might well ponder the Gospel message that all the willpower in the world and all the well doing it produced never cured a person of creatureliness, but a joy and delight in being might graciously well up within him, making life a little more divine so long as it lasted.

John Dewey. The work of John Dewey was the brunt of much of Santayana's criticism. From the standpoint of Santayana's aesthetic spirituality, Dewey's writings looked like efforts to transform philosophy into an institution for social engineering. Santayana claimed that Dewey's lectures were so focused on social problems that they eclipsed the old Christian concern for the soul in its solitude.

This picture of Dewey's work has more than a grain of truth about it. Social engineering was, indeed, a part of his vision of the tasks of theory and criticism. But Dewey's metaphilosophy was more complex than that. In fact, such central works as *Philosophy and Civilization* (1931) and *Art as Experience* (1934) suggest that his vision was very much informed by the same sort of aesthetic spirituality seen in Edwards, Emerson, James, and Santayana: beauty was to duty as grace was to law. To be sure, Dewey was quick to insist that theological problems had never bewitched him. But he was concerned, much like Santayana, to safeguard elements of religious life consonant with republican institutions while sloughing supernaturalism.

Like Santayana, James, Royce, and Peirce, Dewey was eager to recommend abandoning the elements of religious life that were superstitious and fanatical. He sided with James in urging religious people to drop their commitment to religious institutions because he thought they provoked tribal fanaticism. He sided with Santayana in arguing that supernaturalism was the outcome of grammatical confusion fueled by wishful thinking. Like Santayana he considered that religious thinking at its best developed imaginative conceptions that celebrated the whole of life.

Dewey argued for these claims in *A Common Faith* (1934). Within the context of a pragmatic conception of knowledge and an understanding of philosophy as culture criticism, he sought to distinguish the "religious" from "religions," recommending maintenance of the former, neglect of the latter; to expose supernaturalism as a piece of vicious intellectualism in order to develop a view of divinity as the consequence of natural processes; and to link his view of the religious to the vitality of democratic republican institutions.

Religions, Dewey claimed, were static while the religious was generative and generational. Religions were closed systems of belief while religious experience stretched people's minds, opening them up to novel expressions of joy and delight in mortal life. Religions appointed special days, places, and officials as exceptionally holy or authoritative; the religious could be discovered anywhere, anytime, by and in anyone. Religions placed their closed systems beyond criticism, while the religious provoked people to seek and find more adequate ways to say and do things humanely. Life, in sum, had a religious quality when people experienced a sense of well-being, "a sense of human nature as a cooperating part of a larger whole."

But, implicitly attacking James and the very idea of a science of religions, Dewey argued that there were no distinctively religious causes of religious qualities. Moreover, there were no special avenues to religious truth outside the bailiwick of science. People who wished to retain God-talk must reconceive divinity in a naturalistic way. Dewey suggested that "God," rectified naturalistically, meant "the unity of all ideal ends arousing us to desire and action," or, better, the "active relation between ideal and actual." Construing divinity this way did not take humanity as an object of worship, as some feared, but underscored humanity's fragile relations with the natural powers on which the unity of ideal ends in actuality depended.

Reflecting on "the human abode of the religious function," Dewey argued that the day of religions had passed, since the emergence of democratic republican assumptions and institutions undercut ecclesiastical polities that were basically aristocratic and/or monarchical in structure. In a society permeated by voluntarism and practical idealism, one that ordered its understanding of goodness from the bottom up, the notion that an unseen king governed the world simply failed to hold sway over the human imagination. The religious function in society was to weld together "impulses toward affection, compassion and justice, equality and freedom."

If churches took it upon themselves to do this, Dewey suggested, they might recover their vitality without sacrificing their diversity. But this would mean giving up deeply embedded traditions. So long as the practical structure of religious institutions conflicted with the assumptions and aspirations of democratic republican people, culture was better off neglecting them.

Because *A Common Faith* was Dewey's only mature work dealing with religion in detail, philosophers and theologians immediately gave it special critical attention. For the sake of understanding the course of religious philosophy in the United States, however, *Art as Experience* is just as important because it clarified the ultimately aesthetic character of Dewey's vision. There, he claimed that the very aim of human praxis was consummatory experiences of quality or value. Such experiences were healing, overcoming feelings of bifurcation and dissonance that individuals harbored; they were experiences of the fittingness of things, and so, of the ideal rendered actual. The upshot of such aesthetic experiences was a "deep-seated memory of any underlying harmony, the sense of which haunts life like the sense of being founded on a rock."

Such claims recapitulated ones made earlier by constituents of the aesthetic tradition of spirituality. But equally significant were things Dewey did not claim. He did not claim that aesthetic experience required or even permitted theistic interpretation; nor that it necessarily revealed things either antecedently or consequentially divine; nor that religious expressions made uniquely valuable contributions to their understanding. Thus Dewey's lectures on art as experience signaled the transformation of distinctively religious philosophy into something else again, not only for Dewey, but for his many followers. Maintaining allegiance to democratic republican institutions, Dewey's community of discourse largely abandoned concern for distinctively religious phenomena, choosing, like Dewey himself, to emphasize the indispensible role that art, especially fine art, had to play in the life of the republic.

ATTEMPT AT SYNTHESIS

Alfred North Whitehead. To be sure, some American religious thinkers, like Henry Nelson Wieman and Bernard Eugene Meland, associated with major liberal divinity schools, not only took Dewey seriously but tried as long as they could to accommodate his naturalism to the concerns of their religious, even theological, communities. But in the long run, they could not escape the radical conclusion to which Dewey's antiessentialism, his view that the notion of "the really real" was more trouble than it was really worth, came: the distinctions on which Christian republican thought depended—eternity and history, virtue and prudence, supernatural and natural, transcendence and immanence—cut no intellectual ice. So, for the most part naturalistically inclined theologians dropped allegiance to Dewey and turned to Alfred North Whitehead for guidance.

If Dewey's work phased out religious philosophy for one community of discourse in the United States, Whitehead's work helped to dissolve it for others. To be sure, Whitehead had—and has—his philosophical champions. A number of very influential philosophers, Charles Hartshorne first among them, have developed Whitehead's process philosophy with much ingenuity and industry. But the community of scholars that canonized Whitehead's work eventually became only marginally associated with the profession of philosophy in the United States. The devotees of Whitehead are characteristically divinity school professors and their students, identified more with theological academies and journals than with professional philosophical associations. Thus, while Whitehead surely must count as an heir to the religious philosophers in America, his own concern with religion eventually led to a brand of theology, not to the maintenance of religious philosophy.

Whitehead's work was received by many as extending, clarifying, deepening, and theologically bettering James's radically empirical theism. Whitehead read James's essays in radical empiricism differently than either Santayana or Dewey had. They had interpreted James's doctrine of pure experience as a warrant for abandoning metaphysics. Whitehead read it as sanctioning one view of the really real. He thought that James had come close to achieving the goal of traditional philosophy by isolating a privileged discourse, neither subjective nor objective but affectional. This discourse, he claimed, rendered an adequate ontology of presence a real possibility. This was good news for liberal Protestant theologians looking for a vision that could overcome materialism the way that idealism had promised without concluding that the only thing worth talking about were ideas.

Whitehead claimed that "the foundations of the world [are found] in the aesthetic experience, rather than—as with Kant—in the cognitive and conceptive experience" (*Process and Reality,* 1924). All order, he claimed, was aesthetic order and that order is "derived from the immanence of God." If this was so, then the traditional post-Kantian problem of finding the "third" world that enveloped both value and fact was solved—and there were no adequate reasons behind historicist revolt.

In the view of Whitehead and his theological followers the elements of the world disclosed in affectional experience vindicated the ideals that federal republicans cherished as well the the God in whom they trusted. In Whitehead's view one out of many was not just a real cosmological principle but an actual process of realization. Indeed it was the process that "implanted timelessness on what in its essence is passing," thus salvaging the Christian republican distinction between time and eternity; it made both principled law and antinomian expression indispensible, preserving "order amid change, and . . . change amid order," thus salvaging the distinction between law and grace; it selectively overcame evil, salvaging the distinction between sin and salvation; it organized things through a sort of charity, salvaging the connection between Jesus the Galilean and the exceptionally spiritual process of life embodied in the motto of the United States.

Sociologically viewed, Whitehead's work gave theologians impressed with James, Dewey, and, less often, Santayana something to do. From the vantage point of Dewey's community of philosophers, however—not to mention Santayana's idiosyncratic perspective—Whiteheadian theologians hardly rescued their hero from the charge of anti-intellectualism. To the contrary, they appeared to conserve a theological tradition that was viciously intellectual, confusing ideals and powers. In any case, scholars who devoted careers to learning and enlarging Whitehead's novel metaphysical language did not help to return the profession of philosophy in the United States to an agenda that gave high priority to clarifying or celebrating religious life. If anything, the efforts of Whiteheadians helped to bring an end to conversation between religious intellectuals and members of a philosophical profession that was no longer centrally interested in religion at all.

After Whitehead. Interest in religion did not vanish entirely from the profession of philosophy, for Whitehead's metaphysical writings were appropriated by members of liberal Protestant divinity schools. Thus, in 1936 two of Whitehead's admirers, Henry Nelson Wieman and Bernard E. Meland, published a celebrated compendium entitled *American Philosophies of Religion* that gave synopses of diverse views of religion and that attempted to introduce the American public to a host of conflicts and debates occurring between and among various intellectual parties concerned with religion.

Wieman and Meland presented four traditions at work in American philosophy of religion: supernaturalism, idealism, romanticism, and naturalism. There were "traditional supernaturalists" like John Gresham Machen and Francis L. Patten as well as "neo-supernaturalists" like John Oman, Paul Tillich, George W. Richards, H. Richard and Reinhold Niebuhr, Wilhelm Pauck, Edwin Lewis, and George C. Cell. Not one of these figures was considered a philosopher by other professional philosophers.

To be sure, some of the "philosophers of religion" associated with the other "traditions" that Wieman and Meland identified clearly contributed to professional philosophical discourse in the United States. Nobody doubted the professional credentials of absolute idealists like Royce, William E. Hocking, or William Urban; nor those philosophers who were categorized, rather strangely, as romantics: D. C. MacIntosh, Eugene Lyman, and George Santayana; nor, finally, naturalists like John E. Boodin, William P. Montague, Whitehead, F. S. C. Northrop, Roy Wood Sellars, or Dewey.

But this meant that, at best, only one-quarter of the thinkers appearing as "philosophers of religion" in *American Philosophies of Religion* could be identified as professional philosophers. The rest were either divinity school professors, literary critics, free-lance political theorists, psychologists, or professors of religion. Moreover, the professional philosophers whose works were considered in the book represented the old guard. They still thought of philosophy as a civic profession, fundamentally geared to serve federal republican institutions.

By 1930 Clarence I. Lewis' *Mind and the World-order* stood as the exemplar of excellence in the philosophical profession. While written, in part, to systematize pragmatism, the work was received as transforming pragmatic philosophy into a technical school of thought, no longer concerned in any essential way with the problems or aspirations of civic life. Lewis' work represented the triumph of philosophy understood as a discipline exploring technical issues in epistemology, ontology, logic, and conceptual analysis. Professionals in this "age of analysis" pictured philosophy as a rigorous science of the sciences, downplayed concern with the history of philosophy on the grounds that prior work in the field had been merely speculative, and replaced an older emphasis on learning foreign languages with a focus on learning logic construed as an acultural and ahistorical calculus of thought.

But it would be a serious historiographic distortion to suggest that philosophy and religion became unhitched simply because philosophy transformed itself into a technical discipline randomly related to America's cultural institutions. Between the world wars three other movements of note contributed to this division. First, Neo-Orthodox Protestants, following the German theologian Karl Barth, turned from philosophy to church dogmatics and tended, as well, to distinguish their own faith from religion altogether. For some very influential members of this movement, anyhow, neither philosophy nor religion was as important as personal commitment to their radically monotheistic God, who eluded the bounds of formal thought and worship.

On the other hand, under the institutional leadership of such figures as Yale Divinity School's Charles Foster Kent religious studies emerged as a distinctive academic profession. Many students who might well have chosen to train in philosophy at the turn of the century because of an interest in problematic relations between religion and other elements of culture started taking degrees in religion. Kent founded the National Council on Religion in Higher Education in 1922 to promote not just the study but the cause of religion in American colleges and universities. The very idea of religious studies was, thus, originally undivided from a quest to show the indispensibility of religion to civilization. As Thornton Merriam put it in his 1951 retrospective on the work of the council, "the essence of the relationship of religion to education is partnership in the presence of staggering forces now threatening our civilization. Its method consists in creating and energizing communities of devoted learners" (Wilder, *Liberal Learning and Religion,* 1951).

For the founders of religious studies as for some religious philosophers from another age, religious faith was the "center around which may be arrayed all the truth seeking disciplines of man and the whole directed toward the improvement of human living" (Wilder, 1951). This sort of rhetoric, suggesting that religious studies was privileged in a way other studies never could be, along with the view of the council that teachers of religion ought to have exceptionally and visibly spiritual personalities, tended to alienate broad segments of the academic community committed to academic pluralism. It led to open hostility and ridicule between philosophers and professors of religion.

Finally, many students who might have followed a James or a Whitehead or even a Dewey into philosophy because of an interest in religion and culture turned away from both philosophy and religious studies. They found the communities of discourse associated with academic departments of literature, history, classics, political theory, anthropology, sociology and, in a few cases, psychology more accommodating than either philosophy, now a technical profession, or religious studies, too self-righteous and unprepared to demand the hard thinking that open-minded inquiry made obligatory.

To be certain, "philosophy of religion" courses still dotted the bulletins of departments of philosophy and of religion in American colleges and universities. But generally speaking, these were courses in divinity, in the epistemology of theistic truth claims, or in the logic of God-talk or the coherence of supernatural metaphysics—topics only tangentially concerned with the role of religion in human culture. Such understanding currently comes more likely from literary critics, cultural anthropologists, and cultural historians than from intellectuals who have made philosophy their profession.

The religious philosophers writing in the United States from the late 1870s through the 1930s neither replicated the theological and moral interests of their predecessors nor determined the future transformation of their profes-

sion into a discipline with religious issues. Nonetheless, their intellectual influence has endured in the United States (and in the cases of Peirce, James, and Santayana, elsewhere), largely through the writings of intellectuals and academicians outside the professional guilds of philosophy, religious studies, and divinity. Their works still guide many efforts, in literature and criticism, to reinterpret culture in ways that suit the expectations and aspirations of a democratic republican people that identifies itself as constituted one out of many, thrives on spiritual diversity, and bridles at both authoritarianism and self-indulgence. In particular, their more or less common view of religion as adding grace to moral experience—as demanding not just a life of obedience or conformity but one of joy and delight—has formed pretexts for such diverse contemporary reflections on religious culture as the poetry of Wallace Stevens and Robert Lowell, the thick anthropological descriptions of Clifford Geertz, and the cultural criticisms of Kenneth Burke. But fewer and fewer teachers currently assign the writings of these religious philosophers to their students, thus making their specific religious claims and sensibilities more a matter of rumor than study.

BIBLIOGRAPHY

Jacques Barzun, *A Stroll with William James* (1983); Richard Bernstein, *John Dewey* (1966); Anne Boydston, ed., *Guide to the Works of John Dewey* (1970); Frederick H. Burkhardt, ed., *The Works of William James* (1975–); Arthur W. Burks, ed., *The Collected Papers of Charles Sanders Peirce,* vols. 7 and 8 (1958); William A. Christian, *An Interpretation of Whitehead's Metaphysics* (1959); Norman Fiering, *Jonathan Edwards' Moral Thought and Its British Context* (1981) and *Moral Philosophy at Seventeenth-Century Harvard* (1981); H. Fisch et al., eds., *Writings of Charles Sanders Peirce: A Chronological Edition* (1982–); Elizabeth Flower and Murray G. Murphey, *A History of Philosophy in America,* vols. 1 and 2 (1977); Charles Hartshorne and Paul Weiss, eds., *The Collected Papers of Charles Sanders Peirce,* vols. 1–6 (1931–1935); Bruce Kuklick, *Josiah Royce: An Intellectual Biography* (1972) and *The Rise of American Philosophy* (1977).

T. J. Jackson Lears, *No Place of Grace* (1981); Henry Samuel Levinson, *The Religious Investigations of William James* (1981) and "Santayana's Contribution to American Religious Philosophy," in *Journal of the American Academy of Religion,* 52 (1984); George R. Lucas, Jr., *The Genesis of Modern Process Thought: A Historical Outline with Bibliography* (1983); John D. McDermott, ed., *The Basic Writings of Josiah Royce,* 2 vols. (1969); William G. McLoughlin, *Revivals, Awakenings, and Reform* (1978); Ralph Barton Perry, *The Thought and Character of*

William James (1935); Herman J. Saatkamp, Jr., and John Jones, eds., *George Santayana: A Bibliographical Checklist, 1880–1980* (1982); Herbert W. Schneider, *A History of American Philosophy* (1946; 2nd ed., 1963); Peter Skagestad, *The Road of Inquiry* (1981); Ignas Skrupskelis, *William James: A Reference Guide* (1977); John E. Smith, *Royce's Social Infinite* (1950); Henry Nelson Wieman and Bernard E. Meland, *American Philosophies of Religion* (1936); Amos N. Wilder, ed., *Liberal Learning and Religion* (1951).

[*See also* CALVINIST THEOLOGICAL TRADITION; ENLIGHTENMENT; NEO-ORTHODOXY; PSYCHOLOGY OF RELIGIOUS EXPERIENCE; *and* TRANSCENDENTALISM.]

RELIGION AND LITERATURE

Lynn Ross-Bryant

BOTH American religious thought and American literature frequently have focused on America itself as symbol. As a consequence, much literature that is distinctively American is also distinctively religious, and explorations of religious issues often overlap explorations of the meaning of America.

Cultural anthropologist Clifford Geertz argues that religious symbols function to bring together the world view and ethos of a culture. *World view* denotes a culture's shared understanding of the way things really are, including the origin and meaning of creation, human life, and death. *Ethos* denotes the shared understanding of the way human beings ought to live in relation to the reality revealed by the world view, including all aspects of life-style from dress to art to ethics. Religious symbols demonstrate the fundamental congruence between the way the world really is and the way people ought to live. Hence religion becomes the integrating force that gives meaning and value to life.

America itself becomes the symbol that integrates meaning and value in the culture. America as "the land of promise," "the New World," and America as a people on an "errand into the wilderness" or with a "manifest destiny" has symbolized the perfect integration of the way the world is and the way we ought to live—heaven and earth brought together.

Even before the New World had been colonized, it provided the occasion for reflection on what the ideal world might be. If the human race could start over, what would it make of its world? Renaissance works such as Shakespeare's *The Tempest* (1611) and Thomas More's *Utopia* (1516) use the image of the New World to explore human potential. They, like Christopher Columbus' and Amerigo Vespucci's reports on their encounters with the New World reveal that America was already operating as an idea as well as a reality. Columbus wrote of the New World, "I deeply feel within me that there . . . lies the Terrestrial paradise." The place itself, emblematic of nature uncorrupted by Old World civilization, is generally instrumental in this development of a new Eden. Occasionally the land is important only as a place to start over, or it may signify an obstacle to overcome, a wilderness to be tamed. *The Tempest* presents both significations: the island is home to Caliban as well as to Ariel, a place that makes possible spiritual renewal, but only through the overcoming of earthly obstacles.

Although a little-known region not surprisingly fired the imaginations of explorers and writers, this same kind of imaginative response less predictably informs writings of the settlers who became Americans. Indeed, America continues to function as both idea and place, and much of the best American literature depicts America as the setting for spiritual struggle and renewal. The land, whether represented as wilderness or as Eden, remains central to a spiritual drama often represented through the struggle of a solitary individual. However, this individual usually joins with others who together form a community of special people chosen to share a common purpose. Echoing its image in the Renaissance imagination, America sees itself in possession of a special errand or destiny that could redeem not only itself but also the whole world.

Such assumptions, intrinsically religious and usually self-consciously so, have remained dominant in American literature. Over the course of American history writers have framed these assumptions in varying ways that reflect the impact of varying religious movements on their world views. The Puritan tradition, undeniably decisive for the colonists of Plymouth and Massachusetts Bay, has continued to influence later writers, so powerful is its vision of America as the ground for understanding the self and its mission in the world. The Puritan vision was adapted, for example, by writers influenced largely by the religious ideas of the Enlightenment and of romanticism, as well as by writers influenced largely by twentieth-century secularism. Thus an examination of Puritan writers—historians and theologians as well as poets—indicates how religion infused all aspects of their intellectual activity and created the paradigm of America as the New Israel, the unifying symbol for world view and ethos.

THE LITERATURE OF THE COLONIES

The Puritan movement in England sought to push the Anglican Reformation further, to eliminate all vestiges of the supposedly unnecessary additions Roman Catholicism had made to the original Christianity of the Bible. Some Puritans separated totally from the English church and were persecuted and forced to flee, first to Holland and then to the New World, where they established Plymouth Plantation in 1620. Other Puritans, who settled in Massachusetts Bay, saw America as an opportunity to establish a proper religious community that by the power of example would prompt the English church to reform.

The Bible was the guidebook for all aspects of Puritan life, including literature. As a literary model the Bible provided the common background, metaphors, and the supreme example of "plain style." Just as the Puritans accepted the senses and emotions only as they worked with reason to lead the individual to serve God better, so too they accepted literary devices only as they served the goal of all literature, to express God's truth. The plain style was intended not to entertain but rather to instruct its audience, the common people. Since no one could rely on priestly authority, all were required both to read the Bible and to deal with quite sophisticated theological issues. The plain style presumably made this possible.

Since the plain style required clear, concrete images in order to communicate to the common people, the particularities of life in the New World immediately made their way into the literature of the sermon, the history, and the poem. The plain style thus encompassed vivid descriptions, colloquial diction, and concrete imagery drawn from daily life. For example, Edward Taylor's poem "Huswifery" uses the imagery of a spinning wheel and loom to dramatize the speaker's desire to conform to God's will:

Make me, O Lord, thy Spining Wheele compleate.
  Thy Holy Worde my Distaff make for mee.
Make mine Affections thy Swift Flyers neate
  And make my Soule thy holy Spoole to bee. . . .
Then cloath there with mine Understanding, Will,
  Affections, Judgment, Conscience, Memory,
My Words, and Actions, that their shine may fill
  My wayes with glory and thee glorify.

All Taylor's poetry, but especially the private poems he wrote as pre-Communion meditations, employs sensuous, emotional language and imagery that at first seem contrary to the Puritan emphasis on plain style and distrust of the senses. When Taylor's poetry was recovered in 1939, scholars first assumed that it had been hidden because it was heretical to the Puritan spirit. More recently, however, scholars have expanded their understanding of the Puritan aesthetic and concluded that Taylor's poetry contains, quite in harmony with its expressive images, the values and concerns of all Puritan literature. The plain style, then, while distinctive, is expansive. It uses a wide variety of literary techniques but always harnessed and disciplined for a certain end: to reveal the glory of God and to hasten the coming of his kingdom in New England.

This theological justification for literature encouraged writing of various kinds, and a surprisingly large body of literature emerged from the difficult and isolated life of the colonies. Sermons obviously were an important form, but histories and biographies too became crucial for these people who saw themselves as on a mission for the God who acts in history. A great deal of poetry was also written, ranging from the didactic verses of Michael Wigglesworth to the personal meditations of Edward Taylor and Anne Bradstreet. But whether sermon or history or poem, the intention behind the literature was religious and the aesthetic that governed it was congruent with Puritan theology.

As a genre history evolved naturally from the early settlers' theology and life circumstances.

RELIGION AND LITERATURE

William Bradford's *History of Plymouth Plantation* (1630–1650); John Winthrop's *Journal*, often called *History of New England* (1630–1649); Edward Johnson's *Wonder-working Providence of Sions Saviour in New England* (1654); and Cotton Mather's *Magnalia Christi americana; or, The Ecclesiastical History of New-England* (1702) exemplify this form. They all are ecclesiastical histories because the writers saw themselves as living out the plan of a God who acts in history. One way to perceive, understand, and help fulfill this plan was through God's statement of the plan: the Bible. Using the interpretive approach of typology—common to the early church fathers, Renaissance theologians, and reformers alike—the Puritans saw in the Old Testament the prefiguration or type that was the promise of what the New Testament brought to fulfillment through Christ as the anti-type. Both promise and fulfillment were understood to refer to actual events in history, while the description of God's kingdom in Revelation was understood to anticipate a future event that would bring an end to history. This eschatological emphasis that examines history for signs of its end typified the Reformation world view. What distinguished the reformers in the New World was seeing the anticipated end close at hand in their own actions since they had been chosen by God and sent on an "errand into the wilderness," as Samuel Danforth proclaimed in his 1670 election day sermon.

This typological approach accounts in part for the recurrent comparisons between the voyagers to the New World and the Israelites who wandered in the wilderness under the leadership of Moses on their way to the promised land of Canaan. Such comparisons point out not simply the similarity between the Israelites' exile and the colonists' exodus from the land of tyranny and their time of trial away from an established civilization. Nor is the point of such comparisons simply to aggrandize the Puritans by their self-comparison to God's earlier chosen people. Rather the implications are typological: the Israelites are the type, the Puritans the anti-type. Although not often stated explicitly, the writers believed that God is bringing his kingdom to fruition through the historical events associated with the New World Puritans. Associating the Pilgrims with the Israelites, Bradford underscores the Puritans' identity as God's new chosen people by adapting the words from the Passover celebra-tion to describe the exodus to New England: "May not and ought not the children of these fathers rightly say: 'Our fathers were Englishmen which came over this great ocean, and were ready to perish in this wilderness; but they cried unto the Lord, and He heard their voice and looked on their adversity' " (Gunn, 1981). Bradford continues his comparison by noting that these New World wanderers, newly arrived on bleak Cape Cod, could not ascend Mount Pisgah, as Moses had, to view the promised land and take hope in their affliction. These Separatists would find no other promised land, and so the land of Canaan became their New Jerusalem. In this way the Pilgrims who cry the coming of God's kingdom are related typologically to John the Baptist who cried his message of Christ's coming. Edward Johnson explicitly connects this hope for the coming kingdom with the migrations to America as he describes the journey of the first of Christ's forces to this New England "where the Lord will create a new Heaven, and a new Earth in new Churches, and a new Commonwealth together."

At the end of the seventeenth century Cotton Mather's history continues the association between the Israelites and the New Englanders and compares Bradford, governor of Plymouth, and Winthrop, governor of Massachusetts Bay, with Moses. Although Bradford's and Winthrop's sense of mission still informs Mather's writing, the discrepancy between the hope and the reality prevents him from viewing New England as the anti-type of Israel, as his grandfather John Cotton might have. Mather presents the history of Christ's work in the settlement of New England in order to inspire the current generation to recapture the piety and enthusiasm of those who set out on the errand. His work belongs to the literary form of the jeremiad, condemning, as did the Old Testament prophet Jeremiah, the apostasy of God's chosen and promising them destruction unless they return to the covenant and fulfillment if only they would. Mather's history attempts to convince the people that they stand in a special relationship to God and that they can live up to the terms of this relationship and perform the errand as their fathers had. His history turns to biography for illustration and inspiration through example. Indeed, he states that the Bible, the "Best of Books," comprises just such history. Bradford also embeds biographies in his histories for this purpose and employs letters to reproduce the urgency of actual lives, to lend the concreteness of the plain style, and to demonstrate that the life of one can speak for many.

This kind of history was needed both for the unbelievers across the sea who had never acknowledged the light of the "city set on the hill" and for the settlers at home who were no longer wanderers and had fallen from the great early days of Massachusetts Bay. Speaking of New England as a spiritual entity, Mather describes the plan for which Christ planted the New World and laments that perhaps all this will now come to nothing. He writes, "But whether New England may Live any where else or no, it must Live in our History!"

This jeremianic tension between what was or might be and what is dominates Bradford's history as well. As Sacvan Bercovitch suggests, the jeremiad did not originate with the third or even the second generation, but appeared almost from the moment the voyagers landed on the shores of the New World. Bradford seems to have been inspired to write Part One of his history in 1630 because of his doubts about the success of the Pilgrim venture begun in 1620. Only when doubts about the living reality arise does it become necessary to write a history. If actions suffice, then interpretations become unnecessary. Bradford's doubts arose from his perceptions of the human failings marking the colonial experience: he saw self-love rationalized under the rubric of necessity as the work of Satan in the colony. In addition, the establishment of new churches in Massachusetts Bay as a result of the 1630s migrations served both to support his view of God's presence in New England and to fuel his doubts about the success of the Pilgrim colony: if God had been totally pleased with the Pilgrims' efforts, then why had he established other churches? Even in 1630 Bradford writes about the past in the hopes of revitalizing the present. His form follows the model of the jeremiad: take up the errand, return to the covenant as it was followed at the beginning, and surely God will use New England to bring the New Jerusalem to earth.

Bercovitch argues that the jeremiad in its special American form exerted a substantial influence on the American character. Although the jeremiad castigates the people and points out their failures, it also asserts the promise of a special relationship to God and a special mission for the chosen people in America. The form fuses the sacred and the profane, the everyday, self-interested life of the colony and the eschatological errand the colonists live out in the New World. Although this fusion frequently results in a sense of disappointment and failure, for not even the first voyagers could live up to its ideal, it also provides an impetus for the sense of mission and self-confidence that have supported America's belief that God's plan will be accomplished.

The early poetry of the colonies presents the individual dimension of America's salvation-history. Although Anne Bradstreet and Edward Taylor both wrote "public" poetry that deliberately dealt with the salvation-history of the world, their best poetry is cast in a more personal, lyric or meditative form. Puritanism and the American sense of space structure their poetic visions. Their visions embrace an appreciation for this world based on a natural typology; an eschatological impetus derived from the specialness of this space and the inadequacy of any space; and an attempted balance between the reality of sin and the hope of election, between this world and the next, between the real and the ideal.

The Puritan aesthetic encouraged an appreciation for the signs of God in natural creation as well as in human language and experience. Believing that God has created all things and provided for their salvation in Jesus Christ and that all levels of reality are meaningfully interconnected in God, the Puritans considered nature and human language and experience as pointers to God, though always limited and finally inadequate. While Bradstreet's poetry focuses on nature and human relationships, Taylor's focuses on language.

Bradstreet came to the New World in 1630 at age seventeen and later moved to new settlements at Ipswich and Andover, thus remaining in the "wilderness" much of her life. However, as her poem "Contemplations" shows, the wilderness was for her much like a garden. In "Contemplations" (published in 1678), her meditations on the beauties of the natural world lead to reflections on God the creator, but her human song fails her and she turns back to the natural world for inspiration, symbolized by the grasshopper. The world of nature, then, not only leads her toward God but also provides an image of an almost Edenic world from which humans seem excluded as a result of both their failings—the poet's inadequate song—and their experience of time and death. Although spring returns each year, "man grows old, lies down, remains where once he's laid." The poem's speaker might prefer to be joined with nature in a perpetual garden, but it is only by looking toward God and the immortality of eternity that she can live with meaning in this world. All history and civilization will perish, "But he whose name is graved in the white stone/Shall last and shine when all of these are gone." The eschatological image of the white stone from Revelation signifies one who is saved by Christ. This image does not turn her from appreciation of the natural world but allows her to live happily in it because of the hope (though not the assurance) of her salvation. The present moment in a New England woods is given meaning by the future eschatological event.

This sense of balance that overcomes the conflict between this world and the next also pervades her short poem "To My Dear and Loving Husband," which begins, "If ever two were one, then surely we," and ends, "Then while we live, in love let's so persevere/That when we live no more, we may live ever." The love she shares with her husband is so great that it can only be possible by the grace of God and indeed seems as sure a sign of God as the sun. Only those who share in God's love—only the saved—could share such love. There is no conflict between this world and the next but rather a correspondence that points to God.

This balance does not pervade all of Bradstreet's poetry. Often her poems display an awareness of the deep conflict between this world and the next, between human hopes and human actualities. The conflict dominates in elegies she wrote for her grandchildren, and it alternates with acceptance in "Upon the Burning of Our House." Here she powerfully evokes the importance of household "treasures," the everyday things that give meaning to everyday lives. But when these treasures are destroyed in a fire, she bids them adieu, commenting, "all's vanity."

She knows that she should not fix her hopes on earthly things and turns to the "Architect" whose mansions will never be destroyed. The ending of the poem—"Farewell, my pelf, farewell my store./The world no longer let me love,/My hope and treasure lies above"—convinces the reader of the depth of her love for the things of this world as well as her love for God and the next world. Much of Bradstreet's poetry mediates the conflict between these loves, reconcilable only through the establishment of a new heaven and a new earth.

Taylor's poetry also responds to the wilderness, the western frontier of the Connecticut Valley. For Taylor, however, the place is important not in itself but as the arena for the saving activity of God. In his long public poem "God's Determinations," Taylor recites the history of humankind from the Fall through the coming of the Savior and the promise of glory, all dramatized through the speaker's attempt to bring one soul into his congregation at Westfield, which becomes the site of God's glory that beckons the pilgrim. Taylor's "Preparatory Meditations," some 200 personal poems written between 1682 and 1725, evidence the same longing for God's glory to find realization at this moment in New England. Here language itself becomes the primary means of grace. Taylor's Christocentric poetic both justifies language as a path to God and shows its inadequacy. Because Christ took on finite human form, he bridges the divine and human. Taylor's joy at this unimaginable gift pours forth in Meditation 1.23, expressed through the graphic language that characterizes much of his poetry:

> I know not how to speak't, it is so good:
>   Shall Mortall, and Immortall marry? nay,
> Man marry God? God be a Match for Mud?
>   The King of Glory Wed a Worm? mere Clay?
>   This is the Case. The Wonder too in Bliss.
>   Thy Maker is thy Husband. Hearst thou this?

Because of the astounding act of Incarnation, we can approach, though never fully know, the Word behind the word. This is the justification for our words in our search for God, which for Taylor are the words of poetry.

But the only perfect metaphor is Christ, who is both fully human and fully divine and in his full humanity reveals his full divinity. All other metaphors fail, including the poet's own. Much of Taylor's poetry concerns poetry's ineffectual attempt to speak the glory of God. In Meditation 2.36 he says:

My Metaphors are but dull Tacklings tag'd
  With ragged Non-Sense. Can such draw to thee
My stund affections all with Cinders Clag'd,
  If thy bright beaming headship touch not mee?

Taylor's recognition of the inadequacy of language may account for the abundant wit and extreme and often humorous or even absurd metaphors in his poetry. For example, the preface to "God's Determinations" queries, "Who in this Bowling Alley bowld the Sun?" Meditation 1.8 proclaims, "This Soule Bread take./ . . . Its Heavens Sugar Cake." Such imagery reminds Taylor of the truth and the falsity of metaphor, the promise and the inadequacy of human language. Since metaphors are a bridge to God, poetry is justified, but no metaphor is ever adequate because the gap can be bridged only by God.

The essence of both Taylor's and Bradstreet's poetry lies in their individual struggles to reconcile the ambiguities and conflicts of human life. Each lives out the story of Israel in the New World, conceived by Taylor more as a wilderness, by Bradstreet more as a garden. Both move away from the primary emphasis on community that characterizes the histories of the founders. In Taylor's case this movement may relate to Puritanism's greater individualism and emotionalism on the frontier. Bradstreet also spent much of her adult life on frontiers. In addition, her partial independence from the community may be because as a woman she stood outside the power structure of the community and as a poet outside the conventional identities of wife and mother. Taylor's and Bradstreet's individual, meditative poetry establishes a significant literary tradition in America.

Both the histories and the poetry of the colonial period are crucial to an understanding of the relation of religion and literature in America. The histories demonstrate the association made between the migrations to America and a providential plan that would save all nations. The poetry reveals the interior, personal version of that same salvation history. The Puritan sense of mission remained even after Puritan society gave

way and the spiritual entity of New England became more generally America. The wilderness was no longer hostile to the project but itself became part of it. The Puritan dream of a New Jerusalem blended with the secular travel descriptions of a New Eden to form a religious world view for which America itself became the primary symbol.

Not surprisingly, this symbol has dominated American literature. The special nature of the people and the place appears again and again in the literature. So too does the other side of this providential calling. "You shall be as a city set on the hill," Winthrop proclaimed, implying that if one doesn't live up to one's calling, one will be despised and cast out. Much of American literature is a jeremiad that reveals belief in that special calling, but gives way to bewilderment and disappointment with the discovery that America is not what it could be. The final reassurance is that even if America fails, at least it has been called, and final victory lies just ahead. At its core the American dream, frequently associated only with secular and material pursuits, envisions the fusion of the ideal and the real, heaven and earth. As such the dream always remains "the Word behind the word," the never-realized vision of how Americans see themselves but know they are not yet. It is for our writers to show us this about ourselves.

THE LITERATURE OF
THE NEW NATION

A theological outgrowth of Enlightenment thinking, Deism strongly influenced the literature of the Revolution and the new nation. Deists considered God to be the "clockmaker" who created an orderly world and charged human beings to keep their part running smoothly. God continues to affect the world as Providence, working through the laws of nature. The task for humans is to use their senses and reason to understand the laws of nature and to create human institutions that mirror the harmonies of nature. This belief that Providence made the world and human nature amenable to reason encouraged an optimistic view of the potential for establishing the good society. Although this optimism countered the Puritan belief that only God could create the good society, it also reinforced the

Puritan belief that the special place of America could make possible the creation of the good society.

Jonathan Edwards stands as the last great thinker in the Puritan tradition, although his thought exercised a continuing spiritual force on the new nation. To Puritan theology he adds and adapts ideas drawn from Lockean psychology, notably that all knowledge comes through sense perceptions. Counting on the presence of the "Word behind the word" that Locke dismissed, Edwards uses vivid imagery to portray for his straying flock the experience that awaited them unless they repented. His sermon "Sinners in the Hands of an Angry God" (1741) exemplifies this technique:

> The God that holds you over the pit of hell, much as one holds a spider, or some loathsome insect over the fire, abhors you, and is dreadfully provoked. . . . You hang by a slender thread, with the flames of divine wrath flashing about it, and ready every moment to singe it, and burn it asunder; and you have . . . nothing to lay hold of to save yourself.

The spiritual energy that Edwards crystallized underlay the Great Awakening, which Edwards describes in *Some Thoughts Concerning the Present Revival of Religion in New England* (1742): " 'Tis not unlikely that this work of God's Spirit, that is so extraordinary and wonderful, is the dawning, or at least a prelude, of that glorious work of God, so often foretold in Scripture. . . . And there are many things that make it probable that this work will begin in America."

Edwards' hopeful expectations found an echo in the political awakening that culminated in the Revolution and the establishment of the republic. The founders did not abandon the Puritan sense of America as the land of a chosen people. Thomas Jefferson and Benjamin Franklin submitted a proposal for the seal of the United States showing Moses leading the chosen people from Egypt. John Adams exactly echoed Winthrop's "City Set on a Hill" speech when he wrote in defense of the Constitution: "The people of America have now the best opportunity and the greatest trust in their hands that Providence ever committed to so small a number since the transgression of the first pair; if they betray their trust their guilt will merit even greater pun-

ishment than other nations have suffered and the indignation of Heaven" (Bercovitch, 1978). The establishment of the nation was the culmination of the process that began aboard the *Mayflower* and *Arbella,* which suggests that the kingdom had now begun. Puritan imagery added to Enlightenment optimism led the American nation to see as its responsibility the establishment of a perfect society not only for Americans but also for all peoples.

Franklin's *Autobiography* (begun in 1771) presents an apt history of his time. Although he emphasizes individual experience, he closely ties his identity to his society. Telling his own story, he acts out America's mission. The reader sees through the eyes of the old and wise Franklin the young man struggling to become himself now: successful, virtuous, living the good life, and instructing others. Franklin shows Providence at work in his life and at the same time displays an awareness of the limits of human understanding. In the end God must direct the affairs of people. Franklin also emphasizes the lessons of human experience: only through trial and error and the discovery of what works can people evolve the rules by which to live. Using the plain style and recounting the ordinary events of his life, Franklin dramatizes the successful resolution of the tension between reliance on Providence and devotion to pragmatic common sense. Franklin went "west" to Philadelphia and in many ways became a model for the individual who succeeds on his own on the border of society. (Yet another part of Franklin—the part that dined with kings —was far from Poor Richard.)

Another model American lived in the South, not in the new urban area but in the country on a farm: Thomas Jefferson adopted the religion of the Enlightenment, an influence that reinforced his belief in America as the place where the good society would become possible. He applauded John Locke's statement that "in the beginning all the world was America." Another influence was the Enlightenment emphasis on nature as the creation the Creator left humankind to enjoy. For many Enlightenment thinkers sublime nature served as an object of devotion indirectly oriented toward God. As Leo Marx notes, nature in this case referred not to the wilderness but to the "middle landscape" of the pastoral or, for Jefferson, to the cultivated land of the farm. Only by keeping literal ties with the land can Americans create the perfect society and make the pastoral literary form a political reality. Jefferson's hero is the independent, rational, democratic husbandman—one of God's chosen people. Interrupting a more prosaic discussion, Jefferson describes the laborer in the fields who maintains his virtue by "looking up to heaven" and down "to [his] own soil and industry." The simple ploughman, America's hero, speaks the simple language of the land. Jefferson affirms the plain style because it can best express the order and simplicity of the world. There is no need for a Word behind the words, for the literal reality that words describe suffices.

Doubleness marks Jefferson's life as well as Franklin's. Jefferson is a gentleman farmer, not a simple ploughman, and he spends most of his life not on the farm but in the public life he forever criticizes. A tension remains, between the unrealized model for the perfect society and the pressing—and exciting—realities of American political life, between America as Eden and America as political institution. The kingdom is not yet actualized.

Although American Transcendentalism diverges in many ways from both its Puritan and Deist ancestors, it nonetheless draws from their affirmation of the created world, whether as a typological sign of God or as the handiwork of Providence. Transcendentalism also draws from the Puritan stress on the reality and mystery of God and the Enlightenment stress on human experience in the world. Emphasizing the individual who is yet part of a community, Transcendentalism concurs with Puritanism and Enlightenment thinking in the belief that the individual and the community possess a special purpose in America.

Freed by Deism from the narrow route to God laid out by Puritan theology, this American form of romanticism recovered the experience of God neglected by Deism and stressed its availability to the individual. The Transcendentalist Oversoul relates and inspires, inhabits and undergirds all aspects of the universe. One must only learn how to see. In his essay "Nature" (1836), Ralph Waldo Emerson reports from the woods: "I become a transparent eye-ball. I am nothing. I see all. The currents of the Universal Being circulate through me; I am part or particle of God."

In the same essay Emerson describes the literary theory that arises from this understanding of nature and the Oversoul: "1. Words are signs of natural facts. 2. Particular natural facts are symbols of particular spiritual facts. 3. Nature is the symbol of spirit." Corrupt societies separate things and language. The American poet knows that "the world is emblematic" and that "the whole of nature is a metaphor of the human mind." Thus, truth and beauty are found not in abstractions but in the given, concrete experiences of the world. "Only so much do I know, as I have lived," Emerson asserts in "The American Scholar" (1837). In *Walden, or Life in the Woods* (1854) Henry David Thoreau notes, "No way of thinking or doing, however ancient, can be trusted without proof." Thoreau makes his home at Walden Pond in order to experience his life, explaining, "I went to the woods because I wished to live deliberately, to front only the essential facts of life, and see if I could not learn what it had to teach, and not, when I came to die, discover that I had not lived." Like Franklin, Thoreau writes an autobiography of an American in the process of becoming himself. However, Thoreau's self-portrait presents an interesting contrast to Franklin's: Thoreau depicts himself not as the prudent and urbane citizen but rather as the individual in nature who creates himself and his world.

"To create . . . is the proof of a divine presence," Emerson writes in "The American Scholar." Like Adam, the American names and creates the world and society. Thoreau's unwillingness to trust the past introduces a model for revolution grounded in the Spirit's continuous creation of the world. Americans are the paradigm for that continuous, universal creation. Emerson closes "The American Scholar" proclaiming that "A nation of men will for the first time exist, because each believes himself inspired by the Divine Soul which also inspires all men."

The hope of creating a new society in the New World originated with the Puritans. They immigrated to a world that was for them literally new and at the same time a promise of the new Canaan and the coming kingdom of God. For the country's founders the Revolution swept clean the past and left the New World a new nation, a political rather than a heavenly state. The new world of the nineteenth century became the creation of the individual American. Emerson advised his contemporaries to slough off the European inheritance and forge an American literature in the American spirit. To be American means to recognize the implications of the universal spirit flowing through all people: each individual becomes the universal human being and creates the world anew.

Walt Whitman's poetry reveals two aspects of this democratic ideal. In "There Was a Child Went Forth" (1855), the Adamic innocent enters his world:

There was a child went forth every day,
And the first object he look'd upon, that object he
    became,
And that object became part of him. . . .
These became part of that child who went forth
    every day, and who now goes, and will always
    go forth every day.

Whitman describes himself as "a child, very old" in "Facing West from California's Shores." This perpetual child shows the political implications of becoming part of the divine spirit in "Song of Myself" (1855):

Walt Whitman am I, a Kosmos, of mighty
    Manhattan the son. . . .
Whoever degrades another degrades me;
And whatever is done or said returns at last to me.
. . . I speak the pass-word primeval—I give the sign
    of democracy;
By God! I will accept nothing which all cannot have
    their counterpart of on the same terms.

Whereas the Puritans' optimism arose from their sense of God's mission and the founding fathers' optimism arose from their belief in the orderliness of creation and the power of human reason, the Transcendentalists' optimism arose from their belief in the benevolence of the universal creative spirit flowing through all people. America again becomes the perfect setting for the realization of these possibilities because of its newness, its continuing revolution, and its democratic ideals.

In spite of their optimism, however, Thoreau, Whitman, and Emerson criticize the way America actually is compared to what it could be. Like other American jeremiads, their writings remind us that we are not living up to our ideals. Yet to recognize this failing deepens the meaning of our actions and reaffirms the struggle toward America's ideals. This literature engages another kind of questioning as well, the questioning of the mission itself. The very title of Whitman's "Facing West from California's Shores" (1860) asks, What do we do when there is no more West, no more New World? "Inquiring, tireless, seeking that is yet unfound," Whitman returns from his journey around the world and asks:

Now I face home again, very pleas'd and joyous,
(But where is what I started for, so long ago?
And why is it yet unfound?)

THE LITERATURE
OF THE DARKER VISION

This questioning of the American mission continued as writers increasingly recognized the discrepancy between rhetoric and reality and increasingly doubted the certainty of God's hand in the mission. Nathaniel Hawthorne presents the darker side of both Puritanism and Transcendentalism. He self-consciously reexamines his Puritan roots, presenting his ancestors' era as a "brighter day" even while condemning their narrowness of vision, a narrowness most glaringly evident in their persecution of witches, but also evident in their presumed scorn for his "story-books" and in their condemnation of individuals like Hester Prynne in *The Scarlet Letter* (1850). In contrast to that "brighter day," the present-day Salem described in "The Custom-House," his introductory essay to the novel, looks darker still, its inhabitants seemingly without spirit or ambition, relying on Uncle Sam, and lacking the commitment to God, community, or even imagination that he saw in his forebears. Hawthorne did see one sign of hope in the Transcendentalist-inspired experiment at Brook Farm, where he lived for seven months. Although the innocence of both the natural world and of human nature appears possible in his novels, his final judgment, embodied in *The Blithedale Romance* (1852), is that Transcendentalism ignores the dark side of both human beings and the natural world.

This darkness pervades Hawthorne's fiction, but never without ambiguity. His world view more resembles Edwards' assessment of human nature as totally depraved than the Deists' and

Transcendentalists' confidence in human progress. Hawthorne's character Young Goodman Brown, in a story of that name, embodies the innocence of a Whitman, but lives in a Puritan society. He leaves his wife, Faith, and goes on an errand into the dark wilderness, not sent by God but called by the devil. He encounters the holy community of Salem engaged in devil worship in the woods. Is this what lies behind the facade of the Puritans' pure hearts? Or is this just a dream of an unsanctified heart? Insofar as even the Puritans remained sinners, albeit saved sinners, they may have harbored secret sins in their lives. But the appearance of their human, sinful nature in a metaphor of such devastating totality may be due to the childish innocence of one who thought people wholly good. "My Faith is gone," Goodman Brown says, referring to both his wife and his belief. Having been initiated into the evil in the world, he commits the worst sin of doubting that there is any good in human beings and ends a broken man.

In *The Scarlet Letter* Hawthorne offers a more complex study of innocence and the mystery of darkness. Darkness is present in Hester Prynne's alienation from her community—both in the harsh punishment that isolates her from the community and in the pleasure that she finds in her estrangement. As she says, her alienation allows her heart and mind to roam "as freely as the wild Indian in his woods." In this "moral wilderness" Hester discovers some new truths, perhaps similar to those the new nation might hope to institutionalize. But since she finds these truths outside the sanctions of society, she pays a price by living as an outcast and as a threat to the social order.

Hester's alienation from social institutions enables her to say to Dimmesdale as they plan, within the forest, their escape from the community: "The past is gone! Wherefore should we linger upon it now? See! With this symbol, I undo it all, and make it as it had never been!" She removes the scarlet letter from her dress, and nature responds by filling their forest glen with sunlight. Like the Transcendentalists, Hawthorne sees nature as a place of restoration and new life. But like the Puritans, he also sees it as a place of danger, both physical and moral, for Hester and Dimmesdale's meeting takes place outside the bounds and protections of civiliza-

tion. Pearl, the living sign of Hester and Dimmesdale's adultery, reflects the same ambiguous duality of darkness and possibility as does the natural world. She embodies innocence, as the child always does for the romantics, but she also reveals a dark knowledge that hurts and punishes and, as Mistress Hibbins says, may make her kin to the dark powers. Or it may make her spokesperson for the wisdom of civilization. When she comes back to her father and mother in the forest, she forces Hester to return her scarlet letter to its rightful place on her bosom.

The dark ambiguity within Dimmesdale results from the tension between his felt hypocrisy as a hidden sinner and his effectiveness as a minister of God. This conflict reaches its climax as he delivers a powerful election day sermon for the successor to Governor Winthrop:

> And, as he drew towards the close, a spirit as of prophecy had come upon him, constraining him to its purpose as mightily as the old prophets of Israel were constrained; only with this difference, that, whereas the Jewish seers had denounced judgments and ruin on their country, it was his mission to foretell a high and glorious destiny for the newly gathered people of the Lord.

Even as he preaches the promise of the New World, he is planning his escape with Hester and Pearl across the ocean to the Old World. He cannot tolerate this hidden darkness, but must make a public confession, after which he dies.

Hester does flee the promised land, but after Pearl has grown she returns, and again takes up her penance on the border of society. The final ambiguity lies in her return to the New World, even though its dream has failed her. As she does, she looks ahead to a new world where "sacred love" can flourish. Has America become this new world in Hawthorne's time? The "surer ground of mutual happiness" Hester sought may find more support in a democracy than in a theocracy. However, Hawthorne's description of contemporary Salem in the introduction to the novel suggests that his society is further from the reality of "sacred love" than Hester's. Her dream of a new world remains only a dream in the dark reality of America.

Darkness and mystery also characterize the

writing of Herman Melville. His novel *Pierre* (1852) is subtitled *The Ambiguities,* and its hopeful protagonist wrestles with the question of whether one can know what is true or good. A pamphlet Pierre reads entitled "Chronometricals and Horologicals" provides a commentary on this question and, indirectly, on America's role as the New Jerusalem or New Eden. Contrasting chronometrical (Greenwich) time with the imperfection of individual clocks, the writer, Plotinus Plinlimmon, asserts that one must not confuse God's time (the chronometer) with this world's imperfect time. Any attempt "practically to force that heavenly time upon the earth" will end in failure. In other words, there is no typological or rational or transcendental correspondence between this world and the next. To try to found the New Jerusalem on American soil is to misunderstand the realities of heaven and earth. Yet, although Melville questions the American mission, most of his characters try in one way or another to force chronometers and horologicals together.

Captain Ahab in *Moby Dick* (1851) and Captain Vere in *Billy Budd* (1891) present two possible alignments of chronometers and horologicals. *Moby Dick,* one of the richest treasures of American literature, explores the meaning of America from a variety of perspectives. Although Ishmael's searching aids this exploration, the towering figure of Captain Ahab dominates the novel and generates its darkness. Neither Ahab nor Moby Dick can be read allegorically, but together they suggest the dark side of the Puritan God and the stern hollowness of his appearance in the residual Calvinism of Melville's day. This darkness corresponds to the dark side of American individualism, seen so pacifically in Franklin and Thoreau, and to the dark power of nature, represented more as an intensified version of the Puritan's wilderness than as the Transcendentalists' Eden or the Deists' orderly creation. Captain Ahab reveals the demonic power of the rugged individual who has cut himself free from the bonds of community. He considers himself the chronometer and intends to impose his will on the world. He is on a new errand to rid the world of all evil by means of his demonic power. Whether this evil originates as the blind forces of nature inimical to human values and human survival or as the workings of a wrathful or indiffer-

ent god, Ahab feels personally wronged by this evil and determines to conquer it. Melville acknowledges the madness of such hubris but also its power. Melville calls the American mission into question—this is the monster it can produce —but he also dramatizes its compelling nature.

Although Captain Vere speaks the last word in Melville's quest, his is not the only word, for Captain Ahab is never silenced. *Billy Budd, Foretopman* presents a much more hopeful alignment of chronometers and horologicals than does *Moby Dick* and reconsiders the Adamic figure who inhabits the American Eden. Although Melville does not portray Billy Budd's innocence as foolish, he shows how the reality of evil in this world dooms such innocence. If Billy is the chronometer, then it is Captain Vere who possesses the wisdom to see how, as Plinlimmon says, though "God's truth is one thing and man's truth another . . . by their very contradictions they are made to correspond." Vere appreciates Billy Budd's innocent goodness, but he also understands the necessity of earthly justice. He has the balance between head and heart that Ahab lacks and thus both can love the boy and fulfill the duties of his office. Although Billy Budd cannot survive long in this world, he shows the reader the possibility of a better world. Displaying a Christ-like forgiveness when he is hanged, Billy ascends, "and, ascending, took the full rose of the dawn." But the novel focuses on Vere, the wise father, perhaps like a wise, loving, and judging father in heaven. In *Billy Budd,* one of the more balanced dramatizations of the American story, Melville affirms the innocence and promise of the New World Adam who nonetheless must fall and the wisdom of the father figure who can acknowledge this inevitable fall yet still affirm the promise: "by their very contradictions" the ideal and the real "are made to correspond."

With Emily Dickinson (who was born in 1830), we move from the epic stage of history back to the personal stage of the inner life explored by Bradstreet and Taylor. In large part her poetry, like her Puritan forebears', struggles with God and searches for the presence of God. She acknowledges her Puritan ancestors and identifies her quest with theirs, but she is also a child of her own age, the age of both Emerson's affirmation of nature and God and of Hawthorne's and

Melville's dark questioning. She says of her ancestors:

> Those—dying then,
> Knew where they went—
> They went into God's Right Hand—
> That Hand is amputated now
> And God cannot be found—
>
> The abdication of Belief
> Makes the Behavior small—
> Better an ignis fatuus
> Than no illume at all—

Although she wills belief in God, she finds, like Melville, that more often than not God either remains silent or operates on the world with apparent malignance. "The Missing All," she writes, "prevented Me/ From missing minor Things." She speaks of God as a sneering "Mighty Merchant," who withholds the one thing for which we will give all. In another poem she writes, "He fumbles at your Soul" and then "Deals—One—imperial—Thunderbolt—/ That scalps your naked Soul—"

The times of joy in Dickinson's poetry almost always occur in connection with nature: "There came a Day at Summer's full," a day that she compares with the resurrection, or "A Light exists in Spring," compared with a "Sacrament." Yet the cruel hand of God is also found within nature. "There's a certain Slant of light,/ Winter Afternoons—" that gives "Heavenly Hurt." And, poignantly, the deception of Indian summer in "These are the days when Birds come back" promises the presence that evokes the rejoicing of a sacrament, even though the speaker remains aware that it is a "fraud."

Dickinson led the life of a recluse in the Connecticut Valley, where Taylor and Edwards before her had struggled with their God. Her poetry speaks with equal power of the promise of faith and the darkness of skepticism, both legacies of the dream of the New World.

THE LITERATURE OF THE TWENTIETH CENTURY

From Bradstreet to Dickinson, American writers have explored various ways that America symbolizes a new society that would bring together heaven and earth. This exploration continues in the twentieth century, significantly influenced by writers from new immigrant groups, despite the increasing secularization of American society. Although religious movements seldom present issues of central concern to American writers, the idea of America still exerts a power that demands a religious framework for interpretation. As contemporary students of American religion like Robert Bellah have shown, American civil religion continues to be a pervasive, unifying force in our culture. The following examples point up varying ways that America functions as a religious symbol in twentieth-century literature.

Hart Crane stands as a twentieth-century Whitman, determined to include all of American life in his poem "To Brooklyn Bridge" (1930) and thereby provide a unity and meaning for America that may "lend a myth to God." Robert Frost is the twentieth-century poet of New England, the New England of the Puritans and Transcendentalists alike. His poetry often focuses on the individual in the natural world or struggling in community. The presence of Emerson's nature is matched by the darkness of the Puritans' and Hawthorne's wilderness both in nature and the human heart. And the dream of the New World persists. In "The Gift Outright" (1960) the promise, the hope, and the ambiguity of the people and their land loom large. "The land was ours before we were the land's," Frost begins. Although living in the New World, Americans were still tied to the Old World.

> Something we were withholding made us weak
> Until we found out that it was ourselves
> We were withholding from our land of living,
> And forthwith found salvation in surrender.

Americans made a gift of themselves:

> To the land vaguely realizing westward,
> But still unstoried, artless, unenhanced,
> Such as she was, such as she would become.

Both our gift and the land—as it is and will become through our imagination—remain ambiguous and unperfected. But at least in this poem Frost seems to accept that imperfection, that discrepancy between the ideal and the real, as the nature of the gift, the land, and the people.

America's novelists also continue to explore

the religious meaning of America. F. Scott Fitzgerald brings the American Adam to life once again in *The Great Gatsby* (1925). Gatsby echoes Hester Prynne, insisting in his innocence that he can undo the past and create himself as he will. He proves not only a failure in this world but also a danger to others. Nick Carraway, the wise narrator, sees the destruction and destructiveness of this American innocence, yet nonetheless muses on its attractions as he stands on West Egg (not perfect "like the egg in the Columbus story"), gazing out at Long Island Sound:

> I became aware of the old island here that flowered once for Dutch sailors' eyes—a fresh, green breast of the new world. . . . For a transitory enchanted moment man must have held his breath in the presence of this continent, compelled into an aesthetic contemplation he neither understood nor desired, face to face for the last time in history with something commensurate to his capacity for wonder. . . . [The dream] eluded us then, but that's no matter—tomorrow we will run faster, stretch out our arms farther. . . . And one fine morning—
>
> So we beat on, boats against the current, borne back ceaselessly into the past.

The hope for the New World still lures us as a marvelous possibility, even after we have recognized its impossibility.

William Faulkner sees the failure of the New World dream not in God's promise to America, but in our failure to fulfill it. The collection *Go Down, Moses and Other Stories* (1942) uses the language of the promised land, as did the Puritan settlers, to tell the story of the corruption of the Old World and the possibilities in the New World. In "The Bear," Isaac McCaslin rehearses the salvation-history to his cousin, explaining why Isaac must give up the land he has inherited. "Dispossessed of Eden. Dispossessed of Canaan," he begins and continues through the downfall of the Romans and Huns, who "snarled in what you call the old world's worthless twilight over the old world's gnawed bones, blasphemous in His name until He used a simple egg to discover to them a new world where a nation of people could be founded in humility and pity and sufferance and pride of one to another." The inhabitants of the New World get a second chance, but almost at once they lose it because of their greed and desire to own land and own peo-

ple. Slavery is the irrevocable curse that has fallen on the South and on America. The story Ike discovers as he searches out his family's history tells of corruption and inevitable decay, of the misunderstanding and loss of the promise.

The power of Faulkner's vision, however, lies not in the portrayal of this inevitable fall, but in the implicit contrast with the promise of America. Although the theme of destruction perhaps dominates Faulkner's work, the theme of the possibility of new life—if America's promise were properly understood—appears as well: in Ike's almost saintly perseverance in "The Bear," in Dilsey's endurance in *The Sound and the Fury* (1929), and in Quentin's negative affirmation when he says of the South, his America, "I don't hate it" in *Absalom, Absalom!* (1936). In so doing Quentin and Shreve together work out a moral vision of history that goes beyond Miss Rosa's apocalyptic vision without redemption, beyond her jeremiad without hope.

Among contemporary writers Thomas Pynchon explores the possibilities of America. In *The Crying of Lot 49* (1966), Oedipa Maas sets out on a quest through the America of the 1960s—an America of rock music and drugs and sex . . . and perhaps miracles. Jesús Arrabal, a Mexican revolutionary, tells her that a miracle is "another world's intrusion into this one." Is this what happens as she encounters one almost surrealistic situation after another, including a possible underground postal service linking all the outcasts of America? Neither Oedipa nor the reader can know whether her discoveries uncover meaningful symbols and reveal connections for the most part obscured in secular lives, whether her experience perpetuates some sort of hoax, or whether she is crazy. But what the reader does know is that she has discovered a sense of possibility and potentiality lying beneath the success-filled yet empty facade that calls itself America. Her legacy is the true America that may exist hidden in the midst of the outcasts from the American dream. She thinks of all those voices of America (as Whitman might) who are searching "for that magical Other who would reveal . . . the Word." In a secular age where relativity reigns, Pynchon gives no certainty of the Word behind the word, but extends the longing for the promise still connected with America.

The rich heritage of America's varied immigrant past informs much contemporary literature. Not surprisingly, the immigrants all adopted the story first told by the Puritans and adapted it to their own religious traditions. Abraham Cahan's *The Rise of David Levinsky* (1917) is a model for presenting both the promise of the New World and its dangers. In the next generation of Jewish-American writers, Saul Bellow peoples his novels with Old World/New World immigrants' sons who struggle with their Jewish culture and with the American promise. In *Herzog* (1964), Moses Herzog is an example of one son who may succeed. His father, a sometime bootlegger who struggles to make a place for his children in America, criticizes his non-European innocence, while his brother, a successful and empty American businessman, criticizes his infection by "Old World . . . feelings like Love— Filial Emotion. Old stuporous dreams."

Herzog's conversations with the reader encompass not only Jewish stories and language, but also the whole tradition of Western philosophy that he studies and teaches. In addition, his conversations flirt with Catholicism and secular humanistic "life options," usually connected with the woman he is currently involved with. Neither his tradition nor his philosophy nor his love relationships can provide the fulfillment he longs for. And so he sets out on a journey through America and visits the various places he has lived. Through reenactment and introspection, he attempts to find the promise that was lost. What he finds is a way of being authentically American that is an alternative to his brother's success story, a way that values human life and believes in a moral universe. At the end he is content to say nothing as he experiences the grace of acceptance: "And inside—something, something, happiness . . . 'Thou movest me.' That leaves no choice." Herzog, alone in the silence of nature, experiences, as so many Americans before him, the Word behind the word.

Black literature in America also employs the symbol of America as promised land, though it cannot ignore the discrepancy between the ideal and real. Ralph Ellison's *Invisible Man* (1952) tells the story of a young black man who believed in the promise of America. During a chapel service at his southern Negro college, the founder of the institution appears as the new Moses: " This barren land after Emancipation . . . this land of darkness and sorrow. . . . into this land

came a humble prophet. . . . And your parents followed this remarkable man across the black sea of prejudice, safely out of the land of ignorance, through the storms of fear and anger, shouting, LET MY PEOPLE GO! " The romantic aura surrounding this chapel speech warns the reader of the illusory nature of this dream of equality through self-improvement. The reader sees that illusion played out through the rest of the novel as the invisible man is betrayed again and again because he lives as if the promise of freedom and equality were true. He finally realizes the futility of the dream and hides in a basement to escape from life. It is from here that he tells the story of his invisibility in the hopes that we might be warned and come to see the reality of the black experience before it is too late. Even though he doubts that we can see, and even though he must remain invisible, he says, "in spite of all I find that I love." And so he ends his hibernation, not giving up the promise in spite of the darkness.

Flannery O'Connor and Walker Percy are Roman Catholics and southerners, two identities that give them a different perspective on the American story. O'Connor uses the Fundamentalist Protestantism of her native South to write a jeremiad on the hypocrisy of offering mere lip service to God when the giving of one's whole life is demanded. Her work mines the apocalyptic tradition of American culture: her characters turn to God only when confronted by a world-shaking, often world-ending revelation. Those who survive such confrontations must live in the apocalyptic moment of a new heaven and new earth that O'Connor only points to but does not try to imagine for us. Like Ellison, she is aware of the dangers of assuming the fulfillment of heaven on earth.

Walker Percy also uses an apocalyptic approach in his novel *Love in the Ruins: The Adventures of a Bad Catholic at a Time Near the End of the World* (1971). As his title suggests, he employs humor to create a somewhat plausible America of the not-so-distant future. Exaggerating and polarizing existing realities, he warns the reader about where America might be heading. Percy imitates Faulkner in both content and style: the protagonist, Dr. Tom More, suggests that the violation of people through slavery symbolizes all the violations that have led America to this moment of disaster. "But wait. It is still not too late. I can save you, America! . . . I can save the terrible God-blessed Americans from themselves! . . . You are still the last hope. . . . Bad as we are, there is no one else." Although Dr. More may possess wisdom, he needs to learn the lesson of humility—perhaps what America needs to learn as well. Over the course of the novel he learns this lesson to some extent by transforming from a "bad" though believing Roman Catholic to a contrite yet joyous communicant in a small chapel, shared in turn by remnant congregations of Jews, Protestants, and Catholics. While the chapel does not typify America, it nonetheless promises hope for America. In the meantime More remains a "sovereign wanderer, lordly exile, worker and waiter and watcher." He says, in the spirit of the new age, which may indeed be the spirit of the New World, "I thought of Christ coming again at the end of the world and how it is that in every age there is the temptation to see signs of the end and that, even knowing this, there is nevertheless some reason, what with the spirit of the new age being the spirit of watching and waiting, to believe that—"

A striking continuity links religion and literature in America as writers, inspired by visions of a new age, have explored the promise of America. In so doing they have searched for a balance or congruence or even merger between the hope and the actuality, between the ideal and the real, between heaven and earth. This promise began with the Word behind the word that inspired Puritan poetry and justified the errand into the wilderness. It is still present in Enlightenment thinking as the earthly word of reason is granted the certainty of the Word. Emerson's dictum that "Nature is the symbol of Spirit" assured that correspondence between the Word and the word, even while again restoring mystery. The writings of Hawthorne, Melville, and Dickinson first reveal the ambiguity and uncertainty that have best characterized American culture. The certainty remains of what we ought to be. Few of our writers question whether America has a special calling; that is usually assumed, even by those who say we have failed it. But when the Word behind the word becomes inaudible or disappears, America itself possesses no justification save its mission. Nonetheless, contemporary American writers continue to seek out the Word and to explore the possibilities and failure of the hope of a New World.

BIBLIOGRAPHY

Robert N. Bellah, *The Broken Covenant: American Civil Religion in Time of Trial* (1975); Sacvan Bercovitch, *The Puritan Origins of the American Self* (1975), *The American Jeremiad* (1978), and, as ed., *The American Puritan Imagination: Essays in Revaluation* (1974); Ursula Brumm, *American Thought and Religious Typology* (1970); Emory Elliott, ed., *Puritan Influences in American Literature* (1979); Charles Feidelson, *Symbolism and American Literature* (1953); Leslie A. Fiedler, *An End to Innocence: Essays on Culture and Politics* (1955); Albert Gelpi, *The Tenth Muse: The Psyche of the American Poet* (1975); Giles Gunn, ed., *New World Metaphysics: Readings on the Religious Meaning of the American Experience* (1981) and *The Bible and American Arts and Letters* (1983).

Howard Mumford Jones, *Belief and Disbelief in American Literature* (1967); Karl Keller, *The Example of Edward Taylor* (1975); R. W. B. Lewis, *The American Adam: Innocence, Tragedy, and Tradition in the Nineteenth Century* (1955); Leo Marx, *The Machine in the Garden: Technology and the Pastoral Ideal in America* (1964); F. O. Matthiessen, *American Renaissance: Art and Expression in the Age of Emerson and Whitman* (1941; rev. ed., 1954); Perry Miller, *Errand into the Wilderness* (1956), *Nature's Nation* (1967), and, as ed. with Thomas H. Johnson, *The Puritans: A Sourcebook of Their Writings*, 2 vols. (1938); Kenneth B. Murdock, *Literature and Theology in Colonial New England* (1949); David W. Noble, *The Eternal Adam and the New World Garden: The Central Myth in the American Novel Since 1830* (1968).

Roy Harvey Pearce, *The Continuity of American Poetry* (1961); William H. Shurr, *Rappaccini's Children: American Writers in a Calvinist World* (1981); Alan Simpson, *Puritanism in Old and New England* (1955); Henry Nash Smith, *Virgin Land: The American West as Symbol and Myth* (1950); Arnold Smithline, *Natural Religion in American Literature* (1966); Randall Stewart, *American Literature and Christian Doctrine* (1958); Tony Tanner, *The Reign of Wonder, Naivety and Reality in American Literature* (1965); Ernest L. Tuveson, *Redeemer Nation: The Idea of America's Millennial Role* (1968); Lois Zamora, ed., *The Apocalyptic Vision in America* (1982); Larzer Ziff, *Puritanism in America: New Culture in a New World* (1973).

[*See also* IMPACT OF PURITANISM ON AMERICAN CULTURE; JEWISH LITERATURE AND RELIGIOUS THOUGHT; RELIGIOUS AUTOBIOGRAPHY; *and* TRANSCENDENTALISM.]

RELIGIOUS AUTOBIOGRAPHY

Robert F. Sayre

BEGINNING with St. Augustine's *Confessions,* the great theme of confessional literature has always been the writer's religious experience. In the Augustinian tradition, the convert to Christianity wrote to confess God's grace and to tell the story that no one else could tell of how this change had come about and how much it meant to the convert. Conversion gave the writer a new perspective on his life, enabling him to organize his past and to select the important experiences, while the story of the conversion could also be made instructive to others—a useful aid in proselytizing. So with few exceptions, all through the Middle Ages, the Renaissance, and the Reformation, the personal and confessional writing that is the foundation of modern autobiography continued to be based on the story of one's Christian religious experience.

The importance of this connection to autobiography in America can hardly be overemphasized. American autobiography, even when it is most professedly secular, often has an underlying religious message; and American religious writers have again and again turned to autobiography to tell their most intimate and often most memorable and appealing stories. To be sure, religious writing has not been the only source of autobiography in America. Early travelers and explorers like John Smith and John Bartram wrote first-person narratives of their experiences, and so laid a foundation for the stories of many later travelers and settlers. But from the 1600s to the present, autobiography in America has shown its religious roots, even while—like American religion—being extremely diverse.

The history begins with the Puritans, who brought from Europe what Perry Miller called an "Augustinian strain of piety" and with it an in-tense interest in self and selfhood. Diaries were kept as records of one's religious experience. Conversion narratives were evidence of the writer's piety and of the workings of Providence. And the histories and journals of leaders like William Bradford and John Winthrop were kept as their personal records of communal enterprises. But perhaps most important, the Puritans' biblical typologies assigned to each individual and the events of his life a potential cosmic significance. John Winthrop was not simply the leader of the Massachusetts Bay Colony and first governor of New England; he was, to his later biographer Cotton Mather, "Nehemias Americanus," the American Nehemiah, and this, as Sacvan Berkovitch showed, has had far-reaching consequences for the American sense of self. The individual, to the extent that he gave a biblical prototype a new American embodiment, had a place in a universal design.

Autobiography was a way of defining and locating the self within the universal designs of God, history, or Providence, and so it became a very important kind of American writing. American literature is, more commonly than English literature, a first-person one: often written from an I-perspective and typically placing the views or conscience of the individual ahead of the values of society. But autobiography in America has broadened its base, spreading far beyond the story of religious conversion. As a result, many of these other stories, like the *Autobiography* of Benjamin Franklin or Walt Whitman's "Song of Myself," also have a profoundly religious function and sacred place. Religious autobiography in America includes both the writings of members of various religious sects and the writings of other men and women who made a religion of

America—of their dedication to it and its ideals, their identification with it—and made its ideals their bond to other people.

We can see this process beginning in the late seventeenth century in the development of that uniquely American genre, the "captivity narrative." These were stories of men and women captured by Indians, and so they focused on the conflicts between Europeans and Indians and the Europeans' inside views of Native American life. But originally, as in *The Captivity of Mary Rowlandson* (1682), they had a specifically religious function. Her story tells of her capture at Lancaster, Massachusetts, in February 1676, during King Philip's War, and her survival of the rigors of winter, hunger, and threatened torture because of her Puritan faith, which grew stronger by the trial. She could even incorporate the Indians within the scheme of Providence: they were devils created to torment and test the elect.

A disproportionate number of the early captivity narratives were written or edited by ministers. The ministers were the most literate members of a community; they also seemed to have the most to fear from their parishioners' going over to the supposedly savage side, as a great number of captives actually did. But as the tradition of the Indian captivity narrative developed through the eighteenth and nineteenth centuries, less stress was placed on these Puritan values and more on violence, terror, and overt propaganda against the Indians. The "redemption" justified not only Christianity but civilization in general. The stories were warnings to others of what might happen to them, thus counteracting the influence of the Indians and French among the English. Later still, they were imitated by popular writers like James Fenimore Cooper and Catharine Maria Sedgwick, both because they were exciting and because captivity proved a hero's or heroine's devotion to English or American civilization.

Outside the captivity narratives, the most revealing eighteenth-century American autobiographers were Jonathan Edwards, John Woolman, Charles Woodmason, Ethan Allen, and Benjamin Franklin.

Jonathan Edwards, the New England leader of the Great Awakening, wrote his "Personal Narrative" in about 1740, testing his own religious affections by the standards he had reached after observing hundreds of his contemporaries and

parishioners. "I Had a variety of Concerns and Exercises about my Soul from my Childhood," he began, "but had two more remarkable Seasons of Awakening, before I met with that Change, by which I was brought to those new Dispositions, and that new Sense of Things, that I have since had." He was rigorously objective with himself, describing examples of his childhood piety, like the making of little altars in the woods, with simple beauty but as if at great distance from his present. He said even less about other people, focusing on his own soul in an almost frightening solitude. But the result was a short essay in self-examination that is at once lean and analytic and also deeply passionate and sensitive. Like the plain white walls and clear windows of a New England church, it is cold and unadorned, but spiritually very moving.

The *Journal* of John Woolman also has a plainness, but in Quaker gray rather than Congregational blacks and whites. His vocabulary alone, with words like "satisfaction," "comfort," "service," and "reverence," induces a calm. The self is less agent of action than disciplined receptor of divine light. And so even Woolman's vigorous challenges to authority, like his advocacy of the abolition of slavery and insistence on the rights of sailors, were utterly lacking in shrillness. He did not wish to arouse anger and resistance but reason and goodwill, and so subdued his own self or ego. But if this was passivity, it was passivity only to the voice of God, and therefore, in the end, it made Woolman all the more determined and persistent in pursuing what he heard as God's will. He has never had as many readers as his two contemporaries Edwards or Franklin, and yet his life and *Journal* were indeed "the finest flower of a unique Quaker culture," as Frederick B. Tolles said. To the alert reader, the *Journal* also contains some of the clearest, most precise, and most remarkable language ever written, a perfect expression of his religious insights.

At roughly the same time that Woolman was subduing his vanity to the service of God and humanity, the itinerant Anglican minister Charles Woodmason was exercising his in trying to overcome what he took to be the abominable crudity and ignorance of the South Carolina backwoods. His *Journal* and other writings were unknown until edited by Richard J. Hooker in 1953. They give a marvelous sense of the religious life of the early backwoods because they are also so expressive of Woodmason himself—his energy, rage, distress, and final affection for his flock. His main antagonists in his errand into the wilderness were New Light Baptists and Irish Presbyterians, along with swamps and swollen creeks, bad roads and trails, whiskey, lewdness, laziness, and greed. From day to day, he seemed only to grow more distressed at the impossibility of converting such folk to a proper Episcopal morality. And yet the more he raged, the more he seemed to become like the people he preached to and the more he sympathized with them against the government on the seacoast. Woodmason is representative, in the extreme, of the Englishman or European acclimatizing himself and his foreign religion to American conditions. The antithesis, in most respects, of Edwards and Woolman, he was nevertheless like them in pushing his religious life to its limits, to the frontiers of culture and knowledge, until it was basically changed. There, as he notes at one point, Presbyterians and Episcopalians agreed "in this Article, . . . That of getting Drunk." It was not the finest of reasons for doctrinal unity. But it also made the finer reasons superfluous.

Ethan Allen and Benjamin Franklin, to some readers, may not seem to be religious autobiographers at all, but they deserve discussion because they also illustrate the transformation of religious writing into a national writing with religious undertones. Allen, the Vermont colonel who captured Fort Ticonderoga in 1775, was later famous again as the writer of a *Narrative* describing his capture by the British at Montreal and imprisonment in Canada, England, and America for two years. At every moment, he went on resisting British tyranny and cruelty, embarrassing his captors by not obeying their orders and standing up for his honor and freedom. But this was not mere boasting. The man who captured Fort Ticonderoga "in the name of the great Jehovah and the Continental Congress" made the American Revolution a kind of religious war, and made his *Narrative* (1779) the story of how he suffered for his faith and how that faith in turn supported him in adversity. As the religious autobiographer wrote from a love of God, Allen wrote from "a sense of duty to my country" and in that way adapted religious autobiography to the service of patriotism.

But it was Franklin who fully secularized au-tobiography, or turned it to the service of a new national mythology. He took the Puritan conversion narrative and story of a pilgrim's progress and made it into the story of worldly work and success. His *Autobiography,* first published in the early nineteenth century, became a bible to ambitious young Americans. Copies were cheaply reproduced (often bound together with "The Way to Wealth," his compendium of the prudential maxims of Poor Richard) and distributed by schools, commercial colleges, banks, and church groups. The tale of how he rose from "humble beginnings" by thrift and industry and "doing good" became the archetype of the American myth of rags to riches. The *Autobiography* also tells of Franklin's particular religious beliefs: his father's Presbyterianism, his youthful flirtation with deism, and his attempt to find a universal creed that would please all sects and offend none. He heard the great revivalist George Whitefield (though he was chiefly interested in measuring the power of Whitefield's voice!). And he found means of soothing Quaker pacifists while still raising funds for the Pennsylvania militia. To detractors like D. H. Lawrence, Franklin is the snuff-colored manipulator and worshiper of the God of businessmen; to others, he is a founder of American religious pluralism and tolerance. Either way, there is no overlooking him.

The period from the 1780s to the 1830s was not rich in American autobiography. Unitarianism in religion and classicism in popular taste did not encourage introspection or self-mythologizing. By the 1830s, however, several forces were at work that would make the 1840s and 1850s extremely creative, in autobiography and American literature generally.

One such force was New England Transcendentalism, which, to quote Ralph Waldo Emerson, relocated the foundations of life in "spirit" rather than "matter." Spirit was accessible to all men and women, if they could regenerate themselves, and such people were "part or particle of God." Emerson's early writings, particularly *Nature* (1811), "The American Scholar" (1837), and "Self-Reliance" (1841), led a new generation to study of nature and self and so to "journalizing," as Henry David Thoreau called it.

The Transcendentalists needed, however, to break free of the directly religious associations of confessional literature, just as Emerson needed to leave the pulpit and church (before going to the lectern and lyceum). Thus their most characteristic form, as Lawrence Buell has noted, was the travel book, not the conversion narrative. Thoreau's *A Week on the Concord and Merrimack Rivers* (1849), *Walden* (1854), *The Maine Woods* (1864), and *Cape Cod* (1865), as well as many of his essays, were all in a broad sense travel writing. But of these the *Week* and *Walden* were the most philosophical and spiritual, two more examples of American "secular" autobiography with profound religious meaning. In the first Thoreau used the occasion of a boat trip with his brother in 1839 to express his dissatisfaction with churches, his discovery of Chinese and Indian religions, and to expound on many other subjects. He wished to grow wild in America, like the "wild" apple trees that had escaped from the settlers' orchards and gone native.

In *Walden,* Thoreau's account of two years beside Walden Pond, 1845–1847, the "extravagance," as he called it, went further. He wrote out his own declaration of independence from Concord village (even though it was only a mile away and he visited it often) and devoted himself to a life of minimal work, reading, observing, and writing. It was a very Emersonian program, learning from nature, the classics, and the necessary action of growing beans, building his cabin, and preserving his life. The more he simplified his physical life, he said, the more the spiritual life grew—and the more sensitive he was in seeing the spirit in nature.

In July 1846, visiting Concord from Walden, Thoreau was arrested by the town sheriff and confined for a night in jail, for not paying the poll tax that every voting male owed to the town and state. This was his protest against slavery and the Mexican War. (He had earlier announced that he was not a member of any church and would not pay a pew tax.) This high-principled refusal was the occasion for his later essay "On Resistance to Civil Government," or "Civil Disobedience" (1849). In this short, electrifying essay, Thoreau gave the major arguments for nonviolent resistance that later influenced Gandhi, Martin Luther King, Jr., and conscientious objectors to military service. The state, he argued, has no conscience; only individuals do; and where a state behaves unjustly, the place for a just man is in jail. The individual must also act as friction to impede the machinery of injustice, interposing himself wherever he is, not running amok, but letting the state run amok against him, "it being the desperate party."

A year after the publication of *Walden,* Walt Whitman published the first edition of *Leaves of Grass,* an even more astonishing product of American "wit and wisdom," as Emerson called it. Many of its great poems are also spiritual travels: "Song of Myself," "Song of the Open Road," "Starting from Paumanok," "Crossing Brooklyn Ferry," "Out of the Cradle Endlessly Rocking," "A Passage to India." But there is a big difference between the stiff-necked Yankee rectitude of Thoreau and the "hankering, gross, mystical, nude" Whitman. Whitman thought of himself as the world's greatest democrat, celebrating his body, his sexuality, his loafing, equality, and diversity. He wished to be the priest of democracy, treating all those before himself as foreground and all poets afterward as his descendants. And so he was—in his poetry. The speaker or singer of "Song of Myself" is an American as hero of a democratic epic. He is the composite of all workmen and regional types, the male and the female, soldiers and savages, president and prostitute. He finds his selfhood in his allegiance to them, expressed with a sort of rowdy mysticism; and they, the Country, will find their voices in his voice.

But Whitman the man, his biographers have shown, was far more troubled, prudential, and unsure of himself than the "Walt Whitman, an American, one of the roughs, a kosmos" invented or discovered in "Song of Myself." He had to hide and sublimate his "male adhesiveness," as he called it, and he had to fight to get his book recognized, even reviewing it himself. In *Democratic Vistas* (1871) he expressed his distress, too, at the failures of American culture. The "self" in the poetry, therefore, might be described as a kind of holy ideal for both poet and readers, the autobiographer as he and his readers would like to be but so far are not. The paradox is that this figure is also so universalized that no particular person could ever become him, except in imagination. Heroic spokesman for the religion of democracy though he was, Whitman also demonstrates the gap that still stands between America and the American as imaginative ideals and the nation or person as realities. Like many others, this religion is difficult to practice.

RELIGIOUS AUTOBIOGRAPHY

A second force that revived autobiography in the 1830s was the growing movement for the abolition of slavery. To gain publicity and sympathy for their cause, abolitionists encouraged escaped slaves to write about their bondage, flight, and freedom. The accounts were of all lengths, from short articles in abolitionist newspapers to long books. They were often dictated to white editors, and a few were later proved fakes. But so developed the slave narratives; and these, like narratives of Indian captivity, are another native American genre. Moreover, because of the piety of both the abolitionists and the ex-slaves, this genre also shows an immense influence from religious autobiography. Christian moral teaching was, to a great degree, the common ground on which the writer wanted to meet with his or her readers. Again and again, the path from slavery to freedom was also allegorized as progress away from sin and bondage to the devil and toward salvation. The North in the slave narratives (as in songs and sermons) was a "promised land"—even though it usually failed to live up to that promise. A great number of the writers, as Gilbert Osofsky has said, "were slave preachers, 'professors,' 'exhorters.' " Many also later became clergymen, among them J. W. C. Pennington and Josiah Henson, to name two of the most famous. But even in other cases, as in Frederick Douglass' outstanding *Narrative* (1845), they write with a religious sense of conviction, mission, and urgency. The authors contributed their share to the Civil War's later becoming a religious crusade. The content of slave narratives was unique; but the structure and language were fashioned from existing religious autobiography. They also laid a foundation for many other black autobiographies, from Booker T. Washington's *Up from Slavery* to *The Autobiography of Malcolm X,* and also for much of black fiction.

The third and largest source of autobiography in the middle of the nineteenth century was the new spaciousness in American life itself. As the country expanded from the Atlantic seaboard into the Mississippi Valley and California and Texas, so did individuals have new experiences to tell, like Richard Henry Dana in *Two Years Before the Mast* (1840), Francis Parkman in *The Oregon Trail* (1847), and Herman Melville in his autobiographical novels of whaling and the South Seas.

Peter Cartwright, an itinerant Methodist minister in the Ohio Valley, is a great example of this new energy. Representative of the hundreds of early frontier clergymen—many of whom wrote autobiographies—Cartwright is also very much his own man. He joined the Methodist Episcopal Church in Kentucky when he was sixteen, became an "exhorter" in the spring of 1802, and a preacher at age eighteen. For the next fifty years he preached at camp meetings and in tiny new churches in Kentucky and Tennessee, Ohio, Indiana, and Illinois, helping "to set the world on fire" (the American world at least) for Methodism. Baptists, Shakers, and the New Lights, in his opinion, were too indiscriminate: they would save and accept everyone. Presbyterians and Congregationalists were too conservative, believing in predestination, fancy pews, and college-trained clergy. Cartwright thought "velvet-mouthed and downy D.D.'s" with eastern manners and written sermons held themselves above their people. They were unsuited to the roughness of the West. He fought with tavern keepers, campaigned against slavery, preached to all who would listen, both black and white, native and immigrant, and so helped to spread not only Methodism but democracy and civil order. His *Autobiography,* first published in 1856, is a remarkable book—a compendium of his yarns and adventures, his pride in his calling, and his original anti-intellectual, muscular Christianity. The records in nearly every chapter of the annual growth in Methodism are also a sign of religion in America becoming a competitive business. Peter Cartwright is Charles Woodmason two generations later, a frontier preacher not just adapting to the country but helping to shape it, a religious pioneer in the most fundamental sense.

Equally illustrative of mid-nineteenth-century religious variety is Orestes Brownson, author of *The Convert* (1857). Born in Stockbridge, Vermont, in 1803, Brownson was raised by foster parents who had forgotten their ancestral Calvinism. His life became a spiritual odyssey, from Presbyterian to Universalist, to world reformer, to Unitarian, to Transcendentalist, to Saint-Simonian, and finally to Roman Catholic. Unlike Thoreau and Whitman, he did not think of himself as a prototype for a new race, and his energy was intellectual rather than physical—hardly like Cartwright. But he was quite similar to many other refined and intelligent Americans in losing faith in American novelty and spiritual independence. He wanted order and an authority higher than himself and the changeable crowd. The spiritual odyssey he reviews is nowhere near as cosmic or dramatic as that of Ishmael in Melville's *Moby-Dick* (1851) or the narrator in Melville's *Clarel* (1871), but it demands attention even so. Rarely did a Yankee of Brownson's generation become a Catholic. His decision was so shocking to many of his former associates among the Unitarians and Transcendentalists that they and proper Boston ostracized him. But his need for stronger traditional authority anticipated those of many later Americans, from the generation of Henry Adams to the times of T. S. Eliot, Dorothy Day, and Thomas Merton.

The Civil War and the Gilded Age that followed it were not very productive of religious autobiography. Veterans of the war and their families wanted to read the memoirs of generals (mostly the victorious Union ones) or they wanted to read sentimental fiction that represented the South as a beautiful but hotheaded, disobedient girl and the North as the patient, suffering suitor that eventually reclaimed her. The true religion of the Gilded Age, it has been suggested, was worship of what William James later called the Bitch Goddess, Success. Even by the 1890s the most popular autobiographies were ones like Andrew Carnegie's uplifting tale of hard work, "How I Served My Apprenticeship," published in *Youth's Companion* in 1896. Yet what made Carnegie a national hero was not only that he had been overwhelmingly successful in business, but that with his famous "Gospel of Wealth" he promoted the idea that successful men should use their money for educational and charitable purposes. Religion kept its hold on the American imagination (and it continued to be honored in autobiographies). The worship of success is like hypocrisy: it still pays its tribute to virtue.

The period also had an abundance of autobiographies by ministers, missionaries, and former abolitionists who saw their work as a religious vocation. In Louis Kaplan's *A Bibliography of American Autobiographies,* "Clergymen" is one of the longest entries in the subject index, and the years between 1850 and 1900 were when American clergymen published the greatest number of their autobiographies. In the large denomina-

tions like Baptist and Methodist the number of clergymen's autobiographies published between 1850 and 1900 is approximately twice the number published between 1800 and 1850 and three times the number between 1900 and 1945.

Generalizations about such a large class of books are risky, but it is interesting that most of them emphasize the writer's good works and public life rather than his or her conversion or doubt and inner experience. Religious belief for these writers (and their readers, presumably) was a given. The focus was on what that person then did with it to spread the faith. Stephen Riggs's *Mary and I: Forty Years with the Sioux* (1880) is about his and his wife's missionary work, his writing of a Sioux grammar and translation of the Bible, and their founding of Santee Normal School. Despite all the hard work and dedication the book records, it is strangely complacent. Riggs never doubts his white man's burden and the value of what he has done for the Sioux. Thus, even while his work was historically very interesting, the book is finally rather dull. It is also troubling to recall his times, even though we might still learn from them. Perhaps the self-satisfaction of Riggs and men like him is what is most troubling.

Somewhat different observations might be made of *An Autobiography: The Story of the Lord's Dealings with Mrs. Amanda Smith, the Colored Evangelist* (1893). A brilliant and energetic woman, with a keen sense of the ironies of racial segregation, Mrs. Smith produced a book that is like a curious antique. It has fascinating angles and episodes, like her defending her dignity and social status when she finds herself the only black on a transatlantic liner. Studying such experiences brings back her time and place; it also partially relates it to our own. But it would require a major research project to examine the hundreds of memoirs and recollections by the clergymen and missionaries and other religious leaders of this period. Who were the publishers and audiences? How popular were these books, and why did people read them? If American religion has changed a great deal since then, how and why did it change?

One series of answers is in *The Education of Henry Adams.* Adams, writing around 1905, presented himself as a seeker and pilgrim alienated from his own time because he could not accept its political corruption, ominous technological power, and religious complacency. Describing his childhood in Boston and Quincy, he sneered at the "eighteenth-century" traditions of his parents and grandparents. Describing his experiences in London as his father's secretary during the Civil War, he made diplomacy sound too corrupt for his refined sensibility. The same was true of life in Washington during the Grant administration. So as time passed, he became a pilgrim to the shrines of the Middle Ages, as described in *Mont-Saint-Michel and Chartres* (1913), where he saw art and religion and reason as fully unified. In *The Education* these contrasting worlds of the Middle Ages and the modern are symbolized by the Virgin and the Dynamo, the one feminine, natural, and unifying, the other masculine, mechanical, entropic, and disunifying. For most of his own nineteenth-century contemporaries Adams had little but contempt. They did not even see the "chaos" that "coal power" and the "dynamo" had thrown up all around them. They pursued only superficial success and display; they did not admit—as Adams did of himself—their cosmic "failure."

For many of the people who read Adams just after World War I (the first commercial publication of *The Education* was in 1918), his sense of prophecy seemed brilliant and his historical analysis certain. He was finally granted, posthumously, the fame he seems to have secretly wanted all his life. But the more perspective we get on Adams, the more the book loses as history and the more it gains as art. For whatever else it is or isn't, it is written with dazzling command of language, irony, and narrative positions. Historical people like his grandfather and grandmother, his sister Louisa, President Grant, and his friends John Hay and Clarence King are used like figures in a novel. They instruct, defeat, or illuminate aspects of the central character. Likewise, the quest of the character "Adams" for order and belief is a narrative technique that threatens to overwhelm the book. He cannot stop or the book and his life would be over. And thus the strong and charming and human side of Adams the man is suppressed. He exaggerated his own "failure" and with it, the "failure" of much of his culture. Early readers of T. S. Eliot's *The Waste Land* (1922) and other members of what Gertrude Stein called the Lost Generation might be convinced that nineteenth-century religion and society were as bad as *The Education* said, but today

we acknowledge the strength and promise of other groups that Adams also scorned, like working-class Jews and immigrants.

Adams was not alone in his generation in using autobiography as a means of reflecting on the changes between the preindustrial world of childhood and the machine civilization of adulthood. In the 1890s and early 1900s William Dean Howells, Mark Twain, and Henry James all turned back nostalgically to boyhood innocence and freshness. Edward Everett Hale, author of *The Man Without a Country,* wrote *A New England Boyhood* (1893), and Charles Eastman wrote *An Indian Boyhood* (1902), about his life as a Sioux before his conversion to Christianity. Perhaps the fear of new waves of immigration contributed to their nostalgia also: pride in one's native heritage, be it New England, Anglo-Saxon, or Indian, was a kind of upper-class ethnic protest against racial and religious as well as industrial and technological change.

Still another instance of the fascination autobiography held for this generation is William James's *The Varieties of Religious Experience* (1902), a study based to a great extent on James's reading of dozens of first-person accounts of conversion, mystical visitations, and other spiritual phenomena. The more James and his contemporaries doubted their own religious faith, the more curious they were about other faiths and what they meant to their adherents. "Autobiographies are my particular line of literature," William James wrote to Henry Adams, "the only books I let myself buy outside of metaphysical treatises." James did not write an autobiography himself. But *The Varieties of Religious Experience,* as a pioneering work in the scientific and psychological study of religious behavior, records, among its other achievements, his own religious quest. The respect with which he approached other people's experience was both scientific and personal. It was the style, also, of a good reader, someone suspending disbelief so as to learn the most from the person he was reading. James's book helped in understanding religion, in building tolerance, and even in the later use of autobiographies as clinical and anthropological documents.

After the religious complacency of the Gilded Age and the uncertainty of the generation immediately after, it is not surprising to find a "social gospel" emerging in the early twentieth century. One sees it in a great number of radicals, reformers, and leaders of the so-called Progressive Era.

Booker T. Washington's *Up from Slavery* (1901) is one illustration. Negroes should improve their lot by a black version of Benjamin Franklin's virtue and thrift and hard work, taking jobs in agriculture and mechanics. W. E. B. Du Bois's various autobiographical essays of the 1900s took the opposite position: blacks should not compromise their pride, should seek political power, and should follow the most talented, who would get work in business and the professions. In most respects, the argument between Washington and Du Bois was political, economic, and educational. Yet something in the conditions of American culture made it a religious argument as well, with Washington gaining support from many white churches and Du Bois answering in *The Souls of Black Folk* (1903), calling on the consciences of both his white and black readers. Moreover, by the very act of writing autobiographically, both Washington and Du Bois interposed ethical proofs for their respective positions. Each invited the readers to judge him as a representative or ideal of the race as a whole, more or less as various white autobiographical heroes like Franklin, Thoreau, and Whitman had asked to be taken as representative Americans. Washington, in particular, was treated as a spokesman for all Negroes. He was more than a leader; he and Du Bois too, in some ways, were messiahs.

But black leaders were not the only ones so deified in the social gospel, whose autobiographies became, to extend the metaphor, more or less sacred texts. Another was Jane Addams, whose *Twenty Years at Hull-House* (1910) was sacred to the settlement house movement. Following the structure of a conversion narrative, it told of her pious upbringing in Rockford, Illinois, where her father was a prosperous Quaker, her college education, and then her travels through Europe, where she was expected to continue preparing to become a wife and society woman. But at a moment when she was disgusted by a bullfight in Spain, she also became disgusted by herself. She wished to escape this "snare of endless preparation," in which all her life was just grooming for what supposedly lay ahead, and begin to live and to serve others, correcting the social conditions that had shocked her in cities like London. Shortly, she and several of her friends opened Hull-House in an immigrant neighborhood in Chicago. Their objective, it should be noted, was in no formal sense religious. Hull-House was nondenominational and open to persons of all religions and nationalities. But any careful reader of Addams can see the enduring influence of her father's Quakerism in her actions and language. Moreover, even as she fought against being popularly canonized as Saint Jane, her skills in uniting people and getting them to work together made her a religious leader in the most fundamental sense. With her the social gospel worked.

Frederic C. Howe's *Confessions of a Reformer* (1925) tells of his early wish to become a journalist. He went from Allegheny College to Johns Hopkins, where he became excited by doctoral studies and the prospect of a scientific approach to government. Like other idealistic men and women of his generation, he was also horrified by the squalor of urban life and the connivance of big-city political machines in gambling and prostitution. His spiritual conversion came in New York, when he discovered that the prominent religious reformers of the city, like the Rev. Charles Henry Parkhurst, indirectly contributed to corruption by driving up the amounts the police charged the prostitutes and saloonkeepers for protection. Machine politics, he discovered, were also practical politics: machines obtained jobs and services for immigrants and the poor; they made democracy work. Serving reform administrations in Cleveland and then in the national government, Howe tested his new theories of government. But as Richard Hofstadter wrote in *The Age of Reform,* Howe and other Progressives continued to have a fundamentally religious dedication to their work—even while denying it and strongly opposing Fundamentalist religion. The reformer was a secular priest. The new professional training that Howe and his contemporaries espoused in disciplines like law, statistics, government, and city planning led also to the establishment, it is sometimes said, of a new priesthood. Howe's very title, *Confessions of a Reformer,* captures this paradox. Howe and Jane Addams were but two of the hundreds of converts.

Almost from its beginnings, therefore, religious autobiography in America has been of two types, what we might call the doctrinal and the national. The doctrinal has been the confessions or memoirs of a religious leader like Edwards or Woolman, Cartwright or Brownson. It recounted the writer's experience within one or more specific Christian sects or denominations. The national autobiographers like Franklin and Allen, Thoreau and Whitman, or Adams and Washington have hardly been less religious, however. They adopted many of the forms of confessions, conversions, and traditional religious autobiography in order to defend, broaden, and champion America as a providential land or ideal: a new Canaan, a wilderness, a Philadelphia, a mystical democracy, or a corrupt land of slavery and oppression needing redemption.

The autobiographer, while not overtly a saint, has also been national hagiographer, autohagiographer, promoting himself or herself in the process or as a way of promoting the vision or prophecy. The history of American autobiography, therefore, is an obvious place in which to study the whole long phenomenon of America as a secular or national religion. And yet the very complexity and diversity of this "religion" has kept the autobiographical heroes from being mere nationalists and patriots in the jingoistic sense. If there have been autohagiographers like the poet of "Song of Myself," there have also been Jeremiahs like the author of *Democratic Vistas* and *The Education of Henry Adams*.

To become "an American" in the secular and social sense, then, has often meant giving up one's Puritanism, Quakerism, or other denominational affiliation. But such a surrender, at least to Franklin, Emerson, Thoreau, Whitman, and even Booker T. Washington and Jane Addams, was not a giving up of religious dedication, spirituality, and brotherhood. It was a finding and fulfillment of them. On the other hand, for writers like Woolman and Brownson and Cartwright religion was a necessary counterweight to the state or addition to it. The variety and tolerance of democracy was a blessing only to a point. After that, it became vagueness and laxness. Religion was above the state, as for Woolman and Brownson, just as the individual conscience was above it for Thoreau. Or religion must tame and redeem it, as it did for frontier evangelists like Cartwright. Nevertheless, only a few of these writers saw their religion as opposed to the state, in open conflict with it. They could be Quakers or Methodists or Catholics and still be Americans, too.

The twentieth-century American who was perhaps most critical of democratic pluralism and secularism was T. S. Eliot, who lamented in "Thoughts After Lambeth" (1929) that "The World is trying the experiment of attempting to form a civilized but non-Christian mentality"— an experiment he believed certain to "fail." His long poem *The Four Quartets* (1934–1943) is a meditative quest that merges elements of his own experience with Christian ritual, symbols, and tradition. For over thirty years, from the late 1920s to the 1950s, Eliot was a leading spokesman for conservative American Protestants and Anglo-Catholics.

Other twentieth-century autobiographers, however, have championed the faiths and the pluralism Eliot feared, while also showing the conflicts that they and their religions and cultures have with existing American society.

One of the most prominent arenas for these conflicts has been Jewish autobiography, a genre, some would say, that is at once religious, national, and ethnic. Mary Antin's *The Promised Land* (1912), one of the first American Jewish autobiographies, told the story of her birth in Polotsk, Russia, her emigration, and her passion to be "made over" into an American. She wished "to forget" her earlier life and her time as "the Wandering Jew," to shed the customs and language of the past, and acquire the education and refined speech of a new "promised land." She gave up the name Mashke to become Mary. She went to Barnard College. And at age thirty she began the writing of this book that confirmed her new identity. In the course of it, she also became a great advocate of America and of assimilation —an example displaying herself to other immigrants. But the reply to *The Promised Land*, as Alvin Rosenfeld has said, was Abraham Cahan's autobiographical novel, *The Rise of David Levinsky* (1917). Levinsky also wished to become an American, and he succeeded in rising from poverty to wealth. But in the course of becoming comfortable and well-off, Levinsky lost his Jewishness and found himself torn apart. "My past and present do not comport well," he mourns. In this cry, said Rosenfeld, "we recognize the tragedy of Jewish irreconciliation with America." The material success that Jews have attained to a greater degree than any other immigrant group does not "comport" with the traditional Jewish "pieties."

RELIGIOUS AUTOBIOGRAPHY

The three volumes of Alfred Kazin's autobiography, *A Walker in the City* (1951), *Starting Out in the Thirties* (1965), and *New York Jew* (1978), draw together both these strands of Jewish autobiography. In the first volume, the young Kazin is just as anxious to shed his immigrant past as Mary Antin was, and in the next two volumes he succeeds like Levinsky. He also tries harder than Levinsky to make his past and present comport with one another. The writer of *A Walker in the City* recaptured the same sights and sounds of the Brooklyn ghetto that the child had escaped. In a roughly similar way, the author of the last volume was not ashamed of being that target of Gentile antagonism, the "New York Jew"; he was proud of it. But that very insistence on his separateness from other Americans (whether causing or caused by their exclusion of him) guaranteed that his story would not become a national exemplary tale like Franklin's, Whitman's, or Thoreau's. He did not wish to become like others or have others become like him. His Jewishness being more ethnic than religious, they cannot, even if they were doctrinally to convert. Thus he does not proselytize either. Kazin did not wish to drop his ancestral past into the great simmering melting pot, like a legendary democrat; he wished to hang on to his particularity as tenaciously as any of the descendants of the *Mayflower* or Daughters of the American Revolution who once dreaded his entry into "their" colleges and clubs.

In *A Walker in the City* Kazin noted that during his childhood "no one around me seemed to take God very seriously. We neither believed nor disbelieved. He was our oldest habit." If this was also true in Allen Ginsberg's childhood in New Jersey, it did not remain so in his adulthood. His two long autobiographical poems *Howl* and *Kaddish* are great religious poetry. When first published in 1956, *Howl* was widely attacked as obscene, repetitious, and formless, but it had the anger and the anguish of prophecy. A young imitator of the Hebrew prophets (and Blake and Whitman, too), Ginsberg moved from relentless enumeration of the destructive "madness" around him to a denunciation of Moloch, the child-eating God responsible for modern materialism and inhumanity. In the third section of the poem he then expressed his own empathy with one of the victims, Carl Solomon, a friend in an insane asylum. In *Kaddish* (1961) he

adapted the Jewish prayer for the dead, traditionally read by sons for their fathers, into a long lament for his mother, a woman who had once been a young, optimistic socialist and had died in a madhouse. The poem is remarkably intimate, even by modern standards, and also remarkably rich in the humorous and pathetic details of Jewish domestic life. It is just as certifiably Jewish as any volume of Kazin's.

In the end *Kaddish* and *Howl* both are more national and universal than doctrinal. They protest a materialism that has consumed children of promise from all religions, Jewish and Gentile; they cry for the defeated dreams of many mothers and sons. In these ways they are also far from the buoyant confidence of earlier national autobiographers. They mix the anger and tragedy of the post-Hiroshima age, of the Beat Generation, as Ginsberg and his early cohorts called themselves. To be "beat" was a way of not taking one's own tragedies too solemnly, of realizing that many others, saints and sinners, were beat, beaten, and beatific also. Finally, the "beat" were seekers, people on a spiritual quest through all great religions, Buddhist as well as Christian or Jewish, Asian as well as Western. Even more devotedly than the Transcendentalists of the nineteenth century, they sought a "Passage to India," and a "passage of the soul to India," to quote Whitman.

American Catholic autobiography has come into its own in the twentieth century just as much as Jewish, although it has not had any writers who have received the widespread celebration that Allen Ginsberg did during the 1960s. In *The Seven Storey Mountain* (1948), Thomas Merton told in fascinating detail his unusual story of growing up in France, England, and America as the son of an American mother and New Zealand father. Both died when he was young, and he was later generously supported by their friends and his maternal grandparents, whose funds and trust funds sent him to Cambridge University and then Columbia University. Oppressed by his excessive youthful dissipation, he gradually found discipline in Catholic ritual. Following his conversion, while at Columbia, he soon wanted to become a priest. "I needed a high ideal, a difficult aim, and the priesthood provided me with one." In December 1941, at the age of thirty-two, he joined the Trappist monastery at Gethsemane, Kentucky. Originally expected to have a sale of a few thousand, his autobiography became a best-seller. It and Merton's many later books, up to his death in 1968, also gave hope to many young Catholics that they could have an intellectual life in America similar to that of European Catholics. They did not have to abandon their Catholicism, as earlier writers like Theodore Dreiser and Scott Fitzgerald had, or limit their activities as Catholics to teaching in Catholic schools and colleges.

Further proof of this acceptance came with the publication of Mary McCarthy's *Memoirs of a Catholic Girlhood* in 1957. At that time McCarthy was already well known as a reviewer and novelist, but the *Memoirs* told of her uniquely Catholic experience: her parsimonious Irish relatives in St. Paul, her generous relatives in Seattle, her experiences with the strict but not very sophisticated nuns in school, and her discovery of her independence from this world and her ability to use it in fiction.

Perhaps the greatest Catholic autobiographer, however, is Dorothy Day, author of *The Long Loneliness* (1952) and another convert. The daughter of a sports reporter, Day went to the University of Illinois and then moved to New York, where she became a radical journalist. She was arrested in demonstrations for women's rights. She had many friends among the artists and intellectuals of Greenwich Village. In the 1920s she and her common-law husband moved to Staten Island, where she wrote fiction and he pursued his research in biology. She was, she says, extremely happy. But slowly this very happiness, accentuated by her husband's love of the natural world, made her long for more knowledge of God as "the Creator." She and her daughter were baptized as Catholics. Her husband, a nonbeliever, could not accommodate himself to her new faith, and she left him. Then in the early 1930s, through friends on *Commonweal* magazine, she met the the radical French Catholic Peter Maurin. Together they founded the *Catholic Worker*, publishing the first issue in May 1933 during the depths of the Depression, as a Catholic counterpart to the Communist *Daily Worker*. By 1936 it had a circulation of nearly 150,000.

"The long loneliness" of Day's title is many things, from the solitude of the individual outside the community of friends and church, to the life of a woman, the life of a martyr, or life itself.

This loneliness seems answered by her pleasure in friends and work. She is also unusual among converts to any faith for turning to religion out of happiness rather than distress or a sense of sin. Not recanting her past, she made her Catholicism a continuation of her earlier pursuit of social justice. Her influence can be found in the liberation theology of today, which her and Maurin's Catholic Marxism anticipated, in the "hospitality houses" that she and Maurin founded, and in the focus that the *Catholic Worker* gave to other movements like pacifism and war resistance. One of its contributors, for instance, was Ammon Hennacy, a socialist who in 1918, while in solitary confinement in a federal prison in Atlanta, was so moved by reading the Sermon on the Mount (the Bible was the only reading he was allowed) that he became a Christian pacifist and anarchist. His autobiographical essays, like "God's Coward" and "Atlanta Prison—1917," were published in the *Catholic Worker* and read by conscientious objectors to World War II and the Vietnam War.

Conflicts between church and state and ethnic groups and state have been even more prominent in twentieth-century Indian and black autobiography. Building upon traditions established in the slave narratives and biographies and autobiographies of famous chiefs, they have become simultaneously more religious and more outspoken.

Black Elk Speaks is the autobiography of a Sioux holy man who as a boy had a vision of being taken to meet the Six Grandfathers who were "the Powers of the World." They represented the four directions, the Sky, and the Earth and gave him agents and symbols to be used in serving the Sioux people. They also gave him ceremonies involving horses, bison, and other animals that Black Elk later performed, when at the age of seventeen he described his vision to older medicine men. In 1890, having been unable to bring his vision to fruition, Black Elk joined the Ghost Dance movement. His autobiography was "given" to John G. Neihardt in the early 1930s, but readership of the first edition was limited.

In 1961 the book was reissued in paperback, having in the meantime been discovered by Carl Jung, and its popularity spread like a prairie fire, among both Indians and whites. It presented a clearer, more accessible account of Plains Indian religion than had ever been presented by anthropologists. It made ceremonies appear beautiful as well as sacred. And so it contributed to many of the Indian and pro-Indian rights movements of the early 1970s.

Before *Black Elk,* the best-known Indian autobiographies had been the stories of warriors like Black Hawk or Geronimo or of converts to Christianity like Charles Eastman. The one emphasized tragic, though heroic, military resistance and ultimate submission. The other praised the white way, even if with many qualifications. In fact, Black Elk had also been a convert to Christianity, accepting baptism in 1904 and serving for many years as a catechist. But Neihardt said nothing about this side of Black Elk's life. He presented him as a spiritual holdout, thereby making the Indian way more compelling.

Black Elk Speaks also generated interest in other Indian religious autobiographies. In 1969 N. Scott Momaday, then a professor of literature at the University of California, Santa Barbara, published an account of his personal journey in pursuit of his father's Kiowa past. Following the route of the emergence of the Kiowa people, who had left the Rocky Mountains and ventured out onto the Great Plains just before the Europeans arrived in America, Momaday learned more about the Kiowa religion, told ancient stories, and recalled his own memories of his grandparents. *The Way to Rainy Mountain* thus reversed the direction of earlier conversion stories. It did not tell of an Indian's submission or conversion to Christianity; it recounted a highly educated "white Indian's" discovery or rediscovery of his Indian religion.

Lame Deer, Seeker of Visions (1972) by John Fire, Lame Deer, and Richard Erdoes gives an often comic account of another Sioux's journey through rodeos, alcoholism, and prison and on to the life of a modern medicine man. What makes his book different from *Black Elk* or from an anthropological study like Paul Radin's *The Autobiography of a Winnebago* (repr. 1963), an account of a convert to the Peyote religion of the Native American Church, is that Lame Deer boldly and proudly preaches to his white readers. The Indian way is best, he says, and he tells funny stories of white incompetence and error to prove it. Like Momaday, he and Erdoes also had to depend to a great degree on information in old anthropological journals; but Lame Deer

made it his own. Autobiography enabled him to be, in effect, a self-made Indian. It also allowed him to voice the anger that made him and other Indians (and their white sympathizers) want to drop out of white America and live a more composed, traditional life. Once having expressed it, however, the book (and one might cynically add, the royalties) partially helped to integrate and establish him in that society.

The search for native or alternative faiths is just as strong, if not stronger, in modern black autobiography. In fact, one could write a whole history of the civil rights movement and black protests of the 1960s and early 1970s as they are reflected in religious autobiography.

During the 1930s and 1940s the angriest black writers were not associated with black churches. In *Black Boy* (1945) Richard Wright scarcely mentions them, and when Wright escaped from Mississippi to Chicago, he became a member of the John Reed Club, the Communist party's artists' cell. His later rejection of communism, described in *The God That Failed* (1949), and his emigration to France did not take him into the church. For Wright and the younger generation of black writers represented by James Baldwin, Christianity meant conciliation with the reigning black authorities, who were, in turn, conciliatory and even obsequious to white authority. In his autobiographical novel *Go Tell It on the Mountain* (1953) Baldwin's young protagonist had to choose between "the church," representing obedience, however angry, and "the jail"—the consequence of rebellion.

But when Baldwin turned to writing autobiographical essays, he used the language of black preachers with superb authority. He began to prophesy white doom, "the fire next time," if white readers did not join with blacks in opposing racial injustice. Then in "A Letter from a Region in My Mind," the longest essay in *The Fire Next Time* (1963), he also introduced his readers to the leader of the Black Muslim movement, Elijah Muhammad.

By the early 1960s, the most vocal leader of the Muslims, however, was Malcolm X. His *Autobiography* (1964), dictated to the black journalist Alex Haley, has become a classic. Perhaps no other book so vividly demonstrates the rage behind black protest and the corresponding appeal that the Muslim movement held. The autobiographical writings of Martin Luther King, Jr., while more attractive to many people on ideological grounds, are not nearly so powerful.

The *Autobiography* ranks with the greatest American autobiographies. In outline, it is a straightforward narrative of Malcolm's conversion, or conversions. He was born Malcolm Little, in Omaha, Nebraska, in 1925, the son of a West Indian mother and a black Baptist minister who supported Marcus Garvey. Harassed by the Ku Klux Klan, the family soon moved to East Lansing, Michigan, where Malcolm's father was harassed again and killed. His mother was sent to the Michigan State Mental Hospital, and Malcolm and his brothers and sisters became wards of the state. In the next ten years, he went through several transformations: popular "mascot" in a white school in Lansing, neophyte "homebody" in Boston pool parlors and dance halls, sandwich butcher on the New Haven Railroad between Boston and New York, "Detroit Red" the Harlem hustler and pimp, and back to Boston as a burglar. Finally caught and sentenced to Charlestown State Prison (not because he had been robbing houses, he says, but because he'd been working with white women), he then became "Satan." He was the meanest, least cooperative prisoner he could be. But his brother wrote to him in prison about the teachings of Elijah Muhammad, whose explanation of the condition of blacks in America became Malcolm's salvation. Overnight, the new Malcolm X set out upon a program of self-education, copying out the dictionary to build his vocabulary and interpreting history and economics from the Muslim perspective, in which the white man was the devil and Allah the savior.

When he left prison in 1952, he went to Detroit and soon became a Muslim minister. In a short while, Malcolm became the movement's most brilliant missionary, founding mosques in many cities and debating on college campuses and television talk shows. His fame, however, raised many jealousies within the Muslim movement, until, despite his sincerest efforts to continue supporting Elijah Muhammad, he was eventually excommunicated.

The remainder of the book tells the equally amazing story of his pilgrimage to Mecca, his founding of a new movement that was to be closer to traditional Moslem religion, and his hope of reconciliation with the most liberated American whites. But at this point, the *Autobiog-*raphy ends—shortly before his assassination in Harlem on February 21, 1965.

It is ironic that works like *Howl*, Malcolm X's *Autobiography*, and *Lame Deer* are on their way to entering the canon of American literature and civilization. Like Thoreau's "Civil Disobedience," they are so widely read in college classrooms that their dissenting message is always in danger of being blunted. They represent the human spirit challenging the injustices of the state, responding to gods that to the mass of Americans are surely false. And yet the most fundamental exercise of freedom of speech and religion is a person's right to tell his own story and speak of God in his own tongue. Religious autobiographers in America have exercised that right repeatedly and in so doing have not only defined the land and its religions but changed them forever.

BIBLIOGRAPHY

Sacvan Bercovitch, *The Puritan Origins of the American Self* (1975) and "The Ritual of American Autobiography: Edwards, Franklin, Thoreau," in *Revue Française d'Études Américaines*, 14 (1982); Warner Berthoff, "Witness and Testament: Two Contemporary Classics," in *New Literary History*, 2 (1971); Mutlu Konuk Blasing, *The Art of Life: Studies in American Autobiographical Literature* (1977); Elizabeth Bruss, *Autobiographical Acts: The Changing Situation of a Literary Genre* (1976); Lawrence Buell, *Literary Transcendentalism: Style and Vision in the American Renaissance* (1973); Stephen Butterfield, *Black Autobiography in America* (1974); Thomas Cooley, *Educated Lives: The Rise of Modern Autobiography in America* (1976); G. Thomas Couser, *American Autobiography: The Prophetic Mode* (1979); Raymond J. DeMallie, ed., *The Sixth Grandfather: Black Elk's Teachings Given to John G. Neihardt* (1984); Janet Varner Gunn, *Autobiography: Toward a Poetics of Experience* (1982).

Richard Hofstadter, *The Age of Reform* (1955); Louis Kaplan, *A Bibliography of American Autobiographies* (1962); David Minter, "By Dens of Lions: Notes on Stylization in Early Puritan Captivity Narratives," in *American Literature*, 45 (1973), and "Conceptions of Self in Black Slave Narratives," in *American Transcendental Quarterly*, 24 (1974); Lynn W. O'Brien, *Plains Indian Autobiographies* (1973); James Olney, *Metaphors of Self: The Meaning of Autobiography* (1972) and, as ed., *Autobiography: Essays Theoretical and Critical* (1980); Gilbert Osofsky, ed., *Puttin' On Ole Massa* (1969); Marc Pachter, ed., *Telling Lives: The Biographer's Art* (1979); Alvin H. Rosenfeld, "Inventing the Jew: Notes on Jewish Autobiography," in *Midstream: A Monthly Jewish Review* (April 1975).

Robert F. Sayre, *The Examined Self: Benjamin Franklin, Henry Adams, Henry James* (1964), "Vision and Experience in *Black Elk Speaks*," in *College English*, 32 (1971), and "The Proper Study: Autobiographies in American Studies," in *American*

Quarterly, 29 (1977); Daniel B. Shea, Jr., *Spiritual Autobiography in Early America* (1968); Sidonie Smith, *Where I'm Bound: Patterns of Slavery and Freedom in Black American Autobiography* (1974); William C. Spengemann, *The Forms of Autobiography: Episodes in the History of a Literary Genre* (1980); Albert E. Stone, ed., *The American Autobiography: A Collection of Critical Essays* (1981) and *Autobiographical Occasions and Original Acts* (1982);

David L. Waddle, "The Image of Self in Jonathan Edwards: A Study of Autobiography and Theology," in *American Academy of Religion Journal,* 43 (1975); Karl J. Weintraub, "Autobiography and Historical Consciousness," in *Critical Inquiry,* 1 (1975), and *The Value of the Individual: Self and Circumstance in Autobiography* (1978).

[*See also* NEW ENGLAND PURITANISM.]

RELIGION AND SCIENCE

Walter H. Conser, Jr.

POPULAR discussion during the 1980s concerning the teaching of evolution and creationism in the public schools has once again raised the issue of the relation between religion and science. Such renewed attention to the controversy is significant; however, the debate concerning the nature of this relation dates back to the fifteenth century and the very beginnings of European settlement in North America, and even beyond that in the history of Western civilization. Nor have historians been the only participants in this discussion. The interpretation of the epistemological status, methods of inquiry, and purposes of science and religion has likewise figured prominently in the discussion of social scientists.

The anthropologist Bronislaw Malinowski, for example, argued in his famous essay "Magic, Science, and Religion" (1928) that science and religion were complementary forms of thought. Science dealt with the knowable and controllable, Malinowski stated, while religion concerned the unknowable and uncontrollable. In the 1960s Anthony F. C. Wallace countered that science and religion are not forms of thought at all. Where science is tied to a kind of empirical knowledge, religion relies upon the congruence between belief and ritual. Here, then, science and religion are seen as radically different and perhaps even antagonistic forms of human experience.

While this theoretical debate shows no signs of abating, the historical contours of the modern relationship between science and religion, and particularly its American aspects, are more settled. For it was in the Renaissance and especially in the work of Copernicus and Galileo that the foundations for the new scientific era were laid. Likewise, it was from their research that religious implications were drawn which set the agenda for several generations of religious, and especially Christian, thinkers. Copernicus revised the older Ptolemaic-Aristotelian view with its immobile earth at the center of the universe and the other planets ringed about it in perfectly concentric orbits. Earth and mankind were the centerpiece of divine creation in the Ptolemaic view, and if there were mathematical or empirical flaws in this system, that seemed a small price to pay. Nevertheless, it was the search for a more mathematically precise description that motivated Copernicus. His findings set the planets and earth revolving around the sun, squared with empirical observations at least as well as the Ptolemaic system, and contained the crowning glory of greater mathematical simplicity. This Copernican revolution continued in Galileo's work, with its further emphasis on the laws of nature expressed as mathematical relationships as well as its extensive use of experimentation, such as with the telescope.

The implications of this new science were widespread for the older scientific view and the medieval religion that rested upon its assumptions. The earth was no longer the center of the universe and mankind no longer the indisputable crown of creation. Indeed, the possibility of other worlds, so long discounted by medieval theologians, now loomed larger. Mankind's cosmological identity had been questioned, and a previously secure, though increasingly inadequate, explanation built on hierarchical design and supernatural purpose had been irrevocably shattered.

During the Reformation the attitude of Martin Luther and John Calvin toward the new science, John Dillenberger has persuasively argued, amounted to a positive view of science, though it placed that science within a distinctly theological context. For Luther and Calvin the Bible was not a book of information, nor were its accounts and stories to be always interpreted literally. Indeed, when the reformers did emphasize a literal meaning in the Scriptures, they did so primarily as a rebuff to analogical interpretations and always within the context of their understanding of the meaning of a Christ-centered faith. Furthermore, both Luther and Calvin repeatedly insisted that while ordinary curiosity about the workings of the natural world was legitimate, excessive attention to such questions could blind one to God's sovereignty over the world and direct attention away from proper praise and adoration of Him. Thus in their own writings they maintained a guarded but essentially positive respect for the new scientific enterprises.

One of the legacies of the Reformation, then, was the perception of a measure of compatibility between Protestantism and the scientific world view. The general Protestant dislike for what were regarded as Catholic "superstitutions" inclined Protestants to search for mundane explanations of the natural world. In its seventeenth-century Puritan form, the Protestant emphasis on orderly work and the speculation that worldly success was a sign of divine favor paralleled the view that the natural world was good and that its study could be beneficial to mankind. Beyond that, investigation of the natural world, the Puritans believed, showed the divine agency behind and within creation and consequently was deserving of further support. Thus scientific investigation was active, orderly, efficient, and at least potentially beneficial to mankind, and as such fit nicely into the Puritan hierarchy of moral values. In this context religion and society interacted, as religious values and understandings validated the scientific enterprise.

The affinity between science and Puritanism can be clearly seen in seventeenth-century England as well as in Puritan Massachusetts Bay. For example, seven out of every ten members of the Royal Society of London were English Puritans. Many of these men were ordained clergymen and either passively or through their own personal work supported and encouraged further scientific investigation. Schools such as Durham University and the various dissenting academies, presenting a range of scientific topics in their curricula, also evidenced Puritan interest in science. Similarly, instruction at Harvard College, the center of learning and the chief training ground for clergy in Massachusetts Bay, included the findings of much of the new science. By the 1650s the Copernican system, for example, was officially sanctioned and taught at Harvard. In addition to this clerical support for the new astronomical findings, physics instructors drew on the work of Robert Boyle, Isaac Newton, and the first-generation New Englander and friend of the John Harvard family Charles Morton. In Massachusetts, as in Puritan England, the religious presuppositions remained constant. As long as scientific investigation revealed the glory of God's creation, it was legitimate and was to be valued and supported. If it led to or actually became unbridled curiosity, then, as John Cotton averred, it was blasphemy.

By the beginning of the eighteenth century, however, New Englanders allowed for increasing latitude in the sphere of scientific investigation. The Dudleian lectures were established at Harvard in 1755, in part to explicate natural religion. And when Edward Holyoke, president of the college, took his turn as lecturer, he both signaled the shift away from arguments grounded in ontology and revelation to those constructed in design and also indicated the secure position of such cosmological defenses with his invocation of Newton's argument for God not "from his Perfection, Nature, and Existence . . . but from his Dominion." Earlier, Cotton Mather, scion of the famous Boston family, combined theological and scientific interests. He was elected to the Royal Society of London in 1713, one of the first Americans so honored. His strong advocacy of smallpox inoculation and his familiarity with health issues have earned him recognition in the history of early American medicine.

Yet if Mather's acceptance of much of the work of Copernicus and Newton indicated his sympathy with important scientific findings, and if his book *The Christian Philosopher* (1721) foreshadowed later themes in rational religion, he was still a figure trapped between allegiance to an older tradition of faith and the new currents of thought. His ambivalent response to the Salem witchcraft trials in 1692—undertaking an allegedly scientific investigation of the suspects, cautioning about the use of "spectral evidence," only to conclude initially that the verdicts were fair and then later to reverse himself and find the entire proceedings unjustified—illustrated the depth of conflict between tradition and modernity.

With less drama, Jonathan Edwards also represents an important transitional figure. Though best known as a revivalist preacher and theologian in the First Great Awakening (1739–1745), Edwards maintained a lifelong interest in science. In several youthful essays, he rhapsodized about natural beauty with a keen eye for botanical detail; other pieces, both early and late, demonstrated his familiarity with Newton's works and sought to explicate both a theological and a naturalistic context for phenomena. Edwards continued to assume that scientific findings were compatible with religious understandings and that science, properly understood, led to and reinforced religious belief. Yet by the second third of the eighteenth century, deeper doubts were being expressed about this traditional assumption of compatibility and new terms were being proposed to account for the relationship of science and religion.

Three broad approaches concerning science and religion characterized the years between the Declaration of Independence and the publication of Charles Darwin's *Origin of Species* in 1859. The Enlightenment perspective championed by Thomas Jefferson, the mediational stance represented by Charles Hodge and James Henley Thornwell, and the romantic attitude portrayed by Transcendentalists such as Ralph Waldo Emerson and Henry David Thoreau were all attempts to redefine the terms of the earlier debate and to do so in a way that would both acknowledge new scientific discoveries and recognize the claims of religion.

The watchword of the Enlightenment was reason, and the implications of this term were as far-reaching for religion and science as they were for politics and society. Reason for the *philosophes* of the Enlightenment meant a mental capacity found in all humanity. Like other physiological features it was deemed to work in a more or less uniform, indeed almost mechanical, manner in all persons. Obstacles to the proper exercise of reason were to be found in the environment and to be eliminated. Archaic laws and institutions, outdated assumptions, and restrictive codes were the principal obstructions in Europe and America, and all were to be done away with in order that reason might flourish and mankind prosper.

And just as reason was universal, so was truth everywhere the same. On this fundamental point the Enlightenment conceded very little to claims for the influence of the environment or for cultural differences of an essential nature. The cosmopolitan nature of reason and truth was the basis upon which the Enlightenment constructed both its ideal of the noble savage—free of artifice, pretense, and vanity—and its conception of a rational society—free of the restraints of tradition, custom, and hereditary privilege. Science was a tool to the ends of authentic humanity and a free society. Scientific progress advanced furthest where the greatest liberty existed; conversely, free inquiry, which was the embodiment of scientific method, produced numberless advances, all of which improved the lot of mankind.

In this perspective religion was to be judged by its conformity to reason. Miraculous stories that ran counter to the dictates of reason were to be disregarded, as were disputatious discussions of dogmatic theology that only served to confuse and antagonize individuals. The enlightened Christianity that resulted from this winnowing process prized the existence of God, the moral example of Jesus, and the probability of future rewards and punishments as the religious beliefs that reason could validate. It was a religion progressive in orientation and optimistic about the accomplishments that human nature and power could achieve. For did not technological progress indicate divine blessings upon human enterprise and symbolize the march of a properly rational Christianity? It was also a religion that assumed an intimate congruity between nature and all that was good in Christianity, for there was a growing suspicion during the eighteenth century that a firmer and more authentic revelation, a message more stirring, more constant, and more orderly, might be available from the scientific investigation of nature than was available in the traditional explications of the Bible.

Throughout his life Jefferson exemplified this Enlightenment concern to distill the pragmatic and morally significant elements out of the contentious sectarian warfare of historic religion. At the same time he participated in discussions about the latest findings in natural history, paleontology, and the differential effects of climate. For in an eighteenth-century update of the Puritan perspective, Jefferson also believed that science provided a crucial window on the workings of the universe. Yet where the Puritans emphasized the majesty, inscrutability, and ultimate sovereignty of divine ways, he chalked up doubt and error to provisional human ignorance. And where the Puritans were ambivalent in their support of scientific investigation—it must be undertaken in the right frame of mind and to display the greater glory of God—Jefferson was unabashedly supportive.

In this context Jefferson sent off the expeditionary team of Meriwether Lewis and William Clark and supported the work of the American Philosophical Society and the American Academy of Arts and Sciences. He maintained a lively correspondence with leaders in the American and European scientific communities, and these efforts merely served to underscore once again the cosmopolitan assumptions of the Enlightenment and the commitment to a knowledge (and derivatively a theory of morals) that was at once national and international, regionally found and universally experienced.

Both Jefferson's *Notes on Virginia* (1785) and his edition of the teachings of Jesus represent his search through free inquiry for practical knowledge, a knowledge confirmed by the faculties of reason and directed to the betterment of the human condition. *Notes on Virginia* was a thin but wide-ranging volume. Under twenty-three different headings Jefferson sketched out the topographical and natural boundaries of the state as well as its legal, social, and religious history. In so doing, he responded both to European charges of biological deterioration and cultural dissolution in the New World and to domestic conservatives skeptical of his democratically inspired plans for broader public education, greater religious freedom, and more equitable laws. Jefferson's concern for a vigorous life of the mind, for a flourishing of arts and letters, was matched by his hopeful observations concerning agriculture, animal husbandry, and uniform weights and measures. In the *Notes*, he combined his fulsome praise for the present gifts and future aspirations of America with his optimistic Enlightenment belief in the efficacy of reason and scientific method. Religion occupied a place

in this scheme, but its rank had been severely demoted.

If it seemed that many traditional religious beliefs were being sacrificed, Enlightenment champions in America such as Jefferson, Thomas Cooper, Ethan Allen, and Elihu Palmer all thought the excision justified and long overdue. For because these enlightened Americans believed religious belief to be a matter of personal conscience and private duty, they contended that too often the power of institutional religion had been used to supress scientific investigation, impede social and political progress, and thereby defeat the creator's rational plan for humanity.

Here Jefferson's espousal of the separation of church and state was indicative of his own fundamental religious beliefs. For truth aided by unimpaired reason will win out, Jefferson maintained, and it will do so without the use of state coercion. Thus church and state should be completely separated, in order that each institution might prosper on its own and avoid any collusion between king and bishop, which Jefferson believed tainted so much of the European experience. And just as free inquiry in the scientific realm would eventually establish the truth or falsity of any of a number of scientific hypotheses, so, Jefferson insisted, would free inquiry in the religious sphere establish the truth or falsity of competing religions. What a person believed was less important in Jefferson's view than how he acted, for, as he put it in the *Notes*, "it does me no injury for my neighbour to say there are twenty gods, or no god. It neither picks my pocket nor breaks my leg."

The stylistic equanimity of the Jeffersonian perspective, highlighted by its classic balance between personal conscience and public action, its blend of knowledge and morals that comprised the Enlightenment approach to the question of science and religion, covered an important fissure concerning the issue of race. Jefferson himself had written that all men were created equal, and as late as 1826 he extolled the achievements of science in dispelling ignorance, defeating tyranny, and arousing hopes. Yet he never accepted the full equality of whites and blacks, and in both the *Notes* and his private correspondence he wavered between caution and ambivalence in his hopes that someday blacks might overcome their inferiority. This inconsistency in Jefferson's rationale for the Enlightenment society was noted, and contemporaries such as Samuel Stanhope Smith and Benjamin Banneker joined the debate.

Banneker, a free black man, was born in Maryland in 1731. His early interest in science and mathematics was nurtured by his Quaker neighbor George Ellicott. In 1791 Banneker began issuing almanacs and sent a manuscript of his first edition to Jefferson. In his letter accompanying the gift, he appealed to Jefferson for recognition of the accomplishments of blacks such as himself and more generally for the eradication of prejudicial attitudes toward his race. Banneker shared the Enlightenment's hope in reason and free inquiry as the vehicles to a better world, and in 1793 in *Banneker's Almanack* he published Benjamin Rush's proposal for the establishment of a secretary of peace in the presidential cabinet. The qualifications Rush named were that the individual be "a genuine republican and a sincere Christian."

Where Banneker directly confronted the issue of racial equality in the Enlightenment cosmology, Samuel Stanhope Smith dealt with it more obliquely, but in so doing illustrated another feature of the complex relation between science and religion during the early federal period. Smith, professor of moral philosophy and later president of the College of New Jersey, (now Princeton), had published an ambitious work in 1787 that attempted to prove the unity of the human species. Although this view had the resources of biblical authority to draw on, several commentators had begun to question the interpretation, pointing to the differences of physical appearance and cultural development. In the face of the obvious diversity within the human race, Smith propounded an environmentalist answer to account for differences of appearance. Beyond that, he chided Jefferson for his reluctance to accept the power of locale and circumstances and to concede that the blacks' impairment was a function of the degradation of slavery or the primitive conditions in Africa. In Smith's accounting, science was called to the aid of biblical reports, but the results, however impressive, would not go unchallenged by scientists and churchmen alike in the continuing debate in America over slavery and race.

The second broad approach during this period, that of the mediational theologians Charles Hodge and James Henley Thornwell, aptly re-vealed other important features of the early-nineteenth-century configuration of science and religion. To begin with, the growing confrontation was not a dispute simply between the findings of natural scientists and the defenders of traditional belief. Indeed, if defenders of religion felt besieged, it was due in part to the fact that their age-old beliefs appeared to be under attack not only from the provenances of geology and biology, but also from the fledgling sciences of anthropology, philology, and history. In this context disputes over the unity or diversity of the human race, the claims of higher and lower criticism concerning the text, authorship, and meaning of the Scriptures, and generally the arguments over biblical chronology and the issue of miracles all fueled as pervasive a set of controversies for religious authority as did the findings of geologists such as James Hutton and Charles Lyell.

The fact that a constellation of disciplines could be called scientific illuminated another key aspect of the period—the conflict over whether science was seen as a method to search for data, an empirical method of critical inquiry applicable to any area of investigation and set of data, or whether science was equated exclusively with the findings of a certain area of inquiry. If science was a method, then perhaps religious claims could be demonstrated to be as scientific as those of the geologist or philologist. Lastly, religious thinkers such as Hodge and Thornwell sought to reconcile the claims of science and religion, as the term *mediational* implies. In so doing, these theologians represented the ruling assumption among American Christians up to and through the Civil War that science and religion, despite any apparent discrepancies, were nevertheless ultimately compatible and reconcilable.

Hodge of Princeton and Thornwell of South Carolina were both Presbyterian clergymen, schooled in Protestant Scholasticism and shaped by Scottish commonsense philosophy. Unconvinced by the Enlightenment's emphasis on rationalism, they sought to reaffirm a more traditional, biblically based faith and at the same time demonstrate the "holy alliance" between such a faith and the new science. Like their Enlightenment counterparts, these mediational theologians also had a firm commitment to reason; however, their understanding of the meaning of this term was significantly different from the

Enlightenment's. Hodge and Thornwell's position shared a commitment to the inductive method and an affirmation of the ultimate infallibility of Scripture, anchored in commonsense philosophy.

This Scottish philosophical movement was originated by Thomas Reid, Dugald Stewart, and William Hamilton and then transported to America by John Witherspoon, president of the College of New Jersey. Scottish common sense was in large measure a response to the Enlightenment and, specifically, the philosophy of David Hume. Hume had taken Lockean epistemology, with its claim that the mind is a blank slate upon which the environment impinges, and radicalized its conclusions. For Hume, all the realities of everyday life—cause and effect, personal identity, the existence of the external world—were epistemologically suspect because they were verifiable only in individualistic terms. And in Hume's account, if cognition devolved into these terms, then morality was nothing better than the individual acting on the perception of momentary self-interest.

These Humean conclusions were unnerving to the reflective portions of the religious population, and it was against this radical skepticism that the Scottish commonsense philosophers devoted all their energies. In short, they countered that there were a priori categories in human consciousness, categories without which human experience would be unintelligible. These categories, such as personal identity, cause and effect, and the existence of moral principles, were known intuitively or through "common sense" to anyone who took the time to examine properly his own self-consciousness. And a correct examination for these philosophers was an inductive examination, one that began from the so-called facts of self-consciousness, and from that basis built up an account of the world and mankind's place in it.

Both Hodge and Thornwell took over this minimal epistemological and moral intuitionism and upon it based their strategy for reconciling science and religion. They argued that both science and religion (or more specifically theology) relied on the inductive method. In an early-nineteenth-century version of a prominent twentieth-century debate, they were arguing for the methodological unity of scientific inquiry. Facts are the basis of inductive conclusions. These

facts are to be collected carefully, diligently, and comprehensively. Every correct theoretical statement is derived from properly assembled factual evidence. This, then, was the rejoinder of Hodge and Thornwell to scientific criticism—scientific method and theological method were the same when both were properly pursued. No radical disjunction existed between the scientist and the theologian, but rather, there was a community of inquiry. And if there were problems, these were due to a misapplication of method and hasty generalization.

This perspective on science and religion traded heavily on the availability of appropriate factual evidence from which to draw generalizations. For Hodge and Thornwell the Bible was a storehouse of facts, and these facts, insofar as they concerned doctrine, were infallibly correct. Again, these theologians sought to draw parallels with science, for just as scientists look to the natural world for their data, so do theologians look to the Bible for theirs. Beyond that, Hodge and Thornwell claimed that the Scriptures authenticated everything found in nature and available to the natural scientist's inspection.

Drawing more directly on Scottish commonsense philosophy than on Enlightenment rationalism, these mediational theologians sought to answer the skepticism of the Enlightenment critics. Their efforts were often scorned by their more progressive and more conservative brethren alike, as liberals and Pietists clung exclusively to either pole of reason or faith. Their attempt was also flawed by their inadequate understanding of the nature of the epistemology upon which they claimed to base their position, as well as their propensity to dismiss as illegitimate any findings that failed to agree with their own. Nevertheless, their attempt at reconciliation was significant within the culture of antebellum America and illustrates that the relation between science and religion had not hardened into the adversarial Maginot-line mentality that would characterize the late-nineteenth- and early-twentieth-century situation in America.

The third approach to the relation between science and religion in this period was that of romanticism. Edward Robinson, professor of biblical literature at Union Theological Seminary in New York City for many years, represented one aspect of this romantic approach. Trained in Germany and influenced by Friedrich

A. Tholuck, Johann August Neander, and Carl Ritter, Robinson, too, sought to reconcile science and religion. For it was Robinson's goal to research the archaeological background of the various biblical accounts as comprehensively as he could. The result of his labors, *Biblical Researches in Palestine, Mount Sinai, and Arabia Petraea* (1841), combined scholarship with his own Evangelical faith. In its acknowledgment of the organic connection between the physical and spiritual, the material and cultural realms of life, its abiding sense of the fundamental mystery of life, and the interrelation between the part and the whole, Robinson's work is testimony to the influence of romanticism. Likewise, with its strong advocacy of historical-critical methods, its deep grounding in the language, literature, and culture of the areas under investigation, one sees in Robinson's writings his equally firm commitment to high scholarly standards. In the end, however, these elements were but vehicles toward his fundamental goal—the full comprehension and empathic understanding of the situation of the Jewish people, so as to show the veracity of the biblical account. Here, then, as with Hodge and Thornwell, there was an attempt to reassert the credibility of biblically based religion, and in so doing to try to demonstrate the amity between science and religion.

If, in their various ways, Hodge, Thornwell, and Robinson all sought to answer the renewed challenges by scientific investigation to traditional Christianity, the Transcendentalists altered the terms of the debate and criticized the scientific spirit as inadequate to comprehend fully the most vital and significant aspects in the human and natural worlds. The Transcendental movement, associated with Ralph Waldo Emerson, Henry David Thoreau, Orestes Brownson, Margaret Fuller, Amos Bronson Alcott, Theodore Parker, Sampson Reed (the New England apothecary and Swedenborgian disciple), and a score of others, was a youthful proclamation of rebellion against the past. A revolt in the name of individualism and self-reliance, it was thus, for better or worse, very much in tune with significant aspects of Jacksonian and antebellum America.

The roots of American Transcendentalism lie in European romanticism and in the nineteenth-century heir of rational religion, New England Unitarianism. A generational revolt against the elders, Transcendentalism was also, as Orestes Brownson put it, an insurrection that championed intuition against the tyranny of the rationalism reigning within Unitarianism. At another level, as a religious movement, it proclaimed that Christianity was essentially about moral and spiritual truths and not about dogmatic propositions or apologetic defenses grounded in rationalistic arguments, historical evidence, or allegations of miraculous occurrences intervening in the natural world. In this way individuals such as George Ripley Parker and Emerson himself sought to demolish the older attempts to reconcile science and religion. In so doing, they allied themselves with the later attempts of language critics, such as Horace Bushnell, who argued for figurative and literal levels of meaning in language as a means by which to reconcile the conflicts between the defenders of religion and the proponents of new scientific findings.

American Transcendentalists were sympathetic to William Wordsworth's adage that we murder to dissect. Their attitude toward science was one of goodwill; however, they construed the role of the scientist as much broader than simply that of an assayer. Thoreau called for the scientist to experience nature fully through sight, sound, touch, taste, and smell. Such direct encounters, rather than rationalist deduction or Baconian induction, would produce not simply knowledge but wisdom and truth. Reed argued that the natural world did not exist merely to excite mankind's quest for knowledge but rather to quicken the fires of imagination and lead one into humble awe before the mysterious majesty of creation. Significantly, he claimed that the true soul of science lay in the poetic spirit.

Similarly, Emerson called for a new seer who recognized the correspondence between the spiritual and physical worlds, who realized the relation of the law of gravity to the purity of the heart, and who perceived the sermon contained in the mud puddle on Boston Common. Nature for Emerson, then, was both a conduit of divinity and a repository of truth, and in his books and essays, especially *Nature* (1836), he articulated a vision of personal identity that dissolved the individual into the divine monism of "the transparent eyeball" comprehending the world and all within it.

Emerson's optimistic conception bore some relation to that of his Unitarian mentor, William

Ellery Channing, especially when Channing stated that "nature breathes nothing unkind." Yet where Channing's view was centered on the sublimity of an aesthetic delight in the natural world, Emerson and the Transcendentalists tended to emphasize the fundamentally spiritual dimensions of nature and to draw optimistically moral lessons from its panoramas. This was the tone of Thoreau's admonition that nature is "mystical and mythical always," and if it fell to Thoreau to gain more firsthand knowledge of nature than his other confreres and to present this experience in the most direct, concrete, and accessible manner, it reaffirms the basic unity of the Transcendentalist approach to the relation of science and religion.

The publication of Charles Darwin's epochal *The Origin of Species* (1859) and *The Descent of Man* (1871), marked a watershed in the history of science and religion in America. Darwin's work drew on a philosophical heritage highlighting the concept of development in the human and natural worlds. It also drew on the researches of two British geologists, James Hutton and Charles Lyell. Where other geologists characterized geological change as an abrupt and catastrophic experience, Lyell and Hutton depicted it as a slow and uniform process of organic transformation. Finally, Thomas Malthus' theory that population often outnumbered available food resources as well as Darwin's own years of field research contributed to his hypothesis.

In *The Origin of Species* Darwin argued that species evolve through variation and natural selection of those individuals best suited to survive in given environmental conditions, but he skirted the issue of human beginnings. In *Descent,* however, he placed human evolution squarely within the field of animal development. His analysis confronted many of the standard assumptions of Americans. Instead of a world of moral freedom in which the individual had an expansive realm for the discharge of his or her responsibilities and the exercise of his or her talents, Darwin seemed to preach a world operating under an iron-clad naturalistic determinism. Moreover, in the Darwinian perspective it was not the individual who occupied center stage at all, but rather the species or type. Second, nature no longer was a showplace for God's plan, no longer an evidence of divine design but rather an accumulation of random modifications that served under the pressure of overpopulation to provide some small edge for survival over the long run. Pastoral landscapes were in fact only facades covering intense conflict, arenas in which species grappled in gladiatorial duels to the death. Finally, Darwin seemed so pessimistic in an American culture that had lived so long on growth, improvement, and optimism. No longer was progress inevitable; instead, uncertainty clouded the horizon, and beyond might only lie mankind's extinction.

These were the initial impressions of Darwin's message, and as commentators on the religious implications lined up to underscore or repudiate his claims, their range showed a remarkable diversity. One group with a tremendous interest in the Darwinian controversy was the scientific community in America. In the conflict over Genesis and geology, Louis Agassiz, Asa Gray, and Joseph Le Conte staked out representative positions. Shortly after its publication, Darwin sent Agassiz, one of America's foremost naturalists and a professor at Harvard, a copy of *Origin.* Agassiz strongly criticized it, finding his own view of "special creation" both scientifically and biblically sounder. For Agassiz, God had intervened often in the course of natural history, geological change was not uniform, and the human species had a distinctive origin in the divine plan. Agassiz's reputation and his strident objections to Darwin made him the champion of those scientists opposed to the Darwinian perspective.

Ironically, Gray, Darwin's chief American defender, was a colleague of Agassiz's at Harvard. Gray wrote one of the earliest American reviews of *Origin* and both shared Darwin's commitment to uniform development and natural selection and sought a means to reconcile Darwinian science and traditional theism. Gray saw in Darwin's presentation nothing incompatible with either the existence of God or the possibility of a divine plan for creation.

Le Conte steered a middle course between condemnation and outright acceptance of Darwin's theory. A professor at the University of California, Berkeley, Le Conte instructed his students that Darwinian natural selection was but one of the mechanisms by which evolution operated. Le Conte emphasized, and here he took his cue from the French naturalist Lamarck, that direction rather than randomness characterized the evolutionary process.

Agassiz, Gray, and Le Conte were not the first American scientists to adjudicate religious issues. They drew on a heritage prominent in which figured Benjamin Silliman, Edward Hitchcock, and James Dwight Dana. Like the later generation of Agassiz, Gray, and Le Conte, Silliman, Hitchcock, and Dana believed that the facts of science had something important to say about the Christian religion. Accordingly, they canvassed their scientific research for religious implications and, in so doing, found a body of evidence reiterating the traditional religious beliefs. Silliman, professor of geology at Yale, saw the harmony between geology and Genesis represented in the similarity between biblical accounts of floods and contemporary geological hypotheses emphasizing catastrophes in the course of geological development. Similarly, Silliman's student Dana argued for a progressive development through six stages, the culmination of which was the age of mankind. Each age after the first had been concluded by a catastrophe, and the succeeding one was inaugurated through a specific creative act. Hitchcock held the chair of natural theology and geology at Amherst. In his major publication, *The Religion of Geology and Its Connected Sciences* (1851), he argued that the biblical account used a different kind of vocabulary than did scientists. Thus the Bible was just as truthful as scientific reports; it merely used a different language.

For all three of these men, then, science and the Bible were compatible. Yet if this earlier generation of scientists was the counterpart to the mediational theologians with their belief in the holy alliance between science and religion, it is still true that the post-Darwinian debate was one in which the issues had changed importantly from their earlier formulation.

Philosophers and theologians joined scientists in interpreting the meaning of Darwin. Four years before his death in 1878, Charles Hodge wrote a repudiation of Darwinism that was both consistent with his earlier thinking and considered by some to represent the standard under which the forces of religious orthodoxy should rally. Hodge's major criticism assailed the methodological implications of Darwin's analysis rather than the theory of natural selection as

such. Hodge found Darwin denying a pattern of design or final causes in nature, and this denial of teleology was enough for Hodge to dismiss the entire Darwinian framework as atheism. More moderate voices, such as that of the theologian James McCosh, sought a rapprochement between science and religion by suggesting that evolution, properly understood, meant "coordinated development" among several independent parts within a given structure. This reintroduction of design into evolution was the basis upon which McCosh could argue for correspondence between the scientific and religious world views.

Henry Ward Beecher and Lyman Abbott provide further examples of theologians trying to tame Darwinism into a Christian evolution. Falling back on an earlier rhetoric of romanticism, Beecher simply called evolution the "divine method," and portrayed scientists as cryptographers deciphering "the hieroglyphics of God inscribed upon the temple of the earth." Indeed, in *Evolution and Religion* (1885) Beecher identified himself with Christian evolution and wrote of two sorts of divine revelations—one in the biblical Scriptures and the other in the rocks of the earth. This balance of revealed law and natural law was underscored in Beecher's rhapsodic identification of the advancement of the human race as the progressive embodiment of the divine plan.

Abbott, in his books *The Theology of an Evolutionist* (1897) and *The Evolution of Christianity* (1892), sought a more empirical basis for reconciling science and religion. Basic to his approach, and typical of the post-Darwinian accommodation of religion and science, was the argument that evolution was not identical with Darwinism. In differentiating Darwinism and evolution, Abbott recognized development as a prominent feature of life; however, he refused to concede that natural selection was the means by which it operated. Instead, in a move that would resonate with later religious liberals, he spoke of the radical immanence of God in the universe and equated the so-called laws of nature with divine laws.

Yet not all attempts to square evolution and religion entirely dispensed with the mechanism of natural selection. Le Conte, as noted previously, in arguing for a variety of evolutionary methods, claimed that natural selection was restricted to the plant and animal worlds. Human evolution, due to the appearance of rationality, raised mankind out of this random process of natural selection.

Drawing on the work of Herbert Spencer, with its aspirations for a synthesis through positivism of every field of knowledge, together with Spencer's own concept of cosmic evolution, as well as the research of Charles Darwin, John Fiske provided a sketch for the harmony of religion with science in his *Outlines of Cosmic Philosophy* (1874). Asserting that "though science must destroy mythology, it can never destroy religion," Fiske, a part-time instructor at Harvard but better known as a popular lecturer and writer, propounded a scientific theism shorn of a personal deity and substituted instead "a wondrous Dynamis." Fiske claimed for evolution a universality in the world of animals equal to that of the law of gravity in the physical world. Yet later in his life, and especially in *Through Nature to God* (1899), he moved toward a more familiar presentation of the compatibility of science and Christianity. Here the evolution of mankind was identified with the process of salvation, while the goal of the ethical processes at work in the world, he argued, was the perfection of the human character. In this way Fiske's cosmic theism took on at least the trappings of an ethical code and the tenor of his message assumed a more pastoral tone.

Fiske's theological revisions were matched by those of the Congregational minister and president of the University of Wisconsin John Bascom. Bascom portrayed Christianity as a spiritual adjustment to the environment, and human history as a seesaw battle to gain control over mankind's animal nature. Bascom's treatise *Evolution and Religion; or, Faith as a Part of a Complete System* (1897) resembled Fiske's depiction of developmental ethical processes with its own presentation of divine moral laws expressing the ultimate fulfillment of human potential. For both Fiske and Bascom evolution became, in a certain sense, a spiritual process.

If Fiske and Bascom sought to accommodate religion to science, Chauncey Wright was prepared to divorce the two entirely, in order that each might be better able to pursue its distinct spiritual and empirical ends. Though he never held a university position, Wright was the leader of an informal discussion group whose members included William James, Charles Sanders Peirce, and Oliver Wendell Holmes, Jr. Wright's sharp separation between science and religion, his willingness to let these bickering contenders part from one another in peace, presaged a later resolution by religious liberals and cultural fundamentalists. Yet Wright, who was a friend of Asa Gray, personally conceded that in the order of the universe there was a sign of the existence of God. Clearly his conception of a divinity was not the traditional one of a personal savior and instead approximated an eighteenth-century representation of a first cause, responsible for the otherwise inexplicable creation of life. Wright had little patience for Fiske's infatuation with Herbert Spencer or for his claim to have established a foundation for scientific theism.

If the range of interpretations of Darwin was diverse, the impact of Darwinism and, more broadly, evolutionary thought in general on social ethics was profound. William Graham Sumner represented an important example. In his discussion of social ethics Sumner focused on the themes of social conflict and individualism that he found in the writings of Darwin and Spencer. For Sumner social life was inevitably one in which conflict between persons, groups, and races remained a constant feature. He depicted such struggle as virtually necessary, and in this context he had only contempt for ameliorative or charitable efforts designed to enable the weak to survive. For Sumner, natural rights did not exist and mankind was not created equal. Invoking Spencer's phrase "the survival of the fittest" (Darwin did not coin it), Sumner championed individual competition and an absence of governmental regulation as the best means to achieve progress. In his panegyric to rugged individualism, Sumner, who had abandoned a career in the ministry for one as a professor at Yale University, voiced the laissez-faire philosophy that dominated Gilded Age pulpits, policy, and public oratory.

Josiah Strong, in his book *Our Country* (1885), also turned this conservative Social Darwinism to discussion of religious purposes. Misinterpreting survival of the fittest to mean survival of the physically strongest, Strong constructed a brief for missionary efforts that blended modern science with evangelical Protestantism, but did so, according to some interpreters, at the cost of nearly sinking the entire enterprise beneath the weight of his racist and imperialist conclusions. In Strong's book justifications for American expansion, previously couched in notions of providential manifest destiny, now took on an evolutionary air of inevitable factuality, as white, Anglo-Saxon, Protestant Americans prepared to incorporate, convert, and conquer the rest of the world.

A more moderate and less individualistic amalgam of evolution and religious ethics can be seen in the work of James Mark Baldwin and Charles Horton Cooley. Baldwin, who studied under James McCosh, construed all his scientific work as an application of Darwinian theory in the fields of psychology and ethics. Tracing the growth of human personality, Baldwin emphasized that man "is a social outcome rather than a social unit." This dialectic process between the individual and society betrayed the influence of G. W. F. Hegel and Josiah Royce on Baldwin's thinking; however, it was the desire to refute the Sumnerian individualistic interpretation of Darwinism that motivated Baldwin's efforts. This concern not only to reconcile evolution and ethics, but the individual and society as well, likewise characterized Charles Horton Cooley's work. Professor at the University of Michigan and author of *Human Nature and the Social Order* (1902) and *Social Organization* (1909), Cooley emphasized the organic unity between the individual and the group, and framed personal growth within social boundaries. He also stressed, as had Baldwin, that cooperative means played an important role in human progress, a point downplayed by Sumner.

If Sumner praised individualism and Baldwin cautiously spoke of social harmony, Thorstein Veblen dreamed of a socialist society. Veblen's checkered academic career included positions at the University of Chicago, Stanford, and the New School for Social Research in New York City. *The Theory of the Leisure Class* (1899), *The Theory of Business Enterprise* (1904), and *The Place of Science in Modern Civilisation* (1919) were among some of his best-known works. Indebted to Darwin for his developmental approach to social questions, Veblen took the measure of bourgeois capitalist society. In a series of scathing analyses, all loaded with empirical data, witty epigrams, and sardonic insights, Veblen dissected individualism, consumerism, and the business entrepre-

neur. He likewise satirized institutional Christianity, but in casting about for ethical resources for a new future, he praised the humility and brotherly love expressed in the Gospels. Veblen, then, countered the encomiums of men such as Sumner and did so by using the same Darwinian resources as his opponents.

Evolutionary thinking and conclusions also had an important influence on religious liberals. This disparate group held a common allegiance to a belief in the immanence of God in the human and natural worlds, an optimistic appraisal of human nature often expressed in ethical preaching, and a postmillennial expectation of the Kingdom of God. Somewhere at the fringe of this large conceptual umbrella were Octavius Brooks Frothingham, Francis Ellingwood Abbot, and Robert Ingersoll. These three were the cultural and organizational leaders of what would become the Free Religious Association. Their books, such as Frothingham's *Religion of Humanity* (1872) and Abbot's *Scientific Theism* (1885), extolled a scientific approach to religious questions and a naturalistic framework for theology.

Frothingham was born in Boston, and he achieved a reputation as a popular preacher in the years after the Civil War. Reared in the traditions and controversies of New England Unitarianism, he was chosen as the first president of the Free Religious Association in 1867, when it broke from the National Conference of Unitarian Churches. Abbot served as editor of the association's journal, the *Index,* beginning soon after the group's formation. Sharply critical of conventional religion, Abbot, in his books and work with the Free Religious Association, sought to promote a brand of religion consonant with the rising scientific spirit of the times. Yet neither Frothingham nor Abbot reached wide audiences, and it fell to Ingersoll to popularize their concerns through his lecture tours and journal columns.

A broader-based and more significant group was composed of modernist liberals such as Newman Smyth and Charles A. Briggs. Smyth expressed his fidelity to science in his claims for the scientific modernity of the Old Testament, its developmental progression past animism and polytheism, and its explicit theory of evolution in the six-day Creation reported in Genesis. This effort to adapt religion to modern science and culture likewise characterized Briggs's contention that theology, properly understood, verified, and examined, is a science. He reflected the environmentalist heritage of Darwin's influence in his insistence upon the cultural conditioning of all religious expression. Recognition of this important contextual dimension, for Briggs and other liberals, presented the only viable avenue for renewal of religion in a modern culture transformed by political upheaval, technological progress, and intellectual revolution.

This effort to explain events, literature, and persons by situating them in their relevant context did not derive exclusively from Darwin; however, Darwinism provided this interpretive strategy with a great deal of intellectual legitimacy and power during the second half of the nineteenth century. And while the agenda of religious liberals contained many more items than the issue of science and religion, their sensitivity to this issue and their willingness, especially by the modernists, to readjust, reinterpret, and refashion religion in the light of new scientific findings was significant.

Even if not all religious liberals shared in their commitment to social change, all who espoused the Social Gospel, such as Washington Gladden, Richard T. Ely, and Walter Rauschenbusch, shared the liberals' basic orientation. Subscribing to the researches of biblical critics such as Briggs, embracing the results of the new historical approach in economics, psychology, and sociology (an approach compatible with the Darwinian developmental method when not directly inspired by it), and rejoicing in the intellectual ferment wrought by the revolution in the sciences, the advocates of the Social Gospel turned a mordant eye on the social injustices of American society. Their interpretation of Darwin saw science reaffirming order and purpose in the universe and thus posing no insuperable barriers to religious faith. Beyond that, as Ely and Rauschenbusch explicitly claimed, evolutionary development and a progressive socialism, correctly understood and patiently carried out, amounted to a Christian socialism, which they heartily advocated. In so doing, they, too, sought to refute the conservative social ethos that Sumner and others drew out of Darwin.

The growth of religious liberalism during the second half of the nineteenth century precipitated an equally vigorous conservative response, a movement that by the 1920s had achieved na-

tional prominence. This conservative and evangelical force, in opposing liberalism and especially its modernist wing, drew on a heritage of complaints, including the significance given to historical criticism, the degree of accommodation to cultural change, and the relative importance of supernatural faith and religious experience. In the years between 1870 and 1920, a number of heresy trials, forced resignations, and summary firings signaled the growing strength of conservatives in their controversy with religious liberals. James Woodrow, uncle of Woodrow Wilson, was dismissed from Columbia Theological Seminary for claiming that evolution was compatible with the teachings of Scripture, while Crawford Toy of the Southern Baptist Seminary at Louisville and Alexander Winchell of Vanderbilt University both lost their academic positions because of their views questioning the accuracy of Genesis. The situation of these three southerners was paralleled in the North by the much-publicized ecclesiastical proceedings against the Presbyterians Charles A. Briggs, Arthur C. McGiffert, and Henry Preserved Smith.

Out of this renewed conservatism developed a militant Fundamentalist movement. Popularly associated with the twelve-volume series *The Fundamentals* (1910–1918), and more narrowly with a five-point declaration of "essential beliefs" drawn up by the Presbyterian General Assembly in 1910 (inerrancy of Scripture, virgin birth of Christ, his substitutionary atonement, his bodily resurrection, the authenticity of miracles), Fundamentalism had a cultural appeal much broader than the number of adherents to its theological manifestos.

While pessimistic about human progress and the technological advancements assumed to represent it, Reuben Torrey and Benjamin Warfield, for example, both agreed, as Torrey once stated in *The Fundamentals,* that "true science does not start with an *a priori* hypothesis that certain things are impossible," but rather remains open to investigation and verification. And once an open mind was adopted, these two insisted, then there was room for acknowledgment of the intervention of the supernatural both at the creation and during the course of natural and human history. Though they challenged the supremacy of naturalist causality, both Torrey and Warfield sought to fashion a version of scientific method compatible with their Fundamentalist beliefs. J. Gresham Machen, first of Princeton and later of Westminster Theological Seminary, also hoped to achieve this end, but he drew the issues in much sharper relief. Dismissing naturalistic claims to empirical knowledge as misguided and repudiating liberalism's claims to true religion, Machen repeatedly asserted the factual basis of the Bible and the ability of science to confirm these facts. Machen censured liberalism for what he considered to be its concessions to modernity, its diminution of biblical authority, and its failure to uphold traditional belief.

Divine agency and biblical inerrancy were but two of the most prominent issues at stake, and not all those gathered under the Fundamentalist banner believed that science was worth saving, even on the terms that Torrey, Warfield, and Machen dictated. Billy Sunday, the preeminent revivalist of the early 1900s and a prime symbol for the shifting values of his era, excoriated "the bastard theory of evolution" and stated that "science and religion can never be reconciled."

A significant variation on the view that science and religion are radically different and perhaps even opposed to one another occurs in the Christian Science and Pentecostal movements. The Church of Christ (Scientist) was founded by Mary Baker Eddy in the 1870s. Prominent among its beliefs was an emphasis on the "science of health." Believing that she had rediscovered Jesus' methods of curing illness, Mrs. Eddy stated that disease and pain were mental states rather than material ones. Her discussion of remedies for illness called for stricken individuals to allow God's presence into their lives, and the tenets of her beliefs were summarized in her book *Science and Health with Key to the Scriptures* (1875). The organized denomination, which developed after Mrs. Eddy's death, allows for medical intervention in childbirth and other special circumstances, yet maintains that even these would not be necessary if Christian Science beliefs were correctly applied on a broader scale.

While the roots of claims for divine healing can be traced back to antiquity, Pentecostal or charismatic churches have been another congenial home in American religious history for such practices. In the context of this essay, the revival of 1947–1958 gave special prominence to reports of divine, nonmedical healing. Associated with individuals such as William Branham, Oral

Roberts, Jack Coe, A. A. Allen, and, more recently, Kathryn Kuhlman, this group of revivalists and healers proclaimed their message of deliverance from physical illness, exorcism from demons, and relief from bodily injury through personal faith. Their relationship to the medical profession and the scientific world in general was rather distant. Coe, for example, rebuked those who consulted physicians for advice and remedies, while Roberts told his followers that they might seek confirmation from medical authorities of their miraculous healing if they wished.

Highly personalized in their style and insisting on themselves as conduits of special curative powers with sensitivity to disease and infirmity, these healing ministers have been characterized by their pragmatic, positive-minded offers and, more recently, by their well-organized use of radio and television. Their claims to physical cures, even to the extent of resurrection of the dead, have brought angry rebuttals from the wider religious community. Yet their particular belief in the existence and availability of spiritual powers outside the empirical realm continues to characterize a portion of religious believers and one of the more extreme positions concerning the relation of science and religion in America.

A high point in the early-twentieth-century Fundamentalist counterattack on liberalism took place in 1925 with the trial of John Scopes for teaching Darwinian evolution in a Tennessee public high school. Scopes was found guilty (only to have the verdict reversed by a higher court on appeal), and his trial gave national prominence to the battle over evolution. With William Jennings Bryan serving as an assistant to the prosecutor and Clarence Darrow the chief counsel for the defense, the Scopes trial riveted media attention on its daily proceedings and its implications for the future direction of American culture and society. Dismissing Darwinism as a "mere hypothesis," Bryan reiterated Christianity's alliance with "legitimate" science. However, Bryan's poor public defense of his beliefs under cross-examination by Darrow reduced the Fundamentalists' prestige.

In the succeeding decades, antievolution statutes were passed in four other states (Oklahoma, Florida, Mississippi, and Arkansas), and the Tennessee law remained in effect for twenty years after the Scopes trial. In at least fifteen more states, however, proposed legislation either failed to pass or was substantially toned down. Despite this flurry of activity, cultural Fundamentalism seemed to go underground, curtailing its efforts to fashion a publicly understood evangelical version of science and, for the moment at least, leaving both the culture and scientific investigation in the hands of liberals.

Neither the controversy between liberals and conservatives nor the debate over the meaning and implications of Darwinism were confined to Protestantism, as both Roman Catholics and Jews in America discussed these issues within their own religious communities. Throughout most of the eighteenth and nineteenth centuries, the attention of the American Catholic and Jewish communities was directed primarily to the problems of settling their new immigrants, coping with the dilemmas of cultural preservation or assimilation, and strengthening their fledgling ecclesiastical institutions. In the wake of Darwin's *The Descent of Man,* Catholic commentators began to take notice, and their judgments were not supportive of Darwin. The Louisville *Catholic Advocate* (January 28, 1871) derisively stated that Darwin's theory taught that "man having first been a tadpole, became a monkey, and then wore off his tail." This hostile reception for Darwin characterized Catholic thought in the 1870s and 1880s.

By the 1890s a change in attitudes was visible within certain circles of the Catholic church. John A. Zahm, professor of physics at the University of Notre Dame, published *Evolution and Dogma* and *Scientific Theory and Catholic Doctrine* (both 1896), in which he gave a sympathetic presentation of Darwin's position and argued more broadly for evolution's basic compatibility with Catholic teachings. Indeed, Roman Catholic thought had always acknowledged theological resources outside of Scripture, nor were Catholics so closely tied to a literal interpretation of the Bible as were some Protestants. Thus, like Henry Ward Beecher or Lyman Abbott, Zahm constructed a case for theistic evolution and found no contradiction between evolution and cosmic design. His efforts were silenced, however, first indirectly by the attack on Americanism in the papal letter *Testem Benevolentiae* (1899) and then more personally with the ruling by the Holy Office that Zahm's *Evolution and Dogma* could not be translated into other languages with its sanction. When Zahm was further threatened

with the possibility of his book being placed on the Index of Forbidden Books, he withdrew it from publication.

Another creative engagement between Roman Catholicism and evolution took place in the work of Pierre Teilhard de Chardin. Born in France, Teilhard was a member of the Jesuit order and a person with international contacts and a deep interest in paleontology and geology. He spent much time after World War II in America and when he died in 1955 he was buried at the Jesuit seminary in New York. In books such as *The Phenomenon of Man* (1955; Eng. trans., 1959) he emphasized the evolution of mankind's creative as well as natural powers and placed this human evolution within the framework of a cosmic Christ who suffused the world. Teilhard's books did not meet with official church approval, however, and it was only in the 1960s that his work gained recognition in both the American church and the wider American culture.

In the wake of the condemnation of modernism in the papal encyclical *Pascendi Gregis* (1907), American Catholicism developed its own fundamentalist movement, dedicated, like its Protestant counterpart, to a broad agenda that included attacking Darwinism. Francis LeBuffe, professor of sociology at Fordham University, was one of this movement's most visible leaders. He denounced Darwin's inclusion of mankind in the evolutionary scheme, rather than reserving a special place for human creation. While he found Darwin's claims theologically disquieting, LeBuffe repeatedly insisted that Darwin's account of human origins should be repudiated as faulty science.

If Catholic fundamentalists could make common cause with Protestants, they did not support the case against John Scopes. Most Catholic editorial writers acknowledged William Jennings Bryan's sincerity, but found his emotional appeal presumptuous. Moreover, the Tennessee law and the climate of opinion supporting the prosecution appeared, to many Catholics, as an attack on the separation of church and state and a latent renewal of Protestant nativism.

For American Judaism, modern science, expressed as historical analysis of sacred texts or geological refutations of biblical chronology, posed many of the same intellectual challenges as it did for Christianity. The Orthodox tradition in America, especially in the nineteenth century, was unprepared to participate in these scholarly debates and sought to ignore the furor and to concentrate instead on the correct practice of Jewish faith and tradition. The Reform movement, however, maintained an openness to scientific analysis and refused to dismiss it simply as a concern of the Gentile community. The Pittsburgh Declaration of 1885 found no antagonism between the "modern discoveries of scientific researches in the domains of nature and history" and Judaism. Jacob Voorsanger, rabbi of a San Francisco congregation and an influential leader of Reform Judaism, sought to adjust Jewish theology to the prominent scientific theories of the late nineteenth century. He characterized Judaism as "divinely evolved" rather than revealed, and this emphasis on gradual and continuous growth appeared throughout his writings.

Conservative Judaism, as a response to both the Reform and Orthodox branches, adopted a more cautious approach to Darwin and the implications of modern science. In 1902 Solomon Schechter was called from England to assume the presidency of the Jewish Theological Seminary in New York City. He gathered together a learned faculty of scholars, one noted for its relative openness to the results of a broad range of scientific studies, yet still dedicated to exposition of the Scriptures within a traditional manner.

The misery and destruction of World War II called into question for many American Jews an earlier faith in science as the road to progress and the wisdom of the Reform movement's interpretive adjustments. Consequently, both Conservative and Orthodox Judaism with their more traditional approach to Judaism and their less accommodating approach to society gained new members and respectability in the postwar decades.

Since the end of World War II, the relationship between science and religion in America has been as complex as in any era of its history. For if Darwinism shattered the eighteenth-century mechanistic world view, the twentieth-century revolution in science, especially in physics and biology, has had equally dramatic consequences. Theoretically propounded in Albert Einstein's theory of relativity and Werner Heisenberg's principle of uncertainty, the new physics posed fresh interpretive problems.

Science had previously been thought to provide accurate pictures of reality, depicting, for example, the dynamic relationships of physical objects in generalizations such as Newton's laws of motion. Yet the new physics proclaimed that time and space were relative concepts and lacked any objective standard applicable throughout the universe. It argued that electrons sometimes acted as waves, other times as particles and thus did not obey Newton's laws of motion. Such findings led some, such as Alfred North Whitehead, into new religious speculations, while for others they opened the door to wide-ranging cognitive relativism. Beyond that, the military use of atomic energy and the unleashing of a power able to annihilate the human species and obliterate the planet raised ethical questions of the first order.

Another significant development in recent decades has been the revival of a creationist, or antievolutionary, movement. In the wake of the Scopes trial debacle, creationist forces went underground until the 1940s. In 1941 the American Scientific Affiliation was formed by a group of conservative Evangelicals, giving creationist believers an organizational base. A major turning point occurred in 1960 with the publication of *Genesis Flood* by Henry Morris and John C. Whitcomb, Jr. Although dismissed by the mainstream scientific community in America, as has been most creationist literature, Morris and Whitcomb's efforts sparked the development of the Creation Research Society in 1963 (membership in which was restricted to holders of a graduate degree in the sciences) and one year later the lay-based Bible-Science Association. Finally, in the 1970s two other organizations, the Creation-Science Research Center and the Institute for Creation Research, were established for the purpose of producing textbooks, offering degrees, and providing popular literature from the creationist point of view.

The antievolutionary movement of the 1960s and 1970s differed from its predecessor in several important ways. Rather than trying to outlaw evolution, these groups sought instead to give the creationist perspective equal time in the classroom. Such a shift in tactics acknowledged several political and social considerations. First, the leaders of the creationist revival argued for the legitimacy of their perspective on the basis of alleged scientific claims as much as by reference to the Bible. Second, after a federal district court in 1968 declared an Arkansas antievolution law unconstitutional, they realized they probably could not expect to win exclusive rights of presentation for their creationist views. Finally, drawing on the relativism injected into contemporary discussions of philosophy of science, they argued that their creationist perspective was just as valid as the evolutionary one. Thus if liberals hoped and conservatives feared that the evolution question had been settled in 1925, a spate of court hearings, publications, and popular discussions demonstrated its lively resurgence.

A third characteristic of the postwar relation between science and religion in America has been a neoromantic rejection of the excesses of technology and a repudiation of the reductionism of scientific method. Popularly associated in America with the counterculture movement of the 1960s, and forcefully articulated by Theodore Roszak in his books *The Making of a Counter Culture* (1969) and *Where the Wasteland Ends* (1972), this perspective echoed Emerson and Thoreau in emphasizing intuition, a holistic and balanced relationship with nature, and a spiritual and mystical approach to religion.

The relation between science and religion has been a complicated one throughout American history. Sometimes seen in conflict with each other, other times interpreted as complements to each other, the history of science and religion provides important insights into the nature of American religious and cultural experience.

BIBLIOGRAPHY

Ian G. Barbour, *Issues in Science and Religion* (1966); John Rickards Betts, "Darwinism, Evolution, and American Catholic Thought, 1860–1900," in *Catholic Historical Review*, 45 (1959); Daniel J. Boorstin, *The Lost World of Thomas Jefferson* (1948); John Dillenberger, *Protestant Thought and Natural Science: A Historical Study* (1960); Ray Ginger, *Six Days or Forever? Tennessee vs. John Thomas Scopes* (1958); Richard Hofstadter, *Social Darwinism in American Thought, 1860–1915* (1944); Herbert Hovenkamp, *Science and Religion in America, 1800–1860* (1978); William Hutchison, *The Modernist Impulse in American Protestantism* (1976).

David C. Lindberg and Ronald L. Numbers, eds., *God and Nature: Historical Essays on the Encounter Between Christianity and Science* (1986); George M. Marsden, *Fundamentalism and American Culture: The Shaping of Twentieth-Century Evangelicalism, 1870–1925* (1980); James R. Moore, *The Post-Darwinian Controversies* (1979); John L. Morrison, "American Catholicism and the Crusade Against Evolution," in *Records of the American Catholic Historical Society of Philadelphia*, 64 (1953); Stow Persons, ed., *Evolutionary Thought in America* (1950); Marc Lee Raphael, "Rabbi Jacob Voorsanger of San Francisco on Jews and Judaism: The Implications of the Pittsburgh Platform," in *American Jewish Historical Quarterly*, 63 (1973); Cynthia Eagle Russett, *Darwin in America: The Intellectual Response, 1865–1912* (1976); Richard S. Westfall, *Science and Religion in Seventeenth-Century England* (1958).

[*See also* MEDICINE AND MEDICAL ETHICS.]

MEDICINE AND MEDICAL ETHICS

Harold Y. Vanderpool

R ELIGION comprises a world view or comprehensive picture and ordering of human existence in nature and cosmos out of a congruent set of symbols that characteristically include beliefs in a superempirical, usually supernatural, Being or Beings. This world view also makes distinctions among sacred, profane, and forbidden objects and aspects of life and instills and maintains characteristic emotions, motivations, and virtues of character and action. It is regarded as singularly or uniquely realistic or true, is enacted and enlivened by rituals and, oftentimes, by sustained reflection and discipline. These enable humans to make sense of and feel relieved or rescued from chaotic and tragic features of life, as well as certain of life's urges, frustrations, and limits. Through religion humans also find measures of peace, significance, pleasure, and empowerment.

Medicine is the art and practice of understanding and treating physical and mental sickness, suffering, and trouble so as to restore health and prolong life (or fend off death). This art and practice relies upon definitions of health, sickness, and infirmity; upon theories regarding the ways to sustain health and the causes of mental and physical sickness (disease etiology); and upon theories and methods of healing (therapy). Medical practitioners also rely upon patterned, ritualized interactions with patients and families, as well as upon symbols that convey the meanings and emotional power of their science and craft.

In light of these definitions, religion and medicine share much common ground. In traditional societies this is evident by their virtual fusion. Yet even when religion and medicine are widely considered as operating in separate realms—as

in America after about 1890—there are still common elements between them. This is true not merely because a certain number of persons continue to cling to beliefs and practices that are out of step with scientific medicine, but because religion, whether traditional or not, and medicine, whether scientific or not, encompass many similar aspects of human existence, which may be divided into seven major subject areas.

First, both religion and medicine within respective cultures and eras provide normative views regarding the value of life, the nature, uses, and taboos of the human body and its functions, the locus or seat of life (in blood, breath, heart, and/or brain), gender distinctions and identity, and the expressions and limits of human sexuality. Second, religion and medicine address and deal with life's significant passages—reproduction, abortion, childhood, aging, care for the dying, definitions of death, autopsies, and the disposal of the dead. Third, they interlink with respect to concepts of health and well-being for both body and mind, including such topics as foods, drinks, stimulants, narcotics, hygiene, positive mental states, and altered states of consciousness.

Fourth, both deal with definitions, causes, and results of sickness, diseases, pain, and suffering. Topics illustrating these include explanations for epidemics, views of drunkenness, tobacco use, masturbation, homosexuality, anger, guilt, stress, and grief. Fifth, counterbalancing explanations for mental and physical disease are numerous therapies, some of which were or are viewed as the particular methods of religion (prayer, healing miracles) or medicine (interventions of scientific specialists), and many of which are controversial because of religious opposition

1253

to medical practices (bloodletting, blood transfusions, sterilization) or vice versa (exorcism,
phrenology, folk remedies, Transcendental Meditation, Rolfing, and so on).

Sixth, religion and medicine establish and
maintain social institutions for health, healing,
and special forms of care, including hospitals,
asylums, dispensaries, and hospices. And finally,
both have long traditions regarding what is or
is not ethically permissible regarding healer-
patient relationships, specific medical interventions, and social responsibilities and policies.

That medicine and religion are connected in
these respects does not settle issues regarding
the extent and intensity of their interrelation-
ships within respective eras and traditions. Historical specificity is imperative.

COLONIAL AMERICA: 1603–1787

Although culturally diverse, America's permanent colonies were settled and developed primarily by Protestant Europeans. Health and
medical heritages were thus indelibly linked to
Continental traditions, especially the legacies of
Martin Luther and John Calvin. Crucially, while
neither Luther nor Calvin denied the devil's role
in grave illness, both delimited or opposed healing miracles because they rejected Catholicism's
cult of saints and belief in the miracle of transub-
stantiation. They also believed that the healing miracles of the apostolic age validated Christianity in ways that were no longer needed or
possible.

As reformist and innovative, Protestantism
furthermore aligned itself with national languages, traditions, and aspirations and with the
developing trends in philosophy (John Locke,
Immanuel Kant), science (Isaac Newton, Joseph
Priestley), and medicine (William Harvey, Herman Boerhaave) within Western culture. In England, Puritans and Anglicans looked forward to
a millennium of better medicine, better health,
prolonged life, and greater benevolence for the
sick and poor. Protestant faith and innovative
medical practice thereby became connected.

Medical knowledge and skill in the colonial
period focused on understanding and manipulating the factors responsible for disease and
health. Many of these were regarded as subject
to natural laws and processes: observed imbal-

ances between bodily humors, mechanical laws
of tension and relaxation, and the chemistry of
digestion and putrefaction, to name a few. The
primary therapies of the time reflect how these
factors were variously understood and interrelated: bloodletting to balance the humors or
relax bodily or vascular tension; purging, vomiting, sweating, or blistering out morbid humors
with purgatives and various laxatives; medications to restore natural strength with tonics or
narcotics like opium; and surgery for wounds,
injuries, and infections.

Although medicine and therapy in the seventeenth and eighteenth centuries focused on a rational understanding of the human body and the
world of nature, religious perspectives were consciously and regularly viewed as compatible with
and at points augmentative of such knowledge.
This is illustrated in George Cheyne's *An Essay
of Health and Long Life* (1724), which was distributed widely in the colonies. Cheyne stated
that his book was based upon rational principles
drawn from two entirely analogous and complementary sources—nature and the Bible. He said,
for instance, that destructive human passions are
best quieted by "the Love of God," a love for a
being who "stills the Raging of the Seas . . . the
Tempests of the Air . . . [and the] overbearing
Hurricanes in the Mind" with equal ease (p. 83).
His recommendations regarding bodily health
also fused rational learning and the Bible; he
opposed laziness, gluttony, drunkenness, and
various sensual pleasures.

Self-help books and pamphlets on medical ailments and cures illustrate a similar combination
of natural and religious understanding. One of
the most popular, *Primitive Physick* (1747) by
John Wesley, the principal founder of Methodism, was published in at least twenty-four
American editions. Wesley expressly advocated
primitive physick (medicine), the characteristic
features of which were parallel to his understanding of the primitive or apostolic church:
ancient, uncorrupted by self-serving theoreticians, plain, inexpensive (like Wesley's free
grace), and efficacious.

Other examples of interconnected health,
medicine, and Protestant-biblical themes in colonial America include a general opposition to
drunkenness—but not the drinking of wine and
ale; the widespread conviction that disease, suffering, and death are due to the judgments of

God upon sinful humanity; an association of defective newborns (regarded as monstrosities) with demonic influences; and the ethics of practitioner-patient relationships. An early view of infant monstrosities is reflected in John Winthrop's graphic description of the severely malformed child born to Mary Dyer, whom Anne Hutchinson assisted as a midwife. Winthrop, the first governor of the Massachusetts Bay Colony, described Dyer as "a very proper and fair woman" who had become "infected with Mrs. Hutchinson's errors" (Cone, 1979, p. 19) and the child as having a face and body similar to the devil's. He later banished both Dyer and Hutchinson from the colony.

Views regarding the ethics of practitioner-patient relationships are exemplified in Nicholas Culpepper's *A Directory for Midwives* (1651). Culpepper was a zealous English Puritan whose publications were widely used in America. He counseled midwives, who almost exclusively supervised childbirths, that their work should be conducted in light of their knowing that "the Creator of Heaven and Earth . . . commits the life of every Child of His to your Charge" and that their efforts one day will be fully reviewed "before Jehovah, the Lord Jesus Christ, and all the Angels" (Poynter, 1962, p. 159). This and other biblical themes pervade the 1769 graduation address of the notable New York physician Samuel Bard on the ethics of the doctor-patient relationship: "thou shalt do no murder"; doctors will be held accountable for every patient "at the awful bar of eternal justice"; dying patients should never be cut off from "the hopes and promises of religion"; and doctors should practice charity medicine for the laboring poor (Burns, 1978, pp. 104–105, 108, 110–111).

These compatibilities between religion and medicine explain in part why many clergy from various Protestant traditions served as doctors in the New World. They did this at a time when medical theory and therapy could be readily learned and when the average person using the loosely regulated title *Doctor* trained by reading a few books on medicine and by serving as an apprentice to a practicing physician for several months or more.

A highly abbreviated listing of colonial American minister-physicians displays something of their denominational and regional diversity. They represent some of the most important figures in America's early religious history. Puritan Congregationalists in Massachusetts included Charles Chauncy, the second president of Harvard, and Thomas Thacher, pastor of Boston's Old South Church and author of America's first medical article. In Connecticut John Winthrop the younger practiced medicine and served as governor and Eliot Jared practiced medicine and trained physicians as a Congregationalist minister. The Presbyterian leader Jonathan Dickinson was well known as the first president of the College of New Jersey (now Princeton); he also practiced medicine and wrote a detailed treatise on diphtheria. In Pennsylvania the influential and colorful Lutheran patriarch Henry Melchior Mühlenberg was active as a medical practitioner and pamphleteer. And in the Middle Colonies Francis Asbury, one of the key founders of American Methodism, regularly ministered to the sick, as did his mentor, John Wesley.

Prospective ministers often studied medicine during theological training in order to render special service in rural or missionary settings. Other ministers practiced medicine for the more mundane reason of needing an alternative source of income. Mühlenberg captured some of the patently unromantic dimensions of the minister's medical roles when he likened himself to a "privy to which all those with loose bowels came running from all directions to relieve themselves" (Duffy, 1976, p. 40). How such experiences related to Mühlenberg's and others' theology remains a curious, open-ended question.

The highly charged controversy between the Puritan divine Cotton Mather and the professionally trained doctor William Douglass over smallpox vaccination illustrates important features regarding the interplay of religion with medical theory and practice in the colonial period. Consider, first, understandings of disease etiology. Terrifying, unpredictable pestilences continually wreaked havoc among the colonists and American Indians. Traditional humoral, chemical, and mechanical medical theory hardly provided convincing explanations for the horror, suffering, and mass deaths caused by successive waves of smallpox, diphtheria, yellow fever, and influenza epidemics. Smallpox, for example, caused thousands of deaths in Boston alone in 1702, 1721, 1730, and 1752. For the colonists, religious explanations seemed to account for these scourges far more than natural explanations—as was captured in these lines of poetry written about 1735:

> What tears apace, run down our Face,
> to hear our Children crying
> For help from pain, but all in vain
> we cannot help their dying.
> New England's Sins have greater been
> than Sins of Heathen round,
> Such breach of Laws, is the grand
> Cause,
> God's Judgments do abound.
> (Parrish, 1956, p. 61)

Interestingly, in his controversy with Mather, it was Douglass—the only physician in Boston at the time with formal medical training—who opposed inoculation by appealing to "the all-wise Providence of God Almighty," while Mather urged inoculation on grounds that any life-saving medical practice had to agree with God's providence and with the means He provided for escaping from sickness and death. Furthermore, Mather knew of the latest reports on the success of variolation (placing pus from an active smallpox postule under the skin). Aided by the expertise and statistical records of Boston's Dr. Zabdiel Boylston, Mather's point of view was eventually adopted throughout the colonies, but not until Douglass and others had for a season successfully outlawed variolation in Massachusetts in the name of God, life-threatening danger, and objections to the clergy's interference in complex medical matters. To his credit, Douglass himself began urging inoculation in 1730, when Boston was threatened by another outbreak of smallpox. Colonial epidemics informed the clergy's jeremiads and likely contributed to America's evangelical awakenings—including the First Great Awakening, which followed upon the heels of the great diphtheria epidemic of the late 1730s.

Douglass' defense of medicine's separate professional status was prophetic of the way doctors eventually came to control medical care as off limits to the clergy. Mather's scientific innovativeness was prophetic of the way American religion increasingly adjusted to the Enlightenment quest for a more accurate knowledge of nature and cosmos. This quest included eliminating traditional medications viewed as magical and ineffective, reassessing and at times adopting certain folk remedies (like the herb belladona), abandoning aristocratic traditions that gave only marginal attention to the needs of the poor, and ardently opposing the use of secret remedies identified with charlatans.

Mather enthusiastically read about recent scientific and medical discoveries, corresponded with notable figures in Europe, made several contributions to the *Transactions* of the Royal Society of London, and was elected a Fellow of that society in 1723. He became America's most innovative medical theorist of his generation. Mather not only advocated inoculation but speculated that germlike creatures ("Little Animals") caused disease. While admitting that sometimes mad persons were "demoniacks," he also held that everyone is "Mad in some One Point" and hence set forth a variety of natural cures for those who faced madness from natural causes.

Enlightenment science was advocated and employed innovatively by many people. Deists like Benjamin Franklin largely replaced revelation with rational and natural knowledge. Avowed "Christian rationalists" like Joseph Priestley viewed the Bible as complementary to inductive science. Yet neither Franklin's electricity and electrotherapy nor Priestley's use of oxygen created breaks with or breakthroughs in colonial health and medical practices. Conventional medicine continued to try to treat disease as if it were caused by a single set of internal factors like too much or too little bodily tension or acidity. Consequently, physicians continued to employ alarming, sometimes lethal, levels of bleeding, vomiting, salivating, and evacuating.

Whether based on "unaided" reason or reason supplemented by revelation, American physicians informed by Enlightenment thought intensely opposed practices associated with superstition and quackery—notably the peddling of secret remedies. They also praised the value of common sense, the worth of the common man, and the virtue of showing concern for the poor. This last emphasis led to the building of almshouses for the sick and poor in Philadelphia (1729 and 1752) and New York (1736 and 1791).

Catholicism influenced colonial American developments from two sources—French Catholicism in Louisiana and Spanish Catholicism primarily from Mexico. Both French and Spanish medical care contrasted in important ways with that of America's predominantly English colonies. Most important, it was viewed as directly under the control of the mother country and hence was far more organized, controlled, and financed. Beginning in 1570, for example, Spain kept careful records of all medical practitioners, established and inspected hospitals, collected reports on local plants, and set up quarantine measures for epidemics. Royal policy also maintained a high level of practitioner expertise. Medicine was a tool in the Counter-Reformation; throughout New Spain, for example, practitioners were prohibited from providing medical care to sick natives unless they first confessed faith in the Catholic church.

Yet this hierarchically organized approach led to the construction of numerous hospitals in the New World (more than 150 in Mexico alone by the end of the sixteenth century). Furthermore, Catholic policies allowed sixteenth- and seventeenth-century European medical theory to adopt certain native Indian remedies and practices. This fusion of humoral theory with folk practice gave rise to *curandería,* the Mexican-American folk healing system that utilizes candles, herbal cures, special rites, and prayers to various saints for healing diseases and ailments.

French medicine was also highly organized and controlled. Hospitals were built in New Orleans and Fort Saint Louis (Biloxi) in the 1720s; by 1731 they were staffed by teams of well-trained Ursuline nuns as well as by Crown-paid physicians and surgeons. Since the French began to settle Louisiana in 1699, two centuries after the earliest Spanish explorations, they fostered a different, Enlightenment-oriented legacy of medical theory and therapy. Indeed, the generally highly trained practitioners of Louisiana used more sensible, more natural, less "heroic" remedies than even their Protestant-American counterparts. ("Heroic" medicine refers to the use of bold and mighty measures for combating disease—notably bleeding repeatedly and copiously and purging with powerful emetics.)

THE NATION'S FIRST CENTURY: 1787–1890

Medical theory and practice were increasingly predicated upon secular foundations in America's first century as a nation. Regular practitioners—those schooled in continental traditions regarding anatomy, materia medica (includ-

ing botany and chemistry), and surgery—were trained primarily by apprenticeship before the founding of medical colleges beginning in 1765, when the school of medicine in the College of Philadelphia (now the University of Pennsylvania) was established. Within three years the first medical degrees in America were granted to eight graduates from this college.

Regular practitioners relied upon natural explanations and therapies, organized themselves into state medical societies, perpetuated themselves through numerous medical schools, closed ranks behind the American Medical Association (founded in 1846), and officially opposed nonregulars (various sects and groups at odds with traditional theory and practice) and secret nostrums. In the process, minister-physicians both withdrew from and were partly squeezed out of medical practice by the early decades of the nineteenth century. By the 1860s ministers, at the urging of denominational leaders, began to cease from publicly endorsing patent remedies.

In the decades following the Civil War, medicine and religion were sometimes viewed as inherently in conflict. The new sciences of geology, evolutionary biology, "scientific" historiography (in the form of biblical criticism), and psychology called into question fundamental biblical assumptions regarding human origins and development, the historical and scientific accuracy of the Bible, and traditional views regarding the nature of the human psyche.

These fundamental challenges to biblical tradition gave rise to opposition and defensiveness by Christian conservatives—heated criticisms of Charles Darwin's evolutionary theories, heresy trials for those advocating the new biblical criticism. Frontal attacks and rearguard action by conservatives contributed to the notion that the sciences upon which medicine was predicated were at loggerheads with biblically informed faith. Andrew Dickson White's influential and popular *History of the Warfare of Science with Theology in Christendom* (1896) displays many of the antipathies a number of physician-scientists felt toward traditional religion. White's thesis is that the church—both Catholic and Protestant—had largely betrayed the moral mission of Jesus and put in its place a benighted and self-serving theology that opposed and thwarted medical progress at numerous points. He applied this thesis to such topics as gross anatomy, mental illness, inoculations, sanitation, and even anesthesia. Still more critical were the works of the American scientist-physician John W. Draper and the founder of psychoanalysis, Sigmund Freud. Draper's *History of the Conflict of Religion and Science* (1889) depicted religion as intolerant, stationary, and restrictive over against the tolerant, progressive, and expansive orientations of science. In *The Future of an Illusion* (1928) Freud analyzed religion's psychological dynamics as rooted in wishful illusion productive of infantile immaturity and regression. White's, Draper's, and Freud's views were adopted by many medical professionals who viewed religiosity as "equivalent to irrational thinking and emotional disturbance" (Foster, 1982, p. 260).

In spite of its alliance with science and professionalism, medicine during the United States' first century offered little by way of effective cures. Consider, for example, the therapies of Benjamin Rush, a physician of immense influence in the first decades of the nation's history. Rush believed that all disease was caused by spasms in the vascular system. He held that these spasms could be relieved by heroic and repeated bloodletting; and blood, he once said, was no longer sacred after Christ died on the cross. In advocating one grand disease cause, Rush followed the precedent of grasping for a ruling disease principle parallel to the role of gravity in the cosmos. In holding to such a cause and in shifting therapy toward heroic extremes, however, Rush became blind to the healing powers of nature, to the complexities of disease etiology, and to the harm that he fostered in the name of science and saving lives.

Conventional medicine perpetuated a variety of traditional religious values. Masturbation was transformed into a disease, replete with physical and psychological symptoms and ghastly results (including death) that sometimes called for drastic therapies like castration and clitoridectomies. A campaign to prohibit abortions at any stage of pregnancy was mounted by regular practitioners —partly as an anti-Catholic crusade (namely, a manifestation of "blatant nativism" fed by Protestant fears over the greater reproductive rates of Catholic immigrants). Traditional gender distinctions and circumscribed roles for women were fostered under the banner of scientific physiology. And medical writers helped fuel the flames of an Evangelical Protestant crusade against the production and consumption of alcohol that began in the 1810s and did not lose its ardor until after the repeal of the Prohibition amendment in 1933.

This partial listing of standard medical values indicates the degree to which medical theory and therapy were interwoven with Evangelical Protestantism during the nation's first century. The majority of regular practitioners were Protestant. Many were regular churchgoers and leaders, and most of the Protestant clergy were "consistent supporters" of conventional medicine. Evangelical views regarding the nature, purposes, and limits of body, mind, and sex became concretely embodied in normative "medical" notions of health and disease.

Partly as a reaction against the questionably effective and often harmful heroic therapies of conventional medical practice, numerous irregular health schemes and schools of medical thought flowered in nineteenth-century America. These were positively nourished by a number of religious influences, notably the ideas and practices of earlier authors like John Wesley, utopian and millennialist expectations, and religious sectarianism. The interpenetration of Thomsonianism, health food campaigns, hydropathy, and mesmerism with three religious traditions originating in America—Mormonism, Seventh-day Adventism, and Christian Science— illustrates the rich and complex interplay of these influences.

Thomsonianism was the creation of Samuel Thomson, whose heat-restoring botanicals like cayenne pepper and lobelia (an emetic) were designed to clean out the digestive tract. Thomson also opposed bloodletting, blistering, and calomel, as well as imbibing alcohol, coffee, tea, and tobacco. Having converted the Restorationist Christian Church leader (and later Universalist) Elias Smith to his cause, Thomson peddled his remedies in an expensive book of secret cures, the buying of which conferred almost immediate "doctor" status.

Thomsonianism became exceedingly popular, especially in frontier settlement areas. Thomsonian doctors were among the closest advisers of Joseph Smith, through whom both botanical remedies and an opposition to tea, coffee, alcoholic beverages, and tobacco became Restorationist principles in Mormonism. Smith also revived the practice of spiritual healing through prayer, anointing with oil, and the laying on of hands. Through Brigham Young these healing and health legacies were passed to generations of Latter-day Saints. Epidemiological research in the 1970s and 1980s has shown that the health traditions of Mormonism contributed to their having lower rates of cancer and cardiovascular disease than Americans generally.

In the eighteenth century George Cheyne and John Wesley had warned against eating salty, greasy, pickled, and highly seasoned foods; and they spoke of the virtues of breads, eggs, milk, and vegetables. In the nineteenth century these and other dietary schemes became virtual crusades in America. No crusader was more fervent and successful than Sylvester Graham, who began his career as a Presbyterian minister and temperance advocate. Through numerous publications and temperance boardinghouses established and regulated by Graham and frequented by many reformers, Graham popularized the view that one's diet should consist solely of vegetables, unsifted wheat bran bread, fruits, and pure water. The foods and drugs that he opposed—meats, alcoholic beverages, tea, coffee, hot chocolate, and tobacco—were regarded not only as responsible for bodily disease, but also as stimulating destructive and unwholesome passions, none more than masturbation and excessive marital sex (which Graham defined as more than once each month).

Graham also championed regular bathing, but others, like Russell T. Trall, who had a regular medical education, and James Caleb Jackson, used internal and external applications of water as a full-fledged therapeutic system, called hydropathy. They also superimposed Graham's dietary regulations upon this system of water cures.

Having frequented Jackson's health and diet center in Dansville, New York, Ellen G. White, the principal prophetess and leader of Seventh-day Adventism, came to believe that the theories and practices of Graham and Jackson comprised an essential component of a fully recovered apostolic Christianity: holy and healthy living in preparation for the Second Coming of Christ and a life in heaven. Through the influence of her surroundings, her prophetic visions, and her close association with Dr. John Kellogg, White inspired Seventh-day Adventists to build numerous health-oriented medical institutions. She

contributed to a long-standing interest among many Americans in whole grain cereals, fresh air, exercise, and natural food products.

Franz Anton Mesmer's hypnotic methods reached New England in the 1830s. Mesmer and his disciples believed that an invisible, magnetic fluid coursed through mind and body, that it was responsible for hypnotic trances, and that trances, séances, and the magnetic emanations from another's hands could be used therapeutically to release disease-causing obstructions of this healing force. A clockmaker from Belfast, Maine, Phineas P. Quimby, became a mesmerist himself and by 1859 was busily treating the sick in Portland. His work as a mesmerist led him to a new discovery: disease is caused by mental error, and if the mind gives no credence to illness or pain, normal bodily health will be restored.

Upon being relieved of much of her invalidism by Quimby, and after advocating his theories in public, Mary Baker Eddy, too, began viewing the mind as the path to freedom from all sickness. Mrs. Eddy, however, set forth Christian Science as the interpretive key to Christ's teachings and hence the one true way of understanding the world. Christian Scientists view physical and emotional well-being as totally dependent upon a mental unification with the single reality of the universe—mind or soul or God. This entails a total denial of the reality of matter, sickness, suffering, and death. A recognition of this leads to a "metaphysical system of treating disease" that is antithetical to illusory, matter-based physiology, pharmacology, or any other belief and therapy of regular medical practitioners. Whereas Mormons and Seventh-day Adventists give great attention to bodily health and appreciate various therapeutic systems, Mrs. Eddy's Christian Science is fundamentally at odds with medical practices that entail recognizing, nurturing, and manipulating the human body.

MODERN AMERICA: 1890 TO THE PRESENT

The fortunes of physicians improved rapidly after the Civil War with the reinstating of state licensure laws (after 1873), the widespread use of anesthesia combined with antisepsis (1880s), the opening of a model medical school at Johns

Hopkins in Baltimore, Maryland (1893), the beginning of clinical and laboratory research (1890s), and the development and use of vaccines, antitoxins, and X rays (1890s). Accompanying these developments, thousands of newly built hospitals (from 178 hospitals in 1872 to over 4,000 in 1910) served as the infrastructure for scientific practice and professional power. Furthermore, through the efforts of the American Medical Association and the Rockefeller Foundation, the profession achieved far greater homogeneity and coherence as medical education was reorganized and standardized and as the profession increasingly controlled public health and pharmaceutics.

Linked to the natural sciences, which were widely viewed as conflicting with traditional religion, these dramatic alterations meant that religion was by and large discounted as a significant factor in defining, diagnosing, and curing physical or mental illness. For example, the focus of clinical medicine at the Boston's Children's Hospital shifted from providing children a supportive, clean, Christian environment to the treating of diseases and injuries. Hospitals became the turf of modern scientific medicine; and the secular world view that brought this medicine into being was widely viewed as the path to human progress.

Organized religion nevertheless participated in these changes by assuming that it could contribute to human well-being and progress by making scientific medicine more available to religious constituents and to the public at large. It sought to accomplish this by building and sponsoring hospitals.

The earliest denominational hospitals were built in the 1820s, and due to the needs of immigrants (especially Lutherans and Catholics) they were constructed in greater numbers in the 1840s and 1850s. Many Catholic hospitals were built because of discrimination by Protestants in settled areas. Irish Catholics in the Northeast, for example, began building hospitals so they would not be the subjects of Protestant missionary efforts, would not be refused extreme unction, and would be comforted by their own historic faith. These hospitals later served as training grounds for Catholic physicians, provided nuns with an opportunity to fulfill the ideals of their callings, and displayed Catholic faith and commitment to outsiders.

Greatly stimulated by the advent of modern medicine, 541 Catholic hospitals were built by 1915, the year the Catholic Hospital Association of the U.S. and Canada was founded. By 1979, 637 Catholic hospitals of various types existed, with a capacity of 166,000 beds—17 percent of the beds in nonfederal, short-term hospitals.

Jewish hospitals were built out of a similar set of dynamics: as a means of escaping Protestant conversion efforts; of honoring Jewish rites (especially ritual circumcision), kosher laws, and prohibitions regarding dissection after death; and of displaying the benefits and strengths of Judaism. The first was the Jewish Hospital of Cincinnati, built in 1850. Additional hospitals were constructed wherever the Jewish population reached some 30,000 persons. The number of Jewish hospitals increased greatly between 1900 and 1910, when immigration mushroomed following pogroms in Central Europe, Poland, and Russia. By 1954 sixty-six Jewish-sponsored hospitals had been built in America's largest cities; these hospitals were the recipients of some 33 percent of Jewish charitable contributions. Presently, about thirty general, all-purpose hospitals are operated under Jewish auspices. Large numbers of Jews entered the medical profession, viewing it as an ideal career for achieving security and upward mobility, and as a way to express treasured religious ideals.

Hospitals were also built in large numbers by Lutherans, Methodists, Presbyterians, Episcopalians, and Baptists. The building of hospitals reflected Protestantism's long-standing identification with scientific progress, but more particularly grew out of the new theological orientation of mainline Protestant traditions after the Civil War—Protestant liberalism. Identifying with progress, modernity, and change, liberals endorsed biological evolution, welcomed and molded the new biblical criticism, and rekindled a commitment to the ethical teachings of Jesus and the Hebrew prophets. They sought to empower these teachings with insights from the emerging disciplines of sociology and economics, so as to humanize and Christianize society by alleviating patterns of poverty, crime, unfair labor conditions, racism, and ill health. The building of hospitals became an essential component in this grand scheme to transform society by means of modern social organizations under the banner of the ideals of the Social Gospel. The impact of this optimistic ideology was all the more important because it was linked to the power and vitality of American Progressivism.

Two additional facets of organized religion accompanied the social and scientific transformation of American medicine: the development of standardized training for hospital chaplains, technically called clinical pastoral education (CPE), and a heightening concern for biomedical ethics. CPE began in 1925 under the leadership of Anton T. Boisen, who combined Protestant theological liberalism with a mystical appreciation of the divine presence. In 1932 Russel L. Dicks began his creative career as a chaplain to patients with religious and psychological problems at Massachusetts General Hospital. Dicks worked closely with Richard C. Cabot, a pioneer in both internal medicine and medical social work.

CPE expanded beyond the confines of New England in the late 1930s. By the early 1950s four national training bodies had been formed, the *Journal of Pastoral Care* was being published, and CPE began to be supported in theological seminaries. The movement remained primarily Protestant until the Second Vatican Council (1962–1965), when Catholic priests and nuns began to be trained in significant numbers. In the mid-1960s a group of ministers, theologians, and medical school deans began sharing common concerns over ethical and theological dimensions of medical education, out of which beginnings grew the Society for Health and Human Values, an active and well-organized society whose some 1,100 members include most of the key figures in biomedical ethics in America.

The impact of Protestant, Catholic, and Jewish chaplains in hospitals, health centers, and mental institutions is exceedingly difficult to assess. Clearly, the religious and psychological needs of many individual patients are being attended to by knowledgeable and trained professionals, the majority of whom now operate out of some 360 accredited centers, many of which are located within large hospitals. Nevertheless, beginning as it did well after the fundamental scientific and social dynamics of modern medicine had been established, CPE remains marginal to the everyday work and concerns of the majority of medical practitioners. This explains in part why chaplains often feel that in spite of their insights and expertise, they live somewhat enigmatically and uncomfortably between two worlds of meaning and practice—medicine and their respective religious traditions.

As for biomedical ethics, its roots lie in longstanding traditions in Judaism, Christianity, and Western philosophy, but it emerged as a specialized discipline and as a social movement within American medicine beginning in the late 1960s. The terms *medical ethics, biomedical ethics,* and *bioethics* are usually used interchangeably, but for historical and analytical purposes they should be distinguished as follows: *medical ethics* refers comprehensively to the ethical principles and positions brought to bear on medical practice past and present; *biomedical ethics* refers more particularly to the engagement between the discipline of ethics and the biomedical sciences over the last twenty years; and *bioethics* to the engagement of ethics with all of the biological sciences in the same time period.

As a social movement, biomedical ethics now manifests itself through journals, standard reference works, several free-standing centers (like the Hastings Center in Hastings-on-Hudson, New York), and courses and programs in nearly all of America's medical schools. Biomedical ethics seeks to discover and utilize rational and theological principles to determine what is or is not permissible regarding medical interventions, relationships, and policies. Modern bioethics now encompasses a great range of issues, including such matters as the nature of practitioner-patient relationships, the ethics of experimental research, definitions of death, interventions in human reproduction, genetic manipulations, and health-care policies. This discussion focuses on a limited set of such issues.

Christian reflection on the ethics of certain medical procedures began in the first centuries of the Christian era—in which, for example, contraception and abortion were prohibited. From this legacy Catholic medical ethics emerged as a subdiscipline of moral theology. In general, great continuity has existed within Catholicism regarding the rightness or wrongness of many medical procedures, even though different types of philosophical principles have been utilized to reach conclusions about these procedures. Abortion, sterilization, and euthanasia, for example, have been viewed as immoral except for certain carefully defined circumstances permitted by natural law. This law, however, has been variously identified with the unchanging purposes of biological processes (Catholic thought prior to 1940), with the authoritative pronouncements of the church regarding the natural order (1940–1960), and with the natural dynamics of humans as physical, psychological, moral, and social beings (post–1960 writings). The last view breaks with long-standing Catholic traditions of ethical reflection and provides modern Catholics with a greater range of exceptions to traditional prohibitions and practices.

In America, manuals regulating the actions and relationships of doctors and patients were regularly translated from Latin, German, and French works. Beginning with the book by the Jesuit Charles Coppens in 1897, manuals were also written by Americans. Between 1850 and 1960 a distinct tradition was sustained: all intended medical procedures must conform with the physical purposes of living biological organisms and the ecclesiastical pronouncements of the church as rooted in the Ten Commandments and Christian Scripture. This tradition, as reflected, for example, in the 1971 code of Ethical and Religious Directions for Catholic Health Care Facilities, prohibited contraceptive devices, sterilization (except for diseased organs), masturbation (including masturbation for seminal specimens for reproductive purposes), artificial insemination by husbands or nonhusband donors, abortion, and euthanasia.

Certain adverse consequences, however, were acceptable as long as the intentions of practitioners conformed with traditional interpretations of the purposes of nature. Thus, a fetus implanted in a fallopian tube could be destroyed as an indirect consequence of seeking to save the mother's life. This line of reasoning also allowed Catholics not to use extraordinary means to extend life and to consent to experimental therapy as long as it was either not injurious or was directed at saving life. Although many of these traditional positions continue to represent official church policy, after 1960 and the Second Vatican Council greater dissent was voiced by Catholic moralists who identified natural law more broadly; that is, with the complex interplay of physical, psychological, and social dimensions of human life. Catholic biomedical ethicists thereby entered a thoroughgoing dialogue with other religious and secular ethicists and, in the process, developed and adopted a variety of ethical vantage points. This methodological pluralism has given rise to defenses of contraception, sterilization, artificial insemination, and active euthanasia under limited circumstances by some Catholics.

Except for the controversial topic of abortion, little is known about the degrees to which Catholic lay persons abide by official church doctrine or by the opinions of Catholic scholars who differ with official teaching on important bioethical issues. Regarding abortion, the attitudes of Catholics differ only marginally from those of their Protestant counterparts, 69 percent of whom believe that a woman's decision to have an abortion "should be left entirely to the woman and her doctor" versus 64 percent of Catholics (*Family Planning Perspectives*, 1980, p. 53).

Jewish bioethics also represents a historic tradition, but one that is less centralized and authoritatively controlled than Catholic ethical teaching. Administered under secular auspices, Jewish hospitals, for example, have no ethical and religious directives similar to those of Catholic hospitals. Their codes are viewed as ethical guidelines for medical professionals and patients. Like Catholic ethics, however, Jewish ethics derives its norms from theistic absolutism as opposed to expediency, individual intuitive judgments, and social relativism; but unlike Catholic biomedical ethics, the positions of Jewish writers display greater variety. Differences in Jewish biomedical ethics reflect different orientations toward Jewish law—orientations calling for strict observance by Orthodox Jews, a willness to make certain changes in the law by Conservative Jews, and, on behalf of Reform Jews, a volunteristic following of the law as long as it accords with the needs and autonomy of the individual.

Jewish law or tradition is commonly understood as preserved (or revealed) in the written law of God to Moses (Pentateuch) and the oral law delivered to Moses (as preserved in the Talmud). Oral law is also viewed as preserved in case-law decisions (called responsa) over time by rabbinic courts and notable rabbis. Responsa have been written down and published over time by the Orthodox, Conservative, and Reform branches of Judaism, and they represent primary sources for Jewish bioethics.

Orthodox medical ethics corresponds to Catholic ethics in many respects: masturbation for the purpose of artificial insemination or test tube babies, artificial insemination by nonhusband donors, homosexuality, sterilization (except for urgent therapy), active euthanasia, transsexual surgery, and most instances of contraception and abortion (including of defective fetuses) are forbidden. Orthodoxy, however, allows for abortion in instances of grave psychological threat to the mother and views oral contraception with greater leniency than does Catholicism. In contrast to Orthodox Judaism, Conservative Jewish authorities are more lenient with respect to abortions to relieve the mental suffering or turmoil of the mother. Reform Judaism by and large leaves abortion decisions to the individual woman. The Reform tradition also permits artificial insemination by nonhusband donors and officially accepts homosexual congregations into the fellowship of Reform Judaism.

Protestant traditions of medical ethics are even more diverse than those of Judaism. As noted earlier, these traditions influenced the way many American physicians understood both their duties to patients and their broader social responsibilities. Unlike both Catholicism and Judaism, however, Protestant denominations did not develop ongoing legacies regarding the rightness or wrongness of specific medical interventions. In fact, pioneering discussions on medical ethics by Protestants began with the books by Willard Sperry (*The Ethical Basis for Medical Practice,* 1950), a Congregationalist minister and dean of the Harvard Divinity School, and by the Episcopalian priest Joseph Fletcher (*Morals and Medicine,* 1954).

By the late 1960s, America's biomedical ethics movement was under way; and active in it were a number of Protestant ethicists, including Fletcher, the Presbyterian theologian-ethicist Paul Ramsey (*Patient as Person,* 1970), the Methodist ethicist Harmon J. Smith (*Ethics and the New Medicine,* 1970), and many others writing from an ecumenical, rather than a strictly denominational, perspective. Beginning in 1967 Episcopalians, Presbyterians, the Lutheran Church in America, and other denominations began to establish commissions charged with reflecting on moral dilemmas raised by technological developments within scientific medicine.

The so-called mainline Protestant churches generally agree with Jewish and Catholic biomedical ethics in opposing active euthanasia and supporting patient-consent guidelines for biomedical experimentation. On other issues many Protestant spokespersons differ from their Catholic and Orthodox Jewish counterparts. Mainline Protestant churches, for example, generally advocate the universal availability of contraception because it promotes marital happiness, curtails abortions, and serves to control world population growth. Abortion is the subject of widespread debate among Protestants; some congregants (like the Southern Baptist Convention) condemn abortion except when the mother's life is at stake. Others (like Presbyterians and Methodists) counsel restraint and recommend that women seek pastoral counseling. Still others, like the Mormons (who resist being identified as Protestants) and the so-called Moral Majority Fundamentalists, steadfastly oppose abortion—the Mormons because it keeps preexistent souls from entering earthly and celestial life, and Fundamentalists because they identify the fetus as a child or person with an immortal soul. On other matters like in vitro fertilization or genetic engineering, positions vary from enthusiastic support to uncertainty to outright opposition. This is in keeping with long-standing emphases within mainline Protestantism on the freedom of the individual's conscience and with the propensity of Protestant sectarians to shun positions identified as "worldly."

Given the limits of hospital chaplains and the lack of consistency in religiously based bioethics, the social impact of particular religious beliefs upon the contemporary practice of medicine has been limited. The interpenetration of shared religious perspectives with the ethics and values of contemporary medicine is nevertheless evident in strong agreement regarding the singular importance of the individual, the incalculable value of the gift of life, the duty of becoming stewards rather than exploiters of natural and human resources, and the necessity of greater social justice. At these points religious and secular medical ethics are virtually inseparable.

Surprisingly, just as modern scientific medicine was securing its enormous power and prestige in the twentieth century, millions of Americans began practicing long-neglected forms of religious healing. Pentecostal and charismatic revivals got under way in the 1890s, expanding rapidly in the 1920s and even more so after World War II. By the end of the 1970s a Gallup poll reported that some 10 million Americans—

among whom were Catholics, Protestants from several denominations, and two large Pentecostal groups, the Assemblies of God and the Pentecostal Fellowship of North America—were practicing faith healing. Although much skepticism existed regarding these cures, M.D.'s and lay people alike wrote books describing how persons with such diseases as rheumatoid arthritis, malignant brain tumors, and multiple sclerosis had been healed. While some small Pentecostal groups consider it sinful to seek any care from doctors, healers like Oral Roberts warmly endorse and support standard medical therapy. (Roberts' $150 million City of Faith Medical and Research Center opened in 1978 in Tulsa, Oklahoma.)

Similar to mainline Protestant tradition, the Jehovah's Witnesses believe that miracles ceased with the apostolic age. In other health and medicine matters they hold that the Bible should be obeyed to the letter. This led to a scrupulous effort to recover exactly what the Bible teaches, while at the same time allowing for freedom of conscience on various issues not directly addressed in the Bible. Witness interpretations include opposition to masturbation, homosexuality, and drunkenness (but not all alcoholic beverages); utilization of most of the treatments of modern medicine; and freedom of conscience regarding contraception, sterilization, and abortion.

In 1927—some fifty-five years after the movement began under the inspiration of Charles Taze Russell—the Witnesses first began setting forth their teachings on the sanctity of blood, in this instance the necessity of abstaining from unbled meat. By 1945 this position was extended to blood transfusions. Witnesses were to refuse transfusions because blood is holy; it is the seat of each creature's life and was used by God to furnish life to others only when Christ was sacrificed for the sins of all. This position put Witnesses in the "spotlight" as a people willing to risk life for a holy cause, the betrayal of which keeps them from eternal life in Jehovah's "new world of righteousness." For this position Witnesses have marshaled evidence regarding the dangers of blood transfusions and have hastened the development of plasma expanders.

Refusals of blood transfusions by Jehovah's Witnesses have been highly controversial and have contributed to ethical and legal reflection regarding the individual's rights of self-determination, in particular, the right to refuse life-saving medical treatment. While the celebrated case *Application of the President and Directors of Georgetown College* (1964) ended with a circuit court judge's authorizing transfusion primarily because of the state's duty to protect the child of a twenty-five-year-old female patient, other cases in 1962 (*Erickson* v. *Dilgard*) and 1965 (*In re Brooks' Estate*) were decided in favor of self-determination for adult patients. Cases involving child refusals, however, have been resolved in favor of the state's right to preserve the lives of those who cannot decide for themselves.

Theories, theologies, movements, and institutions tell us much about medicine, bioethics, and religion in America. As we have seen, in the twentieth century organized religion became less influential as matters of health and medicine were increasingly secularized by scientific medicine and its accompanying world view. Nevertheless the degree to which religion is less of a factor in the experiences of patients remains an open question. The control of most healing by scientifically trained practitioners largely segregated from public view in hospitals surely makes it appear that health and disease have been largely secularized. This segregation also extends to theological education, where scant attention has been focused on the dynamics between medicine and religion and where courses on medical ethics have only recently been introduced. Yet the suffering, the sense of frailty and finitude, and the self-examination that accompany much sickness and injury raise ultimate questions of meaning, as well as everyday quandaries regarding the body, sexuality, human relationships, and ordinary habits. Many Americans continue to turn to religion when grappling with these issues.

BIBLIOGRAPHY

Erwin Ackerknecht, *Therapeutics* (1973); Chester R. Burns, ed., *The Quest for Professional Ethics in American Medicine: Source Book* (1978); H. Richard Casdorph, *The Miracles* (1976); James H. Cassedy, "An American Clerical Crisis: Ministers' Sore Throat, 1830–1860," in *Bulletin of the History of Medicine*, 53 (1979); "Catholics Agree with Protestants," *Family Planning Perspectives*, 12 (1980); George Cheyne, *An Essay of Health and Long Life* (1725); Thomas E. Cone, *History of American Pediatrics* (1979); Charles E. Curran, "Roman Catholicism," in *Encyclopedia of Bioethics,* 4 (1978); Robert T. Divett, "Medicine and the Mormons: A Historical Perspective," in *Dialogue: A Journal of Mormon Thought,* 12 (1979); John Duffy, *The Healers* (1976) and, as ed., *The Rudolph Matas History of Medicine in Louisiana,* vol. 2 (1958); Mary Baker Eddy, *Science and Health with Key to the Scriptures* (1875); H. Tristram Engelhardt, "The Disease of Masturbation: Values and the Concept of Disease," in *Bulletin of the History of Medicine,* 48 (1974).

Daniel W. Foster, "Religion and Medicine: The Physician's Perspective," in Martin E. Marty and Kenneth L. Vaux, eds., *Health/Medicine and the Faith Traditions* (1982); Richard T. Fox, William R. Walker, and Mark Unger, "Changes in Numbers of Hospitals and Beds," in *Hospital Progress,* 63 (1982); I. S. Geettler, "Historical Development of Hospitals Under Jewish Auspices," unpublished paper, Conference for Presidents and Executives of Jewish Federations and Hospitals, Philadelphia, 1954; Francisco Guerra, "The Role of Religion in Spanish-American Medicine," in F. N. L. Poynter, ed., *Medicine and Culture* (1969); John S. Haller and Robin M. Haller, *The Physician and Sexuality in Victorian America* (1974); David Edwin Harrell, *All Things Are Possible* (1975); Seward Hiltner, "Fifty Years of CPE," in *Journal of Pastoral Care,* 27 (1975); Lawrence E. Holst, "The Hospital Chaplain Between Worlds," in Martin E. Marty and Kenneth L. Vaux, eds., *Health/Medicine and the Faith Traditions* (1982).

David F. Kelly, *The Emergence of Roman Catholic Medical Ethics in North America* (1979); N. H. Knorr, "Acts of Jehovah's Witnesses in Modern Times," in *1975 Yearbook of Jehovah's Witnesses* (1974); Cotton Mather, *The Angel of Bethesda,* Gordon W. Jones, ed. (1972); James C. Mohr, *Abortion in America: The Origins and Evaluation of National Policy, 1800–1900* (1978); Ronald L. Numbers, *Prophetess of Health: A Study of Ellen G. White* (1976), with Ronald C. Sawyer, "Medicine and Christianity in the Modern World," in Martin E. Marty and Kenneth L. Vaux, eds., *Health/Medicine and the Faith Traditions* (1982), and, with Darrel W. Amundsen as eds., *Caring and Curing: Health and Medicine in the Western Faith Traditions* (1986); Henry M. Parrish, "Contributions of the Clergy to Early American Medicine," in *Journal of the Bowman Gray School of Medicine,* 16 (1956); F. N. L. Poynter, "Nicholas Culpepper and His Books," in *Journal of the History of Medicine and Allied Sciences,* 17 (1962).

Fred Rosner and J. David Bleich, eds., *Jewish Bioethics* (1979); Richard Harrison Shryock, "The Medical Reputation of Benjamin Rush: Contrasts over Two Centuries," in *Bulletin of the History of Medicine,* 45 (1971); Paul Starr, *The Social Transformation of American Medicine* (1982); Isaac N. Trainin and Fred Rosner, "Religious Directives in Medical Ethics: Jewish Codes and Guidelines," in *Encyclopedia of Bioethics,* 4 (1978); Harold Y. Vanderpool, "Miracle and Faith Healing: Conceptual and Historical Perspectives," in *Encyclopedia of Bioethics,* 3 (1978), "Protestantism: Dominant Health Concerns in Protestantism," in *Encyclopedia of Bioethics,* 3 (1978), and "The Holistic Hodgepodge: A Critical Analysis of Holistic Medicine and Health in America Today," in *Journal of Family Practice,* 19 (1984); Morris J. Vogel, *The Invention of the Modern Hospital, 1870–1930* (1980); Brigham Young, *Discourses of Brigham Young* (1954).

[*See also* CHRISTIAN SCIENCE AND HARMONIALISM; *and* RELIGION AND SCIENCE.]